The PC BIBLE

ROBERT LAURISTON

Peachpit Press

The PC Bible, Third Edition

Edited by Robert Lauriston

Peachpit Press
1249 Eighth Street
Berkeley, CA 94710
510/524-2178
800/283-9444
510/524-2221 (fax)

Find us on the World Wide Web at:
http://www.peachpit.com and www.thepcbible.com

Peachpit Press is a division of Addison Wesley Longman

Project Editor: **Corbin Collins**
Production: **Mimi Heft**
Copyeditors: **Carol Henry, Lysa Lewallen, Vivian Perry, Judy Ziajka**
Compositor: **Maureen Forys, Happenstance Type-O-Rama**
Cover design: **Mimi Heft**
Tecnical editors: **Dick Hol, Lenny Bailes, Bill Karow**
Interior illustrations: **Bud Peen**
Interior design: **Mimi Heft**
Indexer: **Carol Burbo**

Colophon
This book was created with QuarkXPress 4 on a Pwer Computing Power Tower Pro 250. The fonts used were Aldine and Letter Gothic 12 Pitch from Bitstream, Myriad from Adobe, and PIXymbols from Page Studio Graphics. Imagesetting and printing were done at Edwards Brothers, Inc., Ann Arbor, MI, on 50# Arbor Smooth.

ISBN 0-201-35382-2

9 8 7 6 5 4 3 2 1

Printed and bound in the United States of America

Kid, it's their job to sell you a line of bullshit. It's your job not to buy it.

—Rolling Stone *co-founder Ralph Gleason to his then-new film critic, Michael Goodwin*

About the Authors

A book like this one would be impossible without the collaboration of many authors with a wide range of experience. Here's the cast of characters that created this edition.

Jim Aikin is the senior editor of *Keyboard* magazine, where he writes regular product reviews of music software. He is also the former technical editor of *Music & Computers* magazine, and the author of two science fiction novels.

Anita Amirrezvani covers the arts as a staff writer for the *Contra Costa Times*. She was a 1998 fellow of Columbia University's National Arts Journalism Program.

Lenny Bailes is a consultant, teacher, and computer journalist who lives in the San Francisco Bay Area. He is the author of *Maximizing Windows 98* and *The Byte Guide to Optimizing Windows 95*, and has written hundreds of articles for computer magazines including *Windows Magazine*, *Computer Shopper*, and *Computerworld*.

Foster D. Coburn III (`www.unleash.com`) has co-authored five books on CorelDraw and is the host of the CorelDraw Unleashed Boot Camps.

Steve Cummings A medical doctor, Steve is the author or coauthor of many computer books, including *VBA for Dummies* and Peachpit's *Jargon: An Informal Dictionary of Computer Terms*.

Alfred Glossbrenner is the co-author of Peachpit's *The Little Web Book* and *Search Engines for the World Wide Web: Visual QuickStart Guide*. He has written more than 30 books and hundreds of articles and columns for numerous publications.

Wendy M. Grossman (`www.well.com/user/wendyg`) is a freelance writer based in London and a regular contributor to the Daily Telegraph's technology section. She is author of two books, *net.wars*, and *Remembering the Future: Interviews from Personal Computer World*, and has also contributed to *Scientific American* and *Wired*.

Galen Gruman has coauthored 11 books on desktop publishing and has covered PC and Mac software and hardware since 1985 for a variety of publications, including *Macworld*, *PC World*, and *InfoWorld*. He is currently West Coast bureau chief at *Computerworld*.

Judy Heim (`execpc.com/~judyheim`) writes *PC World*'s monthly "Internet Tips" column and is the author or coauthor of several computer books including *The Needlecrafter's Computer Companion, The Quilter's Computer Companion, Free Stuff for Quilters on the Internet, I Lost My Baby, My Pickup, and My Guitar on the Information Highway*, and *Internet for Cats*.

Eric Knorr is a freelance writer, editor, and Web site design consultant. He was formerly editor of *PC World* and *Computers.com*, to both of which he remains a frequent contributor, and edited the first and second editions of *The PC Bible*.

Maria Langer (`www.gilesrd.com`) is the author of 22 computer books, including many titles in the Peachpit's Visual QuickStart series. She also writes for a variety of computer magazines, including *FileMaker Pro Advisor*, *NetProfessional*, and *Computer User*.

Robert Lauriston (`www.lauriston.com`) is a Berkeley-based freelance writer and editor who has written and edited hundreds of hardware and software reviews and how-to features for computer publications including *PC World*, *Windows Magazine*, *CNET*, and *Computers.com*.

Robert Luhn is editor-in-chief of *Computer Currents*, a biweekly national magazine. His work has appeared in *Omni*, the *Christian Science Monitor*, and *Mother Jones*.

Richard Scoville is a software training consultant based in Chapel Hill, North Carolina. From 1989 to 1997 he wrote *PC World*'s monthly spreadsheet column, and he testified as an expert witness in Lotus v. Borland.

Scott Spanbauer is a freelance writer and editor, a contributing editor for to *PC World* and author of its "Bugs and Fixes" column, and the author of *The No B.S. Guide To Windows 95*.

Daniel Tynan is executive editor for features at *PC World*. He has received three Neal Awards, and his work has appeared in *Newsweek*, *Sports Illustrated*, *US News and World Report*, and *Men's Journal*.

Sean Wagstaff has written several books, including *3-D Starter Kit for Macintosh* and Peachpit's *Animation On the Web*. He is a frequent contributor to *eMediaweekly*, *DCC*, and numerous other magazines.

Jake Widman is the former editor in chief of *Publish* magazine, for which he continues to write regularly as a contributing editor. He has also written a book on the use of personal computers for graphic design.

Naomi Wise is a freelance writer whose work has appeared in *PC World*, *Family Circle*'s Computers Made Easy, the *Washington Post Magazine*, the *Village Voice*, and the *San Jose Mercury News*. She also has four cookbooks and a biography to her name, and is the restaurant critic of *SF Weekly*.

Kathy Yakal is a freelance writer specializing in personal finance and accounting software. She writes columns and reviews for several business and computer publications, including *Barron's* and *PC* magazine.

Acknowledgements

The person most responsible for *The PC Bible*'s existence is Eric Knorr, who in editing the first edition invented the model that this third edition merely follows. Credit is also due to Neil Salkind, who originally proposed a reference that would provide the same wealth of information to PC users that *The Macintosh Bible* has provided to the Mac community, and to Rick Altman, TJ Byers, George Campbell, Scott Dunn, Michael Goodwin, Gregg Keizer, Celeste Robinson, Steve Sagman, and Daniel Will-Harris, whose contributions helped make the first and second editions a success.

In addition to the freelancers and Peachpit Press staffers credited on the copyright page, who did a great job of putting this book together and making it look good, I'd like to thank Peachpit managing editor Marjorie Baer for her help solving a couple of tough problems. Not to snub anyone else's contribution, but I'd especially like to thank Peachpit's project editor Corbin Collins and freelance Quark maven Maureen Forys for putting in the unreasonable hours required to get the book to the printer on time.

With the completion of this book, it's ten years almost to the month that I've been in the computer journalism business, so I'd like to take this opportunity to thank all the editors and other magazine staffers who have made it possible for me to make a living in such a pleasant and intellectually stimulating manner. In particular, thanks to Michael Goodwin, who suggested the idea in the first place and gave me my first assignment for a national publication, to Cathy Smith and Richard Dalton for recommending me to magazines that became major clients, and to Richard Landry, Robert Luhn, Steve Fox, Eileen McCooey, Sandra Rosenzweig, Dominic Milano, Eric Knorr, and Nancy Ruenzel for abundant supplies of nice, fresh work.

Table of Contents

Chapter 8: **Upgrade It Yourself • 145**

Chapter 9: **Protect Your Data • 185**

Chapter 10: **How To Choose and Buy Software • 211**

Chapter 16: **Databases • 495**

Chapter 17: **Painting, Drawing, and Other Graphics Software • 537**

Chapter 18: **Sound and Video Editing • 577**

Chapter 19: **Getting on the Internet • 605**

Introduction

Welcome to the third edition of *The PC Bible*, the only book that dares to cover the whole universe of PC hardware, software, and communications in a single volume. Like the previous editions, this book delivers a truckload of tips, tutorials, overviews, and buying advice on everything from using Quicken to balance your checkbook to choosing the fastest Internet connection. Due to the big changes in PC technology since the last edition, every chapter has been completely revised—in fact, most have been rewritten from scratch, and several are new additions to the family.

Yes, this is a monster of a book, but a big, friendly monster. Every effort has been made to strip out jargon, and every necessary technical term has been explained in context and in the glossary. Just as important, all 27 chapters have been organized to provide both quick tutorials for beginners and easy access to hundreds of tips and product evaluations for people who already know what they're doing. In other words, you can browse randomly for tidbits, read sequentially to get a working knowledge of a given area, or use the index to zero in on exactly the information you need.

The secret to this book is in the expertise of its authors. Obviously, there's no way to cover everything about PCs in fewer than 1000 pages. So each of this book's 20 experts had the same mandate: Use the benefit of experience to tell people what they most need to know. With this book, you can get up and running fast with Excel, the most popular spreadsheet—but you won't learn about advanced statistical functions or get more than a brief overview of macro programming. You can discover how to create your own Web page or connect several PCs to share files and printers—but if you want to set up your own Web server or manage a network, look elsewhere. Instead of truly advanced stuff, you'll find concise primers and frank opinions about products, plus some of the hottest tips around.

We hope this book's breadth, usefulness, clarity, and logical organization earn it a place right next to your PC. *The PC Bible* is a work in progress that will hopefully go through many editions. To make it a more effective reference, we invite you to send in your comments when you visit our Web site at **www.thepcbible.com**.

How to Use This Book

The PC Bible is loosely divided into three parts: hardware, software, and communications. Chapters 1 through 9 are largely devoted to helping you select and install the right hardware. Chapters 10 through 18 cover software: buying it, mastering Windows, and using major applications from word processing to video editing. Chapters 19 through 23 tell you how to get on the Internet and what you can do while you get there, and chapters 24 and 25 cover your PC's other communications capabilities: faxing, voicemail, and connecting to other PCs on a local network. Rounding out the book, Chapters 26 and 27 explain how to keep your PC from making you sick, and what to do when your PC is under the weather.

Beginners and Raw Beginners

This book is intended for people at various levels of computer expertise. After all, no one knows everything about computers—you may be a spreadsheet wizard, for instance, but be completely at sea when it comes to printers. That's why each chapter has been carefully designed so that you can plunge right in without knowing much about the subject—and usually get the information you need without resorting to the glossary.

However, if you're new to the entire subject of PCs, and terms like "RAM" or "hard disk" leave you scratching your head, go directly to Chapter 1: For Beginners Only. There you'll find the basic explanations that will help you understand the rest of this book. If you're a raw beginner and already have a PC, then the next step is Chapter 11: Windows 95, 98, and NT, where a fairly complete tutorial and Cookbook reference will get you acquainted with your PC's most essential software.

Software Assumptions

This book takes for granted that you're running or are about to upgrade to Windows 95, Windows 98, or NT Workstation 4.0. For emergencies we've included some of the most important tips for DOS and Windows 3.1 from the second edition in the Survival Guide appendices, but if you're actually using them full-time, this edition's not for you.

Those Little Icons

For those who like to browse, we offer icons to call attention to passages in text and make the browsing more fun. With icons and an abundance of little subheads as signposts, you may not even need to bother with the index when you search for specific information.

If you're already a PC user, try this experiment: Turn to the chapter that covers the type of software you use most. Then check out the **tip icons** in the margin (when a whole block of tips runs together, you'll see a vertical line next to the icon). Chances are you'll find some tips worth trying.

Knowing what you shouldn't do—buy a bad product, press a wrong key, touch a sensitive component—is every bit as important as knowing what you should do. The **danger icon** is this book's red flag. It's reserved for important warnings that might frighten an ostrich.

Certain facts should take up residence in the back of your mind as you shop or as you work. This icon highlights these important points. For example, this whole discussion about icons could easily get its own **remember icon**, but that would look pretty weird.

Note that the icons merely call out some of the most important information—but there's useful stuff on almost every page. If you have a special interest in a subject, checking for tips may not be the best strategy, since information valuable to you may lack an icon entirely.

Typographic Conventions

Throughout this book you'll find keycaps, characters in a special font used to represent keys on the PC keyboard. Keycaps indicate the keys you should press when you enter a command or execute a keyboard "shortcut"—Ctrl B for boldface, for example. However, when you're supposed to type a whole string of characters into a dialog box, we set them off with quotes: for example, 'type "regedit" and press Enter'. When commands are entered at the DOS prompt, or in a search engine, we indicate them with a special font: `copy *.*`.

Menu choices in a sequence of commands are separated by slashes, like File/Save As. When multi-word menu commands or dialog box choices are shown on screen without initial capital letters, we set them off with quotes, as in "Use large icons."

Web addresses (URLs), which you type into a browser to view a particular Web page, are shown in a special font (**www.peachpit.com**). To minimize your typing, we've stripped these addresses to their essentials, so for example instead of **http://www.pcworld.com/top400/index.html** we show only **pcworld.com/top400**.

Whenever a technical term is introduced, you'll find it italicized and defined in context. Thereafter the term won't be italicized, so if you forget what it means, you can either flip backward in the chapter or check the glossary.

In most cases, acronyms are usually explained on their first occurrence, as in TCP/IP (Transport Control Protocol/Internet Protocol). However, in cases where properly explaining the acronym would result in a confusing and pointless digression, we've moved that discussion to the glossary.

Products, Prices, and Resources

Information on products, particularly pricing, versions, and models, is subject to swift and sweeping change. We did our best to get the latest data for products in this book, but it will age quickly. Use the Web addresses (URLs) throughout the book and in the Resources sections at the end of each chapter to check manufacturers' sites for updated information. We'll also be posting new product recommendations regularly to this book's Web site, **www.thepcbible.com**.

Wherever possible, we've indicated street prices. That is, instead of using whatever suggested or estimated price the manufacturer publishes, we checked advertised prices, and used the lowest we could find. See the "Official Price vs. Street Price" section of Chapter 10: How to Choose and Buy Software for more on this topic.

1

For Beginners Only

by Eric Knorr, Naomi Wise, and Robert Lauriston

This chapter was originally written by by Eric Knorr and Naomi Wise, and updated for the third edition by Robert Lauriston.

In This Chapter

A personal computer is just another appliance, like a blender or a microwave oven. If you want to do something with a PC—write a letter, get the latest stock-market quotes, play solitaire—you click the right buttons and the job is done. True, it's not always obvious where the right buttons are. But the most important thing to realize is that you'll find them eventually, without having to learn sleight of hand or mind-bending secret codes.

The main difference between a PC and other appliances lies in the variety of jobs it can do. The PC's closest relative is the VCR: Every time you pop in a new videotape, the VCR shows a different movie. Just like a VCR, a PC is merely the required electronic equipment—the hardware. Without software—the PC's equivalent of the feature film—you wouldn't be able to do anything useful or entertaining with a computer.

When you buy a PC, it comes with a little software for word processing, doing calculations, and playing games, to get you started. But these simple pieces of software—each one a small application because it applies to a specific job—are only the beginning.

This book will introduce you to hundreds of the best applications you can buy, help you choose among them, and even lead you step by step through the process of using many of them. You'll also learn how to pick hardware to run that software—Chapter 2, for example, explains how to choose a PC. But if you're really a raw beginner, you need to understand a few things first. Where to start? Well, imagine you just bought a PC and brought it home...

Unpacking and Getting Settled

The best way to unpack new hardware is to get a friend to help. While unpacking, the aim is to place all the components on a desk without destroying the boxes, the styrofoam, or your spine. Remember to keep the packing materials in case you have to return your PC or send it in for repairs, or if you move.

1. **Find a good home.** If you're setting up a PC at work, hopefully your company has prepared a proper work area (see Chapter 26: Health and Safety). If you're setting up at home, choose a large desk near an AC outlet with enough space not only for the PC and printer, but also papers, reference materials, and so on (avoid those tiny "computer desks"). The desk should be low enough so your forearms are parallel to the floor when you type—failing that, a keyboard drawer (available at most office supply stores) should do the trick

2. **Unpack the PC.** Take your PC out of its box, carefully following any instructions printed on the box itself, or any posterlike "boxtopper" diagram, or "read me first" card. If you have a helper, the weaker person should hold the box while the stronger yanks out the PC, which will probably be surrounded by styrofoam. The monitor will probably be heavier and harder to lift. With 17-inch or larger monitors, it's often easier to fold back all four top flaps, carefully turn the box over so the styrofoam packing inserts are resting on the floor, and then lift the box off the monitor.
3. **Prepare to connect.** Carefully set the PC and monitor on your desk. Both the monitor and PC should be angled away from the wall so you can access their backs and connect various cables. Look for your floppy disk drive (see "The ABCs of Hardware" later in this chapter for its location), check inside it, and remove any paper, cardboard, or plastic packing material.
4. **Prepare your printer.** Printers often come with a special set of unpacking instructions that tell you how to remove plastic spacers that prevent damage during shipping. A certain amount of assembly will be required. The user manual will have instructions and a diagram.
5. **Take inventory.** Make a final search of each box (and the indentations in the styrofoam blocks) for additional documentation—not to mention software, cables, or other parts, which are frequently packed in baggies or in small boxes. Check packing lists—especially if you bought the hardware by mail order—and make sure all the listed items are there. If anything is missing, immediately call the vendor that sold you the equipment.

Now's an excellent time to put every piece of documentation you've found into a manila folder labeled ***PC Survival Kit***, and stash it in a place where you'll find it easily. Add the PC manufacturer's technical support number to your Rolodex for good measure.

In some cases you may need to unpack and connect other *peripherals* (the word for any hardware devices besides the PC itself), such as a modem, which enables you to hook your PC to your phone line and communicate with other computers. The section "Making the Right Connections" will explain what plugs into where.

The ABCs of Hardware

To start computing, all you need is a PC with a monitor, keyboard, and mouse. The nice little setup shown here also includes a printer for putting your thoughts on paper, and a modem for communicating with other computers over the phone lines.

Figure 1

The ABCs of Hardware.

System unit. Sometimes called the system or the machine, this is the PC itself (although without a keyboard and monitor you couldn't do anything with it). This is where the computer's brains are. Inside, you'll also find the hard disk—a small, sealed mechanical device that stores huge quantities of software and data, whether the PC is turned off or on (see Chapter 4: Disks, Hard and Otherwise).

Monitor. Also called the display or the screen, this device is what your system uses to show you what you're doing and what it's doing. A monitor is much like a TV without the ability to receive broadcasts, but the picture tube is of a much higher quality (see Chapter 5: Monitors, Etc.).

Printer. The printer makes paper copies of documents, called printouts or hard copies. Shown here is a laser printer, which produces documents using a technology similar to that of a photocopier (see Chapter 6: Printers).

CD-ROM drive. This device spins CD-ROMs, plastic discs that look just like regular audio CDs. Commercial software like Windows and Microsoft Office usually comes on CD-ROM.

Floppy disk drive. This device spins floppy disks, inexpensive little magnetic disks that you use to transport small quantities of data or to install software onto your hard disk. (Software occasionally comes on floppy disks instead of the usual CD-ROM.)

Keyboard. With a design similar to a typewriter, the keyboard enables you to type data into your PC and tell your software what to do (see "The Keyboard and the Mouse" later in this chapter).

Mouse. So called because of its small size and tail-like trailing wire, the mouse is used to point at parts of the screen and issue commands (instructions) to make software do your bidding. Move the mouse, and the mouse pointer moves in the same direction on the screen. An inexpensive mouse pad, which is just a piece of plastic over a foam backing, can make mouse operation smoother.

Making the Right Connections

Let's say everything is out of its box and sitting on the desk, waiting for you to put it all together. Your PC's manual will tell you how to hook things up, but seldom will you find everything explained step by step in one place, as you will here.

Don't be thrown by the fact that there are multiple names for everything—for example, the connectors on the back of your PC are also called ports. Note that connectors are either male or female—that is, they have either small pins or sockets to accommodate those pins.

To help you along, your PC may have small text labels, color-coded dots, and/or universal symbols alongside the ports on your PC—then again, it may not. And the placement of connectors varies from PC to PC, so you should check out the basic diagrams of connectors (coming up) to see which is which.

1. **Plug in the keyboard and mouse.** Most likely they will both have round *PS/2* plugs about a quarter-inch in diameter. If the matching ports on the back of the PC aren't clearly labeled or color coded, you may have to look in the manual to figure out which is which.

   Increasingly, keyboards and mice use USB (Universal Serial Bus) connectors, which are small boxy plugs that fit into matching rectangular ports on the back of the PC. A USB keyboard may have a port on it, in which case you can "daisy-chain" the mouse to the keyboard instead of plugging it into the back of the PC.

   Some keyboards use the old-style *AT* plug, which is about a half-inch in diameter; in that case, you'll have no trouble telling which port it fits into.

   Some mice have 9-pin plugs that fit the PC's serial port; some of those include an adapter cable to let the mouse fit a PS/2 port. Attach that and plug it in; otherwise, connect it to the serial port (there's normally only one that will fit).

2. **Hook up the monitor.** The monitor has two cables: an AC power cord and a video cable. The video cable is as thick (or thicker) than the power cord and ends in a 15-pin female connector known as a *D-sub,* so called because of its D-like shape that keeps you from plugging it in backwards. The 15-pin male video port will probably be located on the rear metal bracket of an *expansion card* (a circuit card that fits inside your PC to give it added capabilities). Connect the video cable using gentle pressure, and screw in the plug's thumbscrews; then plug the AC cord into the back of the monitor.

3. **Connect the speakers** and microphone (if any), which may be part of the monitor. Speaker setups vary, but usually you need to plug one speaker into the other (sometimes using two plugs, one for power and one for sound), and then plug the other speaker into the PC's speaker jack. The microphone jack is always close to the speaker jack, though there may be a similar jack in between the two. If it's not clear what goes where, or if your PC has more than one set of sound jacks, check the manual.
4. **Hook up the printer.** The printer has a thick cable that plugs into the PC's parallel port, with a male D-sub connector with holes for 25 pins (sometimes labeled LPT1 or PRN). If your printer didn't come with a cable, you'll have to buy it separately. If you don't have a favorite computer store, try Radio Shack. (As USB ports become more common, printer manufacturers may start switching to it. But as this book goes to press, parallel's still the unchallenged standard.)

Figure 2

Plugging it all together.

Every PC has most of the connectors shown in this rear view, although their locations vary from model to model.

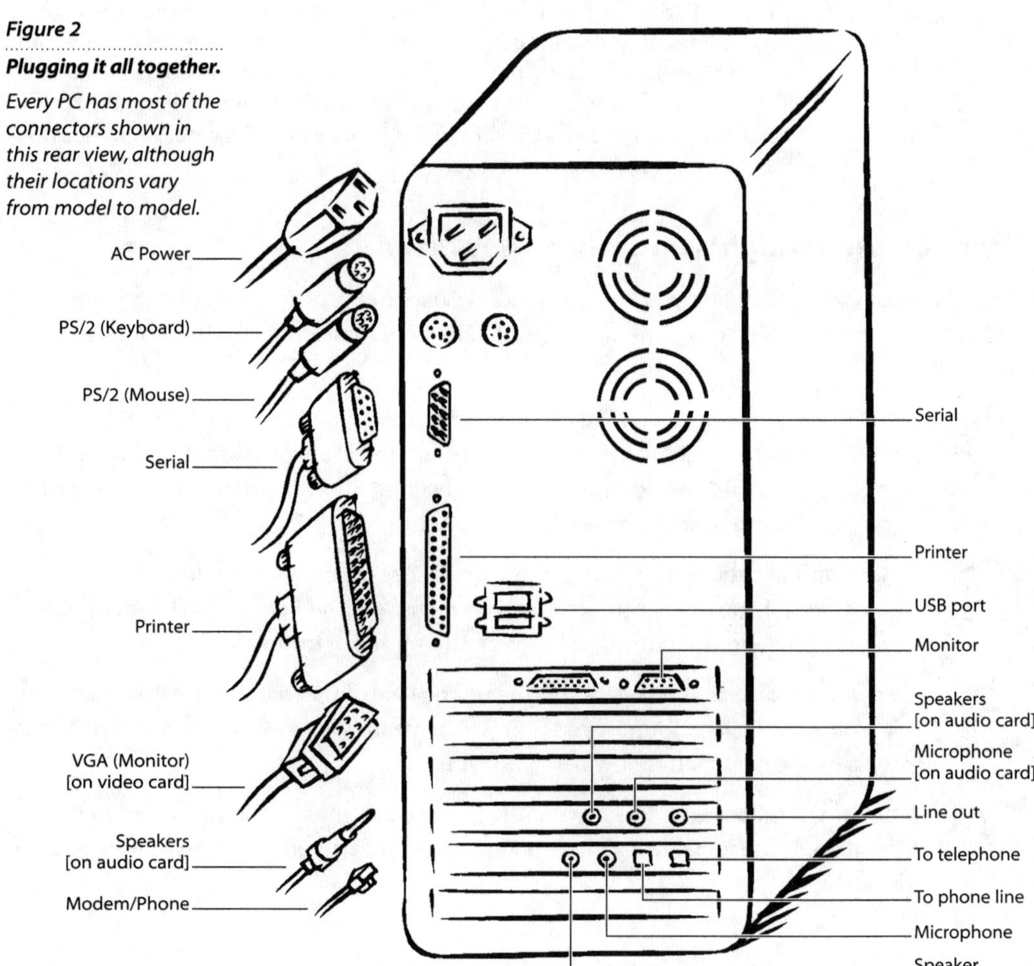

5. **Connect the modem to the phone line.** Assuming you've got a built-in modem (a standard feature in new PCs), connect the *line jack* on the back of the modem to the *phone jack* on the wall with the telephone cord (normally included). If you have a telephone or fax sharing the same line, plug it into the modem's phone jack. You may need to check the manual if all these jacks aren't labeled clearly. Some modems have only one jack that won't fit a phone cord; in that case, there should be a little plastic box with two phone jacks, which plugs into the modem. In the unlikely event that the modem wasn't installed at the factory and you have to install it, see Chapter 8: Upgrade It Yourself.
6. **Position the PC.** Now that the parts are all connected, you can place your PC in its work position. If you have a desktop or minitower PC, you can leave it on top of the desk. Or—if the keyboard, mouse, and monitor cables are long enough—place it underneath to save desk space. If you have a full-sized tower PC, keep your desktop free and find a home for the tower under your desk (see Chapter 2, Figure 5).
7. **Plug in the power cords.** Your PC and printer plug into a surge protector, outlet strip, or wall outlet. Your monitor may be designed to plug into the back of the PC; if so, the monitor will have a funny-looking plug with a sort of cuff around it that matches the equally funny-looking socket next to where the PC's power cord is attached. Otherwise, plug the monitor into the surge protector too.

Your PC's Status Lights and What They Mean

On the front of your system unit you'll see several small icons and/or lightsflthe exact number and type depend on the make and model of the PC. Here are some common icons and what they indicate:

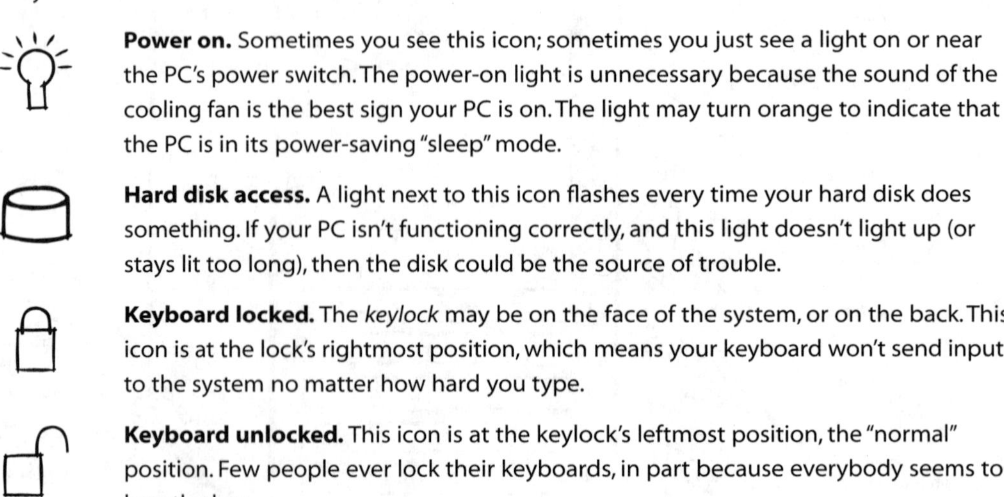

Power on. Sometimes you see this icon; sometimes you just see a light on or near the PC's power switch. The power-on light is unnecessary because the sound of the cooling fan is the best sign your PC is on. The light may turn orange to indicate that the PC is in its power-saving "sleep" mode.

Hard disk access. A light next to this icon flashes every time your hard disk does something. If your PC isn't functioning correctly, and this light doesn't light up (or stays lit too long), then the disk could be the source of trouble.

Keyboard locked. The *keylock* may be on the face of the system, or on the back. This icon is at the lock's rightmost position, which means your keyboard won't send input to the system no matter how hard you type.

Keyboard unlocked. This icon is at the keylock's leftmost position, the "normal" position. Few people ever lock their keyboards, in part because everybody seems to lose the key.

Flicking the Power Switch

Now it's time to *boot up*—computerese for starting your PC. Turn on the monitor first (the On button is usually in front under the screen). The screen won't light up until you turn on the PC, but its power light should turn to green right away and then switch to orange to show it's in power-saving mode. Next, look for the PC's power switch. On many models, it's a button or a switch on the front panel. On other PCs, it may be a switch at the rear of the chassis on the right side—or on the back of the machine, out of sight completely. If you have a printer, look for its power switch, too—but be aware that many inkjet and inexpensive laser printers don't have power switches at all. They turn themselves on when you print from an application, and off when you don't print anything for five minutes or so.

If you're using a power strip and nothing happens when you flip all the switches, ask yourself: Is the power strip turned on? If you hear something but see nothing, check your monitor's brightness and contrast controls, usually located below the screen or on the right side, to make sure they're not turned all the way down.

What's It Mumbling to Itself?

The term *booting* or *booting up* derives from "pulling oneself up by the bootstraps." Every time you turn on your PC, the system BIOS (basic input/output system)—a smidgen of software permanently stored on a chip inside the computer—checks the computer over. You don't have to do anything while the BIOS does its stuff, but you'll hear all sorts of sounds (whirs, beeps, clicks, grinds) and may see a fair quantity of incomprehensible gibberish scrolling quickly on the monitor. Here's what the typical PC is doing:

1. It checks to see if it has power.
2. It does a self-test of its components. Many PCs display messages on screen that explain what's being tested, so if anything fails, you know immediately. You may also hear a grinding noise from the floppy drive and a whirr from the CD-ROM drive as the PC checks them out.
3. It looks for an operating system in the floppy and/or CD-ROM drives (which may make some more noise). The operating system is the software that enables your PC to run. On a new PC, your operating system is almost certainly Windows 98, and the manufacturer has already loaded it on your hard drive. (See the beginning of Chapter 11: Windows 95, 98, and NT, for more on what an operating system does). If there's no disk in either drive—and, except in emergencies, there shouldn't be—the PC continues searching.

4. It looks for an operating system on the hard disk and most probably finds it there. Strictly speaking, booting is the process of loading the operating system into memory—that is, taking the operating system out of storage on disk and making it active. *Memory* (also called *random access memory* or *RAM*) is an array of chips into which the computer puts everything it's actively handling (programs and data). *Storage* refers to data and programs on disk that the computer isn't using for the moment. When the PC boots successfully, it beeps.

The point to remember here is the practical difference between memory and storage: When you turn off your PC, everything in RAM vaporizes, while everything stored on disk stays the same. Whatever you're working on as you compute is held in memory. So if you don't want that work to go to waste, you must copy it from memory to disk before you turn off your PC—a process called saving your work.

What You See After Your PC Boots Up

Your machine has finished booting. So what will you see on screen? That depends on what company made your PC, but in most cases you'll encounter some more-or-less self-explanatory messages. They'll ask you to enter the serial number from your Windows Certificate of Authenticity, select your time zone, and confirm the kind of printer you're using. (See the "How To Set Up Windows" section of Chapter 11 for more details on this routine.)

You may also get a sound test, modem test, mouse tutorial, and/or an opportunity to register your computer online. If, during the registration routine, the PC asks you any nosy personal questions (like your age, income, or fax number), you can just leave the answers blank and click the Next button. All this stuff should be self-explanatory. If it's not, check the manual, and if that doesn't set you straight call the company's 800 number.

If you don't see anything, your PC may be malfunctioning. Check to make sure all the cords are connected and everything's plugged in. If that's not the solution, call the manufacturer's technical support number, which should be on the "boxtopper" or in the manual.

Once you get to Windows, you'll find yourself looking at its *desktop*, which looks something like Figure 3.

Feel free to explore or run the offered tutorials, or turn to Chapter 11 for an in-depth look at your new operating system.

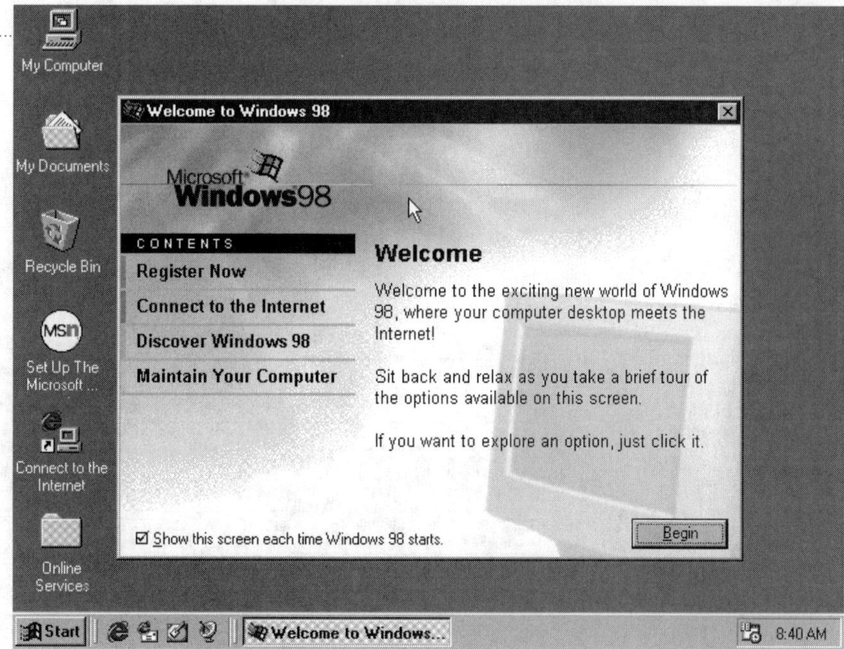

Figure 3

The Windows Desktop.

The Keyboard and the Mouse

To talk to your PC properly you need two input devices: the keyboard and the mouse. Here's a quick look at both these devices and a few hints on how to use them.

A Tour of the Keyboard

A computer keyboard has all the characters of a typewriter keyboard and then some—101 keys in all (see Figure 4). A few keyboards have nonstandard layouts, but the basic key placements are pretty much the same. Several keys have the same labels as typewriter keys but have slightly different functions. Some examples:

- Caps Lock works like the typewriter key—except that you only get capital *letters* when Caps Lock is on. The *number* keys are not affected by Caps Lock. To get the asterisk (*) on the 8 number key, for instance, you still have to press the Shift key. On most keyboards, a little light stays lit while Caps Lock is on.

- Tab jumps several spaces at a time, according to where you set the tabs, just as with a typewriter. In Windows, Tab moves you to the next choice in a dialog box, and Shift Tab moves to the previous one.
- Bksp goes backward one space at a time, as you'd expect,; but unlike a typewriter's backspace key, the PC version destroys everything in its path. Held down, it keeps deleting.

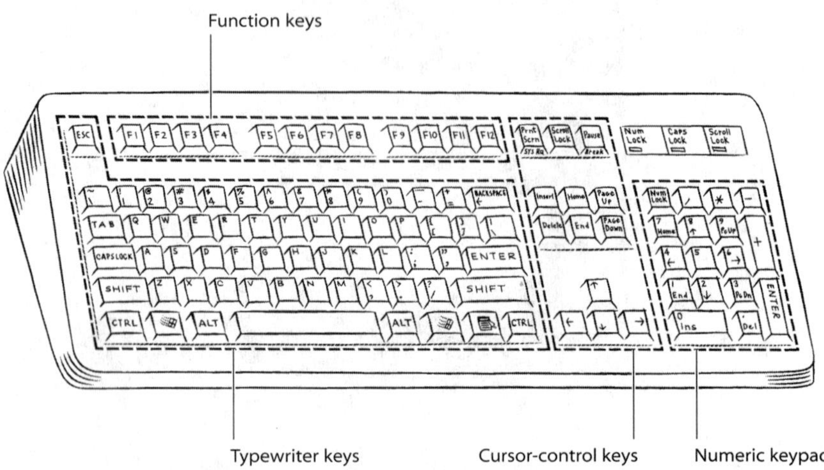

Figure 4

More than a typewriter.

The vast majority of PCs come with a keyboard that looks just like this, with 101 keys arranged in four basic groups.

The Four Most Important Computer Keys. Here are the four most important keys on a PC keyboard that you won't find on a typewriter:

- Enter starts a new paragraph by moving the cursor down one line. (You don't need to use it to start a new line in the middle of a paragraph, however; all applications wrap the lines automatically.) Enter also tells the computer that you've completed a command and that it's time to take action.
- Esc, the Escape key, is used in most applications to tell the computer, "Cancel that last command" or "Stop that right now!" or "Let's blow this joint." A very useful key.
- Ctrl, the Control key, is used in many programs as part of a command formed by pressing Ctrl and another key at the same time. For example, in Windows word-processing programs, pressing Ctrl I italicizes text.
- Alt, the Alternate key, activates the menu bar, so you can access menu commands using the computer's cursor-control keys instead of with the mouse. Alt is often used in combination with other keys to form commands, just as Ctrl is.

If your computer "freezes" or "hangs" when you're trying to make it do something, and it just won't unfreeze, simultaneously pressing Ctrl Alt Del will usually give you a chance to get out of it.

The Microsoft Advertisement on Your Keyboard

Many keyboards these days have three extra keys squeezed in at the right and left ends of the spacebar, between Ctrl and Alt. Basically, these are just free advertisements for Microsoft. The last thing PC keyboards needed was more keys, given that of the 101 already there, a dozen are rarely used. But if you've got them, you can use them.

The Windows keys. Pressing either of the Windows keys brings up the Start menu. (You can also do that by pressing Ctrl Esc.) In combination with other keys, the Windows key does other system-level functions. (See Chapter 11 for a list.)

The Application key. Pressing is like right-clicking with the mouse: It brings up the pop-up menu, if any, for the currently selected item. (You can do the same thing with Shift F10.) In some programs, the Application key it has other special functions.

Three Special Key Groups. There are three groups of PC keys that don't appear on typewriters:

- **Function keys.** Numbered F1 through F10, the function keys line the top edge of the keyboard. In some applications, pressing a function key issues a command specific to that program, such as "print this document" or "go back to the beginning of this line." However, in most situations, pressing F1 gets you help with what you're doing, in the form of instructions that pop onto the screen—which is why F1 is often called "the Help key."
- **Cursor keys.** The four "arrow keys," arranged in an upside-down T formation, move the cursor up, down, and sideways, as indicated by the arrows. In most Windows applications, Home takes you to the beginning of a line, and End takes you to the end of a line; holding down Ctrl while pressing Home or End takes you to the beginning or end of the document. Pg Dn advances you one screen's worth, and Pg Up goes backwards by the same amount. Ins toggles between overtyping characters and pushing them to the right as you insert other characters. Del erases the character after the cursor, or any highlighted item (such as a block of text).
- **Numeric keypad.** With the Num Lock key on, the numeric keypad is like the keyboard of a 10-key adding machine, enabling you to enter numbers and mathematical signs (into a spreadsheet, for instance). The +, -, and = signs have standard roles; the asterisk (*) is the multiplier, and the slash (/) indicates division. With Num Lock off, the numeric keypad becomes an alternate cursor control pad—that is, it duplicates the functions of the cursor control keys, but in a different layout that some users find more comfortable.

Three Keys You May Never Use

Typically, three other keys reside above the cursor pad:

- Prt Sc copies a picture of whatever is on your screen into the Windows Clipboard, from which the image can then be pasted into another document (go to Chapter 11: Windows 95, 98, and NT, to see what this is all about). Alt Prt Sc copies only the front window if you have multiple windows displayed. "SysRq," which is usually printed on the Prt Sc key in a different color, is short for "System Request." It's a holdover from mainframe terminal days. Ignore it.
- Scroll Lock changes the way the cursor keys work in some programs. You'll probably never need it.
- Pause normally has no function in Windows, but you can use it before Windows loads—for example, if during startup something scrolls by too fast for you to read it. Press Pause to pause, and Enter to make it go again. "Break" also appears on the Pause key; accessed by pressing Ctrl Pause, it's a holdover from the old days, when it served as a kind of emergency brake, enabling you to stop what DOS was doing and return to the DOS prompt. ("Break" was never used much, since Ctrl C, which you can press with one hand, does the same thing.)

Using a Mouse

You use the mouse to execute commands, to jump around in documents, highlight blocks of text, and what have you. As you roll the mouse on your desk, an arrow-shaped pointer moves on screen in the same direction your hand moves. The leading end of the mouse device is divided into two (or in some cases three) buttons, but the left-hand button is the one you'll use most by far. (If you're left-handed, see Chapter 7 to learn how to swap the primary button).

If you don't press any buttons, the pointer just floats on top of the application displayed on the screen. Press a button, and things happen (see Figure 5). All applications use roughly the same vocabulary to describe mouse actions:

- **Click** means to press the leftmouse button once. Depending on where the pointer is, clicking may execute a command, cancel a command, or move you to a different location in a document. Often, to perform a specific action, you click on an item listed on a menu (a list of commands).
- **Double-click** means to click something with the left mouse button twice in very quick succession. Depending on what's beneath the pointer, double-clicking may start an application, execute a command, or call up a menu.

Many people have difficulty double-clicking at first, because they don't click fast enough. When working with text, double-clicking selects a whole word; in some programs, triple-clicking selects a whole paragraph.

- **Right-click** means to press the right mouse button once. In most applications, right-clicking brings up a menu of commands relating to whatever you clicked on.
- **Click and drag** means to hold down the left mouse button and move the pointer at the same time. You can click and drag to highlight text or graphics as if you were using a highlighter pen (usually in preparation for another action, such as deleting).
- **Drag and drop** is a variation on click and drag: You click something and hold down the button while you move mouse, and then release the button to drop whatever you clicked somewhere else. You can drop a file icon on an application's title bar to open it, or onto a printer icon to print it, or you can delete something by dropping it into the Recycle Bin. In some applications, you can also drag text or graphics out of one position and drop them in another.

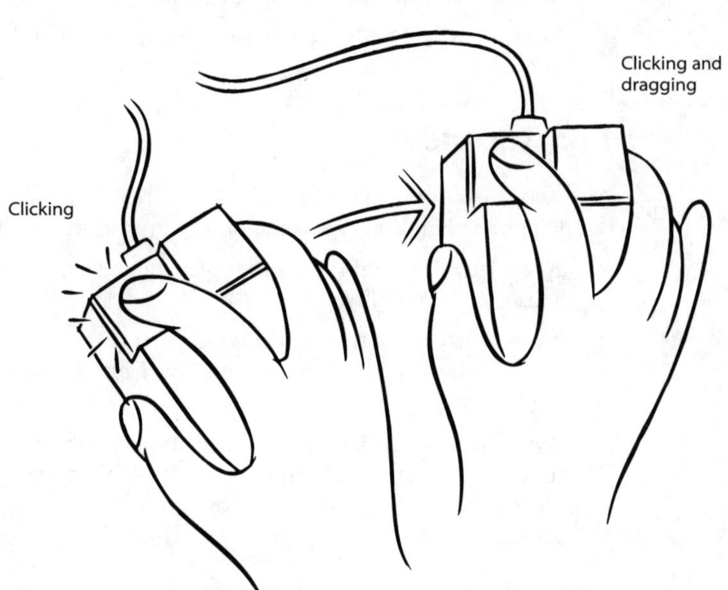

Figure 5

Mouse moves.

Click the left mouse button to select an object or perform an action. Click and drag to select text or move graphics or text.

CD-ROMs and Floppies

Your PC should have a CD-ROM drive and a floppy drive (see Figure 6 and Figure 7). Either drive can be used to install more software (like a new word processor or game) on your computer, although most stuff these days comes on CD. Usually you only need the CD or floppy the first time you run the program, but in some cases—particularly with games and reference CDs—you may need to insert the disk every time you use it.

Floppies (also called *diskettes*) are also a handy way to transport data from one computer to another. If you don't have a modem or if you're not hooked up to a network, floppies are far and away the most convenient way to get data on and off your computer.

Here are a few tips to keep the data on your disks safe:

For both floppies and CD-ROMs:

- **Avoid temperature extremes.** No dashboards or windowsills in summer, no car trunks in the dead of a Minnesota winter.
- **Don't lube.** Don't spray lubricants (such as WD-40) into your drives, no matter what horrible noises they make.
- **Don't crush.** Don't place heavy objects on top of disks—this can scratch the surface.

For floppies:

- **Avoid magnets.** This includes not only refrigerator magnets, but also telephone handsets, speakers, or anything with an electric motor.
- **Keep 'em dry.** Liquids and floppies don't mix. If you spill your drink on a disk, kiss it goodbye.
- **Never pull back the metal cover** that protects the disk itself. The cover keeps dust out and prevents you from damaging the disk by touching its surface.
- **Avoid working directly on data that's on floppies,** beyond what's necessary. It's faster, easier, and quieter (and causes less wear and tear on both drive and diskette) to copy files to the hard disk and work on them there.

For CD-ROMs:

- **Handle the discs only with clean hands,** and then only by the edges. Fingerprints on the surface of the disc can cause read errors—i.e., the disc won't work.
- **Don't leave CD-ROMs lying around** unprotected. Always return them to their protective cases.

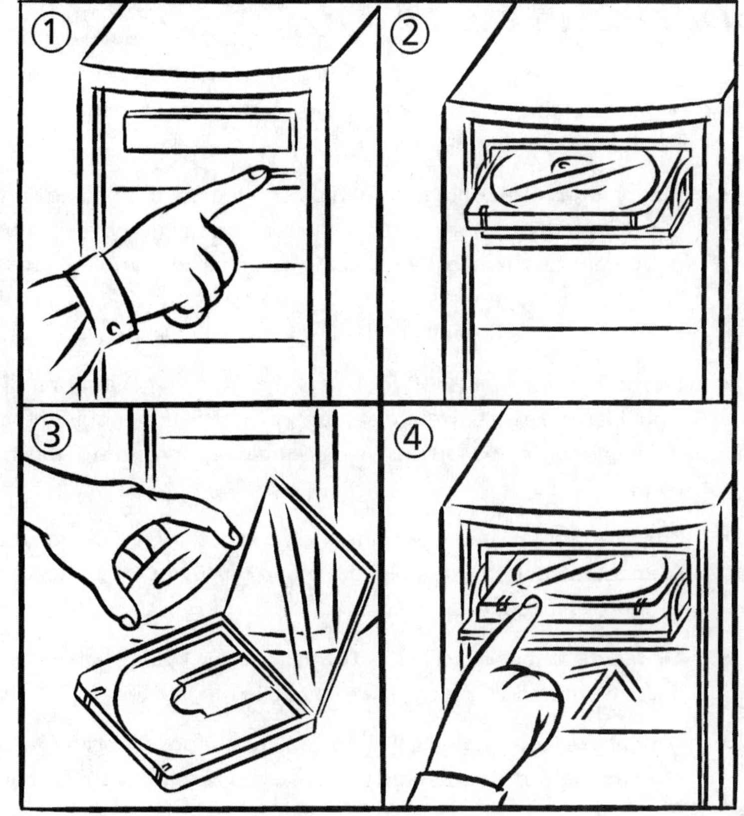

Figure 6

Using a CD-ROM drive.

When you need to insert a CD, first put away any CD that's already in the drive. (1) Press the button on the front of the drive to make the tray pop out or the caddy eject. (2) Remove the old disc and store it in its protective sleeve. (3) Take the new disc out of its protective sleeve and place it in the tray or caddy. (4) Gently press on the tray or caddy (or its button) until the drive activates and sucks in the disc.

Figure 7

Using a 3.5-inch floppy drive.

To insert a 3.5-inch floppy, slip the shiny metal edge into the drive first, with the hub side of the disk down. To remove the disk, push the button on the drive. Always wait until the drive light goes out before removing a diskette!

Bits and Bytes Defined!

Everyone tosses around *bits, bytes, binary,* and related terms without knowing their true meanings. Remember these definitions, and you can amaze your friends—and maybe get a little better of an idea how computers work:

- **Binary logic.** Most of us automatically do our "math thinking" in the decimal system, which is based on the number 10 (based, in turn, on the number of fingers our species can count on). Computers use a *binary* system, which makes complete sense for an electronic brain: The two binary numbers are 0 and 1, representing "off" and "on." Counting in binary goes like this: 0, 1, 10, 11, 100, 101, 110, 111, 1000, 1001, and so forth.

- **Bits and bytes.** A *bit* (short for binary digit) is the smallest unit of computer information. Eight bits make one *byte*, the amount of information required to store a single letter or number in plain text format. We measure memory and storage in bytes or multiples of bytes.

- **Kilobyte** (abbreviated K) sounds like it ought to be 1000 bytes, but it's actually 1024 bytes. From there on up, all multiples are based on 1024. One K equals approximately half a page of double-spaced text.

- **Megabyte** (abbreviated MB) is 1024K or about 1.05 million bytes (1,048,576, to be exact). Your PC's memory capacity is expressed in megabytes.

- A **gigabyte** (abbreviated GB) is 1024MB or about 1.07 billion bytes (1,073,741,824) of hard-disk storage The biggest hard disks you can buy today store about 20GB of data.

Data, incidentally, is a slippery term. To your computer, data is simply anything that takes up bytes, including software. From your perspective, data means information you've created or want to changeflas opposed to software, the tool you use to create or alter information.

Application Basics

Some programs will be ready to use the first time you turn your computer on—if you don't see their icons on the desktop, you can find them by browsing the choices on Windows' Start menu. For example, you'll probably find WordPad (a limited but functional word processor) and Paint (a simple graphics program) in the Accessories submenu. Depending on where you bought the PC and what options you ordered, you may find other programs like Microsoft Office or Quicken. (For instructions on adding more programs to the menu, see Chapter 11: Windows 95, 98, and NT.) Once you've found or installed a useful application, you're ready to do something meaningful with your new PC.

Almost everything you create on a computer will be called a *file*. Files are the basic units that hold data of any sort. A file can be a five-word note to your neighbor or a gigantic collection of information about your business's customers. There are two general types of files:

- **Program files** contain all or part of a program or application (applications are usually big programs made up of many program files).
- **Data files** contain information you've created or want to manipulate, rather than software. A customer file, your latest novel, and a spreadsheet full of meaningless projections are all data files.

Each file should have a unique, descriptive name. (Windows imposes a few restrictions on how you can name files—for example, you can't use colons or question marks. See Chapter 11 for a more detailed discussion.)

Opening, Storing, and Abandoning Files

On a very basic level, every application handles files in the same way, using the File menu located in the upper-left corner of the application's window. (You click on the word File with your mouse to display the menu.) Learn your way around this File menu, and you can immediately begin work in any application. Here's what the commands on the File menu do::

- **New** starts a new file, whether a word processing document, a blank spreadsheet, or an empty database. This is your blank slate. Do what you will. Sometimes before the new file appears you'll get a choice of *templates*, which are various preformatted files for various purposes. If you can't find the template that's appropriate for what you're doing, there's usually a generic template you can use, like the Word application's Blank Document.
- **Open** loads an existing file. That is, you pick a file by name from a list, and the application copies the file from storage (the hard or floppy disk) into memory, your computer's work area.
- **Save** copies a new file (or an existing file that you've changed) from memory to the hard disk for safekeeping. If you've created a new file, you give it a name when you save for the first time.
- **Save As** lets you make a second copy of the open file, only you must give it a different name (or store it in a different location).
- **Print** lets you send all or part of your file to the printer.
- **Close** abandons a new file or any changes you've made to an existing file. Use this option instead of Save when you've messed up an existing file and want to restore the file to its original condition.
- **Exit** gets you out of the application. Remember to save your changes before you exit.

Remember that you must save an open file before you exit your application or turn off your PC, or you lose any changes you've made. Save your work every few minutes—someday, that portable heater will trip the circuit breaker, or the computer may freeze up for no reason at all. Experienced PC users get into the habit of saving their work every 10–15 minutes, or they use automatic options that save the current file at regular intervals.

Data Safety Tip #1

A hard disk acts as an electronic filing cabinet, storing data and keeping it safe and sound even when you turn off your PC... that is, it *usually* keeps your data safe. Hard disks have moving parts that wear out. Computer viruses can do terrible mischief. And sometimes, lightning really does strike. The only way to keep your data totally safe is to create a copy of it—called a *backup*—and store it in a safe place. Before you get very far in your computing career, turn to Chapter 9: Protect Your Data, and learn how to develop your own daily backup program. Someday, guaranteed, you will need that backup copy.

Bye for Now (Shutting Down)

When you're done working, don't just switch off the computer. (Life should be simpler than this.) Here's your basic shutdown procedure:

1. **Save your work.** The file you're messing with is in memory while you're working on it, and as you know by now, anything in memory disappears when you turn off your PC. If you don't save the file before you shut down, you'll lose any changes you made, back to the point when you last saved the file.
2. **Choose Shut Down from the Start menu**, select the option to shut down the computer, and click Yes. This will automatically close any applications you have open, and you'll be asked if you want to save any documents you've modified but didn't save. Depending what model of PC you have, you'll either get a message on screen telling you it's okay to turn off the power, or the computer will simply shut itself off, in which case the screen will go blank.

3. **Turn off your monitor, too.** This step isn't necessary if the monitor is plugged into the back of the PC, or if you use the power switch on an outlet strip shared by the PC and monitor.

Your computing session is now officially over. Easy, right?

If you don't agree with that sentiment, remember that making mistakes is one of the most popular computing activities, and no one has ever damaged the hardware by pressing the wrong key. True, you can completely destroy your data, but if you're a beginner, destroying the small quantity of data you've accumulated probably won't be too tragic. If, on the other hand, your PC didn't work properly—say, it wouldn't boot, it froze up, or it stubbornly refused to cooperate in some other way—then you should call your PC manufacturer's technical support line immediately.

If you have all the hardware you think you'll need, and it seems to work all right, then the next logical step in completing your basic training is to turn to Chapter 11: Windows 95, 98, and NT, where you'll learn the ins and outs of your most basic and essential software. Continue with chapters 12 through 18 to learn about word processors, spreadsheets, and other key applications, or turn to Chapter 19: Getting on the Internet, to get yourself online. This book is intended to be browsed rather than studied, so kick back, skim a few pages, and see what happens.

Don't Try This at Home (or at Work)

Nothing's worse than damaging equipment because you broke some dumb rule about basic system care that you didn't even know about. So here are the rules. Now you don't have an excuse.

- Don't place any piece of hardware in direct sunlight.
- Don't leave anything on the vents atop your monitor. Without circulating air, your monitor's innards won't last as long (confine your rubber alligator to an unvented section.)
- Don't place your PC so that its back is less than two inches from a wall, because your PC needs air circulation, too.
- Don't turn on your PC if it's too cold in the room. Warm the room to a comfortable temperature before flipping the switch, so any water vapor condensed inside the chassis can evaporate.
- Don't place open containers of liquid (or frozen yogurt bars) on top of or even very near to any of your equipment. Liquid, especially sugary stuff, can severely damage hardware.
- Don't use an extension cord if you can avoid it. Disastrous disconnections may result.
- Do use a power strip—device with a row of AC outlets—preferably one with surge suppression, which dampens potentially damaging fluctuations in electric power (see Chapter 9: Protect Your Data). Plug into a power strip, and you can leave your PC, monitor, and printer switches turned on and instead control everything with the flick of a single switch. Remember to plug the power strip into a three-prong, grounded outlet to guard against problems caused by static electricity and the remote hazard of electric shock.

Resources for PC Beginners

- ***PCs for Dummies***, Dan Gookin (5th ed., 1998: ISBN: 0789716887). We'd like to think *The PC Bible, 3E* will give beginning PC users all the help they need, but if you want more help with the basics, get yourself a copy of Gookin's book. We hate to plug other publishers' books, but Dan Gookin—who in 1992 wrote the first in the now seemingly infinite line of *Dummies* books—is the best. Luckily for us, most of the other *Dummies* books aren't nearly as good as Gookin's, and you'd have to buy a dozen of them to cover half the topics we get into in *The PC Bible*.
- ***How Computers Work***, Ron White (ISBN: 1562765469). This unique volume uses scores of detailed illustrations to show visually how the stuff inside your computer works. There's nothing in it you *need* to know, but if you're curious and if verbal explanations leave you puzzled, this book's for you.

2

How to Buy a PC

by Robert Lauriston

In This Chapter

This is, by far, the easiest time in history to buy a new PC. The computer industry's ongoing trend toward ever-faster, ever-cheaper hardware has reached the point where even the cheapest systems from most manufacturers are overkill for the average person.

If you run only mainstream applications like Microsoft Office, Netscape Navigator, Quicken, or their counterparts, there's really no reason to pay more than around $800 for a basic PC. (That price includes the modem, keyboard, and mouse, but not the monitor and printer.) Granted, such low-end models won't generate very impressive numbers on the benchmark programs computer magazines use to compare systems, but in day-to-day use you'll seldom notice any difference between a basic machine and a high-end system costing five times as much.

Of course, such inexpensive systems aren't the best deal for everyone. If you plan to use software that will make heavy demands on your PC's hardware, like action games, Photoshop, AutoCAD, or Visual C++, it may be worth your while to spend more. If a faster computer will speed up your work substantially, it might not take long to recover the cost of a top-of-the-line workstation costing $5,000 or more.

In this chapter I'll tell you how to figure out what you need, and how to get the best deal. First I'll give a quick overview of what to look for in a basic PC. We'll go through the laundry list item by item (CPU, memory, hard disk, etc.), discussing what each component does and when it's worth spending extra for more speed or higher capacity. Then we'll take a look at some of the accessories and options you might want to buy along with your PC, either for convenience or to take advantage of special bundle prices.

The Basic PC

In past years, it often made sense to buy more PC than your immediate needs required, on the theory that you'd save money in the long run by not having to upgrade as soon. But that doesn't make much sense any more. The most expensive systems used to be three to five times as fast as the cheapest models, and were priced accordingly. Today's top-of-the-line PCs, however, are only around twice as fast as entry-level models—not enough to justify their much higher prices. Moreover, there's nothing on the horizon that seems likely to make current PCs obsolete any time soon. Microsoft and other companies have ideas about futuristic interfaces where running your computer will be more like talking with an assistant than operating a machine, but that stuff is still years off—and when such sophistication does arrive, there's a good chance that *none* of today's PCs will have the horsepower to handle it.

Thus, unless you've got special needs (discussed later in the chapter), there's no compelling reason to spend more than $800 on a PC (not including the monitor and printer). But watch out—although many inexpensive PCs have everything you need, manufacturers occasionally cut corners by leaving out important items or using obsolete components. Here's a quick rundown on the minimum you should get for that money. (See Figure 1 to get an idea of where these things are and what they look like, and check out this book's Web page at **www.peachpit.com/pcbible** for updates.)

- CPU: 300MHz or faster
- L2 (secondary) cache: at least 512K (kilobytes)
- RAM (memory): at least 32MB (megabytes)
- hard disk: 2GB UDMA (aka "Ultra-ATA" or "Ultra IDE")
- CD-ROM (or DVD-ROM) drive
- video card: at least 2MB memory
- modem: "56K" that supports V.90 standard
- slots and bays: sufficient for future expansion
- mouse
- Windows 98
- one-year warranty on parts and labor

If you're new to computers or don't want to be bothered with technical details, most of this list is probably incomprehensible". Let's take a close look at each of the items in turn, and I'll explain what each one does and what the numbers mean.

CPU

The CPU (Central Processor Unit) chip is your computer's brain. All CPUs in today's PCs are basically interchangeable, in the sense that they can all run the same software. The only significant difference is that some are faster than others.

Almost everything your PC does involves the CPU in one way or another, which means that a faster CPU will speed up everything else. Whether you'll notice that difference is another matter. I recently upgraded from a 100MHz Pentium to a 200MHz K6, and about the only difference I've noticed in my everyday work is that sorting the Filemaker database I use for my business accounts now takes two seconds instead of four.

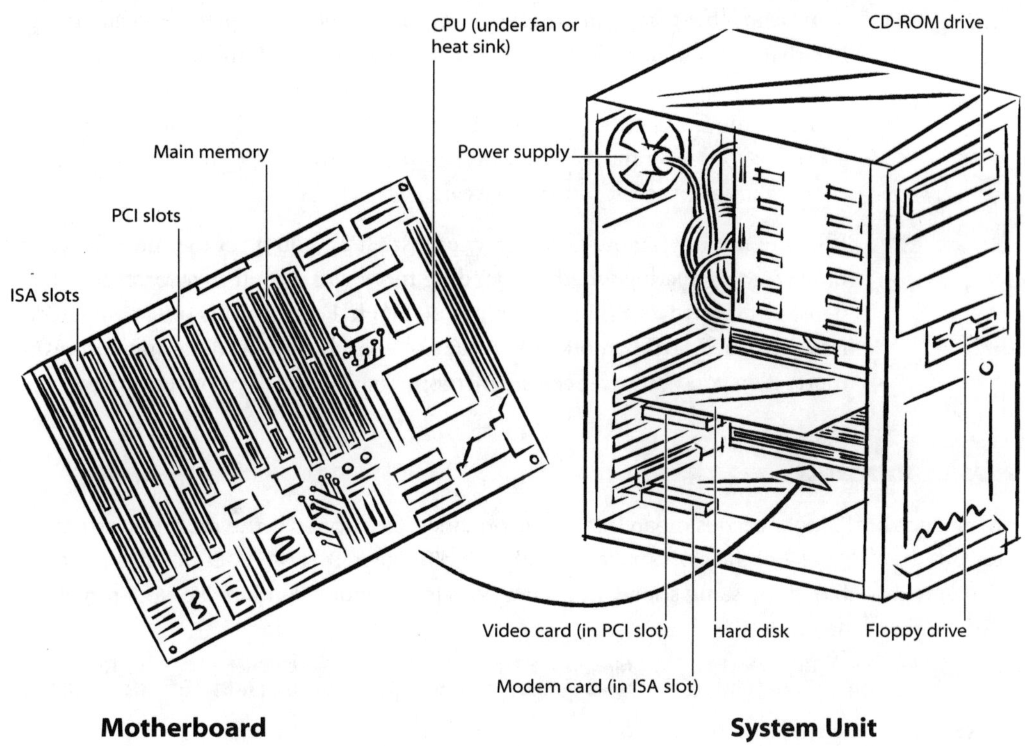

Figure 1

Your PC and its motherboard.

Welcome to the inside of a typical PC. Choose components wisely, and you'll get more performance and capacity for your buck.

The primary indicator of CPU performance is its *clock speed,* which is roughly equivalent to the revolutions per minute (rpm) of a car's engine. A K6 running at 300MHz is roughly 50% faster than one running at 200MHz; a Pentium II running at 300MHz has about 75% the horsepower of one running at 400MHz. But when comparing *different* chips, like a 300MHz K6 and a Pentium II, that have the *same* clock speed, it's not so easy to generalize—relative performance usually depends on what software you're running.

CPU prices vary more than any other PC component, which makes it easy to waste money by choosing the wrong one. For example, the day I wrote this paragraph, AMD's 200MHz K6 chip was going for $60, while Intel's 400MHz Pentium II cost around $700. It sounds kind of crazy to spend ten times as much for a chip that's only twice as fast, but for some people it makes sense. Programmers compiling large applications, engineers working on complicated blueprints, and graphic artists creating realistic 3-D objects often execute commands that take many minutes or even hours to complete. In a situation like that, $600 spent on a faster CPU may be recovered quickly through improved productivity. In fact, it may even make sense to get a system with two or more CPUs (though only if you run Windows NT). But those people are exceptions—on most PCs, action games are the only software that will ever make the processor break a sweat.

If you're not buying the fastest or cheapest CPU, you'll get the most for your money by calculating whether spending more will pay off in a corresponding boost in performance. For example, a 300MHz Pentium II is only about 13% faster than a 266MHz model (300 / 266 = 1.13). If the 300MHz unit costs 10% more, it's a good buy; if it costs 20% more, the 266 is more cost-effective.

CPUs Compared

Faster speeds and bigger caches mean better performance. CPU speed is the most important factor, but the L1 and L2 cache sizes make enough of a difference that an AMD will often outperform an Intel chip of the same speed. The same goes for a regular Pentium II or Celeron vs. one of the no-cache models.

	CPU "clock" Speed (MHz)	Memory "bus" Speed (MHz)	L1 Cache Size (KB)	L2 Cache Size (KB)	L2 Cache Speed (MHz)
AMD K6	166 to 300	66	64	External	66
AMD K6-2	266 to 400	100	64	External	100
AMD K6-3	TBA	100	64	TBA	100
Cyrix 6x86MX	120 to 300	66 to 83	64	External	Same as memory
Cyrix M II	300 and up	66 to 75	64	External	Same as memory
Intel Pentium MMX	166 to 233*	66	32	External	66
Intel Pentium II	233 to 333	66	32	512	Half CPU speed
Intel Pentium II	350 to 600	100	32	512	Half CPU speed
Intel Celeron	266 to 300**	66	32	None	n/a
Intel Celeron	300** and up	66	32	128	Same as CPU
Intel Xeon	400 and up	100	32	512 to 2MB	Same as CPU

*"Mobile" version used only in notebook PCs goes up to 266MHz.
**The Celeron "300A" has a 128K integrated L2 cache, the "300" model does not.

L2 Cache

The L2 (secondary) cache is a small amount of very fast, very expensive memory that sits in between your computer's CPU and its main memory (RAM), playing some rather clever tricks that improve performance significantly. Currently, buying a PC without an L2 cache is a waste of money—you'd be better off knocking the CPU speed down a notch and using the savings to pay for a cache. (Don't be confused by ads that refer to "primary" or L1 cache. That's a small amount of ultrafast memory built into every CPU.) A new technology called Direct Rambus may eventually eliminate the need for L2 cache, but it will probably take a few years to filter down from high-end servers to average desktops.

That's all you really need to know about L2 cache size to help you decide on the right PC. Read on for the technical details, or skip ahead to avoid them.

The L2 helps compensate for the difference between the enormous speed with which CPUs can process information, and the RAM's somewhat slower rate of sending and receiving that information. For example, my PC's 200MHz K6 CPU can chew through almost 800MB of data in a second, but the RAM chips that feed the CPU that data can process only a little over 100MB a second.

The L2 helps bridge that gap by taking advantage of the CPU's tendency to read the same data over and over again. Every time the CPU gets a chunk of data from memory, the L2 makes a copy. Then, if the CPU fetches that same chunk of information again, the L2 sends the copy. Since the L2 cache is faster than RAM, the CPU doesn't have to wait as long, so it can finish whatever task it's working on that much sooner (see Figure 2). On my PC, the L2 can feed data to the CPU at over 200MB per second—twice the speed of RAM alone. (Since the L2's storage is limited, it constantly has to throw out old copies to make room for new data. However, every time the CPU calls for a particular copy, the L2 puts it back on top of the stack; so as long as the CPU keeps accessing it frequently, that copy will be in the L2.)

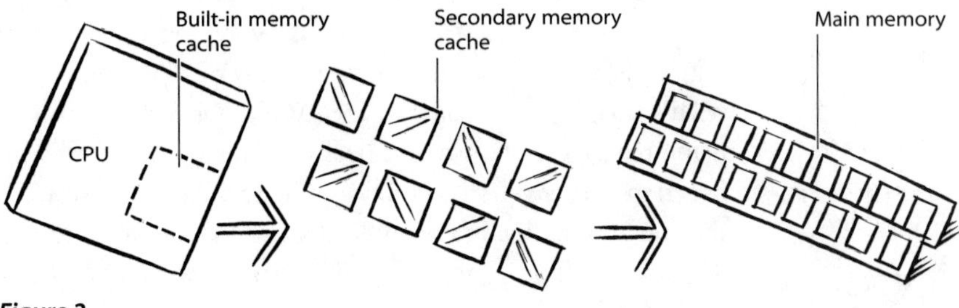

Figure 2

Why you need cache memory.

Main memory is too slow for the CPU to access quickly so most CPUs have their own fast, on-chip memory cache. If the CPU can't find what it needs in that cache, it turns to the secondary cache before resorting to main memory. A larger secondary cache can yield better performance.

The faster the CPU, the larger the cache required to get this effect. PCs with 486 CPUs typically had 64K of L2, older Pentiums usually had 256K, and current models generally have 512K, though high-end workstations may have 1MB or more. Pentium II and Xeon CPUs (like the obsolete Pentium Pro) come in a sealed cartridge containing both the CPU and its L2 cache; with other CPUs, the cache chip(s) are on the motherboard.

The effects of L2 cache size and speed vary wildly from one application to another. Programs and processes that are small enough to fit entirely within the cache may run more than twice as fast as they would with no cache. (This category includes most CPU benchmark utilities, which explains why benchmark scores don't map very closely to real-world performance.) On the other hand, with operations that pump large amounts of data through the CPU (like many database operations), the L2 cache may actually cause a minor slowdown. The common generalization that an L2 cache will give an overall performance boost of around 15% is a simplification of this complicated situation.

Memory

When you're choosing a PC, memory (RAM) is one of the simpler decisions. You definitely want at least 32MB for running Windows 98—otherwise, your PC may feel sluggish. If you plan to run Windows NT, get at least 64MB. If you're running a memory-hungry app like Photoshop, you may need more, but you can always add it later.

Memory comes in little strips called DIMMs that plug into sockets on your PC's motherboard; usually you can install up to three. It's a good idea to insist that all of your memory be on *one* DIMM. That will give you more flexibility if and when you upgrade. Although there are lots of different kinds of DIMMs on the market, you don't need to worry about that when buying a new PC. (See Chapter 8: Upgrade It Yourself, for more about variations in memory chips.)

Why does more memory make your PC run faster? Well, it doesn't, precisely—it just makes the PC less likely to slow down. When you load more applications and documents than will fit in memory, Windows doesn't make you stop working; it just offloads some of the contents of RAM onto your hard disk, into what's called *virtual memory*. Since Windows offloads stuff that isn't currently being used, you often won't be aware this has happened until you switch to a program you haven't used for a while and have to wait for a few seconds while the app and its documents are reloaded from disk. The more RAM you have, the more stuff you can load before virtual memory kicks in.

In an emergency, you can also use virtual memory to run tasks that require more RAM than you have installed in your system, but performance in this mode is dreadful. A command that normally takes an imperceptible fraction of a second to execute in RAM can easily take ten seconds or more if the application is using virtual memory.

Hard Disk

Choosing a hard disk is another easy task for most PC buyers. The smallest drives currently being produced can hold so much data that you'd have trouble filling one up. A 4GB (gigabyte) drive, for example, could hold 30 copies of this book in its native Quark XPress format. What's more, almost all of that space would be taken up by graphics. If you stripped them out and saved this book as plain text, you could store more than 2000 copies on that 4-gig drive.

Getting enough speed isn't a big issue for average users, either. These days, even entry-level drives are extremely fast: Just be sure you get a UDMA (aka Ultra-ATA or Ultra-IDE) model. Figure 3 shows you how far I am from filling my own hard drive.

Please verify label placement

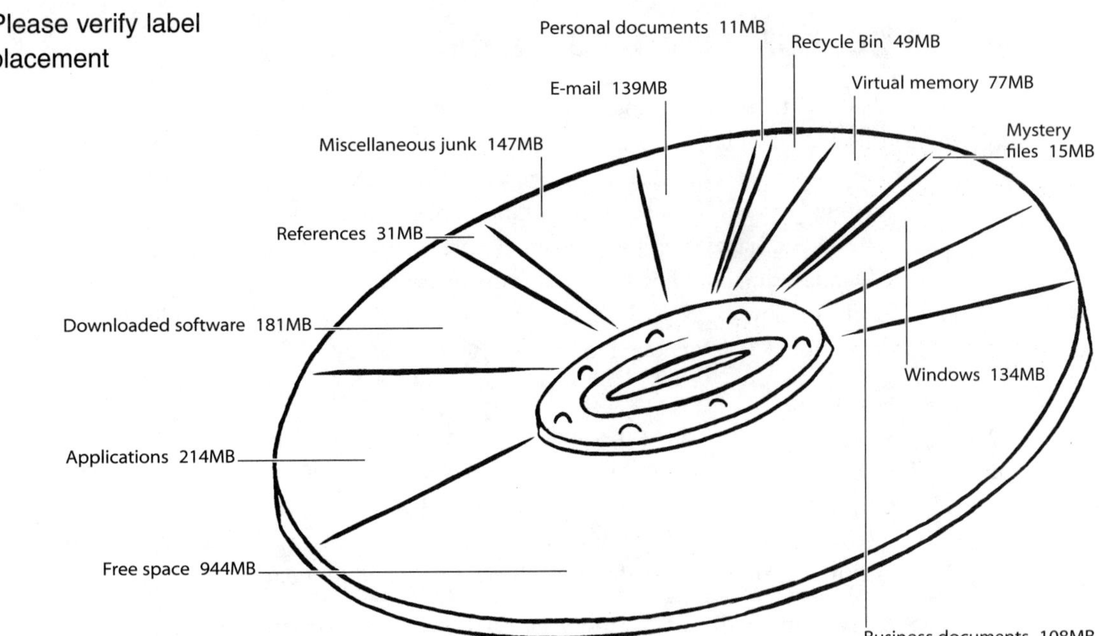

Figure 3

Hard Drive Usage Map.

It's not easy to fill a multigigabyte hard drive. I've been accumulating documents, e-mail, and applications for more than ten years, and despite being pretty lax about cleaning out old junk, I'm nowhere close to filling up my 2GB hard drive.

If you do lots of jobs involving very large files, like generating magazine covers in Photoshop, or very many small ones, like creating large Web sites, you will eventually fill up even the biggest drive. In that case, however, before spending money on a larger hard disk, you'll do better to buy an inexpensive high-capacity removable drive like a SparQ or Jaz. That will allow you to offload an unlimited amount of data from your hard disk but retrieve it quickly if you need to revise something or use it in a new project. See Chapter 4: Disks, Hard and Otherwise, for a look at the pros and cons of various removables.

Two things that really demand larger hard drives are digital audio and video. One CD's worth of music can take up two-thirds of a gigabyte, and for many projects you might find you need three or four times that as workspace. Video is even more of a disk hog: For high-quality results, dumping a videotape to your hard disk may require from 150MB to 600MB per minute.

Depending on what format you use, a gigabyte may hold from five minutes to half an hour of digitized video. See "When To Spend More on a PC" later in the chapter for advice on what to look for in a PC for that kind of work. Chapter 18: Sound and Video Editing, offers more on the topic.

CD-ROM / DVD-ROM Drive

I have yet to hear a convincing argument for spending extra to get a CD-ROM drive with a higher "X" speed rating(32X, 40X, etc.). For most tasks, like looking things up in a CD encyclopedia or loading the next scene in a computer game, the improvement in speed is pretty much obscured by the wait for the drive to spin up and start pumping out data. A faster drive will install applications from CD in less time, but how much time do you spend doing that, anyway? You may need a minimum "X" rating to run certain games, but any new PC's CD-ROM drive should be fast enough to run any game currently on the market.

One thing that *is* worth a little extra money is a multi-disc changer. These let you load three or more CDs and switch between them without having to keep swapping discs in and out of the machine. As with audio CD players, you can only access one disc at a time. Note that CD-R and CD-RW drives (discussed in Chapter 4: Disks, Hard and Otherwise) can also play CD-ROMs, so if you plan to buy one of these drives, a changer may be redundant.

A DVD-ROM drive is basically a CD-ROM drive that can also play DVD videos. A DVD drive can also play DVD-ROM data discs, but as this book goes to press there are still only a handful on the market, even though the drives have been around for more than a year—so there's not much reason to buy one. See the *PC Bible* Web site at **`www.peachpit.com/pcbible`** for updated recommendations on DVD.

Video Card

Here's another component where even entry-level models are overkill for average users. If you're not doing professional graphics work or playing action games, even the cheapest video card currently on the market will be so fast you'll never know the difference.

The main spec to watch out for is the amount of memory on the card. That determines how large a desktop you'll be able to use without compromising color quality. Generally, you want at least 2MB with a 15-inch monitor, at least 4MB with a 17- or 19-inch, and 8MB for anything larger. Personally, given the modest price difference, I recommend getting 8MB, and then you'll be set if you ever upgrade your monitor. (See Chapter 5: Monitors, Etc., for more detail on this stuff.)

When shopping for a PC, you may see both PCI and AGP boards in various models' spec lists. PCI is the current standard high-speed expansion slot—most PCs have at least three. AGP is a special slot, just for video cards, that's found mostly in Pentium II systems. Intel, which invented AGP, claims it will allow higher performance, but tests have found no significant difference between PCI and AGP cards currently on the market. (That may change in the future, as faster versions of AGP are in the works.)

Another video card enhancement is 3-D acceleration: There's no reason to pay extra for it unless you're going to play action games that require or benefit from it. See the "Video Cards" section of Chapter 5: Monitors, Etc. for more on that topic.

Video card technology evolves so fast that buying tips are out of date almost as soon as they're written. However, one thing has remained constant over the last few years: A card that costs over $400 today will cost less than $200 within a year. In other words, today's high end is next year's low end. Unless you're a really fanatical gamer or are making money using your PC with a high-end graphics program like Photoshop or AutoCAD, it doesn't make much sense to spend a lot on the latest video technology. You'll get more for your money buying more software or other goodies.

Modem

Your computer's modem is the device that connects it to your telephone line and from there to the Internet. Modems are standard equipment in new PCs (though if you've already got a good one that you want to transplant, you may be able to order your PC without one).

The current official modem standard you want a modem to support is V.90; most modems will also support either X2 or K56flex, older semistandards that are now obsolete. Modems of all three standards are referred to as "56K" modems, so make sure the one you get can handle the V.90 standard. Watch out for modems that are "upgradeable" to V.90 but don't support it out of the box.

The "56K" refers to the theoretical 56 kilobits (6.8K) per second of data they can theoretically download when you're surfing the Web and so on. When you're uploading (sending e-mail, for instance), the modem can handle 33.6K per second—the download speed can be higher because your Internet service provider has a digital connection to the phone system. I always put quotation marks around "56K" because the number seems to be grossly inflated; the highest transfer rate I've seen in tests so far is 47K. The 33.6K upload number is much closer to reality; a number of modems can do over 31K.

These days, all modems are fax modems—that is, they can all send and receive faxes. A "voice" modem will let you use your computer as a speakerphone and answering machine. See Chapter 24: Use Your PC as a Phone or Fax, for more details on using your modem for those purposes.

Chapter 19: Getting On the Internet, offers a guide to faster alternatives to modems: ISDN, DSL, and cable modems. In that chapter you'll also find some explanation of V.90 and other cryptic modem jargon.

Sound and speakers

Unless you custom-order a system without a sound card, you'll normally get a pair of speakers and support for the following three kinds of audio (discussed in more detail in Chapter 18: Sound and Video Editing):

- **Digital audio** (.WAV files), used for Windows's own sounds, for live radio and TV broadcasts on the Web, and for sound effects in games. This is the digital equivalent of a tape recorder—.WAV files can contain any sound, and the PC's mic and line inputs let you record your own.
- **CD audio tracks,** used in some games and educational CDs. You can also use this feature to play regular audio CDs (see "Playing Audio CDs with Your PC's CD-ROM Drive" in Chapter 4: Disks, Hard and Otherwise).
- **MIDI music** (.MID files), used mostly for soundtracks in games and by music software. Software or a special chip emulates a wide variety of musical instruments.

You'll notice a difference between sound cards primarily when playing MIDI music: Some cards have more realistic instrument sounds than others. (Note that an increasing percentage of PCs don't have sound cards—instead, audio chips are built into the motherboard.)

If you only run Windows and Windows apps, you can skip this paragraph, but if you run old DOS games or experiment with different operating systems, I recommend buying a board made by Creative Labs. This company's original Sound Blaster is the de facto standard for PC sound, and in my experience boards that emulate Sound Blaster are a lot less likely to work than the real thing.

In terms of speaker quality, you'll encounter a much wider range than for sound cards. Cheap PCs are typically bundled with speakers that would cost $20 if purchased separately; as you might expect from the price, they're tinny and have no bass. For better sound, look for name-brand speakers by Altec Lansing, JBL,

Yamaha, Boston Acoustics, or Cambridge Soundworks. If you spend over $50, expect to get a subwoofer to make up for the desktop speakers' lack of bass.

Slots and Bays

One of the benefits of generic PCs is that you can add new capabilities by installing optional equipment. Want to edit video? Install a video capture card. Looking to make your own CD-ROMs? Add a CD-Recordable drive. Need to speed up your Internet connection? Install an ISDN adapter. (See Chapters 4 and 8 for more on those and other possibilities.)

Many of these options require an empty *expansion slot*, a socket on the PC's motherboard (Figure 1) that a small circuit card plugs into; or an open *drive bay*, an empty rack into which you can slide a drive (see Figure 17 in Chapter 8: Upgrade It Yourself). If you want the widest choice of options, buy a PC with plenty of empty slots and bays.

- **PCI slots.** Today's motherboards typically have three or four high-speed PCI slots, which are appropriate for devices that pump a lot of data. This includes video cards, 100-megabit network cards, and SCSI adapters. One slot will likely be occupied by the video card; the other two are usually free, unless you buy your PC with Ethernet or SCSI built in. If you have an AGP video card, all the PCI slots may be free.
- **ISA slots.** Most motherboards have two or three slower ISA slots. These are used for devices like modems and sound cards, which pump relatively small amounts of data. ISA slots are also used for things that don't deal with data at all and only need power, including internal UPS and cooling-fan cards. PCs with no ISA slots at all are starting to appear, which isn't necessarily a problem so long as they have modem and sound built into the motherboard.
- **"PCI/ISA" slots.** Most motherboards have at least one combo slot that can take either a PCI or an ISA card. (Figure 4 shows how that works.) Typically you get one or two ISA-only slots at the bottom, two or three PCI-only slots at the top, and one combo slot in the middle. Sometimes PC vendors count both of the connectors in a combo slot; so a PC that's advertised as having three PCI and three ISA slots, for example, may be able to hold a maximum of only five cards.
- **External drive bays.** "External" means the bay can hold a drive that is accessible from the outside of the PC, like a Zip, CD-Recordable, or tape drive. You can get PCs with up to eight bays (at least two of which will be occupied by floppy and CD-ROM drives). See Figure 5 for a look at some common configurations.
- **Internal drive bays.** These are strictly for hard drives. Most PCs have one or two empty internal bays, so if you run out of disk space you can install a second or third drive. PCs designed for use as servers may have half a dozen or more internal bays. Note that if you don't have an internal bay free, you can use an external bay (see Chapter 8: Upgrade It Yourself).

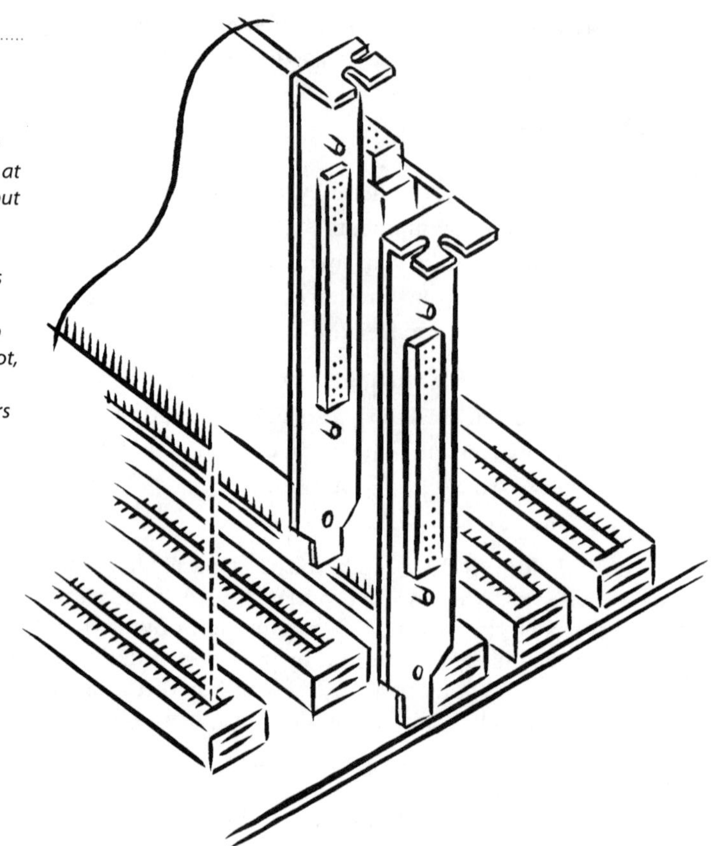

Figure 4

PCI and ISA slots.

Both PCI and ISA expansion boards hook onto the same rectangular cutouts at the back of the PC, but the boards' brackets bend at opposite angles. This prevents your accidentally plugging a card into the wrong kind of slot, and allows motherboard manufacturers to put both PCI and ISA sockets in the same slot space.

Desktop or Tower?

In recent years, the horizontal, under-the-monitor "desktop" design of the original IBM PC has been largely supplanted by vertical "tower" cases, which have several big advantages:

- They take up less space on your desk.
- You can put them on the floor.
- They have more room for expansion. A standard desktop case has only three external drive bays; since two are taken up by floppy and CD-ROM, that leaves only one free for expansion. Towers have up to eight external bays, which gives plenty of room to grow (see Figure 5).
- A standard desktop case raises the monitor about six inches off the desk. If you have a small monitor, this may be a plus, but with larger monitors putting the display right on the desk usually makes for a more comfortable viewing angle—and with the monitor on the desk, you're better off with a tower case.

If you do plan to put your PC on the floor, I recommend getting a "full tower" case. The extra height (around 25") makes the CD and floppy drives easier to reach.

Figure 5

PC case types and drive bays.

The bigger the case you get, the more room you'll have to add drives. Many cases have special miniature drive bays that hold only floppy or Zip drives, or (if you've got two bays free, one on top of the other) certain tape drives.

Keyboard and Mouse

The keyboard and mouse are not significant issues when buying a PC. Most PCs are bundled with cheap keyboards you could buy separately for less than $30, and there's seldom a choice of models—but if you don't like the one you get, it won't cost much to replace it. You're more likely to get a quality mouse, but again, if you don't like it, there are lots of inexpensive alternatives for less than $30. See Chapter 7: Input Devices, for an in-depth look at these components.

Windows 98

Virtually all PCs on the market these days are bundled with Windows 98. If you prefer Windows NT (see Chapter 11: Windows 95, 98, and NT for the pros and cons), it's cheaper to buy it when you buy your PC. Windows NT often adds only $100 to the cost of a new PC, but upgrading from Windows 95/98 costs around $140.

Some PC vendors offer a choice of Windows 98 configurations, and there are also some differences among vendors. Most notably, you may be able to get a system with Netscape Communicator installed in place of Microsoft Internet Explorer, or with Internet Explorer installed but with its intrusive Active Desktop feature disabled. (See Chapter 21: The Web and Browsers, for more on that.)

Currently, Windows 98 and Windows NT are the only operating systems available that make sense for average PC users. IBM's OS/2 isn't compatible with much current mass-market software other than games. There aren't many apps available for Linux and other flavors of UNIX, either—despite ongoing efforts to make it more user-friendly, UNIX is still strictly for geeks and Web servers. BeOS has the same problems as UNIX, only worse.

When to Spend More on a PC

If you're going to run nothing more than business applications, a Web browser, and e-mail—all that most people ever do with their computers—there's no good reason to spend more than the minimum for your PC. Today's entry-level PCs do all that stuff without even breathing hard. However, if you're going to play action games, do professional-quality graphics or publishing work, or work with audio or video, you'll need more than the minimum capabilities. Here's a rough guide of the specs to look for.

	CPU Speed	RAM	Hard Disk	Video	Monitor	Other
basic, under-$800 PC	300MHz	32MB or more	2GB	2MB	15-inch	
gamer PC	300MHz or higher	64MB or more	4GB or larger	8MB, 3D accelerator	15-inch or larger	Fancy joystick and/or flight-stick; sub-woofer
digital audio production	400MHz or higher	64MB or more	6GB or larger	4MB or more	17-inch or larger	Pro-level audio card; CD-R or CD-RW drive; cartridge hard disk
digital video production	400MHz or higher	64MB or more	16GB or larger (drive array preferred)	8MB	20-inch or larger	Video capture; 1394 interface; cartridge hard disk
professional graphics/ publishing	400MHz or higher	128MB or more*	8GB or larger	8MB	20-inch or larger	Windows NT; scanner; CD-R or CD-RW drive; Zip drive

*Large color graphics for prepress work require 256MB or more.

See Chapter 18: Sound and Video Editing, for additional tips on choosing hardware for special tasks.

Warranty, Service, and Tech Support

Most PCs come with either one-year or three-year warranties on parts and labor. The one-year warranties can almost always be extended to three years, often for as little as $100—a wise investment, given that you probably expect your PC to last at least that long. You can usually get another two years (total of five) for the same amount, though many vendors don't advertise that option very loudly.

It's also a good idea to get on-site service—sometimes that's included in the warranty, other times there's an extra annual fee. Without on-site service, fixing problems can be an annoying time-sink. When something goes wrong that the company can't resolve over the phone, you might have to pack up the system and ship it to the manufacturer, or haul it back to the store or a service center.

Many PC manufacturers these days provide free technical support by telephone 24 hours a day, 7 days a week. Going with a vendor who doesn't answer the phone at 3 a.m. might work out fine for you, but avoid those who charge for support after an initial period (typically a year). In addition, it's a good idea to check out a vendor's Web site before you buy, to see how extensive their FAQs and driver libraries are. (You'll find more pointers in Chapter 27: HELP! Where To Turn When Things Go Wrong.)

Other Stuff You Might (or Might Not) Want to Buy with a New PC

There are a number of options you might want to purchase along with your PC, either to get a better price, to avoid a tricky installation, or to have a single place to complain if something goes wrong. However, not all of the stuff that PC vendors may try to sell you will be a good buy. Here's a quick rundown of the good and the bad:

Applications

Many PC vendors either bundle Microsoft Office "free" with certain models, or offer it pre-installed for an extra $185 or so. That's the lowest price I've ever seen for the product, and having it preloaded saves you a little work. IBM offers even better deals on Lotus SmartSuite.

Keep in mind that bundled software you won't use doesn't justify paying a higher price for a PC. Also be aware that some bundled software isn't as full-featured as the versions you'd buy in the store. See the upcoming sidebar, "Possibly Worthless Stuff You Might Get with a New PC" for a list of frequent offenders.

Monitor

I don't know whether they're selling at cost or what, but some PC vendors offer unbeatable deals on monitors when you get them with a new PC. As I write this, for example, Dell is charging $255 for a 17-inch monitor that's part of a package, but sells the monitor separately for $429—and it's not a bad deal even at that price. Bundled monitors aren't always the ones you'd pick out of a lineup in a store, but when the price is that low you might as well give it a shot. If you don't like the monitor, you shouldn't have much trouble turning around and reselling it for what you paid.

Printer

Computer retailers often bundle a printer with a PC and monitor to make a complete package. Sometimes these are great deals, but more often the printer is a supercheap model, or an outdated model that might not be adequate for your needs. Mail-order vendors like Dell usually offer a choice of printers as options with a new PC, but their prices are seldom the best. (See Chapter 6: Printers, for tips on picking the right printer.)

Scanner

The caveats that apply to bundled printers also apply to scanners. There's one exception: a scanner built into the keyboard may save you a few bucks, provided you don't need a flatbed model and scanner output quality isn't a high priority. (See Chapter 7: Input Devices, for more about scanners.)

Zip Drive

Zip drives, a higher-capacity alternative to floppy drives, are ubiquitous in desktop publishing and many other arenas. (See Chapter 4: Disks, Hard and Otherwise, for details and a comparison of zip drives and other removable media.) A zip drive built into your new PC will cost you less (under $100), and you won't have to deal with the cables, power supply, and sometimes-problematic drivers of the external version (which connects to the PC's parallel port). Another advantage of the internal Zip drive is that you may be able to boot your PC from it, though that's probably useful only to nerdy types who experiment with operating systems and/or do their own maintenance.

Tape Backup Drive

Installing a tape drive is a relatively difficult upgrade. You have to install the drive itself, usually an expansion card as well, connect the drive to the card or motherboard with a cable, and hook the drive to the power supply (which may not have a spare plug). Unless you enjoy fiddling with computer hardware, you might as well get the drive built in. Another plus: If there's any problem, you won't have to worry about the PC and tape drive companies blaming each other and leaving you stuck in the middle. In most cases, a tape drive that can hold the entire contents of your hard disk on a single tape will add no more than $200 to the price of the system. (See Chapter 9: Protect Your Data, for a comparison of tape and other backup options.)

Network Adapter

More and more people are setting up networks at home to share peripherals and play network games. If you think you might eventually hook your PC to a network, you might as well get a 10BaseT Ethernet card built in. Get one of the 10/100 megabit combo models—they cost only a little more and will allow you to set up a network that's ten times as fast. Such a card should add no more than $50 to the system cost.

SCSI Adapter

SCSI (pronounced "scuzzy") is an alternative interface for connecting hard drives (and occasionally other devices) to your PC. SCSI has several advantages over EIDE, the standard PC drive interface. If you aren't sure whether you need SCSI, you most likely don't, but Chapter 4: Disks, Hard and Otherwise, will help you decide for sure. If you do need SCSI, you might as well get an adapter built into your PC. You probably won't save any money (in fact, it may cost more than adding a card yourself), but you won't have to deal with installing the card and you'll have a single point for support if anything goes wrong.

UPS (Uninterruptible Power Supply)

If you live in an area prone to power blackouts or brownouts, a UPS card is a worthwhile investment. (When a blackout crashes your PC, you lose any unsaved data. With some applications you might even find that the files you're working on were damaged beyond repair. Brownouts can damage your hard disk and other components.) A UPS card protects your data from such events by switching the PC to battery power and sounding an alarm to warn you to shut down manually before the battery runs out. External UPS devices with larger batteries are available, as well, but if you want one of those you can probably find a lower price by purchasing it separately. See Chapter 9: Protect Your Data, for more on UPSs.

Possibly Worthless Stuff You Might Get with a New PC

In an attempt to make their PCs look good against the competition, vendors often bundle any software they can get cheap or free, resulting in an impressively long list of goodies. However, unless you would have paid money for that stuff anyway, it adds nothing to the value of the PC, so you shouldn't let it influence your buying decision. Here's a guide to several basic categories of junkware and some common examples:

- Stuff you can get for free, such as Microsoft Internet Explorer, Microsoft Outlook, Microsoft Netmeeting, and Netscape Communicator; and the client software for fee-based services like America Online, CompuServe, and Connected Online Backup.
- Apps that aren't what you really want. Microsoft Works, for example, is better than nothing but it's no substitute for the full-featured Microsoft Office suite. And Works is outclassed in most respects by its major competitor, AppleWorks. Lotus SmartSuite and Corel's WordPerfect Suite are good products, but they're not 100% compatible with Microsoft Office and thus not always good substitutes. (Of course, the different versions of Office are annoyingly incompatible, as well.)
- Crippled versions of popular products like Quicken SE or Basic, HyperTerminal PE, and Adobe Photoshop LE.
- Educational or game CD-ROMs you've never heard of.
- Promotional stuff, like DVD samplers from movie studios.
- Outdated versions of popular programs. (I've seen bundles that included Corel CD-ROMs for a program that was two revs out-of-date.)

What Brand to Buy

So much for what to look for in a PC. Now the really tough question: *Which brand*? The great thing about writing a book rather than a magazine article is that I can tell you all the stuff the magazine editors cut out of my manuscripts for fear of annoying their advert...—I mean, in the interest of fairness and journalistic impartiality.

Dell

If money were no object, I'd tell everyone to buy from Dell. This mail-order-only vendor has the best reputation in the business. They're always at the top of *PC Magazine*'s service and reliability polls, and I've rarely heard a complaint about their telephone support—which is available 24 hours a day, 7 days a week, for the life of the machine.

There's just one problem: Dell's systems are expensive. At the high end, their prices are reasonably competitive, at least with other major brands—which is one reason Dell is so popular among programmers and engineers. Unfortunately, there's no such thing as a low-end Dell. As I write this, their least expensive system costs $1,800 (including monitor), almost twice the price of entry-level models from most other vendors. The Dell is more generously configured, with lots more RAM, a much bigger hard disk, a 17-inch monitor, a copy of Microsoft Office, and a longer warranty. That said, you can still save hundreds of dollars by going with another brand.

Compaq

Around 15 years ago, Compaq held the role that Dell has today. It was common knowledge that Compaq's PCs were the best, and those who had enough money to find out for themselves expressed few complaints. Times change, though, and more recently Compaq has become the biggest PC manufacturer in the world by focusing on inexpensive PCs for the mass market.

You have to watch the specs and components carefully with Compaq's Presario models (the inexpensive mass-market line). I've frequently found them to have slightly outdated video boards, smaller hard disks, or less memory than their competitors. On the other hand, they're sometimes discounted so heavily by retailers that they're still good values.

Hewlett Packard

You could think of Hewlett-Packard as the Avis to Compaq's Hertz—except Compaq often seems like the one that's trying harder. HP's home-oriented Pavilion PCs are comparable to Compaq's Presarios, and the eternal price war between the two brands was the main force behind mainstream PC prices' dropping below $1,000.

HP's reputation is one of the best in the industry. The company had some problems when it first entered the consumer PC market a few years ago but has applied the lessons learned from selling zillions of LaserJet and DeskJet printers. HP was one of only three vendors to rate an A in *PC Magazine*'s last annual service and reliability poll (the other As were Dell and IBM). The company does not, however, back up that reputation with a longer warranty: You get the same one year on HP machines as you do with most other consumer-oriented PCs. Still, given a choice between an HP and a Compaq with the same specs and price—a common real-world choice in many consumer electronics stores—I'd take the HP.

About "Business" PCs

Many PC vendors sell two different lines of computers: one for consumers, one for business. The consumer models, like the Dell Dimension, Compaq Presario, HP Pavilion, and IBM Aptiva, are the ones most people reading this book will want to buy.

The business counterparts of these popular machines (Dell Optiplex, Compaq Deskpro, HP Vectra, IBM PC) are designed for companies that buy lots of PCs and hook them together on networks. Business PCs include extra features, like support for remote management software, that are of no value to home and small-business users—typically making these machines more expensive than consumer-oriented PCs. If you find a great deal on a business PC, there's no reason *not* to buy one, but check carefully to make sure the price includes any multimedia features you're expecting (sound card, speakers, 3D video, etc.).

IBM

There's an old saying that nobody ever got fired for buying IBM. There was a period in the late '80s and early '90s when anyone who bought IBM *should* have been fired, but in recent years the company's got its act together and is once again one of the best PC manufacturers. *PC Magazine*'s user poll has given IBM an A grade for the past six years, and the company's phone support is legendary for its dogged pursuit of customers' problems.

IBM's consumer-oriented Aptivas are fairly similar to their main competitors, the Compaq Presarios and HP Pavilions. IBM is more of a follower than a leader when it comes to pricing, so if you notice that Compaq has dropped its prices, expect matching prices on comparable IBM models within a month or so.

Gateway 2000 and Micron

These two mail-order-only vendors both focus on giving customers a lot of bang for the buck. The PCs you get from these vendors aren't the absolute cheapest, but compared with other major brands they tend to deliver more features and/or better performance for a given price. Both Gateway and Micron tend to bundle mediocre monitors with their systems.

Packard Bell NEC

A few years back, Packard Bell was the Valujet of the PC industry. The company left no corner uncut in its goal of selling the cheapest PCs around, and the results were predictable. PB's systems were more prone to software configuration problems and hardware failures than other brands', and the company's telephone support lines were always jammed, frustrating customers with busy signals and long hold times.

Then NEC bought Packard Bell and has had some success in trying to turn it around, but the job's not done yet. Recently I've seen PB systems that seem a huge improvement over earlier models, but the company's still ranked near the bottom of *PC Magazine*'s service and reliability poll. And the Web is still peppered with sites with names like "Boycott Packard Bell" and "Packard Bell Is Evil."

The merged company also sells systems under the NEC label, which doesn't have the same bad rep of Packard Bell. The NEC systems I've seen have been on the expensive side but otherwise fine, except that some of the bundled monitors' displays weren't sharp enough.

Sony (and Toshiba?)

Sony is the most recent major brand to enter the PC market. I've been very impressed by Sony's Vaio line, mostly due to the quality of its monitors and their built-in speakers—not surprising for a company better known for TV sets and stereos. I expected Sony would gain an edge over older computer manufacturers as PCs have become more appliance-like (that is, inexpensive and interchangeable), but so far that doesn't seem to have been the case.

Although Toshiba's been selling laptops for years, it only recently entered the desktop PC market—but for the moment, at least, seems to have backed right out again. Toshiba has pulled its consumer-oriented Infinia line and is now selling only the corporate-oriented Equium line. (See "About 'Business' PCs" for an explanation of the difference between consumer and corporate models.)

Generic Clones: Parts in a Box

There are scores of other PC vendors, but there's less difference among them than among the above-mentioned major-brand models. Almost all sell generic *clones*—what I call "parts in a box." That is, they buy a bunch of components from other companies, assemble them into a PC, (maybe) stick a label on the front, and toss it all into a box with some software and accessories.

Not that all these vendors are alike. Selecting good, compatible components while keeping prices down is an art, and some companies are much better at it than others. I hesitate to recommend any particular vendors, since these companies come and go and the quality of their PCs and service tends to vary over time. For example, in the latest *PC Magazine* user survey, Midwest Micro got a B, up from a D two years before. Quantex also got a B, up from a C the previous year (the first in which Quantex made it into *PC Mag*'s survey).

In addition to nationally advertised brands, there are hundreds (maybe thousands) of small clone shops that assemble no-name or house-brand computers according to local customers' specifications. If you live near a good one, a local shop can be a great deal: I've bought all my PCs from such shops, always at prices lower than any nationally advertised brand. Of course, you don't have the benefit of comparative reviews in computer magazines, and tech support is only available during store hours. Like brand-name clones, these shops vary in quality, so it's best to shop only at stores recommended by satisfied recent customers. A shop chosen at random may indiscriminately buy whatever components are cheapest, a process that typically results in unreliable PCs.

Getting the Best Deal

Plenty of different kinds of places sell PCs, and each place has its own advantages and disadvantages. The bigger the selection, the less likely all the products will be on display for you to give them a hands-on tryout. Outside of mail-order vendors and local clone shops, you can't usually specify a custom configuration (more RAM, larger hard drive, etc.), although the service department in a computer superstore will probably upgrade the computer for a small fee. Here's a quick rundown on the four different places where you're most likely to buy a PC.

Wherever you buy, the following tips will help you get the best deal.

- **Check prices online first.** Assuming you already have access to a computer, it's easy to get a rough idea of street prices without leaving home; just browse some online hardware retailers and see what they're asking. Or just use CNET's **Shopper.com**—a Web site that consolidates price information from dozens of mail-order vendors. Enter the product you're interested in, and **shopper.com** will bring up a list of all the vendors it knows are selling your product, and what they're charging. Note that the best prices aren't always available online; I've frequently found that Costco has stuff cheaper than anyplace else.
- **Shop around.** Computer product pricing is weird. Some stores may ask the full suggested retail price for a product that's routinely discounted up to 40% someplace else. On top of that, some retailers are better than others at tracking manufacturers' price reductions and remarking products on the shelves. The same goes for discontinued products—it's not unusual to find one store's closeout specials still being sold by a competitor at the regular price.
- **Buy discontinued models.** People are so hot for the latest gadget that trailing-edge technology is often marked down way below its actual worth. There are a number of retailers who specialize in unloading last month's models at a fraction of the original cost. Two that have been impressed me are J&R Computer World (**jandr.com** or 800-221-8180) and the Onsale Auction Supersite (**www.onsale.com**).

Type of Store	Prices	Selection	Custom Configuration	Try Before You Buy	Support	Return Policy
Web/mail-order PC vendor	Often low	Moderate to large	Yes	No	Usually 24/7	Often 30-day, no questions (but you pay shipping)
local generic clone shop	Usually low	Small	Yes	Yes	Store hours only	May charge restocking fee
shopping mall*	Vary	Small to moderate	No	Yes	Depends on brand	Varies; ask
warehouse membership store	Low	Tiny	No	Maybe	Depends on brand	Usually liberal

*Computer superstore, office supply superstore, consumer electronics store, etc.

- **Shop at factory outlets.** Some vendors of brand-name computers have stores and/or Web sites where you can buy discontinued and refurbished models. Dell, for example, has an outlet store in its hometown of Austin, Texas, as well as a Web page, the Dell Online Outlet (**`dell.com/outlet`**). These are the only places where you can get a Dell for a price comparable to other vendors' entry-level models—though the outlet's PCs still come with the same three-year warranty as Dell's other products.
- **Watch out for bait-and-switch.** It's fairly common for retailers to tell customers looking for a heavily advertised entry-level PC that they're out of stock, and then try to persuade the customer to spend another $100 or so on a comparable model with slightly better specs. Even mail-order companies sometimes have similar lines: "We can't ship X for two weeks, but I can get Y out to you tomorrow." Don't fall for these ploys. Make the dealer give you a rain check, try another store, or buy later. (The dealers aren't necessarily lying about being out of stock, but I'm quite sure that some intentionally don't order enough low-end models to meet demand.)
- **Check the return policy.** You should be allowed 30 days to return the product, no questions asked, if you're not satisfied (that is, a 30-day, money-back, unconditional guarantee). Ask about refunds—it's common for mail-order companies to make you pay for return shipping, but avoid vendors that will refund only a percentage of the price, keeping the rest as a "restocking charge." Also make sure you get the refund in cash, not credit.

- **Pay with a credit card.** Never order by mail, phone, or the Web except by using a credit card. That way, if the product doesn't show up or it doesn't work, you can refuse the charge.

PC-Buying Resources

www.pcmag.com/special/reliability98/pcs.html Every August, *PC Magazine* publishes the results of an extensive survey of its readers, who rate the reliability of the products they've purchased and the quality of service and technical support they've received from various PC vendors. (After July 1999, I imagine the **98**" in that URL will be replaced by **99**.)

pcworld.com/top400/ibg This questionnaire-driven "interactive buyer's guide" from *PC World* may help you find some PC models that meet your criteria.

computers.com CNET's hardware site has a product-finding tool much like *PC World*'s. In the left column, click "Desktops" on the main page, then "PC," and then fill out the form and click "Filter."

shopper.com I always check this site before buying any computer hardware or software. The compilation of price info from multiple online vendors doesn't always turn up the best deals, but it lets you know immediately how much is too much. (Watch out for vendors whose low prices are offset by exorbitant shipping fees.)

www.pricewatch.com Another price-comparison site. I like shopper.com better but the more price information you can compare, the better.

www.onsale.com This online auction is a great source for discontinued brand-name systems, particularly IBM models, that usually carry full warranties.

3

Notebook PCs

by Robert Lauriston

The sections "Durability and Security" and "Service" and portions of "About Batteries and Power Management" and "Ten Tips for Mobile Computing" were written by Steve Cummings and updated for the third edition by Robert Lauriston.

In This Chapter

Notebooks, aka laptops, raise a whole extra set of issues on top of the ones you have to consider when choosing, buying, and using a regular desktop PC. The good news is that falling hardware prices mean that these two types of computers are more alike than they used to be—laptops now have plenty of RAM, big hard disks, and decent-sized color screens. The bad news is that notebooks still cost considerably more, and to get one for a reasonable price you have to make additional compromises, as well.

In this chapter, we'll review the things to consider when picking a notebook and choosing what options you want it to have. We'll also give you some tips for getting the most out of your notebook, both at home and on the road.

Six Basic Notebook Types

Choosing and configuring a notebook means striking a balance between features, size, weight, performance, battery life, and price. A faster CPU runs the battery down sooner; a bigger screen weighs more; a more comfortable keyboard makes a bulkier notebook; a four-pound notebook can cost up to 50% more than a seven-pound version with the same features; and so on.

With the huge number of notebook models and configuration options available, there are many different ways you can work this balancing act. Here are some descriptions of more-or-less distinct varieties to help you sort out the market confusion.

- **Budget models.** This is the notebook equivalent of the basic PC we discussed in Chapter 2. These are low-cost, no-frills machines, but they'll do everything most people need. The screen and hard disk are (relatively) small, the CPU and modem are (relatively) slow, battery life and weight are average (two hours and seven pounds) or worse, and you might have to upgrade to bring the system up to 32MB of RAM. Cost: from around $1,500 for top brands like IBM and Toshiba, down to less than $1,000 for off-brands.
- **Performance models.** These models make sense for programmers and other types for whom a faster CPU pays off in improved productivity. Typically, the fastest notebooks are not terribly expensive (by notebook standards)—they're just heavy and have short battery life. Cost: varies radically depending on CPU market.
- **Full-featured heavyweights.** These moderately priced models are aimed at people who use notebooks in place of desktop PCs and don't lug them around much. Since size and weight aren't a consideration, they typically have a CD-ROM, floppy, and modem all permanently built in, and a full set of PC ports on the back. The trade-off is that they weigh more than

eight pounds, and battery life may be short. Cost: around $1,500 and up, depending on brand and configuration.

- **Thin models** weigh four pounds or less. These are aimed at people for whom toting around a machine of average size and weight would be a constant annoyance. Thin models have regular-sized screens (12.1 inches or more) and keyboards, and the floppy and/or CD-ROM drive may be an external unit that hooks up with a cable. Cost: varies depending on configuration, but expect to pay about $1,000 more than you'd pay for a notebook with similar specs that is two or three pounds heavier.
- **Ultralights,** weighing two pounds or less, take portability to the max. They use small screens and cramped keyboards (on which touch-typing is difficult or impossible) to fit a full-featured PC into an undersized case (see Figure 1). All drives are external and can be left behind. Don't confuse ultralights with Windows CE computers, which are quite limited in features and functionality as compared with PCs.

Figure 1

Different sizes, different weights.

Today's notebooks come in several flavors. Most measure about 12 inches wide by 9 inches deep—about what will fit on a standard airplane tray table. Regular models are about 2 inches thick and weigh around 6 to 9 pounds; "thin" models are about half that thickness and weight. Ultralights typically compromise on features and keyboard comfort in order to fit into a smaller, lighter package.

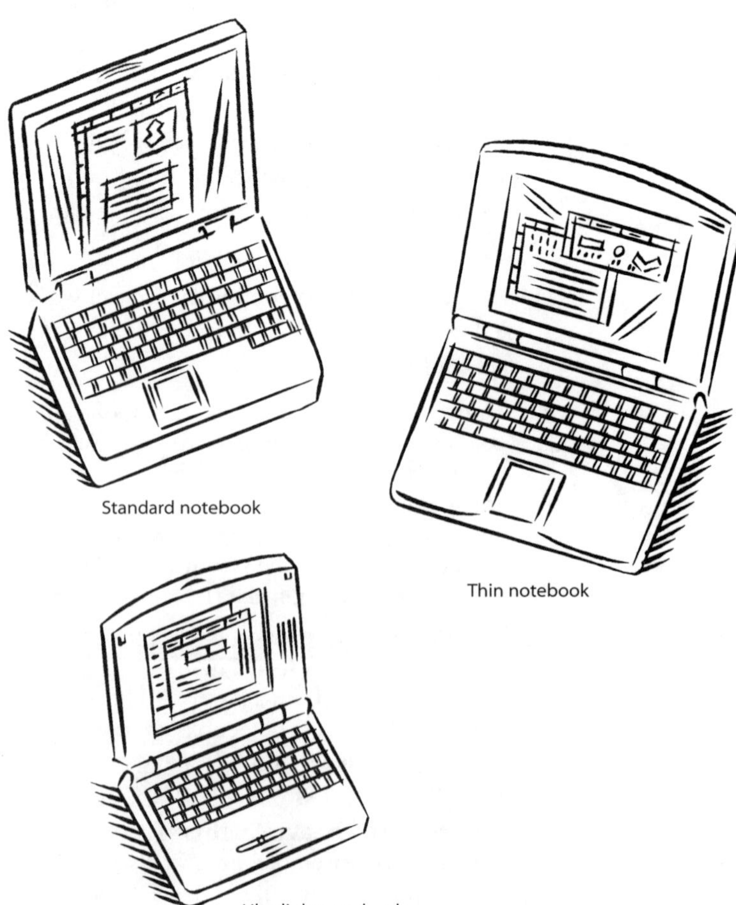

- **Executive models.** These notebooks are the PC equivalent of a Porsche—they have the fastest CPU, biggest hard disk, maximum battery life, and every feature yet invented, useful or otherwise. (If the notebook doesn't impress people, just show them the invoice.) Naturally, as with any status symbol, brand names are all-important—top-of-the-line IBM ThinkPads and Toshiba Tecras dominate this fashion-conscious niche. Price: if you have to ask, you don't wanna know ($5,500 to $7,000).

There are also a lot of notebooks that fall into the nebulous "mid-range" category—not cheap enough to be budget items, but not fast, light, or full-featured enough to fit into any of the other categories, either. Generally they're not great values when compared with budget models.

How Do They Weigh Notebooks, Anyway?

There's no consistent definition of what notebook weight includes. Magazine comparisons often refer to "travel weight," which includes the notebook, the external power supply or charger, and both floppy and CD-ROM drives—a combined number that might more reasonably be called "suitcase weight." Magazines may also refer to "system weight" or "base weight," which may or may not include removable floppy or CD-ROM drives.

If you're going to be using the notebook on airplanes, what you really want to know is the *minimum weight:* your computer with one battery and a minimum of options installed, plus, for long flights, the weight of the spare battery. (Some notebooks include bay covers so you can have no drives at all.)

As an example of how misleading these varying definitions of weight can be, consider the Dell Latitude M166ST (long since discontinued, but a good example nevertheless). Stripped for flight—with one battery and the included protective cover installed over the empty floppy-drive bay—it weighed only 5.3 pounds; with the optional second battery installed in the floppy bay, only 6.1 pounds. However, the only number mentioned in *PC Magazine*'s review was a "travel weight" of 7.7 pounds.

Screen Considerations

These days, all notebooks have color displays—a good thing, since the Windows interface is ugly and sometimes hard to navigate when displayed in shades of gray, which used to be the rule for all but the most expensive notebooks. And you no longer have to pay a steep premium to get a first-rate color screen. The better-looking *active-matrix* (aka TFT) screens are now the norm; dimmer, duller-looking *passive-matrix* (aka DSTN, HPA, or MLA) screens are found only in the cheapest models. (Useless translation: TFT means

Thin-Film Transistor, DSTN is Dual-Scan Super-TwistedNematic, HPA is High Performance Addressing, and MLA means Multi-Line Addressing.)

The ideal way to choose a notebook is to line up several units side by side and have a close look at their screens. Selecting the right one is an important decision, because generally the screen can't be changed. The following buying tips may help you narrow down your choice:

- **Active vs. passive.** Why are active-matrix screens faster and better looking than passive-matrix screens? With passive-matrix, electrodes transmit pulses to liquid crystal molecules, which line up to either block backlight or let it through, depending on the polarity. The same process occurs with a TFT screen, except that transistors do the work of electrodes—resulting in a faster, sharper, higher-contrast display that rivals the quality of a desktop monitor. Unfortunately, all that silicon is expensive, so it increases the system cost by $300 or so.
- **Size.** Three screen sizes dominate the notebooks currently on the market: measured diagonally, they're 12.1, 13.3, and 14.1 inches. A few models have 15.1-inch screens, but they're huge, heavy, and too big to fit on standard airplane tray tables, and thus unlikely to catch on. Bigger isn't always better: Some 12.1-inch screens actually display larger, more readable text than 13.3- or 14.1-inch models. See "Notebook Screen Readability" for an explanation.

Notebook Screen Readability

Screen Size (inches)	Desktop Size (pixels)	Pixels per Inch
11.3	80 x600	88
12.1	800x600	83
12.1	1024x768	106
13.3	1024x768	96
14.1	1024x768	91
15.1	1024x768	85

Larger notebook screens give you a bigger desktop, but they can actually be harder to read than smaller screens (see Figure 2). For example, a 12.1-inch, 800x600 screen has 83 pixels per inch (ppi), about the same density as a 17-inch monitor running at 1024x768—a resolution most people find comfortable. In contrast, 13.3- and 14.1-inch screens, thanks to their larger 1024x768 desktops, have 91ppi and 96ppi, respectively, which is about the same as a 15-inch monitor running at 1024x768—a resolution that makes print unacceptably small for many people. Notebooks' liquid crystal displays (LCDs) are much sharper than the' cathode ray tubes (CRTs) of regular monitors, so on your notebook you may be able to tolerate more closely-spaced pixels.

Figure 2

Bigger screen, but harder to read?

Though you might not expect it, a 1024x768 13.3-inch screen is actually harder on your eyes than an 800x600 12.1-inch screen. These two windows, which are both 3 inches wide, illustrate this difference. Note that those 12.1-inch screens that use 1024x768 resolution are harder *on your eyes than 13.3s.*

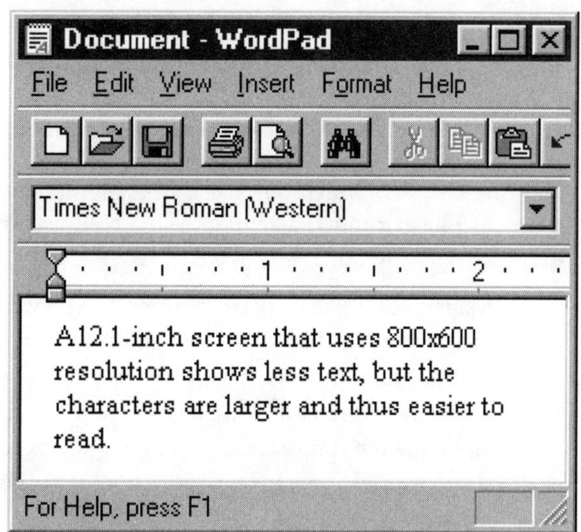

12.1-inch 800x600 screen

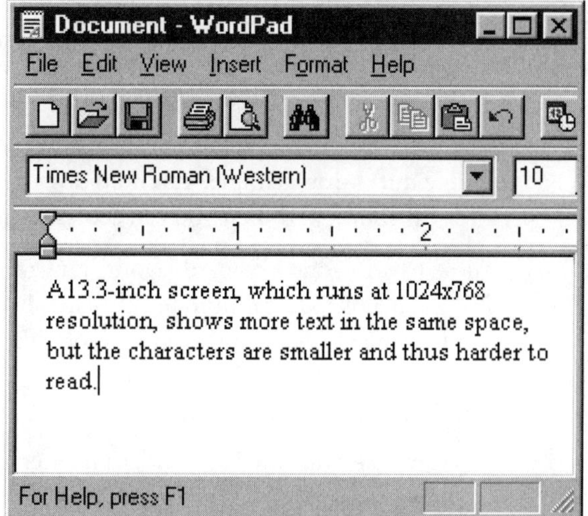

13.3-inch 1024x768 screen

- **Viewing angle.** Passive-matrix screens become unreadable when viewed at an angle, while active-matrix can be viewed at up to 35 degrees or more off center. If you want to be able to use your notebook for multi-player games or for running PowerPoint slide shows, you definitely want to choose active-matrix. On the other hand, if you'll often be using this computer in public places such as airplanes, you might prefer the extra privacy afforded by a passive display.

- **Color depth.** Most notebook screens these days are *16-bit high color*—they can display around 65,000 different colors simultaneously. Some can display *24-bit true color,* which allows more than 16 million colors. With most applications, you'd never notice the difference. If you're creating color graphics, however, 24-bit color may be important, and for color publishing work it's essential—though flat-panel displays can't match the color range or accuracy of tube monitors.

- **Brightness and contrast controls.** Best case for these controls: Slide controls or knobs mounted right next to the screen. Worst case: Weird key-combinations you'll never remember. (Note that TFT screens don't have a contrast setting, so if a contrast control is provided, it won't do anything.)

Many people like to hook up their notebooks to desktop monitors—either for a bigger view of their own applications, or for presentations to a slightly larger group. Many notebooks can run external monitors at higher color depths or higher resolutions than are supported by the built-in display; if that's an important issue for you, ask the vendor about that feature. The color depth/resolution combinations the notebook can support are also limited by the amount of video memory it has. See Chapter 5: Monitors, Etc., for details.

Keyboards and Pointing Devices

No notebook has as many keys as a desktop keyboard. Thus some keys must do double duty—for example, you hold down a special key (usually labeled Fn or F for function), and then you can access such keys as Home, End, and so on.

These two-for-one keyboard layouts range from ingenious to very awkward. The main alphabet and number keys are always in the usual places, and the first ten function keys are always on top, but placement of other keys varies from model to model. Personal taste will guide you here, but these rules of thumb may make your evaluation easier:

- **Key size and spacing.** The main letter and number keys are almost always spaced the same as on desktop keyboards—that is, the distance from the center of the A key to the center of the " ' key is a hair short of 7.5 inches. Other keys are sometimes much smaller than usual. For instance, watch out for too-narrow Shift, Enter, and Bksp keys, which can result in a lot of typos. On ultralights, the keys are placed closer together—another source of more typing errors, at least while you're getting used to the keyboard.

- **Emulated keys.** Prt Sc, Scroll Lock, and Pause can disappear for all we care. But it's a constant annoyance to have to press Fn to access Home, End, Pg Up, and Pg Dn. This is rare on notebooks with regular-sized keys, but it's a common problem on ultralights.
- **Cursor keys.** Most users are more comfortable with a notebook that has cursor keys in an inverted T configuration, the same arrangement as on a desktop keyboard.

- **Key placement.** You should be able to reach Ctrl, Alt, and Fn easily with your hands in the standard typing position. Having Ctrl and Alt in their usual locations is also a plus.
- **Windows 95 keys.** Watch out for notebooks that dedicate keys to these Microsoft advertisements—er, innovations—by moving more important keys such as Ctrl and Alt to awkward positions, or by making the spacebar so narrow that you might miss it.

As you type, don't expect the same sensation you get on desktop keyboards. Notebook keyboards are thinner, so the *key travel*—the distance the key moves when you press it—is always less than on a desktop keyboard. This may cause you to repeat characters accidentally. The additional miniaturization in ultra-lights worsens the problem.

Pointing Devices

All notebooks today come with a built-in pointing device, either a touchpad below the keyboard or a little joystick-like gizmo resembling a pencil eraser between the G and H keys (see Figure 3). Most people seem to prefer the latter device, but some folks are quite partial to the touchpad. There's also substantial variation in design within each type:sensitivity, position and shape of buttons, etc.

Figure 3

Notebook pointing devices.

There's often no place to put a mouse when you're using a notebook, so it'll come with a built-in pointing device. This is most commonly a touchpad—a little touch-sensitive rectangle below the keyboard. More expensive models sometimes have a little pencil-eraser kind of thing in the middle of the keyboard.

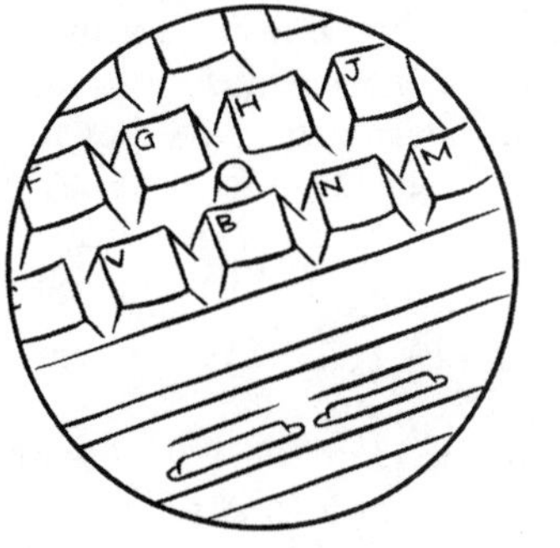

Pointing Stick

Touchpad

Try a variety of notebooks before you commit yourself. Pay close attention to the position of the pointer's two buttons. Do your thumbs rest comfortably on them while you're typing? Is there a ridge that cuts into your thumb? Can you use the pointer easily while touch-typing?

Almost all notebooks include a port for hooking up a standard, full-size PC keyboard and mouse when you're at home or at the office. That's a real plus if you plan to use your mobile machine as your sole computer. If that's a big issue for you, avoid the models on which you have to disable the modem in order to hook up an external mouse.

Notebook Modem Choices

When you're on the road, you'll surely want to keep in touch by e-mail, and you may want access to the Internet or to your company's network as well. That means you'll need a modem—preferably a 56K V.90 model. (See the "Modem" section of Chapter 2: How to Buy a PC, for an explanation of those terms.) For notebooks, which can't use the same internal modems that are standard in desktop PCs, there are three basic options (see Figure 4) to choose from:

- **Built-ins.** This is the most convenient choice. There's just a standard phone jack in the side of your notebook. You can't accidentally leave the modem at home or in your hotel room, and the only accessory you need to pack is a phone cord to connect the modem to the wall jack. The drawback is that built-in modems are usually more expensive than other options. (That's because there's no standard, and thus little or no competition to drive down prices.)
- **PC Card (aka PCMCIA) modems.** This is the most popular kind of notebook modem in use today. Since PC Card slots are standard, the competition is healthy, which means plenty of modems to choose from at reasonable prices. Unfortunately, PC Card modems aren't quite as trouble-free as built-ins. For instance, they're small and thus easy to lose, or lose track of in a messy suitcase or hotel room. Some have tiny tail-like cords that are easy to break or misplace; you're better off with one of the models that has a flat jack which pops out of the side.

- **External modems.** This is the cheapest option. An external modem costs less than a PC Card model—and when you're not travelling, you can use it with a desktop PC. The trade-off is that, in addition to the phone cord, you've got to pack the modem, its power supply, and a serial cable to connect the modem to the notebook. Forget or lose any one of those, and you're incommunicado. The 3Com (formerly US Robotics) Sportster 56K (around $150) is a good choice.

For the ultimate in mobile communications, consider a *cellular fax modem*—they're available in all three types (though built-ins are rare). This device works in concert with cellular phones, so you don't have to hunt for a phone jack in order to link up. However, cellular modems are expensive, they only work with certain cellular phones, and you can expect dropped connections when you drive under a bridge or across cellular communications zones. But the kinks in this technology are being worked out, and prices are dropping rapidly.

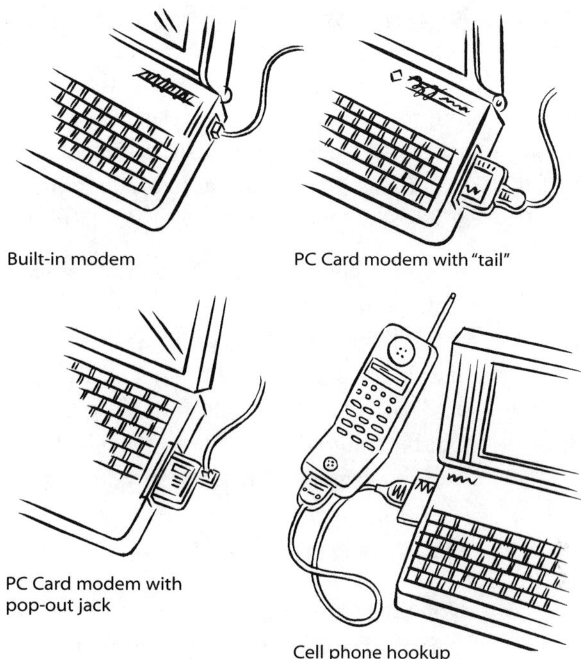

Figure 4

Mobile modem options.

The most convenient notebook modem option is a built-in; you just plug the phone jack into the side of the notebook. Next easiest is a PC Card modem. Both built-ins and PC Card modems may have special connectors for connecting to cell phones. An external modem's cheap, but you have to carry around a lot more stuff.

Other Notebook Components

When it comes to mobile PCs, you often pay more for less. Cramming all that technology into such a small space costs money—notebooks with the fastest CPUs and biggest displays are particularly pricey, and the fastest notebook always lags behind the fastest desktop. Expect to pay nearly twice as much for the same speed and capacity in a mobile PC as in a desktop; the same inflation applies to pricing for such mobile add-ons as fax modems, memory modules, hard disks, and so on.

CPU

Notebooks mostly use chips specifically designed for mobile use (lower power consumption, extra power-saving features), and performance of those chips is typically so far inferior that entry-level desktops have clock speeds similar to top-of-the-line notebooks. Still, any notebook currently on the market has more than adequate CPU horsepower for Windows 98 and popular apps. As with desktops, it doesn't make much sense to spend a lot on a faster CPU unless you frequently run unusually demanding applications like Photoshop, AutoCAD, or action games. Likewise, it doesn't make sense to buy a notebook without an L2 (secondary) cache (see Chapter 2: How To Buy a PC for a technical explanation).

Memory

Notebooks are sometimes shipped with 16MB of RAM—half the 32MB minimum generally required to keep Windows applications from bogging down. In addition, inadequate RAM reduces battery life, because when Windows runs out of real memory it automatically switches to virtual memory—i.e., the hard disk—which burns up power a lot faster than RAM does.

Most notebooks these days can hold at least 128MB of RAM, usually in two or three standard SO-DIMM memory modules. The guideline here is the same as for desktops: It's a good idea to insist that your new notebook's memory be in a single module, so the other socket(s) will be free for future upgrades if necessary. (Pointless technical detail: SO-DIMM is short for Small Outline Double Inline Memory Module. The letters SO distinguish SO-DIMMs from the larger DIMMs used in desktop PCs.)

Drives and Bays

Notebooks typically come with at least 2GB of **hard disk** space, much more than most people are likely to need during a business trip. If you plan to use your notebook as your primary system, you might want to order a 4GB or larger drive—but first compare the extra cost with the price of a cartridge hard disk such as a SparQ or Jaz, which (as discussed in Chapter 4) is more flexible.

Most notebooks have **removable hard disks** that can easily be pulled out and replaced with larger models. (This is also a useful arrangement for companies in which people share a pool of notebooks. It's much cheaper to buy each user their own hard disk than their own computer.) Some notebooks will let you install a second hard disk in place of the CD-ROM drive, floppy drive, or battery. There are also hard disks that plug into a pair of PC Card slots. These PC Card hard disks have three big disadvantages, however: They're more expensive, they have less capacity, and they're not as fast as ordinary notebook hard disks.

Just as on desktops, **floppy and CD-ROM drives** are standard equipment for today's laptops. On heavier notebooks, both drives may be built in; on lightweight notebooks, one or both may be external, connected by a cable. Average-weight notebooks often have a single bay that can hold either a floppy or a CD-ROM; for these models, it's a big plus if one drive (usually the floppy) can be hooked up by cable when it's not in the bay.

Most notebooks these days have one or two **modular bays** (see Figure 5) that can hold a variety of devices. What these bays can hold varies between vendors and models, but options include floppy or CD-ROM drives, second battery, second hard drive, Zip or LS-120 drives (discussed in Chapter 4), and DVD-ROMs. On notebooks with two bays, usually only one can hold the CD-ROM drive, and this can limit the possible configurations.

Figure 5

Modular bays.

Most notebooks have modular bays, which let you reconfigure the system with various devices depending on your needs of the moment. Some allow you to hook up the floppy or CD-ROM externally when it's not installed in the bay.

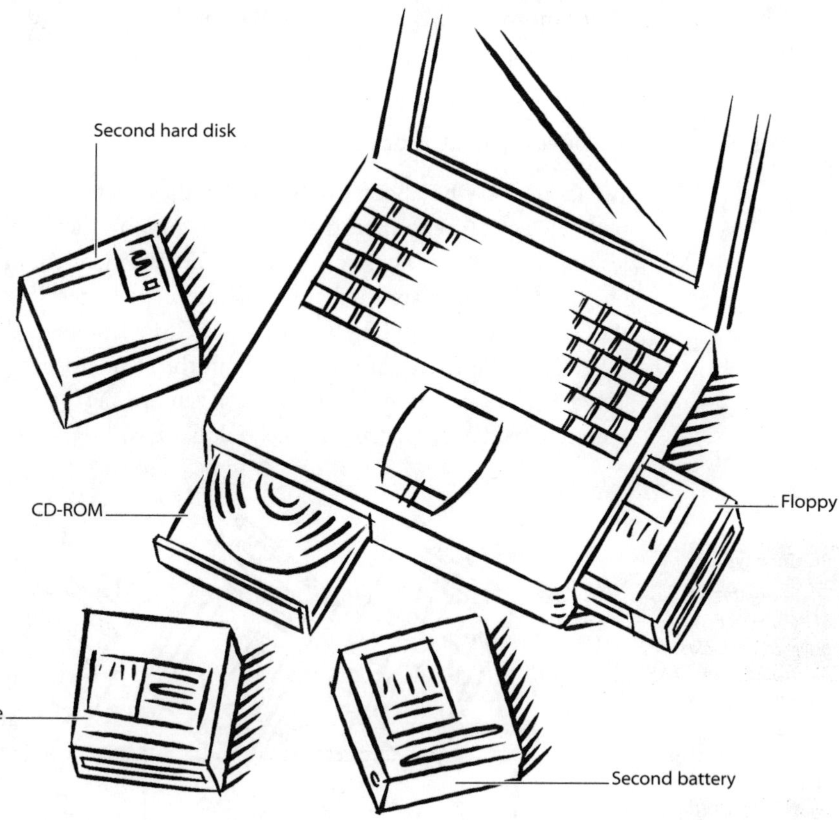

Ports and Slots

Here's a list of the **ports** you should expect a notebook to have, and what they let you connect to your notebook:

- **one parallel:** for printers, external drives, desktop computer (see "Exchanging Files with Your Desktop PC," later in this chapter)
- **one or two serial:** for external modem, mouse
- **one or two USB:** for any USB device (keyboard, mouse, drive, speakers, etc.)
- **one SVGA out:** for external monitor
- **one or two PS/2:** for mouse, keyboard
- **two or three audio jacks:** for microphone, headphones, external speakers

Here are some other ports that aren't essential but may be useful:

- **infrared:** for printer, desktop computer (for file transfer)
- **composite or S-video inputs:** for video camera

- **composite or S-video outputs:** for TV or VCR
- **joystick** (sometimes requires breakout box)
- **Ethernet:** for network
- **port replicator** or docking station

Just about every notebook on the market these days has two PC Card (formerly PCMCIA) **expansion slots** (see Figure 6), the notebook equivalent of desktops' PCI slots. These can hold a wide variety of credit card-like devices. The most common are modems and Ethernet adapters, but there are all kinds of other add-ons including hard drives, SCSI adapters, and wireless networking gizmos. For more information about the standard, see **`pc-card.com`**. To see what you can put in the slots, check out **`mplanet.com`** and **`warrior.com`**, two retailers that specialize in notebook hardware.

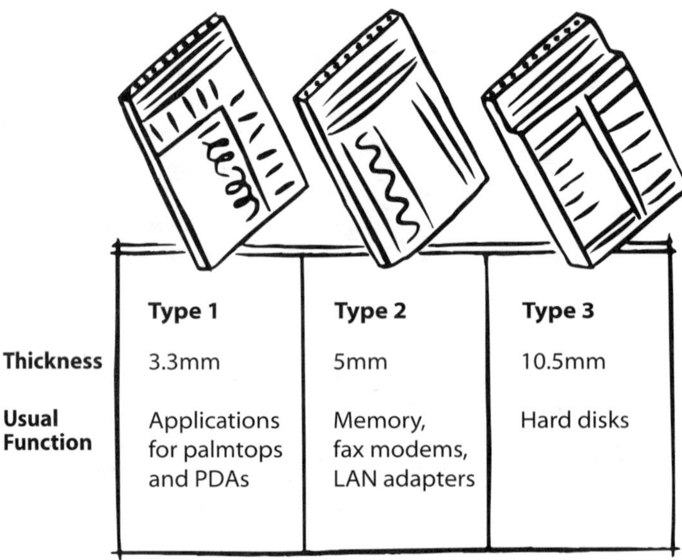

Type 1
Type 2
Type 3
Thickness
3.3mm
5mm
10.5mm
Usual Function
Applications for palmtops and PDAs
Memory, fax modems, LAN adapters
Hard disks

Figure 6

PC Card types.

There are three types of PC Cards, distinguished by thickness. Almost all notebooks have two Type II slots, stacked one on top of the other, which can hold all three types of PC Card (though there's only room for a single Type III). Ultralights may have only a single slot.

Speakers

Stereo speakers are the norm in notebooks today. Generally they sound fine, but they have no bass and can't be turned up very loud without the sound being distorted horribly. A few heavier models have slightly larger speakers, allowing you a little more volume; and in rare cases you'll get enough bass for decent music played on the built-in CD player. However, in almost all cases you'll get better results with headphones or a pair of powered external speakers—the kind you get at a stereo store to plug into a Walkman.

About Batteries and Power Management

The big power question is, how many hours will the battery last on a full charge? The range is enormous. When a notebook is away from the wall socket, it may run from two to eight hours, depending on the model, configuration, power management settings, and the unit's typical use.

Notebook batteries can be removed easily, so you can replace them yourself when they wear out, or charge up a couple in advance and then swap them during a long airline flight. There are two main types of batteries; many notebooks support both, and you may get a choice when you order.

- **Nickel metal-hydride (NiMH).** Batteries using this technology are on the way out. They cost less but don't last as long.
- **Lithium ion storage (LIS).** This is today's mainstream battery technology. LIS batteries last about a third longer than NiMH batteries. They also cost more, but they take longer to die permanently. NiMH batteries last for about 500 charges, but LIS batteries can be recharged approximately 1200 times before they go belly up. LIS batteries also contain fewer toxic substances.

Remember, though, no matter which type of battery you buy, you should always send it back to the manufacturer for recycling when it has exhausted its usefulness. You wouldn't pour used oil from your car into the gutter, would you?

Power Management

All notebooks have *power conservation features* that extend the length of a battery charge by powering down the components when you're not actively using the computer. Commonly, if the hard disk isn't being used, the computer turns it off automatically; and if you stop typing for a minute or two, the screen backlight turns off. Options are also available to reduce power consumption while you're using the computer, such as setting the CPU to a lower speed and dimming the display's backlight—things you might or might not be willing to put up with.

After a few minutes of inactivity, the notebook goes into suspend (aka "sleep") mode: Everything shuts down except for the bare minimum required to keep any unsaved data alive. Press the "resume" button, and within five or ten seconds the unit comes back to life right where you left off. On most notebooks, you can initiate suspend mode manually by pressing a button or key-combination.

On some systems, closing the cover immediately suspends the unit, and opening it resumes normal operation. This is convenient and intuitive, and has the added advantage of keeping you from losing data if you accidentally pack the thing up while it's still on.

The period of time varies for how long you can leave your notebook in suspend mode without losing data—sometimes it's hours, sometimes weeks. Check the manual to see how your machine behaves.

Many notebooks also have another, deeper level of sleep called "hibernation" or "suspend to disk." This mode saves the contents of memory and the current state of the machine to the hard disk. Put the machine in this mode, and you can leave it off indefinitely without worrying about the battery running out and losing your data. The best level of power management will let you set the inactivity period that will trigger regular suspend mode, and how long after that the suspend-to-disk mode will kick in (see Figure 7).

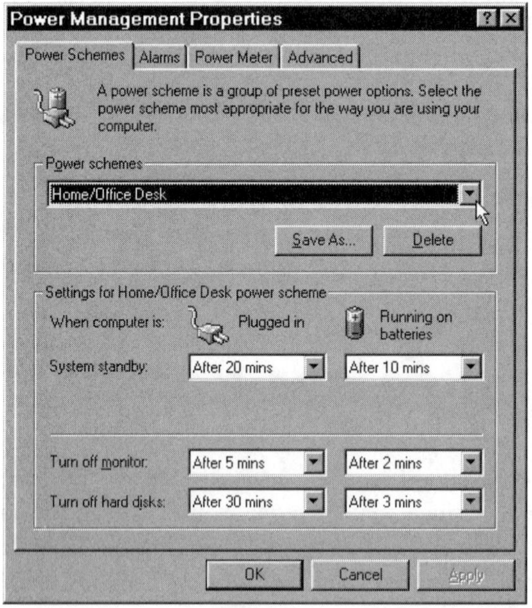

Figure 7

Notebook power management.

Some notebooks have very flexible power-management features that let you fine-tune battery use to suit your personal needs.

Bear in mind that Windows NT 4.0, unlike Windows 95 and 98, has no power-management support built in. If you want to run NT on your notebook, make sure the vendor provides an NT-compatible power-management utility. Dell, IBM, and Toshiba notebooks have good reputations among NT users, but not all their models are necessarily compatible with NT.

Convenience Features

Ideally, you should be able to swap batteries while you work, so that you don't have to shut the computer off to do the job. To let you know when batteries are low, most notebooks feature a blinking light, which sometimes blinks faster as doom approaches; and sometimes an alarm indicates that you should save immediately while there's still time. Best of all is a gauge (either a software utility or an array of lights) that shows how much juice you have left—unfortunately, these devices aren't always accurate.

The AC Power Supply

In terms of AC power supply, the main things to consider are size and weight, because you'll be taking the power supply with you. Expect anything from a few ounces and the size of a cigarette pack, to over a pound and the dimensions of a small book. Notebooks occasionally have the power supply built in, which adds a little weight to the base unit but eliminates the clutter of the "brick."

The cord connecting the AC power supply to your laptop should be long enough for you to put the power supply on the floor when the computer is in your lap. And give the power connectors a close look, too—flimsy connectors are a frequent source of breakdowns for otherwise hardy portables.

Going abroad? Then the power supply should be able to adapt automatically to 220-volt operation. If it can't, and you accidentally plug the power supply into the wrong voltage, you may burn it to a crisp. Just try replacing one of those in Estonia!

Off-the-Road Connections

Notebooks usually have one parallel port, one serial port, one USB port, a video connector for hooking up an external monitor, and a PS/2 connector that can handle a mouse or a keyboard (or, using a Y adapter, both). That's enough to let you hook up an external monitor, keyboard, mouse, and printer for more comfortable working off the road.

If you need to hook up to a network when you're off the road, you'll need an Ethernet port. Some high-end notebooks have them built in, but that's fairly rare. There are lots of PC Card adapters on the market. Standard 10-megabit models start around $80, and combo 10/100-megabit versions cost about twice that. A few companies (including 3Com and Xircom) make PC Cards that do double duty: On the road, they're modems; at the office, they're Ethernet adapters.

Thinking about making a notebook your primary computer? Consider buying one of the following manufacturer options, which can make using a notebook at your desk as easy and as comfortable as using a desktop PC:

- **Port replicators** are simply two-sided strips of connectors. On the back, you plug in your desktop monitor, mouse, and keyboard, along with a printer if you have one. When you return from traveling, you plug your road machine into the connectors along the front of the replicator—and hook to all the desktop devices in one fell swoop. Port replicators are usually quite inexpensive.
- **Docking stations** offer duplicated ports, expansion slots, and sometimes as much room for disk drives as a desktop PC (the notebook still provides all the processing power). With a well-designed docking station, you keep the cover on your notebook closed, slide it into a bay beneath the monitor, and everything comes up just as if you'd turned on a desktop PC. Predictably, most docking stations are expensive.

Not all manufacturers offer these options, so if your notebook will be doing double duty as a desktop, make sure before you buy that the features you want are available.

Durability and Security

Yes, do kick the tires. More than desktop computers, portables are prone to physical breakdowns (as opposed to electronic ones) because they get banged, bumped, dumped, and dropped. Make an overall judgment about how sturdy the whole unit is, and watch out for these trouble spots:

- Avoid hinged compartment doors; they break off too easily. Look for sliding compartment covers instead. Metal and rubber hinged doors are generally sturdier than plastic.
- Avoid switches and knobs that project past the main outline of the case—a forceful whack is bound to knock them off eventually.
- Avoid keyboards that flex when you type, or that seem too fragile to take the punishment endured by desktop keyboards.
- Avoid flimsy-looking power connectors and cords on the computer and on the AC adapter.

As for those less-accidental disasters, some machines have key locks that will at least keep out casual snoopers. Some let you set up a password that you must type in to use the computer—without it, the machine refuses to start. Other models come with built-in metal brackets, so you can cable-lock them to a desk.

Service

"Service" is a euphemism for what usually happens when a mobile computer stops working: The manufacturer simply swaps a new machine for the sick one. At wholesale prices, these computers apparently cost less than a technician's time, and most of the broken computers just get junked.

Nevertheless, be sure you check out the service policy carefully. Find out how many service centers there are and where they're located. If a traveling computer is critical to your business plan, you want guaranteed on-site service within 24 hours, or a guaranteed overnight exchange/loaner policy. Also, ask if you'll need a credit card in order to exchange the system via Federal Express or another courier when you're not near a service center. (This is common practice among many vendors who want to protect themselves until they can definitively say whether the failure was their fault or yours.)

Falls kill more portables than anything else. As a result, it's becoming increasingly popular for the vendor to offer extra-cost accident insurance. But check out the rates before you buy.

Exchanging Files with Your Desktop PC

If you have a desktop PC and use your laptop when you're on the road, you'll need some way to get files from your desktop to your notebook and vice versa. Here are several different methods; the one that will work best for you depends on how much data you need to take along and how organized you are.

- **Floppy "sneakernet."** Fast and simple, but there's not much room on a floppy, and it's a big pain to have files scattered over a bunch of floppies.
- **Zip "sneakernet."** Like floppies, but you get almost 70 times as much space. [This is the method I use, partly because I'm often running late. I've got an internal Zip drive in my PC, so I can just copy whatever I need onto a Zip disk. Then I throw the disk into the bag with my notebook and parallel-port Zip drive, and sort it all out when I get to where I'm going. —RJL] Any other parallel-port drive will work as well or better than a Zip.
- **E-mail.** This is easy if you just have a few files—you can e-mail them to yourself, and download them from the road when you need them. You should be able to set your notebook's e-mail program to leave attachments on the server until you want them, so you won't clog your modem with a huge download until you really need the files. For tips on those settings, see Chapter 20: E-Mail.

- **Briefcase.** This Windows utility is supposed to simplify "sneakernetting" between laptop and desktop PC (or between home and office PCs) by automatically synchronizing files. Unfortunately, if you exceed the capacity of the disk, it fails in such a way that you might accidentally lose data, or go off without important files. [I only mention this Microsoft utility to warn you not to use it. —RJL]
- **Direct Cable Connection.** This Windows utility lets you set up a network connection between laptop and desktop by connecting their parallel ports with a special cable—no Ethernet cards required. This arragement is harder to use than it ought to be, but once you've got it figured out it's a fast way to transfer large quantities of data. (If you have trouble getting it working, you may need to install the IPX protocol using the Network control panel.)
- **Laplink.** If you move files back and forth a lot, this utility can't be beat. You connect your notebook and desktop (or any two PCs) over whatever connection is most convenient (a cable connecting the serial or parallel ports, or infrared, modem, Ethernet, or Internet). Then select the folders and files you want to appear on both systems, and Laplink does the rest. You can also use the modem or Internet link feature to pick up files from your home or office PC while you're on the road. See the Resources section at the end of this chapter for information.

Duplicating your desktop's e-mail setup on your laptop can be painless, difficult, or impossible—depending on what progam you use. Chapter 20: E-Mail, offers tips on that sometimes complicated task.

Ten Tips for Mobile Computing

The following free advice may save frustration when you're traveling with a mobile PC in tow. Note that some of these suggestions may add to the traveling weight—another reason to go with the lightest system you can find that has the features you need.

1. **Back up before you go.** No matter how durable your mobile PC, its data is always at greater risk than a deskbound PC's. Before you pack up and move on, at the very least copy the files you've updated to a floppy, and keep that disk in a safe place separate from your computer.
2. **Bring an extension cord.** In some hotel rooms, the phone jack is a mile away from the AC outlet. You want to make both connections simultaneously, since modems suck battery power like crazy.
3. **Carry a spare boot disk.** Any system, mobile or otherwise, should have a nearby floppy disk to boot from should anything go wrong with the hard disk. To learn how to create a boot disk, see "Safety Check" in the last section of Chapter 11: Windows 95, 98, and NT.

4. **Take your Windows CD** along with you when you travel. If you have access to a printer on the road, you'll be able to install the necessary drivers from the CD.
5. **Don't forget tech support numbers.** If your hardware is on the fritz, you won't want to be wracking your brains trying to remember the city where the manufacturer is so you can call 555-1212 to find help. Keep those 800 tech support numbers in your carrying case.
6. **International tip.** You probably know that much of the world uses 220-volt instead of 110-volt AC power. But did you know that Europe alone has more than a dozen types of power plugs? If you're going abroad, make sure you have the correct adapter plug. Specialty travel stores often sell "universal" kits that fit five or six types of sockets.
7. **Don't sweat the airport X-rays.** Some people say you're risking data if you run your mobile PC through a security check's X-ray machine, but that's just a myth.
8. **Print by fax.** If you don't have access to a printer, use your computer's fax modem to send the document to the nearest fax machine. The document won't look great, but you'll have a paper copy.
9. **Improve your Windows cursor.** On some screens, the mouse pointer gets lost when you move it, becoming a blurry gray streak. To help combat this, check the "Show pointer trails" option in the Mouse control panel (see Figure 8).

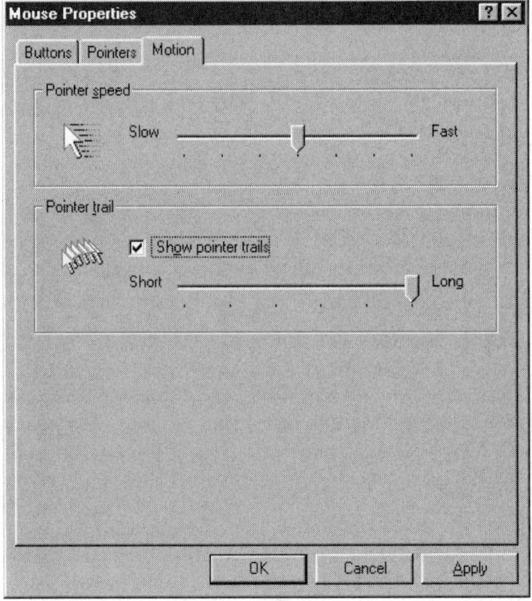

Figure 8

Mouse pointer trails.

If you have trouble seeing the mouse pointer on your notebook's screen, check this box in the Mouse control panel. The "trail" of ghost images, as illustrated in the graphic next to the checkbox, makes it much easier to follow the pointer as it moves around the screen.

10. **Enlarge Windows text.** Notebook screens are too small for many people to read comfortably. One solution is to choose a larger font in the Display control panel (see Figure 9). If you're not happy with the results (some stuff may look weird), try the Zoom option in your application's View menu. If the application doesn't have Zoom, you can try choosing a larger font (usually in the Font or Character dialog on the Format menu), but this approach can screw up the line breaks in your document

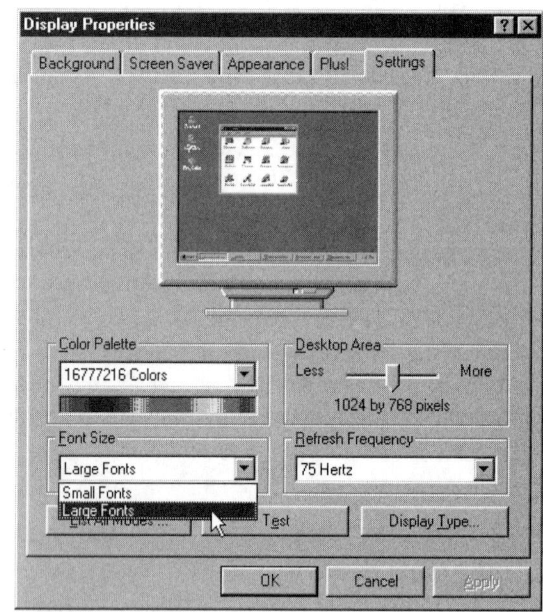

Figure 9

Using larger fonts.

If it's too hard to read the text on your notebook's screen, try switching the Font Size choice to "Large Fonts" in the Settings tab of the Display control panel.

Printers to Go

Most of the time, taking a printer on the road makes about as much sense as stuffing your suitcase with a brick. With floppies available for backup copies of your work, and electronic mail for communicating, printing can usually wait until you get back home. In some cases, though, you really do need a printed paper copy of that contract, invoice, or estimate.

You'll want a plain-paper ink-jet printer, because they consume the least battery power, supplies are relatively cheap, and print quality is great. (For more on ink-jets, see Chapter 6: Printers.) As this book goes to press, the best portable on the market is probably Canon's BubbleJet BJC-80, which weighs three pounds and cranked out four pages a minute in *PC Magazine*'s tests. According to the magazine, the BubbleJet's main competitor—the HP DeskJet 340—weighs more, is only about half as fast, and can't print envelopes. On the bright side, however, the DeskJet has an infrared port, so (assuming your notebook has one, too) you don't have to carry a printer cable. Both printers cost around $250 on the street.

Notebook Resources

Computer magazines tend to promote the latest technology regardless of whether it's cost effective, but the magazines are still the best source of information about notebooks. Here are three that do a better-than-average job. The section "How Do They Weigh Notebooks, Anyway?" near the beginning of this chapter will help you make sense of the conflicting and sometimes odd standards for comparing these products. (Full disclosure: I used to review notebooks for CNET and I've written about other topics for *PC World,* and other contributors to this book write regularly for *PC Magazine.*—RJL)

www.pcmag.com *PC Magazine* devotes most of its August issue to notebooks, and throughout the year does smaller roundups and covers new products. You can find all of this on the magazine's Web site. The magazine's battery-life tests attempt to simulate how people use notebooks in the real world. From the main page, click "PCs" under the "PC Labs Reviews" heading, and then click "Notebooks." Every July, *PC Magazine* publishes the results of a subscriber "PC Service and Reliability" survey; it rates various brands based on their reliability and the quality of the manufacturer's service; pay particular attention to the "would buy again" figures. The front page of the Web site usually has a link to this article; otherwise, click "Issue Archives" and find the July issue.

www.pworld.com/top400 *PC World* takes the approach of listing, every month, the top 10 or 20 products in each of a dozen or so categories. Under "Hardware," click "Notebooks." That will bring up a list of the latest notebook reviews, including the magazine's most recent Top 10 lists, as well as individual reviews of new products.

computers.com CNET's hardware site intermittently updates its reviews in five categories:

- "Ultralight notebooks"—by CNET's definition, those under five pounds. (In this book, we use the term to mean less than *two* pounds.)
- "Bargain notebooks"—low-cost models.
- "Leading-edge notebooks"—those with the fastest CPUs.
- "Executive notebooks"—fast, lightweight, full-featured, expensive.
- "Workhorse notebooks"—whatever doesn't fit into one of the other four categories.

To get a full list of reviews, click "Notebooks" on the front page, then "All Notebook Reviews." (Be aware that **computers.com** also has a lot of raw data about products it hasn't reviewed; that stuff's just taken from manufacturers' spec sheets, so it's not necessarily reliable.)

yahoo.com Yahoo! has a page where you can find lots of other notebook reviews. Go to Computers and Internet : Information and Documentation : Product Reviews : Laptop Computers. If you have trouble finding a particular vendor's site, try Business and Economy : Companies : Computers : Hardware : Personal Computers.

4

Disks, Hard and Otherwise

by Robert Lauriston

In This Chapter

Disk drives are essential components of every PC—without them, when you shut off the computer, all your data would disappear into the ether. Actually, you wouldn't have any data, because without an ample hard disk to hold your word processor and so on you wouldn't have been able to enter any data in the first place.

In this chapter, we'll take a look at the hard, floppy, and CD-ROM (or DVD-ROM) drives that come with virtually every PC. We'll also take a look at other drives you might find useful, like CD-R, CD-RW, Zip, and SparQ, and compare their pros and cons. (Tape drives, since they're normally used only for backup, are covered in Chapter 9: Protect Your Data.)

Hard Disks

Shopping for a hard drive is a lot easier than it used to be—for most of us, the entry-level models are overkill just as they are with CPUs. The capacity of hard disks currently on the market ranges from around 2GB (found mostly in notebooks) to more than 20GB (found mostly in network servers). At the time this book was printed, most entry-level PCs came with 4GB drives, but by the time you read this the norm may have risen to 6GB or 8GB, or even more.

Any of these number represents a huge amount of storage: A single gigabyte would hold seven copies of this book—500 copies if you stripped out the graphics. I see no reason to pay extra for a larger-than-average hard drive unless you're going to be working on projects involving massive amounts of data, like editing high-quality digital video. Otherwise, you'd be better off with a removable hard drive or some other type of removable storage, which will let you add space inexpensively a gig or so at a time, as you need it.

- **EIDE vs. SCSI.** There are two basic types of hard drives on the market these days: EIDE, which is standard in mass-market PCs, and SCSI,

Tech Note: Playing Loose with "Gigabyte"

Strictly speaking, a gigabyte is 1024 megabytes. (A megabyte is 1024 kilobytes, and a kilobyte is 1024 bytes, so a gigabyte is thus 1024 x 1024 x 1024, or 1,073,741,824 bytes.)

Though all drive and PC manufacturers are aware of those facts, they usually pretend that "gigabyte" means a billion bytes, which is to say they overstate drive capacity by 7.4%. Thus if your PC has, for example, a drive advertised as having a capacity of 6.4 gigs, you will likely find that the real capacity is only 6GB.

Some vendors strike a balance between that bogus definition and the truth, claiming that a gigabyte is 1000 megabytes. That overstates real capacity by only 2.4%.

which is common in servers and high-end desktop PCs used for special tasks like professional publishing and video editing. SCSI's main advantage is that it allows the creation of high-performance "drive arrays," configurations in which two or more drives act as a single unit. SCSI will also let you hook up a much larger number of drives to a single PC. The downside is that configuring a SCSI system properly can be difficult, and errors or crashes may occur if you don't get it right. See "SCSI Advantages" for a detailed comparison of EIDE and SCSI. (Tech note: To be precise, SCSI and EIDE describe not the drives themselves but rather the "bus" that connects the drives to the other components in the PC. There's a third bus on the market, Fibre Channel, which is even faster than SCSI, but it's found only in high-end servers.)

- **Average Access Time.** One of two key specifications for comparing hard disk performance is the *average access time*: the number of milliseconds (ms) that elapse between Windows asking a drive to read a file and the moment the drive actually starts pumping out the data. Since that interval can vary substantially depending on where the file is stored on the disk, the advertised spec is the *average* access time. Access times typically range from 8ms (better) to 10ms (worse). You won't notice this difference in most tasks, but certain large operations like hard-disk searches and database queries can benefit a lot from a shorter access time.

SCSI Advantages

When discussing drive interfaces, "multitasking" means two or more devices can work at the same time. For example, your PC could be reading from a SCSI CD-ROM drive while simultaneously writing to the hard disk, or reading from or writing to all the SCSI drives in an array at the same time. With EIDE, only one device at a time can be active, so the PC has to read from the CD-ROM, then write to the hard drive, then read some more from the CD-ROM, etc. Hence EIDE is not suitable for drive arrays, which depend on all drives working simultaneously.

	EIDE	SCSI
maximum bandwidth	33MB/sec	40MB/sec
supports hard drives	Yes	Yes
supports CD-ROM drives	Yes	Yes
supports tape drives	Yes	Yes
supports drive arrays	No	Yes
supports scanners	No	Yes
supports external devices	No	Yes
maximum number of devices	4 per PC	15 per adapter
multitasking	No	Yes

Gory Technical Details: UDMA vs. EIDE

Earlier versions of EIDE had a theoretical top speed of 16.7MB. Actually, due to signal overhead and other constraints, this speed topped out at a real-world transfer rate of something less than 8MB/second, which eventually became a bottleneck on hard disk performance. UDMA was a fairly simple and inexpensive modification to EIDE that doubled the theoretical speed of the interface to 33MB/second. I'm not sure what the real-world limit is, but to date it's still fast enough so that it's not a bottleneck even on the fastest drives.

- **Sustained transfer rate**, aka throughput. The second significant hard-disk performance specification is the *throughput*: It tells you how many megabytes a second the drive can pump out. (Don't confuse this factor with the *burst transfer rate,* which tells you how fast the drive can read data out of its on-board RAM buffer—a matter of mostly academic interest.) Entry-level drives currently pump around 5MB/second; high-end drives about twice that. Faster drives are sometimes noisier because their platters (see Figure 1) spin faster. Most mass-market drives spin at 5400 rpm; drives used in servers, where noise isn't such an issue, often spin at 10,000 rpm or faster.
- **UDMA** (aka Ultra-ATA) is sometimes incorrectly called Ultra-EIDE). You don't really have to worry about the alphabet soup: Just be aware that to get top performance, your hard drive and motherboard both need to support this specification.

Windows includes several utilities to help keep your hard drive running smoothly. For tips on where to find them and how to use them, see "Safety Check" in Chapter 11: Windows 95, 98, and NT.

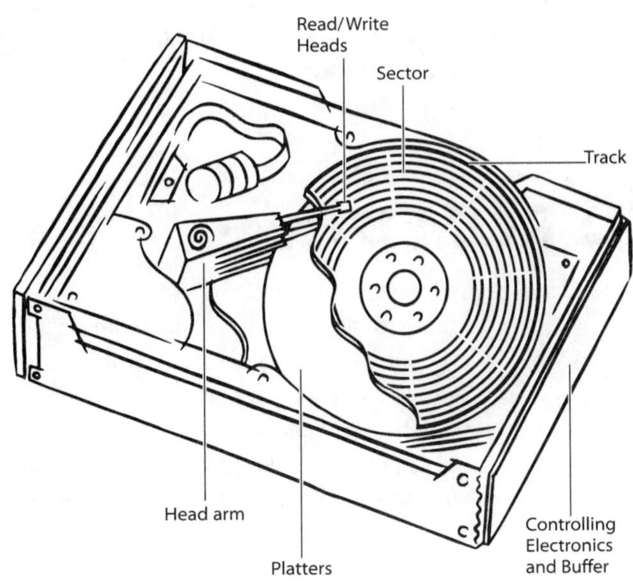

Figure 1

Inside a typical hard drive.

Covered with a thin film similar to the coating on magnetic tape, a hard disk's platters spin at 5000–10,000 rpm. Acting on instructions from Windows, the drive's controlling electronics tell the read/write heads (two for every platter, one for the top surface and one for the bottom) to seek for or deposit data in specific locations. The buffer *(a small amount of RAM) in the drive's circuits improves performance by allowing the drive to send and receive data when the PC is doing something else, and vice versa. (Functionally, this is very similar to the L2 cache memory between the PC's CPU and memory, as explained in Chapter 2: How To Buy a PC.)*

Floppies

The floppy (or diskette) drives that are standard equipment in today's PCs are fairly interchangeable. They all take the same 3.5-inch disks with the hard plastic shell, and all are equally slow. The disks are commonly referred to as "1.44MB," but in fact they normally hold only 1.39MB. There's a special read-only DMF format occasionally used to distribute software that packs 1.7MB onto each disk, and floppy capacity can also be increased by using the DriveSpace utility bundled with Windows 95 and Windows 98.

A number of drives on the market today can handle both standard floppy disks and special higher-capacity disks holding 100MB or more, and some PC vendors will let you order one of these drives in place of the regular floppy drive. See "Zips and Other Removable Media" later in this chapter for more information.

If you need to exchange data with 286 PCs and other funky old systems from the DOS era, you might need an old-fashioned 5.25-inch floppy drive as well. These outmoded drives use disks protected by a flexible plastic sleeve—the origin of the term "floppy." The lower 1.25MB capacity of the 5.25-inch disk means you can't necessarily copy the entire contents of a 3.5-inch diskette to the older format. An even older type of floppy looks the same but holds only 360K—however, you can read from and write to those with the 1.2MB models. These drives have been obsolete for years, so few PC vendors offer them as factory options. You can still buy them, though—check out **floppydrive.com**, an online vendor who carries these and other obscure models.

Tech Note: Playing Loose with "Megabyte"

Like hard disk vendors, floppy-drive manufacturers overstate the capacity of their products through creative redefinition. Their "1.44MB" measurement pretends that a megabyte is 1000 kilobytes (1,024,000 bytes); actually, it's 1024 kilobytes.

CD-ROM Drives

Since virtually all software (including Windows itself) is now distributed on CD, a drive that can read CDs is an essential component for every PC. In most cases today, that component is a CD-ROM drive (Figure 2), but a DVD-ROM, CD-R, or CD-RW drive will do just as well. (There's a comparison chart coming up, in the "CD-ROM Plus..." section.) The following sections tell you what to look for in a regular old CD-ROM drive.

Figure 2

The inner workings of CD-ROM.

Unlike a hard disk drive, which stores data magnetically and enables you to save or alter data, a CD-ROM drive uses a laser beam and photocell detector to read data only—up to 650MB of it on a single, replaceable disk.

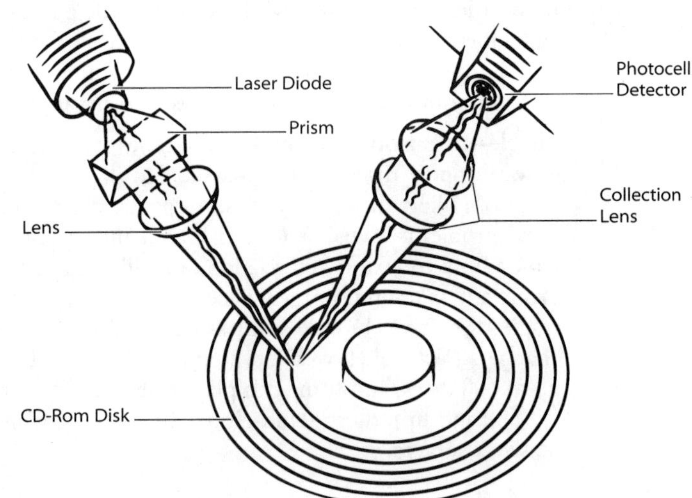

- **Speed.** Advertised "X" speeds (see the upcoming Tech Note) might give you the idea that some CD-ROM drives are much faster than others, but the difference isn't always noticeable. With many tasks, like looking something up in an encyclopedia CD, differences in speed are outweighed by a delay of a few seconds while the drive spins up. (The drive stops spinning the disc when it's not in use, to save power and stop the annoying whine.) Thus you'll mostly notice speed differences when installing applications. When searching encyclopedias and similar online references, you'll likely notice more of a benefit from a drive with a faster access time than one with a higher "X" rating. That spec typically ranges from less than 100ms (better) to more than 150ms (worse).

Tech Note: Understanding CD-ROM "X" Ratings

The original CD-ROM drives in PCs about ten years ago spun discs at the same rate as audio CD players. This resulted in a maximum transfer rate of about 150K per second; that is, it would take at least one second to read a 150K file. After a while, it occurred to drive manufacturers that they could improve the transfer rate by spinning the discs faster, so they made newer drives to spin two and then four times as fast. People started calling these "2X" and "4X" drives, and the term stuck.

Thus, multiplying the "X" number by 150kbps will give you a drive's theoretical maximum transfer rate. A 32X drive, for example, could in theory pump out up to 4800K every second. But in fact, you'll often get only half that rate or less, due to differences in a drive's rate of reading data from different parts of the disc (and other variables, like buffer size and driver efficiency).

For example, a while back, PC Labs (the testing lab used by *PC Week* and other Ziff-Davis magazines) found that 12X drives were only about 20% faster than 6X drives. Some vendors have started acknowledging that disparity by citing a range of speeds. A 14–32X drive, for example, is supposed to pump between 2100K and 4800K of data per second—a much more realistic estimate of its performance than a simple 32X label.

- **Controls.** Most CD-ROM drives have only a button to eject the disc and a knob to adjust the volume of the drive's front-panel headphone jack. Some also have audio CD controls, which you can use to play music CDs without having to load any special software on your PC.
- **Single-disc models vs. changers.** If you use more than one CD regularly, swapping discs can be a hassle, and the more you handle the discs the more likely they are to get smudged and cause errors. You can avoid those problems by using a multi-CD changer. The less expensive models, which hold four or five discs, look just like regular internal CD-ROM drives and take up no more space. They typically cost a little more than single-disc drives but are still less than $200. Stand-alone CD-ROM changers (aka "jukeboxes"), which require a SCSI card in the PC, hold up to 100 discs, and some can play several discs at once. Due to their cost ($1,500 and up), these stand-alone changers are generally used only with network servers.

Playing Audio CDs with Your PC's CD-ROM Drive

Windows has an audio CD player built in, so all you need is a pair of speakers in order to use your PC as a stereo system. If your PC's speakers are decent, the results are usually acceptable, though on some PCs you may notice an annoying hum at high volume.

Personally, I much prefer to use a separate stereo, even an inexpensive boom box. The controls are much more convenient, I can easily adjust the volume without accidentally setting myself up to get blasted by one of Windows's alert sounds, and I don't have to interrupt the music when I need to look something up on one of my reference CDs.

Figure 3

The Windows CD Player utility.
This has one nice feature you don't get in your stereo system: You can enter the names of CDs and their tracks, and it will show them as the disc is playing. I have no idea how the utility knows which disc is which, but it recognizes them and displays the right titles.

CD-ROM Plus: CD-Rs, CD-RWs, and DVD-ROMs

Once upon a time, if you wanted to play a CD in your PC, you had to use a CD-ROM drive. Today there are several other choices that do more or less everything a CD-ROM drive can, plus other stuff. Here's a quick look at the major contenders, as well as some likely losers to avoid. (Flip to the end of this section for a summary chart comparing the various capabilities of these CD-plus drives.)

CD-R Drives

CD-R (for Recordable) drives look and work like CD-ROM drives, except you can also use them to create your own data CDs. Your "home brew" CD-ROMs will play back fine on almost any 6X or faster CD-ROM drive. Play back on 4X and many slower drives, though, and you may experience problems. With the right software, a CD-R drive can also produce audio CDs, which will play on most CD players.

Blank CD-R discs are quite cheap—around $1 a disc. Good thing, too, because CD-Rs are a "write-once" medium. That is, once you write a file to the disc, it can't be erased; and if there's an error while you're burning an audio CD, you have to toss the disc and start over.

Using Adaptec's DirectCD and similar special software, you can treat a CD-R like any other disc, adding, updating, and deleting files at will. Any files you delete or copy over, however, are simply hidden and will still take up just as much space on the disc. For example, if you copy the same file to a CD-R over and over, the free space on the disc will get smaller and smaller as it gets eaten up by successive hidden copies of the same file, and will eventually run out.

CD-RW Drives

CD-RW drives can do everything CD-R drives can, plus one extra capability: They can write to CD-RW discs, an erasable CD format that can be used over and over, like a floppy. Compared with a Zip disk, a $20 CD-RW disc is a pretty good deal. For around twice the price you get five times the storage. After you've saved data to a CD-RW, you can read it using some newer CD-ROM drives or any DVD-ROM drive—which can be useful since some DVD-ROMs can't read CD-Rs.

CD-RW speed ratings are kind of confusing. Some, like CD-Rs, have just read and write ratings. Others have separate "X" numbers for reading, for writing CD-Rs, and for writing CD-RWs. The fastest CD-RW drives on the market as this book goes to press are supposed to read at 6X, write CD-Rs at up to 4X, and write CD-RWs at 2X. In fact, however, I've found they write at only about 200K/second—that is, it takes about five seconds to copy a 1MB file. Also there's apparently something weird about the DirectCD format that makes CD-RW drives slow to a crawl (20–30K/second) if you try to edit a file directly on the disc, instead of copying it to your hard drive first.

A Glossary of CD Terminology

CD-ROM: Compact Disc-Read Only Memory. This is the factory-produced CD format that is used for almost all commercial software. At this point, we're obviously stuck with this term, but it's a lousy choice of words. The significant difference between the original CD format and the computer industry's variation is that the former held audio and the latter held data. Both formats are read-only (i.e., you can't record to them), and "memory" is a term that should be reserved for RAM. Personally, I tend to use "CD" or "data CD" when I can get away with it.

CD-R: Compact Disc-Recordable. This format is "recordable" in the sense that you can use it to make your own data or audio CDs. CD-WORM (Write Once Read Many), an early term that didn't catch on, was more accurate: Once you fill up a CD-R, it's as unwritable as a regular CD-ROM.

CD-RW: Compact Disc-Rewritable. This relatively recent addition to the family is basically an erasable version of a CD-R. You can use a CD-RW disc over and over indefinitely, like a giant floppy.

DVD-ROM: Digital Versatile Disc-Read Only Memory. This is the data counterpart of the format used in DVD video players.

MultiRead: A drive that can read CD-ROMs, CD-Rs, CD-RWs, and audio CDs.

DirectCD: An Adaptec format that allows you to access CD-R and CD-RW discs on the Windows desktop and from applications, just like any floppy or hard drives. This format reduces the disc's capacity from the usual 650MB to 493MB.

I expect that CD-RW drives eventually will completely replace CD-R drives in the marketplace. In the meantime, the RWs cost only around $100 more—a reasonable price for the extra capabilities, unless you already own a removable hard drive or something similar.

DVD-ROM Drives

The computer industry has been pushing the DVD-ROM format, which can hold 4.7GB, as the successor to CD-ROMs. So far, however, CD-ROMs seem to be solidly entrenched favorites.

As I write this, DVD drives have been on the market for a year, but there are only half a dozen DVD-ROM titles you can buy—and those are all just variations on stuff already available on CD-ROM. So, really, the only thing you can do with a DVD drive that you can't do with a CD drive is play DVD movies—which, if you're like me, you'd rather do in the living room on your TV set.

DVD technology seems to be caught in the old chicken-and-egg bind. Most PCs don't have DVD-ROM drives, so software companies have little motivation to abandon the CD-ROM format that everybody can read. Since there's so little software on DVD-ROM, consumers don't have much reason to pay extra to buy a drive that can read them. I expect DVD-ROM won't really take off until after the drives are as affordable as CD-ROMs. And that probably means not until after 400MHz CPUs are considered entry-level, since slower PCs require a special "decoder" card to decode the DVD movie format and that card drives up the price.

DVD "X" ratings aren't directly comparable to those used with CD-ROMs. From test results to date, a 2X DVD drive's rating is similar to a 20X CD drive.

Recordable DVDs: Too Many Cooks Spoil the Alphabet Soup

To date, there's no recordable DVD-ROM format—that is, no counterpart of CD-RW. Hitachi is selling a so-called DVD-RAM drive that can read DVD-ROM discs and record 2.3GB on a special disc, but you can't read that disc on a DVD-ROM drive. Sony, Philips, and Hewlett-Packard (which, with Yamaha and Ricoh, dominate the CD-R and CD-RW markets) are working on another format called DVD+RW. Pioneer is working on yet another, DVD-RW. This insane proliferation of incompatible formats with similar names seems likely to confused consumers to the point where they won't want to buy any of these products.

There is a write-once DVD-R standard, but it creates DVD videos, not data DVDs. Even if you want to make video DVDs, that technology's not likely to filter down to the consumer level for a few years. The only drive available as I write this lists for $16,995.

CD Format Compatibility Chart

Drive Type	CD-ROM	CD-R	CD-RW	DVD-ROM
max. capacity	650MB	650MB	650MB	2.6GB
read CD-ROM	yes	yes	yes	yes
play audio CDs	yes	yes	yes	yes
read CD-R	yes*	yes	yes	varies
read CD-RW	varies	varies	yes	yes
read DVD-ROM	no	no	no	yes
play DVD movies	no	no	no	yes
write CD-R	–	yes	yes	–
write CD-RW	–	no	yes	–

*All drives manufactured in recent years can read CD-R; some older models may have problems.

The plethora of CD media and formats currently in use has led to some confusing compatibility issues. The easiest way to avoid them is to get a drive with a "MultiRead" sticker, which means it can read CD-ROMs, CD-Rs, and CD-RWs, and play audio CDs.

Zips and Other Removable Media

Compared to other components in today's PCs, the floppy drive is a Stone Age relic. The computer I used to write this book has 100 times the memory, 300 times the hard drive space, and a CPU around 100 times faster than the 286 I was using in 1987—but the floppy disks I use today can hold only 20% more data than their predecessors.

That disparity means floppy disks are no longer suitable for many of the tasks for which they were once used. For years I backed up my hard disk to a stack of floppies; if I tried that today, I'd need a stack about eight feet high. I still regularly use floppies for "sneakernet," to transfer files to and from computers without Internet connections. Increasingly, however, the files I'm moving are too big to fit on a floppy.

Enter the Iomega Zip drive, a floppy drive scaled up to match other contemporary components. The Zip disk, which is only slightly bigger and thicker than a regular floppy, can hold 95.7MB (the "100MB" in Iomega's ads is 100 million bytes), making Zip disks suitable for passing around large files or whole projects. Purchased in bulk, the disks cost $10 each, so you're not going to hand them out like floppies, but they're still cheap enough for lending to clients or delivering desktop-publishing jobs to a print shop. If you're buying a new PC, I strongly recommend getting a built-in Zip drive. They're affordable (less than $100), you don't have the cable and power-adapter clutter you get with the parallel-port model, and you don't have to worry about the drivers messing up your printer.

For backing up multigigabyte hard drives, however, Zips aren't an economical or practical medium. For example, backing up 2GB of data storage would take between 10 and 15 Zip disks ($100 to $150), which you'd have to spend half an hour or so swapping in and out of the drive. A better solution is tape backup.

You can back up over 5GB to a single $25 tape, and the backup can run unattended while you're at lunch or sleeping. See Chapter 9: Protect Your Data, for an in-depth discussion of tape drives and other backup topics.

The Zip isn't the only "superfloppy" on the market. The LS-120, aka SuperDisk, drive (sold by various vendors) can handle both 120MB proprietary disks (around $80 a 10-pack) and regular floppies. Sony and Fuji have announced a similar product called HiFD that will hold 200MB. The main disadvantage of these formats is they're nowhere near as popular as Zips, so they're less useful for "sneakernet" file transfer.

Another removable-media alternative is the cartridge hard drive, like the Syquest SparQ and Iomega Jaz, which are sort of like Zips on steroids. These are basically just small hard disks built into hard-shell cartridges. Install one of these drives in your PC and you can swap cartridges in and out, just like floppies. One of these drives will cost you more than a superfloppy drive, but in the long run they're cheaper, since (as you can see from the "Removable Media Comparison" chart) the cost per gigabyte of storage is much lower. After the first few gigs, cartridge drives are also cheaper than regular hard disks—though they're not as fast. Their lower capacity makes them less convenient for backup than tapes, but they're the next best thing. For the best performance in a cartridge drive, get a SCSI model.

Removable Media Comparison

The removable drive that's right for you will depend on how much data you need to store and what you want to do with the discs. The low unit cost of CD-Rs means you can practically hand them out like business cards. The low cost of CD-RWs is offset by how slow they are. Removable hard drives are more prone to damage from being knocked around in transit.

	Drive Cost*	Media Cost (each)	Claimed Capacity	Cost per GB	Versions
Zip	$100	$10 (in 10-pack)	100MB	$100	EIDE, SCSI, parallel
LS-120	$100	$8 (in 10-pack)	120MB	$70	EIDE
Iomega Jaz 2GB	$325	$75 (in 3-pack)	2GB	$37.50	SCSI
Syquest SparQ	$175	$24 (in 10-pack)	1GB	$24	EIDE, parallel
Syquest SyJet	$250	$50 (in 3-pack)	1.5GB	$33	EIDE, SCSI, parallel
CD-R	$325	$1 (in 10-pack)	493-650MB	$2 (write-once)	EIDE, SCSI, parallel
CD-RW	$400	$10 (in 3-pack)	493-650MB	$20	EIDE, SCSI, parallel

*Street price, cheapest internal model.

Disk Drive Resources

www.computershopper.com Most computer magazines don't do a very good job of covering hard disks and other drives. One exception is *Computer Shopper*, a catalog-like monthly with a lot of ads for mail-order houses that sell components. (One assumes a lot of readers want to buy them.) Look for the "Storage" section on this Web site.

www.tdl.com/~netex Net Express is a computer retailer that sells exclusively over the Web. I've never bought anything from them, but I've found a lot of useful information about drives, CPUs, and motherboards on their site. Their catalog includes tons of specs and is peppered with useful links to FAQs, technology white papers, and vendor sites. Note: Although their selection of products is always current, the technical explanations are sometimes out of date, and the product recommendations are aimed at hardcore Silicon Valley geeks.

www.fadden.com/cdrfaq This is a slightly disorganized but comprehensive guide to not just CD-R, but also CD-RW, DVD, and the contending writable DVD specs.

www.onlineinc.com/emedia/index.html EMedia Online (no relation to *e/media weekly*) is the Web site of *EMedia*, a monthly magazine aimed at professional media types who use CD-ROM, CD-R, CD-RW, DVD, and so on. This publication is the best source I know for news of evolving standards and the latest CD-related products. Unfortunately, not everything that appears in the print edition is provided online, and the subscription price is pretty steep if you're not in the business.

www.adaptec.com/support/faqs/dcdissues.html The DirectCD format supported by many CD-R and CD-RW drives can be kind of confusing. This page is a good place to start if you have questions or problems.

5

Monitors, Etc.

by Robert Lauriston

In This Chapter

How important is your monitor? Ask someone who just spent 12 hours suffering in front of a crummy one. Paying extra for a monitor that's easy on the eyes makes sense—even if it costs half the price of the PC itself. And when you're talking that kind of money, it's worth getting educated about the specifications to look for when you go shopping. That's what this chapter is about, mostly.

Remember, though, that the monitor you buy won't work without a graphics card, a small cluster of circuits residing on an expansion card (or occasionally built into the motherboard). The monitor itself is pretty dumb. If the monitor is a movie screen, then the graphics card is a projector—it regulates the monitor's resolution, the number of colors displayed, and several other key factors.

If you already have a PC, then buying a new graphics card will be an upgrade for you. The "Installing Expansion Cards" section of Chapter 8: Upgrade It Yourself, will tell you what's involved in that. If you're buying a whole system, monitor included, use this chapter in conjunction with Chapter 2: How to Buy a PC, to get the best deal. Just remember: Don't scrimp on the monitor, or your eyes will regret it.

Monitor Buyers Guide

The monitor's the most expensive component in many PCs, and the one that has the biggest effect on your everyday computing experience. Yet many people spend more time deciding what CPU to choose than on selecting the best display. Don't make that mistake. Whether you spend less than $250 or more than $1,000, this chapter will help you get the most for your money.

Monitor Size

The bigger the screen, the less time you'll spend scrolling through documents and switching between applications, and the more time you spend actually working. Desktop monitor sizes range from 14 inches to 21 inches, with prices rising along with tube size from less than $150 to more than $2,000. Note that the number of inches in the screen size is actually the diagonal measurement of the tube, and there's an unused border around the edge. So the screen area is always smaller than the number of inches suggested. For example, a typical 17-inch monitor's viewable area is about 12-1/2 inches wide by 9-1/4 inches high.

I don't recommend 14-inch monitors for everyday use. Good monitors of this size haven't been manufactured for several years. Consider using them on servers, when you only need to look at the monitor for occasional maintenance tasks, or as a cheap emergency spare while your main display is in the repair shop.

- **The 15-inch minimum.** A 15-inch monitor with an 800x600-pixel desktop is acceptable for Windows use. Some Web pages are a little cramped at this resolution (see Figure 1), but millions of people get along with it just fine anyway. If you're going to be doing a lot of page layout or other graphics work, get something larger. Street prices start around $150, and few models cost more than $250.

Figure 1

Resolution, screen size, and image size.

Generally speaking, a larger monitor will let you run Windows at a higher resolution, which means you'll get a larger desktop to work on. This illustration gives a rough comparison of the different monitor sizes. See "How Big Is Big Enough?" later in the chapter for more details on resolution settings.

- **The 17-inch comfort zone.** A 17-inch monitor with a 1024x768 desktop is big enough to give Windows some breathing room. It also gives you plenty of room for viewing bloated Web pages or for cutting and pasting between windows. This is the minimum size I recommend for people whose eyesight isn't so good. Models aimed at regular users generally cost between $250 and $475 on the street; more expensive models are designed for graphics professionals who need more precise color.

- **The 19-inch maybe.** For most people, a 19-inch display doesn't make much sense. As you can see from the "How Big Is Big Enough?" table in the upcoming sidebar, a 19-inch isn't quite big enough to display a 1280x1024 desktop comfortably—and many of the models we've seen aren't sharp enough at that resolution anyway. Most 19-inchers can handle an 1152x864 desktop just fine, but that's not enough compared to what a 17-inch can handle to justify the higher price: around $600 to $800 on the street.

How Big Is Big Enough?

My monitor recommendations reflect the resolutions most people seem to prefer. If your eyes aren't so good, you may want to select a lower desktop area setting (resolution) in Windows's Display control panel; if your eyes are really good, you might want to knock it up a notch or two. Or, to turn that around the other way, the worse your eyes are, the bigger the monitor you'll need to run Windows with any given desktop area. This table sorts various combinations of monitor and desktop sizes into groups with similar pixel spacing. (The most popular settings are displayed in bold.)

Pixels per Inch	Monitor Size / Desktop Size
40–45	19"–21" at 640x480
51–58	15"–17" at 640x480
	19"–21" at 800x600
65–67	17" at 800x600
	20"–21" at 1024x768
72–76	**15" at 800x600**
	19" at 1024x768
	20"–21" at 1152x864
81–84	**17" at 1024x768**
	19" at 1152x864
	20"–21 at 1280x1024

Pixels per Inch	Monitor Size / Desktop Size
90–93	15" at 1024x768
	17" at 1152x864
	19" at 1280x1024
95–97	21" at 1800x1440
101–105	15" at 1152x864
	17" at 1280x1024
	20"–21" at 1600x1200
113–116	15" at 1280x1024
	19" at 1600x1200
121–127	17" at 1600x1200
	21" at 1920x1200 (letterboxed)
	21" at 1800x1440 (side borders)

Most people are comfortable with their monitors set to display somewhere between 72 and 84 pixels per inch. Fewer than that, and the image starts to look grainy; more than that, and smaller text gets too hard to read. People with below-par eyesight typically prefer fewer pixels per inch, while people with exceptionally sharp eyes often prefer higher settings.

If you know what desktop area setting you like on a particular size monitor, it's a safe bet that on a larger monitor you'll want a setting that gives roughly the same number of pixels per inch. Note, however, that monitor sharpness varies, and on a sharper monitor you may well be able to tolerate more closely-spaced pixels. For example, I have an exceptionally sharp17-inch monitor on my Mac and a mediocre 20-inch monitor on my PC, and I run them both at the same 1024x768 resolution.

- **The jumbos.** The 20- and 21-inch monitors are still too expensive for most people, but they're essential tools for desktop publishers, architects, and other graphical types who need a big, sharp view of their work. These jumbo monitors are also essential for Web designers and other programmers who need to be able to see lots of windows at a time. There's a wide range of quality and price—you can get a 21-incher for less than $700, but first-rate models cost more like $1,000 to $1,500. Eizo, Mitsubishi, Nokia, and Sony are brands favored by graphics professionals. These displays are large enough to run 1280x1024 resolution without giving most people eyestrain.

If you choose a monitor larger than 17 inches, make sure you have a place to put it. The 17-inch models are already big and heavy; they average 40 pounds and 17 inches deep (from screen to rear end). Larger models are 18–20 inches deep and weigh 50 to 65 pounds—enough to buckle the chassis on some compact PCs. Don't forget to calculate for the extra height of a tilt-and-swivel stand, and make sure there's enough space for twisting and turning.

If you're a graphics pro or serious amateur planning to do color prepress work, be sure the monitor you buy is among those supported by any and all color-management systems you need to use. See Chapter 17: Painting, Drawing, and Other Graphics Software, for more on this topic.

Monitor Image Quality

Three basic specifications affecting image quality can help you narrow your choice of monitors; you'll find these specs here in this section. Specifications don't tell the whole story, though: there's no substitute for going to the store and look at several prospective buys side by side (just as you'd compare, say, stereo speakers).

- **Maximum resolution.** Much as a photographic image is produced by strategically arranged dots of ink, the image you see on your screen is created by *pixels* (short for picture elements). The *resolution* of an image is its width and height in pixels (controlled by the "image size" or "desktop size" setting in Windows's Display control panel), which are arranged and sent to the monitor by the graphics card. The lowest resolution you're likely to encounter today is 640x480 pixels; the highest is 1600x1200. Raise the resolution and you can see more at once: more paragraphs of a letter, more cells of a spreadsheet, etc. The trade-off is that since the monitor stays the same size, the text, icons, and window controls all get smaller in order to fit more on the screen. At a certain point, they get too small and blurry to read and manipulate comfortably. See the sidebar, "How Big Is Big Enough?" to get an idea of what resolution you need.
- **Dot, aperture, or stripe pitch.** The image on a color screen is made up of tiny triads of red, green, and blue phosphor dots. Dot pitch—the distance in millimeters between phosphor dots of the same color—is a major factor in determining the sharpness of a monitor. Generally, the smaller the dot pitch, the sharper the image (see Figure 2). As a rule of thumb, you should never consider a monitor with a dot pitch larger than .28mm.
- **Vertical refresh rate.** This is the number of times per second the tube's electron gun can produce a full-screen image. A faster refresh rate means less flicker and less eye fatigue. A refresh rate that updates the screen 85 times a second (85Hz) is ideal. At 75Hz, you may see some flicker, especially if there's a lot of fluorescent light in the area. If the refresh rate drops much below that, some flicker is likely, and at around 60 to 65Hz it's likely to be intolerable. Most monitors today will do 85Hz at their recommended resolution, but may drop off to 60Hz at their highest possible resolution—but you probably won't use that mode often, if at all, anyway.

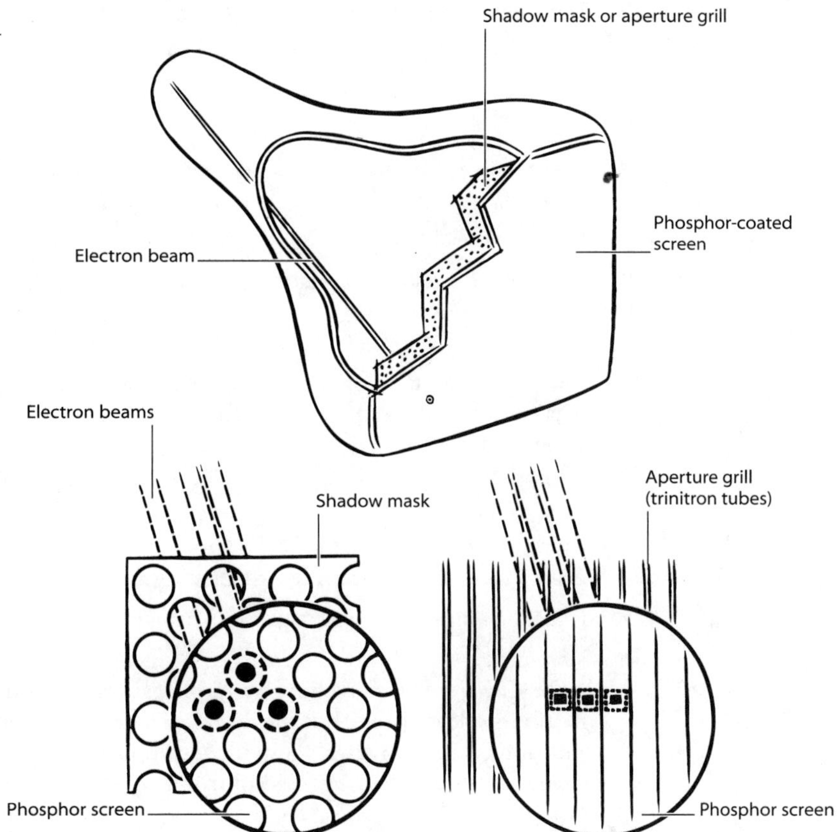

Figure 2

A cathode-ray tube (CRT) and all those dots.

Inside a monitor's tube, an electron gun sweeps the phosphor-coated inner surface of the screen, illuminating the dots it lands on. The closer together the dots are (that is, the smaller the dot pitch), the sharper the image generally is, regardless of the resolution.

Controls and Adjustments

At the factory, your monitor should have been fine-tuned to produce the best possible image, and it contains circuits that will automatically adjust it to whatever signal it gets from your video card. Thus, ideally, all you will ever need to adjust are the brightness and contrast.

However, if your monitor gets knocked around in shipment, the factory adjustments can go out of whack—or (especially with a cheap off-brand monitor) it may never have been adjusted to its optimal settings in the first place. Here's a glossary of the controls you may need to adjust. Generally speaking, the less expensive monitors have a more limited set of controls. (Your monitor's manual should tell you which controls it has.)

- *Degauss* removes random color swirls caused by changes in the earth's magnetic field. To avoid putting a strain on your monitor, wait at least 10 minutes before pressing the degauss button a second time.
- *Horizontal position* moves the image from side to side.

- *Horizontal size* increases or decreases the width of the image.
- *Vertical size* increases or decreases the height of the image.
- *Vertical position* moves the image up or down.
- *Pincushion* and *barrel distortion* correct for the sides of the image being bowed inward or outward. Adjust the control until both sides are straight.
- *Rotate* (or *Tilt*) turns the image clockwise or counterclockwise so its edges line up parallel with the edges of the bezel (the "frame" around the screen).
- *Trapezoid* adjusts for the sides of the image not being parallel (i.e. the top of the image is wider than the bottom, or vice versa). Adjust until the sides are parallel.
- *Parallelogram* adjusts for the sides of the image being parallel but tilted, so that the top is not centered over the bottom. Adjust until the corners are at right angles.
- *Convergence* corrects the annoying separation of white dots into their red, blue, and green color components. The distortion is caused by a misalignment in either the vertical or horizontal convergence, or both. You need a special test pattern to properly adjust this.
- *Focus* (*Sharpness*) works just like in a camera—it makes the dots on the screen sharper or blurrier.
- *Moiré Cancel* helps make wave or ripple patterns—which occur in all monitors—less visible, but the trade-off is that the image is less sharp. Adjust to your own taste. (You can accomplish much the same thing by a slight adjustment to the focus control.)
- *Color Temperature* (aka *White Balance* or *White Point*) affects the overall color balance of the image. The most common settings are 9300°, which gives white a slight bluish tint, 6500° (yellowish), and 5000° (reddish). Many monitors also allow you to create a custom color balance by setting red, green, and blue values manually. Adjust to your own taste, or as recommended by your color-management system.

All this button punching could strand you with a screen that looks nothing like what you intended. If you end up in that situation, use the Recall or Reset control to bring the screen back to its factory defaults. Finding the optimal settings for many of these controls requires the use of test patterns. See the following sidebar, "Give Your Monitor a Tune-Up with DisplayMate," for a tip on where find them.

Give Your Monitor a Tune-up with DisplayMate

Optimizing your monitor's settings is impossible without the right test patterns (see Figure 3). DisplayMate from Sonera Technologies gives you all the patterns you need, organized into an easy-to-follow, do-it-yourself tune-up utility with ample explanations and tips. You can download a free trial version containing the most important tests from **sonera.com**; if you like it, you can download the full version for $69.

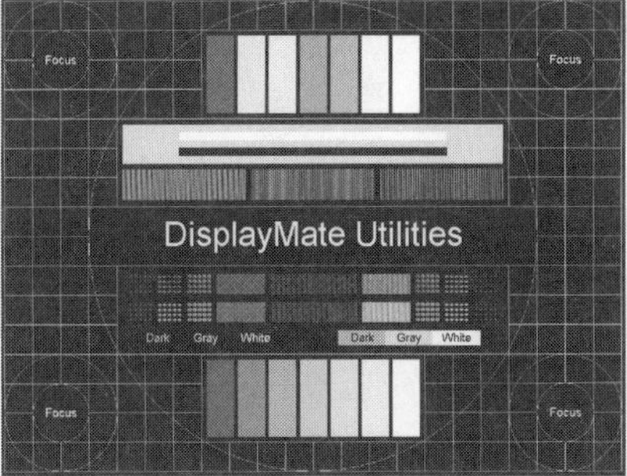

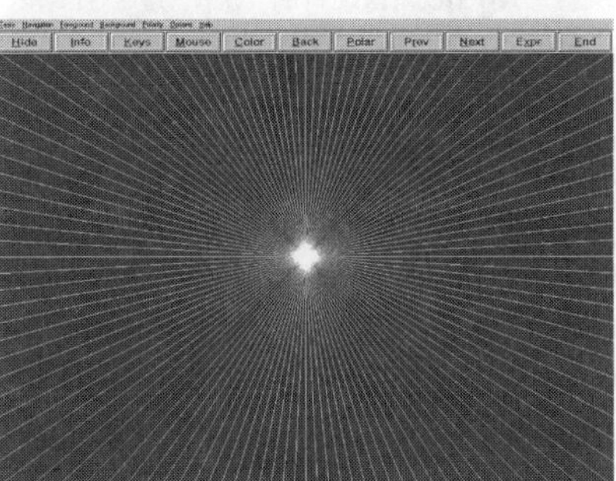

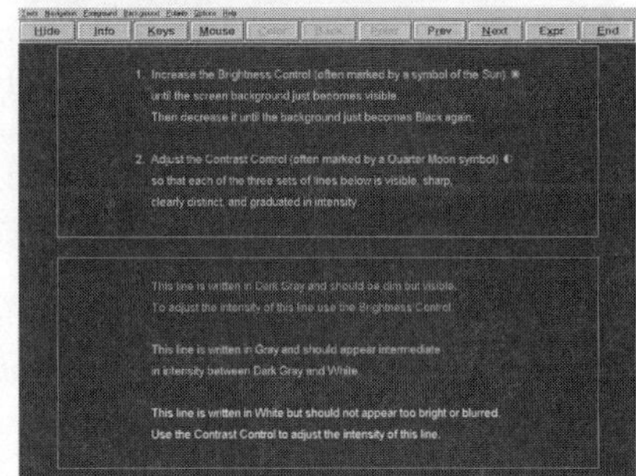

Figure 3

These four test patterns are just a sample of the dozens included in the DisplayMate monitor tune-up utility.

Monitor Buying Tips

Since monitors are mass-produced, name-brand products, it doesn't really matter where you buy. Once you figure out which one you want, you might as well shop around for the best price. Web price-comparison services like **`computershopper.com`** can be very helpful in comparing mail-order dealers, but be sure to add in shipping charges.

The normal warranty period for monitors is three years parts and labor, so don't buy one with only a one-year warranty, or with three years parts and one on labor. If you're not buying a cheap low-end model, ask if an extended warranty is available.

You can often find exceptional prices on recently discontinued models, which are typically 90% as good as their successors at 50%–60% the price. The Web's a great place to find such deals—check out auction sites like onsale.com. Just be sure you get the full manufacturer's warranty.

Don't buy a used monitor unless you get a really great price, because you won't have any warranty. Use DisplayMate (see the "Give Your Monitor a Tune-Up with DisplayMate" sidebar) or a similar utility to align the monitor, *before* you write the check.

Health and the Environment

Monitors produce electromagnetic emissions, which some studies suggest may pose a serious health hazard and/or cause birth defects. Although monitor manufacturers have steadfastly denied such effects, they have radically redesigned their monitors to reduce emissions. In addition, monitors account for a large share of the power consumed by PCs, which indirectly creates pollution by raising demand for electricity. Manufacturers have responded to both problems (see Chapter 26: Health and Safety, for more on these topics).

- **Monitor emissions.** Studies have yet to prove that electromagnetic radiation (EMR) produced by monitors constitutes a health hazard, yet public concern has grown, prompting monitor makers to adopt the strict Swedish MPR-II emissions standard defining exposure limits. In fact, you'll be hard pressed to find a monitor today that doesn't meet the standard. Nonetheless, remember no one claims to have established "safe" limits. It's best to keep your monitor at (literally) arm's length when you compute, and—more importantly—to make sure no one is exposed for long periods of time to the back of a monitor, the strongest source of emissions.
- **Low power.** The Environmental Protection Agency's Energy Star guidelines suggest no monitor or PC should draw more than 30 watts of electricity when idle. The monitor industry has responded by creating the DPMS (Display Power Management Signaling) standard. Essentially, DPMS defines four descending levels of power below full on, with a final level of 5watts or less. Again, it's unlikely you'll find a monitor that doesn't support this standard.

Flat-Panel Displays

Flat-panel displays, which use the same liquid crystal (LCD) screens found in notebook PCs, are superior to regular monitors in several ways. Because the pixels are like tiny light bulbs, each the exact same size and permanently fixed in its correct position, the image is perfectly sharp and stable—the focus and geometric distortion problems common on other monitors are physically impossible. Flat panels take up less desk space (they're only a few inches thick), so they can fit in locations too cramped for tube displays; some can even be hung on the wall. They only weigh 10 or 12 pounds (half the weight of a 15-inch tube monitor), so they're easier to move around. The absolutely flat surface is less susceptible to glare than any tube—if there's a light source reflecting off the screen, you just tilt the display a few degrees and it's gone.

So what's the catch? The price. They're more affordable today than ever before, but they still cost up to four times what a roughly comparable monitor will set you back. As this book goes to press, the cheapest off-brand models cost around $850, and their major-name counterparts are more than twice that.

Another catch is that LCDs can't match a tube's color accuracy. Because of the way the image is generated on LCD, if you change the viewing angle slightly the colors you see will change. The effect is subtle enough that average users won't notice it, but it makes flat-panels unsuitable for graphics professionals.

Picking a flat-panel is easy. The desktop size is fixed, so what you see is what you get. The most important thing to look for is even backlighting: Watch out for dim or bright areas, especially along the edges and in the corners. You should also watch out for defective pixels, which will be permanently stuck on one color or dark. A good way to locate them is to display an all-white or all-black image in Paint. LCDs frequently have defective pixels, and since they aren't always very noticeable and the displays themselves are so expensive, vendors often refuse to exchange them unless they're particularly bad (a certain number of bad pixels in a row, or a larger number scattered across the screen).

Note that flat-panel displays are so sharp, they are comparable to tube monitors with larger diagonal measurements. For example, a 14.1-inch flat-panel displays a 1024x768 desktop, and looks as good or better than a 17-inch monitor at the same resolution.

Video Cards

Your PC's video card creates the image you see on your monitor. The video card includes a graphics chip, which in response to commands from the PC creates desktop elements like windows and text. The card also has its own memory, where it stores the image you see on your monitor. Every pixel on the monitor has its own chunk of the graphics card's memory—though it's a very small chunk, 1–4 bytes.

For most people, choosing a graphics card is easy. It's one of those PC components today whose entry-level standard is overkill for most people. Any entry-level model from a proven company like ATI, Matrox, or Number Nine should do just fine. A basic card should cost less than $150 with 4MB RAM, less than $200 with 8MB. Special features like a TV tuner, video capture, or 3-D acceleration raise the price. Here's a quick rundown on the specs and features that matter:

- **Video memory.** The amount of memory on your video card determines how many colors Windows can display (see Figure 4). Use the table, "Video Memory, Desktop Size, and Color Quality," to figure out how much memory you need.

Gory technical details: If there's enough memory for the card to give each pixel on the screen only 1 byte (8 bits), it can't display more than 256 colors. With2 bytes (16 bits) per pixel, it can display 65,536 colors; with 3 bytes (24 bits), 16,777,216 colors. Color professionals typically refer to these settings by *bit depth*—8-bit, 16-bit, or 24-bit color.)

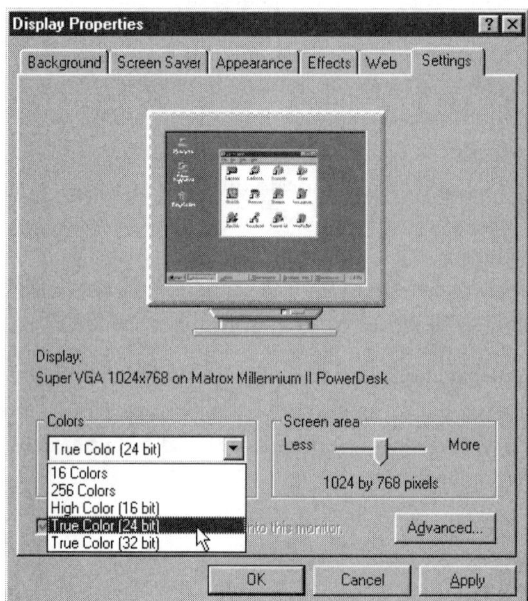

Figure 4

Setting color depth in Windows.

The number of colors Windows can display depends on what resolution you're running and how much memory your video card has. Best case, you'll get all the choices shown here; if there's not enough memory, the higher color settings will be missing, but you can make them appear by reducing the resolution (aka screen area or desktop size).

- **Slot type (PCI vs. AGP).** These days, video cards come in two basic flavors. PCI boards plug into the PCI slots found in all motherboards; AGP boards plug into the Advanced Graphics Port slot found mostly in Pentium II motherboards. Theoretically, AGP boards can run faster, but to date the test results I've seen don't show any big practical advantage over PCI. In any case, both PCI and AGP are so fast that, unless you play action games, you might never notice the difference anyway.
- **2-D acceleration.** This used to be something to worry about, but it's now a standard feature on video cards. Once upon a time, the image you saw on your monitor was created mostly by the PC's CPU, which wasn't especially fast at the job. Video card vendors figured out they could speed things up radically by creating most of the image on the card. At first, such cards were called "Windows accelerators," but after a while they became the only kind of video card left on the market, so the term no longer has much meaning.

- **3-D acceleration.** If you play action games, you'll probably want a 3-D accelerator. Sometimes they're built into the video card; sometimes they're on their own separate card. These cards speed up the calculations required to simulate three-dimensional objects in games—characters, buildings, vehicles—and to apply colors and textures (skin, fur, scorched metal) to their surfaces. 3-D cards require more memory than 2-D cards, since they store not just what's showing on screen at the moment but things that are hidden (i.e. behind other objects in the card's imaginary space), which can thus reappear instantly when the objects obscuring them move away. You can find a good technical explanation of 3-D issues in the "Perfect PC" feature on *PC Magazine*'s Web site (**`www.pcmag.com`**).
- **TV Tuner.** Some video cards have tuners built in, or available as add-ons, so you can hook up an antenna or cable and watch TV in a little window on your PC's monitor. Some tuners can do cool things with closed captions, like save the text to files (so you can make your own transcripts of favorite shows), or pop up the video window when certain keywords are detected (for instance, CNBC pops up if it has news about a stock you're thinking of buying or selling).
- **Video capture.** A few video cards include jacks for hooking up video cameras, but in the less-than-$200 price range, don't expect to be impressed by the quality. If you really want to capture and edit video on your PC, see Chapter 18: Sound and Video Editing.

Video Memory, Desktop Size, and Color Quality

The more video memory you have, the larger you can make the Windows desktop before color quality starts to degrade. You don't want to spend much time in 256-color mode—most images look lousy, and Windows itself looks a lot better in the 16-bit "High Color" mode it was designed for. The difference between High Color and 24-bit "True Color" is so subtle that, unless you're a graphics professional, you may never notice it (except occasionally in scanned photographs or other graphics with very subtle color gradations).

Desktop size	**640x480**	**800x600**	**1024x768**	**1152x864**	**1280x1024**	**1600x1200**
Recommend Monitor Size	**-**	**15-inch**	**17 to19-inch**	**19 to 21-inch**	**20-21 inch**	**-**
1MB	True Color	High Color	256 colors	256 colors	–	–
2MB	True Color	True Color	High Color	High Color	256 colors	256 colors
4MB	True Color	True Color	True Color	True Color	True Color	High Color
8MB	True Color	True Color	True Color	True Color	True Color	True Color

True Color = 16.8 million colors (24-bit)

High Color = 65,536 colors (16-bit)

256 colors = 8-bit

Monitor and Video Card Resources

Computer magazines have an unfortunate tendency to recommend the latest technology rather than the most cost-effective. In the case of monitors, that may mean they dismiss 15-inch monitors as obsolete when in fact for many people a larger display is just a waste of money and desk space. In the case of graphics boards, the reviews may come up with farfetched reasons for you to demand features you don't really need, like the recent *PC Magazine* article that suggested 3-D graphics might soon be essential for spreadsheets.

Despite those faults, magazines are the only reliable source for comparative information on displays. Here are the three I think do the best job. (Full disclosure: I've written for *PC World* and CNET, and some contributors to this book write regularly for *PC Magazine*.)

`www.pcmag.com` *PC Magazine* reviews more products than any other computer magazine, and monitors are no exception. Every October they round up 50 or more of what they consider to be the most mainstream displays, and throughout the year they have smaller comparisons of particular types of displays and graphics cards, as well as coverage of individual new products—all of which you can find on the magazine's Web site. From the main page, click "Peripherals" under the "PC Labs Reviews" heading; then click "Displays."

`pcworld.com/top400` *PC World* takes a different approach: Every month they list the top 10 or 20 products in each of a dozen or so categories. To find the latest recommendations, on the main page click "Top 400 Products," then click "Monitors" or "Graphics Boards." That will bring up a list of the latest reviews, including the magazine's most recent top 10 lists, as well as individual reviews of new products.

`computers.com` CNET's hardware site intermittently updates its reviews in three size categories; check the date at the top of each review to see how current the information is. One nice feature is that if you find a product you like, you can jump directly to a comparison of the latest prices from various mail-order vendors. To get a full list of reviews, click "Monitors" on the front page, then "All Monitor Reviews." (Be aware that **`computers.com`** also has a lot of raw data about products it hasn't reviewed; that stuff's just taken from manufacturers' spec sheets, so it's not necessarily reliable.)

`yahoo.com` Yahoo! has a page that lists lots of information about monitors, graphics cards, and their manufacturers available on the Web. Go to Computers and Internet : Hardware : Peripherals : Monitors or Computers and Internet : Hardware : Components : Cards : Video.

`sonera.com` Sonera Technologies makes the extremely useful DisplayMate test-pattern utility (see "Give Your Monitor a Tune-Up with DisplayMate," earlier). If you don't have Internet access, you can reach Sonera at 800-932-6323 or 732-747-6886 (voice), or 732-747-4523 (fax).

`onsale.com/category/monitors.htm` This auction site sells discontinued products from major manufacturers, often at incredibly low prices. Be sure to check out the "Warranty" link for a product before you put in a bid. You can find similar sites on Yahoo at Business and Economy : Companies : Auctions : Online Auctions.

6

Printers

by Steve Cummings and Robert Lauriston

This chapter was originally written by by Steve Cummings, and updated for the third edition by Robert Lauriston.

In This Chapter

How do you pick the right printer out of hundreds on the market? The easy answer: Buy a Hewlett-Packard LaserJet.

If you print standard documents like letters, reports, and maybe some newsletters and forms, and as long as you don't need color or portability, then choosing a LaserJet is a no-brainer. No, they didn't pay us to say that, and we're not saying LaserJets are the very best printers at the best possible price. It's just that you can't go wrong with a LaserJet.

LaserJets produce excellent print quality and are extremely reliable. Compared with other printers, LaserJets work with more software and more add-on devices. Supplies, parts, and repair services are widely available. And even if they're not the rock-bottom cheapest printers, LaserJets are reasonably priced.

Nonetheless, laser printers can't satisfy everyone's printing needs. If you need inexpensive color, or if even the cheapest laser is too much for your budget, you want an inkjet printer. Is tight desk space your determining factor? Consider one of the multifunction products that combine a printer, scanner, copier, and sometimes a fax in a single unit.

Then, when you've made your choice, turn to the "Printing Advice" section at the end of this chapter to get the most out of your machine.

Laser Printers

Why do they call them *laser* printers? Because inside the machine, a tiny laser beam scans across a rotating, electrostatically charged drum to create an image of the printed page. Toner sticks to the scanned image on the drum, which in turn rolls onto the paper, where the toner is fused at about 400 degrees to create hard copy. The quality produced by this process is so good, and the cost of laser printers has fallen so low, you need a good excuse *not* to buy one.

- **Personal lasers** cost less than $500 and take up about as much desk space as an open magazine (see Figure 1). They print relatively slowly—four to eight *pages per minute (ppm)*—and generally hold only 100 to 200 sheets of paper at a time. Despite their name, most personal laser printers can be shared over a network; they're just not designed to hold up under heavy use.
- **Workgroup lasers** are a step up in speed (around 12 ppm). They hold more paper and can be connected directly to a PC or a network, so they're good for small groups and individuals who print a lot. They're usually a bit bigger than personal lasers and cost less than $1,000.

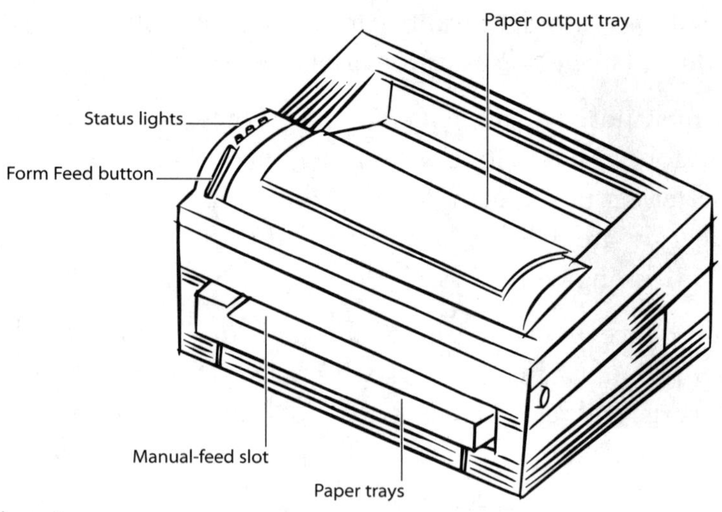

Figure 1

A typical laser printer.

Most laser printers are laid out more or less like this one, with a U-shaped paper path (the paper's fed in the front, makes a U-turn in the printer, and comes out on top.) Some use the L-shaped paper path of the typical inkjet printer shown in Figure 4. Some under-$500 laser printers have no manual-feed slot.

- **Network lasers** need to be fast—16 to 30 ppm and up—and to hold plenty of paper, because they're designed to serve a whole office. They're big and expensive ($1,500 to $4,000, or even $10,000 for some with special options); price and size vary widely according to the expected printing volume. And, of course, they come ready to hook up to a network.

There's no hard line between these three categories—some vendors' workgroup models are basically the same as their personal printers, with additional paper trays, a network card built in, and more RAM. See the later section "Serious Color Printers" for a look at **color lasers** and the like.

Print Quality

Now for the technical stuff. Laser print quality depends on three factors, all of which depend in turn on the basic element of a laser-printed image—that humble speck of toner known as the *dot.*

- **Resolution** is measured in *dots per inch (dpi).* It's the key factor in determining print quality. The current resolution standard for laser printers is 600 dpi, which produces much better output than older 300 dpi printers. Text looks considerably sharper, and when you print scanned photos, the improvement is dramatic (see Figure 2). You can get 1200 dpi printers—near-typeset quality—starting around $1,000. (When you see specs like "1200 x 300 dpi" or "1200 x 600 dpi," the lower number is the one to pay attention to.)

300 dpi

600 dpi

Figure 2

The benefits of higher resolution (dpi).

- **Resolution enhancement** simulates higher resolution by strategically sizing and offsetting dots to give fonts and line graphics smoother curves and sharper edges. "Resolution enhancement" is a Hewlett-Packard term, but other companies offer similar technologies. The simulation works, but watch out for manufacturers who use resolution enhancement to claim "1200 dpi quality," when in fact they're enhancing 600 dpi output.
- **Blacks and grays** must be seen in print in order to judge a printer's ability to render them. Black areas should be solid and dark—otherwise, large characters and block graphics alike will look weak. Ask to see printed output before you buy. Watch out for unwanted bands in solid shades, or hairlines that mysteriously break up. The more shades of gray a printer can simulate, the more lifelike printed photos will look. In general, higher resolution means more available gray shades.

Print Speed

Manufacturers routinely exaggerate ppm speed ratings by not counting the time it takes a printer to generate the page image in memory—in other words, the ppm number usually tells you how fast the printer can move blank sheets of paper into the out-tray. The ppm rating is often not that far off for printing plain text documents, but when it comes to printing graphics, huge differences emerge. When comparing printers of the same ppm rating, you'll typically find that some machines print graphics twice as fast as others.

Likewise, the various kinds of graphics take different amounts of time to print. You may encounter a rating called *gppm* (for *graphics pages per minute*), but this measurement is absolutely useless out of context. For a meaningful comparison between two printers, you must test them with the same graphics files. Do this yourself if the dealer will let you, or check out the latest computer magazine speed tests. See "Printer Resources" at the end of this chapter for help finding those reviews on the Web.

Paper Handling

Every printer comes with a *duty cycle* rating, a recommended maximum number of pages a printer should print each month. It's hard to tell what this number means, since each company seems to estimate duty cycles differently. Just don't make a personal laser your network printer, okay? And be sure to check these important features:

- **Paper sizes.** Desktop laser printers usually have two paper trays, so you can easily switch between legal- and letter-size paper. Personal models generally have a single tray that you can adjust to hold legal-size paper, and/or they offer a feeder slot into which you slip single sheets. Only big, relatively expensive printers can handle 11-by-17-inch paper, useful for large spreadsheets, poster-size graphics, page proofs, and the like.
- **Capacity.** No one likes to fill the paper tray. Personal laser paper trays typically hold 100–200 sheets. Optional, extra-cost trays let some personal lasers hold up to 400 sheets, putting these models in the same range as workgroup models. Network paper trays typically hold 500–750 sheets. With many of these models, you can configure a second tray to kick in when the first is empty, or load two or three different kinds of paper.
- **Envelopes.** Envelopes have long been the bane of laser printers. The laser printer's physical design makes envelope printing awkward. On personal printers, you may have to manually change the paper path to get a single envelope through the mill. Desktop and network printers generally offer optional bulk-envelope feeders that can hold up to 70 envelopes—but many have an unfortunate tendency to jam. (You can sometimes resolve that by experimenting with different envelopes until you find one that makes the printer happy.)
- **Sorting and stapling.** The most expensive network printers, especially from copier companies like Canon and Xerox, have paper-handling features similar to those of professional photocopiers. These features may include capacity for half a dozen different kinds of paper, collating of multiple copies, and even automatic stapling of multipage documents.
- **Duplex printing.** A boon to the environmentally conscious, the ability to print on both sides of a page is a $400 to $600 option on most network models. Of course, you can always do it the manual way, by flipping one-sided pages over and putting them back in the paper tray, but a paper jam can make a mess of things. And if somebody else's job slips into the network print queue, you're really in trouble.

Built-in Fonts

Every laser printer comes with at least a handful of fonts built in—but if you use Windows, who cares? Windows makes handling fonts so easy, and the selection of fonts is so vast, that the number or quality of a printer's built-in fonts shouldn't determine whether you buy it or not. (See Chapter 12: Windows Add-Ons, for tips on choosing and adding more fonts to Windows.)

But there are exceptions: Sending fonts from an application to a printer across a network can bog down performance, and built-in fonts may deliver much better performance. Some network models offer optional hard disks that hook right to the printer and store as many fonts as you'd like.

Compatibility

Every printer you can buy today is compatible with PCs running Windows. If you never use other platforms, compatibility is a nonissue. Of course, if you're buying a printer that's going to be used with other operating systems (like DOS or UNIX), or with other kinds of computers (Macs, UNIX workstations, and minicomputers), you need to make sure your printer will be compatible.

In that situation, LaserJets are a safe choice because they set the standard for compatibility. Every DOS application or UNIX flavor will work with a LaserJet—which is another way of saying they all have a LaserJet *driver*, a little program that tells the printer what to print and where to print it.

On the other hand, drivers for Epson, Panasonic, Lexmark, Canon, and other brands are less common. If you don't have a driver for your printer, you have to select a LaserJet driver instead. As long as your printer claims to be "LaserJet compatible"—as most do—you have reason to hope the thing will work properly. ("PCL support" is geek jargon for LaserJet-compatible.) In practice, results with simple text are usually good, but with graphics or heavily formatted documents things may get dicey.

If you want a printer that will work with both Windows and Macintosh computers, get one that supports **PostScript**, a hardware-independent standard developed by Adobe and originally popularized by the Apple LaserWriter. Most network lasers will work with both LaserJet and PostScript drivers, switching between the two automatically.

Controls

Always check out the printer's front panel readout and controls. Is it easy to figure out what's going on? Many printers have little displays and buttons to help you manually adjust toner density, resolution enhancement, paper feed, and so on. Better yet, most now come with software to let you configure such things from your PC instead of having to fiddle with buttons. For example, when the printer runs out of paper or encounters some other problem, a message pops up over your application letting you know what's wrong (see Figure 3).

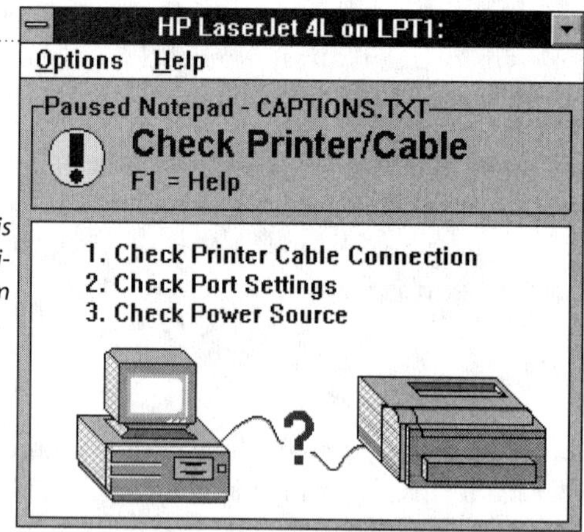

Figure 3

On-screen printer warnings.

Many printers come with software that provides on-screen status reports, like this pop-up Alert box indicating that a problem has occurred.

Memory

Laser printers generally need 2MB of RAM to print a full page of 600-dpi graphics. Most come with that much installed; others don't and make up the difference with memory compression.

Sufficiently complex pages, like newsletters with lots of fonts, columns, and graphics, will overload the printer's memory. You can work around that by lowering the resolution to 300 dpi (some printers will do so automatically), but the results are inferior.

To eliminate such problems, you'll need to upgrade the printer's memory. Even the cheapest laser should be upgradeable to at least 5MB. Some printers take inexpensive standard memory modules used in PCs; others use more expensive proprietary modules. In either case, you can usually get memory upgrades from mail-order specialty dealers for lower prices than the manufacturer offers.

PostScript laser printers need more memory, simply because you're more likely to do complex desktop publishing jobs with one. How much more depends on the number and type of fonts you plan to use at one time, and the complexity of your layouts, but 4MB (3MB with memory compression) is about the minimum. With the exception of some personal PostScript models, you'll find most PostScript printers come with enough memory for both font processing and a full page of graphics.

Some very organized companies load blank electronic forms into printer memory so applications merely need to send form data to the printer, vastly speeding print time. Depending on the number of forms, this can hog quite a bit of RAM. Fortunately, this is only an issue with network printers, which can all be upgraded to hold more than enough RAM for the job.

Operating Costs

Per-page costs for laser printers vary radically. Personal lasers cost from two to three cents a page, workgroup and network lasers from one to two and a half cents. If that doesn't sound like much, consider that it means spending $5 to $15 for every 500-page ream of paper.

You can get operating cost estimates out of computer-magazine printer reviews, but it's not hard to calculate them yourself, and the results may be more accurate. (Reviewers sometimes neglect to add in the cost of print drums for those printers that use them.) The manufacturer's spec sheet

Top Five Toner Tips

Most of the time, laser printers quietly and efficiently crank out page after page without any intervention from you. The only thing you have to maintain regularly is the toner.

1. Use print quality as your guide for knowing when to replace the cartridge. When the printer gives you a "toner low" message, you can keep right on printing as long as the pages look good.
2. When the print starts to look washed out, pull out the cartridge, rock it gently from side to side, and put it back—this may redistribute the remaining toner enough to give you many more good printouts.
3. Use remanufactured print cartridges to save money and reduce waste. They work just as well as the brand-new ones (though they may produce fewer pages), as long as you get them from a reputable remanufacturer that guarantees its work. Before using them, though, check your printer's documentation to make sure that using third-party cartridges won't void the warranty.
4. Don't worry if the first pages you print after changing a print cartridge look too light or uneven. It takes awhile to break in a new cartridge. To speed the break-in process, try printing four or five sheets of solid black.
5. To get more pages out of a toner cartridge, turn down the print density (darkness) setting. Most laser printers have a "draft mode" setting that basically does the same thing, which gives your proof printouts a wan look but lets you easily bump up toner density for your final copies.

should tell you how many pages you get from each toner cartridge, and how often you need to replace the drum (if any). Here's the calculation:

1.	cartridge street price	$68
2.	cartridge estimated page life, 5% density	2500
3.	divide (1) by (2) for cartridge cost per page	$0.0272 (2.7 cents)
4.	drum street price	$95
5.	drum estimated page life	20,000
6.	divide (4) by (5) for drum cost per page	$0.00475 (0.5 cents)
7.	add (3) and (6) for total cost per page	$0.03195 (3.2 cents)

Replacing toner cartridges, drums, and belts can be tricky, but perhaps the biggest trick of all is finding replacement consumables for an off-brand laser. You'll always find toner cartridges for popular LaserJet models at a nearby Costco or office supply store—in fact, there may even be third-party cartridges that cost less. And the other guys? You may have to order from the manufacturer. (See Chapter 26: Health and Safety for tips on recycling and recycled laser cartridges.)

Inkjet Printers

Inkjets are color printers for the masses, and laser printers for the budget-conscious. Instead of transferring toner, they use tiny nozzles in a movable print head to squirt precisely aimed streams of ink onto the page. They're slower than lasers—typically turning out only one or two text pages per minute—but the best match laser print quality, and the cheapest start at not much more than $100.

Inkjets share two laser printer limitations: Few accept anything but letter- and legal-size paper, and since there's no impact against the page, they can't print on multipart forms. But they have one important advantage over lasers. Many inexpensive models can print in color, and even upscale inkjets designed for high-volume color printing top out at around $500–$800. By contrast, the cheapest color laser printer costs around $3,000–$4,000.

There are only a few companies who make inkjet printers. So you won't find an overwhelming number of inkjet manufacturers to choose from, making comparison shopping is a little easier than with lasers. The major manufacturers are Canon, Epson, Hewlett-Packard, and Lexmark (IBM). The market is extremely competitive, so products come and go constantly, but typically each has four consumer models selling for around $100, $200, $300, and $400 on the street, plus some more expensive products aimed at networks and graphic professionals. (The high-end products are discussed "Serious Color Printers" below.)

Print Quality

You really can't predict the quality of an inkjet printer's output by looking at the spec sheets. You'd think a 1200 dpi printer would surely print better text than a 600 dpi model, but that's not always the case. You might think a printer with a seven-color ink cartridge would do a better job than one using only four colors, but that's not always true either. You're really dependent on personal observation and computer-magazine comparisons here.

Inkjets in the $100 price range sometimes have lousy color graphics but decent or even nice-looking text. If you want a cheap printer just for correspondence and other plain text jobs, one of these might do the job. Be sure to buy plain-black rather than color print cartridges.

After you buy an inkjet, there are a number of factors that can affect print quality. Here's a rundown:

- **Paper type.** Many inkjets produce better results when you use coated "inkjet paper," which typically costs 10-15 cents a page. (Plain white bond costs as little three pages a penny.) Ink, print heads, and paper are all designed to work together, so you may get the best results from the brand recommended by the manufacturer, but at those prices it's worth experimenting with generic inkjet paper as well. Note it's not unusual for inkjets to print text better on plain paper and graphics better on coated paper, or vice-versa. Some printers' output just doesn't look good enough on coated paper to justify the extra cost.
- **Ink cartridge type.** Most inkjets can take a variety of ink cartridges: some may produce sharper or blacker text, others better graphics. You'll have to experiment with different combinations of ink and paper types to find out what combinations work best. You may find one cartridge's printouts are more waterproof than others, too.
- **Software settings.** Most inkjets have an extensive set of settings available through dialog boxes under Windows. Sometimes the printer's default settings don't produce the best results, so experiment with these as well.

Paper Handling

Inkjet printers aren't as flexible as lasers when it comes to paper handling—in fact, some practically make you pull the paper across the print head yourself. On the other hand, you can get inkjets that handle oversize paper for a fraction the price of an equivalent laser. Here are a few things to look for:

- **Manual feed slot.** Some inkjets don't have a manual feed slot, which means you have to unload the paper tray to feed envelopes. Others don't make you remove the paper but still make you flip a lever to switch between automatic and manual feed.

- **Output tray.** The cheapest inkjets sometimes have no output tray (see Figure 4)—pages just spew out onto the top of the desk, or the floor. Avoid these models.

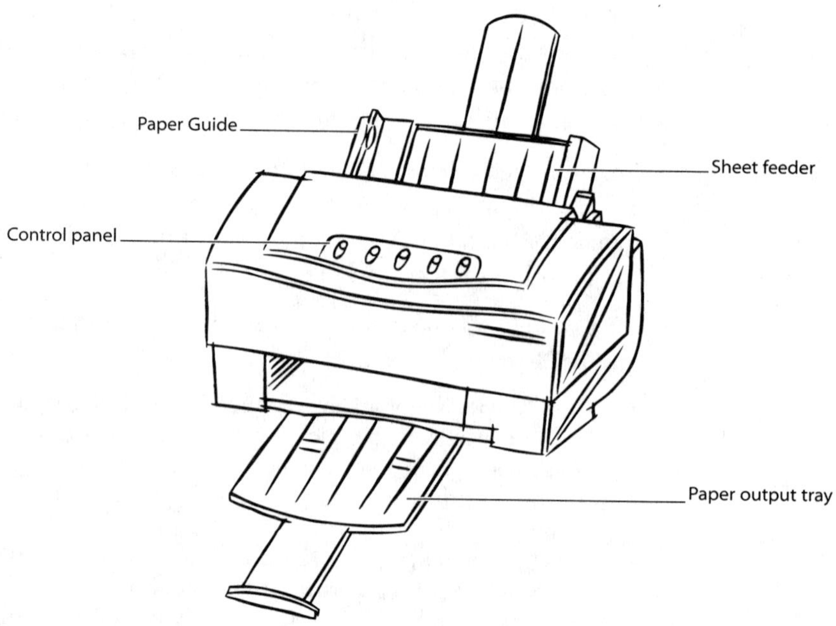

Figure 4

A typical inkjet printer.

A good inkjet printer will have a paper output tray, like this one. In many models, the sheet feeder doubles as a manual-feed slot—you just push a button, or slip the single sheet into a special guide. This inkjet has an L-shaped paper path, which takes up more space; some models have the space-saving U-shaped path of the typical laser printer shown above in Figure 1.

- **Tray capacity.** Some inkjets' input trays hold as few as 30 sheets, others as many as 150, but for most people this isn't a big issue. If you're doing a lot of big jobs, you really want a laser, and inkjets are so slow it takes them a long time to go through even a small stack of paper.
- **Paper source.** This is a driver issue—if you set the first page of a document as "manual feed" in your word processor's page setup, the printer should pause for you to insert letterhead or whatever into the manual feed slot. Some inkjets don't support this feature, which means more paper shuffling.
- **Envelopes.** Some inkjets can feed multiple envelopes, others make you feed them one by one—a pain if you're doing a bulk mailing or sending out a bunch of invitations.

- **Duplex printing.** You'll have to do this manually, though some inkjets' printer drivers will help manage the task.
- **Large-size paper.** This is one place where inkjets beat lasers. Canon sells an inkjet that can handle 11" x 17" paper for less than $300, and Epson has one that can do 17" x 22" for less than $750.
- **Banners.** A minority of inkjets support continuous gatefold banner paper, so for example you can print out a 10-foot "Happy Birthday" sign for a party.

Compatibility

Most (not all) inkjets will emulate LaserJets for use with DOS applications, but some will do so only when you run the DOS apps under Windows. Read the spec lists carefully or call the manufacturer to ask if this is an important issue for you.

Epson's the only company currently making moderately priced inkjets that work with both PCs and Macs. (The professional-graphics-oriented inkjets discussed in "Serious Color Printers" below usually handle both.)

Operating Costs

The cost to print an ink-jet page varies wildly depending on the model and what you're printing. Plain text will cost between 2.5 and 13 cents per page, but printing a full-page color graphic could use $5 worth of ink! Obviously, if you want to print a lot of color graphics, you'll want to take a close look at ink costs. Read manufacturers' cost-per-page claims carefully, and compare them with those in computer magazine reviews.

Be sure to pay particular attention to "coverage" figures. An estimate of 45 cents a page for 15% coverage means a full-page graphic (100% coverage) would cost three bucks. (100% divided by 15% equals 6.66; 45 cents times 6.66 equals $3.00.)

Dot Matrix Printers

Dot matrix printers, which were once the only kind of printer most PC users could afford, are nearly obsolete. They're noisy, they're slow, and the print quality's lousy. Now that you can get an inkjet for $100, what reason do most people have to buy a dot matrix? None.

But there's still one task at which they excel: printing continuous forms. Their tractor-feed mechanism (see Figure 5) means they can crank out reams of paper without getting out of alignment, and the physical impact of the print head can carry all the way through to the bottom of a stack of carbon or carbonless copies.

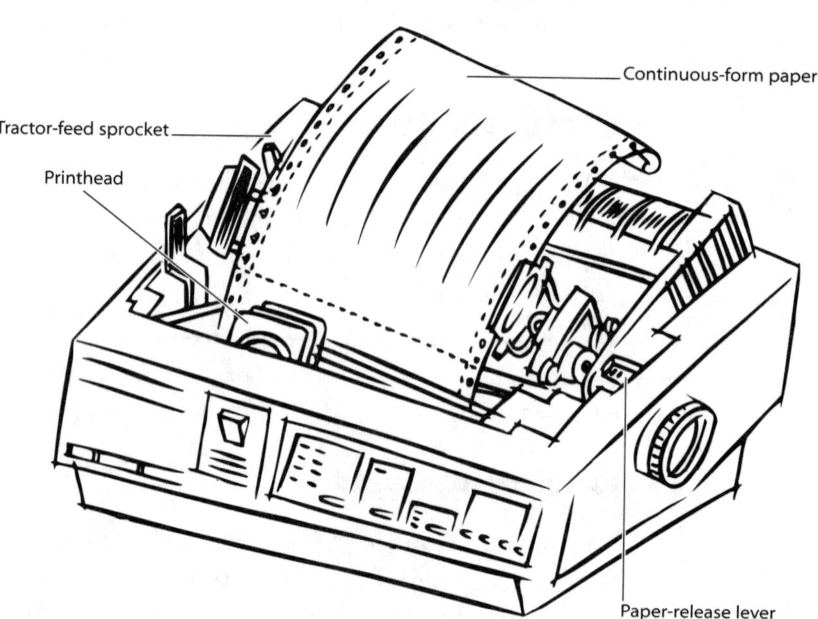

Figure 5

A typical dot matrix printer.

This typical dot matrix is shown here with its cover off, so you can see the guts, but in real life you'd want to keep it on, to quiet the racket a bit.

There are only two major companies left in the dot matrix market: Epson, which practically invented it, and Okidata, its major remaining competitor. You can find a list of the various models they offer on their Web sites, listed in the "Printer Resources" section at the end of this chapter

Instead of pages per minute, dot matrix printers go by the *characters per second (cps)*. You can be sure the printer's low-quality *draft mode* will be promoted, which is usually three times faster than its *letter quality* mode, the only mode you'd want to use for printouts you expect someone will read. For a rough estimate of pages per minute, divide the characters per second by 70—for example, 75 cps is roughly one page a minute.

If you need a printer that will bang its way through multipart forms, check the specs. Some dot matrix models can only handle forms with three or four parts, while others grind their way through five-part forms. Also look for *paper parking*, which keeps continuous-feed paper queued up when you need to insert single sheets or envelopes one at a time. Add-on feeders for stacks of single sheets are widely available.

Multifunction Printers

If you're very short on desk space, you might want to consider a multifunction printer. These gadgets combine a printer (usually inkjet), scanner, faxmodem, and sometimes an answering machine, all in one box, for around $500.

Depending on how you set it, when you feed a document into the box it can act as a copier (route it to the printer), a fax machine (send it to the faxmodem), or scanner (send it to the attached PC). Like a standalone fax machine, it can route received faxes straight to the printer.

This is a nice concept, but if you're not cramped for space it doesn't make much sense. You can get an inkjet with better print quality for $250, a scanner with higher resolution for $150, and a much faster faxmodem for $100. That setup will do everything the multifunction box will (except answer the phone), only better, and you can upgrade any of the three components when something better comes on the market.

Serious Color Printers

The inkjets discussed above are good values, and some produce really great looking color output, but they're not right for everybody. In this section, we'll take a look at some more expensive color printers, and discuss when you might want one.

- **Color lasers.** These are similar to the regular network laser printers discussed above. Quality's not as high as the best inkjets or other "serious" color printers, but color lasers are fast (one to two pages per minute vs. 5 to 10 minutes per page for inkjets), and their operating costs are low (35-50 cents per full-page graphic vs. $1 to $5). Prices start around $3,500, so you need to print a lot to make them cost-effective—which explains why they're found mostly on office networks. They use separate black and color cartridges, so you can use them for regular text jobs, too.
- **PostScript inkjets.** Designed for professional graphics types, these printers support PostScript and color management, both essential for proofing documents that will eventually be sent out for printing. Most support tabloid (11" x 17") or larger formats, and/or let you print "full-bleed"—all the way to the edge of the paper. Prices range from over $500 to less than $2,000.
- **Thermal dye (dye sublimation), thermal wax, solid ink.** These printers cost more than $5,000 (sometimes more than $15,000), and with the advent of cheap color lasers and high-quality inkjets are now of interest only to graphics professionals. Thermal dye printers are of

particular note because they produce photograph-like "continuous tone" images (i.e. no visible dots), which look great for posters, banners, trade-show displays, and so on. However, if you don't need that stuff several times a week, it's likely more cost-effective to pay by the print at a laser parlor or service bureau. Service bureaus usually offer color duplication, too, which beats waiting for one of these printers to crank out a bunch of copies. See Chapter 17: Painting, Drawing, and Other Graphics Software for more on getting color output from service bureaus.

Printing Advice

Because printers are such durable beasts, you can get healthy-looking pages month after month without doing much but changing the toner, ribbon, or ink cartridge, and maybe dusting the innards with a lint-free cloth now and again (with lasers, you may also have to replace the drum, eventually). Nonetheless, I've pulled together a few tips about software, consumables, and printer sharing that will hopefully make your printing experience a happier one.

Speed Printing

Well, you can't really speed up your printer, but you do have some control over how quickly the printing process goes. With an inkjet, using the printer's draft mode or a lower resolution will usually speed things up, but at a price in print quality. With lasers, those settings may not make any difference, at least with documents that are mostly text.

Most of the time, how long a printer takes to finish printing your document doesn't matter much. What's more important is how soon you can use your computer again after you start a print job, so you can get work done while the printer does its business. Windows speeds that up by using a *print spooler*, a chunk of software that lets applications spew out print data as fast as they can. Generally, you'll get the best results by leaving the spooler at its default setting (see Figure 6), but with some applications you may find you get a speed boost by bypassing the spooler and printing directly to the printer.

To get to the settings for Windows 95 print spooler, right-click the printer located under the Settings/Control Panel option of the Start Button and choose Properties. In Windows 98, click the Details tab, then click Spool Setting; in Windows NT, click the Scheduling tab.

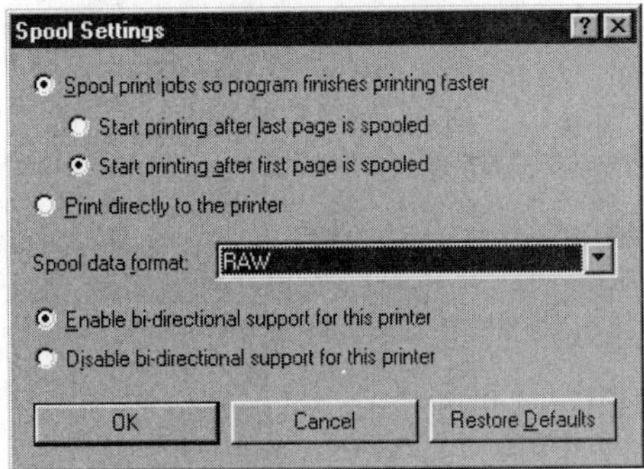

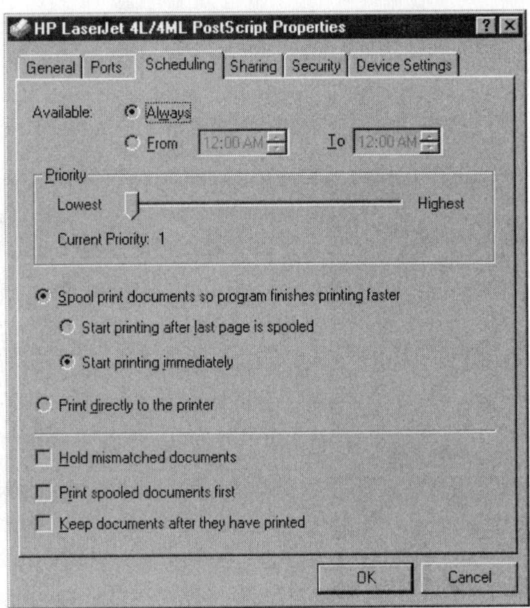

Figure 6

Windows' print spooler.

Windows' print-spooler settings are usually best left at their defaults, but in some cases fiddling with them may speed up printing. Exactly what settings are available will depend on what printer you have and which version of Windows you're running. (The spooler dialogs shown here are for an HP LaserJet 4ML printer under Windows 98, and under Windows NT).

The Stuff You Print On

Here's what you need to know about paper, labels, and transparencies for lasers and inkjets. Continuous-form paper for dot matrix printers can be bought at any office supply store, and differences in paper thickness and quality don't mean much. Paper thickness seems to have little effect on whether dot matrix printers jam (which they tend to do) and you wouldn't want to print your résumé with a dot matrix, anyhow.

Paper. For everyday printing chores, ordinary 20-pound copier paper works just fine for both lasers and inkjets, and you can get it for less than $20 a box (5,000 sheets) at warehouse stores. Expect to pay more for recycled stock. For a huge selection of interesting colored and patterned papers that work well in lasers, call PaperDirect (800/272-7377) for a catalog.

Regular bond paper not intended for copiers isn't so good, because it may leave too much paper dust behind in your printer. Paper that's too thick or too thin will jam (depending on the model, the acceptable range is typically between 16- and 24-pound paper). Preprinted forms or letterhead are usually OK, but they can cause trouble—unless the inks can withstand the heat, they'll melt and muck up your laser printer. Perforations may cause jams, and you should never pass stapled paper through your machine.

With inkjet printers, although regular copier paper works well, special clay-coated papers produce noticeably better results—especially when printing in color. Clay-coated paper for printers is the same type used in glossy magazines. The heavier the weight, the greater the clay content (usually between 15 and 25 percent) and the sharper the image. Beware: Clay has a low melting temperature, and should never be used in a laser printer.

Labels. Never use ordinary label stock in a laser printer. The printer's heat can melt the glue, which can damage the printer's insides. Labels made specifically for laser printers are sold everywhere.

Laser printers can't print reliably on partly used label sheets—passing the sheet through again often leads to jams. You can minimize the risk by printing the bottom labels of the sheet first, and by straightening the sheet as much as possible. But a more reliable solution is smaller sheets of labels; you can cut your own or buy Mini-Sheets from Avery.

For inkjet printers, the main problem is that the ink tends to smear on the smooth surface of standard label paper. Special label stock for inkjets is also available, though it's a little difficult to come by.

By the way, you can buy specialized printers just for producing labels. These little units, like the CoStar LabelWriter and Seiko Smart Label Printer, are inexpensive, can print individual labels as well as large runs, and even work with Windows scaleable fonts.

Transparencies. When you print transparencies with an inkjet, the main thing to remember is to hold the transparency by the edges until it dries or it will smear. With lasers, you usually have to feed transparencies one at a time into a manual feed slot. You'll get different results with different types of transparencies, so you may have to experiment—more *character voids* (blank spaces in characters) crop up on some than on others. But the big question to ask is: Can it take the heat? The last thing you need is a melted transparency in your laser, so make sure you buy transparencies approved for laser *printer* use (never try to use transparencies designed for use with laser *copiers*).

Printer Sharing and Switching

If you want to share one or more printers among a few PCs in the same space, the best solution is to use Windows' built-in networking. The hardware to set up a small network will only set you back around $50 a PC, and it'll let you move files around as well as share printers. (See Chapter 25: Networks to learn how to set up such a mini-network.)

If you're just sharing one printer among a few PCs, a switchbox will save you some money. A bidirectional electronic "autoswitch" box automatically switching among up to four PCs will set you back only around $30, plus the cost of an extra printer cable for each PC.

Printer Resources

www.pcmag.com *PC Magazine* is the king of computer magazine printer reviews. They review more printers, more often, and have more money to spend on extensive lab tests. They also review all *kinds* of printers, from $100 inkjets to $7,500 dye-sublimation printers to $15,000 network printers. Watch out for *PC Mag*'s per-page cost estimates on color printing, though—usually they're just extrapolated from manufacturer estimates, which are sometimes overly optimistic. From the main page, click "Peripherals" under the "PC Labs Reviews" heading, then click "Printers."

computers.com CNET's hardware site doesn't trust inkjet manufacturers' estimates of ink consumption—the site's lab actually runs off test pages until the color starts to degrade. (At least, that's how they did it when Robert was writing those reviews.) To get the latest review, click "Printers" on the front page, then on the right side of the page under "Printer Reviews" click "Inkjet Printers." (Be aware that computers.com also has a lot of raw data about products it hasn't reviewed; that stuff's just taken from manufacturers' spec sheets, so it's not necessarily reliable.)

www.publish.com *Publish* is a magazine aimed at graphics professionals, so it reviews some esoteric products the mainstream computer magazines might miss, like wide-format inkjet printers that use rolls of three-foot-wide paper. Click the "Search" button; click "these collections"; uncheck everything except "Reviews" and "Buyer's Guides"; enter "printers" in the search field and click "Seek."

Freeware/shareware

There are some useful freeware and shareware printer utilities that can add features your printer may not have, like printing multiple reduced pages on a single sheet or labels. An easy place to get them is to go to **download.com**. Under the Categories list click "Utilities," under Subcategories click "Printers." Click "downloads" to sort the list by popularity—if a program turns up at the top of the list, that's a good sign a lot of people have found it useful.

Recommended Printer Manufacturers

Canon (inkjet) **www.ccsi.canon.com/printers/color.html**

Epson (inkjet, dot matrix) **www.epson.com/printer**

HP (laser, inkjet, color laser) **hp.com/cgi-bin/peripherals/pandi.pl**

Lexmark (laser, inkjet) **www.lexmark.com**

Okidata (dot matrix) **www.okidata.com/mkt/html/nf/Products.html**

NEC (laser) **www.nec.com/cgi-bin/list.exe?product=printers**

7

Input Devices

by Scott Spanbauer and Robert Lauriston

This chapter was originally written by Scott Spanbauer, and updated for the third edition by Robert Lauriston.

In This Chapter

Too bad computers aren't telepathic yet. You still have to get the data in there and tell the computer what to do with it, which usually means banging away on the keyboard and whisking a mouse around your desktop. But thanks to PCs' appetite for graphics, and some of the alternative technology available today, letting your fingers do the talking isn't the only way to supply your computer with the data it craves.

Scanners scoop up graphics like digital vacuum cleaners, enabling you to add photolike images to newsletters and presentations, or to use simple line art for letterhead and other decorative applications. Run *optical character recognition (OCR)* software on scanned documents, and you can produce megabytes of reasonably accurate electronic text without lifting a finger.

Then there are the more exotic technologies, such as *digital photography, voice recognition,* and *pressure-sensitive tablets* for artists. This chapter covers them all: from the mundane keyboard, to PCs that respond to spoken commands. If you're in the market for any of these devices—particularly scanners—then you'll find plenty of buying tips here.

Keyboards

Your PC came with a keyboard, and you've likely not given the thing a second thought since the first time you used it. In fact, however, switching to a better one could improve your typing efficiency and accuracy and even prevent injury. Consider these simple improvements and extras:

- **A better feel.** Don't believe your fingers can tell the difference? Then try this sometime: Walk around a superstore (or a large office) and try a bunch of different keyboards. Some keys click crisply when you press them, others feel like marshmallows, many are in between. You may well find a keyboard that feels a lot better than the one you use, and it will probably cost no more than $50. Your hands are important. Why not buy it?
- **A built-in pointer.** Hate meeces to pieces? Desk space already cramped? Then consider a keyboard that includes a built-in pointing device. There are models with trackballs, touchpads, and eraser-head pointers like the ones you find on laptops. (Trackballs and touchpads are discussed below; eraser-head pointing sticks are covered in Chapter 3: Notebook PCs.)
- **Another layout.** Most typewriters place the Caps Lock key below the Shift key, but on most PC keyboards you'll find Caps Lock above Shift, and Ctrl below. If you don't like your current keyboard layout or would like to experiment, try a keyboard that lets you swap keys—such as any of Northgate's

Omnikey models. If you don't mind re-labeling the keys on your current keyboard, you can swap key assignments easily using a shareware or freeware keyboard utility. (See Chapter 21: The Web and Browsers, for more on finding shareware.)

If you want to change layouts to something other than U.S. English, you can do so easily with Windows. In the Keyboard control panel, click the Language tab (in NT it's labeled Input Locales); then click Properties. A dialog box will pop up with a list of 70 different keyboards—including some English-language alternatives that use the Dvorak layout, which rearranges the keys to allow the fastest possible touch typing. (The standard QWERTY layout was actually designed to slow down people using early manual typewriters, which had a tendency to jam if users typed too fast.)

Ergonomic Keyboards

Fast typists who spend long stretches at the keyboard are prime candidates for repetitive strain injury (RSI), particularly carpal-tunnel syndrome. If you've experienced wrist or hand problems or if you're bound and determined to prevent them, you might want to look into one of the many ergonomically designed keyboards on the market (see Figure 1).

Figure 1

Alternative keyboards.

You don't have to stick with a stock keyboard. Look around and you'll find plenty of alternatives, with integrated pointing devices, injury-preventing designs, and better responsiveness overall.

Ergonomic keyboards break the keyboard into two angled sections, or otherwise fit the keys to your hands' natural resting position—rather than the other way around. Microsoft's so-called Natural Keyboard (around $50) separates the keyboard into two halves, one on each side of a sort of hump. For some people this may be better than the normal flat design, but it's no more adjustable. The Kinesis Maxim (around $150 without optional numeric keypad) is a more flexible product that lets you adjust the width and height of the split. The Health Care Keyboard Company's Comfort Keyboard System (around $450) goes even further, splitting the keyboard into three sections, each of which can be adjusted to a different height and angle. See "Input Device Resources" at the end of this chapter for information on finding these and similar products, most of which are seldom seen in major computer stores.

Remember, though—an ergonomic keyboard by itself is no guarantee against injury. Regular breaks and a properly configured workspace are most important. See Chapter 26: Health and Safety, for some basic strategies for avoiding RSI.

Talking Instead of Typing

If handwriting recognition still has a few kinks, then voice recognition is downright experimental. However, there's no dearth of products out there competing for your dollars. Voice recognition products fall loosely into two categories:

- **Voice control systems.** You say "File, Save," into the microphone, and the software executes the command—sometimes—*if* you talk slowly, pause between words, and repeat yourself.
- **Dictation systems.** Designed to convert speech into text, dictation systems such as 'Naturally Speaking, by Dragon Systems, seem like the nontypist's dream come true. These systems generally come with large libraries of known words, often targeting specific professions. Unfortunately, even the best dictation systems have trouble understanding what you say—an accuracy rate of 90% is about the best you can hope for.

Many voice recognition systems require that you spend quite a bit of time "training" them to recognize your specific enunciation, which means that no one else can use the system (nor can you if you have a bad cold). Some may require an unnatural pause after every word; those are called "discrete," as opposed to "continuous-speech" products.

In the final analysis, both types of recognition systems are best for people who can't use a keyboard, either because they're disabled or because their hands are otherwise occupied as they work. For other people, a typing tutorial program like *Mavis Beacon Teaches Typing* is probably a better investment than voice recognition software.

Keep Those Keys Clean

You may like your current keyboard just fine, except that sometimes characters repeat when they shouldn't, keys don't work unless you really pound them, and the letters on the keys have all but disappeared. No wonder—you've had your dirty hands all over that keyboard for years! Worse, you've nibbled donuts, sipped coffee, and ripped open envelopes over the thing, to the point where the key mechanisms don't work like they should. Here are some quick cleaning tips:

- **The dry method.** Turn off the computer, disconnect the keyboard, turn it over, and give it a good shake. Buy a can of pressurized air (available at photo shops) and try blowing detritus out. Canned air is also good for cleaning out individual stuck keys: Pry off the offending key's cap with a pen or screwdriver, being careful not to lose any moving parts under the cap (those springs can get away easily!), and give the hole beneath the key a couple of quick blasts. You can also vacuum a keyboard, but when you do, use a new vacuum bag. If any loose parts get sucked up, you really don't want to have to pick through a pile of household dirt to retrieve them.
- **The wet method.** A damp rag will do—avoid abrasive cleaners or scrubbers. If you've spilled something sticky on your keyboard, you can even take the whole thing into the shower with you for a thorough cleansing (as a last resort). The water won't hurt it. But be sure the keyboard is thoroughly dry before you plug it back in. (You may have to dismantle it to get it completely dry.)

To prevent sticky keyboard situations to begin with, avoid eating, drinking, and smoking around your computer, and keep the keyboard covered when not in use. You'll find hard plastic keyboard covers at most office supply stores, although a plain dishtowel works just as well.

For unavoidably grungy settings such as a factory floor, use a soft plastic-membrane cover that protects your keyboard against dirt as you type.

Pointing Devices

Is "pointing device" just a fancy name for a mouse? Yes, but the phrase also applies to other cursor-moving tools. *Trackballs* are basically upside-down mice—instead of moving the whole device around the desktop with your arm, you move the ball itself with your thumb or fingers. *Touchpads* are small touch-sensitive rectangles that let you move the mouse pointer around with your finger. *Graphics tablets* let you point and click, too, but their real benefit is for drawing, as anyone who's tried a freehand sketch with a mouse can tell you.

A Plague of Mice

You can get RSI from using a mouse just as you can from using a keyboard, so if your mouse doesn't fit your hand well, find a model with a more comfortable shape. And try a few clicks before you buy—mouse buttons that are too stiff cause unnecessary strain, and loose buttons can be clicked accidentally. (For a tutorial on mouse basics see Chapter 1: For Beginners Only.) Here are some other criteria to help you find the best mouse:

- **Connections.** Many mice come with two connectors: a PS/2-style plug for the standard mouse port built into most systems, and a 9-pin serial connector for a serial port. You can also buy mice with a bus mouse-interface card, which adds to the price. If your PC has a mouse port, use it—using the other two connections will waste either a serial port or an expansion slot.
- **Extra buttons.** Most mice have only two buttons, but some have three or more. Few applications recognize more than two, but mice with more usually with software that lets you assign application commands or command sequences to the extra buttons.
- **Scroller wheel.** An increasing number of mice let you control the current window's vertical and (sometimes) horizontal scroll bars, with a little thumbwheel or miniature joystick between the two buttons. You may find these handy for Web surfing, because you won't have to move the mouse to scroll through pages too big to fit in your brower's window.

- **Resolution.** If you work with graphics, kern type, or perform other kinds of detailed screen work, be sure to consider *mouse resolution,* which varies from 150 to 500 dots per inch (dpi) depending on the model. The higher the resolution, the better you'll be able to pick on-screen nits.
- **The wireless option.** Your mouse doesn't have to have a tail. Cordless mice (see Figure 2) use one of two transmission methods: infrared or radio frequency. Infrared mice require a direct line of sight between the mouse and its receiver unit. Radio mice work fine with under-the-desk computers, but they may conflict with similar mice in a roomful of computers. Both types of receivers require a serial port.
- **Size and shape.** Mice come in many sizes and shapes. The one most comfortable for you depends on the size of your hand and other highly personal factors—the best thing is

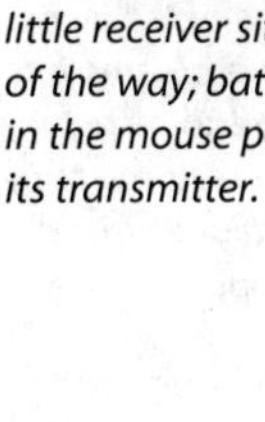

Figure 2

Wireless mice.

If your mouse's cord gets in your way, you can switch to a cordless model. A little receiver sits out of the way; batteries in the mouse power its transmitter.

to just try lots of different devices and see which you like the best. Some mice are available in left-handed versions (although any mouse's button functions can be swapped using Windows's Mouse control panel, as shown in Figure 3).

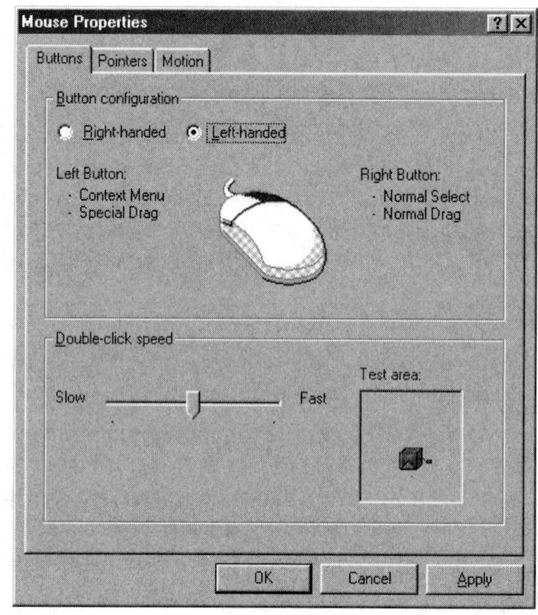

Figure 3

Swapping mouse buttons.

If you want to use the mouse with your left hand, change the "Button configuration" setting in the Mouse control panel, as shown here.

Like keyboards, mice start acting funny when they get dirty (see "Keeping Your Mouse Clean"). One good way to prevent grungy buildup is to buy a mouse pad—it won't magically repel dirt, but you'll be less likely to set your morning donut down on it, and your mouse performance will be smoother in the bargain. If you're worried about RSI, consider a mouse pad with a wrist rest (see Figure 4); it will keep you from bending your hand upward and causing strain.

Figure 4

Mousepad with wrist rest.

Because of the increasing occurrence of RSI and similar problems, lots of mouse-pad manufacturers have come out with models that feature built-in wrist rests made of foam or gel. There are also stand-alone wrist rests you can use with any mouse pad.

Keeping Your Mouse Clean

Over time, your mouse can get dirty , giving you poor control over the cursor. To clean it, follow the procedure shown in Figure 5.

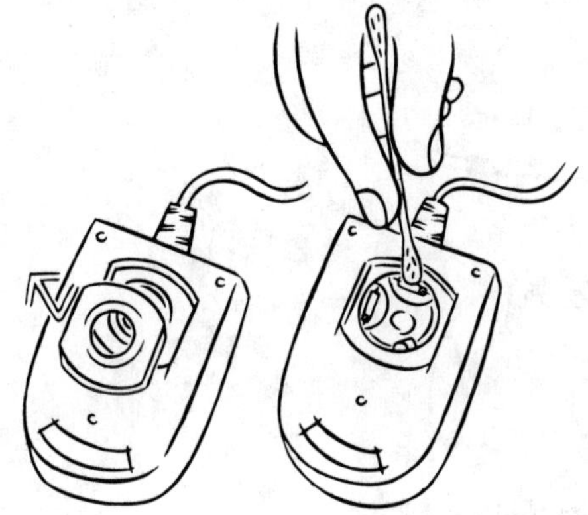

Figure 5

Here's how you clean a mouse.

Remember to use alcohol on the cotton swab as you wipe the rollers. The ball inside the mouse should be removed, cleaned with lukewarm soapy water, and dried thoroughly.

Getting on the Trackball

Why use a trackball instead of a mouse? Yes, a trackball has the advantage of using much less desk space—but other than that, the choice is a matter of taste. Some people hate trackballs; other people love 'em. Trackballs come in an even greater variety of designs than do mice, so you should really get your hands on a few before deciding which one to buy.

All the buying issues for mouse pertain to trackballs as well: hardware and software compatibility, resolutions, and extra buttons (trackballs normally duplicate the mouse's two-button arrangement). Likewise, a trackball can hurt your hand or wrist, so a wrist rest might be a good idea for you. And most people agree: The bigger the ball, the easier a trackball is to use.

Clicking and dragging can be tricky with a trackball because you have to hold down a button with one finger or your thumb, and then rotate the ball with another finger, your thumb, or your other hand. In some models this issue is addressed with a *drag-lock button,* which maintains the left button in the clicked position until you punch drag-lock again. 'Try several different types of trackballs (see Figure 6) to see which you find most comfortable to use.

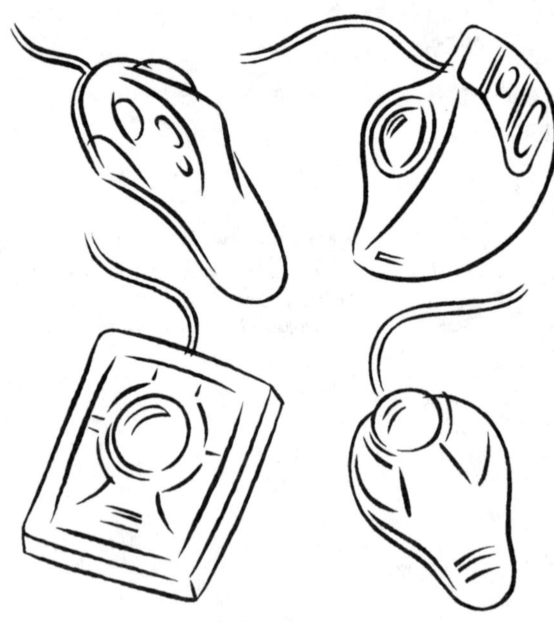

Figure 6

Trackballs.

You'll find a wide variety of trackball designs on the market. Some people prefer to click the main button with their thumb and move the ball with their fingers; some people do the reverse. Try a few and see what you like.

Touchpads: Let Your Fingers Do the Mousing

Another common alternative to a standard mouse is a *touchpad*, a small touch-sensitive rectangle the shape of your computer's screen. You move your finger around on the pad and the mouse moves accordingly. A touchpad is the same gizmo you find on most notebook PCs, except it's packaged in a small box with a cable so you can hook it up just like a mouse or trackball, to the same PS/2, serial, or USB port.

If you've tried a touchpad and didn't like it, you might want to give them another try. Newer models can detect when you tap on them, so instead of having to push buttons you can click things by just tapping your finger. Given the choice, though, it seems like most people prefer a regular mouse or trackball over a touchpad.

Drawing Tablets

Whether you're a budding computer artist or a high-tech design professional, you need a flat input surface on which to paint or draw, just as you do when using paper or canvas (close to it, anyway). The range in price and capability of these *digitizing tablets* (aka *graphics pads)* is enormous: You can pay more than

$1,500 for tablets up to 44" by 60 inches", or not much more than $100 for a 4 by 5-inch sketchpad (see Figure 7). Here are a few quick buying tips:

- **Size and resolution.** If you plan to use the pad with a low-end paint or draw program, a small pad is fine, and even the lowest-resolution pads (500 dpi) will be plenty accurate.
- **Pressure sensitivity.** You draw on a tablet with a stylus—it's like a pen, only there's usually a battery instead of ink. A sensor in the stylus detects how hard you're pressing and sends a signal to the tablet, which passes it on to your compatible paint or draw program, which makes its line thicker or thinner in response. (Some large tablets designed for AutoCAD users don't have this feature, but it is essential for good results with paint and draw programs.)
- **Other features.** These days most styli have "erasers." The tablet can tell which end of the stylus you're using and will tell compatible applications to switch tools—from pen/brush/pencil/whatever—to eraser and back again. Some styli can communicate with compatible applications just by the angle at which the stylus is held. In response, the application will dynamically vary the angle of the pen tool or other settings.
- **Connections and compatibility.** Graphics tablets connect to your PC's serial port, which can make installing them a hassle if your mouse is connected to a serial port and you have a modem. Two ways to free up a serial port are to move the mouse to a PS/2 port, or replace it with a USB mouse. (Tablets will likely move to USB in the near future, eliminating this potential problem, at least for Windows 98 users.)

Figure 7

How large a drawing space do you need?

You can get tablets the size of notepads, easels, or anything in between. Note that the document size isn't limited by the size of the tablet; you can use even the smallest pad to create a large drawing by working on small sections at a time, or zooming out so the whole document fits within the tablet's workspace.

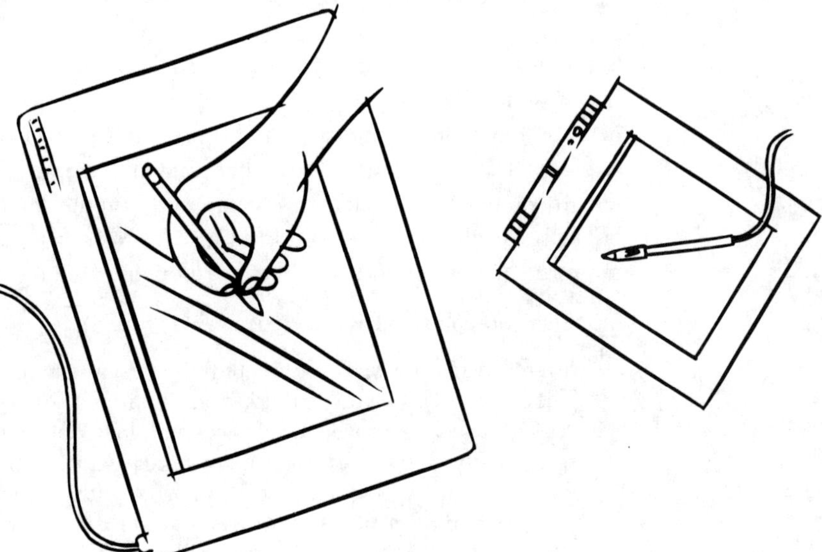

If CAD is your thing, you'll need a digitizing tablet large enough for you to trace blueprints and undertake very detailed work. Expensive tablets come with a *puck*—a transparent, circular sighting window with crosshairs that lets you work more precisely than you could with a pen. Many digitizing tablets accommodate menu templates that work with specific programs, so you can click zones on the surface of the pad to execute commands quickly.

Are Pens Mightier Than the Keyboard?

Your tablet may come with some sort of *handwriting recognition software,* which can supposedly convert handwriting to editable text. Hunt-and-peckers may see this as a sign of imminent liberation from the keyboard, but they shouldn't.

Even after training the software to recognize your writing, you'll probably experience a 90% success rate at best, which means you'll spend quite a bit of time correcting errors. For now, handwriting recognition makes sense only in a few specialized applications (such as collecting data in the field using hand-held computers). However, if you have a fax modem card, note that a tablet is a great way to annotate faxes right on the screen—without the tedium of printing them out, scribbling on them, and scanning them before you return them to the sender.

Scanners and Scanning

Scanners are among the most versatile peripherals you can add to your system. In addition to their obvious use for scanning art and photographs, most scanners come bundled with capable OCR programs that let you turn mountains of press releases, legal papers, or other printed matter into searchable, editable text. If you use a fax modem, a scanner gives you the ability to send hard-copy originals. Finally, if you have a printer attached to your system, adding a scanner can turn your system into an effective (though extremely slow) photocopier.

Scanners come in two basic varieties (see Figure 8):

- **Sheetfed scanners.** These accept full pages, much like a fax machine. Pros: They're very easy to use and don't take up much desk space—you can even get keyboards with sheetfed scanners built in. Cons: Resolution (and hence scan quality) is typically lower than similarly priced flatbeds. Also, sheet feeders have a tendency to tilt the paper slightly (which produces skewed images), and they can't scan books or other three-dimensional objects. Price: $100–$200 depending on resolution and bundled software.
- **Flatbed scanners.** These work like photocopiers—you put the document to be scanned face down on a glass panel. Pros: Images scan straight; you can photocopy anything you can fit on the glass; and with many models

you can add optional sheet-feeders or slide scanners. Cons: They're a little more work than sheet feeders, and at about 12 by 18 inches they take up more desk space. Price: Consumer models are $75 to $300, depending on resolution, speed, and software bundle. The sky's the limit for professional models—Scitex's top-of-the-line EverSmart Pro lists for $40,000.

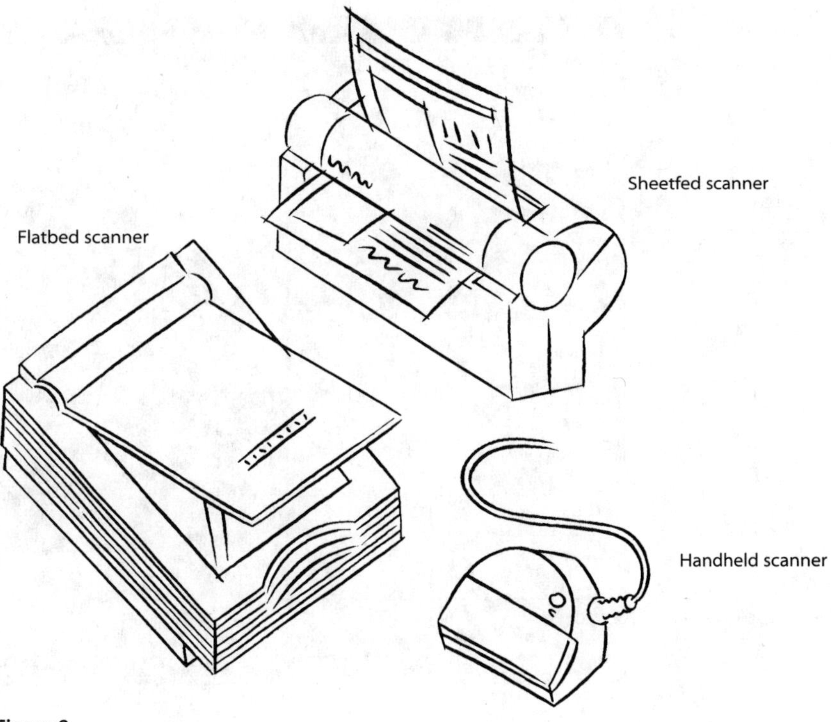

Figure 8

Flatbeds and sheet feeders.
There are two basic kinds of scanners: flatbeds, where you lay the document face down on a sheet of glass (as on a copy machine); and sheet feeders, where you feed in one end of the document and the device pulls it through automatically. Handheld scanners, which produce inferior results, have become almost extinct as prices on the other two types have dropped.

Most desktop scanners connect with your computer via the parallel port, though they'll probably all be switching to USB during the next few years. Some models use SCSI, but it's best to avoid those unless you "have a SCSI adapter in your system already."

On the software side, you can control scanners from within some Windows applications. In a TWAIN-compatible image editor like PhotoShop or Paint Shop Pro, you just choose "Acquire" or "Import" from the File menu, and the scanner's control panel (see Figure 9) pops up for you to choose scan settings and launch the scan. When the scan's complete, it appears as a new file in the program. (See Chapter 17: Painting, Drawing, and Other Graphics Software, for more on image editing software.) Many scanners include a software utility that lets you OCR text right into your word processor. ("TWAIN", by the way, is one of those joke acronyms that computer geeks love to play on a public inured to incomprehensible jargon: It stands for Technology Without An Interesting Name.)

Figure 9

A typical scanner control panel.

This is the window that pops up when Robert activates his scanner from within any TWAIN-compatible application, like Photoshop or the OCR program that came with the scanner. There are controls for all the basic image settings, as well as a "Prescan" button that does a fast, low-res scan to put an image of the document in the window at right. Using a selection box tool (visible as an outline), you can then select only a portion of the prescanned image to be scanned at the desired higher resolution, speeding up the scan and reducing file size.

How to Pick a Scanner

Scanner technology has progressed to the point that even under-$100 flatbeds now produce excellent results. Watch out for these features, to make sure you get the most for your money:

- **Optical resolution.** Expect 1200 x 600 dpi or higher. Don't be misled by "interpolated" or "enhanced" resolution, which is typically 9600 x 9600.
- **Scan mode.** Expect 30- or 36-bit. (Output will still be 24-bit.)

- **Maximum document size.** Some scanners can handle 14-inch paper, some are limited to 11-inch.
- **Operating system support.** Most any scanner will support Windows 95 and Windows 98. If you want to use the scanner with Windows NT, make sure the drivers (including TWAIN) are available, and that the company offers technical support for them. (You can usually figure that out from the company's Web site.)
- **Automatic scanning.** Some scanners have a button that launches the scanner software in Windows, or a switch that does the same thing when you open the lid. It's not a big thing, but it's convenient.
- **Software bundle.** The software bundle should include an image editing application (like PhotoDeluxe, Picture Publisher, or iPhoto Plus) and an OCR program (like TextBridge or OmniPage). A program for managing scanned images and documents may also be part of the bundle. The software you get with your scanner will typically be a pared-down version or older release of a popular product, and maybe a coupon for a cheap upgrade to the full version or latest release.

Halftones and Scanning Resolution

Laser printers and even professional imagesetters, unlike monitors, are basically 1-bit devices. Because they can only print black dots (or leave white spaces), these devices can't reproduce the grayscale and color data captured by the scanner—at least, not by themselves.

Borrowing a trick from traditional printing technology, programs capable of printing graphics (image editors, word processors, and desktop publishing applications) convert continuous-tone images into a printer-friendly format using a *halftone.*

The halftoning process filters original tones, converting darker tones to larger dots, and lighter tones to smaller dots (for evidence, examine any photograph in a newspaper or magazine under a magnifying glass). The fineness of the halftone screen (called the *halftone screen frequency* or *linescreen*) is measured in lines per inch (lpi), and the fineness of the screen depends on printer resolution. Because digital halftoning discards much of the original image's data, you can get away with a scanning resolution far lower than the output device's resolution (see the "Matching Scan Resolution with Print Resolution" table coming up).

As a rule of thumb, choose a halftone frequency that matches your printer, and then scan at a resolution roughly one-and-a-half to two times the halftone frequency. Scanning at a higher resolution won't hurt your final image, but it won't help it either and will simply chew up disk space unnecessarily. If you'd rather not do the math, just double it, or get Lightsource's superior scanning program *Ofoto* (415-925-4200), which automates the entire process.

Don't forget that line art consists of only two colors—black and white—and therefore doesn't require halftoning to print on laser printers and phototypesetters. As a result, you'll get the best results if you match scanning and printer resolution as closely as possible. For phototypesetter output, however, you may find that the quality is sufficient if you scan at half the printer's resolution.

OCR: From Hardcopy to Editable Text

You're probably surrounded by valuable data trapped in hard copy—newspaper clippings, white papers, correspondence, whatever. Someday you may need to search through all that text or borrow chunks of it. When that day comes, you can spend hours fishing through files and typing away—unless you've scanned those documents and converted them to editable text using an OCR program (see Figure 10).

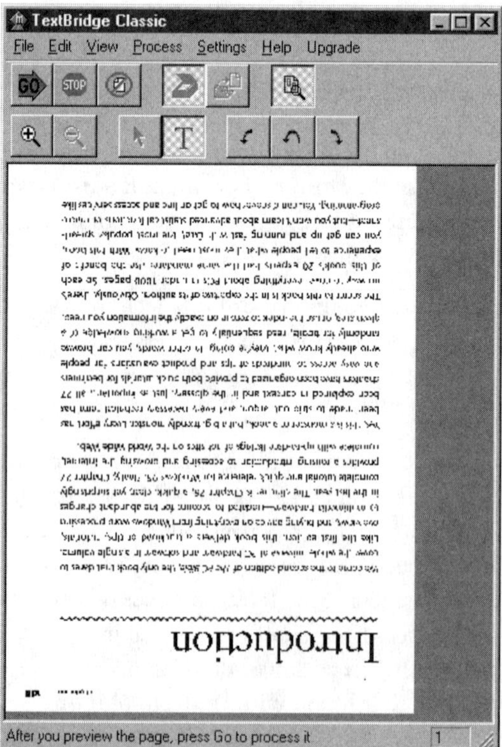

Figure 10

A basic OCR program.

This is a bare-bones but functional OCR program that came with Robert's inexpensive scanner. The actual scanning is done with the same TWAIN control panel shown earlier in Figure 9. You can OCR direct to a file or to the Windows' Clipboard or, if you prefer, into this window, where you can rotate or flip the scanned document, select only a portion to be OCR'd, and define multiple text fields (as in a multicolumn document). The better the OCR software, the more of those tasks it can handle automatically.

OCR runs document image files produced by your scanner through a special recognition routine that—depending on the print quality of the original document—can produce text files fairly low in errors. As with other recognition technologies, this is not an exact science. But it's generally quicker to correct errors in an OCR'd document than to type in all that information by hand; and storing searchable documents on disk or tape takes far less space than using a filing cabinet. If you find that the OCR software bundled with your scanner doesn't do a good enough job or is too awkward to use efficiently, you can replace it with something more powerful and user friendly. See "Input Device Resources" at the end of this chapter for specific recommendations.

Top 10 Scanning Tips

Getting images into your PC is easy, if you have the hard disk space. Here are a few tips to help you get the best scans with the least effort and the fewest wasted megabytes:

1. **Fix the original.** It's often easier to correct your original than it is to edit a digital image. Unless the original is a precious antique, clean up scratches, dirt, too-light lines, and the like before scanning. Use a pen, eraser, pencil—whatever works.
2. **Learn to edit images.** Teach yourself to use the scanning software. No scanner does a great scanning job using default settings. For best results, you may need to adjust brightness, contrast, and other exposure controls.
3. **Don't scan photos at maximum resolution.** As you can see from the "Tones, Resolution, and Disk Space" chart just below, scanning at maximum resolution will usually give you an unmanageably huge file, and you don't need a file that big anyway. For Web graphics and other stuff to be seen on screen, you want the final image to be 75 dpi (the average screen resolution); for laser printer output, you want 106 to 170 dpi.
4. **Experiment with different resolutions.** What scan resolution will give you the best output? That depends on what combination of scanner and photo-editing software you use. If your software's lousy, you'll get the best results by scanning at the resolution you want—say, 75 dpi for Web

Matching Scan Resolution with Print Resolution

Most printers use halftones to print scanned photos. The printer's resolution determines the optimal halftone screen frequency, which in turn determines the best scanning resolution. Scanning at a higher resolution simply wastes disk space.

Printer Resolution	Halftone Screen Frequency	Optimal Scanning Resolution
300 dpi (laser printer)	53 lpi	106 dpi
600 dpi (laser printer)	60–85 lpi	120–170 dpi
1270 dpi (phototypesetter)	120–133 lpi	240–266 dpi
2450 dpi (phototypesetter)	133–150 lpi	266–300 dpi

graphics. If you've got PhotoShop or another good image-editor, you'll get the best results by "overscanning" at a resolution at least twice what you're going to end up with.

5. **Use higher resolutions for line art.** When scanning line art (black-and-white, no grays or colors) to be laser-printed, you'll probably get the best results by scanning at the same resolution as the printer. If you're scanning line art for display on screen, however, you may get better results by using the maximum optical resolution of the scanner, then reducing the size of the resulting image to the desired dpi in your photo-editing application.
6. **Don't scan the whole thing.** You might be tempted to scan that entire color map of Central Asia, but don't—it'll take up 30MB of hard disk space. Instead, scan just the part you need.
7. **Use drawing tools to correct tilted scans.** If your photo-editing application can display the angle of a line when you're using the straight-line tool, you can use that feature to measure the amount a scan is skewed off vertical and then straighten it precisely. Draw a line parallel to a straight vertical or horizontal line in the image; note the angle; use the Rotate command to turn the image the same number of degrees in the opposite direction.
8. **Recover disk space by using compressed image formats.** Some graphics file formats use tricks to compress graphics into less space. Try saving copies of scanned images as .tif (check any compression options in the Save dialog) or .jpg (with quality set to maximum) files, and see if they take up less space than the originals.
9. **Clean the platen.** Like copy machines, flatbed scanners must be cleaned regularly. Wipe dust, gunk, and ink stains from the scanner's platen using glass cleaner—but spray the cleaner on the towel, not on the glass.
10. **Mess around.** Scanners are lots of fun, and the best way to learn to use them is to play around. Don't feel limited to photos or line art—you may not be free to use them in your publications without paying royalties anyway. Try scanning household objects, leaves, and other bits of nature (fabrics, woods, whatever).

Tones, Resolution, and Disk Space

Your PC probably doesn't have enough memory or disk space to handle the highest-resolution images today's scanners can produce, but if you're not doing professional color publishing, that probably doesn't matter. Most scanned graphics get uploaded to the Web, where 75 dpi (average resolution for computer screens) is all you need.

Size (Inches)	Number of Tones	75 dpi	150 dpi	300 dpi	600 dpi	1200 dpi
2 by 4	2 (line art)	5K	22K	88K	352K	1.4MB
2 by 4	256 (grayscale)	44K	176K	703K	2.7MB	11MB
2 by 4	16.7 million (color)	132K	527K	2.1MB	8.2MB	33MB
5 by 7	2 (line art)	48K	192K	769K	3MB	12MB
5 by 7	256 (grayscale)	192K	769K	3MB	12MB	48MB
5 by 7	16.7 million (color)	577K	2.3MB	9MB	36MB	144MB

Digital Cameras

If your main use for a scanner is to take pictures of people or things and post them directly into Web sites, into documents that are going to be output on laser printers rather than professionally printed, or into an employee or inventory database, you may be better off with a *digital camera* (see Figure 11) instead of a scanner. Look for these at consumer electronics stores—prices start around $150 and there are dozens of different models for less than $500. (Professional models can cost up to $25,000.) Here's what to look for:

- **Image size.** Inexpensive digital cameras typically take images of a maximum size between 640x480 and 1280x960. You can set them to take smaller images to conserve memory.
- **Image quality.** There's no simple spec to indicate quality; and it's impossible to compare in a store, where the cameras aren't hooked to a computer. The best comparison is available in online reviews that provide actual images for you. (For pointers, see "Input Device Resources" at the end of the chapter.)
- **Storage medium.** Most digital cameras store images on flash memory cartridges, which you can swap in and out like film. Usually you can just plug the memory cartridge into a laptop's PC card slot and copy the images directly. (A compatible slot for your PC should cost only $50–$75.) A few cameras use regular 1.44MB floppies. Some save images only in permanent, built-in memory, which means you'll have to keep going back to your PC to transfer, using a bundled cable, the shots you want to save.
- **Number of images.** How many images a camera can store varies depending on what image size you're using. Some cameras can store less than five images at maximum resolution, others more than a hundred at minimum res.
- **Shutter delay time.** Most digital cameras need to charge up before they take the picture, so there may be a delay of several seconds after you push the button. Avoid these models if you can't depend on your subjects' sitting still.
- **Recovery time.** A digital camera needs some time after the shot is exposed to process and store the image.
- **Viewfinder.** An optical viewfinder doesn't drain the batteries and can be easier on the eyes; a digital viewfinder lets you browse the images in memory without downloading them. It's best to have both types.
- **Optics and flash.** These issues are just the same on digital cameras as on regular film cameras. Cheaper models are fixed-focus; expensive models have autofocus. Zoom raises the price. If you need to do extreme closeups, check the range. Red-eye reduction helps avoid those weird space-alien eyes with flash photos.
- **Video output.** This lets you display the stored images on a TV.

Figure 11

A typical digital camera.

Instead of taking pictures, then developing them, and then scanning the prints, you can save those intermediate steps by using a digital camera. The picture is stored in digital format in the camera's memory card or disk, from which you can transfer it directly to your PC and into a document or Web page.

You can get digital images out of regular film cameras, too: When you take your film in for processing, order a PhotoCD. All graphics applications now support PhotoCD images, and unless you live in Outer Mongolia, there's a PhotoCD-capable lab nearby.

Input Device Resources

Keyboards

`yahoo.com` You can get a list of programs that will teach you to touch-type, or just raise your typing speed, on Yahoo! at Business and Economy : Companies : Computers : Software : Training : Typing. *Mavis Beacon Teaches Typing* is excellent and costs only $25–$35. (We'd give you the program's URL, but it's one of those long, ugly strings of random-looking characters; it's only a few clicks from that Yahoo! page.)

Yahoo! also has a comprehensive list of keyboard manufacturers at Business and Economy : Companies : Computers : Hardware : Peripherals : Input Devices : Keyboards.

`cvtinc.com/avant.htm` Creative Vision Technologies sells a clone of the Northgate Omnikey, thought by many old-time geeks (but few others) to be the crème de la crème of keyboards. Check it out.

www.safecomputing.com/keyboard.htm If you want an ergonomic keyboard, check out Safe Computing. This online retailer specializes in ergonomic computer accessories, including a large selection of hard-to-find keyboards.

comfortkeyboard.com An expensive but ultra-adjustable ergonomic keyboard.

Manufacturers that make keyboards with built-in pointing devices.
www.keytronic.com/lifetime.htm
www.pc.ibm.com/us/accessories/family/fokeypt.html
www.focustaipei.com/products.htm
www.cherrycorp.com/gp_kbd2.htm

Voice Recognition

www.dragonsys.com Dragon Systems has been the leader in voice-regognition systems for years. The company sells a variety of voice software for various purposes.

Pointing Devices

www.kensington.com/products/mice Kensington makes a wide variety of pointing devices, including the excellent Turbo Mouse—a trackball, despite its name.

logitech.com/en/mice+trackballs Logitech makes some of the best mice around, as well as some rather eccentric trackballs.

Drawing Tablets

www.wacom.com/productinfo/showcase.html Wacom is the most popular manufacturer of pressure-sensitive drawing tablets for artists. They offer a slew of models across the price range to suit amateurs and professionals alike.

www.calcomp.com/p_tablets.htm The other major vendor of graphics tablets focuses more on AutoCAD users and other engineering types, but the company has some models aimed at hobbyists and artists too. (Calcomp makes the SummaSketch tablets.)

Scanners

www.visioneer.com/products/software If you find the software that's bundled with your scanner too hard to use, check out Visioneer's extremely user-friendly PaperPort Deluxe.

`caere.com/products` This is another alternative if you find your bundled scanner's software difficult to master. Caere's OmniPage offers industrial-strength OCR and is priced to match, but your bundled OCR software should qualify you for a cheap, competitive upgrade offer.

Digital Cameras

`pcmag.com` *PC Magazine*'s online editions of its major digital-camera comparisons include the actual test image files, so you judge them for yourself (but you have to click around a lot to gather up all the ones of interest). On the front page, click "Peripherals" under "PC Labs Reviews"; then click "Digital Cameras" for a list of all reviews. The links to the full-size images, when they're available, are under the individual product reviews.

`computers.com` The digital camera reviews on CNET's hardware site include reduced test images so you can compare image quality and color accuracy. Unfortunately, they don't provide the original images themselves. On the site's front page, click "Cameras," and then "Snapshot cameras" on the right side of the page under "Camera Reviews."

`shopper.com` A lot of different companies are making flash memory cards for digital cameras. You can find a lot of them and compare prices on **`shopper.com`**. See the categories under "Mass Storage Devices: Flash RAM Cards (blank) & Drives." The shopper.com site also has a section on cameras themselves—click on "Digital Cameras" on the front page.

`yahoo.com` It seems everybody wants to make digital cameras: camera companies like Minolta and Olympus, film companies like Fuji and Kodak, printer companies like Epson and HP, scanner companies like Mustek and Umax, consumer electronics companies like Casio and Sony. You can find a fairly comprehensive list of manufacturers at Business and Economy : Companies : Photography : Digital : Supplies and Equipment : Manufacturers.

8

Upgrade It Yourself

by Eric Knorr and Robert Lauriston

This chapter was originally written by Eric Knorr, and was updated for the third edition by Robert Lauriston.

In This Chapter

Once you get accustomed to your PC, you don't want to do without it. That's the real reason for you, rather than a service person, to add or replace hardware in your PC. Who wants to work around someone else's service schedule and lose the use of a PC for days? And of course, you save money when you do it yourself—for example, having a superstore add a hard disk to your system usually costs around 50 bucks.

Another reason to entrust your PC's innards to no one but yourself is that *you* control the quality of the components and the work. Most upgrades are easy to do if you have good information, something not all service people avail themselves of. And what better way to ensure that top-of-the-line parts are used than to install them yourself?

If you're new to PCs, you should give Chapter 2: How to Buy a PC a close look before getting too deep into this chapter. The terms and concepts explained there will help you understand what's going on here.

Except where specified otherwise, the upgrades in this chapter refer to Pentium PCs. We also discuss some possible upgrades for late-model (66MHz or faster) 486 PCs, but with today's low-priced basic Pentium PCs it doesn't make much sense to spend a lot of money upgrading them.

What Every Upgrader Should Know

PCs were designed to be upgraded by their owners—that's why they have standard slots into which you plug expansion cards. You don't need a degree in rocket science, a working knowledge of hexadecimal, or the cunning to build a transistor radio out of several digital watches. A little bit of manual dexterity can help, but otherwise, we're talking cookbook stuff. As Eric's high school geometry teacher used to say whenever someone screwed up, "Can you bake a cake?" In other words, follow the instructions, and you should get the right results.

Tools of the Trade

Unless you make a point of avoiding hardware stores, you probably already have on hand the necessary implements for performing almost any upgrade:

- one medium flat-head screwdriver
- one small flat-head screwdriver

- one medium Phillips screwdriver
- one small Phillips screwdriver
- tweezers
- flashlight

Those are all the tools you need to get going. To avoid stripping screw heads and to give yourself a little extra torque, buy a couple of hex nut drivers, one 3/16" and the other 1/4". Hex screws are often used to hold down expansion cards and fasten system casings, so if you strip a hex screw head with a screwdriver, a nut driver can keep you from standing there wondering what to do.

A hemostat—a locking, scissorslike pair of tongs used by surgeons and potheads—is handy for retrieving screws and other small parts that sometimes fall into inaccessible corners in your PC. And if you work on an old Compaq system (they just keep going and going), you'll need two Torx wrenches, one T-10 and one T-15. Finally, a chip puller (available at any electronics store and illustrated in Figure 21) helps you replace older CPUs without damaging them.

As for software, all you really need is an emergency boot disk, which you should have anyway. (To learn how to create one, see "Safety Check" in Chapter 11: Windows 95, 98, and NT.) A boot disk can help you install a hard disk, or get things up and running if things go wrong.

Disassembly without Destruction

Is this the place where you're going to read all the boring stuff about how to avoid hurting yourself or your PC as you take it apart? You bet—but we'll keep it short, and along the way we'll explain how to get your PC open and ready for work:

1. **Back up before you start.** You *should* back up your hard disk regularly. And if you're adding or changing a hard disk, you *must* do this backup. In the unlikely event you accidentally disable your system while fishing around inside it, having a backup copy of your data before you start means you can restore the data to another system and minimize downtime (see Chapter 9: Protect Your Data).

2. **Stop that static.** Delicate circuitry, like CPUs, RAM chips, and expansion boards, can be damaged by static electricity. To minimize the chance of that happening, touch your hand to a grounded object before beginning your upgrade.' If your outlets are properly grounded, touching your PC's metal fan grille while your PC is still plugged in will do the trick,. Don't wear polyester when you work, because moving around in polyester generates static. For maximum safety, wear a static-discharge wristband (around $3 from Radio Shack or any well-stocked electronics supply store), which prevents any charge from accumulating while you work.

3. **Power down.** Turn off your PC and monitor. If your PC has a regular on/off switch, you can leave it plugged in so you can continue to discharge static if necessary. If the power switch is a doorbell-type button, it's not safe to leave it plugged in, since accidentally tapping the button can turn on the power at the wrong moment, resulting in a nasty shock or burned-out component. *Never* open up your PC's power supply or stick any object inside one of the vents, because there's enough current running around in there to knock you for a loop, permanently.
4. **Remove the cover carefully.** Some computer cases are easy to open—you just flip a couple of toggles or remove a thumbscrew or two, and the cover or a side panel flips off easily. Other models may remind you of childproof bottle caps: You remove a few screws on the rear of your system, try to pull the cover back, and—hey, what's the problem here? For some reason, on these boxes you sometimes need to give the cover a little yank upward before you slide it forward and remove it completely from the chassis (see Figure 1). If the cover snags as you pull, don't force things—just reverse direction, lift up a little more, and try again. Otherwise, you may tear a wire or cable.

5. **Keep parts organized.** This usually means the screws. Keep a roll of clear 2-inch packing tape handy. Tape related screws together while you're working, and stick them on the side of the chassis where they'll be handy for reassembly later on.

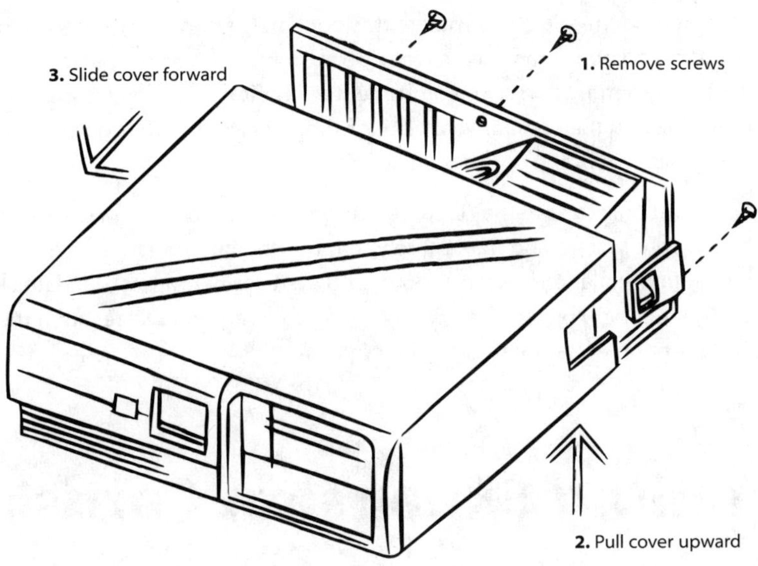

Figure 1

Removing the cover.

Old-fashioned desktop (as opposed to minitower) cases are often among the most difficult to remove. First remove any screws that hold the cover on the case, but don't unscrew the fan by mistake. You may need to pull the cover up before it will slide forward and off. In some cases, you pull the cover forward only an inch or two, and then lift it off.

6. **Write stuff down.** This will form the thread that you unroll to get yourself back out of the labyrinth. If you panic and suddenly realize you don't know what you're doing, having those notes will help you quickly put things back the way they were.' Even if you've just sketched it out with paper and pencil, it'll show you how cables, expansion cards, jumpers, switches, and so on were arranged to begin with.

Everyone needs a clean, well-lighted place to work but this goes double when you're playing ace mechanic with your PC. Nothing is more uncomfortable (or more likely to make you lose or drop components) than working on the cramped corner of a desk. If you don't have access to a work table, any wide, clean, flat surface with a nearby high-intensity lamp will do. One of those cantilevered reading lamps that let you move the light around independent of the base is very useful.

Save That Manual!

If you've just bought your PC, then I'm getting to you at exactly the right time. The documentation that came with your machine is your ticket to doing things right. It tells you how to use your all-important system setup software, needed for any configuration changes, and covers other basic maintenance tasks specific to that product. In short, that documentation gives you a lot of specific information about your model of PC that this chapter can't tell you.

Your system may also come with separate manuals for such components as the graphics card, hard disk, and modem—you accumulate this documentation every time you buy hardware. Documentation on boards and drives may be even more important than the manual for the PC itself, because settings on such components are often both complicated and critical. If you run into trouble and the company you bought the device from has gone belly up, you may have to simply *get rid* of the mystery device if you've lost the docs.

My advice is not only to save the documentation, but also to do a quick inventory of the boards and drives in your system and make sure you have documentation on everything. If you don't, call the manufacturer and request a copy—and do it sooner rather than later. In the dog-eat-dog world of high tech, you never know when calling that number will result in the dreaded "We're sorry, but that number has been disconnected."

Installing Expansion Cards

The physical part of installing an expansion card—whether a graphics card, fax modem, sound card, or whatever—couldn't be easier. A single screw holds each card in place (see Figure 2). And aside from making sure the card is inserted all the way into the expansion slot, there's not much at all to the whole deal (unless cables connect to the card, which may make things somewhat tricky). Here are a few general tips on installing expansion cards:

- **Find all the documentation.** Flip through *all* the papers that came with the product you're installing to make sure you've found all the instructions. In addition to the manual, there may be newer information in a printed addendum sheet or pamphlet. Also, load any floppies or CDs that came with the product and check for any files with names like Readme or Read Me First. Take a look at these files and print out any relevant portions.
- **Handle with care.** Of course you shouldn't toss cards around, but you should also avoid touching them against any conductive surface. A card lying flat on a metal surface (such as the top of a power supply) could spell disaster. Your hands are somewhat conductive, too, so make a practice of holding cards by their edges—but *not* by their edge *connectors* (the part with the little gold strips that plugs into the slot). A rubber mouse pad is an excellent nonconductive surface on which to set down parts.

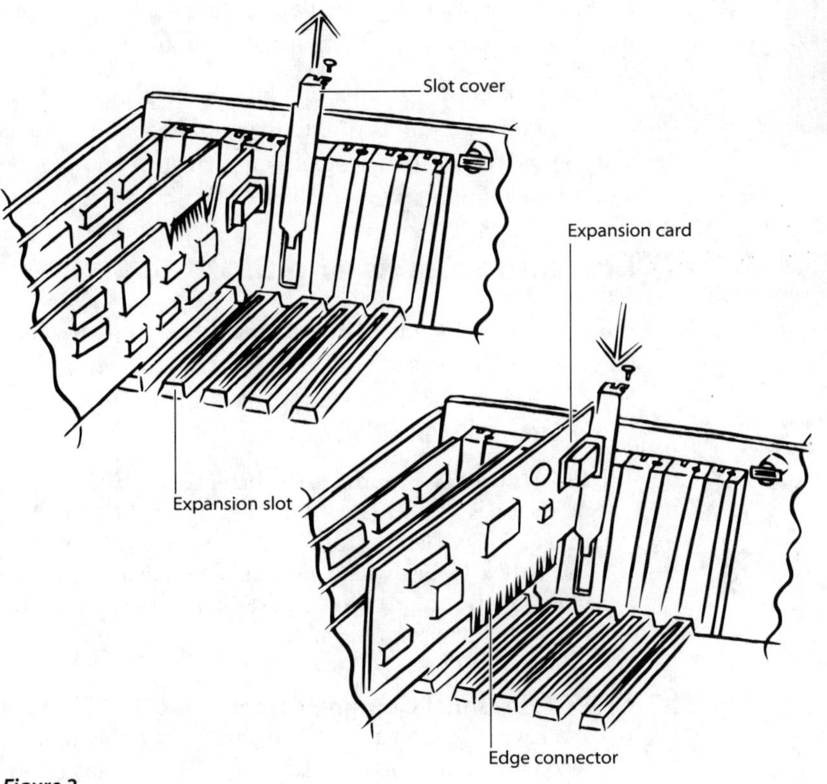

Figure 2

Installing an expansion card.

A single screw holds a standard expansion card in place. Don't use brute force to remove or insert cards—"work" the card back and forth a little if the fit is tight. At all times, avoid touching the gold tines on the edge connector that plugs into the slot.

- **Log those connections.** Before you remove boards with cables connected to them—typically, hard disk interface cards—disconnect the cables. Before you do *that*, though, make a note of how the cables were connected so you don't plug something in wrong later. If one side of a flat cable has a red line or other distinctive marking, note which side of the plug it's on. When you do reconnect, don't force a connector if it doesn't slip on easily—you've probably got it the wrong way around.
- **Don't *lean* on it; *rock* it.** Sometimes a card fits very tightly in a slot. If you yank too hard to remove it, you could damage the motherboard, the most important component in your PC. Rock the board slightly back and forth as you pull, and it should come loose without too much force. The same gyrations make inserting the cards easier, too. Snug-fitting leather gloves can be a help for getting a grip on expansion cards, which often have sharp little wire stubs sticking out of one side.

Reading the manual for an expansion card before you attempt to do anything with it is not an optional undertaking. It may be a legitimate test of software to see how far you can get without hitting the Help button, but it's a really bad idea to approach hardware installation in the same lighthearted way.

With some products, you have to install things in a very particular order or they won't work right. If you don't go to school on the documentation first, you run the risk of frying something permanently or, more likely, rendering your system temporarily unusable.

Matching Cards and Slots

When you shop for an expansion card, step 1 in narrowing down your selection is easy: The slots in your computer can only accept certain types of boards. Here are the three kinds of slots and boards (see Figure 3) used in PCs manufactured in recent years:

- **ISA (Industry Standard Architecture).** These slots are a variation on the ones that were used in the original 1981 IBM PC. They normally run at a poky 8MHz (although a few systems run them as fast as 12MHz) and have a 16-bit-wide data path. The maximum bandwidth of the bus is under 5MB/second, which makes it appropriate only for components with relatively low data rates, such as modems, sound cards, and 10-megabit Ethernet cards.
- **PCI (Personal Computer Interconnect).** These slots run at 33MHz and have a 32-bit data path, for a maximum theoretical capacity of 132MB/second. PCI supports *bus mastering*, which means it can improve performance by cutting the CPU out of the loop and transferring data directly from one component to another (for example, hard disk to memory, or CPU to video card). PCI's higher bandwidth makes it preferable to ISA for devices with high data rates, like video cards, SCSI adapters, and 100-megabit Ethernet boards.

Figure 3

ISA, PCI, and AGP slots.

This diagram shows the usual positioning of ISA, PCI, and AGP slots on a motherboard. There's usually at least one slot space with connectors for both ISA and PCI slots, so it can hold either kind of board.

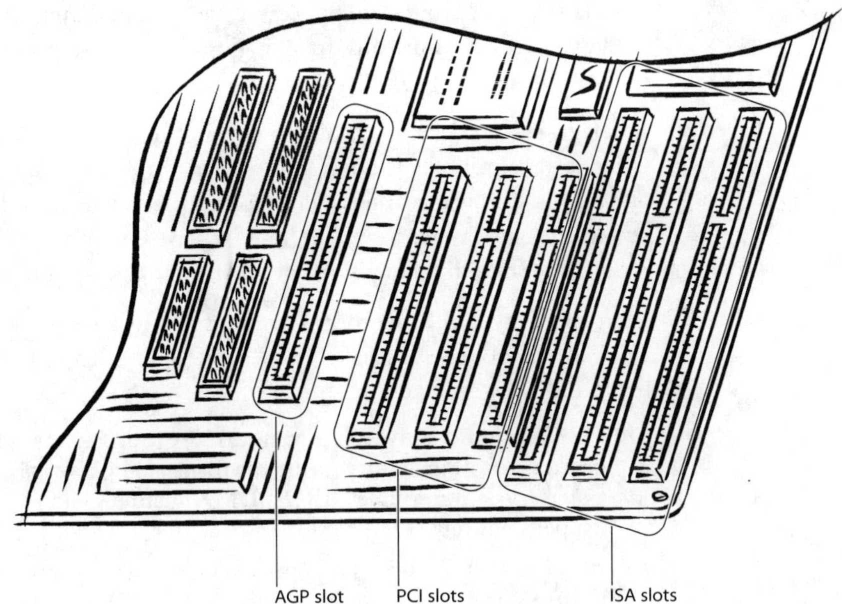

- **AGP (Advanced Graphics Port).** This special-purpose slot is strictly for video cards. Current AGP slots are 32-bit but run at 66MHz, so they've got twice the bandwidth of PCI. And future variations on AGP are supposed to allow that to be doubled or quadrupled. The AGP bus also allows game programmers to use the PC's memory to store 3-D data.

Almost all systems come with both PCI and ISA slots; Pentium II systems and some others also have a single AGP slot. If both ISA and PCI versions of a card are available, there's not necessarily any advantage to getting the latter—modems and standard sound cards, for example, have such low data rates that ISA doesn't impose any bottleneck on performance. Tests so far haven't shown that AGP video boards are faster than their PCI counterparts, but if you've got an AGP slot you might as well get an AGP board and keep your PCI slots free for other uses.

If you've got a PC with a 486 CPU, it probably has VLB (VESA Local Bus) rather than PCI slots. There are still a few VLB video, EIDE, SCSI, and Ethernet adapters on the market, but given how cheap entry-level Pentium PCs are these days it doesn't make sense to spend much upgrading an old 486.

Plug and Play

Until a few years ago, upgrading your own PC meant mastering the black art of troubleshooting hardware conflicts. When you installed a new sound card, for example, your network connection might disappear, your video card might go crazy, or your hard drive might refuse to boot until you pulled the card out again.

Resolving such problems was often a major challenge even to experts like us. Often it was a painfully tedious process of trial and error: Shut down the PC, pull boards, flip switches and/or change jumpers, put the boards back in, and power up again, over and over for hours or days until you finally hit on a combination of settings that allowed the new hardware to coexist happily with the old.

Plug and Play (aka **PnP**) has made things much easier, at least sometimes. Plug and Play technology is actually two separate things that get lumped together under the same moniker:

- **PCI Plug and Play.** When you turn on your PC's power, the motherboard takes an inventory of the boards in its PCI slots, and automatically assigns system resources (IRQs, DMA channels, etc.) as necessary. This happens entirely at the hardware level.
- **Windows Plug and Play.** When Windows 95/98 launches, it scans to see if there's any new hardware it doesn't recognize. If it finds something, it checks the inventory of hardware in the system and changes system settings as necessary to make everything work harmoniously. If needed, Windows will prompt you to insert a disk including the new device's software. (Windows NT is scheduled to get this feature in version 5.0.)

When it works, Plug and Play is wonderful. You don't need to know anything about your PC's IRQs and whatnot—you just plug stuff in and it works without a hitch. Unfortunately, PnP doesn't always work, so you may still need to do some manual troubleshooting. The newer your PC is, the less likely that is to be the case.

Troubleshooting Conflicts

When Plug and Play fails, you may have to manually *configure* the expansion cards in your PC—that is, adjust software settings, flip switches, or move jumpers—to make the cards work properly.

Why the complication? Because your system has limited resources—not just memory and disk space, but hardware resources, too, that enable cards and drives to interact correctly with your system and with Windows. In a correctly configured system, the cards, drives, system, and Windows all share resources in an orderly way, like children contentedly passing the fish sticks, string beans, and potatoes around the table. In a badly configured system, you've got a food fight.

The Four Types of Hardware Configuration Conflicts

If you have only Plug and Play devices in your system, you should not encounter any conflicts, but if you've got some older hardware they're almost inevitable. There are four basic types of potential hardware configuration conflicts:

Fighting for the Same IRQ. When a card installation problem occurs, it's most often a *hardware interrupt* problem. A hardware interrupt is a top-priority message from a card (or other device) to the CPU that says "I need service immediately!" Nearly every card needs to send interrupts, and in so doing requires its own *interrupt request (IRQ)* line, which is a sort of personal hotline to the CPU.

Unfortunately, there are a limited number of IRQ lines (a mere 16 in every system) and several of them are already hogged by the PC itself for the keyboard, the communications (COM) ports, the parallel (LPT) ports, and so on. By the law of averages alone, many boards default to the *same* IRQ. Two boards can't contend for one IRQ without making your system go haywire.

Standard and Common IRQ Assignments

IRQ0	system timer
IRQ1	keyboard
IRQ2	free (actually used by IRQ8-IRQ15)
IRQ3	serial mouse or modem on COM2 (shared by COM4) or free
IRQ4	serial mouse or modem on COM1 (shared by COM3) or free
IRQ5	sound card, second parallel port (LPT2), or free
IRQ6	floppy controller
IRQ7	parallel port (LPT1) or free
IRQ8	system clock
IRQ9	redirected IRQ2
IRQ10	free
IRQ11	free
IRQ12	PS/2 mouse or free
IRQ13	floating-point math unit
IRQ14	primary EIDE channel
IRQ15	secondary EIDE channel

The above list shows the standard and most common optional IRQ assignments. As you can see, there usually aren't very many free IRQs to choose from.

When Plug and Play can't resolve conflicting IRQ settings correctly, the results can be pretty bad. Your computer may not boot at all, or it may hang when you try to install the conflicting device.

Vying for the Same I/O Address. IRQs aren't the only bones of contention. Sometimes, two cards try to use the same *I/O (input/output) address*, which tags a few bytes of memory the CPU uses to zap instructions to a specific device. All devices should have their own individual I/O addresses.

And if they don't? Nothing bad happens, if they don't use the address at the same time—which is why I/O address conflicts are so insidious. You may not experience a system crash for some time, and then poof! I/O address conflicts occur most often between like devices, such as two hard disk interface cards or two graphics cards.

Battling Over DMA. Do you want to add a SCSI or network adapter? Then there's a good chance you'll be installing a device that uses *direct memory access (DMA)*, whereby a device improves performance by doing an end run around the CPU and writing directly to system memory.

Your system has eight *DMA channels*, each one a kind of data expressway to memory. Channel 0 and Channel 4 are sometimes used by the system, the floppy drive uses Channel 2, and your sound card probably uses two channels. The rest may be up for grabs.

Commonly Available DMA Channels

If you're installing a card that uses DMA—say, a sound card or a hard disk interface—then you have several free channels to choose from. Some cards may perform better if assigned 16-bit rather than 8-bit channels.

DMA Channel	Bits	Typical status
0	16	sometimes used by system or sound card
1	8	most often used by sound card
2	8	used by floppy disk controller
3	8	sometimes used by serial port
4	16	used by DMA controller
5	16	most often used by sound card
6	16	free
7	16	free

Two devices shouldn't use the same DMA channel, but if they do, the outcome won't be as severe as that caused by a conflict between IRQs or I/O addresses. Instead of crashing the system, a DMA conflict usually prevents one device from completing its task while the other device takes over the channel. Nonetheless, a conflict will, at the least, hobble performance and—with so many channels to choose from—can be easily avoided.

Some cards can live without DMA if no channel is available. Thus you can sometimes resolve tough DMA conflicts by disabling one board's DMA access entirely.

Living at the Same Address. Video cards, as well as some SCSI and network adapters, include a ROM (read-only memory) chip containing code that helps the card do its chores. Your system reserves an area in memory for ROM starting addresses. Similar types of devices tend to take the same addresses and stay away from the territory of other types of devices. The symptoms of an unresolved ROM address conflict resemble that of an interrupt conflict: Your system locks up at boot and you can't do anything with it.

Resolving Conflicts

When Plug and Play fails, resolving conflicts becomes your job. The good news is that you can often solve problems without cracking the PC's case. The bad news is that figuring out exactly what's conflicting can be a real puzzle.

One thing that's extremely unintuitive: Thanks to Plug and Play, resolving conflicts may involve changing settings on things that are *working just fine*. For example, if you install a new voice modem and your scanner stops working, the solution could be to change the settings on your sound card. (Explanation: The new modem's voice circuits conflict with your sound card; Windows Plug and Play changes the sound card's settings; new sound card settings create a conflict with the scanner's SCSI adapter, which Windows can't detect because the card's from the pre-Plug and Play era.)

Obviously, given this kind of complexity, we can't give you an exhaustive guide to do-it-yourself device conflicts, but here are some things you can try.

Check the Windows 95/98 Device Manager. Windows 95 and Windows 98 are sometimes able to identify conflicts they're not smart enough to resolve. You'll find any such conflicts marked with an exclamation-point icon in the Device Manager (see Figure 4). Double-click any such icon. and look at the Device Status message in the dialog box that appears (see Figure 5) for tips on what's wrong. Click the Troubleshooter button for more detailed suggestions on what to try next (see Figure 6).

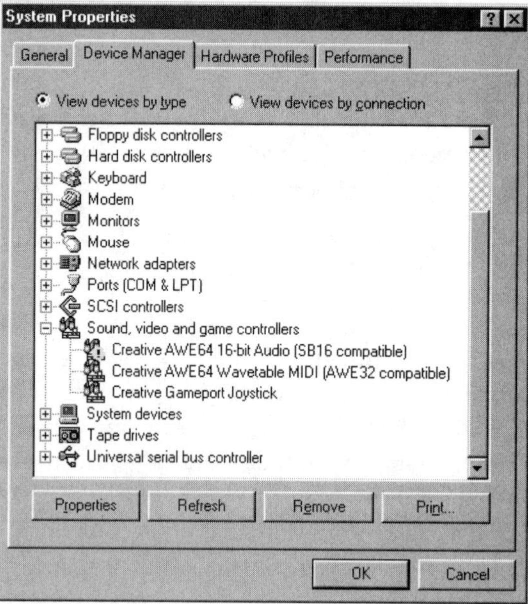

Figure 4

Device Manager.

In Windows 95 and 98, you can identify many conflicts by looking for exclamation-point icons in the Device Manager tab of the System control panel.

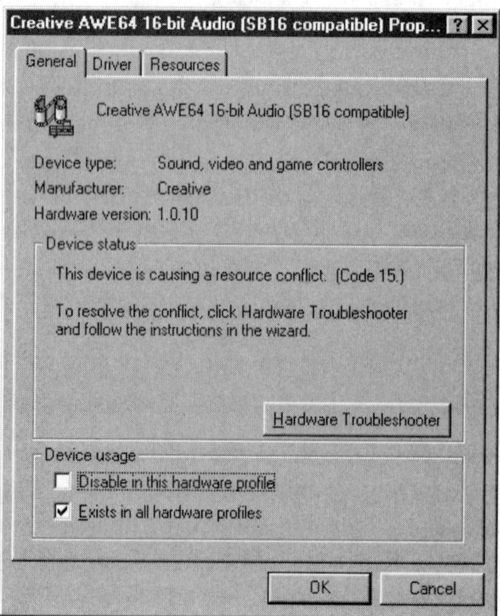

Figure 5

Device status report.

Double-clicking on an exclamation-point icon in Device Manager brings up the troubled device's property sheet, which includes a device status report about the problem and a recommendation for what to do about it.

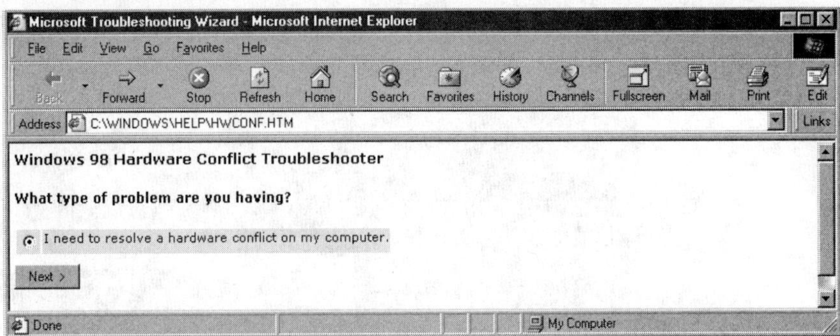

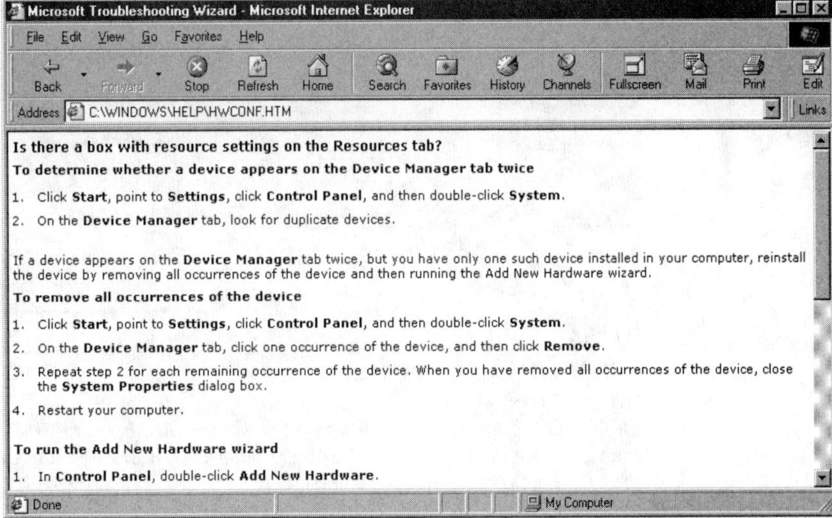

Figure 6

Device troubleshooting wizard.

In Windows 98, clicking the Hardware Troubleshooter button brings up a troubleshooting wizard in Microsoft Internetnet Explorer. (If you use Netscape Navigator or some other browser, in order to use the troubleshooter you may have to temporarily make MSIE your default browser—assuming the U.S. Department of Justice hasn't forced Microsoft to redesign this "feature.")

If Windows isn't smart enough to detect a conflict, you may still be able to use the Device Manager to manually override device settings. (See Figure 7).

Check with the Manufacturer. The company may already be aware of the problem you're experiencing, and if you're lucky will already have a fix—which is often as simple as downloading and installing an updated driver. Check the FAQ on the company's Web site or call their 800 number and ask. (See Chapter 27: HELP! Where to Turn When Things Go Wrong, for tips on navigating tech support.)

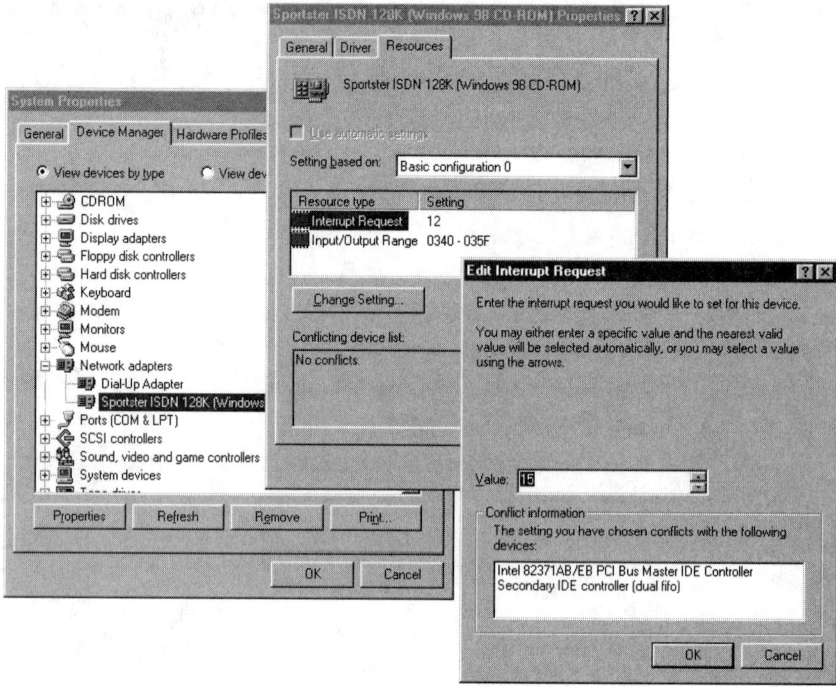

Figure 7

Adjusting settings manually.

The conflict shown in Figures 4, 5, and 6 was actually the result of an incorrect IRQ setting in the PC's ISDN adapter. Although it might have been possible to resolve it by changing the sound card's settings (shown in the other figures), the most elegant solution was to change the ISDN adapter to a nonconflicting IRQ.

Run Setup. Sometimes a motherboard can't tell that an ISA board is using an IRQ or DMA channel, and the motherboard provides a conflicting IRQ to a PCI board. In such cases, you can often resolve the conflict by using the motherboard's built-in setup utility (see the sidebar "Accessing Your PC's Setup Routine"). There's no standard menu command for this function—look for options that reserve specified IRQ/DMA numbers for ISA cards, or that affect the order in which the numbers are assigned to PCI devices. **Always write down current settings** before changing them so you'll be able to restore them if you make matters worse.

You may also be able to resolve conflicts by disabling unused hardware built into the motherboard. For example, modem conflicts can often be fixed by using setup to disable any unused serial ports.

Install Windows NT's Plug and Play Driver. Officially, Windows NT 4.0 does not support Windows Plug and Play (though hardware-level PCI Plug and Play still works). Microsoft does, however, include a Plug and Play driver.

Accessing Your PC's Setup Routine

Some upgrades require that you access your PC's setup routine (sometimes called "CMOS setup"; see the glossary for an explanation). Your system manual explains how to do this—if you still *have* your system manual. Well, you can always call tech support... if you can get through. When you can't reach tech support, or if the manufacturer has gone out of business, try these tricks:

- Press the "magic keys." In almost all systems, the setup routine is accessible during startup if you tap a particular key or combination of keys. Often the key is indicated by a message on screen, like "Press Del to run setup." If there's no message, popular keys for invoking setup include the aforementioned Del, Ins, and F10.
- Reboot and lean on it. Sometimes holding down the Esc key while your system boots will return a message saying something like "Keyboard error; would you like to configure your system?" Choose Yes and you'll bop right into the setup routine. If Esc doesn't work, reboot and try other key combinations.

Still no luck? Well, now you know why you should stash your manual in a safe place. If you really can't raise the manufacturer's tech support, check the FAQs on the company's Web site.

To install it, load the Windows NT CD-ROM, and find the following Setup Information file. (You'll see the .inf only if you have Show All Files selected in Windows Explorer's View/Options dialog box.)

```
\drvlib\Pnpisa\X86\Pnpisa.inf
```

Right-click the file, choose Install from the pop-up menu, and reboot. If this doesn't help, or if the driver causes problems, you can remove it by deleting Pnpisa.sys from the System32\Drivers subdirectory of your Windows NT folder (by default, that's C:\Winnt).

Try Trial-and-Error. If the foregoing doesn't get you anywhere, you're left with the old trial-and-error method. We can't give you much advice on that, since every situation is different, but we can tell you where to look for ideas.

First, dig out the manuals for whatever non-Plug-and-Play "legacy" boards you have in your system. Find the sections that discuss the available IRQ, I/O address, DMA channel, and memory address settings. Compare those with the resources currently in use to figure out where the conflict might be. To get a list of resources in use:

- **In Windows 95**, open the System control panel, switch to the Device Manager tab, and double-click the Computer icon to bring up the Computer Properties box (see Figure 8). This will let you view lists of all four system resource types—IRQs, I/O addresses, DMA channels, and memory addresses. Unfortunately, this utility doesn't have a Print button, but you can print out summary or detailed configuration information by clicking the Print button in the Device Manager proper.

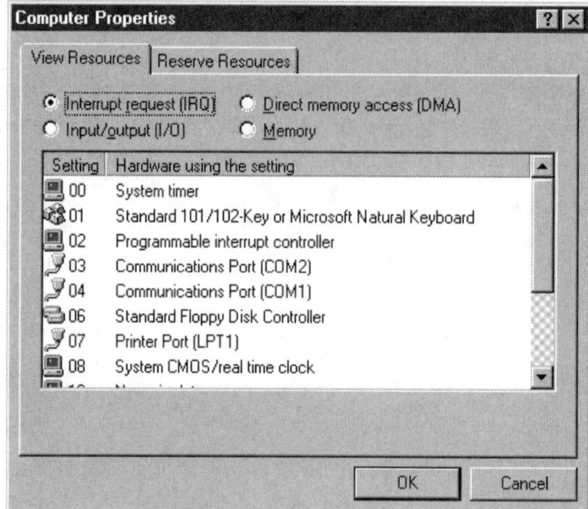

Figure 8

Windows 95's Computer Properties.

This feature displays all the hardware settings the operating system can detect.

- **In Windows 98,** use the System Information utility in the Programs/ Accessories/System Tools folder on the Start menu (see Figure 9). In addition to the four system resources, this utility can also display "forced hardware" (any manual changes you've made that are overriding Windows Plug and Play), shared resources, and any conflicts that Win98 is aware of. Use the Print button if you want a hard copy.

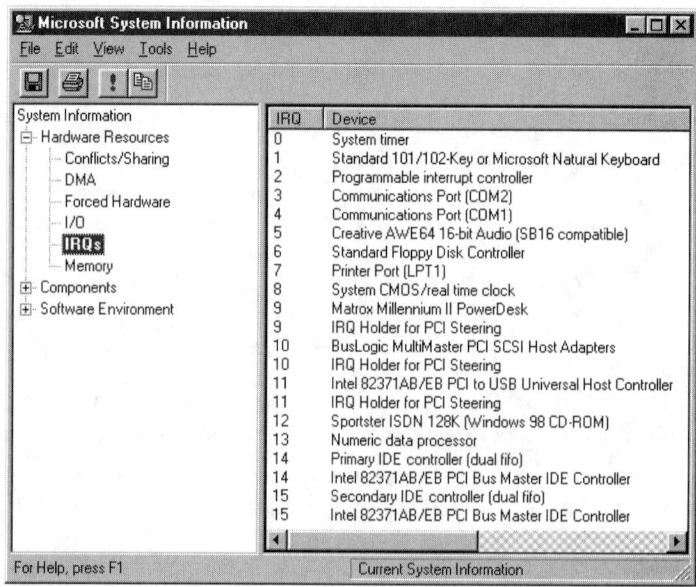

Figure 9

Windows 98's System Information.

Windows 98 displays considerably more hardware settings than Windows 95 does. Win98 also displays manual settings you've made with Device Manager, and any actual or potential conflicts it detects.

- **In Windows NT,** use Windows NT Diagnostics in the Programs/ Administrative Tools folder of the Start menu (see Figure 10). Click the Print button for a hard copy.

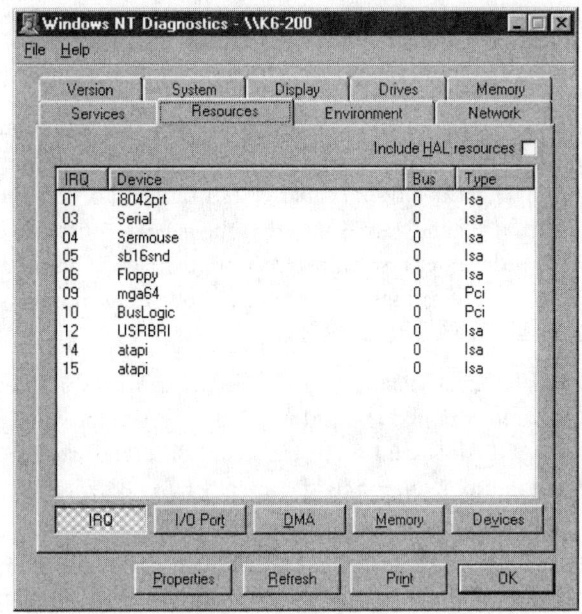

Figure 10

Windows NT Diagnostics.

WinNT's settings display isn't as exhaustive or helpful as Windows 98's. Notice there's no indication that the parallel port is using IRQ7.

- **In Windows 95 and 98,** non-Plug-and-Play boards can sometimes be configured using Device Manager, using the same process described above (see Figure 7). In Windows NT, you may be able to adjust them using software that came with the board. If the settings aren't accessible there, you'll have to crack the case and change the jumper or switch settings (see Figure 11).

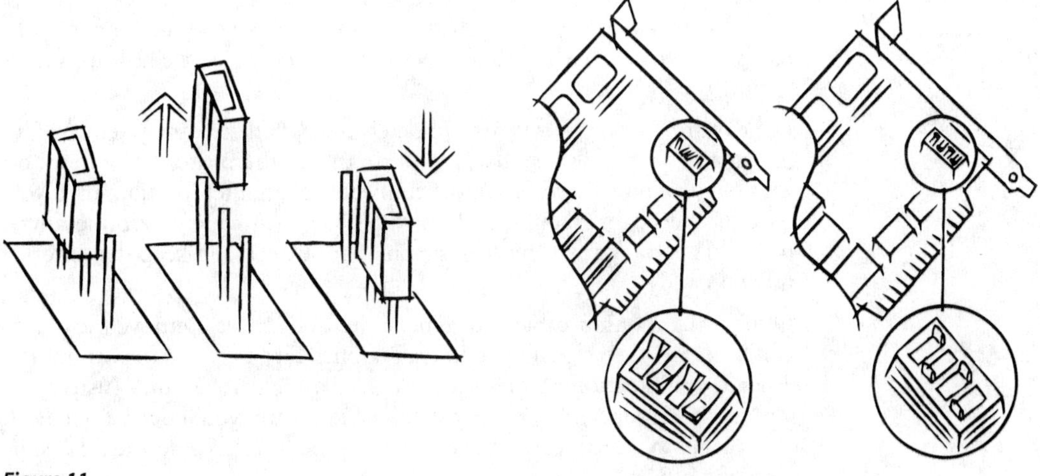

Figure 11

How to set jumpers and DIP switches.

Here's what a typical jumper block looks like. To change your configuration, you move the jumper from one pair of pins to another, or remove the jumper entirely. It all depends on what you need to do and how the manual says to do it. Often, to change a card's I/O address or other settings, you move a DIP switch—a tiny slide or rocker switch on a small switch block. If you've got big fingers, try flipping the switch with a pen.

Upgrading Your Video Card

Most people replace their current graphics *controller* (the monitor's controlling electronics, which may be either on a card or on the motherboard) because they want 3-D acceleration, higher resolution, and/or less flicker. But before making such a change, remember that the *monitor* must also be able to handle less flicker and higher resolution. You can damage a monitor by trying to drive it beyond its specifications. (For more on matching monitors and graphics cards, see Chapter 5: Monitors, Etc.)

If your PC has an AGP slot, buy an AGP card. You won't necessarily get better performance than you would with a PCI card, but you can't put anything else in the AGP slot—and there are lots of different uses for PCI slots. With either version, upgrading the video card is fairly easy.

1. Read and follow all the instructions in "Installing Expansion Cards" earlier in this chapter. Be sure you know which floppy or CD holds the board's drivers; you might also check the manufacturer's Web site and see if there are newer drivers you could download. (See Chapter 21: The Web and Browsers for help with that task.) Note that any special instructions from the manufacturer take precedence over what's in these steps.
2. If you're running Windows 95 or 98, skip to step 3.

   In Windows NT, run the Display control panel. On the Settings tab, click Display Type, then Change. In the Manufacturers (left) column, select "Standard display types"; in the Display (right) column, select "VGA compatible display adapter." Click OK, and then follow the prompts.
3. Shut down Windows, switch off the power if necessary, touch the PC's fan grille to discharge any static electricity you may have picked up, and unplug the PC.
4. Look at the back of your system to determine whether your system's existing graphics controller is on a card or on the motherboard. If the monitor isn't plugged into a card but into a connector in another location, then you have motherboard graphics. Check your PC's manual to determine how to disable your system's built-in graphics controller, and keep that information handy.
5. Unplug the monitor cable and remove the PC's cover. Remove the old graphics card—or, if you're adding a graphics card to a system with motherboard graphics, follow the procedure to disable that circuitry (usually you move a jumper). If you're installing a PCI card, you'll need a free PCI slot. Install the card, reaffix the cover, plug the monitor into the card, and turn on your system.
6. Under Windows 95 and 98, if Plug and Play works properly, Windows will detect the board and set it up. If it asks for a disk, give it the one where you found the drivers.

Under Windows NT, you may get a series of prompts to set up your new card. If not, run the Display control panel. On the Settings tab, click Display Type, then Change, then Have Disk. Insert the driver disk, browse to the folder containing the drivers (or type its path into the "Copy manufacturer's files from" field), click OK, and follow the prompts.

7. Finally, run the Display control panel, and on the Settings tab select the resolution and color depth you want to use. For recommended settings, various monitor sizes, and additional information about these settings, see "How Big Is Big Enough" and "Video Memory, Desktop Size, and Color Quality" in Chapter 5: Monitors, Etc.

If Windows 95/98 does not prompt you for a driver, and the card doesn't seem to be working well, run the Add New Hardware control panel. When you reach the part where Windows offers to let you choose from a list (see Figure 12), do so, and follow the Windows NT instructions in step 6.

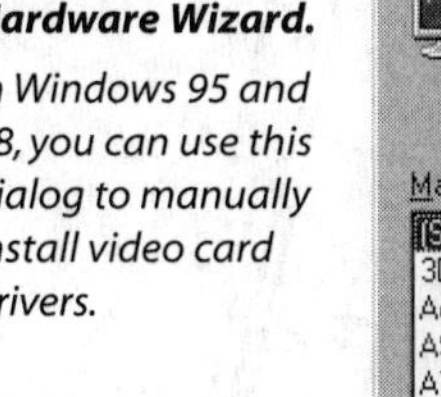

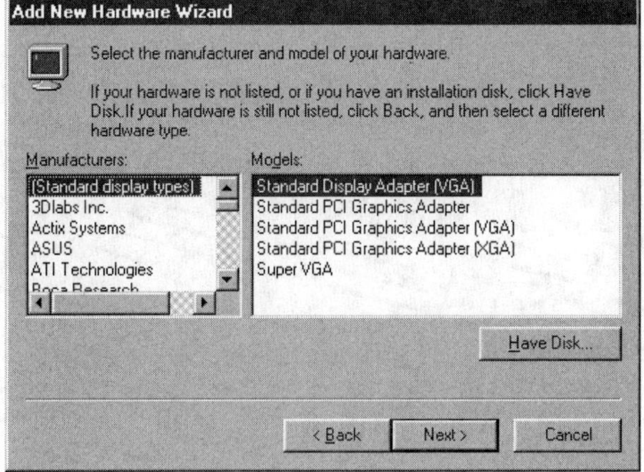

Figure 12

The Add New Hardware Wizard.

In Windows 95 and 98, you can use this dialog to manually install video card drivers.

If that doesn't work, check with the card manufacturer and see if you have the latest Windows drivers—they sometimes go through many bug fixes and revisions. Most companies make their drivers available on their Web sites (see Chapter 21: The Web and Browsers, for help with finding and downloading drivers). If you don't have access to the Web, you should be able to get drivers on diskette for free or a nominal charge.

Adding Video Memory

All graphics cards come with *video memory*, a relatively small quantity of RAM in which the image on your screen is created. The more memory on the card, the more colors and the higher the resolution the card can produce. (See "Video Memory, Desktop Size, and Color Quality" in Chapter 5 for details.)

Many cards come with less video memory than they can hold, so you can add more later. To do this, check your card's documentation and see what kind of memory chips the card uses. Buy those chips at a discount electronics store or through a mail-order memory specialist and plug them into the open sockets on the card.

Turn off your PC and remove the video card, following the instructions in "Disassembly without Destruction" at the beginning of the chapter. Add the chips or memory modules (see Figure 13), and check the card's documentation to see if you need to do anything to make the card recognize the new memory. (You probably won't have to do anything—most cards automatically sense the memory, and their drivers adjust accordingly.)

Reinstall the card, and turn on your system. The card's new capabilities should appear in the Display control panel's Settings tab.

Figure 13

Video memory upgrades.

Many graphics cards enable you to add memory to bump up resolution and colors. Just buy the appropriate chips as cheaply as you can and plug them in.

Installing a Modem

To "install" an **external modem,** all you do is find a free serial or USB port, connect the modem to it, and plug in your phone line(s)—see Figure 14. Then you run the Modem control panel, click Add, and follow the prompts. That's all there is to it.

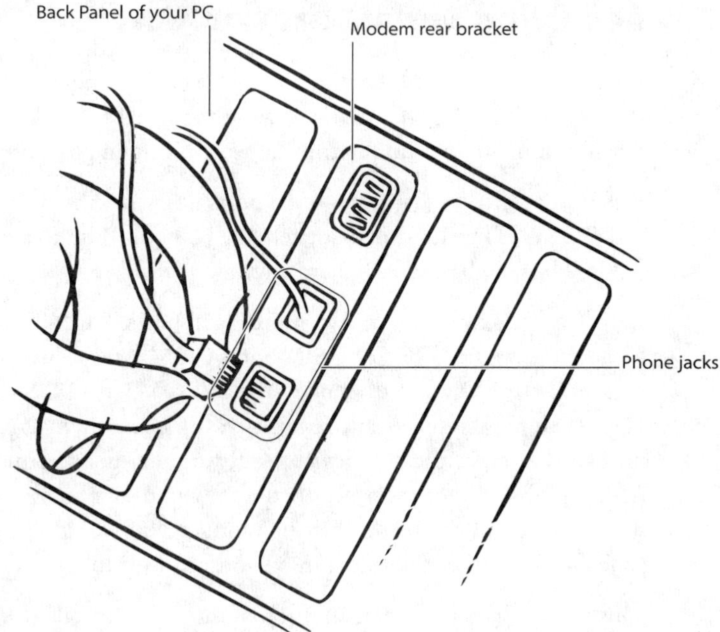

Figure 14

Hooking a modem to the phone lines.

Most modems come with two phone jacks—one for the phone line itself and another for your telephone. If you're using the same line for both voice and data, you need to make both connections.

With some luck, installing an **internal modem** won't be much more difficult:

1. If you're upgrading an old modem, first look in the Modem control panel and see what COM port it's set to, so you'll know to set the new modem to the same one. Also, make sure you've written down all the information about your Internet dial-up account: user ID, password, access number, DNS server IP number. Windows sometimes reacts to a change in modem drivers by throwing out your Internet configuration, after which you have to reinstall from scratch!
2. Read the cautions in "Disassembly without Destruction" at the beginning of the chapter. Then follow the instructions in "Installing Expansion Cards" to remove the old modem (if any), put the modem in any available slot, and plug in the phone line.
3. When you restart your PC, Windows Plug and Play may detect the modem and set it up automatically. If it doesn't, run the Modem control panel, click Add, and follow the prompts.

If Windows doesn't detect the modem or it doesn't work, the most likely explanation is a serial port conflict. See "Resolving Serial Port Conflicts" just below for some tips on troubleshooting and resolution.

Another common problem is a wrong or outdated driver. If Windows didn't prompt you for a disk when installing the modem, open the Modem control panel, select the modem you just installed, click Remove, and then Yes to confirm removal. Then click Add, check "Don't detect my modem," click Next, click Have Disk, and follow the prompts to load the drivers that came with your modem.

Resolving Serial Port Conflicts

Serial (COM) ports can be one of the most confusing components of your PC. Here's a brief guide to how they're supposed to work in theory, their practical limitations, and the things that most often go wrong.

PCs normally come with two serial ports built into the motherboard: COM1 and COM2. The latter may not actually be hooked up to a port on the back of the PC, but the hardware's there anyway.

In theory, PCs can support two more serial ports, COM3 and COM4. These, however, share the IRQs of COM1 and COM2, respectively—which means you can't use COM1 at the same time as COM3, or COM2 at the same time as COM4. In fact, practically speaking, even using them at *different* times is problematic, since the two devices' software may conflict and make one or both unusable. Since most people use only two serial ports at most (one for the modem, and maybe one for the mouse), you wouldn't expect this to be a problem—but in fact it's a common source of trouble.

This usually happens when an internal modem is installed, which adds a third serial port to the PC. Logically, you'd expect that you could set the modem to COM2 if the serial mouse was on COM1, or set it to COM1 if the mouse doesn't use a serial port. But often this doesn't work.

The reasons are too arcane and complicated to explain, but the fix is simple: Disable any unused serial ports using the motherboard's setup utility, and don't leave any "holes"—that is, use COM1 first, COM2 next, and so on. If the modem's the only serial device in the computer, disable both ports on the motherboard. For a serial mouse, enable the motherboard's COM1 and disable its COM2. (The same general principle applies with other serial devices, like a graphics tablet or UPS.)

If you want to use more than two serial devices and have trouble getting them to coexist, you may be able to get them to work properly by switching COM3 and COM4 to unused IRQs. There are also special serial port boards specifically designed for people who need to use more than two ports simultaneously.

Adding Memory

The less often Windows has to access the hard disk—accessing memory instead—the better your computer's performance. That's why you shouldn't run Windows with less than 32MB of main memory. And if you run several big applications at once, 64MB can't hurt. Fortunately, standard SIMMs

(Single Inline Memory Modules) and DIMMs (Double…) are now used in nearly every system. Not only are these modules easy to install—they snap right into sockets on the motherboard—but they're cheap, too (usually no more than $2 a megabyte).

Buying the Right Kind of Memory

Memory comes in several different varieties. Everything except the capacity of the SIMMs or DIMMs you install is determined by your PC's memory specifications, so check your manual carefully to see which kind you need.

- **SIMMs vs. DIMMs.** Older Pentium PCs mostly use 72-pin SIMMs; more recent ones use 168-pin DIMMs. A few motherboards have sockets for both types. SIMMs must be installed in pairs; DIMMs you can add one at a time. (486 PCs mostly use 30-pin SIMMs, installed in matching groups of four.)
- **ECC (DIMMs only).** DIMMs come in two types: regular and ECC (Error Code Correcting). The latter costs more, but (when used with a motherboard that supports ECC) brings the likelihood of data-corrupting memory errors a hair closer to zero.
- **Parity and EDO (SIMMs only).** SIMMs come in three types: parity, non-parity, and EDO. Check the manual to see if your system requires a particular type. If it supports more than one, don't mix types; if it supports both parity and non-parity, the latter costs less and has no significant disadvantages unless you crunch a lot of extremely important numbers. (Parity is very slightly less prone to errors; for a technical discussion, go to **www.kingston.com/king/mg4.htm**.)
- **Capacity.** You can get both SIMMs and DIMMs in 8, 16, 32, 64, and 128MB capacities. There are also 256MB DIMMs. Not all motherboards support all capacities—check the manual to see which combinations yours allows, and if there are any constraints on how you can combine them.
- **Speed (SIMMs only).** SIMMs come in 60, 70, and 80 nanoseconds (ns) flavors—the lower the number, the faster the memory and the higher the price. Check the manual to see what speed your motherboard requires. There's no problem in buying SIMMs faster than your system requires (in fact, that may be unavoidable if your manual calls for the nearly extinct 80ns modules), but the faster SIMM won't improve performance. Whatever you do, however, *don't* buy a SIMM rated slower: that invites memory errors that could trash your data. Avoid mixing memory of different speeds—often it works fine, but it's been known to cause problems.

- **High-end DIMMs.** Most PCs that use DIMMs require the standard 5-volt, 60ns variety, but Pentium IIs running at 350MHz or faster (those with 100MHz motherboards) require one of a confusing variety of 3.3-volt DIMMs rated at 10ns or faster. A good dealer should be able to help you figure out which type of DIMM your system requires.

Installing Memory Modules

If all the sockets in your motherboard are full, you'll have to remove some of your modules to make room for the upgrade.

About the height and width of a stick of chewing gum, your average SIMM snaps into its socket fairly easily (see Figure 15). But remember—your motherboard is *not* the place to use force. Break a SIMM socket, and you may as well have your motherboard replaced. The trick is to lightly spread the delicate plastic side brackets as you extract or insert SIMMs.

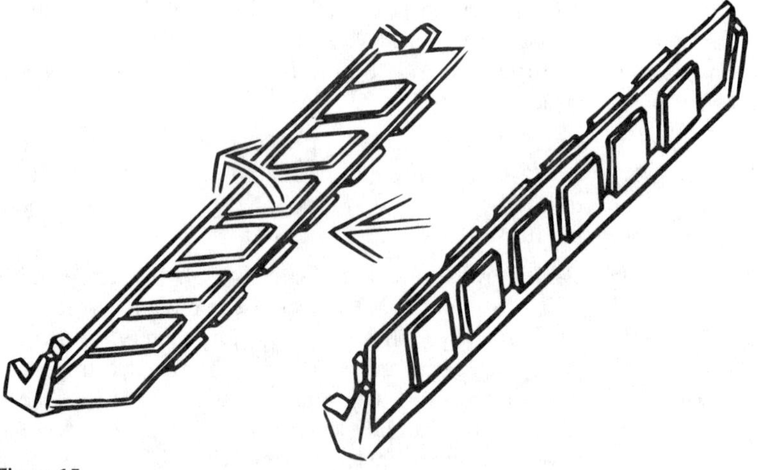

Figure 15

How to install a SIMM.

Begin by sliding the SIMM into the socket at approximately a 45 degree angle, until the edge of the SIMM is flush with the bottom of the socket. (If it won't fit, you may need to turn the SIMM around, or try a different angle). Then gently tilt the SIMM up to a vertical position, until the brackets on the side snap in to lock it in place. To remove a SIMM, spread the brackets, tilt the it down to 45 degrees, and slide it out of the socket.

Installing DIMMs is easier. You just flip a lever on the socket, drop in the DIMM, and flip the lever back to lock the module in place (see Figure 16).

Installing EIDE Drives

With today's PCs, adding or replacing a hard disk, CD-ROM, tape backup, Zip, or other EIDE drives is easier than you might think—certainly much easier than it was a few years ago. Your motherboard handles the hardware setup, and Windows does the rest. There's not much for you to do except plug in the drive and work your way through a few simple menus.

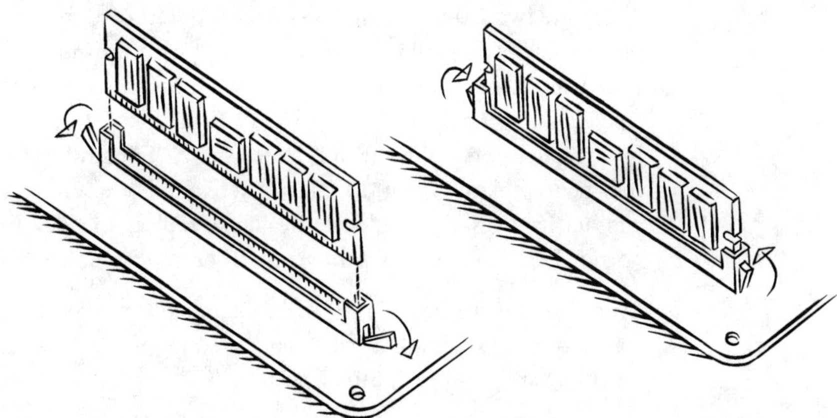

Figure 16

Installing DIMMs.

To install a DIMM, you just flip the lock lever on the DIMM socket, drop in the DIMM, and flip the lever back to lock it in place. To remove a DIMM, reverse the process.

As noted at the beginning of this chapter, before replacing a hard drive you *must* back up your entire hard disk, preferably to tape. The possibility of something going fatally wrong is slim, but there's no need to take even a small risk with your data. Moreover, if you're replacing a hard disk, backing up the old one and restoring the backup to the new drive is the safest and easiest way to transplant your old data to the new drive.

Finding a Drive Bay for the Upgrade

The first thing you need to determine is whether you have room for your new drive—that is, whether you have a free *drive bay* (an empty area in your PC for mounting a drive). Some compact PCs have only three bays (for the floppy, the CD-ROM, and the hard disk), so you'll have to replace an old device to make room for a new one.

CD drives always need a 5.25-inch external bay. Tape drives usually do too, though some will fit in two 3.5-inch bays. Internal Zip drives and other superfloppies will generally fit a 3.5-inch bay. Hard drives come in both sizes, but the internal drive bays in most consumer-oriented PCs hold only 3.5-inch hard disks. The 5.25-inch drives are usually designed for the server and workstation markets.

If necessary, you can always install a 3.5-inch device in a 5.25-inch bay. Any well-stocked computer store should have the inexpensive mounting bracket that's required. You can also install a hard disk in an external bay if your internal bays are full or not big enough.

EIDE Configuration Issues

Configuring your motherboard's EIDE adapter and the devices connected to it isn't rocket science. It's a little complicated, but if you pay attention to the details you should have no problems.

There are two EIDE channels on your motherboard, the primary and the secondary. Each can hold up to two devices, for a maximum of four. Thus, if you've already got four EIDE drives (say, a hard disk, CD-ROM, Zip, and tape backup), there's nowhere to add a fifth device. In that situation, you look into parallel-port, USB, or SCSI alternatives. Sometimes the best solution may be to replace one of the existing devices. For example, if you want to add another hard disk, it would be cheaper to replace the Zip drive with a parallel-port or USB model than to buy a SCSI hard drive and adapter.

Every EIDE drive has two or three possible jumper settings. If they're not set correctly, your system may not boot, or some of the drives may be inaccessible. Here are the three jumper positions:

Stand-alone (aka master, no slave)	The drive is the only device on the ribbon cable. This is usually the way hard disks are set at the factory.
Master (aka master, slave present)	There are two drives on the cable, and this one is the master. This is usually the way hard disks come from the factory. (On some drives, the same jumper is used for both master and stand-alone configurations.)
Slave	There are two drives on the cable, and the other one is the master. When you add a slave drive to a cable, it's often necessary to change the jumpers on the existing drive from stand-alone to master.

Keep these considerations in mind when adding EIDE devices:

- Your boot drive must be the master, or the only drive on the primary EIDE channel.
- If you're installing a second hard drive and it's faster than your existing drive, you might want to make the new drive the boot drive (that is, make it the master, and your old drive the slave) so that Windows will launch faster. That would mean setting your old hard disk to slave mode. For the new disk to be the boot drive, it has to be the master on the primary channel. (Actually, this isn't *always* necessary—some PCs' setup menus have an option that lets you change which hard disk is the boot device.)
- A CD or tape drive can impose a performance bottleneck with a hard disk on the same channel. To eliminate this possibility, put those devices on the secondary channel, and your hard drive(s) on the primary channel.

- Operating systems other than Windows (such as Linux) may not recognize devices on the secondary channel unless the primary channel is full.
- Adding a new drive to your system can rearrange drive letters, which can interfere with CD-ROMs that have installed icons in your Start menu. Some discs are smart enough to fix themselves by giving you a dialog box to browse to the CD's new location. With others, you can edit the Target

and Start In properties of the CDs' shortcuts on the Start menu. (See Chapter 11: Windows 95, 98, and NT, for tips on editing shortcuts.) If you're an advanced user, you can search the Registry for paths pointing to the CD-ROM's old drive letter, and manually edit the paths to reflect the new drive letter. (If you're not sure what that means, you probably don't want to mess with the Registry.)

In some cases when upgrading, you may want to shuffle existing devices around from one EIDE channel to another.

Installing the Drive

Now you're ready to physically install your new drive. It probably has its own detailed installation instructions, but here's a general description of the process:

1. Turn off your PC, unplug it, and open it up. To access the drive bay where you're going to install the new drive, you may need to temporarily unplug and clear away the flat, gray ribbon cables that connect other drives. If so, make sure you write down exactly how those cables were hooked up, so you can reconnect them later.
2. If you're *replacing* a drive, unplug the cables connected to the drive you're replacing, remove it, and set the new drive's jumpers to match the old drive's settings.

   If you're *adding* a drive, examine the configuration of the existing drives. Decide on the channel into which you're going to install the new drive, and adjust its jumper settings and those of any other drives), as necessary.
3. If you're installing a 3.5-inch drive in a 5.25-inch bay, attach the mounting bracket (see Figure 17).
4. Slide the new drive into the bay and use the four screws that came with it to secure it to the drive cage (see Figure 18).
5. Attach the EIDE ribbon cable to the drive and, if necessary, plug the other end of the EIDE cable into the secondary EIDE socket on the motherboard (see Figure 18). Usually the EIDE cable's plugs and sockets are "keyed," that is, they will only connect in one direction. If they're not, look for the red stripe or other distinctive marking on one side of the cable, and plug it in so that it's on the side marked "Pin 1." (You may need to look in the drive and/or motherboard manuals to find out where Pin 1 is.)
6. Now look for an unconnected white plug at the end of a bundle of four wires sprouting from the power supply. (If you're replacing a drive, it's the smaller of the two plugs you unplugged from the old drive.) That's a power connector, and you should plug it into the power socket on the back of the new drive. Power connectors are always keyed so you can't reverse them accidentally, but they can be a little stiff to plug in. If you *don't* have a spare power connector, you'll need to buy a Y splitter cable (a couple of bucks at a computer store). Unplug a power connector from a drive near the one you're installing, plug it securely into the socket of the Y cable, and plug the other two ends of the Y into the two drives' power sockets.

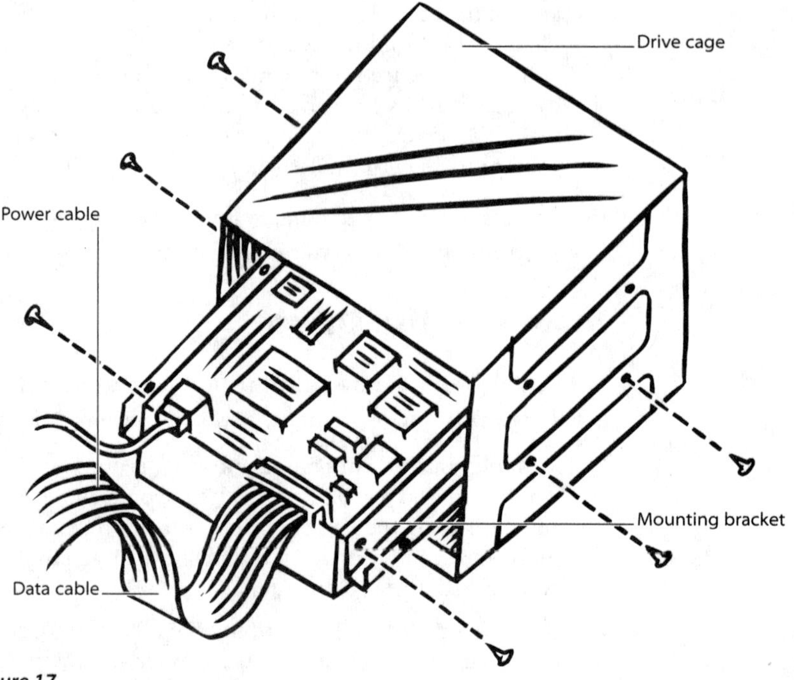

Figure 17

Mounting a drive in a bay.

This diagram shows how you install a drive (EIDE or SCSI, it doesn't matter) into a bay. In this example, we've also shown where you attach the mounting brackets to put a 3.5-inch drive in a 5.25-inch bay. If you're mounting a drive in the matching-sized bay, ignore that part of the diagram and just attach the screws on the outside of the bay directly to the drive.

7. If you're installing a CD-ROM or DVD-ROM drive, connect the audio cable to the appropriate input on your sound card. The drive's manual should have instructions. If the cable doesn't match, call the drive vendor's tech support number about getting a replacement.
8. Replace your PC's cover, but don't screw it in just yet. You may want to check a few things if you run into trouble later.
9. Plug your PC back in, turn on the power, and run the setup utility. The menus should include a choice called something like "IDE Setup," "Hard Disk Detect," or "Auto HDD Configuration." Run that utility, and your motherboard will automatically configure all installed EIDE devices. If all the devices show up correctly, save the changes and exit setup.

If you're installing a CD-ROM or tape drive, you're almost done. Just turn on the PC, and follow the installation instructions to install whatever software came with the drive.

CD-ROM drives don't always come with software—Windows 95 and 98 detect them automatically. In Windows NT, you may need to install a driver manually (see Figure 19).

Figure 18

Connecting an EIDE cable.

An EIDE ribbon cable connects to the motherboard at one end, and to an EIDE drive at the other. If the cable has a third plug, it can connect to a second drive as well. (If your existing cable has only two plugs, you can replace it with one that has three—EIDE hardware is standard and compatible.)

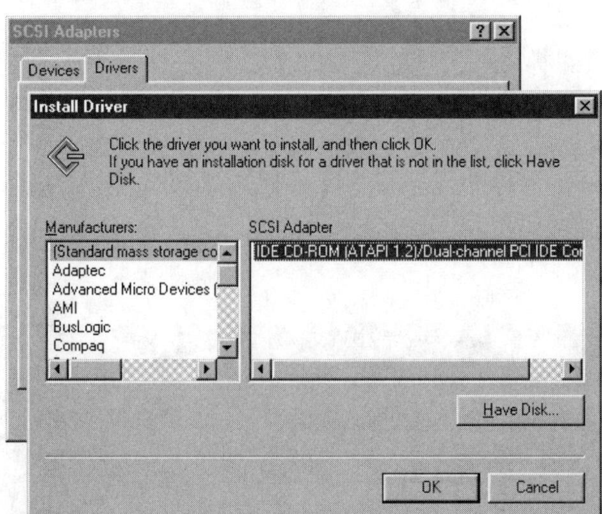

Figure 19

Installing Windows NT's EIDE CD-ROM driver.

If Windows NT doesn't recognize your new CD-ROM drive, you may need to install the driver manually. Open the SCSI Adapters control panel (even if you don't have a SCSI adapter—go figure). Click the Drivers tab. If IDE CD-ROM doesn't appear on the SCSI Adapter list, click Add, click "Standard mass storage controllers" in the Manufacturers (left) column, click "IDE CD-ROM..." in the "SCSI Adapter" column, and click OK. Follow the prompts, and your new drive should appear after your computer reboots.

Setting Up a New Hard Disk

There are two steps in setting up a new hard disk: partitioning, which makes the drive visible to Windows; and formatting, in which Windows sets the disk up for use. Your new drive may have come with easy-setup software that automates one or both tasks; if it didn't, here's how to do them yourself.

If you've replaced your boot disk, Windows Setup can handle both jobs. Put your Windows CD-ROM in the PC's CD drive, boot from the Setup disk, and follow the prompts. (See the installation section of Chapter 11: Windows 95, 98, and NT, for more details.) Then restore your old data from the backup you made before installing the new disk.

If your backup software has a DOS Restore utility, you probably don't need to install Windows before restoring. You can just partition and format the new drive, as described in the steps coming up. Then follow the Backup utility's instructions to restore your old Windows installation, applications, and data. One extra step: After you partition the drive, use the Set Partition Active option in FDISK to make the first volume active.

If you've added a second disk, you'll have to partition the drive manually:

1. If you're running Windows NT, skip down to the next set of instructions. If you're running Windows 95 or 98, choose Run from the Start menu, type fdisk, and click OK. (FDISK is a funky old DOS-style program, so you'll have to do everything with the keyboard.)
2. If asked whether you want to "enable large disk support," press Y for "yes," unless you want to access the new disk from an operating system other than Windows 95 or 98, or you have some other reason for not using FAT32 (the Windows disk format that supports volumes larger than 2GB.)
3. Press 5 for "Change current fixed disk drive" (see Figure 20), then type 2 and press Enter.

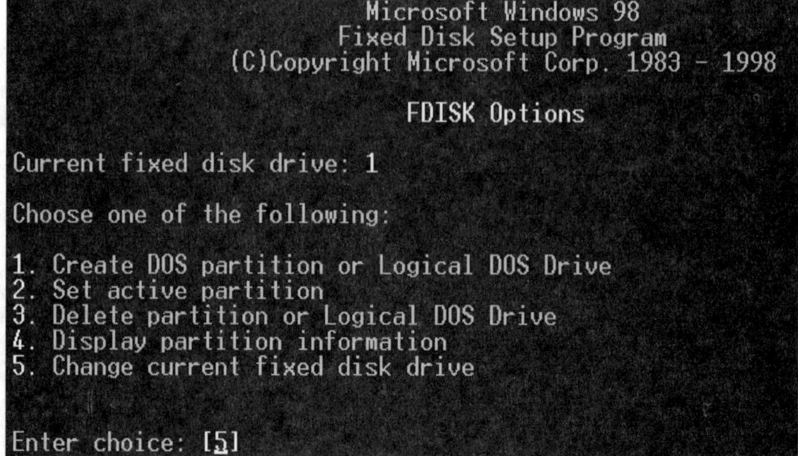

Figure 20

FDISK with two hard disks.

When you have two hard disks in your PC, a fifth choice appears on the FDISK menu, allowing you to choose which one you want to partition.

4. Press 1 for "Create DOS partition or logical DOS drive."
5. Press 1 for "Create primary DOS partition." There will be a pause while Windows inspects your new hard disk.
6. Press Y to create a single partition on the disk.
7. After FDISK reports that the partition is created, press Esc, and your system will reboot.
8. After the system reboots, open My Computer or Windows Explorer, right-click the new drive's icon (normally D), and choose Format from the pop-up menu.

For Windows NT only:

1. On the Start menu, choose Disk Administrator from Programs/Administrative Tools.
2. Right-click the large Free Space block of the new disk (probably Disk 1, since your existing drive will be numbered Disk 0), and choose Create.
3. On the Start menu, choose Shut Down, then Restart, and click Yes.
4. After the system reboots, open My Computer or Windows Explorer, right-click the new drive's icon (normally D), and choose Format from the pop-up menu.

Tool-Free Upgrades: USB and Parallel-Port Devices

An increasing number of upgrades don't require you to open the case. Instead, you just plug the new device into the PC's parallel or USB port.

Parallel Port. This port was originally intended to support only a single printer, so getting it to support multiple devices has been somewhat problematic. Nevertheless, it has still become the most popular way to connect scanners and removable-media drives (Zip, SparQ, Jaz, CD-R, etc.).

Some of these devices may require an updated port, either an EPP (Enhanced Parallel Port) or an ECP (Extended Capabilities Port). A *pass-through* port allows you to connect your printer, or other parallel-port devices. Unfortunately, the more stuff you hang off the parallel port, the more likely it is that one device's software will conflict with another's. Also, many parallel-port device drivers are not compatible with Windows NT.

USB. The problems in using parallel ports with devices other than printers have led Intel, Microsoft, and Compaq to develop the Universal Serial Bus specification (now administered by an independent industry committee).

USB can handle up to around 1.5MB of data a second, and you can daisy-chain multiple devices off a single port.

In theory, USB could handle all of a PC's peripherals except those requiring higher data rates (notably video, hard drives, and 100-megabit Ethernet). Your mouse, keyboard, printer, microphone, speakers, modem (or ISDN adapter), and joystick; the tape backup, floppy, CD-ROM, other removable-media drives; your videophone camera and scanner—all could be attached to a single USB port. In fact, USB may eventually make ISA slots obsolete: Microsoft and Intel have both been pushing that concept, although it doesn't seem to have yet caught on with PC manufacturers.

Windows 95's USB support is so problematic that it's a good idea to upgrade to Windows 98 before installing any USB devices. Windows NT 4.0 doesn't support USB at all—that's on the feature list for 5.0.

Adding USB Ports to Your PC

If your PC doesn't have USB ports, it's cheap and easy to add them. There are two ways you can do this.

The first step is to run setup to see if there are any settings for USB ports. If there are, your motherboard has USB circuitry built in, and you may be able to buy a kit to add the physical ports to the back panel. There's no standard motherboard connector, so check with the PC vendor or motherboard manufacturer to get the kit.

Otherwise, you can add a USB "hub" expansion card. These are available in both ISA and PCI versions, starting at around $15 for models with two ports.

CPU Upgrades

Nothing gives a PC a new lease on life like a new CPU. A faster processor will speed up performance of almost all other components in your system: memory, video, hard disk, in fact just about everything but your modem. In many cases, you can simply swap in a new CPU chip, an upgrade that takes only slightly longer than opening and closing your PC's cover. If that's not practical, you can usually do a motherboard transplant—remove the PC's main circuit board and replace it with a modern one.

CPU Chip Swaps

A PC upgraded with a new CPU chip will not necessarily perform as well as a PC that was designed for that CPU. As PCs evolve, their memory, video, and disk drive subsystems all get faster, so installing an up-to-date CPU in a three- or four-year-old motherboard is a little like strapping a jet engine onto the Wright brothers' biplane. As a rough rule of thumb, a reasonable CPU upgrade for an old system should double the speed of the CPU and cost significantly less than a full motherboard transplant done in a shop.

The upgrade options and issues will vary depending on what CPU your PC came with, and what motherboard you have. There are so many variations that your best bet is to check out some vendors specializing in CPU upgrades to see what they have to offer. Here are some general tips:

- **486s.** These old PCs aren't worth putting a lot of money into, but at this writing there are still some inexpensive upgrades on the market. See the "Upgrade Resources" at the end of this chapter for pointers. Some have "upgrade" or "OverDrive" sockets, which let you upgrade the CPU by simply plugging in a new chip (the old one goes to sleep). With others, you'll probably need a tool called a "chip puller" (Figure 21).

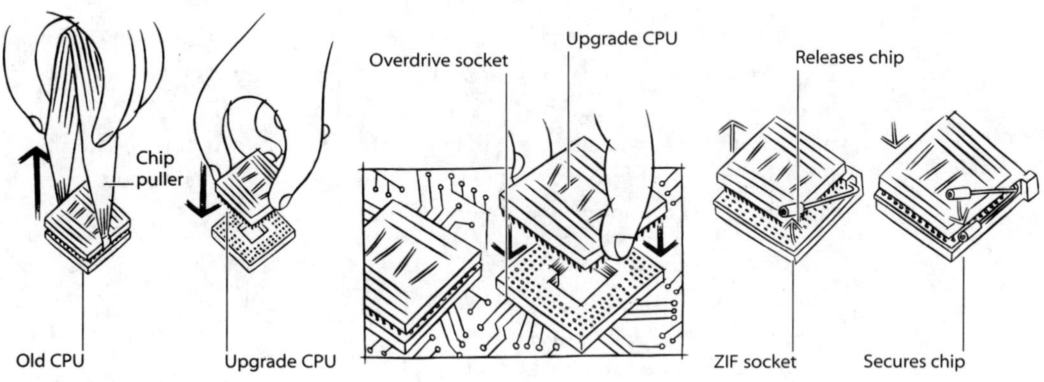

Figure 21

How to upgrade your CPU.

At left, the old-fashioned method—pull out the old CPU by force with a chip puller, and plug in the new one. At center is a method used in some 486 motherboards, where you just plug the upgrade chip into a socket dedicated to the purpose. (The original CPU stays in place but is disabled.) Finally, the modern solution on the right: a lever-operated zero-insertion-force (ZIF) socket makes swapping chips a breeze.

- **60–66MHz Pentiums.** These first-generation Pentiums used a higher voltage and different socket than later models, so they're not compatible with other Pentium and clone chips. Whatever CPU upgrades were once available seem to have been discontinued, though if you shop around you might find some still in stock. (Intel's 120/133MHz OverDrive kit is one possibility.)
- **75MHz and faster Pentiums and clones.** Most of these systems have "zero insertion force" (ZIF) sockets, which make them very easy to upgrade. You flip up the lever, the old chip slips out easily, you pop in the new chip and flip the lever down to lock the new chip in place. (See Figure 21.) Most Pentium motherboards can be upgraded with chips that run at 200MHz

or faster—but note you'll probably have to replace your old fan with a stronger model, or your upgrade chip will burn up. MMX CPUs and their clones generally require motherboards that can supply two different voltages to different parts of the chip. AMD's K6 chips are the best upgrade if your motherboard can handle them—you can get a 300MHz model for not much more than $100.

- **Pentium IIs.** As we go to press, the potential for upgrading Pentium IIs is still unclear. The 350MHz and faster CPUs require a 100MHz bus, so they won't work in slower models that use a 66MHz bus. It seems likely that Intel will offer 400MHz and faster upgrades for 233MHz to 333MHz systems, but the company has made no announcement yet. Intel has some patents on the Pentium II's slot technology, and some aspects of its design are trade secrets, which are major obstacles to other companies producing compatible upgrades.

Motherboard Transplants

If you can't find a compatible CPU upgrade, you can always do a motherboard swap: Just take out the PC's main circuit board, and replace it with a modern model. Generally this will give you a whole bunch of other advantages, including a bigger L2 cache, faster memory subsystem, support for faster hard disks, improved setup utility, and so on.

The downside is that you may then *have* to upgrade other components as well. Your new motherboard may not be compatible with your old memory modules, and if you're upgrading from a 486 you may have to replace your video board, too. In a case like that, you're probably better off just buying a barebones new system, and selling the old system or passing it along to a poor friend or relative.

Doing your own motherboard transplant is a lot more practical than it used to be. Motherboards themselves are cheap enough that you're not risking a big investment (Robert recently upgraded his PC with one that cost only $90), and the technology's improved so that making all the connections is a lot easier than it used to be. If you go that route, get a model that has all of its sockets keyed so you don't have to work hard to figure out which way the ribbon cables for EIDE, ports, and so on plug in.

If you are going to replace your motherboard, consider upgrading your hard disk at the same time. With 4GB UDMA drives selling for less than $150, why not take advantage of your new motherboard's faster drive interface?

In motherboard upgrades, there are too many variables to give a precise step-by-step guide. Instead, here's a general outline of the process that should help you figure out if its the kind of project you'd want to do yourself, or if you'd rather pay a shop to do it:

- Make a full backup of your hard disk in case something goes wrong.
- Run the PC's setup utility and make notes of any important configuration settings, like hard disk cylinders, heads, and sectors (which must be input manually in some old hardware).
- Power off, unplug, and open the PC as described in "Disassembly without Destruction" at the beginning of the chapter.
- Unplug all the cables from the motherboard and its expansion cards, labeling or making detailed notes about where and how each one was connected. You may need to refer to the old motherboard's manual to figure out what some wires are for (particularly the ones that go to the buttons and lights on the front of the case).
- Remove all expansion cards from the motherboard. See the earlier section on "Installing Expansion Cards" for tips on getting cards out and putting them aside without damaging them.
- Some of the old cards may not be used in the transplant. For example, your new motherboard will surely have serial, parallel, USB, and EIDE built in, so any cards you're currently using for those purposes won't be needed. The new motherboard might also have sound, video, SCSI, and/or Ethernet built in. If you're upgrading a 486, it probably has a VL-Bus video card, which won't work in current motherboards.
- Remove any back-panel serial or parallel ports that will be replaced by new ones included with the new motherboard.
- Remove the old memory modules, if they're compatible with the new system.
- Remove any components blocking access to the motherboard, like drive cages.
- Remove the screw(s) holding the motherboard in place. If it uses only screws, you can then just lift it out. If it uses spacers, slide the board an inch or so to unhook the spacers from the notches they fit into, and then lift out the board.
- Compare the holes in the old motherboard with those in the new one and figure out how you're going to mount it. You may need to reposition the threaded metal rods that the screws came out of; occasionally this may even require drilling new holes in the case.
- If spacers are necessary, mount them on the new motherboard and slide it into position. (If the old motherboard used unusual spacers, you may need to recycle them. Removing them may require a delicate struggle with a pair of needle-nosed pliers.) Otherwise, just place the new motherboard in position, with the screw holes lined up on top of the threaded rods. Screw the motherboard in place.

- Install any new back-panel ports, and any ports mounted on slot-cover brackets.
- Install the new CPU, its new fan, and the memory chips.
- Connect all the cables to the motherboard. If the motherboard included new cables, you may want or need to replace the old ones—for example, if there are keyed EIDE cables in the motherboard package, it's a good idea to use them to replace any old unkeyed cables.
- Install the expansion cards and connect their cables.
- Close up the case, plug in the PC, and turn on the power.

Windows may go a little nuts trying to identify and configure the new hardware, and it may take some fiddling to get it running smoothly. Worst case, it may not work at all, and you'll have to reinstall Windows from scratch. That's one more incentive to upgrade your hard disk at the same time you do the motherboard transplant.

Upgrade Resources

sysdoc.pair.com Tom's Hardware Guide is a geeky Web site devoted to reviews and tips about component-level PC upgrades. Aimed at performance freaks, it may be the only place that regularly reviews new motherboards, and it also covers CPUs, memory, disks, video cards, and more.

Video Cards

gamecenter.com CNET's gamer site regularly reviews 3-D video cards and other gamer-oriented upgrades.

Memory

shopper.com As we go to press, this is the best of the memory price guides. Click "Memory - RAM" on the front page, then click on the type of RAM you want to price.

yahoo.com Yahoo! has a list of other memory price guides at Business and Economy : Companies : Computers : Hardware : Components : Memory : Retailers : Price Guides.

www.kingston.com/king/mg0.htm This is a great memory FAQ put together by a major RAM vendor. If you've got technical questions about memory that weren't answered in this chapter, you'll probably find an explanation here.

www.kingston.com The sponsor of the FAQ site mentioned just above, and the Mercedes of RAM vendors, Kingston isn't the cheapest place to buy—but if you've got a weird system that doesn't take standard SIMMs or DIMMs, these folks are the ones most likely to come up with the correct part.

EIDE Drives

www.maxtor.com/technology/q&a Maxtor FAQs and pointers to some useful third-party FAQs elsewhere on the Web.

support.quantum.com/menus/faq_menu.htm Quantum FAQs.

www.seagate.com/support/disc/faq/faqtop.shtml Seagate FAQs.

www.wdc.com/support/FAQ Western Digital FAQs (you must type FAQ in all caps for the URL to work).

www.storage.ibm.com/storage/hardsoft/stortek.htm A library of technical backgrounders and white papers from IBM, which among other things is a major manufacturer of hard disks.

news:comp.sys.ibm.pc.hardware.storage This Usenet newsgroup is devoted to discussing all kinds of PC drives. The group maintains a FAQ, which is available on the Web. The URL's too long to type, but you can find it at the bottom of Maxtor's FAQ menu.

USB Ports and Devices

www.usbstuff.com This USB specialty retailer has the best selection of USB products. If it exists, it'll likely be in this catalog.

usb.org This is the Web site of the official USB standards organization. It's a good source for technical information, but their product list doesn't seem to be as up-to-date as USBStuff's.

CPU Upgrades

www.evertech.com Evergreen Technologies specializes in CPU upgrade kits for older systems.

www.kingston.com/prod/procesor Better known as a RAM vendor, Kingston sells CPU upgrades as well. (Don't add the missing **s** to **procesor**, or the URL won't work.)

intel.com/overdrive You can find a guide to Intel's current CPU upgrade products on this page. Take any claims about the advantages of their upgrades relative to other vendors' with a grain of salt—in truth, AMD's CPUs usually perform better than Intel's at a given clock speed, and cost less.

`shopper.com` They're kind of hard to find, but some CPU upgrades are listed at this price-comparison site. Under "Memory & CPU" on the front page, click "more," then "Processors/Math Coprocessors," then "Processor Upgrades." The page will be cluttered with a lot of expensive upgrades for servers, but it includes desktop-oriented upgrades as well. You may get better sections by going to the front page of the site and searching for "evergreen," "kingston," or "overdrive."

Motherboard Transplants

`sysdoc.pair.com` As noted above, Tom's Hardware Guide regularly reviews new motherboards.

`yahoo.com` Yahoo! has a page with miscellaneous motherboard-oriented sites: Computers and Internet : Hardware : Components : Motherboards.

9

Protect Your Data

by Dan Tynan and Robert Lauriston

This chapter was originally written by Dan Tynan, and was updated for the third edition by Robert Lauriston.

In This Chapter

Forget what anybody else tells you. The most important part of your PC isn't your hard disk, your monitor, or those overpriced bits of silicon under the hood—it's your data. Why? Because it's the one thing you can't replace.

Yet your data is in jeopardy this very minute. Sooner or later, your hard disk will die. At any time, viruses—those lethal little programs created with evil intent—could infect your PC and turn your files to oatmeal. If your PC is in an office, careless or disgruntled employees could steal your data or use it for target practice. Thieves could walk off with your hardware. Power surges and failures can wipe out hours of work; fires, floods, earthquakes, and other disasters of Biblical proportion do strike.

Feeling paranoid yet? Don't sit there worrying—do something! You can prevent many of these calamities, and you can recover from the rest. This chapter will show you how. Skip it at your own peril.

Back It Up or Lose It All

You've probably heard this before: The best way to protect yourself against disaster is to have an up-to-date copy of your data, called a *backup*, on hand. Even if your machine goes belly up, you can transfer the backup data onto another computer's hard disk and be up and working again in no time.

If you want to gamble, go to the racetrack. If you want to keep your data safe and sound, back up your hard disk. Here's how.

Backup Basics

The task is simple: You want to copy data from your hard disk to some kind of removable media—tape cartridge, removable hard drive, CD-R or CD-RW, whatever. You want this copying stuff to be painless, with as little intervention from you as possible.

Backup software is designed to make the whole process pretty much automatic. You pick the files you want to back up, and the software starts filling up tapes or disks, prompting you for new ones as needed.

But backing up is only half the story. Eventually, you'll need to reverse the process and restore those files, by copying part or all of your backup data back to your hard disk. Backup software's ability to *restore* comes in handy when

- Your hard disk bites the dust or becomes infected by a virus.
- You accidentally delete a file or directory and can't undelete it.
- You need to revert to an earlier version of a file.

People often forget that backup programs create a handy index of all the files in your set of backup disks or tapes. So if you accidentally delete a single file, you can just scan the index, find the file, and restore it quickly—without having to restore other data in the process.

Backup Hardware

Think you can back up your hard disk to floppies? Sure thing. To back up 500MB (a fairly modest amount of software and data by today's standards), all you'd need would be 250 or 300 floppies and at least four hours of your time feeding disks into the A drive. Then you'd only have to label and store all those disks. I live for this kind of scut work, don't you?

Obviously, to make backup easy you need something with higher capacity than a floppy—ideally, something big enough to hold the entire contents of your hard drive. There are several practical alternatives:

- **Tape drives.** These are often called "tape backup drives" because most people don't use them for anything else. (Like any other backup medium, you can also use them for archiving old data you don't need to access but aren't ready to throw away.) Luckily, tape drives are now cheap enough for that single use to justify the modest expense: So-called 5GB models start around $150 for an internal EIDE model, or $200 for an external version that hooks to your parallel or USB port. And the tapes cost $15 to $25, less if you buy in quantity. The main brands you should check out are Hewlett-Packard's Colorado, Iomega's Ditto, and Seagate's TapeStor.

  Why "so-called" 5GB? Because you probably won't be able to get 5GB on a tape. The physical capacity is actually only 2.5GB.The 5GB reflects an extremely optimistic estimate of how much the backup software will be able to compress your files. (A more realistic estimate is that the compression will allow around 60% more than physical capacity, or about 4GB.)

  Higher-capacity drives and tapes cost a bit more, but it's worth spending extra to be able to start a backup running, walk away from your PC, and come back to find the job complete.

- **Zip disks and other superfloppies.** These are an inconvenient and relatively expensive way to back up your hard disk. The disks cost at least $8 each even in quantity, and you'll need six or more for every gigabyte of data you want to back up. During the backup you have to sit there swapping them in and out of the drive every few minutes. On the plus side, they are a cheap and handy way to back up a single project—just drag the folder to your Zip disk icon, wait for the light to go out, and put the disk away in its protective case.

- **SparQ, Jaz, and other cartridge hard drives.** If your hard disk's small enough to back up to a single cartridge, cartridge drives are an extremely fast and easy backup medium. For larger drives, they're not as convenient, and at $25 or more per gigabyte (uncompressed) the cost can add up fast.

Backup Media Comparison

This chart gives an idea of the costs for various kinds of removable-media drives for backup. The amount of data you can actually fit on each tape or disk, and thus the actual media cost for a full backup, will depend on how deeply the backup software can compress the files on your hard drive.

Drive Type	Internal EIDE Drive Cost	Media Cost	Uncompressed Capacity	Cost per GB	Notes
HP Colorado 5GB	$150	$22	2.5GB	$9	
Iomega Ditto Max 7GB	$150	$15	3.5GB	$4	
Seagate Tapestor 8GB	$200	$23	4.0GB	$5	
Iomega Zip	$100	$8	96MB	$85	
Syquest SparQ	$175	$30	1.0GB	$30	
CD-R	$250	$1	500–650MB	$2	Write-once
CD-RW	$300	$10	500–650MB	$16–$20	Can also write CD-R

- **CD-R.** With CD-R blanks going for $1 a pop, backing up to CD-R would be even cheaper than tape—except you can use a tape over and over but a CD-R is write-once. That means CD-Rs make sense only if you like to archive your backups indefinitely. The CD-R's 650MB capacity (uncompressed) means most people will need several CDs for a full backup.
- **CD-RW.** This rewritable CD format is relatively slow and, at around $10 per 650MB (uncompressed), relatively expensive. On the other hand, the same drive can also write CD-Rs, so you can do an occasional full backup to CD-R and supplement it with an incremental (changed and new files only) backup to CD-RW.
- **DVD-R Whatever.** As this book goes to press, rewritable DVD drive technology is in a state of flux, but it sounds pretty good. The discs should cost around $25 and hold 5–6GB of data (though you may have to flip them over halfway through).
- **A second hard disk.** Backing up to a second hard disk of the same or higher capacity of your primary one is extremely fast and easy. There's just one problem: Anything that damages the first hard drive might also trash the second, and then you'd have no backup. Tapes and other removable media, on the other hand, you can put in a fireproof safe or the trunk of your car, store them at home or office or at a friend's house to protect them against fires, lightning, earthquakes, and other disasters that can destroy your PC.

Backing Up without Hardware

The latest thing in the world of data safety is online backup. You install some special software on your PC, and once a day (or however often you like) it connects via modem or securely encrypted Internet connection to a remote server and uploads all new or changed data. For a modest monthly fee ($20 and up), your home or small-business PC can have the same secure, redundant backup you'd have if you were working on a netowrk at a big corporation. If anything goes wrong with your PC, you get immediate access to your files from any computer equipped with a modem or Internet connection.

For a modest additional charge, you can get the company to send you an archive CD of all your files. See "Data Protection Resources" at the end of this chapter for pointers to online backup services.

Backup Software

Commercial backup utilities, at least those intended for use by individual users rather than corporate networks, are practically extinct. A few years back, Symantec bought the three best-selling products—Central Point Backup, Norton Backup, and Fastback—but didn't update *any* of them for use with Windows 95.

Well, no matter—that's one less thing to spend money on. If you buy a tape drive or most any other removable, you'll probably get some perfectly adequate software: Colorado Backup with an HP drive, Backup Exec with a Seagate, Iomega Backup with a Ditto or Zip, etc.

If you don't buy a drive that comes with software, you can probably use the Windows backup utility (see Figure 1). The utilities in Windows 95 and 98 work with a variety of tape drives and any kind of removable disk. Unfortunately, the backup utility in NT works only with tape drives and does not compress data.

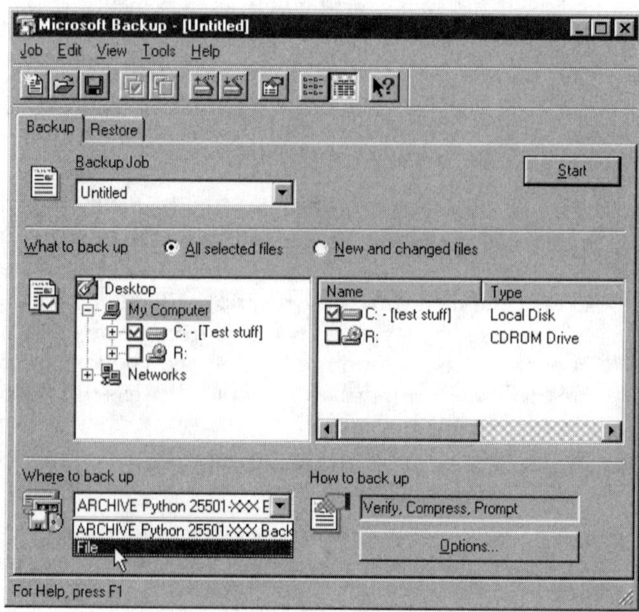

Figure 1

Windows 98's backup utility can back up to tape or to a file, which can be on any disk: Zip, removable hard disk, CD-R or CD-RW in DirectCD or some other random-access format, etc. The program will automatically prompt you to insert more tapes or disks, but it won't remind you to label and number them sequentially.

If the Windows built-in utility doesn't work for you, there are a few commercial backup utilities still on the market. See "Data Protection Resources" at the end of this chapter for pointers.

Backup Strategies

Backing up is like flossing: A little each day is more effective than a lot every six months. Nothing's more frustrating than needing to restore a file and discovering you never backed it up, or that your only backup copy is hopelessly out of date. The answer is to set up a schedule for doing backups and then stick to it.

Here's the tricky part: There are actually three different kinds of backup techniques, each with its own pluses and minuses.

- **Full.** Backs up all files in whatever drives or directories you've specified. Full backups are the safest route for protecting your data, but they take the most time and storage space. Unless you're backing up a network server's hard disk, you'll rarely perform a full backup more than once a week.
- **Incremental.** Backs up only files that have changed since the last full or incremental backup. Incremental backups are the fastest kind and are best for daily backups.
- **Differential.** Backs up every file that's changed since the last time you did a full backup. Since you only need to keep the latest copy (as opposed to each day's incremental copy), differential backups are easier to restore.

The most efficient backup strategy mixes regular full backups with *either* daily incrementals *or* differentials, but *never* with both.

Remember: Incremental and differential backups go together like gasoline and matches. There's a chance you'll miss or overwrite a file, and attempting to restore from both kinds of backup can be a nightmare.

Not everyone needs to follow the same backup strategy. The main question you need to ask is "How much data can I afford to lose?" Here are some basic approaches.

The Bare Minimum

So you have a fair-size hard disk but you don't want to buy a tape drive? To cut the time spent shuffling floppies, you can ignore your program files (since you can always reinstall them from their original disks) and focus on your data.

Back up all your data files once a month. To do this, you'll have to tell your backup software to copy only those files of specific types (Word, Excel, and so on).

Better yet, store data files in a drive or directory (such as C:\DATA) separate from your program files; within that directory, set up data file subdirectories for word processing, spreadsheets, databases, and so on. Then you can simply tell the software to back up only those directories. (The problem with this latter approach is that after restoring, you may find that some programs stored data in places you didn't expect, and—ZAP—there go your macros, e-mail address book, or who knows what.)

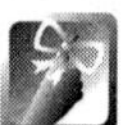

Every day, do either a differential or incremental backup of your modified data. You can't get away with less.

Backups by the Book

The problem with the data-file-only approach is that it could take forever (longer, if you lost the original disks) to reinstall your software if everything goes kaput. And full data-file backups a month apart can be risky (since you may not discover in time that one of your backup floppies was marinated in coffee). The solution: Buy a tape drive and do a full backup of all files (programs and data) once a week, and incrementals each day. Then create two backup scripts—one for full backups, another for daily incrementals—and use the software's scheduling module to run them automatically.

The Anal-Retentive Backup

If losing even an hour's worth of data is a potential disaster, modify your backup schedule to perform several incremental backups per day.

On Windows, you can run these backups in the background as you work. Most Windows backup programs won't back up a file if it's being used by another program, so you'll have to close the file before you start the backup.

Storing and Labeling Backups

Doing regular backups earns you plenty of good computer karma, but it's not worth much if you misplace or mislabel your backup disks or tapes, or if your only copies are destroyed in a fire.

Rotating Media

The bunch of tapes or disks you use to back up your data is collectively called a *backup set*. Always use at least two sets and alternate between them. If one set gets damaged or lost, you can restore your data using the previous set. You'd still lose a few days' work, but it's better than starting from scratch.

The E-Z Disaster Protection Plan

On Monday do your first full backup using Set A. Tuesday through Friday, use another batch of disks or tapes (Set B) to perform incremental or differential backups of modified files. The following Monday, do another full backup using a third set (Set C), and move Set A into off-site storage for safekeeping. Then repeat the process, erasing and reusing Set B for modified files, and alternating between Sets A and C for full backups and off-site storage.

Monday	Tuesday	Wednesday	Thursday	Friday	Monday
full	modified	modified	modified	modified	full
backup	files only	files only	files only	files only	backup
(Set A)	(Set B)	(Set B)	(Set B)	(Set B)	(Set C)

Depending on your business, once a month, quarter, or year you may want to archive a backup set (that is, keep it on hand for several years, or indefinitely) to provide a long-term or permanent record of the data. In some cases, this may be required by law.

Storage

Observe these three Golden Rules for storing backups:

1. Store backup disks separately from other floppies, preferably in their own disk caddy, away from dust, moisture, and smoke.
2. Keep backup sets away from phones, monitors, power supplies, and anything else that gives off a magnetic field that can erase their contents.
3. Always keep one recent full backup copy in a secure place off site.

A backup set is worthless if your computer has been stolen or destroyed in a fire and you don't have another system where you can restore your data. So scout out a compatible system before disaster strikes.

Backing Up Forever

Who wants ancient files rattling around a hard disk? No one—especially if disk space is at a premium. If you need to keep those files for history's sake, you can use backup software to archive them. Just back up the files as you normally would, use the software's Compare option to ensure that the backups are valid, and erase the originals from your hard disk.

Be sure to store archive media separately from your backup sets. If you're using tapes, be sure to flip the write-protect switch (see Figure 2).

Figure 2

When you archive old data remember to flick the write protect switch to keep yourself from accidentally using the disk or tape.

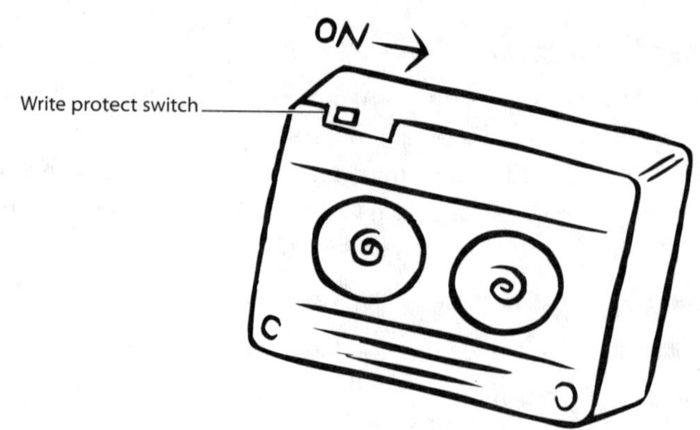

Backup Labeling

Labeling is the most tedious part. But believe me, you don't want to sit there staring at a disk trying to remember which backup is on it. So label each backup disk and cartridge with the following:

- **The date** the disk or tape was first formatted
- **The type** of backup (full, incremental, differential)
- **The drives** or directories backed up (C and D, C:\DATA, etc.)
- **The date** of the backup
- **The number** of the disk or tape in the set ("Set A/Disk 5")

Why bother with the date of the first format? Because most disks and tapes wear out after about two years, and you'll want to know when to think about replacing them.

If you're religious about regular backups, you can label disks or tapes with "Daily" or "Weekly" (or the day of the week when you do it) instead of the calendar date. Add your name or initials if your backup sets are stored in the same place as other people's sets.

Killer Viruses

A software virus is a program whose sole purpose is to wreak havoc with your system—a technoweenie's idea of a practical joke. Viruses range from annoying but harmless creatures that pop up stupid messages on your screen, to malevolent beasts that can trash all the data on your hard disk—and crash your computer so badly that it could take a techie all day to bring it to life again.

A Brief, Disgusting Guide to Viruses

Thousands of known software viruses exist, with new ones born every day. Essentially, there are three different types:

- **Boot sector viruses** take up residence in the part of your hard disk where the computer stores the files it needs in order to start up (the boot sector). They become active each time you turn on or reboot your computer. Boot viruses spread via infected floppy disks.
- **Program infectors** attach themselves to any file that runs a program (or part of a program); these files have the extensions .exe, .com, .dll, and .drv. They are activated whenever the file is run, or they install themselves as terminate-and-stay-resident (TSR) programs that hang around in your PC's memory and infect other programs. Program viruses can be contracted from floppies, electronic bulletin boards, and networks.
- **Macro viruses** take advantage of Microsoft's bad decision to allow macros to be stored in Word and Excel files. Starting with Office 97, the programs warn you that files contain macros and offer to strip them out. The nastiest macro viruses propagate by using the ability to send mail from Word; they send themselves to a few people chosen at random from your address book.

Some viruses attack both the boot sector and program files.

And here are a few especially pernicious subspecies:

- **Stealth viruses** attempt to escape detection by undoing any changes they've made to a file's size, creation date, or other attributes (factors that usually indicate the presence of a virus).
- **Polymorphic (or self-mutating) viruses** continually change their internal code so that they look different with each infected file, making the virus harder to identify.
- **Trojan horse** programs pretend to be legitimate software (typically games) while secretly infiltrating files on your hard disk, causing either mischief or serious damage. A Trojan horse is not a true virus because it doesn't replicate itself. Some antivirus programs detect and destroy Trojan horse programs anyway.

Viruses are nasty business. Once it gets into your system it can replicate, hide inside other programs, and spin off new viruses. It can lurk silently on your hard disk for months and suddenly strike when the PC's internal clock reaches a certain day (like Friday the 13th).

Fortunately, your system can't develop a virus spontaneously on its own—it can only catch one from infected floppy disks or files or through network connections. Your odds of contracting a virus increase if you engage in any of the following activities:

1. You exchange floppy disks or Microsoft Word or Excel documents with other users.

2. You download program files from amateur Web sites or bulletin boards.
3. You purchase software that has been returned to the store and repackaged.
4. You share program files via electronic mail or across a LAN.

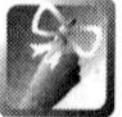

You probably belong to group #1, and you probably don't know whether or not you belong to group #3. There's also a slim chance your new hard disk was infected at the factory. That's why, to be on the safe side, everyone should employ some kind of strategy for detecting and eradicating viruses.

Antivirus Software to the Rescue

Fortunately, there's a cure for these vile creatures: *antivirus utilities.* They're often bundled with new PCs, or you can buy one for less than $50. (See "Data Security Resources" at the end of this chapter for pointers.) The following sections describe how they work.

Detection

Antivirus utilities use three methods to diagnose viral infection:

- **Signature Search.** Every antivirus program begins by scanning your PC's memory and hard disk for hundreds of virus "signatures"—telltale strings of text that inform the utility a known virus is present. Because saboteurs are constantly cooking up new viruses, you'll need to update your antivirus software regularly. The best programs will automatically offer to update themselves from the vendor's Web site on a regular basis.

The Seven Warning Signs of Viruses

Has your system been infected? If you notice any of these symptoms, grab the nearest antivirus program, run a virus scan, and keep your fingers crossed:

- Your PC is inexplicably slow.
- Files suddenly disappear from your disk.
- Program files increase in size.
- You have trouble opening or saving Word documents.
- Your computer crashes repeatedly or reboots unexpectedly.
- Odd messages appear on your screen (like "Your computer is now stoned").
- The same problems occur on several computers in your office.

Of course, you could have some of these problems and still not have a virus. And some of the most successful viruses show no outward signs at all. That's why, to be safe, you should run an antivirus scan every time you start your PC.

- **File Snapshots.** When program files change, trouble may be afoot. Most virus scanners take mathematical snapshots of the files right after a program's installation, and sound the alarm if changes occur.
- **System Watchdogs.** The best method for detecting new or unknown viruses is to look for "viruslike" behavior, such as attempts to format your hard disk or change program files.

Disinfection

Once antivirus software detects a virus, it pulls out the scalpel and goes to work. Depending on the kind of virus and the extent of its destruction, it may

- **Remove** the virus and perhaps even repair the damage.
- **Delete** the file and instruct you to restore a previous version (another good reason for doing regular backups).
- **Tell you to restart** your PC with a clean boot disk in drive A. Many antivirus programs will create a disk (sometimes called a "rescue" or "emergency" disk) that you can use to restore your hard disk's original boot sector files.

Make sure you write-protect this floppy after creating it, so it doesn't also become infected.

Prevention

Modern antivirus utilities don't just sit around waiting for your system to get infected: If you let them, they'll inspect every disk, file, e-mail message, and Web page coming into your computer to make sure no virus is hitching a ride.

Tips for Fighting Infection

- Set up your antivirus program to do a quick scan of your system every morning when you turn on the computer.
- Schedule weekly virus scans of all the executable files on your disk.
- Scan any boot disks you've created and write-protect them.
- Scan any floppies you receive before copying files from them to your hard disk.
- Scan any network drives you use. (Better yet, have your LAN administrator scan all network drives each day.)
- Scan any program files attached to e-mail messages or downloaded from the Internet or a BBS. File-library sysops normally scan files before uploading them, but it never hurts to double-check.
- Update your antivirus software's virus database every month or so—sooner if you notice symptoms but your utility hasn't detected anything.

This stuff can be intrusive, so you may prefer to leave the utility switched off and just check manually when a risk of infection presents itself.

There's one thing *you* can do that will drastically reduce the risk of infection. Run your PC's setup routine (see "Accessing Your PC's Setup Routine" in Chapter 8: Upgrade It Yourself) and find the menus that control boot options. Change the "boot sequence" or "boot order" so that during startup the computer boots directly from your hard disk (C), bypassing the floppy drive (A) entirely. This arrangement prevents infection by "boot-sector" viruses; If left in the drive when you power down or reboot, these viruses will subvert the PC's floppy-boot process to infect your hard disk.

PC Security: Who Needs It?

The scariest threat to your data isn't hardware failure or software viruses; it's other humans. When *you* screw up—deleting an important file or accidentally reformatting your hard disk—you realize it immediately and can usually undo the damage. But if somebody else screws up your system, accidentally or otherwise, you may not find out until it's too late.

Do you really need to worry about security? You do, if

1. You share a computer with someone else (like a child or coworker).
2. You keep confidential or personal files on your PC at work and you want them to stay that way.
3. You maintain sensitive company files and need to prevent tampering or damage.

Keeping data secure means controlling access—to your files and directories, your hard disk, and your PC itself. How much security do you need? If you're in group 1, you can probably get by with the simple techniques outlined in the following section. If you're in group 2 or 3, you'll need to look at the options discussed in the section "More Stringent Measures."

Minimum Security PCs

Unless you're a work-at-home hermit or you keep your office door locked at all times, it's a safe bet that other people have access to your PC when you're not around. Fortunately, there are several things you can do to protect yourself against accidental damage or unwanted intrusion—and, best of all, they won't cost you a dime.

- **Use the system lock** on your desktop PC to prevent the computer from accepting keyboard input.

- **Define a system password** using your PC's setup program (see "Accessing Your PC's Setup Routine" in Chapter 8: Upgrade It Yourself). For the system to load, you have to type the magic word. (You usually can't get past this one without opening the case and flipping a switch or moving a jumper.)
- **Define a Windows NT startup password** via the User Manager (in the Administrative Tools folder of the Start menu). Windows 95 and 98 have a similar feature, but you can get past it by just hitting Esc.
- **Lock Windows NT** to make your PC inaccessible when you leave your desk. Press Ctrl Alt Del and click the Lock Workstation button.
- **Password-protect Windows NT's screensaver** (see Figure 3) to invoke the Lock Workstation command automatically when your screensaver goes on.

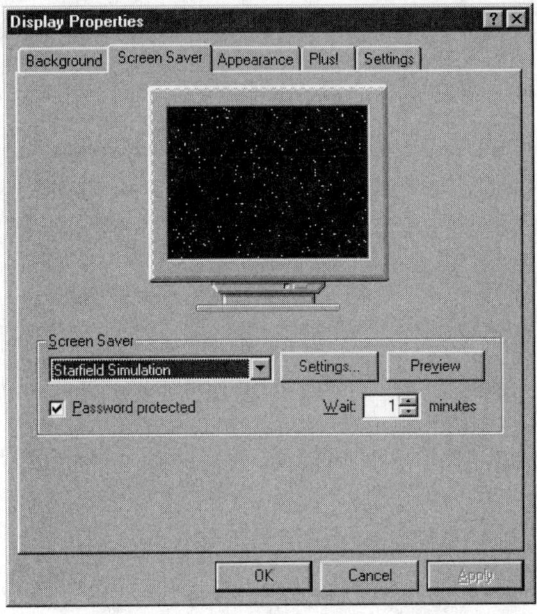

Figure 3

Windows NT's screensaver passwords.

To block users from getting out of screensaver mode, just check the "Password protected" box on the Display control panel's Screen Saver tab.

- **Password-protect Windows 95/98's screensaver** to keep your PC secure when you escape from your desk. First, define the password at startup or with the Users control panel; then check the password box in the Screen Saver tab of the Display control panel. A password prompt (see Figure 4) comes up when anyone touches your mouse or keyboard. (This isn't very secure, since you can get past it by rebooting the machine.)

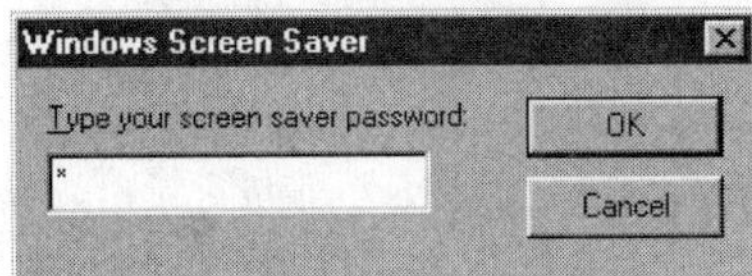

Figure 4

Screensaver password check.

If you password-protect your screensaver in Windows 95/98, you'll get this dialog box when you interrupt the screensaver by pressing a key or moving the mouse.

- **Use built-in password protection** in Microsoft Word, Lotus 1-2-3, and other popular applications that let you limit access to a particular file. (Of course, that won't prevent anyone from *deleting* the file.)
- **Don't save your Internet access password,** so no one who doesn't know it will be able to log on to your Internet account.
- **Log off e-mail** when you leave your desk. If you don't, anyone can read your private mail and send messages to other people in your name.

- **Make important files read-only,** so they can't be changed or deleted. Right-click the file's icon, choose Properties, check the Read-only box, and click OK.

Naturally, you need to find the right balance between security precautions and ease of use. You wouldn't want to lock every door in your house, and you don't want to hide every file on your disk.

More Stringent Measures

A skilled PC sneak can easily find his or her way around most of the simple techniques discussed above. To protect against deliberate damage, you'll need to spend a little money on one (or more) of the kinds of products listed in the following sections.

Floppy Drive Locks

A drive lock will keep potential vandals from booting up your system with a floppy disk to bypass the password protection on your hard disk. These devices slide into your floppy drive and lock with the turn of a key. Drive locks cost from $13 to $50. "Data Security Resources" at the end of the chapter tells you where to buy them.

Data Encryption Software

Even hidden and password-protected files can be read using a utility like *The Norton Utilities*. With data encryption software, you can scramble your files so that no one can read them—at least until you issue the password (called a *key*) that unlocks their secrets. Encryption is particularly useful for

- Sending confidential files via electronic mail, where privacy is less than assured
- Protecting sensitive company data on notebook PCs, lest the little machines fall into the wrong hands

Most encryption programs use a *public/private* key approach. To send your best friend Ted a scrambled file, you'd run the file through an encryption program and assign it the key that Ted has provided (the public key). Ted would then unscramble the file using a private key that only he knows. The same is true in reverse—for Ted to send you an encrypted file, he'd have to know your public key. Sort of like two halves of the same password.

For less than $100 you can get an encryption program like Symantec's Norton Your Eyes Only, which lets you secure your files with CIA-level encryption without having to master any complicated technology.

If all you want to do is scramble selected files on your hard disk, you can use the password option in WinZip or whatever compression utility you use. But remember: If you forget the password, there's no way to decompress the file.

The Password Is...

Even the best data security system is only as secure as the passwords you choose. Here are some quick do's and don'ts for selecting passwords:

Do

- Use passwords of seven characters or more.
- Use a mix of letters and numbers.
- Change passwords every three months or so.
- Store a written copy of your password in a safe place, such as a locked drawer—away from the computer.

Don't

- Use your name, or that of your spouse, child, or pet.
- Use "password" or "mypassword."
- Use your phone number, street address, or other easily accessible personal information.
- Write your password on a Post-it note stuck to your desk, or file it in your Rolodex under *P*.

Access Control

With access control software, you can password-protect just about anything from floppy drives to individual directories, files, and applications. You can even block access to potentially damaging applications and commands, or design a menu system that allows access only to a few authorized programs and subdirectories. You can also encrypt data, create an audit trail of attempts at unauthorized entry, and assign a single password to whole groups of protected applications.

If your job is to safeguard the PCs for an entire department or organization, you may want to roll out the heavy artillery: access control software. These top-to-bottom security utilities let you assign different levels of security for each user, and they are usually designed to work on a LAN.

For more information about keeping a network's data secure, check out the International Computer Security Association's Web site at **www.icsa.net**. The ICSA is a clearinghouse for information about all kinds of security products and computer security issues.

For individual users, the best way to get access control is to switch to Windows NT. It's not proof against a well-equipped industrial espionage specialist, but it does allow a high degree of control. You can designate the files, directories, and programs to which users (identified by password-protected userids) have access. See "Server Operating Systems" in Chapter 25: Networks: Connecting PCs for additional information.

Removable Storage Devices

An easy way to keep your data safe is to store it on removable media and keep it under lock and key at night. In addition to the removable-media drives discussed in Chapter 4: Disks, Hard and Otherwise, you can also get inexpensive mounting kits that turn any hard drive into a removable unit. A key lets you lock the drive in place while it's in use. If your local computer stores don't stock these, flip through the ads in *Computer Shopper* or in the back of *PC Magazine* or *PC World* to find a dealer.

Avoid Power Struggles

Too much AC power surging from the wall socket can cause hard-disk data errors, as well as damage to your modem, motherboard, and other system components. Likewise, not enough juice can instantly shut down your PC, obliterating any data you haven't saved. AC power can be affected by faulty wiring, blackouts and brownouts, and lightning storms. Fortunately, there are dozens of devices designed to sit between your PC and the wall socket, smoothing out power problems. They fall roughly into three camps:

- **Surge suppressors** protect against power *spikes* and *surges*—sudden increases in voltage passing to your computer. Because spikes can cause catastrophic damage, every user needs a good surge suppressor. The simplest models are power strips with sockets for plugging in your PC, monitor, and other devices.
- **Line conditioners** (sometimes also called *voltage regulators*) protect against power sags, which account for more than 80% of all power problems.

Most also defend your system against surges and interference generated by other electronic devices. If you live in an area where brownouts are frequent or the lights flicker every time you crank up the air conditioner, you'll want a line conditioner.

- **Uninterruptible power supplies** (UPSs) are battery-powered expansion cards or boxes that give you enough juice to safely shut down your system in case of a total blackout. They also protect against power surges and are a must for LAN servers and other PCs on which critical data is constantly updated.

Some UPS vendors claim their products will protect your system when lightning strikes. But do you really want to find out? To be safe, turn off and unplug your PC, printer, and modem during electrical storms.

Power Shopping

You don't have to be an electronics whiz to figure out which suppressor, line conditioner, or UPS to buy. But you will need an idea of what PC devices you'll be plugging into it, and how much power they consume.

Surge Suppressors

Most people go to their local hardware store and buy a cheapo power strip. Pay a bit more for a power strip with surge suppression, and you'll be protected against surges and spikes. Prices start at around $20, but plan on paying about $50 for a good one. Here's what to look for:

- **Energy dissipation.** A suppressor's ability to dissipate power surges is rated in *joules.* Generally, the higher the joule rating, the more likely your suppressor will filter out power problems. But joule ratings can vary depending on the manufacturer. A more reliable measure is Underwriters Laboratories (UL) specification 1449, which gauges the maximum surge power the device will let through. The rating is expressed in peak volts, so lower numbers are better—the best suppressors have a UL 1449 rating of 330 volts.
- **Power control features.** Better surge suppressors provide LEDs that alert you to problems on the line. Some models are designed to sit under your monitor, and you can turn everything on and off with a single switch. Others let you plug in phones and other devices as well as your computer equipment. All of these features boost the quality (and cost) of the model.

Line Conditioners

Line conditioners use a special ferromagnetic transformer to maintain a steady flow of power, so you can keep computing even when the lights dim. As with surge suppressors, you'll want to get a model that comes with enough outlets and protects against voltage spikes as well as power sags. Prices range from $130 for an LC with two outlets, to more than $500 for one with 14 sockets.

The main issue is *capacity*: how much of a power load the LC can handle. Unfortunately, some vendors measure an LC's capacity in wattage, while others do it in volt-amps (VA). Here's the quick way to figure out how big an LC you need:

1. Make a list of every device you plan to plug into the line conditioner.
2. On the back of each device, you should find a metal plate listing its maximum power needs in amps (1A = 1 amp). Write down all the amp figures and add them up. For example:

   System unit (1.0A) + Monitor (1.5A) – 2.5 amps
3. Multiply the total amps by 120. This gives you your VA rating.

   VA rating – 2.5A x 120 = 300 VA
4. To translate this figure into wattage, take the VA rating and multiply it by the device's power factor (which indicates how much of the juice flowing to the machine provides useful energy). With PCs, the power factor is typically .6 (or 60%).

   Wattage rating = 300 x .6 = 180 watts

Most PCs have VA ratings between 300 and 400, which means wattage ratings from 180 to 240. If you plan to add peripherals, you'll need to add in the VA or wattage figures for the printer, external tape drive, and so forth. Then buy a line conditioner with 20%–25% more capacity than you currently need, to leave room for adding new devices.

Uninterruptible Power Supplies

UPSs are designed with one thing in mind—to let you save data and exit applications gracefully during a total power failure. There are several types of UPSs, but most fit into three genres: *standby* (aka *offline*) models, where there's a lag of a few milliseconds between the moment everything goes dark and the instant the battery kicks in; *online* models, where there is no time lag; and *line interactive* models, a sort of in-between technology that can use line conditioning to handle extended brownouts without draining the battery. Prices range from less than $70 for individual PCs, to several thousand dollars for units that can handle multiple network servers. The cheapest models usually fit right inside your PC.

- **Capacity**. Figuring out what capacity UPS you need involves the same mathematical process as for line conditioners. Fortunately, UPS vendors make life simpler by measuring everything in VA units. Some have even done the math for you, providing VA ratings for popular brands of PCs. But don't factor a printer into your UPS plans; although printers suck huge amounts of power, an interrupted print job is no disaster.
- **Shutdown time.** The capacity of your UPS also determines how much time you'll have before shutdown. At full load (when your system's power needs match the capacity of the UPS), you'll get at least 5 minutes of power. At half load you could get 20 minutes or more. Longer battery life means a higher price.

- **Power features.** Some UPSs come with built-in line conditioning, providing full blackout and brownout protection. Others feature their own lighting systems, so you can see your keyboard in the dark. Online UPSs provide a continuous power source, minimizing the chance of data loss due to a power glitch. More advanced models have built-in hardware and software that automate shutdowns during unattended operations, such as overnight backups of a LAN.

Almost every UPS vendor carries a full line of surge suppressors and line conditioners; for information about specific products, contact the manufacturers listed at the end of this chapter.

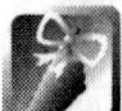

Whether you're buying a suppressor, line conditioner, or UPS, a five-year warranty (or better) is your best indication of product quality. The best products boast lifetime warranties and insurance policies against damage caused by power problems.

Power Insurance: How Much Time Are You Buying?

	Volt-Amp Rating of UPS					
	250	**400**	**450**	**600**	**900**	**1250**
Your Power Load (in VA)	**Typical UPS Run Times (in minutes)**					
75	29	72	88	105	155	210
100	23	47	65	79	110	160
150	14	30	41	54	83	115
200	8	19	32	41	65	92
250	5	13	24	31	47	75
300	-	9	18	22	40	64
350	-	7	14	17	35	54
400	-	5	11	13	29	46
450	-	-	8	10	24	40
500	-	-	-	7	20	34
600	-	-	-	5	15	25
700	-	-	-	-	13	22
800	-	-	-	-	11	17
900	-	-	-	-	10	13
1200	-	-	-	-	-	9

Source: American Power Conversion

Buying a UPS with a higher volt-amp rating gives you more juice when the lights go out—so you can keep on working, even in the dark.

Burglar-Proof Your PC

Today's PCs are smaller and more portable than ever—which makes them prime candidates for theft. Short of strapping your PC to a pit bull, the best solution is an antitheft device. Some devices work like car alarms, guaranteed to deafen (if not deter) would-be burglars. Others are the PC equivalent of The Club, designed to make pilfering your PC more trouble than it's worth.

Most antitheft devices require that you attach brackets to your desktop CPU, monitor, keyboard, and printer, and then feed a steel cable through each bracket and into a padlock (see Figure 5). On laptops and notebooks, you plug the cable into a special slot or a port in the back of the machine and then loop the cable around something heavy, like the desk. With other devices you put your computer inside a box that attaches to your desk with heavy-duty adhesives. Both kinds can be a hassle to dismantle when you need to pop the PC's hood and install something new, or when you just want to move the machine—but not as much of a hassle as replacing your computer. A third type of antitheft device is a simple motion-detector burglar alarm: Try to move the PC, and the unit keeps shrieking until you enter a code in its keypad.

The "Data Protection Resources" section coming up includes a list of retailers that sell antitheft devices.

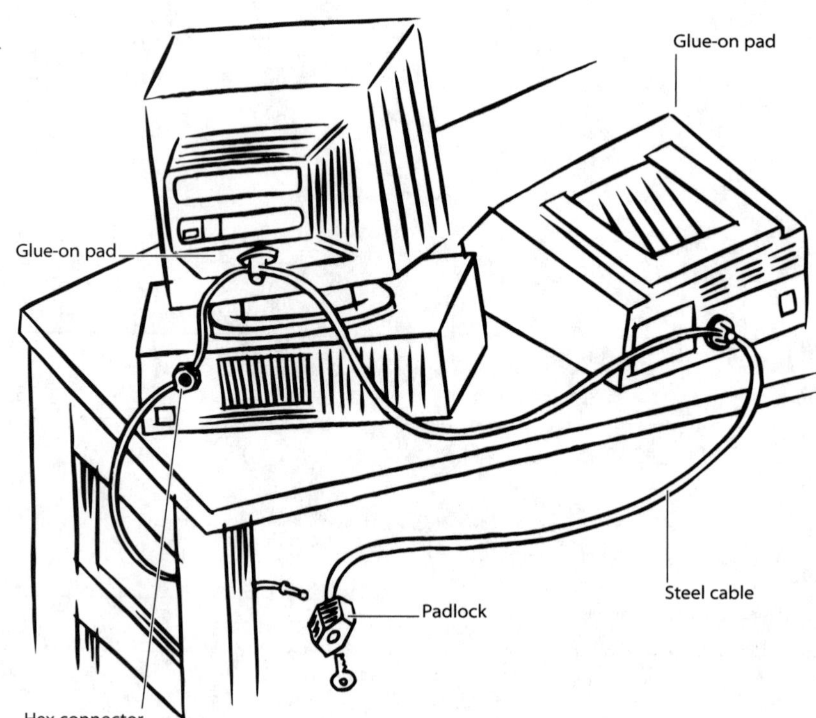

Figure 5

With this typical $50 security system, you attach brackets to your PC and its expensive friends, and string together the whole deal with steel cable. One look at this setup and most burglars will head straight for your VCR.

PC Insurance: Are You Covered?

Homeowners and renters insurance policies typically have a $5,000 liability limit on computer hardware and software, and the policies rarely cover damage from power surges and other common computer ills—not to mention losses outside the home (like your notebook PC's getting stolen at the airport). If you use your PC to run a home business, your homeowners policy may not cover you at all. The following agencies offer separate policies that specifically cover your computer:

The Computer Insurance Agency	Data Security Insurance	Safeware, The Insurance Agency
6150 Old Millersport Rd. NE	4800 Riverbend Rd!.	5760 N. High St.
Pleasantville, OH 43148	Boulder, CO 80301	Columbus, OH 43085
800-722-0385	800-822-0901	800-800-1492
614-781-2585	303-442-0900	614-781-1492
www.computer-ins.com	**data-security.com**	**www.safeware.net**

These companies provide the full replacement value for hardware and software up to the amount of coverage, including losses from power surges, lightning, viruses, and theft of your notebook on the road. Annual premiums range from $50 to $130, depending on the policy.

Regardless of what insurance you get, remember to keep good records of all equipment and software purchased, including serial numbers and date purchased, as well as all invoices, canceled checks, and credit statements. Be sure to register your software, too (some policies won't cover the loss of programs that aren't registered). Finally, take photos or videotape of your equipment to help substantiate your claim.

Data Protection Resources

Backup Hardware and Software

shopper.com For the latest prices on tape drives, go to the main page, click "tape" on front page, then "DOS," and then "external" or "internal."

www.seagatesoftware.com Seagate's software site covers separate versions of BackupExec for Windows 95/98 and Windows NT. The backup utilities included with Windows are based on this software.

novastor.com BackupExec's main competitor, NovaBackup, supports all versions of Windows—no separate versions are needed if you run both 95/98 and NT.

microsoft.com/hwtest/hcl Check the Windows NT hardware compatibility list to see what tape drives are compatible with NT's built-in backup utility.

Online Backup Services

www.connected.com Connected Corp. was one of the first companies to offer online backup services to average users and got the nod from CNET in a 1997 comparison of five such services. It also got an endorsement from HP, which preloads Connected's software on its Brio line of small-business PCs.

atbackup.com @Backup claims to be the #1 online backup service.

sgii.com Safeguard Interactive claims to be the most secure online backup service.

www.atrieva.com Atrieva doesn't make any grandiose claims, but it seems to be fairly similar to Connected, @Backup, and Safeguard Interactive.

cnet.com/Content/Reviews/Compare/Backup Unless it's been updated since we went to print, this comparison of online backup services is out-of-date, but the features and issues it discusses are still timely.

yahoo.com Yahoo! lists online backup services, most of which are oriented toward high-volume corporate accounts. Go to Business and Economy : Companies : Computers : Services : Backup.

Antivirus

symantec.com/nav Norton AntiVirus is widely regarded as the best on the market. It won the most recent antivirus comparisons in both *PC Magazine* and *PC World*.

www.mcafee.com/products/virusscan/virusscan.asp McAfee's VirusScan is another popular antivirus utility. If a copy came with your PC, you should log onto the Web site every month or two and download an update to the utility's virus signature file.

Removable Hard Disk Mounting Kits

starpower.com/QuickDraw.html This inexpensive kit for turning a regular hard drive into a removable unit isn't necessarily better than any others, but the illustrations on the Web site give you a good idea of how these products work. Most of them are made by obscure Taiwanese companies you've never heard of. You'll usually find ads for a few retailers selling these products, in the back of any computer magazine.

Surge Suppressors, Line Conditioners, and UPSs

www.pcmag.com/features/ups/upss2.htm A *PC Magazine* review of five UPSs aimed at home and small business users; out-of-date, but a good introduction to the technology.

shopper.com This price-comparison site is a good place to identify affordable UPSs. Click "Backup Power Supplies" on the main page.

www.apcc.com/english/power/glossary A handy reference to some of the arcane terms used by UPS manufacturers; compiled by American Power Conversion, a major UPS manufacturer.

pcpowercooling.com PC Power and Cooling makes power supplies with line conditioning built in, and also sells base PCs (power supply, case, motherboard) from which you can assemble your own system.

Antitheft Devices

pc-security.com Business Protection Products claims to be the biggest provider of computer antitheft devices. True or not, its Web site has a lot of useful info in addition to a product catalog.

computersecurity.com Computer Security Products is another retailer with a huge selection of, obviously enough, computer security products.

c-si.net Computer Security International sells a variety of desktop and notebook locks and cabling systems.

10

How To Choose and Buy Software

by Robert Lauriston

In This Chapter

Chapters 11 trhough 18 of this book are devoted to close-up looks at the most popular and useful kinds of software: word processors, spreadsheets, personal finance programs, and so on. In this chapter, I'm going to zoom out for a quick overview of three big-picture issues. First I'll outline the central role Microsoft plays in determining what software you can buy today, and look at some possible ways you might deal with that situation. Then we'll take a brief look at the software "suites" that account for the bulk of software sales today. Finally I'll give some tips on how to make the most of your software dollar.

Microsoft

Do you need more than one software company? An increasing percentage of PC owners answer that question "no," at least when it comes time to put their money on the table. The result is a software market increasingly dominated by Microsoft, a trend that has reduced consumers' software choices, slowed the pace of innovation, and effectively raised prices by allowing Microsoft to stop offering competitive-upgrade discounts for users of competing programs.

"The customer can have any color he wants, so long as it's black."
—Henry Ford

On the other hand, Microsoft's dominance has some big advantages, not just for the company's stockholders but for consumers as well. With everybody running Windows, software companies don't have to spend time and money developing versions for different operating systems, and when you shop for software you don't have to worry about picking the right version. With most companies using Microsoft applications, you don't need to learn new software when you take a new job, and your employer doesn't have to spend as much money on training.

Also, Microsoft was one of the leaders in driving software prices down to their current level. It pioneered the "suite" approach, where you get four or five major apps for less than you used to have to pay for just a word processor and spreadsheet. Microsoft's aggressive pricing on Access helped pushed the price for PC database software down from the $800–1500 range to $100–300. The $0 price tag for Microsoft's Web browser eventually forced Netscape to give its browser away free, too.

How Did Microsoft Get So Big?

Of course, those lower prices may have had something to do with Microsoft's former competitors going out of business. If Microsoft used the profits from its cash cows (Windows and Office) to enter new markets by undercutting its competitors' prices and driving them out of business, in the long run that's bad for consumers—but it's not clear that the company's actually done that.

Most of Microsoft's former competitors are out of business or heading that way thanks more to their own mistakes than as a result of anything Microsoft did to them.

Operating systems. Up until 1981, Microsoft's main business was producing BASIC and other programming languages for the personal computers of the day—most notably for the IBM PC. Despite a total lack of experience with operating systems, Microsoft persuaded IBM to give it that contract as well. To deliver on schedule, Microsoft bought a program called QDOS (for Quick and Dirty Operating System) from one Tim Patterson for $50,000, and hired him to help adapt it to run on IBM's new computer. Though PC-DOS wasn't the only OS available for the PC, it was the cheapest, and it was required by Lotus 1-2-3—a program many, many people wanted so badly that they bought PCs just to run it—so it became the standard.

In perhaps the smartest deal in the history of computers, Microsoft retained the rights to sell its own version of DOS to other companies. Within a year other manufacturers figured out how to "clone" the hardware in IBM's PC, and with MS-DOS their computers could run 1-2-3 and other PC applications. However, instead of simply selling DOS to the cloners, Microsoft negotiated "per processor" license deals in which a manufacturer paid X amount for each PC it sold. This effectively shut out Microsoft's competition, since a manufacturer that offered a choice of OSs would end up paying twice when a customer chose, for example, DR-DOS instead of MS-DOS. In 1994, Microsoft agreed to abandon such practices as part of the settlement of an antitrust action, but by then DOS had long since been supplanted by Windows.

Windows itself has yet to face any significant competition. Despite media portrayals of an "OS war" between Windows and OS/2, the latter wasn't a practical alternative for average users until version 3.0 shipped in 1994, and there were never any compelling OS/2 applications to give Windows users a reason to switch.

"In this issue you'll find 55 reviews of general-purpose word processing programs. Another 18 reviews of integrated programs will follow in our next issue."

PC Magazine, ***February 29, 1988***

Word processing. Toward the end of the DOS era, WordPerfect was the #1 word processor, with over 60% of the market; Microsoft Word was a distant second with around 15%. That their positions reversed was largely due to WordPerfect Corp.'s bad guesses. In the late '80s WPC bet that OS/2, rather than Windows, would be the successor to DOS. When Windows sales took off in mid-1990, the company was caught by surprise, and it didn't get a Windows product out the door until the end of 1992. That version was crippled by the company's decision to make it 100% compatible with the existing DOS version, which meant that it had few of the advantages Word for Windows offered, like WYSIWYG editing and zoom. By the time WordPerfect got its Windows act together, it was behind, and it never caught back up.

Spreadsheets. Lotus 1-2-3 was even more dominant in the DOS era than WordPerfect, and Excel, which was #2 by the end of the 80s, had only 10–15% of the market. (There was never a DOS version of Excel—until Windows 3.0 came out, it included a "runtime" version of Windows that let it run on DOS.) 1-2-3 had many of the same problems as WordPerfect: Lotus bet wrong on OS/2, its Windows version didn't ship until late 1991, and the first release was crippled by the company's decision to make it 100% compatible with the DOS product. Microsoft had been shipping Excel for Windows since 1987, making it the most polished Windows app of the time, so a lot of people who switched from DOS to Windows switched from 1-2-3 to Excel as well.

Suites. Microsoft's embrace of the software-suite concept—bundling a word processor, spreadsheet, and other software in a single package—may be the main reason they've been #1 in application sales since 1993. That year, the company knocked the list price of its Office suite down to $750 (at the time, WordPerfect listed for $499, 1-2-3 for $599), and sales skyrocketed. If Lotus had succeeded in its 1994 attempt to acquire WordPerfect Corp., the duo might have given Microsoft some competition, but WPC's owners decided to sell to Novell instead. Bundled with the unpopular programs Quattro Pro and Ami Pro (which peaked at around 15% and 2% market share respectively), WordPerfect and 1-2-3 just didn't have the one-two punch of Office's Word-Excel combination, so Microsoft's had 80-90% of the suite market ever since.

Is Microsoft a Monopoly?

So is Microsoft a monopoly? As Bill Clinton might say, that depends on how you define "monopoly."

"I did not have sexual relations with that woman, Miss Lewinsky."

—Bill Clinton, January 26, 1998

According to the definition in my copy of Microsoft Bookshelf, no, because Microsoft doesn't have "exclusive control" over any market. Even in operating systems, where the company's dominance is the greatest, buyers have lots of choices: OS/2, BeOS, Linux, FreeDOS, Solaris, and dozens of others. Is it Microsoft's fault that most people prefer Windows?

The Encyclopedia Britannica, on the other hand, says one generally accepted definition of a monopoly is a company that controls at least a third of the supply of something, "with a view to restricting competition." Microsoft definitely controls over one-third of the supply of operating systems, word processors, spreadsheets, PC databases, office suites, and Web browsers—but does it control them "with a view toward restricting competition"?

As far as Office applications go, none of the stories I've ever heard (for example, Microsoft programmers supposedly saying, "Windows ain't done till Lotus won't run") seem very credible. The notion that the popularity of Word and Excel depended on Microsoft leveraging its control of the operating system doesn't make a lot of sense given that they're even *more* popular on the Mac, where Apple is in charge.

With regard to operating systems and Web browsers, on the other hand, that question may be answered by the courts. Caldera Inc., the current owner of DR-DOS (a competitor of MS-DOS), is pursuing a lawsuit claiming that sales of DR-DOS were harmed by alleged illegal practices by Microsoft. Meanwhile, the Justice Department has taken Microsoft to court alleging that bundling MS Internet Explorer with Windows was a violation of the consent decree that settled an antitrust case in which Microsoft agreed (without admitting guilt) not to engage in some of the practices Caldera is complaining about in its lawsuit.

"You are free to infer that my testimony is that I did not have sexual relations, as I understood this term to be defined.... If the activity you just mentioned would be covered in number (2), and number (2) were stricken, I think you can infer logically that paragraph (1) was not intended to cover it."

—Bill Clinton, August 17, 1998

The Internet Explorer case may actually be influencing Microsoft's software development. According to the deposition of a Compaq executive taken by Justice Department investigators and made public in a 1997 court filing, when Compaq removed the Internet Explorer icon from the desktop of some of its PCs to replace it with one for a Netscape browser, Microsoft canceled its license for Windows 95, and offered to reinstate the license only on condition that Compaq restore the icon.

The Justice Department says that cancellation violated the consent decree, which specifically prohibits Microsoft from requiring its Windows 95 licensees to bundle other products; Microsoft disputes that on the grounds that Internet Explorer and Windows 95 were not separate products. Given how negative beta testers and the press were about Microsoft's more extensive integration of Internet Explorer in Windows 98, I suspect the company was more concerned about putting the product out of reach of the consent decree than with making useful improvements.

Will You Be Assimilated?

Whether you call Microsoft a monopoly or not, its position gives it a disproportionate influence over your software choices. I think it's important to be aware of that influence and make a conscious decision about whether one software company is really enough: that is, whether you're comfortable trusting Microsoft with the future of computing, or if you want to use your buying power to help steer things in some other direction.

If you don't think too much about what software you'll use, chances are you'll end up with a matching ensemble of Microsoft apps. In theory, at least, there's nothing wrong with that: the single-vendor approach *should* have some significant advantages:

- **Compatibility.** If everybody's using Microsoft apps and e-mail, you can just pass documents around to friends and coworkers without having to worry about file formats, whether WordPerfect or 1-2-3 supports a particular feature, or whether file attachments will come through intact—right?

- **Reliability.** Microsoft knows Windows better than anyone else, so their programs will run better—right?
- **Convenience.** Microsoft's browser and e-mail come with Windows, so you don't have to download or install any new software—right?

In practice, these benefits often don't pan out. If you're not lucky, you'll end up more like this:

"You're keeping an 800-pound gorilla in your apartment? Where does it sleep?" "Anywhere it wants."

—punch line of an old joke

- **Compatibility problems.** Exchanging files between different versions of Microsoft apps is sometimes more of a headache than exchanging them between programs from different companies. Word 95 and 97 are a classic example: both programs use the same .doc extension, which is supposed to indicate that they have the same file format, but if you open a Word 97 file in Word 95 you just get a bunch of garbage. (Many other programs, like WordPerfect, will give you an error message warning you that you're trying to open a file created by a later version of same the program.) If you try to fix that by using Word 97's Save As command and choosing the "Word 6.0/95 (*.doc)" format, you get (despite the .doc extension), a file in Rich Text (.rtf) format, which can cause worse problems, like lost data. Microsoft apologized for the screwup and posted a free workaround on its Web site, but since it has had similar problem with previous releases, I won't be surprised if it happens again.
- **Unreliability.** Of the 20 applications I use on a regular basis, only three tend to crash. One is Netscape 3.04, which (like the Microsoft browsers I've tried) regularly chokes on certain pages. The other crashers are the only two Microsoft apps I use: Word 95 and Excel 95. They don't crash very often, maybe once a month, but that's still more often than the rest of my apps, which are rock-solid. Microsoft's programs also seem to be susceptible to "bit-rot," a mythical disease that eats away at program files, making them more and more unreliable until they finally stop working entirely. More than once I've had to reinstall Word or Windows after they stopped working or started behaving erratically—not an uncommon experience. Obviously, this is just one user's experience, but I've heard similar reports from other nerdy types I've talked with online.
- **Convenience.** Score one for Microsoft. Having a Web browser on the Windows CD is actually pretty great: you can use it to download another browser, a better e-mail program, and updates to fix some of the bugs Microsoft found since it pressed the CD.

Resistance Is Not Futile

Don't get the idea from all this Microsoft-bashing that I'm making a general argument against using the company's software. To the contrary: I've tried lots of different operating systems and applications, and use Windows NT 4.0, Word 95, and Excel 95 because I prefer them to the competition. Given the overwhelming popularity of Microsoft Office, in this edition of *The PC Bible* we've revamped the word processing and spreadsheet chapters to make more room for helpful tips on using Word and Excel.

I'd just like Microsoft to have *some* competition. In recent years, it's been steadily diminishing. I hope to see that trend halted and eventually reversed. To that end, I have a few recommendations.

- **Check out the competition.** Most people who use Word, Excel, or Access have never tried the alternatives. On the Web, you can get a free CD with a trial version of SmartSuite by filling out a form. Corel doesn't have any freebies as this book goes to press, but check out their Web site to see if they've followed Lotus's lead. Frustrated with Access? Download a trial version of FileMaker Pro (see Chapter 16: Databases) from their site. (See the "Software Buying Resources" section at the end of this chapter for all three URLs.)
- **Use at least one major non-Microsoft product.** I particularly encourage people to use Netscape or another non-Microsoft Web browser (see next item). Personally, I would not use both Word and a Microsoft e-mail program. Word files are susceptible to infection by macro viruses, Word macros can access e-mail to send messages—and there's at least one virus out there that took advantage of this capability to propagate itself by e-mail. While Word 97's not susceptible to that particular one, I fear some determined hacker will eventually find and exploit a security hole.
- **Avoid Microsoft's Web software.** Microsoft's Web strategy seems pretty clear: support standards like HTML and Java long enough to get control of them, then gradually incorporate proprietary elements that require Microsoft products like Windows, MS Internet Explorer, and NT Server. Microsoft has a particularly pernicious habit of not clearly documenting where it parts from established standards, so if you create a Web site using FrontPage you may not realize it won't work with a non-Microsoft browser. Reports on betas of Office 2000 suggest its HTML export feature may have such problems.
- **Don't buy buggy upgrades.** There's no reason that users should put up with the kind of compatibility problems I discussed above. If enough customers had passed on upgrading to Office 97 until the Word 95 export problem was worked out, Microsoft would have fixed it ASAP. (This goes for other companies' upgrades too, of course.)
- **Don't buy unnecessary upgrades.** If the software you've got is doing what you need, be wary of upgrades without clear and significant advantages. For example, I think Windows 98's minor improvements over Windows 95 (discussed in the next chapter) aren't significant enough for most people to justify paying $90 to upgrade.

Software Suites

Software "suites" including a word processor, spreadsheet, and several other programs have accounted for the bulk of business application sales for most of the 90s. By far the most popular—by most surveys accounting for over 80% of suite sales—is Microsoft Office; its two competitors are Lotus SmartSuite and Corel WordPerfect Suite.

One big difference between the three is operating system support. Corel still sells older DOS and Windows 3.1 versions, and Lotus an older release for OS/2. Microsoft recently released a new version for the Mac, and has promised to keep it current with the Windows version at least through 2002.

In this section, I'll briefly compare the contents of the big three suites and their variations. For a more in-depth discussion of the suites' components, see Chapter 13: Word Processing and Desktop Publishing, Chapter 14: Spreadsheets, and Chapter 16: Databases.

Microsoft Office

Microsoft Office comes in several different "editions." (See "Office Suites Compared" later in this chapter for a chart that shows the key differences at a glance.) **All versions** have the following three components in common:

- **Word and Excel**, the most popular word processor and spreadsheet around (around $300 each, if purchased separately).
- **Outlook**, the big brother of Outlook Express, the free e-mail program bundled with Windows 98. This version ($100 separately) adds enhanced PIM and fax capabilities (see Chapter 16: Databases and Chapter 24: Use Your PC as a Phone or Fax).

Only the **Professional Edition** includes:

- **Access**, Microsoft's powerful but somewhat user-hostile database.

The **Standard Edition** and **Professional Edition** also include **Powerpoint**, a presentation package used for creating slide shows or their virtual desktop equivalents. Unless you're in sales, marketing, some sort of bureaucratic management position that involves a lot of meetings, or a college or graduate student in a department where presentations are common, you probably won't have any use for this program.

That's probably why Microsoft came up with the **Small Business Edition**, which replaces Powerpoint with **Publisher**, a simple desktop publishing program. Actually, Word can handle most of the jobs you'd be likely to use Publisher for just fine, but it's still more useful for most people than Powerpoint. Office SBE includes a few other little business-oriented widgets that don't strike me as terribly useful or valuable.

If you add up what it would cost you to buy the Office components individually, the suite seems like a great deal. Word, Excel, Access, and Powerpoint all go for around $300 each on the street, and Outlook and Publisher for around $100. Thus the Standard and Small Business editions, which cost around $450 on the street, theoretically include $800 and $1000 worth of software. The Pro edition sounds like an even better deal: for $525 you get software that would cost $1,300.

There is, of course, another way read those numbers: as part of a calculated strategy by Microsoft to get everyone buying Office instead of individual apps. Every person who might have gotten by with just Word or just Excel, but goes for Office instead because the price difference is so small, spends an extra $125 on Microsoft apps—and is less likely to buy 1-2-3, WordPerfect, or other competing applications.

Microsoft Home Essentials

Some new PCs come with a sort of starter version of Office called Microsoft Home Essentials. The only major component the two packages have in common is Microsoft Word. The rest of the Home Essentials bundle is Works (discussed later in this chapter), which gives you a basic spreadsheet and database applications, Encarta (one of the better CD-ROM encyclopedias), Money (see Chapter 15), Hallmark Greetings Workshop (for printing your own greeting cards), and some games. Owning this package does qualify you for the upgrade price on Office.

When you consider the competition, Office starts to seem downright overpriced. You can get a whole suite from Lotus or Corel for about the price of a single Microsoft app—or, if you already own a major application from any of the three companies, you can get a competitive upgrade for a mere $130. That's half what Microsoft (which no longer offers competitive upgrades) charges its own users to upgrade from one version of Office to the next. Given this gross disparity in price, it's kind of puzzling that Microsoft's sales have remained so high.

Corel WordPerfect Suite

This suite traveled a pretty rocky road to get where it is today. It started out in 1993 as Borland Office for Windows, a joint venture that combined WordPerfect Corp.'s popular word processor with Borland's Quattro Pro spreadsheet and Paradox database program. After WPC's 1994 merger with Novell, the suite was redubbed Perfect Office, but Novell's attempt to enter the desktop software market was a disaster, and in 1996 it sold the product to Corel.

The suite comes in two main versions, regular and Professional, whose components track those in Microsoft's Standard and Pro editions. (See "Office Suites Compared" later in this chapter for a chart highlighting the differences.) Corel also produces a "Legal Edition" which is the Pro version bundled with legal references and tools for creating legal documents.

Perhaps the most interesting thing about this suite is Corel's plan to develop a version for Linux, an increasingly popular free version of UNIX. Linux currently has two big drawbacks compared with Windows: it's considerably harder to install and maintain, and it doesn't have any applications comparable to those in the three big Windows suites. Volunteers are working away steadily on the first problem, and this might solve the second, giving Microsoft some heavy competition for the first time in years. I take Corel's plans with a grain of salt, since it has a history of announcing products it never ships—like Corel Office for Java, a suite it worked on for a while in 1996-97.

Lotus SmartSuite

Lotus launched SmartSuite in 1992 with the popular spreadsheet 1-2-3, its well-regarded Freelance presentation package, and the generally unknown word processor Ami Pro (predecessor to today's Word Pro). The following year it added Organizer, a personal information manager a lot of people seem to like, and Approach, a database program that's easier to use than Access or Paradox but not nearly as friendly as FileMaker. That's basically been the package ever since. IBM bought Lotus in 1995, which doesn't seem to have changed things much, except that it gets more copies of the suite in circulation since they're often bundled with IBM's PCs.

Mini-Suites: AppleWorks and Microsoft Works

If your needs are simple enough that a full-blown suite seems like overkill or a waste of money, there are a couple of good alternatives. AppleWorks ($80, formerly called Claris Works) and Microsoft Works ($50) are what in the pre-suite era were called "integrated packages": single applications combining basic word processing, spreadsheet, and other functions. These programs are particularly well suited for underpowered or older PCs, for example one with only 8MB memory or a 100MB hard disk. In my opinion, AppleWorks is by far the easier to use and the more powerful of the two, particularly for database, page-layout, and graphics tasks. (Microsoft hasn't released a major upgrade to Works since 1995. I suspect that's because Works was mostly distributed as "free" software with new PCs, and that role has been taken over by Microsoft's Home Essentials package.)

Office Suites Compared

	Corel WordPerfect Office	Corel WordPerfect Office Professional	Lotus SmartSuite	Microsoft Office, Standard	Microsoft Office, Small Business	Microsoft Office, Professional
word processor	WordPerfect	WordPerfect	WordPro	Word	Word	Word
spreadsheet	Quattro Pro	Quattro Pro	1-2-3	Excel	Excel	Excel
PIM	Corel Central	Corel Central	Lotus Organizer	Outlook	Outlook	Outlook
presentation graphics	Corel Presentations	Corel Presentations	Freelance	PowerPoint		Access
desktop publishing	—	—	—	—	Publisher	—
database	—	Paradox	Approach	—	—	Access
street price, full version	$285	$325	$325	$450	$450	$525
street price, competitive upgrade	under $100	$130	$130	n/a*	n/a*	n/a*

*Microsoft offers competitive upgrades ($225 Standard and SBE, $350 Pro version) only for owners of long-outdated versions of 1-2-3 and WordPerfect.

Buying Software

The economics of software are funny: while creating a good program and its documentation is an expensive endeavor, the per-unit cost of producing the package you buy in the store is minuscule. Combine that with brutal competition both in manufacturing and retailing, and it's not surprising that costs vary wildly.

Take Adobe Photoshop, for example. The program's official list price is $999; on the street you can find it for under $600; special academic discounts knock the price down to $259. If you got a copy of Photoshop LE (a stripped-down starter version) bundled with your scanner, you can get the latest version for $300, and the upgrade price drops to under $200 if you already own a copy of Photoshop proper.

In the remainder of this chapter, I'll discuss these and other pricing variations to help you get the most for your software dollar.

Software Return Policies

When shopping for software, the main thing you want to compare is price. All dealers sell the same mass-produced products, and since you get technical support from the company that makes the software, one dealer's about like another.

Return policies are the one significant difference between retailers. Some stores will give you your money back with no questions asked; others offer only store credit. Since software often doesn't perform as advertised, and sometimes won't work at all, I buy only from dealers that offer cash refunds.

Note that some software companies have their own money-back guarantees. Microsoft, for instance, has a 30-day money-back guarantee displayed prominently on some of its programs' boxes. Since to take advantage of such refunds you have to pay to ship the software to the manufacturer, it's not as good a deal as a retailer refund, but it's a lot better than store credit.

Official Price vs. Street Price

Manufacturers use different methods for calculating their official, published prices, and as a result some programs are discounted much more heavily than others. Some use *list prices* that are inflated by almost 75% over the street price. The lowest street prices on these programs will usually be 42 to 43% off their official price: Photoshop, for example, lists for $999 but as I write this it's being advertised for as little as $577.

Other manufacturers use *estimated* or *suggested retail* prices, which are usually only a bit higher than the actual real-world cost. For example, the lowest price I could find on Microsoft Office was $428—less than 15% off the official estimate of $499.

Finding the Best Price

Among the most useful tools on the Web are *price guide* sites, searchable databases that collect the latest price information from many different mail-order companies and generate lists that let you compare price, shipping charges, availability, and other options for whatever products you're interested in buying. See "Software Buying Resources" at the end of this chapter for pointers to the three that are currently the best for comparing software prices. Note that some

mail-order vendors try to make themselves look better on price-check sites by lowering their software prices but making up the difference by inflating shipping charges.

Many software retailers will match any advertised price, so you may be able to use the data from the price-check sites to get a lower price from the dealer of your choice. Note, however, that retailers usually call to make sure an item is in stock at the advertised price, so a low price from a store that's sold out is useless.

Academic Discounts

Most software companies offer extremely deep discounts for students, teachers, and schools. As I write this, for example, the student store at UC Berkeley is selling Microsoft Office for $150 and Photoshop for $259. If you're planning to buy a lot of software, it might be worth the money and trouble to enroll as a full-time student in a local community college just to take advantage of such discounts.

Note, however, that academic prices are not always better than what you can find by shopping around. For example, the student store is selling the upgrade version of Photoshop for $198, only $1 off list price, while regular retailers nearby have it for $175.

Rebates

Most software manufacturers occasionally offer rebates to try to increase their market share or spike sales of a slow-selling new release. Retailers aren't always up to date on what rebate offers are available, so it's a good idea to check the manufacturer's Web site for any announcements. Look both in the section of the site devoted to the product in question and in the section where the company posts press releases. The trade publication *Computer Retail Week* (**crw.com**) is also a good source for information on rebates and other special offers.

Closeouts and Free Upgrades

Most large software stores have a closeout bin where you can sort through marked-down copies of discontinued and unpopular software. Occasionally you'll even find popular, current programs that get tossed in the bin because their packaging has been damaged. Online software vendors also have closeout sections, and some even offer e-mail newsletters to let you know about special deals.

Software manufacturers frequently offer free upgrades to customers who buy the current version of a program after the next version has been announced. In itself that's no big deal, unless for some reason you actually want both versions,

but if you can find a cheap closeout copy of the old version a free upgrade can make it a great deal. Years ago I bought a copy of the recently discontinued Microsoft Word 3.0 for the Mac for $25 and got a free upgrade to 4.0, which cost around $250. Note that there's usually an expiration date on such free offers, so check carefully before you buy.

Buying Software by Mail or on the Web

Mail-order software dealers are just like any other retailer: just be sure to add in shipping charges when comparing prices with local stores. In some cases, you may be able to avoid having sales tax added to the bill by ordering from an out-of-state dealer, but be aware that you may be legally required to pay the tax yourself and could conceivably be assessed a penalty if you're audited. As always when ordering by mail, protect yourself by paying with a credit card, so if you don't receive your order you can refuse the charges.

Shareware

The line between *shareware* and regular commercial software has blurred in recent years. Traditionally, shareware worked on the honor system: you could download and try the product for free, then pay the author only if you liked it. If you didn't like it, you were usually obliged by the terms of the license to stop using it after a set evaluation period, but outside of potentially guilt-inducing dialog-box messages ("you have exceeded your free trial period by 42 days—register now!") there was nothing to force you to stop using the program.

Increasingly, however, the free versions of shareware programs are limited-function trial versions rather than the actual program, and/or they self-destruct after a set trial period. Since many commercial software vendors also offer crippled or time-limited trial versions of their products, there's no longer much of a distinction.

The main difference with shareware is that you're buying direct from the developer—the software equivalent of a farmers market. That means you can't shop around for a discount.

Freeware vs. Public-Domain Software

Freeware is just what it sounds like: free software. Somebody creates a program, then gives it away, no strings attached. Microsoft Internet Explorer and Netscape Communicator are probably the most prominent examples of this phenomenon.

Public domain software is slightly different. Freeware authors retain copyright and control of their work, typically allowing free distribution and use, but prohibiting the sale or modification of the program. Programmers who put their work in the public domain relinquish all rights to their programs—you can modify them, sell them, whatever you like.

Piracy

Since it's so easy to copy software, people often give in to the temptation to borrow a copy rather than buy their own. While this is always illegal, some kinds of software piracy are much more likely to get you in trouble than others. (Note that legally speaking, software piracy is not theft but copyright infringement.)

- **Individual** software piracy—borrowing software from the office or a friend to install on your home PC—is about as likely to get you in trouble as making a cassette copy of a friend's CD. Frankly, since software vendors could easily make their software much harder to copy, I suspect many see this kind of low-level piracy as a marketing tool: I've seen lots of people start out with a pirated copy of a program and then eventually upgrade to a new version. Note that some software licenses permit users to make certain kinds of copies that are usually illegal. The most liberal I've seen allow you to install as many copies as you like (for example, on your home, office, and notebook PCs) so long as only one is used at a time.
- **"Warez"**—pirate copies of software collected and traded by hacker teenagers (of all ages), just like baseball cards—are, despite the claims of the Software Publishers Association and other industry groups, generally harmless. They displace few if any actual sales, since most of these kids don't have the money to buy software and, except for games and programming tools, don't really use it anyway. Nevertheless, due to heavy lobbying by software companies, trading warez now constitutes criminal copyright infringement under federal law.
- **Corporate** piracy—typically, buying one copy of a program and installing it on every PC in the office—is surprisingly common given the potential penalties and how easy it is to get caught. There are a number of 800 numbers unhappy employees can call to blow the whistle, and companies that have been caught have frequently been hit with heavy fines. Note that breaking up a software bundle contrary to the terms of its license may constitute piracy: for example, you can't buy one copy of Microsoft Office and use it to install Word on one PC and Excel on another.
- **Commercial** piracy—that is, selling counterfeit or illegally copied software—can lead not just to fines but to a jail sentence. Watch out for cheap software sold at flea markets or computer swaps: if it's pirated, you won't get any tech support and the purchase won't qualify you for upgrade pricing on future versions.

Software Buying Resources

Microsoft

yahoo.com/Full_Coverage/Tech/Microsoft Pointers to lots of sites with court documents, news, and opinion regarding the antitrust actions pending against Microsoft.

Gates: How Microsoft's Mogul Reinvented an Industry—and Made Himself the Richest Man in America, Stephen Manes and Paul Andrews (ISBN: 0671880748). This well-researched and entertaining unauthorized biography of Bill Gates is also the best history of Microsoft written to date.

Hard Drive: Bill Gates and the Making of the Microsoft Empire, by James Wallace and Jim Erickson (ISBN: 0887306292). Not as good as the Manes & Andrews book, but if you're looking for embarrassing dirt about Microsoft, this is the place.

pbs.org/nerds/transcript.html The transcript to the television program *Triumph of the Nerds* gives a good history of Microsoft and the rest of the software industry.

library.microsoft.com/mshist/mshist.htm Microsoft's own official corporate history, in timeline format.

Software Suites

www.lotus.com/home.nsf/tabs/sswin You can get a CD with a 30-day trial version of SmartSuite by filling out a form on Lotus's Web site.

www.corel.com/products/wordperfect You can find information about Corel's various suites by picking from the menus on this Web page.

microsoft.com/products For info about Microsoft Office, pick the edition you're interested in from the menu on this page.

microsoft.com/office/000/productcklist.htm Microsoft's own chart comparing what you get in the different versions of Office. (Doesn't display correctly in Netscape Navigator 3.0.)

www.filemaker.com/products/trialsoftware.html Download a free trial version of FileMaker Pro, a database that's a lot friendlier than Microsoft Access.

Price Guides

`shopper.com` I usually check CNET's price guide first. I think it's easier to use than the competition, but it could be that I've just gotten used to its design since it's been around longer. It was the first big price guide on the Web—prior to its purchase by CNET it was called ComputerESP.

`www.pricewatch.com` This price guide's operated by CMP, best known as publisher of *Windows Magazine*. This hardware-centric site isn't very well organized for comparing software prices.

`computershopper.com` *Computer Shopper* is a unique monthly magazine that's comprised mostly of ads from a zillion mail-order companies. Its Web price guide is the worst-organized of the three sites listed here, and you have to wade through a lot of ads to get the information you want. Choose "software" from the category list, click on the kind of software you're interested in, and use the search form that appears to generate a list of the products you want to price.

Academic Discounts

`www.tsw.berkeley.edu/pricing/software/software.html` UC Berkeley's student store maintains this software price list. You can't buy from them if you're not enrolled, of course, but it's an easy way to keep tabs on what deals are available for students.

11

Windows 95, 98, and NT

by Robert Lauriston

In This Chapter

Windows, your computer's operating system, is a sort of digital office building—the place your applications (word processor, spreadsheet, e-mail, etc.) do their work every day. Windows has almost everything ready that the applications need to do their work: a filing system (disks), an inbox (for input from the keyboard, mouse, and scanner), an outbox (for output to printer and fax), communications with the outside world (e-mail, network), even an interoffice communication system so the apps can talk with each other (the Clipboard). Since Windows handles all the basics, all an application needs to manage are its own special functions. As a result, all Windows applications work similarly.

In this chapter, first I'll compare Windows 95, 98, and NT 4.0 to help you decide which is best for you and whether you should upgrade from your current version. (Unless specifically noted otherwise, everything in this chapter applies to all three versions.) Then, after a quick visual tour to get beginners oriented, you'll find the Windows Cookbook, a step-by-step guide to performing common tasks.

The rest of the chapter's sections are organized roughly in the order a new user might refer to them. There's a guide for folks who are facing the often daunting task of installing, re-installing, or upgrading Windows. Then I've got some tips for organizing your hard drive and keeping it running smoothly. Next comes an exhaustive field guide to the hundred-odd programs, utilities, widgets, and thingamabobs you get with Windows, followed by tips on customizing Windows to make it work better. Rounding out the chapter are tables of mouse tricks and keyboard shortcuts to help you work efficiently, and a list of Internet and other resources where you can find additional information about Windows.

I've tried to write this chapter in such a way that it's equally comprehensible to novices and more experienced users, but if you come across any unfamiliar terms or concepts, be sure to consult the Glossary or Chapter 1.

Which Windows Is Right for You?

If you're buying a new PC, or considering upgrading an old version of Windows, you have to choose between two flavors: 98 and NT. The easiest way I know to outline the major differences between the two is to trace the history of Windows, which will also explain *why* Microsoft's operating systems split off on two different paths.

A Brief History of Windows

Version	Shipped	Major Additions/Changes
	11/83	Windows announced at COMDEX
"Premiere" pre-beta	8/84	Demo distributed to major retailers
Windows 1.0	6/85	Beta
Windows 1.01	11/85	Graphical interface using titled windows; swapping of inactive apps to disk; Clipboard; Reversi game; may have had multitasking for Windows apps; task-switching for DOS apps; DDE
Windows 1.02	8/86	International versions
Windows 1.03	10/86	PostScript; 101-key and foreign keyboards
Windows 1.04	4/87	VGA; 3.5" floppies; PS/2
Windows 2.0	10/87	May have been a runtime version shipped with the first PC release of Excel
Windows 2.01, 2.02	?	May have been late betas
Windows/386	12/87	New interface with overlapping windows; EMS support; DOS multitasking
Windows 2.03	12/87	Same as Windows/386 except no DOS multitasking
Windows 2.1	7/88	Increased maximum application size by 50K, using himem.sys to access HMA
Windows 2.11	3/89	Updated drivers; bug fixes
Windows 3.0	5/90	Program Manager, File Manager, and Task List; SmartDrive; virtual memory; XMS for Windows apps and DPMI DOS apps; EMS emulation for DOS apps; 3-D look and 8-bit color; Solitaire game (runtime version discontinued)
Windows 3.1	4/92	OLE; drag-and-drop; scalable fonts; multimedia; pre-emptive multitasking and virtual memory for DOS apps; improved disk performance (32-bit disk access); application hot-keys; split-window File Manager; StartUp program group; easier installation; faster and more stable; ability to kill hung app without rebooting; Minesweeper game
Windows for Workgroups 3.1	10/92	Built-in peer-to-peer networking; e-mail; group scheduler; TCP/IP and NetWare drivers; shared Clipboard
Windows NT 3.1	8/93	Long filenames; preemptive multitasking of Win32 apps; built-in networking; security; high-performance file system; video-driver preview
Windows for Workgroups 3.11	11/93	Improved disk cache performance (32-bit file access); lawsuit-proof NetWare drivers; icon bar in File Manager

A Brief History of Windows (continued)

Version	Shipped	Major Additions/Changes
Windows 3.11	2/94	Updated drivers; minor bug fixes; hologram on box
Windows NT 3.5	9/94	OLE 2.0; long filenames on FAT volumes; preemptive multitasking of 16-bit Windows apps; animated cursors; lower RAM requirements; interoperable with NetWare
Windows NT 3.51	6/95	NTFS file compression; multithreaded OLE; license manager; PowerPC version
Windows 95 (aka 950; aka 4.0)	8/95	Mac-style desktop; long filenames; taskbar and Start menu; MS Internet Explorer; built-in Internet dialer; Plug and Play
Windows 95 OSR1 (aka Service Pack 1; aka 950a)	2/96	Bug fixes; MS Internet Explorer 2.0; distributed only with new PCs and as free download
Windows NT 4.0	8/96	Windows 95 interface; modem pooling for faster Internet access
Windows 95 OSR2 (aka 950B)	12/96	FAT32; wake-on-ring power management; IrDA and CardBus support; Online Services folder; Internet Explorer 3.0; sold only with new PCs
Windows 95 OSR2.1	8/97	USB support; shipped only with new PCs
Windows 95 OSR2.5	12/97	MS Internet Explorer 4.0; shipped only with new PCs
Windows 98 (aka 4.1)	6/98	New system maintenance utilities; improved power management; support for DVD
Windows 2000 Professional	TBA	Windows NT plus "the best of Windows 98"

Windows 3.1 (1992) had some very serious limitations. Most notably, filenames could not exceed eight characters; a misbehaving application would often crash the system; the file system was prone to data-damaging errors; and due to some arcane design defects it was common to get "out of memory" errors that limited the number of applications you could run, even when there was in fact plenty of free RAM.

Windows NT (1993) pretty much solved the problems of 3.1. Unfortunately, the solution came at the cost of compatibility: Many DOS applications and even some Windows applications ran poorly or not at all. Moreover, memory prices had dropped much more slowly than Microsoft had anticipated when it began working on NT in 1989, so few users had the required 16MB RAM. Developers therefore had little incentive to write applications for NT; and with few applications available, users would have no reason to switch. Microsoft didn't even try to sell this version to end users—it was marketed strictly as an operating system for servers.

Windows 95 was sort of halfway between 3.1 and NT. It was essentially a much-improved version of Windows 3.1, with the old DOS-era limitations eliminated or at least significantly eased, and a new interface that incorporated many good ideas from other operating systems—particularly the Mac and NextStep. It wasn't as bulletproof as NT, but it was much more compatible with older apps, and despite widespread reports to the contrary it really required no more hardware than Windows 3.1. (Many Windows 95 *applications* were major memory hogs, but that's another issue.)

Windows NT 4.0 (1996) put the improved Win95 interface on the much more robust NT foundation. NT4.0's ability to run almost all apps written for the extremely popular Win95 has largely eliminated the software compatibility problem—in over two years of running this OS, I've found only a handful of programs it wouldn't run. Some minor hardware compatibility issues still exist, though—NT won't run on all laptops; support for Plug-and-Play boards is problematic; there's no USB support; and not all hardware comes with drivers for NT. This is the first version Microsoft has actively marketed to end users: They knocked the price of the upgrade down to around $140, and now provide the same 90 days of free tech support you get with Windows 98. (Note that when I talk about NT in this chapter, I'm referring to NT Workstation, not NT Server. The two are basically identical except that Microsoft disables or limits most of the server functions in NTW, and charges a lot more for NTS.)

Windows 98 is a fairly minor upgrade that replaced Windows 95. The differences between the two are modest enough that I don't see much reason to upgrade unless you want to buy some new hardware or software that requires 98. Microsoft's performance claims for Win98 have for the most part not been confirmed by independent lab tests. In fact, CNET found that Windows 98 was actually a bit slower than Windows 95 when the latter was tested without Microsoft Internet Explorer 4.0 installed. Here's a URL for CNET's test results if you want to check them out for yourself:

`cnet.com/Content/Reviews/Compare/Win98/ss08b.html`

Windows 2000 Professional, the successor to Windows NT, will supposedly add most of the features of Windows 98, and may be sold as an upgrade for *both* NT 4.0 and Windows 98. This is such an ambitious undertaking that I won't be surprised if doesn't ship until 2000.

Bottom line: if you're choosing a new operating system or considering an upgrade, your current choices are Windows 98 and NT 4.0. The following table compares their advantages and disadvantages.

Windows 98 vs. Windows NT Workstation 4.0

	Windows 98	Windows NT Workstation 4.0
Bare minimum RAM to boot	4MB	12MB
Practical minimum RAM for marginally acceptable application performance	8MB	16MB
Recommended RAM for good performance	32MB	64MB
OS detects and recovers from drive errors automatically	No	Yes
Supports drive spanning and arrays (makes multiple drives appear as one; improves drive performance)	No	Yes
Preemptive multitasking for DOS and 32-bit Windows applications (helps prevent misbehaving applications from crashing system)	Yes	Yes
Preemptive multitasking for 16-bit Windows 3.1 applications	No	Yes
Can kill misbehaving application without rebooting	Sometimes	Yes
Can run DOS games	Yes	Some
Automatically resolves hardware conflicts	Usually	No
Supports Windows Plug and Play devices	Yes	Some
Supports USB devices	Yes	No
Supports multiple CPUs (improves performance)	No	Yes
Secure file system (can password-lock selected drives, folders, or files)	No	Yes
Price with new PC	No extra charge	Typically $100
Upgrade price	$90	$135
Free tech support	90 days	90 days

Generally, I recommend Windows 98 for home users. Pretty much any software or hardware you buy will work with it, it handles more of the hardware-configuration chores, and it's better for games and entertainment.

On the other hand, if your PC is essential to your work or business, I think NT's a better choice. The more reliable NTFS disk format alone is worth the price of the upgrade. Note that to get the full advantage of NT's security and greater reliability, you'll need to choose that format during installation, or convert your drives later. (See "More Stuff Worth Knowing About" below for instructions.)

If you're already running Windows 95 and have no specific reason to upgrade to Windows 98, you might as well stick with what you've got.

The 10-Minute Windows Tour

The latest versions of Windows are the friendliest yet—but if you've never used a computer before, they can be baffling. And if you already know Windows 3.1, things are pretty different from what you're used to. In this quick tour, we'll take a look at the basic components of Windows:

- **The desktop** is a sort of virtual work surface. Windows puts some important tools here, and you can use it to store frequently used files and folders, just like a regular desktop. (There's a good chance Microsoft and/or your computer manufacturer has already cluttered it up with a bunch of useless junk.)
- **The taskbar** keeps track of the stuff you're actively working on at the moment, and often includes controls for components such as the speakers and monitor.
- **The Start menu** lets you access Windows's various components, and any applications that you've installed or that came with your PC.
- **Windows Explorer** is the most efficient of the various Windows tools for managing files and folders.

In addition to a quick look at each of these four primary components, our 10-Minute Windows Tour will cover the basics of Windows navigation and file management. Of course, you'll need to have Windows already installed on your computer; in the unlikely event that it hasn't been, see the "How to Install" section later in this chapter.

The images in the tour were taken from Windows 98, but at this basic level it is quite similar to Windows 95 and NT 4.0. We'll note in passing a few minor differences.

The Tour Starts Here

When you turn on your PC, it will klunk and whir a bit, but eventually you should end up at the Windows desktop. (If you're turning on the PC for the first time, you'll be asked for your registration number and time zone, as discussed in the "How to Install" section.) The desktop will look something like the following illustrations:

This is the *mouse pointer*. Read "Using a Mouse" in Chapter 1: For Beginners Only if you haven't used one before and aren't sure about the differences between click, double-click, right-click, and so on.

The *Channel Bar* is a special Microsoft Internet Explorer window that's basically an advertisement for Web sites operated by Microsoft and companies with which it's made deals.

This blank area is the *desktop*. You can store frequently used documents, folders, and programs on this virtual surface.

These are *icons*: They can represent programs, folders, documents, and services (like printers or the Recycle Bin). When you first run Windows, in addition to the useful icons for My Computer, Network Neighborhood, and the Recycle Bin, you'll see some icons that are just ads for Microsoft products or services, like the MSN icon here.

The first time you run Windows, you'll get a Welcome display something like this. Once you've explored it to your satisfaction, uncheck the "Show this screen each time Windows 98 starts" box.

This is the *Start button*. Clicking on it brings up the *Start menu*, from which you can access programs, recently edited files, Windows settings and online Help system, and various other things.

This is a *toolbar*, a customizable portion of the Windows 98 taskbar where you can store icons for quick access to your favorite programs.

This strip across the bottom of the screen is the *taskbar*. Every time you start a program, a button for it appears on the taskbar; clicking the button takes you back to the program. As you'll see shortly, the desktop can get pretty cluttered; but the taskbar ensures that beginners won't get lost (a common complaint in Windows 3.1).

Move the mouse over the X at the upper-right corner of the Welcome display (if you see one), and you'll see a little yellow Tooltip *box pop up to let you know that's the Close button. Click the button to close the Welcome window. Do the same to the Channel Bar and any other open windows, so you have a nice clean desktop for the tour. Windows and its applications have so many buttons for so many different tasks, that the Tooltip labels are often essential to keep everything straight.*

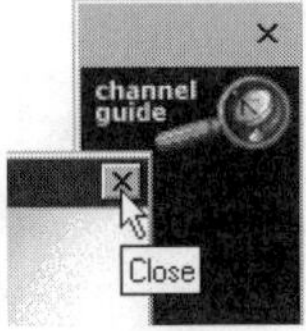

If Windows doesn't respond to your mouse as described in this tour, you may need to turn off Active Desktop, as described on page 329.

Move the mouse over the My Computer icon and double-click (click the left button twice in quick succession). Depending on the speed of your PC, an hourglass may appear next to the pointer for a second or so—Windows's way of telling you to wait.

The My Computer *window contains icons for all the drives in the PC, plus folders for printers, control panels, dial-up networking settings, and (in Windows 98 only) scheduled tasks. You can use My Computer for file management tasks, but I strongly recommend the more-efficient Windows Explorer instead. The browser-type toolbar buttons at the top and the Weblike message at left appear only in Windows 98.*

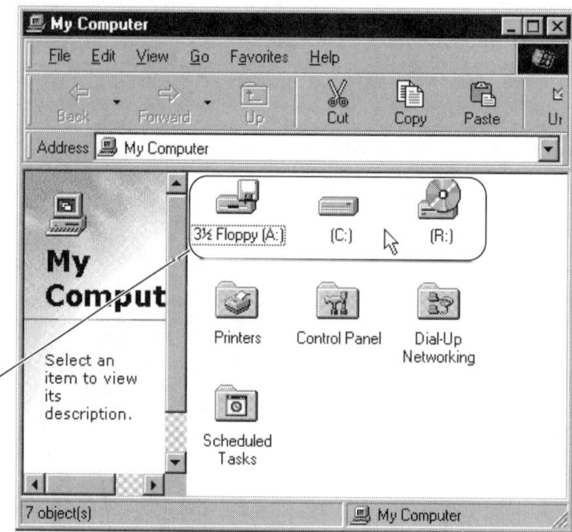

These are your PC's *drives*. Usually, A is the floppy disk drive, B is reserved for a second floppy drive (increasingly rare), and C: is the hard disk. By default, the CD-ROM is usually D: but, as discussed later, you can avoid potential problems by setting it manually to a higher letter. To complicate matters, a single hard disk may be divided into several logical drives (or volumes) instead of one big C: drive, so you have C:, D:, E:, and so on, each with its own folders and files.

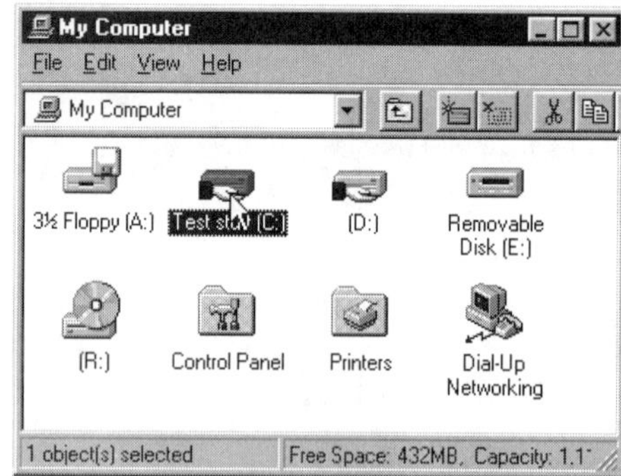

Here's how My Computer looks in Windows 95 and NT. Functionally it's almost identical to the Win98 interface; in fact, I'm pretty sure the main reason Microsoft changed the interface was to support the claim that Internet Explorer is part of Windows. Notice how this computer has a couple of extra drive icons—the hard drive has two volumes, C: and D:, as well as a Zip drive (E:).

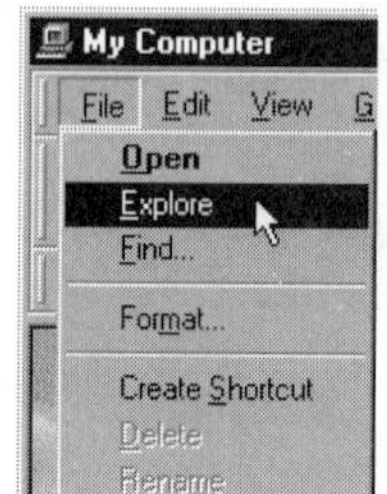

No matter what view you're looking at, click the C: icon to highlight it. Then choose File/Explore:—that is, click File to pull down the menu, move the mouse down to highlight Explore, and click again. This basic process—selection followed by a menu choice—is the basic pattern for most Windows commands.

This is Windows Explorer, *Windows' tool for manipulating the basic elements of computing on a PC:* files, folders, *and* drives. *We'll use the Explorer to take a look at the components of a Windows window.*

The *control box* contains a menu of commands that affect the window itself. It's something of a Windows 3.1 holdover, with most of its functions duplicated elsewhere. But it's useful if you don't have a mouse or prefer not to use one, because it lets you move and resize windows from the keyboard.

The *title bar* tells you the name of the program, and sometimes other information, like the name of the file being edited or the address of the Web page being browsed.

This is a *toolbar;* you can click its buttons instead of choosing commands from the menus. (You'll see these big buttons only in the Windows 98 version of Windows Explorer; Windows 95 and NT have smaller ones, as pictured here.)

Scroll arrows steadily move the contents of a window in the direction indicated. Just put the pointer on the desired arrow and hold down the left mouse button.

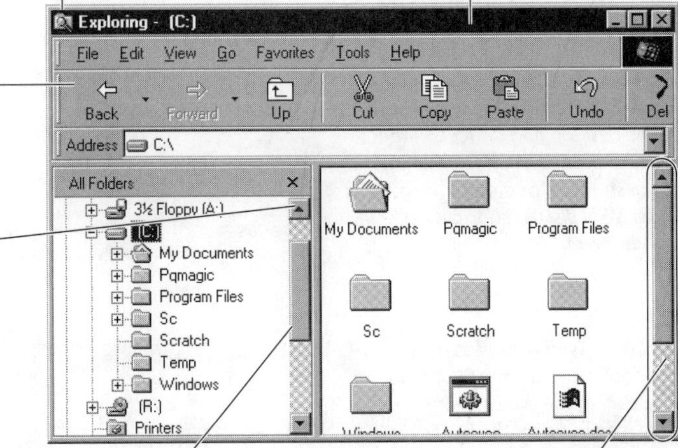

Scroll boxes provide the fastest way to scroll. Move the pointer to one, hold down the left mouse button, and drag the button along the scroll bar in the desired direction.

The *scroll bars* let you view information you can't currently see on screen. All Windows applications have them. Clicking in the empty part of the bars, on either side of the scroll box, jumps one screenful in that direction.

Click the Maximize button *to enlarge the window. Make sure you click Windows Explorer's Maximize button, and not the one on the My Computer window behind it.*

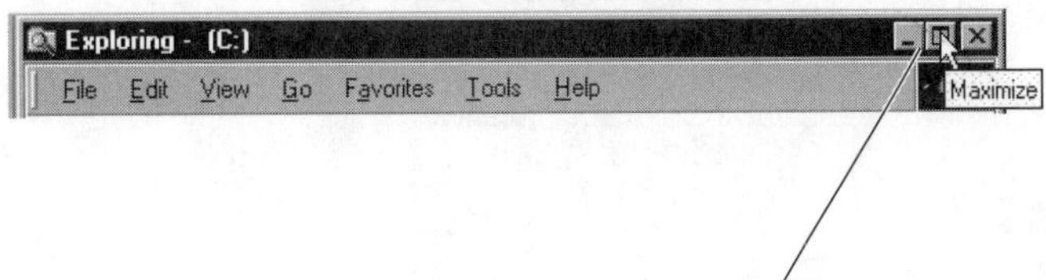

From left to right, these are the *Minimize, Maximize,* and *Close* buttons. Minimize hides the window temporarily when you need to clear clutter off the screen. Maximize expands the window to fill the screen, so you can see more files at once. Close makes the window go away.

At the left, Windows Explorer displays the folder tree: *a hierarchical display of all the drives, folders, and files on your PC. The tree is another way of representing nested windows on the desktop: Folders and files are below/inside drive C:, which is below/inside My Computer, which in turn is below/sitting on the desktop. If you're on a network, its servers will appear in the tree as well, one level below the Desktop, under Network Neighborhood. (You may wonder why My Documents shows up both on the desktop and under C:—that's because the one on the desktop is just a "shortcut" or alias to the actual folder. We'll discuss shortcuts later in this chapter.)*

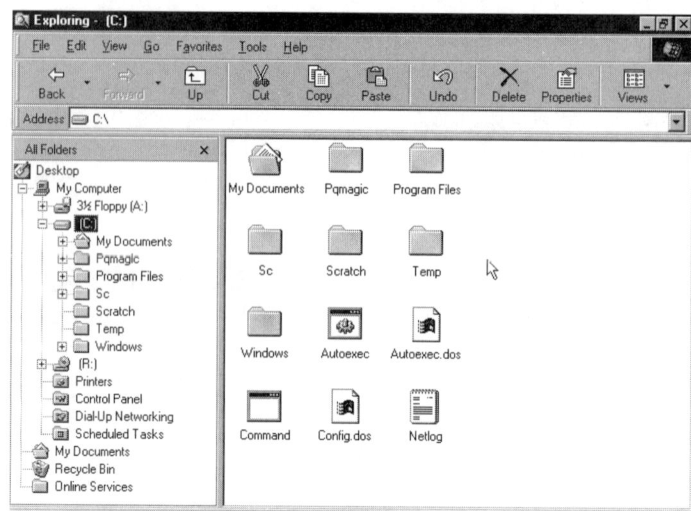

Click the + symbol next to a folder to "expand" it and see the folders inside. (The stuff inside the Program Files folder shows up on the Start menu, which we'll get to presently.) Click one of the folders in the tree, and the files inside it will appear in the right-hand window. Try using the scroll bars, boxes, and arrows to view various parts of the folder tree.

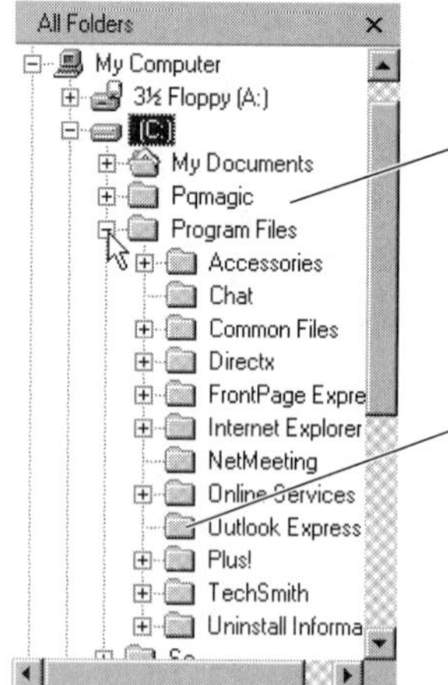

This display of folders, which shows where each is in relation to the others, is called the *folder tree* (or *directory tree*), so named because the lines showing folder locations branch like the limbs of a tree.

This is a *folder* (sometimes called a *directory* or *subdirectory*). It looks like a file folder and, just like the real thing, you use it to store files and other folders. Double-click any folder, and all files and folders inside it appear. In a given folder, each file must have a different name.

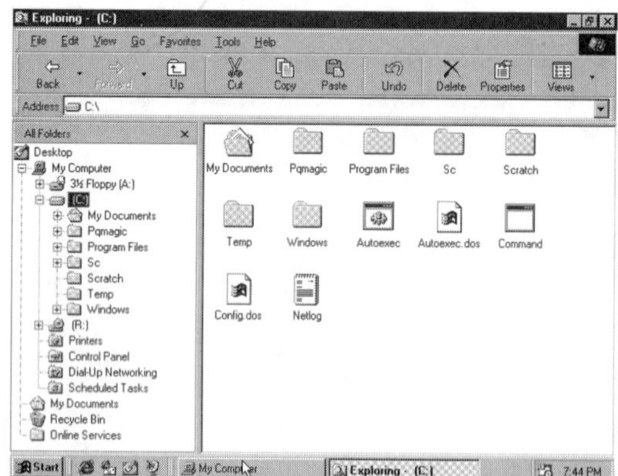

Now lets get into window navigation. *If you look at the taskbar at the bottom of the screen, you can see that My Computer is still open; it's just obscured by the expanded Windows Explorer. Click the My Computer button on the taskbar to bring that window to the front.*

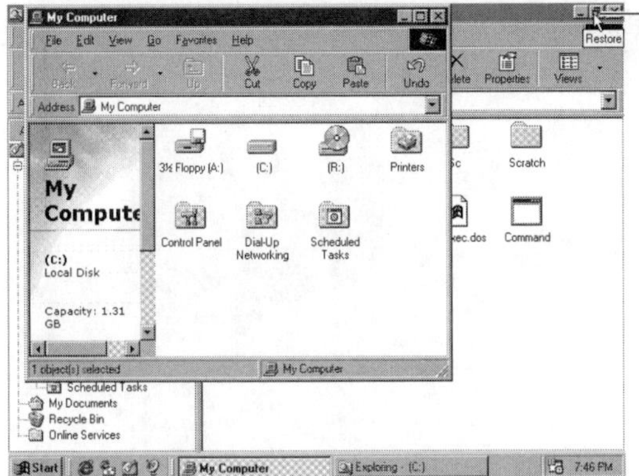

This is the *Restore* button, which appears when you maximize a window. When you click it to restore the window to its original size, Restore turns back into the Maximize button.

When you can see a window, you don't have to use the taskbar to bring it to the front—you can just click anywhere in the window. Click Windows Explorer's Restore button to bring it to the front again.

Those big icons don't really tell you much about what you're looking at, so let's get more information by choosing Details from the View menu. To see all the file details, you need a wider window—but instead of maximizing, this time let's adjust the window manually. Position the cursor over the right edge of the window until it turns into a sort of double-headed arrow (the sizing pointer*). Then* click and drag *to widen the window—that is, click and hold the mouse button, move the mouse to the right until the border reaches the edge of the screen, and let go of the button.*

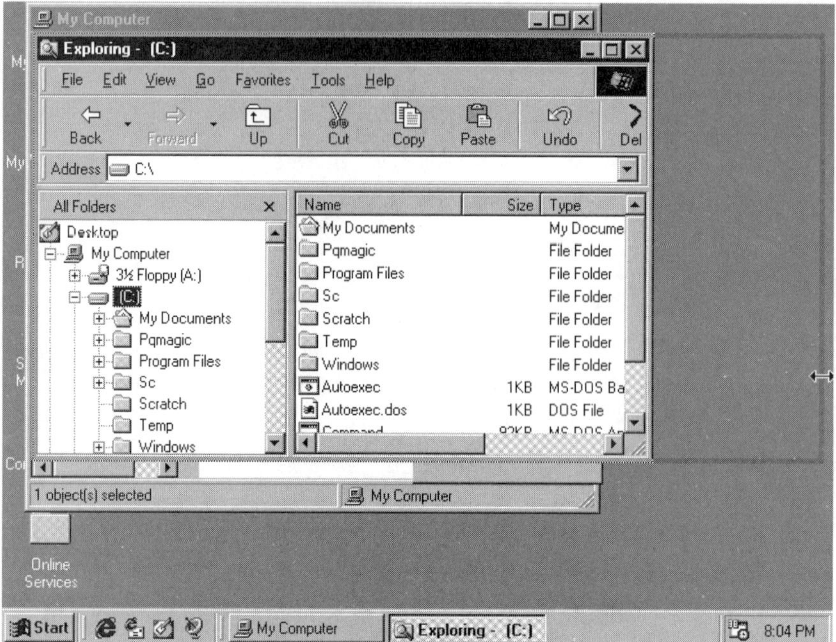

Using click and drag, you can resize *windows in any direction, or in two directions at once by dragging any corner. You can also* move *windows around using a similar technique: Click the title bar—the (usually) blue strip at the top of the window—drag the window to the bottom, almost off the screen, and then let go.*

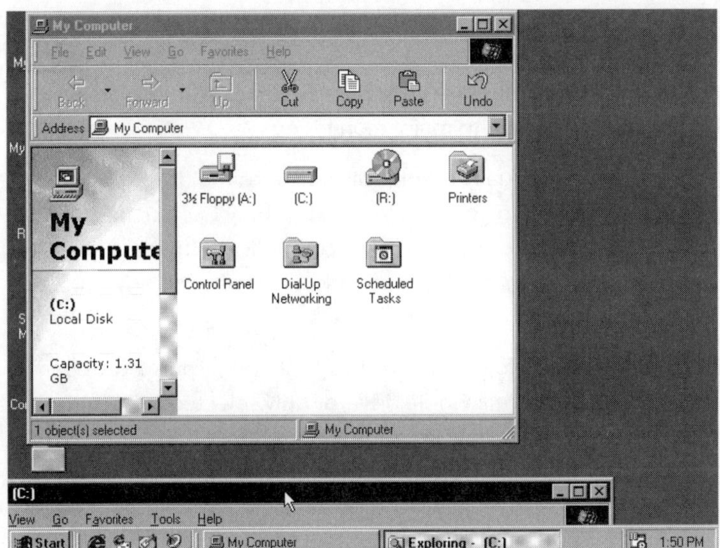

Obviously you can't do much work on the window while it's off the screen like this, but having the title bar visible means you can drop things on it, which is sometimes useful. The title bar's useful for one other thing—double-click it and you'll see . . .

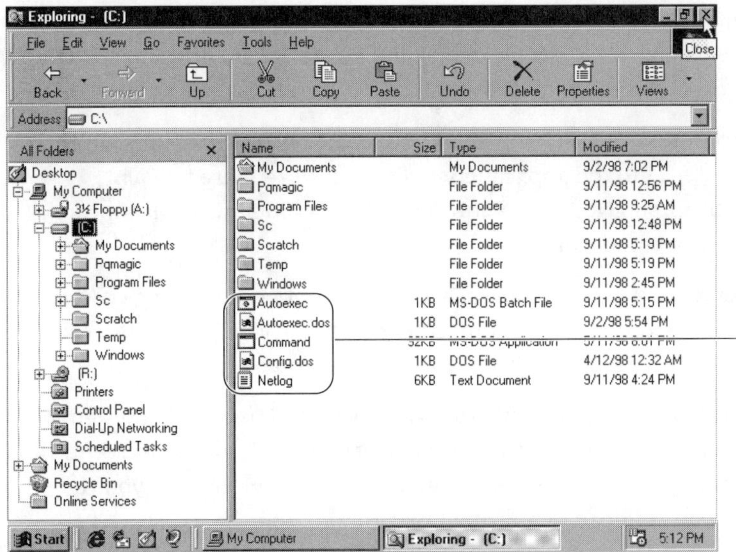

. . . that it does the same thing as clicking the Maximize/Restore button. This is particularly useful if you're clumsy and find yourself regularly clicking the wrong buttons.

These are *files*. In Windows Explorer's Details view, the Type column gives you a brief description of what each file is—although, as you can see, those descriptions are not always very helpful. In other views, you can get some idea of what a file is by its icon (see the sidebar "Field Guide to Windows Icons").

We'll get into a lot more detail about Windows Explorer in the Cookbook section of this chapter. For now, click the Explorer's Close box, and then the one on the My Computer window, and let's move on to the Start menu.

Field Guide to Windows Icons

A file's icon often gives some indication of its purpose—a paintbrush icon for Windows Paint, a sheet of paper for Notepad, etc. Here's a quick guide to major icon types:

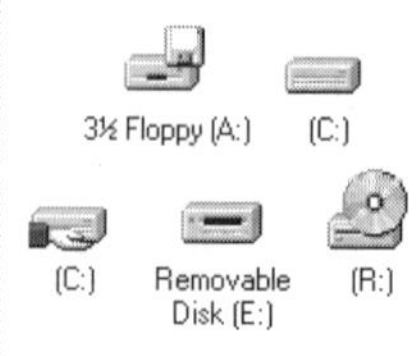

Drives. A drive's icon usually graphically indicates the drive type: a floppy, a big slot for a Zip (Removable Disk), a shiny CD, a sealed box for a hard drive. A hand under the drive icon indicates that sharing is turned on, so other users on your network can access the drive, at least they can be set to open access.

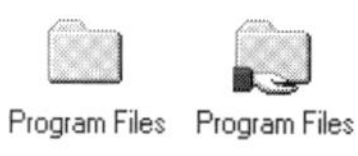

Folders. A hand on the folder shows that its sharing option has been turned on. (You can share a whole drive, or only selected folders; the hand appears on a folder only in the latter case.)

Applications. Most applications have their own distinctive icons, like Microsoft Paint, WordPad, and Notepad here. (As you can see, the names of actual program files are often abbreviated.) Those that aren't get just a generic icon representing a program window, like the Route command here. A generic program icon with a gear in it represents a DOS batch file—a text file containing a series of DOS commands that are executed one after the other.

Documents. A document of a known type normally appears with an icon similar to the application that opens it, like these for Paint, WordPad, and Notepad. Normally, any file saved as text will appear with a Notepad icon.

Shortcuts. A shortcut (aka *alias*) is recognizable by the little curved arrow in a box at the bottom left corner of the icon. These Start menu shortcuts have the familiar names for the programs shown above.

System files. A generic file icon with gears on it indicates a system file, which you should always leave alone if you aren't sure what you're doing. Gears on a text file icon indicate a configuration file you can edit with Notepad or any other text editor.

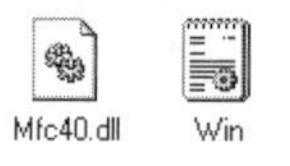

Unknown/garbage files. When Windows doesn't recognize a file's type, or if it considers the file to be garbage (like this temp file, which it will delete automatically when the program that created it closes), it shows this generic Windows logo icon.

Move the mouse pointer to the lower-left corner of the window, click the Start button, and this menu pops up.

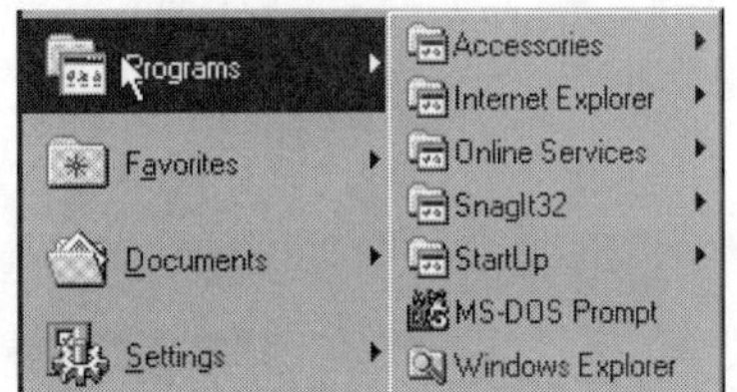

Move the mouse pointer up the menu until it's over Programs…

…then to the right until it's over Accessories, further right until it's over Communications, and then down until it's over WordPad. Click on WordPad. All the Windows menus work similarly—and if you're as clumsy as I am, it may take a while to be able to navigate them accurately. If you get frustrated, after you click the Start button you can switch to the keyboard arrow keys to navigate the menu hierarchy.

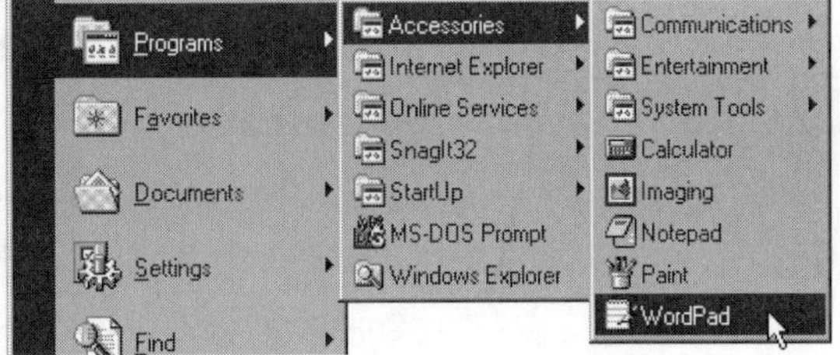

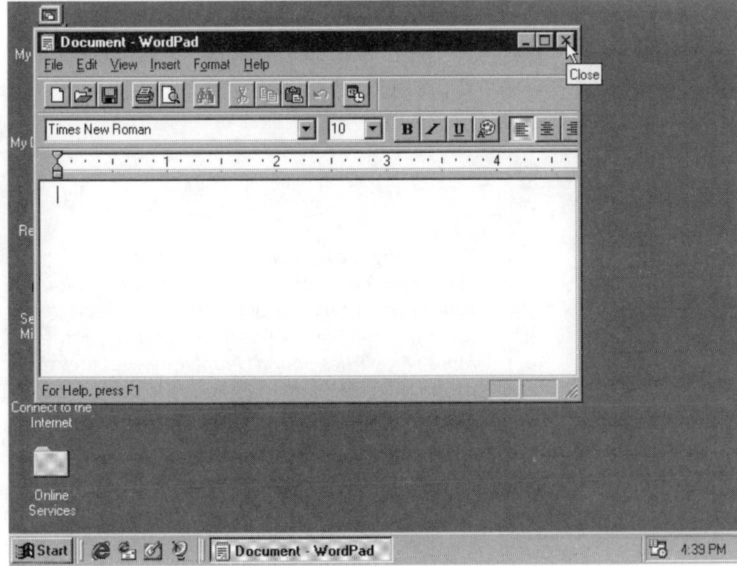

The Start menu goes away and WordPad, a simple word processor that's bundled with Windows, appears on the screen. Click WordPad's Close box to get rid of it.

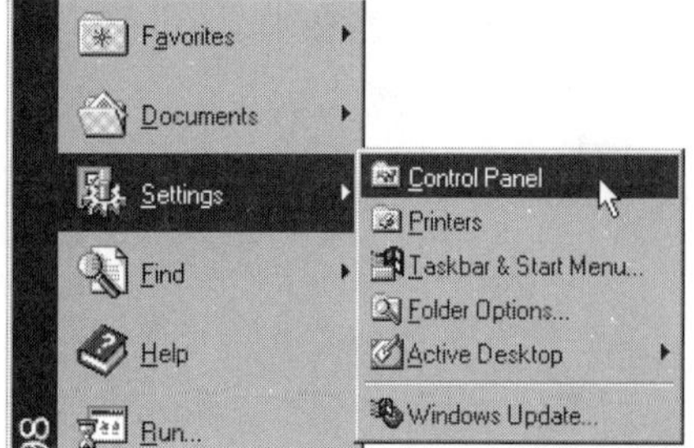

Click the Start menu again, move the pointer over Settings, then to the right and click Control Panel. (Elsewhere in this book, we describe this action as "Choose Settings / Control Panel from the Start menu.")

You use Windows's Control Panel to adjust all sorts of software options, and occasionally hardware settings as well. The Web-page-like explanation appears only in Windows 98, but that's no big deal—the information's seldom helpful enough to justify use of the screen real estate it takes up.

If necessary, move down in the window by clicking in the right-hand scroll bar until you see the Mouse control panel, then double-click it. (Technically the widgets in the Control Panel are called properties*—Mouse Properties, Sounds Properties—but they're commonly referred to as* control panels.*)*

We'll use the Mouse Properties to look at some controls customarily found in dialog boxes. *Feel free to play with the controls—none of your changes will be saved unless and until you click the OK button. Click the tabs at the top of the dialog to switch among properties for Buttons and Pointers and Motion.*

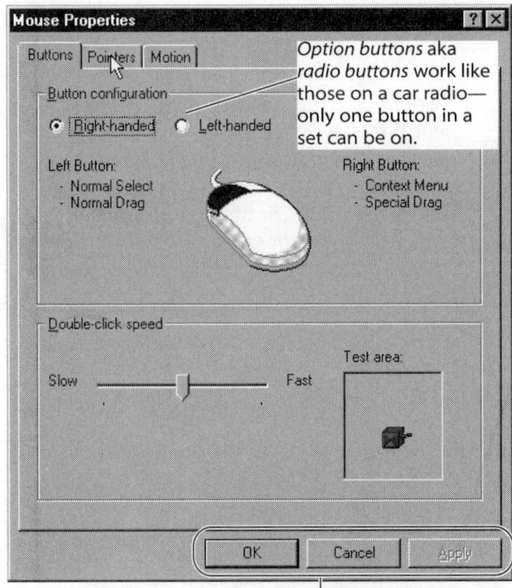

Option buttons aka *radio buttons* work like those on a car radio—only one button in a set can be on.

Command buttons are in every dialog box. Cancel and OK are universal. Buttons that aren't currently usable are grayed out. Apply, for example, can't be used until you've made some changes in the dialog's options. None of the selections you make take effect until you click OK or Apply.

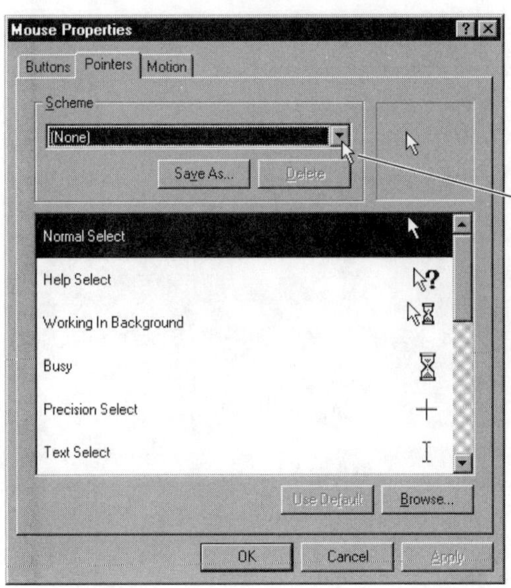

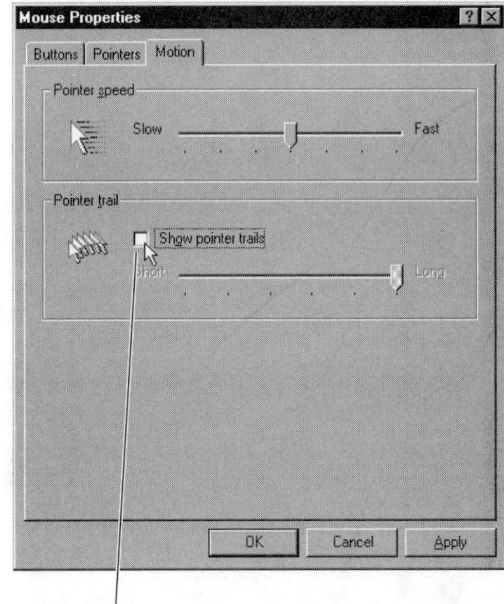

Check boxes work like on/off switches. If you click this one, the check mark appears. Click again, and it disappears. Notice how the slider is a sort of ghost image until you check the box; controls that are dependent on other controls are often "grayed out" like the one above to let you know they're not available.

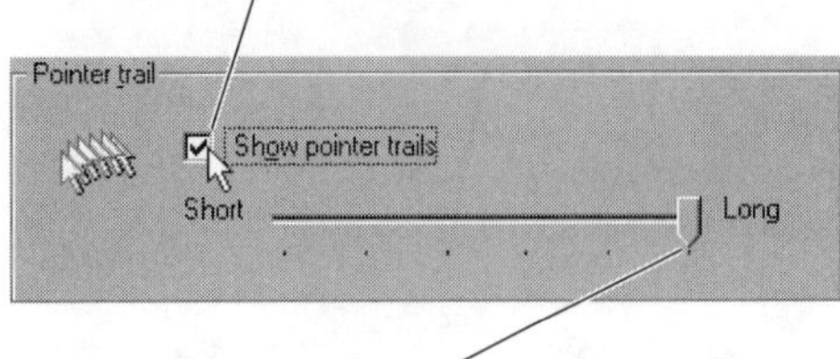

Sliders are used to set options with a continually variable range, like cursor blink speed, sound volume, or brightness.

List boxes work like option buttons, only you make your choice from the list that drops down.

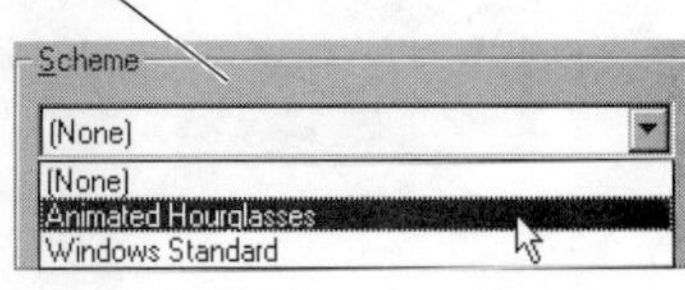

When you're through checking out the Mouse properties, click Cancel to throw away any changes you made. (If you wanted to save them, you'd click OK.)

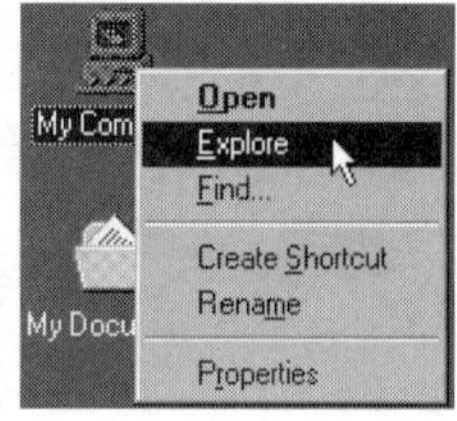

One last thing for you to try before we end this tour: Put the mouse pointer over My Computer, but click with the right button instead of the left. Right-clicking *on almost any object on screen pops up a menu of commands that can be used on that object. Choose Explore and you'll get a Windows Explorer window with My Computer selected in the folder tree.*

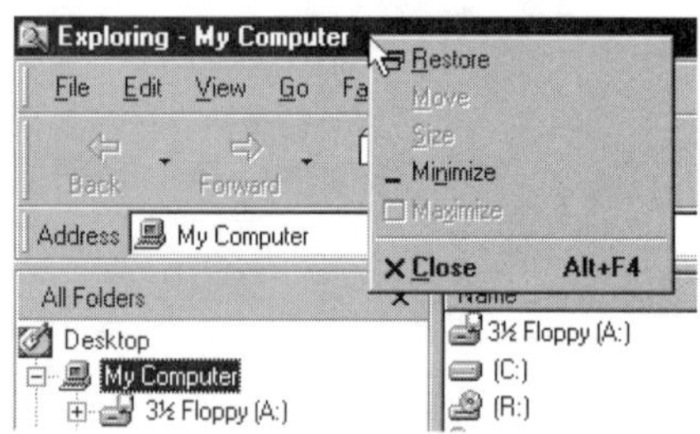

The right-click menu (aka pop-up or shortcut menu) varies wildly depending on the object. Right-click Windows Explorer's title bar, for example, and you get Restore, Minimize, and Close commands. Choose Restore and then right-click the title bar again, and the choices are Move, Size, Minimize, Maximize, and Close.

It's not very logical, but when you want to shut down your PC, or exit Windows to run DOS (necessary for some games) or some other operating system, you have to go back to the Start menu—that's where you'll find the Shut Down command. If you've had enough of Windows for the moment, choose Shut Down now. Otherwise, you might want to check out the tutorials on the Help menu, or read through our next section here—the Windows Cookbook—which gets into more depth about most of the topics we touched on in this tour.

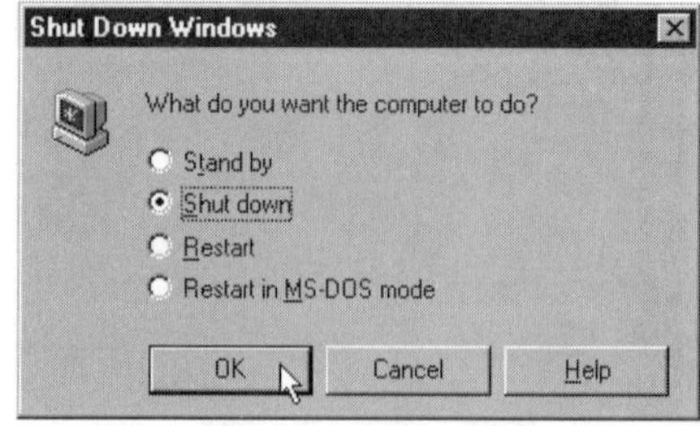

So long!

A Quick Summary of What You Just Saw. The preceding "10-Minute" tour gives you a brief hands-on experience with many of the fundamental concepts of using windows. Here's a quick review:

- Double-click to open document or application icons.

- Most commands are a two-step process: *First* select what you want to affect, *then* click a button or choose a menu command.
- To bring a window to the front, click any part of it, or click its taskbar button.
- Use the Minimize, Maximize/Restore, and Close buttons to manage windows.
- Drag a window's title bar to move it, or double-click the title bar to maximize or restore it.
- Drag a window's sides or corners to resize it in any direction.
- To scroll a window, click a scroll arrow (to scroll slowly), click in the blank part of the scroll bar (faster), or drag the scroll box up or down (fastest).
- Right-click to get a pop-up menu; what's on the menu varies depending on what you click.
- Windows almost always offers multiple ways to do things—from the pull-down menus, the toolbar buttons, the right-click menus, the keyboard, etc.

The Windows Cookbook

The step-by-step instructions in the Windows Cookbook assume that you're using the "classic" interface, in which you double-click on an icon to open it. If you have Active Desktop (see pages 328-329) turned on and its single-click option enabled, you will have to adjust some of these instructions accordingly to get the expected results.

File Tasks

See what files are in a folder...

You need to see where a file is before you can open it in an application, move it, or otherwise work with it. Files live in folders, so that's where you need to look for them.

Basic Method

1. Start Windows Explorer. (Click the Start button, then Programs, then Windows Explorer.)
2. In the folder tree display (the left window), click the folder you think contains the files you want. The files in that folder will appear in the right window.
3. If there are more files in the folder than the right-hand window can display, you can enlarge it by maximizing the Explorer. (To maximize, double-click the menu bar; then double-click the menu bar again when you're ready to return the Explorer to its original size.)

By default, Windows Explorer displays only filenames and icons. If you want to see more information, including the type of file, its size, and the date it was last modified, choose View/Details (see Figure 1).

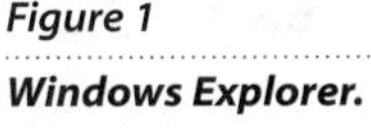

Figure 1

Windows Explorer.

There are minor variations among the Windows Explorers that come with different versions of Windows: This one, from Windows 98, can display text labels on its toolbar buttons. Here it's set to Details view.

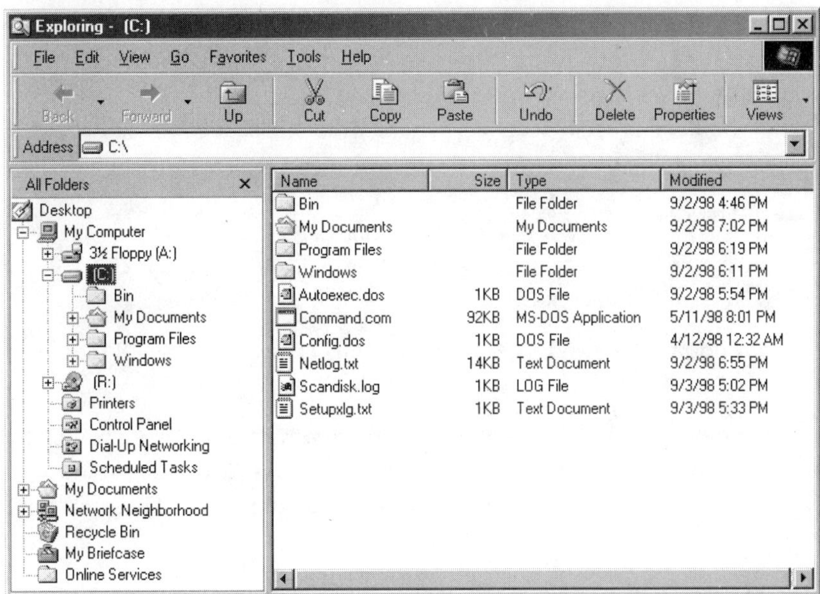

To get still more information about an individual file, right-click the file icon or name, and choose Properties from the pop-up menu. The property sheet will include the date the file was created, the name under which it will appear to DOS and 16-bit Windows applications, and file attributes. (The latter are discussed in "About File Attributes" later in this chapter.) The property sheet is supposed to include the date the file was last accessed, but that information is often the current date and time. Other information is available depending on the type of file.

By default, Explorer displays files in alphabetical order. If you want to change that, pick one of the other options in the View/Arrange Icons submenu. If you're in Details view, you can resort simply by clicking on a column heading (Name, Size, Type, or Modified); click again to sort in reverse order.

Other Ways to Do It

- **In My Computer or in Open view:** Nearly everything you can do in Windows Explorer, you can also do in My Computer or the Open view of a drive or folder, for the simple reason that they're the same program. When you double-click My Computer or a folder on the desktop, what you get is Windows Explorer minus the folder tree window.

Danger Zone: Hidden Files

Normally, Windows does not display *hidden files,* which are special files that Windows, or some other operating system you've installed, or an application needs to operate properly. Hiding the files is the Windows equivalent of the CONTAINS NO USER-SERVICEABLE PARTS sticker on the back of a TV set. If you rename, delete, or move these files, you may lose data, crash your system, or both! Outside of a few special tasks, like enabling the Windows 95/98 boot menu, there's no reason you need to see hidden files. On the other hand, once you know Windows well enough to avoid damaging them accidentally, there's no particular reason to hide these files, either.

To reveal hidden files:

- In Windows 98, select View/Folder Options, click the View tab, check the Show All Files radio button, and click OK.
- In Windows 95 and NT, select View/Options, check the Show All Files radio button, and click OK.

In the same way, you can reveal file name *extensions*, so that a Word file, for instance, would appear as My File.doc instead of My File. (Windows uses extensions to track file types.) To make extensions visible, uncheck the "Hide file extensions for known file types" option in the View tab.

- **From the Open and Save dialogs:** When you choose Open or Save within an application, you'll get a display that's similar to the one in Windows Explorer (see Figure 2). These windows don't have menus or a toolbar, but most of the file commands are available from the pop-up menus that appear when you right-click a file icon or name. The same goes for folder commands, which appear when you right-click the blank space below or to the right of the files.

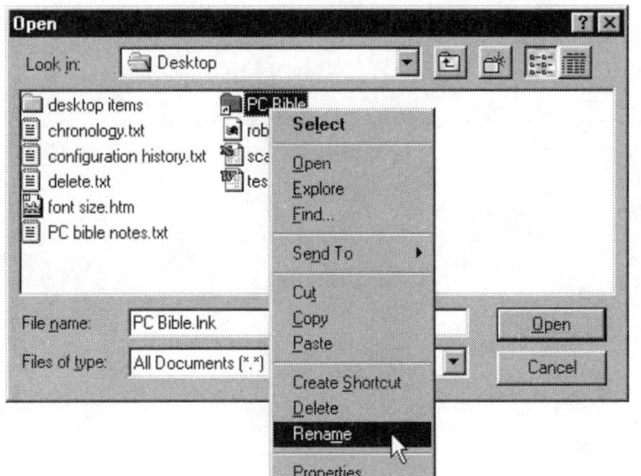

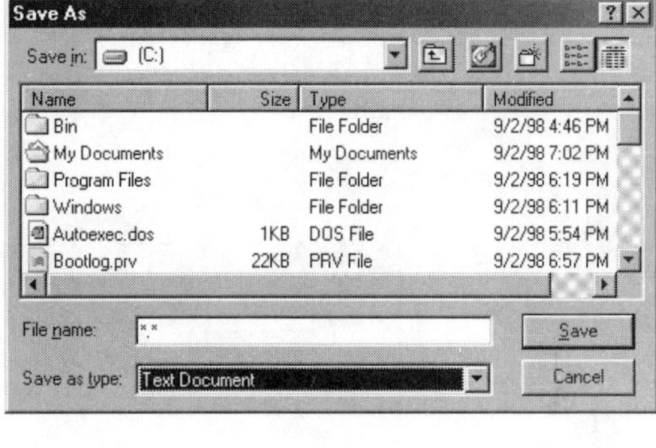

Figure 2

Windows's standard file dialogs.

The File/Open and File/Save dialog boxes give you most of the tools of Windows Explorer. For access to menu commands, right-click a file, folder, or the blank space behind them to get a pop-up menu (shown here at left); to see file details, click the button at the right of the toolbar. The Windows 95 and NT (left) and Windows 98 (right) dialogs are pretty much identical except for the latter's Go to Desktop button.

- **At the MS-DOS prompt:** While Windows has largely made DOS obsolete, there are still a few things you can do at the command line that you can't do in Windows proper, at least not without adding some extra software. One of those things is display the last-accessed date for all the files in a folder at once.

  In Windows 95 and 98, use:

  ```
  dir /v/p
  ```

  In Windows NT, use:

  ```
  dir /ta/p
  ```

  To see more options for the DIR command, in any version of Windows use:

  ```
  dir /? | more
  ```

See Appendix A: DOS Survival Guide for general instructions on using the command prompt.

To move from one folder to another...

The file you want to do something with often resides in a folder other than the one you're in—so you need to look in another folder to find the file.

Do This in Windows Explorer:

1. Scroll the folder tree (left-hand window) up or down so you can see the drive that has the folder you want to view.
2. If necessary, "expand" the disk's folder tree to show the folders inside it, by clicking the + symbol to the left of the drive icon (see Figure 3).
3. Expand nested folders as necessary until you find the one you want, then click on it.

Figure 3

Navigating the folder tree.

To see the folders on a drive, click the + symbol to the left of its icon. Do the same to see folders inside of another folder.

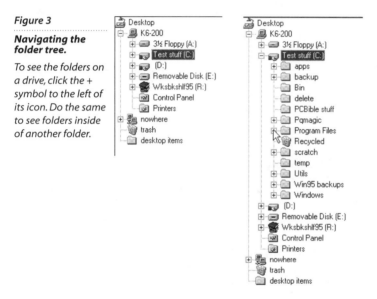

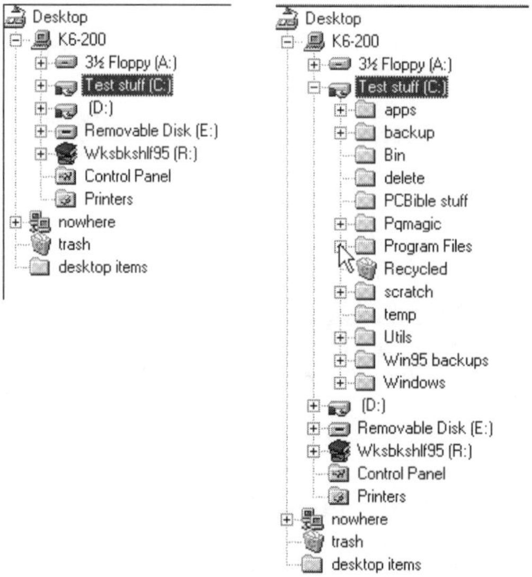

If you prefer, you can navigate the folder tree with the keyboard:

- [↑][↓] Highlight the folder above or below the current one in the tree.
- [↑] Takes you up one level of the hierarchy, to the parent (enclosing folder or drive) of the current folder.
- [→] Expands the current folder.
- hold [Ctrl] while using the arrow keys Scrolls the window without changing the current selection.
- [Home] Takes you to the top of the tree (the Desktop).
- [End] Takes you to the bottom of the tree.
- [Tab] or [Shift][Tab] Switches among the two windows and the "Go to a different folder" drop-down list.

Do This in the Open or Save Dialog:

When you choose File/Open or File/Save, you may not be in the right folder. Here's the least-confusing way to get there when you're not sure where you are.

1. **In Windows 98,** click the View Desktop button. (If you don't see one, follow the instructions for Windows 95 and NT.)

   In Windows 95 or NT, click the Look In menu to drop it down, tap Home, and press Enter.

2. The Desktop is at the top of the folder tree, above both My Computer (your PC's drives) and Network Neighborhood (your network's drives, if any). So from here you can navigate your way down to the correct folder. For example, double-click My Computer, then on C:, then on My Documents.

Another Way to Do It

Using the Find Command: Instead of rummaging around on your hard drive, you can use the Find command to locate a specific folder, then go straight to it. (See the upcoming Cookbook item, "To find files or folders…".) When you've found the folder you want, right-click its icon, and choose Explore from the pop-up menu (see Figure 4).

Figure 4

Opening a folder from the Find dialog.

After you've located a folder with the Find command, you can use the Explore command on the right-click pop-up menu to browse its contents in Windows Explorer.

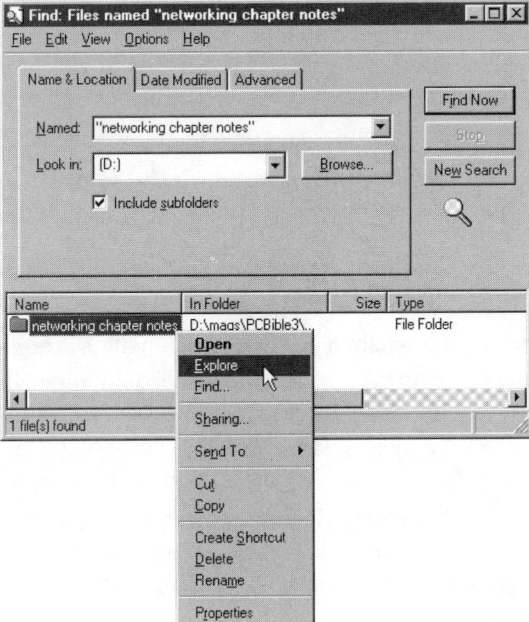

To copy or move files or folders...

Copying and moving files and folders are part of routine disk housekeeping. There are a million reasons to perform these tasks—to copy files from your hard disk to a floppy so someone else can use them, to move files from a working folder to one that contains finished work, and so forth.

When you need to copy a file to a floppy or Zip disk but it's too big to fit, you can use WinZip to split it across two or more disks. See Chapter 12: Windows Add-Ons.

Basic Method

In Windows Explorer, you copy and move using basically the same mouse movements. Dragging and dropping a file from one folder to another on the same disk moves the file; dragging from one disk and dropping onto another copies the file.

1. In Explorer's *right* window, find and select the files and/or folders you want to copy or move. (To select a folder, you must first select the drive or folder that contains it, in Explorer's *left* window. This is traditionally called the *"source" folder.*)
2. Scroll Explorer's *left* window until you see the folder to which you want to copy or move the selected items. (This is traditionally called the *"target" folder.*) Alternatively, you can arrange the windows on screen so that the folder (or a shortcut to it) is visible on the desktop or in another window.
3. Click on the selected files and drag them over the target folder.
4. If you want **to move files around on the same disk**, or **copy them from one disk to another**, just drop the files into the target folder.

Danger Zone: Moving Program Files

When you attempt to copy or move program files, Windows sometimes creates a shortcut to the original .exe or .com file for the program proper, rather than copying or moving the program file. Windows is trying to be helpful—although many old programs written for DOS and Windows 3.1 don't care what folder they're run in, programs designed for Windows 95, 98, and NT typically won't work if they're not run from the folder in which they were installed. The other files in the program's folder, however, will copy normally, and there's no error message. This can lead to unpleasant surprises when you really want the actual program file—for example, when you copy a utility from your PC onto your laptop and don't discover until you're a thousand miles from home that you don't have the complete program.

If you're sure you know what you're doing, and you want to override Windows's helpfulness, use the Alternate Method 1 above for copying/moving program files. If you're moving the program, you'll probably still get a message about how the change may "impact one or more registered programs," but if that's the case you can always move or copy it back.

If you want **to copy files on the same disk**, hold down Ctrl until a + appears on the pointer's tail (see Figure 4); then drop the files onto the target folder.

If you want **to move files from one disk to another**, hold down Shift until the + *disappears* from the pointer's tail, then drop the files onto the target folder.

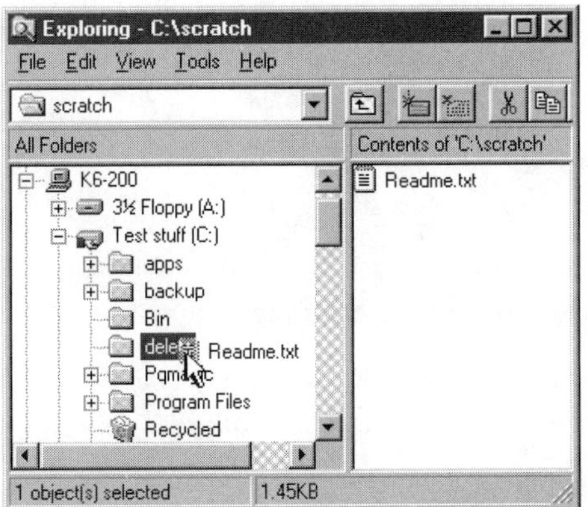

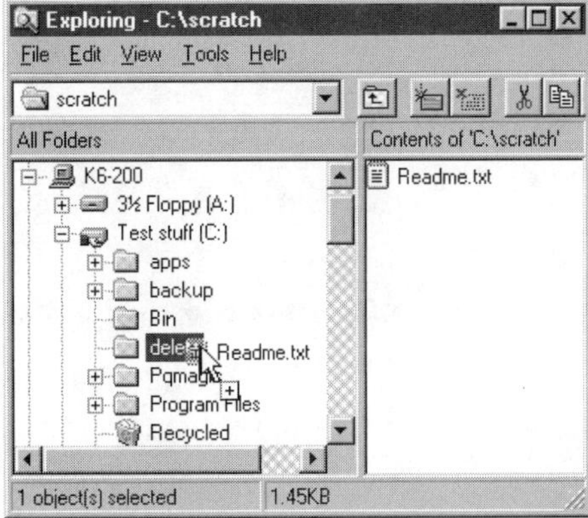

Figure 4

Overriding Windows's move/copy behavior.
Normally, when you drag a file over a folder on the same disk, you see something that looks like the image on the left: the regular mouse pointer, with a ghost image of the file icon and the file's name appearing behind it. If you drop the file, it will be moved to the folder. However, if you press Ctrl*, a + appears on the pointer's tail, indicating that when you drop the files they'll be copied rather than moved.*

Alternate Method 1 (Mouse Only)

When you want to copy files on the same disk, or move them from one disk to another, there's a simpler method. Follow steps 1 and 2 above, for the source and target; then

3. *Right*-click the selected files, drag them to the target folder, and drop.
4. A pop-up menu (see Figure 5) will appear at the cursor position, from which you can choose either Move or Copy files.

Danger Zone: Overwrite Confirmation

If you copy or move a file from one folder to another, and there's a file in the target folder that has the same name, Windows will ask you whether you want to replace the file in the target folder—that is, if you want to *overwrite* the file in the target folder with the file of the same name from the source folder. If you don't want this to happen, you need to rename one of the files before proceeding.

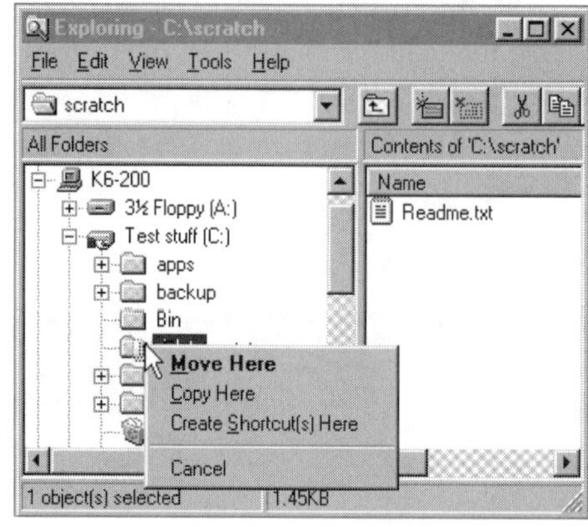

Figure 5

Right-drag-and-drop.

If you drag and drop files or folders with the right mouse button, a menu like this appears. From here you can choose on the fly whether to copy or move the files.

Alternate Method 2 (Keyboard Copy, Cut, and Paste)

A lot of people find the following combination of mouse and keyboard commands to be the most efficient method for copying and moving files.

1. Find and select the files and/or folders you want to copy or move.
2. Press

   Ctrl C (for Copy) if you want to copy

   Ctrl X (Cut) if you want to move

   (Warning: If you use Ctrl X, don't get distracted at this point or you might accidentally delete the files.)
3. Select the target folder, and press Ctrl V (for Paste).

Still Other Ways to Do It

- **Use the Send To menu:** An alternative way to copy selected files or folders to a floppy is to right-click the selection, choose Send To, and then choose 3½ Floppy (A:). You can add folders or other drives to the Send To submenu by creating shortcuts to them in the SendTo folder. (In Windows 95 and 98, the SendTo folder is inside the Windows folder. In NT, it's in the folder that matches your login name, inside the WinNT\Profiles folder.)
- **In My Computer or in the Open view:** To move and copy in My Computer or the Open view of a drive or folder, you can use pretty much the same commands described throughout this section. For drag and drop, open a second window for the target folder. You can also mix and match Windows Explorer and Open view windows—for example, it's often faster to bring up the My Computer window and use its floppy and Zip drives as targets.
- **Shortcuts as targets:** You can use a shortcut to a folder or drive as the target for any of these approaches, and it'll work just as if you'd used the regular icon. You may find it convenient to create shortcuts on your desktop to frequently used folders.

To select multiple files or folders...

If you need to perform the same task (move, copy, delete, etc.) to an entire group of files or folders, you can often avoid time-wasting repetition by selecting all the files first and executing the command once.

Basic Method

1. Start Windows Explorer and go to the folder containing the files you want to select.
2. What you do next depends on which files you want to select:

   To select multiple files manually, hold down Ctrl and click the files one after the other.

   To select several adjacent files, click the first file, hold down Shift, and click the last file. To select adjacent files from a particular range of dates or of a particular type, choose View/Details, click the label at the top of the Modified or Type column, then click and Shift-click to select the desired files (see Figure 6).

   To select everything in a folder, choose Edit/Select All or press Ctrl A.

   To select everything *except* certain files, press Ctrl A; then hold down Ctrl and click the files you want to exclude from the operation ("deselect" them), one after the other. You can also deselect adjacent files by Ctrl-clicking the first file and then Ctrl Shift-clicking the last.

Other Ways to Do It

- **In My Computer or in Open view:** You can use the same multiple file-selection techniques in these windows, which are really just Windows Explorer without the folder tree.
- **With the Find command:** You can use the same multiple file-selection techniques on files displayed in the window at the bottom of the Find dialog. This is handy when you want to **select files in different folders or on different disks.** See the Cookbook task, "To find files or folders" for more on using the Find command.

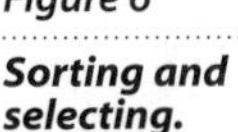

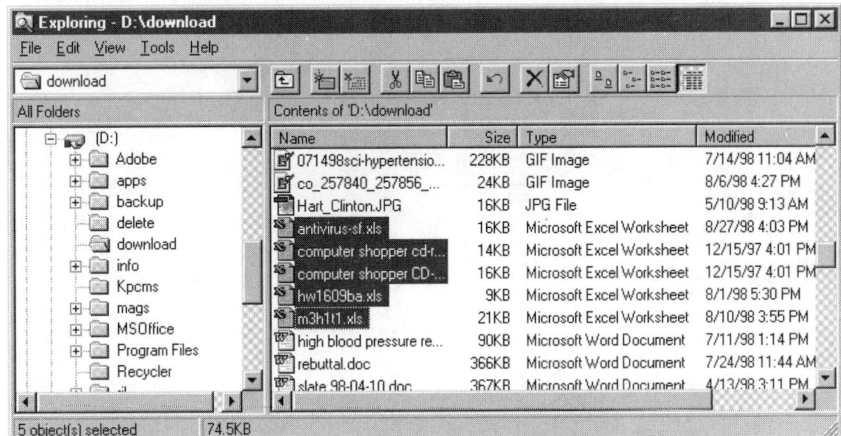

Figure 6

Sorting and selecting.

You can use Windows Explorer's Sort option to make it easier to select a group of files that meet certain criteria. Here I first clicked on the Type button to re-sort the folder. With the files sorted by type, I used click and Shift-click to select all the Excel files.

To create a new folder...

It's faster and easier to find files if you organize them into folders, just as you would papers in a filing cabinet.

Basic Method

1. Start Windows Explorer and go to the drive or folder where you want to create the new folder.
2. Choose File/New/Folder.
3. Type a descriptive name for the folder and press Enter.

Other Ways to Do It

- **Using right-click pop-up menus:** Instead of using the File/New/Folder command, right-click someplace in the blank area of the *right* window, and choose New/Folder.

  You can use this technique to **create a new folder on the desktop.**
- **From the Save or Save As dialogs:** When you choose Save or Save As within an application, the resulting dialog has a Create New Folder button (see Figure 7). Navigate to the folder where you want to create the new folder, and click the button. You can also right-click in the blank space in the file list, and chose New/Folder from the pop-up menu.
- **In My Computer or in Open view:** You can use the same menu or right-click techniques in these windows, which are just Windows Explorer minus the folder tree display.

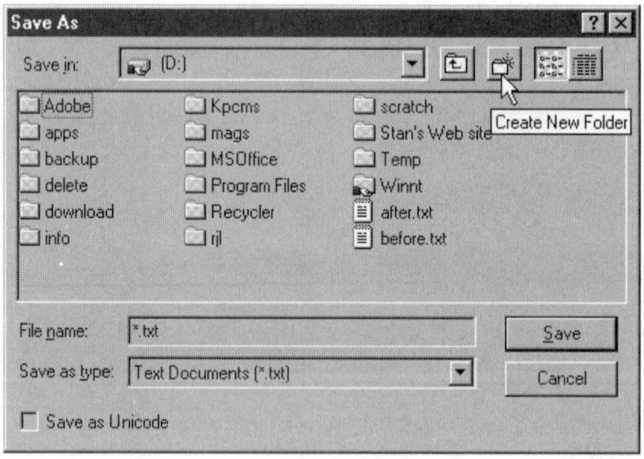

Figure 7

Creating new folders on the fly.

Windows Save and Save As dialogs include a handy Create New Folder button, which you can use on the fly, as you're saving documents.

To delete files or folders...

Old, useless copies of files often confuse matters and always take up disk space unnecessarily. The general rule: if you don't need it, delete it.

Basic Method

1. Start Windows Explorer and select the files or folders you want to delete.
2. Choose File/Delete or press Del.
3. Click Yes if you get a dialog asking if you're sure you want to delete the files.

If you want to **destroy the files immediately**, rather than have Windows keep them in the Recycle Bin for a while in case you change your mind, hold down Shift while choosing File/Delete, or press Shift Del.

Other Ways to Do It

- **Use the right-click pop-up menu**: Right-click the files you've selected for deletion and choose Delete. If you only want to delete one file or folder, there's no need to select it first. To **destroy the files immediately**, hold Shift while you choose Delete.
- **Use the Recycle Bin**: Drag the files you've selected and drop them on the Recycle Bin. To **destroy the files immediately**, hold Shift while you drop the files.
- **In the Find, Open, Save, or Save As dialogs**: You can use the right-click pop-up menu to delete files within any of these dialogs.
- **In My Computer or in Open view**: You can use all the same file deletion techniques in these windows that you use in Windows Explorer.

Danger Zone: File Confirmation

Windows asking "Are you sure?" every time you want to delete a file can get annoying fast. You can switch off this confirmation request in the Recycle Bin's properties dialog (see Figure 8)—but then you'll have no warning if you delete something accidentally.

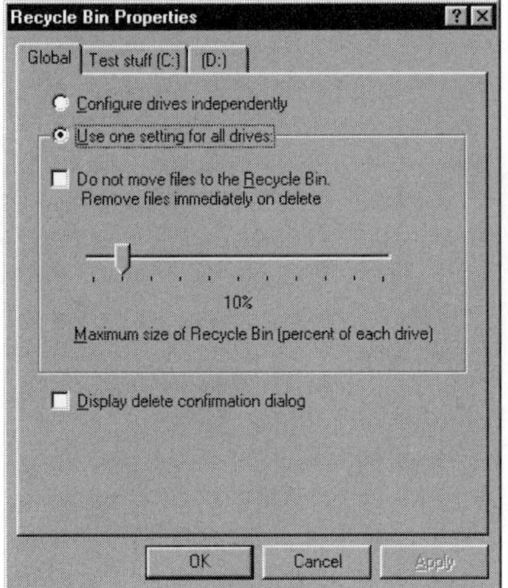

Figure 8

Recycle Bin properties. *Right-click the Recycle Bin and choose Properties to bring up this dialog, where you can switch off the annoying file-deletion confirmation dialog. You can also disable the Recycle Bin entirely by checking the "Do not move files" box—however, unless you're facing an emergency disk-space shortage, that's not such a good idea.*

To rename files or folders...

The usual reason you need to rename a file or folder is to correct a typing mistake you made when you originally named it. But there are a zillion other reasons—for example, to give a document a more descriptive name before you e-mail it to somebody.

Basic Method

1. Start Windows Explorer and select the file or folder you want to rename.
2. Choose File/Rename or press F2.
3. Edit or retype the name as you wish, and press Enter when finished.

You usually can't rename a file if it's currently open (some applications will let you, some won't), and you can't rename a folder if the files in it are open. Sometimes you have to close not just the files but also the application that had them open, before Windows will let you rename.

Danger Zone: Renaming Folders

Renaming applications' folders can cause big problems. Some programs expect to find files in certain places and won't run properly, if at all, when you rename the folder in which they're stored. Unless you really know what you're doing, avoid renaming folders unless they contain data files only.

Other Ways to Do It

- **Use the right-click pop-up menu:** Right-click the file and choose Rename.
- **In the Find, Open, Save, or Save As dialogs:** You can use the right-click pop-up menu to rename a file within any of these dialogs. This is particularly useful when saving, if you want to keep an older version of the file under a new name, like "My File (first draft).doc".
- **In My Computer or in Open view:** You can use the same file renaming techniques in these windows as in Windows Explorer.

To find files or folders...

Even if you're better organized than anyone else, you'll occasionally forget where you saved a file. Other times, it's useful to be able to search more than one folder to find similar or related files.

Finding by Name

1. Start Windows Explorer and go to the drive or folder you want to search.
2. Choose Tools/Find/Files or Folders, or press Ctrl F or F3.
3. If capitalization in the filename will make a difference (usually it doesn't), choose Options/Case Sensitive.
4. Type part or all of the filename, and click Find Now.

Any files whose names contain the search criteria you typed will appear in the window at the bottom of the Find dialog (see Figure 9). You can do most of the tasks discussed in this Cookbook directly on files in that window: Just double-click to open the file and right-click it. Then you can choose a command from the pop-up menu, drag and drop the file onto a printer icon, folder, or application window, etc.

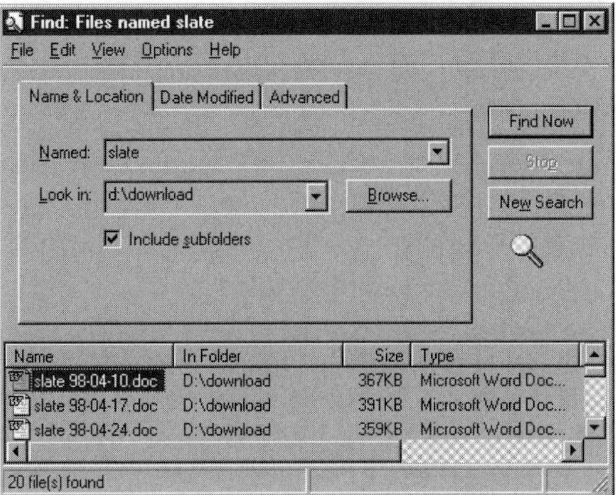

Figure 9

The Find dialog.

After you've found some files, an Explorer-type window appears at the bottom of the Find dialog. Many of the commands discussed in this Cookbook will work right in this window. (The Windows 98 dialog looks slightly different.)

If you don't find the files you're looking for, you can pick another location to search by selecting it from the Look In menu. Choose any disk drive, or choose My Computer to search all drives. If you have more than one hard drive, the Look In menu will contain a Local Hard Drives choice, which skips the floppy, CD-ROM, and any other removable drives. You can also manually type into the Look In field any drive letter (followed by a colon) or the path of any folder.

Finding by Date Modified

To search for files by the date they were last modified, first follow steps 1 and 2 above to get to the Find dialog. Then

3. Click the Date Modified tab.
4. Click the "Find all files created or modified" radio button.
5. Check one of the three date options (see Figure 43), enter the desired range of dates or number of days or months, and click Find Now.

Finding by Type

To search for files of a particular type (Microsoft Excel, Netscape Hypertext, etc.), first follow steps 1 and 2 above to get to the Find dialog. Then

3. Click the Advanced tab.
4. Choose a file type from the "Of type" menu and click Find Now.

Finding by Contents

To search for files containing a particular word or phrase, first follow steps 1 and 2 above to get to the Find dialog. Then

3. In Windows 95 or NT only, click the Advanced tab.
4. In the "Containing text" field, type the word or phrase you want to search for. Click Find Now.

Finding by Size

Searching for files of a particular size is most useful when you're looking for large files that you might be able to delete in order to free up disk space. First follow steps 1 and 2 above to get to the Find dialog. Then

3. Click on the Advanced tab.
4. Click the drop-down "Size is" menu. Choose one of these options based on whether you want to find files over ("At least"), under ("At most"), or of a certain size (leave "Size is" blank).
5. In the box labeled KB, type the file size you want to search for, in kilobytes (or use the arrow buttons to "spin" up the number. Then click Find Now.

Combination Searches

When it's useful, you can use two or more of the Find criteria in a single search. For example, if I've just created and misplaced a spreadsheet containing tax information, I might search my C: drive for all Excel files created in the past day containing "1999" (see Figure 10).

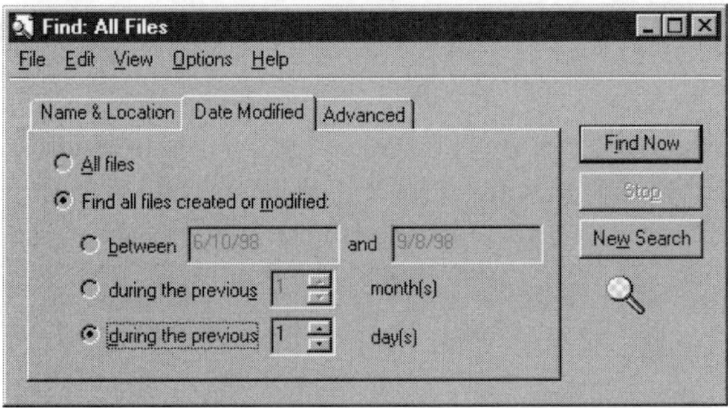

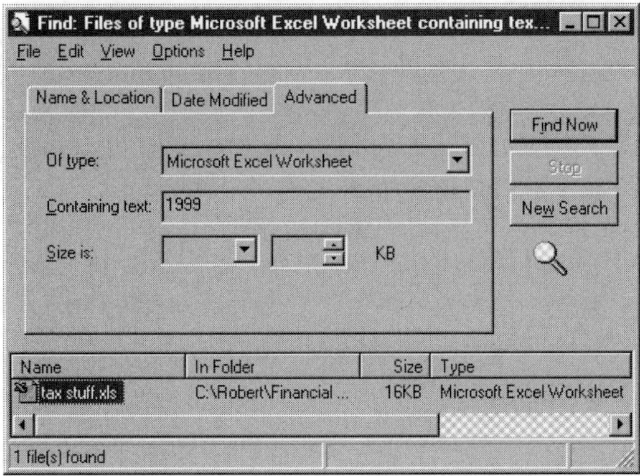

Figure 10

Complex searches.

You can combine any or all of the Find criteria, from all three tabs, into a single complex search. Note that the "Containing text" option will only find plain text. Thus Find was able to detect "1999" in this Excel file because it appears in a cell formatted as text, but Find would miss the same number if it appeared only in cells with number formats. You can hit the New Search button at any time to clear all search criteria and start afresh.

Other Ways to Do It

- **On the Desktop.** You can search My Computer, Network Neighborhood, or any drive or folder for which you've created a desktop shortcut by right-clicking on the desktop icon and choosing Find.
- **In My Computer or in Open view:** Select a folder and choose Find/ Files or Folders, or use the keyboard commands or right-click menu as described above.

To retrieve accidentally deleted files or folders...

Sooner or later, every one of us will accidentally delete a file or folder. Fortunately, you can always retrieve them easily from the Recycle Bin—provided you catch your mistake soon. (Windows constantly deletes the oldest files in the bin to make room for new arrivals.)

Restoring a folder also restores its contents, including any folders within it.

Basic Method

1. Double-click the Recycle Bin on the desktop, or click on it in near the bottom of Windows Explorer's folder tree (left window).
2. Select the files or folders you want to retrieve (see Figure 11).
3. Choose File/Restore (or right-click the files and choose Restore).

Figure 11

The Recycle Bin.

Windows's handy Recycle Bin lets you retrieve files and folders you delete accidentally.

Note that the Recycle Bin does not contain items deleted with DOS commands or by DOS or Windows 3.1 applications.

Another Way to Do It

With the Undo Command: If you catch your mistake immediately, just choose Edit/Undo (or press Ctrl Z) to reverse the deletion. You have to do this immediately, before performing any other Windows operation, and it will undo only the very last command you executed.

Bigger Recycling Bin = Safer Files

If you have a lot of free space on your hard drive, you might as well increase the percentage of the disk Figure allowed for Recycle Bin's storage of files for possible undeletion. (See Figure 12.) The more space Recycle Bin can use, the longer the files can hang around, and the more time you have to notice your mistake. To increase the size of the Bin, right-click the Recycle Bin icon, choose Properties, and move the slider to the right.

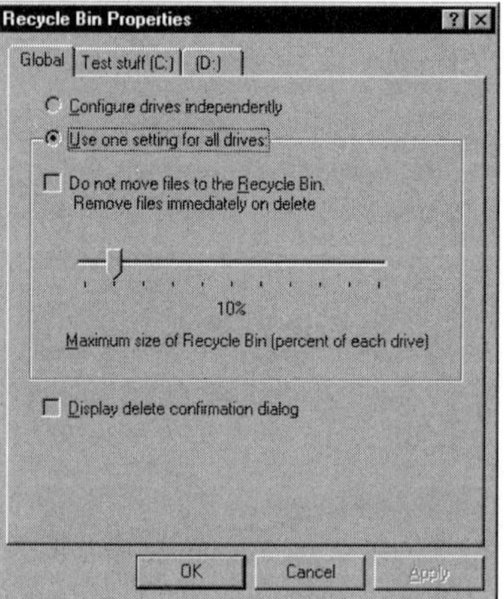

Figure 12

Recycle Bin Settings.

If you've got disk space to spare, drag the slider to the right and the Recycle Bin will hang on to deleted files longer.

Disk Tasks

To format a floppy or other removable disk...

You need to format a new floppy disk before you can use it; the same goes for some other types of removable disks. Formatting lays down the basic information necessary for storing files. It's also the fastest way to erase everything from a floppy or most other kinds of removable disks.

Basic Method

1. Insert the floppy or other removable disk to be formatted.
2. Start Windows Explorer and scroll the folder tree (left) window until you see the drive's icon ("3½ Floppy (A:)" in the case of a floppy).
3. *Right*-click the drive icon and choose Format. If you inserted a brand-new, unformatted disk, Windows 98 may show the hourglass for a long time before the Format dialog appears. (In 95 and NT, the dialog normally appears in a few seconds.)
   - If you're erasing an already formatted disk, check Quick Format.
   - If you're formatting a new disk for the first time, in Windows 95 or 98 check the Full radio button; in Windows NT, make sure the Quick Format box is unchecked. (See Figure 13.)
4. When formatting is done, click OK, then Close.

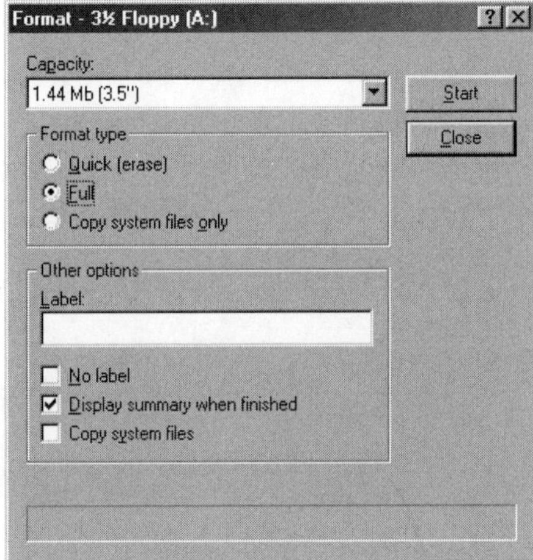

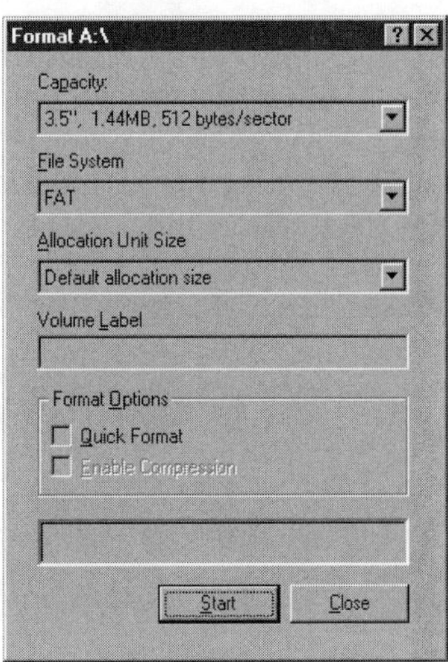

Figure 13

Windows Format dialogs.

To format a brand-new floppy, this is how the Format dialogs in Windows 95/98 (on the left) and NT (on the right) should be set. The Quick Format option does a much faster job of erasing already-formatted floppies, but if you try to use it on a new disk Windows will just spin the hourglass for a while and then offer to do a Full format.

If the Format command fails, close any files you have open on the disk and try again; if the command still fails, you may also need to close the applications in which you opened the files. In some cases, you may have to select another drive in Windows Explorer, and/or close any My Computer or Open windows that are viewing the disk you want to format.

In Windows 95 or 98, you can make the disk bootable by checking the Copy System Files option. However, you'll get a more useful boot disk (particularly in Win98) by using the Startup Disk tab of the Add/Remove Programs control panel. See the "Safety Check" section later in this chapter for more about that function, plus instructions on using Windows NT's closest equivalent, the Repair Disk Utility.

Other Ways to Do It

- **From the Save or Save As dialogs:** You can format a floppy on the fly in the Save or Save As dialog by right-clicking on the 3½ Floppy (A:) icon and choosing Format.
- **In My Computer or in Open view**: Click the floppy icon and choose File/Format (or use the right-click menu).

To copy a floppy or other removable disk...

Sometimes you need to duplicate an entire disk, either to make a backup copy or a copy to give to someone else.

Basic Method

1. Insert the floppy or removable disk you want to copy (the "source disk") into the drive. Have ready the disk that will receive the copy (the "destination disk"). Note that any files on the destination disk will be permanently erased, so if there's anything on the disk you want to keep, make a copy first or grab another disk.
2. Start Windows Explorer, right-click the drive's icon, and choose Copy Disk.
3. Select the drives you want to copy from and to. Unless you have two drives of the same type (an unusual situation), both source and destination drives will be the same (see Figure 14).
4. Click Start, then OK. Windows will display a progress bar as it reads the source disk.
5. When prompted to insert the destination disk, take the disk you're copying out of the drive, insert the blank disk you're copying to, and click OK.
6. If the disk is large or if you're short on memory or disk space, you may have to swap source and destination disks several times. Follow the prompts; when the copy is complete, click Close.

Figure 14

Copying a floppy.

These dialogs show the steps in the Copy Disk command. Note that even though all the removable drives in the PC show up—here, the floppy (A) and a Zip drive (E:)—you can't use this command to copy from one type of disk to another.

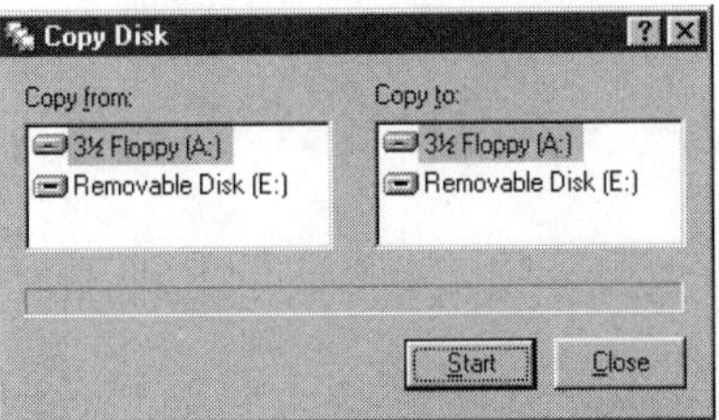

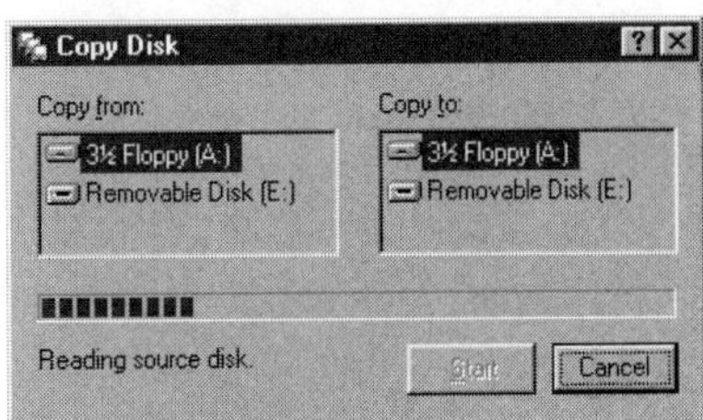

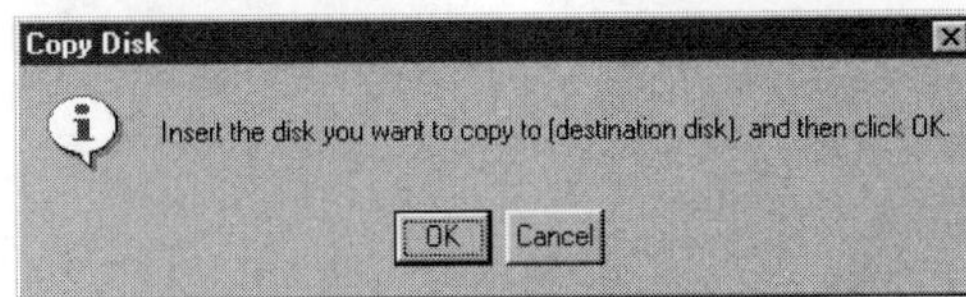

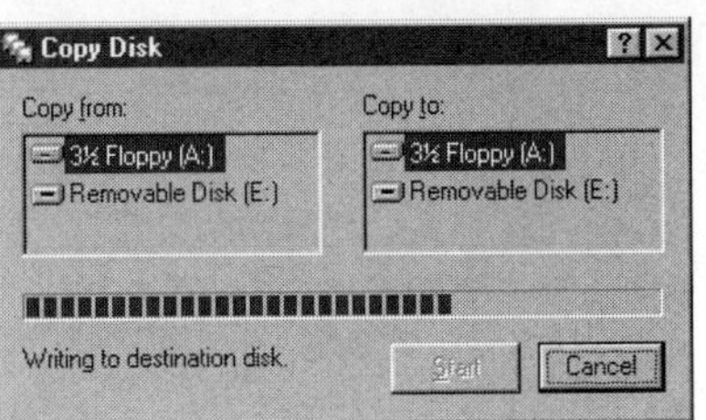

If the copy operation fails, close any files you have open on the disk and try again; if the command still fails, you may also need to close the applications in which you opened the files. In some cases, you may have to select another drive in Windows Explorer, and/or close any My Computer or Open windows that are viewing the disk you want to format.

Other Ways to Do It

- **In My Computer or in Open view:** Select the removable drive's icon and choose File/Copy Disk (or use the right-click menu).
- **From the Save or Save As dialogs:** You can copy a removable disk on the fly in the Save or Save As dialog by right-clicking on the drive's icon and choosing Copy Disk.

Application Tasks

To install an application...

These days, most Windows applications pretty much install themselves, but the process isn't always obvious.

Basic What-the-Heck Method

Stick the CD-ROM in the drive, click whatever button installs the program, and follow the prompts.

Alternate Better-Safe-Than-Sorry Method

1. Look through any printed documentation that came with the program and read any installation instructions. If there are hardware requirements, make sure your PC meets them.
2. Load the application's CD in the drive.
3. A setup menu may appear at this point. If it doesn't start Windows Explorer, right-click the drive and choose AutoPlay. If there's no AutoPlay choice, press Esc to get rid of the menu, and go on to step 5.
4. If the CD's setup menu (see Figure 48) contains an option to view last-minute installation notes that didn't make it into the printed documentation (which is almost always prepared before the programmers have finished writing the program itself), read them. If the instructions are complicated, you might want to print them out before continuing.
5. Start Windows Explorer, and search the disk for files with names like Readme or Read Me. If you find any, open them and see if they have any special installation instructions; again, you might want to print these out.
6. If the CD has a setup menu, click whatever button launches the install routine (see Figure 15).
7. If there's no setup menu, use Windows Explorer to find an application on the CD named Setup or Install, and double-click it.
8. Follow the prompts to install the program.
9. Unfortunately I can't give you much help from that point on, since every application is different. I can give you three tips:
   - You can usually skip over any request that you register electronically; some installation routines, however, insist that you fill out some of their forms before you can cancel the registration.
   - If you do register, don't agree to enter any information other than your name, address, and maybe the program's serial number.
   - If the program asks for your e-mail address, there should be a box you can check (or uncheck) to tell the vendor not to send you junk mail.

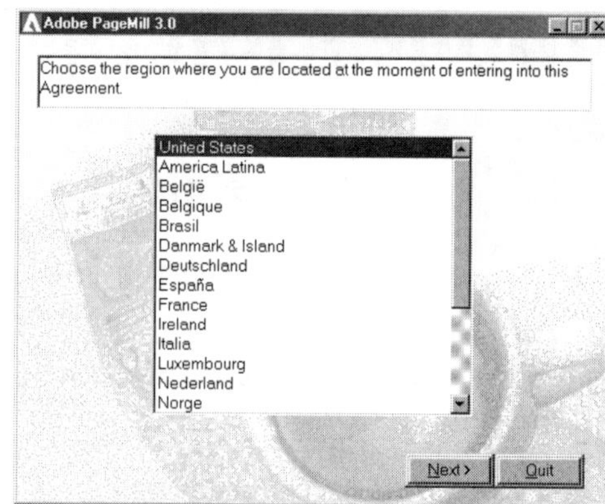

Figure 15

Application setup menus.

You never know what you'll see when you load an application's setup CD—software vendors do all sorts of different things. Often there will be a simple dialog with a Setup, Install, or Continue button. Or sometimes you may get a fancy menu like FileMaker Pro's (left), which includes a button to view the Readme file. Or even something that doesn't relate directly to the program at all, like Adobe PageMill's "where are you" dialog (right).

Other Ways to Do It

- **Installing programs from floppy:** It's increasingly rare, but some small programs are still distributed on floppy disks. Follow step 1 in the Better-Safe-Than-Sorry method, put the diskette in the drive, and then follow steps 5 and 7–9.
- **Using the Add/Remove Programs control panel:** Open the Control Panel, double-click Add/Remove Programs, click Install, and follow the prompts. I don't recommend this approach for beginners because it's too often more confusing than the other methods outlined here.
- **Installing DOS programs:** If there's a Setup or Install application or batch file on the program disk, you can follow the instructions for installing from floppy; otherwise, you'll probably have to install the app manually. For instructions, turn to Appendix A: DOS Survival Guide, and read "Installing an Application" from the DOS Cookbook.

To start an application...

You have to start an application before you can use it.

Basic Method

The standard way to start applications is about as simple as it gets:

- Choose the program from the Start menu.

At least, it's simple if the program's *on* the Start menu. If it isn't, see "Customizing the Start Menu" later in this chapter.

Other Ways to Do It

- **Double-click the program's icon:** Many programs put shortcuts on the desktop. Double-click one, and it'll launch the program. If you want to create your own, see "Using Shortcuts" later in this chapter.
- **Open a document:** When you open a document by double-clicking it, the program that created it will start automatically. See the "To open a file" task later in this Cookbook for useful alternatives to double-clicking.
- **Use a shortcut key:** You can assign a shortcut key (see Figure 16) to any of the items on the Start menu; then you can launch the program from the keyboard at any time. For example, I use Ctrl Alt W for my word processor, and Shift Alt B for my Web browser.

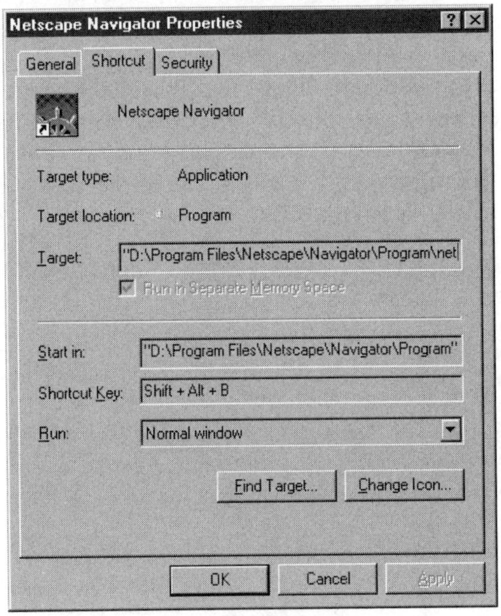

Figure 16

Assigning shortcut keys.

By editing the properties for an application's entry on the Start menu, you can assign a shortcut key combination that will launch the program from the keyboard. See "Customizing the Start Menu" later in this chapter for details on assigning shortcut keys.

To open a file...

To read, edit, or do other work on a file, you need to open it.

Basic Methods Windows provides two basic methods for opening files:

- **Within an application**, choose File/Open, find the file you want, and double-click to open it.
- **Elsewhere**—in Windows Explorer, My Computer, Open view, or on the desktop—just double-click the file you want to open.

Other Ways to Do It

- **On the File menu:** In many applications, a list of recently edited documents appears at the bottom of the File menu. Choose one of the files to open it.
- **With the Documents menu:** The Start menu's Documents submenu contains a list of recently opened documents. Click a file to open it.
- **Drag and drop:** This option is particularly useful when you want to open a document in a program *other than* the one it opens in when double-clicked—for example, let's say you want to open a Web page in an editor rather than your browser. First start the application. Then start Windows Explorer and find the file you want. Rearrange the windows on screen so you can see the application; then drag the file out of Explorer and drop it on the application's title bar (the strip at the very top of the window that shows the program's name).
- **Use the Send To menu:** This is an even easier way to open documents in programs other than the ones they open in when double-clicked. Right-click the file (or a selected group of files) and choose one of the programs on the Send To menu (see Figure 17). To add a program to the Send To submenu, create a shortcut to it in the SendTo folder. (In Windows 95 and 98, the SendTo folder is inside the Windows folder; in NT, it's in the folder that matches your login name, inside the WinNT\Profiles folder.)

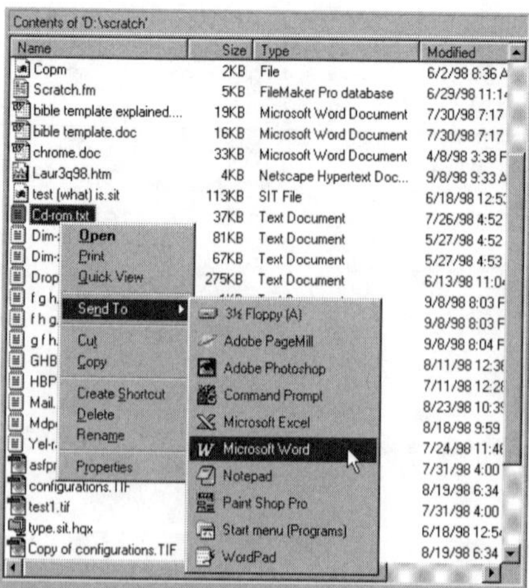

Figure 17

The Send To menu.

The Send To section of the right-click pop-up menu is a great tool for opening a file in an application other than the one that opens when you double-click the file. For example, if I double-clicked this text file, it would open in Notepad; but with Send To, I can open it in Microsoft Word or WordPad. I've also got the menu configured so I can open graphics in Paint Shop Pro or PhotoShop instead of in Paint, and open Web pages in PageMill (my HTML editor), instead of in Netscape Navigator (my browser).

To save a file...

In most programs, if you don't save your work in a file, it'll be gone forever if the power goes off.

Saving a New File

1. After creating a new file in an application, choose File/Save.
2. Navigate to the folder where you want to save the file (see the "To move from one folder to another" task earlier in this Cookbook).
3. Type a name for the file and press Enter.

Saving a Copy of a File

When you want to start a new document by modifying an existing one, and you want to keep the original, follow the above instructions for saving a new file, except in step 1 choose File/Save As instead of File/Save.

Saving as You Work

When working, it's a good idea to save regularly in case of a crash or other data-threatening event. In many programs, you can do that by just pressing the keyboard shortcut Ctrl S. Otherwise, choose File/Save.

Rules for Naming Files

Characters: When naming files, you can use any characters on the keyboard except the following (which have special meanings as noted):

< > Angle brackets (used to redirect command-line program output)

* Asterisk, often called "star" (a wildcard character at the command line)

" Double-quotation marks (used to bracket long filenames that contain with spaces)

? Question mark (wildcard character)

/ Slash (indicates command-line options)

\ Backslash, properly called a "virgule" (separates folders in paths)

: Colon (indicates a disk drive in paths)

| Pipe (redirects command-line program output)

Although you can type both uppercase or lowercase letters in filenames and Windows will (generally) display them the way you typed, it does not otherwise distinguish case. So you can't have a file named MyFile and another named myfile in the same folder.

Windows 3.1 and DOS Compatibility: If for some reason you want to assign filenames that will work in DOS, you must limit the names to eight characters plus the three-letter extension (by default, the extension is hidden by Windows). You can't use spaces (traditionally, underscores are used instead) or any of the following punctuation:

[ ] Square brackets

; Semicolon

+ Plus symbol

. Period (except the one between the filename and the extension)

Windows assigns DOS filenames automatically, but they sometimes can be very confusing. For example, if you save a Word file named Star Wars 4, the DOS name will be STARW~1.DOC; if you then create one named Star Wars 1, its DOS name will be STARW~2.DOC. See Figure 18 for some other examples.

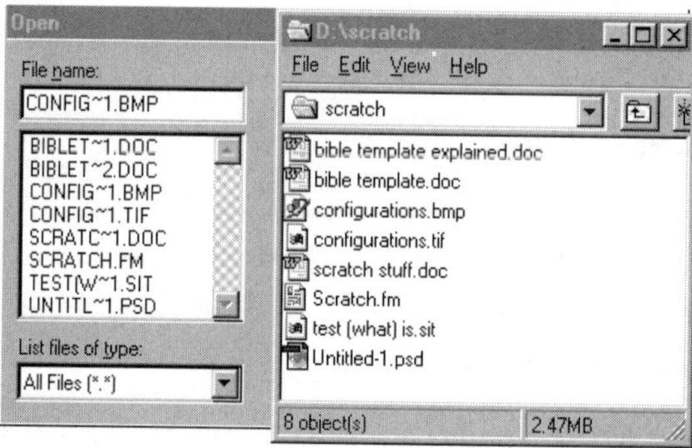

Figure 18

Old applications vs. long filenames.

These two windows are listing the same files. The one on the right is the way they look to modern Windows applications; the one on the left shows the 8-dot-3 names Windows automatically generates for use by old Windows 3.1 and DOS apps.

Maximum Length: Theoretically, Windows filenames can be up to 255 characters long, including spaces (though the actual limit seems, for reasons unknown, to be slightly lower). You'd probably never have a use for such a long filename—however, since that limit is imposed on the full path (for example, C:\My Documents\My File.doc is 27 characters, not 7), it does restrict the number of folders you can nest one inside the other, particularly if each folder has a fairly long name.

To print a file...

Use the Print command to get a paper copy of the current document from your printer. In some cases, you may also use Print to send a fax.

Basic Method

1. Choose File/Print, or press Ctrl P.
2. If you have more than one printer available, on the Printer Name menu choose the one to which you want to send the print job.
3. Set any relevant print options—selected pages, number of copies, etc. (see Figure 19)—and click OK.

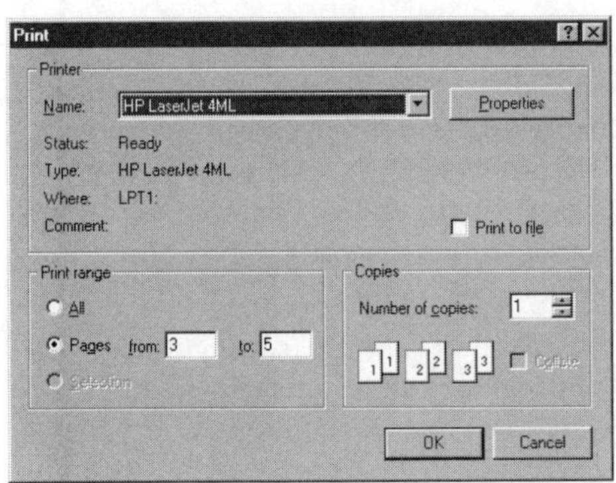

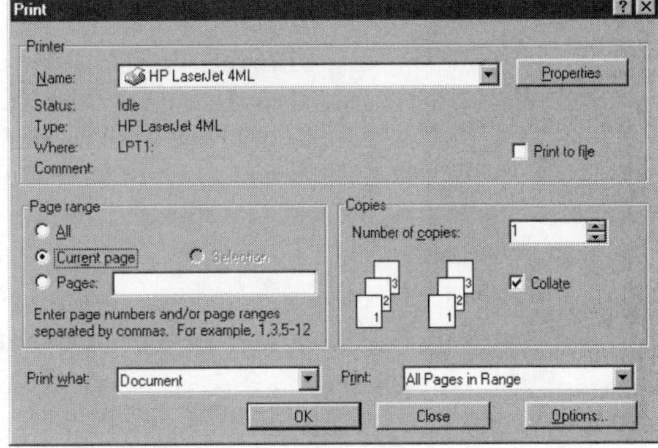

Figure 19

Windows Print dialog.

Exactly what options you get in the Windows Print dialog depends on which printer you've selected; it also depends on the application you're working in, since some programs add their own options to the dialog. At left is the basic dialog I get in most applications; at right is the fancier one I get in Word 95.

Certain applications, like Notepad, will print only to the default printer. In some of these programs, you may be able to change the default printer with File/Print Setup or File/Page Setup. If these dialogs don't have a menu of available printers, you'll have to select Settings/Printers from the Start menu in order to change the default printer., Select the printer you want, and choose File/Set As Default. And don't forget to reset the default printer when you're through.)

Other Ways to Do It

- **Drag and drop:** You can create a shortcut to a printer on the desktop, by dragging the printer icon out of the Printers folder and dropping it on the desktop. Then you can drop files on the shortcut, and they'll print. How useful this is to you will depend on the printer and application: In some cases all you can do is print the whole document to the default printer with the current settings. Experiment with short documents before trying a long one.
- **Use the right-click pop-up menu:** You can right-click a document and choose Print, but this method has the same problems as drag-and-drop.

To switch between programs...

Windows is expressly designed to let you run multiple applications at the same time, so that, for example, you don't have to close your word processor to read your e-mail.

Basic Method

1. Start one application.
2. Start another application.
3. Click the appropriate button in the taskbar to switch back to the first application.

Other Ways to Do It

- **Use shortcut keys:** If you start an application with a shortcut key (discussed in the earlier task, "To Start an Application"), you can switch back to it at any time with the same key-combination. Note, however, that if you start a program using another other method, like the Start menu, and then use its shortcut key, it may start a second copy of the program.
- **Use Alt-Tab:** Hold down Alt and tap Tab, and you bring up a window showing icons for all the programs currently running (see Figure 20). Tap Tab or Shift Tab repeatedly until the program you want is circled, then release Alt to switch to your program. Pressing Alt Tab once switches you back to the last program you left; that's usually the fastest way to switch back and forth between two programs.

Figure 20

Alt-Tab switching.

Holding down Alt and tapping Tab brings up a window with an icon for each program currently running.

Control Panel

- **Navigate the taskbar from the keyboard:** If you prefer the keyboard, or for some reason find yourself without a mouse, you can navigate the taskbar from the keyboard. Press

  Ctrl Esc (or ⊞), Esc, Tab, and →. (If you're using Windows 98 and have toolbars on the taskbar, press Tab to jump from one toolbar to the next, or from the last toolbar to the application buttons.)

  The first application button on the taskbar should be highlighted; tap → to move to the one you want, then press Enter to switch to it.

How to Install Windows

When you bought your PC, unless it was a supercheap no-brand clone it probably came with Windows already installed. Unfortunately, there are all sort of reasons you might end up having to re-install it yourself anyway. A hardware failure or virus might wipe out your original setup, or you might upgrade your hard drive. Sometimes you might even want to start from scratch to purge your system of old, unused software.

In this section, I'll walk you through the steps for installing Windows 98. The process is pretty much the same for Windows 95, so you'll be able to get the idea of what's expected from the outline of the Win98 Setup process. The main difference with Windows 95 is that there's a good chance you'll have to format the hard drive and load CD-ROM drivers manually. (See "Preparing a Hard Disk Manually" for instructions.) During installation, Win95 will prompt you to install a printer, which you can put off 'til another time by clicking Cancel.

Setting up NT is superficially similar. However, it has some radical differences, so I'll discuss those separately in "A Few Notes on Installing Windows NT."

Preparing a Hard Disk Manually

If you're installing Windows 95 or NT, you may have to set up your hard disk and CD-ROM manually before you can install Windows. Unfortunately, there are too many variables for me to provide an exact step-by-step guide, but you'll find an outline below, with tips on getting past the more difficult parts. Do this *only* if you can't get Setup to run any other way.

If you're not familiar with DOS, you might want to read Appendix A: DOS Survival Guide, to familiarize yourself with command-line basics. (This is a fairly advanced task, so if you're new to PCs you might want to get a more experienced user to help.)

1. Get hold of a boot disk. You should have been given one with your PC; if you didn't, get somebody to make you one. You'll need the following files from the same version of DOS or Windows that made the boot floppy:
   - FDISK.EXE (prepares a new hard disk for formatting)
   - FORMAT.COM (formats the disk)

   You'll also need the DOS drivers for your CD-ROM drive. A diskette containing them should have come with your PC.
2. Put the boot disk floppy in the PC's drive and turn on the power.
3. When you see the A: prompt, type `fdisk` and press Enter. Use the menus to create a primary partition and set it active. (Read "Danger Zone: Drive Converter and Large Disk Support (FAT32)" coming up, before enabling large disk access.)

(continued on next page)

Preparing a Hard Disk Manually (continued)

4. When you've finished with FDISK, restart the PC by pressing Ctrl Alt Del (all at once).
5. When you see the A: prompt again, type `format c: /s` and press Enter. Respond to the prompts as necessary to format C:. Once formatting is complete, take the boot floppy out of the drive and press Ctrl Alt Del to restart.
5. When you see the C: prompt, install the CD-ROM drivers. Usually you can do that by typing `a:install` or `a:setup` and pressing Enter. After the drivers are installed, take the floppy out of the drive and press Ctrl Alt Del to restart.
6. Load the Windows installation CD in the drive, type `r:setup` (or for Windows NT, `r:\i386\setup`), press Enter, and Windows Setup should start.

If step 5 doesn't work, you can copy the drivers from diskette and install them manually using the following series of commands, replacing "whatever" with the name of the CD-ROM driver (usually something like cdrom.sys or atapicd.sys). Be sure to type the commands exactly as shown:

```
copy a:whatever.sys c: Enter
copy a:mscdex.exe c: Enter
copy con c:\config.sys Enter
device=whatever.sys /d:cdrom001 Ctrl Z
copy con c:\autoexec.bat Enter
mscdex /d:cdrom001 /L:r Ctrl Z
```

Installing on a Brand-New Drive

If you're upgrading from an existing version of DOS or Windows, skip ahead to "Upgraders Start Here." Use the following steps 1–5 only if you're installing Windows 98 on a new, unformatted hard drive.

1. **Boot the PC.** Put the Windows 98 boot disk that came with your PC into the floppy drive and turn on the power. You'll get a menu with "Start Windows 98 Setup from CD-ROM" highlighted. Put the Windows 98 Setup CD into the CD-ROM drive and close the drawer; then press Enter to continue.
2. **Microsoft Windows 98 Setup.** Read the help text if you want; then press Enter to continue.
3. **Configure unallocated disk space.** Nothing you need to do here. Press Enter to continue.

4. **Enable large disk support?** See "Danger Zone: Drive Converter and Large Disk Support (FAT32)," coming up, to decide which option you want. If necessary, use the arrow keys to change the option, and press Enter to continue.

Danger Zone: Drive Converter and Large Disk Support (FAT32)

During installation, or if you upgrade your system with a new hard drive, you might encounter a dialog asking, "Do you wish to enable large disk support?" You might also encounter the Drive Converter tool on the Start menu. Both of these do the same thing: convert your hard drive into a format called FAT32. The FAT32 format—at least, as this book goes to press—can be read only by Windows 98 and the OSR2 versions of Windows 95, which were only sold installed on new PCs.

Obviously, if you *ever* want to run any other operating system on this PC, you *don't* want to enable large disk support or run Drive Converter.

Like most people, you'll probably find one operating system more than enough. So you might want to consider using FAT32 because it will allow you to format your entire hard disk as a single C: volume. Without FAT32, Windows can't format drives larger than 2GB; for example, you'd have to set up a 10GB hard disk as five logical volumes.

Another FAT32 plus is that on a smaller drive that's quite full, running Drive Converter may increase the amount of free space available. Microsoft also claims that upgrading a drive to FAT32 will improve performance, but in fact it actually makes things run more slowly in many cases.

Drive Converter is a one-way tool: If you try FAT32 and don't like it, Drive Converter can't get you back where you started. If you want to experiment with FAT32, you might consider buying a copy of Partition Magic, a third-party utility that can convert in both directions. (See Chapter 12: Windows Add-Ons, for a little more about this geeky tool.)

5. **Setup is now going to perform a routine check on your system.** Press Enter to start the ScanDisk utility, which will run automatically. (ScanDisk is discussed later in the "Safety Check" section.)

After ScanDisk completes, Setup will copy some files and reboot. From then on, the process is identical to that described in "Upgraders Start Here."

Re-installing from a Restore or Recovery CD

Some brand-name PCs, including most consumer-oriented models from Compaq, HP, IBM, and Sony, come with a CD that will restore the original factory-loaded contents of your hard drive. In most cases, these PCs can boot directly from the CD; sometimes there's a special boot floppy that launches the CD. Typically you get two choices:

- One option restores Windows and preloaded programs to their original state but doesn't touch your data. After you restart, you'll do the last few steps of Windows Setup, just as you did when the PC was new—entering your product key number and your name, setting the time zone, etc. After using this option you'll likely need to re-install most or all of the applications you added to the PC.
- A more drastic option formats before reloading, destroying all files you've created. Obviously this option is best reserved for emergencies, preferably after copying your data files to another disk.

Upgraders Start Here

If you've already got DOS or an earlier version of Windows on your PC, there's no need to boot from a floppy or set up your hard disk: Just run Setup right off the CD.

- **In Windows,** putting the CD in the drive may bring up a "Would you like to upgrade?" dialog box, in which case you can just click Yes. If not, look at the CD with File Manager or Windows Explorer, and double-click on the Setup application.
- **At the DOS prompt,** enter `x:setup` (replacing the `x` with your CD-ROM's drive letter).

Then pick up with step 6, as follows.

When an Upgrade Goes Wrong

When an upgrade to Windows 95 or 98 goes wrong, you can use the Uninstall option to put things back the way they were before. If Windows is running well enough to get to the Add/Remove Programs control panel, open it, select "Uninstall Windows" (see Figure 21), and click Add/Remove. If you can't get into Windows or it's acting too crazy to get to the control panel, boot from a floppy and type this as the command line:

`c:\windows\command\uninstal.exe` [Enter]

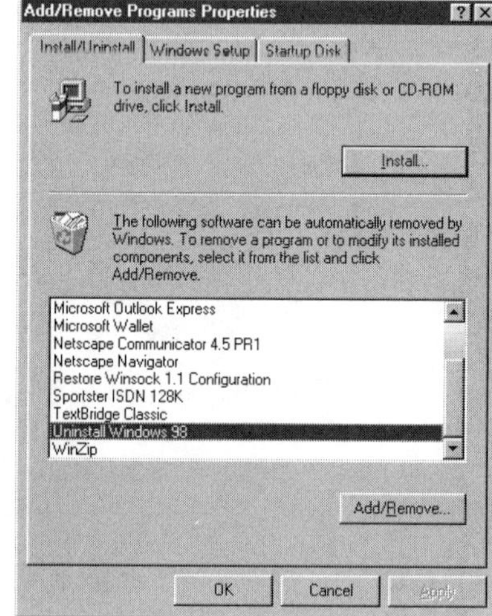

Figure 21

Uninstalling Windows.

6. **"Welcome to Windows 98 Setup…":** This is just an explanatory message from Microsoft. There's nothing you need to do here, so just click Continue.
7. **License Agreement:** Who knows what rights you're signing over to Bill Gates et al. with this lengthy bit of legalese, but if you don't accept it, you can't install the program. Click "I accept the Agreement" (see Figure 22), and click Next to continue.
8. **Product Key.** Here you need to enter the long string of semirandom characters that you'll find either on the back of your Windows CD's case or on the authenticity certificate that came with your PC. (If you don't have either, you may have a pirate copy of Windows, which you can

check by calling Microsoft at 800-RU-LEGIT or sending e-mail to **piracy@microsoft.com**.) You don't have to type the hyphens or worry about capitalization in the product key, and if you get it wrong Setup will give you a warning message and a chance to correct it. (I regularly misread "8" as "B" when typing these things.) After you've entered the number, press Enter to continue.

9. **Upgrade Compliance Check.** You'll get this only when installing an *upgrade* version of Windows onto a hard drive that does *not* have Windows installed already. Stick the original Setup floppy or CD from the earlier version of Windows (or one of the versions of OS/2 that includes Windows) into the PC's drive, and type the drive letter followed by a colon. Press Enter to continue.

Figure 22

Windows 98 License Agreement dialog.

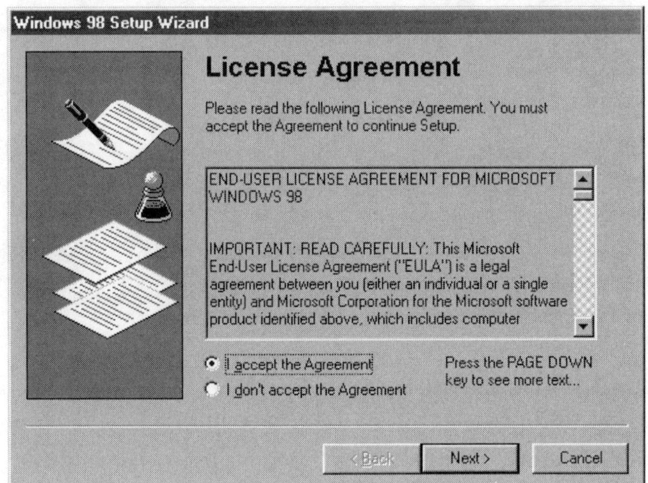

10. **Select Directory.** You can use this option to install Windows someplace other than the default location, c:\windows. ("Directory" is another term for a folder.)

    The main reason you'd want to do that would be to preserve an existing Windows 3.1 installation, so you could still use it sometimes. (Switching between Windows 95 and 98, or between multiple installations of 98, takes more juggling than simply installing them in two different folders. If that's what you want to do, see the discussion of System Commander in Chapter 12: Windows Add-Ons.)

11. **Setup Options.** This dialog determines which set of Windows components will be selected for installation. If you're installing on a laptop, choose Portable; if you're really short on disk space, choose Compact. Choose Custom if you know exactly which components you want to install. Otherwise, stick with Typical. Press Enter to continue.

Saving Uninstall Information

If you're upgrading from an earlier version, Win98's Setup Wizard will offer (see Figure 56) to save the old version, so that if the upgrade doesn't work you can uninstall Win98 and go back. In the event anything goes wrong, having this backup will save you so much time that you should check No only if you simply won't have enough disk space otherwise-in which case you probably shouldn't be upgrading anyway.

Figure 23

Enable Win98 Uninstall.

If upgrading from an old version of Windows, make sure the Yes box is checked so you'll be able to uninstall Windows 98 if it doesn't work.

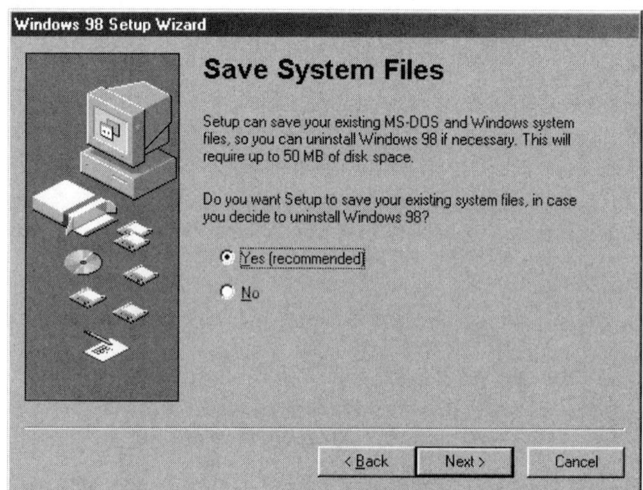

12. **User Information.** Type your name; optionally, press Tab and type your company's name. Press Enter to continue.
13. **Windows Components.** If you want to manually override the component selections of step 11, click "Show me the list of components so I can choose" and press Enter. See the sidebar "Relatively Useless Windows 98 Components" for a discussion of components you might want to dump, and "All That Windows Stuff" later in this chapter for descriptions of all the components. When you've finished making your selections, or if you don't want to make any, press Enter to continue.
14. **Identification.** These three fields distinguish your computer from others on a local network. If you are, ask the network administrator for advice. If you're not, it doesn't really matter what you put here. Press Enter to continue.
15. **Establishing Your Location.** Select your location from the menu, and press Enter to continue.
16. **Startup Disk.** Click Next. If you have a spare floppy handy, follow the prompts to make a startup disk.

If you don't, go ahead and click Cancel to skip this step—but be sure to get a floppy and create a startup disk later, using the Add/Remove Programs control panel.

17. **Start Copying Files.** Click Next, and take a break. It may take Setup half an hour or longer to build your Windows installation, during which time it may reboot your PC one or more times.

18. **Date/Time Properties.** Choose your time zone from the list. I recommend unchecking the "Automatically adjust for daylight savings changes" box, which in some versions of Windows doesn't work right if your PC is running at the moment the clock is turned back. (Windows sets the clock back an hour, then an hour later sets it back again, and so on.) You can click on the Date & Time tab to set the correct date and time if you wish. Click Close to continue, and Setup will spend a few more minutes copying files and configuring Windows.

19. **Enter Windows Password.** Or don't. Unless you plan to share your PC with one or more people, and you all want to have your own settings for desktop colors and so forth, you're better off without a password. (It doesn't make your system any more secure, since you can get past the password dialog by simply pressing Esc, and it delays startup waiting for you to enter the password.)

    Type both a username and password if you want the feature, otherwise type neither; then press Enter to continue.

That's about it. After your PC reboots, you may be prompted to insert diskettes for any hardware for which drivers aren't included on the Setup CD. Outside of that, the next thing you see should be the Windows 98 desktop. "Optimizing Windows" later in the chapter offers some suggestions for changes you might want to make.

Relatively Useless Windows 98 Components

Personally, I have no use for the following Windows 98 components. They're mostly Microsoft Internet products, or add-ons for them, which (as discussed in Chapter 10: How to Choose and Buy Software) I deliberately avoid. You can always add components back in later, using the Add/Remove Programs control panel.

Communications Group. Microsoft NetMeeting (see "What's All That Stuff on the Start Menu?").

Internet Tools. Microsoft FrontPage Express, Personal Web Server (see "What's All That Stuff on the Start Menu?").

Microsoft Outlook Express. This is the basic e-mail program bundled with Win98. There's no reason to install it if you're planning to use other e-mail and fax software. (See Chapter 20: E-mail and Chapter 24: Use Your PC as a Phone or Fax for details.)

Multimedia. Macromedia Shockwave Director, Macromedia Shockwave Flash. I wouldn't install these browser add-ons even if I did use MS Internet Explorer, because I don't find that animation or sound effects contribute anything useful to the Web pages I visit, especially since they tend to crash if I run them.

Online Services. America Online, AT&T, CompuServe, Prodigy, The Microsoft Network. There's no reason to install any of these you don't plan to use. In fact, even if you do plan to use them, you might check first to see if more recent software is available.

A Few Notes on Installing Windows NT

Installing NT is superficially similar to installing Windows 95 or 98, but it's actually a very different operating system. Here's a list of the key differences. (If the technical details make you want to throw up your hands, you'd probably be better off getting a PC with NT already installed, or paying a shop to do the upgrade.)

- NT is so picky about hardware that you have no guarantee whether a system that can run Windows 95 or 98 will be able to run NT. Thus it's always a good idea to check your components against the Hardware Compatibility List on **microsoft.com** before deciding to upgrade. (See the "Windows Resources" section at the end of this chapter for a pointer.)
- NT can't access FAT32 drives. If you've formatted your C: drive as FAT32, you'll have to convert it or re-create it as FAT16 before you can install NT. (See "Danger Zone: Drive Converter and Large Disk Support (FAT32)" for more about that issue.) Alternatively, you can use System Commander (see Chapter 12: Windows Add-Ons) to hide the FAT32 partition from NT—but in that case you'll be unable to see NT's files when running Windows 95/98, and vice versa.
- Only NT can access NTFS drives, so don't format a drive with NTFS unless NT is the only OS that will ever need to access that drive.
- NT sometimes loses track of the CD-ROM partway through the installation process. If you encounter this problem, the simplest workaround is to copy the i386 folder from the NT CD to your C: drive. Then start installation by double-clicking on the Setup application in the folder on the hard disk (or with the DOS command `c:\i386\setup`). If you use this workaround, you may need to set up the CD-ROM drive manually within NT before you can access it.
- If you install NT 4.0 on a machine that's already running Windows 95 or 98, NT Setup will automatically create a dual-boot menu that lets you switch between the two operating systems. It will do the same if you install on a Windows 3.1 machine, but you have to choose to do a new installation (which installs NT into a new folder) rather than an upgrade (which overwrites your existing Windows 3.1 files).

- If you do have a dual-boot setup, I recommend disabling NT's startup disk-check routine for FAT volumes. When NT finds errors on FAT drives, it sometimes "fixes" them by removing whole folders—a cure that's usually worse than the disease. Windows 95/98's ScanDisk, in contrast, usually repairs such errors without losing any of your data (see "Safety Check" section). To exclude drive C: from NT's startup check, run Command Prompt from the Programs section of the Start menu, and enter the following command:

  ```
  chkntfs /x c: [Enter]
  ```

  Repeat the command for any other FAT drives in your system, replacing the `c:` with the appropriate drive letter.

How to Organize Your Hard Disk

Though Windows and its applications pretty much install themselves, they don't give you much help in organizing the contents of your hard disk. You can save yourself a lot of confusion later if you figure out how you want to arrange your folders—*before* you start creating them wholesale.

A well-organized hard disk starts with an uncluttered *root*—that is, the top level of the drive, where Setup puts the Windows and Program Files folders. I've been using variations on this basic top-level plan for years, never creating more than a dozen or so folders in the root so its contents always fit in a single window.

Segregate Data and Applications

Many applications these days are helpful enough to install themselves out of the way, under the Program Files folder. There are still plenty that don't, however, and nine times out of ten such a program will suggest putting the folder that contains its program files right in the root. In the long run, it will be easier to navigate your drive if you use the manual-override option (see Figure 24) to reroute such apps into the Program Files folder. If you run many DOS or old Windows 3.1 programs that can't read long filenames, it's a good idea to create an Apps folder for them.

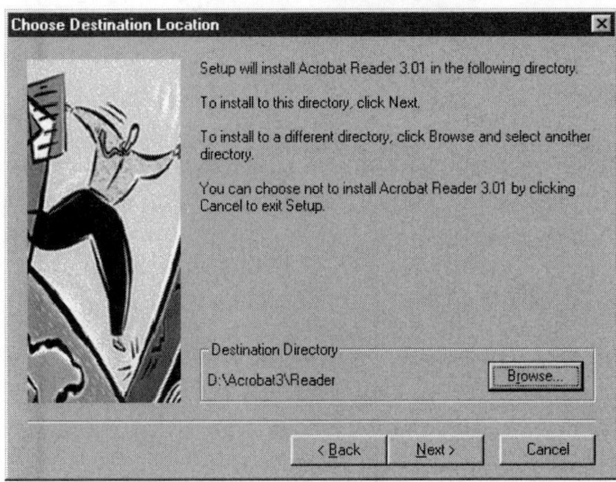

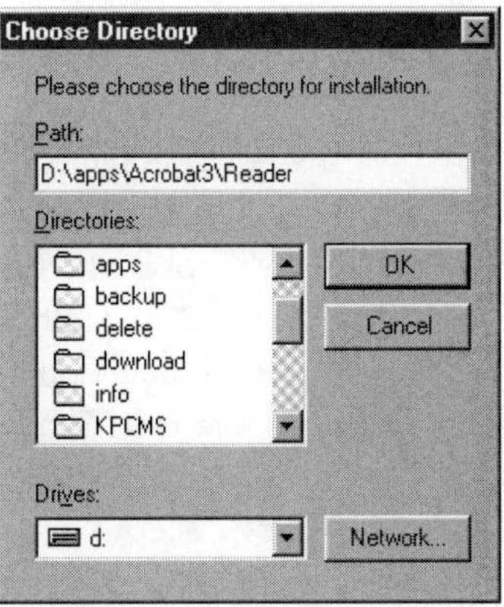

Figure 24

Rerouting program files.

By default, many applications create folders in the root of your hard drive, cluttering it up and making it pointlessly hard to navigate. You can keep things clean by manually rerouting setup utilities and putting programs under the Program Files folder or, in the case of programs that have trouble with long filenames, in an "apps" folder. In this case, clicking the Browse button (left) brings up the manual-override dialog (right). (My main work disk is D: because I reserve C: for testing applications and operating systems.)

Microsoft is increasingly nudging users toward segregating program and data files by creating a My Documents folder and having its applications save documents there by default. However, just dumping everything into My Documents is the digital equivalent of throwing all your papers in a drawer. A better approach is to create a number of folders within My Documents, just as you'd organize papers in folders within your filing cabinet.

Organize by Project

How you organize your business documents depends on what kind of work you do, but you'll be able to find what you need faster if you create a new folder for each project you work on. For example, as a writer it makes the most sense for me to create a folder for each magazine I write for (see Figure 25). Each magazine's folder contains a separate subfolder for each article. Sometimes I create additional folders within a single project—for example, to keep the various drafts of this book's chapters straight, and to keep its hundreds of illustrations out of the way of my word processing documents.

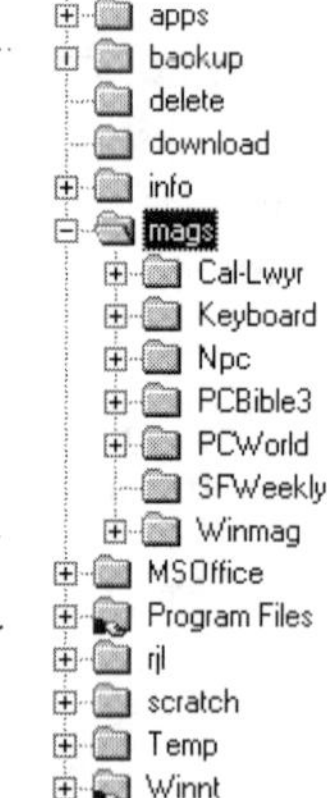

Figure 25

Robert's hard disk.

This section of Windows NT's folder tree is where I keep all my important files. From top to bottom, I've got DOS and 16-bit Windows apps (which don't know about long filenames), backups of software I've downloaded from the Internet, files to be deleted, miscellaneous downloads, files with useful information I refer to frequently, business files ("mags," since I mostly write for magazines) with separate subfolders for each client, MS Office, other program files, personal files (my initials are RJL), scratch files, temp files, and Windows NT.

Here's a setup that might make sense for an accountant: Create a folder for each client, then create a new subfolder for each year's files. Depending on your application, it might make more sense to use dates in filenames instead of subfolders.

If you track clients or projects using account numbers, using the same numbers on your hard drive may make sense. This example is from some attorneys I know: The first level is the four-digit client number, and the second level is a four-digit case number. This approach means temps and people sharing computers don't get confused about where to look for files relating to a particular case. When you're using your employer's computer, it's a good practice to keep your personal files separate from business stuff. That way it will be easier to pack up and move if you change jobs or want to transfer the files to a home computer. Similarly, on your home computer you might want to create separate folders for each business you're involved in (for example, putting work you bring home from the office in one folder, and stuff related to your spouse's self-employment in another).

Temporary Holding Areas

It's a good idea to create folders in which to hold files temporarily, before you know where they should go or after it makes sense to care. For example, all my communications programs dump incoming files into a "download" folder, which serves as a kind of in-box. A "scratch" folder contains files I don't need to keep but don't feel absolutely safe about deleting yet. A "delete" folder contains files that I can trash as soon as I'm finished with them, like files I download only to print out. (One big advantage of multi-GB hard disks is that most of us no longer need to worry about wasting storage space.)

All by themselves, applications often create temporary files, which are supposed to be deleted automatically but often aren't. When they aren't deleted, serious problems can occur: Even a 10GB disk will fill up in a few months if a misbehaving program leaves a 50MB pile of garbage on the disk every time you run it—and if there's no space on the hard disk, Windows tends to run slowly and crash a lot. Whenever possible, I set up applications so that they create their temporary files in the Temp (c:\temp) folder, from which I occasionally delete any accumulated garbage files. (Windows 98's Disk Cleanup tool supposedly handles this automatically.)

None of these organization strategies is likely to be a perfect fit for you, but the basic ideas should help you figure out your own plan of attack. One thing's for sure: Don't accept the dump-everything-in-My Documents default. Eventually you'll end up with a zillion documents and a very cumbersome, slow-scrolling folder. Trying to figure out what you have to keep and what you can purge or archive in a folder that large will be a huge headache.

Using Disk Compression

If you're running short on hard disk space, you can use Windows's built-in data compression to fit the same data in less space. There are two different approaches to this task.

Volume-Level Compression. Used by the DriveSpace utility (see Figure 26) in Windows 95 and 98, volume-level compression is basically like moving everything on your C: drive into one single giant .zip archive. (See the WinZip discussion in Chapter 12: Windows Add-Ons, for a discussion of .zip files.) The archive file lives on a normally invisible "host" volume, which DriveSpace uses to create a virtual C: drive. From your point of view, it seems you've magically gained more free space on C:.

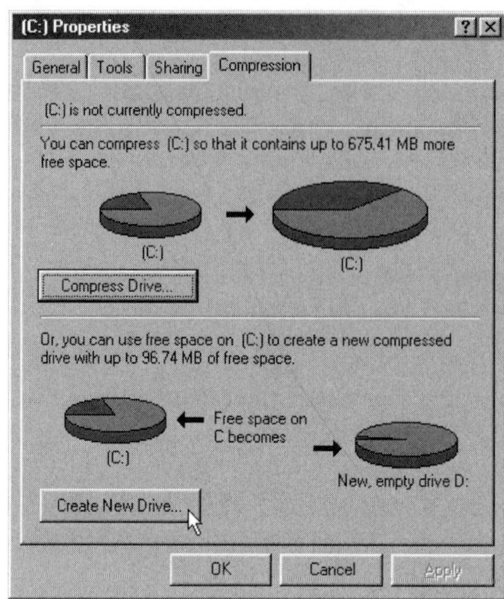

Figure 26

Drive Space.

DriveSpace's cons are that the initial compression can take hours, and other operating systems (including DOS, Windows 3.1, and NT) can't read compressed drives. Also, it's one more thing that can go wrong: In my experience, disk errors on drives compressed with this method are likely to damage a larger number of files, more seriously, than they would on regular uncompressed drives. Consequently, I recommend putting only backed-up files on a compressed drive, and leaving new files on an uncompressed volume until they've been backed up.

1. **To run DriveSpace,** right-click on the drive you want to compress, and click the Compression tab.
2. **To compress the whole drive**—which I don't recommend—click Compress Drive. The system will run a disk test, then chug along compressing files, probably for some hours, and will finally prompt you to reboot.

   To create a new, empty compressed drive using some of the drive's free space, click Create New Drive, type the amount of space you want to use in the "Using… MB" field, and click OK. Leave at least 100MB free space on the uncompressed drive for virtual memory and temp files.

3. **You can increase or decrease the size of the compressed drive** (that is, reallocate space between the uncompressed and compressed drives) at any time by running DriveSpace (in the System Tools section of the Start menu) and choosing Drive/Adjust Free Space. Just like initial whole-drive compression, this process can take hours.

4. **Run Compression Agent** (Start/System Tools) to use alternate compression methods that fit the same data into less space. The trade-off is that these methods take more CPU horsepower and might result in a noticeable slowdown on older PCs—but if you do notice that performance degrades, you can always switch back.

File-Level Compression is built into NT and is a much cooler approach. You can compress a whole drive, the contents of selected folders, selected files, or any combination. This feature is only available on NTFS drives (see "Which Windows Version Is Right for You?" earlier), which is kind of annoying, although it ensures that you won't accidentally make files on FAT drives unreadable by Windows 95 or 98—an easy mistake if, like many NT users, you dual-boot back and forth regularly. I don't know of any downside to NT's compression—in my experience it's been 100% reliable. And since other operating systems can't access NTFS drives anyway, it doesn't make any difference whether the files are compressed or not.

To use it NT file compression, just right-click on the file, folder, or drive you want to compress, check the Compress box, and click OK (see Figure 27). If you want to compress a whole drive or a set of nested folders, check the "Also compress subfolders" option in the dialog box that appears, and click OK. Check "Display compressed files with alternate color" in Windows Explorer's View/Options dialog to make it easy to tell which files are compressed and which aren't. If you want to use compression but your drive's not formatted with NTFS, see the discussion of the Convert command under "More Stuff Worth Knowing About" later in the chapter.

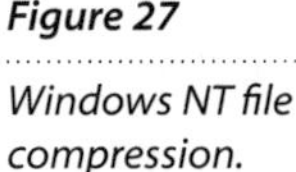

Figure 27

Windows NT file compression.

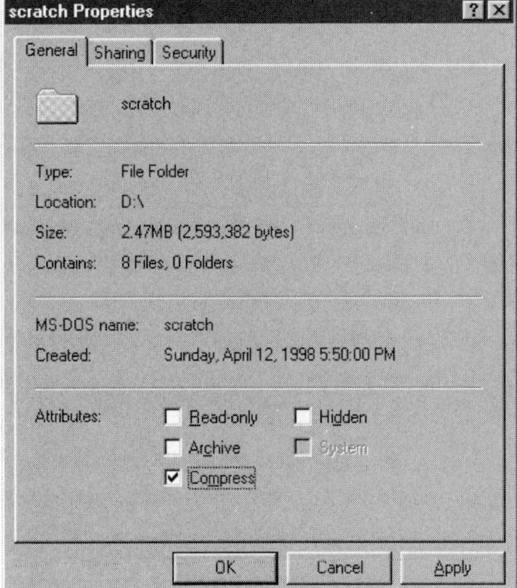

Safety Check

Windows includes important tools for keeping your system running smoothly and your data safe. Here, you'll find out how to use them.

Create an Emergency Boot Disk

If your computer fails to start normally, you'll need a floppy disk to stick in drive A and boot from, so you can assess the problem. If you didn't create a startup disk when Setup gave you the option during installation, here's how to make one. First, make sure you have a high-density floppy disk that is either blank or that you don't mind erasing (you needn't format it first). Then follow these steps:

In Windows 95 or 98

1. Choose Settings/Control Panel from the Start menu.
2. Double-click Add/Remove Programs.
3. Click the Startup Disk tab and then click Create Disk. Insert the diskette when prompted.

When Windows finishes creating the disk, you can use the floppy to boot your computer, whereupon you'll land at the DOS prompt. The disk includes DriveSpace drivers to let you access a compressed hard drive, along with the command-line tools you need to format, partition, and add system files to a drive. Also included are utilities for editing text files, correcting disk errors, changing file attributes (so you can modify a read-only file, for example—see "About File Attributes" later in this chapter), and importing and exporting system Registry files (complicated settings files you'll hopefully never need to touch).

In Windows NT

You can't boot NT from a floppy the way you can Windows 95 or 98. NT does, however, let you create a *repair disk*.

1. Choose Run from the Start menu.
2. Type `rdisk` and press Enter.
3. If you didn't just install NT, click Update Repair Info. This updates files in the Repair folder (under Windows NT's own folder) to reflect any new hardware or other relevant configuration changes you've made.
4. Click Create Repair Disk. Insert the diskette when prompted.

When you boot from the repair disk, it uses the files in the Repair folder and on the NT Setup CD to attempt to rebuild your damaged NT installation.

Regular Maintenance Checklist

To keep your computer running at its best, you need to clean up and tune your system regularly. Windows 95 includes a few simple utilities for the purpose. Get into the habit of following the regimen below on a regular basis and in the order shown.

1. Scan for viruses.
2. Check your hard drive.
3. Back up your hard drive.
4. Defragment your hard drive.

Step 1: Scan. Windows doesn't come with a virus scanner, though many PCs ship with one installed, and Microsoft bundles one with the Plus! 98 package. See Chapter 9: Protect Your Data, for some recommendations.

Step 2: Check. Glitches happen. When applications crash or otherwise flub up, your disk drive's file structure and even the files themselves can be damaged. ScanDisk (CheckDisk in NT) looks for and corrects these problems. Here are the basic steps. (If you have both Windows 95 or 98 *and* NT installed, follow steps 1–4 in Windows 95/98 first to run ScanDisk. Then reboot to NT and repeat the same steps to run CheckDisk.)

1. Right-click on the drive's icon in Windows Explorer or My Computer and choose Properties.
2. Click the Tools tab and click Check Now (Figure 28).

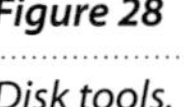

Figure 28

Disk tools.

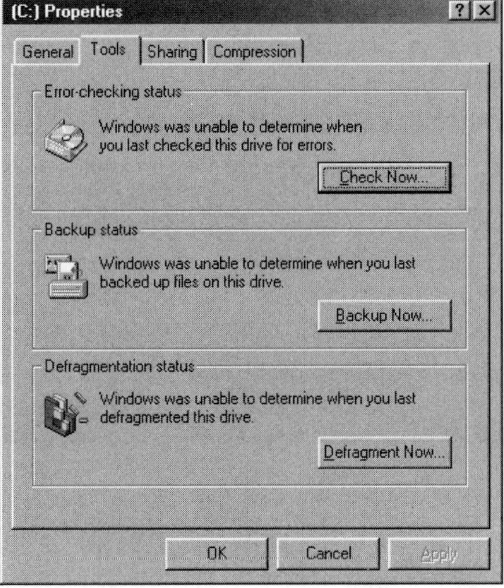

3. Set the options (see Figure 29). Make sure "Automatically fix errors" has a checkmark. The "Thorough" option (listed as "Scan for and attempt recovery of bad sectors" in NT) checks the disk for physical defects—use this option occasionally to prevent errors from happening in the first place.

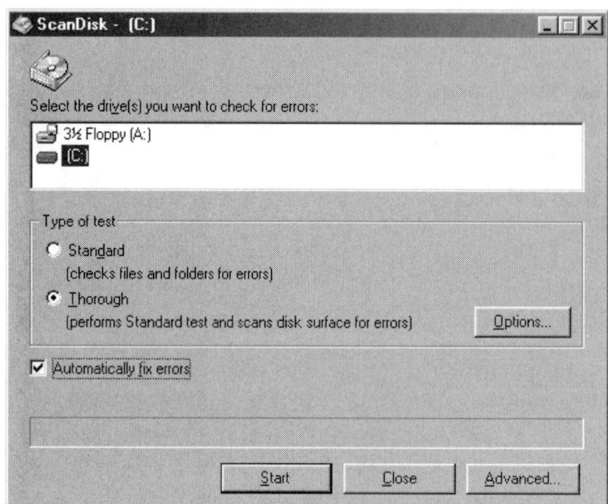

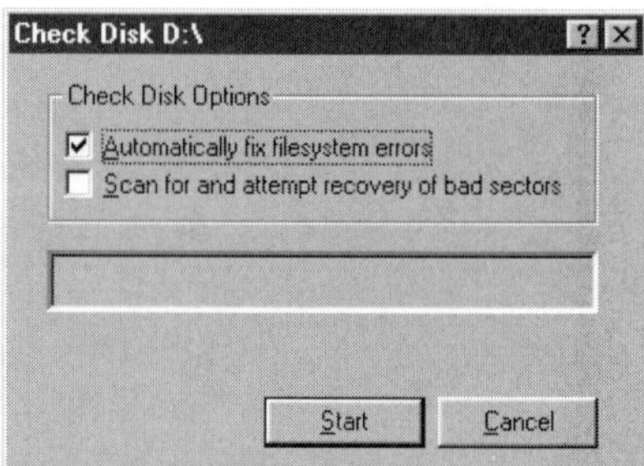

Figure 29

ScanDisk and CheckDisk.

4. Click Start. If you chose the Standard option, the process should take no more than a few minutes. If you chose the Thorough option, the process will take a while—as much as an hour or more if you have a huge hard disk. While it's running, Windows NT can't scan drive C: or the drive NT's own program files are stored on; instead, it runs a check the next time you restart it.

When the check is done, the utility will present a summary of its work. For example, by default, ScanDisk converts lost file clusters into files and stores them in your top-level folder (root directory) with names like FILE0000.CHK, FILE0001.CHK, and so on. If an application crashed recently, you can try opening those files to see if there's anything worth salvaging inside. If they're garbage, throw them in the Recycle Bin.

Step 3: Back Up. The version of Microsoft Backup that comes with Windows 95 and 98 can back up to tape or any kind of removable disk; the one in NT is tape-only. If you have some backup software that came with your tape or removable drive, it's probably a better tool, but Backup will get the job done. (See Chapter 9: Protect Your Data, for more about backup drives and software.) Using Windows's Backup is simple:

1. Insert a formatted tape or disk in the drive you're going to back up to.
2. Right-click on the drive's icon in Windows Explorer or My Computer and choose Properties.
3. Click the Tools tab and click Backup Now.

After this, continue with the steps that match your Windows version:

In Windows 95:

4. If necessary, click OK to get past the "Welcome..." and "Backup has created..." messages.
5. Choose File/Open File Set and double-click on Full System Backup.
6. Click Next Step, select the tape or drive you want to back up to, and click Start Backup.

In Windows 98:

4. Choose "Create a New Backup Job," click OK, choose "Back Up My Computer," click Next, choose "All selected files," and click Next.
5. Specify the tape or drive you want to back up to. (Select a drive by choosing File and using the Browse button to create the backup file on the appropriate disk.
6. Make sure "Compare..." and "Compress..." are checked, click Next, and click Start.

In Windows NT:

4. Click the checkbox next to the drive(s) you want to back up.
5. Check "Verify After Backup" and "Backup Local Registry"; then click OK.

A big downside of the Backup utility versions in Windows 95 and NT is that they work only in those operating systems. If you have a complete disk failure and have to reformat your hard drive, you have to re-install Windows from the Setup CD before you can run Backup and use its Restore option to restore your files.  Windows 98 has a more efficient method for restoring: You can boot from the Startup Disk (see "Create an Emergency Boot Disk") and then run the System Recovery utility right off the CD. When you see the A:> prompt, enter the following commands to start the utility (replace the `d` in the first command with your CD's drive letter):

```
d: [Enter]
cd tools\sysrec [Enter]
pcrestor [Enter]
```

This will create a minimal Windows 98 installation and then restore your files automatically.

Step 4: Defrag. Unlike real filing clerks, computers don't store files all in one place—they store bits and pieces of them anywhere they can find free space. Eventually this *fragmentation* can slow disk performance as your computer jumps all over the drive to access all of one file. Disk Defragmenter reverses the problem by consolidating both files and free disk space. Here's how it works in Windows 95 and 98:

1. Right-click on the drive's icon in Windows Explorer or My Computer, and choose Properties.
2. In the Tools tab, click Defragment Now. If you're running Windows 98, it starts defragging immediately; if you're running Win95, click Start to begin the process (see Figure 30).

Windows NT doesn't have a defrag utility built in, but you can get one by buying Norton Utilities for NT, discussed in Chapter 12: Windows Add-Ons.

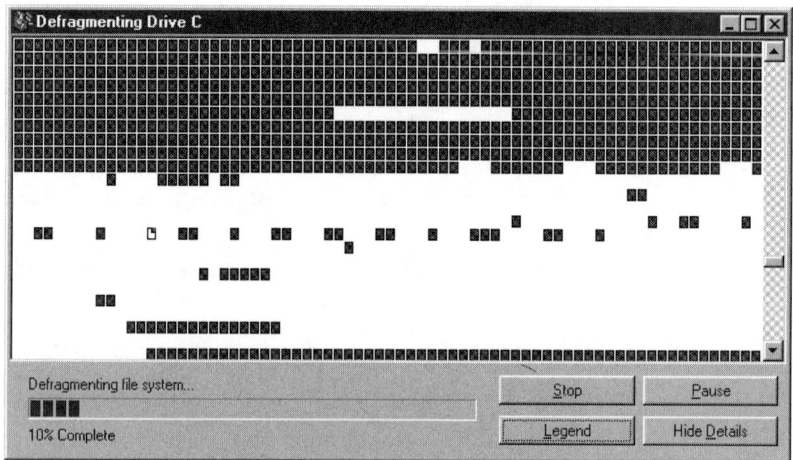

Figure 30

Disk Defragmenter.

All That Windows Stuff

Windows is nominally an operating system, but it's also an ever-expanding bundle of programs, utilities, reference documents, and less categorizable goodies. A full installation of Windows 98, for instance, has a dozen items on the desktop, over 50 programs on its Start menu, another 20-odd in the Control Panel, and yet more hiding on the hard disk or awaiting manual installation from the CD.

Here's a brief guide to help you figure out what you've got and what you can do with it (or do without). The most useful tools are discussed in depth elsewhere in the book. Some oddball ones are discussed only here, so in a few cases I'll go into some detail.

What's All That Stuff on the Desktop?

Microsoft keeps changing what it sticks on the desktop, and PC vendors often add extra stuff, so there's no telling exactly what you'll see when you first turn on a new PC or install a new version of Windows. It's fairly likely you'll see most of the following (and most of which are pictures in "The 10-Minute Windows Tour" earlier in this chapter).

- **My Computer.** Double-click and you'll get a window showing your PC's drives and a few special folders, like the Control Panel and Dial-Up Networking. You can manage your PC's files and folders by double-clicking on the drive icons to open them, but Windows Explorer is considerably more flexible and powerful. Right-click and you'll bring up the System control panel.
- **Recycle Bin.** See the "Delete files or folders" and "Retrieve accidentally deleted files or folders" tasks in the Cookbook.
- **Network Neighborhood.** The network counterpart of My Computer. See Chapter 25: Networks: Connecting PCs.
- **My Documents.** A shortcut to the folder where Microsoft applications save their files by default. See "How to Organize Your Hard Disk" for tips on using it intelligently.
- **Inbox** or **Outlook Express.** The basic e-mail program bundled with Windows 98. See Chapter 20: E-mail.
- **Connect to the Internet.** (Windows 98 only) Launches the Internet Connection Wizard; see Chapter 19: Getting On the Internet.
- **Internet Explorer.** Microsoft's Web browser. See Chapter 21: The Web and Browsers.
- **The Internet.** (Windows 95 and NT only) Initially, runs the Internet Setup Wizard (see Chapter 19: Getting On the Internet). Once a dial-up connection is set up, runs Internet Explorer.

The following three items are basically clutter and can be safely deleted.

- **Set Up the Microsoft Network.** An advertisement to encourage you to use Microsoft as your Internet service provider. Before you buy, see Chapter 19: Getting On the Internet.

- **My Briefcase.** This widget's supposed to help you transfer files between desktop and laptop, or between work and home PCs, but it doesn't work reliably. For alternatives, see "Exchanging Files with Your Desktop PC" in Chapter 3: Notebook PCs.
- **Channel Guide.** A sort of electronic billboard Microsoft hopes to use to advertise its Web sites and those of companies with which it has made various technology or marketing deals.

Some PC vendors put the company logo on the desktop. See "Customize the Desktop" for instructions on changing it.

What's All That Stuff on the Start Menu?

The Start menu is a sort of filing system for applications: Almost any program you install in Windows will add at least one icon to it, and more complex programs may add a whole set of menus. The following is a guide to the parts of the Start menu that belong to Windows. If something doesn't appear in your menus, you may be able to add it using the Windows Setup tab of the Add/Remove Programs control panel.

- **Windows Update.** (Windows 98 only) If you've got an Internet connection, choosing this item takes you to a Web page (Figure 31) with downloadable upgrades and bug fixes that Windows will install automatically. If you let it, the Update page will check your system to see what hardware and software you've got, and create a custom menu containing only things you haven't installed.

Upgrades are sometimes buggy, so it's a good idea to get a recommendation from an expert or a good computer magazine before installing; it's also wise to check your PC manufacturer's Web site for recommendations and alternative updates that may be more suitable for your hardware.

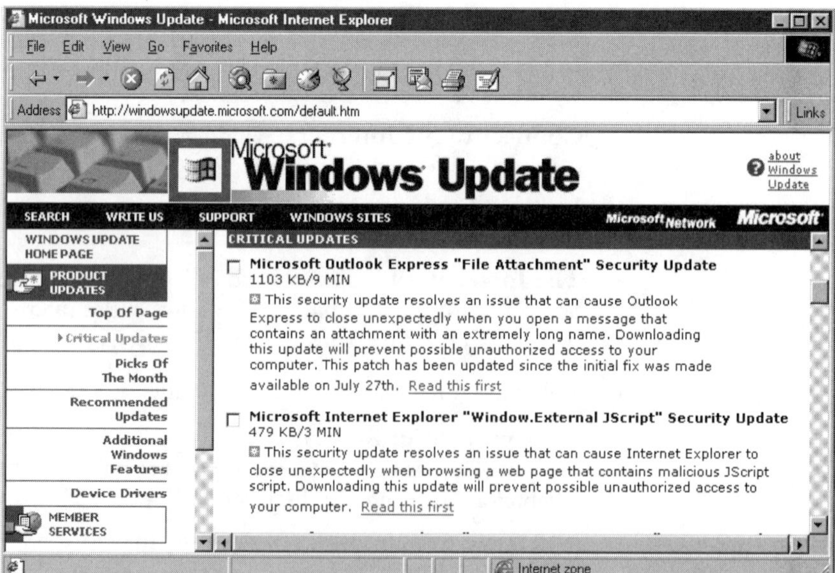

Figure 31

Windows Update.

- **Programs.** A folder where well-behaved programs install themselves. We'll look at its contents below.
- **Favorites.** If you use Microsoft Internet Explorer as your Web browser, you can access your bookmarks from this menu. It also doubles as yet another place where Microsoft can clutter up your computer with plugs for its other products and services.

- **Documents.** The 15 documents you most recently opened appear in this menu, where you can easily get to them even if you're not sure where they are.
- **Settings submenu.** Access to the Control Panel and other basic Windows settings. We'll look at its contents shortly.
- **Find.** See the "Find files or folders" task in the Windows Cookbook for tips on using the Find Files or Folders command. "Find Computer" is similar except it looks for servers on a local network.
- **Help.** Windows's online Help system. Sometimes helpful, too often not. In Windows 98, the Help appears in a variation of the Internet Explorer browser, and often includes links to Web pages.
- **Run.** Lets you enter text commands, as you would at the DOS prompt. Sometimes useful for starting programs that Windows doesn't show on the Start menu, like the Registry Editor (`regedit`) or the System Configuration Editor (`sysedit`).
- **Log Off.** (Windows 98 only; in Windows 95 and NT, this is an option in the Shut Down dialog.) If you've configured Windows (via the Users control panel) to be shared by two or more people, this item lets you switch from one user's settings to another.

Unlike Windows NT's similar feature, logging off Windows 98 does nothing to secure your computer—anyone with access to the PC can access any of its files, with or without a password.

- **Suspend.** (Windows 95 only. In Windows 98, use the "Stand by" command on the Shut Down menu.) Puts your PC into power-conserving standby mode; the screen will go black. Press any key or move the mouse to turn it back on. It may take a few seconds for the screen to come back, and there may be another delay of a few seconds when you enter a command that accesses the hard drive.
- **Shut Down.** Lets you turn off or restart your computer.

  In Windows 95 and 98, also lets you switch to MS-DOS mode for running DOS apps that don't behave under Windows.

  In Windows 98, also lets you put the system into power-saving mode (see "Suspend" above).

  In Windows 95 and NT, also lets you log off and log on as a different user.

In Windows NT, a logged-off workstation is secure, and if necessary it can be configured so that users can't access other users' files.

Settings Submenu

- **Control Panel.** See "What's All That Stuff in the Control Panel?"
- **Printers.** Open this folder to add another printer to your system, change your default printer, or adjust the settings of your printers. To pause or purge printing jobs or tweak a printer's properties, right-click on the printer's icon and make your choice from the pop-up menu. To see a window from which you can manage a list of currently printing jobs, double-click on the printer's icon.

- **Taskbar.** See the "Customize the Taskbar" section coming up later.
- **Folder Options.** (Windows 98 only) Same as choosing View/Options in Windows Explorer or My Computer. See "Customize the Desktop."
- **Active Desktop.** (Windows 98 only) Opens up the Display control panel with the Web tab selected. See "Customize the Desktop."

Programs Submenu

- **StartUp submenu.** Any program you add here will be run automatically when Windows starts. If you're trying to get rid of something that's loading at startup, however, you won't always find it here—apps can also be started from the Registry. In Windows 98, you can stop those programs from launching by using the System Configuration Utility, which is part of the System Information utility (discussed in the Accessories submenu section below). In 95 and NT, you have to edit the Registry manually. (See Figure 32.)
- **Microsoft Exchange.** (Windows 95 only) See "Inbox" under "What's All That Stuff on the Desktop?"
- **MS-DOS Prompt.** Opens a DOS session. If a DOS program won't run properly, try using the Shut Down menu's option, Restart in MS-DOS Mode, instead (not available in NT).
- **Windows Explorer.** Runs the Windows File Manager. See the Windows Cookbook for detailed instructions on using it.

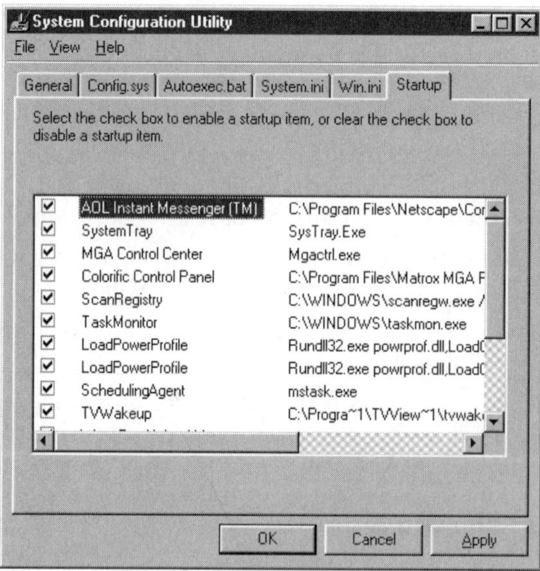

Figure 32a

Blocking Startup apps.

If an application starts when Windows does, but there's no icon for it in the StartUp folder, it's probably being launched from the Registry. In Windows 98, run System Information from the Start menu, choose Tools/System Configuration Utility, open the Startup tab, and uncheck any programs you don't want to run.

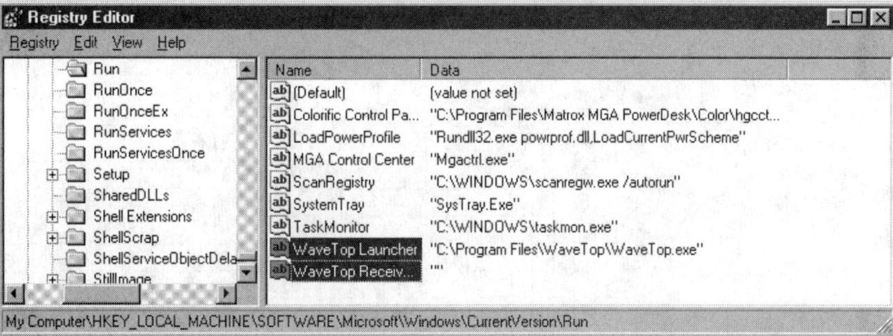

Figure 32b

Blocking Startup apps.

In Windows 95 and NT, choose Run from the Start menu, type `regedit` *and press* Enter. *Just as if you were navigating nested folders in Windows Explorer, open HKEY_LOCAL_MACHINE, SOFTWARE, Microsoft, Windows, and then CurrentVersion. Look in the folders whose names start with Run. Select the offending program(s), press* Delete *and click OK. Close RegEdit and your changes are saved automatically.*

Accessories Submenu (under Programs). The items under Accessories vary from one version of Windows to another, and reflect whatever other Microsoft products you may have installed. Here's an alphabetical list:

- **ActiveMovie Control.** (Windows 98 and Windows 95 OSR2.5 only) An audio and video player that can handle various formats, including *streaming* ones designed for playing over the Internet or private networks. In this context, the word "Control" is Microsoft-speak for a program that can add capabilities to another program such as a Web browser.
- **Accessibility Wizard.** (Windows 98 only) Helps set up special Windows options for people with impaired vision or physical limitations.
- **Backup.** Back up your hard drive. See Chapter 9: Protect Your Data, for more details. (In Windows NT, Backup is in the Administrative Tools submenu.)
- **Calculator.** Works like a pocket calculator. Choose View/Scientific if you want access to trig and binary math functions.
- **CD Player.** See "Playing Audio CDs with Your PC's CD-ROM Drive" in Chapter 4: Disks, Hard and Otherwise.
- **Character Map.** Helps you find special characters (accented vowels, bullets, and so on) and paste them into documents. Choose the font you want from the Font list box, double-click on the character you need, click the Copy button, switch back to your document, and choose Edit/Paste. You can also use Character Map to find out how to input special characters from the keyboard: Click the character you want, and look for its keystroke in the window in the bottom-right corner.

If the characters in the Character Map window are hard to make out, click and hold down the mouse button to get an enlarged view (see Figure 33).

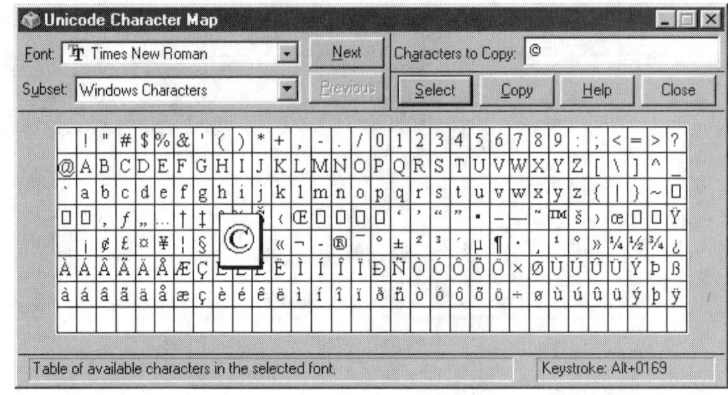

Figure 33

Character Map.

Holding down the mouse button pops up a larger image of the selected character.

- **Clipboard Viewer.** Shows the contents of Windows' Clipboard, where things are stored when you use the Copy or Cut command. In Windows NT, this utility also includes the ClipBook, a sort of clippings file that can store the Clipboard's current contents for retrieval later. (If you've used a Mac, you're probably familiar with this feature already.)

You can install ClipBook in Windows 95. In the Add/Remove Programs control panel, display the Windows Setup tab and click the Have Disk button. Use the Browse button to install the ClipBook from the Other\Clipbook folder on the Win95 Setup CD.

The ClipTray utility in the Windows 98 Resource Kit (discussed later in this chapter) is somewhat similar.

- **Compose New Fax.** (Windows 95 and 98 only.) Launches Microsoft Fax. See Chapter 24: Use Your PC as a Phone or Fax.
- **Cover Page Editor.** (Windows 95 and 98 only.) A utility that's installed with Microsoft Fax. See Chapter 24: Use Your PC as a Phone or Fax.
- **Compression Agent.** See "Using Disk Compression" in this chapter.
- **Dial-Up Networking.** Contains your Internet dial-up connection settings (sometimes called "DUN connectoids"). Even though DUN looks like a folder in Windows 95 and 98, and the connections look like files, they don't actually exist as such on your hard disk. Windows NT organizes connections in a more logical dialog box (Figure 34).
- **Direct Cable Connection.** This Windows utility lets you set up a network connection between laptop and desktop by connecting their parallel or serial ports with a special cable—no network required. It's harder to use than it ought to be, but once you've got Direct Cable Connection figured out it's a fast way to transfer large quantities of data.

If you have trouble getting Direct Cable Connection working, you may need to install the IPX protocol using the Network control panel.

- **Disk Cleanup.** (Windows 98 only) Deletes junk files from your PC's hard disk.

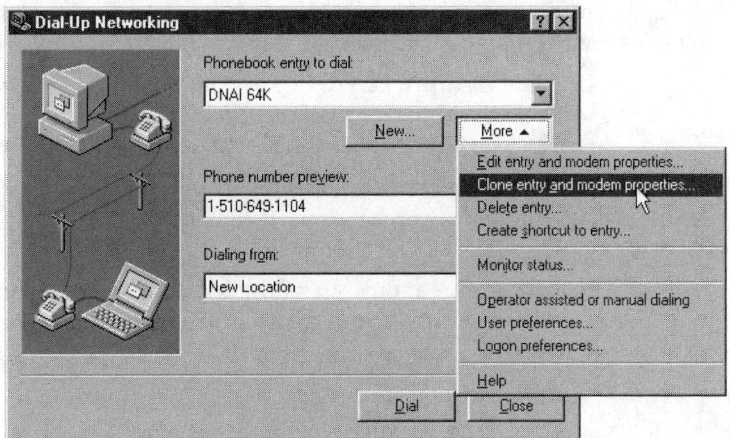

Figure 34

Windows NT's Dial-Up Networking dialog.

- **Disk Defragmenter.** (Windows 95 and 98 only; see discussion of Norton Utilities in Windows Add-Ons for an NT defragger.) Reorganizes files scattered around your hard disk to improve performance. See "Safety Check" in this chapter.
- **Drive Converter (FAT32).** See "Danger Zone: Drive Converter and Large Disk Support (FAT32)" in the "Installing Windows" section.
- **DriveSpace.** See "Using Disk Compression" in this chapter.
- **FreeCell.** Solitaire card came: a more difficult version than the basic Solitaire.
- **Hearts.** (Windows 95 and 98 only) A digital version of the popular card game. You can play it with other users over a local network.
- **HyperTerminal.** You can use this basic modem communications program to access old-fashioned dial-up BBS systems (now nearing extinction thanks to the Web) and Internet servers that require telnet (ditto).

You can download a free upgrade with improved features at **`hilgraeve.com/htpe.html`**.

- **Imaging.** This program does double duty as the control panel for some scanners (though it doesn't work with mine), and as a fax viewer and annotation tool for later versions of Microsoft Fax (see Chapter 24: Use Your PC as a Phone or Fax). It also has some basic graphics file-conversion capabilities that might be helpful if there's nothing else available.
- **Inbox Repair Tool.** (Windows 95 only) Windows 95's bundled e-mail program was apparently so buggy that it needed its own repair tool. See Chapter 20: E-mail, for better alternatives. [[Migrated to Win98 if previously installed under Windows 95]]
- **Interactive CD Sampler.** Another batch of advertisements from the friendly folks at Microsoft. Also includes some trial versions you can install and check out.

- **Internet Explorer.** If it appears in the Accessories submenu, this is probably a long-outdated version that was bundled with Windows 95 or NT.
- **Internet Setup Wizard.** If it has this name and appears in the Accessories submenu rather than the Internet Explorer submenu, this wizard is probably an outdated version that was bundled with Windows 95 or NT.
- **ISDN Connection Wizard.** Helps you get a supported ISDN adapter up and running, if you have one. (See Chapter 19: Getting On the Internet.)
- **Magnifier.** (Windows 98 only) A sort of virtual magnifying glass for the visually impaired. Puts a window at the top of the screen with a zoomed-in view of the area currently under the mouse (see Figure 35).

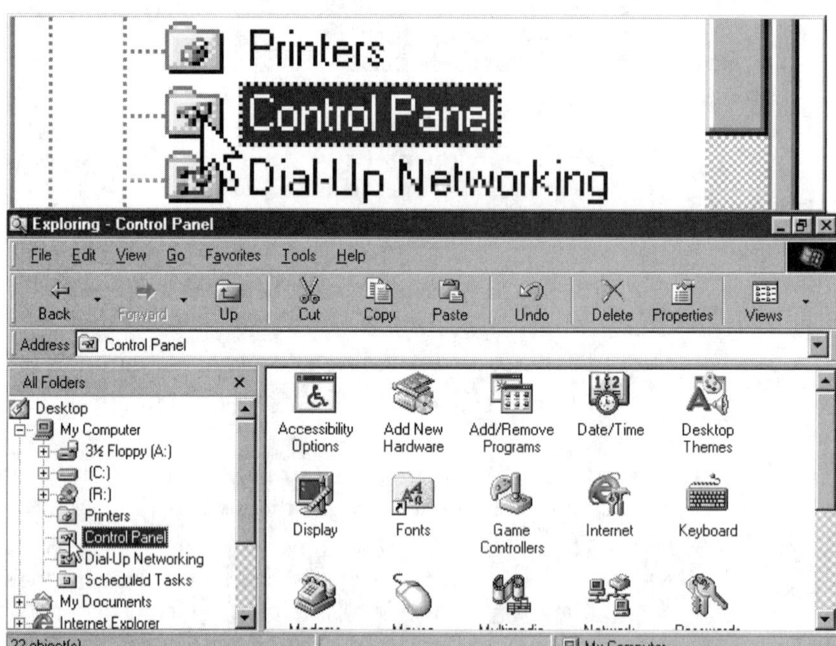

Figure 35

Windows 98's Magnifier.

- **Maintenance Wizard.** (Windows 98 only) Sets up your system to run Disk Cleanup, Disk Defragmenter, and ScanDisk automatically at specified times. Really useful only if you leave your computer on all the time; if you turn it off when you're not working, the scheduled tasks are likely to interrupt your work. Would be much more useful if it could run an unattended Backup as well.
- **Media Player.** Lets you play multimedia files—exactly which file types you can play will depend on what hardware and software are in your system. Choices typically include digital audio, MIDI music, and digital video in Microsoft's AVI format.
- **Minesweeper.** A digital version of the Submarine board game. Challenging; some people find it addictive.

- **Net Watcher.** Displays network activity. May be useful for troubleshooting.
- **Notepad.** A text editor sometimes useful for editing configuration files.

WordPad is more useful than Notepad—especially because you can't open files larger than around 50K in Notepad. (The NT version of Notepad doesn't have that limitation.)

- **Online Registration.** (Windows 95 only) Lets you register your copy of Windows with Microsoft over the Internet rather than by mailing back the registration card. There's no great advantage to doing either, unless you want to get Microsoft advertisements in the mail.
- **Paint.** If you've never used a paint program before, you might find Microsoft Paint a lot of fun, but it's not a serious graphics tool—in fact, it's not even much of a toy. See Chapter 17: Painting, Drawing, and Other Graphics Software, for a look at some real paint programs.
- **Phone Dialer.** Lets you dial phone numbers from the computer's keyboard. Only works if you have your telephone on the same line as your modem, and even then it's not as handy as a PIM or contact manager that lets you look up a name in an address book and push a button to dial the phone. (For more about such programs, see Chapter 16: Databases.)
- **Pinball.** (Windows NT and Plus! versions of Windows 95 only) This game is a virtual pinball machine designed to show off Windows' s graphics and audio capabilities.
- **Request a Fax.** (Windows 95 and 98 only) Launches Microsoft Fax. See Chapter 24: Use Your PC as a Phone or Fax.
- **Resource Meter.** (Windows 95 and 98 only; NT's equivalent is the Performance tab in Task Manager) Displays memory usage. May provide an early warning if you're getting out-of-memory errors.
- **ScanDisk.** Finds and repairs any errors on your hard disk. See "Safety Check."
- **Scheduled Tasks.** Launches programs automatically at specific times. Not very useful because it can't automatically run Backup, the single most important task for programs like this. (It launches the program fine, but Backup then just sits there waiting for you to start it manually.) If you want to do this kind of thing, consider getting a copy of Unisyn's AutoMate (**`unisyn.com/automate`**), which can schedule just about any task.
- **Solitaire.** e: The popular card game pastime. Choose Game/Deck and select the palm tree design for a cute surprise.
- **Sound Recorder.** Use this basic audio tool (see Figure 36) to record from a microphone, audio CD, or other sound source to digital audio (.wav) files on your hard drive, which you can use as custom system-event noises selected in the Sound control panel. See Chapter 18: Sound and Video Editing, for a detailed look at the kind of audio tasks you can perform on your PC, and a discussion of the more sophisticated sound-editing tools available.

To chose which sound source (microphone, audio CD, sound card's aux input) gets recorded, double-click on the volume control on the taskbar, choose Options/Properties, click Recording, and click OK.

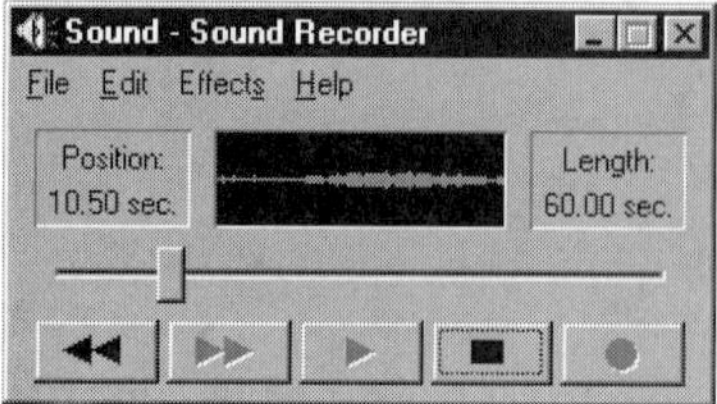

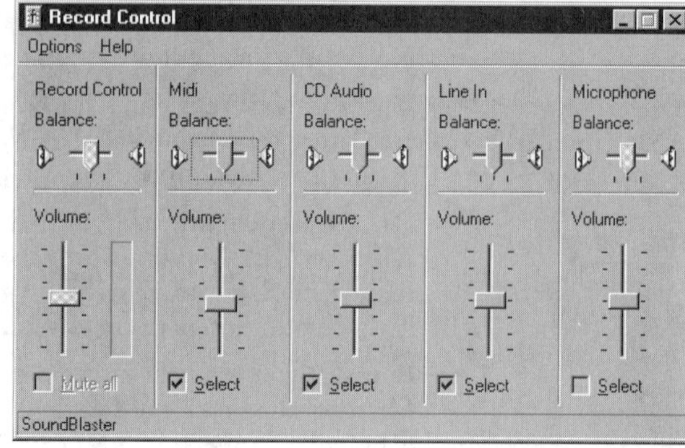

Figure 36

Sound Recorder and Audio Mixer.

The controls for this simple audio recorder (left) work like a tape deck. Press the red button to start recording, the square button to stop. To control the inputs for the recorder, use the Record section of the Volume Control's mixing console (right). Always uncheck the microphone's Select box to turn it off when you're recording from another source.

- **System Information.** (Windows 98 only) An enhanced version of the tool that comes with Microsoft Office, this utility not only displays all sorts of useful info about your PC and its software, it also includes a menu of useful troubleshooting and configuration tools. Unless you're a hard-core Windows geek, you generally won't want to run these except when instructed to do so by a tech support agent, but here are a couple of exceptions:

To tell the Add Hardware Wizard to take another stab at configuring a hardware device after you've told it to stop trying, choose Tools/Automatic Skip Driver Agent and re-enable the device.

To stop the "fast shutdown" feature if it doesn't work right on your PC, choose Tools/System Configuration Utility, click Advanced, check "Disable fast shutdown," and click OK twice.

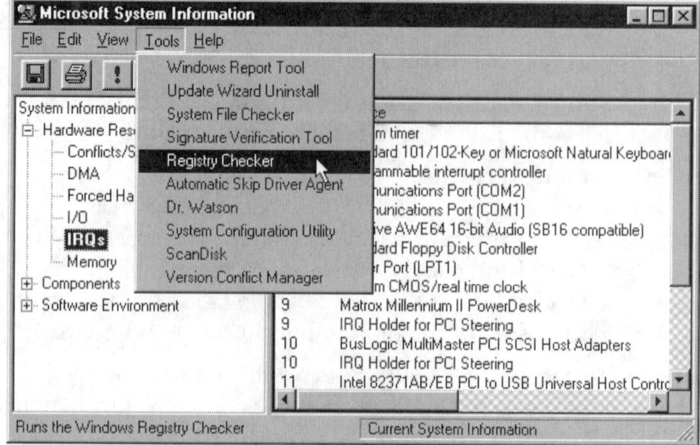

Figure 37

Microsoft System Information's Tools menu.

- **System Monitor.** Useful for troubleshooting performance problems.
- **Trial Programs.** Advertisements for more Microsoft products you can spend money on.
- **Volume Control.** A mixer you can use to adjust the balance between the three different kinds of sound—digital audio files (.wav), MIDI music files (.mid), and CD audio tracks—used by Windows.
- **WaveTop.** If your PC has a TV tuner card (like the ATI All-In-Wonder), you can download pages from certain Internet sites without using your modem. There's no charge to you—I assume WaveTop makes its money by either selling ads or charging the companies whose content it transmits. To use WaveTop, your PC's tuner must receive PBS via broadcast, cable, or analog satellite dish; digital satellite services (DirectTV, Dish Network, or Primestar) won't work. See **wavetop.net** for more details.
- **WebTV for Windows.** If your PC has a TV tuner card (like the ATI All-In-Wonder), you can use this to watch television on your PC's monitor. The viewer hooks into the TV program guide at **broadcast.microsoft.com**, which lets you pick programs from a menu (see Figure 38) just as you can on a digital satellite system. The service is free; Microsoft hopes to make money by selling ads. Note, however, that your tuner card may be able to hook into other program listings, some of which may have advantages. Check out the competition at **yahoo.com** at Business and Economy : Companies : News and Media : Television : Program Guides.

Figure 38

WebTV for Windows.

The original WebTV lets you surf the Internet on your TV screen; WebTV for Windows lets you watch TV on your computer's screen.

- **Welcome To Windows.** The tutorial/advertisement thingy that starts automatically when you first run Windows 98.
- **WordPad.** If your word processing needs are very simple—no fancy stuff like multiple columns, footnotes, or mail merge—you might get by with this basic word processor. You can insert graphics; format text with a variety of fonts; set tabs, line spacing, and justification; and define headers and footers with automatic page numbers. WordPad can read and saves files in several formats: .txt (ASCII text), some versions of .doc (Microsoft Word), and .rtf (Rich Text Format). It can also read (but not write) files in the .wri format used by Microsoft Write, the Windows 3.1 precursor to WordPad.

Internet Explorer Submenu (under Programs)

- **Address Book.** Brings up the address book for Outlook Express, the basic e-mail program bundled with Windows 98. See Chapter 20: E-mail, for more details.
- **Connection Wizard.** Sets up Internet access on your PC. See Chapter 19: Getting On the Internet.
- **FrontPage Express.** A starter version of Microsoft's toolkit for building and managing your personal Web site. See Chapter 21: The Web and Browsers, for a comparison with other do-it-yourself Web tools.
- **Internet Explorer.** Microsoft's Web browser. See Chapter 21: The Web and Browsers, for a comparison with Netscape Navigator.
- **Microsoft Chat.** Microsoft's tool for the popular Internet activity of communicating with friends or strangers by typing messages into a shared window. See Chapter 24: Internet Live: Chat, Etc.
- **Microsoft NetMeeting.** Allows you to communicate with other users over a local network or the Internet using text "chat," a virtual whiteboard, audio, and even video if you've got a camera connected to your PC. At least, that's the theory: In practice, live audio over the Internet is highly problematic, and videoconferencing is next to impossible. See Chapter 23: Internet Live: Chat, Etc. for more on those and related topics.
- **NetShow Player.** Microsoft's wannabe competitor for the far more popular RealPlayer, which receives live audio and video broadcasts over the Internet. See Chapter 21: The Web and Browsers.
- **Outlook Express.** The basic e-mail program bundled with Windows 98. See Chapter 20: E-mail, for more details.
- **Personal Web Server.** Turns your PC into a Web server. Run the program and the online help for more information.
- **Web Publishing Wizard.** A utility for uploading Web pages created on your PC to a server.

Online Services Submenu (under Programs). These menu choices let you choose America Online, AT&T, CompuServe, Prodigy, or Microsoft as your Internet service provider. Convenient options, yes—but since they're really just advertisements I strongly recommend you inform yourself of other options before choosing to use one. (The other companies "pay" Microsoft for the space on your menu by making MS Internet Explorer their default browser.) See Chapter 19: Getting On the Internet, for help in picking an ISP.

Administrative Tools Submenu (under Programs; Windows NT only)

- **Backup.** Backs up your hard disk to a tape drive. See Chapter 9: Protect Your Data.

- **Disk Administrator.** Partitions and formats hard drives, and configures drive arrays. (Windows NT only.)
- **Event Viewer.** A log of system events and errors. It's a good idea to check this once a week to see if your system's doing anything weird—errors in the log can indicate impending hardware failures (see Figure 39).

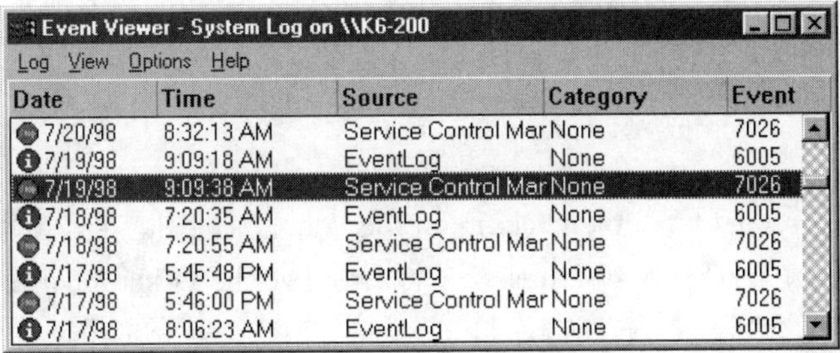

Date	Time	Source	Category	Event
7/20/98	8:32:13 AM	Service Control Mar	None	7026
7/19/98	9:09:18 AM	EventLog	None	6005
7/19/98	9:09:38 AM	Service Control Mar	None	7026
7/18/98	7:20:35 AM	EventLog	None	6005
7/18/98	7:20:55 AM	Service Control Mar	None	7026
7/17/98	5:45:48 PM	EventLog	None	6005
7/17/98	5:46:00 PM	Service Control Mar	None	7026
7/17/98	8:06:23 AM	EventLog	None	6005

Figure 39

Windows NT's Event Viewer.

When all the entries have blue **i** *icons, everything's fine, but a red stop-sign icon is a sign that something's not quite right. Double-clicking on a log entry brings up some additional information, which in this illustration led me to a loose cable on my tape backup drive.*

- **Performance Monitor.** Tracks system performance. May help sophisticated users diagnose problems.
- **Remote Access Admin.** A tool that lets network managers change settings of other computers on a network, without having to leave their desks.

- **User Manager.** Lets you control what other users can do if they log onto your PC. Unlike Windows 95 and 98, passwords set up here in User Manager can, if implemented correctly, actually keep your files secure. See the Network Resources section at the end of Chapter 25: Networks: Connecting PCs for recommendations of some books that can help you master NT's powerful but unfortunately difficult security features.
- **Windows NT Diagnostics.** Nerdy troubleshooting tool. See the Resources tab if you want a readout of IRQs, DMA channels, and other hardware settings.

What's All That Stuff in the Control Panel?

You can adjust most of Windows's settings through the applets in the Control Panel.

- **Accessibility Options.** Lets people with impaired vision or other physical challenges adjust Windows so it's easier to use. For example: If you're hearing impaired, you can display the usual audio alerts visually. If you can't use a mouse, you can use the keyboard, instead, to move the pointer and click. Folks who can only type one character at a time can set the Ctrl, Shift, and Alt keys to toggle on and off; so, for example, you could get Ctrl S by tapping Ctrl, S, Ctrl.
- **Add New Hardware.** (Windows 95 and 98 only.) Searches for any new hardware and installs the necessary drivers. You can also use this tool to install devices manually if Windows doesn't detect them.
- **Add/Remove Programs.** Lets you add or remove Windows components, and uninstall Windows upgrades or applications. In Windows 95 and 98, there's also a tab for formatting emergency boot diskettes (see "Create an Emergency Boot Disk" in the "Safety Check" section).
- **Console.** (Windows NT only) Changes settings for DOS (Command Prompt) windows.
- **Date/Time.** Lets you set the date and time. You can also access this dialog by double-clicking on the taskbar's clock.
- **Desktop Themes.** See "Customize the Desktop" in this chapter.
- **Devices.** (Windows NT only) This geeky tool may be useful for troubleshooting hardware problems.
- **Dial-Up Monitor.** (Windows NT only) Displays configuration and traffic statistics for Dial-Up Networking connections during use. May be useful for troubleshooting Internet connection problems.
- **Display.** Lets you adjust video board settings (see "Optimize the Display"), select screensavers, and change Windows's appearance (see "Customize the Desktop").
- **Find Fast.** Installed not by Windows but by Microsoft Office, this utility is supposed to speed up hard-disk searches in Office applications. Whether it does, I'm not sure—but its habit of making the hard disk thrash at unpredictable times drives me nuts, so I've disabled it. If you want to do the same, double-click Find Fast, select the index (see Figure 40), choose Index/Delete Index, and click OK several times. If there's more than one index in the list, repeat the process to delete them all, and then close Find Fast. Finally, delete the Microsoft Office Find Fast Indexer shortcut from the Startup submenu (see "Customize the Start Menu").

- **Fonts.** This folder displays all the fonts installed in your system. See Chapter 12: Windows Add-Ons, for instructions on adding fonts.
- **Game Controllers.** (Windows 98 only; in Windows 95 it's called Joystick.) Lets you install and configure joysticks, flightsticks, and the like.

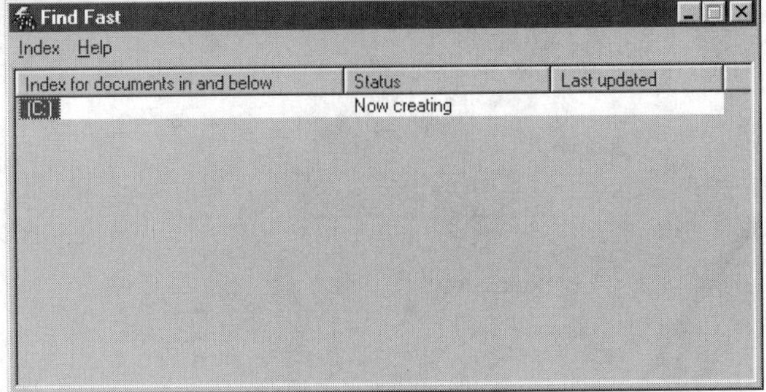

Figure 40

Find Fast.

- **Internet.** All kinds of settings for Internet connections and access. See Chapter 19: Getting On the Internet, and Chapter 21: The Web and Browsers.
- **Joystick.** See "Game Controllers," just above.
- **Keyboard.** Lets you set keyboard repeat delay (the interval for which you have to hold a key before it starts to repeat), repeat speed, and the insertion point's blink rate. Also lets you choose a different keyboard layout if you type in another language.
- **Mail and Fax.** Configures Microsoft Exchange, the e-mail/fax program bundled with Windows 95 and 98. (See Chapter 25: Networks: Connecting PCs, for setup instructions.)
- **Microsoft Mail Post Office.** (Windows 95 and 98 only.) Create or administer a Microsoft Exchange post office.
- **Modems.** Lets you set up your modem and configure it. See Chapter 19: Getting On the Internet, and Chapter 24: Use Your PC as a Phone or Fax.
- **Mouse.** Lets you adjust how fast you need to click to register a double-click, and how far the screen pointer moves relative to the distance you move the mouse. If you handle the mouse with your left hand, you can swap the function of the buttons, so the left button does the right-clicks. Some mice have special drivers that add other functions to this control panel.
- **Multimedia.** Adjusts settings for audio and video playback and recording. If the speaker or microphone volume is way too low or high, you might need to adjust it here (see Figure 41); otherwise, this stuff usually doesn't require any user intervention.
- **Network.** Install, configure, or remove network services. See Chapter 25: Networks: Connecting PCs.
- **ODBC.** A tool for setting up and configuring access to various databases. ODBC (Open Database Connectivity) doesn't come with Windows, but it's installed by many applications. If you need to do anything with it, the program that installs it should give you instructions.

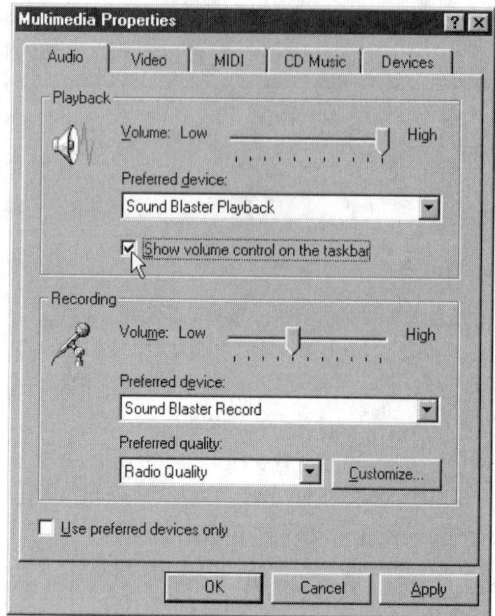

Figure 41

Multimedia.

If you don't have a volume control on your taskbar, check the "Show volume control on taskbar" box on the Audio tab.

- **Passwords.** (Windows 95 and 98 only; NT's equivalent is the User Manager, in the Administrative Tools section of the Start menu) Lets you enable the feature that allows people sharing a single PC to save individual preferences for desktop appearance, etc.

Don't get the idea that setting a password makes your data secure—you can get past the password dialog by just pressing Esc. All a log-on password will do is keep others from using any network or Dial-Up Networking passwords you've saved.

- **PC Card (PCMCIA).** Configures your PC Card slots and any PC Cards currently installed.
- **Ports.** (Windows NT only; in 95/98, these settings are in the Device Manager tab of the System control panel) Configures serial ports. Generally, manual intervention will be unnecessary—you probably won't ever have to touch this except perhaps at the request of your modem manufacturer's tech support staff.
- **Power** or **Power Management.** (Windows 95 and 98 only) Lets you turn power-saving features on and off. In Windows 98, you can set "timeouts" (length of inactivity required before a device shuts down) individually for the monitor, hard disk, and the whole system.
- **Printers.** See "Printers" entry under "Settings Submenu" in the earlier section on the Start menu.
- **Regional Settings.** Adjusts system for local variations in format of things like dates and numbers. For example, in some countries Christmas falls on 99-12-25 instead of 12/25/99, and the role of periods and commas in numbers is reversed (1.000,05 instead of 1,000.05).

- **SCSI Adapters.** (Windows NT only; in Windows 95 and 98, these settings are in the Device Manager tab of the System control panel) Despite its name, this item displays both EIDE and SCSI adapters and the drives connected to them. Use the Drivers tab to install or upgrade adapter drivers. You can view adapter and drive configuration information (IRQs, SCSI ID numbers, etc.), but you can't change anything.
- **Server.** (Windows NT only) Lists what devices are being shared with the network and who, if anyone, is logged on at the moment; lets you stop sharing devices or disconnect users.
- **Services.** (Windows NT only) The software counterpart of the Devices control panel discussed in this section. Lets you control what services are initialized at startup; may be useful for troubleshooting.
- **Sounds.** Controls the sounds—if any—that are associated with system events like error dialogs and closing windows. Tired of the whooshy musical fanfare when Windows starts up? Turn it off here (see Figure 42). Check the Multimedia section in the Windows Setup tab of Add/Remove Programs to see more sound files that may not yet be installed on your PC.

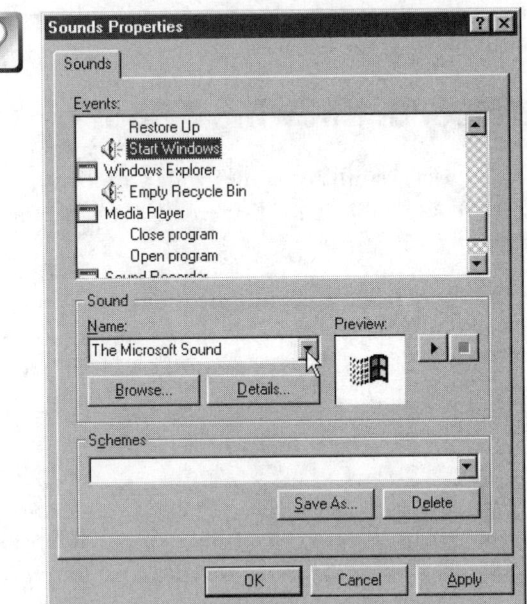

Figure 42

Silence squeaky Windows!

That musical fanfare Windows plays when it starts up is pretty cool the first time you hear it, but when it gets old you can shut it off with the Sound control panel. Click on the Start Windows item in the Events menu, change the entry in the Name menu from "The Microsoft Sound" to "(None)," and click Apply. To stop the shutdown music, do the same to the Exit Windows event.

- **System.** Lots of stuff in this one. The General tab tells you how much memory's installed in your system and precisely what version of Windows you're running. Hardware Profiles let you configure sets of drivers for various situations—for example, a notebook you take on the road, or one that's attached to its docking station. The Performance tab has settings that you may need to adjust if your system runs slower than it should. In Windows 95 and 98, the Device Manager displays all the hardware in your PC and lets you resolve hardware conflicts.
- **Tape Devices.** (Windows NT only; in Windows 95 and 98, tape drives appear in Device Manager) Similar to the SCSI Adapters control panel discussed above. Displays settings of any tape drives in your PC and lets you install or upgrade drivers.
- **Telephony.** (Windows 98 and NT only) See Chapter 24: Use Your PC as a Phone or Fax.
- **Users.** (Windows 98 only) Lets you set up a shared PC so everyone can have their own personal settings. See "Passwords" in this control panel section.
- **UPS.** (Windows NT only) Lets you configure how the system responds to signals from an Uninterruptible Power Supply (discussed in Chapter 9: Protect Your Data).

More Stuff Worth Knowing About

Finding some of the useful stuff that comes with Windows takes a little extra digging. Here are a few valuable items that aren't accessible through the usual channels.

Convert. This Windows NT command-line utility lets you convert drives from the FAT format used by Windows 95 and 98 to the more secure and reliable NTFS format, which is also a prerequisite for NT's drive compression and array features. Choose Command Prompt from the Programs section of the Start menu, and enter the following command:

```
convert c: /fs:ntfs [Enter]
```

Be sure to back up your PC before converting—there's little chance anything will go wrong, but in that unlikely event you may have to reformat the drive.

Emergency Recovery Utility (ERU). (Windows 95 only) Lets you back up your Windows 95 configuration information. It's a good idea to run ERU before adding any new hardware or software to your PC, so if anything goes wrong you can easily restore the previous, good configuration. This utility's in Other\Misc\Eru on the Windows 95 Setup CD; read the text file in that folder for more info on using it.

By default, the utility wants to save to diskette, but the data probably won't fit on one. I've always just pointed it to a folder on my hard drive and never had a problem. To restore your old configuration, run the ERD program that's created with the configuration backup files.

ERU may not work properly if you don't have DOS AUTOEXEC.BAT and CONFIG.SYS files in the root directory of your boot drive. Some PCs don't have these files, since they aren't strictly required.

Hover. (Windows 95 only) An action game (nonviolent) designed to show off Windows's graphics capabilities. You can play it right off the Windows 95 CD, or copy the Hover folder (under Funstuff) to your hard drive for better performance.

Old DOS Commands. (Windows 95 and 98 only) In the versions of DOS built into Windows 95 and 98, many commands are absent that old-time DOS users might miss. Some of the deleted commands are on the Windows CD. On the Win95 CD, look in Other\Oldmsdos; in Win98, tools\oldmsdos. To use the commands, copy the commands you want from the CD to the Command folder under the Windows folder on your hard disk.

Quick View. This file viewer appears on the right-click pop-up menu for certain types of files. Open it, and a preview of file's contents appears (Figure 43), usually in a fraction of the time it would take to actually open the document. Quick View isn't always installed with Windows, so if you don't find the choice on your right-click menus, open the Add/Remove Programs control panel, click the Windows Setup tab, double-click on Accessories, check Quick View, and click OK.

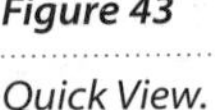

Figure 43

Quick View.

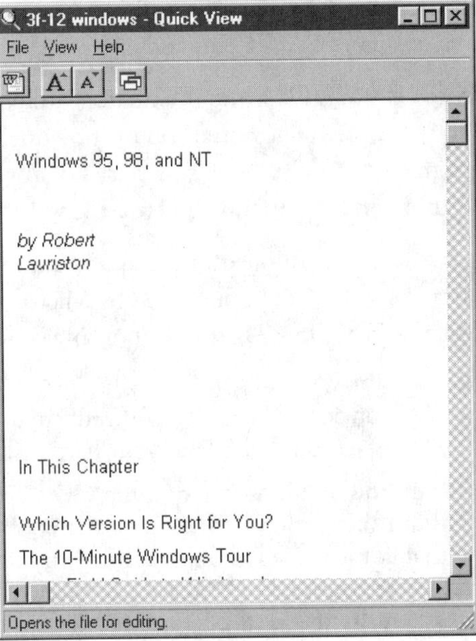

Repair Disk Utility. (Windows NT only) See "Create an Emergency Boot Disk" in the "Safety Check" section.

Rollback. *DO NOT RUN THIS PROGRAM!* It is an undocumented utility hiding in an obscure folder of early copies the Windows NT 4.0 Setup CD, intended for use only by PC manufacturers. It will thoroughly trash your Registry and make your NT installation unusable. The only way to recover from the damage is to re-install NT and restore from a backup. Microsoft corrected the mistake and removed the file shortly after NT shipped; if your CD's files are dated 10/14/96 or later, you've got the clean version.

System Configuration Editor. An easy way to edit the configuration files used by DOS and Windows 3.1 programs: CONFIG.SYS, AUTOEXEC.BAT, WIN.INI, and SYSTEM.INI. (See "Tuning AUTOEXEC.BAT and CONFIG.SYS" in Appendix A: DOS survival guide.)

Task Manager. The version in Windows 95 and 98 is pretty useless—it basically just duplicates some of the functions of the taskbar. The one extra trick it offers is the ability to Ctrl-click on multiple applications and then choose End Task or Minimize from the Windows menu to kill or hide all of them at once. Not on the Start menu; choose Run from Start menu and enter `taskman`.

Windows NT's Task Manager, in contrast, is an essential troubleshooting tool. The Processes tab (see Figure 44) displays all kinds of information about running programs (for instance, the amounts of CPU time and memory they're using)—including hidden programs that don't show up in the taskbar—and allows you to kill misbehaving programs that refuse to shut down normally. There's also a Performance tab that graphs CPU and memory usage. Not on Start menu; choose Run from Start menu and enter `taskmgr`.

Welcome to Windows 95. This is the orientation utility that appears when you first run Windows 95. If you've gotten rid of it by unchecking the option to "Show this Welcome Screen next time you start Windows," you can bring it back by choosing Run from Start menu and entering `welcome`.

Windows Resource Kit. The full text of the appropriate Windows Resource Kit, a series of fat, nerd-oriented books published by Microsoft Press, is included on the Windows 95 and 98 Setup CDs (but not on NT's, sorry).

- In Windows 95, look for Win95rk (the one whose icon looks like a book with a question mark on the cover) in the Admin\Apptools\Reskit\Helpfile folder. You might want to copy the file to your hard disk for faster searches.
- In Windows 98, run the Setup program in the CD's Tools\Reskit folder. This will install both the text of the Resource Kit book and a "sampler" of the software that comes on the book's accompanying CD. Included are the TweakUI utility mentioned in "Customize the Desktop," and the rest of the Power Toys kit discussed in Chapter 12: Windows Add-Ons.

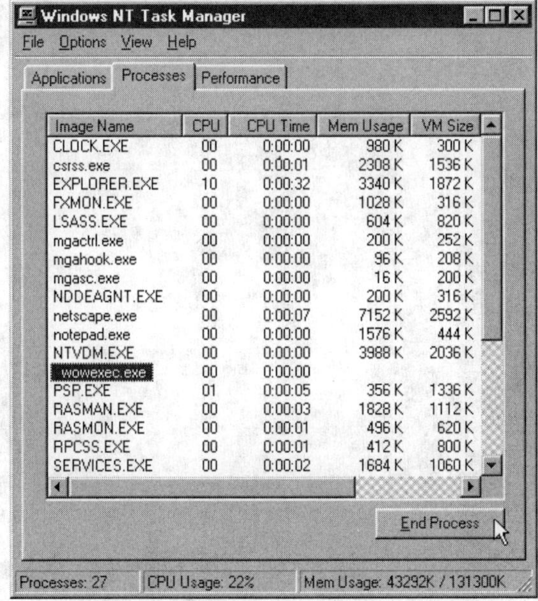

Figure 44

Windows NT's Task Manager.

You can use NT's Task Manager to see and terminate any program, even those that don't show up on the taskbar. For example, the highlighted process (wowexec.exe) is NT's Windows 3.1 subsystem, which remains active even after you close the Win31 program that launched it; ending the process frees up some memory. The version of Netscape I use regularly also has a bad habit of leaving a hidden process (netscape.exe) behind after I close the program. Sometimes it hogs so much memory that it affects performance, in which case I use Task Manager to kill the process.

Optimizing Windows

Windows works okay as installed, but there's plenty of room for improvement. In this section, I'll give you a boatload of tips for making it better.

Optimize the Display

If Windows can't identify your monitor, it sets your video card to the lowest common denominator: 640x480 resolution, 256 colors. (Resolution, colors, and other display concepts are discussed in Chapter 5: Monitors, Etc.) This default ensures that the display will work, but it's not likely the best you can do. Even if Windows does recognize your monitor and uses higher settings, they're often not optimal for your monitor. You can check by experimenting with the settings in the Display control panel, as follows.

Figure 45

Improve the display, step 1.

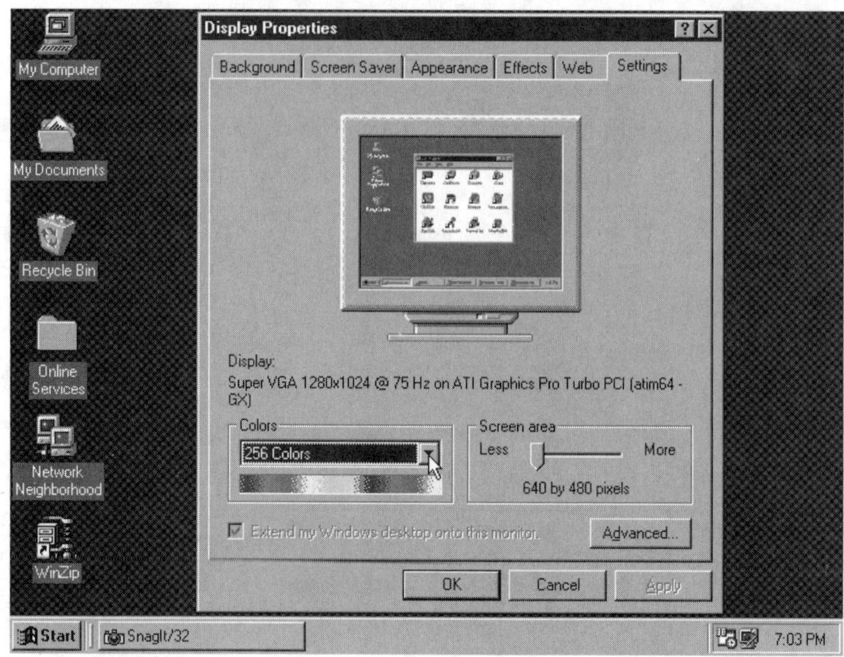

Open the Control Panel and double-click on Display (or right-click on a blank spot on the desktop and choose Properties). Click the Settings tab. If any of the settings matches the above illustration, you can probably do better.

Figure 46

Improve the display, step 2.

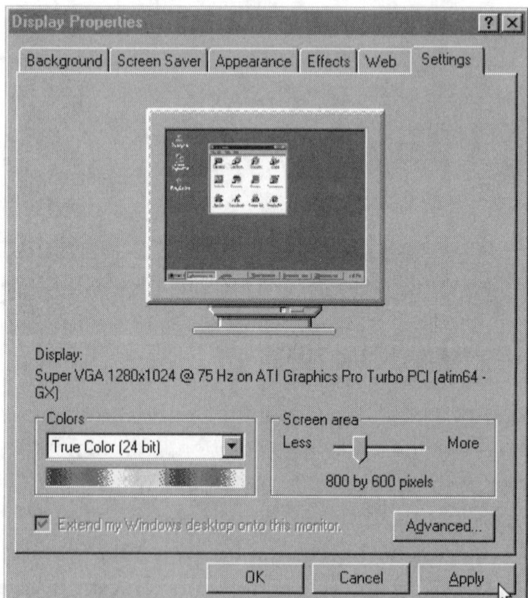

Try setting color to 24-bit and the screen slider to 800 by 600, then click Apply.

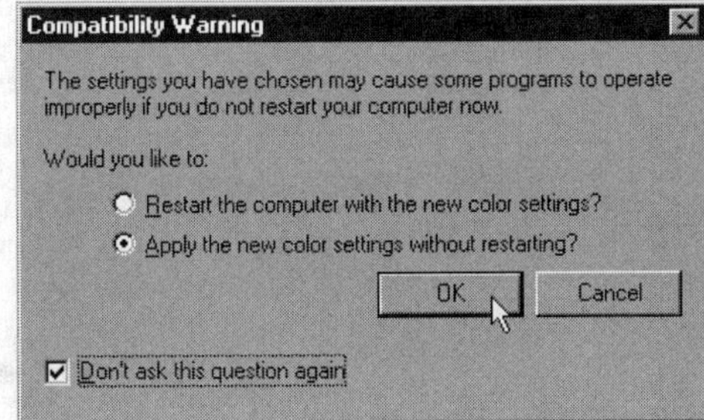

Figure 47

Improve the display, step 3.

If this is the first time you've changed the display settings, you'll probably get the dialog in Figure 47. The settings shown here allow you to change video resolution quickly, without rebooting your PC. Since the default is to reboot, I assume some PCs have a problem with that, but I've used these settings on over a hundred PCs and have yet to encounter a problem.

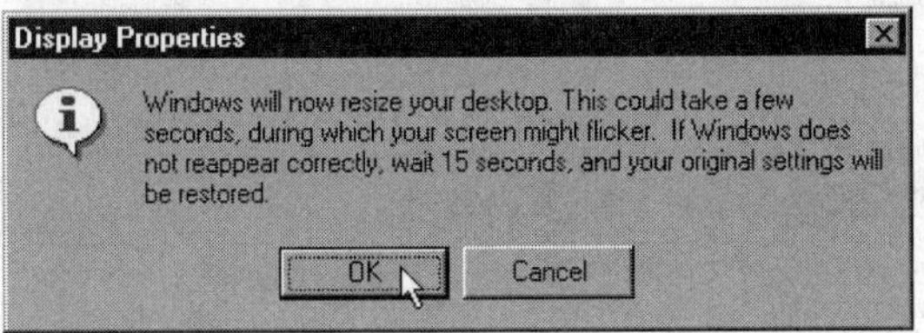

Figure 48

Improve the display, step 4

Click OK. If the screen goes black, just wait, and in 10 or 15 seconds the display will return with your old settings restored. Try some other settings and see if they work better.

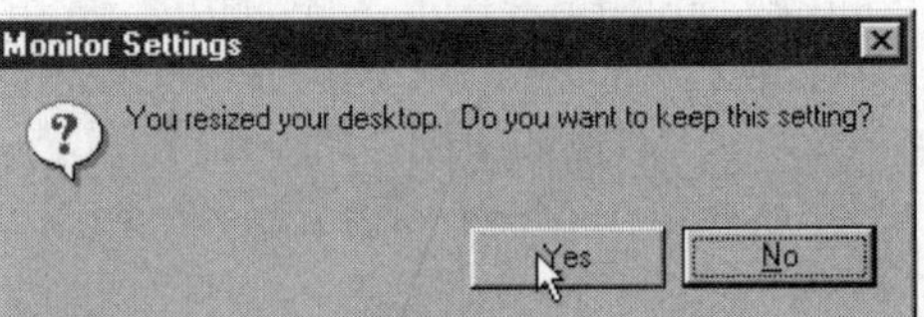

Figure 49

Improve the display, step 5.

If you see the dialog in Figure 49, and the image looks okay, click Yes.

Experimenting with these settings can often give you a bigger desktop to work on, as shown just above, and in some cases you'll notice significantly better colors. See Chapter 5: Monitors, Etc. for tips on optimizing your display further.

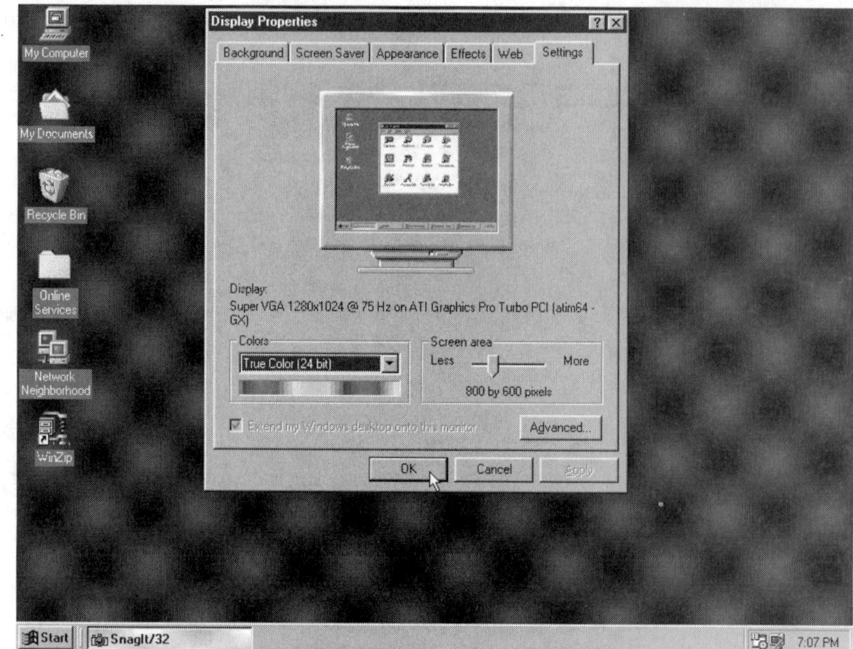

Figure 50

Improve the display, step 6.

Customize the Taskbar

The taskbar's not a bad tool right out of the box, but there's still room for improvement. Try some of these tips to make it work better.

Hide the Taskbar. The taskbar's defaults are designed to prevent one of the most common problems encountered by beginners and the chronically inept in Windows 3.1: losing applications and programs. Somebody accidentally clicks the wrong button or presses the wrong key-combination, and suddenly their work is no longer visible on screen. Maybe it got minimized to an icon, maybe one window's obscuring another—regardless, to the unsophisticated eye, the document has just "disappeared." By making the taskbar always visible at the bottom of the screen, Microsoft makes it next to impossible for new users to get lost.

Once you're used to the way Windows works, though, you probably have better ways to use the desktop space taken up by the taskbar when you're not using it. To recover that space, right-click on the taskbar, choose Properties, and check "Auto hide." The taskbar will now appear only when you drag the mouse to the bottom of the screen. The rest of the time, it's reduced to a single-pixel line.

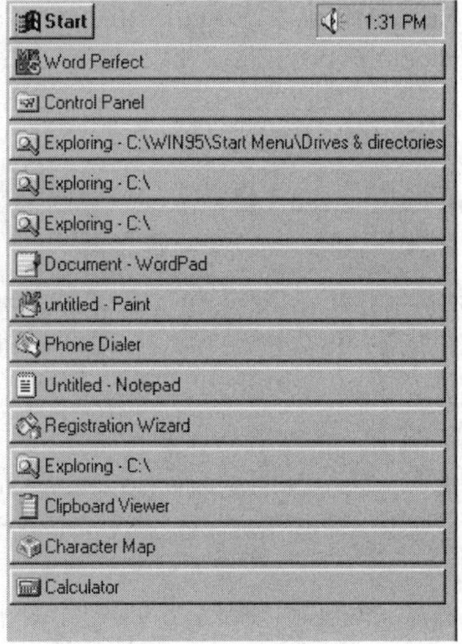

Figure 51

After:

Taskbar Vertical.

Move the Taskbar. Once you've got the taskbar into hiding, it makes more sense to put it on the side rather than the bottom of the workspace, and widen it a bit. This makes room for a lot more buttons (Figure 51), and the text doesn't get cut off the way it does when buttons are squeezed onto the default horizontal taskbar (Figure 52). To move the taskbar to the side, click on an empty area of the taskbar, drag it up and to the left until the outline moves, and let go. To make the taskbar wider, position the pointer over the edge so it turns into a double-headed arrow, and then click and drag.

Figure 52

Before:

Taskbar Horizontal.

Other Taskbar Settings. In addition to "Auto hide," there are three other settings in the taskbar properties:

- Check "Show small icons in Start menu" if you'd like to reduce the size of the jumbo icons in the top level of the Start menu to match those in the other menus. This option also gets rid of the Windows banner that runs alongside the menu.
- Uncheck "Show Clock" if you don't want the taskbar clock.
- Uncheck "Always on top," and the taskbar appears in front of an application window only when you press the keyboard shortcut Ctrl Esc. This option is useful if you often bring up the Start menu by accident.

Add Volume and Power Controls. If your taskbar doesn't have a volume control (the little speaker icon shown in Figure 51) in its "tray," see "Multimedia" under "What's All That Stuff in the Control Panel." There you'll find instructions on making this control show up. It also includes a Mute checkbox, which lets you switch the sound off quickly if you need to answer the phone.

There's a similar option in the Power Management control panel that will put a power control in the tray. This option's particularly useful on a laptop—if you hold the mouse pointer over the icon for a second, it'll display a Tooltip with an estimate of how much battery life is left.

Quick-Change Video Resolutions. If you like to change video resolutions frequently, you can add a video mode control (like the one shown in Figure 53) to the taskbar's tray. Some video cards add such a control automatically; if you don't see one, here's how to add it:

- **In Windows 98 and Windows 95 OSR2** (an updated version of Windows, never sold separately, that was loaded on new PCs from December 1996 on): Choose Start/Settings/Control Panel, double-click on Display, click the Settings tab, click Advanced, check "Show settings icon on taskbar," and click OK twice.
- **In Windows 95:**, Install the QuickRes portion of Microsoft's PowerToys kit (discussed in Chapter 12: Windows Add-Ons).
- The **Windows NT** version of QuickRes is, so far as I've been able to determine, distributed only on the CD that comes with the Windows NT Resource Kit book.

Toolbars on the Taskbar. In Windows 98, you can create toolbars—like the ones in Microsoft Internet Explorer—on the taskbar for quick access to icons (see Figure 53). The taskbar's pretty small, so if you do want to put a toolbar there, you'll probably want to reserve it for only your most often-used programs.

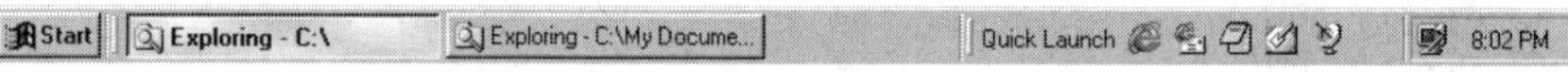

Figure 53

A taskbar toolbar.

- To get rid of the toolbar Windows 98 creates by default, right-click on the taskbar and choose Toolbars/Quick Launch.
- To add a program to a toolbar, find it in the Start menu. Then right-click on the icon, drag it over the toolbar and drop it, and choose Copy from the pop-up menu. (See "Customize the Start Menu" in this chapter if you have trouble dragging program icons.)
- To delete a program from a toolbar, right-click on the program's icon and choose Delete.
- To move a toolbar, click and drag it to a new location. You can drag toolbars onto the desktop, but that doesn't make much sense to me—you can already create icons there, and it's usually faster to use the Start menu anyway. It makes more sense to dock toolbars on the edges or top of the desktop, where they act like the taskbars, and turn on the "Auto hide" option to get them out of the way when not in use.
- To change icon size or turn text labels on or off, right-click on a blank portion of the toolbar and choose View/Large, View/Small, or Show Text.
- To create a new toolbar, first create a new folder on your hard disk to hold its shortcuts. Then right-click on a blank portion of the taskbar, choose Toolbars/New Toolbar, select the folder you just created, and click OK.
- To hide a toolbar, right-click on the taskbar and uncheck the toolbar in the Toolbars submenu.

Customize the Desktop

Change Windows's Appearance. Windows 95 gives you a lot of control over the way it looks on screen. Using the Appearance tab of the Display control panel (see Figure 54), you can not only change colors and window border widths, but also adjust the fonts to suit your screen resolution and eyesight. Try the different choices on the Scheme menu to get an idea of the options, and then make your own custom scheme. Most of the options are self-explanatory, but following are a few things that are less than obvious:

- The font settings for the Icon item help you control not just labels of icons on the desktop, but also the text used in My Computer and Windows Explorer. Similarly, settings for "Active Title Bar" also affect Taskbar buttons.
- You can select *most* configurable items by clicking on the examples in the preview window, but there are additional elements you can adjust *only* by picking them from the Item list. These include vertical and horizontal icon spacing, palette title bars, and Tooltips (the yellow explanatory labels that appear when you hold the cursor over an icon on a toolbar or the like).

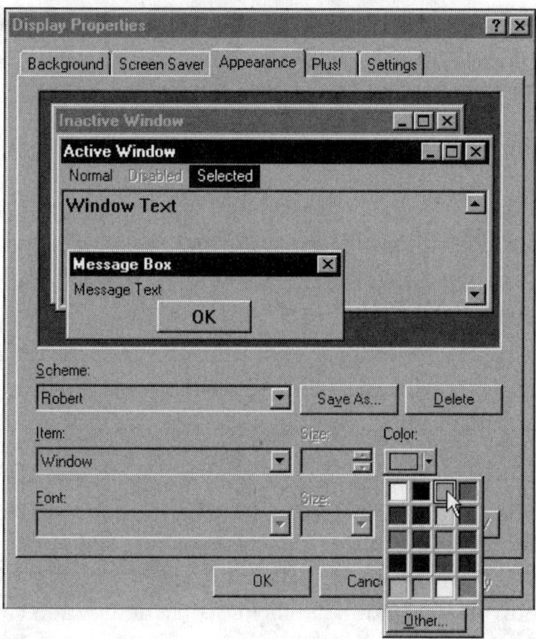

Figure 54

Display appearance.

Personally, I find the glaring white background in most of Windows's stock color schemes unbearable. To avoid eyestrain, I always change it to light gray. If you don't like the 20 choices in the pop-up color palette, choose Other to pick from the full range of colors your video card can display.

- Perhaps most confusing is that if you want to change the size of the default font (the one used in Notepad), you have to switch to the Settings tab and use the Font Size command. Windows Help has its own font setting: open any Help topic and click the Options button.

When you've set the Appearance options to your liking, click the Save As button and enter a name to add your settings to the Scheme menu.

Decorate the Desktop. You can decorate the blank desktop with a variety of patterns or with a picture of your choice. using the Background tab of the Display control panel. Click the Tile button, and then try some of the choices in the Wallpaper menu. Click the Apply button to update the desktop with the currently selected pattern.

To display a picture on the desktop, first save the image to your hard disk in .bmp format. Then set the Display option in the Background dialog to Center, click the Browse button, select the file, click Open, and click Apply. You can also drag and drop a bitmap file from Windows Explorer onto the Background list.

Most Web browsers offer a simpler way to change the background. Just right-click on the picture you want, and choose Set As Wallpaper.

Windows 98 also lets you use whole Web pages as the background. It's an interesting idea but requires you to enable Active Desktop, which I don't recommend (see the description of Active Desktop coming up).

Change the Screensaver. Use the Screen Saver tab in the Display control panel to select a screensaver. Check out Flying Through Space (sometimes called Starfield Simulation) and 3D Pipes (not in Windows 95). If you don't see these choices, run the Add/Remove Programs control panel, click the Windows Setup tab, double-click Accessories, check any unchecked screen savers, and click OK twice. The Scrolling Marquee (or Marquee Display) option is useful to leave a message visible on your screen for coworkers, family members, or roommates—like "Don't turn me off—I'm waiting for a fax." Click the Settings button, type your message in the Text field, and click OK. If the preview of the text shows it zipping across the screen too fast to read, click Settings again and adjust the Speed slider.

Change the Mouse Pointer's Appearance. The Pointers tab in the Mouse control panel offers a variety of alternative mouse pointers. You can change pointers individually by double-clicking on a description (Normal Select, Help Select, etc.), or use the Scheme menu to change all pointers at once. If you don't get a choice of schemes, open the Add/Remove Programs control panel, click the Windows Setup tab, double-click Accessories, check Mouse Pointers, and click OK twice.

Change Sounds. The Sounds control panel (see Figure 42 earlier in this chapter) lets you assign noises to different system events. It works very much like the Mouse Pointers dialog: You change individual sounds by selecting an event (Close Program, Exit Windows) and then picking from the Name menu. Or you can change all sounds at once by choosing a scheme. If you don't have a choice of schemes, open the Add/Remove Programs control panel, click the Windows Setup tab, double-click Multimedia, check one or more sound schemes, and click OK twice. To make Windows shut up, choose the "No Sounds" scheme.

Change Icons. Though icons for Windows applications and their documents are fixed, you *can* change the icon used by their shortcuts on the desktop. Right-click on the icon, choose Properties, select the Shortcut tab, and click Change Icon. By default, the Change Icon command displays the icons in the program or in shell32.dll (in the Windows\System folder in Windows 95 and 98, Windows\System32 in NT). But there are additional icons in moricons.dll (in the Windows folder in Windows 95 and 98, Windows\System32 in NT). This moricons file will only appear in the Browse dialog if you've checked the "Show all files" setting in Windows Explorer's options, but you can still load it by typing `moricons.dll` in the Filename field of the Change Icon dialog box (see Figure 55). You can also download all kinds of other icons from the Internet (see Chapter 21: The Web and Browsers).

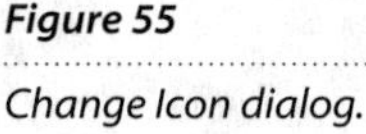

Figure 55

Change Icon dialog.

All of the Above. Windows 98 (and Windows 95 with the Plus! add-on) have a Desktop Themes control panel that changes *all* the foregoing desktop options at once, and offers a wider choice of desktop pictures and patterns, icons, screensavers, and sounds. Personally I find these themes *way* too distracting for a work environment, but some people like them.

Rename, Delete, or Hide Desktop Icons. Most desktop icons can be renamed by right-clicking them and choosing Rename. For the Recycle Bin and other ones that have no Rename command, you can use TweakUI (discussed in Chapter 12: Windows Add-Ons).

You can delete most desktop icons by right-clicking and choosing Delete or Remove from Desktop. When you want to get rid of an icon you can't delete, like My Computer or the Recycle Bin, use TweakUI to hide it.

Change Folder and File Display: By default, Windows hides a lot of things in order to avoid confusing new users. If you want to change that, run Windows Explorer or My Computer, choose Options or Folder Options from the View menu, and click on the View tab (Figure 56). You'll have these options:

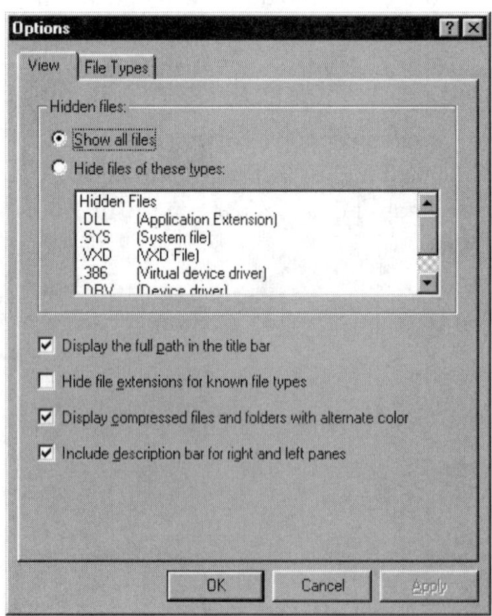

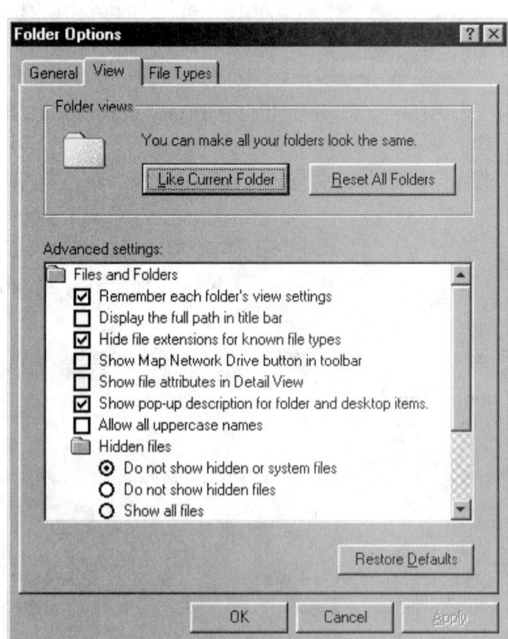

Figure 56

View options.

- To see files Windows normally keeps hidden, check Show All Files. (First read "Danger Zone: Hidden Files" in the Windows Cookbook section for some warnings about this option.)
- To see the filename extensions (so a Word file, for instance, will appear as My File.doc instead of My File), uncheck "Hide file extensions for known file types."

- To see the full path, check "Display the full path in title bar" (so when browsing the System folder, for instance, the window will show "C:\windows\system" instead of just "System").
- To add file attributes to the Details view in Windows 98, check "Show file attributes in Detail view." (Windows 95 can't do this, and NT always does.)

After making the changes you want, click OK.

Another way to get more information is to choose View/Details in the Windows Explorer or My Computer windows. Read the "See what files are in a folder" task in the Windows Cookbook for more about that.

View as Web Page. This Windows 98 innovation (which you may also get if you install Internet Explorer 4.0), on the View menu of Windows Explorer and My Computer, basically puts a little Web-browser window to the left of the file listing. This strikes me as a pointless waste of screen space. (If Microsoft weren't basing its defense against the antitrust case on the claim that MS Internet Explorer 4.0 and Windows 98 are not two separate products, I'd

About File Attributes

When you right-click on a file and choose Properties, you'll find that the dialog includes checkboxes for four *attributes* (see Figure 57). Here's a brief guide to what they mean and why you might want to change them.

Read-Only. You can open the file, but if you try to save it you'll get an error message. Marking a file read-only gives an extra warning dialog if you try to move or delete the file.

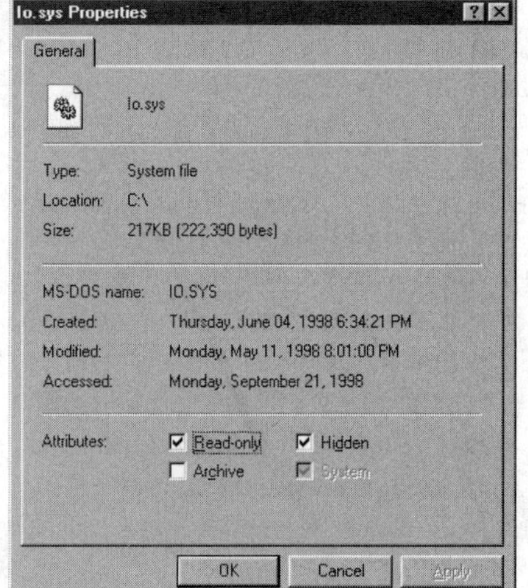

Figure 57

File attributes.

Hidden. The file is invisible—it doesn't show up in the file lists of Windows Explorer or File Open.

System. Functionally the same as Hidden, except that Windows won't let you change the setting.

Archive. In theory, means that the file is not backed up yet, which allows programs to do incremental backups by backing up only those files with the Archive property set. Not all backup utilities use the attribute, however, so it doesn't necessarily tell you anything. See Chapter 9: Protect Your Data for more on incremental backups.

In Windows Explorer (when shown) and at the DOS prompt, attributes are indicated by single-letter codes: R for Read-only, H for Hidden, S for System, A for Archive.

wonder whether they would have added this odd feature at all.) Other weird items that fall into the same category are the Address bar and the File menu's Work Offline command—these make sense in a Web browser, but they have nothing to do with your hard disk.

Active Desktop (Web Style): If you have Microsoft Internet Explorer 4.0 installed (which, if you're running Windows 98, you do whether you want it or not), you can choose to make both the desktop and Windows Explorer behave like a Web browser. That is, instead of double-clicking on a file to open it, you single-click, as if it were a link on a Web page. To make this change, select Start/Settings/Folder Options, and choose Web Style. However, I don't recommend you do this.

Some Words of Caution About Active Desktop. For over 15 years, people using computers with graphical interfaces have clicked files to select them, and double-clicked to activate them. That was a logical decision on the part of the people who designed those interfaces: The two kinds of clicks make it fast and easy to open a particular file, but just as easy to select one or more files for other operations, like moving, copying, or rearranging. The distinction between clicking and double-clicking is hardly intuitive, but it's easy to learn and has been consistently implemented not just in Windows and its applications but in almost all other mouse-driven interfaces as well.

Now, in a Web browser, the use of single clicks makes good sense. In a browser, you don't move links around on a page or edit them. Around 99% of the time you'll always be doing the same thing with a link—clicking it to go to another page—and you can only follow one link at a time. Hence it would be unnecessarily awkward to have to click once to select a link, then double-click to follow it.

On the Windows desktop, though, the single-click approach creates problems. If you use single-click instead of double-click to open a file, how do you select it so you can use a menu command? Microsoft's solution is to have you pause the cursor over the file for a second, until it highlights. To select multiple files, you hold down Shift or Ctrl and pause the pointer over the files to select or deselect them. These techniques work, but they're slow and awkward compared with the usual method.

There are several other drawbacks to enabling Active Desktop:

- **Performance.** A number of published benchmark tests have found that enabling Active Desktop slows things down—though if you've got a 166MHz or faster PC with plenty of RAM, it might not *feel* any slower. (Benchmark scores reflect the total amount of time it takes to perform thousands of commands, most of which a fast PC seems, from the user's perspective, to execute instantly.)

- **Instability.** Some users have reported that turning on Active Desktop makes Windows crash more. Given that Web browsers in general are one of the more crash-prone categories of software, that's not particularly surprising, since using Active Desktop is equivalent to running MS Internet Explorer all the time.
- **Inconsistency.** With Web Style turned on, some things, including Windows Explorer and the Find dialog, switch to single-click. But similar interfaces in other programs still use double-click.
- **Inaccurate help.** Windows's online Help generally assumes that you're not running Active Desktop, so Help's step-by-step instructions don't always work. The same goes for this and most other computer books.

Put all that together, and I think you've got a very strong argument against Active Desktop. I see no reason to switch it on, and if your PC came with it enabled, I recommend you turn it off. Right-click on the desktop, choose properties, click the Web tab, uncheck "View my Active Desktop as a Web page," and click OK.

Customize the Start Menu

The average Start menu, even on a brand-new PC, is typically a mess. Most applications create their own submenus, which is easy for their programmers but not a very efficient way to organize your apps. It makes more sense to put the dozen or so apps you use most often in the top-level Start Menu folder, or to group them in the Programs folder, and collect the stuff you use less often into logical submenus like Business, Games, Taxes and Finance—whatever makes sense to you. All the stuff you seldom or never need to use—Readme files, setup utilities, online registration routines—you can simply delete; the originals will still be on your hard drive if you need them.

How you edit the Start menu depends on which version of Windows you're running. In all versions, you can right-click on the taskbar, choose Properties, and click the Start Menu Programs tab. There you'll find buttons for Wizard-type dialogs that will walk you through the process of adding or removing individual items—but I've found the alternatives discussed below to be significantly more straightforward and efficient.

In Windows 98, you can edit the Start menu directly. Just drag icons from one submenu to another, or use right-click menus—just like manipulating files with Windows Explorer. The process is a little fussy.

To move, rename, delete, or edit a menu entry:

1. Click the Start button, but don't hold down the mouse button. (Usually, when navigating the Start menu, it doesn't make any difference whether you hold the button down or let it go, but in this case it does.)
2. Leaving the mouse button up, navigate your way to the icon for the submenu or folder you want to change.

3a. To move the icon, click and hold it. Keeping the mouse button down, navigate to the submenu where you want to put the icon, then to the precise position on the submenu where you want the icon to appear (which will be indicated by a black bar like the one in Figure 58). Drop the icon in place. You will have to pause the pointer over a submenu's icon longer than usual before it pops open.

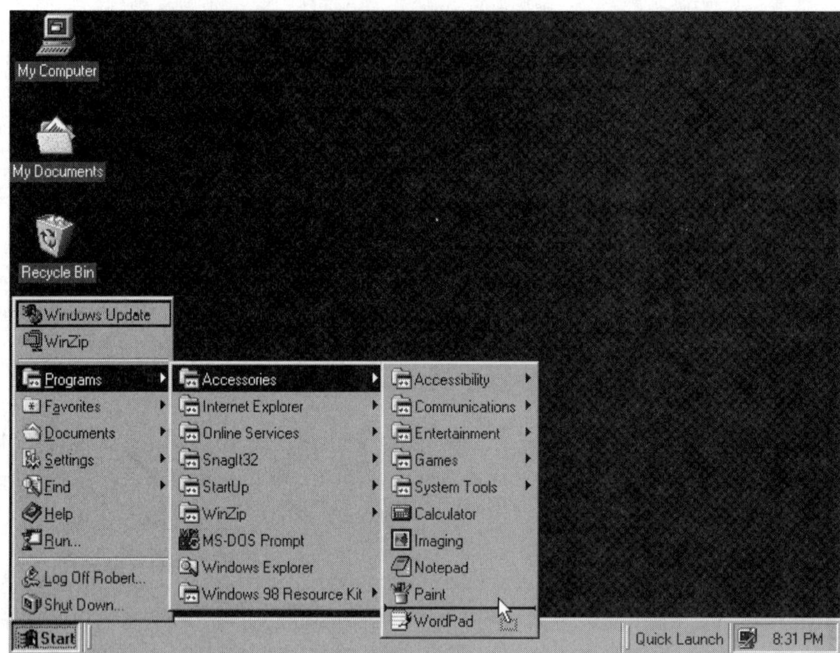

Figure 58

Editing the Start Menu in Windows 98.

3b. To rename or delete the icon, right-click on it and choose the appropriate command.

3c. To change what happens when you choose the icon from the Start menu, right-click on it and choose Properties. See the upcoming section "Using Shortcuts" for instructions on changing settings.

To add a new program to the menu, first create a shortcut (see "Using Shortcuts"). Then drag the shortcut onto the Start button, then to the submenu where you want it, and drop it at the exact position where you want it to appear (which will be indicated by a black bar).

To add a new submenu, use the procedure described just below for Windows 95/NT.

In Windows 95 and NT, you can't edit the Start menu directly. Instead, you revise the Start Menu *folder* (under the Windows folder), which contains a shortcut for every program on the Start menu, organized into folders that match the submenus. (See "Using Shortcuts.") When you change those folders and shortcuts, the Start menu changes to match—although sometimes you may have to press F5 or restart your computer before the changes appear.

The easiest way to start editing is to right-click on the Start button and choose Explore. This brings up Windows Explorer with the focus on the Start Menu.

To copy, move, delete, or rename the Start menu's entries, just use the same techniques you would use for managing files. (For detailed instructions, see the relevant sections of the Windows Cookbook earlier in this chapter.)

To add a new submenu, just create a new folder in the position on the folder tree that matches the place on the Start menu where you want the submenu to appear. Give it the name you want to appear in the Start menu.

To add a new item to the menu:

1. Create a shortcut for the item you want to add to the menu (see "Using Shortcuts" just below).
2. Drag the shortcut to the taskbar and drop on the Start button. This will add the program to the top level of the Start menu, above the Programs submenu.
3. Right-click the Start button and choose Explore.
4. If you wish, rename the new shortcut.
5. Click on the Start Menu folder icon in the folder tree (left window), and press * on the numeric keypad. This will expand all the subfolders so you can see the whole structure of the Start menu (see Figure 59).
6. Drag the new shortcut to the folder that matches the submenu where you want it to appear, and drop it.

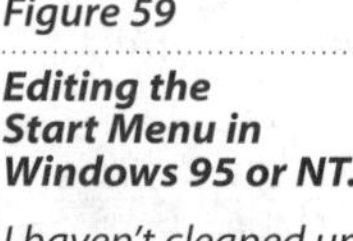

Figure 59

Editing the Start Menu in Windows 95 or NT.

I haven't cleaned up my Start menu in a few months (I've been too busy writing a book…), so it's a perfect example of the kind of mess that occasionally needs cleaning up.

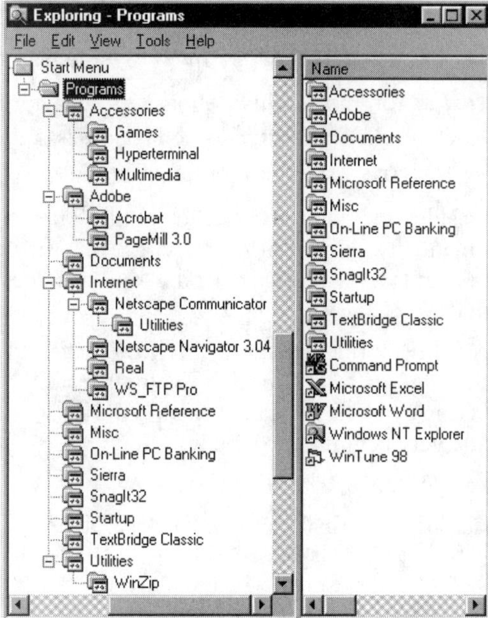

Using Shortcuts

Windows makes heavy use of *shortcuts*, which are basically files that don't do anything except point to other files—they're kind of like links on a Web page. You can recognize them by the little curved arrows that appear on the lower-left corner of their icons. (In other operating systems, shortcuts are usually called *aliases*.)

Shortcuts' most important function is to launch programs: Most Windows applications won't work if they're moved out of the folder where they were installed, but you can put shortcuts to an application anywhere you like. The Start menu is made up mostly of shortcuts, and program icons on the desktop are usually shortcuts as well.

Shortcuts can point not just to programs but to almost anything else in Windows: documents, folders, disk drives, printers, dial-up networking connections, and control panels, among other things. It's often handy to create desktop shortcuts to documents or folders you're using a lot. When you're not using them so much any more, you can delete the shortcut to get it off the desktop, but the actual document or folder remains undisturbed on your hard disk.

As usual in Windows, there are a number of different ways you can create shortcuts. The main ones:

- Right-click an icon and choose Create Shortcut.
- Right-drag on an icon, drag it to the place where you want the shortcut, drop it, and choose Create Shortcut(s) Here.
- Right-click where you want a shortcut to appear and choose New/Shortcut. (This method will only let you create shortcuts to program and document files, but not to folders, drives, printers, or other objects.)

Shortcut Settings. You can modify a shortcut's behavior by changing its settings. Right-click on the shortcut, choose Properties, and click the Shortcut tab (see Figure 60). Here's what the various settings do:

- The Target field is the pointer to the actual file. There's generally no need to edit this manually—if you move the target file, the next time you use the shortcut Windows will offer to find it, and if it does will offer to fix the shortcut.

The main reason you might want to edit the Target field is to make a folder or drive's shortcut open in Windows Explorer instead of the default My Computer view. Click in the Target field, press Ctrl← until the insertion point is at the very beginning of the line, and type

```
explorer.exe /n,/e,
```

with no space after the final comma. Click Apply to save the change.

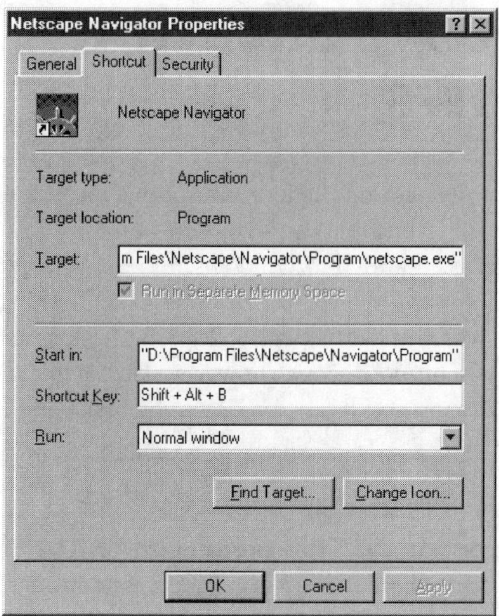

Figure 60

Shortcut properties.

- The Run in Separate Memory Space checkbox is available only in Windows NT, and only when running 16-bit Windows 3.1 applications. Turning on this option may occasionally help old programs to run smoothly; otherwise, leave it off to avoid wasting memory.
- The Start In field determines the default folder for the File/Open and File/Save dialogs. Some older applications may require it to be set to the program folder.

- The Shortcut Key setting lets you launch or switch to a program from the keyboard. Click inside the field, press the desired combination of keys, and click Apply to save the shortcut key selection. To remove a shortcut key, click in the field, press Bksp, and click Apply.
- The Run setting lets you set the target program to be launched maximized, minimized, or in a regular window.
- Clicking the Find Target button opens a My Computer view of the folder where the actual target file lives.
- Change Icons button: Instructions for using this button to change the shortcut's appearance are in the "Customize the Desktop" section.

Running DOS Applications under Windows

There are lots of reasons you might want to run a DOS application under Windows. Your job or business might require you to run an obscure old program that's never been ported to Windows. You might have a favorite DOS program you don't want to give up, or one that can do things Windows alternatives can't. Maybe you have a large collection of games and like to play the oldies sometimes. For most people, however, there aren't any compelling reasons to run DOS apps, so I'll just run down the basics and a few key tips here.

To install a DOS app, follow the instructions in the DOS Cookbook in Appendix A: DOS Survival Guide.

To add a DOS app to the Start menu, run Windows Explorer, and change to the folder where the app is installed. Find the application's icon (switch to Details view and look in the Type column), and drag it to the Start button. This will create a shortcut to the program in the top level of the Start menu. Follow the instructions in "Customize the Start Menu" earlier in this chapter to move the icon to the appropriate subfolder.

To adjust the way a DOS app runs, edit the shortcut's properties. Here's a brief rundown of the most important settings:

Program Tab. This is functionally quite similar to the Shortcut tab in a Windows program's properties, discussed just above in "Using Shortcuts," and the same instructions apply—just substitute Cmd line for Target, and "Working" for Start In.

- **Batch file** points to a file containing any DOS commands that need to be executed before Windows starts the program itself.
- **Run** works as it does with Windows apps, except that the Maximized setting doesn't expand the window to fill the desktop—it just makes the window as large as necessary to get rid of any scroll bars. Maximized is generally the setting you'll want.

- Check **Close on exit** to make the window close automatically when you exit the DOS app—otherwise you get an "inactive" window that you have to close manually.
- **Advanced** (not available in Windows NT) brings up a dialog that lets you have Windows automatically switch to MS-DOS mode when you run the program. Use this for DOS apps that won't run under Windows.

Note: Although this looks just like full-screen mode discussed under "Usage" just below, MS-DOS mode actually shuts down Windows before launching the DOS app.

Screen Tab. Lets you adjust the way a DOS program appears on screen.

- **Usage** determines whether the program takes over the full screen or appears in a window on the desktop. If a DOS program won't run right, try changing this setting. (You can toggle between window and full-screen mode while running a DOS app by pressing Alt Enter.)
- **Display toolbar** turns a toolbar at the top of the DOS window on or off. The toolbar's handy for adjusting the display font and copying text.

Misc Tab. Various random settings.

- Check **QuickEdit** only for DOS programs that don't use the mouse. It reserves the mouse exclusively for selecting and copying text from the DOS window, so you can just click and drag without having to hit the Mark button first.
- Check **Exclusive mode** only when a DOS program isn't responding to the mouse the way it's supposed to.
- Uncheck any **Windows shortcut keys** required by the DOS app. While you're working in the app, those key-combinations will be ignored by Windows.

The Windows 95/98 Boot Menu

If you work in DOS a lot, you might want to enable the Boot menu in Windows 95 and 98. It lets you get straight to DOS when you turn on your PC, without having to wait for Windows to load first.

1. Start Windows Explorer and turn on the Show All Files option. (See "Danger Zone: Hidden Files" in the Windows Cookbook.)
2. Click on the C: drive icon in the folder tree pane (left window).
3. Right-click on MSDOS.SYS and choose Properties.
4. Uncheck the Read-Only and Hidden boxes, then click OK.
5. Right-click on MSDOS.SYS and choose Open With.
6. If "Always use this program…" is checked (it shouldn't be), uncheck it.
7. Scroll down until you see Notepad and double-click on it.
8. Add `BootMenu=1` on a line by itself after `[Options]` (see Figure 61).
9. Choose File/Save; then File/Exit.

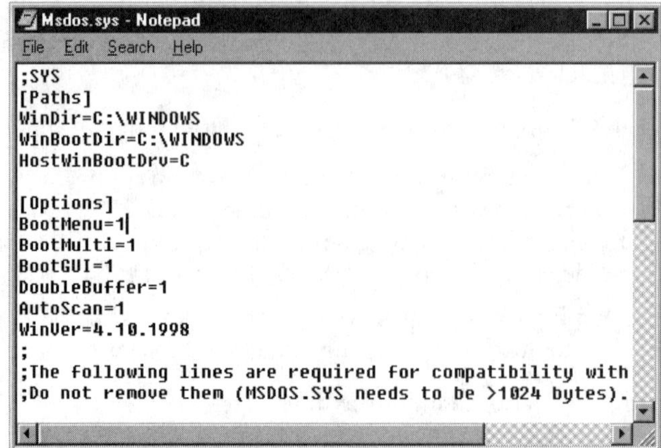

Msdos.sys - Notepad
File Edit Search Help
;SYS
[Paths]
WinDir=C:\WINDOWS
WinBootDir=C:\WINDOWS
HostWinBootDrv=C

[Options]
BootMenu=1
BootMulti=1
BootGUI=1
DoubleBuffer=1
AutoScan=1
WinVer=4.10.1998
;
;The following lines are required for compatibility with
;Do not remove them (MSDOS.SYS needs to be >1024 bytes).

Figure 61

Enabling the Windows 95/98 Boot menu.

The next time you start your computer or restart Windows, you'll get a menu of boot options. Choose "Command prompt only" to boot directly to MS-DOS mode without loading Windows.

If you upgraded to Windows 95/98 from DOS or Windows 3.1, you can choose "Previous version of MS-DOS," instead, to run your old version of DOS. (You'll be able to run Windows 3.1 only if you installed Windows 95/98 in a separate directory rather than upgrading your existing Win31 installation, and only if you did not convert the drive to FAT32.

Mouse Tricks and Keyboard Shortcuts

How to do what you want to do with the least hassle isn't always obvious in Windows. This quick reference will help you out, whether you want to teach your mouse a few tricks or you prefer keeping your hands on the keyboard.

Mouse Tricks

Mouse Tricks: General	
Maximize or restore a window	Double-click on the title bar.
Suppress AutoPlay when loading a CD	Hold down Shift while inserting the disc.
Mouse Tricks: Taskbar	
Display the Mixer	Double-click on the Sound icon.
Display the Date/Time control panel	Double-click on the clock.
Display the date and day of the week	Hold the pointer over the time display until the yellow Tooltip appears.
Arrange all open windows	Right-click on the taskbar and choose the Tile or Cascade command. (If you don't like the new arrangement, right-click again and choose Undo Tile.)
Minimize all open windows	Right-click on the taskbar and choose Minimize All Windows. (To restore minimized windows, right-click on the taskbar again and choose Undo Minimize All.)
Edit the Start menu	Right-click on the Start button and choose Explore.
Mouse Tricks: Desktop	
Display the Display control panel	Right-click on the desktop and choose Properties.
Display the System control panel	Right-click on My Computer and choose Properties.
Display the Network control panel	Right-click on Network Neighborhood and choose Properties.
Mouse Tricks: Files, Folders, and Drives	
Erase files immediately, bypassing Recycle Bin	Hold down Shift when you drop the file in the Recycle Bin.
Display properties	Alt-double-click on the icon.
Display the Open With command for any file	Click once to select, then Ctrl Shift-right-click.
Open a folder or drive in Windows Explorer	Shift-double-click the icon.
Change sort order in Details view	Click any column header; click again to reverse the order.
Mouse Tricks: Drag and Drop	
Drop into a minimized window	Drag to the taskbar, hold icon over button until the window restores, then drop in window.
Display a pop-up menu	Drag with the right mouse button, or hold Ctrl and Shift while you drop.
Copy a file to another folder on the same drive	Hold Ctrl while you drop.
Move a file from one drive to another	Hold Shift while you drop.
Type a file's path and filename in a DOS window	Drag and drop the file's icon onto the DOS window.

Most keyboards don't have the [Windows] or [Menu] keys. For a table of some other things you can do with them, search for "Using the Windows key" in Windows 98's online Help.

Keyboard Shortcuts

Keyboard Shortcuts: General	
Pop up the right-click "shortcut" menu	Shift F10 or [Menu]
Move from one dialog-box tab to another	Ctrl Tab or Ctrl Shift Tab
Close the current application window	Alt F4
Close the current document window	Ctrl F4
Switch to the next document	Ctrl F6
Keyboard Shortcuts: Taskbar	
Navigate the taskbar buttons for running applications	Press Ctrl Esc, then Esc, tap Tab repeatedly until the app you want is highlighted, and press Enter.
Minimize all open windows	Press Ctrl Esc, then Alt M. To undo, press Ctrl Esc, Esc, Ctrl Z. Or press [Windows] D to minimize; [Windows] D again to undo.
Keyboard Shortcuts: Files, Folders, and Drives	
Erase files immediately, bypassing Recycle Bin	Shift Del
Rename a file or folder	F2
Search (run Find on) the selected drive or folder	F3
Display a selected file's properties	Alt Enter
Keyboard Shortcuts: Windows Explorer	
Open new Explorer window	[Windows] E
Navigate the "Go to a different folder" drop-down list	F4
Move to the other pane	Tab or F6
Move up one level	Bksp
Move down one level	→
Expand next level of folders	→ on numeric keypad
Expand all subfolders	* on numeric keypad
Collapse subfolders	- on numeric keypad
Scroll the tree pane without changing the selected folder	Ctrl ↑ or Ctrl ↓.

Windows Resources

winmag.com *WINDOWS Magazine* has the best Windows tips and technical information of any publication, and it's usually ahead of any other U.S. magazine with news of major Windows bugs and sneak-peek reports on future releases. Most of their articles are aimed at advanced users, but John Woram's column, "Optimize Windows," is a great source of info for beginners. Keep an eye out for articles by *PC Bible* technical editor Lenny Bailes.

annoyances.org/win95 The Windows 95 Annoyances site is one of the best places for answers to questions that begin, "How can I make Windows stop…" The same folks also have a Windows 98 site, but unlike the original, which was a labor of love devoted to giving away information, the new site seems more oriented toward promoting their book.

www.pcmag.com/pctech *PC Magazine*'s Web site has a handy collection of tips from the publication's advice columns. After navigating to this page, click the link for your flavor of Windows under the "Tips" heading.

support.microsoft.com/support Microsoft's database of support documents has a wealth of information, but there's something flaky about its search engine. My searches frequently fail to turn up documents that I know for a fact *are* in the database and *do* contain the keywords I was searching for. (Sometimes a different browser, or the same search performed the next day, gets better results. Go figure.) You may need to fill out a registration form before you get access to the full library. If you have a CompuServe account, you might try using their MSKB (Microsoft Knowledge Base) service instead. I usually get more hits there for the same searches than I do on **microsoft.com**.

yahoo.com You'll find pointers to hundreds of Windows-oriented sites—some good, some bad, some no longer available—on Yahoo! under Computers and Internet : Software : Operating Systems : Windows. Click the Windows 95, Windows 98, or Windows NT links for a list specific to the version you're using.

12

Windows Add-Ons

by Robert Lauriston and Galen Gruman

Galen Gruman wrote the Fonts section of this chapter; the rest is by Robert Lauriston.

In This Chapter

Over the years, Windows has evolved to handle more tasks with its ever-growing toolkit, and Microsoft has improved the operating system to eliminate some of its former defects. As a result, the need for utilities and other add-on programs has shrunk substantially. However, that's had little effect on the *supply*: there are literally tens of thousands of programs (mostly free or distributed as shareware) you can install to add features to Windows or change its appearance or behavior in various ways.

Unfortunately, many enhancement slow Windows down. Also, if you install a lot of them, or even just one particularly bad program, Windows may start crashing or behaving erratically. Thus, I recommend installing a minimum number of add-ons and choosing the ones you do use very carefully.

In this brief chapter, I offer a highly opinionated guide to the few add-ons I can't do without, plus some that, while not essential, are more useful than most.

For those interested in experimenting further, see the "Windows Add-On Resources" section at the end of the chapter, where I provide some pointers to additional information and places where you can download enough software to choke your hard drive.

Note that several kinds of software that in previous editions of *The PC Bible* were discussed in the chapter on utilities are in this edition discussed elsewhere:

- File-transfer utilities in the "Exchanging Files with Your Desktop PC" section of Chapter 3: Notebook PCs.
- DisplayMate, a monitor-tuning utility, in Chapter 5: Monitors Etc.
- Anti-virus and backup software in Chapter 9: Protect Your Data.
- Windows' built-in disk utilities in the "Safety Check" section of Chapter 11: Windows 95, 98, and NT.
- Personal information managers (PIMs) in Chapter 16: Databases.
- Web browser plug-ins in Chapter 21: The Web and Browsers.
- Macintosh diskette readers and file converters in Chapter 25: Networks: Connecting PCs.

You won't find any discussion of third-party memory optimizers, disk caches, or disk compression utilities in this edition as Windows 95, 98, and NT handle those tasks well enough without help. There are some products on the market that may provide marginally better performance, but in my experience the potential compatibility problems introduced by such utilities outweigh any minor speed increase.

Essential Add-Ons

There are only two Windows add-ons that I absolutely couldn't get along without. If you use e-mail or surf the Web, you'll probably need them too.

WinZip: Compress and Consolidate Files, Span Disks

WinZip is my favorite *zip utility*, a class of programs that create and read *zip archives* (aka *zip files*). Zip archives do three useful things:

- **Compress files.** "Zipped" files take up less space on disk and take less time to transmit or receive as e-mail attachments. Zipped files also download faster, which is why electronically distributed software is almost always in .zip format. How much a file can be compressed depends on its format: some graphics files may compress 95%, while program files or a compressed .tif file may hardly compress at all. My Word files are usually a third their original size after zipping.
- **Consolidate files.** One .zip file can hold any number of other files, or even a set of nested folders. If you have to e-mail someone a number of files, it's usually faster (at both ends) and more convenient to zip them into a single file first.
- **Span disks.** Most zip utilities will automatically *span* multiple disks if the archive is too large to fit on a single disk. You can use this feature to split a 5MB file between several floppy disks, or a 500MB file between several Zip disks. (There's no special connection between .zip files and Zip disks; Iomega apparently just liked the name.)

From the user's point of view, a .zip file acts a lot like a floppy disk. When you zip files, nothing happens to them; instead, you get a new .zip file with compressed copies of the files inside of it (see Figure 1). Once you've created a zip archive, if you extract a file from it, the zip utility creates a copy on your hard disk, and the compressed copy stays in the archive. You can add more files to the archive, or delete selected files from it, at any time.

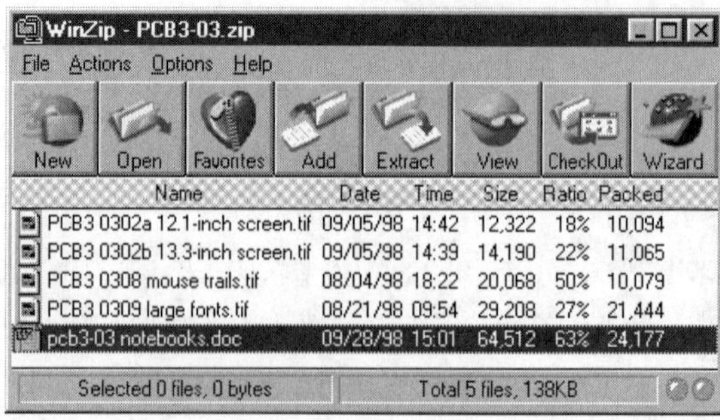

Figure 1

This WinZip archive contains five files that total 138K, but thanks to compression, the .zip file takes up only 76K on disk.

WinZip adds several commands to Windows right-click pop-up menus that make common zip tasks fast and efficient:

- **New/WinZip File** creates a new, empty .zip file; when creating an archive, I often use this command, double-click to open the file, and then drag and drop the files I want to add from Windows Explorer into the WinZip window.
- **Add To Zip** creates a new archive for the selected files and prompts you to enter a name for the new file. If you right-click a single file or folder, a second Add To Zip choice appears that automatically creates a .zip file with a matching name (see Figure 2).
- **Extract To** prompts you for the name of a new folder into which the .zip file's contents will be copied. A second Extract To choice will automatically create a folder based on the name of the .zip file (see Figure 2).
- **Create Self-Extractor** converts a .zip file to a self-extracting program that can be opened on any PC running Windows, whether or not it has a zip utility installed.

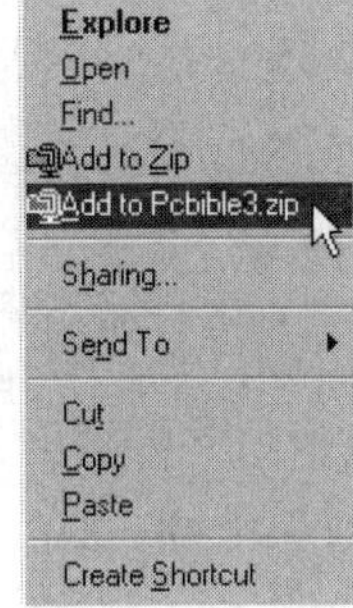

Figure 2

WinZip's pop-up menus include choices that create a .zip file with a name that matches the selected folder or extract a .zip file to a new folder with a matching name.

One WinZip feature I use all the time is the Install button, which appears when you open a .zip file containing a program with a Setup utility. Click Install, and WinZip automatically extracts the archive to a scratch directory and runs Setup; after the program's installed, or if install fails, WinZip automatically deletes the temp file.

Another feature I occasionally find useful is WinZip's support for various other popular archive formats, including .uue, .z, and .tar. I've had little success in using WinZip with the .hqx files I occasionally get from Mac users; to open those files, I use Aladdin Expander, a free utility you can download from **www.aladdinsys.com/expander/#win**.

WinZip's process for spanning disks is not entirely intuitive, but it's explained clearly in the online help. The trick is that you must start by creating a *new* .zip file on the first disk (you can't just copy an existing .zip file to the disk). Then you just add files as usual. When the first disk is full, WinZip will prompt you to add another, and it will keep on prompting for new disks as necessary until you've added all the files.

I have no idea whether WinZip's the best zip utility around—all I know is that it's good enough that I paid the $29 shareware registration fee, and I've had no motive to try another. A lot of other people seem to like it, too: it's always near the top of shareware library sites' most-downloaded file lists. You can find it anywhere, or get it straight from the vendor at **www.winzip.com**. If for some reason you need a DOS zip utility, the classic is PKZip (**www.pkware.com**).

Acrobat Reader: View and Print Online Documents

Adobe's Acrobat technology does one thing really well: it turns any document into a digital form that can be viewed onscreen on just about any Windows PC, Macintosh, or Unix workstation, and printed on any printer. You don't need a copy of the application that created the document; all you need is a copy of Acrobat Reader, a free view-and-print utility.

This has made the Acrobat format (aka PDF, for Portable Document Format) the Internet's standard for the distribution of documents that can't easily be converted to HTML, or where high-quality printouts are more important than Web access. It's increasingly common for computer hardware manuals to be distributed in Acrobat format—this cuts down manufacturers' printing costs, but still allows users to print pages as they need them.

You can find a copy of the reader on most CD-ROMs that include Acrobat documents. If you don't have a copy, or if you want to get the latest version, you can download it for free from **www.adobe.com/acrobat**.

Installing Acrobat Reader adds a plug-in to your Web browser so that when you click a link to an Acrobat document, it will open right in your browser. I've found it faster and more reliable to download Acrobat documents to my hard drive and then open them in Acrobat Reader, which works better as a stand-alone application than as a browser add-on.

To disable the plug-in in Netscape browsers, delete the file nppdf32.dll from the Plugins folder. In Microsoft Internet Explorer, follow the instructions on the following Web page (be sure to capitalize "solutions" or Adobe's server won't find the page), but stop at step 10.

www.adobe.com/supportservice/custsupport/SOLUTIONS/98fe.htm

If you want to create your own Acrobat files, you need a copy of Adobe Acrobat (list price $295; around $175 on the street). Once you've installed it, you can create an Acrobat file by simply "printing" any document to the

Acrobat PDFWriter, a special object Acrobat adds to the list of available printers. If you have a scanner, you can also convert paper documents; the resulting file can maintain the original image, but you can search the file for words or phrases (see Figure 3), something you can't do in a normal scanned image file.

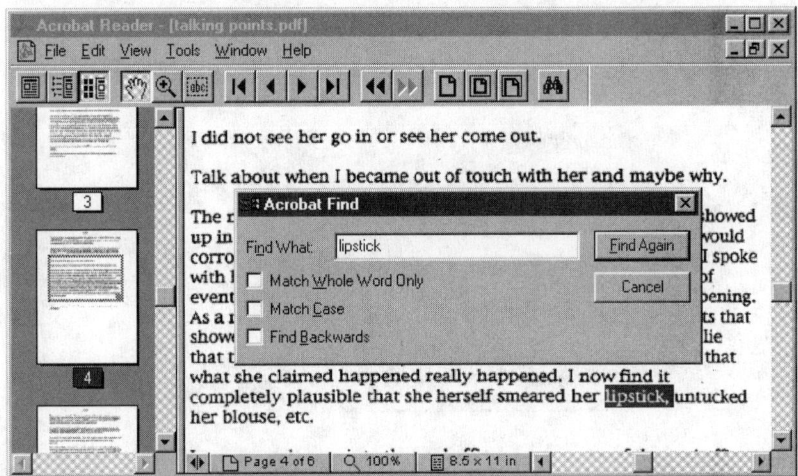

Figure 3

Adobe Acrobat.

Options and Enhancements

The following add-ons aren't by any means essential, but they enhance Windows significantly. I don't use any of them regularly myself.

TweakUI: Change Windows' Look

TweakUI, an optional control panel available for free from Microsoft, is the answer to a lot of questions that start with, "Why won't Windows let me...." With it, you can, among other things:

- Hide or rename any of the icons on the desktop except My Computer, including the normally uncooperative ones like the Recycle Bin and Network Neighborhood (see Figure 4).
- Stop Windows from adding "Shortcut to" at the beginning of shortcut names and/or get rid of the little arrow at the lower-left corner of shortcut icons.
- Turn AutoPlay on or off independently for audio and data CDs.
- Change the location of special folders, like My Documents and Favorites.

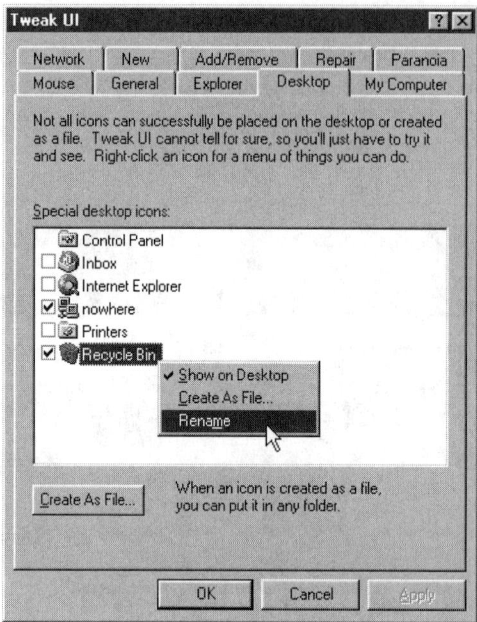

Figure 4

TweakUI.

- Turn the Start menu's "Click here to begin" and the "Tip of the Day" displays on or off.
- Automatically clear file history lists, like the Documents menu and the drop-down list in the Find Files dialog box, every time you restart Windows.
- Remove nonfunctional entries from the Add/Remove Programs list.
- Set your computer to log onto a network automatically at startup.
- Disable Windows 98's Active Desktop and/or the integrated copy of Microsoft Internet Explorer 4.0.

Depending on exactly what version of Windows you have, there may be a copy of TweakUI on the setup CD, but to minimize the chance of bugs, it's a good idea to download the latest version from Microsoft.

- **For Windows 95 or NT**, go to `microsoft.com/windows/downloads`. Choose your version of Windows from the "Select a Product" list and choose Power Toys from "Select a category"; then click Go. Click the TweakUI entry and follow the download and installation instructions on the page that appears.
- **For Windows 98**, there should eventually be a TweakUI update available at the Windows Update site (accessible from the Start menu), though as we go to press, there's not one there. In the meantime, you can install TweakUI from the Windows 98 CD. Open the \tools\reskit\powertoy folder, right-click the Tweakui Setup Information file (tweakui.inf), and choose Install.

Note that TweakUI is, as Microsoft warns you when you install it, unsupported. In other words, if it doesn't work, or of it somehow screws up your system, you won't get any help from Microsoft's tech support.

QuickRes: Fast Access to Display Options

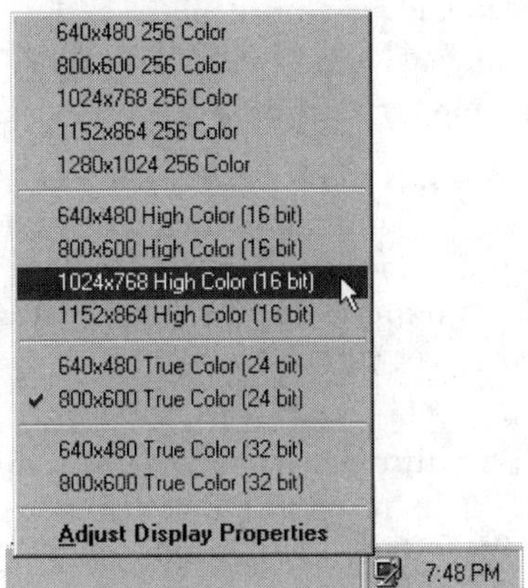

Figure 5

The QuickRes menu.

QuickRes puts a little icon in the taskbar's "tray" that you can click to pop up a menu where you can instantly change your display's resolution and/or color depth (see Figure 5). This feature is quite useful if you're designing Web pages and want to test the look of your pages in different video modes. Some video cards install QuickRes automatically. Otherwise, here's how to get it:

- **For Windows 95**, follow the same instructions as for TweakUI, except click the QuickRes entry.
- **For Windows NT**, QuickRes is currently available only on the CD that comes with the Windows NT Workstation Resource Kit, an expensive book from Microsoft Press that I haven't found terribly useful. However, the NT drivers for my video card install something that looks and works just like it.
- **For Windows 98**, there's nothing to install—QuickRes is built in. Just open the Display control panel, click the Settings tab, click Advanced, check "Show settings icon on taskbar," and click OK twice.

Other Power Toys

There are some other interesting goodies in the Power Toys pages for Windows 95 and NT—for example, a "Send To X" addition to the right-click pop-up menu that lets you pick a target for the Send To command on the fly. Windows 95 and NT users can check out all of them on the same Power Toys page with the link to TweakUI. I'm not sure whether Microsoft plans to offer more Power Toys for Windows 98.

Norton Utilities: Improved Disk Tools, NT Defragger

The Norton Utilities dates all the way back DOS 1.0. Perhaps the biggest problem with that sorry excuse for an operating system was how easy it was to accidentally delete files—and once they were deleted, they were gone. Peter Norton wrote a little program that added an undelete command, which a huge percentage of PC owners bought. As Microsoft improved DOS and later Windows, the Norton Utilities kept a step ahead, offering essential tools like a defragger and a disk repair utility.

Eventually, however, Microsoft added almost all the really essential tools to Windows, so Norton's no longer the must-have product it used to be. However, it's still worth buying for a couple of tasks:

- **Emergency disk recovery.** If a disk becomes unreadable or starts behaving too erratically to use, Norton can often get it working again, at least for long enough to copy any important data to another disk. The less you do to the disk *before* running Norton's Disk Doctor utility, the more likely you'll be able to recover your files, so it's nice to have a copy on hand just in case.
- **Defragmenting NTFS volumes.** While Windows 95 and 98 have defragmenters built in (as discussed in the "Safety Check" section of Chapter 11: Windows 95, 98, and NT), Windows NT 4.0 doesn't. If, like most NT users, you have your system set up so it can dual-boot between Windows 95/98 and NT, you can use the former's defragger for FAT volumes, but this doesn't do anything for NTFS drives, since only NT can see them. The solution: buy a copy of Norton Utilities for NT, which includes an NTFS-compatible defragger, Speed Disk (see Figure 6).

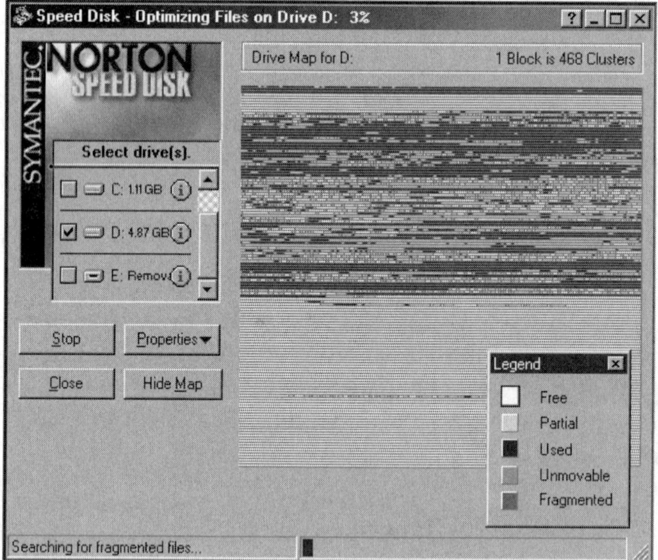

Figure 6

Norton Utilities for NT's Speed Disk..

Unfortunately, the NT version of Norton is kind of buggy, and Symantec isn't in any big rush to fix things. I purchased a copy a while back when I was having some problems with one of my hard disks (which, as it turned out, was going bad and eventually had to be replaced). One of the main reasons I bought the program was to detect disk errors as they happened, before they had time to cause problems, but I wasn't able to use that feature because of a bug that caused the program to report an empty Zip drive as a hardware failure. At this point, Symantec has known about that bug for at least ten months without coming up with a better workaround than keeping a disk in the drive at all times (which is contrary to Iomega's recommendations for maximizing Zip disk life).

Also, I'm currently unable to use the NT defragger, which chugs along for a minute or so and then stops with an error message about "metadata corruption." Symantec's one possible workaround for that problem is to copy all the folders on the drive, compare them with the originals, and rename or delete any files that didn't copy.

Quick View Plus

The original QuickView is a file viewer built into Windows. Right-click a file and choose Quick View, and an image of the file will appear in a special window. A toolbar includes buttons that let you change the font size for text files or open the document (see Chapter 11, Figure 43). This is a particularly handy tool when you have several large files and aren't sure which one to open: previewing a large file with Quick View really is quick compared with opening it.

Unfortunately, Quick View doesn't know how to open most kinds of files. That's where Quick View Plus comes in: it enhances Quick View so it can display over 200 popular file formats. You can download a free 30-day trial version at **www.inso.com/qvp/qvptrial.htm**; if you like it and want to keep using it, the regular version will set you back $45 to $50.

Alternative File Managers

Personally, I find Windows Explorer a perfectly adequate file-management tool, at least if you use the efficient techniques I describe in the *Windows Cookbook* in Chapter 11. While I do have some complaints about it, like its inability to rename a group of files in one operation, I'm satisfied enough that I can't be bothered to experiment with other programs.

The people I know who really dislike Windows Explorer generally aren't happy with the current alternatives. Most of them complain that there's nothing as good as Norton Commander, PC Tools, or XTree, old DOS and Windows 3.1 file managers—all of which were purchased by Symantec, which never upgraded *any* of them for use with Windows 95. Commander and XTree are popular enough that there are a number of shareware clones; to find one, search for "commander" or "xtree" at **shareware.com** or any large shareware library.

One of *The PC Bible's* technical editors, Lenny Bailes, uses a couple of alternative file managers. Here's what he had to say about them:

"Drag and File offers all the features that Microsoft left out of Windows Explorer: side-by-side file listings for multiple drives, horizontal and vertical tiling of file windows (see Figure 7), extensive sorting options, and multiple file display filters. You can use it to create or edit multiple program associations for registered file types, print directory listings, or synchronize the contents of two file directories. Drag and File also includes a built-in FTP client (for downloading files from the Internet), customizable taskbars for launching applications, and more. Drag and File Gold also includes Drag and Zip, one of WinZip's most popular competitors.

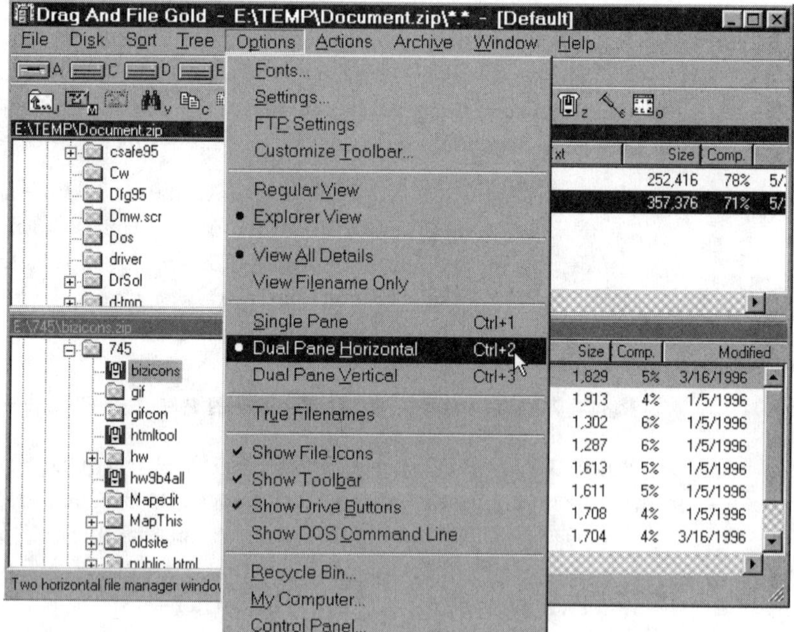

Figure 7

Drag and File Gold is one of the many alternative file managers that old Norton Commander or XTree users might prefer to Windows Explorer.

"TurboBrowser 98 is handy if your work involves viewing and manipulating word processing, spreadsheet, or graphics files for which you don't own the creating applications: it has a variety of file-preview features like those in QuickView Plus. For me, though, there's one TurboBrowser feature that's worth the price all by itself: the intelligent 'PrintQ' lets me select 50 or 60 files, click the Print button, and go out for a cup of coffee with the assurance that all the printouts will be ready when I return. Left to its own devices, Windows would get part way through and then halt with an 'out of memory' error."

For Nerds Only

Most people don't need the three programs discussed in this section. Given the broad focus of *The PC Bible*, normally that would exclude them from the book, but if your job requires you to install a lot of software, or if you just like to install software for fun, these nerd-oriented tools are so useful that I'm making an exception.

Partition Magic: Resize and Convert Disk Partitions

If you experiment with different operating systems, Partition Magic (around $60) is extremely useful. It allows you to make the following changes to your hard disks without having to back up and restore the data the way you would if you used Windows' own tools:

- **Resize disk partitions.** You might need to do this if, for example, your whole hard drive is formatted as a single C: drive, and you want to make room to install BeOS or Linux or to create an NTFS drive for use by Windows NT.
- **Convert disk partitions.** This is useful if you've converted a drive to FAT32, which can be read only by Windows 95 OSR2 and Windows 98, and decide you want to run DOS, Windows 3.1, an older version of Windows 95, or Windows NT. The same is true if you've converted to a NTFS, HPFS, or Linux partition.
- **Change the FAT32 cluster size.** This is a fairly arcane change that in some cases may improve performance substantially.

When you add new logical drives, drive letter assignments can change, which means that applications on those drives may stop working. Partition Magic includes DriveMapper, a utility that fixes most such problems by editing Windows' registry and substituting the new drive letter for the old one (see Figure 8).

Figure 8

Partition Magic's DriveMapper.

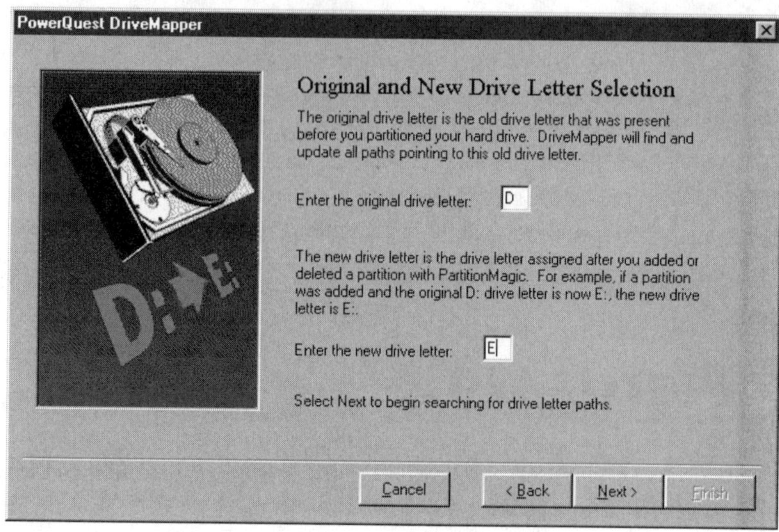

You can get information about Partition Magic's other features at **`www.powerquest.com`**. The latest version of the program adds a utility that competes with System Commander, but the latter's still the best at what it does.

System Commander: Manage Multiple Operating Systems

If you just want to run one copy each of DOS and Windows 3.1, Windows 95/98, and NT, the boot-menu features in Windows are all you need (so long as you install them in the right order and in the right directories). However, if you want to run *both* Windows 95 and 98, or multiple copies of a single version of Windows, or a variety of operating systems, you probably want a copy of System Commander.

To simplify a bit, System Commander's basic trick is that it makes and hides copies of your operating system's boot files. Then, when you install a new operating system, it copies the boot files for that operating system as well. Whenever you start or reboot your computer, System Commander displays a menu from which you choose which operating system you want to run; after you make your choice, the program copies that OS's files to the hard disk, and the OS starts as if it had the PC to itself.

The program has a lot of other utilities and options you can use to work around the various conditions that make it difficult to get operating systems to coexist peacefully. For example, if you have two operating systems that both need to boot from C:, but they can't share the same partition, you can install them on separate partitions, and System Commander will hide one from the other so that both think they're booting from drive C.

Depending on exactly what you want to do, using System Commander can be pretty difficult. The manual's confusing, and I've seldom found the FAQs at the Web site helpful. A number of times I've run into problems I couldn't resolve and have had to call tech support or start over—though in the end, I've always managed to get the program to do what I wanted.

System Commander costs around $30 to $40. System Commander Deluxe, which adds a built-in partition manager (not as powerful as Partition Magic), costs around $60. System Commander 98, a single-purpose, stripped-down version of Deluxe, costs only $20, but it's a one-trick pony: it lets you upgrade to Windows 98 in such a way that you can switch back to Windows 3.1 or 95 as needed. You can find more information about all three versions at **www.v-com.com**.

CleanSweep Deluxe: The Ultra Uninstaller

In theory, all current Windows apps should let you uninstall them using the Add/Remove Programs control panel. In practice, they often leave garbage behind, and if enough of that garbage accumulates, your system can become sluggish or unreliable. If you install beta programs or other imperfect software, even a small amount of garbage left behind can be big trouble.

Hence the popularity of commercial uninstaller utilities. Many of these don't work so well: typically, they use a sort of educated-guess approach to figure out which files to keep and which to throw out, and as a result, they sometimes delete stuff you really need or don't do a very thorough job of taking out the garbage.

CleanSweep Deluxe (around $50) is the best of the bunch. It monitors application setup routines, tracking every file they add and every registry change they make. Thus, when you undelete something, CleanSweep knows exactly what to remove—but it will still warn you before deleting things that might cause trouble. For a detailed description of the program's capabilities, you can download an Acrobat copy of the program's manual from **www.qdeck.com/products/cleansweep**.

Personally, I prefer simply testing software in a scratch installation of Windows or on a separate PC and reinstalling Windows when necessary. If I had to test software on the same Windows installation I use for business, though, I'd definitely use CleanSweep.

Fonts

Even if you have no idea what they are, you're relying on fonts. Text, whether on screen or on paper, comes in a variety of shapes and forms. Those differently shaped types of text are called fonts, and they provide the visual variety that lets you add emotion, authority, whimsy and just plain interest to your words.

Windows comes with a basic set of fonts for text (Arial, Times New Roman, and Courier New) and for symbols (Symbols, such as αγ∃ιε4, and Wingdings, such as ♋♑♌♓♏🗐). These cover the bases of basic communication: staid Times for business communication, neutral Arial for headlines and flyers, and Courier for people who just love their own Remingtons and want that sense of "I'm too retro to admit I use a computer" in their documents. The symbols fonts, of course, let you use special-purpose characters, such as Greek letters for math and whimsical characters such as starbursts for the pure fun of it.

But just as the world long has gone beyond vanilla, chocolate, and strawberry, so too can you go beyond these basic fonts. In fact, there are thousands of fonts available, each with a distinctive look and feel. Windows is designed to let you add these fonts to your repertoire, so you can make the text of your documents have precisely the look you want. You can also use these fonts to change the appearance of the text in Windows' menus, desktop, and dialog boxes, as well as the appearance of Web pages you view or create. Look at this book, almost any other book, and almost any magazine: see the variety of fonts and how they help give each publication its distinctive look? That's why you'll want to add at least a few fonts to what Windows provides.

Font Formats

If you're new to fonts, you'll quickly discover that there are three types: TrueType, System, and PostScript. This is key, because Windows knows how to handle two of them, but not the third. But you can't ignore that third format if you produce documents for output at commercial printers or desktop-publishing service bureaus.

TrueType. The native Windows font format, this is the format that Arial, Courier New, Times New Roman, Symbol, and Wingdings come in. If you get nerdy and look to see the filename extension for these files, you'll see that it is .ttf. You'll also often see a double-T icon in font menus in programs like Microsoft Word to let you know you're using a TrueType font (see Figure 9).

System. Also known as bitmap fonts, these fonts are relics, used for compatibility with very old versions of Windows and with DOS. Basically, don't worry about this format, which was designed for onscreen display. Windows has several System fonts installed in case they're needed by old programs, or in case somehow Windows has trouble with TrueType and needs a backup font to display its menus and so forth. The most common System fonts are Modern, MS Sans, MS Serif, and Terminal. They have the filename extension .fon. Most programs won't even display these fonts in their font menus. If you have a program that does let you use them, you'll know you're using one if you get blotchy-looking text when printing—these fonts were never designed for the fine resolution of a printer.

PostScript. The standard format in the publishing and Macintosh worlds, these fonts won't work in Windows unless you have the program Adobe Type Manager installed. (That program, commonly called ATM, will let you use PostScript fonts even with non-PostScript printers.) Each font is composed of two files, one with the filename extension .pfb and the other with the extension .pfm. Some programs, like Microsoft Word, display a printer icon next to PostScript fonts' names in font menus, while others, like QuarkXPress and CorelDraw, display a T1 icon. (The T1 comes "Type 1," the variation of PostScript now standard.) It's fine to use both TrueType and PostScript fonts

in documents to be printed on a local printer, but don't use TrueType fonts in documents that will be output on a high-end PostScript device, such as a film recorder, imagesetter, or proofing printer-even if you are using Adobe Type Manager. These devices will often substitute an incorrect font for your TrueType fonts or simply refuse to print the pages using TrueType.

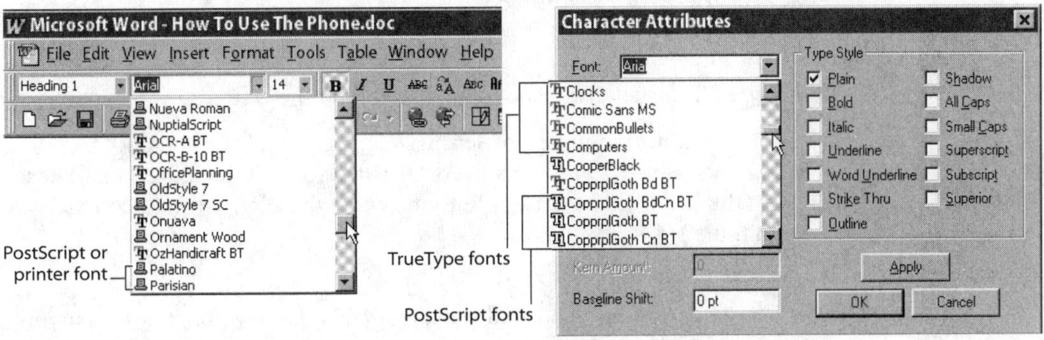

Figure 9

The indicators in common programs (Microsoft Word, left; QuarkXPress, right) to show whether a font is in TrueType (TT) or PostScript (printer icon or T1) format. The printer icon also appears next to the names of fonts built into your printer.

How to Install Fonts

Because fonts are so basic a necessity, Windows makes it easy to install them. That wasn't always true, but it is today, since Windows 95, 98, and NT 4.0 all use the same font-management system.

One caveat before you start: the variations within a font—such as bold, italic, bold italic, light, semibold, and so on (see Figure 10)—are each stored in a separate font file. (These variations are called *faces*.) So, for example, to install the font Times, you need to install four fonts: Times, Times Bold, Timed Italic, and TimesBold Italic. Most fonts have the four basic variations of regular (also called roman or medium or book), bold, italic, and bold italic. Most programs let you specify these variations through menus, buttons, and shortcuts, so to boldface a word in a sentence, you just highlight and click the Bold option, rather than having to go to a font menu and find the bold version of the font. With other variations like semibold, heavy, and ultra, you'll almost always need to select each variant from a menu.

Figure 10

Font variations.

Cheltenham Light *Light Italic* Roman **Bold** *Italic* ***Bold Italic*** **Ultra** ***Ultra Italic*** Condensed **Bold Condensed** **Ultra Condensed**

Bauhaus Light Medium **Demi** **Bold** **Heavy**

Esprit Book *Book Italic* **Medium** ***Medium Italic*** **Bold** ***Bold Italic*** **Black** ***Black Italic***

Poppl Laudaito Light Light Condendsed *Light Italic* Regular *Italic* Condensed **Medium** **Medium Condendsed** ***Medium Italic*** **Bold** **Bold Condensed** ***Bold Italic***

TrueType. To install TrueType fonts, just follow these steps:

1. From the Start menu, select Settings/Control Panel and then double-click the Fonts folder. You'll see a list of installed fonts (see Figure 11). (Those with the TT icon are TrueType fonts, while those with the A icon are system fonts.)
2. Select File/Install New Font.
3. Navigate to the disk and folder that contains the new fonts, just as if you were using the regular File/Open dialog box. In a few seconds, the dialog box will display all the fonts in that folder (see Figure 11). Select the ones you want to install (click Select All to quickly select them all), make sure "Copy fonts to Fonts folder" is checked, and click OK. Your new fonts will appear in the Fonts window and be available to your programs.

To see what the new TrueType fonts look like, just double-click them in the Fonts menu; You'll see a display that shows all characters in several sizes (see Figure 12).

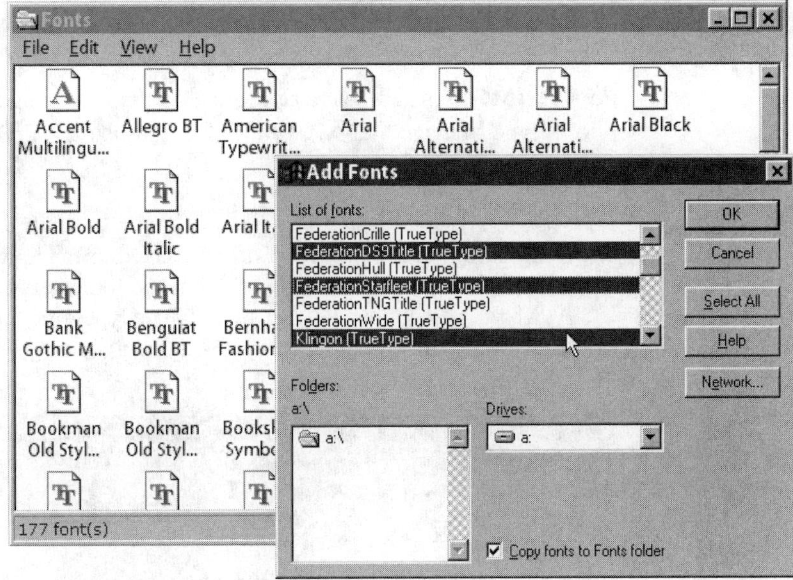

Figure 11

Installing TrueType fonts.

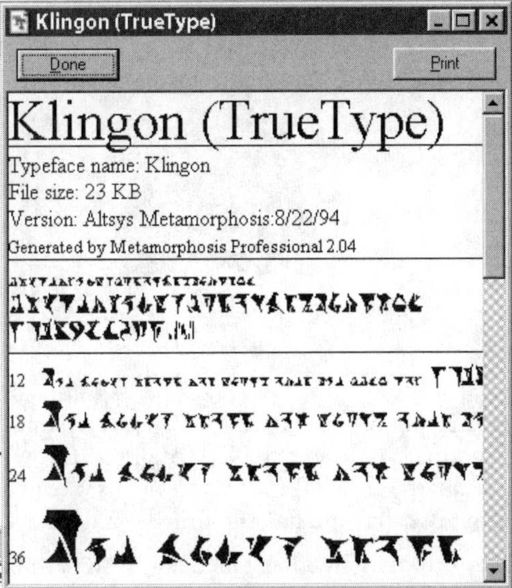

Figure 12

Windows' font display.

If you don't check "Copy fonts to Fonts folder" when installing TrueType fonts, your PC will still use those fonts, but they won't be copied to the Fonts folder. That means you won't see them in that folder later, but having them in their own folders can be handy if you like to keep fonts organized by project or other concept. Be sure to check "Copy fonts to Fonts folder" when installing fonts from a floppy drive or CD-ROM—otherwise, you'll have to have that disk in the drive to use those fonts.

To remove fonts from the menu, open the Fonts folder, select the fonts you want to get rid of, and choose File/Delete (or just press Del).

PostScript. To install PostScript fonts, do the following after you've installed Adobe Type Manager (ATM). Notice how similar the process is to the TrueType installation process.

1. Open Adobe Type Manager and click the Add Fonts tab.
2. Make sure that Browse for Fonts is selected in the Source pop-up menu, and select the drive and folder that has the fonts you want to add. Note that ATM will install both PostScript and TrueType fonts. In a few seconds, a list of fonts will appear. Select the ones you want to add. (See Figure 13.)

Figure 13

Adding fonts in Adobe Type Manager.

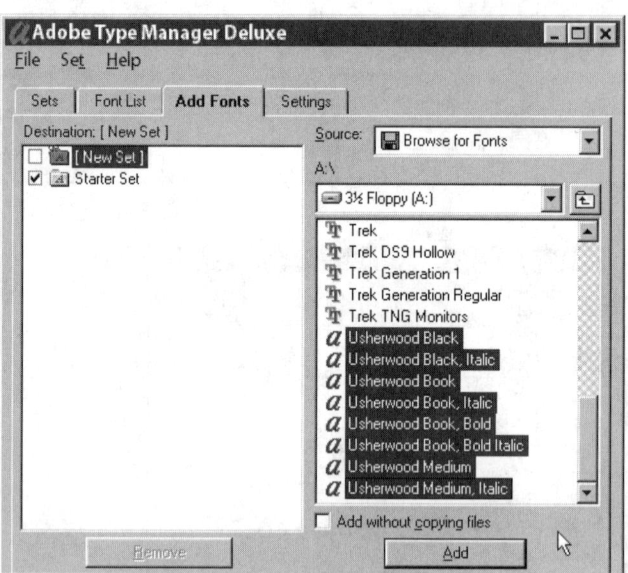

3. Check a set (a group of fonts that can be activated and deactivated together) from the window at the left, or check [New Set] [note to production: use square brackets] to create a new set containing these fonts. The Starter Set usually contains the fonts you'll always want available.
4. Click Add. Your fonts will be installed and made available to your programs. (Note that PostScript fonts are copied to a folder, usually called PSFONTS, that you designated when you installed ATM. TrueType fonts are copied to the Windows Fonts folder.) Close ATM when you're done.

To see a preview of PostScript fonts, go to the Font List pane in ATM and double-click the font you want to see. A window will pop up showing you what the font looks like in several sizes.

To remove fonts from your menu, go to the Font List pane, which displays all installed fonts, no matter what sets they reside in, select the fonts you want to delete, and click Remove. You can also select fonts within their sets in the Sets pane and use Remove to delete them.

Where to Find Fonts

Fonts come from many sources—big companies that sell packages for $100 or more each, little companies that sell collections of fonts at lower prices, big companies that give away a ton of fonts when you buy their other products, and hobbyists who make and sell them for a few dollars or simply give them away over the Web.

The fastest and cheapest way to start a font collection is to buy a program like CorelDraw (around $400 on the street). It comes with hundreds of TrueType and PostScript fonts, so the fonts alone may be worth the purchase price.

Adobe is not quite as generous, but it usually includes a copy of Adobe Type on Call in its programs (Photoshop, PageMaker, Illustrator, PageMill, Premiere, and others), which includes a few dozen free PostScript fonts. You can then buy additional fonts electronically from Adobe for anywhere from $29 to $219 and, when you get an unlock code, install them from the Type on Call CD. You can buy also Type on Call for $50. You can preview Adobe's fonts at **www.adobe.com/type**.

Microsoft's programs tend to install new fonts, especially several optimized for use on the Web (Verdana, Minion Web, and Trebuchet MS are ones that current Microsoft programs add to Windows). You can download several free Web-oriented fonts (Webdings, Trebuchet MS, Georgia, Verdana, Comic Sans MS, Arial Black, Impact, and Monototype.com) from **microsoft.com/truetype/fontpack**.

There are dozens of font makers who'd be happy to sell you fonts. You can get a list—including Web links—from *Publish* magazine's Web site (**www.publish.com**) at the Software Closet. You need to register to use the site, but there is no fee. Established, popular firms include The Font Bureau (**fontbureau.com**), Fonthaus (**www.fonthaus.com**), and Bitstream (**bitstream.com**).

Finally, you can find some free or nearly free fonts online. *Publish*'s Web site has some free fonts, as does the Yahoo site (**www.yahoo.com**), if you follow the trail Arts & Humanities: Design Arts : Graphic Design : Typography: Typefaces. If you use America Online, use the keyword Fonts to get to the Desktop and Web Publishing forum's font library, which offers many free and inexpensive TrueType and PostScript fonts.

It used to be that everyone and his mother was in the business of creating fonts, and many were poorly constructed, resulting in poor-quality output at large or very small sizes and flaws that sometimes prevented pages from printing. But things have settled down in recent years, and you should feel confident in using fonts from any of the commercial sources. If you use shareware or freeware fonts, you likely will have no trouble, but test them first before relying on them for publications you have output at a commercial printer or service bureau.

Using Fonts Effectively

It's easy to get carried away with fonts once you start collecting them. In the early 1980s, when the Macintosh first introduced fonts to the general public, professionals sniffed about "ransom-note typography," popular with amateurs, where it seemed as if every word was in a different font. That's definitely overkill.

The secret to using fonts effectively is to use them sparingly and with purpose. You rarely will have more than four fonts in a publication (not counting things like ads, of course). Typically, you will have the following:

- **Body text.** This is the standard text in a document, used for the basic text (called *body copy*), like the text you're reading right now. The font for this text sets the basic visual tone for all of your copy.
- **Title text.** The headlines, titles, and other such titling in a document typically use variations of the same font, although sometimes you may use one font for the headlines and another for titling inside the text (such as in subheadlines).
- **Sidebar text.** For separate stories that appear as adjuncts to your main story, it is common to use a different font to help separate the two kinds of stories. However, there are many techniques to distinguish such elements (such as different column widths); there's no rule saying a sidebar or other separate content must use a different font.
- **Ancillary text.** Captions, page numbers, credits, and so forth usually use variations of one font or end up being variations of other fonts. For example, credit lines can either be a variation of the body text font or a separate font that may also be used for other ancillary elements like captions.
- **Display text.** Not everything you create is a report or newsletter. If you create posters, flyers, ads, or other such materials, you'll want a sampling of display fonts—those fonts designed to have high impact when used sparingly. They're typically too weird or bold to use as body text, but in an ad or logo, they catch people's eye in a flash.

While no document must follow this typical breakdown, it's a good place to start if you're uncertain when to use different fonts. But no matter how you decide to use fonts for different kinds of text, be sure to create some sample documents so you can see whether the fonts look good together and whether the result ends up being chaotic rather than helpful. Unfortunately, there's no magic formula to tell you what fonts look good together—as with fashion and furnishings, rely on someone with good aesthetics (who may be yourself).

When in doubt, use fewer fonts. While using separate fonts can make different kinds of content clearly distinct, overdoing it can simply be jarring. This advice also applies to the use of font variations: use boldface and italics only for consistent, infrequent uses; for example, use italics to stress a word in a sentence (the visual equivalent of raising your voice or enunciating a little more slowly to emphasize something when speaking) and boldface for the first few words after a bullet (·).

Remember that every font or font variant used should *mean* something: don't throw fonts around at random just for variety's sake.

As you get familiar with fonts, you'll quickly discover two terms: serif and sans serif. Serifs are the doohickeys that come out like flanges from the tops and bottoms of most letters (such as at the bottom of a *p* or top of a *b*). They help give the characters a distinctive look and help people recognize the shapes more easily. Fonts that don't use these serifs are called sans serif (*sans* is French for *without*). Times New Roman is an example of a serif font, while Arial is an example of a sans serif font.

There's an old saw that you should use serif fonts for body text and sans serif fonts for title and ancillary text (sidebars can use either). While that's a common approach, it's not a rule. With the right fonts, you can create very effective all-serif and, although it's harder to pull off, all–sans serif documents.

Because of the oddities of copyright law, it's legal to duplicate a font and sell it under a new name so long as you don't copy the mathematical code that makes up the fonts (and tells the printer how to print it). Thus, you'll find many fonts with different names that appear to be the same. They probably are, or at least are close copies.

Font Gallery

While taste in fonts is personal, I do recommend some as the building blocks of a must-have collection. If you see some you like, refer to "Where to Find Fonts" earlier in this chapter to find out where to get them.

For Publications:

Charter (Bitstream)—This clean, crisp, serif face works well almost anywhere:

ABCDEFGHIJKLMNOPQRSTUVWXYZ

abcdefghijklmnopqrstuvwxyz 1234567890

abcdefghijklmnopqrstuvwxyz

Cheltenham (many companies)—Its wider, more squared look makes this serif great for books and other wide-column documents:

ABCDEFGHIJKLMNOPQRSTUVWXYZ

abcdefghijklmnopqrstuvwxyz 1234567890

abcdefghijklmnopqrstuvwxyz

Garamond (many companies)—This popular 1980s serif font is both serious and legible:

ABCDEFGHIJKLMNOPQRSTUVWXYZ

abcdefghijklmnopqrstuvwxyz 1234567890

abcdefghijklmnopqrstuvwxyz

Gill Sans (many companies)—This versatile sans serif font works well for small blocks of body text such as sidebars and captions:

ABCDEFGHIJKLMNOPQRSTUVWXYZ

abcdefghijklmnopqrstuvwxyz 1234567890

abcdefghijklmnopqrstuvwxyz

New Baskerville (Adobe Systems)—This dainty font works well in narrow columns, although the italic is sometimes odd looking:

ABCDEFGHIJKLMNOPQRSTUVWXYZ

abcdefghijklmnopqrstuvwxyz 1234567890

abcdefghijklmnopqrstuvwxyz

News Gothic (many companies)—This slightly compressed sans serif font is legible in body copy and captions:

ABCDEFGHIJKLMNOPQRSTUVWXYZ

abcdefghijklmnopqrstuvwxyz 1234567890

abcdefghijklmnopqrstuvwxyz

Poppl-Laudatio (Adobe Systems)—This is a clear, easy-to-read, distinctive sans serif font:

ABCDEFGHIJKLMNOPQRSTUVWXYZ

abcdefghijklmnopqrstuvwxyz 1234567890

abcdefghijklmnopqrstuvwxyz

Poppl-Pontifex (Adobe Systems)—This is a clear, distinctive serif font:

ABCDEFGHIJKLMNOPQRSTUVWXYZ

abcdefghijklmnopqrstuvwxyz 1234567890

abcdefghijklmnopqrstuvwxyz

Stone Serif (many companies)—This is a classically clear serif font:

ABCDEFGHIJKLMNOPQRSTUVWXYZ

abcdefghijklmnopqrstuvwxyz 1234567890

abcdefghijklmnopqrstuvwxyz

Times Ten (Adobe Systems)—This is a more readable version of the classic serif font Times.

ABCDEFGHIJKLMNOPQRSTUVWXYZ

abcdefghijklmnopqrstuvwxyz 1234567890

abcdefghijklmnopqrstuvwxyz

Veljovic (Adobe Systems)—This sharp, condensed serif font gives a feel of a bygone era.

ABCDEFGHIJKLMNOPQRSTUVWXYZ
abcdefghijklmnopqrstuvwxyz 1234567890
abcdefghijklmnopqrstuvwxyz

For Use as Display Text:

Americana (many companies)—This widened serif font has a laconic feel that works well for logos and large, short headlines.

ABCDEFGHIJKLMNOPQRSTUVWXYZ
abcdefghijklmnopqrstuvwxyz 1234567890
abcdefghijklmnopqrstuvwxyz

Caslon (many companies)—A real nineteenth-century feel permeates this serif font:

ABCDEFGHIJKLMNOPQRSTUVWXYZ
abcdefghijklmnopqrstuvwxyz 1234567890
abcdefghijklmnopqrstuvwxyz

Copperplate (many companies)—This font has the look of a sans serif engraving that is simple and classic:

ABCDEFGHIJKLMNOPQRSTUVWXYZ
ABCDEFGHIJKLMNOPQRSTUVWXYZ 1234567890

Eras (many companies)—This slightly slanted sans serif font has a modern look that isn't dated like other "moderns:"

ABCDEFGHIJKLMNOPQRSTUVWXYZ
abcdefghijklmnopqrstuvwxyz 1234567890

Machine (many companies)—This bold, compressed all-caps serif clearly evokes industrial strength:

ABCDEFGHIJKLMNOPQRSTUVWXYZ
1234567890

For Fun:

Anna (Adobe Systems)—This decorative sans serif font has a real 1930s feel to it:

ABCDEFGHIJKLMNOPQRSTUVWXYZ
123456789

Bauhaus (many companies)—This funkily curved sans serif font says "art deco:"

ABCDEFGHIJKLMNOPQRSTUVWXYZ
abcdefghijklmnopqrstuvwxyz 1234567890

Wingdings (comes with Windows):

✌👌👍👎☜☞☝☟✋☺😐☹💣☠⚐🏱✈☼💧❄✞✝✠✡☪
♋♌♍♎♏♐♑♒♓🙰🙵●❍■□◻❑❒⬧⧫◆❖⬥
⌧⍓⌘🗁🗎🗏🗐🗄⌛🖮🖰🖲✇🗀

Windows Add-On Resources

`download.com` This CNET site is a sort of library of software libraries. Its search engine hooks into servers all over the Internet, from huge archives of hundreds of thousands of programs to vendor sites that have only a single program. When you decide to download something, it often gives you a choice of sites, each rated for reliability. Reviews, download statistics, and regularly updated Top 10 lists help you figure out which programs might be winners, and the site offers its own Download Manager utility to help software junkies manage their habits.

`www.pcmag.com/downloads` *PC Magazine*'s software collection is one of the biggest on the planet, and it includes a lot of utilities that were written especially for the magazine—stuff you won't find anywhere else. This page consolidates links to all the magazine's various libraries, plus it provides a monthly Top 10 list and other download-promoting features.

`pcworld.com/fileworld` *PC World*'s site is similar to *PC Magazine*'s, with links to categorized file collections, a Top 10 list, regularly changing editor's picks, and a daily download.

yahoo.com If you're not happy with the preceding three sites, go to Yahoo and find your way to Computers and Internet: Software: Shareware for a list of dozens of other software libraries.

www.pcmag.com/features/utilities98 Once a year, *PC Magazine* publishes a special issue devoted to utilities. This one covered over 225 different products. (I assume that the "98" at the end of the URL will change to "99" after the 1999 edition hits the newsstands.)

Fonts

America Online The Desktop and Web Publishing forum on America Online (keyword: DWP) has a collection of free and sample typefaces in its Fonts, Font Utilities & Clip Art section (keyword: FONT). There's also a set of useful definitions in the Reference: Fonts & Utilities folder.

publish.com The online site for Publish magazine has a collection of fonts for download in its Software Closet. There's also a directory of 90 typeface makers that will help you find both mass-market font makers like Fonthaus and Adobe Systems and special-purpose font makers like San Gabriel Custom Fontologists.

yahoo.com Go to Arts & Humanities: Design Arts: Graphic Design: Typography: Typefaces for pointers to a number of sites from which you can download free fonts. For commercial font companies, click the Fonts@ link above the list (which jumps to Business and Economy : Companies: Communications and Media Services: Desktop Publishing : Software).

13

Word Processing & Desktop Publishing

by Maria Langer and Galen Gruman

In This Chapter

Word processors take textual communication far beyond the capabilities of typewriters. They make it possible to create documents that include not only formatted text, but graphics and other elements that Herman L. Wagner (inventor of the modern manual typewriter in 1896) never dreamed were possible: information that automatically updates, portions of other documents, and hyperlinks.

What's the benefit of all this? Well, when properly constructed, a word processing document gets noticed by its intended audience—and maybe even read! That's the goal, isn't it?

Think about it. How many printed documents do you see in a day? Which ones do you remember? Which ones do you read? Chances are, the documents that get your attention are the ones that look good and are well organized.

This chapter explains how you can use any word processor to create documents you can be proud of—without spending a lot of time and effort. It will also provide some tips for using WordPad, a free word processor that comes with Windows, and Microsoft Word, the most powerful Windows word processing package, as well as recommendations for desktop publishing programs to consider when your needs exceed Word's capabilities.

Anatomy of a Word Processor

Let's start with a very quick tour of the most popular word processor, Microsoft Word (Figure 1). All the basic components discussed here are shared by most other Windows word processors, including two you might consider: Lotus Word Pro and Corel WordPerfect.

You'll find title, menu, and scroll bars in almost any Windows program, and all three Windows word processors support the usual Windows conventions—for example, pressing Alt activates the menu bar. But Windows word processors have other key components in common:

- **Toolbars,** sometimes called *button bars* or *icon bars*, provide access to commonly used commands. They take up very little room and are quick and easy to use—simply click a command's button to activate the command. Most programs offer several toolbars, each designed for a group of specific tasks—for example, the lower toolbar in Word offers buttons for formatting text. To show or hide individual toolbars, just right-click any toolbar and choose from the pop-up menu.

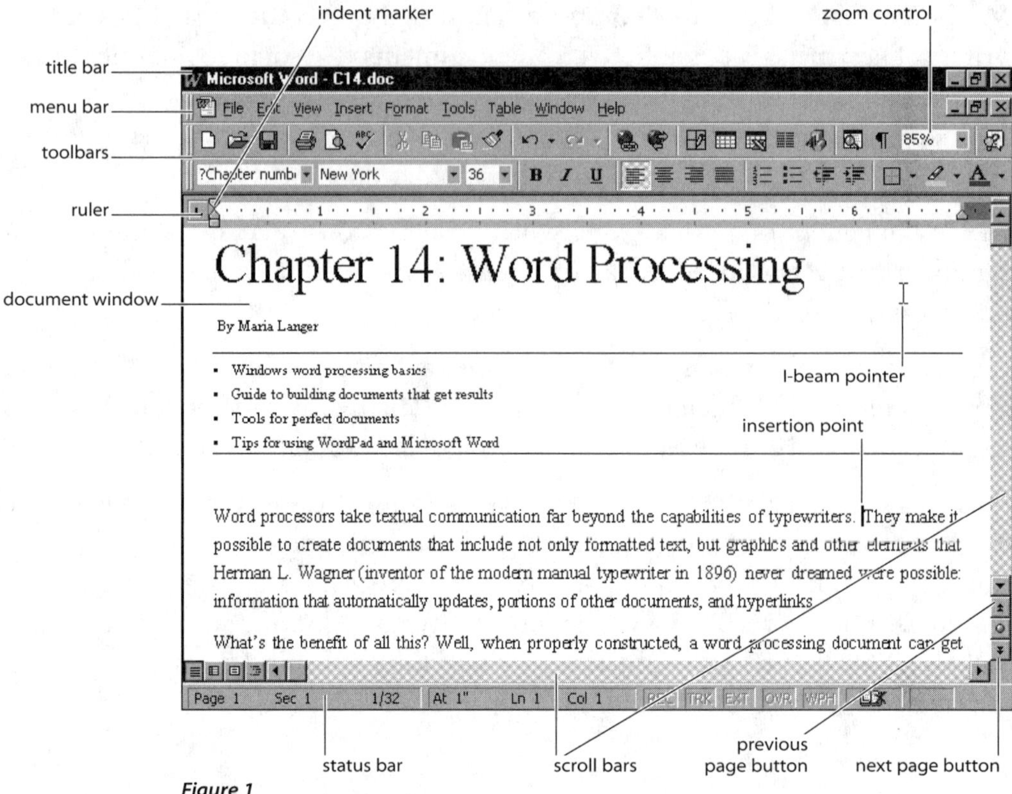

Figure 1

The anatomy of Microsoft Word.

- **The ruler** does more than show you how wide your page is. If you drag an indent icon with your mouse, you can adjust the indentation for a paragraph or for a whole document. Setting tabs is as easy as clicking the ruler. To adjust a single tab stop, for example, to change it from a regular tab to a decimal tab or to set its position precisely, double-click it.
- **The document window** gives you various views of your document, including a *normal view* for fast typing and scrolling and a *page layout view* that closely approximates the look of the final page. These are just two of the views Word offers from its View menu.
- **The zoom control** in the View menu lets you adjust the size of text on the screen to help you work with small text more easily and to help make sure that the page's margins fit within your screen. You can select any zoom percentage you want from 10% to 500%, but the most useful choices are Page Width and Whole Page, which adjust the page to fill the window. (Whole Page appears only when you're in page layout view.) If you want to see even more, you can turn off all the Word menus by using the Full Screen command in the View menu.

- **The I-beam pointer appears as you move the mouse over text, and it** looks like a large capital I (or construction I-beam—which is where it got its name). Click the mouse button to position the pointer wherever you want to insert text. The insertion point will appear, letting you know where the text will be added. The insertion point looks like a blinking vertical bar. The I-beam pointer turns into a regular arrow pointer when you move it out of the text area and pass it over toolbars, menus, scroll bars, rulers, and dialog boxes.
- **The status bar** indicates the current page and section number, insertion point position, and status of certain features.

Building Documents that Get Results

When you create a document, you have a primary goal: communicate information. But you probably have some secondary goals, too:

- Make your document look interesting so people *want* to read it.
- Make your message easy to read and understand.
- Make sure your document is error free to avoid embarrassment.

Word processors make it easy to do all of these things. Start by organizing your document so it makes sense and breaking up large blocks of text with headings and subheadings. Use bulleted or numbered lists to avoid long lists in boring paragraph format. Include graphics to illustrate points within the text. Use spelling and grammar checkers to make sure your ninth-grade English teacher would approve of what you've written.

With all this in mind, here's how you can create documents that achieve all your goals.

Think It Through

Planning your document should be your first step. What do you want to say? What topics do you want to cover? In what order do you want to cover them?

You may want to begin by jotting down a few notes on a piece of paper, just to make sure you won't forget to cover something important. Or just type your ideas in your document as notes—you can always delete them later.

For long documents, consider using your word processor's outlining feature to organize your document before you begin writing it. In Word, you switch to outline view by choosing Outline from the View menu or clicking the Outline View button on the left end of the document's horizontal scroll bar. You can then enter headings and subheadings by typing them. Press Enter after each heading you enter. Press Tab to indent or demote a heading or Shift Tab to unindent or promote a heading. Figure 2 shows the original outline for this chapter. You can add body text to the document at any time in any view—even while you're still building the outline.

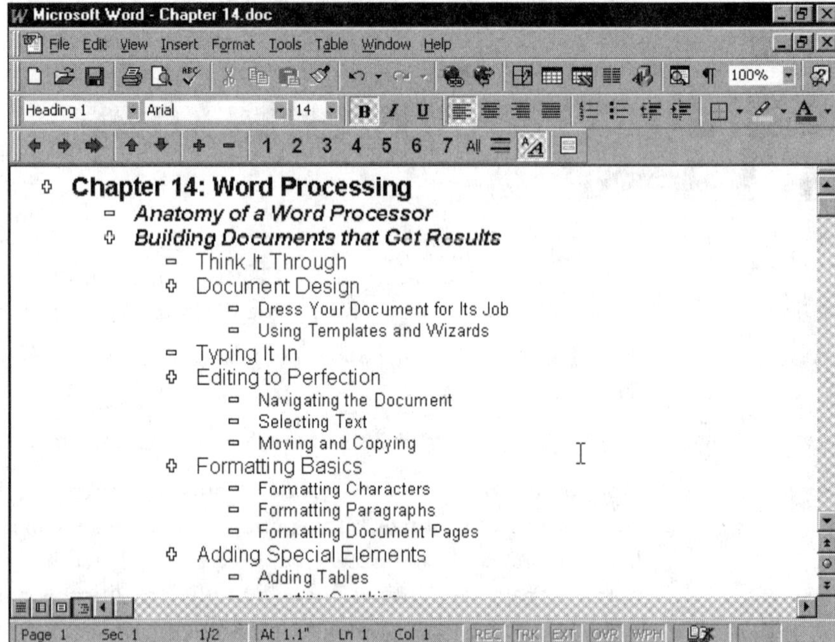

Figure 2

The original outline for this chapter, in Word's outline view.

The best thing about using outlines is that they enable you to organize your thoughts while automatically providing formatted headings that break up your text so it's easier to read. You can add, remove, or modify headings and body text as you write. You can even rearrange an entire document by dragging a heading to a new position in the document. If you do this in outline view, any body text or subheadings that belong to the heading are moved with it.

Word can automatically create a table of contents for a document based on its outline headings. This is a big time-saver, especially for very long documents. The trick is to use the Heading 1, Heading 2, and Heading 3 styles for the headlines in your document—they are what tell Word's outline feature what should be in the table of contents, Of course, you can use any paragraph styles you want to make up the TOC, but to use any but these three, you'll need to override Word's defaults. Choose Insert/Index and Tables and click Options) and then put a "1" next to the name of the style that you want to be the first-level head in the table of contents, a "2" next to the style for the second level, and a "3" next to the style for the third level (see Figure 3). (There is more information on styles later in this chapter.)

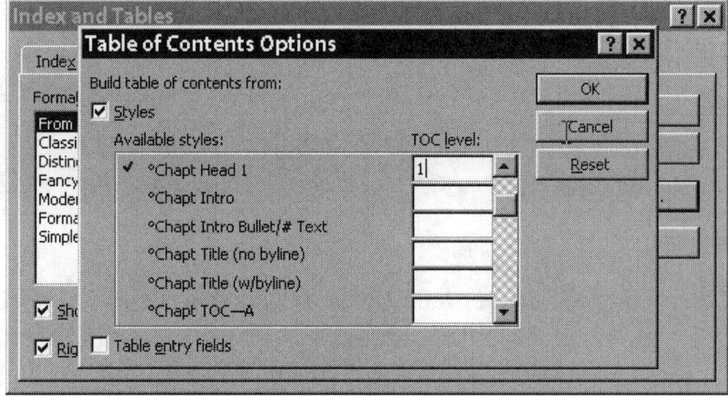

Figure 3

You can have Word generate a table of contents automatically, even if you use your own custom styles for section headings.

No matter what you're doing, there's a shortcut that can save you lots of time: Ctrl Y will repeat the last action, so you can use it to repeat almost any command—for instance, to apply text formatting to several separate paragraphs or insert rows in a table.

Templates and Document Design

When you open a new word processing document, some very basic design decisions have been made for you: margins, half-inch tab settings, a typeface for body text, and so on. The word processing program stores these settings in a special kind of file called a *template.* Unless you specify otherwise, a simple *default* template, which is called the *Normal* template in Word, automatically attaches itself to every new document, controlling its basic look.

You might want to accept the default template, but chances are you shouldn't. Why? Because your word processor has templates for all occasions: letters, memos, invoices, fax cover sheets, business cards, you name it. With most Windows word processors, when you choose File/New, you can choose a template you prefer (Figure 4).

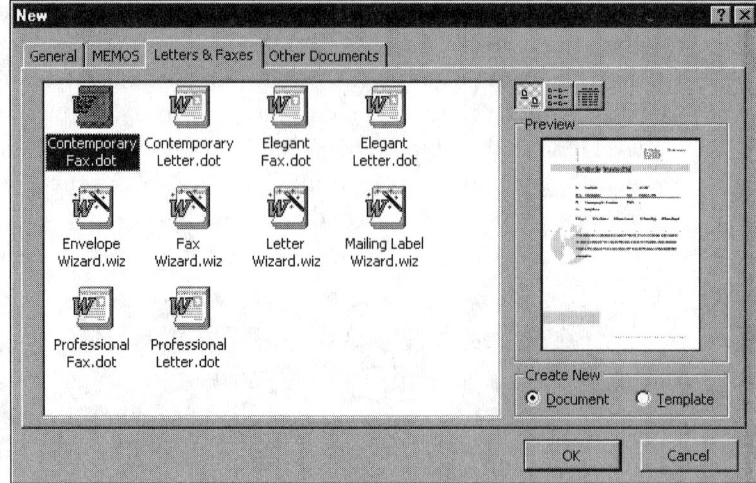

Figure 4

You can choose a document template from Word's File/New dialog box

Say you load a letter template. You'll see places for the address, the salutation, and so on blocked out with the correct margins and formatting. If it's a *wizard* or *automated* template, you will be prompted for information to be entered in the document (Figure 5). You can save the finished letter as a document, or customize the template to include your address and preferred formatting, thus saving time and effort the next time you use the template.

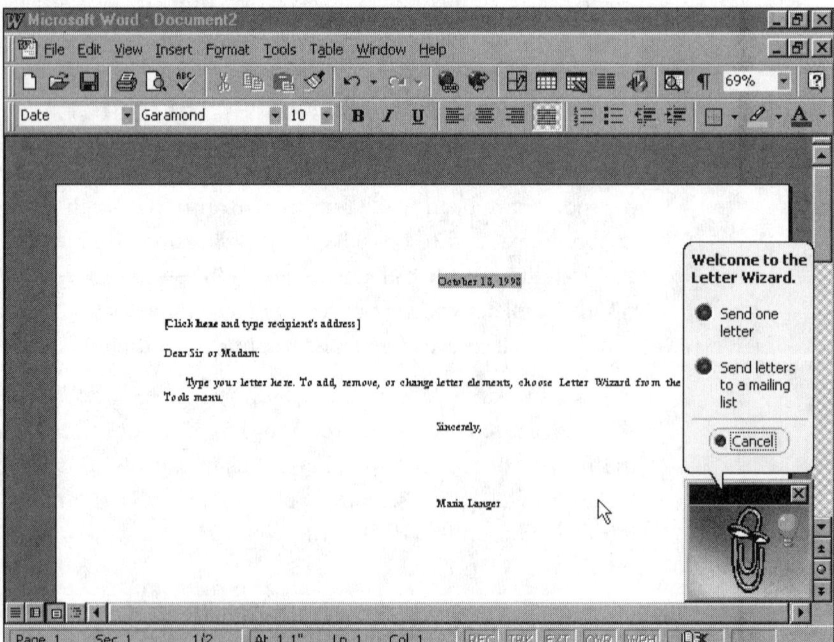

Figure 5

Word's wizards prompt you to provide information in a document.

You can also create your own templates from scratch and save them with their own names so they appear along with the other templates the program offers. Saving a template is easy. After you've set up things like margins and paragraph styles, just save the file as a document template (choose File/Save As and choose Document Template (.dot) in the Save as Type menu. If you want the template to appear in the list of templates displayed when you choose File/New, save it in the Templates folder (usually either c:\Program Files\Microsoft Office\Templates or c:\MSOffice\Templates).

Be careful when saving a file as a template in Word. If you save a file you're working on as a template by accident, you can't resave it or otherwise change it back to a regular document.

Typing It In

You're ready to type your document's text. Nothing could be simpler, really. Simply position the I-beam pointer where you want the text to appear, click, and type. The characters you type appear before the insertion point. (You can use this technique to insert text while editing, too.)

Here's some additional advice to save you time:

- Just type the text and worry about choosing fonts, changing margins, and making other formatting changes later. Formatting as you type interrupts thinking and slows writing. Really.
- Indenting with spaces is never a good idea. Use the Tab key instead. Or, if you want to get fancy, use the indent marker on the ruler to set indentation—but that's part of formatting, which you really should save for later!
- There's only one correct time to press the Enter key: when you want to end one paragraph and start a new one. If you want to shorten lines, change the indentation or margins (preferably by using styles, which we'll get to later in this chapter).
- Press Enter only once at the end of each paragraph. To create space between paragraphs, use Word's paragraph spacing formats (discussed later). The exception to this rule is when preparing documents for text-only applications, like Internet newsgroup postings and most e-mail programs.

Use the word processor's *AutoText* or *glossary* feature to enter commonly used text, such as your name, your address, or the closing lines on a letter. All major word processors offer this feature for collecting repeated words and phrases, which you can then insert into your document by simply typing an abbreviation and pressing a key. Word makes using AutoText very easy by displaying available entries on the screen as you type (Figure 6); just press Enter when an entry appears to insert it.

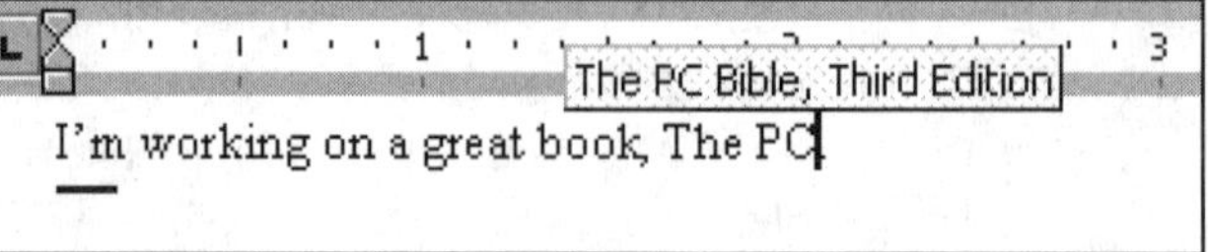

Figure 6

Word's AutoText feature literally jumps out at you, making it extremely convenient to use.

Although Word can automatically add bullets, typographic quotation marks, and dashes as you type (see the next section, "When Word Gets in Your Way"), there are times when you want to insert these characters—or others—yourself. Choose Insert/Symbol to display the dialog box shown in Figure 7. On the Special Characters tab, you can select all characters available in the Normal style's font, or pick characters from a specific font by selecting that font from the Font pop-up menu. The Special Characters tab gives you quick access to common text symbols and punctuation not shown on the keyboard, like ©, ®, ™, and em and en dashes (— and –). While you have a character selected in this dialog box, you can click Shortcut Key to assign a key combination to any character (for example, you might set Shift Alt M to insert an em dash), or you can click AutoCorrect to assign a keyboard sequence to be replaced by a symbol (such as "/c" for "©"). Other word processors offer similar features.

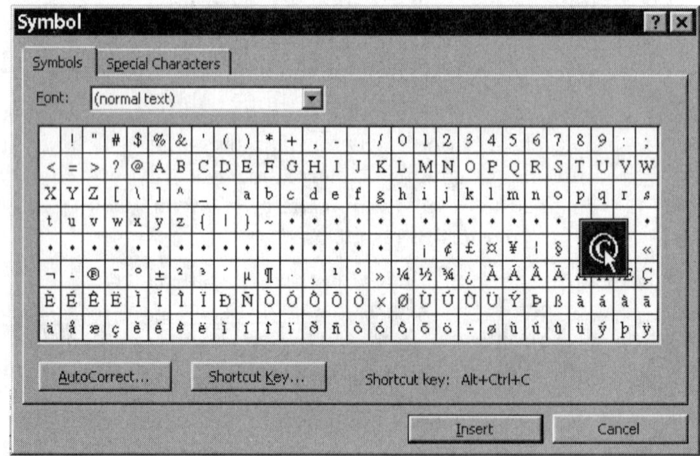

Figure 7

The Symbol dialog box in Word. Click to get an enlarged view of any character.

You don't always have to type to enter text—you can also copy it from other programs or other documents. Copy (Ctrl C) or cut (Ctrl X) text from another source, click your current text to place the insertion point at the location where you want to add the text, and then paste the text (Ctrl V). That's all there is to it.

Well, most of the time. When you copy information that isn't textual, such as cells from a spreadsheet or graphics from an illustration program, you may get unexpected results. For graphics, you will get a copy of the graphics—sometimes at a lower level of quality than in the original—inserted into the document. For spreadsheet cells, you will probably get a table inserted, but you may just get the data separated by tabs, or possibly an uneditable picture of the cells. The Edit/Paste Special command will let you determine exactly how the element is pasted. For example, if you paste cells from an Excel spreadsheet and use Paste Special, you can choose to paste the cells as formatted text (using the same fonts and so on as in Excel), as plain unformatted text, as a piece of the original spreadsheet (which, if double-clicked, will open Excel so you can edit it), or as a picture. Figure 8 shows the dialog box.

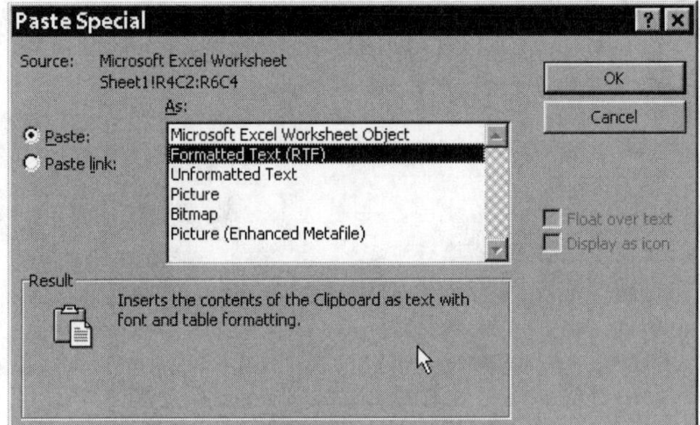

Figure 8

The Paste Special dialog box lets you determine how copied elements are treated.

When Word Gets in Your Way

In recent years, Microsoft's been gung-ho on the concept of "active assistance"—features that, at least in theory, watch what you do and figure out ways to help you. Unfortunately, the examples in Word often go so far in their efforts to be helpful that many users find them an annoying distraction, or worse. Here's a quick guide to what they do and how to get them out of your way.

AutoCorrect. This feature automatically fixes spelling and other common errors as you type. This is great in concept, but the feature needs some work, and if you're a good typist, it may cause more problems than it fixes.

For example, Word doesn't know many acronyms, so with the default setting of correcting two capital letters in a row (a common typo), Word will change "INstead" to "Instead," but it will also change "PCs" to "Pcs." If you immediately catch the error and backspace, Word will add "PCs" to its list of exceptions to the two-capitals rule, but if you're a fast typist and fix it later, you have to add the exception manually by choosing Tools/AutoCorrect and clicking Exceptions (see Figure 9).

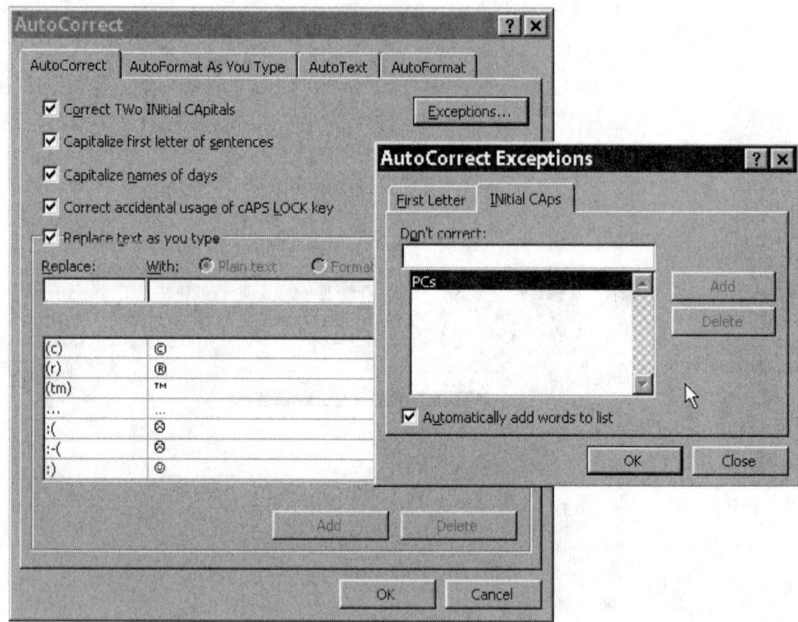

Figure 9

Word lets you decide what it automatically corrects for you in the AutoCorrect dialog box. Click the Exceptions button to stop Word from changing things you don't want changed.

Some of the "corrections" in the Replace With list at the bottom of the AutoCorrect dialog box can also cause trouble. For example, if you're using Word to compose an e-mail or newsgroup message, it will turn :-) into J, a character that won't necessarily be displayed correctly when other people read your message. Other potentially problematic changes are (C) to ©, (R) to ®, and (TM) to ™. To disable any of these changes, just select them from the list and click Delete.

AutoFormat as You Type. This presumptuous feature works just like AutoCorrect, but affects punctuation and formatting. The default settings will, among other things:

- convert keyboard quotation marks (' ") to curved quotation marks ('hey' " and ")
- turn typed fractions (1/2 3/4) into built fractions (½ ¾)
- turn typewriter-style dashes (--) into em dashes (—)

- replace e-mail and Internet newsgroup text conventions (*italics* and _underline_) with font formats (**bold** and underline)
- format the text in ordinal numbers (1st, 2nd, 3rd, 4th) as superscript (1st, 2nd, 3rd, 4th)
- format Web addresses (URLs) as underlined blue text and turn them into hyperlinks, so clicking them opens the referenced page in your default Web browser
- add bullets, numbers, indents, and borders to certain paragraphs

With the exception of the Web addresses, these changes are great for printed documents, but they can cause problems when you're using Word to create a document for the Web, e-mail, or a newsgroup, where these special characters may not be supported. You can disable any or all of these changes on the AutoFormat As You Type tab of the dialog box shown earlier in Figure 9. (In Word 95, choose Tools/Options and click the AutoFormat tab.)

Continuous spell and grammar checking. Also potentially distracting are those squiggly lines that appear under your text as you type it. Squiggly red lines indicate words that Word doesn't recognize as correct, which include not just typos and misspellings but any correctly spelled word that's not in the spelling checker's dictionary. Squiggly green lines indicate sections of text whose grammar Word questions. Again, it may be wrong, so use it only as a guide. If you just can't stand these squiggles, choose Tools/Options, click the Spelling & Grammar tab, and uncheck "Check spelling as you type" and "Check grammar as you type." See the section "Finding Your Goofs" for more on these features.

Office Assistant (the paper clip). Perhaps the worst way Word gets in your way is with Office Assistant, the animated paper clip character that appears when you first start and interferes with your work by asking you questions or engaging in pointless antics. This may be helpful for some people, but most find it simply annoying. Fortunately, you can turn off this critter: Click its close box to get it out of the way until the next time you use Word, or double-click the critter and choose Options. This will give you a dialog box where you can decide when—if ever—you want it to appear.

Editing to Perfection

It's editing time. Here are a few tricks that'll help get the job done in just about any word processor.

Finding what you want to change. If the place you want to make your change is within sight, navigation isn't really necessary—you're already there. But if the place you want to make your change is off the screen, you'll have to display it before you can change it. The easiest way is to use the scroll bars, Previous Page or Next Page button, or Pg Up or Pg Dn key to get to your destination. But if your destination is more than a couple of pages away, the following methods may be quicker:

- Use your program's search feature—probably by choosing Edit/Find—to find any unique word or phrase you can remember that is at or near your destination.

If you're a touch typist, press Ctrl F to bring up the Find dialog box without taking your fingers off the keyboard, and then type the word or phrase to look for, press Enter, and use the cursor keys to move the insertion point where you want it.

- Use Edit/ Go To or Ctrl G to jump to a specific page or other place in the document (Figure 10). And don't forget Ctrl Home and Ctrl End, which take you to the beginning and end of a document, respectively. In Word, you can also go to a specific page using the scroll box: as you drag it, page numbers appear next to the box.

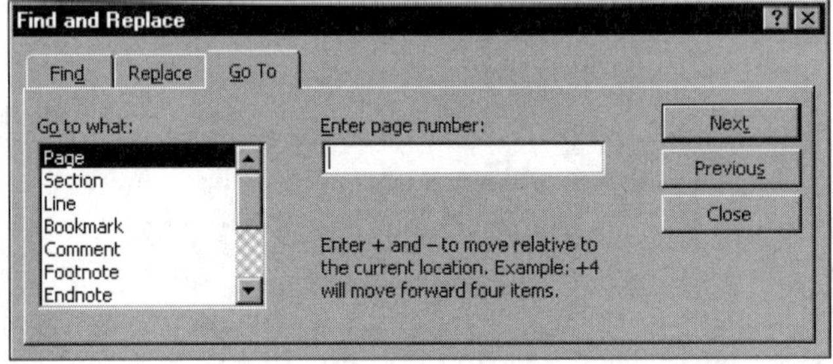

Figure 10

Word's Find and Replace dialog box is three dialog boxes in one: Find, Replace, and Go To.

- Use *bookmarks,* which let you mark one or more locations in your document and return to them in a flash. To set up a bookmark in Word, click in the document where you want the bookmark to go, choose Bookmark from the Insert menu to display the Bookmark dialog box, enter a name for the bookmark, and click Add. To find the bookmark, use the Go To command to enter the bookmark name.

Quick selection. Select it first. That's good advice for almost anything you do with any program. For example, rather than using Bksp, it's almost always faster to use your mouse to highlight the offending text and zap it with the Del key. These text selection shortcuts work in all Windows word processors:

- To select a word, double-click it.
- To select a sentence, hold Ctrl and click the mouse button.
- To select a paragraph, triple-click anywhere inside it or double-click in the left margin.
- To select a block of text fast, click the beginning of the block and then hold down Shift and click the end of the block. (This is often called shift-clicking.)

Beyond this, each Windows word processor has its own mouse shortcuts for selecting lines, paragraphs, and so on. Learning the shortcuts can save you time.

By default, Microsoft Word will automatically select entire words when you begin to drag over them. This feature can be handy if you want to select only entire words, but it is downright annoying if you want to select a few entire words with part of another word. It also sometimes will include punctuation along with the word, even if you don't want the punctuation selected. To turn it off, choose Tools/Options, click the Edit tab, and uncheck "When selecting, automatically select entire word." Don't confuse this option with the similar-sounding, "Use smart cut and paste." The smart cut-and-paste feature will delete extra spaces when you cut words from text and add any necessary space before or after pasted words.

Moving and copying. There are four ways to move or copy selected text: with menu commands, your keyboard, your mouse, or the keyboard and mouse together.

Using menu commands is effective but time consuming. You select the text you want to move or copy, choose Cut (to move) or Copy (to copy) from the Edit menu, position the blinking insertion point where you want the text to appears, and choose Paste from the Edit menu. The text is either moved or copied to the position you indicated.

That's a lot of work! So consider one of the following approaches (or a combination of them) instead, to speed things up:

- Use the keyboard shortcuts: Ctrl X for Cut, Ctrl C for Copy, and Ctrl V for Paste. When editing, try keeping your left hand on the keyboard to type these shortcuts and your right hand on the mouse to move through the document and reposition the insertion point.
- Drag and drop. (This method requires a steady hand.) To move text, first select it; then press and hold down the mouse button until a little box appears at the bottom of the pointer. Keeping the mouse button held down, position the insertion point at the exact spot where you want to move the text. When you release the mouse button, the text moves. Cool—though not very efficient if you're moving it very far in a long document.

  To copy text, you do almost exactly the same thing. Just hold down the Ctrl key as you drag to the new position. When you release the mouse button, the text is copied.

If you want to quickly alphabetize a bullet list or series of paragraphs (usually bulleted, but not always), select the paragraphs you want to alphabetize and choose Table/Sort (you don't have to be working on a table). If you choose Ascending in the dialog box, you'll sort from A to Z; Descending sorts from Z to A. You can also sort by number and date, if that's what's in your paragraphs. This feature also works with rows and columns in a table, which is why it is in the Table menu.

Use revision marks. When you're collaborating on a document with other people, Word's revision marks can track who made what changes. Additions are underlined, deletions are struck out, and each person's work appears in a different color. This makes it easy when, for example, you're revising a document written by someone else and want that person to check and approve the changes. To turn this feature on for the current document, choose Tools/Track Changes/Highlight Changes and check "Track changes while editing."

Formatting

Even if you use a template, you may decide to change the whole document's margins or tabs. Maybe you'll indent a paragraph here and there, and certainly you'll want to boldface or italicize *something.* These touches fall into the broad category of formatting, which different word processors tend to handle in different ways. As throughout this chapter, we'll focus here on Microsoft Word, but most of the concepts and tips are applicable to other word processors as well.

Word Formatting Basics

Microsoft Word has three levels of formatting: character, paragraph, and section. To use the program efficiently and avoid problems, it's important that you understand all three levels and how they interact.

Character-level formats. **Bold**, *italic*, underline, font, font size, and other formats that affect the fundamental appearance of the text are applied at the character level. Applying these formats is simple: just select the text you want to affect, right-click, and choose Font. The Font dialog box that appears (see Figure 11) has a handy preview window at the bottom so you can experiment with various formats without having to close the dialog box to see the results. Click the Character Spacing tab to squeeze letters closer together or stretch them apart. For tips on using fonts and adding a wider selection to the menu, see the "Fonts" section of Chapter 12: Windows Add-Ons.

Note that it's often more efficient to define character styles and use them to format your text. See the "Using Styles" section later in this chapter for more on that topic.

Paragraph-level formats. Formats that affect the way characters are arranged to form paragraphs, like line spacing, alignment (align left, center, align right, justified), indentation, and tabs, are applied at the paragraph level. To apply them, right-click anywhere in the paragraph you want to format and choose Paragraph. To format a series of paragraphs at once, select them, right-click, and choose Paragraph. (The selection can start anywhere in the first paragraph and end anywhere in the last paragraph.)

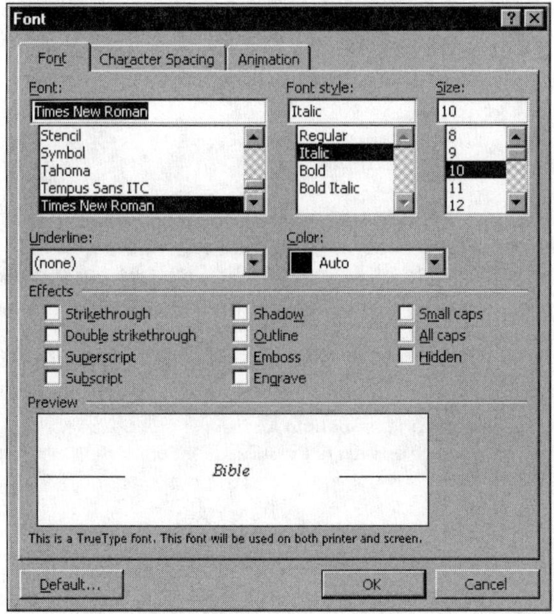

Figure 11

Word's Font dialog box offers dozens of formatting options.

The sections "Indents and Margins," "Bullets and Numbering," and "Line and Paragraph Spacing" discuss paragraph formats in detail.

Formats Revealed!

Word can tell you exactly what formats are applied to text or paragraphs. Press Shift F1 to activate the What's This help cursor and then click any characters in the document to display their formats and those of the paragraphs in which they appear (Figure 12). When you're finished, press Esc to switch back to the normal mouse pointer.

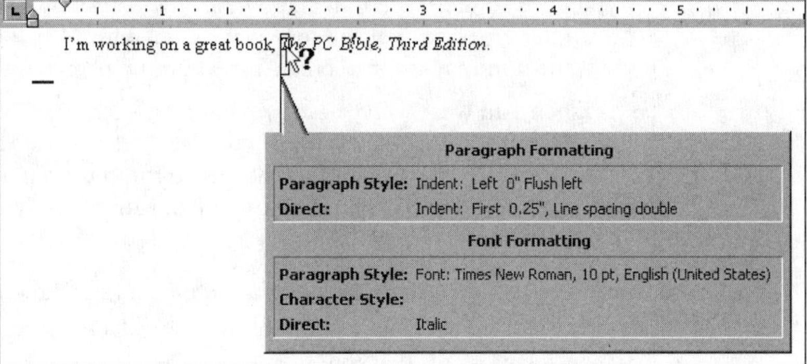

Figure 12

Here's a trick to impress your friends: reveal text formatting in Word.

Word's paragraph-level formats are stored in markers at the end of each paragraph (see Figure 13). Here are a few tips to avoid common problems resulting from that somewhat unintuitive design.

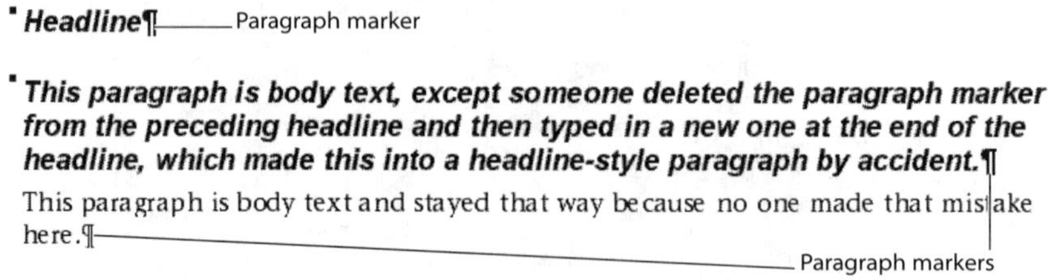

Headline¶ — Paragraph marker

This paragraph is body text, except someone deleted the paragraph marker from the preceding headline and then typed in a new one at the end of the headline, which made this into a headline-style paragraph by accident.¶

This paragraph is body text and stayed way because no one made that mistake here.¶

Paragraph markers

Figure 13

Paragraph markers store the formatting for the text that precedes them, which can cause incorrect formatting to be applied to the subsequent paragraph when you delete such a marker, as shown here.

- When you delete the marker separating two paragraphs, the formatting of the first is applied to the combined paragraph. If you do that by mistake, press Ctrl Z to undo the deletion; then select more carefully to avoid deleting the marker.
- When you cut or copy text from the end of a paragraph, if you copy the marker, its formatting will be applied to the paragraph where you paste the text. To avoid that, select carefully to be sure you select only text and not the marker. One easy way is to Ctrl-click to select the first sentence you want to cut or copy and then Shift-click to select the last sentence.
- It's easier to avoid accidentally deleting or copying markers when you can see them. You can make them visible temporarily by pressing Ctrl Shift *; press again to turn them off. To make them visible permanently, select Tools/Options, click the View tab, and check Paragraph Marks.
- When you cut or copy a section of text that includes a paragraph marker and paste it in the middle of a paragraph, the marker's formatting is applied to the preceding text, while any text following the marker picks up the formatting of the rest of the paragraph. If that's not what you want, you may want to create a new empty paragraph before pasting.
- When you want to type a new paragraph between two paragraphs with different formats, you can put the insertion point at the end of the first paragraph and press Enter, or at the beginning of the second paragraph and press Enter ↑, depending on which format you want the new paragraph to use.

Note that it's often more efficient to define and use paragraph styles rather than formatting paragraphs directly. See the "Using Styles" section later in this chapter for more on that topic.

Section-level formats. In Word, formats that affect groups of paragraphs, like margins and columns, are applied at the section level. So are formats that affect whole pages or the entire document, like paper size and page numbering.

This dual function can lead to trouble. If you don't understand how sections work or are used to another word processor that works differently, it's very easy to create multiple sections in a document without realizing it. As a result, the document may not print the way you expect it to, and trying to figure out why may be quite frustrating.

One place it's easy to accidentally create a new section is in the File/Page Setup dialog box, which allows you to apply page formats like paper type and orientation to the entire document, from the insertion point forward, or to selected text only. Applying any of these formats to less than the entire document—for example, applying new margins using the This Point Forward option instead of Whole Document as shown in Figure 14—creates a multiple-section document.

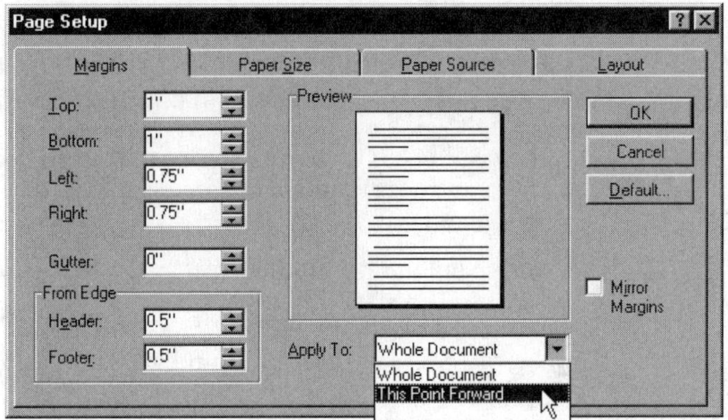

Figure 14

When applying Page Setup formats in Word, choosing This Point Forward instead of Whole Document will create a new section.

If that's what you mean to do, that's fine, but if you do it by accident, when you print you'll find that only part of the document has the margins you expect, and if you don't know what the problem is, you may find that your efforts to correct it have no effect.

To avoid trouble, when using Page Setup always check to make sure the Apply To settings are what they should be.

Here are some examples of formatting actions that will create *section breaks* (a marker that appears on the screen to show you where one section ends and the next starts):

- switching paper sizes or orientation, as when you have an envelope at the end of a letter or a landscape table in the middle of a report
- using columns (discussed later in this chapter)
- restarting page numbering or changing the place on the page where page numbers appear (discussed later in this chapter)

To check whether you've accidentally created any sections, press Ctrl End to move the insertion point to the end of the document. If there are no sections, you'll see "Sec 1" to the right of the page number display. If instead you see "Sec 2" or some other number, you'll know you have multiple sections (the number tells you how many sections there are).

Indents and Margins

Many people find the distinction Word makes between margins and indents confusing. That's not particularly surprising. There's a lot of overlap between their functions, and if you don't understand the difference between paragraph- and section-level formats, they sound like the same thing.

- Margins are section-level settings that are relative to the edge of the paper. The top and bottom margins affect all the pages in the section, and the left and right margins affect all the paragraphs in the section.
- Indents are paragraph-level settings that are relative to the margin setting.

The two versions of the same document shown in Figure 15 illustrate the difference between margins and indents. On the top, the margins are 1½ inches; on the bottom, they've been reduced to only ¾ inch. The various indents, however, all stay the same relative to the margins.

Except when you change paper size or orientation, it's bad practice to change left and right margin settings at the section level—that is, using Edit/Page Setup. Instead, use one margin setting throughout the document, and when you want to vary the margins, use the indent settings in Format/Paragraph instead. The latter approach is essential for formatting with styles and setting up documents with dual-sided pages.

To set margins, choose File/Page Setup and click the Margins tab. To set indents, use Format/Paragraph or drag their markers on the ruler.

When you drag the bottom (square) part of the left indent marker, the first-line marker moves as well; drag the top (triangular) part, and the first-line marker stays where it is.

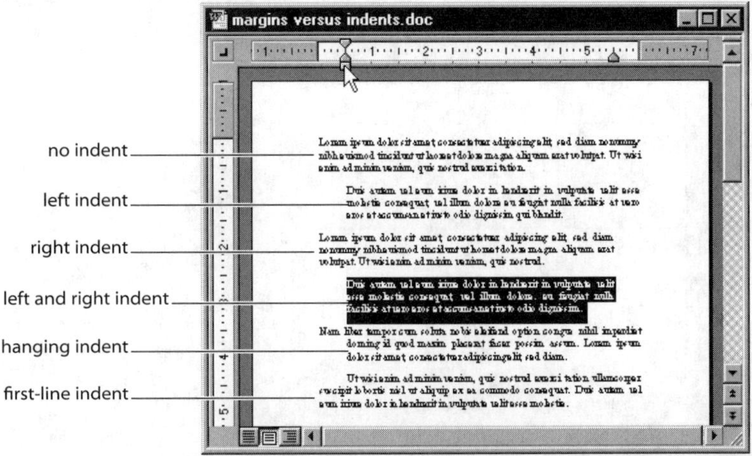

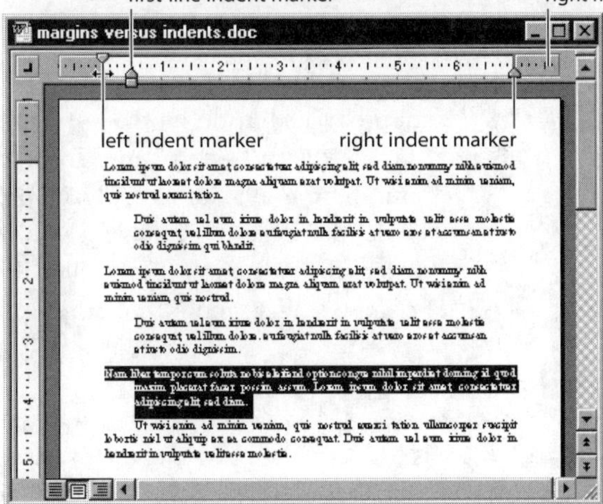

Figure 15

The margins in the document on the top are 1½ inches, and on the bottom, they've been changed to ¾ inch; the indents remain the same relative to the margin. Note how the controls in the ruler reflect the currently selected paragraph; also notice that on the bottom, the mouse pointer has turned into a double-headed arrow because it's positioned over the left margin boundary.

Bullets and Numbering

Another useful paragraph-level format is Bullets and Numbering. This tricky format automatically creates bullet lists or numbered paragraphs, with or without hanging indents, and automatically renumbers list entries or paragraphs as you add, remove, or rearrange them. You can also use this formatting tool to number headings hierarchically according to various legal and academic outline standards (see Figure 16), provided you format the headings with styles.

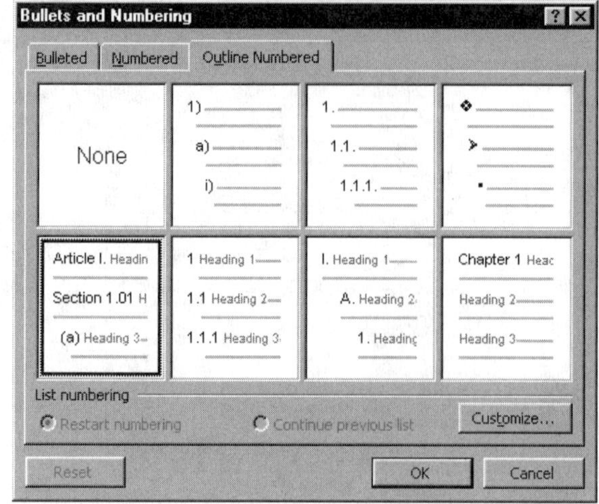

Figure 16

Word's outline numbering dialog. Click the Customize button if you want to apply the numbering to your own styles rather than the default Heading 1, Heading 2, etc.

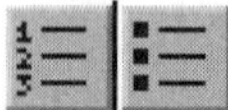

Figure 17

Word's Numbering and Bullets buttons.

To start a bulleted or numbered list, just click the appropriate button on the Formatting toolbar (see Figure 17) and start typing. To change the bullet or numbering style, or to apply a bullet or numbering style to a series of paragraphs you've already typed, select the paragraphs, right-click the selection, and choose Bullets and Numbering..

Line and Paragraph Spacing

How much space there is between lines and paragraphs has a big effect on how your document looks. Double-spaced text looks like a draft or legal document. Small spaces between paragraphs look right for letters and longer documents; bigger spaces may seem more appropriate for flyers and announcements. Subtle differences in these settings is one of the elements that distinguish professionally designed documents from the ones we crank out with our word processors.

When you create documents using Word's templates, line and paragraph spacing are already set, so you don't have to worry about them. The one exception is the Blank Document template, which sets all the spacing options to something resembling old-fashioned typewriter output.

That's appropriate when you're creating a plain text file, for example, to paste into an e-mail message or newsgroup posting. When working on such documents—and *only* then—you should press Enter twice at the end of each paragraph (except the last) to leave blank lines between them.

When preparing documents for printing, there's no need to leave blank lines. Instead, you set the Spacing After paragraph format, as shown in Figure 18. To bring up the dialog box, choose Format/Paragraph (or right-click where you want to apply the format and choose Paragraph). Here's a rundown of what that and the other spacing settings do:

- **Spacing After** does just what it sounds like it does: it puts blank space after the paragraph. A setting of six points is typical in Word, but what looks best depends on what font you're using. A *point*, a measurement adapted from old-fashioned mechanical typesetting and still used by publishing professionals, is 1/72 of an inch. You can enter settings in inches or centimeters if you prefer: just type "in" or "cm" after the measurement.
- **Spacing Before** does the same thing at the top of the paragraph. This setting's useful for headings. For example, if you want a half inch of blank space between chapters in a report, you would format the chapter headings with a Spacing Before setting of 0.5in.
- **Line Spacing** adjusts the space between the lines of the paragraph (often called *leading*, another term from the old lead-type days). The settings Single, 1.5 Lines, and Double adjust automatically as you change the size of the font. Sometimes the results don't look very good—for example, if there's one outsized character from a symbol font in a line, it will be spaced differently from the other lines in the paragraph. And for a lot of fonts, Word simply doesn't choose the spacing that looks best. You can set the line height manually by choosing Exactly and setting a point size: try one about 15% larger than the font size.

Note that once you understand how these formats work, it's usually best to set them using styles, discussed next, rather than by applying them to paragraphs directly.

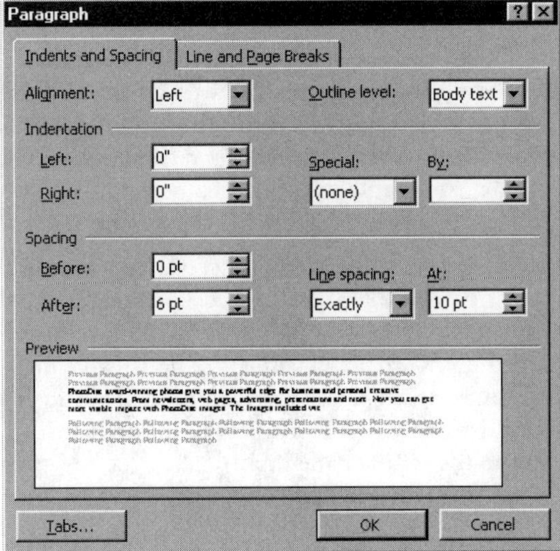

Figure 18

The Spacing section of the paragraph format dialog lets you adjust line and paragraph spacing.

Using Styles

Styles are the biggest formatting time-savers ever invented. Each word processing program handles them a bit differently; here's a basic idea of how they work:

Say you're working on a document and decide to use 18-point Arial bold headings. Why choose the font, set the size, and boldface the headings every time? Instead, you can save those settings as a style. You can then pick the style from a list to apply it to selected text any time you want to. In that way, you can create a complete set of styles for your document.

Not only does using styles save time, but it ensures consistent formatting in your document. If you change the definition of a style, the formatting applied with that style changes automatically throughout your document.

In Word, you use the New Style dialog box shown in Figure 19 to create styles. A similar dialog box lets you modify styles. To get to either, choose Format/Style. Click New to create a new style or Modify to modify the style whose name is selected in the dialog box's left-hand list. Here are some basics of the New Style and Modify Style dialog boxes:

- You set the formats for a style with the options in the Format button menu, which correspond to the choices on the regular Format menu.
- Use "based-on" formatting whenever possible. From the Based On list, pick a style to start with to define a new style. For example, suppose you're creating a style for long quotations, and you want everything the same as your regular body text except the indent and point size. Why set all the formats from scratch when by choosing Based On/Body you can just modify the point size and indent? Even better, if you change the font in the Body style, all styles based on it will change to the new font, too.

- Use "Style for following paragraph" whenever possible. Often, styles follow one another in a predictable sequence; for example, in a newsletter, article headlines may always be followed by the author's byline. With this feature, you would set Byline as the style to follow Headline, so when the writer applies the Headline style to a paragraph, types a headline, and presses Enter, the next paragraph is automatically put in Byline style. Similarly, heading styles should usually be followed by body text.
- Not all styles apply to full paragraphs. Maybe you use a few words of bolder, larger type at the beginning of a paragraph as a form of headline within your body text. You might think you have to manually set the boldness and point size every time you do this—which could lead to mistakes. But there's a better way: choose Character from the "Style type" list, and Word will know to apply the style just to selected text rather than to the whole paragraph.

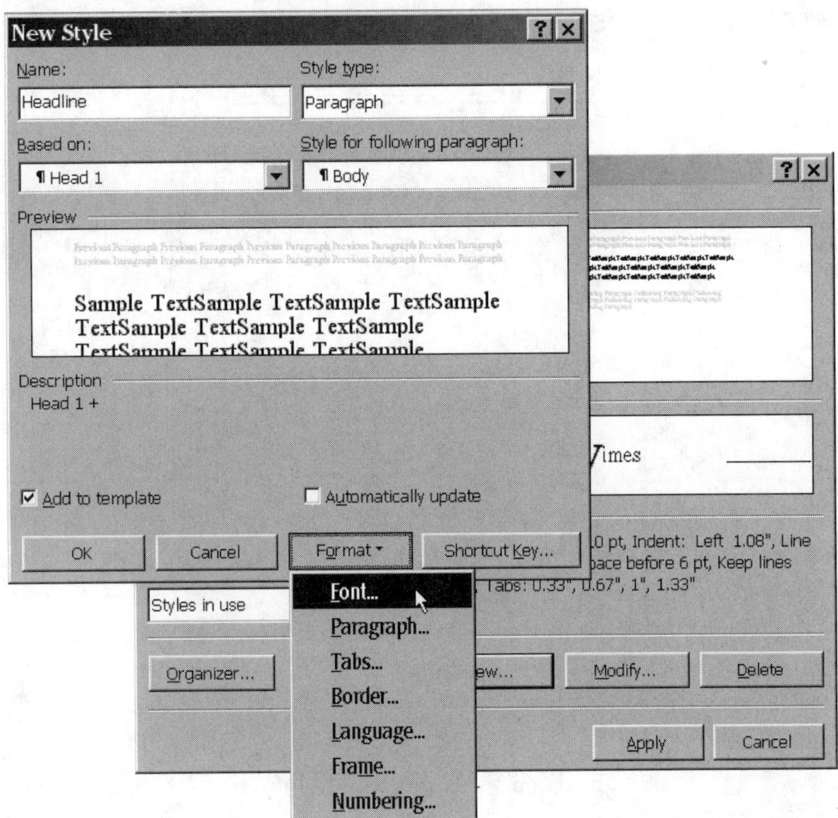

Figure 19

The New Style dialog box, where you define styles.

- If you check the "Add to template" option, the style you create is added automatically to the document template used by the current document and will thus be available to all other documents created using this template. If you're not using templates and you check this option, all future documents will have this new style (since you actually are using the global template, called Normal.dot).

- If you *always* use styles for formatting, and nobody else works on your documents, you might find the "Automatically update" option useful—if it's checked, any time you change the formatting of a paragraph in Word by highlighting text and applying, say, other font or indent settings, Word will change the style to reflect those changes. The danger is that you may really just want to apply the style to that one paragraph or piece of text and not realize that Word will now change all other text, too.
- To apply a style, use the Style drop-down menu from Word's button bar, as shown in Figure 20. (If that button bar doesn't appear, choose Tools/ Customize and check the Formatting option on the Toolbars tab.) For faster access, assign a shortcut key, like Alt F3 to a style to make it easy to apply that style.

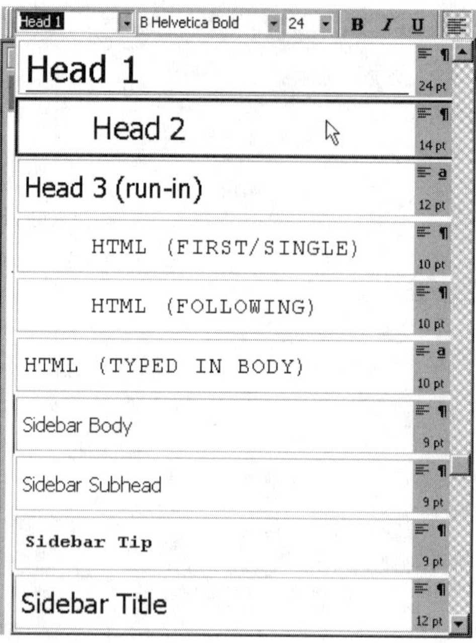

Figure 20

*The Formatting toolbar lets you apply styles from a pull-down list that shows sample text. The ¶ symbol indicates a paragraph style, and the **a** indicates a character style.*

Word has a confusing way of working that could make you change your style by accident. If you make some formatting changes to a specific paragraph or text selection and decide you want to undo them, the fastest way is to reapply the original style to that paragraph or selection. So far so good. But be careful. When you do that, Word displays the dialog box shown in Figure 21. Notice that the default option is to update the existing style with the changes you made in that text—even though that's not usually what you'll want Word to do. So make sure you choose "Reapply the formatting of the style to the selection?" option rather than hurriedly just press Enter or click OK. And *never* check the "Automatically update the style from now" option—that is the same as the "Automatically update" feature in the New Style dialog box mentioned earlier.

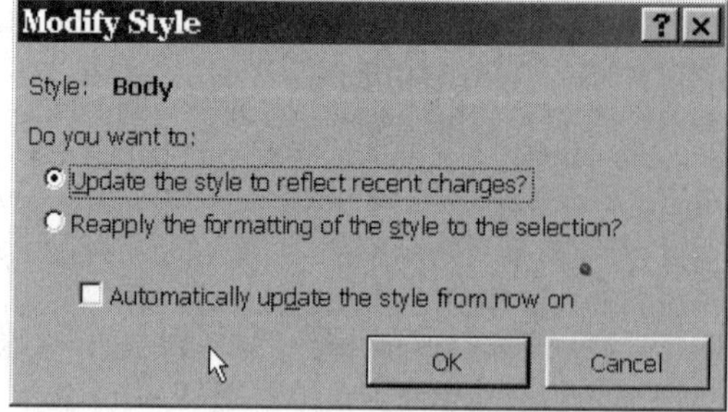

Figure 21

If you're not careful, you can accidentally overwrite a style definition when this dialog box appears, since that's its default setting—even if you're trying to reapply the original formatting.

Styles can be *global* (available in all documents) or *local* (attached to a specific document). Document templates usually include a handful of useful styles. If you create custom styles for a document, you can save that document as a template so you can use the styles the next time you create a similar document. And if you want to use a style in another document or template in your current document, choose Format/Style and click the Organizer button to display the dialog box shown in Figure 22, which lets you copy styles between any two documents or templates.

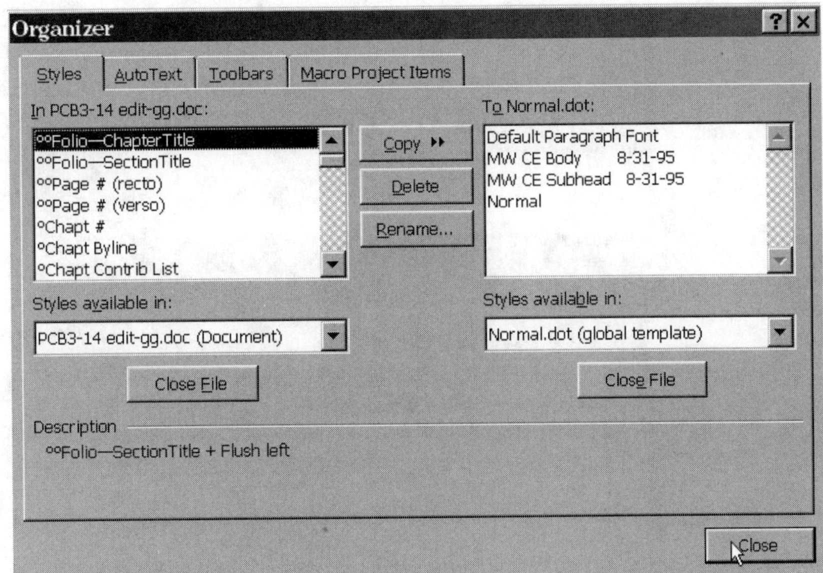

Figure 22

Use the Organizer dialog box to copy styles among documents and templates.

If you're really lazy about formatting and you use Microsoft Word, you can use Word's AutoFormat feature to apply formatting throughout your document for you. This feature applies styles based on rules programmed into it. Just choose AutoFormat from the Format menu, set options in the dialog box that appears, and let Word go to work. If you don't like what Word did, don't worry—Undo (Ctrl Z) will restore your document to the way it was.

Columns

As noted earlier, text may sometimes be laid out in more than one column. Sometimes that format's dictated by the content of the document: for example, if you're comparing the pros and cons of two or three proposals. Other times, it's just a matter of style: smaller text (around 9 points and under, depending on the font) is hard to read if it's stretched across the page; breaking it into two or three columns makes it more readable. You can save a lot of paper by formatting long documents as two-column, 8-point text instead of full-page, 10- or 12-point text. (Try the Bookman font for such jobs.)

Figure 23 shows the Columns dialog box, which you display by choosing Format/Columns. The dialog box does a good job of showing you the effects of the various options. The ones to pay attention to are the Spacing settings (which determine how much space there is between columns; the default half inch is often more than necessary) and the Apply To setting, where you determine whether these column settings are for the entire section or from this point on (basically, a subsection). You can use one of the preset column settings (the icons at the top) or build your own. If you want to get fancy, for example, when laying out a newsletter, you can make each column a different width and put vertical lines (*rules*) between them. Usually, though, you just want your columns evenly sized.

Figure 23

The Columns dialog box.

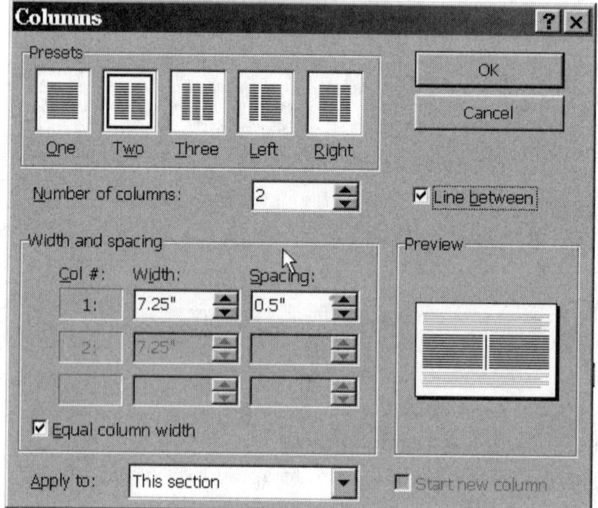

Page Numbering

To add page numbers, choose Insert/Page Numbers. If you don't want the numbers to appear in the bottom-left corner, change the position and/or alignment settings (see Figure 24). If you just want straight numbering starting from 1, click OK. If you want something fancier—for example, to use roman numerals in a preface or to switch to regular numbering beginning from 1 after the preface—click Format and adjust the appropriate settings (see Figure 24). Note that when you have multiple sections, the insertion point must be in the section whose page numbering you want to change.

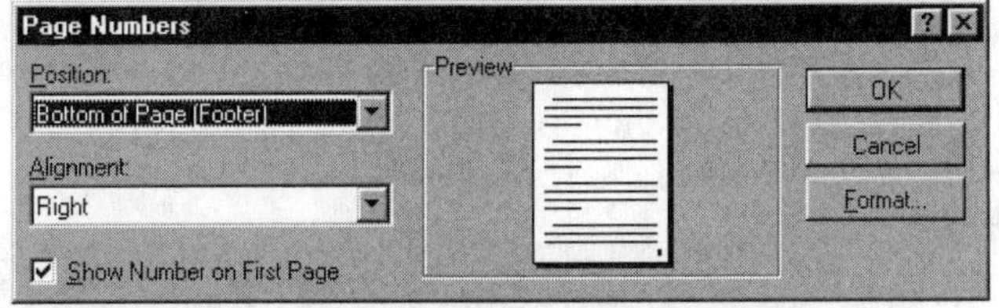

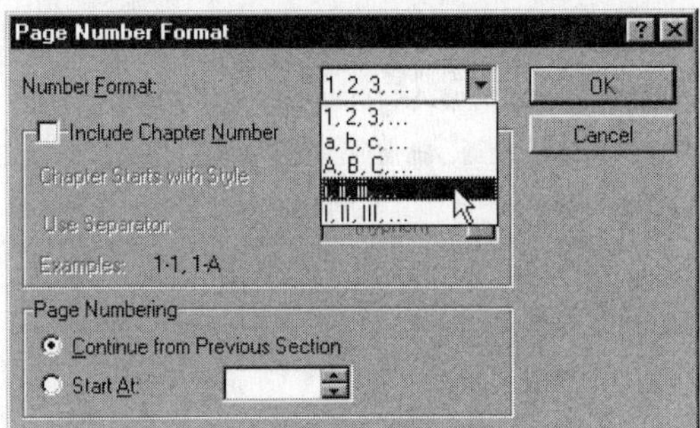

Figure 24

Word's page numbering dialog boxes.

You can't change the *character* format of page numbers—font, size, and so on—in the page numbering dialog boxes. Instead, you have to edit the header or footer in which the page numbers appear.

Headers and Footers

Elements that you want to appear on every page, which commonly include page numbers, document and chapter titles, author, revision or print date, and confidentiality notices, live in headers or footers, special areas at the top and bottom of the page.

To create or edit headers or footers in Word, choose View/Header and Footer, or if you're in page layout view, just double-click the top or bottom margin. You'll get a floating palette as shown in Figure 25, as well as outlined boxes at the top and bottom of your pages (one for the header and one for the footer). Your regular text will turn gray to alert you that you have switched to headers and footers. The header and footer you create here apply to the current section or, if you have defined no sections, the entire document. If you previously inserted page numbers as described earlier, you will see them here.

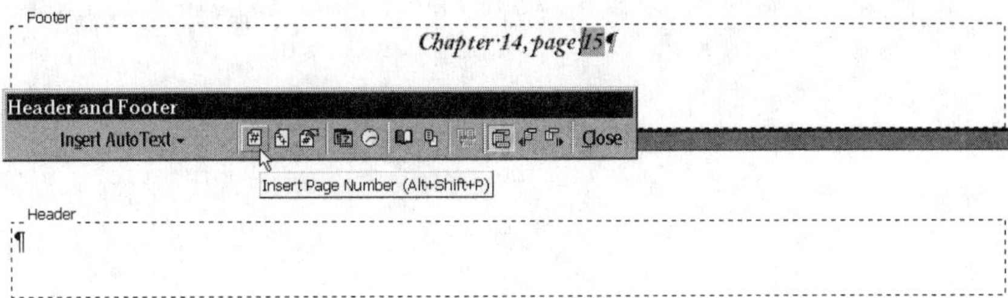

Figure 25

The footer at the bottom of one page, and the header at the top of the following page.

The icons on the Header and Footer toolbar aren't exactly self-explanatory, and the tooltips (the text that appears when you hold your mouse over an icon) isn't always that helpful either. Here's a rundown of the elements, from left to right, as shown in Figure 25:

- Insert Auto Text is a menu of common text phrases, such as "Page X of Y" and "Saved By X." Word will fill in the X's and Y's with actual page numbers, the author's name (as set in File/Properties), current date, and so on.
- current page number
- total number of pages in the section or document
- open the Page Number Format dialog box
- current date
- current time
- open the Page Setup dialog box
- hide or show the document's text (you toggle between the two settings)
- make the current header or footer the same as the previous section's header or footer
- switch between the header and footer
- go to the previous section's header or footer
- go to the next section's header or footer
- close the floating palette (you can also just double-click the document itself)

You can type any text you want in the header and footer regions. If you enter more text than fits those boxes, the region depth will automatically increase. You can also format the text and AutoText elements using the standard menu and button bar commands for formatting—you can set anything from the point size and font to the alignment and indentation. As far as Word is concerned, the text is like any other text, and you can do the same things to it as you can to regular document text.

Dual-Sided Pages

Here's one task that usually sets the office experts apart from the rest of us: dealing with dual-sided pages. You know how you never could figure out how to get the photocopier to make double-sided documents copy correctly? Well, fortunately Word (like its competing word processors) knows how to handle them. It won't help you copy them correctly—you'll still need to get Mrs. Sneadly down the hall or the kids at Kinko's to do that for you—but at least it will produce the pages correctly so you can print them two-sided (if you have a printer that can do that) or have them ready for two-sided copying.

The key to working with two-sided documents is in the Page Setup dialog box, which you saw in Figure 14. If you check the Mirror Margins options, the dialog box changes to the one in Figure 26. Instead of having settings for left and right margin, you now have settings for inside and outside margins. That's a subtle but key difference.

Think of it this way: in a one-side document, the left margin is often a little wider than the right margin so you can put holes in the left side for your ring binder and have enough room so the holes don't go into the text. But on a two-sided document, that wouldn't work, because on the back sides of the page, it's the right side of the margin that's close to the holes. You don't want to have each page be its own section, so you can adjust the left and right margins appropriately based on whether the page is a front-side page (an odd-numbered page usually) or a back-side page (usually an even-numbered page). That's where Inside and Outside comes in. The inside margin is the one closest to the holes (or whatever you're binding your document with), while the outside margin is the one on the, er, outside edge.

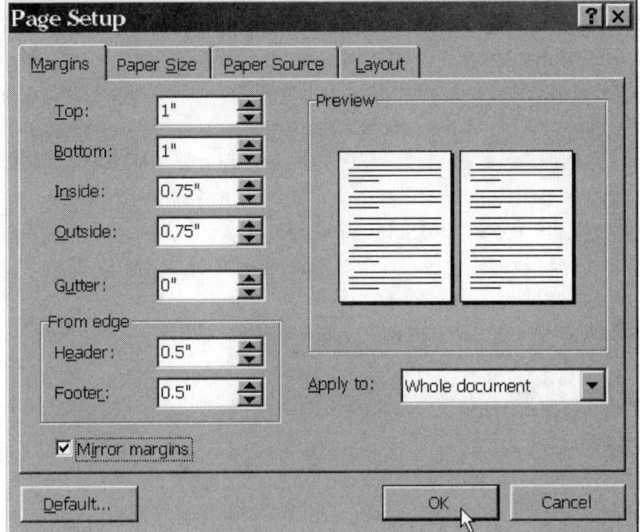

Figure 26

The Page Setup dialog box changes to a two-sided-page mode (Inside and Outside replace Left and Right) when you check "Mirror margins."

Other formats you may want when working with double-sided documents are different odd and even headers (choose File/Page Setup and click the Layout tab), inside and outside page number alignment (choose Insert/Page Numbers), and two-page view (choose View/Page View or File/Print Preview and then choose Two Pages from the Zoom menu).

Including Other Elements

As powerful as they are, words aren't always enough. To get the attention of potential readers, your documents can often benefit from other elements that help you get your message across, such as tables and graphics. Here's a quick overview of how you can include these elements in your documents.

Tables

Although you can create a simple table by setting up and using tabs, a word processor's table feature is far more powerful and flexible. With it, you can build a table of nicely lined up rows and columns of information, apply borders and shading, and even add column totals.

With Word, you can create a table by either inserting (choose Table/Insert Table) or drawing a table (choose Table/Draw Table). Although drawing a table is kind of fun—you use a pencil-like tool to draw table borders and an eraser-like tool to remove them—it's more efficient to position the insertion point where you want the table to appear, choose Table/Insert Table to display the Insert Table dialog box (see Figure 27), and enter the number of columns and rows you want to start with. (You can always add more later if you need them.) Once the table is in the document, enter information into each cell and format it as desired. Each cell's text can be formatted like any paragraph text can—you can specify the font, size, alignment, and so on—using the standard formatting functions for text and paragraphs. Cells automatically expand vertically to accommodate text; you can drag to resize columns and rows manually if desired.

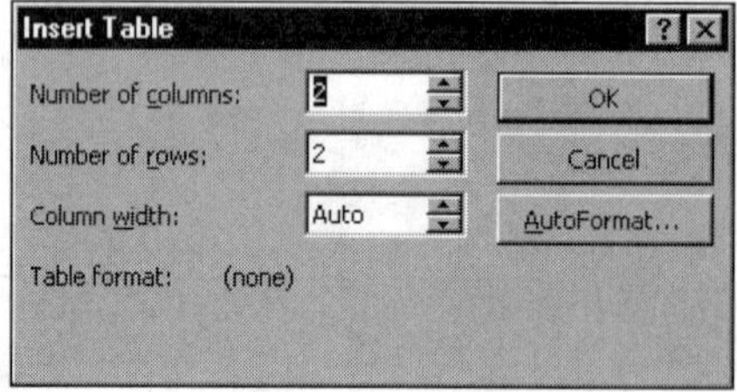

Figure 27

Use Word's Insert Table dialog box to specify table settings.

If you have to work on tabular text created by someone who didn't know how to use tables, you aren't necessarily stuck with it. Select the whole tabular text and then choose Table/Convert Text to Table. If you're lucky, the result will be a nice table, or at least one that's good enough that you can whip it into shape. If the results are unacceptable, just press Ctrl Z to undo the conversion.

Inserting rows and columns is easy. To insert a new, blank row, select the row *below* where you want the new one to appear by clicking in the margin just to its left. Right-click the selection and choose Insert Rows from the pop-up menu. To insert additional rows, press Ctrl Y to repeat the command as many times as necessary. To add a row at the bottom of the table, put the insertion point at the end of the last row, *outside* the border of the table, and press Enter. A new, blank row will appear at the end of the table.

To insert a column, hold the mouse pointer just over the top of the column to the right of where you want the new one to appear. When the pointer turns into a down-pointing arrow, click to select the column and then right-click the selection and choose Insert Columns. Use Ctrl Y to insert more columns. To insert a column at the end of the table, move the down-pointing arrow past the right edge of the table and then click. Right-click the narrow black selection bar that appears to the right of the table and choose Insert Columns.

You can select multiple rows or columns by first selecting a range of cells that include all the desired rows or columns and then choosing Table/Select Row or Table/Select Column. If you use the down-pointing mouse pointer to select columns, hold down the Shift key and select the next column(s).

To move rows and columns, select the row or column as just described and then press Ctrl X. Select the new row or column location, right-click the selection, and choose Insert Columns. To copy rather than move, use Ctrl C instead of Ctrl X.

However you create your tables, you may wonder how to make them look right. Word has a feature called Table AutoFormat that will apply a variety of common styles to a table, as Figure 28 shows. (It's in the Table menu.) It does a decent job, but not always the best job. For example, a common problem is that it will take a small table—say, one with just a few columns of numbers—and make the table as wide as the page, so the numbers are inches apart from each other: basically, an illegible result.

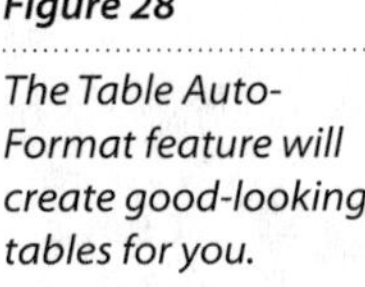

Figure 28

The Table Auto-Format feature will create good-looking tables for you.

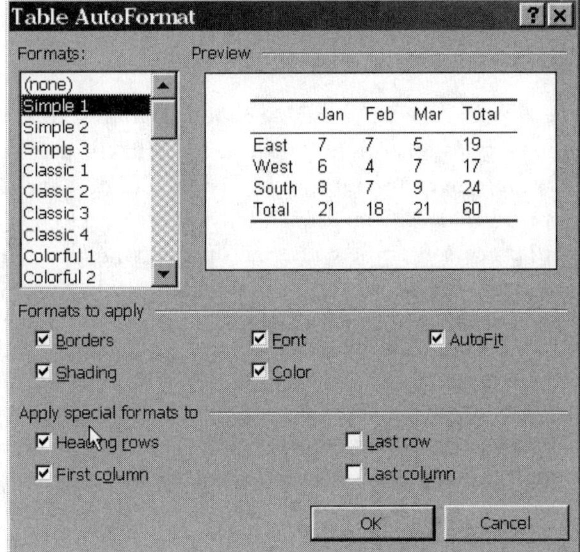

Also, if you incorrectly estimate the column widths when you use the Draw Table feature, you have to resize the columns—there's no obvious function to do this. Figure 29 shows one way to handle this problem: when your mouse hovers over the boundary between cells or at the edge of a cell, the mouse pointer changes to the shape highlighted in the figure. When that happens, you can drag that boundary wider or narrower, thus resizing the column or row. If you move the outer boundaries, you make the table smaller or bigger.

Item	Estimate	Actual
Chocolate bars	$43,000	$45,674
Ice cream sandwiches	$14,500	$12,347
Hard candies	$24,000	$24,424
Sodas	$109.00	$128.53

Figure 29

The special mouse pointer here lets you resize columns, rows, and table boundaries.

You can also resize columns with the Table/Cell Height and Width dialog box, either manually or with the AutoFit button, which sometimes makes good guesses about what will look best. To make columns the same width, select them, right-click the selection, and choose Distribute Columns Evenly.

If you're working with columns and rows of numbers, Word can save you some of the hassle of doing math. If you select an empty cell and choose Table/Formula, you'll get a dialog box that will perform mathematical calculations on other data in the table. For example, if you choose the last cell in a row or column that is full of numbers, Word will assume you want to total those numbers and insert the result in that cell. Of course, you can override that assumption and have Word give, say, the average value of the data in a row or perform some other calculation on the data you select. See the "Perform calculations in a table" entry in Word's online help for more information.

Graphics

When we say graphics, we're talking about artwork: scanned photos for newsletters, illustrations for technical documents, and clip art for any document that you want to liven up. Unless you have talent or you're doing something simple, create graphics from scratch only if you have to. Even though all Windows word processors come with their own drawing programs (see Chapter 17 for more on drawing software), they also come with extensive clip art collections that are much quicker and easier to use.

To use Word's clip art, put the insertion point where you want the graphic to appear, choose Insert/Picture/Clip Art, insert the CD if prompted to, and then find the image you want and double-click it to paste it into your document. To use other artwork, choose Insert/Picture/From File and then find the image you want and double-click it to insert it into the document (see Figure 30). Word can open most graphics formats, but only if you installed the graphics filters when you installed Word. If Word won't place all of your graphics files, rerun setup from the Office or Word CD to ensure that all graphics translators you may need were, in fact, installed.

Figure 30

In Word, you can use this dialog box to insert a graphic.

A third way to add graphics is to have Word scan an image directly from a scanning device attached to your PC. To use this command, you must have installed the Microsoft Photo Editor program that came with Word; if you installed it, you'll have the option Insert/Picture/From Scanner. Make sure that your scanner is turned on and that the image you want to scan is positioned correctly in it. You'll see a dialog box that controls the scan operation. When the operation is done, the scanned image will appear in your document where the text pointer was. (The other options when you choose Insert/Picture are for drawing tools within Word.)

Finally, you can use the Copy and Paste commands to get images from other programs. First, open the image with a graphics program, select the portion you want to add to your document, and press Ctrl C to copy. Then switch to the word processing document, position the insertion point where you want the graphic to appear, and press Ctrl V to paste. Note that the resulting image is often of lower quality than it would be if you used the Insert/Picture method.

If, after you get the graphic in your document, you decide it's not in exactly the right spot, you can simply drag it to the position where you want it to appear. Click the Text Wrapping button on the Picture toolbar (which appears when you click a graphic) to adjust the flow of the document's text around the image.

Embedded Objects

Embedded objects are other files (or portions of other files) incorporated into the document using Microsoft's Object Linking and Embedding (OLE) technology (see Figure 31). The embedded document is linked to the original document; double-clicking it launches the program that created it so you can make modifications. Similarly, if you open the embedded document and make changes to it, when you save it, those changes are reflected in the word processing document in which it is embedded. As you can imagine, this is a great way to include information that's likely to change.

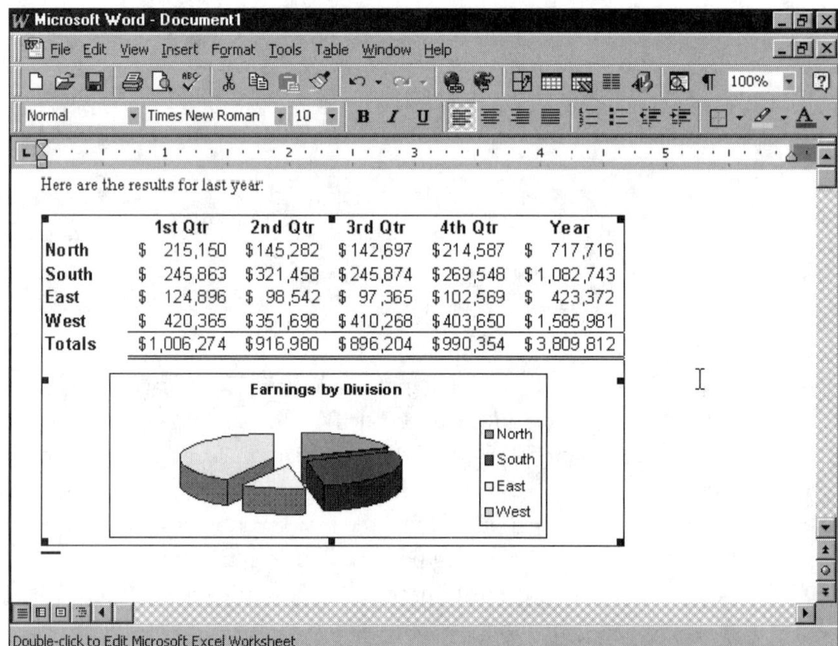

Figure 31

A Microsoft Excel worksheet and chart embedded together in a Word document. In this illustration, the Excel information is selected.

There are two ways to embed an object in a word processing document: copy it and paste it in or insert it as an embedded file. Here's a little more information about how each method works in Word:

- To use the Copy and Paste commands, open the file you want to embed with the program that created it, select all or part of the document, and use the Edit menu's Copy command to copy it. Then switch to the word processing document, position the insertion point where you want the information to appear, and choose Paste Special from the Edit menu. Select an object option in the Paste Special dialog box that appears and click OK.
- To insert an object, choose Insert/Object, click the Create from File tab, and use the Browse button to locate the file you want to insert. Then click OK to insert the file as an object.

If you choose Insert/Object and use the Create New tab, you can create new objects within the document you're working on. This can be confusing, so it's best reserved for objects that can't be created as separate files, most notably WordArt and Equation objects.

WordArt

If you're into having fun with fonts, check out WordArt, which creates a variety of wild type effects, as you can see in Figure 32. You can rotate text, bend it in a curve, create 3-D block letters, add shadows and crazy color effects, and more. WordArt's particularly useful for creating greeting cards and flashy flyers or invitations.

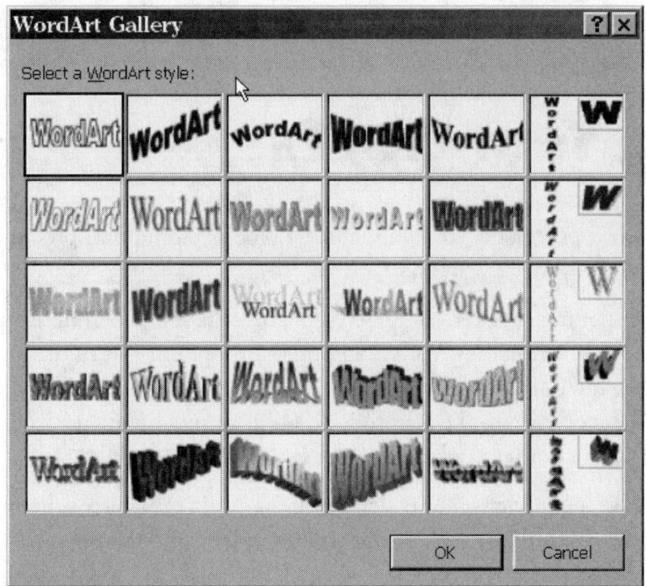

Figure 32

The WordArt feature lets you create very fancy type.

To use WordArt, choose Insert/Picture/WordArt or click the WordArt button on the graphics toolbar (it looks like a 3-D letter "A"). Enter your text in the dialog box, choose a font and size, and then click OK. Now you can use the WordArt button bar to play around with various effects. If you want to change the text, double-click the WordArt object.

Note that what WordArt creates is a graphic, so to edit the text, you'll need to select the WordArt graphic and double-click it to display the WordArt dialog box, where the text can be edited. Because the WordArt result is a graphic, you can move it, resize it, wrap text around it, or do anything else to it that you can to a graphic. Since each WordArt object can have only one set of effects, for some projects you may want to create several objects—for example, an arch-shaped banner over a block of straight horizontal text.

Equations

Word also has an optional Equation Editor that may be useful if you're working on scientific documents, economics papers, or maybe business reports that include advanced mathematical formulas. Adding an equation is not an obvious process: choose Insert/Object and then scroll down the list of object types until you see Microsoft Equation 3.0. You're actually launching a program to create the equation, which is then inserted as an OLE object into your Word document.

If Equation Editor crashes when you try to use it, launch your Web browser and go to **microsoft.com**. Click Search, enter "Q167958" in the search field, click the Support & the Knowledge Base radio button, and click Search Now. That should bring up a page with a link to WD97: Invalid Page Fault Typing Symbol in Equation Editor 3.0; click it to bring up the article and then follow the instructions for fixing the bug.

Finding Your Goofs

Word processors usually include two tools to help improve your prose: a spelling checker and a grammar checker.

A spelling checker compares the words in your document to the words in one of the dictionaries maintained by the program. If it finds a word that's not in the dictionary, it tells you about it. You can then either correct the word or, if the word is correct, ignore it or add it to the dictionary so the spelling checker doesn't bother you again about it.

The spelling checker is definitely the most valuable of the three writing tools, and it should be run before you complete any document. But don't rely on it to find all your errors! If you make an error that spells another word (like *form* instead of *from*), the spelling checker won't catch it. Proofread your document the old fashioned way—by *reading* it—before you print it or forward it to someone else.

A grammar checker looks at your sentences and compares them to a set of rules. Although grammar checkers are a lot better than they were when the second edition of this book went to press, they're still not good enough to rely on. In fact, if you know grammar, you may realize that a lot of the advice a grammar checker gives you is wrong. For this reason, many good writers never use them.

They do have one good feature, however: the readability indexes. These use established formulas to tell you how easy your prose is to read. Big words and long sentences give high (bad) scores, so (depending on your audience) a high score may mean it's time for a rewrite.

Word can automatically check both grammar and spelling as you type, putting red squiggly lines under possible spelling errors and green ones under possible grammar errors. Right-click one of these squiggly-underlined words to display a menu you can use to act on the problem (Figure 33). If you find this as-you-type approach too distracting, disable the feature as discussed in "When Word Gets in Your Way" earlier in this chapter.

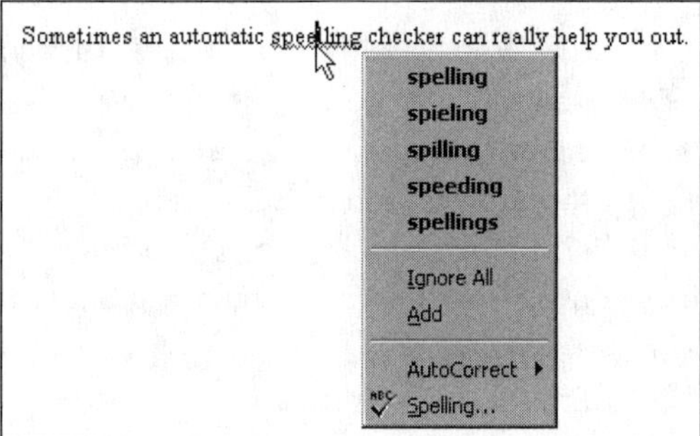

Figure 33

"As you type" spell checking in Microsoft Word.

Printing

When you're finished creating, editing, formatting, and checking your masterpiece, you may want to print it. But wait! Is the document really picture perfect and ready to print? You can tell by using the Preview feature offered by most word processors. It displays complete pages on the screen so you can look at them (To view Word's version, choose File/Print Preview). You may have to magnify the image to read it, but you should get a good idea of its overall appearance before you print. Using this feature can save paper—you can gauge whether text is too long, margins too narrow, and so forth in the context of your content, fix any problems, and then preview again to make sure the problems are fixed before you print.

In theory, print preview should show you exactly what you'll see in the printed document, or at least the closest approximation the PC is capable of displaying. Page numbers and other text in headers and footers appear in solid black, any nonprinting elements such as revision marks are removed, and on-screen guidelines like section breaks and table outlines disappear. Word will let you change margins in print preview; to make other format changes, press Esc to switch back to edit mode.

With most documents, there's not much to printing. Just choose File/Print, set any of the self-explanatory options, and click OK.

If you're printing two-sided documents, choose Odd Pages or Even Pages from the drop-down Print menu at the bottom-right corner of the Print dialog box. Depending on how your printer works, you may want to click the Options button and check Reverse Print Order for the second pass through the printer.

Printing Envelopes

In some word processors, notably old versions of Word, printing envelopes was a tough process that even for expert users involved a lot of experimentation. These days, your word processor will handle the task automatically. Word will even copy the address from a letter: here's how to do it—if you can figure out where the envelope should go in your printer (newer printers usually have nice icons on their paper trays to help you figure that out):

1. If the address is already typed in your document, put the insertion point in the first line of the address block.
2. Choose Tools/Envelopes and Labels. The Envelopes tab should be visible; if it isn't, click its tab.
3. You'll see the address in the dialog box that appears (see Figure 34). Modify it as needed. If you didn't select any text to begin with, type the address here. If you're using Outlook or some other compatible contact manager, you can pick an address from its address book by clicking the Book button above the "Delivery address" field.

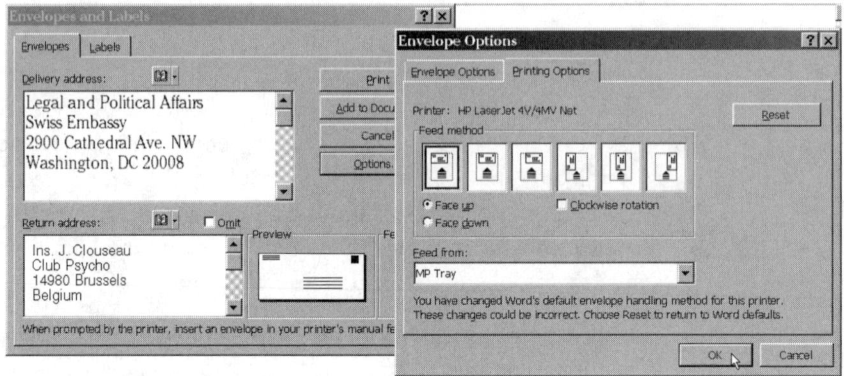

Figure 34

The dialog boxes used in setting up an envelope for printing.

4. Insert the return address, if you want it printed, in the dialog box. (The first time you add an address here, you'll be asked if you want to use this as the default; if you say yes, that address will appear here automatically from then on.) If you don't want the return address to print, check Omit.
5. Click the Options button and make sure the right paper tray, envelope size, and envelope position are selected. You can also set the mailing address and return address formatting here as well (separately, if you wish, from each other). You'll likely have to experiment a few times to make sure you

have the right settings. Word will use the last settings you used (it saves them in the current template), so once you have figured these out, they'll always be there—at least for documents using the current template. Click OK to close the Envelope Options dialog box.

6. Click Print to print the envelope. Cross your fingers!

If you use a laser printer, note that some envelopes may seal themselves when they pass through the device. That's because laser printers use a heating device to dry the ink, and for some envelopes, it's hot enough to melt the glue and seal the envelope. But *don't* put your letter in the envelope first just in case—it will likely then be too thick to go through the printer and could cause a paper jam.

The conventional way to solve the heat-sealing problem is to experiment with different envelopes until you find one that works right with your printer, but here's a funky but functional alternative. Tear the glossy cover off a magazine, and from it cut out a rectangular strip about 2½ inches wide and an inch shorter than the length of the envelope—around 8 inches for standard size-10 envelopes. Slip this strip under the envelope's flap, tuck it up against the fold, and try printing. With any luck, the coating on the paper will keep the envelope's adhesive from sticking, and after it cools, it will seal normally.

Printing Labels

In Word, the process for printing labels is similar to that for printing envelopes. Use the same dialog box, but click the Labels tab. In its Options dialog box, make sure you select the correct type of label (check it against the box the labels came in—standard labels all have a code that you can match to the list in this dialog box). Note that you can have Word print just one label or print the same address on a whole sheet of labels—the latter is handy for printing a batch of return-address labels.

Use only labels designed for use with your type of printer. Otherwise, with an inkjet printer the labels may smear, and with a laser printer the labels' glue may melt and jam the printer.

Customizing Word

No program is designed exactly for how you work. That's why most programs let you customize at least some of their options. Word is particularly customizable, from the buttons that appear on the button bars to the meaning of keyboard shortcuts to the commands that appear on the menus. You can even make Word behave (more or less) like a previous version that you may have used for years, so you don't have to learn the newest version's interface.

It's amazing what you can customize. The flip side, of course, is that the more you customize your copy of Word, the more trouble anyone else will have making it work. Thus, these tricks are mostly useful if you don't share your PC.

You can find these customization options by exploring the tabs of Word's Tools/Customize and Tools/Options dialog boxes. There are far too many options to go into detail about them here. Instead, we'll just give you suggestions of particularly useful changes and warnings about things best left alone.

- **Save your screen space** for displaying documents by turning off toolbars you don't use often. Right-click any toolbar, choose Toolbars, and uncheck the ones you don't use.
- **Disable fast save.** This shaves a bit off the time it takes to save files, but it results in larger files that other programs may have difficulty importing. Choose Tools/Options, click the Save tab, and uncheck "Allow fast saves."
- **Don't turn off Automatic Save** (on the same tab as the fast save feature). This feature automatically backs up your documents every ten minutes (or however often you set it), so in the event you forget to save for a while and your computer crashes or the power goes out, you'll still have most of your work. The one time you might want to turn off this option is when editing a huge document that takes a long time to save.
- **If you find yourself constantly repeating** a long series of mouse actions or keystrokes to use a hard-to-reach command, you can add it to a menu or toolbar or create a keyboard shortcut. First, choose Tools/Customize and click the Commands tab.

  To add a command to a menu or toolbar, in the left (category) pane, select the category to which the command belongs. If you don't know, choose the All Commands category. Scroll down the right pane until you find the command (see Figure 35) and then drag its icon to the exact spot on the menu or toolbar where you want it to appear. To remove commands you add in this way, choose Tools/Customize/Commands and drag unwanted icons off the menus or toolbars.

  To create a keyboard shortcut to a command, click the Keyboard button (see Figure 35). For some strange reason, this brings up another category/command menu that duplicates the one in the previous dialog box (see Figure 36). Select a command in the same way as before, click the field under "Press new shortcut key" and press the combination of keys you want to use to activate the command. If that combination is already assigned to something else, Word will display a "currently assigned to" message. (Word has a zillion predefined keyboard shortcuts, for mostly obscure, little-used features.) If you don't use that key combination and don't share your copy of Word with someone who might, click Assign. If you'd rather leave that key combination assigned to its current command, press Bksp to clear the box and press another key combination.

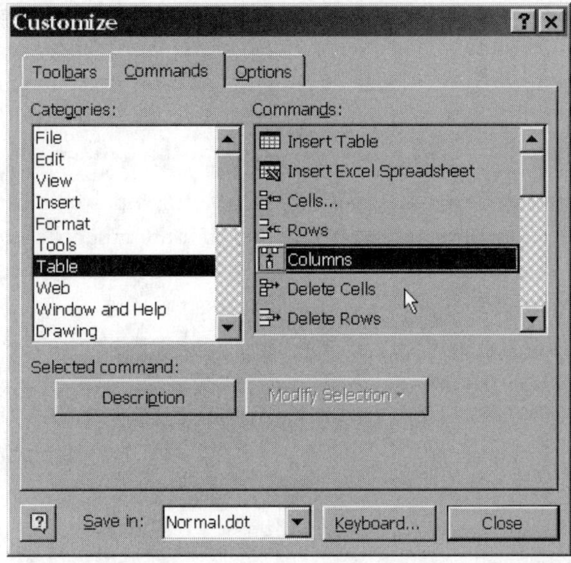

Figure 35

Word's Customize dialog box lets you add commands to any menu or toolbar by dragging icons to the spot where you want them to appear.

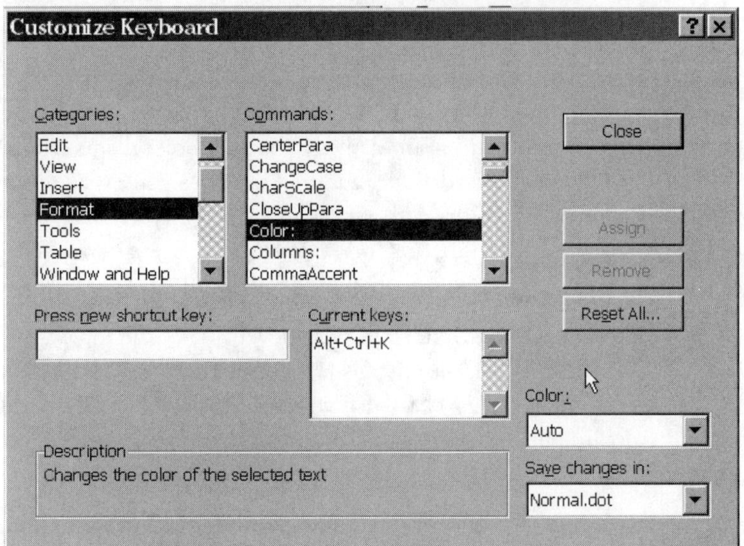

Figure 36

The Customize Keyboard dialog box lets you assign a keyboard shortcut to any command.

Choosing a Word Processor

Nowadays, word processors are most often purchased as part of *suites*—software collections that include a word processor, spreadsheet, personal information manager, and other programs useful in a work environment. Although word processors are also available separately, suites are priced so it's cost-effective to buy the entire suite if you use at least two of the packages. Of the three main office suites—Microsoft Office, Corel WordPerfect Suite, and Lotus SmartSuite—Microsoft Office is by far the most popular, which makes Microsoft Word the most popular word processor. (See Chapter 10: How to Choose and Buy Software, for a comparison of the three suites' contents and prices.)

"Most popular" doesn't always mean best for you, so if you don't already have a word processor, you should take a look at the others before simply buying the one that won the popularity contest. Here's a little more information about each of the major word processors.

Microsoft Word. Microsoft Word is undoubtedly top dog. Regularly revised and updated, it's very powerful and has far more features than the average person could use in a lifetime. Microsoft is currently working on another major revision that should be available not long after this book hits the stores. The cheapest way to buy Word is as part of the Microsoft Home Essentials bundle, which is supposedly sold only with new PCs but is sometimes available for around $100. Otherwise, expect to pay about $450 for Microsoft Office, and $300 for just Word.

Corel WordPerfect. WordPerfect was top dog back in the DOS era, but it's been a distant number 2 for years, and its market share seems to be declining steadily. Popularity aside, WordPerfect for Windows is powerful, flexible, and customizable. It's also relatively cheap: Corel sells its whole suite for the price of Microsoft Word alone, and that includes voice recognition software that can help you enter text without typing. (See Chapter 10: How to Choose and Buy Software, for more on Corel's prices.)

Lotus Word Pro. Lotus Word Pro (like its predecessor Ami Pro) is part of the Lotus SmartSuite. This was never one of the top dogs—just a companion for Lotus 1-2-3, the spreadsheet counterpart to WordPerfect back in the DOS era. Still, Word Pro has what you need to create picture-perfect word processing documents and, like WordPerfect, it supports voice recognition for text entry. Expect to pay about $325 for Lotus SmartSuite or $70 for just Word Pro.

If you're on a budget, you might consider two other options: WordPad and the word processing component of an integrated software package.

WordPad. Don't laugh. Sure, WordPad is a simple freebie that comes with Microsoft Windows. But let's face it: it has all the basic features of a word processor, including the ability to format text and insert objects. If you write only simply formatted documents, like letters and memos, it might be all you need.

Word processors in integrated software. Integrated software such as Microsoft Works (about $50) or AppleWorks (formerly ClarisWorks, about $80) include word processing components. These word processors don't have all the features of the big three word processors, but you get a lot of software for a lot less money. (See "Mini-Suites: AppleWorks and Microsoft Works" in Chapter 10: How to Choose and Buy Software, for more on these two products.)

Desktop Publishing

Desktop publishing (or DTP, if you're into acronyms) refers to the process of designing, creating, and printing complex documents composed of multiple elements (both stories and graphics) right from your desktop. While it doesn't sound like a big deal today, it was a big deal years ago. You see, before computers started popping up on desks everywhere, the only way to create a complex document like a newsletter, flyer, or catalog was to have it typeset by a printing professional. The process was time consuming and costly. Any changes had to be made by the typesetter, who might or might not do exactly what you wanted.

The desktop publishing revolution began when computers could include both formatted text and graphics in the same document and print that document on a high-quality laser printer. This cut the typesetter from the loop and gave computer owners a relatively low-cost, fast turnaround method for creating complex documents to communicate with customers, sell products, or just get the word out. It also created a brand-new job category: desktop publishing professional.

Today's full-featured word processors can handle many basic desktop publishing tasks, such as formatting text, adding graphics, and creating multicolumn text blocks. This makes them useful tools for creating simple newsletters, flyers, and other documents that are more than just text on a page.

As documents get more complex, word processors become less useful. Despite the addition of desktop publishing features, they still tend to see documents as one long series of paragraphs. While you can use paragraph formatting, columns, and text boxes to create newsletter-like and magazine-like layouts, you'll find that it starts getting very labor intensive to set up such documents, and even harder to modify them. That's when you'll want a DTP program, which is designed from the get-go to handle multiple independent elements easily.

If you have more sophisticated needs than your word processor can easily support, Microsoft Publisher is a great, inexpensive option (less than $100). It's a desktop publishing program that has wizards and templates that help you create many kinds of documents.

There's a giant step up from Microsoft Publisher to QuarkXPress (around $700 on the street), the standard industrial-strength DTP program used by graphics pros for things like magazines and books produced on printing presses and distributed to thousands or even millions of people. For most people reading this book, Quark is total overkill. Graphics pros demand a very high level of precision, formatting, and text and graphics manipulation, but if you're not a pro, many of the program's features are just baffling, and not of much use anyway if your output device is a laser printer. The same goes for Adobe Photoshop, Corel Ventura Publisher, and Adobe FrameMaker, DTP programs popular in certain niches.

Word Processing Resources

***Word 97 Bible*,** Brent D. Heslop (ISBN: 0764530380); *Corel WordPerfect Suite 8 Bible*, Stephen E. Harris and Elizabeth Olson (ISBN: 0764530585). These books are comprehensive guides to Word and WordPerfect. Although they cover the basics, they also go far beyond to offer the detailed information that a power user needs.

***Word for Windows 95: Visual QuickStart Guide*,** David Browne (ISBN 0201883627); *WordPerfect 6 for Windows: Visual QuickStart Guide*, Webster & Associates, (ISBN 1566091098). These books teach the basics of Word and WordPerfect using a step-by-step approach with lots of screen shots that keep you on track.

***Microsoft Word 97: Visual Basic Step by Step*,** Michael Halvorson and Chris Kinata (ISBN 1572313889). To take full advantage of Word's powerful macro feature, you'll need to know Visual Basic. This book will teach you how to create macros and custom Word applications.

www.zdjournals.com/msw The Web site for *Inside Microsoft Word*, a monthly newsletter for Microsoft Word users, offers free access to a few articles each month, but a $59 per year subscription (excluding discounts) will get you access to all new articles each month as well as all back issues.

pcworld.com/software/word_processing PC World Online's word processing section includes reviews, buyer's guides, and tips and tricks.

www.hic.net/goliad/wordbk.htm A collection of links to Web sites with information about a variety of word processors, including Word, WordPerfect, and WordPro.

14

Spreadsheets

by Richard Scoville

Portions of this chapter first appeared in PC World *magazine.*

In This Chapter

Crunch, crunch. What's that noise? It's the sound of 38 bazillion spreadsheets out there crunching numbers, doing everything from abscissas to zymosis. Now that the dust has settled from the spreadsheet wars of the early '90s, the spreadsheet that all these diligent electronic laborers are using is—you guessed it—Microsoft Excel. Interestingly, the spreadsheets these hard workers create boil down to just two basic types:

- **Templates** are what most people think of as spreadsheets—kind of custom calculators that you plug numbers into. You can use a template to automate reports like an expense voucher or a sales report, or you can use a template for a "what-if?" model like a budget, where you try out alternative sets of data to gauge their effects on the bottom line.
- **Lists** are for keeping records—invoices receivable, vehicle maintenance records, sales receipts, whatever. A list is actually a database: you can use it for reference and just print it, but more likely you'll want to use the program's database features to select items from the list, calculate group totals and other statistics, and generate graphs.

The trick in using spreadsheet software is not in getting started—the basics are simple enough that most people can be up and running (well, jogging) in an hour or two. The problem is that most people who use spreadsheet programs exploit only a tiny fraction of the power these tools have to offer. This chapter can help you create:

- **Error-free templates.** A template can be a tremendous timesaver, because it frees you from the drudgery of arithmetic, and it can help you make better business decisions because it lets you look at all the options before you leap. But if it gives you wrong answers, it's worse than useless—it's dangerous. I'll show you step by step how to set up a representative template and give you a set of techniques that will help you avoid career-threatening mistakes.
- **Lists done right.** I've heard it estimated that two thirds of all spreadsheets (that's about 25 bazillion) are lists—which is fine, except that most spreadsheet users set them up wrong, fail to use the tools provided by the software, and then get frustrated because they can't rearrange the data into a new pattern. In this chapter, you'll set up a typical list spreadsheet and use some of Excel's spiffy database features to analyze it.

Of course, I can't make you an instant spreadsheet guru, but I can help you become a very savvy learner by getting you off to a quick start, giving you a sense of direction, and pointing out some major pitfalls to avoid. In addition, by comparing the quality and capabilities of today's popular spreadsheets, I'll help you decide which one has the right stuff to best solve your business problems.

Spreadsheet Basics

Using a spreadsheet is a bit like working in a machine shop. The software provides you with components—cells, formulas, functions, etc.—and tools in the form of commands and other features. Your job is to use the tools to assemble the components into a custom calculation machine: your template or list worksheet. In this section, we'll take a tour of the shop. I'll point out some of the essential components, the basic tools, and give you a sense of the basic procedures.

A Walking Tour of the Spreadsheet Shop Floor

All of today's spreadsheet programs, Excel foremost among them, provide the same basic set of number-crunching tools. In addition to basic calculation capabilities, all of the major products provide the following:

- **Functions** to perform calculations that would be difficult or impossible using simple arithmetic. Functions include everything from sums and averages to internal rate of return, statistical distributions, and specialized engineering functions (You need Bessel functions? We have Bessel functions—three kinds!)
- **Formatting tools** for turning tables of data and formulas into attractive reports. These include fonts, shading, colors, cell borders, and other fancy gewgaws.
- **Graphs** to display the data visually.
- **Printing routines** to put the worksheet or graphs on paper in a readable way.
- **Macros** for automating repetitive operations and creating custom applications such as data-entry screens or "executive information systems."
- **Database features** for managing, summarizing, and viewing lists of data and tapping into external data sources.
- **Specialized analytical tools** for answering more specialized business questions, ranging from statistical tests and forecasts ("What will our inventory needs be in six months?"), to linear programming solvers ("What product formula most reduces waste?"), to systems for managing alternative data scenarios ("How much can we budget for R&D given our rosiest sales projections for next year?").

This section and the next stress the components that are common to every spreadsheet application. Later, we'll look at a few of the more specialized Excel tools.

Anatomy of a Workbook

Excel documents are called *workbooks.* A workbook is like a loose-leaf notebook, with multiple pages.

A *worksheet* is one page in the workbook, a sort of electronic grid where you assemble numbers, text, and formulas. To select a sheet, click the *sheet tabs* at the bottom of the workbook window. The grid is composed of *cells*, arranged in *rows* and *columns*.

- **Rows** are identified with numbers down the left edge of the worksheet *frame*.
- **Columns** are identified with letters across the top edge of the frame.
- **Cells,** which contain the worksheet's data and formulas, are boxes created by the intersection of a row and column.
- **The cell pointer** is the spreadsheet's cursor; it highlights the worksheet's *active cell*.
- **The mouse pointer** appears as a fat cross: click a cell to make it the active cell; drag it to select a *range* of cells.
- **The formula bar** displays the contents of the active cell and also the cell *address*, which is a combination of the cell's column letter and row number: for example, B8.
- **Scrollbars** let you view the entire grid: 256 columns by 65,536 rows.
- **Toolbars** give you short-cut access to Excel's menu commands.

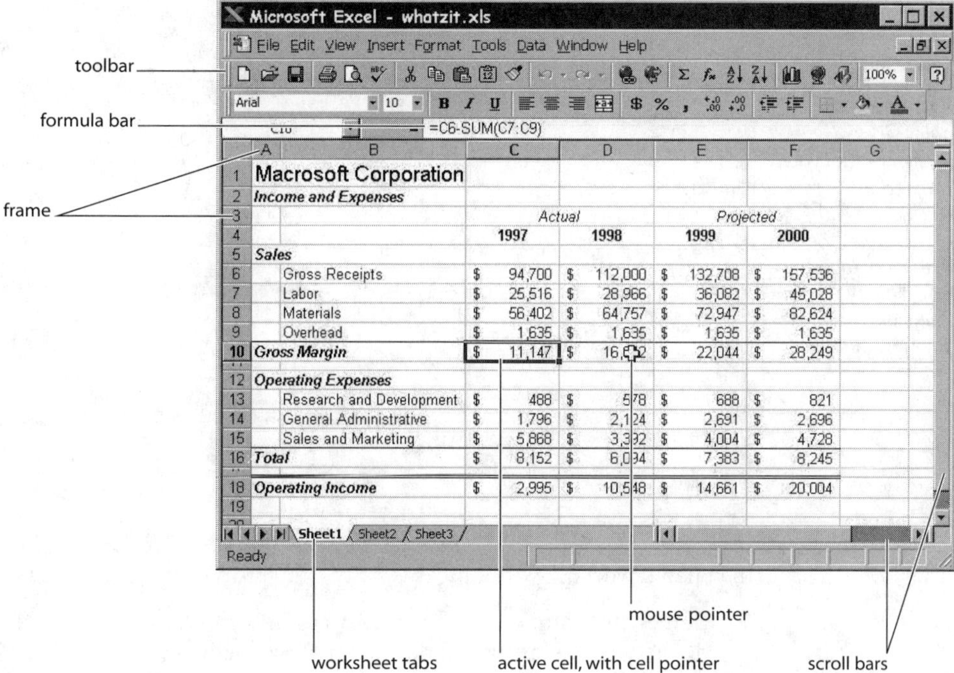

	A	B	C	D	E	F
1	Macrosoft Corporation					
2	*Income and Expenses*					
3			*Actual*		*Projected*	
4			**1997**	**1998**	**1999**	**2000**
5	*Sales*					
6		Gross Receipts	$ 94,700	$ 112,000	$ 132,708	$ 157,536
7		Labor	$ 25,516	$ 28,966	$ 36,082	$ 45,028
8		Materials	$ 56,402	$ 64,757	$ 72,947	$ 82,624
9		Overhead	$ 1,635	$ 1,635	$ 1,635	$ 1,635
10	*Gross Margin*		$ 11,147	$ 16,[illegible]2	$ 22,044	$ 28,249
12	*Operating Expenses*					
13		Research and Development	$ 488	$ 578	$ 688	$ 821
14		General Administrative	$ 1,796	$ 2,124	$ 2,691	$ 2,696
15		Sales and Marketing	$ 5,868	$ 3,392	$ 4,004	$ 4,728
16	*Total*		$ 8,152	$ 6,094	$ 7,383	$ 8,245
18	*Operating Income*		$ 2,995	$ 10,548	$ 14,661	$ 20,004

Figure 1

Like every spreadsheet, Excel 97 shows the address and contents of the active cell in its formula bar. In this case, cell C10 contains a formula that takes the Gross Receipts value from cell C6 and subtracts the sum of the direct costs in cells C7, C8, and C9.

So much for the parts list. You have the workbench, you have the material (data), but you need tools to do the work. You can access them all—from the Print command, to options for creating graphs, to trigonometric functions, to a choice of colors for text—by pulling down menus, the names of which lie in a neat little row on the *menu bar* at the top of the screen.

But why dig around in menus when you don't have to? Most of the commands you need are at the ready, represented by icon buttons on the *toolbar* immediately beneath the menu bar. In Excel, you can even customize the toolbar so your favorite commands are always available at a single mouse click. If you ever forget what an icon does, just drag the cursor over it and pause for a second or two on the icon, and an explanatory message will appear in a pop-up balloon called a *tooltip*.

Ranges and Range Names

A *range* is a rectangular block of cells that contains something you want to work on: perhaps a set of numbers that you want to sum or a group of labels that you want to print in italics (see Figure 2). A range may be as small as a single cell or as large as the entire worksheet. A range *address* is composed of the addresses of two of a range's opposing corner cells: for example, B1:C5.

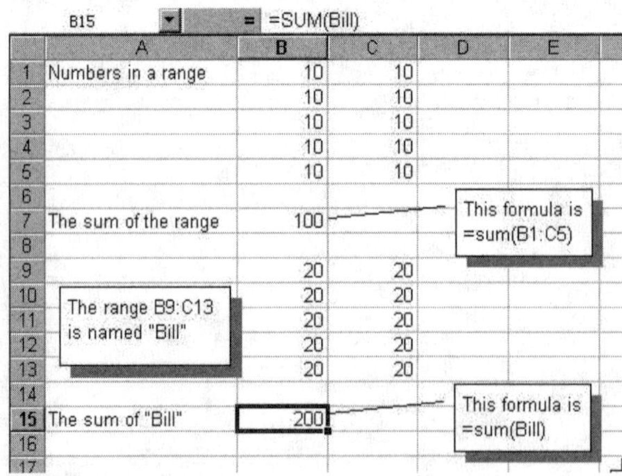

Figure 2

A range is a rectangular block of worksheet cells that you can perform some calculation with or perform some action on. You can give a range a meaningful name to make your formulas easier to interpret.

In general, working with ranges is a two-step process:

1. **Select the range** first, either by dragging with the mouse or holding down Shift while you use the cursor-movement keys.
2. **Do something**: click a button on the toolbar, drag the range to a new location, right-click to choose a pop-up menu option, etc.

Since cell and range addresses are meaningless and hard to remember (Quick, without peeking, what was the range that held the Gross Margin values in

Figure 1?), and because they change when you move things around the worksheet (see "Copying and Moving" later in this chapter), it's best to *name* ranges that you will use often in commands and formulas. Thereafter, you can substitute the name for the cell addresses in formulas, as shown in Figure 2. The more ambitious and complex your worksheets, the more important it is to make systematic use of range names to keep things orderly and sensible.

Cell Values: Formulas Versus Data

The cells of a spreadsheet contain either *data*—simple numbers or text—or *formulas* that perform calculations on the data cells (see Figure 3). The *value* of a cell is "how much it's worth": a data cell that contains a 2 has the value 2; the value of a formula depends on the value of the cells it refers to.

Parts of a Formula. In Excel, every formula begins with an equal sign (=). Formulas have four possible components:

- **Cell addresses** of the cells that contain the numbers or labels you want to crunch.
- **Functions**, which are really prepackaged formulas: for example, the SQRT() function calculates the square root of a number, and the PMT() function calculates the payment on a loan. Some functions, like PROPER(), work with text instead of numbers.
- **Constants:** numbers or text strings enclosed in quotation marks.
- **Operators,** which are the glue that binds the cell addresses, functions, and constants together into a formula.

formulas.xls:2 [Shared]

	A	B	C
1		Numbers	Text
2	Data	12	CAT
3			
4	Formula	12	CAT
5			
6	Formula with constant	48	CATNIP
7			
8	Formula with function	3.46410162	Cat
9			
10	Date	3/16/1948	
11	Date function	10/20/1998	
12	Difference (days)	18480	
13			
14	Logical Formula	TRUE	
15	Conditional Formula	Low	
16			

formulas.xls:1 [Shared]

	B	C
1	Numbers	Text
2	12	CAT
3		
4	=B2	=C2
5		
6	=B2*4	=C2&"NIP"
7		
8	=SQRT(B2)	=PROPER(C2)
9		
10	17608	
11	=TODAY()	
12	=B11-B10	
13		
14	=B2=12	
15	=IF(B2>50,"High","Low")	
16		

Figure 3

Two views of the same Excel worksheet containing a variety of data and formulas. The left window shows the values of the cells; the right window reveals the underlying formulas and data. The formula in cell B8 uses a numeric function to calculate the square root of the value in B2; C8 uses a string function to capitalize the initial character of the label in C2.

Have You Been Born Yet? Excel versus the Year 2000

Just about everyone is familiar with the basic outline of the Year 2000 bug, or, Y2K for short. But in the event you have just returned from a long space flight or have been trying really, *really* hard not to think about it, the story goes something like this:

Back in the halcyon days when "computer" referred to a sheet metal and Plexiglas behemoth kept in an air-conditioned room processing financial transactions with programs written in COBOL, storing data on punch cards, tapes, or disk packs was cumbersome and expensive. So to economize, programmers decided to record only the last two digits of the year: 1968 became just 68.

By itself, that wouldn't matter, except when it comes to doing arithmetic with those dates. For example, a program might subtract the year of your birth (let's say it's '48) from the then-current year ('68) to get your then-current age (20). The problem, of course, occurs on January 1, 2000, when the now-current year becomes 0, and the age calculation yields –48.

Strictly speaking, Excel is not susceptible to the Y2K problem, because of the serial date system employed by most PC applications. Instead of separating the month, day, and year, Excel represents a date as the number of days elapsed since December 31, 1899. For instance, July 11, 1998, is day number 35,987. Excel can display the serial date in various formats—7/11/98, 11-Jul-98, and so on—but in each case, the underlying number is the same.

With serial dates, the original Y2K problem is moot. For instance, to calculate age, just subtract two serial dates, and you get the difference in days; then divide by 365 to get the age in years. There is no Y2K barrier: January 1, 2000, is just day 36,526, and from there, the serial date numbers just keep rolling on into the millennium.

Does all this mean that Excel users are off the Y2K hook? Unfortunately, no. Since Excel permits you to enter dates using just two digits for the year, there is a cutover year that determines the century. In Excel 95, entering 12/31/19 yields the serial date for 2019; entering 1/1/20 yields a twentieth-century date. In Excel 97, the cutover year is 1929.

For most business users, this arrangement makes a lot of sense: the advantage of entering January 12, 2003, as 1/12/03 is obvious. But for users who deal with more historical data—say health care analysts storing or importing the birth dates of elder citizens—this shortcut can lead to errors: a patient born in 2012 instead of 1912.

The fix? Enter early-century dates using all four year digits.

Data Types. Cell values come in three basic flavors, or *data types*: *numeric*, *string* (or text), and *logical*, plus dates, which are actually a special kind of number. See Figure 3 for examples.

- **Numeric** data cells contain numbers; numeric formulas use numeric operators (+, -, *, /, and ^ for addition, subtraction, multiplication, division, and exponentiation, respectively), and numeric functions, which compute numeric values.

- **String** data cells contain text: they're often called *labels*. String formulas use the string operator &, which pastes two strings together to form a longer string, and string functions like PROPER(). So if cell C2 contains the label "cat," the formula UPPER(C2&"nip") has the value "CATNIP."
- **Logical** formulas render true-or-false comparisons of values. They employ *logical operators* (=, >, <, and so on) as well as the *Boolean functions* AND() and OR() for more complex constructions. In Excel, logical formulas have their own special data type, with logical values TRUE and FALSE.

  Examples: The formula =A1=25 is true when a number in cell A1 is equal to 25; the formula =AND(A1>=20,A1<30) is true when the number is between 20 and 29. Logical formulas have a variety of uses, notably in the conditional function IF(). For example, the formula =IF(A1>400,A1-400,0) calculates the amount the number in A1 exceeds 400.
- **Dates** have a special format, but they're really ordinary numbers, which means you can use them in calculations. A spreadsheet may *display* 3/16/48 but it *thinks* of that date (my birthday) as the 17,608th day of the century. To find out my age in days, if you're interested, you'd use the formula =TODAY()-17608 to calculate the number of days elapsed from 3/16/48 to today. The most recent spreadsheets include a greatly expanded set of functions for performing such date calculations.

Copying and Moving

When you get right down to it, the most powerful tool that a spreadsheet program provides is the ability to quickly copy and move cell values and formulas.

Copying: Shifty Business. Copying data values is easy to understand: a number or label is simply duplicated from one cell to another. But when you copy a formula, you don't get an exact duplicate; instead, you get a similar formula that's appropriate to its new location. Thus, if you have a formula in cell A7 that sums the numbers in column A and you copy it to B7, the new formula will sum the corresponding numbers in column B (see Figure 4).

A7 = =SUM(A1:A6)

	A	B	C	D
1	1	6		
2	2	7		
3	3	8		
4	4	9		
5	5	10		
6				
7	15			
8				

B7 = =SUM(B1:B6)

	A	B	C	D
1	1	6		
2	2	7		
3	3	8		
4	4	9		
5	5	10		
6				
7	15	40		
8				

Figure 4

When you copy a formula, its cell referents adjust to the new location. Cell A7 shows a simple =SUM( ) formula that adds the numbers in the range A1:A5. When the formula is copied to B7, the copy is adjusted: the new formula sums B1:B5.

However, in certain situations you'll want to override this automatic adjustment by using an *absolute cell address*: for example, when you want a series of cost formulas for various items to refer to a single cell that contains a universal markup rate (see Figure 5).

absolut.xls:1

	A	B	C	D	E
1	1	2	2	2	
2	2		0	4	
3	3		0	6	
4	4		0	8	
5	5		0	10	

absolut.xls:2

	A	B	C	D
1	1	2	=A1*B1	=A1*B1
2	2		=A2*B2	=A2*B1
3	3		=A3*B3	=A3*B1
4	4		=A4*B4	=A4*B1
5	5		=A5*B5	=A5*B1

Figure 5

Sometimes, you will need to prevent formulas from shifting their referent when you copy them. Here are two views of the same worksheet: the left window shows the values; the right shows the formulas. The formulas in C2:D2 have been copied into C3:D5. In column C, the reference to B1 has shifted, so the values of the formulas in C3:C5 are zero. In D1, the dollar signs make the reference to B1 absolute; *when copied, it doesn't shift.*

Moving Things Can Be Dangerous. Superficially, moving cells is similar to copying them, but this action has a very different effect on the worksheet and especially on formulas. Instead of merely duplicating a cell entry, moving relocates a cell and eliminates the destination cell in the process. The effect on formulas, as shown in Figure 6, can be devastating.

- When you move a cell that lies at the corner of a range, you change the size of the range; a formula that refers to that range can end up referring to the wrong set of values.
- When you move a cell onto a cell that a formula refers to, the formula ends up displaying an error message, because you've destroyed one of the data cells it needs for its calculations.

In addition to using a two-step cut-and-paste procedure, you can quickly move things via the *drag-and-drop* method: just select a cell or range, move the mouse pointer to the edge of the selection where the cursor changes from a plus sign to an arrow, and then drag the selection with the mouse to a new location.

Cell Formatting

There is an important difference between the contents of a cell—its data or formula—and the *format* of the cell, which determines how its value is displayed. Think of the cell format as the packaging of the cell value. You can manipulate the format of a cell separately from it contents: for instance, you can copy just the formatting from one cell or range to another, without disturbing the contents of the destination cell or range. This provides a great shortcut for formatting a large worksheet. And to save time, you get convenient toolbar access to the major formatting features.

Book3: 1

	A	B
1	1	6
2	2	7
3	3	8
4	4	9
5	5	10
6		
7	15	40

Book3: 2

	A	B
1	1	6
2	2	7
3	3	8
4	4	9
5	5	10
6		
7	=A1+A2+A3+A4+A5	=B1+B2+B3+B4+B5

Book3: 1

	A	B
1	1	6
2	2	7
3	3	8
4	4	9
5		5
6		
7	15	#REF!

Book3: 2

	A	B
1	1	6
2	2	7
3	3	8
4	4	9
5		5
6		
7	=A1+A2+A3+A4+B5	=B1+B2+B3+B4+#REF!

Figure 6

When you move a cell that a formula refers to, the formula changes to track its movement. In two views of this simple worksheet, formulas appear in the right-hand window. After cell A5 is moved to B5, the formula in B7 is damaged, because one of its referents has been eliminated.

Formatting includes:

- **Alignment.** You can left-, center-, or right-justify cell values, wrap text within a cell, or display it at an angle. In addition, Excel can *merge* a range of cells into a single cell—perfect for creating report titles or setting up forms.
- **Number format.** For clear reports, it's important that the numbers appear with the proper decimal places, commas, currency symbols, and so on. Excel offers a basic selection of number formats and makes something of an advanced art out of them by letting you create your own customized formats.
- **Fonts and text attributes.** To add emphasis, you can print your cell entries in boldface, underlined, italicized, and so on, and even change the color of the onscreen text to emphasize the distinction between formulas and data cells.
- **Cell shading and border lines.** How about hot pink cells in a fish scale motif, edged with a Baroque gilt frame? Doable, yes, but maybe it's not you. At least you can emphasize the current totals of your humdrum reports by letting them appear in a lightly gray-shaded row—or make a tidy line across the worksheet to separate the total formulas from the data cells.
- **Drawing elements.** Excel includes a drawing toolbar that lets you add shapes such as circles, arrows, and callout boxes to annotate your worksheets. You can store cell format settings as named *styles* and then apply the same formatting to a new range by invoking the style. Styles speed things up a lot. You can even save styles in a *template file* and pass them to anyone with the same spreadsheet program—a good way for a company to give worksheets a consistent look.

Windows spreadsheets all provide some form of "automatic," "intelligent," "speedy" formatting—but it's none of the above. Usually, you end up with a mess that you'll spend more time on than you would have if you formatted the worksheet from scratch. Automatic formatting makes the product reps look great at trade shows, but in real life, it's worse than useless. Just do it yourself.

Graphs

There are two kinds of people in the world: those who really enjoy staring at tables full of numbers in search of The Meaning of Life, and those who would rather glance at a well-designed graph, get the gist, and boogie on. Excel's graph module lets you satisfy the latter group: you can make graphs a regular feature of your reports, and because the graphs reflect up-to-the-moment changes in the data, you can use them as part of your "what-if" analyses.

It's easy to whip up a basic graph with a spreadsheet. You just highlight a range and pick a toolbar option, and Excel will launch a wizard to guide you through the steps to create the chart. In a graph, the cells containing the numbers you want to chart are known as a *data series*. For example, in a bar graph, each series appears as a separate cluster of bars. When the data values in the series range change, the shape of the graph changes to match. Graph titles and legends can be entered directly into the chart or linked to cells on the worksheet so that they display values from the cells, as illustrated in Figure 7.

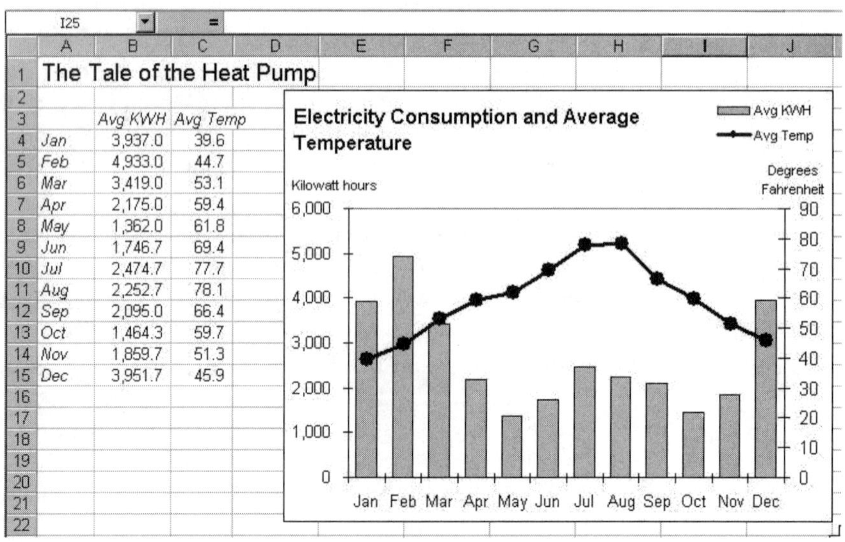

	A	B	C
1	The Tale of the Heat Pump		
2			
3		Avg KWH	Avg Temp
4	Jan	3,937.0	39.6
5	Feb	4,933.0	44.7
6	Mar	3,419.0	53.1
7	Apr	2,175.0	59.4
8	May	1,362.0	61.8
9	Jun	1,746.7	69.4
10	Jul	2,474.7	77.7
11	Aug	2,252.7	78.1
12	Sep	2,095.0	66.4
13	Oct	1,464.3	59.7
14	Nov	1,859.7	51.3
15	Dec	3,951.7	45.9

Figure 7

This combination Line-Column chart is tied to the data values shown at the left. One series (B4:B15) produces the bars showing average monthly electricity consumption in a southeastern home; the other series (C4:C15) produces the line showing the average monthly temperature. The legend titles, Avg KWH and Avg Temp, are linked to the labels in B3:C3.

To let you customize your graphs, Excel provides an editing environment where you can adjust the position and size of the graph elements, scaling of the axes, gridlines, fonts, colors, and so on. You can also add trend lines, error bars, and the like as well as your own annotations, such as text, bitmap clip art, arrows, etc.

Today's spreadsheets offer a wide selection of chart types to cover just about any conceivable need. The basic repertoire includes the ones shown in the "Chart Types" table.

Chart Types

Today's spreadsheet programs offer a variety of chart types tailored to typical business and technical needs.

Chart Type	Example	When to Use
Bar Chart	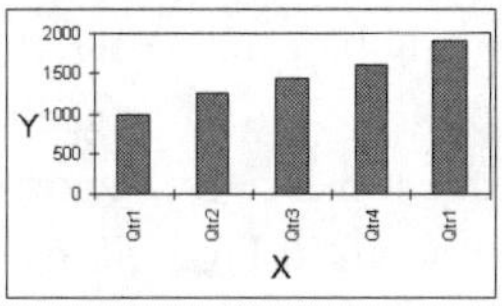	Use to show changes in a countable quantity over time.
Line Chart	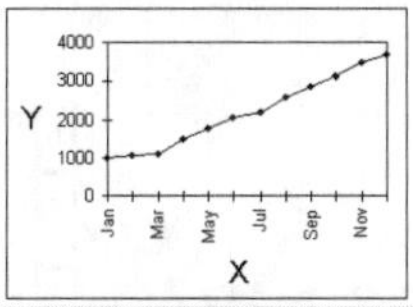	Use to show changes in a continuous variable or index over time.
Column Chart	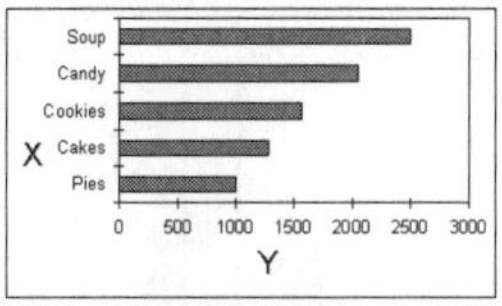	Use to compare quantities across categories.
Pie Chart	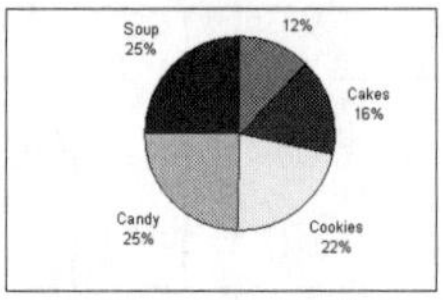	Use to show simple proportions.
Scatter Diagram	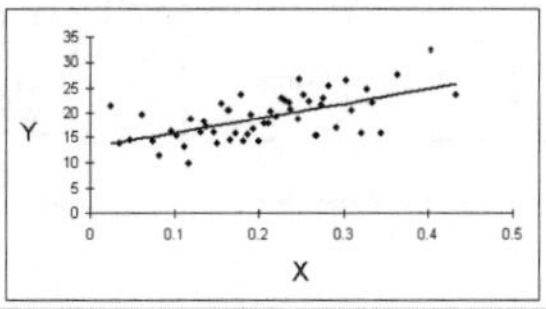	Use to show correlation: the relationship between two variables.
Radar Chart	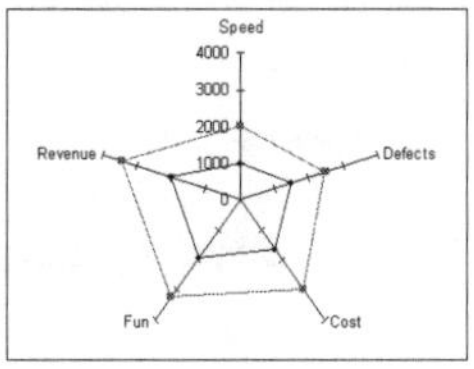	Use to compare entities on several dimensions.

Printing

Printing a small worksheet is simple. When you click the Print tool, Excel automatically prints all of the data on the current worksheet; if you want to be more discriminating, you can select File/Print to find an option to print just a selected range. Use the print preview feature to check the page layout, adjust the margins, maybe set up a page header and footer, and then, when the worksheet looks right, send it on to the printer.

If your worksheet is larger than a single sheet of paper, things get more complicated. When confronted with a print area that is larger than the page, Excel slices it into vertical strips, each one page wide, and then slices the strips into pages, as shown in Figure 8. If the result isn't acceptable, you can adjust the page margins and orientation or use the auto-compression feature to shrink the worksheet onto a single page.

However, if your worksheet is really big, shrinking to a single page is not a practical option, and you must produce a multi-page report. Now the problem is making sure that every page looks right. A normal, everyday, garden-variety spreadsheet like the one shown in Figure 8 has labels in the top row

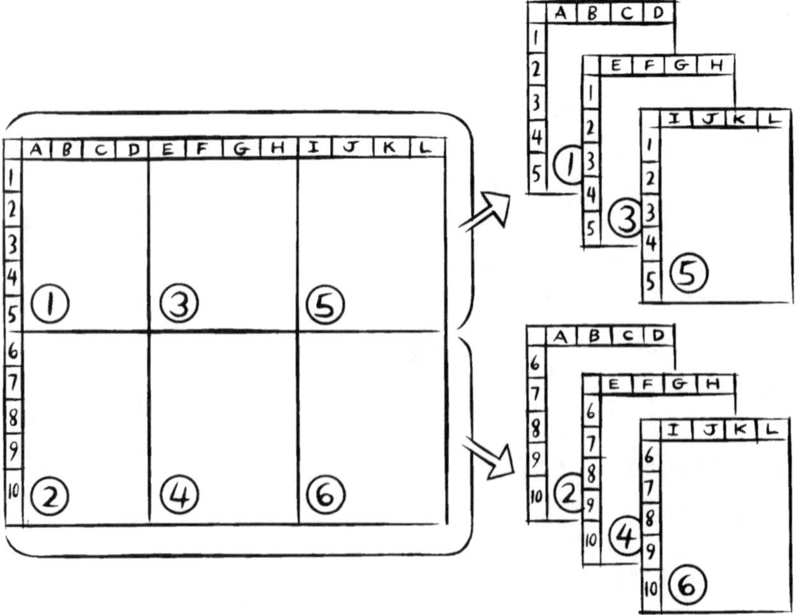

Figure 8

When you print a big worksheet, Excel slices it into multiple pages automatically. If that's not okay, you can compress the report to fit on a single page or use print titles to make sure the column and row headings are repeated on every page. In this example, pages 3 and 4 use the same column headings, and pages 2, 4, and 6 use the same row headings.

and left column to identify the values in the cells. In such worksheets, the slicer, left to its own devices, quickly renders the report indecipherable: page 4 in the example shown in the figure would appear with no headings at all. So Excel lets you set up print titles—rows and columns that contain the needed headings—and the print routine duplicates them on every page of the report.

Macros

A *macro* is a prerecorded series of spreadsheet actions that you can "play back" to quickly to automate some repetitious operation. Since version 5.0, Excel's macros have been based on Visual Basic, a programming system that now animates all the programs in the Office Suite as well as other Microsoft products. VB allows sophisticated users to quickly write applications that integrate the functionality of multiple products using a common language and programming interface.

To create an Excel macro, you can either use the macro recorder to record a sequence of actions or enter code into the VB editor. Most macro writers routinely employ a combination of these methods, recording basic building blocks with the recorder and then knitting them together and revising them with the editor.

It's useful to think of three distinct types of macros, each with its own purpose:

- **Construction macros** automate the routine tasks of setting up or manipulating any worksheet. Thus, you might create a macro to convert all the labels in a column to uppercase. Since construction macros are all-purpose tools, you'll want to store them independent of any individual worksheet, in a personal macro workbook, so you can use them with any worksheet.
- **Production macros** automate the routine tasks associated with an individual worksheet, such as the preparation and printing of a multi-range report or the management of data entry. These macros are stored within the individual worksheet rather than in the personal macro workbook. They're meant to be used by experienced users who simply want to speed up repetitive operations.
- **Application macros** are designed to automate a worksheet for use by an unskilled user. Writing application macros is definitely a professional skill, not to be attempted by the spreadsheet dabbler. Application macros typically provide a customized interface, extensive error checking, custom help, and all the accouterments of a well-built computer application.

In all macros, the statements often refer to actions that occur in specific ranges of the worksheet. To write macros that function reliably, it is imperative that you use range names to refer to any cell or range addresses that the macro must deal with.

Databases

Most people use spreadsheets for keeping records, and when you organize those records into a list, it's called a *database*. More precisely, a database is an organized body of facts about people (employees, customers, etc.), things (inventory items, assets), or events (financial transactions, visits from your mom) that you can set up and manage with your spreadsheet, with a specialized database program like Access or Paradox—or with a shoe box full of index cards, for that matter. If your data is already stored in a database program somewhere (say, on a mainframe or minicomputer system), it's likely that you can import all or part of it directly into your worksheet to play with.

First, some jargon: A database consists of one or more *tables*, which in a spreadsheet program means a range. The data is arranged in *fields* (columns) and *records* (rows). The first row of a table contains unique *field headings* that identify the contents of that column. If more than one table is involved, the database is called a *relational* database, where the tables are cross-referenced by *keys*—and see; you're already in over your head. To find out more about database concepts, check out Chapter 16: Databases. For now, think of a spreadsheet database as a simple list like the one shown in Figure 9.

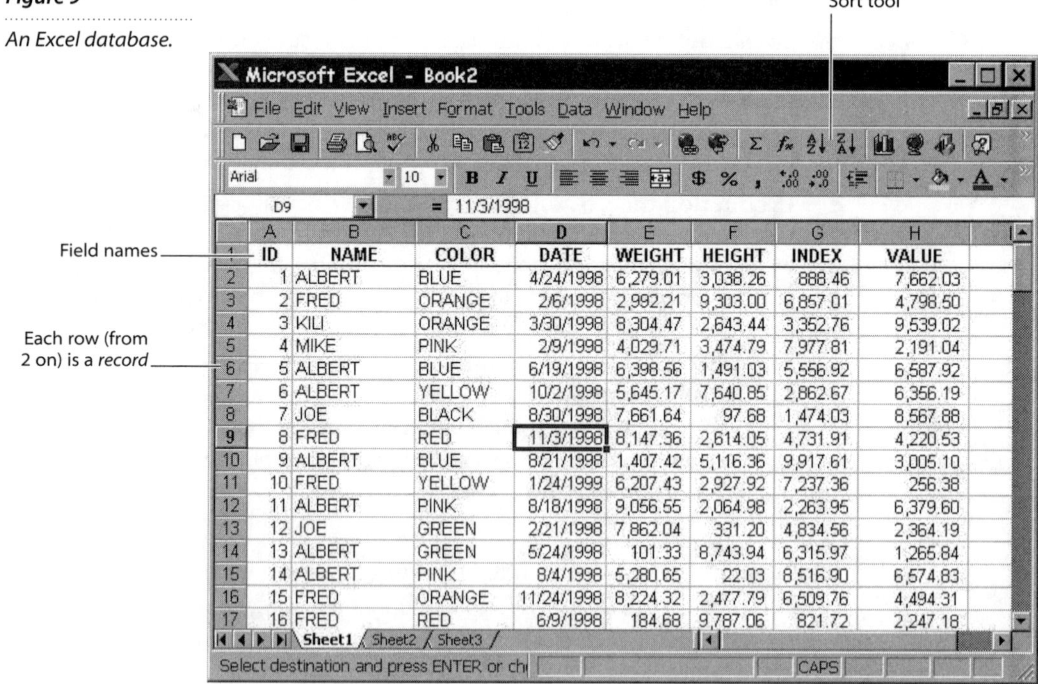

	A	B	C	D	E	F	G	H
1	ID	NAME	COLOR	DATE	WEIGHT	HEIGHT	INDEX	VALUE
2	1	ALBERT	BLUE	4/24/1998	6,279.01	3,038.26	888.46	7,662.03
3	2	FRED	ORANGE	2/6/1998	2,992.21	9,303.00	6,857.01	4,798.50
4	3	KILI	ORANGE	3/30/1998	8,304.47	2,643.44	3,352.76	9,539.02
5	4	MIKE	PINK	2/9/1998	4,029.71	3,474.79	7,977.81	2,191.04
6	5	ALBERT	BLUE	6/19/1998	6,398.56	1,491.03	5,556.92	6,587.92
7	6	ALBERT	YELLOW	10/2/1998	5,645.17	7,640.85	2,862.67	6,356.19
8	7	JOE	BLACK	8/30/1998	7,661.64	97.68	1,474.03	8,567.88
9	8	FRED	RED	11/3/1998	8,147.36	2,614.05	4,731.91	4,220.53
10	9	ALBERT	BLUE	8/21/1998	1,407.42	5,116.36	9,917.61	3,005.10
11	10	FRED	YELLOW	1/24/1999	6,207.43	2,927.92	7,237.36	256.38
12	11	ALBERT	PINK	8/18/1998	9,056.55	2,064.98	2,263.95	6,379.60
13	12	JOE	GREEN	2/21/1998	7,862.04	331.20	4,834.56	2,364.19
14	13	ALBERT	GREEN	5/24/1998	101.33	8,743.94	6,315.97	1,265.84
15	14	ALBERT	PINK	8/4/1998	5,280.65	22.03	8,516.90	6,574.83
16	15	FRED	ORANGE	11/24/1998	8,224.32	2,477.79	6,509.76	4,494.31
17	16	FRED	RED	6/9/1998	184.68	9,787.06	821.72	2,247.18

Figure 9

An Excel database.

The number of records you can include in your list is limited by the number of rows in a single worksheet: 65,536 in Excel 97, 16,384 in Excel 95. Actually, deduct one from those figures, since you'll need the first row to store the *field headers*.

Sorting, Selecting, and Summarizing. Excel provides several tools for organizing, culling, and summarizing lists of data.

- **Sorting**. First is the sorting tool, which lets you rearrange the records (rows) of the table according to the entries in one or more of the columns. The database in Figure 9 is sorted by [ID]; the sort operation would let you reorder the database, for instance, by [NAME] and then by [COLOR] when the names are the same.
- **Filters**. Next is a handy gadget for selecting subsets of records to answer questions like "Which customers bought pink?" Excel's AutoFilter feature turns the field headings in the top row of a worksheet into selection controls that list the unique entries in the column (see Figure 10). When you make a selection, Excel hides the rows that lack a corresponding entry in the column.

Figure 10

Excel's AutoFilters let you select specific rows in a list for display.

	A	B	C	D	E	F	G	H
1	II	NAME	COLOR	DATE	WEIGH	HEIGH	INDEX	VALUE
3	2	FRED		2/6/98	2,992.21	9,303.00	6,857.01	4,798.50
4	3	KILI		3/30/98	8,304.47	2,643.44	3,352.76	9,539.02
16	15	FRED		11/24/98	8,224.32	2,477.79	6,509.76	4,494.31
21	20	ALBERT		10/19/98	4,574.98	7,948.09	300.33	1,635.19
26	25	FRED		3/17/98	220.61	8,787.70	6,094.24	3,672.67
38	37	ALBERT		6/6/98	5,865.64	6,633.91	3,740.33	5,882.25
46	45	ALBERT		11/3/98	2,734.95	5,596.37	4,108.54	2,060.35
55	54	TED		8/21/98	6,637.60	4,947.79	4,324.03	8,421.94
71	70	ALBERT	ORANGE	1/21/99	8,615.17	8,204.24	5,988.91	9,190.18
72	71	JOE	ORANGE	1/4/99	3,785.28	3,907.78	429.73	2,467.62
81	80	FRED	ORANGE	2/24/98	774.14	7,102.02	1,100.44	9,557.16
89	88	FRED	ORANGE	7/6/98	6,475.71	6,126.84	3,815.49	4,007.40
92	91	TED	ORANGE	10/1/98	8,730.13	2,434.26	9,000.42	5,273.43
98	97	KILI	ORANGE	5/11/98	9,960.19	3,952.49	9,559.24	3,433.92
101	100	FRED	ORANGE	1/9/99	3,140.06	695.64	3,984.90	7,784.49
103	102	MIKE	ORANGE	3/17/98	8,760.68	1,425.87	5,595.39	4,434.88
112	111	MIKE	ORANGE	4/3/98	7,315.11	3,910.17	3,937.63	3,562.37
114								

- **Summarizing: functions, subtotals**. Excel provides a set of sophisticated tools for summarizing the data in groups of records: for instance, to count the number of records in each group or produce group subtotals. The most basic tools for this purpose are the *database statistical functions* DSUM(), DCOUNT(), etc., which let you use a summary statistic. These functions yield summary statistics for the values selected from specified records and fields in a database. *Subtotals* automatically insert rows of formulas into your sorted list to sum, count, or average subgroups of records (see Figure 11).

Figure 11

Subtotals (in the bottom-right corner, above the grand total) display summary information in a sorted list.

	A	B	C	D	E	F	G	H
1	ID	NAME	COLOR	DATE	WEIGHT	HEIGHT	INDEX	VALUE
11			**BLACK Total**					62,493.99
27			**BLUE Total**					78,821.81
43			**GREEN Total**					77,366.74
44	2	FRED	ORANGE	2/6/98	2,992.21	9,303.00	6,857.01	4,798.50
45	3	KILI	ORANGE	3/30/98	8,304.47	2,643.44	3,352.76	9,539.02
46	15	FRED	ORANGE	11/24/98	8,224.32	2,477.79	6,509.76	4,494.31
47	20	ALBERT	ORANGE	10/19/98	4,574.98	7,948.09	300.33	1,635.19
48	25	FRED	ORANGE	3/17/98	220.61	8,787.70	6,094.24	3,672.67
49	37	ALBERT	ORANGE	6/6/98	5,865.64	6,633.91	3,740.33	5,882.25
50	45	ALBERT	ORANGE	11/3/98	2,734.95	5,596.37	4,108.54	2,060.35
51	54	TED	ORANGE	8/21/98	6,637.60	4,947.79	4,324.03	8,421.94
52	70	ALBERT	ORANGE	1/21/99	8,615.17	8,204.24	5,988.91	9,190.18
53	71	JOE	ORANGE	1/4/99	3,785.28	3,907.78	429.73	2,467.62
54	80	FRED	ORANGE	2/24/98	774.14	7,102.02	1,100.44	9,557.16
55	88	FRED	ORANGE	7/6/98	6,475.71	6,126.84	3,815.49	4,007.40
56	91	TED	ORANGE	10/1/98	8,730.13	2,434.26	9,000.42	5,273.43
57	97	KILI	ORANGE	5/11/98	9,960.19	3,952.49	9,559.24	3,433.92
58	100	FRED	ORANGE	1/9/99	3,140.06	695.64	3,984.90	7,784.49
59	102	MIKE	ORANGE	3/17/98	8,760.68	1,425.87	5,595.39	4,434.88
60	111	MIKE	ORANGE	4/3/98	7,315.11	3,910.17	3,937.63	3,562.37
61			**ORANGE Total**					90,215.68
85			**PINK Total**					114,396.47
100			**RED Total**					55,308.69
120			**YELLOW Total**					90,201.53
121			**Grand Total**					568,804.91

Slicing and Dicing with Pivot Tables. The features just described are quite cool and very easy to use, but it's *pivot tables* that really make your spreadsheet databases sing. Pivot tables cross-tabulate a list to tally or summarize data in groups. The result is a flexible display that you can rearrange with the flick of a mouse pointer, and which provides a host of flexible tricks for turning those boring lists into illuminating results. An example of a pivot table is shown in Figure 12.

Figure 12

A pivot table summarizes records from a database list according to the categories that appear in one or more fields. This example shows summary sales figures for two products, organized by color and sales rep.

	A	B	C	D
1			Data	
2	COLOR	NAME	Sum of VALUE	Count of ID
3	BLACK	ALBERT	29337.82	4
4		JOE	26921.98	4
5		TED	6234.19	1
6	BLACK Total		62493.99	9
7	BLUE	ALBERT	26355.28	5
8		FRED	25789.24	5
9		JOE	2669.56	1
10		MIKE	16117.49	2
11		TED	7890.24	2
12	BLUE Total		78821.81	15
13	GREEN	ALBERT	14933.82	4
14		FRED	16116.73	3
15		JOE	21298.53	4
16		MIKE	9100.57	2
17		TED	15917.09	2
18	GREEN Total		77366.74	15
19	ORANGE	ALBERT	18767.97	4
20		FRED	34314.53	6

Importing Data. When it comes to using data from external sources, Excel can open just about any kind of common data format, from delimited text files to database tables. Then, depending on the data structure, you may need to supply some information to the Text Import Wizard to help it decide how to transfer the data into worksheet cells. If your data resides in a relational database system such as Access, SQL Server, Oracle, or the like, you can establish a live link via a Database Query, so that every time you open your workbook, you get the current version of the data at that time.

Spreadsheet database tools are great: they let you store your data in a standard format and then flexibly select, sort, subtotal, slice, and dice it into the final form you need for your reports. The problem, as we'll discuss later in this chapter, is recognizing when you need to use them.

Step This Way for Lesson One

Now that you've survived your tour of how the spreadsheet works, it's time to roll up you sleeves and do a little work yourself. The next two sections show you the procedures for setting up a basic template worksheet and a representative database worksheet. Along the way, you'll learn the operations that are essential to every spreadsheet apprentice.

Building a Template Worksheet

Template worksheets are used for modeling (playing the "what-if?" game) and for automating printed paper forms. Our first hands-on example is a simplified travel expense voucher, the kind you might submit to your comptroller (bookkeeper, spouse, etc.) after a long and dusty week on the road (see Figure 13). Of course, you can set up this kind of a report with any spreadsheet software, but we'll illustrate this exercise with Excel.

Figure 13

This simple expense report is a typical template worksheet.

	A	B	C	D	E	F	G
1	McBlast Bros. Inc. Travel Expense Voucher						
2							
3	Name:			Date:		Mileage:	$ 0.100
4		MON	TUE	WED	THU	FRI	
5	Date						
6	Location						TOTAL
7	Hotel	1.00	1.00	1.00	1.00	1.00	$ 5.00
8	Breakfast	1.00	1.00	1.00	1.00	1.00	$ 5.00
9	Lunch	1.00	1.00	1.00	1.00	1.00	$ 5.00
10	Supper	1.00	1.00	1.00	1.00	1.00	$ 5.00
11	Airline	1.00	1.00	1.00	1.00	1.00	$ 5.00
12	Rental Car	1.00	1.00	1.00	1.00	1.00	$ 5.00
13	Taxi	1.00	1.00	1.00	1.00	1.00	$ 5.00
14	Tips	1.00	1.00	1.00	1.00	1.00	$ 5.00
15							
16	Vehicle Miles	1	1	1	1	1	5
17	TOTAL	$ 8.10	$ 8.10	$ 8.10	$ 8.10	$ 8.10	$ 40.50
18							

You work as a U.S. rep for McBlast Brothers Pyrotechnic Emporium. (based in Loch Enlode, Scotland, and manufacturers of fine fireworks since 1535). You want to create an expense form than computes running totals, including personal vehicle cents-per-mile calculations.

Step 1. Enter the Labels

Your current expense report resembles the one shown in Figure 13. To set it up in Excel, your first step is to enter the labels that give your template its basic shape. Launch Excel (or execute File/New) and take a look at Figure 14. Put the cell pointer on cell A1, type "McBlast Bros. Travel Expense Voucher," and press Enter. Notice that the label you just entered is much longer than the cell you put it in. That's okay: a label, unlike a number, can spill out onto adjacent empty cells. Repeat the process to enter the "Name:" label in A3. Now for a small shortcut: put the cell pointer on A5, type "Date," and instead of Enter, press [Key Caps: Cursor Down]. You've entered the label and moved to the next cell, all in one step.

	A	B	C	D	E	F	G
1	McBlast Bros. Inc. Travel Expense Voucher						
2							
3	Name:			Date:		Mileage:	
4		MON	TUE	WED	THU	FRI	
5	Date						
6	Location						TOTAL
7	Hotel						
8	Breakfast						
9	Lunch						
10	Supper						
11	Airline						
12	Taxi						
13	Tips						
14							
15	Vehicle Miles						
16	TOTAL						
17							

Figure 14

The first step in building a template is to enter the labels, to give shape to your new worksheet.

If you need a set of labels that fall into some common patterns (MON, TUE, WED..., January, February..., etc.), your Windows spreadsheet can help you enter them quickly. Put the cell pointer in B4 and enter "MON." Then select B4:F4 and choose Edit/Fill/Series. Click the AutoFill button in the Type box and click OK. Excel obligingly fills in the remaining days of the week. You can also execute AutoFill by dragging the *AutoFill handle*, the small black rectangle in the lower-right corner of the current selection (see Figure 15). Now continue until your worksheet looks like Figure 14.

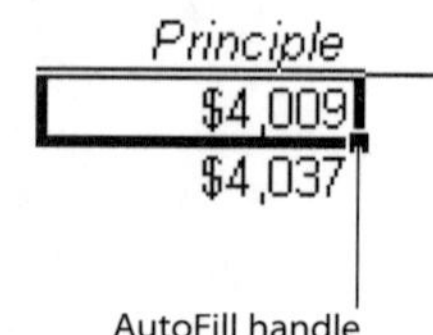

Figure 15

Excel's AutoFill handle.

Step 2. Build and Check the Formulas

Let me say this real loud, so you'll be sure to hear me:

Never, ever sign your name to a piece of paper printed from one of your spreadsheets without making sure that the results are correct.

Spreadsheets make it very easy to perform complex calculations—and even easier to perform them incorrectly, if your formulas contain either logical or careless errors. The most important way to prevent errors is to avoid using real data (in the current example, real expense amounts) as you construct the formulas. Instead, follow rule 4 in "Avoiding the BIG MISTAKE" later in this chapter: in place of real-life numbers, enter dummy data values that make it easier to spot errors. Later, once you're sure the formulas are working properly, erase the dummy data and enter the real data. We'll follow this procedure as we enter and copy the formulas for our expense voucher. (Even though the formulas we're building here are so simple that the whole ritual seems perversely obsessive, it's good for you. So just do it.)

Sums and Copies. Start by entering ".1" in cell G3 (no, we don't really reimburse just 10 cents per mile; it's a dummy data value). Next, enter "1" in cell B7 and select B7:F7 and execute the command Edit/Fill/Right. Now you have your dummy data for the hotel expenses, so let's use the SUM() function in a formula to find the total. Put the cell pointer in G7 and click the AutoSum button on the toolbar (see Figure 16). All by itself, Excel enters =SUM and selects B7:F7. Click the AutoSum button again, and Excel enters the formula and displays the result: 5.

Figure 16

Excel's AutoSum button.

Now, every expense item needs a similar formula and its own set of dummy values: select the range B7:G13 and execute Edit/Fill/Down. Select B13:G13 and execute Edit/Copy. Select B15, execute Edit/Paste, and press Esc to cancel the selection (denoted by the "Vegas lights" around the range), and you have a set of formulas for the vehicle miles. Just to be sure you understand what's happened, click each formula in column G and notice that each copy of the original formula refers to its own row: the one in B8 sums the 1's in row 8, the one in B9 sums row 9, and so on.

Absolute Cell Addresses. Finally, select B16, type "=SUM(," select B7:B4, type ")," type "+," click cell B15, type "*," click G3, and press Enter. The formula appears as =SUM(B7:B13)+B15*G3 on the formula bar and displays 7.1 in the worksheet. Is it correct? Let's see, 7 ones is 7, and 1 mile times 10 cents per mile is .1, so it looks okay.

Congratulations! you've just entered your first erroneous formula. Don't believe it? Just use Edit/Fill/Right as described earlier to copy the formula into C16:G16 and then look at the results. Although the original formula was correct, the copies you made have adjusted all their cell references: the one in column C sums the values in column C and then adds the product of C15 times H3. But H3 is empty, so its value counts as a zero.

Let's fix the original formula so that the reference to cell G3 is absolute; that way, it won't change when you make copies. Select cell G3 and then click the mouse pointer on the formula bar just to the left of the G in G3. Type a dollar sign there and then type another one between the G and the 3. Press Enter. The formula now reads =SUM(B7:B13)+B15*G3. Copy it again into C16:G16 and note that all the results are now correct. Examine the formulas and observe that each one multiplies the mileage by the rate in cell G3, as required. Your worksheet now looks like Figure 17

Figure 17

The formulas in B16:G16 all include a absolute reference to the mileage rate in cell G3.

B16 = =SUM(B7:B13)+B15*G3

	A	B	C	D	E	F	G
1	McBlast Bros. Inc. Travel Expense Voucher						
2							
3	Name:			Date:		Mileage:	0.1
4		MON	TUE	WED	THU	FRI	
5	Date						
6	Location						TOTAL
7	Hotel	1	1	1	1	1	5
8	Breakfast	1	1	1	1	1	5
9	Lunch	1	1	1	1	1	5
10	Supper	1	1	1	1	1	5
11	Airline	1	1	1	1	1	5
12	Taxi	1	1	1	1	1	5
13	Tips	1	1	1	1	1	5
14							
15	Vehicle Mi	1	1	1	1	1	5
16	TOTAL	7.1	7.1	7.1	7.1	7.1	35.5
17							

Inserting a Row. Oops! You may not have noticed, but if you compare Figures 13 and 14, you'll see that your worksheet is missing a row to hold the car rental information. Start by selecting the entire row at the point where you want the new row to appear (see Figure 18). Now, execute Insert/Rows. Notice that everything below row 11 just moved down one row. Click the formula for Monday's total, now in cell B17: it has adjusted to accommodate the new row you inserted, so that the SUM function now includes B7:B14. This universal feature of spreadsheet programs is very important; it means you don't have to keep fixing your formulas after you adjust your worksheet.

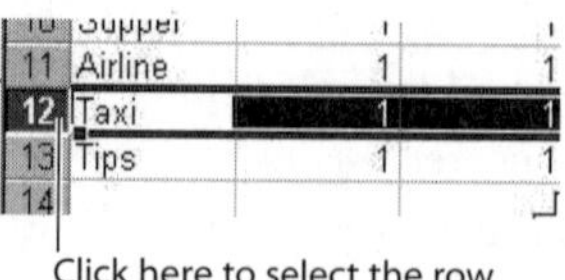

Figure 18

Selecting a row.

Enter "Rental Car" in cell A12 and copy a set of 1's and a row formula into the new row. Your worksheet should now resemble Figure 19.

Figure 19

When you insert a row, the daily total formulas (now in row 17) adjust to make room for the Rental Car data.

B17 = =SUM(B7:B14)+B16*G3

	A	B	C	D	E	F	G
1	McBlast Bros. Inc. Travel Expense Voucher						
2							
3	Name:			Date:		Mileage:	0.1
4		MON	TUE	WED	THU	FRI	
5	Date						
6	Location						TOTAL
7	Hotel	1	1	1	1	1	5
8	Breakfast	1	1	1	1	1	5
9	Lunch	1	1	1	1	1	5
10	Supper	1	1	1	1	1	5
11	Airline	1	1	1	1	1	5
12							
13	Taxi	1	1	1	1	1	5
14	Tips	1	1	1	1	1	5
15							
16	Vehicle Mi	1	1	1	1	1	5
17	TOTAL	7.1	7.1	7.1	7.1	7.1	35.5
18							

Step 3: Format Your Template

At this point, your template is mechanically complete: the labels are in place, and the formulas are correct and ready to go. But it doesn't look very snazzy, to say the least. Let's dress it up. We'll use a technique that's standard for all Windows spreadsheets—namely, using the right mouse button to change the properties of elements on the sheet. We'll also use some common toolbar shortcuts.

The aim is to get the template to look like Figure 20.

Figure 20

Formatting makes the spreadsheet more appealing and helps reduce the probability of careless errors: with the data cells shaded, the data won't be confused with formulas.

I20 =

	A	B	C	D	E	F	G
1	McBlast Bros. Inc. Travel Expense Voucher						
2							
3	Name:			Date:		Mileage:	$ 0.100
4		MON	TUE	WED	THU	FRI	
5	Date						
6	Location						TOTAL
7	Hotel	1.00	1.00	1.00	1.00	1.00	$ 5.00
8	Breakfast	1.00	1.00	1.00	1.00	1.00	$ 5.00
9	Lunch	1.00	1.00	1.00	1.00	1.00	$ 5.00
10	Supper	1.00	1.00	1.00	1.00	1.00	$ 5.00
11	Airline	1.00	1.00	1.00	1.00	1.00	$ 5.00
12	Rental Car	1.00	1.00	1.00	1.00	1.00	$ 5.00
13	Taxi	1.00	1.00	1.00	1.00	1.00	$ 5.00
14	Tips	1.00	1.00	1.00	1.00	1.00	$ 5.00
15							
16	Vehicle Miles	1	1	1	1	1	5
17	TOTAL	$ 8.10	$ 8.10	$ 8.10	$ 8.10	$ 8.10	$ 40.50
18							

Set the Column Width and Row Height. Start by adjusting the width of the columns and height of the rows. At the top of the worksheet frame, find the line that divides columns A and B. Drag that line to change the width of the column until there's room to display all of the labels (see Figure 21). Use a similar procedure to adjust the height of rows 2, 4, and 15 as shown.

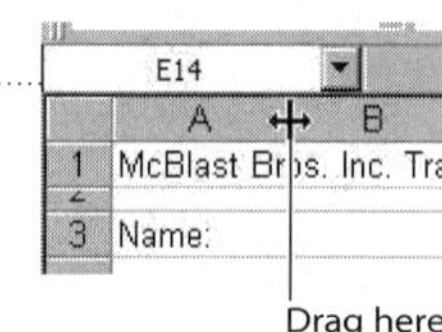

Figure 21

Changing the column width.

Aligning Cell Entries. First, we'll align some labels. Select cell A3 and click the Right-align button (see Figure 22), and Excel puts the text on the right side of the cell. Repeat the process for cells D3 and F3.

Figure 22

Excel's Right-align button.

To center all the labels in row 4, select the whole row by clicking the row number on the left side of the worksheet frame; then click the Center-align button on the toolbar (see Figure 23). Next, center the title in cell A1 across the top of the spreadsheet. Select A1:G1 and click the Merge and Center button.

Figure 23

Excel's Center-align button.

Font and Colors. Make the title bold: select A1 and click the Bold button (see Figure 24). Now make the title bigger: right-click A1 and select Format Cells from the pop-up menu. Click the Font tab at the top of the dialog box to display the font controls. Now scroll through the Size list, click 12, and then click OK. (You can also find this list of font sizes on the toolbar; notice that the dialog box gives you lots of additional choices that are not on the toolbar.)

Figure 24

Excel's Bold and Italic toolbar buttons.

Italicize the daily column headings: select row 4 again as described earlier and click the Italic button (see Figure 24).

Shade the data cells. Another important error-avoidance technique (rule 5 in the BIG MISTAKE sidebar) is to make the data cells look different, so you don't confuse them later with cells that contain formulas. To select all of the data cells at once, start by selecting B3:C3. Now press and hold Ctrl and select E3, G3, B5:F14, and B16:F16. Right-click anywhere inside the selected cells (on D10, for instance) and select Patterns from the menu. Select a light gray or yellow color in the Cell Shading box and then click OK.

Number Formats

You want your numbers to have a neat, conventional appearance: two decimal places, dollar signs on the row and column totals, and if, heaven forbid, you should spend more than $1,000, you want the value to include a comma between thousands and hundreds.

Select B7:F7, then right-click the selection and choose Format Cells from the menu. Click the Number tab and then click Number in the Category list. On the right side of the dialog box, confirm 2 decimal places and select Use 1000 Separator. Click OK and notice the tidy appearance of your dummy data.

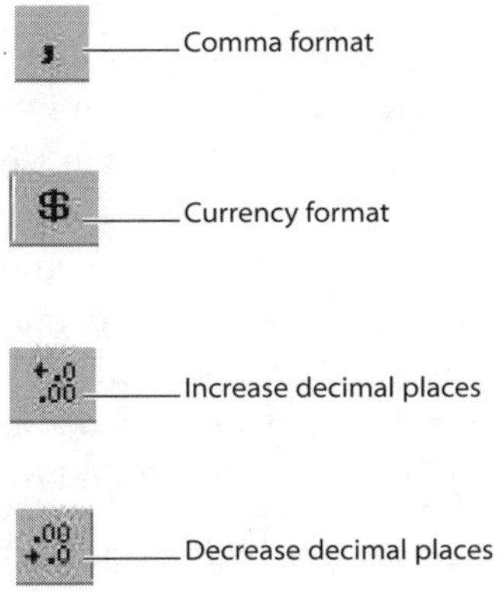

Figure 25

Excel number format buttons

Comma format

Currency format

Increase decimal places

Decrease decimal places

Now complete the formulas: select G7:G17, press and hold Ctrl, and select B17:F17, too. Repeat the above procedure, but select the Currency category instead.

Finally, assign cell G3 the Currency format, but choose 3 decimal places.

Note that you can use the format toolbar to set several basic number formats (see Figure 25).

Lines. Finally, add a couple of lines to separate the major sections of the template. Select Row 6; then right-click the selection and choose Format Cells. Click the Borders tab in the dialog box and click Bottom in the Border box. Click OK. Repeat the procedure to create the line between rows 16 and 17.

Step 4: Finish Up

The template is nearly complete. All that remains is to clear out the dummy data values, set up the page for printing, and save it.

To clear the dummy data values, select all the 1's and press Del.

Now for the page setup. Execute File/Page Setup and click the Margins tab. In the Center on Page box, click Horizontally. Click the Header/Footer tab, click the scroll button beside Header, and choose an appropriate heading from the list. Do the same for the Footer. Click OK to return to the worksheet.

Finally, name the worksheet page and save the file. Double-click the notebook page tab at the bottom of the worksheet. Type "Expense Voucher" on the Page tab and press Enter. Then execute File/Save As. Click the scroll button next to Save File As Type and choose Template. In Excel, when you save a template file, the Save As dialog box always appears, meaning that later, when you're using the template to file expense reports, you won't carelessly overwrite your template with one week's worth of data. Enter a name like "EXPENSES" and click OK.

To use the template, select File/New and then select EXPENSES.XLT, and you'll get a new workbook EXPENSES1.XLS. Fill in a week's worth of data, click the Print button (see Figure 26) on the toolbar to print the file, and then execute File/Save As and save the file under a new name.

Figure 23

Excel's Print button.

Avoiding the BIG MISTAKE: How to Build a Spreadsheet and Survive to Tell the Tale

James Abbott, who has been teaching people in the Southeast about spreadsheet software since VisiCalc days, tells the story of a guy he met once who was living in a cardboard box in Central Park, eating out of dumpsters, and mumbling to himself a lot. Seems this guy had been a golden boy general manager for a Fortune 100 company—you know, the Jaguar, the kids in prep school, the yacht, the penthouse, etc.—who leveraged the buyout of a major competitor with *123* release 1A. After the deal was consummated and the cash flows turned out very red instead of just black enough, the auditors examined our hero's spreadsheets and discovered that everywhere he intended to erase a cell, he had instead entered a space. Thus, all those @AVG functions and @COUNT functions upon whose results our hero had invested so many important people's dollars gave the wrong answers. The rest, as they say, is history.

Here are six spreadsheet rules to help you avoid a similar fate, beginning with the one that snared our hero:

1. **Never erase with spaces.** Never try to clear out a cell's contents by pressing Spacebar and then Enter. In 123 and QuattroPro, this practice causes certain statistical functions—notably @AVG, @COUNT, @STD, and @VAR—to give invalid answers. For instance, the formula @AVG (A1:A5) is equivalent to the sum of the values in A1:A5 divided by the number of nonblank cells in that range. In this scheme, a cell containing a space is equivalent to a zero: the formula divides by one more for the space, and the average is too small. While this problem has been much reduced in Excel, erasing with spaces can still cause wrong answers. Remember: you too could end up in a cardboard box in Central Park...
2. **Point, don't type.** That is, never type cell and range addresses when you build formulas. If the formulas are complex, you will invariably, if only occasionally, type the wrong address, and you may not discover the error before the pink slip arrives. Instead, use the arrow keys or the mouse to select the cells you want to include in a formula. If the spreadsheet is large, give important cells meaningful range names. Then, as you build formulas, use F3 to select the names rather than typing the cell addresses.
3. **Never move data cells.** In any spreadsheet, the data cells are the ones you fill in with data—numbers and text—as you work. The other cells contain formulas that refer to the data cells, static text, or nothing at all. When you move a data cell, whether by dragging and dropping, cutting and pasting, or whatever, any formulas that refer to that cell change to refer to the cell's new position. For instance, if cell A1 contains the formula =SUM(B1:B50), and you move B1 to B2, the formula will change to =SUM(B2:B50). Now a number you put into B1 will not be included in the sum. Such a change can be easy to overlook when you're in a hurry, but don't worry: you'll have plenty of time to reflect on your error while panhandling passersby in the park.
4. **Build formulas using dummy data values.** Never build complex formulas based on real data values: it's too easy to miss careless errors in formulas. Instead, fill in the data cells with dummy values—1's, 10's, 100's—anything that makes it easy to spot incorrect calculations. When you're done and you're sure the formulas are okay, erase the dummy values and enter your own.

5. **Make the data cells look different.** When you're playing the "what game in a dense spreadsheet, it's easy to enter a data value into a cell that contains a formula. This kind of error breaks the chain of calculations so that subsequent changes may yield wrong answers, and such errors are notoriously hard to detect. To avoid such errors, do something systematic to make the data cells look different: format the cells so that data cells have a lightly shaded background or different-colored text. If you can distinguish a formula cell from a data cell, you won't carelessly overwrite it.
6. **Never sign off on a spreadsheet you don't understand.** Today's spreadsheet programs contain lots of exotic analytical tools: statistical tests, solvers, forecasting functions, you name it. Don't simply use this stuff and assume that the answers are truth! Get professional advice, double-check your setup and your formulas, test your model with a textbook example, do whatever it takes. Think it through. Remember the guy in the park.

Spreadsheets, bless 'em: they make it so easy to get answers to sophisticated analytical questions that any fool can do it. And any fool can just as easily get the wrong answers. In spreadsheets as in life, there's no alternative to knowing what you're doing.

Building a Database Worksheet

If you plan to accumulate data in your worksheet over time (as opposed to modeling or filling in a simple form), then you'll probably want to set up your worksheet as a list, or database. A database worksheet gives you the best combination of convenience and flexibility: you can generate the reports you need using the pivot tables and filtering features of your worksheet program. But you'll also be able to do a lot more with the data, by generating alternative pivot tables, extracting groups of records for list reports, creating subtotals, and so on.

Step 1: Is Your Spreadsheet Really a Database?

Often, the hardest part of setting up a database worksheet is knowing when you need one instead of a template-style spreadsheet. The trick is to look beyond the superficial layout of your customary reports and envision the structure of the data that underlies them.

Spreadsheet Makeover. Consider a typical worksheet like the hospital quality report shown in Figure 27. Each unit (department) in the hospital reports several quality indicators, and each indicator has a minimum permissible threshold percentage (T%) of cases that must meet standards. Every quarter, the unit records the number of acceptable cases (the numerator, N), the total number of cases in that category (the denominator, D), and the percentage of acceptable cases (%).

Figure 27

This hospital quality performance worksheet looks like a template, but it's really a database in disguise.

	A	B	C	D	E	F	G	H	I	J	K	L
1	**Hospital Quality Assurance Survey**											
2			**Performance**									
3			Jan-93			Apr-93			Jul-93			
4	**Indicator**	*T %*	*N*	*D*	*%*	*N*	*D*	*%*	*N*	*D*	*%*	*Comments*
5	Unit 1											
6	1. Effectiveness of therapy	90%	24	27	89%	71	72	99%	28	29	97%	
7	2. Maintenance	95%	28	31	90%	78	86	91%	79	80	99%	
8	3. Physical problems	100%	33	33	100%	76	79	96%	95	96	99%	
9												
10	Medical Unit											
11	1. Documentation	100%	92	93	99%	3	4	75%	82	87	94%	Review w/ unit
12	2. Patient falls	5%	54	2	4%	42	3	7%	72	1	1%	Follow up scheduled
13	3. COPD Patient management	95%	35	37	95%	23	25	92%	80	84	95%	
14												
15	Long Term Care											
16	1. Diabetic patient mgmt.	95%	73	78	94%	53	54	98%	53	54	98%	
17	2. Maintenance	100%	69	71	97%	30	32	94%	8	9	89%	

But the worksheet is awkward to use: to include a new quarter's data, the user must add columns to hold it; and it's all but impossible to rearrange the data to summarize the results by unit and print a report of just the indicators that are below threshold.

This application works much better as a database, as shown in Figure 28. Each record holds a numerator (N) and denominator (D) for a single indicator for one quarter.

Figure 28

Here's the worksheet from Figure 27 reorganized as a database. Each record represents one indicator from one department for one quarter. Column H contains a series of logical formulas that signal whether the percentage of acceptable cases is below threshold: cell H2 contains =G2<D2.

	A	B	C	D	E	F	G	H
1	**Unit**	**Indicator**	**Qtr**	**T_Percent**	**N**	**D**	**A_Percent**	**Too Low?**
2	Long Term Care	Diabetic patient mgmt.	Jan-93	95%	73	78	93.6%	TRUE
3	Long Term Care	Maintenance	Jan-93	100%	69	71	97.2%	TRUE
4	Medical	COPD Patient mgmt.	Jan-93	95%	35	37	94.6%	TRUE
5	Medical	Documentation	Jan-93	100%	92	93	98.9%	TRUE
6	Medical	Patient falls	Jan-93	5%	2	54	3.7%	TRUE
7	Unit 1	Effectiveness of therapy	Jan-93	90%	24	27	88.9%	TRUE
8	Unit 1	Maintenance	Jan-93	95%	28	31	90.3%	TRUE
9	Unit 1	Physical problems	Jan-93	100%	33	33	100.0%	FALSE
10	Long Term Care	Diabetic patient mgmt.	Apr-93	95%	53	54	98.1%	FALSE
11	Long Term Care	Maintenance	Apr-93	100%	30	32	93.8%	TRUE
12	Medical	COPD Patient mgmt.	Apr-93	95%	23	25	92.0%	TRUE
13	Medical	Documentation	Apr-93	100%	3	4	75.0%	TRUE
14	Medical	Patient falls	Apr-93	5%	3	42	7.1%	FALSE
15	Unit 1	Effectiveness of therapy	Apr-93	90%	71	72	98.6%	FALSE
16	Unit 1	Maintenance	Apr-93	95%	78	86	90.7%	TRUE
17	Unit 1	Physical problems	Apr-93	100%	76	79	96.2%	TRUE
18	Long Term Care	Diabetic patient mgmt.	Jul-93	95%	53	54	98.1%	FALSE
19	Long Term Care	Maintenance	Jul-93	100%	8	9	88.9%	TRUE
20	Medical	COPD Patient mgmt.	Jul-93	95%	82	87	94.3%	TRUE
21	Medical	Documentation	Jul-93	100%	80	84	95.2%	TRUE
22	Medical	Patient falls	Jul-93	95%	71	72	98.6%	FALSE
23	Unit 1	Effectiveness of therapy	Jul-93	90%	28	29	96.6%	FALSE
24	Unit 1	Maintenance	Jul-93	95%	79	80	98.8%	FALSE
25	Unit 1	Physical problems	Jul-93	100%	95	96	99.0%	TRUE

Pivot Table Redux. It's easy regenerate the original report with Excel's pivot table feature. Here, Unit and Indicator are specified as the row headings, QTR as the column heading, and N, D, A_PERCENT, and T_PERCENT as the data fields (see Figure 29). In addition, the pivot table is flexible: it allows you to create other reports that summarize the data in different patterns, for example, showing the lowest value of each indicator by unit for the whole year, and easily select indicators below threshold.

Figure 29

Excel's pivot table feature reconstructs the original unit-by-unit report from Figure 27. The "Too Low?" values are specified as the Page variable for the pivot table, allowing you to selectively display results for only the TRUE or FALSE values.

	A	B	C	D	E	F
1	Too Low?	(All)				
2		(All)				
3		TRUE		Qtr		
4	Unit	FALSE / Indicator	Data	Jan-93	Apr-93	Jul-93
5	Long Term	Diabetic patient mgmt.	Numerator	73	53	53
6			Denominator	78	54	54
7			Threshold %	95%	95%	95%
8			Actual %	94%	98%	98%
9		Maintenance	Numerator	69	30	8
10			Denominator	71	32	9
11			Threshold %	100%	100%	100%
12			Actual %	97%	94%	89%
13	Medical	COPD Patient mgmt.	Numerator	35	23	82
14			Denominator	37	25	87
15			Threshold %	95%	95%	95%
16			Actual %	95%	92%	94%
17		Documentation	Numerator	92	3	80
18			Denominator	93	4	84
19			Threshold %	100%	100%	100%
20			Actual %	99%	75%	95%
21		Patient falls	Numerator	2	3	71
22			Denominator	54	42	72
23			Threshold %	5%	5%	95%
24			Actual %	4%	7%	99%

Why go through all the trouble to enter the data into a list and then use pivot tables to create the report? Because you can very quickly generate a new report by merely reconfiguring the pivot table (see Figure 30).

Figure 30

Pivot tables prove their worth when you need to rearrange the report to answer a different question. Here, the data is arranged by indicator, with results grouped according to whether or not standards have been met.

3				Qtr	Too Low?				
4				Jan-93		Apr-93		Jul-93	
5	Indicator	Unit	Data	TRUE	FALSE	TRUE	FALSE	TRUE	FALSE
6	COPD Patient mgmt.	Medical	Numerator	35		23		82	
7			Denominator	37		25		87	
8			Threshold %	95%		95%		95%	
9			Actual %	95%		92%		94%	
10	Diabetic patient mgmt.	Long Term Care	Numerator	73			53		53
11			Denominator	78			54		54
12			Threshold %	95%			95%		95%
13			Actual %	94%			98%		98%
14	Documentation	Medical	Numerator	92		3		80	
15			Denominator	93		4		84	
16			Threshold %	100%		100%		100%	
17			Actual %	99%		75%		95%	
18	Effectiveness of therapy	Unit 1	Numerator	24			71		28
19			Denominator	27			72		29
20			Threshold %	90%			90%		90%
21			Actual %	89%			99%		97%
22	Maintenance	Long Term Care	Numerator	69		30		8	
23			Denominator	71		32		9	
24			Threshold %	100%		100%		100%	
25			Actual %	97%		94%		89%	
26		Unit 1	Numerator	28		78			79
27			Denominator	31		86			80
28			Threshold %	95%		95%			95%
29			Actual %	90%		91%			99%
30	Patient falls	Medical	Numerator	2			3		71

Step 2: Set Up the Database Table

Now that you have a pretty good idea of what a list worksheet is, let's get started setting one up. The exercise employs a tiny personnel database, which lists the department and location of a small group of employees, plus four reports. One report is a simple list that selects items in groups. Next is a subtotal report that lists the employees from a selected department or location along with their total salaries. A pivot table summarizes the total salaries by department and location. Finally, another pivot table organizes data for a chart.

Organizing Data and Reports. The best arrangement is to keep your table of data on one sheet and put the pivot tables and charts on separate sheets. That way, you can freely edit and format everything without worrying about messing up the other areas. Figure 31 illustrates a typical setup: the database is on the first sheet of the workbook (shown in the top window of the figure). On the second sheet (named TotalByLocation and shown in the bottom window) is a pivot table report, which summarizes the data by location and department. The third sheet (TotalsChart) contains a chart that summarizes the results, and the fourth sheet (ChartData) holds another pivot table that prepares the data for the chart.

Figure 31

This database worksheet puts the data on the sheet named Employees and a pivot table report on the sheet named TotalByLocation.

Listdemo.xls:1

	A	B	C	D	E	F
1	SSN	Employee	Location	Department	Salary	Date_Hired
2	801-99-4394	Manuel	Charlotte	TRAIN	$ 80,056	10/6/87
3	324-73-0119	Helm	Charlotte	TRAIN	$ 77,730	7/19/85
4	216-77-0522	Dylan	Raleigh	SALES	$ 73,952	11/29/89
5	239-37-6483	Fogerty	Charlotte	SALES	$ 64,306	1/17/90
6	771-38-7240	Danko	Raleigh	TRAIN	$ 92,058	11/3/92
7	145-60-2806	Clifford	Raleigh	SALES	$ 58,752	2/9/86
8	264-00-2799	Hudson	Raleigh	TRAIN	$ 70,488	10/31/88

TotalByLocation / **Employees** / TotalsChart / ChartData

Listdemo.xls:2

	A	B	C	D	E	F
1			Department			
2	Location	Data	SALES	TRAIN	Grand Total	
3	Charlotte	Number of Employees	1	2	3	
4		Sum of Salary	$64,306	$157,786	$222,092	
5		Latest Hire Date	32890	32056	32890	
6	Raleigh	Number of Employees	2	2	4	
7		Sum of Salary	$132,704	$162,546	$295,250	
8		Latest Hire Date	32841	33911	33911	
9	Total Number of Employees		3	4	7	
10	Total Sum of Salary		$197,010	$320,332	$517,342	
11	Total Latest Hire Date		32890	33911	33911	
12						
13						
14						

TotalByLocation / Employees / TotalsChart / ChartData

To build the model, open a new worksheet, double-click the Sheet1 tab at the bottom of the window, type "Employees" on the tab, and press Enter. In row 1, enter the field headings shown in the top panel in Figure 31. Select row 1 and click the Bold and Center buttons on the format toolbar (see Figure 24 earlier in this chapter).

Figure 32

automatic column width adjustment.

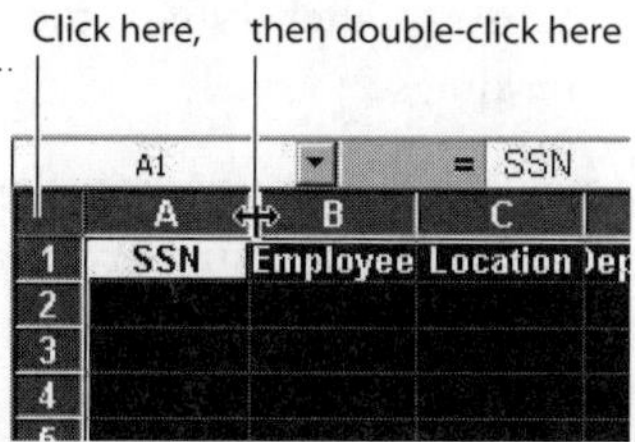

Adjust the column widths: click the square at the corner of the worksheet frame and then double-click the line separating two columns in the top part of the frame (see Figure 32). The widths adjust automatically to accommodate the longest entry in each column.

Finally, use *panes* to keep the field headings in view should the number of records in your database grow beyond the size of the screen: click within the frame to select row 2 and then select Window/Freeze Panes. A line appears on the sheet between rows 1 and 2. Notice that if you scroll down the worksheet, row 1 always remains visible.

Designating Field Types and Data Validation. Next, designate the type of data you'll put into each field. Right-click within the worksheet frame to select column A and click Format Cells to display the Format Cells dialog box. Click the Number tab, select Text in the Category list, and click OK. Repeat the procedure to format column F for dates (select the format 3/4/97). Now right-click column E, set the numeric format to Currency, and specify "0" as the number of decimal places.

Excel can help prevent typographical errors in the values you enter in your database with a feature new to Excel 97 called Data Validation. Let's use it here. Click within the worksheet frame to select column A. Then select Data/Validation. In the Allow box, select Text Length. Then select "equal to" in the Data box and enter "11" as the Length value. Click the Error Alert dialog box tab and enter "Social security numbers must have exactly 11 characters" in the Error Message box. Click OK. In column F, use data validation to allow only Date values greater than 1/1/1985 and to display an appropriate error message if the rule is violated.

Now (sigh) enter the data shown in Employees:A2:F8 in the top pane of Figure 31. It's dull and repetitious work, I know, but someone's got to do it. When you're done, readjust the column widths.

Figure 33

Excel's database sort buttons.

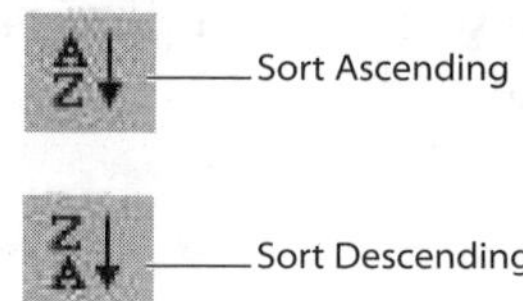

Sorting the Data. Excel makes it really simple to reorder the records in a list. Click a cell in the database in the column you want to sort by. Then click the Sort Ascending or Sort Descending button on the standard toolbar (see Figure 33).

Step 3: Build the List Report

Now that we've created the database and entered data, we can start setting up our reports.

Turning on the Filter. This is pretty simple: click a cell anywhere in the database range and select Data/Filter/AutoFilter. Notice the drop-down controls that appear next to the field headings in row 1.

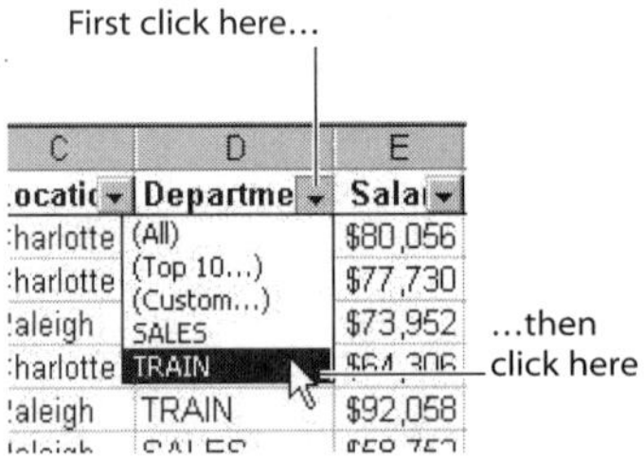

Figure 34

Using Excel's AutoFilter.

First click here...

...then click here

Next, click the drop-down list button beside Department and in the list, select TRAIN (see Figure 34). Excel promptly hides all of the rows that do not contain TRAIN in the department column. (Notice that the field with the active filter displays a blue arrow on its drop-down control.)

Click the Print Preview button (see Figure 26) on the standard toolbar to see what the report will look like when you print it (see Figure 35).

SSN	Employee	Location	Department	Salary	Date_Hired
801-99-4394	Manuel	Charlotte	TRAIN	$80,056	10/6/87
324-73-0119	Helm	Charlotte	TRAIN	$77,730	7/19/85
771-38-7240	Danko	Raleigh	TRAIN	$92,058	11/3/92
264-00-2799	Hudson	Raleigh	TRAIN	$70,488	10/31/88

Figure 35

This report, filtered to display only the employees in the training department, was printed using the database on the Employees sheet.

When you want to clear the filter to ask a different question, click the drop-down list button for the active filter and select ALL.

Asking Questions with Custom Criteria. The whole reason for setting up a database is so that you can easily and flexibly select groups of records that answer interesting questions. First, note that you can set criteria in more than one field: to find out which employees from Raleigh are in the training department, select the appropriate criteria in both columns.

When simple selections can't do the job, you can escalate to custom criteria. Suppose you want to know which employees earn $70,000 or more? In the criteria list for Salary, select Custom. Click the drop-down list button beside Salary and select "Greater than or equal to"; in the field to the right, enter "70000." Click OK, and you'll see the answer in the list.

To turn off the filters, select Data/Filter and click AutoFilter once again.

Step 4: Create the Subtotal Report

Subtotals provide a fast way to summarize your data. The report shown in Figure 36 displays the total salaries by department. Subtotal reports are quick and easy to create, and they let you hide the details to show just the totals.

	A	B	C	D	E	F
1	SSN	Employee	Location	Department	Salary	Date_Hired
2	216-77-0522	Dylan	Raleigh	SALES	$ 73,952	11/29/89
3	239-37-6483	Fogerty	Charlotte	SALES	$ 64,306	1/17/90
4	145-60-2806	Clifford	Raleigh	SALES	$ 58,752	2/9/86
5				SALES Total	$ 197,010	
6	801-99-4394	Manuel	Charlotte	TRAIN	$ 80,056	10/6/87
7	324-73-0119	Helm	Charlotte	TRAIN	$ 77,730	7/19/85
8	771-38-7240	Danko	Raleigh	TRAIN	$ 92,058	11/3/92
9	264-00-2799	Hudson	Raleigh	TRAIN	$ 70,488	10/31/88
10				TRAIN Total	$ 320,332	
11				Grand Total	$ 517,342	

Figure 36

This subtotal report includes special formulas automatically inserted by Excel. The outline structure in the left frame lets you collapse levels of detail for a summary view.

Figure 37

Excel's Subtotal dialog box.

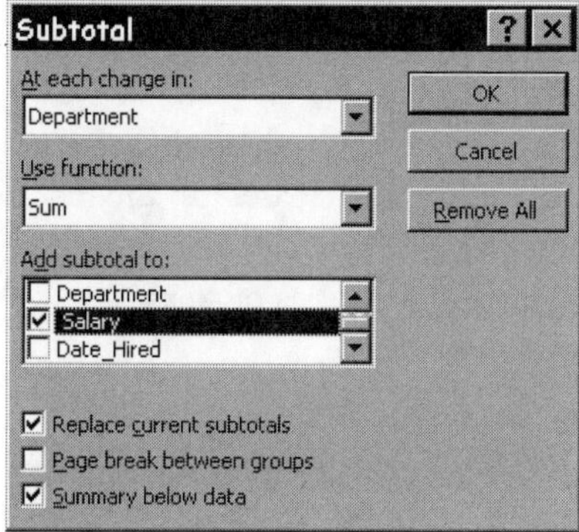

First, sort the database by department: click a cell in the database in the Department column and then click the Sort Ascending button on the standard toolbar.

Next, select Data/Subtotals. Configure the dialog box as shown in Figure 37 and then click OK.

The subtotal feature inserts a row between each subgroup in the database and enters a special =SUBTOTAL() function into each one. It also creates an outline structure on the left side of the worksheet frame that you can use to collapse the report to show only the totals (see Figure 38).

Figure 38

Excel's outline controls.

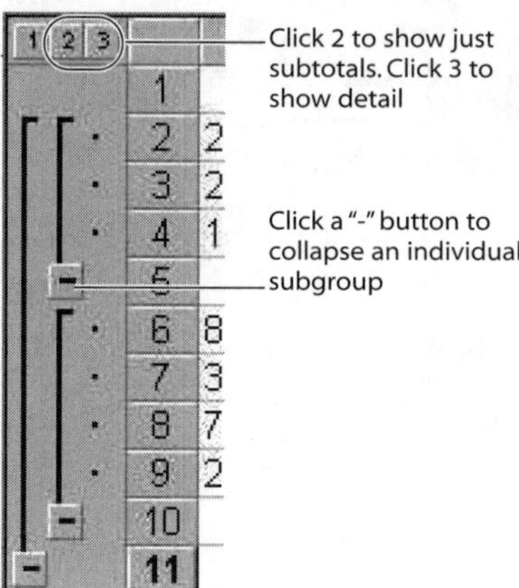

You can clear the subtotals from your list anytime you want (and, since they're so easy to set up, it's no big deal if you do). Select a cell in the subtotaled database and choose Data/Subtotals. Click Remove All, and they're outta there.

Step 5: Create the Pivot Table Report

Subtotal reports are really easy to create, but they're limited to a single statistic and a single grouping field. But those of you with pluralistic needs, take heart! Pivot tables can do everything subtotal reports can do and a whole lot more besides. Skip ahead and take a look at the report shown in Figure 41. It was produced by a pivot table that shows the total salaries, number of employees, and most recent hire date of employees in each location, by department—all at the same time!

To create the pivot table, make sure any filters or subtotals you may have set in the previous exercises are cleared. Select Data/Pivot Table Report to launch the wizard.

In Step 1, Excel asks where your data is located. For this example, it's in an Excel list or database, but pay attention to the other possibilities. We'll be using one of them later. Click Next.

In Step 2, Excel automatically selects the entire database as the input for the pivot table. Verify the range address and corresponding selection (it will include all of your data, unless your database includes some blank rows or columns). Click Next.

Arranging the Pivot Fields. Step 3 is the heart of the pivot table, the place where you actually lay out the report. On the right are a series of field headings taken from the top row of your database. On the left are four layout regions. To set up a pivot table, drag the field headings into the layout regions. We'll work up to the final layout in a series of steps. To begin, arrange the fields as shown in Figure 39.

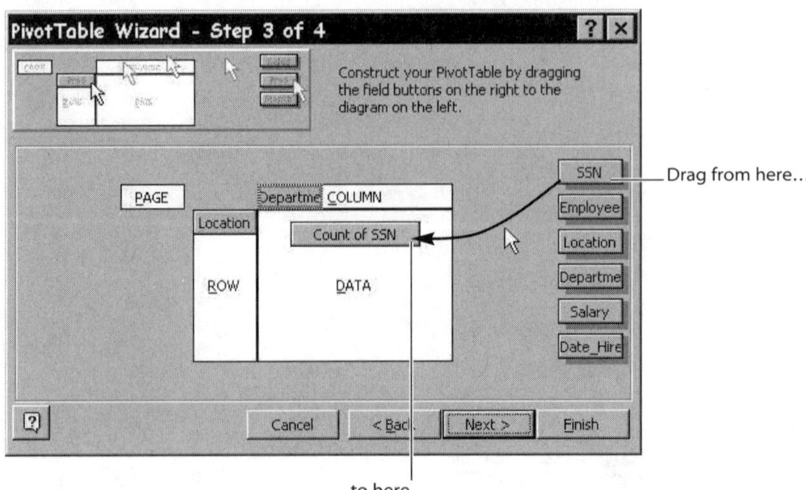

Figure 39

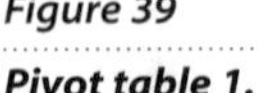

Pivot table 1.

To set up a pivot table in Excel, drag the field headings from the list at the right of the Step 3 dialog box into the layout regions on the left. With the fields shown at this stage of construction, the pivot table will show the number of employees by location and department.

To give the data field a more descriptive label, double-click the Count of SSN field to edit its properties. In the Name box, enter "Number of Employees." Click OK.

Next, add the salary and hire date data: Drag the Salary field into the data area and then double-click it. In the Name box, enter "Total Salaries." Click Number, and in the Format Cells dialog box select Currency in the Category list and zero decimal places. Click OK to close the Format dialog box and click OK to close the Pivot Table Field dialog box.

Now for the dates: Drag the Date_Hired field below Salary, double-click it, and enter "Latest Hire Date" in the Name box. Select Max in the Summarize By list. Click Number and select Date in the Category list and 3/4/97 in the Type list. Click OK twice. The dialog box should now look like Figure 40.

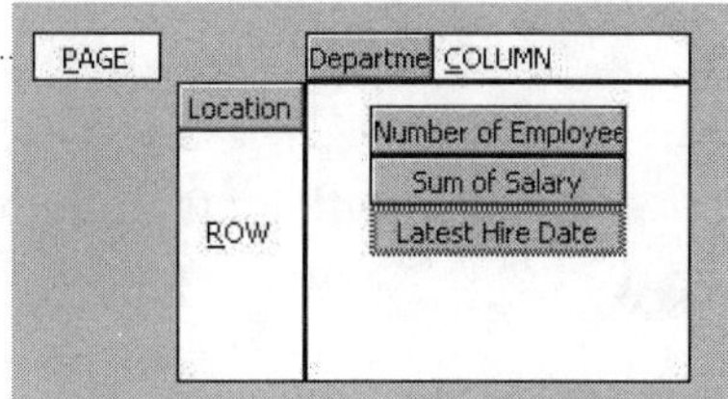

Figure 40

Pivot table 2.

Click Next and notice the alternatives: whenever you create a new pivot table, you should place it on a new worksheet (the default selection in Step 4 of the wizard). That way, your tables will be easy to keep organized in the event you have many reports in the same workbook.

Click Finish. Your pivot table report appears on a new worksheet. Double-click the page tab and enter "TotalByLocation" to identify the sheet. Now just take a moment to admire your work (Figure 41).

	A	B	C	D	E
1			Department		
2	Location	Data	SALES	TRAIN	Grand Total
3	Charlotte	Number of Employees	1	2	3
4		Sum of Salary	$64,306	$157,786	$222,092
5		Latest Hire Date	1/17/90	10/6/87	1/17/90
6	Raleigh	Number of Employees	2	2	4
7		Sum of Salary	$132,704	$162,546	$295,250
8		Latest Hire Date	11/29/89	11/3/92	11/3/92
9	Total Number of Employees		3	4	7
10	Total Sum of Salary		$197,010	$320,332	$517,342
11	Total Latest Hire Date		1/17/90	11/3/92	11/3/92

Figure 41

Pivot table 3.

The finished pivot table report shows the number of employees, their total salary, and most recent hire dates by location and department.

Rearrange the Pivot Table. One of the best features of pivot tables is their malleability. You can work directly with the pivot table report to rearrange column and row headings, select data, and drill down to selected records. Here are a few moves to try:

Drag the Department field over to the left of Location. Watch for the mouse pointer to change shape (see Figure 42).

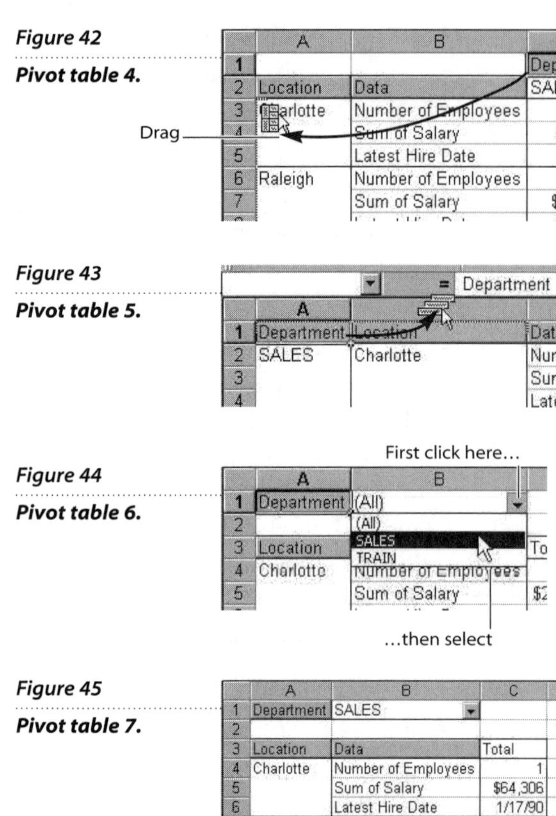

Figure 42

Pivot table 4.

Figure 43

Pivot table 5.

Figure 44

Pivot table 6.

Figure 45

Pivot table 7.

Now, you have a report that has two levels of row headings: Location within Department.

Suppose you want to see separate reports for each department. No problemo. Drag the Department field up to the top of the pivot table sheet (see Figure 43).

At this point, Department becomes the Page field, and a drop-down list button appears beside it. Click the button, select SALES in the list, and pouf!—your report shows just the from the sales department (see Figure 44).

Finally, let's say that when all is said and done, you'd really like to discover who those two employees from Raleigh with combined salaries of $132,704 really are. Double-click the data cell, and Excel copies the corresponding records from the database onto a new sheet that it inserts into the workbook (see Figure 45).

Step 6: Make a Chart from a Pivot Table

Since it's usually a lot easier to interpret a graph than to peruse a raw table of numbers, let's do your boss a favor and prepare the bar graph shown in Figure 48 to summarize the employee salaries. Pivot tables are an ideal tool for organizing the information that you need for charts, so we'll start with a very simple pivot table.

Create the Pivot Table. Click the Employees sheet tab to go back to the database. Click a cell in the table and select Data/Pivot Table Report. In Step 1 of the wizard, select Another Pivot Table as the source of the new pivot table data. Why? Because Excel constructs a pivot table by copying all of the table data into a specially structured *cache* in your computer's memory. From there, Excel can quickly rearrange the data when you drag the field names. If your database is large and you build many independent pivot tables, each with its own cache, you'll quickly exhaust your computer's memory space. When you base a new pivot table on an old one, the new pivot table shares the same cache as the old pivot table. This allows you to easily put dozens of pivot tables in one workbook should you desire. Click Next to advance to Step 2. There, select PivotTable1 as the data source and click Next.

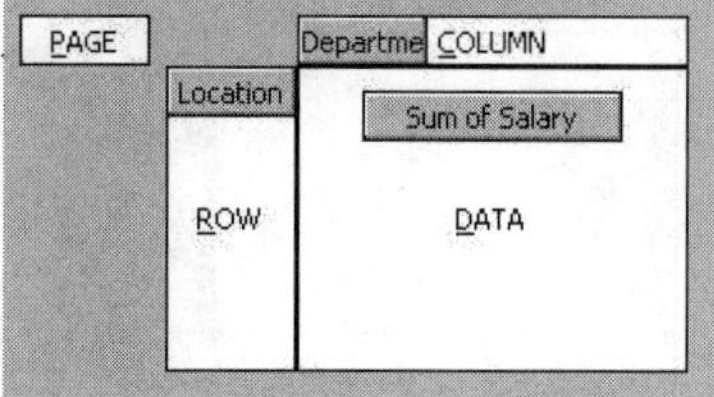

Figure 46

Layout for the new pivot table.

In Step 3, lay out your pivot table as shown in Figure 46.

Click Next; then, in Step 4, click Options. In the Format Options group, deselect Grand Totals for Columns and Grand Totals for Rows. Click OK and then Finish. You end up with a simple pivot table that summarizes the salary data by department and location. Double-click the sheet tab and enter "SalaryChartData."

Build the Chart. Click a cell in the new pivot table and click the Chart Wizard button to create a new chart (see Figure 47).

Figure 47

Excel's Chart Wizard button.

In Step 1, select Column Chart in the Chart type list and select the first subtype option. Click Next. Notice that Excel has automatically selected the data series and formatted the chart. Click Next.

In Step 3, make your formatting selections: On the Titles tab, enter "Total Salaries by Department and Location" in the Chart Title box. On the Legend tab, select Bottom in the Placement group.

In Step 4, select As New Sheet. Click Finish to create the chart. Name the new chart sheet "SalaryChart."

Now for the finishing touches. Right-click the y-axis and choose Format Axis. Click the Number tab and choose Currency with zero decimal places. Then click the Scale tab. In the Maximum box, enter "200000." Enter "0" as the Minimum value. Specify "25000" as the Major Unit value and "5000" as the Minor Unit value. Click the Patterns tab and select Inside as the Minor Tick Mark Type value.

Notice that you can right-click any object in the graph window to display a pop-up menu that lets you change the properties of that object. So, for example, you can right click a series of bars and change their color or shading, or right-click the Plot Area and change its color. You can right-click the legend and change its font, and so on. You may want to try to emulate the example shown in Figure 48. To print a full-page version of the graph, execute the command File/Print in the Graph window and follow the prompts you find there.

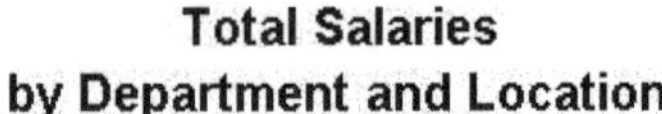

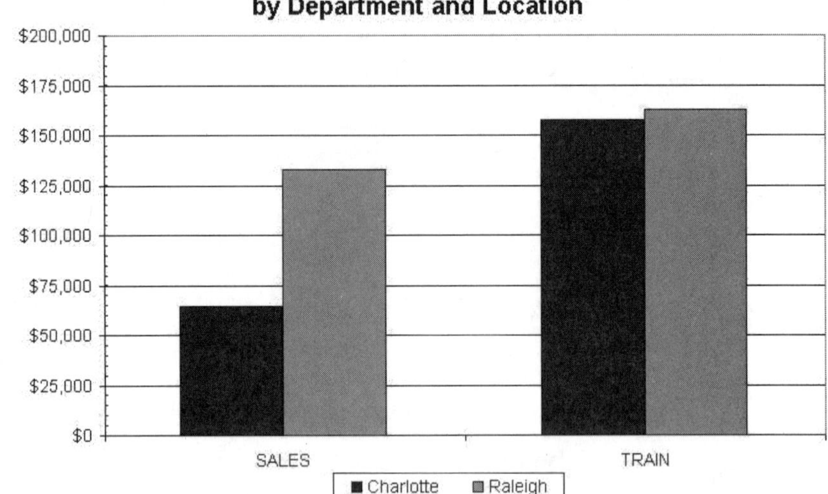

Figure 48

This bar graph is based on a pivot table that aggregates data from an Excel database. The graph changes automatically to accommodate changes in the pivot table.

Updating the Chart with New Data. As time goes by, you may add new employees to your list, and you'll want them to show up in the chart. Use the following procedure to accommodate them.

Select the Employees sheet, click within the frame to select one of your existing records, and select Insert/Rows to insert a new row. Enter the data for the new employee in the blank row.

Figure 49

Adding data.

7	771-38-7240	Danko	Raleigh	TRAIN	$	92,058	11/3/1992
8	123-45-6789	Bernstein	Durham	TRAIN	$	90,000	10/10/1998
9	264-00-2799	Hudson	Raleigh	TRAIN	$	70,488	10/31/1988

Insert row here before entering data

Next, select the worksheet SalaryChartData (the one with the pivot table). Click a cell in the pivot table and select Data/Refresh Data. This command causes Excel to refresh the pivot table cache with the latest data from the worksheet.

Now click your chart sheet, SalaryChart. The new data is already there (Figure 50).

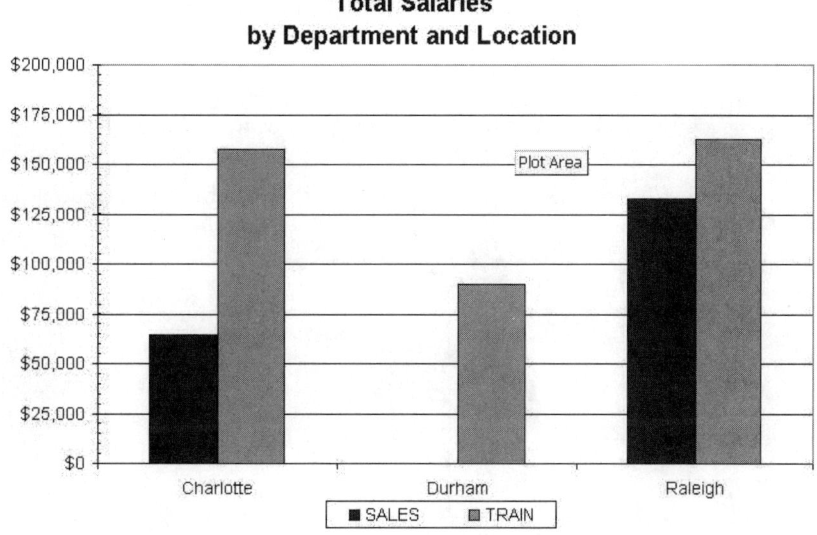

Figure 50

Here's the bar graph showing a new record that was entered in the database.

More Excel Features to Explore

Excel emerged from the intense competition of the spreadsheet wars of the early '90s as the undisputed market leader, and for good reason. Excel 97 has everything: a smooth, intuitive interface, an extensive feature set, a good help system, and tight integration with other Microsoft applications.

In the previous section of this chapter, we delved in depth into what is probably Excel's most generally useful gadget: pivot tables. There isn't space to cover every feature of the program in such detail, but the following should give you a pretty good feel for the range of Excel's capabilities. Later, I'll provide a cookbook of a few selected Excel templates.

Right-Click Tricks

Excel's interface reflects the state of the art of GUI programming. In particular, the right mouse button has emerged as a general "change it" tool:

- You can click the right mouse button on most Excel objects and get a menu of appropriate operations.
- If you select a range and right-click the selection, you can clear the selection, copy it, move it, delete it, insert cells there, or change the properties of the cells or their entries.

- To edit a chart, right-click its components and pick from the menus.
- Drag the AutoFill handle (shown in Figure 15) with the right mouse button, and you get a menu that offers a variety of options for copying cells or building series of cell values.

Also notable are the tear-off palettes for colors, cell borders, drawing tools, and so on. For instance, to work on cell borders, you click and hold the Borders button to display the palette and then drag the palette into the workspace (see Figure 51).

Figure 51

Excel's tear-off palettes.

Click here...

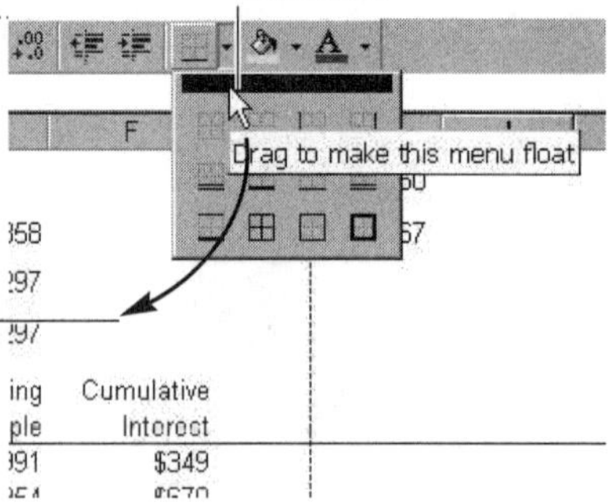

...and drag the palette into Excel's workspace

You can zoom your view of your worksheet or chart pages from 10 to 400 percent (select View/Zoom), and you can select a special full-screen view (View/Full Screen) that removes all unessential screen features to show the maximum amount of worksheet territory.

AutoFill. Excel's cell pointer has a small square at its lower-right corner, called the *AutoFill handle*. AutoFill provides a whole range of techniques for duplicating and filling cells. For instance, as illustrated in the template example earlier in this chapter, if you enter "Monday" in a cell and then drag the AutoFill handle, Excel continues the series with "Tuesday," "Wednesday," and so on. The same is true for the months of the year. Or enter two numbers, select them both, and then select AutoFill; Excel continues the series.

You can even define your own series. How about filling in the name of your first regional office and letting AutoFill list the rest of them automatically? Just enter the items in a range of cells and then select Tools/Options, click the Custom Lists tab, and click Import.

The AutoFill feature exemplifies the best aspects of Excel's interface. It is quick and smooth, and the tiny AutoFill handle offers a constant reminder that it's available. And if you know exactly what you're doing, combining AutoFill with various key combinations lets you work really quickly. For instance, hold down Alt while you drag the AutoFill handle, and you get copies of the original cells instead of a series; hold down Shift, and you'll insert a set of cells into the column or row. If you're not sure what you want, drag with the *right* mouse button, and a pop-up menu lets you choose (see Figure 52).

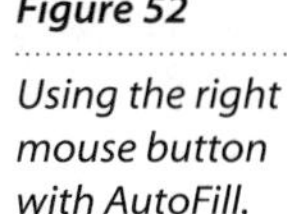

Figure 52

Using the right mouse button with AutoFill.

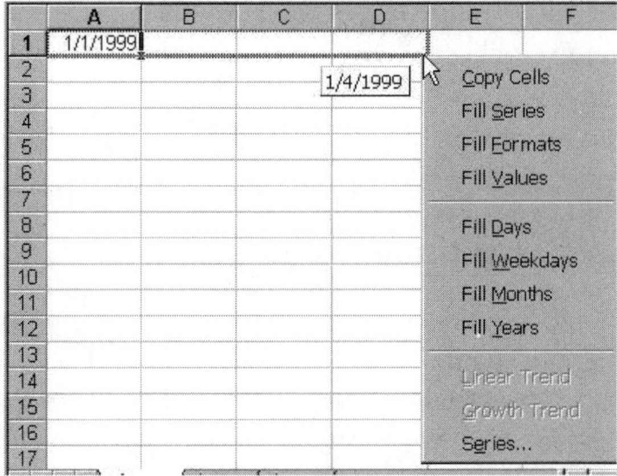

Comments. Excel also lets you insert annotations into your worksheets, for the benefit of your boss and colleagues who must figure out what exactly your cryptic labels and formulas really signify. To create a comment, right-click a cell and select Comment. A little Post-It note (identified with your name) appears on the worksheet. Enter some helpful text. Later, when you move your mouse pointer over the cell, the comment pops up as a reminder (see Figure 53).

Figure 53

Excel's pop-up comment feature.

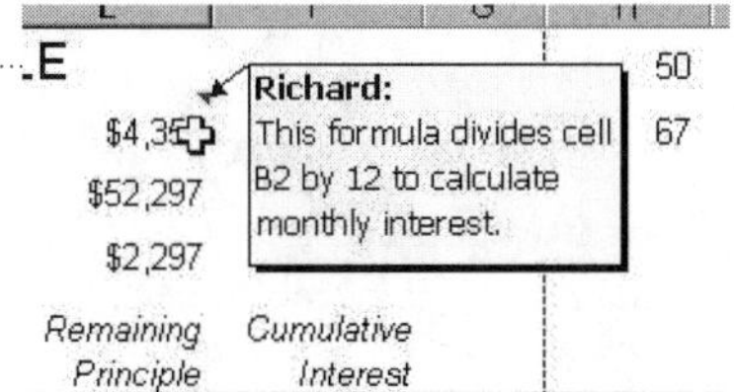

Formatting Tricks

For formatting numeric values, Excel provides a wide range of alternatives, but manages to put the essential elements within easy grasp. A set of four toolbar buttons combine to provide the most common numeric formats (see Figure 25 earlier in this chapter).

For more exotic-looking numbers, the menus offer a large array of standard formats, including most standard accounting formats, and once you master the notation, you can build your own. If you are so inclined, you can format a formula so that a value above 100 appears green, one between 0 and 100 appears yellow, and one less than 0 appears as the word "Gotcha!" (As noted in the preceding exercises, select Format/Cells, click the Number tab, and explore. For custom formats, select Custom in the Category list and study the notation in the right-hand panel. Press F1 and search the Help system for "custom number format codes" for details.)

The Format Painter. Finally, the totally nifty Format Painter button (see Figure 54) lets you instantly copy the formatting from one cell or range to another: select a cell that has the look you want, click the button, and then select the cells you want to change.

Figure 54

Excel's Format Painter button.

The Drawing Layer

You don't think of your spreadsheet as a place to draw pictures, but Excel provides an extensive, serviceable set of drawing tools. The drawing toolbar (see Figure 55) lets you put rectangles, circles, polygons, arrows, lines, and freehand shapes right on the worksheet or on a chart. Then you can size and move them, format them with fill patterns and colors, group them into complex objects, and arrange their vertical priority. Text boxes are like Post-It notes: they're great for annotating a worksheet, and you can format the text inside them.

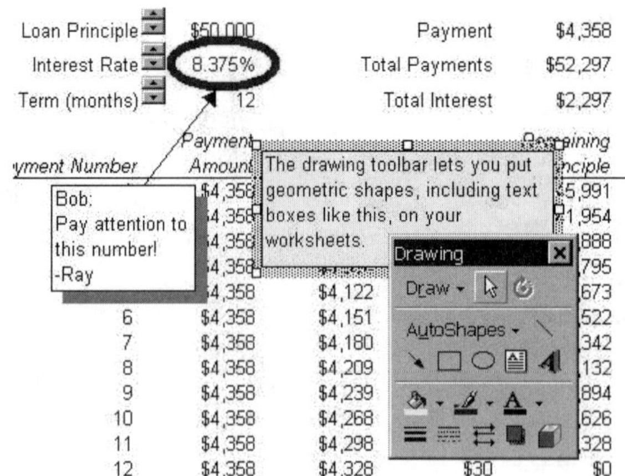

Figure 55

The drawing toolbar provides a host of tools for annotating your worksheets, including callout boxes and a serviceable set of flowchart tools, complete with connector lines that stick to the shapes.

Here is a smattering of tips for working with drawing shapes:

- Right-click a line or freeform shape and select Edit Points to adjust the shape of these elements.
- For a really quick way to duplicate shapes, hold down Ctrl while you drag a shape, and you'll get an instant duplicate.
- If you hold down Alt as you draw and size objects, Excel attaches the objects to the worksheet grid, which lets you draw precisely aligned shapes.

Advanced Analysis

Today's spreadsheets are not just for budgets. Excel is not alone in offering a whole slew of statistical functions, for everything from forecasting and regression, to analysis of variance and other inferential statistics, to nonparametric descriptive statistics. For engineers, there's Fourier analysis, engineering and trigonometric functions, and other mathematical goodies. Financial analysts will find a passel of goodies for them as well. To explore Excel's functions, use the Function Wizard, which you can summon with the Function button (see Figure 56).

Figure 56

Excel's Function Wizard button.

And all this is to say nothing of a host of features that are beyond the scope of this chapter: a solver for analyzing systems of nonlinear equations, basic statistics, a sampling add-in that generates random numbers to conform to a variety of distributions, and so on.

Just to tantalize you into exploring further, I'll give one easy example that hints at the power we're talking about here.

Figure 57 shows a very simple business application called a break-even analysis. It answers the question: "How many widgets do we have to sell before we can begin making money?" Cells B3:B5 contain the data about sales: the number of units, the cost to produce each unit, and the price we'll charge. Cell B8 contains the fixed cost: the amount we must spend each month whether we sell any widgets or not (light bill, CEO's salary, etc.).

	A	B	C	D	E
1	Break Even Analysis				
2					
3	Units Sold	100			
4	Price	$ 10		Formula is =B3*B4-B5*B3	
5	Cost Per Unit	$ 8			
6	Revenue	$ 200			
7					
8	Overhead	$ 10,000			
9				Formula is =B6-B8	
10	Gross Margin	$ (9,800)			
11					

Figure 58

A simple break-even analysis. When gross revenue is zero, you've sold enough units to overcome your overhead. The Goal Seek feature of Excel makes short work of figuring out just how many units that is.

Now the fateful question: how many widgets must we sell before we begin to make money—that is, until the gross margin is zero? To find out, build the model as shown; then select cell B10 and select Tools/Goal Seek. Enter "0" in the To Value box and "B3" in the By Changing Cell box (see Figure 58). Click OK, and the Goal Seeker seeks the solution: 5,000 units. Nifty, huh?

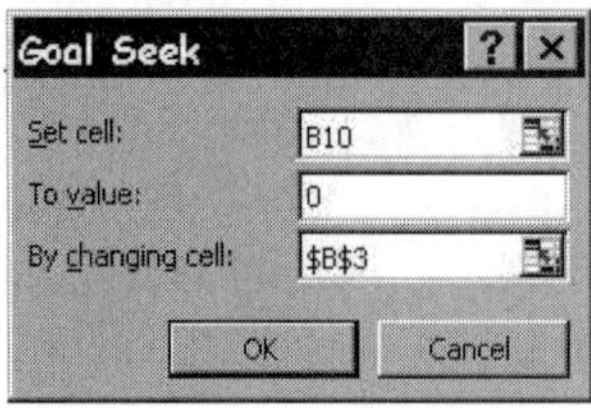

Figure 58

Excel's Goal Seek dialog box.

Arrays

Arrays are one of Excel's least understood, least used, but most elegant features. An array formula lets a single formula do the work of many.

Figure 59 shows one example of how arrays work. In column A is a list of employees; column B shows their department assignments. Suppose you want to know the number of employees in the TRAIN department. You could use a database statistical function, but that would require setting up a criteria range just for that formula (see "Building a Database Worksheet" earlier in this chapter). The formula shown in cell E3 of Figure 59 performs the same calculation, all in one cell: {=SUM((B2:B15=D3)*1)}. The core of the formula, (B2:B15=D3), compares each label in B2:B15 with the label in D3, "TRAIN." That's the equivalent of 14 separate logical formulas, but everything occurs in just one cell. Multiplying the result by 1 converts the TRUE logical values to the numeric value 1; the sum function adds up the 1's to obtain the value shown in cell E3. In Excel, you must enter the formula by pressing Ctrl Shift Enter, whereupon Excel marks the formula with the brackets {} that denote an array formula.

E3 = {=SUM((B2:B15=D3)*1)}

	A	B	C	D	E
1	Employee	Department			
2	Aldo	TRAIN		Department	Number
3	Frodo	SALES		TRAIN	3
4	Jerusco	MARKET		SALES	6
5	Mambo	TRAIN		MARKET	5
6	Kalko	SALES			
7	Iago	MARKET			
8	Credo	SALES			
9	Gumbo	SALES			
10	Heraldo	TRAIN			
11	Numero	MARKET			
12	Bilbo	SALES			
13	Elbo	SALES			
14	Limbo	MARKET			
15	Dumbo	MARKET			

Figure 59

Arrays, one of Excel's least understood but most powerful features, allow one formula to do the work of many.

Intelligent Data Import

Excel is the first spreadsheet program to really put effort into making it easy to import data from text sources, a common need when you have legacy computer systems that can't create PC-format files. To open a text file, select File/Open and select Text Files in the Files Of Type box. The Text Import Wizard then steps you through the process. First, you specify whether the data is in delimited or fixed-width format (see Figure 60); if it's fixed width, you specify the width of the fields by dragging the borders to mark the columns. Then you specify whether the data in each column is numeric, text, or date data.

Figure 60

That perennial pain in the spreadsheeter's neck, importing data from ASCII sources, is made easy with Excel's new Text Import Wizard.

External Data Access

If your data resides in a PC database such as dBASE or Paradox or on a database server such as Oracle or another SQL database, the MS Query add-in program can tap into it. MS Query, which ships with Excel but can work with other Microsoft products such as Word, uses an interface similar to Microsoft Access to let you view the data in external tables, set up relational queries, and then paste or hot-link the results back into Excel.

Macros

Excel had long been famous for its powerful but esoteric macro language. The power is still there, but now it's accessible to mere mortals. Starting with release 5.0, Excel introduced a new macro language, Visual Basic for Applications (VBA), based on Visual Basic, its user-friendly programming language. Starting with Office 97, VBA is the common macro language for all Microsoft applications. Macros appear as *modules* in a special macro editor, which you can launch by pressing Alt F11. Each module can include several separate macros, called *procedures*.

The usual way to create a procedure is by first recording a sequence of actions with the macro recorder and then touching up the macro on the module page. For example, the simple template shown in the top panel of Figure 61 lists occasional expenses for a small business. I've set it up to be expandable: to add a new item to the list, you insert a row just above row 6 (which is short so you won't enter data in it). Row 6 has the range name InsertHere, so the macro can select it. Notice that the sum function in C3 covers cells C5:C6, so it expands to include the new rows you insert. This a repetitive chore, so I created the macro shown in the bottom panel to automate it.

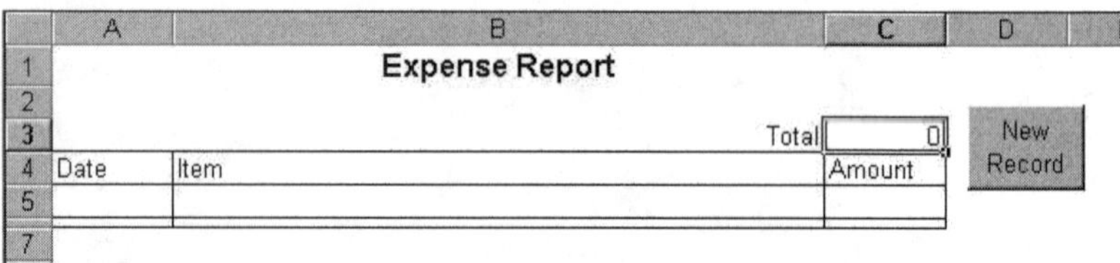

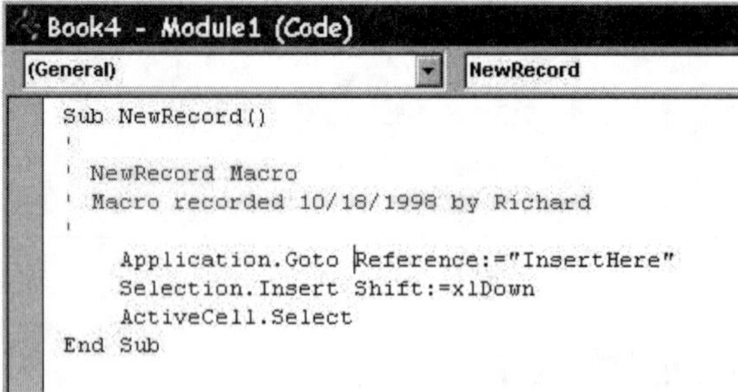

Figure 61

Excel's new macro language is based on Visual Basic, it's Windows-based programming language. The top panel shows the simple expense sheet. Row 5 has the range name InsertHere. When the user clicks the New Record button, the macro shown in the bottom panel selects the named range, inserts a row, and selects the first cell in the new row, so the user can enter data.

To create the macro, use the following procedure: execute Tools/Record Macro/Record New Macro, enter "NewRecord" in the Macro Name box, and click OK to turn on the recorder (Notice that the macro is stored in the current workbook). A toolbar appears with a single button to stop recording. Now record the steps: execute Edit/Goto and select InsertHere. Then execute Insert/Rows. Click the Stop button to halt the macro.

Press Alt F11 to fire up the VBA editor. In the Project window in the upper-left part of the screen, double-click Modules and then double-click Module1 to reveal the code. Insert the statement that appears just above the End Sub line. Now close the VBA editor to return to Excel. Select View/Toolbars and then select Forms to reveal the worksheet controls toolbar. Click the Create Button button (see Figure 62) on the standard toolbar and draw a button like the one shown in Figure 61. The Assign Macro dialog box appears. Select the macro NewRecord, click OK, and you're in business with a button that inserts a new record in your list.

Figure 62

Excel's Create Button button.

Spreadsheet Resources

Excel for Windows 95: Visual QuickStart Guide, Maria Langer (ISBN: 0201883724). If you're brand-new to spreadsheets, this book provides careful, self-paced tutorials for learning the basics.

Excel 97 Bible, John Walkenbach (ISBN: 0764530364); *Special Edition Using Microsoft Excel 97,* Ron Person (ISBN: 0789709600). Once you've got your feet wet, you'll want to obtain one of the comprehensive user guides to Excel. These aren't books to curl up with in front of the fire, but they can answer many of your routine questions, and provide examples of how to apply the many features of this powerful program.

Microsoft Excel 97: Visual Basic Step by Step, Reed Jacobsen (ISBN: 1572313188). If you're a more advanced user trying to figure out how to use Excel's macro language, track down a copy of this excellent book. Reed has an uncanny knack for introducing the intricacies of programming using Excel examples that make you say "Aha!"

Business Analysis with Excel, Conrad Carlberg (ISBN: 0789703823). When you're trying to figure out how to build an Excel model to solve a specific business problem, you don't need to start from scratch. There are many books available to show you how to set up models for almost any conceivable financial, statistical, or engineering solution. This is one of my favorites, with lots of practical examples for small business owners.

`zdjournals.com/ime` *Inside Microsoft Excel*, a monthly newsletter ($59 a year before discounts), is a treasure trove of tips, tricks, and techniques for intermediate to advanced Excel users, and it includes advice from Excel professionals on such topics as setting up flexible charts and advanced data management. Subscribers have access to a full back-issue library at the Web site; other visitors can access only one sample article per issue.

j-walk.com/ss *PC World* spreadsheet advice columnist John Walkenbach's Web site contains everything from tips to complete applications that you can download—even spreadsheet jokes!

www.baarns.com Anyone who aspires to guru status with Excel, or who's looking for specialized Excel applications to solve specific business problems, should spend some time at Don Baarns's Web site. A professional Excel consultant and developer since Release 2.1, Don now leads a team of developers who create customized Office solutions and are happy to share their insights online.

15

Personal Finance and Tax Software

by Kathy Yakal

In This Chapter

In this chapter, we'll explore:

- Why you should use a personal finance program
- How Intuit's Quicken and Microsoft's Money have evolved from checkbook managers to full-service financial managers
- The ever-deepening relationship between financial software and the Internet
- Five reasons why some taxpayers should use tax preparation software, and what's available

You've doubtless heard pitches over the years from software publishers that claim you *must* use their software. In some cases, depending on who you are, that may be true. But no matter who you are, you get income. You pay bills. You pay taxes. Maybe you invest in the stock market, and you probably feel that you should be making financial plans for your future instead of just staying afloat from month to month. If you've never considered buying software that will automate your personal finances and tax preparation process, you absolutely should. These programs can help you get organized and stay organized—and may improve your financial bottom line in the process.

A tax program or a personal finance package won't create that organization for you. But if you take the time to pull your records together and set up some simple procedures, good software can cut the number of evenings and weekends devoted to paperwork, particularly around tax time.

If a CPA already does your books, your financial situation may be too complex for a tax or finance package alone to handle. But even in that case, you might consider using one. At worst, you'll have coherent records, so your CPA won't have to unravel your paperwork—and bill you for doing so. At best, you'll be prompted to dig in and start creating budgets, turning up new tax deductions, figuring mortgage payments, and even paying bills electronically.

Personal Finance Basics

Don't let anyone tell you otherwise: What you don't know *can* hurt you, at least in terms of your personal finances. The explosion of enormously useful and incredibly banal information that we call the World Wide Web has given us way more financial data than we could ever hope to absorb. Which can be both a blessing and a curse.

In your excitement over finding that you can stay up to speed on the closing prices and number of shares traded for Sonargaon Textiles Limited on the Dhaka Stock Exchange, you might miss the fact that mortgage rates just dropped. Or you might let a checking account balance drop below zero or a credit card balance soar over the maximum because you've forgotten to track all the $5, $15, and $35 monthly charges for Web site subscriptions. You may miss a major investment opportunity because you were too busy giggling and ordering fake teeth for all of your co-workers from the Billy Bob Teeth site.

You need serious organizational help. You need PC software that's a cross between a college math instructor, Andrew Tobias, and your mother. You need a personal finance manager, and you need it integrated with the Web.

Intuit's Quicken has been almost as synonymous with personal finance software as Kleenex is with facial tissue—until recently. Two other programs, Managing Your Money and Simply Money, made serious runs at the market leader and finally turned away, grumbling. Microsoft shyly threw its hook in the water several years ago, but forgot to bait it: Its Money title lacked teeth, and just about everything else that was necessary to snag the interest of American consumers.

Microsoft's introduction of its 1995 version of Money was overshadowed by the garish party the company threw to christen Windows 95, but for the first time, Money looked like it actually might be a contender. In 1999, it is. After spending five times the development time and money it had on previous versions, Microsoft finally had something that could compete with Quicken—and that actually beats it in some areas.

More Than You'll Ever Need

Quicken was a hit from the time it was born 15 years ago. It was an electronic checkbook and nothing more, but people loved its simplicity and precision. Today, checkbook management is a very small part of what both Quicken and Money do. It's unlikely that you'd ever use absolutely every feature of either, but these programs are so well-designed that the extras shouldn't get in the way of your regular tasks.

Here's what you'll get with either program:

- **Account management.** Even if you have a meticulous recording-keeping system on paper, betcha you can't always lay your hands on the simplest details related to your financial accounts. Personal finance software lets—nay, *encourages*—you to fill in all those little fields describing all of your accounts of any type: checking, savings, loan, credit card, 401(k) or whatever. You'll use the groundwork you lay here in other parts of the program.
- **Bill-paying.** Personal finance software offers two ways for you to pay one-time and recurring bills. You can print checks and dispatch them, or

sign up for online bill-paying. No matter what bank you use, there'll be a way for you to join in the fun. It's likely, too, that you'll be able to tap into your bank accounts online, through your personal finance software. You can check balances, see if transactions have been posted, and authorize payments, 24/7.

- **Portfolio tracking.** Even if you've sworn to ride out these volatile months in the stock market without altering your portfolio, you still probably want to keep an eye on your investments. Both Quicken and Money do a stellar job of providing tools to keep your portfolio updated.
- **Short- and long-term planning.** What good does it do to know where you are financially if you can't use that information to gauge where you'll be a few years down the road? Personal finance software helps you develop a plan to get out of debt (see Figure 1) and save for big expenses like college educations and retirement.
- **Tax relief.** When tax time rolls around, you won't have to root around records that should have been in order to begin with. Personal finance software encourages you to flag tax-related categories so you can run summary reports of tax-related transactions that match the order of IRS forms and schedules—or export the data directly to a tax program.
- **Instant reports.** Once you assign categories (such as food, clothing, medical, charitable donations) to transactions, you can quickly run reports that show where all the money is going, get precise income and expense breakdowns, and review any account balance whenever you like. If rows and columns of figures are Greek to you, pour them into charts and graphs.

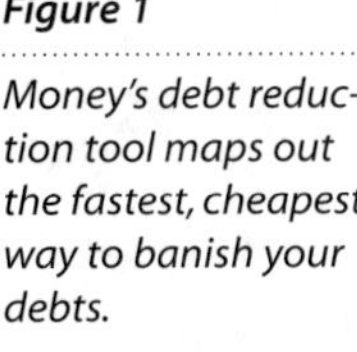

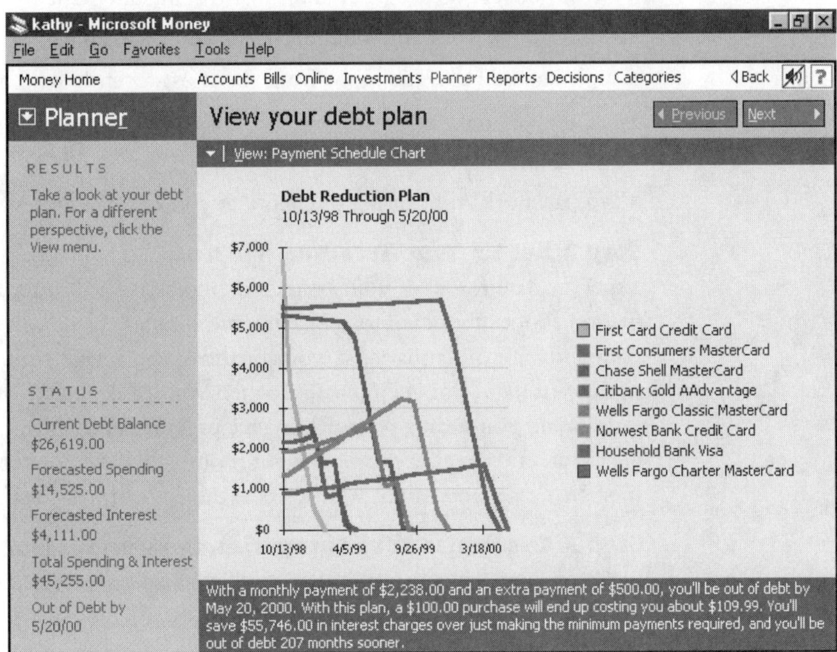

Figure 1

Money's debt reduction tool maps out the fastest, cheapest way to banish your debts.

- **Focused Web connectivity.** The Web serves as a willing partner in all of these financial endeavors. both Quicken and Money have built-in links for tasks like updating stock prices, finding better rates for mortgages and other types of loans, and reading related news and feature articles. It's hard to imagine now how personal finance software existed without its Web partnerships—the timeliness of the financial data it pulls in makes it a far more powerful consumer resource.

Setting Up Shop

Setup is the biggest stumbling block for people who keep haphazard manual records. Personal finance software cannot automatically "get you organized." If you constantly forget to enter your ATM withdrawals, stuff unopened bank statements in drawers, and misplace receipts for tax-deductible purchases, using a personal finance program will seem like twice the work.

You *must* change your ways and enter every check and every deposit, categorize every transaction, reconcile your accounts regularly, and earmark tax-related items. Otherwise, none of the reports or other helpful output will be accurate.

Step 1: Prepare for Setup. You'll breeze through your sessions a lot faster if you set up as much as you can up front. So grit your teeth and get through this unpleasant task in a few sessions—before you start entering transactions. To prepare for this first step, gather up:

- your checkbook register and most recent statement
- passbooks from any other accounts you might have
- all unpaid bills, and stubs from the most recently paid bills
- loan payment books
- investment paperwork
- a paycheck stub (or list of clients, if you're self-employed)

Step 2: Set Up Your Accounts. You'll have to enter opening balances as of a specific date for all of your bank and credit card accounts, along with information about other creditors and income sources. You don't have to start using your software on January 1st, your birthday, the vernal equinox, or any other significant date. But keep in mind when you think about a start date that if it's August and you want a personal finance program to help you prepare your taxes next year, entering the previous eight months' transactions may be too tedious. In such a case, you might want to save the tax features for the next tax year.

Step 3: Customize Your Categories. Every personal finance program includes a generous list of income and expense categories for classifying transactions. Each transaction must be categorized as you enter it so you can take advantage of the two biggest benefits of personal finance software: Categories enable you to group transactions for tax purposes and run reports that show you how much money you're spending on what—.

While the predefined category list may work fine for you, cruise through it before you start to see if any categories or subcategories are missing and then add them. If you're planning to use the program to run a small business, you may want to enlist the services of an accountant to help with this part of the process; if you have your taxes prepared professionally, you definitely want the person who does them involved in this process.

Step 4: Back Up Your Data. This isn't a "You might want to..." kind of thing. You *must* back up your financial records. Period. Businesses have folded because no one backed up a hard disk that later decided to give up the ghost. All personal finance products instruct you how to back up your files, and some won't let you exit without reminding you to do so (See Chapter 9: Protect Your Data for more information on backing up).

Also, keep a well-organized paper backup. Keep receipts, statements, check stubs, and so on in folders labeled by category or by month—you'll need the paper trail if you're ever audited. And if you run a detailed transaction report once a week, you'll have a last line of defense if your backup disks fry.

Quicken 99

Years ago, before Intuit introduced its popular small business accounting program, QuickBooks, accountants told tales of million-dollar businesses that were tracking their books using the personal finance application Quicken. Some may still be doing so, but there are better solutions for business accounting (see "Business Accounting Applications" in Chapter 16: Databases for some suggestions). Though one of its many versions is an edition geared to very small businesses, Quicken is definitely aimed at the individual, not the corporation.

As Quicken has grown, taken on more and more tasks, and added links to the Internet, it's grown a tad unwieldy. For that reason, Quicken 99 instituted a brand new, alternative navigational device, the Quicken Home Page (see Figure 2). It's totally optional—if you're an experienced user you might prefer to keep using Quicken the way you always have, but this new customizable convention may be just the thing to help you keep track of whatever it is you're keeping track of.

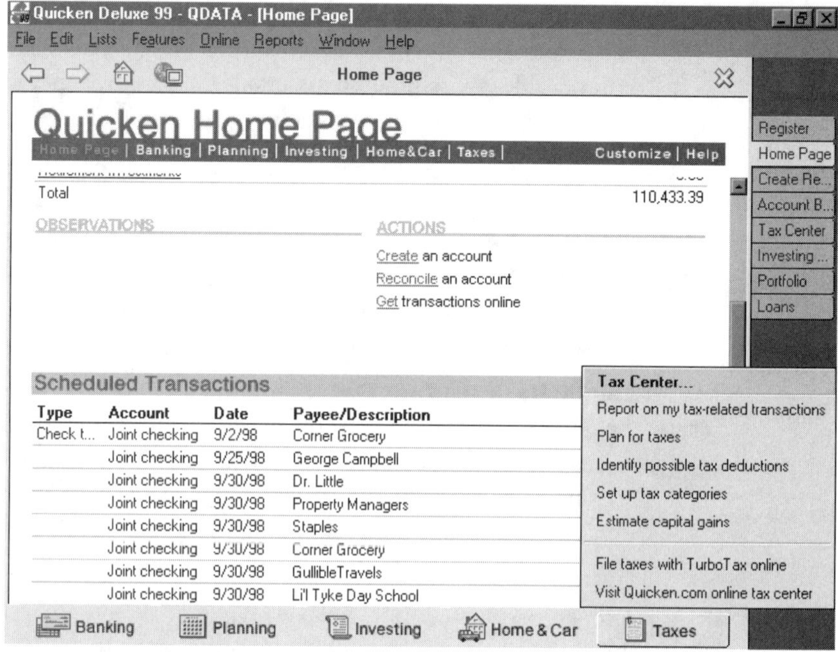

Figure 2

Quicken 99's new Home Page joins other navigational tools from earlier versions, like book-marks and pop-up task lists.

Let's Get Started

Easier said than done, and one of the reasons why people eschew personal finance software. How in the world do you get all of the information scattered around your home into the right places in Quicken?

It's not at all difficult, but it *is* time-consuming. Quicken can help you save time down the road—in areas like electronic bill-paying—but it will bore you to tears up front, unless you get a sense of satisfaction out of putting things into order.

You could actually do all of your setup (as well as much of your related financial activity) from Quicken's Home Page and its counterparts called "Activity Centers", which are similar pages for Banking, Planning, Investing, Home and Car, and Taxes. These screens function much like Web pages, with many of their links taking you to different functional areas of Quicken. You can select up to 16 elements of your financial picture to appear on the home page, things like account details and activity, auto expenses, credit card analysis, tax-related expenses, and your portfolio.Each subsection contains links to data entry and informational pages. For example, the My Accounts section's links take you to:

- individual account registers
- an account creation screen
- the account reconciliation screen
- the online banking center

But there are other ways to get around in Quicken that you might find more efficient. Buttons along the bottom of the Quicken screen are divided into the same categories as the Activity Centers, though each houses only a handful of task areas, like "Write a check to print," or "Track my 401(k)." The old-fashioned drop-down menus at the top of the screen work just fine, too. And once you've visited an area during the current session, you can return to it quickly by clicking one of the labeled tabs at the screen's right edge.

Setting up accounts. However you get around, you'll enter transactions and other data the same way, since your setup and transaction screens and dialog boxes will be the same. If you've ever used Windows software, you shouldn't have any trouble here, since Quicken's operations are as simple and understandable as any other applications, more so than most. Just enter data in each field or register as it's requested, or access drop-down list boxes where they're available. Help is always a click away: Press [Key caps: F1], open the Help menu, or click on any Help button that's available.

Many of Quicken's setup operations are facilitated by wizards, series of screens that walk you through a process by asking you questions and dropping your answers in the right place within the program (see Figure 3). For example, to set up an investment account, you'll be asked for the following information, screen by screen:

- account name and description
- whether you've applied for online services

Figure 3

Wizards in Quicken help you set up things like investment accounts and related securities.

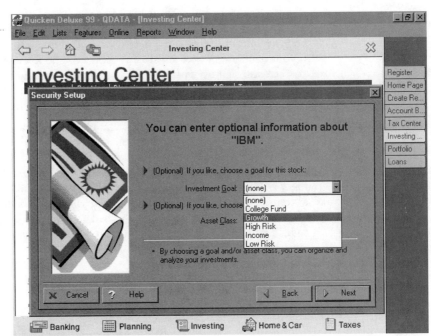

- whether you can write checks or use a debit card against the balance
- what type of securities will be tracked (stocks, bonds, and mutual funds; or a single mutual fund)
- whether the account is tax-deferred or tax-exempt

Once you've created at least one investment account, you can continue on with the wizard and define the securities you hold in each, following a similar process. Your options here include the ability to assign an investment goal (like growth or high-risk) to each security.

Other setup options. If all you're going to do with Quicken is write checks and run reports, your setup chores are almost complete once you've established all of your accounts. But you'll be wasting a lot of the program's hidden talents. There are other setup tools you should consider.

- The **Paycheck Setup Wizard**. Unless you're a human resources expert, you may not know exactly where all of that money that gets deducted from your paycheck is going, or how to keep a running record—you just know that there's a lot of it, and it goes away every pay period. Entering all of those deductions every pay period can be a major pain. Use the Paycheck Setup Wizard to enter all the numbers from your paycheck stub once, and Quicken can automatically enter all of those numbers for you every paycheck and can even record it as a direct deposit.
- The same goes for the envy of all self-employed people, your 401(k). The **401(k) Setup Wizard** helps you create an ongoing 401(k) account. You can then track how your investment is distributed among all of the available choices, and see how it's behaving.
- If you haven't set up accounts to participate in **online banking and bill-paying**, you should. Click the Get Started With Online Financial Services button to find out what services your financial institution offers. If your bank has not yet enlisted (most major and many minor ones have), you can still sign up with Intuit Online Payment, which will serve as a middleman between your bank and your payees. Costs range from free to about $10/month.
- Good software not only does what you tell it to, but it reminds you of things you might otherwise have missed. So check out Quicken's **Alerts**. There are 14 available out of the box, and Intuit is constantly adding more, which are automatically grabbed whenever you do an online session (see Figure 4). Click on one of the four tabs in the setup dialog box: Accounts, Investments, General, and New. You can ask for an onscreen remainder of events like accounts that have reached a maximum or minimum limit (which you set), high/low price limits for selected securities, and important tax dates.

Quicken*'s* ability to analyze your income and spending patterns and give you insightful information in reports depends largely on your willingness to assign **categories** to transactions like checks and deposits. Quicken comes with its

Figure 4

When Quicken grabs a new alert during a download session, it will appear when you click the New tab in the setup dialog box.

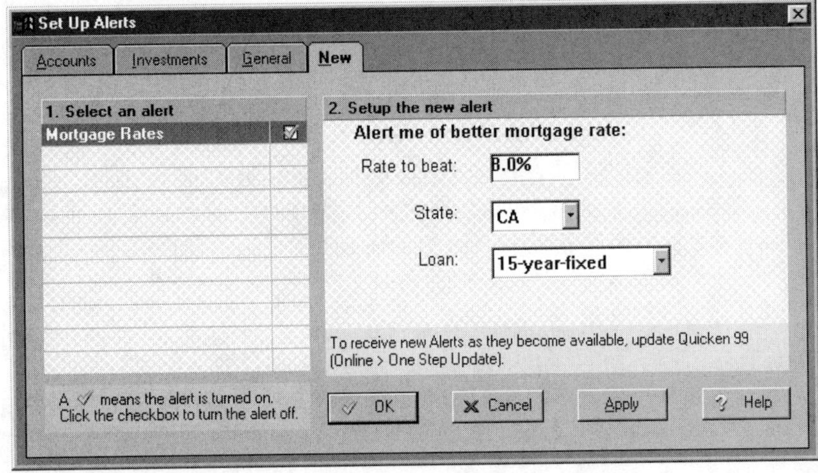

own set of income and expense categories—things like rent income, salary, child care, and groceries—but you are encouraged to tailor these to better meet your individual situation. You can build subcategories to flesh out the detail, and tag categories as tax-related to make your tax preparation process more organized.

This same level of simplicity follows you all around Quicken. Transaction screens are designed to draw on information you've already entered, to ease and speed up data entry, and to collect enough detailed information to make reports thorough and meaningful. Most of the day-to-day transactions you'll be creating lie in two main areas: banking and budgeting, and investments.

Banking and Budgeting

Sorry. This is the ugly part. Unless you're doing your banking and bill-paying online, this is where you'll be pounding keys the most. But it's not really that bad. It's just tedious and repetitive. And there's more than one way to enter those transactions in Quicken, depending on what they are.

Quicken tracks six kinds of transactions: checks, deposits, ATM withdrawals, transfers between accounts, electronic funds transfers, and online payments. You can print checks using special computer paper available from Intuit and third-party vendors.

But if you're like most people, the lion's share of your transactions will be checks. You can select your modus operandi here from the following options:.

- **Entering hand-written transactions.** If you've written a check in your checkbook, you're going to also have to enter it in Quicken to keep your records current. You'll do this in the register, a screen that looks just like a paper check register. You'll enter the date, select the type of transaction from a drop-down list, enter the recipient's name and the amount of the check, assign a category and enter a note in the memo field if you want. Quicken can memorize information you enter here, so the next time you start to type, "Corner Grocery," it will finish it for you, as well as filling in details of the last transaction to that payee (these entries can be overridden).

- **Entering a check to be printed.** One of the things that made Quicken an early success was the familiarity of its interface. Even in the DOS days, a check looked like a check blank on the screen. The check register looked like its paper counterpart. When you're entering a check you want to print, you can fill in the blanks on the register, or you can enter the same information on *Quicken*'s graphic representation of a check blank of the screen (see Figure 5).

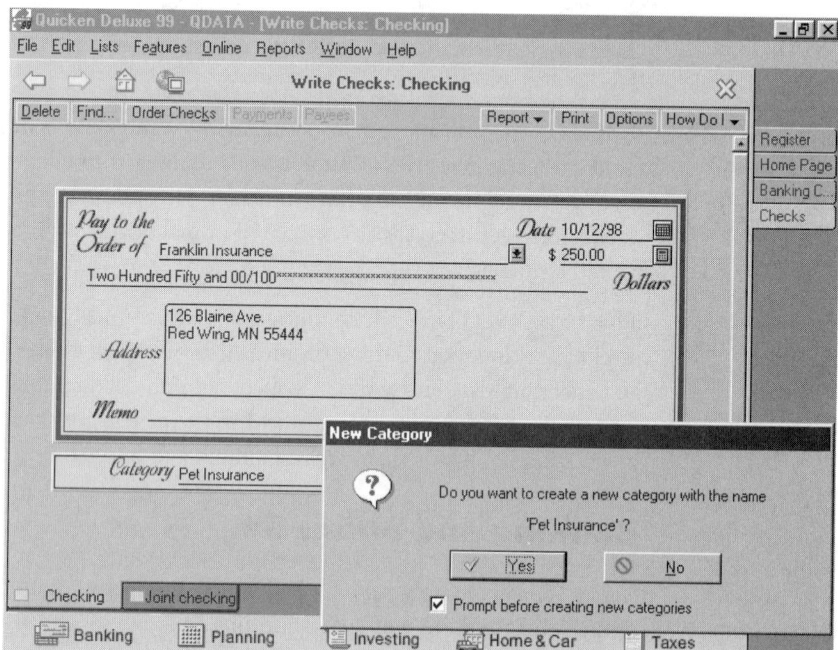

Figure 5

Look familiar? Quicken combines the look of a paper checkbook with its fancy electronic tools.

- **Entering an online transaction.** Dispatching a payment electronically is no more difficult than using Quicken's other options, once you've done your initial setup. You can enter an electronic transaction in the register, on the check blank graphic, or in Quicken's Online Center. The latter displays a graphical check blank that functions like other parts of Quicken—you fill in the check blank by pulling information from drop-down lists or typing in words and numbers.
- **Quick entry.** A new tool in Quicken 99, Quick Entry is a separate mini-application designed for fast data entry only, a simple register that stores entries for classification later. Open it and type in your transactions, and they'll greet you the next time you open Quicken itself, ready to move into your registers.

Once Is Not Nearly Enough: Automating Quicken

If Quicken stopped there, it would be saving you time. But the idea behind personal finance software is for you to save time doing the little stuff so you can spend more time thinking about the big stuff. So Quicken helps you automate many of the repetitive actions you take every month to keep your finances copacetic.

Recurring transactions. Yes, those are expenses that occur every month or at some other predictable interval without fail. Mortgage payments, or rent. Car—and other loan—payments. Utility bills. Day care bills. Insurance payments. Ugh. Quicken can't banish them, but it can remind you when they're due, and even ready the checks for printing or dispatch the electronic payments. On the flip side, you can also tell Quicken about regularly occurring deposits.

Even better, Quicken can politely remind you when specific bills or deposits are due, without you even needing to open the program itself. No more clipping bills to calendar pages or just hoping you'll remember to dash off the checks in time.

It's easy. Head for the **Scheduled Transactions** list. You'll find it in the Lists menu. Click on it, and an empty register screen opens. Click New to open the data entry dialog box and get the ball rolling. By making selections from drop-down lists or entering new data, you'll define the scheduled transaction. (see Figure 6) The fields you'll fill in include:

- account name
- type of transaction (payment, deposit, printed check, online payment)
- payee

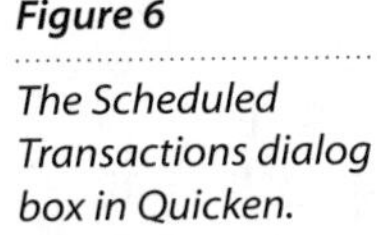

Figure 6

The Scheduled Transactions dialog box in Quicken.

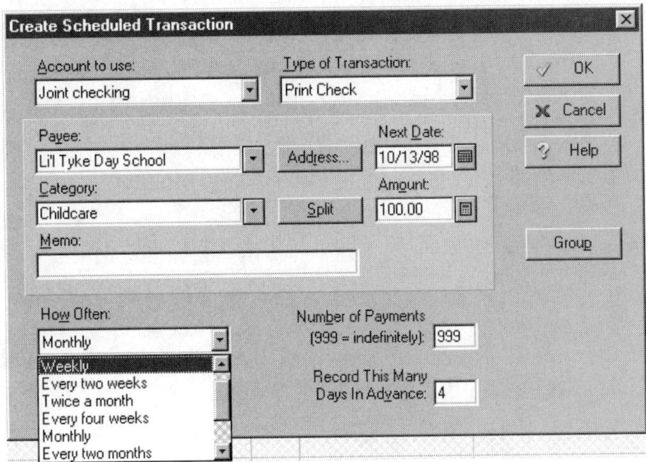

- category
- amount (if the amount varies, simply enter an average and type in the correct amount every month)
- next payment date
- how often? (once, weekly, every two weeks, twice a month, every four weeks, monthly, every two months, quarterly, twice a year, yearly)
- number of payments
- record in register (prompt before entering or automatically enter)
- record (how many?) days in advance

Grouping transactions. You probably don your lucky bill-paying hat at least once or twice a month for bill-paying sessions, depending on when your debts fall due. Quicken makes it easy for you to approve payments in clusters. Click New again, then click the Group button in the Scheduled Transactions dialog box. From the fields offered, select an account to use and give your group a name. Then answer some of the same questions asked when you set up a scheduled transaction.

Click OK, and a dialog box containing memorized transactions appears (memorized transactions include any that you've already entered, unless you've opted not to have Quicken memorize your transaction for fast recall). Select the ones you want in your group (like all bills with due dates during the first three days of each month), and then click Done.

Ready to send them off? Highlight the group you want paid and click the Pay button. Click the Record button if you don't want to add or delete transactions from the group. If you need to change a payment amount before the check is printed or the payment sent electronically, you can do so in the register.

Create a calendar; never forget. There's another way to keep track of what's due when: Quicken's Financial Calendar (see Figure 7). Memorized transactions appear in a vertical window to the left of a graphical calendar. Scheduled transactions appear on the correct days within the calendar itself. To schedule a new transaction, just drag and drop a payee from the list onto a specific day and edit the transaction in the dialog box that appears, if necessary. You can drop unrelated reminder notes onto calendar days, and easily jump to individual transaction records and registers.

Manual reminders. If you've set up automatic online payment of recurring bills that generally require the same amount of payment, like your cable TV bill or car payment, you don't have to worry about actively processing them every month. Your financial institution will send the payment regularly, by the date requested, until you tell it to stop. It sends a notice of the impending payment 30 days ahead of time, just to remind you.

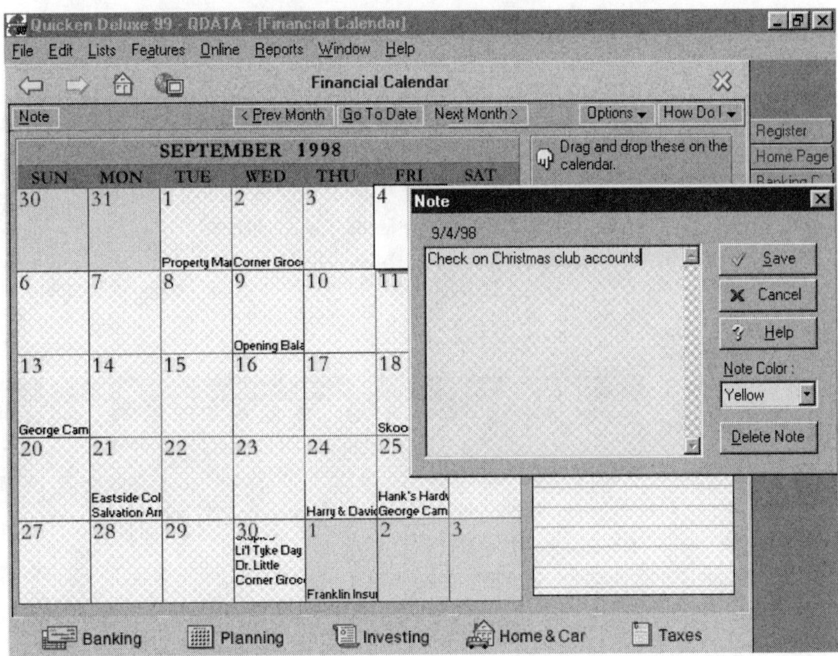

Figure 7

Quicken's Financial Calendar.

But if you print checks to send as payments, write them by hand and enter them in the Quicken register, or dispatch online payment instructions for bills, you're responsible for remembering to process them, just like you are when you send bill payments manually.

Quicken lends a hand here, in more than one way:

- **Your home page.** If you've set up your Quicken home page to include scheduled transactions, you'll be greeted with the news of your impending payments.
- **Reminders.** Open the Features menu and click Reminders/Reminders. This screen can display a number of upcoming financial events, including online payment instructions, notes added to your Financial Calendar, and checks that need to be printed. You can set Quicken to open to this page automatically, or you can reach it from the menu.
- **Billminder.** if you're not one of the many Quicken addicts who must pore over the program daily, you can set up the Billminder to open when you run Windows, reminding you of bills that need to be paid and other financial transactions that require your attention.

By clicking the Options menu with the Reminders screen open, you can select which financial events should be displayed, and for what time period (last month, next seven days, etc.).

Investing with Quicken

Understanding the intricacies, the language, and the tools of the stock market is certainly a more formidable task than keeping track of a checking account, but Quicken makes investment transactions easy. When you use Quicken's investment register entering a buy or sell or any of the other cash movements you need to orchestrate is no more difficult than writing a check. (see Figure 8). Use your existing portfolio information and make selections from the drop-down lists provided.

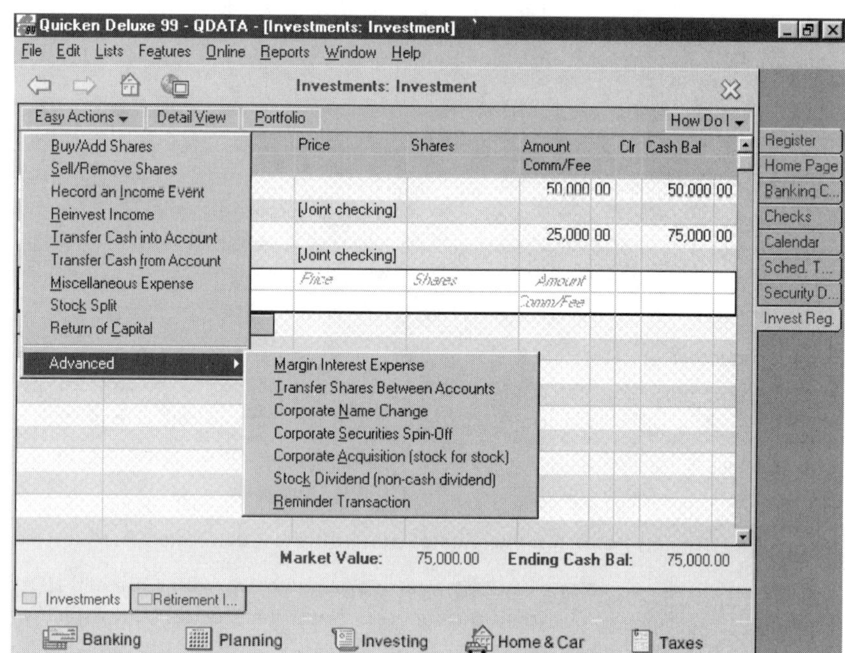

Figure 8

Quicken's investment register.

Updating your data. There's probably no other element of your personal finance machinations that needs current data more than your investment portfolio. And Quicken is up to the task. With one mouse-click, Quicken will connect to the Internet and update the security prices in your portfolio, grab any related news stories, and pull historical data if you need it, dropping each piece of information in the appropriate place.

Quicken's new One Step Update feature makes your online time more economical (see Figure 9). If you'd like to exchange other data with the Web while you're connected to get stock prices, select the One Step Update item from the Online menu. Up pops a dialog box that lets you tag the items you want grabbed. These include, in addition to the security information:

- **Portfolio data.** You can export your portfolio to the portfolio tracker on Intuit's Web site, Quicken.com.
- **Quicken reminders.** You can export reminders about things like scheduled transactions to the Web, where you can view them while you're online.
- **Statement download.** If you're set up with a financial institution that allows statement download (banks, brokerages, credit card companies), One Step Update will grab these. too.
- **WebEntry downloads.** Another new feature in Quicken 99, WebEntry lets you enter Quicken transactions from any computer onto a private page at Quicken.com. The next time you open Quicken, you'll see these transactions and be asked if you want them transferred into your register.

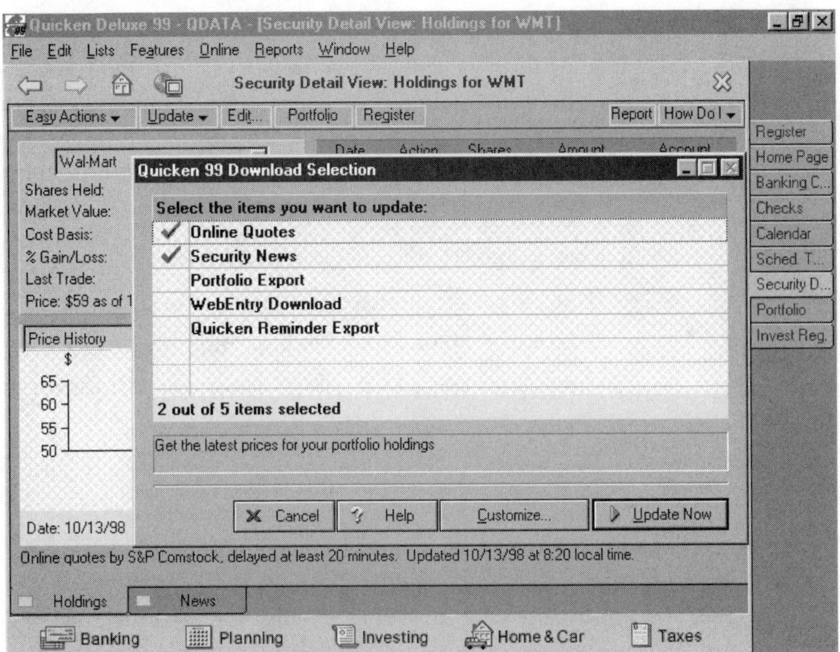

Figure 9

Whoa! What's up with the market? One Step Update helps you find out quickly and can grab other financial data at the same time.

Planning. Having a handle on your current financial picture can help you plan for your future, but Quicken packs in lots of extra horsepower to help you assess your needs and resources and put together a workable, specific blueprint. Here's how.

- **Quicken Financial Planner.** Intuit developed this as a stand-alone application years ago, and now a junior version of that product is an offshoot of Quicken. QFP walks you through dozens of screens, asking for information on income, expenses, savings, taxes, and retirement benefits. It evaluates your answers ands tells you whether your current plan is working toward meeting your goals. If not, it makes concrete suggestions for change.

- **Debt Reduction Planner.** Some financial experts say that one of the best financial moves you can make is to get rid of outstanding credit card balances. If you have credit card debt that runs into the thousands and you can't easily see the end of it, Quicken's Debt Reduction Planner can help you pay your credit cards off in the most lucrative way possible—that is, paying the least amount of interest and zeroing out your cards in the minimum amount of time.
- **Budgeting. Ugh.** Yes, ugh is right. Budgeting isn't practical for some people, but it's a must for others. Quicken provides an easy path for you to build a budget and track it. You can even turn on a progress bar at the bottom of the screen so you're constantly reminded of how you're doing.

Reports and graphs. So you're conscientiously entering transactions and planning for big events like college educations and retirement—how do you know how you're doing? By generating the numerous reports and graphs that Quicken makes possible. You can customize your home page to display some of these every time you call it up, or you can just run reports when you need to know how you're doing in a specific area.

Quicken's prefab reports fall into five categories:

- **Banking.** Account balances, missing checks, etc.
- **Planning.** Net worth, cash flow, monthly budget, etc.
- **Investment.** Portfolio value, investment performance, capital gains, etc.
- **Taxes.** Tax summary, tax schedules, etc.
- **Business.** Profit and loss, accounts receivable by customer, balance sheet, etc.

Quicken sets up the report framework for you so all you have to do is click and run, but you can also customize these reports to contain the specific information you want. For example, you can choose which accounts and payees and categories to include, what range of dates to look at, and take out a slice that only grabs tax-related transactions. You can "memorize" customized formats you use regularly so you can call them up quickly. And Quicken's Easy Answer reports let you create some of the program's reports by selecting English-language questions, like, "What are my investments worth?" (See Figure 10) Several of Quicken's report formats can also be displayed as graphs. These are also customizable.

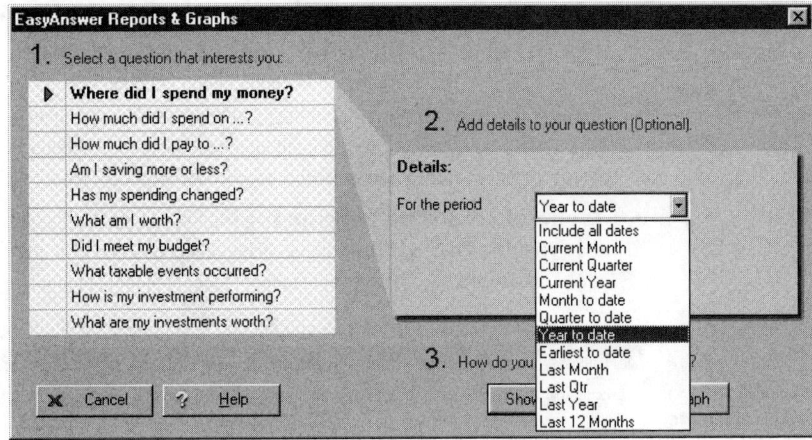

Figure 10

Take your pick: Customize one of Quicken's many report templates, or use its Easy Answer reports.

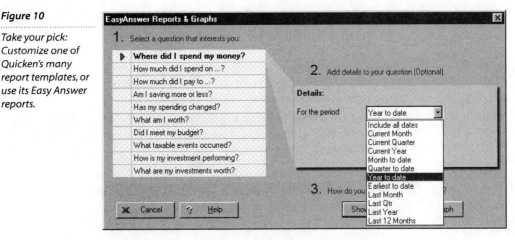

Microsoft Money 99

Microsoft Money, barely a blip on the radar screen a few years ago, has emerged as a serious competitor to the dominant Quicken. It provides a similar set of tools to the befuddled consumer: account management, online banking and bill-paying, investment management, planning, and reports. And it does so within a very elegant, understandable interface.

While Money does the same kinds of things that Quicken does, more or less, it does them differently. Unlike Quicken, Money does not have individual pages for all of its sections. But its sole home page is a bit more functional than Quicken's. It's not designed so much as a navigational tool as it is a clearinghouse for things you should know about your own finances and about what's happening in the outside financial world.

You can design your own home page by selecting from the options Money gives you, like looming bills, an investment summary, reminders, and a daily chart. Another of those options, Financial Readings, is also customizable. You can choose from a list of publications and subjects, and Money will grab articles related to your interests, dropping them onto your home page.

Money's Advisor FYI alerts are powerful tools. Select the ones you want displayed on your home page, and Money will keep them updated for you, from within the program itself and using its Web updates (see Figure 11). Your options here include:

- **Account balance limits.** Tell Money to tell you when any of your account balances reach a minimum or maximum that you specify.

- **Monthly spending by category.** Want to keep an eye on your dining out expenses or your bookstore spending? Set limits here, and Money will let you know when you've reached them.
- **Investment prices.** If you regularly update security prices in Money using the program's automatic update, you can ask to be notified when your securities have reached a specified high or low.
- **General advice on specific topics.** Want guidance from Money and Microsoft personal finance resources on things like investing, reducing debt, and taxes? Click the boxes.

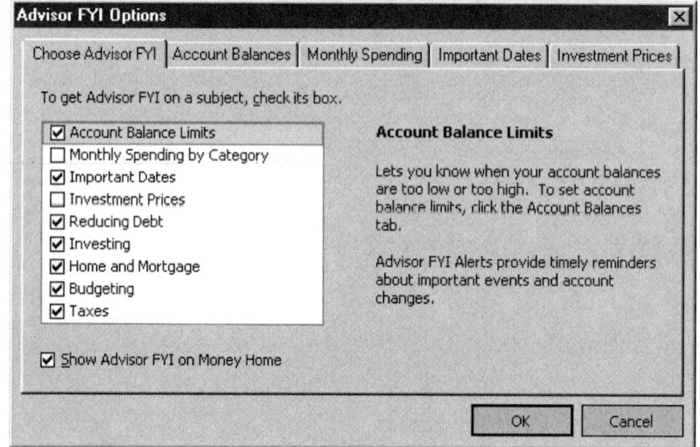

Figure 11

It's easy to customize Money's home page and its FYI Advisor Alerts.

Easy Setup

Money's setup operations are similar to Quicken's, often using wizards for common tasks, and supplying clear, understandable navigation buttons. Though you'll always be adding to your Money file, creating new accounts and payees and the like, at the least you'll need to perform minimal setup procedures before you start using Money.

Unlike Quicken, Money doesn't provide links on its internal home page for internal operations like setup. But the process is just as easy. When you click the Accounts link at the top of the page, any accounts already created will appear as icons. Buttons at the bottom the page will take you to wizards that let you create, edit, or delete accounts (see Figure 12).

Like Quicken, Money lets you set up many kinds of accounts—savings and checking, loan and mortgage, investment, credit card, etc. And you can establish online accounts with banks that support electronic banking. Money's internal Web browser connects you to financial institution Web sites so you can explore what's available and get started.

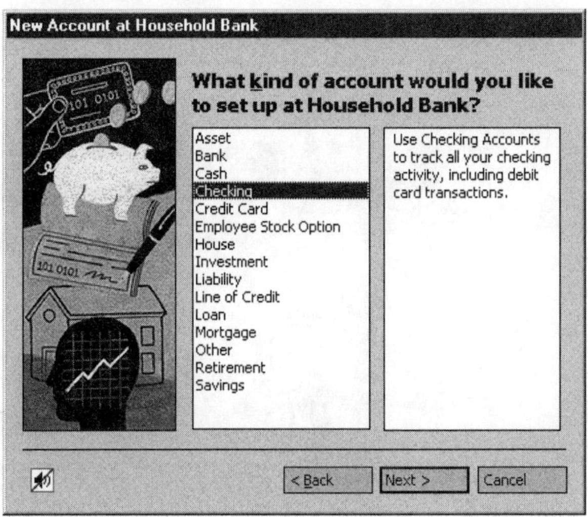

Figure 12

The Microsoft Money Account Setup Wizard.

Tackling other setup tasks early on will make your life easier once you get rolling with Money. For example, you may find it useful to peruse the list of prefab categories and modify it for your own use or set up your paycheck for regular deposits. You may want to let Money help you remember what bills need to be paid when.

Flexible Bill Paying

No matter what the frequency and amount of a bill you have to pay, Money's flexible bill-paying tools can help make sure you don't forget it. Click the Bills button, and then select from the options Money offers here. You can:

- set up bills and deposits that will occur just once or regularly
- look at a list of recently paid bills
- look at a graphical calendar displaying due dates for bills
- pay bills
- see a chart that forecasts your checking account balance based on scheduled bills
- sign up for e-bills (receiving bills electronically—this practice is still in very limited use, but both Money and Quicken are prepared for it)

Money's Scheduled Payment Wizard is painless (unless you think about the money it represents). It walks you through the process of defining the payment(s), and then drops those payments into the Upcoming Bills screen, so you always know what's coming up (see Figure 13). If a payment amount changes every month, like your phone bill, Money will indicate that the amount is an estimation. You can request reminders of bills due either when you start up Money or boot Windows, or both.

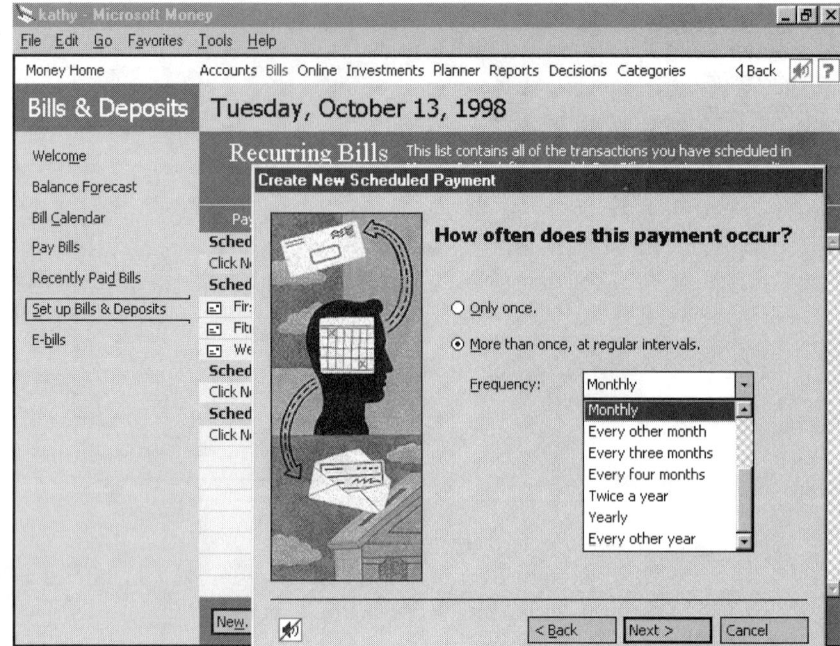

Figure 13

Money helps you keep track of your upcoming financial obligations with its bill payment tools.

You can also enter transactions directly on the form that lies below each account register. It doesn't look like a check blank, like the one in Quicken, but it's just as easy to use. You can record checks, deposits, withdrawals, and transfers here. Click Balance This Account, and Money opens a bank reconciliation screen. Both Quicken and Money help you through the reconciliation process. If the account doesn't balance, you can either ask for more help tracking down the problem or ask that an adjusting entry be made to manually balance the account.

Investing with Money

If you've set up investment accounts to track your securities holdings, you'll find Money a good tool both to keep track of those holdings and to record your buys and sells and other related transactions. Many Web sites now offer portfolio trackers, but it's hard to find one that's as flexible and sophisticated as those included in Quicken and Money.

Just like you have to record a check you've written manually, you'll have to create a transaction for every securities action you take. Money makes this as easy as recording an ATM withdrawal. Just fill in the blanks on the transaction screen, and your portfolio will be updated automatically (see Figure 14). Click a button, and the quotes you're tracking within Money will update. Quicken and Money both do a good job of drawing information into themselves from

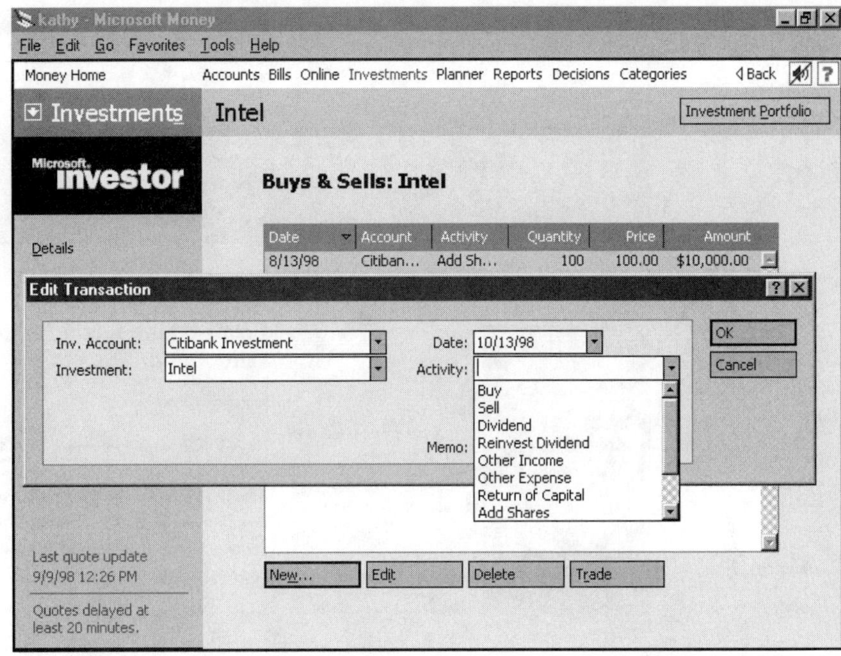

Figure 14

Buy? Sell? Whatever. Money helps you track your market moves.

the Web where appropriate and of bringing the Web to you when that works better. For example, each has an embedded browser that opens when you want to go to a Web site.

Microsoft has done an especially good job of hooking Money's internal investment capabilities to its investment Web site, Microsoft Investor. You can easily move from within Money to use Investor's numerous resources, which include stock screening tools, analysis, and in-depth market research (see Figure 15). One click and you're back in Money itself. And you can synch your portfolio between Money and the Web site.

Budgeting. Money uses a multi-screen, step-by-step process to drag you kicking and screaming through this painful process. You'll be asked to classify every account by its use (long-term savings, daily expenses, etc.), specify how much Money you set aside for those uses, factor in your debts and loans, and provide budget numbers for applicable categories. Money then provides a forecast given your input and offers to monitor your budget, warning you when it slips.

Planning. Microsoft Money's Lifetime Planner asks specific questions about your income, tax rate, retirement accounts, expected rate of return, assets, debts, and expenses. Then it delivers the verdict: Is your plan going to work or will you be eating cat food when you're 70? Suggestions for improving your chances of financial success are offered, and Money will remind you periodically of how you're doing at staying on track (see Figure 16).

Figure 15

The Microsoft Investor Web site viewed from Money's internal browser.

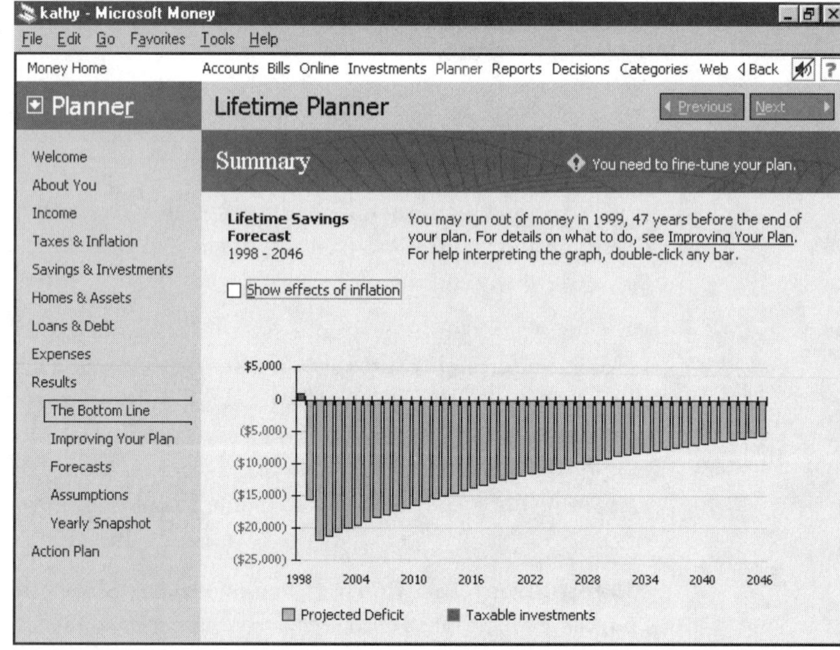

Figure 16

The Lifetime Planner tells you how your plan should work—and when it needs more information to decide that.

Debt reduction. Anyone who's ever watched a financial talking head expound on the evils of credit card debt knows that the best investment you can make is to get rid of those nasty 18% finance charges. If you have much outstanding debt, Money will show you just what a bad idea that is by showing you how much you could save in interest by paying off those cards, and the right way to do it. Enter information about your debts, and Money will spit out the most efficient payment plan to get you out of debt sooner, with less money going to interest.

Reports. Like Quicken, Money includes multiple customizable report formats. One that debuted in 1997 is particularly innovative: the monthly report. Typical personal finance reports include laundry lists like income and expenses for a given period, or investment performance by account. This new, lengthy report outlines all major financial events for the previous month, like the top five expense categories, a graph of your net worth, a budget forecast, and progress on your debt reduction (more on that later). Very useful. Very smart. Very overdue.

Quicken 99 vs. Money 99: A Quick Recap

Quicken and Money are so evenly matched in terms of what they do that it may well be the *how* they do it that helps you decide which is best for you. Here's a quick recap of what they both do:

- Keep track of all financial accounts you have.
- Let you record related transactions.
- Depending on what banks and brokerages you use, let you transact your business with them online.
- Remind you of financial transactions due before it's too late.
- Help you prepare for tax time by categorizing transactions and other tax-related tools.
- Create customizable reports on every aspect of your financial picture.
- Help you budget, get out of debt, and plan for the future.
- Pull related information from the Web and plop it in the right places within the programs.
- Include an embedded Web browser that lets you do Web work without leaving.
- Guide you with informative help files, exceptional navigational tools (including Web-like forward and back buttons), and data entry tools every step of the way.

Quicken and Money were built with the consumer in mind, so naturally both deal primarily with issues you face in your personal finance dealings. Intuit recognized that many small businesses—especially those that don't have extensive payroll or inventory-processing needs—don't necessarily need the power of small business accounting programs like QuickBooks or Peachtree. So in 1997 the company introduced Quicken Home and Business, a version of Quicken that incorporates some of the tools most commonly needed by very small businesses, like invoicing and expanded accounts receivable reporting. As this book goes to press, Microsoft is expected to introduce a similarly expanded version of Money, Microsoft Money Personal and Business.

Tax Software

Really, the question isn't why you should use tax preparation software, but why not? There are only two reasons why you shouldn't: Your tax return is too complicated or your tax return is too simple.

Tax software:

- cuts the time it takes you to fill out forms
- prevents avoidable and potentially costly errors
- may help lower your liability
- is easy to use and inexpensive
- gives you a better understanding of the U.S. tax code, which helps you to plan better for future tax years

If you can fill out a 1040 on a lunch break, you don't need tax software. But if doing your taxes manually takes too much time, or you think you may be missing some deductions, tax software can help. The typical profile of a tax software user is a homeowner who has W-2 income, simple investments, and standard deductions (medical, day care, and so on). Self-employed people, those with substantial investment income, and others with potentially complicated tax situations may want to think twice about using tax software. Likewise, complex issues like depreciation and rental property aren't always handled thoroughly or understandably by tax software, and obscure forms you might need to deal with, for example, those reporting foreign income, are sometimes missing. No software is as flexible as a professional preparer or as savvy about potential deductions as the best accountant.

If you're currently using the services of a tax accountant but want to take a crack at using tax software to reduce billable hours, ask your accountant how he or she would feel about checking over your return after you've completed it. If your accountant finds a missed deduction, you'll still be ahead, since reviewing your return should take fewer hours than doing it from scratch. Alternatively, you might figure your own return using tax software *and* have your accountant prepare it, too. Then compare the results.

Your choices for commercial tax preparation software are two: Intuit's TurboTax and Block Financial Software's TaxCut. You can also now do your tax preparation on the Web. The Intuit and Block sites offer secure Web-based preparation for a small fee, as do several others, like SecureTax (**www.securetax.com**).

If you opt to do your taxes on the Web, be advised that this option lacks the depth of guidance and informational resources that are packed into the shrink-wrapped tax packages. You can find lots of tax help online, scattered among dozens of other sites, but the tax prep sites don't pull it all together like shrink-wrapped software. You can also find lots of sites hosted by accountants that basically use the Web as a point of contact. They'll ask you a series of questions at the site, talk to you by phone, and then prepare your taxes—for fees starting at $75-150, depending on complexity.

The Interview Interface

While the neatly aligned little rows and boxes on the 1040 would lead you to believe that tax preparation is a linear process, if you've ever done anything more than a 1040EZ, you know that's not true. Tax software takes what is a decidedly non-linear process and makes it linear. TurboTax and TaxCut do this through what's called the "interview" method of entering tax data. In other words, they ask you a series of questions that, based on your responses, progressively home in on your specific tax liabilities, just like a good CPA would do. When you're done you have a filled-in form—or forms, depending on your tax profile.

If this creeps you out, you can always fill in onscreen facsimiles of IRS forms, entering data as you would on paper. If you come to a line on the 1040 that requires a supporting document, the program will shunt to it and let you enter figures there. When you're finished, you can jump back to the 1040, and the total from the document you just completed will tag along with you. Even

if you opt for the straight data-entry option, it's a good idea to run quickly through the interview questions before you finish working on your form, just in case you missed a deduction or some income you must claim. The interview identifies any additional worksheets, forms, and schedules you may need.

As you go, instead of moaning about IRS instructions, you can pop up explanations of deductions, calculations, and exemptions that actually read like plain English. Again, neither the programs nor their technical support staff can give you tax advice. All they can do is ensure that you understand what's being asked and suggest outside resources to consult for further clarification.

Once you've completed your return, though, TurboTax and TaxCut comb it for errors and omissions and alert you to them, helping you fix them before you file.

While the best tax programs offer dozens of IRS forms, you may need one that's not supplied. Or you may be warned that a particular calculation—like depreciation—may be too complex to handle. Be forewarned that even if you choose to use tax software you may still need to pick up some extra forms, talk to a CPA, or consult other IRS documentation.

Reducing Your Tax Bill

If all tax preparation products did was automate the process of filling out tax forms, they would still be worth the money (usually less than $50) for all but the simplest returns—but they do more. Here's how they can actually help you cut your tax bill:

- **Hidden deductions.** If you select the interview option, the program may guide you toward deductions you're entitled to but haven't previously taken.
- **What-if scenarios.** It's too much paperwork for most of us to explore different ways of filing, such as comparing the merits of Married Filing Separately to Married Filing Jointly. Tax software makes it easy.
- **Tax forecasting.** Every program gives you some idea of your tax liability for the upcoming year based on your current income and expenses, along with projected tax rates, amounts, and regulations.
- **Built-in auditing.** This function checks for any discrepancies in forms and schedules, for fields that were left blank, and for figures that seem unusually high or low. The latter could save you the hassle of an IRS audit or the pain of a penalty if you entered a figure incorrectly.

Filing

You have a couple of different options for filing. Some people use their tax package like a souped-up calculator and fill in the actual IRS form by hand. Who knows why, since you can also print IRS-approved forms all filled out and ready to sign. If you have a modem, you can file your return electronically, speeding up your refund (if any). E-filing is free if you use TurboTax or TaxCut, though you'll have to pay a small fee (less than $20) if you use a tax prep Web site.

Once you've filled out your federal form, you can export the pertinent data right into the appropriate state module (a state-tax add-on that usually costs extra).

TurboTax vs. TaxCut

Tax software, like personal finance, is dominated by two programs: TurboTax and TaxCut. Here's a quick rundown on their pros and cons.

TurboTax. Intuit's TurboTax, the most popular tax program, has traditionally been just a smidge ahead of TaxCut in terms of its power and usability. The version available for the 1998 tax year took on a more Web-like appearance, as it added frequently asked question links to many of its hundreds of screens, making it easier to get help quickly to the most common quandaries (see Figure 17). It also brought every important element of the program together skillfully. As you work your way through the interview, you can see the current question, the related form or schedule, and an outline of the interview topics.

Figure 17

TurboTax, always good, is better than ever for the 1998 tax year thanks to a major interface overhaul.

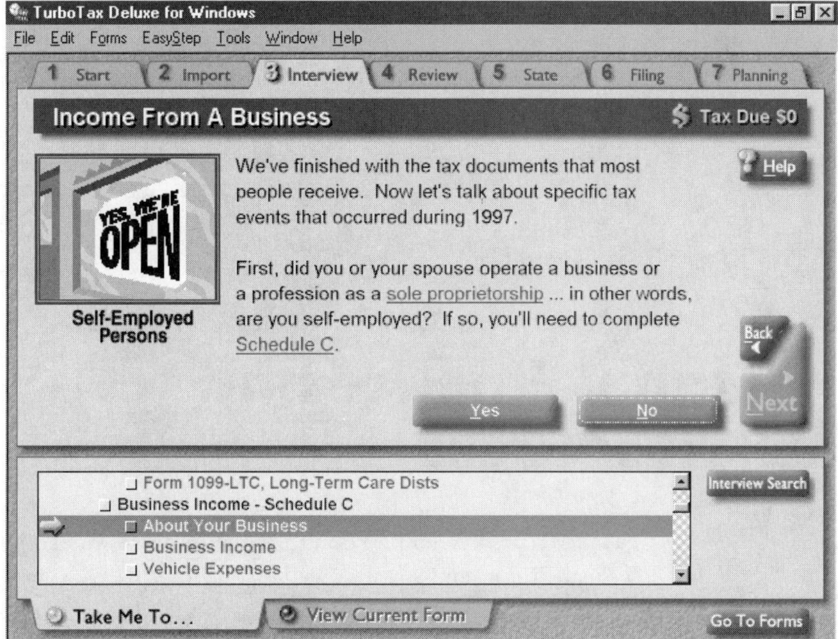

TurboTax has made the interview process even easier with its Fast Track feature. If you know up front that you're not likely to need to go through a good portion of the interview questions, you can select from a series of boxes the issues that are likely to apply to your return, and the interview will only go through those portions.

Another recent innovation from Intuit is an IRA Planner that lets you know if you're eligible to contribute to the new Roth IRA and whether you can roll over funds from a traditional IRA. In an effort to encourage taxpayers to file electronically, Intuit is allowing households with incomes of $20,000 or less to prepare and file electronically absolutely free.

Intuit continues to support sole proprietors with its TurboTax Home & Business, which contains all the features of the original TurboTax along with extra help related to the Schedule C, an interview designed to help you maximize deductions for your home office, and a business tax planner. You can also print 1099s and W-2s, as well as W-3 and 1096 forms.

TaxCut. Block Financial Software's Kiplinger TaxCut has been duking it out with Intuit's TurboTax for years. It contains the same core elements found in TurboTax. Quicken and Money differ mostly not in what they do but *how* they do it; the same goes for TaxCut and TurboTax.

TaxCut offers a similar set of forms and schedules, and lets you import files from last year's program or from Quicken and Money. It gives you the option of filling out the IRS forms themselves or being led by the hand through the interview. It checks your return for errors and lets you file electronically or in hard copy.

Block introduced a new product for the 1998 tax year: Kiplinger TaxCut for Business. It looks and works like the original product, but with many more forms and schedules: over 400 in all, including Forms 1120 and 1120-S, 1065, 940, and 941.

Personal Finance and Tax Resources

`quicken.com` Even if you don't use the software, you should check out the Web site. Quicken 99 grabs a lot of data from the Web anyway, but the Quicken.com site offers a lot of tools, data, and related links to anyone needing help with personal finance issues. Topics include investments, home and mortgage, insurance, banking and credit, retirement, saving, and taxes. Focused forums are available. All site content is free.

`www.moneycentral.com` Microsoft used to maintain separate sites for personal finance and for investments, but they recently combined these into a personal finance supersite. It also incorporates Microsoft HomeAdvisor, a one-stop shop for finding, financing, and buying a home. Some of the investment features require a $9.95/month subscription fee.

www.bankrate.com Want to find out the best rate today on a five-year CD? What is today's average for home equity loans is? Bank Rate Monitor is a great site for that kind of information. Updated daily, it's a collection of non-investment financial rates for services like mortgages, credit cards, auto loans, money market accounts and CDs, checking and ATM fees, home equity loans, and online banking. BRM staff members monitor related rates nationwide and help you find the best deal locally or nationally. A free service. Articles and news stories augment the numbers.

financenter.com This useful little site does only three things, but it does them well. Over 100 calculators in areas like IRAs, credit lines, and mutual funds are joined by links to other financial service providers (car-shopping, loan exploration, financial advice via e-mail, etc.) and answers to questions about personal finance issues. Free.

investorama.com Investorama offers free tools and data for investors, but its best feature is its directory to investment-related Web sites, organized by category.

www.turbotax.com Like its sister site Quicken.com, the TurboTax Web site is a combination of support resources for the shrink-wrapped product and tools, informative articles and forums, and related links for anyone struggling with tax issues.

www.irs.ustreas.gov *The Digital Daily*, hosted by the IRS, is chock full of the kinds of things you need during tax season: official forms and schedules, statistics, news, and answers to questions about the 1040 and its close friends.

el.com/elinks/taxes Search engines can be great tools sometimes, but they often return a lot of junk. Try a targeted link page like this to get a list of tax-related sites that someone has actually looked at, instead of an undigested list of sites that contain the word "tax."

Personal Finance for Dummies, Eric Tyson (2nd ed., 1996: ISBN 0764550136). Frankly, Quicken and Money are competent enough tutors that you can probably learn all you need to know from reading their help files and grabbing articles from their Web sites. But if you'd rather hold a book in your hands and take a more linear approach to your education, this *Dummies* book is worth your time and money.

16

Databases

by Robert Lauriston, Richard Scoville, and Kathy Yakal

The sections "What Is a Database?" "Database Do-It-Yourself Basics," "Using Microsoft Access," and the first two sections of "The Relational Database Debate" are by Richard Scoville. "Accounting Software" and "Contact Managers and PIMs" are by Kathy Yakal. The rest of this chapter is by Robert Lauriston.

In This Chapter

A lot of people hear "database" and think of a program like Microsoft Access, but that's mistaking the tool for the task. A database is really the information itself: your check register, a library catalog, a warehouse's inventory, an airline's schedule and reservations.

In many cases, the best tool for managing such databases is not a programmable database manager like Microsoft Access or FileMaker Pro, but an off-the-shelf program like Quicken, ACT!, or PeachTree Accounting. For other tasks, the spreadsheet or word processor you already own may be plenty. When off-the-shelf programs can't cut it, you may be better off hiring a professional database programmer to create a custom application than trying to create your own.

In this chapter, we'll describe the various software tools available to help you figure out the most appropriate approach for the data management tasks you have in mind. We'll also give you quick tutorials in creating your own database applications with the two most popular programs, Access and FileMaker, and offer some tips on when and how to call in a professional.

What Is a Database?

Damn! Aunt Lizzie's birthday was yesterday, and you really need to send her a card. Now you remember she's moved to a condo somewhere in Florida. Good thing she sent you that postcard with her new address. It's right here in this box, somewhere amidst the old Christmas cards, family photos, high school report cards, those letters from that guy that used to hang around at the shore, papers from last semester's creative writing class, old Halloween candy, and a lot of other stuff. Now if you can just find it.... Maybe what you need is a database.

Database, shmatabase—what are we talking about here? A *database* is simply a collection of facts that's been organized (*structured*) in some way so that you can use it to answer questions. Your box of junk is definitely not a database. But a phone book is: it's arranged in alphabetical order so you can get answers to questions like "What's Joe Smith's address and phone number?" So are everyday lists such as bus schedules or an old-fashioned library card catalog.

Obvious? Yes, but reflect for a moment that the questions you can answer with a database depend upon how the facts have been structured: a phone book is great for finding someone's phone number if you have the person's name, but it's lousy at answering questions like "Who lives at 100 Oak Street?" or "Who's phone number is 919-555-1234?"

The appealing thing about computerized databases is that they let you organize lots of facts in various ways and then search them very quickly. Your business and personal life is no doubt replete with facts that would be a lot more useful if they were organized into a PC database: recipes, check register, family budget, household inventory, business contacts, etc., etc. ("What can I make with this half-empty jar of artichoke hearts?")

Alas, there is a price to pay. When you're thinking of creating a PC database, consider these somewhat disheartening facts of life:

- The structure of a database determines its ability to answer your questions. The more involved the questions, the more intricate the structure has to be.
- Designing a good database structure is difficult. Designing one that will answer every question you might ever feel like asking may be next to impossible.

So what's a poor PC pilgrim to do? Take heart! And follow these guidelines:

- **If possible, buy instead of build.** There are lots of specialized database programs out there that have anticipated your impulse to organize. Personal financial managers, household inventories, computerized cookbooks, business contact managers—the list goes on and on. Don't waste time building a shoddy imitation of something you can purchase for fifty bucks. See "Off-the-Shelf Data Managers" later in this chapter for an overview of several major options.
- **A database doesn't necessarily require database software!** If all you need is a list of club members for the annual fund-raiser mailing, you can do the job perfectly well with your word processor. If you need a simple list of assets with subtotals by category, use your spreadsheet. See "Using Your Spreadsheet" and "Using Your Word Processor" later in this chapter for more details.
- **Keep it simple!** If you must build your own database, think carefully and realistically about the questions you'll need to ask, and don't design the database to make it any more complex than absolutely necessary.
- **Ask for help.** It's nothing to be embarrassed about. If the questions really are complicated ("Which employees reported to supervisory positions that were vacant during the month of December?") and purchasing a solution is not feasible, then don't just hack it. Get help from someone who really understands database design and can create a structure that is equal to the task.

Off-the-Shelf Data Managers

When you buy an off-the-shelf data manager, you can expect a program that's much more powerful and polished than anything you could afford to hire a programmer to create from scratch. If the program does everything you want, that's a great deal—but if it doesn't do everything you *need*, it may be just a waste of money. Here's a quick overview of four categories of off-the-shelf data managers to consider.

Personal Finance Programs

If what you need to manage is your checkbook, credit card accounts, or investment portfolio, Quicken or its competitor, Microsoft Money, may be the best tools. See Chapter 15: Personal Finance and Tax Software, for an in-depth discussion of these two programs.

Contact Managers and PIMs

Computers are quite good at providing storage and retrieval services for all of the minutia in your personal and business life. The trick is to build a software framework that makes it easy to enter and find that information when you want to, quickly—so you're not spending so much time maintaining your information organization software that you don't have time to *use* the organized information.

Two specialized kinds of database programs work well here: contact managers and personal information managers (PIMs). They include similar features. Both have scheduling and task list tools (so you can keep track and be reminded of appointments and other things you're supposed to do) and a specialized database for storing names, addresses, phone numbers, and other information about your friends and business associates. You can use PIMs and contact managers out of the box or change some of the prefab fields to better meet your needs (like labeling a field "Favorite Beverage" or "Type of Industry"). Most have at least a notepad for storing random bits of information and let you run searches and build groupings of people to create mailing lists, for example.

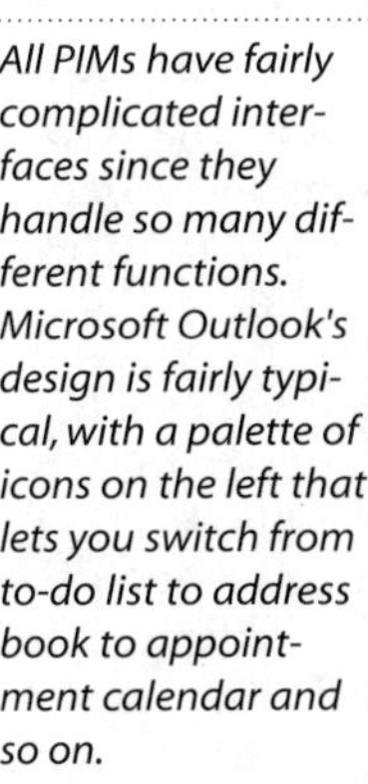

Figure 1

All PIMs have fairly complicated interfaces since they handle so many different functions. Microsoft Outlook's design is fairly typical, with a palette of icons on the left that lets you switch from to-do list to address book to appointment calendar and so on.

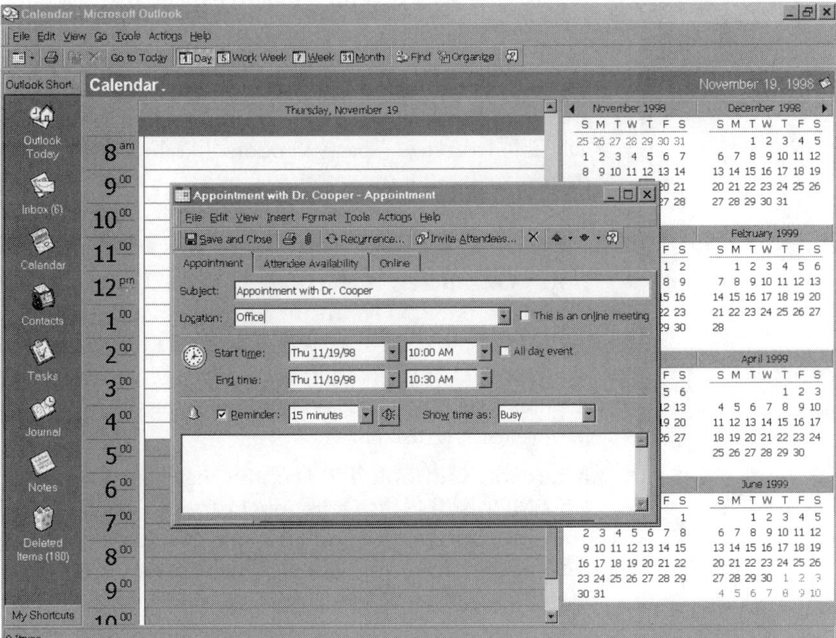

The biggest difference between PIMs and contact managers is this: Contact managers are designed to help professionals coordinate their ongoing, intricate business relationships with their clients, to both keep them copacetic and bring in sales, so tasks and appointments can be tied to clients or groups of them; some offer additional tools geared to sales and marketing professionals, like telemarketing scripts. PIMs are built for more personal use. Prices range from under $100 for PIMs to $200 to $300 for contact managers.

- **ACT!** Symantec's ACT! may or may not have been the first contact manager to market, but it was the first one that really caught on. Today, it's still a favorite, especially among sales professionals. ACT!'s simplicity and usability, as well as its customizability (which makes it a good tool for people in many professions) contribute to the product's success. It's available for several platforms, including Windows CE and the Apple Newton. Symantec also sells a link to the PalmPilot. ACT!'s popularity over the years has prompted Symantec and other companies to create compatible products and links that extend ACT!'s reach, like an expense tracker, business card scanner, and real estate manager software.
- **Day-Timer Organizer.** From the people who brought you that huge line of paper organizers comes an electronic version. Day-Timer Organizer is best-suited for personal or casual business use, owing to its emphasis on easy operation and the absence of the sales automation features found in more traditional contact managers. Naturally, data collected can be transferred to paper Day-Timer products and handheld PCs.
- **GoldMine.** GoldMine, from GoldMine Software, is a heavy-duty workgroup contact manager and sales force automation package, arguably the best for serious business use because of its superior networking capabilities. Going well beyond standard contact management requirements, GoldMine packs on tools for sales forecasting and analysis, history tracking, and lead source analysis. Its portability also makes it a good choice for a big sales organization; you can synchronize local and remote databases and links to PDAs. Like ACT!, GoldMine has many add-ons and services available from third-party vendors, like links to accounting software and project managers, programs that enhance existing GoldMine functions (like caller ID and mass-mailing creation), and e-mail/fax/Web-related add-ons.
- **Lotus Organizer.** If you don't need the latest whiz-bang features and just want a simple PIM for maintaining your address book, calendar, and to-do list, Organizer will serve you well. Its tabbed notebook look is friendly and familiar, and operation is a no-brainer. Lotus has added groupware features in recent years and plopped it into its SmartSuite, but it still works best as a single-user PIM.
- **Microsoft Outlook.** It's a contact manager! It's a PIM! Actually, it's both. This Microsoft Office component tries to play both sides of the fence and doesn't excel at either. Still, it sports standard scheduling, e-mail, and contact database features, with some competent groupware functions, and costs you nothing if you already have Office.

Accounting Software

A few years ago, there were over a dozen Windows-based small business accounting programs. Today, you need seriously consider only three companies' products. They all handle the group of procedures known as double-entry accounting—otherwise known as the rules you must follow to keep your accountant and the IRS happy. They help you set up a core group of accounts, process your receivables and payables, track your inventory and employee payroll, and perform other money-related tasks, like basic job costing and time billing. They also create and print forms, like invoices and checks and purchase orders, and generate myriad reports. And they're all network capable. The average cost is between $150 and $200.

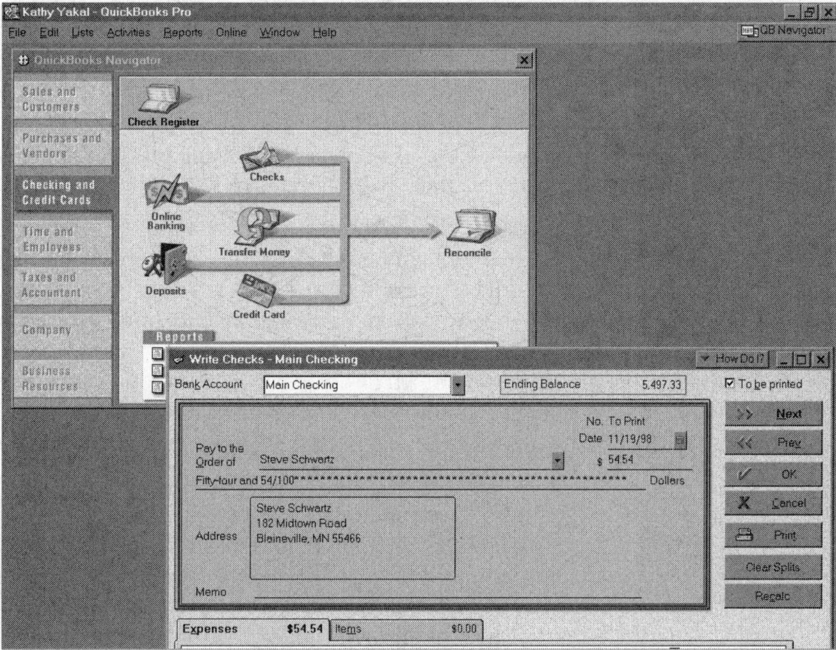

Figure 2

QuickBooks uses the same kind of easy-to-understand checkbook metaphor as Quicken.

Accounting software can help you improve your financial bottom line and make your accounting chores easier and less error prone. Rather than just managing your cash flow day to day, you can get a clearer sense of how your business is doing and where your financial logjams are.

You can use these products as is, out of the box, or customize some of their elements to better meet your individual needs. The three market leaders have varying degrees of usability, power, and flexibility, and each has its own way of doing the same thing. Still, they're fairly evenly matched. Unless you have particularly demanding needs in one area or another, especially inventory, any of them will serve you well. These products are best suited to businesses with only a few million dollars in revenue (or far less) and fewer than roughly 25 employees. Larger or more complex companies must step up to the next class of accounting products.

- **M.Y.O.B. Accounting Plus.** The original Windows-based small business accounting program, M.Y.O.B. has always been simple enough for the beginner to use, but powerful enough to handle the bookkeeping tasks required by small businesses. The most recent version, 8.0, contains time billing tools suitable for the professional. Links to Excel, Microsoft Word, and WordPerfect let you easily move your accounting data into other applications for additional analysis and marketing development. M.Y.O.B. pioneered some of the standard interface features that other accounting programs now use.
- **Peachtree Accounting.** Peachtree Software's flagship Windows program, Peachtree Accounting for Windows, is roughly comparable to M.Y.O.B. and Intuit's QuickBooks in power and usability. It has several sister programs, two of which are of particular interest to the small business community. Peachtree Complete Accounting Plus Time and Billing is probably the most robust accounting product available in this price range, and is thus overkill for many small businesses.
- **Peachtree Office Accounting**, the most recent entry from Peachtree Software, is roughly equivalent to Peachtree Accounting for Windows, with a unique twist: it comes with several "EZ Add-Ins," small applications that help you move Peachtree data into Microsoft Office applications and further manipulate it. Peachtree Office goes further with this integration than M.Y.O.B. For example, you can have reminders sent from Peachtree to Outlook, or make global price changes in Excel.
- **QuickBooks.** Intuit's QuickBooks incorporates the same usability that made its sister product, Quicken, so popular with personal finance software users. It comes in two flavors: QuickBooks, the basic small business accounting product, and QuickBooks Pro, which adds time tracking, estimating, and job costing. The latter is also network ready. Like the Peachtree products, QuickBooks lets you do your banking and bill-paying chores online. Intuit recently introduced an integrated online payroll service that handles your tax payments and direct deposits and prints and mails W-2s.

Industry-Specific Software

Depending on your business, there may be industry-specific database programs out there that will meet your needs. For librarians, there are card-catalog programs; for realtors and landlords, property management programs; for lawyers, calendaring programs and deposition summary catalogers; for physicians, special programs for managing HMO paperwork.

There are literally thousands of such programs, all mostly unknown outside of their target industry, and often not very well known even there. The best way to find out what's good is to get recommendations from other people in your business. Failing that, check out articles in trade publications, and check references before investing in the software. Note that such products are often sold by consultants who expect to be paid well; check their references, too, and see "The Consultant from Hell" later in this chapter for additional warnings.

Create Your Own Database

If off-the-shelf products won't handle your data management tasks, it's time to consider creating your own. We'll first cover the basic concepts involved in designing a custom database; then we'll get into the specifics of creating one using:

- **Your spreadsheet.** You might be surprised what a powerful database manager is built into Excel and its competitors.
- **Your word processor.** No good for most tasks, but if your only data management task is maintaining a mailing list, you may need nothing else.
- **FileMaker Pro.** The one database manager that's truly easy to use, this program (still owned by Apple Computer as this book goes to press) should be able to handle any task you'd want to tackle without the assistance of a professional database designer.
- **Microsoft Access.** The most popular database manager, while not nearly as friendly as FileMaker, has few limitations that can't be overcome with sufficient time and money.

The Also-Rans

Access and FileMaker aren't the only databases around, but they're by far the most popular: according to market research firm PC Data, they accounted for 90 percent of PC sales in 1997. The next three, Alpha Software's Alpha Five, Lotus Approach (bundled with Lotus SmartSuite), and Corel Paradox (bundled with some versions of Corel WordPerfect Suite), had only a few percent each.

In addition, of the five programs, FileMaker's by far the easiest to use, and Access is the most powerful. Hence, there didn't seem to be much point in discussing the also-rans in detail, the way we did in previous editions. We figured the space would be put to better use by devoting it to the software people are actually using.

Database Do-It-Yourself Basics

In today's database software, structure follows a standard scheme. An excellent analogy is a filing system based on index card files, as shown in Figure 3. In this system, a *database* consists of at least one *table*, where a table is like a box of index cards that all store information about a single kind of item or event. Take one card from one of the box, and you'll be holding a *record* of data. Imagine that the cards have been printed especially for this project, and each has predefined slots to hold data. Each slot is called a *field*, and each field has certain *properties*, including, most important, a name and a *data type*, which determines the kind of data that you can put in the field. (The basic data types are text, number, and date, with special variations for specific purposes.) The actual data that you enter into a field is called a *value*.

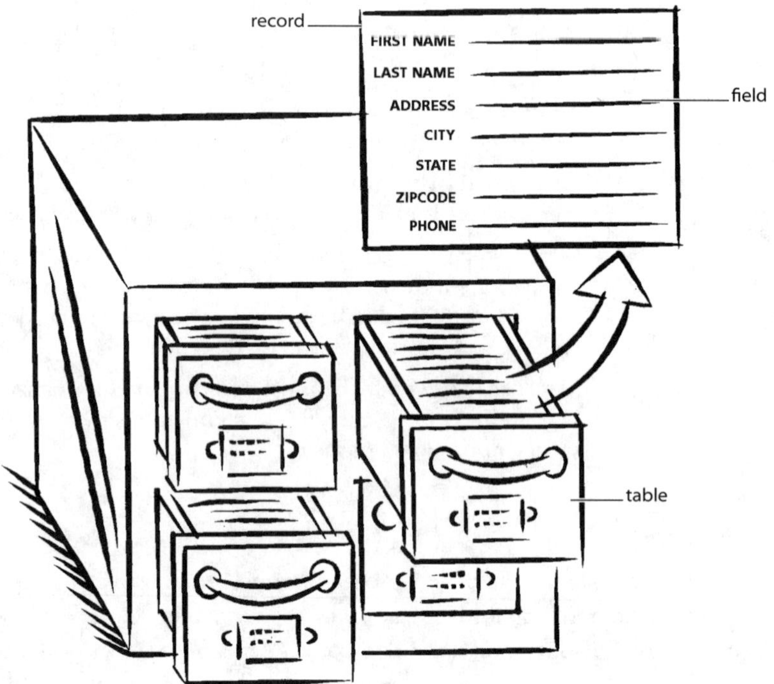

Figure 3

A database is like a card filing system. Each box of cards is a table. Each card is a record, and every line on the card is a field.

The problem that the database builder faces is how to take a higgledy-piggledy heap of facts and organize them into tables, records, and fields. Database design, as you might imagine, can be a highly technical discipline, but if you're determined to build your own database, we can at least offer a few rules of thumb to get you started:

- **When in doubt, break it out!** In general, it's better to break big facts down into small ones and create fields to hold the pieces. For instance, instead of a single field called NAME, it's almost always preferable to create separate fields for first and last names; that way, you can easily sort or select the data based on either the first or last name alone. And if you need to print a list that combines the first and last names, its easy to do, as you'll see later in the Access tutorial (see the section "Using Microsoft Access"). Similarly, addresses are customarily broken out into street address, city, state, and zip code.

- **Avoid redundancy.** Don't enter the same fact in more than one field. Let's say you're tracking people's body density. You create a database with fields for weight in pounds, height in inches, and body density. But if you have the height and weight, you don't need to store the density, because you can have your software calculate and display it whenever it's needed. [The formula is $702*(W/H^2)$. The ideal is somewhere around 22. Go figure—then get some exercise.]
- **Store the raw numbers; use the software to calculate results.** Let's say you're a teacher using a database to automate your grade book. You set up a field for the mid-term examination. Should you make it a text field and put in A, B, C, etc.? Or should you create a numeric field and enter the raw test scores? If you follow the latter approach, you get a lot more flexibility: you can combine the scores with others to create an average score; you can weight the scores, or grade on the curve, changing the threshold score required for an A. If you just enter A's and B's, you're stuck.

  Similarly, if you need to track people's ages, don't create a number field and enter the ages as 17, 21, 39, and so on. That way, the data is accurate only until someone has a birthday. Instead, set up a date field and enter birth dates. You can subsequently calculate people's ages by subtracting the birth date from any reference data you like.
- **Use text fields for phone numbers, zip codes, Social Security numbers, and the like.** These numbers aren't actually values: they're just arbitrary sequences of characters used for purposes of identification. They must be stored as text, since they sometimes begin with trailing zeros that would be stripped from a number field, and they may include punctuation that would be invalid in a numerical value.
- **Every table needs a key.** A *key* is a value that uniquely identifies each record in the table. Keys can help prevent duplicate entries in a table and avoid ambiguity when you're working with the data; they are essential elements in a relational database (which we'll discuss in a second). A table key is like the call numbers of the books in a library: a unique identifier that controls the ordering and storage of the books, identifies duplicates, and avoids confusion when two volumes share the same author or have similar titles. When you're selecting keys for your tables, it's usually best to create a numeric field and simply number the records sequentially. In fact, most database managers have a special field type or other feature that accomplishes this trick.

The Relational Database Debate

Editor's note: As you'll see from the following, Richard thinks the only good database is a relational database. I, on the other hand, used FileMaker happily for years before the program got relational capabilities, and I still haven't found them useful.

We argued about how to deal with that disagreement at some length but never managed to reconcile our positions. That argument may go on forever, but this book has to go to the printer—so we've come up with a point-counterpoint approach where we each lay out our arguments. First, Richard describes a classic database design challenge; then we each explain how we'd solve it, Richard with relations, I without.—Robert Lauriston

So what's this "relational" stuff all about? It may sound esoteric and daunting, but the essential concept is easy to grasp. Let's say that you've been assigned to create the student directory for your child's elementary school. You need a list that shows the teachers' names, room numbers, and grade levels, along with the students' names and home phone numbers (I know, I know: you've *done* your school's student directory, and it needs a lot more stuff in it. For discussion's sake, I'm keeping this very schematic. Just trust me.)

The many to one problem. "A no brainer," you tell yourself—you've been flexing your database muscles, and you're ready for anything, especially an obvious task like this. You roll up your sleeves, set to work, and soon produce a database table that looks like the one in Figure 4. In this table, each row represents a student. You begin to enter data into the table, but in a few minutes you realize that you're duplicating a lot of effort. You have to repeat all of the teacher information for each student record. It seems like a real waste of time and disk space. Also, when teacher Linda Black marries her beau Billy White, you have to make sure that you track down every one of her students' records and change "Black" to "White."

Figure 4

In this (poorly designed) table, all of the teacher information must be repeated for each student. That means wasted effort and increases the likelihood of inconsistent data.

Teacher Name	Room	Grade	Student	Phone
Patricia Smith	121	4	Bill Jones	840-3875
Patricia Smith	121	4	Mary Kendall	497-3328
Patricia Smith	121	4	Edsel Ford	516-6791
Patricia Smith	121	4	Donna Summer	517-2335
Preston Willis	201	5	Joe Schmo	961-4156
Preston Willis	201	5	Fred Freighlode	273-5543
Preston Willis	201	5	Denzel Weisel	788-4366
Preston Willis	201	5	Betty Blue	447-2690
Linda Black	145	3	Danny Deever	987-1234
Linda Black	145	3	Annie Alois	523-9812
Linda Black	145	3	Lenny Plucher	873-9492
Linda Black	145	3	Tom Crumb	482-7234

"Aha!" you think, "maybe I could do this more efficiently if I organized my data by teacher." A few more minutes with your trusty flat-file database software, and you come up with the database shown in Figure 5. At this point, you've created a whole other set of problems. First, you have to decide in advance the maximum number of students you can have in a class. If you've allowed for 25 students and you get a class with 27, you have to change the database structure to accommodate the larger number. Second, and worse, while it's easy to find a teacher, you can find students only by searching individually through the fields Student1, Student2, and so on. This is clearly not the right way to go.

Teacher	Room	Grade	Student1 Name	Student1 Phone	Student2 Name	Student2 Pho
Patricia Smith	121	4	Bill Jones	840-3875	Mary Kendall	497-3328
Preston Willis	201	5	Joe Schmo	961-4156	Fred Freighlode	273-5543
Linda Black	145	3	Danny Deever	987-1234	Annie Alois	523-9812

Figure 5

The equally poor converse of Figure 4. Here, you need separate columns for each student, and the table is almost impossible to search.

The problem with these two flat-file solutions is that your database is trying to keep track of two fundamentally different things, students and teachers, and those things have a *many-to-one* relationship: that is, there are many students for every one teacher. It's this many-to-one problem that relational databases were invented to solve.

Richard's solution: use a relational database. It's simple: Whenever you discover a many-to-one relationship in your facts, put the one and the many into separate tables and use a *key* to relate them. Figure 6 illustrates the layout for this example. The Teachers table includes the field TeacherID as the key, a unique identifying number for each teacher. The Teachers table stores only facts about the teachers. Likewise, the Students table stores data about the students, including each student's teacher, represented by the teacher's key value.

Figure 6

In this relational design, teachers and students go into separate tables, related by the Teachers table's key, TeacherID, in the Students table.

Teachers table

Teacher ID	Teacher	Room	Grade
1	Patricia Smith	121	4
2	Preston Willis	201	5
3	Linda Black	145	3

Students table

Student	Teacher ID	Phone
Bill Jones	1	840-3875
Mary Kendall	1	497-3328
Edsel Ford	1	516-6791
Donna Summer	1	517-2335
Joe Schmo	2	961-4156
Fred Freighlode	2	273-5543
Denzel Weisel	2	788-4366
Danny Deever	3	987-1234
Annie Alois	3	523-9812

Your relational database software automatically matches the key values to let you work with students and teachers together so you can enter data, ask questions, and produce reports. Such key matches are commonly referred to as *links* or *joins*.

Notice just a few benefits of this arrangement:

- Each teacher fact is stored just once. When Ms. Black marries Mr. White, you need change the teacher's name in only one place.
- A teacher can have many students or few; just put the appropriate number of records in the Students table and keep the key values straight.
- The system is modular, so you can easily expand it to include new data. If, later on, you need a directory that shows grade parents along with teacher information, you can create a new GradeParents table, mark each record with the corresponding TeacherID, and you're off and running.

And there you have it: the gist of the relational database concept. The rest is mere details (but remember, that's where the devil is!). Relational databases can get really complex: when you begin to think about the one-to-many relationships in, say, an invoicing system, things can quickly become overwhelming. Figure 7 shows a just barely sufficient set of tables for such an application, taken from Microsoft's simplified help system. In real life, the required data structure would likely be even more complex.

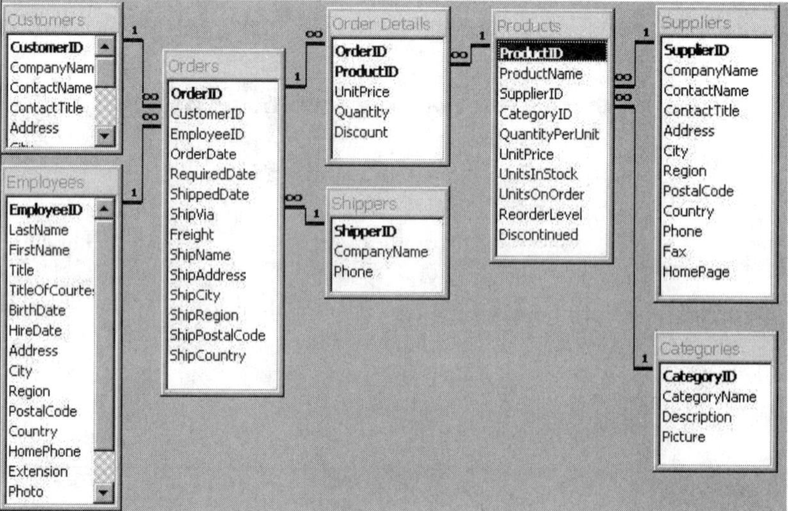

Figure 7

Tables in a slightly complicated relational database. The lines indicate many-to-one relationships between the tables.

Robert's solution: problem? what problem? Richard's student directory is a good example of how relational databases can turn simple tasks into complicated programming puzzles. In FileMaker, I'd simply put all the data for both students and teachers in the same file, just as if I were using index cards.

To avoid having to retype the teacher info over and over, I'd enter each teacher's data once, press D (Duplicate Record) repeatedly to create as many copies as there are students in the class, and enter the student data in those copies. Alternatively, I might use FileMaker's Ctrl ' keyboard shortcut, which copies the contents of the matching field from the last record you browsed. To copy a series of fields, you just press Ctrl ' and then Tab, which moves you to the next field, repeatedly until you've copied all the duplicate data.

For a big school with many teachers, I might take the time to create a separate file of teacher info, and define a *lookup* (see Figure 8) in the student directory file so that I could pick the room number from a pop-up list, and all the other teacher info would be copied automatically. (The room number's unique, so there's no need to complicate things by defining a separate key.) Creating the teacher info file and adding the pop-up list to the student directory is no more than five minutes' work in FileMaker, and I wouldn't need to redo any of the records I've already created.

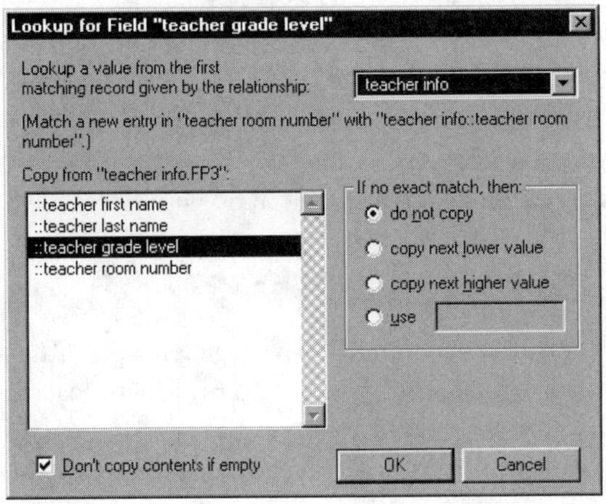

Figure 8

This Lookup dialog box tells FileMaker to copy the grade level from the "teacher info" file into the "teacher grade level" field of the student directory.

When Linda Black marries Billy White—well, here in Berkeley, she'd still be Ms. Black, so there'd be nothing to do, but if she changed her name to Starchild, I'd just do a search and replace, much as you would in a word processor. Choose Mode/Find, type "Linda" in the teacher-first-name field and "Black" in the teacher-last-name field, press Enter to display only matching records, select Black in one record, type "Starchild," and choose Mode/Replace.

FileMaker has supported relational links since version 3.0 came out in 1996, but personally I have yet to encounter a task where they seemed useful. Those data management tasks I haven't been able to handle with the kind of simpler, nonrelational approaches just described have all exceeded my database design skills.

There are data management projects that absolutely require relational links, but I think they're characterized not by many-to-one but many-to-many relationships. For example, even a small inventory management and billing database will probably have at least a dozen products and several hundred customers; each customer may have several invoices; each invoice may list several products; shipping charges will vary with the zip code; sales tax rates will vary with the state—we're probably talking about at least a dozen tables, with many different relations between them.

Sure, you'll need a relational database to handle that job. You'll also need a professional database programmer or be willing to put in long hours of study and practice to become one yourself—not a very practical option if you're busy running a business.

Using Your Spreadsheet

A spreadsheet is very similar to a database table and can be used as one, with each row's cells acting as the fields of a record, and column headings serving as field labels. All three major spreadsheets have fairly sophisticated database tools. See the "Building a Database Worksheet" section of Chapter 14: Spreadsheets, for an example of what you can do with Excel's.

Using Your Word Processor

If your database needs are limited to managing mailing lists, you may have everything you need in your word processor. A mail-merge data source (aka secondary merge document) is composed of a series of records, each with an identical set of fields (first name, last name, address, etc.), just like a database table.

Word's database tools are part of Mail Merge, perhaps the most complicated feature in the program. Unfortunately, Mail Merge is not explained terribly well in Word's online help, and we don't have the space in this book to get into the necessary detail to clear things up. I can, however, point you to Word's data-entry and query (record selection) forms. They're easy to miss, and without them Word's database features aren't much use.

1. Choose File/New, click the Letters & Faxes tab, double-click Mailing Label Wizard, and choose the mailing-list option in the next dialog box. Then choose "Create labels for a mailing list" and click OK.
2. In the Mail Merge Helper, click Get Data, choose Create Data Source, and click OK. Then type a name for the file (like "address database") and click OK to save it.
3. Click Set Up Main Document. Select the kind of labels you want to use (if you're not sure, or if you don't want labels, just pick a label type at random) and click OK.

4. Using the Insert Merge Fields button, create a mailing label field layout that looks something like the one in Figure 9, adding spaces and punctuation from the keyboard as necessary. Click OK and then click OK again to close the Mail Merge Helper.

Figure 9

Word's Create Labels dialog box.

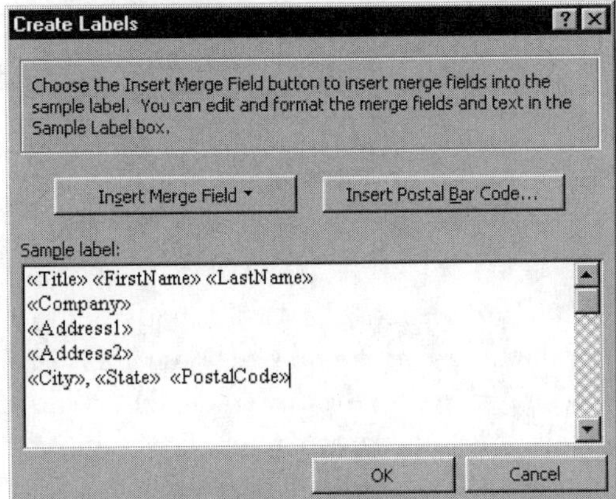

5. Click the Data Form button on the Database toolbar, as shown in see Figure 10. (If you don't see that toolbar, right-click any toolbar and choose Database.)

Figure 10

Word's Database toolbar.

Now you have access to Word's Data Form window, the data-entry interface with Word's built-in database (see Figure 11). The buttons at the bottom let you browse through records, and those at the right let you add or delete records.

Note that any changes you make to the current record are saved automatically, without a confirmation prompt, when you page to another record or click Add New—even if you close the Data Form dialog box without clicking OK.

You can use the Data Form window to edit and search any Word table, whether or not it was created with the Mail Merge Helper. Just put the insertion point in the table and click the Data Form button. You can also use this button with any Word table. The Data Form dialog box will automatically use the contents of the cells in the first row as field names.

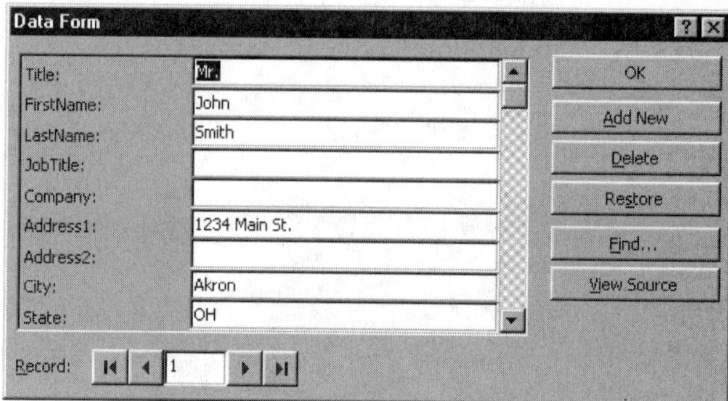

Figure 11

Word's Data Form dialog box.

Word also has a tool for selecting the records you want to use in a merge operation. Close the Data Form window, choose Tools/Mail Merge, and click Query Options. This brings up the dialog box shown in Figure 12, which you can use to select records for a particular job. For example, you can choose a range of zip codes to generate direct-mail form letters for a particular area.

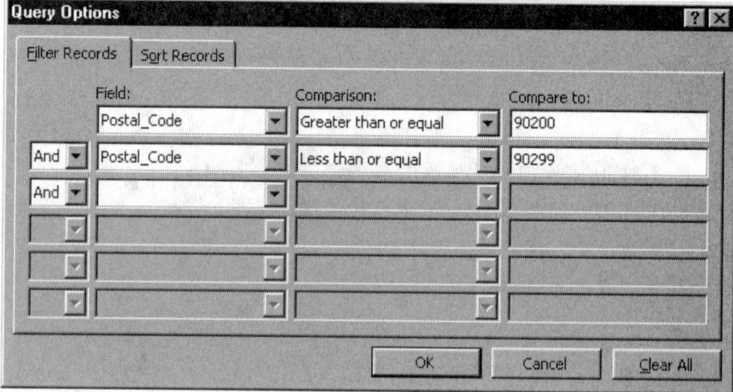

Figure 12

Word's Query Options let you select records from a mailing list.

Using FileMaker Pro

FileMaker has been one of my favorite programs for over ten years. (I started using it on the Mac in 1988, five years before the first Windows version came out.) It's one of the simplest, best designed, most elegant programs yet created. Its long history has given it a polish matched by few other Windows applications, and so far it has not succumbed to the kind of creeping featureitis that has tarnished other masterpieces of the art of programming, like Excel and Photoshop.

I've always been able to get FileMaker to do what I want it to. Two or three times I've had to call technical support to find out how to work around the program's limitations, but otherwise, I've been able to find everything I've needed to know in the excellent manual (a rarity these days) or online help—which quite definitely has not been the case with its current main competitor, Microsoft Access, or with any of the other database programs I've encountered over the years.

Bottom line: I'm convinced FileMaker can do everything most people ask of a do-it-yourself database manager. While there are projects big or complex enough that you'd be better off with Access or an industrial-strength database program like Oracle's or Sybase's, such projects are best left to professional database programmers.

The rest of this section gives you a quick overview of how FileMaker works and offers a few tips for making the most of it. If you'd like to learn more, you can download a free trial version at **`www.filemaker.com/products/trialsoftware.html`**. If you like it, you can get the full program for around $175.

FileMaker basics. One reason FileMaker's so easy to use is that it has fewer parts than other database managers. FileMaker has fields, records, and tables, though to make things easier for new users to understand, it calls the latter "files" and doesn't display them in the usual unwieldy spreadsheet-like grid. It does not, however, make the usual distinction between data-entry forms, queries, and reports: all of those functions are handled by *layouts*.

A layout can be either a single-record form or a columnar list. Most often you'll use the former type for entering data, finding records (queries), and reading individual records, and the latter for browsing records and printing, but you can use either type for any purpose by switching modes:

- To use a layout as a data-entry form, press Ctrl B (or choose Mode/Browse). To create a new record, press Ctrl N and start typing your data into the fields, as shown in Figure 13. To edit an existing record, just bring it up on the screen and make your changes. (FileMaker has various options for protecting selected fields or entire databases to prevent unauthorized users from making changes.) Changes are saved automatically as you make them, though so long as a record remains on the screen, you can undo all changes with Mode/Revert Record.

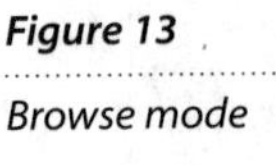

Figure 13

Browse mode

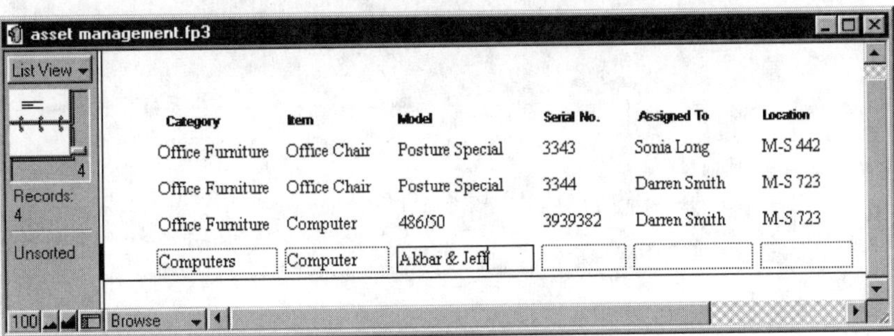

- To use a layout as a search form, press Ctrl F (or choose Mode/Find), type your search criteria into the appropriate field(s) as shown in Figure 14, and press Ctrl Enter (or click Find). Records that match the search criteria will appear in the same layout.

Figure 14

Find mode

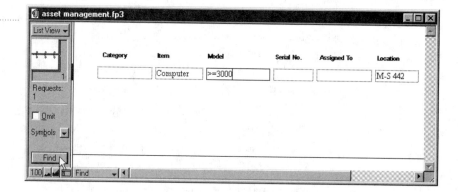

- To modify a layout, press Ctrl L (or choose Mode/Layout). Drag fields and labels around to move them, resize them by dragging their corners, add new fields by dragging the Field button from the tool palette (shown at the left of Figure 15) onto the layout.

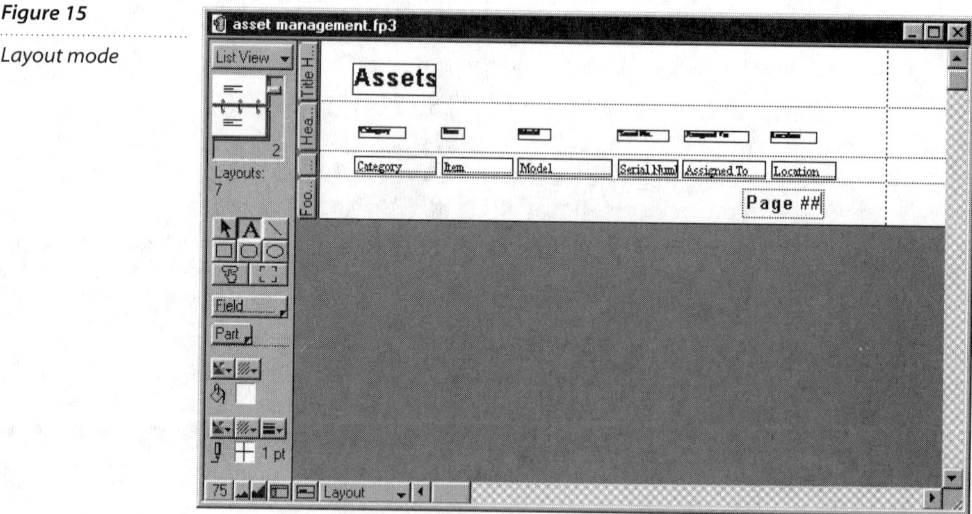

Figure 15

Layout mode

- To use a layout as report, press Ctrl U (or choose Mode/Preview) to switch to page preview mode (see Figure 16) and make sure the formatting is correct. If it is, press Ctrl P to print.

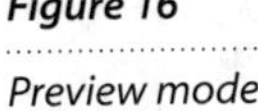

Figure 16

Preview mode

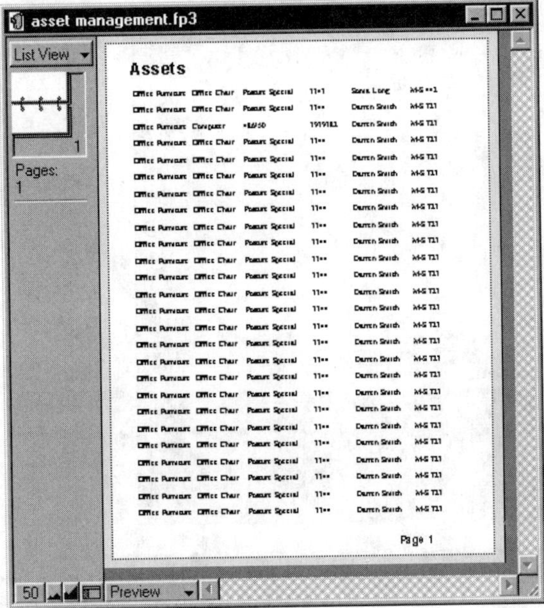

In a single-page layout, you can page through records using the Rolodex-type flip book tool or by pressing Ctrl ↓ and Ctrl ↑. In a columnar layout, you can flip through records a screenload at a time with the scroll bar or by pressing Pg Up and Pg Dn. If you want to see the details of a particular record, just click it with the mouse and switch to a single-page layout.

Defining fields. When you create a new file, FileMaker prompts you to define the fields that will store your data. For example, in a contact list, the fields might include name, telephone number, title, company name, street address, city, state, postal code, and perhaps even a scanned photograph. You can avoid this step if one of the 50-odd templates bundled with the program suits your needs, but for the purposes of this chapter, we'll assume you want to create a new file.

FileMaker makes creating fields very easy. You just type a name for each field and then check off entry options in a dialog box (see Figure 17). When you finish defining fields, FileMaker creates a basic layout containing all the fields you defined. If you wish, at that point you can immediately begin entering information into the database (see Figure 17).

If you discover that your layout doesn't hold all the information you need, you can quickly add more fields. For example, if while entering data to your contact list you realize you need a field for fax numbers, you simply choose File/Define/Fields, type "Fax number," and press Return. The Fax number field appears in the layout, and you go on entering data.

Figure 17

After you enter the field names in the Define Fields dialog box (left), FileMaker creates a basic data-entry layout (right).

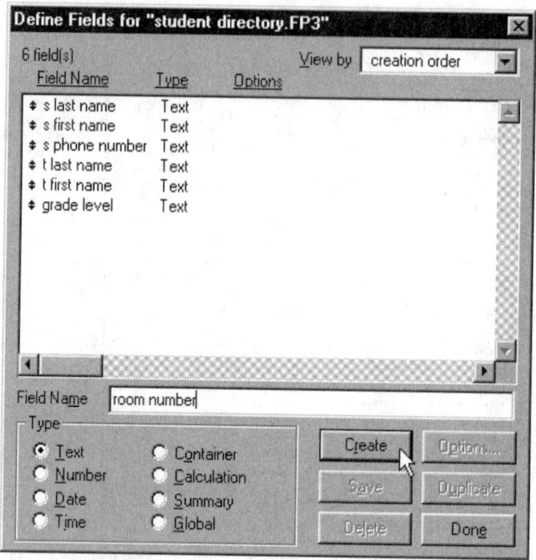

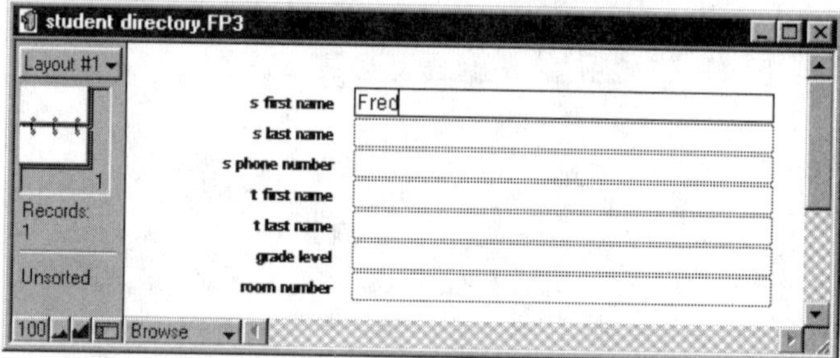

You can *validate* data entry—that is, prevent input of unacceptable data—by performing a calculation or by checking against a list or range of acceptable values, and you can write a custom message for FileMaker to display when validation fails. For example, you can prevent a record from being saved if a field is empty, require that a date be within the current year, make sure only a number is entered in a number field or that dates entered in a date field are valid, and/or allow only entries that are unique. A particularly clever validation option is Existing, which checks to make sure an entry already exists in some other record in the database.

When useful, you can define *value lists*, a list of entries for a particular field (see Figure 18). If you wish, you can block users from modifying the value list, or you can add an Other choice to the list that allows users to add new values during data entry. To make data entry easier, you can use a value list to turn a field into a drop-down menu. Press Ctrl L to switch to layout design mode, select the field, and choose Format/Field Format. Click the radio button to the left of "Pop-Up list," make the appropriate choice from "using value list," and click OK. Press Ctrl L to switch back to browse mode, click the field, and your menu appears. (See "Formatting the display of a value list" in FileMaker's online help for an explanation of additional menu options.)

Figure 18

A FileMaker value list.

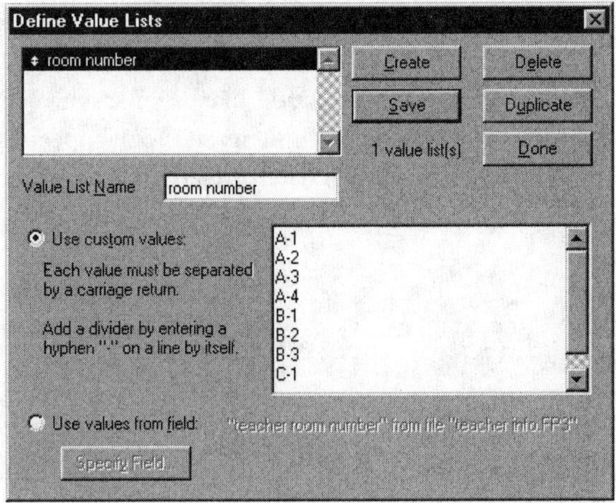

When defining fields, you can tell FileMaker to automatically enter values when a record is created or edited. For example, you can automatically insert today's date in the Date field of a new record, create fields to track the date and time a record was created and last modified, or set the default choice for a field with a value list.

One weak point in FileMaker is its lack of *masks*, which ensure that data conforms to a particular format. For example, the mask (###) ###-#### would ensure that phone numbers have ten digits and also automatically format 8005551212 as (800) 555-1212. You can accomplish the same end by using three fields and setting validation options to make sure they have 3, 3, and 4 characters, respectively, but masks are a faster and easier way to handle such tasks.

Creating and using layouts. Once you've entered data in your file, you will want to create additional layouts for various tasks. For example, for a contact list you might want to print a list of people's names, companies, and telephone numbers. Press Ctrl L to switch to layout-design mode. Then press Ctrl N and select "Columnar report" from the dialog box, and a list of all fields appears. Double-click the fields you want in the report, in the order you want them to appear, and click OK.

This new layout automatically includes column headings for each field at the top of the screen. (They'll also appear at the top of each page if you print the layout.) To add a document title above those headings on the first page, click the Part tool, drag it to the top of the layout, and select Title Header from the

Parts Definition dialog box that appears. As shown earlier in Figure 15, the layout moves down to make room for the title header, where you can type your title and any other necessary information about the report.

Other options in the Parts Definition dialog box allow you to create multipart reports. For example, you can create a contact list printout with a separate section for each state and have each section start at the top of a new page. When a report contains numerical information like expenses or revenues, each section can end with its own subtotal, with the grand total appearing on the last page (see Figure 19). (In conventional database jargon, this is a *band-oriented report generator*.)

Figure 19

The multipart layout at the top produces the report shown in part below.

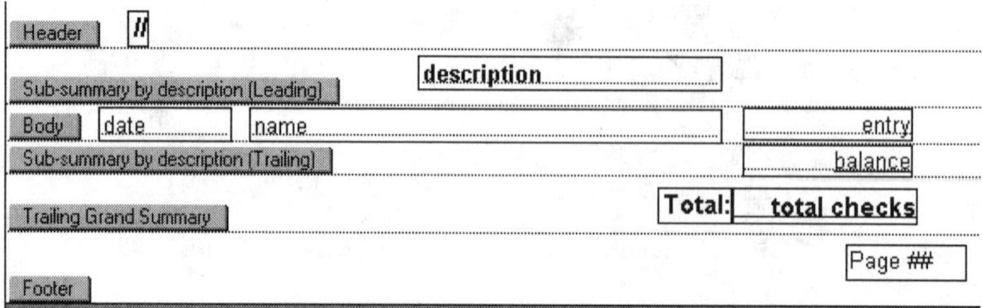

11/16/98

software

3/15.98	Office Depot	-$140.71
1/22/98	Costco	-$189.43
2/4/98	TSI*Digital River	-$37.50
4/3/98	Microsoft	$140.71
4/12/98	Magnum Commerce Services	-$29.00
4/16/98	Ipswitch Inc.	-$37.50
4/16/98	TSI*Digital River	-$99.00
6/9/98	TSI*Digital River	$99.00
		-$293.43

software rebate

6/3/98	Intuit	$50.00
		$50.00

Before you print your telephone list, you will want to put it in alphabetical order. Press Ctrl B to switch from layout-design mode to browse mode. Then press Ctrl S (or choose Mode/Sort), and you get a dialog box with a list of all the fields that appear in the current layout. To display a master list, you double-click the Last-Name field and then the First-Name field and then click Sort.

You can format a layout's text and field borders with any combination of fonts and colors you like. Fields and text labels can be easily moved and resized by dragging them with the mouse, and an Align to Grid option helps give the layout a sharp, professional appearance. FileMaker includes a line-drawing tool to help you make your layouts look more like printed forms, and you can decorate them further by pasting in graphics created in other programs.

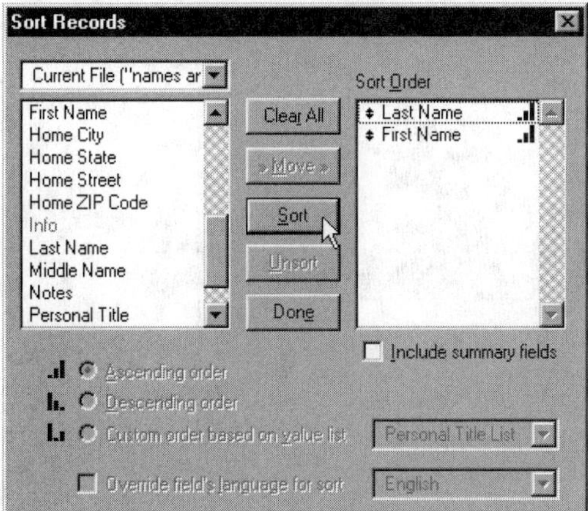

Figure 20

A FileMaker sort.

Searching a database. Once you have stored your information in a FileMaker database, it's usually easier and faster to look up something on your computer screen than to page through a printout. For example, to find all the Peachpit Press employees in your contact database, press Ctrl F, type "Peachpit" in the Company field, and click the Find button (or press Return): FileMaker hides all the records in your database except those for the people who work for this book's publisher.

By entering Find criteria in several fields, you can quickly locate just the information you need. For example, if you keep your business expenses in a FileMaker database, you can easily find all costs incurred during the past six months for clients with currently overdue accounts. Once you find the desired data, you have many options. Among many other possibilities, you can display the total expenses for each month on the screen, print a detailed list of all items, save the data to a spreadsheet file, or delete the records from the file.

Labels, envelopes, and form letters. FileMaker makes it easy to generate labels and envelopes from names and addresses in a database. Just press Ctrl L to switch to layout-design mode, press Ctrl N, select Labels or Envelope, and click OK. If you're creating labels, pick the Avery or CoStar label type from the menu and click OK. Double-click the fields in the list in the top-left part of the dialog box to format an address block similar to the one shown in Figure 21 and then click OK. Press Ctrl N to switch back to browse mode.

As you page through the records in the database, you'll see that each now has a properly formatted label or envelope. To see how labels are arranged for printing, press Ctrl U to switch to page preview mode.

To print, switch to your data-entry layout and use the Find command to bring up the records for which you want envelopes or labels. Then switch back to the envelope or label layout and print.

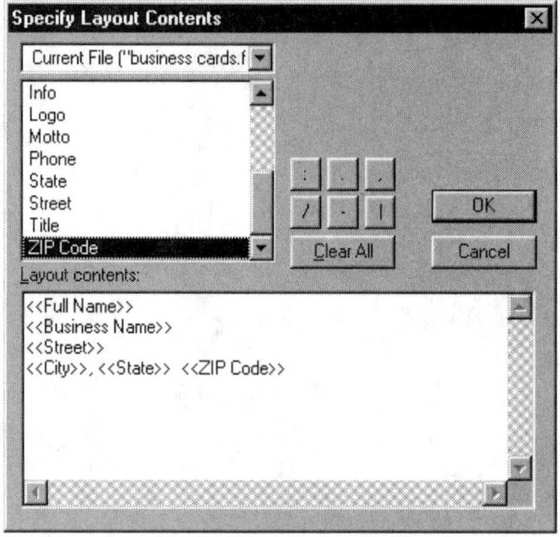

Figure 21

To print labels or envelopes, create an address block like this one. Notice how it's basically almost identical to the one shown in Figure 9—FileMaker and Word use the same double angle brackets to indicate merge fields.

FileMaker has another special layout type, "Single page form," which you can use to create form letters. The program's word processing capabilities are fairly limited, however, so you'd probably be better off handling such tasks in your word processor. Use the Find command to select records and then choose File/Import/Export/Export Records. Choose a format your word processor can merge with from the "Save as type" list (the default, tab-separated text, should work), type a name in the "File name" field, and click Save. In the left column of the dialog box that appears, double-click the fields you want to use in the merge operation (or just click Move All); then click Export. Now set up the merge operation in your word processor and use the file you just created as the data source.

Automating FileMaker with scripts. If you discover you are using the same Find or Sort criteria over and over, you can turn them into a menu or keyboard command by using a FileMaker script. You can use scripts to automate any sequence of FileMaker commands. For example, in the database I use to track my financial records, I have a script that finds all my business-related expenses, sorts them by category and date, and switches to an expense-list layout in preview mode, where I can see the category titles and subtotals. I've also defined a number of simple scripts so I can switch between various layouts and sort operations by just pressing Ctrl 1, Ctrl 2, and so on.

FileMaker on a network. FileMaker lets you share your files with up to 25 other users on a local network. (You need to buy a copy of the program for each user.) If that's not enough, you can buy FileMaker Pro Server (around $850, runs only on Windows NT), which supports up to 100 users.

Each file's creator can define different access rights for different users. For example, for an employee records database, you can specify that only members of the personnel department can create new records, and only senior management can view or change salaries.

The Macintosh and Windows versions of FileMaker not only use compatible files: they are also compatible on networks. When you have both Macs and PCs on a local network, users on both platforms can share the same file.

FileMaker on the Web. You can share a FileMaker database over the Internet or an intranet with very little effort, using any Web browser, without having to purchase any additional software. All you have to do is open the database you want to share and check the Web Companion box in its Sharing settings: instantly, your PC or Mac becomes a Web database server.

To access the database, all the other users on the network have to do is enter the IP address of your PC into any Web browser. That brings up a Web Companion page with a list of all the shared databases currently open on your computer; clicking a database on the list opens it.

The browser view of a FileMaker database is quite basic—it uses a simplified interface that's fairly similar to the database portion of Microsoft Works (see Figure 22). In place of the multiple layouts you'd see in FileMaker itself, the browser interface has only three fixed-format pages. The Table View page shows multiple records as a table; the Search page lets you find information using a typical Web-style data-entry form; and the Form View page (see Figure 23) displays a single record in a simple list format, lets you page through the database one record at a time, and changes to a data-entry form when you edit or create a record. Unlike in FileMaker itself, which saves changes automatically, you have to click a Save button when you're finished editing or entering data.

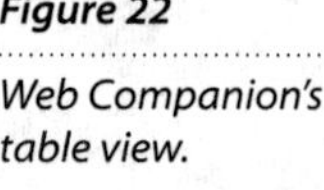

Figure 22

Web Companion's table view.

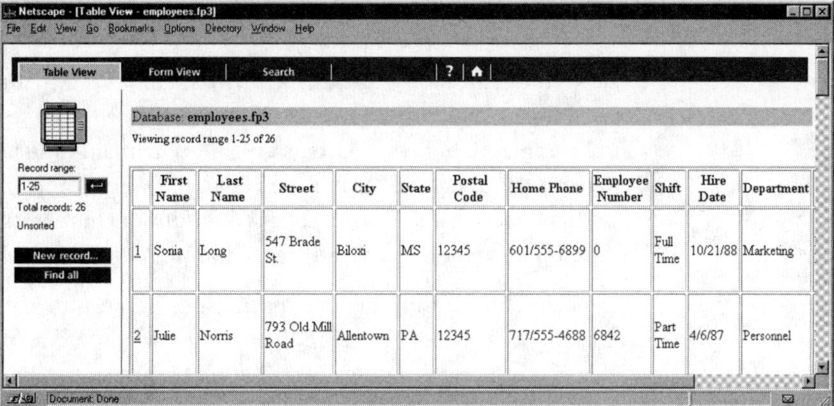

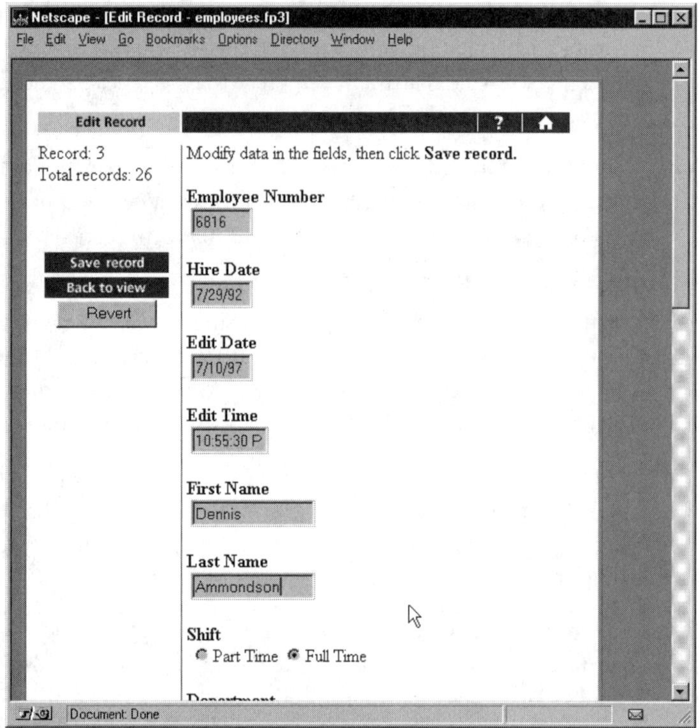

Figure 23

Web Companion's edit record form.

By default, the table, form, and search layouts display all fields. If your database has more than about six fields, this will probably be inappropriate, but it takes only a few seconds to reconfigure a layout to display only selected fields. All you have to do is select a layout for each view in the Edit/Preferences/Web Companion dialog box, and the views will change to display only the fields on those layouts. Often the database will contain appropriate layouts—if not, you can simply create new layouts or copy existing layouts and add or delete fields as necessary.

The Web Companion's Search form (which looks pretty much like the edit record form) is different from the form you get with the regular FileMaker Find command, but it's almost as capable. The main limitation compared with the regular FileMaker Find feature is that the Web Companion won't let you search for records that contain one word but not another in a particular field—for example, you can't set up a search to find "Mexico" but not "New Mexico."

The Web Companion's big drawback is that you can't change the format—for example, you can't close up the empty space in the form view to fit more fields in a browser window. Users with Web programming skills can work around this limitation using Claris Dynamic Markup Language (CDML), a set of proprietary HTML extensions, but that's way beyond the capabilities of the average FileMaker user.

Relational links. As noted earlier, FileMaker supports relational links. As you can see from Figure 24, using them is very similar to using the lookup technique mentioned toward the end of "The Relational Database Debate" (and shown in Figure 8). As I said, though, I personally have never found a need for them.

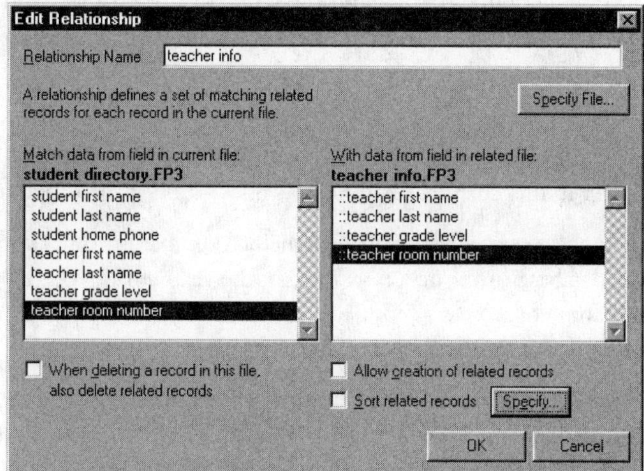

Figure 24

This simple dialog box lets you create relational links between tables and set various link options.

The "Planning a Relational Database" section of the FileMaker manual contains a decent introduction of the subject, but it doesn't explain all key concepts in the depth required to do any real work. The manual contains instructions for creating one sample relational database, but since some steps are described very vaguely and there's no explanation for any of them, it offers little help in understanding the process. The many sample databases on the CD are not much help for learning either, as none of them include explanations of why they were designed the way they were.

If you've created relational databases with other programs, you'll find FileMaker's table-linking tools easier to use and fairly self-explanatory. If you have no experience, before trying to create a relational database much more complicated than the student directory example presented in this chapter, I recommend you take a class or find a good book on database design. The class or book doesn't have to be specifically about FileMaker: the concepts are the same regardless of what program you use.

Don't let the foregoing give you the impression that Microsoft Access is any different. While its relational tools are more powerful than FileMaker's—for example, it can graphically display the database's structure (see Figure 7)—Access is much harder to use, and beginners will definitely need training or a good how-to book.

Using Microsoft Access

Yes, Microsoft Office dominates the desktop—so if you have a database program already sitting around on your PC, it's probably Access. Access serves as both a hands-on-the-data tool set for managing data and an application development environment for creating custom database solutions. Application development goes far beyond the scope of this chapter (and there are many excellent resources out there to help you if you want to move in that direction). Here we'll focus on the basics of setting up and using a simple interactive database with this powerful relational tool.

We'll use the student directory example from "The Relational Database Debate" earlier in this chapter. First, however, let's look at the program interface.

Launch Access, and you'll see a dialog box that prompts you to open an existing database or create a new one. In the real world, you might want to check out some of Access's templates to see if they can handle your task, but for this tutorial, select Blank Database and click OK.

You'll see a dialog box that prompts you to save the database file. In the File Name box, enter "StudentList." In the folder list, navigate to a folder where you'd like to store the new file and click Create. Note that, unlike most other database programs, Access stores all of the component parts of a database in a single file, with the extension .mdb. That's very convenient when you want to move the database around.

At this point, you confront a blank database window (Figure 25). There's not a whole lot to see, since your database is empty, but we can pause a moment to review the components of an Access database.

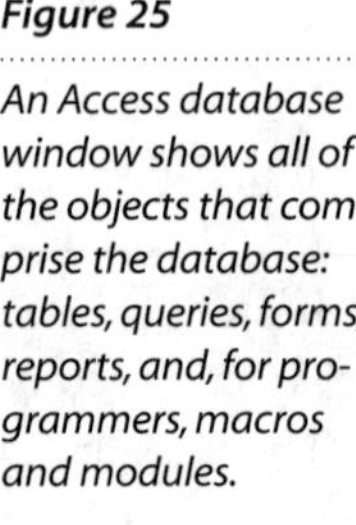

Figure 25

An Access database window shows all of the objects that comprise the database: tables, queries, forms, reports, and, for programmers, macros and modules.

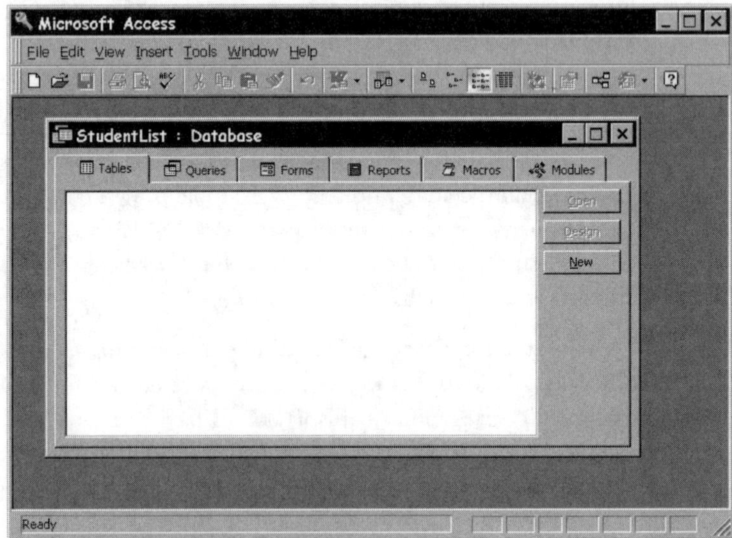

Think of a database as composed of several kinds of *objects* organized on pages that you select with the six tabs along the top edge of the database window:

- **Tables**, as discussed before, are where the data records physically reside.
- **Queries** ask questions about the data in the tables. It's useful to think of queries as filters: they let you join related tables and filter particular rows and columns for display.
- **Forms** help you enter data into the tables. You can design a form to portray the records in a sensible way, help ensure that the data you enter is correct, and help you efficiently locate records you need to edit. Forms can even work with data in more than one table at once. Professional database builders spend about half of their time carefully designing forms for their users.
- **Reports** take data from the tables, often by way of a query, and put it on paper. Report design is a necessary evil: usually, you can get a usable report by simply printing a query. Messing around with fancy report designs is usually a waste of time, unless, of course, your boss or customer requires it.
- **Macros** and **Modules** are used by database developers to automate Access applications. We won't be talking about them in this chapter.

Creating the tables. The first thing we'll do is create a couple of tables: one for the students and another for the teachers. Click the Tables tab and then click the New button on the right side of the database window. In the dialog box, select Design View and click OK.

What you see next is a new table, displayed in design view (see Figure 26). This is essentially a list of the table fields and their properties. I'll step you through the creation of the first field; you can do the rest on your own. In the first Field Name box, type "TeacherID." Then press Tab to move to the Data Type column. A drop-down selector appears; click it and select AutoNumber from the list. Now designate TeacherID as the key for this table: choose Edit/Primary Key and notice the small key symbol that appears next to the field name in the list. Also notice that the list of available properties shown in the bottom pane of the window changes as you choose different data types.

Fill in the field names for the teachers table as shown here:

Field	Data type	Field properties
TeacherID	AutoNumber	
T_LastName	Text	
T_FirstName	Text	
RoomNumber	Number	Field Size = Integer
Grade	Text	Field Size = 5

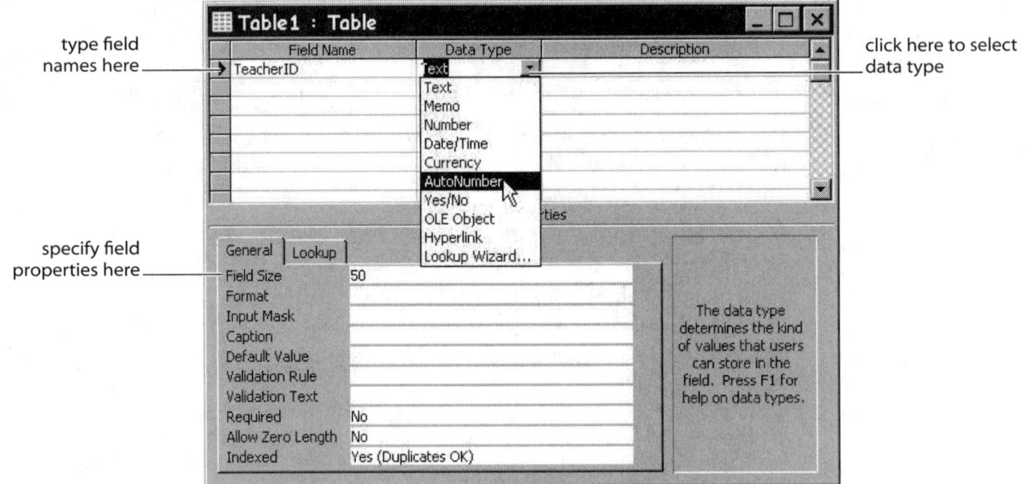

Figure 26

The top pane of the table design view contains a list of fields; you can use the drop-down list to select the data type. The bottom pane lists properties appropriate to the data type.

Before we proceed, note the following:

- The field size limits the maximum length of an entry in a text field. For numbers, it indicates the amount of storage space required for the number. Number sizes control the number of significant digits and the number of decimal places allowed.
- The AutoNumber type is actually a number field with the field size Long Integer. When you add new records to the table, Access increments AutoNumber fields automatically—just what you need for key values like TeacherID.
- We've designated the room number as a number but the grade as text because we know that grade level values will include "K" for kindergarten.

When everything's tidy, choose File/Save, name the file "TEACHERS," and click OK. Close the table.

Now for the students. Repeat the preceding procedure and set up the students table as shown in the following table. Make StudentID the key and save the table under the name "STUDENTS."

In the following table, notice that TeacherID is specified as a long integer because it must match up with the AutoNumber field in the TEACHERS table. ZipCode is a text field, perhaps counter-intuitively, because you never perform calculations with ZIP codes.

Field	Data type	Field properties
StudentID	AutoNumber	(make this field the key)
TeacherID	Number	Field Size = Long Integer
S_LastName	Text	
S_FirstName	Text	
S_BirthDate	Date/Time	
S_PhoneNumber	Text	Field Size = 14
S_ZipCode	Text	Field Size = 5

Now let's do a couple of tricks with the STUDENTS table that begin to hint at the power of Access: We'll specify the format of the phone numbers and create a lookup link between the TEACHERS and STUDENTS tables.

With STUDENTS open in design mode, select the field S_PhoneNumber. (If you get a message instructing you to insert the Office 97 Setup CD and install the Access Advanced Wizards, do so.) In the properties list at the bottom of the screen, click the Input Mask property and then click the button that appears to the right of the property name (see Figure 27). In the Input Mask Wizard, select Phone Number in the list, and in the next-to-the-last step of the wizard, select "With the symbols in the mask." Click Finish.

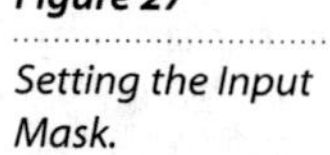

Figure 27

Setting the Input Mask.

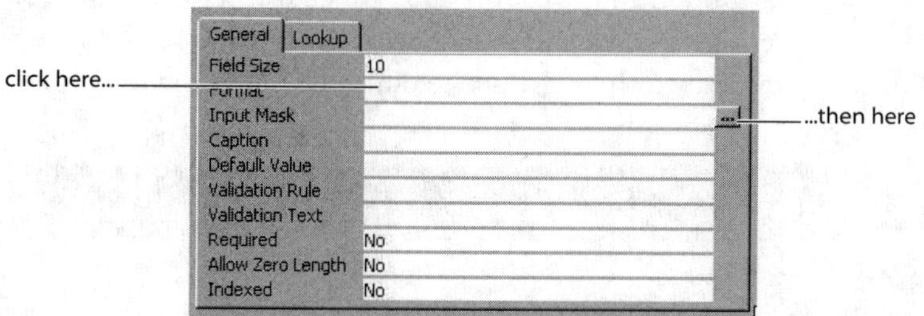

Next, select the TeacherID field. Click the Lookup tab in the properties list at the bottom of the window. Configure the dialog box as shown in Figure 28. This arrangement will allow you to select students' teachers from a list and will prevent you from assigning a student a nonexistent TeacherID. Save and then close the STUDENTS table.

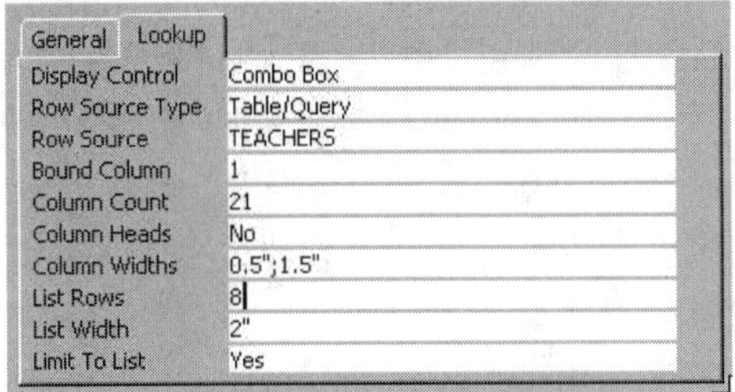

Figure 28

Setting up a lookup between STUDENTS and TEACHERS will let you pick a student's teacher from a list, instead of having to remember each teacher's ID.

Entering data. Now for the fun part: typing!

In the database window, select the TEACHERS table and click Open. You'll see an empty grid where you can enter some data. Use the Tab key to move forward from field to field and Shift Tab to move backward. Notice how when you begin to type in the name field, Access automatically enters a number in the AutoNumber TeacherID field. Enter the data shown in Figure 29. Then close the table.

	TeacherID	T_LastName	T_FirstName	RoomNumber	Grade
▶	1	Smith	Patricia	121	4
	2	Willis	Preston	201	5
	3	Black	Linda	145	3
*	(AutoNumber)			0	

Figure 29

Enter the teacher data. Use the Tab key to move from field to field.

Open the STUDENTS table and for the first student, click the drop-down list button and select the appropriate teacher (see Figure 30). Then fill in the remaining student data as shown in the figure. Notice how the input mask automatically formats the phone numbers. When you're finished, close the table.

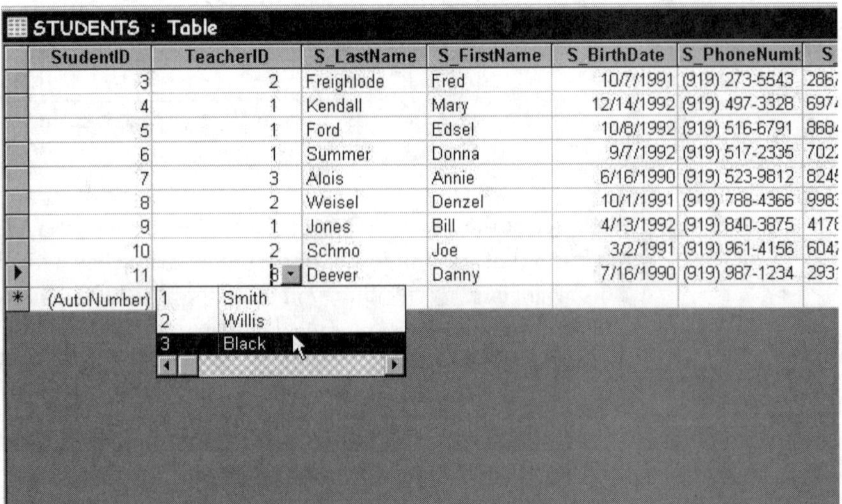

	StudentID	TeacherID	S_LastName	S_FirstName	S_BirthDate	S_PhoneNumb	S_
	3	2	Freighlode	Fred	10/7/1991	(919) 273-5543	286
	4	1	Kendall	Mary	12/14/1992	(919) 497-3328	697
	5	1	Ford	Edsel	10/8/1992	(919) 516-6791	868
	6	1	Summer	Donna	9/7/1992	(919) 517-2335	702
	7	3	Alois	Annie	6/16/1990	(919) 523-9812	824
	8	2	Weisel	Denzel	10/1/1991	(919) 788-4366	998
	9	1	Jones	Bill	4/13/1992	(919) 840-3875	417
	10	2	Schmo	Joe	3/2/1991	(919) 961-4156	604
▶	11	3	Deever	Danny	7/16/1990	(919) 987-1234	293
*	(AutoNumber)						

Figure 30

Enter the student data.

Selecting data with queries. Since a database is not supposed to be a black hole into which you pour data never again to be seen, we need to spend some time thinking about how to get the data back out when we need it. This is where queries come into play.

In the database window, click the Queries tab. Click New, choose Design View, and click OK. You'll see a new query shown in design view, and in the foreground you'll see a dialog box where you can select the tables from which the query will draw its data. Select STUDENTS, click Add, select TEACHERS, click Add again, and then click Close. A list of fields from each table is added to the top pane of the Query window, along with a line that joins them by TeacherID (see Figure 31)

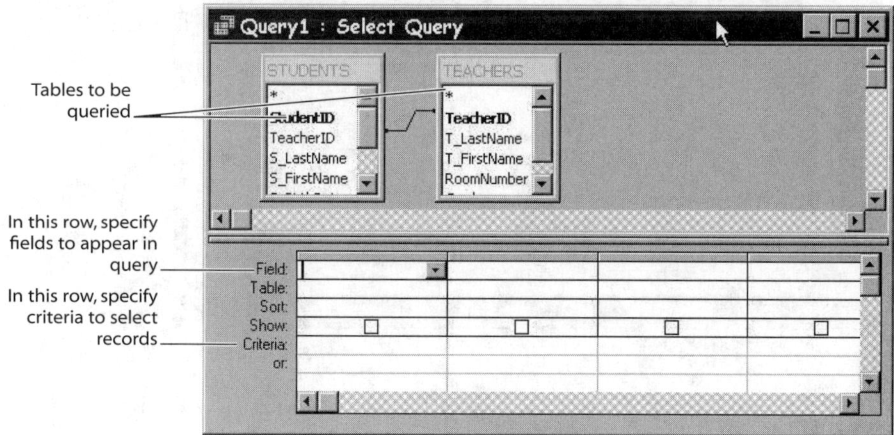

Figure 31

An Access query in design view. The top pane shows the tables that contribute data, with lines showing the links between them. The bottom pane lets you select rows and columns to appear in the query.

Notice in Figure 31 that Access has assumed that it should join the tables by matching TeacherIDs. That's because TeacherID is the key in the TEACHERS table, and because Access found the same field name, with the proper data type, in the other table. In case Access cannot select the proper linking field on its own, you can do it yourself: just drag the field name from one list to the corresponding field name in the other list. The fields you use need not have the same name, and neither needs to be a key, though they must share the same data type (remember that Long Integer matches AutoNumber), and of course, they must share data values among matching records. Incidentally, you can remove a join by clicking the line between the tables and pressing Del.

Now specify the fields you want to appear in the query: select the first field in the query grid, click the drop-down list button, and select Grade. Repeat the process to select T_LastName, S_FirstName, S_LastName, and S_PhoneNumber. Click in the Sort row under Grade and select Ascending. Repeat this procedure for S_LastName. Your query will look like Figure 32. To see the results of your query, choose View/Datasheet View.

Figure 32

The query at the top produces the list of teachers and students shown below.

Field:	Grade	T_LastName	S_FirstName	S_LastName	S_PhoneNumber
Table:	TEACHERS	TEACHERS	STUDENTS	STUDENTS	STUDENTS
Sort:	Ascending				
Show:	☑	☑	☑	☑	☑
Criteria:					
or:					

Query1 : Select Query

Grade	T_LastName	S_FirstName	S_LastName	S_PhoneNumb
3	Black	Danny	Deever	(919) 987-1234
3	Black	Annie	Alois	(919) 523-9812
4	Smith	Bill	Jones	(919) 840-3875
4	Smith	Donna	Summer	(919) 517-2335
4	Smith	Edsel	Ford	(919) 516-6791
4	Smith	Mary	Kendall	(919) 497-3328
5	Willis	Joe	Schmo	(919) 961-4156
5	Willis	Denzel	Weisel	(919) 788-4366
5	Willis	Fred	Freighlode	(919) 273-5543
*				

Record: 1 of 9

Now you're ready to select a subset of records. Choose View/Design View. Suppose you want to see just the third graders: enter "3" in the Criteria row under Grade and choose View/Datasheet View, and your query displays just the records that meet the criterion. In case you want to ask the same question again later on, you can save your query object: choose File/Save, enter a name like "MyFirstQuery," and click OK.

That's basically it for queries. Here are a few concepts for your further consideration:

- **A query does not contain data.** Rather, the query object is a set of instructions (expressed in Standard Query Language, or SQL) for asking a question that draws data from the tables. So let's say the data in the tables has changed. Next time you open your saved query, you'll get an answer that reflects the changes. If you're curious, you can choose View/SQL View in a Query, and you'll see the SQL statement that "really is" the query.
- **A query is a virtual table.** Once you've created and saved a query, you can use it like a table in almost all circumstances. For instance, you can build forms or reports based on either tables or queries, and you can even build a query based on another query.

- **You ain't seen nothin' yet.** Queries are where the action is in any database system. We've just scratched the surface of Access's query system: there are queries to create totals and subtotals, queries to delete or change data in the tables, and an intricate set of procedures for controlling what gets displayed when you join two tables.

Back in Design View, notice that Access has added quotation marks around the 3 you entered as the criterion. That's because Grade is a text field, and whenever you enter a specific text value into an Access property, the entry has to be enclosed in quotation marks to distinguish it from named objects such as variables or table names. In most cases, Access will oblige by adding the quotation marks, but you should be aware of them in case you need to add them yourself.

Once you get the hang of things, you can begin to ask some interesting questions (OK, maybe *interesting* is pushing it. At least you're starting to figure out how Access queries select data.) Try a few of the examples shown in Figure 33 (notice that I've added BirthDate to the field list in the query).

Field:	Grade	T_LastName	S_FirstName	S_LastName	S_BirthDate	S_PhoneNumber
Table:	TEACHERS	TEACHERS	STUDENTS	STUDENTS	STUDENTS	STUDENTS
Sort:	Ascending					
Show:	☑	☑	☑	☑	☑	☑
Criteria:		"Smith"				

Field:	Grade	T_LastName	S_FirstName	S_LastName	S_BirthDate	S_PhoneNumber
Table:	TEACHERS	TEACHERS	STUDENTS	STUDENTS	STUDENTS	STUDENTS
Sort:	Ascending					
Show:	☑	☑	☑	☑	☑	☑
Criteria:	>"3"					

Field:	Grade	T_LastName	S_FirstName	S_LastName	S_BirthDate	S_PhoneNumber
Table:	TEACHERS	TEACHERS	STUDENTS	STUDENTS	STUDENTS	STUDENTS
Sort:	Ascending					
Show:	☑	☑	☑	☑	☑	☑
Criteria:						Like "(919) 987*"

Field:	Grade	T_LastName	S_FirstName	S_LastName	S_BirthDate
Table:	TEACHERS	TEACHERS	STUDENTS	STUDENTS	STUDENTS
Sort:	Ascending				
Show:	☑	☑	☑	☑	☑
Criteria:					Between #1/1/1990# And #12/31/1990#

Figure 33

From top to bottom, these four queries answer these questions: "Who are the students in Smith's class?" "Which students are in grades higher than 3?" "Which students have phone numbers in the 987 exchange?" and "Which students were born in 1990?"

For more information on query criteria, choose Help/Contents and Index. Click the Find tab in the dialog box. In the first text field, enter "Examples of criteria expressions for queries." In the third box, choose "Examples of criteria expressions for queries and filters" and click Display. Then follow the links to explore the topic.

Lots of times, the tables don't contain data in the exact format you'd like to see in the query results. But if the raw material is there, you can create an *expression* to get what you need. Try the query shown in Figure 34 as an example; it takes the students' first and last names, combines them in the format "Smith, John," and calls the new field "Name."

Figure 34

The expression shown in the third column composes students' names in the format "Smith, John."

Field:	Grade	T_LastName	Name: [S_LastName] & ", " & [S_FirstName]	S_BirthDate
Table:	TEACHERS	TEACHERS		STUDENTS
Sort:				
Show:	☑	☑	☑	☑
Criteria:				

Database reports. There are two ways to create Access reports. There's the easy, direct, straightforward, get-it-on-paper-and-get-on-with-the-job approach. Then there's the difficult, tedious, error-prone, gotta-do-it-this-way-cause-the-boss-said-so method. You choose.

Quick and dirty does the trick. The fastest way to get data from an Access database onto paper is to print a query. Do this: Create a query. View it in datasheet view. Choose File/Print Preview. If what you see looks okay, choose File/Print and print it. If the preview reveals that all of the data won't fit on a single sheet, then choose File/Page Setup. On the Margins tab, decrease the size of the left and right margins. Click the Page tab and choose Landscape. You can also adjust the widths of the columns in the query's datasheet view to help squeeze things onto the sheet.

If a printed query is just too rough for your sensibilities, you can take one more step before the going gets ugly. Use the Report Wizard to let Access format your report using one of its standard layouts. You may get something that's acceptable.

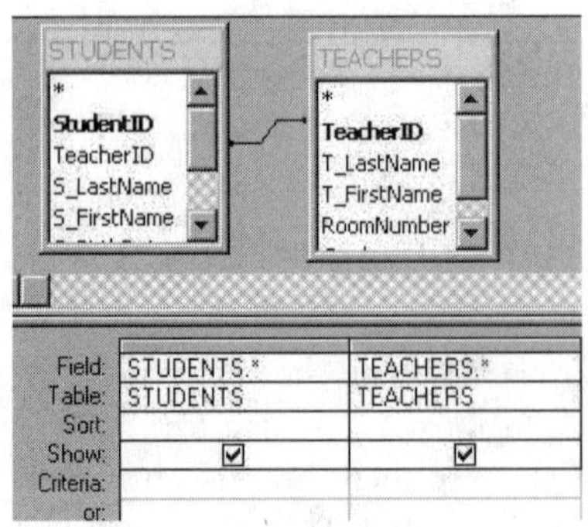

Figure 35

For this query, add both tables to the query and then choose STUDENTS. and TEACHERS.* as the fields. The asterisk stands for "all fields" in the table.*

To start with, lets quickly create a query to support the report. In the Queries window, set up a query that includes all of the fields from both the STUDENTS and TEACHERS tables. Hint: choose the asterisk instead of individual fields, as shown in Figure 35, and your query will include all fields. Save the query with the name "AllData" and then close it.

Next, click the Reports tab in the database window. Click New, select Report Wizard from the list, choose AllData as the record source, and click OK. Now select, in turn, each of the fields you'll need for the report in the Available Fields list and click the top button to move the fields to the Selected Fields list. When you're done, the dialog box should look like Figure 36.

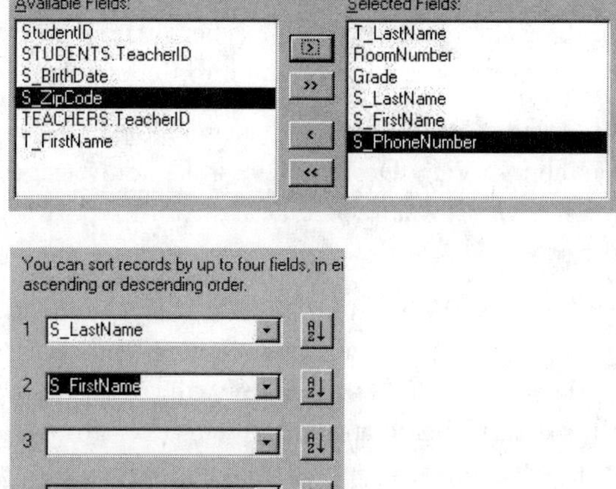

Figure 36

Selecting the fields and sort fields for the report.

Click Next and, in the next step of the wizard, select T_LastName as the grouping field. Click Next and choose S_LastName as the first sorting field and S_FirstName as the second. Click Next.

In the Layout step, select Stepped and click Next. In the Style step, since I'm a soft, gray kind of guy, I chose Soft Gray style. You can choose what you want: the styles are all about equally ugly. Click Next.

In the final step, enter a suitable name for your report and click Finish; you'll see your new report, as shown in Figure 37. Choose File/Save and save the report as "MyReport."

Figure 37

This is what you get when you use Access's Report Wizard. It's not bad, but it needs further refinement. For that, you need to work with the report in design view.

Student Directory

T_LastName	S_LastName	S_FirstName	omNumber	Grade	S_PhoneNu
Black					
	Alois	Annie	145	3	(919) 523-98
	Deever	Danny	145	3	(919) 987-12
Smith					
	Ford	Edsel	121	4	(919) 516-67
	Jones	Bill	121	4	(919) 840-38
	Kendall	Mary	121	4	(919) 497-33
	Summer	Donna	121	4	(919) 517-23
Willis					
	Freighlode	Fred	201	5	(919) 273-55
	Schmo	Joe	201	5	(919) 961-41
	Weisel	Denzel	201	5	(919) 788-43

Not bad for wizard work, but the report would look better if you could put the room numbers and grades up with teachers' names where they belong. For this, you will need to descend briefly into Report Hell. Follow me!

Welcome to Report Hell. Open your new report in design view: if your report is open, choose View/Design View; if it's not, select if from the Report tab of the database window and click Design. Your report will open and spill its guts on the screen.

Like most modern reporting systems, Access uses a band-oriented report generator. You put things on the report by including field objects and text in the bands, which determine where these items will appear on the page. So to get the grade number and label to appear in the teacher group band instead alongside the student details, you simply drag them into the proper position, as shown in Figure 38. In addition to moving things around, you can click twice in a text box to edit the text and select fields and use the formatting toolbar to change their alignment, font, and so on.

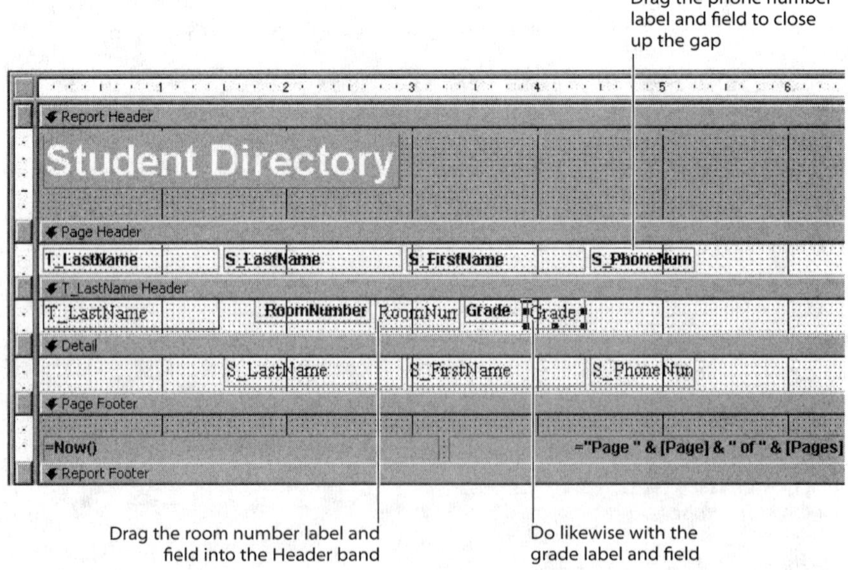

Figure 38

By rearranging and editing the report elements in design view, you can customize your reports. The band in the report design determines where each report element will appear.

Really, it's not that bad, given a little practice. Mess around with your report and choose View/Layout Preview to see the results. Just don't put this off until 20 minutes before the big deadline.

Know Your Limits: When To Call in the Pros

Every experienced database consultant knows the scenario. Somebody has a copy of Access, reads Microsoft's claims about how easy it is to use, dives into a major development project, and months later has a mess of a program that nobody, including the author, can get to work right—but the company can't just chuck it, because it contains lots of important data that the company doesn't have anywhere else.

The moral of that story: just because you *can* design your own database, it doesn't necessarily follow that you *should*. Designing a custom database to hold important information like orders, inventory, accounts receivables, or payroll information is seldom a do-it-yourself job. As we said earlier, when the questions you want your database to answer get really complicated ("Which employees reported to supervisory positions that were vacant during the month of December?"), you shouldn't be afraid to ask for help.

One good way to avoid trouble is to sketch out your database design in detail on paper before you begin. Figure out what tables you need, what fields each should contain, which fields will be the keys, which tables will be linked, and what kind of links you need to use. Consider what data-entry forms and reports you need, and how you'll generate them.

If you're not sure how to handle some features ("How can I let users invoice items from the parts catalog?"), that's a good sign that you need professional help. If you have the same field appearing in more than one table and can't figure out how to work around it, that's another warning sign.

If you do conclude that you need professional assistance, or that you need to farm out the project entirely, ask around for recommendations of good database programmers and check references carefully. Keep in mind that you don't want just a database expert: you want someone who will understand your particular business, ideally someone who's done a lot of database work for other companies in the same field.

Make sure that whoever programs your database, whether an outside professional or an in-house expert, fully documents the project so that you won't be dependent on that same person for future modifications. That means that any code (like macros in Access) should be *commented*: that is, peppered with text explaining what the code does, step by step.

The Consultant from Hell

He talks a good game. He seems to know exactly what you want in a multiuser (check one) order-entry system, accounting application, or customer database. But you're never really happy with the program he ends up writing. Then, after tens of thousands of records have been entered, the program starts crashing all over the place. *And the consultant from hell is the only one who can fix it. Again, and again, and again.*

The moral is: Always, always check references before you hire a consultant to write a network application. Also, ask the vendor, consultant, or programmer if the software has any special requirements, so you don't end up having to replace software or hardware later. Note that when you hire a database consultant to write a custom application, you may *not* need to buy a copy of the database program itself, since the consultant may have already paid for the right to distribute applications written in the program's language.

Database Resources

`www.filemaker.com` FileMaker's Web site has add-on programs and lots of tips, plus links to training materials, consultants, and ready-to-use database applications you can buy.

`microsoft.com/products/prodref/3_faq.htm` Microsoft's Access FAQ.

`advisor.com/av.html` Web site of an Access newsletter.

`comp.databases.ms-access` Busy Usenet newsgroup devoted to Access programming.

17

Painting, Drawing, and Other Graphics Software

by Foster D. Coburn III and Jake Widman

Portions of this chapter were adapted from material originally written by Rick Altman for a previous edition.

In This Chapter

Scanners for less than $100? Digital cameras that cost little more than a good 35mm single-lens reflex? It was hard to imagine a couple of years ago that the barriers to entry to the world of digital imaging would ever fall this low.

At the same time, the World Wide Web offers PC users an unprecedented medium for distributing their images. Today it seems like everybody has a personal Web page with photos of themselves, their friends, and their family; every cult TV show spawns dozens of Web sites with photos of its stars; and even the smallest businesses use a Web site to promote their products, often with an online catalog.

This chapter outlines what you need to know to get started creating your own digital images. We'll discuss the difference between paint programs and drawing programs, tell you what you need to edit scanned photographs, describe some of the specialized graphics programs you can use for out-of-the-ordinary purposes, and show you how you can get digital images if you don't feel like creating them yourself. We'll also discuss the difference between the ways your monitor and your printer handle color (and how you can help make sure they match) and give you some pointers on preparing color images for output on a printing press. Finally, we'll point you to some online resources for trial versions of graphics software and sources of digital images.

Working with images is about the most fun you can have with your PC. (Well, maybe aside from games.) Read on to discover a world where what you can do is limited only by your imagination.

The Two Types of Graphics

Most graphics programs fall into one of two loose groups: paint programs and drawing programs. *Paint programs* produce images made up of dots or squares of various colors arranged in a rigid rectangular grid; *drawing programs* assemble images out of curves, circles, lines, and rectangles. That's it—dots and geometric shapes.

The grid of dots created by a paint program is called a *bitmap*. (The term refers to the way the image is stored; one bit or group of bits in memory describes each dot in the picture.) The image created by a scanner, the output of a inkjet or laser printer, and the image Windows displays on your monitor are all bitmaps. When you create a circle with a paint program, the circle is nothing more than a ring of dots of a particular color. The program doesn't know it's a circle; if you want to change the circle's size or give it a heavier outline, it's probably easiest just to draw a new one.

The geometric shapes created by drawing programs are called *objects* (or sometimes *vectors*). When you create a circle in a drawing program, the program remembers its center point and radius, the thickness and color of its outline, and its *fill* (interior) color, and it uses that information to draw the circle on the screen or print it on a piece of paper. At that point, the circle is represented by a bitmap, but the program still knows it's a circle. You can go back and move the circle around on the page, make it larger or smaller, or change any of its other attributes—but it will always remain a perfect circle.

Generally speaking, if a graphic looks like a photograph or a painting, with smooth transitions between colors and detailed textures, it's a paint image. Drawings tend to look more like pen-and-ink illustrations or cartoons, with sharp outlines and flat colors. Here's a brief overview of the relative advantages and disadvantages of paint and drawing programs.

	Paint programs	Drawing programs
input	You don't have to know anything about art to make realistic-looking bitmap images: all you need is a scanner or digital camera. If you're a good artist, creating a bitmap is very much like sketching or painting on paper, especially if you have a drawing tablet (see Chapter 7: Input Devices).	It's easy to create very simple drawings, like flowcharts and block diagrams, but creating complex images in a drawing program is like assembling a complicated wire sculpture. Some programs have tracing programs that convert scans to draw format, but getting a good result can be tricky.
freehand drawing	Getting a flowing line requires skill and practice, just as when drawing on paper (see Figure 1). If you don't get the line right the first time, undo your work and try again.	If you wish, the program can smooth out the rough edges of your line (see Figure 1). If the line's not quite right, you can fine-tune it rather than starting over.
editing	*Layers*, which let you paint or paste into an image without replacing the pixels underneath, provide some flexibility in making changes to an image, but many changes will still require you to redo whole sections of the image from scratch.	Every element of the image is "live" and can be modified at any time. Need to straighten out that curve a little? Just click and drag one of the control points (see Figure 2). On the other hand, complex images may contain hundreds of elements, and selecting the one you want to modify can be tricky.
resizing	When you enlarge an image or a portion of an image, the original pixels become visible, as though you're zooming in on the dots. Smooth lines and curves become jagged, and faces and other elements start to look grainy (see Figure 3).	You can resize endlessly without damaging the image. You can enlarge a tiny object to fill the screen, and its lines and curves will still be perfectly sharp, because the program simply redraws the object at the new size (see Figure 4).

	Paint programs	Drawing programs
file size	The file size varies with resolution and image size.	The file size varies with the image's complexity, but it is usually much smaller than that of the equivalent bitmap.
printing	You may get jaggy lines or *pixelation* if the image resolution (pixels per inch) is not a good match for the printer's resolution..	The lines are always sharp, because the printer renders the objects at its maximum resolution.

Figure 1

Using a drawing program, you can create accurate, easily manipulated shapes quickly. The perfect curve at the bottom took less time to create than the sloppy one above

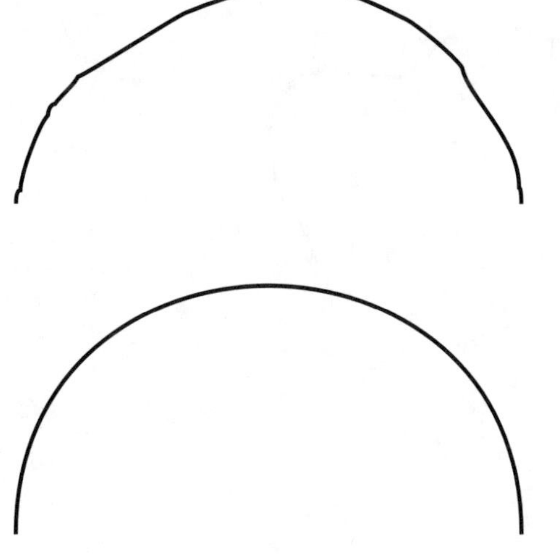

Figure 2

In a drawing program, you can change the shape of an object by dragging its control points.

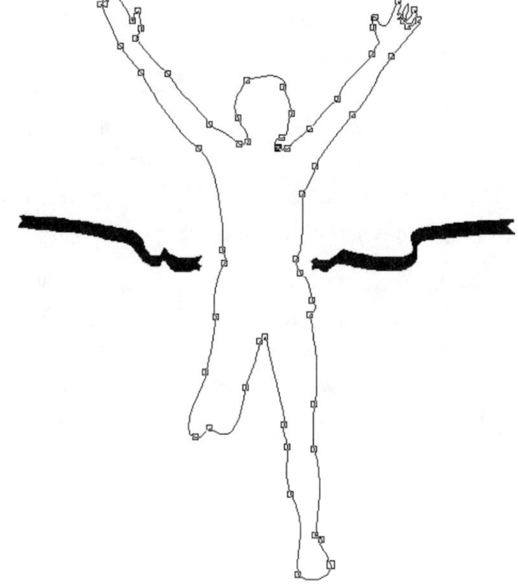

Figure 3

At the left you can see the original photograph. On the right is a blowup of the fisherman's back and head that clearly shows each pixel.

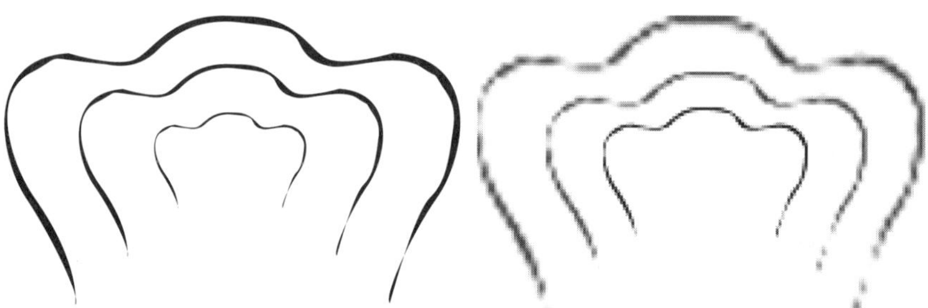

Figure 4

In a drawing program, you can make an object any size you want, and the edges remain perfectly sharp. Enlarging objects in a paint program creates a grainy, blocky look.

Paint Basics

Say you have a scanned photograph and you need to adjust the colors—to make the sky bluer, for instance. Maybe you just need to take the red out of a person's eyes or adjust the overall contrast. Or you need to repair tears and scratches that were on the original. All of these are the kinds of tasks commonly performed in an image editing or paint program. You can also use a paint program to composite multiple photos into a single image or to create Web graphics. And some of the programs have natural media tools like airbrushes and water droplets that let you treat your computer like an electronic canvas (see Figure 5).

When you work with a bitmap image, you alter the color of its pixels—to take the red out of eyes, for instance, you change red pixels to another color. With small areas like eyes, you can work pixel by pixel, but to make changes to larger areas like a sky, you generally want to select the area first and change it all at once.

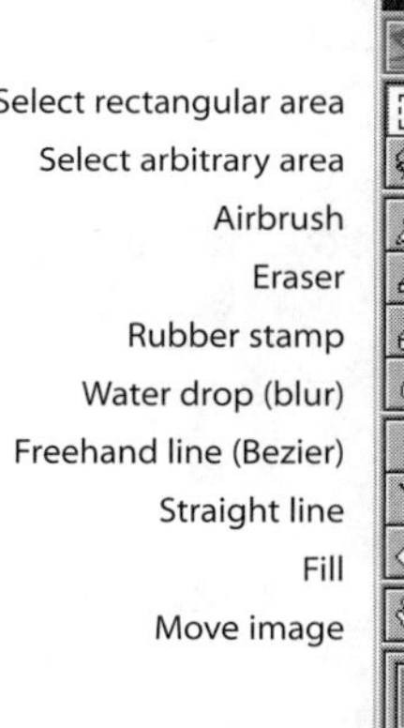

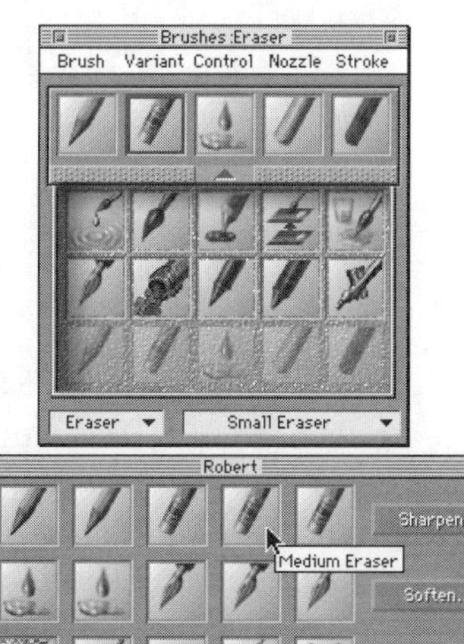

Figure 5

Most of the tools on Adobe Photoshop's palette are common to all paint programs. Painter's brushes palette makes it easier to tell what each tool does.

The tools that allow you to select a certain area to work on are commonly called *masking* tools. The most basic allow you to select an elliptical or rectangular area; more advanced tools allow you to select an area by drawing a line around it or by painting on it. You can also use a so-called *magic wand* tool, which selects all the contiguous pixels of colors similar to the one you click (see Figure 6).

Figure 6

After you use the magic wand to select the water in the background of this image, the rest of the image is masked, so you work on only the background. Here we're using the Dodge tool to make the water brighter.

You can modify the mask so that you're working on the area selected or the area outside the selection, and sometimes it's easiest to select the area you *don't* want to work on. For instance, if you have a picture of a person standing against a background of solid blue sky, you can't use the magic wand to select the person; but rather than laboriously outlining the figure, you could use the magic wand to select the sky and then reverse the selection to work on the figure.

Most current programs take masks one step further and allow you to "float" certain areas of pixels above the background, so you can work on them and move them around without affecting the underlying image. You'll hear this feature called *layers*, *floaters*, or *objects*, depending on the program you're using. Being able to move just certain pixels without affecting anything else makes compositing images easy. Other options include altering the floating object's transparency and the way the object interacts with the background image by specifying a *blend mode* or *merge mode*.

Once you've selected the area you want to work on, the ways you can alter the image are virtually endless. You can easily make overall changes by applying an effect filter to make the colors lighter or darker, adjust the contrast or brightness, or sharpen or blur the image. (You'd probably apply many of these effects to the entire image rather than to just a selection.) Filters can also go far beyond these basics to produce fancy effects that simulate 3-D or a light source or make the image look like it's behind a glass. Some programs allow you to create floating effects called *adjustment layers* or *lenses*. With these, the effect is applied to the area beneath the lens without actually altering the pixels (see Figure 7).

Figure 7

In this Photoshop image, a brightness/contrast adjustment layer lightens the background in front of the girl's face.

Most paint programs include a basic set of filters, but different software offers different sets. If your program doesn't give you the exact filter you want, you can buy products (usually called *plug-ins*) from third parties to use with your program. Some of the most interesting of these are described at the end of the "Paint Programs" section later in this chapter. The plug-in standard was created by Adobe for Photoshop; all the paint programs described here support this standard.

For local, subtle changes—to change the color of the sky or a sweater, for instance—you can use a fill or a brush tool after you've masked the area. First you choose the new color you want from a color palette or by sampling it from another area of the image with what's usually called an *eyedropper* tool. Then you can fill the entire area with the new color or use a brush to paint the color in, changing the color but not the texture, if you want. You can change the size and angle of the brush tip, specify whether the brush tip has a hard edge or a soft edge, determine the transparency of the paint, and more (see Figure 8). Some paint programs even allow you to load a series of images and paint with them, so you can paint butterflies into the sky if you like.

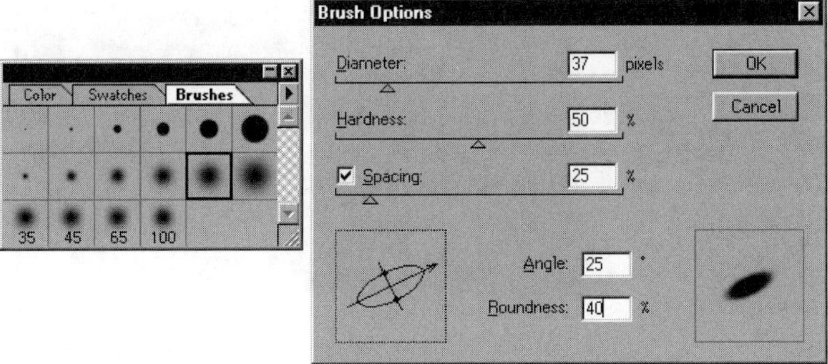

Figure 8

Brush settings in Photoshop

Making changes like these to all the individual pixels in an image places a big demand on your computer's processing power and memory, so when you use paint programs, it is extremely important that you work with files that aren't larger than you need for your output device. Frequently, someone buys a 600 dpi scanner and then scans everything at that resolution, thinking it will produce the best image. That's true if the original art is a line drawing, but if it's a photograph, scanning at that resolution creates a file much larger than is necessary, and the printed result may look worse than if the image had been scanned at a lower resolution. See "Matching Scan Resolution with Print Resolution" in Chapter 7: Input Devices, for tips on choosing the right dpi setting.

Paint Programs

Adobe Photoshop

Adobe Photoshop ($550) is the package against which all other paint programs are measured—it basically defined the field. It's also priced much higher than the competition. You'll find that for some tasks, such as creating Web graphics or simulating a painting environment, Photoshop isn't as strong as other programs, but for most paint and photo-editing projects, it's tops.

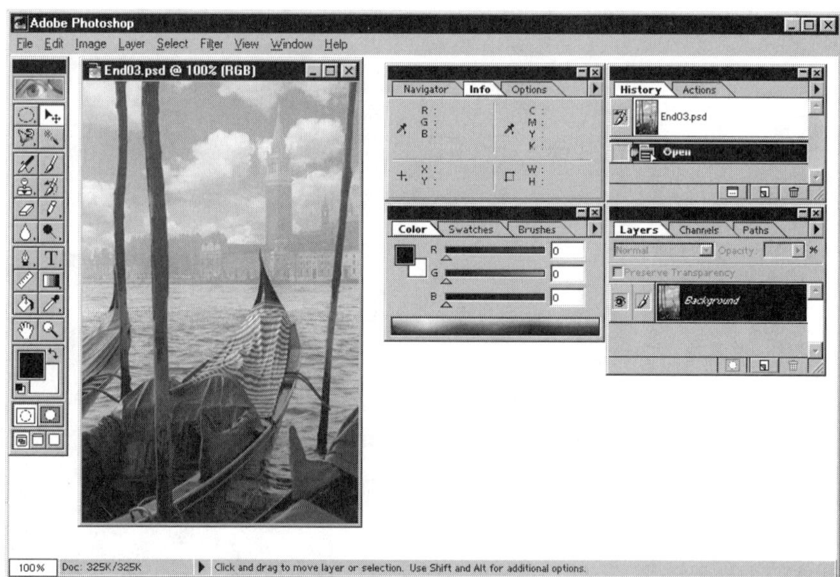

Figure 9

Adobe Photoshop

In addition to the standard selection tools (geometric shapes, freehand outlines, and magic wand), the latest version of Photoshop has added a "magnetic" lasso, a tracing tool that automatically snaps to the edge of an object (by following the border between colors). The current version also handles text better than the other products: with most programs (and earlier versions of Photoshop), once you add text to your image, you can't go back and edit it or change fonts, as you now can in Photoshop.

Another great new feature is Layer Effects, which lets you apply effects to a layer rather than to objects and then manages the effects dynamically; because the effects are separate from the objects on the layer, if you change the contents of the layer (if you edit the text, for instance), the effects are automatically reapplied. Unfortunately, there are only a handful of layer effects, although they do handle some of the most common tasks, such as creating drop shadows..

Photoshop stores most of its tools and information in palettes. The latest version includes a History palette, which presents a list of all recent operations (up to a maximum of 20, depending on how much memory you have) and makes undoing one or all of them very simple. It even allows you to undo operations outside of the order they were originally processed—in other words, you can undo operation 3 without undoing operation 4 first. Other programs allow multiple undo operations, but Photoshop currently has the best implementation.

Photoshop also lets you record sequences of actions so that you can reapply them as a sort of macro to other images: for instance, you can use this feature to reduce several images to the same size and change them all to black and white. You can export these actions from one document to another, and you'll find that people even trade useful Action scripts over the Internet.

Since Photoshop is the current standard in many high-end graphics shops, you may want to use it for compatibility, especially if you're preparing images for prepress separations. However, many other packages offer similar tools for a lot less money and are more than adequate for home and small business use—and if you'll primarily be working with Web graphics, you will be better served using one of the other programs.

Corel Photo-Paint

Corel Photo-Paint ($300 if purchased separately) is a complete package, with excellent tools for photo editing, painting, and Web graphics. The price is relatively reasonable, and owners of CorelDraw get it as part of that suite. And since it shares a number of features with CorelDraw, the learning curve can be less steep.

Figure 10

Corel Photo-Paint

Photo-Paint has the best masking tools of all the products in this roundup. Once a mask is created, it can easily be edited and even aligned to various parts of the image. For floating effects, the mask can even be converted into a lens for the application of special effects just within that area. You can also make the masked area a floating object. Floating objects can be managed quite easily in the Objects Docker, which provides settings for altering the layer's opacity and determining its merge mode.

Photo-Paint's painting tools aren't as complete as those in Metacreations Painter (discussed later in this section), but they are more than adequate for nonartists. You'll find such natural media tools as crayons, markers, and pencils, and if you have a graphics tablet, you can choose from a number of settings to make your painting experience feel even more real. You'll also find two innovative painting modes, called *orbits* and *symmetries*, with which you can create intricate, kaleidoscopelike patterns out of simple strokes, and you can magnify the benefits of these modes even further by using them with the Image Sprayer tool, which lets you paint with an entire image as your brush; with this combination, you can easily create the appearance of rope or phone cord, for instance.

Photo-Paint also does a good job with Web graphics. If you're creating GIF files—one common image file format for the Web—Photo-Paint gives you powerful features for optimizing them, including a zoomable preview window. You can even create a GIF animation by adding frames to a base image. It's not the most elegant implementation, but it's functional.

For export operations, Photo-Paint provides a number of options for controlling the speed and quality of animation. If you're exporting JPEG files—a Web format commonly used for compressing photographic images to manageable size—you also benefit from a before-and-after preview window that helps you choose the best trade-off between file size and image quality. You can even assign URLs (Web addresses) to any floating object to create an *image map*, a Web graphic that functions as a group of links.

In contrast to Photoshop's Actions, which you can edit only with program's dialog boxes, Photo-Paint makes all of its commands available to an internal script recorder and editor or to the programming language of your choice. The openness of the scripting language has enabled developers to create some wonderful scripts. Another time-saver is the ability to perform all of your editing on a low-resolution (and, therefore, smaller) proxy version of your actual image. When you've finished, the changes are automatically applied to the high-resolution original.

For most users, Photo-Paint offers the best balance between cost and features—and since it is bundled with CorelDraw, there is no reason for CorelDraw owners to use any other package.

JASC Paint Shop Pro

Paint Shop Pro ($70) began life as shareware but has grown into a commercial product that provides most of the functionality of more expensive products and even some features they don't include. One of Paint Shop Pro's biggest benefits, compared to its competition, is speed. Many people use a more advanced product, such as Photoshop or Photo-Paint, for their big jobs but also have a copy of Paint Shop Pro for small tasks because of its speed. [Editor's note: I'm one of those people, and have stuck with version 4.0 because 5.0 seems almost as complicated as Photoshop. You can find the older version by searching for `psp4` on **`shareware.com`**. —RL]

Figure 11

Paint Shop Pro 4.0's interface is as simple as the program is efficient.

Paint Shop Pro offers full support of layers and masks, though you won't find the kind of floating effects filters that Photoshop calls adjustment layers and Photo-Paint calls lenses. You'll also find many natural media painting tools—brushes, pens, pencils, markers, crayons, chalk, charcoal, and an airbrush. Paint Shop Pro also has Picture Tubes that allow you to paint with pictures the way you can with Photo-Paint's Image Sprayer and Painter's Image Hose.

For Web graphics, you'll find full support for GIF, JPEG and the new PNG graphics file formats, complete with previews. There is even a batch converter included if you just want to convert a bunch of files from one format to another—several scanned TIFFs to JPEGs, for instance. A separate Animation Shop utility, based on a filmstrip-like interface, is included for creating and optimizing GIF animations.

Paint Shop Pro doesn't contain all the features of Photoshop or Photo-Paint, and its support for color separations is not strong, but if you don't need all the bells and whistles of the high-end packages, Paint Shop Pro gives you an excellent program for a very nice price.

Metacreations Painter

Are you an artist who paints with oils, watercolors, pencil, or chalk—or do you wish you were? If so, Metacreations Painter ($250) is the perfect package for you. It provides a staggering number of natural media tools, all endlessly customizable, as well as the ability to mimic natural painting surfaces like canvas or various kinds of paper. The combination of tool and surface lets you paint with almost any texture you can imagine, and other tools allow you to easily apply textures to objects you've already painted. Other programs have similar features, but they don't come close to the quality and variety of those in Painter. The vast array of settings gives you great control, but the interface can be confusing.

Figure 12

Metacreations Painter

One of Painter's strengths is in animation. You can easily edit both Video for Windows and QuickTime movies to enhance the current frames of a movie or even to create your own frames. Painter also includes the ability to composite two movies into one: to take a foreground image from one movie and place it against the background of another, for example. And, of course, you can output your animation as a GIF file for the Web.

Painter also includes a number of Web-related features such as image maps, image slicing, JavaScript rollovers, and the tools needed to create all types of buttons and backgrounds. With these tools and a very good tutorial, you can soon be creating great graphics for the Web.

Using Painter to create your own original artwork will feel very much like painting on canvas or sketching on paper. Painter introduced the idea of the Image Hose, which allows you to paint by spraying pictures onto your graphic. And if you want to mimic the styles of the masters, the various clone brushes can make your image look like it was painted by Van Gogh or Monet. If your main purpose is photo editing, Painter should not be your first choice, but if you want to be an artist, Painter is a perfect fit.

Micrografx Picture Publisher

Like Paint Shop Pro, Picture Publisher ($100) provides a wealth of features for a bargain price. It is also the easiest-to-use application in this category. It offers a number of wizards and other automated effects that help the user automate the task at hand, though printed documentation is minimal.

Figure 13

Micrografx Picture Publisher

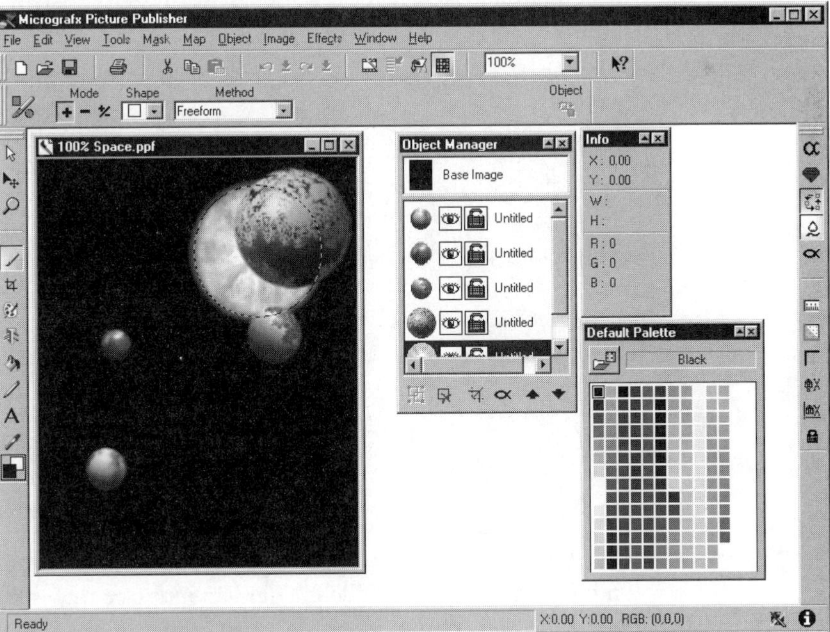

The objects in Picture Publisher work much like the layers found in other applications, and the masking tools are as strong and easy to use as those in Photo-Paint; however, you can't create an empty layer for painting new brush strokes, and you won't find Adjustment Layers or Layer Effects features as in Photoshop. You can record a sequence of effects in a macro, and like Photo-Paint, Picture Publisher allows you to work with a low-resolution proxy image and then apply all changes to the original high-resolution image.

Picture Publisher is on a par with Painter, Photo-Paint, and Paint Shop Pro in the number of paint brushes it offers, and a drop-down list of all the brushes and their variants makes it easy for you to choose the brush that achieves the exact effect you want. You'll even find an Image Spray, similar to Photo-Paint's Image Sprayer and Painter's Image Hose. Again, changing the settings is easy with the drop-down list of files and previews.

Special effects are abundant and easy to use, with over 140 filters in the package and wizards to help you apply them. The Lens Flare, Light Studio, and Camera Aperture filters—which mimic effects and settings a photographer might use—are more flexible than similar filters in other packages.

Web support is where Picture Publisher really shines. GIF and JPEG export filters provide a wealth of options and previews that help you get exactly what you want. The Animation FX Wizard makes it simple for even newcomers to create snazzy GIF animations, and creating image maps is easy. One of the most interesting features is the Web Styles Wizard, which helps you create all of the elements you need for a Web site.

For new users who don't need all of the features found in other packages, Picture Publisher is a great choice. Experienced users of other programs will find Picture Publisher easy to learn, and some of the filters will be welcome additions to their toolboxes.

Plug-Ins

As mentioned earlier, if your favorite program doesn't have a particular feature or effect, you can probably buy a plug-in that provides it. I've listed a few of the top sets of plug-ins here, but this is far from an exhaustive list.

Alien Skin's Eye Candy ($65) provides 21 different filters, each with a number of presets and variations. These include not just flashy effects that you use on rare occasions, but filters that help you complete your everyday projects.

Kai's Power Tools ($110) has been widely praised for its powerful filters, but unfortunately they are hidden behind an interface that is baffling at best (see Figure 14). The quirky interface is even more difficult if you are using a graphics tablet, to the point where getting something you like tends to be a happy accident. Many artists enjoy experimenting with these filters, though, so you might want to give them a try.

Figure 14

Kai's Power Tools

For adding innovative edges and borders to images, you'll want Auto F/X's Photo/Graphic Edges ($149 from **autofx.com**), an older version of which is included with Corel Photo-Paint. With this filter, you can choose from a huge variety of edges for your photos (or create your own) and apply additional special effects to them. Another package, called Typo/Graphic Edges ($99), does similar things for text.

If it is Web graphics that you want, SPG's Web Tools ($200 from **www.spg-net.com**) gives you a phenomenal group of tools for creating and optimizing your graphics. And just when you think that it would be nice to have a new feature, they provide you with a free update and add that missing feature.

Drawing Basics

As discussed in the section "The Two Types of Graphics," drawing programs work very differently from paint programs. If you need to create an organizational chart, draw a map, design a symbol for your logo, or set type along a curving path, one of the programs discussed in this section will do the trick.

All of the programs offer a set of basic tools for creating shapes, including ellipses and circles, rectangles and squares, and polygons (see Figure 15). They also have tools for drawing freehand shapes and flowing lines, or *paths*, as well as for setting text. All of the shapes are defined by the placement of *nodes* or *anchor points*—which sit on the line—and *control points*, which determine the direction of the line away from the anchor point. (You don't need to define control points manually—you can draw any line, and the program will determine the points.)

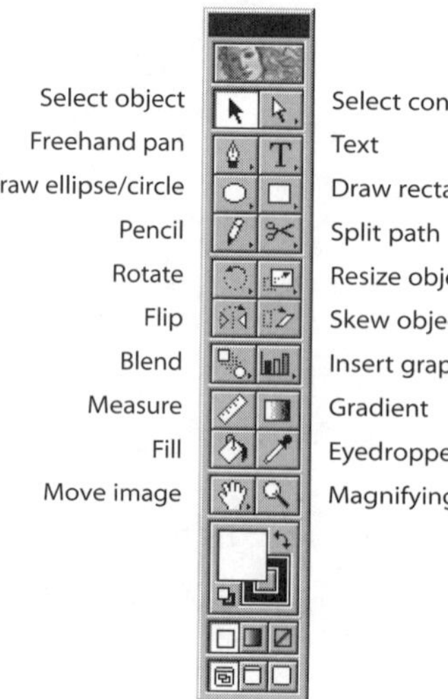

Figure 15

Most of the tools on Adobe Illustrator's palette are common to all drawing programs.

You can then modify the shape of each element by moving the nodes, adjusting the anchor points, or, in some cases, by dragging the line itself. Each shape you draw is a separate, individual object (though several objects can be grouped and handled as a single item) and can be rotated, skewed, moved, placed in front of or behind other shapes, and filled with any of a number of colors. Although these simple shapes and colors may not seem like much, they can be combined to create almost any image you can imagine (see Figure 16).

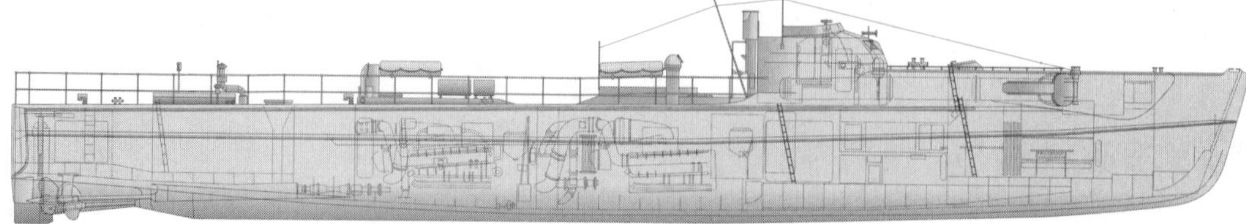

Figure 16

In drawing programs, you create complex images by combining many simple elements, like lines, rectangles, and curves.

Like paint programs, drawing programs offer layers that let you isolate certain objects to work on them independently. Otherwise, it can be difficult in a complex drawing to select just the object you want to modify. If you were making a map, for instance, you might put the streets on one layer and the landmarks on another, so you could label the landmarks without the street names getting in the way.

Other common tools to make the job of drawing easier include alignment commands and guides. You can usually align selected objects vertically or horizontally, by their centers, sides, or tops. You can also set up guide lines based on rulers or existing objects to aid in positioning. When you move an object, it will tend to "snap to" a guide. Finally, to prevent accidents, you can also lock selected objects, which means they cannot be altered or moved until you unlock them.

The most common fill in a drawing program is a flat color, which you choose from a color palette, select from a list of predefined colors, or mix yourself. (See "An Introduction to Color" later in this chapter.) You're not limited to these options, however. You can, for example, fill an object with a gradient that blends between two or more colors to achieve a textured effect.

One of the most common uses for a drawing program is to set text: to add your company name and phone number to your logo, for example. You can use any font available (and most programs come with a good selection), and usually you have control over such typographic adjustments as kerning, spacing, and justification. In addition, you can control the outline color and thickness and the fill color of the letters. If you're using PostScript Type 1 fonts, you can even convert the text to outlines and then modify it just like any other object by adjusting the curve points.

You can run your text along a curve or wrap it around a circle, or you can warp it to make the word *love* look like a heart, for instance (see Figure 17). Some programs allow you to edit the text or the formatting after such modifications, while others don't offer that capability.

Other effects include control over how overlapping objects interact. For instance, if you overlap a circle on top of a square, you can make the circle cut out the overlap area, leaving a square with a bite taken out of it, or you can combine the two shapes into a single object, creating a square with a bump on one side.

The current crop of applications is starting to blur the line between drawing and painting programs. Most drawing programs now allow you to import images from your paint program so that you can mix photos with type or other elements. You won't be able to mask areas and perform pixel-level editing, but you can easily apply an effect filter to the whole image, making it easy to perform a quick color adjustment or apply a special effect.

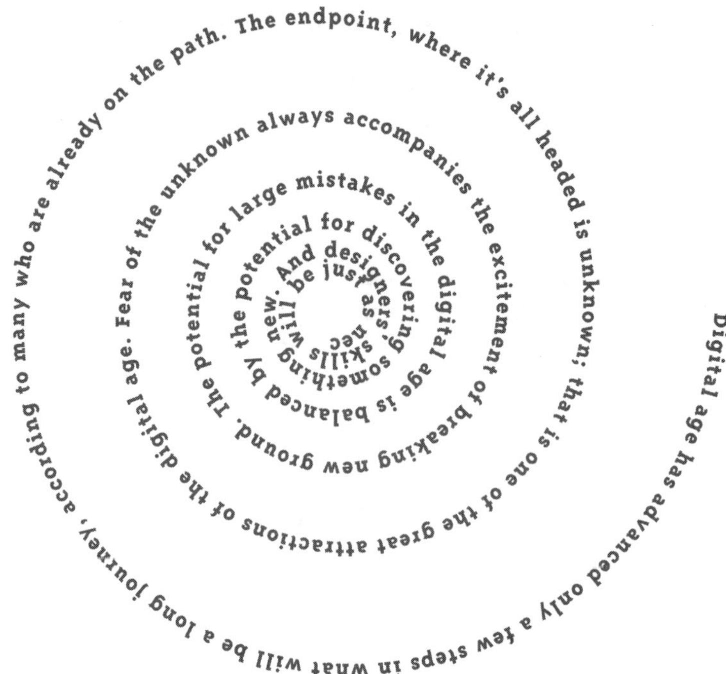

Figure 17

Drawing programs can twist text into shapes.

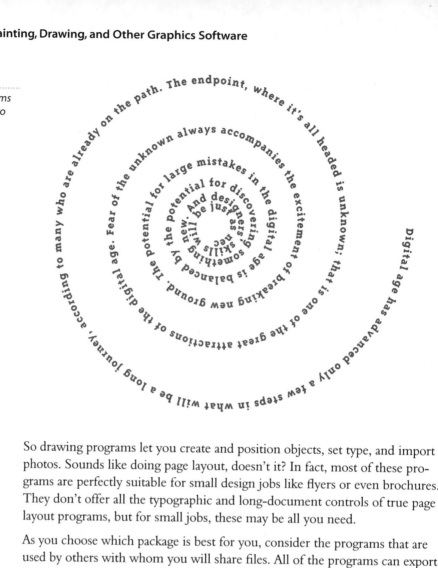

So drawing programs let you create and position objects, set type, and import photos. Sounds like doing page layout, doesn't it? In fact, most of these programs are perfectly suitable for small design jobs like flyers or even brochures. They don't offer all the typographic and long-document controls of true page layout programs, but for small jobs, these may be all you need.

As you choose which package is best for you, consider the programs that are used by others with whom you will share files. All of the programs can export and import files in standard formats, but some handle the standards better than others. If everyone you work with uses CorelDraw, for instance, you'll save yourself some headaches by choosing that program as well.

Drawing Programs

Adobe Illustrator

Adobe Illustrator ($350) was the first high-end drawing program, and it immediately won the favor of graphics artists on the Macintosh. Over the years, however, Illustrator has lagged behind other products in this category on the PC platform, and only recently has it come close to matching the features in CorelDraw and Macromedia FreeHand.

Figure 18

Adobe Illustrator

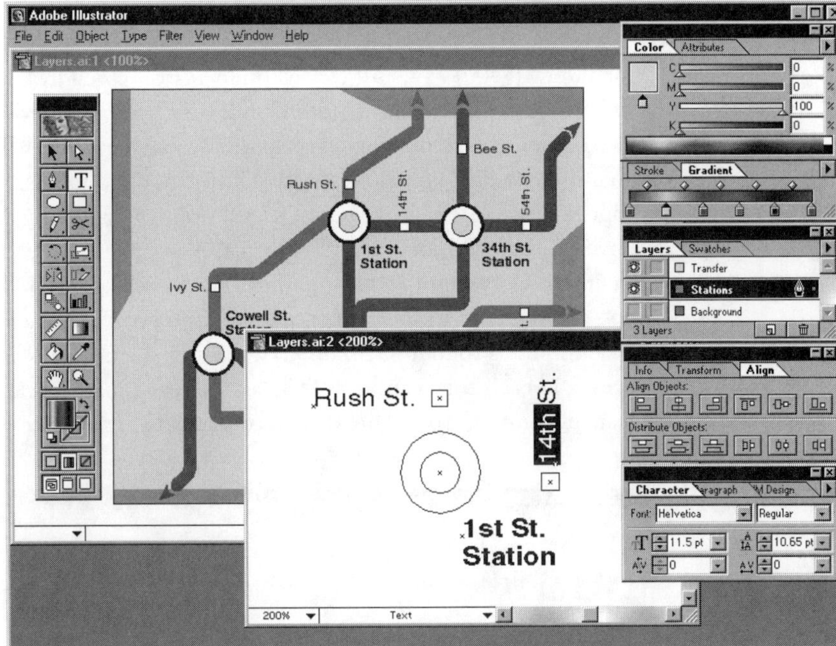

If you are already using Photoshop, you will immediately notice a similarity in the interfaces, including a lot of identical tool palettes, which should make Illustrator easier to learn. Illustrator also works well with Photoshop in other ways; for instance, a layered file in Illustrator will open with layers intact in Photoshop.

The gradient mesh tool in the latest version of Illustrator offers a whole new way to fill objects. This tool overlays a grid on the selected object, and you can drop any color on any part of the grid. This allows you to achieve painterly effects that would have been extremely difficult to create in the past. Another innovative feature lets you easily convert a scanned image into a cross-hatched sketch.

One of Illustrator's traditional strengths has been its solid support for high-end devices. You'll also find that Illustrator files work well with a wide variety of other programs on the Macintosh or PC. Illustrator's cross-platform support and its popularity among graphic artists makes getting output at service bureaus relatively painless.

What Illustrator doesn't have is many of the special effects and fancy fills found in CorelDraw. If you work with other Adobe products and need the cross-platform support, Illustrator may be the product for you. If you're just interested in a program for your own use, on the other hand, you may be better served by CorelDraw.

CorelDraw

CorelDraw ($400)—or, as the label loudly reads, CorelDRAW—is not just one program but a suite that includes CorelDraw itself, the drawing program; Photo-Paint, the paint program discussed earlier; and CorelDream 3D, a three-dimensional graphics program similar to the ones discussed later in this chapter. It also offers a number of useful utilities, including a tracing tool that converts scanned photos to draw format, over 1,000 fonts, and 40,000 pieces of clip art. CorelDraw with or without the bundle, CorelDraw, the program, is no slouch, with more features and greater ease of use than any other drawing program in this roundup. CorelDraw allows a document to span multiple pages, and each page can be as large as 150 feet square, making it possible to create everything from a life-size floor plan to a newsletter or catalog.

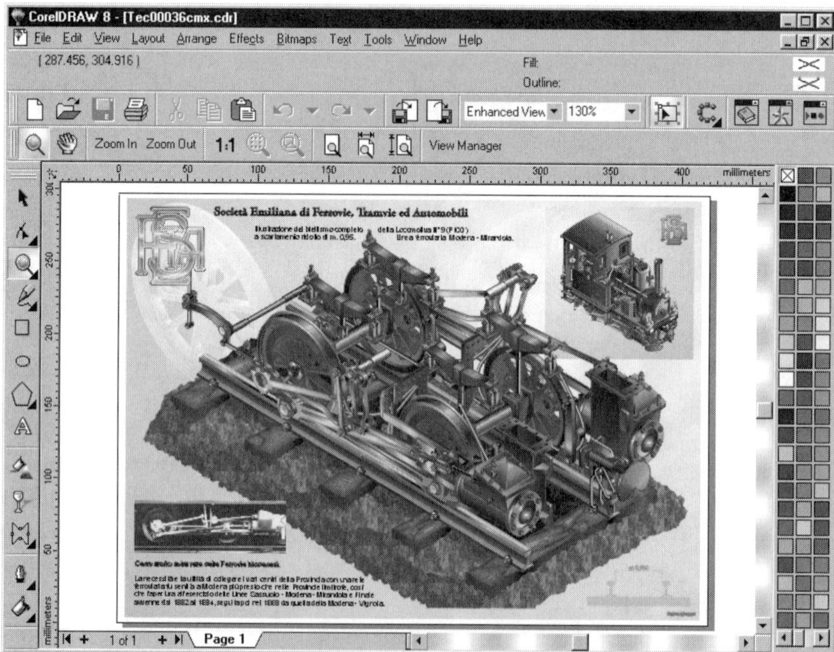

Figure 19

CorelDraw

One reason CorelDraw is so easy to use is its Property Bar. As you select tools or objects, the Property Bar changes to reflect the choices available to you for that selection. Similarly, a right-click on the selected object often brings up a context-sensitive menu that saves you a trip to the menu bar. You can customize the menus and toolbar so that they contain the commands you use regularly. Corel even provides predefined workspaces that make the program work like Adobe Illustrator or Macromedia FreeHand, if you're already familiar with the shortcuts in one of those programs.

If you want special effects, there are plenty to go around. You can warp any shape, including editable text, with the Interactive Envelope tool. If you want something to look three-dimensional, use the Extrude tool. Area filters called *lenses* allow you to use bitmap-like effects on any type of object. You can even add a soft, transparent drop shadow to any object, a feature that's usually the province of paint programs.

When you are finished creating, you can export your drawing in any of a huge variety of file formats. If you're printing directly from the program, you get complete support for color separation, page imposition, and other output tasks.

Corel started bundling other applications with CorelDraw many years ago. The bundle now includes separate utilities for font management, texture creation, screen capture, media management and more—and you also get full-featured applications like Corel Photo-Paint and Corel Dream 3D. With all these tools, there are very few graphics tasks that you can't tackle. Unless you specifically need another package for compatibility purposes, CorelDraw is the best buy of all programs for graphics.

Corel Xara

Corel doesn't promote Xara ($95) as heavily as CorelDraw, so it may be hard to find, but it's worth seeking out. No product listed in these pages is faster. None provides a better looking, fully anti-aliased image on the screen, and none takes up less space on your hard drive (only 10 MB). And while Xara doesn't have all the features of the larger programs, it certainly has its share of outstanding features.

Xara introduced the concept of an Infobar (which became the Property Bar in CorelDraw), and it also boasts transparency functions that many thought couldn't be achieved in a drawing program. All of the tools you need for single-page graphic design jobs are in Xara, and if you're familiar with CorelDraw, you'll pick up Xara quickly.

Where Xara really excels is at creating graphics for the Web. Since the screen display is already anti-aliased (meaning the jagged edges of the bitmap lines are softened by blending with the background color), converting an image to GIF or JPEG format is simple and yields spectacular results. You can even specify a background color or texture for creating the anti-aliased edge. The background isn't exported with the image, so you can specify the same background color for your Web page and have the image blend smoothly into it. Creating an animated GIF image is simple—you just create each frame and change animation settings in the Frame Gallery.

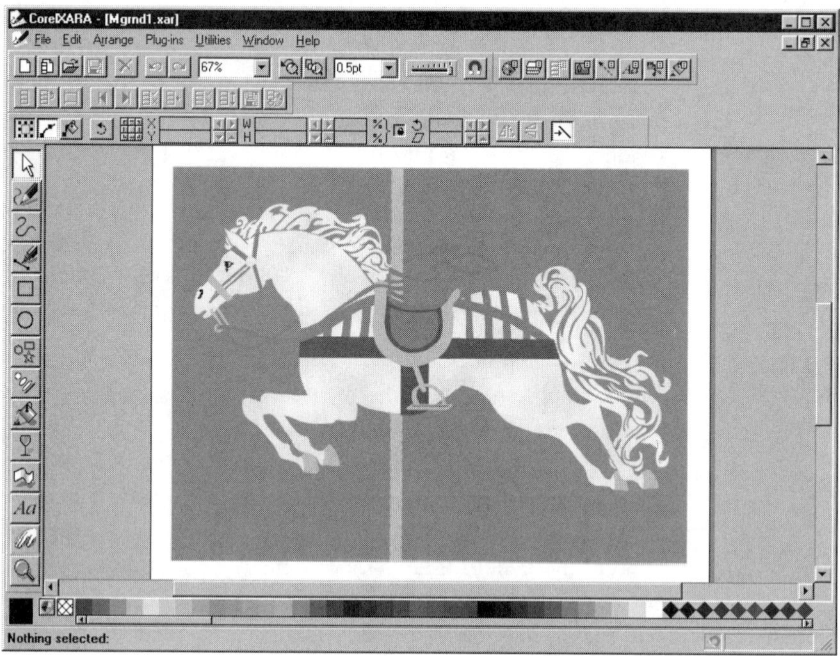

Figure 20

Corel Xara

Fewer people use Xara than any of the other products in this category, but they are very loyal and provide plenty of community support on the Internet. You will run into problems if you need to share your files with other users, since Xara is available for Windows only, and no other program supports the Xara file format, but if you work alone, Xara may be perfect for you.

Macromedia FreeHand

FreeHand ($360) is generally considered one of the big three Windows drawing programs, along with Adobe Illustrator and CorelDraw. The program's two biggest strengths over the years have been its color reproduction capability and the ease with which you can switch platforms from PC to Mac.

Innovative features in the current version include the Graphics Hose, which allows you to spray a series of drawings across your page. This feature is now common in paint programs (such as Painter, Photo-Paint, and Paint Shop Pro), but it is new to the world of drawing programs. The program offers a search-and-replace capability that extends far beyond that of other packages and allows you to search for objects with a specified outline width or color, fill color, path shape, and more and change the selected attribute globally. You'll also find a slew of features included as Xtras (Macromedia's term for plug-ins), including embossing and drop shadows. Third parties can also create Xtras to add a feature not included in FreeHand, and you can use Photoshop-compatible plug-ins on any imported TIFF images.

Figure 21

Macromedia FreeHand

Another feature that sets FreeHand apart from the competition is its excellent support for the creation of files in the Flash format, a format Macromedia has proposed as a Web animation standard. Macromedia has recently been emphasizing its programs' Web capabilities, and although the company sells a separate program for creating Web animations (Flash, described later), the drawing tools in FreeHand enable you to create some great artwork for the Web. You can also export your drawings in GIF, JPEG, or PNG format, as well as create Shockwave files (discussed in Chapter 21: The Web and Browsers).

For those who want to create quick Web page mock-ups, Macromedia also offers Insta.HTML which can reliably convert a FreeHand document into a Web page. This utility can be bought separately, and it's bundled with FreeHand and Flash in the Design in Motion Suite ($435). Included in that package are 493 fonts, 10,000 pieces of clip art, and 370 project templates.

Other Graphics Software

Paint and drawing programs are the main products in graphics software, but they are certainly not the only ones. This section provides a brief overview of several other categories of graphics software.

Web Graphics

The explosion in popularity of the World Wide Web has been matched by an increase in the number of programs aimed at creating Web graphics. From shareware utilities for creating GIF animations to graphics conversion programs to full-fledged image creation packages from leading vendors, you can find something for any task. This section will just mention some of the best-known packages.

Adobe ImageReady ($175) is intended primarily for those who are already familiar with Photoshop. It incorporates many of Photoshop's standard features and borrows its interface. (In fact, many feel that ImageReady's tools should simply have been added to Photoshop.) You can use ImageReady to convert an image to GIF, JPEG, or PNG format, with different settings for compression and number of colors; the program shows you a preview of the results right on the editing screen. You can also set the program to preview the image as it will appear on a Mac or PC, with or without dithering. With all these controls, you'll get a near-perfect look at your graphics as they will appear to your Web visitors. Support for animation creation is strong, and the program can even create the intervening frames between a beginning and ending frame. Another tool allows *image slicing*, which you can use to divide a large graphic into a series of smaller images that are then reassembled in an HTML table. This allows you to treat each section of an image as a separate graphic (to add links, for instance) while retaining the appearance of a single whole image in the browser window.

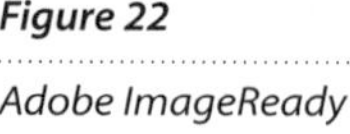

Figure 22

Adobe ImageReady

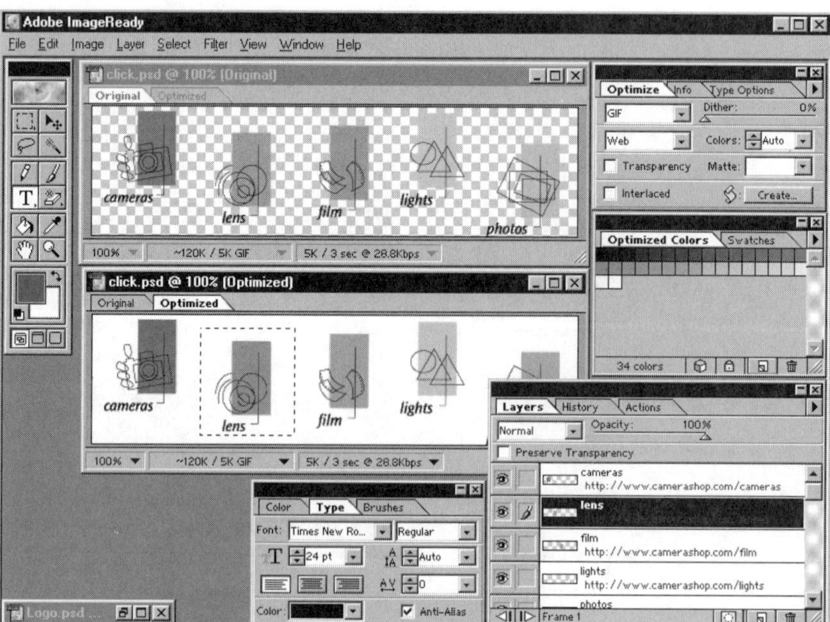

If you use Photoshop as your basic graphics program , ImageReady is a good addition for creating Web graphics. However, you'll also find other packages in this round-up that serve both purposes at a price that is lower than that of either Photoshop or ImageReady.

Macromedia Fireworks ($200) is also designed for creating Web graphics, but unlike ImageReady, Fireworks integrates both drawing and painting tools. You will find more features in Fireworks, but this also makes the program more difficult for the new user. As you might expect, similarities to FreeHand and Flash (described later in this section) make learning Fireworks easier if you're familiar with one of those programs.

Fireworks puts its image previews in the Export dialog box, which displays up to four different previews of the same image so that you can see the effects of different color palette and compression settings. Fireworks supports image maps as well as image slicing. For GIF animations, you'll find a number of innovative features that make it easy to create an animation as well as to keep its file size small. If you're looking for one program to do all your design work for the Web, then Fireworks, with more Web-related features than any other product in this round-up, is a great choice.

Figure 23

Macromedia Fireworks

Macromedia's Flash ($260) allows you to not only create drawings but also animate them. While it works best with FreeHand, it can easily import popular drawing file formats so that you can create graphics in any editor. You can use Flash to animate graphics using several different methods. For instance, objects can move or morph and have actions assigned to them. Visitors to your Web site will need the Flash plug-in for their browsers, but Macromedia has struck deals with browser vendors to automatically include the plug-in. Macromedia has even made the Flash file format available to other vendors to ensure its popularity. A utility included with Flash, called Aftershock, can automatically create HTML code that will play your animations with the Flash plug-in if it's available, play a Java variation if it isn't, or play an animated GIF file for older browsers. The Standalone Player utility will take a Flash file and convert it to a self-running program that can be run by anyone with Windows.

If you are a Web designer and want to create an animated interface for your site, Flash is exactly what you need.

Figure 24

Macromedia Flash

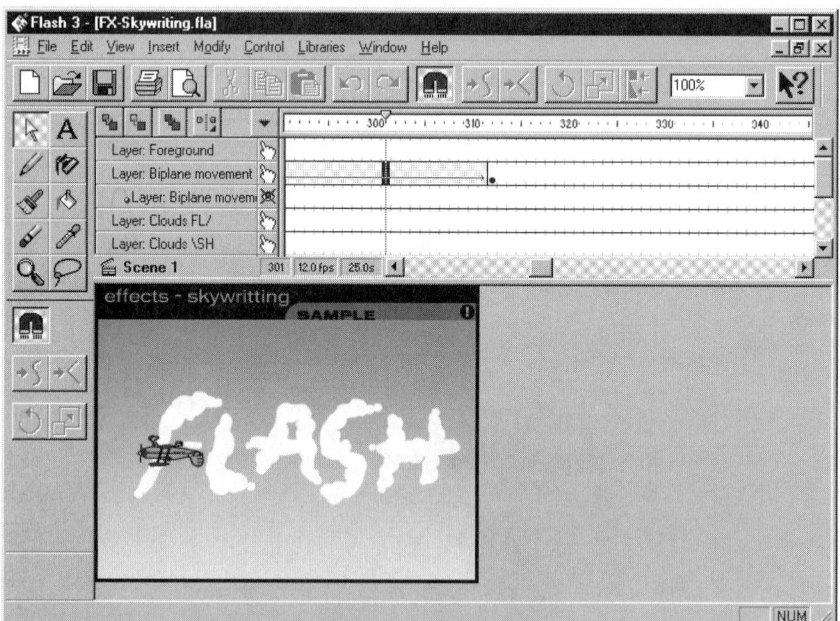

3-D Rendering

If you want a true 3-D image—not just the appearance of 3-D, but something you can actually rotate and view all sides of—you can create it on a PC, but you need specialized software. I'll concentrate on some of the basic packages that create the basic 3-D effects that people use the most.

Within minutes of installing U-Lead's Cool 3D ($50), you'll have created some amazing images and may feel you know the program well enough that you'll never read the manual. Cool 3D lets you add a number of 3-D effects and textures to text by dragging a thumbnail image of the preset you like onto your text. You can take the effect even further by adding fire, explosions and animation. When you're happy, just export the image as a single frame, a movie, or an animated GIF file. This program only does one thing and does it extremely well for a very low price.

Another option is Micrografx Simply 3D ($85). It isn't quite as simple to use as Cool 3D, but it does allow you to work with more than just text. By using a series of wizards, you can work with existing project templates or generate artwork of your own. There are plenty of predrawn objects and textures to aid in putting together an attractive scene. When you're finished, you can export the image to a number of bitmap and animation formats. The program also provides full support for the Web's VRML standard for viewing 3-D images on line.

Metacreations Bryce 3D ($160) is great at rendering lifelike landscape scenes (see Figure 25). It has tools for creating all types of land formations and a multitude of climates. Add a sky and water, and your scene is complete. By defining keyframes, you can bring the scene to life with rolling waves, moving land masses, a rising sun, or changing phases of the moon. The final rendered images are nothing short of stunning.

Figure 25

Bryce 3D

CAD

CAD (computer-aided design) programs are similar to drawing programs but have a specialized purpose. They are designed for creating very detailed technical drawings in three-dimensions. The drawings look like the kind of outlines you can create with CorelDraw or Illustrator, but they can be rotated in 3-D space. CAD programs also offer such features as *dimensioning*, the automatic labeling of a line with its actual length determined by the scale you set, and extensive layer control.

You can find low-end programs that allow you to easily create a basic floor plan or landscape design for personal use, but on the high end, you'll find that Autodesk's AutoCAD ($385 and up, depending on the version) owns the market. AutoCAD requires a lot of training, but it's the program that architects and engineers use.

Diagramming

If you spend a lot of time creating drawings like flowcharts, office layout diagrams, or organizational charts, you'll find that a specialized diagramming package will save you a lot of time. For instance, while you can certainly draw boxes connected by lines in any drawing package, moving the boxes around requires you to redraw the lines that connect them. With diagramming software, on the other hand, the lines connecting the boxes "stick" to them and move and stretch as needed.

The leader in diagramming software is Visio ($135 and up, depending on the clip art included). It comes in several versions; the one you choose depends on the type of diagrams that you need to create. Supplied with the software are collections of special clip art called Smart Shapes. These shapes can be easily connected using Connectors; all you have to do is drag the appropriate Smart Shapes into your editing window and then connect them with Connectors. Wizards can help you create some of the more complex diagrams and even automatically generate a diagram from a database.

Screen Capture

Screen-capture utilities take a picture of your computer screen—the whole thing, just the active window, or whatever part you draw a selection box around—and either save it to disk as a graphics file or copy it to the Clipboard so you can paste it into a graphics program. The cheapest utility, and often the only one you'll need, is the PrintScrn key on your keyboard, which places an image of the whole screen on the Clipboard. (If you want only the active window, hold down the Alt key while pressing PrintScrn.)

Paint Shop Pro and the CorelDraw suite both include screen-capture tools. For tough jobs, like capturing special cursors or other nonstandard interface items, try Techsmith's SnagIt ($40 shareware from **www.techsmith.com**).

Figure 26

Visio Professional

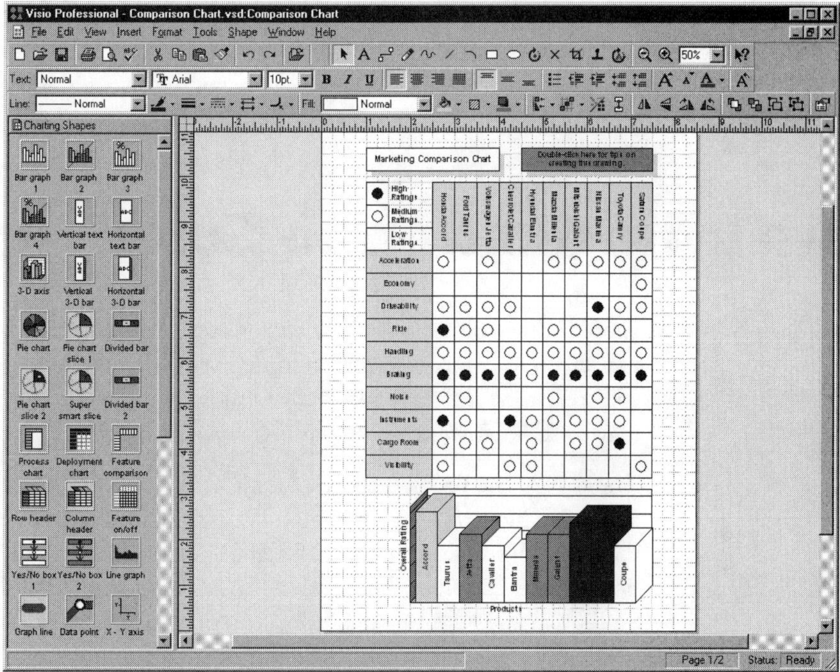

Clip Media

Not everyone has the time or talent to create artwork from scratch. That is where clip media, also known as stock images, can come to the rescue. These are illustrations or photographs that you can buy on disk or CD and use as is or modify to suit your purposes. Sometimes you can purchase just a single image, while other times you'll get thousands of images bundled together in a collection. You do have to pay attention to the licenses that come with the images to make sure you use them in an acceptable fashion, but in general, so long as you don't resell the images and don't use them for illegal or pornographic purposes, you're free to use the images wherever you like.

Collections of drawings are commonly called clip art, and photos go by the name of stock photos. These days, you can also get clip Web graphics with predrawn buttons and so on. Almost all of the programs described in this chapter come with a collection of clip media.

You can find bundles of clip art that offer a huge number of graphics (often in the hundreds of thousands) for a very small price, but you should be aware that you get what you pay for. These collections are known more for their quantity than their quality. The drawings may be tiny images that don't look that good when enlarged, or the photographs may have been scanned sloppily (or may be mediocre photographs to begin with). See the "Graphics Resources" section at the end of this chapter for pointers to some good clip art.

An Introduction to Color

People who produce color publications often have trouble matching colors on the screen to colors in print. A shining yellow gold may transmute into straw-colored tan, vibrating red may turn to mud—and your hot color brochure may look like it was colored with Crayolas.

The root of the problem is that monitors display colors by mixing red, blue, and green light, while printers use cyan, magenta, yellow, and black ink, and these two processes produce a different range of colors. Add in minor variations among monitors and printers, and it's not surprising that what you see on the screen is only an approximation of what comes out of the printer (or back from the print shop).

RGB vs. CMYK

The colors you see on your monitor are created in the RGB (red, green, blue) model. In other words, all the colors are created by combining red, green, and blue light (the three primary colors your monitor can display) in varying intensities. All three colors at full intensity make white; no color equals black. Fifty percent red and fifty percent blue gives a purple; 75 percent blue and 75 percent green gives turquoise. You may also hear RGB referred to as an *additive* color model since you create colors by combining the three primary colors. RGB is also commonly called *radiant* color because the color is actual light coming from your monitor.

Color printers and printing presses, on the other hand, use the CMYK (cyan-magenta-yellow-black) model, which mixes inks in the secondary colors of cyan, magenta, and yellow (*process colors*) to create all the other colors. This is also called a *subtractive* color model—because ink works by absorbing (subtracting) color from white light—or a *reflective* color model. If something looks red, it's because the ink has absorbed all the colors of the spectrum except red, which is reflected to your eye. Since cyan ink absorbs red, and magenta ink absorbs green, when you mix these inks together, they reflect only blue. Magenta and yellow make red; yellow and cyan make green. And opposite from the RGB model, in the CMYK model, all the colors together make black, and no color at all leaves only white (or the paper color). The black you get from mixing the three inks is muddy (brownish rather than pitch black), so color printing uses black ink as well.

Figure 27 shows the same color in the RGB and CMYK models.

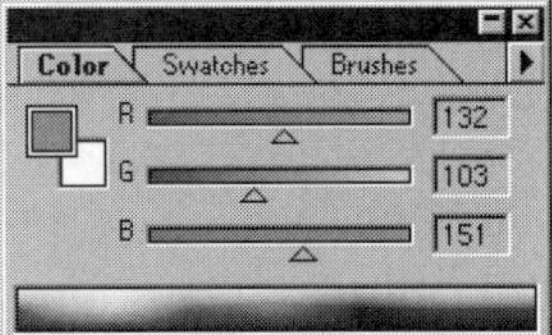

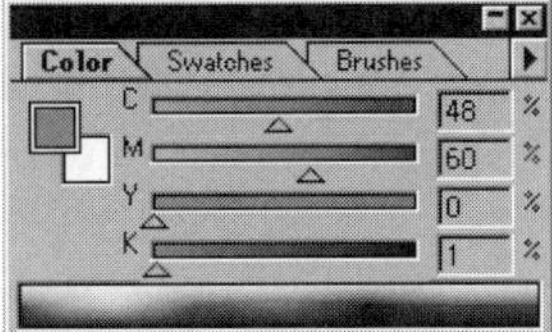

Figure 27

These two Photoshop color palettes show the same color in RGB and CMYK models.

Most graphics software supports both of these color models, and often a few others besides. You can create a new color by mixing proportions of RGB or CMYK colors. Breaking down other colors into their CMYK components for printing—which also has to be done for scanned photographs—is called *color separation*.

Spot Color

In the CMYK color model, you create a given color by mixing percentages of the base colors. The other way to print a specific color is by using what's called *spot* color. Spot colors are used in projects that will be printed in only two or three colors (rather than the four needed for CMYK), or that need a particular color matched exactly, such as the blue in IBM's logo. Some product packaging and screen printing jobs use as many as 8 or 10 spot colors to produce the desired result. You may also see one or two spot colors used along with the process colors so that photographs and a corporate color can both look good. Spot color is really only an issue if you're having your documents printed on a press—desktop printers can use only the CMYK inks that they come with, although you can define a color in your document according to one of the spot color systems, and your printer will do its best to reproduce it.

In a drawing program, you typically specify a spot color by choosing it from a display of sample colors in one of the *color matching systems* and telling the program not to separate it. (Paint programs have very limited or no spot color support.) At output time, the program will put everything of that color on its own sheet, and you can tell your printer what color those elements should be printed in. The most common system is the Pantone Matching System, and you'll hear its colors referred to as PMS colors or Pantone colors.

Color Management

As mentioned earlier, the difference between colors on the screen and in print can be frustrating to users of graphics software. Many brilliant backlit RGB colors just can't be reproduced in CMYK. The range of colors that each color model can reproduce is called its *color gamut*, and while the CMYK gamut encompasses most of the RGB gamut, there are still millions of colors you can see on your monitor that you just cannot print.

There's no way to force your printer to print colors outside of its gamut, so the alternative is to make your software display the image as it will print. One solution is to turn on your software's *gamut alarm* if it has one (Adobe Photoshop and Corel Photo-Paint do, for instance). The program will then warn you if you try to use a color that can't be printed and make its best attempt to find a similar color that's within the CMYK color gamut.

That works for colors you create yourself, if you're painting, for instance, but it won't help if you're trying to print a scanned photograph that contains colors outside the CMYK gamut. The solution in that case is to use *color management* software, which enables your graphics software to mimic your printer's gamut when displaying the image. You still won't be able to print the colors, but at least you'll avoid being surprised when the image comes out of your printer. Most of the professional level graphics software has built-in color management (see Figure 28). You'll also find some form of color management on most color printers.

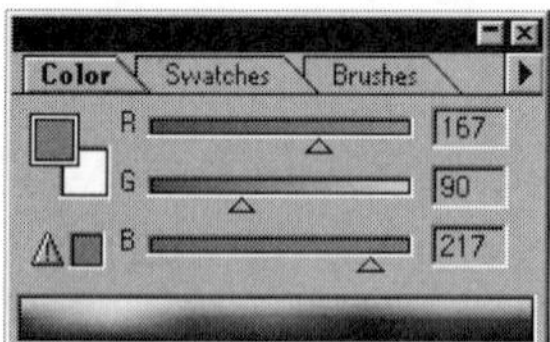

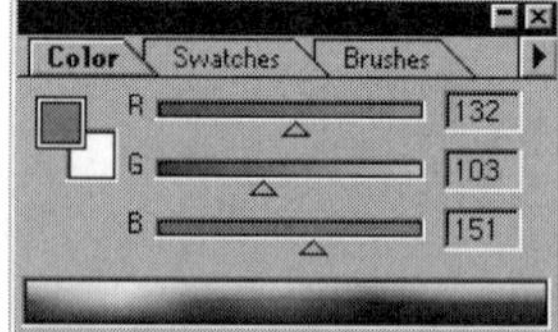

Figure 28

The little triangular button with the exclamation point in the Photoshop color palette at the left is the out-of-gamut warning. Click it, and the program automatically adjusts the sliders to the closest color your currently selected output device can print, as shown at the right (which is also the same color shown in Figure 27).

Color management software relies on *profiles* of the various components of your system—your scanner, monitor, and printer. Your software probably comes with generic profiles for some of the most common input and output devices. To use color management, you select the appropriate profiles in the relevant dialog box, and your software then knows how to alter your monitor display to reflect your scanner's and printer's capabilities.

To increase the accuracy of this process, several companies have come out with color profiling software, which enables you to create a custom profile of your particular monitor or printer to use instead of the generic ones that came with your program. Various factors, such as the age of your equipment and the humidity of your office, can alter the color capabilities of your specific unit from the "ideal" unit the generic profile was based on. A custom profile makes color management that much more accurate. Profiling tools range from simple monitor profiling utilities to elaborate and expensive hardware/software combinations that allow you to make a profile for every piece of equipment you use.

Color management also works better if your monitor is *calibrated*. Calibrating your monitor ensures that its display looks the same from day to day and the same as it did when you profiled it. To really make this work, you need a monitor that comes with calibration software and a special device that attaches to the surface of the monitor to measure its display. Systems like this cost a lot, so for most people, just profiling your monitor from time to time is a good place to start.

Color management is one area in which the Macintosh still has advantages over Windows systems. Apple ColorSync provides color management at the system level so that different applications can all draw on the same profiles and use them in the same way. Microsoft's Image Color Management (ICM) brings this capability to Windows, and ICM 2.0, introduced in Windows 98 (see Figure 29) and due to be included in Windows 2000 Pro, extends its coverage to the CMYK color space. At present, though, ColorSync is a more mature and flexible tool and is supported by more applications.

Figure 29

To use Windows 98's color management, you must add the correct profiles on the Color Management tabs of both the Display control panel and your color printers' properties dialog boxes.

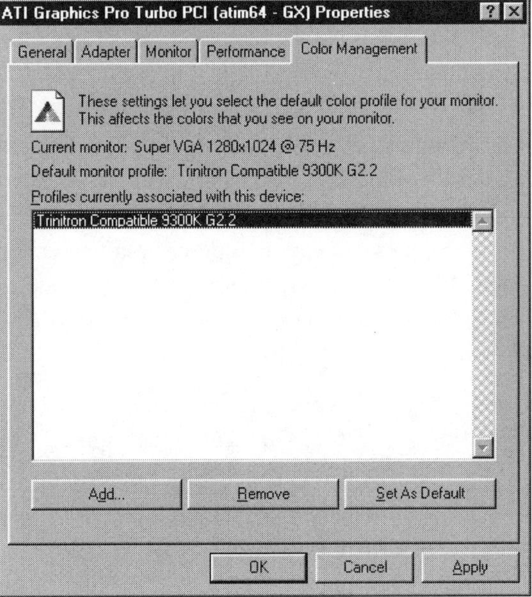

The simplest way to use color management is to test the quality of output yourself. Try using only the color management in your software and turning off that found in your printer. Print something. Now turn off the color management in your software and turn on the color management in your printer. Which method produces the result which most closely matches your screen or makes you the happiest? That is what should be used.

If you're planning to produce really color-critical publications on a printing press, you'll want to explore monitor calibration and profile-based color management in greater depth. It's a complicated subject, and we've only scratched the surface here.

Service Bureaus

Most people have some sort of printer connected to their computer that serves for the vast majority of their work. But there are times when you'll need a special type of output that your own printer doesn't provide. If you're planning to get hundreds or thousands of copies printed at a print shop, for instance, you may need to provide high-resolution film. Or perhaps you want to print a composition at poster size or get a photographic-quality reproduction. For output like this, you'll want to turn to a service bureau.

The most common use of service bureaus is for creating film to be used for offset printing. A bureau takes your files, prints them on an imagesetter, and gives you back high-resolution film and some sort of color proof. In these situations, you will be best served if you are in close contact with both your service bureau and your printer so that the output is to everyone's liking. You'll need to find out what type of film the printer needs and what type of file your service bureau prefers and how you can provide it—over the Internet, on some kind of removable hard disk, or whatever. It is also a good idea to study a book on your graphics software that describes the creation of color separations and potential problems. Many printers these days offer their own imagesetter service or subcontract the work themselves, so if you work with one of these, you'll need to deal with only one person.

Film separations are only one option, though. A bureau may also offer large-format poster prints, color transparencies, vinyl signs, T-shirts, coffee mugs, and much more. You can also have a service bureau scan high-resolution images or provide high-quality, color-corrected proofs. Talk to your bureau to learn its list of services and fee structure.

Most service bureaus are set up to work with Macintosh files, because over the years the Mac has been the most popular computer among graphic artists.

There are ways for PC users to work with such bureaus, and these days, the PC is gaining much greater acceptance as a graphics platform. If you find that your service bureau seems biased towards Mac users, keep looking. More service bureaus are installing PC systems so that they can work with the growing number of PC-using publishers and graphic artists. Remember that they are there to provide a service, and that you are paying to receive the service. It may be helpful to contact the manufacturer of your graphics software to find out which service bureaus have been authorized to work with your favorite software.

Field Guide to Graphics File Formats

In most software categories, there are only a small number of important file formats, but graphics software manufacturers seem to invent new formats all the time. I'll list the formats that you'll see most often and tell you where they may have originated or why that particular format should be used. Many of these formats have several variants, and a program may support a particular file type without supporting all versions of it.

Bitmap File Formats

BMP: Microsoft's format for bitmaps. It doesn't have all the features found in other formats and is not supported well on non-Windows machines.

CPT: Corel's proprietary format for Photo-Paint. It is an extension of TIFF that supports alpha channels and floating objects and retains layers and masks in working files You can also import CPT files into CorelDraw to get nonrectangular bitmaps.

EPS: Encapsulated PostScript. An EPS bitmap essentially packages the PostScript code necessary for printing a file along with a preview that allows you to place and view it in other programs. An EPS file can also contain printing instructions, which makes it most useful for professional graphics. A DCS file is a type of EPS file that has already been color separated.

GIF: Graphics Interchange Format. GIF is a compressed format that was originally developed by CompuServe to speed up image downloads, and it's still widely used on the Web. The format supports no more than 256 colors, though one color can be designated as transparent, and multiple images can be stored to create animations.

JPEG: Joint Photographic Expert Group. JPEG is a way of compressing photographic images and is widely used on the Web for full-color photographs because of the resulting small file sizes. It's a lossy format, meaning that a file saved as a JPEG file loses some data—more compression means greater loss, and at some point (depending on the image), you can start to see the effects.

PCX: Originally the proprietary format of an early paint program. PCX was once a popular bitmap format but is now losing favor as newer formats support more features.

PNG: Portable Network Graphics. The PNG format was designed to replace GIF, providing support for more colors and increased transparency options. There is no direct support for animation, but this is supported in the sister MNG (Multiple Network Graphics) format. Once browsers support PNG, the format will become very popular on the Internet.

PSD: Adobe's native format for Photoshop. It retains full support of layers, channels, and other effects.

TIFF: Tagged Image File Format. This is usually the best format for sharing bitmap images between programs on the Mac or PC. There are many subformats that support various features, and not all programs support all subformats. Using an LZW subformat (which uses the same Lempel-Ziv-Welsh data compression algorithm as GIF files) will greatly reduce file size.

Draw File Formats

AI: The native format of Adobe Illustrator and one of the better ways to transfer drawings between programs. Unless you're going to open the file in Illustrator at some point, though, you might as well use the essentially identical EPS format.

CDR: The native format of CorelDraw. Each version of the program has produced a new version of the format. While non-Corel programs claim to support the format, such support is usually imperfect or quite limited.

CGM: Computer Graphics Metafile. CGM files were very popular in the early days of graphics and are still supported by most programs. Unfortunately, they usually don't work well with the newer programs, and there's no real reason to still use them.

EPS: Encapsulated PostScript. EPS files are the best way to transfer graphics from any of the drawing programs for use in a page layout or word processing program. The biggest limitation is that you *must* print to a PostScript printer to realize all of the advantages of the format unless you're using Photoshop or Illustrator, which can interpret the PostScript files themselves.

WMF: Windows Metafiles. This is the native drawing format of Windows. There is also EMF, or Enhanced Windows Metafiles, which offers more features. Most programs now support both flavors.

Graphics Resources

`www.i-us.com` The i/us site offers something for everybody, including tutorials, discussion groups, product reviews, shareware, plug-in collections—it's a great place to explore all aspects of digital imaging.

`graphicssoft.miningco.com` The Mining Co. Web catalog's graphics section is a good jumping-off place for product information, tips, and shareware.

Paint Programs

`www.adobe.com/prodindex/photoshop` The main page for Adobe Photoshop offers information on the latest features, an art gallery, and free trial software.

`jasc.com` The JASC site offers tips, links to user forums, downloadable Picture Tubes, and free trial software.

`micrografx.com/webgraphics/ppublisher.asp` Micrografx loads the Picture Publisher site with downloadable effects and image sprays as well as an online user forum and free trial software.

`www.metacreations.com/products/painter55/weave.html` More promotional than user-oriented, the Painter page does have links to sources for training.

Drawing Programs

`www.adobe.com/prodindex/illustrator` Like the Photoshop page, Adobe's Illustrator page offers tips, case studies, an image gallery, and free trial software.

`www.corel.com/products/graphicsandpublishing/draw8` The CorelDraw page has lists of training resources (including a list of Corel-approved service bureaus) as well as case studies and a suggestion box.

`www.macromedia.com/software/freehand` The FreeHand page has a gallery, extensive technical notes, a directory to Macromedia Authorized Graphic Imaging Centers, links to training and other resources, and free trial software.

Web Graphics

www.adobe.com/prodindex/imageready Adobe's ImageReady page has tips and an overview of the product in PDF (Acrobat) format and free trial software.

www.macromedia.com/software/fireworks The Fireworks page has a gallery, a training video offer, and free trial software.

www.macromedia.com/software/flash The Flash page offers extensive information about the Flash format, which Macromedia pushes for use on the Web, and a free trial version of the program.

Clip Media

Below are listed only a few online sources for clip art and stock photography, though these offer a wide range of high-quality images. A quick Web search would turn up dozens more, many with highly specialized content.

photodisc.com Photodisc is one of the largest online vendors of royalty-free stock photographs. You can buy images online or download versions for free.

corel.digitalriver.com The Corel site offers images from the Corel Photo Studio collection in Photo CD format. You can download images in various sizes ranging from free thumbnail previews through $40 photos suitable for full-page reproduction.

artville.com The Artville site offers photographs and illustrations you can search for by subject, concept, metaphor ("busy as a beaver"), medium, or artist's name.

www.eyewire.com/eyewire.html Eyewire, formerly Adobe Studios, carries illustrations, photographs (including a nice collection of vintage photos), and even fonts.

18

Sound and Video Editing

by Jim Aikin (sound) and Sean Wagstaff (video)

In This Chapter

In the mid-1980s, revolutionary computer technology gave average people the power to publish their own newsletters, magazines, and books. To be a publisher, you no longer had to spend a small fortune on an expensive typesetting machine and a printing press: all you needed was a computer, a desktop publishing program, and a laser printer.

In recent years, similar developments have brought audio and video production to the desktop. If you own a PC with a sound card, all you need is software to turn it into a recording studio, and the hardware required to let it produce professional-sounding CDs will set you back less than $1,000. If you have a camcorder and your PC has a big, fast hard disk, for under $200 you can turn it into a video editing system, and if you buy a one of the new DV digital camcorders, you can produce videos that may look as good or better than a local TV news broadcast.

In this chapter, we'll describe the tools and techniques, first for audio production and then for video. Note that if you're ambitious, you can use the software described in the audio section to produce more sophisticated soundtracks for your homemade videos. See the "Audio and Video Editing Resources" section at the end of the chapter for pointers to Web sites where you can find additional information about the technologies and products discussed.

Sound Basics

As chips get faster, more and more of the audio in the world—from music to movie soundtracks—is being recorded, stored, and played back digitally. The Macintosh enjoyed an early lead among professionals as the preferred platform for digital audio, but by now the PC has largely closed the gap: many important music and audio applications are cross-platform, and there may now be more PC-only programs than Mac-only programs. While audio editing was once a fairly esoteric activity, with the advent of the Web and cheap CD-R drives (which can create audio CDs), all kinds of people are getting into the act.

To work with audio (that is, digital sound) on the PC, you first need a way to get the audio in and out of the computer. If you purchased a typical consumer PC, you have basic audio capability already in the form of speakers, a microphone, and a *sound card*. The sound card digitizes the analog electrical signals coming from the microphone—that is, it translates them into data that the computer can store, display, and manipulate (see Figure 1). When you click the Play button on your digital audio software, the sound card changes the audio data back into a form that you recognize as music or speech when it comes from the speakers.

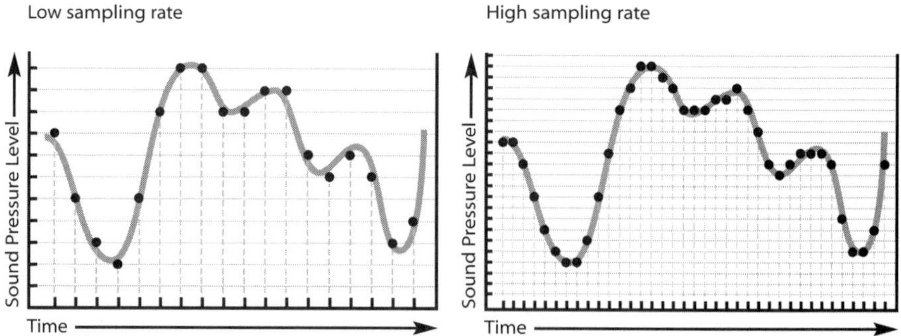

Figure 1

*A microphone converts sound waves into an electric current with a continuously fluctuating voltage, shown here as a curving line. For the computer to deal with the sound, that voltage is measured (*sampled*) periodically, and the voltage levels converted to a series of numbers, which can be stored on disk and used to recreate the sound later. The higher the number of samples that are taken each second (the* sampling rate*) and the larger the number of bits that are used to measure the voltage level (the* sampling resolution*), the more accurately the original sound can be recreated. In other words, a more accurate sampling process translates directly to higher audio fidelity.*

There are a number of ways you might want to take advantage of your PC's ability to record and edit audio and other forms of musical data:

- To re-record old LPs or cassette tapes onto CDs
- To reshuffle songs from your CD collection and burn new CDs to play in the car
- To add sounds to your Web site
- To create and record your own original music or publish it on a CD or as sheet music
- To clean up the soundtrack on a home video or to add music
- To provide musical accompaniment for practicing a musical instrument or for playing or singing along with for fun
- To custom-tailor sounds that will be played back on a digital *sampler*, a type of electronic musical instrument that (to simplify a bit) plays back prerecorded sounds (A lot of the orchestral music you hear in pop music and movies these days is played not by an ensemble of musicians, but by the composer working alone on a keyboard.)

In this chapter we'll explain the various types of audio and music software you may find, show how it's used, point out the most important features to look for, clear up a couple of common misconceptions about computer audio systems, and mention a few of the technical pitfalls that the serious audio geek has to be wary of.

Audio Hardware Options

The sound card found in a typical consumer PC doesn't perform well enough to produce professional-quality sound. This is not just because the components are inexpensive. The interior of a computer is an electromagnetically noisy environment. This noise is not a problem for digital data, but the audio enters and leaves the computer in analog form and can easily be contaminated. Contamination takes the form of *hiss* and *hum*.

Audio professionals generally use multichannel audio interfaces like the Event Electronics Gina and Layla interfaces (**event1.com**), which cost around $400 to $1,500. Multichannel hardware has both a card that fits into a slot in the computer and a *breakout box* with a number of jacks (see Figure 2). Often, the analog-to-digital conversion of the audio takes place in the breakout box, eliminating much of the contamination that would occur inside the computer. A separate analog audio signal can be routed in or out of the computer through each jack on the breakout box. A 2-in, 8-out (two inputs and eight outputs) configuration is common, but there is no standard feature set. (In a recording studio, the eight outputs would normally be plugged into a mixer (also called a console), though in a home studio, all the mixing might be done in software. Often these interfaces also have digital inputs and outputs to connect DAT recorders or proprietary digital multi-track systems like the Alesis ADAT.

Figure 2

The Gina. The Event Electronics Gina audio interface has two 20-bit analog inputs and eight 20-bit analog outputs, plus stereo digital I/O. It requires a PCI bus slot and Windows 95.

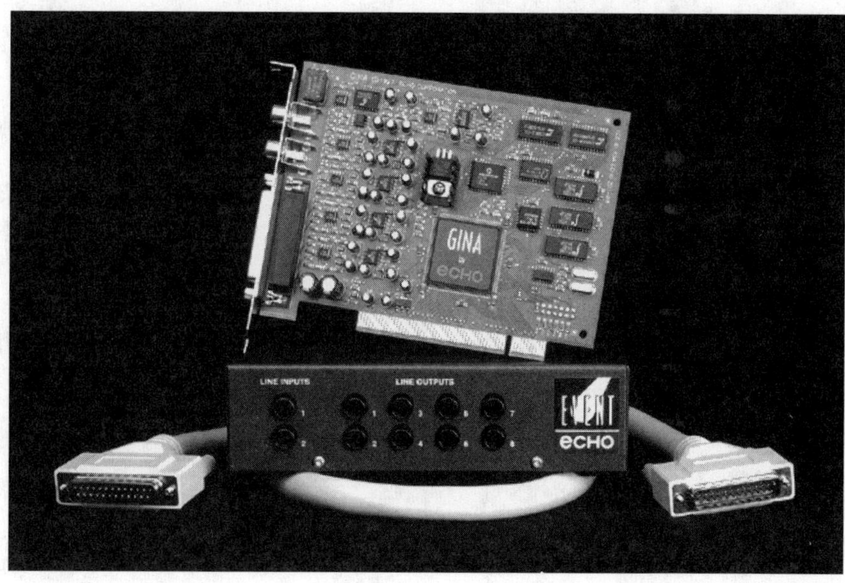

If you're shopping for an upgrade for your audio hardware, at the very least you should check to make sure the sound card has *full-duplex* capability. This means that it can record and play back at the same time. (A card that can't play back while creating a new recording is called *half-duplex.*)

This is necessary if you want to *overdub*: a recording technique in which you record new audio while simultaneously listening to material that was recorded earlier—adding guitar on top of a drum track, for instance.

Some audio hardware is general purpose and can be used with any compatible software. All sound cards are in this category, as are more sophisticated audio interfaces from Event Electronics, Yamaha, and other companies.

Other hardware is sold with proprietary software in a bundled system. A bundled system will often give you superior performance and fewer setup headaches, but down the road your system is likely to be less expandable and harder to keep updated with the latest expansion options.

Audio Specs

The standard in digital audio is 16-bit, 44.1kHz recording. This means that the incoming audio signal is *sampled* 44,100 times per second, and each sample is stored as a 16-bit *word.* Sixteen-bit, 44.1kHz recording is referred to as "CD quality," since this rate is used in ordinary music CDs. CD-quality audio takes up 10MB of hard disk space for each minute of stereo recording. The term *CD quality* is sometimes abused by manufacturers to hype inferior audio formats.

If you're satisfied with less fidelity, or if you lack storage space on your hard drive, you can record at 8-bit resolution, with a sampling rate of 22.05kHz, 11kHz, or even less. Recording at a lower rate will cut some of the high frequencies out of the recording, which may make it sound muffled, and using 8-bit resolution will add noise. Another way to create smaller audio files is by using some form of *data compression.* Some audio data compression is lossless, but most is *lossy,* which means that some fidelity is sacrificed for convenience. Audio that is sent over the Internet in real time is always in a lossy, compressed format.

Professionals often use higher-fidelity sampling formats. Some pro-oriented audio hardware can now record with 20-bit or 24-bit resolution at sampling rates of up to 96kHz. The additional data improves the quality of the final recording by allowing more precise calculations when two or more tracks are mixed.

Audio vs. MIDI

Because many sound cards have both audio and MIDI (Musical Instrument Digital Interface) capabilities, it's easy to confuse the two types of sound data. While an audio (.wav) recording of a real musical instrument playing a note will take (depending on the sampling rate and resolution) 20 to 170 kilobytes per second of sound, the MIDI equivalent of the same sound takes only a few bytes: one set of commands to tell the sound card's synthesizer to start playing a certain note at a certain volume, and another set to stop the note (sort of like the holes in a player-piano roll).

MIDI thus requires less than 1% the bandwidth that audio does, which means that even a slow PC can record and play back complex MIDI performances perfectly. MIDI song files occupy only a tiny amount of disk space compared to audio files, and MIDI data is much easier to edit.

The tradeoff is that with MIDI you get only the limited selection of sounds the synthesizer can make: A vocalist singing a song, for instance, cannot be recorded in MIDI format. A digital audio recording, on the other hand, can contain any imaginable sound—but you'll need a fast computer and lots of storage space.

MIDI recording and playback is done with a *sequencer* (a program that creates *sequences* of MIDI commands). Many of today's sequencers, such as Cakewalk Pro Audio, Steinberg Cubase VST, and Emagic Logic Audio (around $250 to $300 on the street) integrate MIDI recording and editing with audio recording and editing. These programs are used by professional musicians, and if you listen to the radio, you've probably heard many songs that were recorded entirely on PCs using this technology.

MIDI Sequencing

A MIDI sequencer is a great way to record and play back music on your PC. You can create a multi-track arrangement (see Figure 3) using many different kinds of instrument sounds—string orchestra, solo trumpet and flute, bass, drums, guitar, and so on. The sounds can be played by the MIDI synthesizer on your sound card or by a higher-quality hardware synthesizer. With a sequencer, you can freely change any aspect of the music, either in a friendly graphic interface using the mouse or in a notation display that shows your input in the form of standard sheet music. The volume, pitch, and duration of notes can be edited with precision. You can add various kinds of *controller* data to add vibrato and other kinds of nuance to the performance, or you can type lyrics into the sheet music and print it.

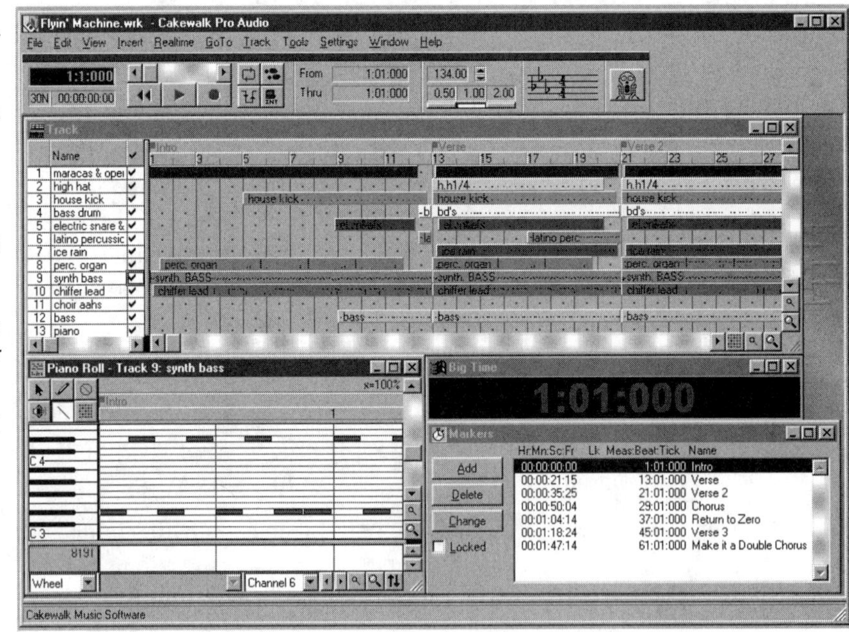

Figure 3

Cakewalk.

MIDI sequencers like Cakewalk let you use your PC to record, edit, and play back music. Chunks of MIDI data are represented by the colored clips in the upper window. The window at lower left is a piano-roll display for editing individual notes. The Markers window at the lower right contains user-defined markers for the various sections of a song.

Editing Audio

In an audio editing program, an audio file is displayed graphically, as shown in Figure 4. When stereo audio is being edited, the left and right channels are normally edited together, but each has its own *waveform* display. To make precise, detailed edits in the sound, you can zoom in the display as far as necessary. After zooming in, you can use a pencil tool to manually draw out clicks and pops in the sound.

An audio editor always has some type of *transport bar* (see Figure 5), usually in the form of a floating window. The transport bar is used for starting and stopping playback of the sound file, rewinding to the start of the file, fast-forwarding to a later point in the file, and so on. The term is taken from the transport mechanisms—motors, hubs, and so on—found on traditional tape decks. The buttons on the transport bar look and operate very much like those on a tape deck, except that when you click the Record button, a file dialog box opens, asking you to name your new recording. One big advantage of computer-based recording over tape-based recording is that on a computer's hard drive you can store an unlimited number of *alternative takes* rather than being limited to a fixed number of tape tracks.

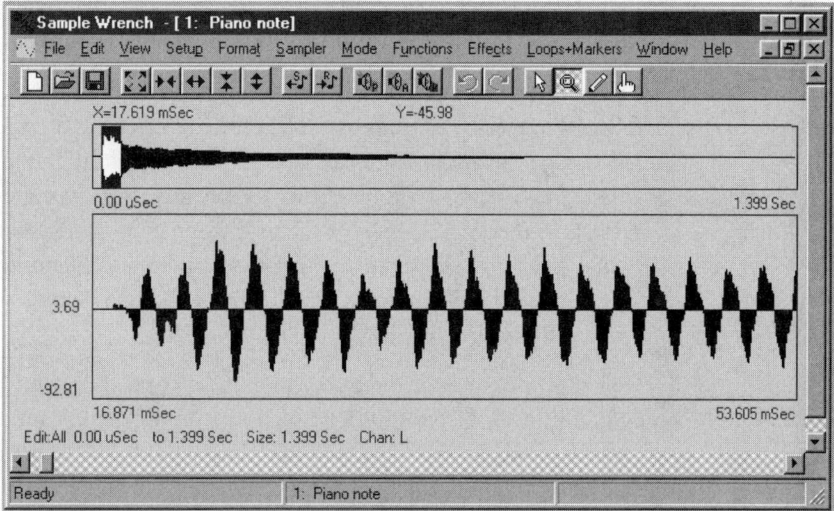

Figure 4

WrenchWave.

An audio recording as it appears on the screen in Dissidents Sample Wrench. The hills and valleys of the waveform correspond to the changes in air pressure that occur when a sound passes through the air and strikes a microphone. The smaller contour in the upper part of the window is an overview of the entire wave. A closeup of the highlighted area fills the larger area.

Figure 5

Steinberg Cubase's transport bar.

In addition to (left to right) the Rewind, Fast-Forward, Stop, Start, and Record buttons, this floating window has one-click controls for looping, automatic punch-in and punch-out recording, turning the metronome on and off, and more. The "OUT" and "IN" indicators at the right end of the bar blink when MIDI data is being sent and received.

Other important convenience features include nameable *markers* and input/output *metering*. After inserting a marker in a sound file (often by typing Ctrl M during playback—this is called inserting a marker on the fly), you can relocate the transport instantly at any marker and start playback from that point. By double-clicking between markers, you can select a region for editing. Input/output metering uses a multisegment loudness meter similar to the one on a cassette tape deck. Watch the meter during recording to make sure you haven't gone into the red. If the top segment (the red one) lights up, you've overloaded the input. This results in a very nasty sound called *clipping* distortion, which can ruin your recording. Since most audio hardware lacks input-level knobs, you'll need to turn down the sound at the source to avoid clipping.

The most basic type of audio editing will be familiar to anybody who has used a word processor or graphics program: you can drag the mouse cursor across a section of the audio, cut or copy it to a buffer, and then paste it back into the file at a different location. This is a great way to produce hilarious stuttering effects in recorded speech or to paste together a conversation that never took place. You can also perform a mix/paste operation, blending the material on the clipboard with the material already in the file, or reverse a section of audio so it will play backward.

For more sophisticated editing, look in the toolbar or pull-down menu. Here you'll find a variety of *DSP* (digital signal processing) options. Some produce results so subtle that only an audiophile would notice them, or care; others are obvious enough to wake the baby. Here are some of the possibilities:

- **Reverb** adds a cavernous echoing quality to the sound, as if it were being heard in a concert hall or gymnasium.
- **Chorus** adds a rich swirling character to the sound.
- **Panning** positions the sound in the stereo field at some point between the left and right speakers, or sweeps the sound from side to side.
- **Equalization** (often called EQ) changes the tone quality by boosting or reducing the overtones within a specific band of frequencies.
- **Normalization** makes the digital recording as loud as possible without overloading.
- **Compression** squashes the loudest signals in a file, boosting the overall level. A compressed sound is often perceived as louder or punchier than the same sound before compression.
- **Distortion** adds a fuzz tone to the sound, changing it from pure to crunchy or downright obnoxious.
- **Noise reduction** is a sophisticated process in which the software creates a profile of the "noise print" of the background noise in a file and then removes this noise throughout the file.
- **Noise gating** finds the quietest sections of the file and squashes them all the way down to silence, eliminating background noise, such as traffic noise or breathing, that might otherwise be heard between words or phrases.
- **Click and pop removal** automatically finds and removes the glitches from an LP recording that has been transferred to the computer.
- **Time compression/expansion** changes the overall length of a file without affecting its pitch.
- **Pitch shifting** transposes a file up or down in pitch without changing its length.

- **Fade in** and **fade out** taper a selected section of a file up from or down to silence.
- **Crossfade looping** creates a smooth *loop* (repeating section) in a sound that will be transferred to a digital sampler. Looping allows even a short sound to be sustained indefinitely.

In general, it's wise to perform no more DSP edits on an audio file than are actually required. Each process adds a tiny amount of noise to the sound, and as edits are piled on top of one another, the tone quality can degrade. To minimize this problem, many digital audio editing programs perform their internal DSP with 24-bit or even 32-bit fidelity, even when the sound is being stored at 16-bit resolution.

Some audio editing programs provide multiple undo/redo buffers. You can use this feature to compare the sound before and after an edit. Each undo buffer will take up its own chunk of disk space, however, because audio files are often too large to reside in the computer's RAM. If you're short of disk space, check the program's Preferences to see if you can limit the number of undo buffers.

The best known general-purpose audio editors for the PC are Steinberg Wavelab, Sonic Foundry Sound Forge, Dissidents Sample Wrench, and Syntrillium Software Cool Edit Pro ($250 to $350). If your main goal is to transfer your collection of old LPs and cassettes onto the computer to save the music as CDs, you can buy a program with limited audio editing and built-in CD-burning capabilities, such as Adaptec Easy CD Creator Deluxe or Steinberg Clean.

Plug-Ins

When buying a digital audio editor, ask what *plug-in* formats it's compatible with. Like Web browser plug-ins, audio plug-ins are small programs that extend the functionality of your main program and are often purchased from a different company than the one that makes the main program. An audio plug-in will usually be found on the Plug-Ins menu in the audio editor. The standard plug-in format on the PC is Microsoft's *DirectX* format. Plug-ins can be used for specialized purposes or to provide higher-quality processing than the host program offers. Some audio plug-ins are found as shareware on the Web. Others are even more expensive than the host programs.

Some plug-ins are *file based,* some function in *real time,* and some can operate in either mode, depending on how fast your computer is. A file-based plug-in, just like an ordinary editing command, makes changes in the audio data stored on disk. If the plug-in's operation cannot be undone, be sure to make a backup copy of your file before processing the sound. A real-time plug-in processes the sound on playback, without making any changes in the file. If you like the results, you can tell the program to overwrite the file. Some plug-ins also offer a preview mode, in which you can listen to the process in real time but with lower sound quality.

Some plug-ins are *CPU based,* which means they use the computer's CPU chip for all of their processing. Others require specialized hardware, such as that found in the Creamware TripleDAT and Soundscape SSHDR-1 PC recorders. Hardware-dependent plug-ins are often in proprietary formats and are offered by the manufacturers of the hardware as optional add-ons. The advantage of a hardware-dependent DSP is that it can perform good-sounding real-time processing even when installed on a slow computer. The disadvantage is that you have to spend extra money on the hardware.

Real-time plug-ins are especially important in multi-track audio recording software. With the right plug-ins, you can independently process many of the sounds in your mix and get truly stunning professional-sounding results—which brings us to the subject of multi-track recording.

Multi-Track Recording

Multi-track audio recording software allows you to record eight or even more separate audio *tracks* and play them back at the same time. This makes it easy to build up and edit a complex musical arrangement on the PC. The tracks always play back in perfect *sync* (synchronization) with one another, just as if they were physical tracks running side by side on a length of magnetic recording tape. On the PC, the tracks are displayed horizontally, as seen in Figure 6.

Every recorder has a limit on how many audio tracks it can record and/or play back at once. Before you purchase a multi-track recorder, be sure you understand exactly how it performs in this important area. A *hardware channel* corresponds to one of the jacks on the audio hardware. Some recorders will play back only one audio track for each hardware channel—for instance, a board with four outputs might play no more than four tracks at a time. More often, several tracks can be routed to a single output or to a stereo pair. For example, your software may be capable of playing 16 tracks at once through the stereo outputs of a standard sound card. In this scenario, the tracks are invisibly *mixed* by the software before being sent to the audio hardware.

In CPU-based recorders, the speed of the CPU and/or hard disk determines the number of tracks you can play back. This is a powerful argument for getting the fastest CPU you can. In proprietary recorders, special audio hardware is required, and the track playback count depends on the add-on hardware, not the CPU. Two of the popular proprietary recorders, Creamware TripleDAT and Soundscape SSHDR-1, were mentioned earlier in the section on plug-ins.

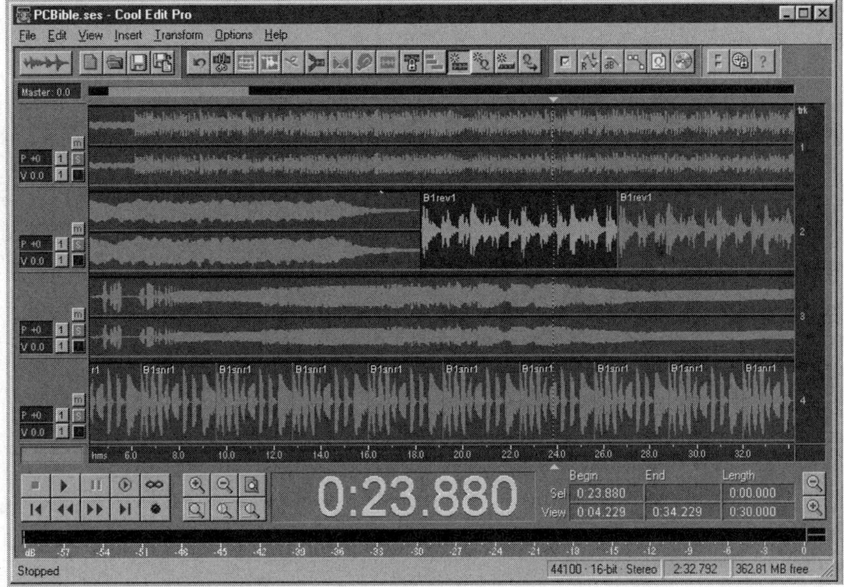

Figure 6

CoolEdit tracks.

In multi-track recording software, audio tracks are displayed horizontally across the screen as small waveforms, as seen here in Syntrillium Cool Edit Pro.

Most multi-track audio software will let you keep adding new tracks—as many as you'd like. Once you pass the maximum number that can be played back at once, however, you won't hear the new tracks unless you *mute* (temporarily silence) previous tracks. Tracks that are not able to play back are called *virtual* tracks. Even though you can't hear them, virtual tracks are very useful. They can store alternative versions of a guitar solo, for example, allowing you to switch back and forth and compare the various takes. Virtual tracks also make handy cut-and-paste buffers for assembling *composite* tracks (tracks made up of many short audio segments). To create a composite track, select the best passages from several other tracks, use a scissors tool to separate them from the surrounding material, and then use constrained vertical dragging to move them into the composite track without changing their time position.

Some multi-track recorders have as many editing options as a stereo audio editor. In addition, most multi-track recorders will let you perform an automated *mixdown,* in which all of the tracks are combined into a new stereo *master.* The master can then be burned onto a CD or sent to a pressing plant for commercial duplication. In a mixdown, the level and panning (left-right stereo positioning) of each track can be independently controlled. Some recorders provide editable graphic envelopes for this purpose, as shown in Figure 7. Others let you record your mix moves from onscreen sliders while listening to playback.

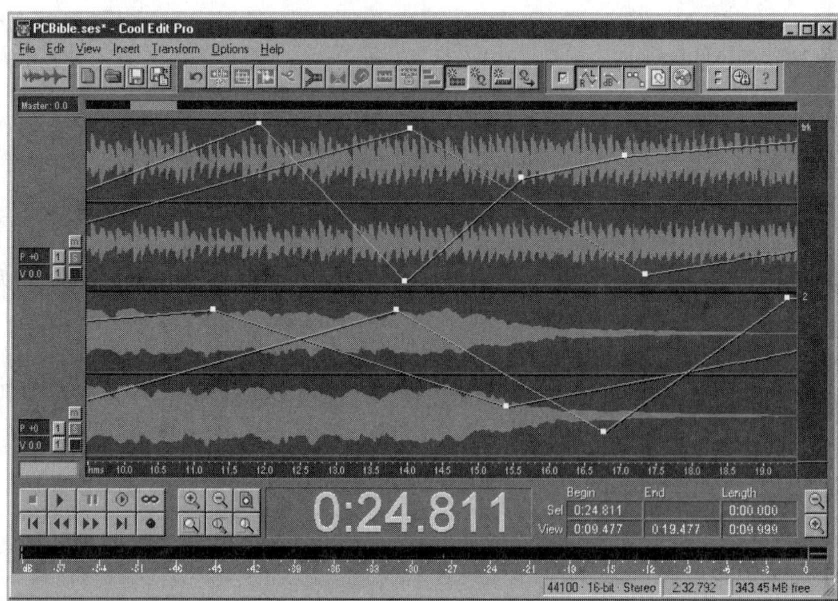

Figure 7

CoolEdit controls.

Here, graphic loudness and panning (left-right stereo positioning) envelopes are displayed on top of the waveforms in two Cool Edit Pro tracks. By clicking and dragging any of the points, you can change the shape of the envelope and thus taper the loudness or smoothly adjust the pan position of the sound. Click a line segment, and a new point will appear.

When a multi-track recorder is used in the studio in conjunction with other devices, such as tape decks and MIDI sequencers, some form of external synchronization is required. When two or more devices are synchronized, one is called the *master* and the others are called *slaves.* The master sends a sync signal of some sort to a slave. The slave uses this signal as a timing reference and is said to be *locked* to the master. Many of the high-end audio interfaces for the PC also include connectors for sending and receiving sync signals.

The important multi-track audio recorders for the PC include Steinberg Cubase and Emagic Logic Audio (both of which are also multi-track MIDI sequencers), Syntrillium Cool Edit Pro, Sek'd Samplitude, and Metalithic Digital Wings for Audio. A slightly different approach is taken by Sonic Foundry Acid. Acid is designed to let you create multilayered, energetic dance mixes quickly with a few clicks of the mouse. It comes with a library of audio rhythm loops in a special proprietary audio format that allows the sounds to be played back at any tempo. This may sound simple, but time-stretching audio in this way usually requires a lot of number crunching and can cause odd little artifacts to appear in the sound, even on a fast computer. Acid bypasses these problems by using a proprietary file format and other tricks.

CD Burning and Web Audio

Audio software often has utility features that go far beyond the editing of audio data. Steinberg Wavelab has a built-in CD burner, for instance. If you plan to burn music CDs, ask whether the CD-burner will support *disc-at-once* mode. Also ask whether the software will let you vary the amount of silent space between music tracks or eliminate this space entirely—a must for good-sounding music CDs. (Less sophisticated CD-burning software often inserts a fixed 2-second gap between tracks.)

If you're preparing audio for a Web site, you'll need to know whether the audio software can *export* a finished file in RealAudio, Shockwave, MPEG, or some other format suitable for *streaming* over the Web. Check with your Internet service provider to make sure its server supports the audio format you want to use. Audio sent over the Web for real-time playback is always *compressed* so that it will take up less bandwidth, and the server will need a particular type of software to be able to stream the audio on demand.

When recording audio on your PC from another source, such as radio or an LP or CD, you need to be savvy about copyright issues. Any audio material that was created by another person is owned by that person or by whomever the creator sold the copyright to. So long as your recording is purely for your own personal use, it's legal to do whatever you like with other people's sounds. However, it's illegal to *distribute* audio or MIDI music that you didn't create unless you have the permission of the copyright owner(s). For instance, if you "borrow" a song from a commercially available CD to use as background music on your Web site, or make a compilation of your favorite songs and burn one-off CDs of the compilation for your friends, you're guilty of copyright infringement. Getting sued for infringement is expensive, and even getting threatened with a lawsuit is an incredible hassle; don't risk it.

Other Ways to Make Noise

Turning into a virtual recording studio isn't your PC's only musical talent: it can also act as a musical instrument, a hip-hop DJ's console, or a band in a can—or it can print sheet music for use by a real band. Here's a brief rundown of software that's available for these tasks.

Software Synthesizers These use a sound card or equivalent for audio output, but they bypass the standard MIDI sound set on the card. Instead, they generate audio within the CPU. Software synthesis is an emerging field: The programs are varied, and most come from small companies. Reality, from Seer Systems (see Figure 8), is aimed at serious musicians and uses an advanced technique called *physical modeling* synthesis. With the far more affordable Mixman Studio ($150), you can assemble your own dance mixes by cueing rhythm loops directly from the PC's keyboard. The most popular soft synth currently is Steinberg ReBirth ($150), which emulates classic beatbox drum and bass hardware from the early 1980s.

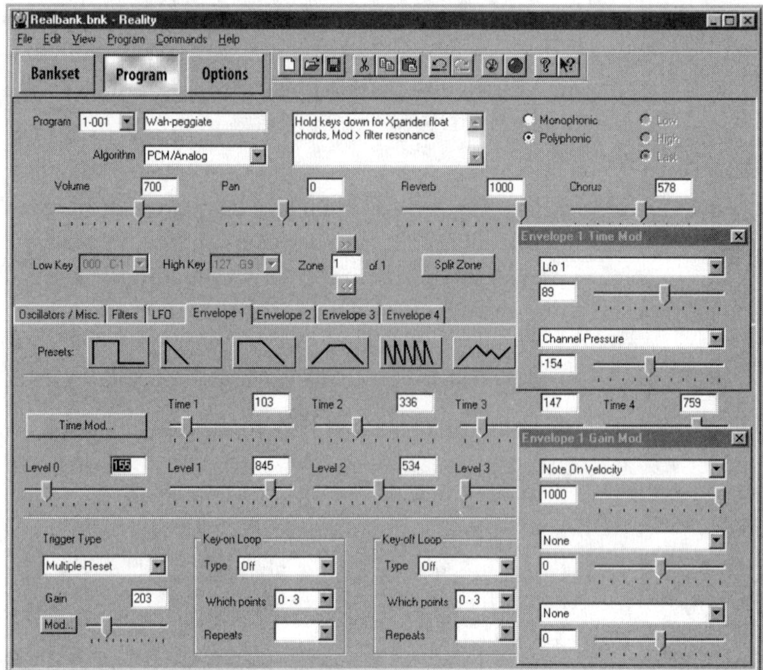

Figure 8

What is Reality?

Seer Systems Reality ($350) can turn your PC into a powerful synthesizer, complete with reverb and resonant filters, all modeled in software. The horizontal sliders are used for editing the parameters that control how Reality sounds. The two floating windows at the right are for adding modulation (expressive changes) to the sound.

Accompaniment Programs These provide a quick, fun way to play professional-sounding MIDI music. All you have to do is enter a chord progression (from a songbook, for instance) and choose a musical style, such as funk, Dixieland, or reggae, and the computer directs the band. PG Music Band-in-a-Box ($88 from **pgmusic.com**) and SoundTrek Jammer (see Figure 9) are the leading accompaniment programs. They duplicate some of the features of a Yamaha or Casio home keyboard, but allow you to customize your music much more freely. Accompaniment software is a better play-along resource for a music student than a CD, because it allows the tempo to be slowed down during practice sessions.

Notation Programs Most MIDI sequencers have some form of score printout for creating your own sheet music. You can play a MIDI keyboard and see a transcription instantly on the screen. Music notation is a surprisingly complex challenge for the computer, however. For true professional-quality notation, you can turn to Coda Finale. Finale lets you do virtually anything with the printed music, from guitar chord diagrams and minute adjustments in spacing to importing your own symbols in custom fonts. Finale can perform MIDI recording and playback, but it lacks many of the MIDI features of a sequencer. Other programs allow you to feed existing sheet music through an optical scanner and create notation files that can be conveniently edited or played back as MIDI music—but this technology is not yet mature, and some manual editing, or a lot, is required after the music is scanned.

Figure 9

Jammer. Jammer Professional ($100) provides many macro-level commands and options for putting together customized MIDI accompaniments. Even if your musical skills are limited, you can create reasonable-sounding music quickly with this type of software.

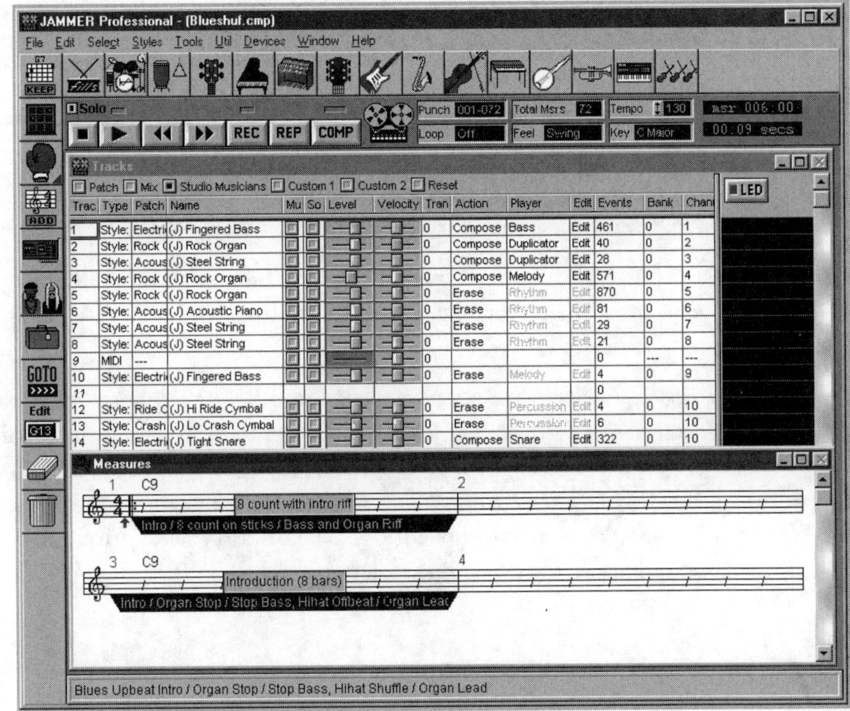

Notation Transcribers The "dream application" for many people is a program that can transcribe music from a CD, either as sheet music or as MIDI data. Emagic Logic Audio can perform this magic with fair accuracy so long as the input is from a clearly recorded *monophonic* (one note at a time) source. But no software yet written is capable of transcribing chords or multi-instrument arrangements. The technical obstacles are simply too formidable.

Musical Clip Art If you're interested in making music with your PC, but your knowledge of music and audio is limited, don't overlook the wealth of musical "clip art"—MIDI libraries and audio files—that are available online, either as free downloads or for a modest fee. MIDI music is distributed in the form of *standard MIDI files* (SMFs), which can be loaded and played back by any sequencer program. Most SMFs take advantage of the *General MIDI* specification, a standardized set of sounds (piano, trumpet, snare drum, etc.) found on all PC sound cards. Audio files are available online and on CD-ROMs as .wav files, the standard PC audio format.

New Sounds You'll also find *SoundFonts* online. These are short audio files that can be loaded into the dedicated RAM of many sound cards, such as the Sound Blaster AWE models. SoundFonts extend the MIDI sound set of the sound card with new types of instrument sounds.

Video Basics

A few years ago, only broadcast professionals and the most enthusiastic amateurs edited their own videos. To get even mediocre results, you had to invest a lot of money in hardware, and if you tried to get by on the cheap, the results were worse than the cheapest local TV show.

As with so many other things, PCs have changed all that: with a fairly modest investment, you can turn your PC into a video production studio. There are basically two ways to do it.

If you have a conventional camcorder, you can hook it to your PC with a *video-capture* device. This is an expansion card and/or external box that turns the analog signal from a camcorder or VCR into a digital format the PC can store on its hard drive (see Figure 10). You can use any camcorder—or for that matter, any conventional video source: a security camera, your VCR's output, whatever. Prices start around $150, including editing software.

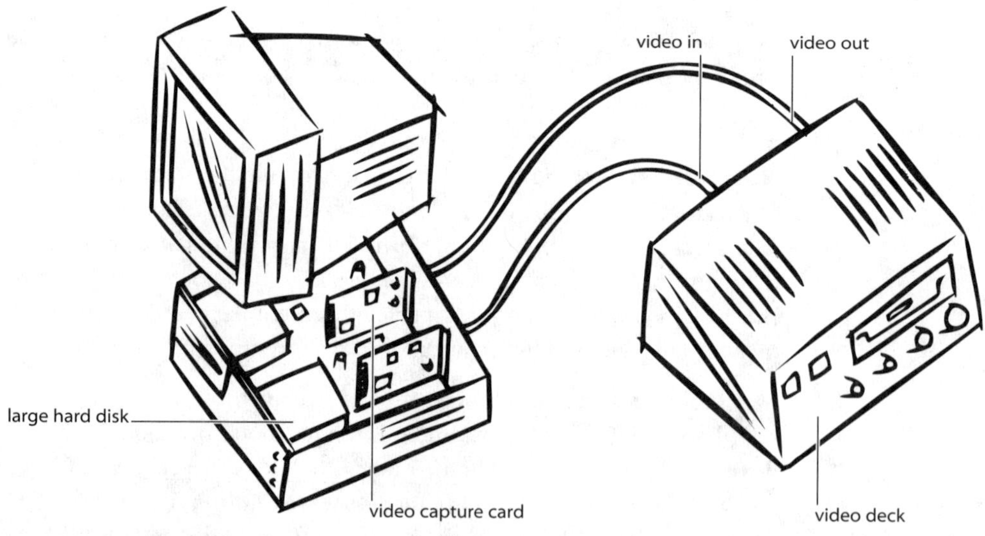

Figure 10

Putting a video-capture card in your PC allows you to transfer videos from tape to your hard drive.

For the highest quality video, get a DV (digital video) camcorder and an IEEE 1394 (aka FireWire or iLink) card to hook it to your PC. As this book goes to press, DV cameras start at $950, 1394 cards with the software necessary to transfer video to your hard drive at around $400, and video editing software costs from $100 to $550. However, camcorder prices are continuing to fall, and PCs with 1394 ports built in are becoming more common, so over the next year or two, the cost of a complete entry-level DV setup may drop to well under $1,000.

Either approach to PC video editing requires a lot of hard disk space. Captured video good enough to output to videotape (a 640x480 pixel image, or larger, at 30 frames per second) typically takes up 4 to 6MB per second, which means each gigabyte of disk space can store around 3 or 4 minutes of video. DV, which has a 720x480 pixel image, takes around 3.6MB per second, or a little under 5 minutes per gigabyte. If this seems like a lot, consider that if you converted one second of video into 30 Windows BMP images, they would take up over 25MB.

Editing video makes substantial demands on your PC's CPU and hard drive. Any Pentium that came with a UDMA drive (discussed in Chapter 4: Disks, Hard and Otherwise) should have what it takes. Older PCs may not have the horsepower to keep up.

Video Capture from Standard Camcorders

Video-capture systems come in a wide variety of configurations and prices, spanning everything from low-cost products for hobbyists and educational media producers to expensive tools aimed at professional videographers. The main differences are in the number and style of the video ports and the quality of the captured video. Pro-oriented boards also offer special features of little interest to the amateur.

Here are several things to look for when comparing video-capture systems:

- **Frame rate** determines how smooth the motion is: 30 frames per second (fps), the broadcast standard, looks best, 15 fps not so smooth, and fewer frames per second is definitely jerky.
- **Resolution** is the size of the captured image in pixels: you want 640 (or 720) by 480 (often called "full-screen") to approach broadcast quality. Note that on some boards you may get the top frame rate only if you use a smaller image, and you may get the largest image only if you lower the frame rate. Television is a standard 640x480 pixels, so you'll want the system to handle this resolution at 30 fps if you want to output your edits to tape.
- **Ports** will always include a pair of composite video input and outputs, which are used by standard consumer video devices, like VHS video cameras and VCRs. Some devices will include a pair of S-video ports, used by SVHS and Hi-8 cameras. Composite and S-video ports don't carry audio; some capture devices have their own audio inputs, while others use your PC's sound card.
- The **interface** affects performance and thus image quality. Your PC's parallel and USB ports can't transfer data fast enough for devices connected to them to capture images larger than 320x240 pixels (often called

quarter-screen images) at high frame rates. Video-capture systems that plug into your PC's expansion slots or connect to a SCSI adapter have no such limitation (though that doesn't necessarily mean they provide better image quality).

- **Single-frame capture** lets you use your camcorder as a digital still camera. You can grab single frames from videos and paste them on your Web page or into your word processing documents.
- The **bundled software** may be a full-featured commercial editing program like Adobe Premiere, a bare-bones capture-to-file tool, or anything in between.

Video-capture technology is evolving very quickly, so the following products may well be obsolete by the time you read this, but they'll still serve as examples of the kinds of products that are out there:

- **Iomega Buz** ($150 street price). The Buz supports video capture at up to 720x480 pixels at 30 fps, making it the closest thing to a professional video-capture device at a consumer-level price. The Buz system includes a card that plugs into a PCI slot and an external box that has all the video connectors (see Figure 11). The card also includes a SCSI port, which is handy if you want to hook up an external drive to offload video files. The Buz is bundled with MGI's VideoWave.

Figure 11

Iomega Buz Multimedia Producer (shown with camcorder and VCR)

- **ATI All-in-Wonder Pro** ($150). This is a regular video card (see Chapter 5: Monitors, Etc.) that also includes video capture at up to 640x480 pixels at 30 fps. This product is bundled with ATI's own software; both PCI and AGP versions are available.
- **Logitech QuickClip** ($60). This input-only box captures video at up to 320x240 at 15 fps. It also captures still images at up to 738x480 pixels. It is bundled with Logitech's own software; USB and parallel-port versions available.

Digital Camcorders

Since digital (DV) camcorders record in digital format, transferring that data onto a PC's hard disk is a relatively simple matter. All you need is a 1394 (aka FireWire or iLink) port, a new kind of serial port that's quite similar to USB except much faster. Your DV camera needs a 1394 port, too, of course—some don't have them.

As noted earlier, as this book went to press an expansion board to add a DV-capable 1394 port to your PC cost around $400, but the price has been dropping quickly as the technology catches on. Within a year or so, I expect it to drop to around the cost of an Ethernet board—not much over $50. Intel estimates that the cost of adding 1394 ports to a PC will be only $15 and expects not just cameras but printers, scanners, DVD players, and eventually hard disks to use the 1394 interface (see Figure 12).

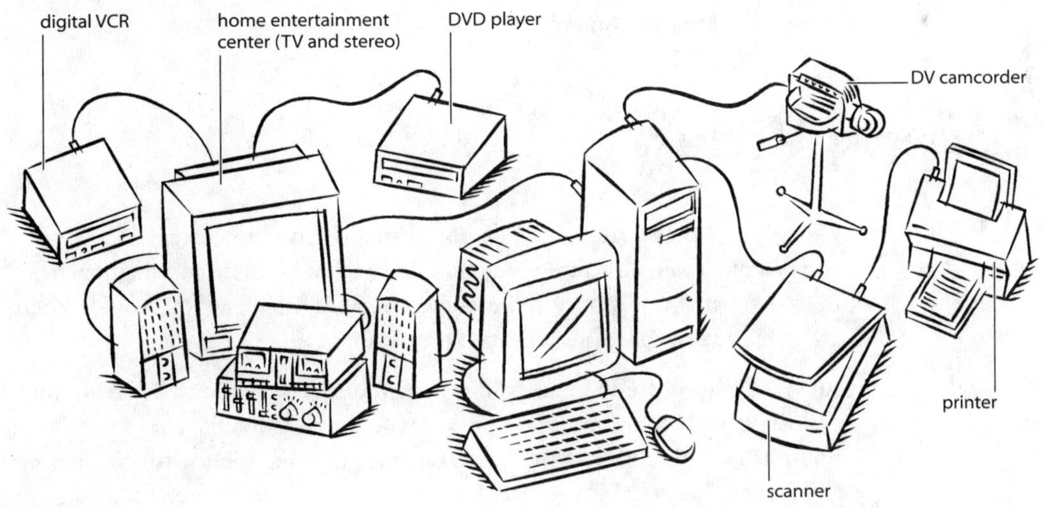

Figure 12

In Intel's vision of the future, 1394 cables link a home PC to a scanner, printer, DV camcorder, and home entertainment center, which in turn uses 1394 cables for high-speed digital connections to a digital VCR and DVD player.

DV camcorders themselves are still pricey compared with their conventional competitors. The cheapest currently available costs around $950—more than twice the price of a comparable analog camcorder. If you want to edit high-quality video, though, that's money well spent.

Here's why. When you transfer a recording from a conventional camcorder to your hard disk, the process of converting it from analog to digital format degrades the image. When you transfer the final edit back to tape, converting from digital back to analog degrades the image again. The better your video-capture system, the less degradation occurs, but the final tape is always going to be inferior to the original.

With DV, the original recording is digital. When you transfer it to your hard disk, no data is lost: the file's an exact copy of what's on the tape. The same is true when you transfer your final edit back to DV tape. The image is degraded only when you transfer your final edit to analog (VHS) tape—though you don't necessarily have to do that, since you can simply play the DV tape. (All consumer-oriented DV cameras have the necessary composite video outputs to connect to your VCR or TV set.)

Even if you do copy your final edit to analog tape, since the quality of the DV recording is higher than you'd get from a conventional camcorder, and the final edit is the same quality as the original, the final results will still be better than you'd have achieved with a conventional camcorder and a video-capture card or with old-fashioned multideck editing. If the VHS tapes you create don't live up to that description, try another deck—early DV users report that transfer results vary from one model to another.

Editing Video

Once you've transferred your tape to your hard drive, it becomes a file. Now you can open it in an editing program like Adobe Premiere and manipulate the video with your mouse and menu commands, much as you would text in a word processor or images in a paint program.

All video editors pretty much follow certain basic conventions. Typically, for each shot (segment of tape) in a project, you drag a video file icon to one of an unlimited number of tracks in a timeline interface and then set the beginning and end (*cut points*) of the segment you want to use (see Figure 13). String together a series of such shots, and you have your edited video.

Figure 13

Most video editors are fairly similar to Adobe Premiere. At the top left, a window displays a list of video files used in the current editing project. At the bottom, a timeline window shows the way the two clips previewed in the top right window will overlap in the edit. The little box between the two long bars indicates a transition, like a wipe or dissolve.

One video clip may start right where the last one ends, or there may be some overlap with a *transition*, like a dissolve or wipe. This can substitute smoothness and continuity for the sometimes jarring effect of "cuts-only" edits. The most common transition is the dissolve, where one layer of video becomes transparent and fades away as the next one appears. Other popular transition effects are the wipe, where one video track slides across the surface of another, and the window shade, where one track opens like a venetian blind to reveal the next. Premiere, for example, provides a rich assortment of transition effects. To use one, all you have to do is drag an icon from the Transitions palette (see Figure 14) and drop it in a track between two overlapping clips (as shown in Figure 13).

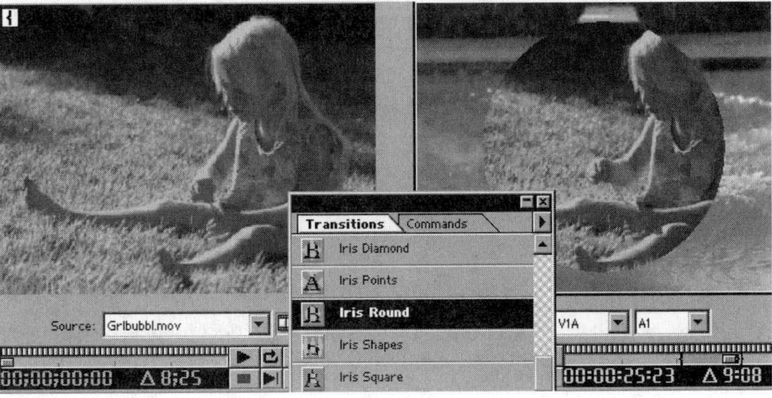

Figure 14

The right window previews a shrinking-iris wipe (popular in silent movies and cartoons) from the little girl to a swimming pool.

After you've finished editing, it's time to create your final product. Usually that means you'll *print* to tape: that is, connect your VCR to the outputs of your video-capture system, start recording, and click the Play button in your editing program to run through the entire project. Alternatively, you can save the final project to a file for playback from disk; if you have a CD-R drive, you may even be able to create a video CD disc for playback on compatible DVD players. Another option is to save in a *streaming* format like RealVideo for playback over the Web.

Animation and Special Effects

Video editing can be as simple as splicing together multiple clips to crop out the bad stuff; however, most desktop producers will want to do much more, including creating animation and special effects. Most video editing software comes with a basic collection of effects; for example, most programs will let you filter your color video to black and white, for that arty look, or composite video clips using blue screen or chromakey effects, to different backgrounds into a scene.

One of the features of most video editing tools is the capability to animate text and other simple artwork, such as logos, to create title effects. To create animation, you generate *key frames* that define the starting and ending points of an object's position over a period of time. For example, in Ulead's Media Studio, you can set key frames to animate an object in an interface that's entirely separate from the editing window's timeline (see Figure 15), or you can paint directly onto layers of video using Photoshop-style brushes and effects, a procedure called *rotoscoping*.

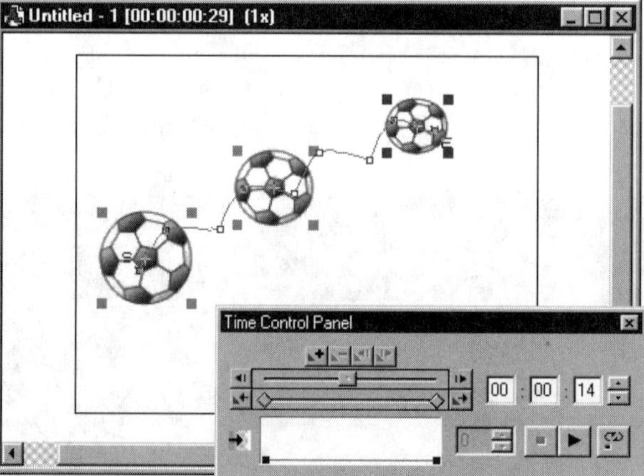

Figure 15

Ulead's Media Studio has an animation interface for titles and other animated objects that's separate from the video editing timeline. This example creates a cartoon soccer ball that bounces across the screen on the path shown, getting smaller to simulate its movement away from the viewer.

There are also a number of special effects and animation tools specifically designed for creating video effects. One of the most prominent examples is Adobe's After Effects, which specializes in video animation and compositing—perfect for combining a character filmed against a blue screen with a background of a bustling news room, for example, and for creating fancy titles (see Figure 16).

Figure 16

After Effects lets you add all sorts of titles to your video projects.

Some video editors, including Premiere and Speed Razor, have plug-in architectures that allow you to add additional effects created by other software makers. Plug-ins are great because some companies specialize in creating tools that generate wild effects, but you get to use them in the familiar environment of your video editing application.

Audio and Video Editing Resources

Audio

`www.emusician.com` *Electronic Musician*, a monthly magazine, is an excellent source for reviews of software, how-to articles on recording, and tutorials on the basics of MIDI. *EM* sometimes shows traces of its roots as a do-it-yourself magazine for the soldering iron set, but this slant has a good side: the coverage is always down to earth and practical.

www.keyboardmag.com *Keyboard*, a monthly magazine aimed at musicians who play all kinds of keyboards, is another excellent source for hard-hitting reviews of software, how-to articles on recording, and tutorials on the craft of making music with computers. *Keyboard* is more performer oriented than *Electronic Musician*, and its coverage of software and digital audio is supplemented with articles on artists and music theory.

Principles of Digital Audio, Ken C. Pohlmann (ISBN 0070504695). If you hanker after a deep technical understanding of esoteric topics like noise shaping, the mathematics of quantization errors, digital tape formats at the bit level, perceptual coding in data compression, and what goes on in the guts of a digital mixing console, this is the reference work to turn to. Its not for the faint of heart, but worth a glance or two purely to catch a glimpse of the wizard behind the curtain.

www.computersandmusic.com and **midi-classics.com** These two mail-order specialty retailers' Web sites offer comprehensive catalogs of the latest music hardware and software.

You can find information about the digital audio and MIDI products mentioned in this chapter at the following manufacturers' Web sites. As you may notice, many of them are German companies.

www.adaptec.com Adaptec, Inc.

cakewalk.com Cakewalk (Twelve Tone Systems)

www.codamusic.com Coda Music Technology

creamware.com Creamware US

dissidents.com Dissidents Software

www.emagic.de Emagic Soft- und Hardware GmbH

event1.com Event Electronics

metalithic.com Metalithic Systems

mixman.com Mixman Technologies

pgmusic.com PG Music

www.seersystems.com Seer Systems

www.sekd.com SEK'D (Studio für elektronische Klangerzeugung Dresden)

sonicfoundry.com Sonic Foundry

soundscape-digital.com Soundscape Digital Technology

soundtrek.com Soundtrek, Inc.

steinberg.net Steinberg Soft und Hardware GmbH

syntrillium.com Syntrillium Software

Video

www.pcgv.com PC Graphics & Video, the Web site of *DCC Magazine*, a tabloid-format monthly, with insightful tips and reviews for digital-content creation professionals.

www.dv.com DV Live, the Web site of *DV* magazine, an industry-leading monthly publication focusing on digital video editing and technology. This is an excellent source of reviews and how-to articles for digital-content producers.

www.eMediaweekly.com The Web site of *eMediaweekly*, a weekly publication by Ziff-Davis that covers industry news about media creation, including video editing and video publishing.

newmedia.com The Web site of *New Media* magazine, a monthly publication devoted to multimedia in general. This is a good source of reviews of digital video products.

www.newmedia.com/NewMedia/97/07/td/Digital_Video_Rev.html The product information in this article is way out of date, but it still gives a good overview of DV technology.

www.adamwilt.com/DV.html An excellent and comprehensive DV FAQ.

www.dnai.com/~zane/dv/dv.html A simpler, somewhat less technical DV FAQ.

www.well.com/user/richardl/SilverListFrameSet.html A DV FAQ devoted exclusively to PC hardware and Windows software.

pentium.intel.com/solutions/archive/issue6/stories/harmony.htm A short essay outlining Intel's vision of how 1394 interfaces will eventually be used to integrate home PCs and entertainment systems.

Here are the Web sites for the video companies mentioned in this chapter:

www.adaptec.com Adaptec, Inc.

www.adobe.com Adobe Systems, Inc.

www.atitech.com ATI Technologies, Inc.

www.canon.com Canon

www.datx.com Data Translation, Inc.

www.digieffects.com DigiEffects Software

www.dps.com DPS, Inc.

www.speedrazor.com in:synch Corp.

www.jvc.com JVC

www.logitech.com Logitech

www.matrox.com Matrox Electronic Systems Ltd.

www.metacreations.com Metacreations

www.mgisoft.com MGI Software, Inc.

www.panasonic.com Panasonic

www.promax.com Promax Technology, Inc.

www.sony.com Sony

www.ulead.com Ulead Systems, Inc.

19

Getting on the Internet

by Robert Lauriston

In This Chapter

Before you can send e-mail, surf the Web, or read newsgroups, you have to get your PC connected to the Internet. In this chapter, I'll briefly describe the pros and cons of the various kinds of connections (modem, ISDN, cable modem, and so on) available, give you tips on choosing the best Internet service provider (ISP), and tell you how to set up Windows to make the connection.

If you're not sure why you would want an Internet connection, browse Chapters 20 through 24 for a look at some of the things you can do with one.

Which Kind of Connection?

You've probably heard the jokes about "World Wide Wait"—the time you spend waiting for Web pages, particularly those with graphics, to appear in your browser, or for software to download to your hard disk. Sometimes that wait's caused by slow Web servers or Internet congestion, which you can't do anything about, but a faster connection to the Internet will speed up many tasks, particularly those that generate traffic only between your ISP's server and your PC, like sending or receiving e-mail. Here's a quick comparison of the five main types of hardware: modems, ISDN adapters, cable modems, DSL, and satellite dishes

Modem

Most people access the Internet through modems. You probably got one with your PC; if not, you can pick up a V.90 (so-called 56K) model for under $100, making a modem the cheapest kind of Internet access hardware. A modem will do double duty as a fax; buy a voice modem and you can use it as an answering machine as well. (See Chapter 24: Use Your PC as a Phone or Fax, for tips.)

All ISPs support modems, and fees for modem connections are less than for any other kind of access: rates start around $15 a month for "unlimited" access, but such cheap accounts are usually limited by busy signals at peak hours. An ISP that makes sure it always has enough lines to handle all its users, and that has a big enough pipe to the Internet that every user gets top performance, will cost more like $25 a month, which will probably include a high but limited number of free hours (my ISP includes 150).

A modem hooks to a regular phone line, so unless you decide to install a second line so you can use the phone and modem at the same time, setup expenses are negligible. Many ISPs charge new users nothing; some even offer a period of free service to attract customers.

Internet Connections Compared

	Modem	ISDN	DSL	Satellite	Cable modem
availability	everywhere	some areas	few areas	anywhere	few areas
hardware cost	under $100	$100 to $200	$500	$300	provided
initial setup cost	$0 to $25	$175	$250	$50	$100 to $175
monthly costs	$15 to $25	$40 to $50	$150 to$400	$30 to $130	$30 to $55
"free" hours*	150 to unlimited	varies	unlimited	25 to 200	unlimited
per-minute telephone charges	none if local call	varies	n/a	none if local call	n/a
charge per additional hour of connect time	50 cents	varies	none	$2	none
top download speed (kbps)**	42 to 47	120	144 to 1500	400	1500 to 3000
top upload speed (kbps)**	30	120	350	30***	500***
minimum 1MB download time	3 minutes	1 minute	5 seconds to 1 minute	20 seconds	5 seconds
minimum 1MB upload time	5 minutes	1 minute.	30 seconds	5 minutes	15 seconds

*Cheaper ISPs with "unlimited" hours often have too few modems for all their customers to connect at peak hours. In other words, your access is limited by busy signals.

**Modem and ISDN figures are from CNET reviews. Others are based on service providers' claims and reports by users.

***Satellites and some cable modems can handle only downloads; your modem handles uploads.

Note that if you live in a remote area, you may have to pay per-minute charges to the phone company. If those charges are steep, you may find that some ISPs offer cheaper access over 800 numbers.

Beyond the way they tie up phone lines, the main disadvantage to modems is that they're relatively slow (see the table "Internet Connections Compared"). See Chapter 21: The Web and Browsers, for some tricks and tips on how to make the most of a slow connection.

When comparing modems with other connection options or evaluating modem upgrades, be aware that the 56K speed rating commonly claimed for today's V.90 modems is misleading. It's supposed to mean 56 kilobits (7 kilobytes) per second, but CNET's lab tests have yet to find a modem that can transfer data at over 47K (though the reported connect speed is often higher). Moreover, you'll get those speeds only when downloading data (getting new e-mail, loading Web pages in your browser, downloading files). When uploading (sending e-mail), the theoretical speed is 33.6K, and actual transfers are more like 30K. Thus, if you already have a V.34 (28.8 or 33.6K) modem, all you should expect from upgrading to a V.90 model is around 50% faster downloads.

All these numbers assume ideal telephone line conditions. If your building has old wiring, or there's old equipment on the line between you and your ISP, you may get much worse performance.

Older 56K modems manufactured before the V.90 standard was approved use one of two proprietary protocols: X2 or K56flex. Many ISPs support only one of these, and those that support both have different access numbers for each type. Most of these modems can be upgraded to V.90, often just by downloading a free firmware update from the vendor's Web site.

ISDN

If you want higher performance than you can get from a modem, the most widely available alternative is ISDN. Whether it's an option for you depends on whether a local phone company offers ISDN service in your area. If it does, you can install a new ISDN line or convert an existing POTS ("plain old telephone service") line to ISDN—at the phone company's end, the two use very different equipment, but at your end, they use the same kind of wires. ISDN lines are usually installed with larger jacks so you won't confuse them with regular phone lines.

Installation, monthly charges, and calling charges vary wildly, so call your local phone company for information. Just as an example, Pacific Bell charges me $26, which includes 200 hours of connect time outside of weekday business hours. All calls over the limit or during business hours are billed at business rates: around one cent a minute.

To use the ISDN line, you need an ISDN adapter ($100 to $275; the most expensive models include a modem for use with fax software and modem dial-up services). Most install in your PC just like a modem (see the "Installing a Modem" section in Chapter 8: Upgrade It Yourself); a few are external boxes that hook to your PC's printer port. There are also external ISDN adapters that connect to your PC's serial port, but they're best avoided: a standard serial port's simply not fast enough to handle the full bandwidth of ISDN. Outside of having to use bigger jacks, connecting the adapter to the ISDN line is just like plugging in a modem, but it won't necessarily work right off the bat. Don't be surprised if you have to make a lot of phone calls to the adapter's tech support people and your phone company before you get everything working (see Figure 1).

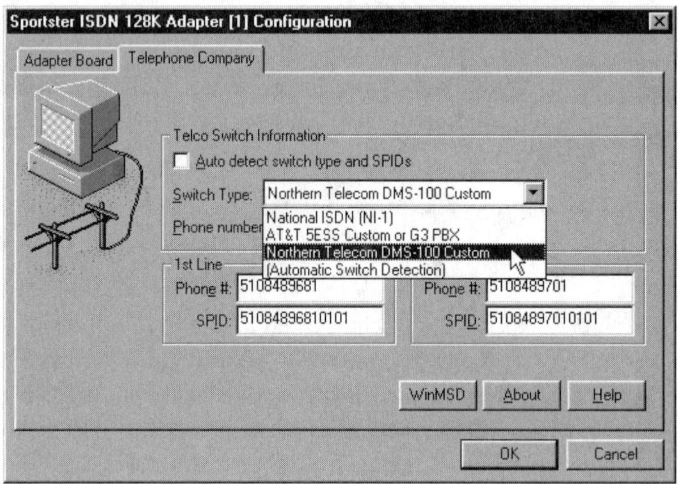

Figure 1

ISDN configuration.

This dialog box from my ISDN adapter's configuration utility gives you an idea of the kind of settings you may have to deal with. In addition to two telephone numbers, my ISDN line has two SPIDs, and all four numbers have to be entered correctly for the board to work properly.

ISDN performance is a complicated topic. An adapter can use either one or two *B channels*, which can run at either 56 or 64 kbps, depending on your phone company's hardware; thus, the maximum transfer rate varies between 56 and 128 kbps. (The numbers in "Internet Connections Compared" reflect the latter.) Phone companies and ISPs sometimes charge separately for each channel, so using only one when you don't need top performance may lower your costs. For example, since Pacific Bell counts each channel as a separate call, during business hours I keep the second channel turned off.

If you want to use your telephone, answering machine, fax, or modem with an ISDN line, buy an ISDN adapter that has one or two regular phone ports. If there are two ports, each will have its own phone number. When your PC's off, the ports probably won't work—and in a power failure, they definitely won't work, which could be a safety concern if you don't have a regular phone line, too. You can use one phone port while you're online if you connect to your ISP with only one channel, but if you use both channels, both ports will be dead until you disconnect. Depending on your telephone habits and your phone company's charges, it may be cheaper to have both regular and ISDN lines than to use the ISDN line for voice calls.

A more expensive but more flexible alternative to an ISDN adapter is an *ISDN router*, a box that connects to the ISDN line and is in turn connected to your PC via an Ethernet cable (which means your PC needs an Ethernet card).

ISDN routers start at around $300, but they can support multiple PCs, and you don't have to leave your PC on to use its phone ports. A router can double as an Ethernet hub (see Chapter 25: Networks: Connecting PCs).

DSL

From the user's perspective, DSL (*Digital Subscriber Line*) connections are quite similar to ISDN connections. As with ISDN, you can use DSL only if a local phone company supports it—and then only if you're within a certain distance of the central office with the phone company's DSL hardware. Like ISDN, DSL uses regular phone lines, and with the right attachments the same line can support regular telephone equipment. You can get either a DSL adapter that goes in your PC or a router that can handle multiple PCs.

The big difference is in performance and cost. There are a number of variations on DSL, which is a fairly new and still evolving technology, but the versions currently in use in my area handle downloading at 144 to 1500 kbps and uploading at 128 to 1100 kbps. Initial installation cost, including the hardware, is around $750. Total monthly charges for the slowest connection start at around $125—but since with DSL you can stay online 24 hours a day without incurring any additional charges, for heavy users that may be cheaper than the fees for ISDN.

DSL is still fairly rare, so there's a good chance it's not available in your area. Prices will likely drop as it becomes more popular.

Satellite

You've probably seen those little DirecTV satellite dishes popping up all over the place. The same company sells DirecPC (**`www.direcpc.com`**), a similar dish you can use to download Internet data to your PC at up to 400 kbps. (You can also get a single dish that handles both TV and data.)

The big drawback to this system is that it's one-way: you can only download from the satellite, so you need a modem and phone line to handle the outgoing data, like the commands that tell the company's servers to send a page up to the satellite when you click a link in your Web browser. Another drawback is the system's $2-an-hour charge after you exceed your monthly allotment (25 hours for $30 a month, 100 hours for $50, or 200 hours for $130), though you can cut that in half by using another ISP to handle the modem connection.

DirecTV's main competitor, Dish Network, reportedly has plans to offer a competing service, which should drive down the price. In the meantime, DirecPC's probably not cost effective unless you live in an area where you have to use a toll call or 800 number to reach a regular ISP.

Cable Modem

If you have cable TV in your neighborhood, you may be able to get a *cable modem*, the fastest Internet connection available at a price most of us can afford. While not yet available in many areas, cable modems are a great deal. The @Home service, for example, costs as little as $30 a month for a 24-hour-a-day connection that's faster than ISDN or DSL. Up-front costs may be as low as $100, since instead of buying the modem, you lease it from the cable company, and the charge is included in the monthly bill.

Cable modems are so new that nobody's sure yet what will happen to their performance as they become more popular. While current subscribers have claimed transfer rates a hundred times faster than you'd get with a modem, all the cable modem users on a particular segment of a cable system share a certain fixed amount of bandwidth, so as more people subscribes to the service, performance may degrade at peak hours. On the other hand, all the users of any ISP share a fixed amount of bandwidth—that of the ISP's connection to the Internet backbone—so this isn't a characteristic unique to cable modems.

Typically, cable modems impose some sort of software or hardware limits to prevent you from using the connection with more than the authorized number of PCs; some work with only one PC—period. Some cable modems are one-way and, like satellite connections, require a regular modem and phone line for uploading.

Get What You Pay For: Choosing the Right ISP

The role Internet service providers (ISP) play in getting you on the Internet is similar to the role local cable TV systems play in the television industry. With few exceptions, neither actually make anything; they just charge you a monthly fee for providing access to services produced by other companies.

Which ISPs you should consider depends on several factors:

- **If you're using a modem or ISDN**, look for an ISP that has a local access number: that is, one where the phone number your modem or ISDN adapter dials to connect to the ISP is a local call. Otherwise, you'll be paying per-minute charges while you're logged on. (Access number are also known as *POPs*, for point of presence.)
- **If you can't find an ISP with a local access number**, compare the toll charges you'd have to pay to connect to the nearest ISPs with the charges of others that offer 800-number access.

- **If you plan to share a single connection with family members or roommates**, check to see how many e-mail accounts are included in the monthly charge and how much extra you'll have to pay for any additional accounts you'll need.
- **If you travel with your notebook PC** and want to access your e-mail or surf the Web while you're on the road, compare rates to see whether the out-of-area surcharges of a local or regional ISP would end up costing you more than the higher monthly rate of a national ISP. If you travel internationally, shop around for the lowest surcharges for the countries you plan to visit.
- **If you plan to use the Internet only for e-mail**, look for an ISP that offers a special light-use monthly rate. Typically, you'll pay around $7 a month for five hours of connect time, with additional time billed at $2 an hour.
- **If you want your own Web site**, compare the number of megabytes of disk storage included in the monthly base rate, the surcharge you'd have to pay for any additional space you will require, and the ISP's support for any special goodies, like RealAudio or FrontPage forms, you want to include at your site. (See "Creating Your Own Web Site" in Chapter 21: The Web and Browsers, for more on this topic.)
- **If you want to use ISDN, DSL, or a cable modem**—assuming any of them are available in your area—you need an ISP that supports that hardware. That may drastically limit your choice.

Online Services: A Dying Breed

America Online (`aol.com`), its now-subsidiary CompuServe, and Microsoft's imitation, MSN (`msn.com`) are national ISPs with a difference. All three began as private online services, which up through 1994 were where average PC users went to exchange e-mail, download shareware, search online reference libraries, and interact with each other. As discussed in more detail in Chapter 21: The Web and Browsers, the explosive growth of the Web from 1994 on forced these companies to reinvent themselves as national ISPs.

For a time, these former online services tried to distinguish themselves by offering their members exclusive services that weren't available on the Internet. For example, America Online used to be the only place online where you could read the current issues and archives of *Newsweek*, *The New York Observer*, and a number of other magazines.

The online services still offer some extra content, but this approach has been dying out due to simple economics. People aren't willing to pay a significantly higher monthly rate for these extra services, so the online services had to move to the same flat-rate pricing as regular, no-frills ISPs. Since the online services can't charge extra, they don't have the money to pay for exclusive content. Even if they did, most companies who own that content would rather put it on the Web, where it gets a bigger audience and they retain control—which is why you can now find *Newsweek* and the *Observer* on their own Web sites (just add .com to those names).

Beyond those basics, the best way to choose an ISP is to pick one that gets high marks from its customers, especially those in your immediate area, using the same version of Windows. Ask about busy signals and server outages and whether people have received good technical support.

If you're using ISDN or DSL, try to get recommendations from users with the exact same hardware as you. Since these kinds of connections aren't as standard as modems, it's usually best to find a good ISP first and buy an adapter or router the ISP recommends rather than to buy the hardware and then shop for an ISP that knows how to make it work.

Beyond recommendations from ISPs' customers, the next best place to get information about them is online. I've listed half a dozen useful Web sites in the "Internet Access Resources" section at the end of this chapter. If your PC's not connected to the Internet yet, check out the sites using an Internet connection at work, school, a friend or relative's house, or a public terminal at a library or cybercafe. You could also just accept one of those free trial offers from America Online and then cancel the account if you find an ISP you like better.

Making the Connection

Compared with deciding which kind of connection you'll use and choosing an ISP, actually connecting your PC to the Internet is painless. If someone's told you it's hard, they probably did it back in the Windows 3.1 days, when it could be a real challenge. (If you want to connect a Windows 3.1 PC to the Internet, by the way, America Online's software is likely to be easier to use than anything else around.)

The following instructions assume that you've opened an account with an ISP (you can usually sign up by phone) and installed your modem or ISDN adapter according to the manufacturer's instructions. If you're using another kind of connection, these instructions probably won't apply.

To connect, you'll need some information your ISP will provide you when you sign up. That should always include:

- your userid
- your password
- your ISP's domain name (whatever.com, or sometimes whatever.net)
- the phone number your modem will dial to connect to the ISP

Your ISP will probably give you the IP addresses of its primary and alternate DNS servers, but you probably won't need that information. In some circumstances, it may assign you a fixed (*static*) IP address for the connection, but this is rare for regular dial-up accounts.

In the rest of this section, I'll give you detailed instructions on how to create new Dial-Up Networking connections in the various flavors of Windows. If you're running Windows 95 and haven't installed Microsoft Internet Explorer 4.0 or a later version, follow the instructions in "Using the Internet Setup Wizard." If you're running Windows 98, or if you have installed MSIE40 or later, skip down to "Using the Internet Connection Wizard." If you're using Windows NT and haven't installed MSIE40, see "Using NT's Dial-Up Networking Phonebook."

Using the Internet Setup Wizard

The following instructions apply *only* if you're running Windows 95 and have not installed Microsoft Internet Explorer 4.0 or a later version.

The obvious way to create a new Dial-Up Networking connection is to double-click the Make New Connection icon, but that method doesn't give you much help. Here's the easy way:

1. From the Start menu, choose Programs/Accessories/Internet Tools/Internet Setup Wizard.
2. Click Next to start.
3. If it's not selected, select "Connect using my phone line"; then click Next.
4. Select "I already have an account ..." and click Next.
5. Select No to tell the Wizard not to set up Microsoft Exchange to handle your e-mail and click Next. (See Chapter 20: E-Mail, for tips on picking a better e-mail program.)
6. Click Next to begin installing files.
7. Type your ISP's name (or whatever you want the connection icon in your Dial-Up Networking folder to be called) and click Next.
8. Enter the area code and phone number the modem is to dial to connect to the IS;, then click Next.
9. Enter your userid and password.
10. Unless instructed otherwise by your ISP, click Next to confirm that it automatically assigns you an IP address.
11. Enter the IP addresses of the ISP's primary and alternate DNS servers (see Figure 2). If you don't have the alternate server's address, you can leave that field blank. Click Next to continue.
12. Leave the Internet Mail entries blank (you can set up your e-mail software later) and click Next to continue.
13. Click Finish to complete the setup.

Your new connection should now appear in the Dial-Up Networking folder, and should be activated and connect you automatically whenever your Web browser or any other program tries to access the Internet. You can also connect manually by double-clicking the icon.

Figure 2

Windows 95's Internet Setup Wizard.

When using this wizard, you always need to enter the IP addresses of your ISP's DNS servers.

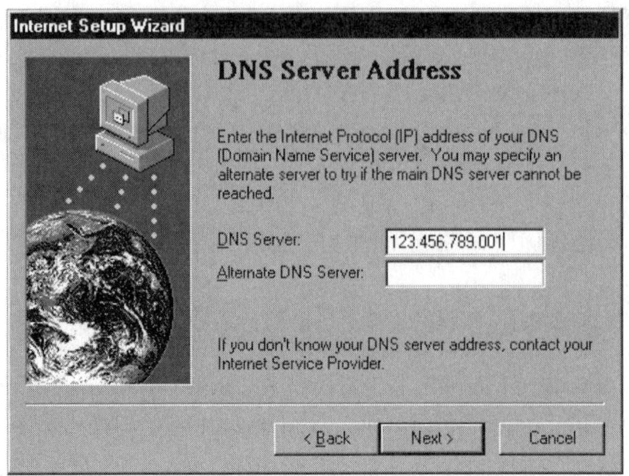

The first time you use your new connection, you'll have to enter your password; if you want Windows to memorize the password, check the Save Password box before clicking Connect.

Using the Internet Connection Wizard

If you're running Windows 98 (or Windows 95 and have installed Microsoft Internet Explorer 4.0 or a later version), the obvious way to create a new Dial-Up Networking connection is to double-click the Make New Connection icon. If you're an expert, that's the fastest approach, but if you're new to the game and want more help, it's easier to use the Internet Connection Wizard.

1. From the Start menu, choose Programs/Internet Explorer/Connection Wizard. That will bring up a screen with three options.
2. If you follow the first option, "I want to sign up and configure my computer for a new Internet account," the Wizard downloads some information from Microsoft and uses it to generate a short menu of ISPs (see Figure 3) available in your area. (Given the names that showed up on my screen, I suspect they're selected on the basis of what kind of deals the companies have made with Microsoft.) If the ISP you want is on the list, you can register directly, without establishing an account first.

   Otherwise, you want the second option, "I have an existing Internet account." Just keep clicking Next to accept the defaults until you get to...
3. ...the Dial-Up Connection screen (see Figure 4). This is an important branching point: from here, you can create a new connection, or you can select an existing ISP and set up its e-mail account or news server for use with Outlook Express. To create a new connection, make sure the settings match those in the figure and click Next.

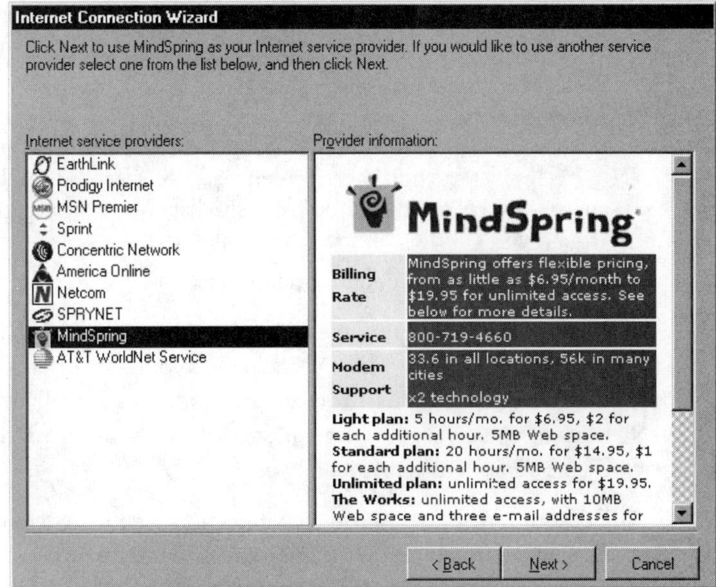

Figure 3

The Internet Connection Wizard offered only ten of the hundreds of ISPs available in my area when I chose the "new account" option.

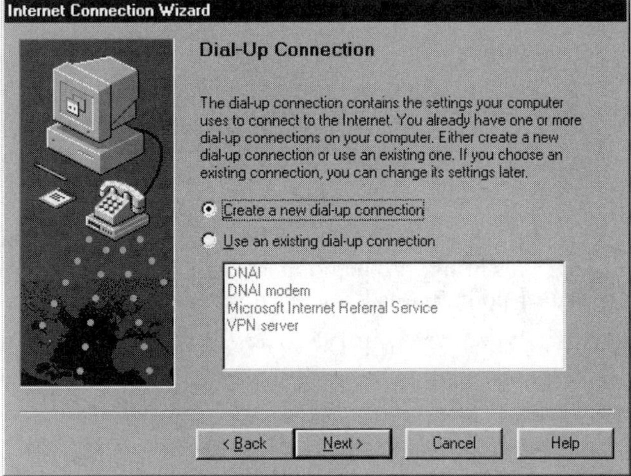

Figure 4

In this screen, you can choose to create a new connection or modify an old one.

4. The next steps are identical to steps 8 and 9 in the previous section. Enter your ISP's phone number and click Next and then enter your userid and password and click Next.
5. Click Next to confirm that you don't want to change the Advanced settings. (In the unlikely event that your ISP does not automatically assign you an IP address and set the DNS server when you log on, you can set those options by choosing Yes here.)

6. Type your ISP's name (or whatever you want the connection icon in your Dial-Up Networking folder to be called) and click Next.
7. Select No and click Next to skip setting up e-mail; then do the same thing again to skip news setup, and again to skip Internet directory service setup. (If you want to use Outlook Express for e-mail and/or news, you can always return to these screens later to set them up, by selecting the name you created in step 6 from the list shown in Figure 4, but I recommend you get the connection working first.)
8. Click Finish to complete the setup.

From now on, Dial-Up Networking should be activated and connect you to your ISP automatically whenever your Web browser or any other program tries to access the Internet. You can also connect manually by double-clicking the icon in your Dial-Up Networking folder, though you may need to reboot your computer before that icon appears.

The first time you use your new connection, you'll have to enter your password. If you want Windows to memorize the password, check the Save Password box before clicking Connect.

Using NT's Dial-Up Networking Phonebook

NT doesn't have a Wizard to automate Internet setup. That's no big deal, though, since its version of Dial-Up Networking is easier to use than the one in Windows 95/98. If you've installed Microsoft Internet Explorer 4.0 or a later version, you can use the Internet Connection Wizard, or this method, whichever you prefer.

1. From the Start menu, choose Programs/Accessories/Dial-Up Networking. This brings up the Phonebook, a dialog box that manages all your dial-up connections. (There's no folder like the one in Win95/98.)
2. Click New. Type your ISP's name (or whatever you want this connection to appear as in the Phonebook list) in the "Entry name" field and type the phone number in the "Phone number" field (see Figure 5).

   Check "Use Telephony dialing properties" if this is a notebook PC and you'll be dialing the same number from various locations defined in the Modems or Telephony control panel. In that case, be sure to add the area code in the "Phone number" field.

   Normally "Use another port if busy" should be unchecked. Check it only if you have more than one dial-up device on your system and want Dial-Up Networking to try another device if the one you've selected is already in use.

Figure 5

The Phonebook's Basic tab.

Enter a name for your connection and your ISP's access phone number in this dialog box.

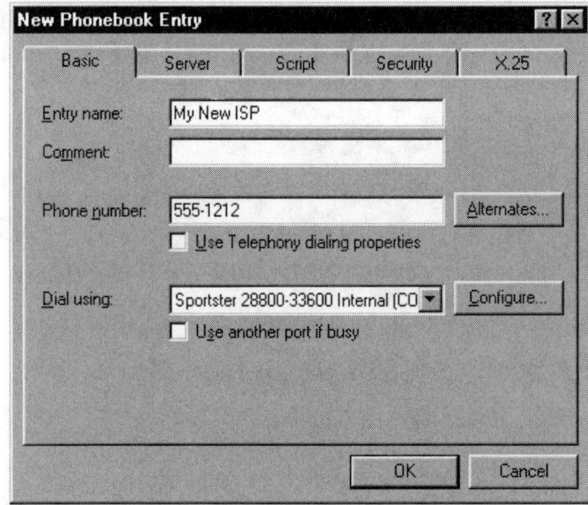

If you're using ISDN and want to connect with both channels, you may need to set "Dial using" to Multiple Lines and then click Configure and check both channels' icons (see Figure 6). If you want to keep your phone bill down by deciding each time you connect whether to use one or both channels, create two Phonebook entries: one for a single channel and one for both. (If you have two modems and two phone lines to connect them to, you can also use Multiple Lines to connect with both at once—provided your ISP supports this feature.)

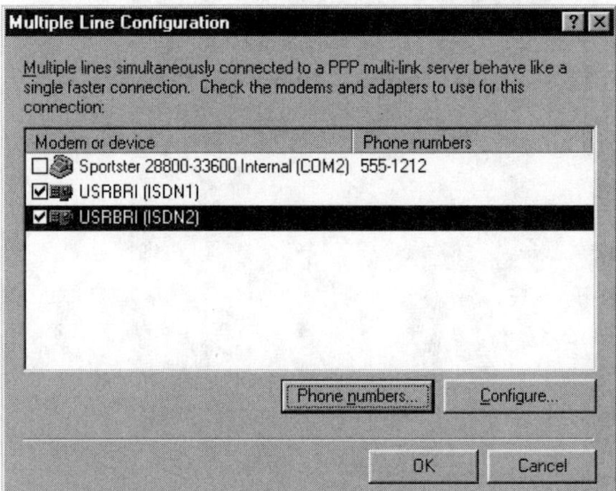

Figure 6

Configuring multiple lines.

NT may see the two channels of your ISDN adapter as separate devices, in which case you need to check both in this dialog box. For each channel, click Phone Number to set the access number (which, unless your ISP tells you otherwise, will be the same for both).

3. Click the Server tab. Unless your ISP has instructed you otherwise, make sure the settings match those shown in Figure 7.

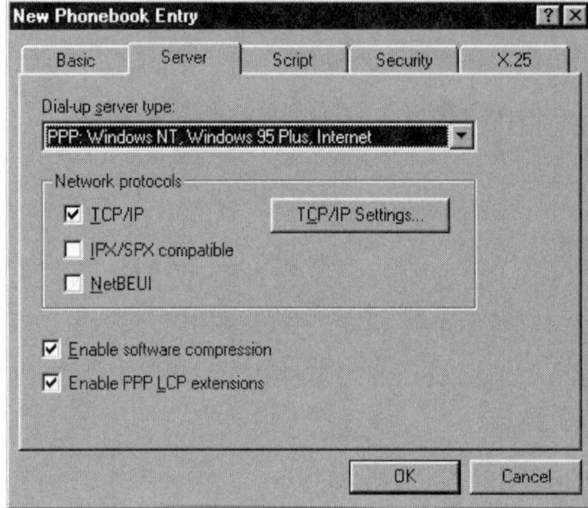

Figure 7

The Phonebook's Server tab.

4. Click the Security tab. Unless your ISP has instructed you otherwise, make sure the settings match those shown in Figure 8 and then click OK to save the new connection.

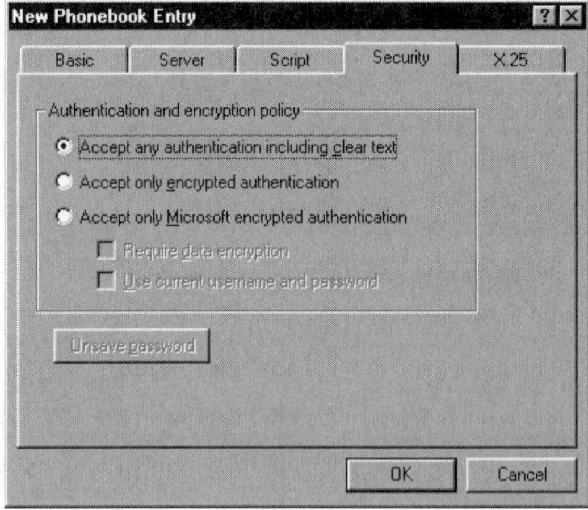

Figure 8

The Phonebook's Security tab.

5. Click Dial to try the new connection. Change the userid (which by default is your NT login name) to the one assigned by your ISP and enter your password (see Figure 9). Leave the Domain field blank. If you want Windows to remember the password so you won't have to enter it every time, check the Save Password box before clicking OK.

Figure 9

The first time you use a new Phonebook entry, you need to replace your NT login name with the userid your ISP assigned you.

6. You'll see a small "Connecting to" dialog box, which should display "Dialing," then "Verifying Username and Password," and finally "Registering your computer on the network." Then the dialog box should disappear, and a small "Connected to ..." message should appear in the bottom-left corner of your screen for a few seconds.

From now on, Dial-Up Networking should be activated and connect you to your ISP automatically whenever your Web browser or any other program tries to access the Internet. You can also connect manually by bringing up the Phonebook and clicking Dial.

Figure 10

Setting name server addresses.

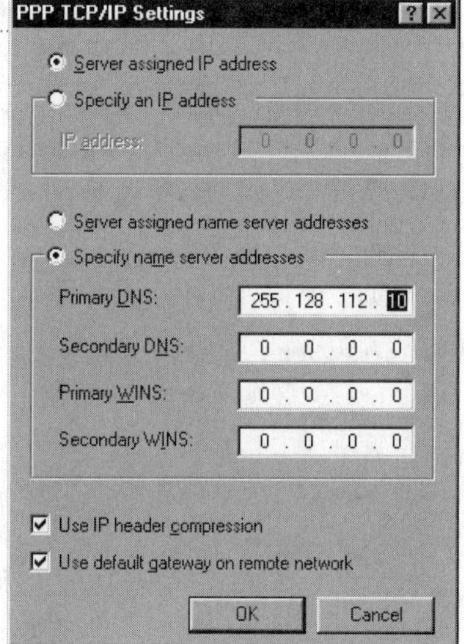

If instead of the messages described in step 6 you get an error message, you may need to enter the IP addresses of your ISP's DNS servers or a specific (*static*) IP address for the connection. In the Phonebook, click More, select "Edit entry and modem properties," click the Server tab, click TCP/IP Settings, click "Specify name server addresses," and enter the numbers you got from your ISP (see Figure 10). If you don't have the alternate server's address, you can leave that field blank. Then click OK twice to save the changes and try step 5 again. If the connection still doesn't work, telephone your ISP's tech support line for assistance.

Internet Access Resources

thelist.internet.com The List is a compilation of user-submitted information on over 5,000 ISPs around the world. You can search for ISPs by telephone area or country code; listings include rates, types of connections supported, links to the ISP's Web site, and the date the entry was last revised (some of the entries I checked were quite out of date).

cnet.com/Content/Reports/Special/ISP This CNET site lets users rate their own ISPs by filling out forms, and averages the results to produce ratings of over 3,500 ISPs. Listings include a letter grade (A to F), the ISP's location, and a link to its Web site. Like any online survey, this one's highly susceptible to ballot-box stuffing, but if an ISP scores a C or lower, I'd want to talk with some users before signing up.

boardwatch.internet.com/isp *Boardwatch* Magazine's ISP directory has some unusual information. ISP entries include the number of ports, which determines how many of the ISP's customers can log on at once, and the bandwidth of the ISP's connection to the Internet backbone, which is shared by all the ISP's customers. Divide the bandwidth by the number of ports to get an idea of relative performance at peak times. To take an example from my area code, an ISP with a single 1.544 megabit-per-second connection and 625 ports will, when all ports are in use, have only 2 kilobits of bandwidth per user—so at peak hours, that ISPs users are getting very slow downloads.

www.barkers.org/online The Online Connection features regularly updated reviews of the major national ISPs and online services.

ipass.com/roaming_providers.html A guide to ISPs worldwide that provide their customers international access through the iPass network.

www.gric.com/frames/about/members_list.htm A list of ISPs that provide international access through the GRIC network.

20

E-Mail

by Judy Heim

In This Chapter

Sending and retrieving e-mail is one of the most useful things your computer can do for you. Not only can you communicate swiftly and cheaply with friends, coworkers, and far-flung relations via e-mail, it can open up new worlds. E-mail-based mailing list discussions are where you'll find all the best information on the Internet, be it on public events, work-related topics, or health and family issues. To join them all you need to know is how to send an e-mail message and how to receive one. You can also use e-mail to retrieve information from the Internet—even text off Web pages and software.

E-Mail for Beginners

In order to e-mail over the Internet your computer needs:

- An Internet connection, either through an Internet service provider (see Chapter 19: Getting on the Internet) or an office network.
- A stand-alone e-mail program, like Eudora or Pegasus, or one built into or bundled with a Web browser, like Netscape Mail, Netscape Messenger, or Microsoft Outlook Express. (There's a good chance one or more of these were loaded on your computer at the factory.)

If your computer's at home you'll need to instruct your e-mail program to dial into the mail server of your Internet provider, check for mail, then download the mail to your computer. You can read and reply to it offline. If your computer's part of an office network with a connection to the Internet, your connection to the Net will be more seamless, although you can still use e-mail programs like Eudora.

For e-mail, an Internet service is superior to an online service like America Online. ISPs handle mail faster, and you can use any mail software you wish to access your mail. But ISPs are not created equal in regard to mail handling. Some are slow as cold bacon fat in shuttling your mail to its destination. Others' mail servers are unavailable at peak Internet traffic times, like after school or late in the evening. If your ISP's mail server suffers frequent downtimes, or if you notice that your mail seems sluggish in getting to its destination, get another ISP, especially if you're using the account for business. It can be mighty embarrassing if mail from clients or customers bounces back to them, even if only once.

What About Free E-Mail Services?

Don't let price deter you. **Free e-mail** services are a great deal. The most popular is Juno (**www.juno.com** or call 800-654-5866). To subscribe, you download its free software, and agree to view online ads in exchange for the ability to send and receive a modest amount of e-mail each day. (The amount changes. It's usually under 100 messages a day.) You don't need an Internet connection to tap in. but the service has limitations. For instance, you need to live in a city where Juno has a local phone access number.

Web-based free e-mail services are a different animal. The mail lives on a Web site, which you can access from any computer with an Internet connection and a Web browser—a computer at work or school, a terminal at a cybercafe, anywhere. These sites are popular among those who don't own their own PCs, or who like to have a second address for public use to avoid cluttering their home account with spam. They're also ideal for those who lead a nomadic lifestyle with ever-changing e-mail addresses.

Popular Web-based free e-mail services are Hotmail (**hotmail.com**), Yahoo! Mail (**edit.my.yahoo.com**), Excite Mail (**mailexcite.com**), and American Express (**amexmail.com**).

The down side to free e-mail services is that a lot of people filter spams based on free e-mail service domain names. In other words, they send mail with addresses from these services directly to the trash.

Anatomy of an E-Mail Program

All e-mail programs have certain elements in common. Here's a quick overview.

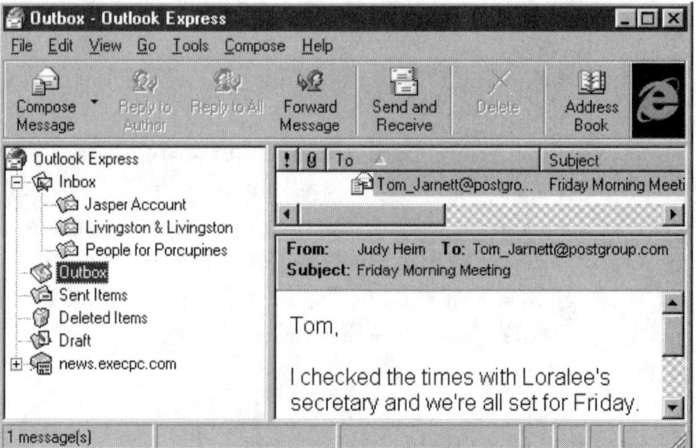

Figure 1

Folders.

E-mail programs let you create folders where you can store messages that you receive, as well as copies of messages that you have sent.

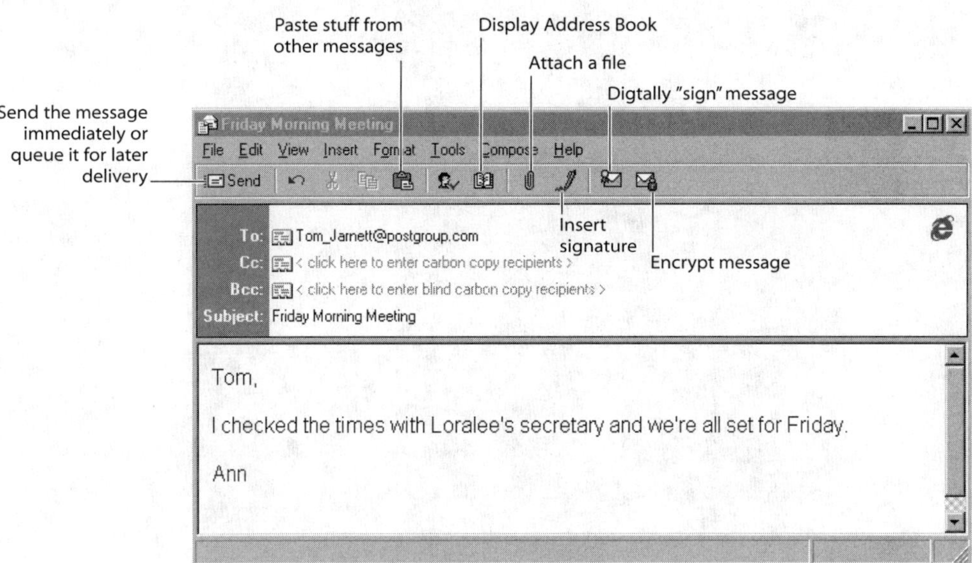

Figure 2

Options.

When you compose a message your mail program gives you many options for how you'd like to send the message, how you'd like it addressed, and what you'd like to attach or insert in the message.

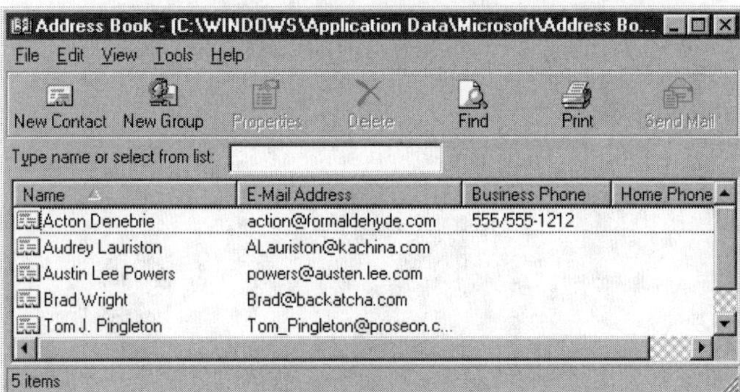

Figure 3

Address Book.

Your E-mail program's address book will probably let you store not only e-mail addresses but other contact information as well, and will let you create mailing lists or define "groups" so you can easily send the same message to a number of people.

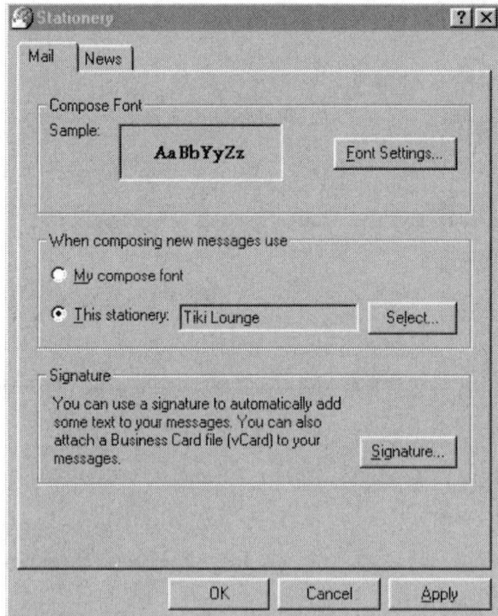

Figure 4

Proprietary Enhancements.

Some mail programs, like Outlook Express and America Online, let you add fancy fonts and "stationery" (shown in Figure 8 later in this chapter) to your e-mail. But in general you want to avoid these features so your recipient doesn't have any problem viewing your message in their mail program.

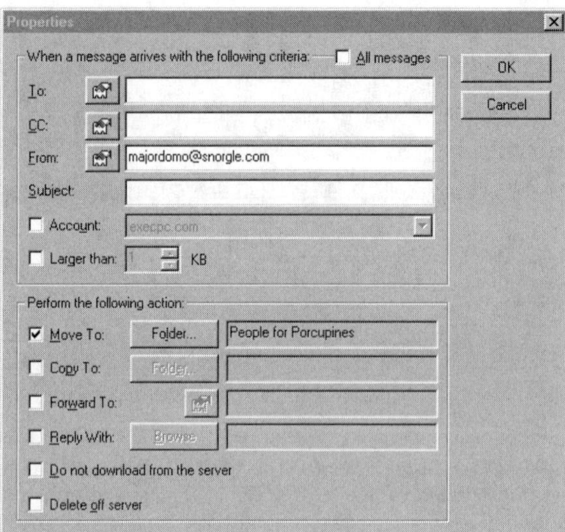

Figure 5

Filters.

You can set up filtering rules for how you would like your mail program to handle arriving e-mail. This rule tells the mail program to siphon all incoming e-mail from the Internet mailing list discussion group run by majordomo@snorgle.com into a folder called People for Porcupines. But you can set other rules to delete mail from certain recipients off your ISP's mail server (so you never have to read it), reply with a canned message, or forward the mail to another account.

Which E-Mail Software for You?

If you're using an online service like America Online, Microsoft Network, or CompuServe you'll need to use their software to send and retrieve mail. It's an unfortunate situation, as the mail software for these services tends to be limited in capabilities.

AOL does have one advantage if you have children: it offers parental controls that let you filter the areas of AOL and the Internet that your children see. But many complain that these controls don't go far enough, and you can't use them to filter the e-mail that your children receive, except to block file attachments (like pictures).

If you're gathering mail through an Internet service you can use the mail software built into or bundled with your Web browser: Netscape's Messenger (or Mail) or Explorer's Outlook Express. These programs are convenient to use, especially since they let you combine retrieval of Usenet newsgroup postings with your regular e-mail.

Outlook Express can easily be set up tohandle multiple e-mail accounts, which is important if you use multiple ISPs or share your computer with people who have different ISPs. It also offers a good selection of mail filtering rules that let you automatically funnel junk e-mail to the trash. Its big-brother e-mail software, Outlook 98 (part of Microsoft Office, or $109 separately), offers personal information management features that make it easy to shuffle mailing lists and contact information between it and other Microsoft products. Although many consider it the best thing since frozen waffles, the product has been prone to glitchiness, especially when used with Microsoft Exchange Server. Still, users flock to it. Go figure.

Netscape Messenger, on the other hand, offers more sophisticated mail filtering rules that make it easier than it is with Outlook to siphon spams (junk e-mail) and automate the handling of a daily e-mail deluge.

But the best mail programs of all are stand-alone mailers. The classic brand-name Internet e-mail program is Qualcomm's no-frills freebie Eudora Light,

Convert Mailboxes and Address Books from One Mail Program to Another

Like to turn that Pegasus inbox into an Outlook Express one? Itching to transform your CompuServe address book into a Lotus cc:Mail one? Head to Interguru's E-mail Conversion Site

(**`www.interguru.com/mailconv.htm`**). For a $20 requested donation you can turn address books and message files from just about any e-mail program, ranging from Pine to Microsoft Exchange, into a format that can be used by just about any other e-mail program.

available at **eudora.qualcomm.com**. A $39 commercial version, Eudora Pro, offers more sophisticated features, especially in regard to mail-handling rules. For instance, you can set it up to automatically send messages to specific addresses. You can also configure it to do things like play specific tunes when mail from specific people arrives. But many find Eudora Pro just a bit too complicated to use and prefer the free version.

Perhaps the best mailer of all, though, is David Harris's freeware Pegasus (**www.pegasus.usa.com**). It offers a full line-up of sophisticated mail handling features. You can preview mail on your ISP's server and delete offensive spams prior to downloading. It's easy to set up for multiple users and to use to create distribution lists. Just about everything in the program is highly configurable, including its mail encryption features.

Configuring Your E-Mail Program

The first step to making an E-mail connection to your ISP is setting up Windows' dial-up networking to call the service and log you on. (See Chapter 19: Getting On the Internet for directions.) Once you have that configured, you'll need to tell your Web browser or your mail program where and how to collect your mail (see Figure 6). Whether you use Outlook Express or Eudora, these are the things you'll need to set:

- **SMTP or Outgoing Mail Server.** This is the computer on your ISP where you'll send mail and which will jettison it out onto the Internet. SMTP is the UNIX mail program your ISP uses. When you sign up, your ISP will send you directions containing the name of this server. It will be something like mailgate.yourisp.com.
- **POP3 or Incoming Mail Server.** This is the computer on your ISP that will hold mail for you until you log on and retrieve it. Your ISP will also give you directions telling you its name. It will be something like mail.yourisp.com. It will be different from the name of the SMTP server.
- **Pop User Name or Shell Login Name.** This is your login name on your ISP.
- **Your E-mail or Shell Login.** This is your e-mail address on your ISP. For example: mary@myisp.com.
- **Your Real Name.** This is the "street name" you want to have appear in your e-mail address. You don't need to use your real name—although you probably should if you're using the e-mail account for business. Your e-mail will look rather silly if you use the name of a Star Trek character, as many people do.
- **Reply-to Address.** This is where you want readers of your e-mail to send their replies. It needn't be the same e-mail address as your regular address.

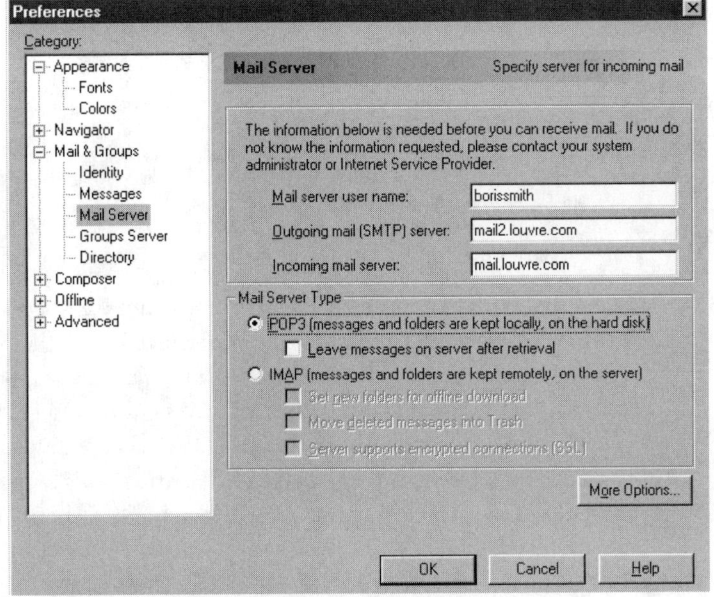

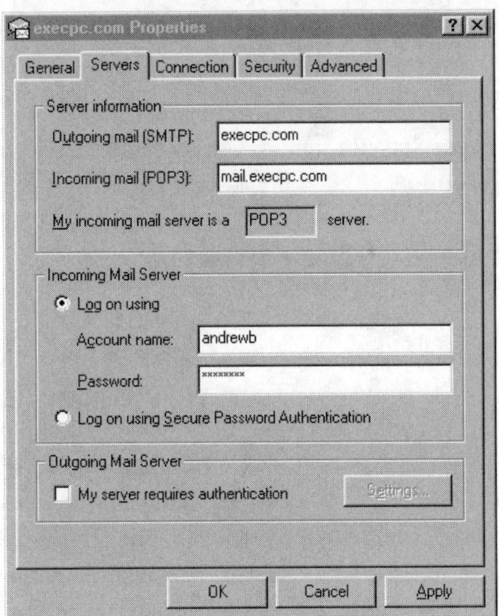

Figure 6

Buried server settings.

The mail server settings can be hard to find in some e-mail programs. In Netscape, head to Edit/Preferences and click Mail & Groups. In Outlook Express, go to Tools/Accounts, head to the Mail tab, and select the account you wish to use.

If you run into any problem with your mail program not sending or retrieving mail the first time you use it, chances are that you have probably not entered the correct POP3 or SMTP mail server name. But here's a rule of thumb: if the mail program has sent and retrieved mail properly once before, but you experience trouble on subsequent connections, it's probably not related to your configuration.

E-Mail Error Messages

`Unable to locate the server. The server does not have a DNS entry.`

`Could not connect. Host is unreachable.`

`The host could not be found. Please verify that you have entered the host name correctly.`

`Timeout waiting for response from server. Unable to send messages.`

Seeing messages like those? If your mail program has successfully connected to your ISP in the past and has sent *and* retrieved mail, the problem is not with your configuration. If you received any of the above messages, it's likely that your mail program simply tired of waiting for a response from your ISP. First ask: Are you connected to the ISP? Was dial-up networking able to log on successfully? If so, is there a chance that your ISP's mail server is overworked or down and is not responding in a timely fashion? Wait a few minutes and try dialing back in.

Also, if several people in your household are using the same PC, but have different e-mail accounts, there's always a chance that their e-mail settings may have invaded your mail program or Web browser. Check those POP3, SMTP, and e-mail account settings.

If your mail program has not sent and/or received mail in the past, and you don't live in a commune, you still need to recheck its settings.

Should It Be POP3 or IMAP?

Buried in the mail server setup box of your e-mail program you'll find an option that lets you configure the program for a POP3 or IMAP server. What's the difference? POP3 is the archaic mail protocol of the Internet. When you retrieve e-mail off your ISP using the POP3 protocol you download the mail from the ISP's server and store it on your computer. But what if you need to access your mail from multiple locations, like your laptop when you're traveling, your PC at home, and the computer in your office? If you download the mail to your office PC it won't be available to you when you log into your ISP from your PC at home.

Sure, you can always set up your mail program to "leave mail on the server" after you download it, but then you need to download it all over again when you want to read the mail on another PC. If your ISP offers an IMAP server you can read the mail on the ISP's server, store it in folders, download only selected messages, and even read a message without downloading that humongous file attachment that comes with it (see Figure 7). IMAP offers other advantages. You can set up mail folders that IMAP users with other e-mail accounts can read. You can search and flag messages for rereading, store message drafts, templates, and sent messages on the server, and synchronize mail folders for use with different e-mail accounts. In other words, IMAP is a sophisticated e-mail filing and manipulation protocol as well as a mail storage one.

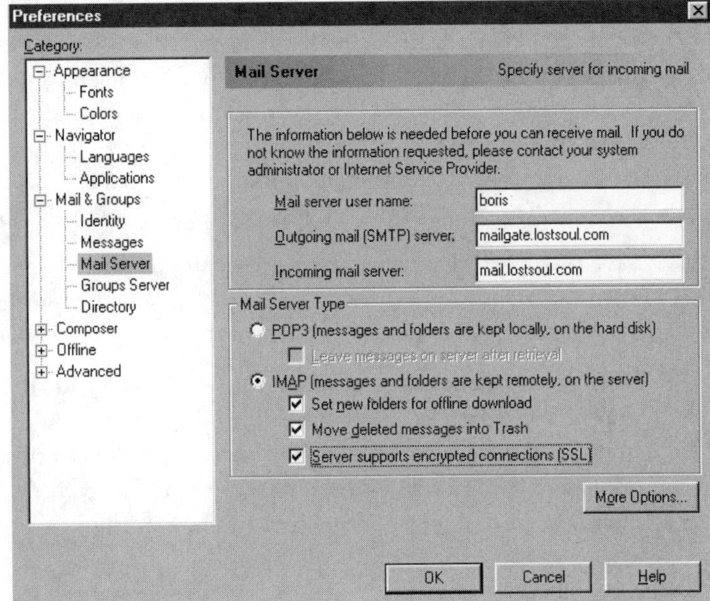

Figure 7

IMAP settings.

If your ISP or employer's mail server supports IMAP, ask what settings you should make in your mail program as many IMAP implementations are quirkily different. If you're unsure of whether your ISP offers IMAP, set up for a POP3 mail server. This is the mail server dialog box in Netscape Communicator.

Not a lot of ISPs support IMAP—yet. More will in the future, since all the major e-mail programs and browsers now support it. Many corporate e-mail servers offer IMAP. If your employer's does, ask the network administrator what IMAP settings to make in your e-mail program. Ask too what is the preferred e-mail program for accessing the company IMAP server—all the e-mail programs have quirks in their IMAP implementations. If neither your company e-mail server or your ISP supports IMAP, then set up for a POP3 server.

Other Things You May Wish to Set

Here are a few other things you may want to set in your mail program. They are not as critical as correct configuration information, but they can make your life easier:

Delete mail from server. If you're not using IMAP, your e-mail program will normally delete e-mail from your ISP's server once you download it. This is not only good housekeeping, but it will prevent an e-mail deluge from

eating up all your disk space on your ISP. In fact, if your e-mail program seems rather slow at downloading mail, it may be because you're letting old e-mail accumulate on the server.

However, if you're sharing an e-mail account with several people, or accessing your e-mail from several different PCs (such as office, home, school, laptop), you may not want your mail program to do this. In one little company, where all the employees shared a single Internet account, all their mail programs were set to delete mail from the server once they downloaded it. It took months before anyone figured out why e-mail marked for specific employees disappeared from the server before that employee logged on to retrieve it. If you do set your software to leave mail on the server, be sure to delete it manually once in a while. (Ask your ISP for help if you're not sure how to do that.)

Save password. Do you want your e-mail program to remember your password to automatically enter it whenever you tap into your ISP? Not if you use a laptop and worry that someone might steal it while you're traveling.

How often to check for mail and how to alert you. You can configure your mail program to check for mail regularly when you're logged on to your ISP. You can also tell it how to alert you to the fact that you have new mail—by playing a tune or flashing an icon. In fact, you can set up Pegasus and Eudora Pro to play specific tunes—or a recording of a coworker's voice—whenever you receive mail from them.

When to delete mail. Do you want your mail program to delete mail immediately when you press Del? Or would you rather send it to a review box in case you hit Del accidentally?

Add a signature. You can set your mail program to add to your messages a standard signature, like your name and business title. You can also create alternate signatures.

HTML, Rich Text, and graphics. Messages formatted with HTML are formatted with the same coding that gives Web pages their glitz. HTML coding is what gives messages its fancy fonts and multi-colored letters. But not all e-mail programs can read HTML-formatted messages; in some they pop up looking like digital goulash. And not all e-mail programs display HTML formatting in the same way. For example, that fancy font you wrote an e-mail message in Outlook Express may appear too tiny to read when your recipient displays it in Eudora (see Figure 8). You should avoid sending HTML-formatted messages at all costs—and that means avoiding Outlook Express's stationery feature—unless you're absolutely sure that your recipient is using a mailer that can display HTML-formatted messages.

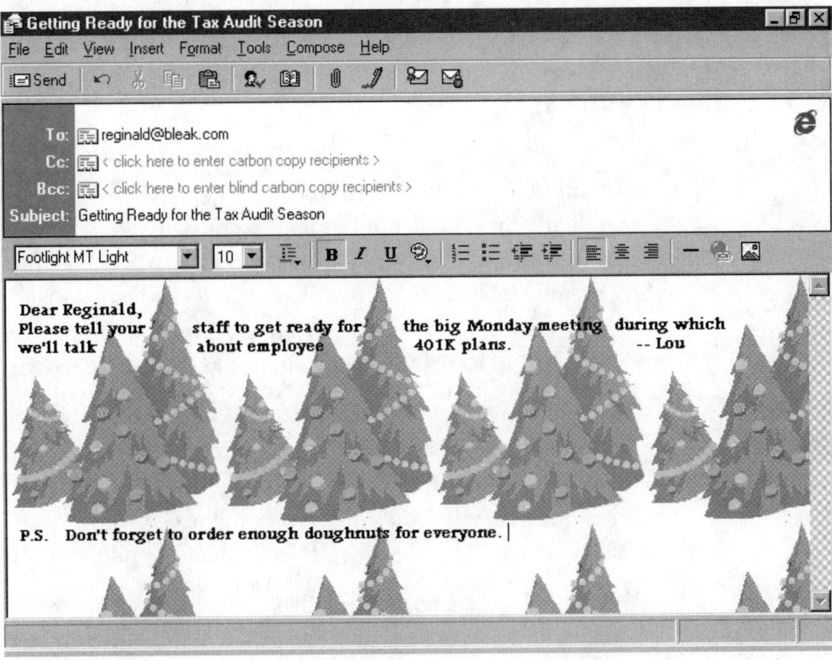

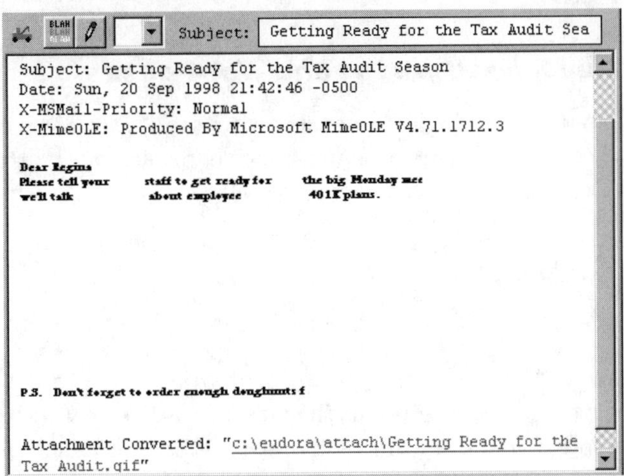

Figure 8

It may look great when you write it in Outlook Express, but how will it look when your recipient opens it in Eudora? As you can see, Eudora received Outlook's festive Christmas tree background as an attached GIF. The recipient will need to open a picture viewing program to view it. Outlook's fonts are nearly unreadable.

Sending Files or Attachments via E-Mail

The Internet and its mail protocols are primitive. They only know how to handle the most basic kind of text (technically it's 7-bit ASCII, a data format that has only 128 different characters). Binary files, like pictures, sounds, and software (which are typically stored in an 8-bit format that uses 256 characters), have to be "encoded" (converted from 8-bit to 7-bit format) before they can be attached to e-mail messages and sent over the Internet.

Mail programs generally give you two encoding options for sending file attachments: MIME (Multipurpose Internet Mail Extension) and Uuencode (UNIX-to-UNIX Encode, an old name that doesn't make much sense today). Sometimes they let you send files in binhex format as well, but that's a Macintosh format. You'd choose this only when sending files to a Mac user.

You should always try sending files as MIME attachments first, as it's the more modern and robust encoding system of the two. If your recipient doesn't receive a file properly as a MIME attachment, then try Uuencode.

How to Read Usenet Newsgroups and Web Pages via E-mail

If your only access to the Net is through an e-mail-only service like Juno, you can still read Web pages and Usenet newsgroups by sending a message to either **agora@dna.affrc.go.jp** or **agora@kamakura.mss.co.jp**.

To retrieve the text of a Web page, type `send . the url/`. For example, to get the text from Peachpit's Web page, you'd type

```
send . www.peachpit.com/
```

To retrieve Usenet messages, in the body of the message type `news:alt.rec.stuff`, where **alt.rec.stuff** is the name of the newsgroup. The message you'll receive in reply will contain a list of message postings. To retrieve them, send a reply message including the numbers of each message on an individual line. For instance:

```
1
2
3
```

To get help, and for more directions on retrieving Web pages and Usenet postings, as well as conducting Internet searches via e-mail, send an e-mail message to **agora@dna.affrc.go.jp** with `WWW` in the body of the message.

How to Send a File Attachment

Create an e-mail message as you normally would, entering the e-mail address of the recipient and a subject. Type a bit of explanatory text if you want. Most mailers have an attach button or feature that you click. Then browse for the file to attach to the message.

How to Read or View a File Attachment You've Received

If someone sends you an e-mail message with a MIME attachment, depending upon your mailer you might first need to save it to disk. You then need to open the file in the appropriate software—a word processor for instance, or a graphics viewer.

If you receive a series of e-mail messages full of gobbledygook, you have probably been sent a Uuencoded file that has been broken into chunks in order to get past a server that imposes a size limit on e-mail messages. In order to read or view it you must piece together the files and then decode them with a program like Wincode, which you can download for free at **`watt.seas.virginia.edu/~bem9q/dwnldme2.html`**.

More E-Mail File Attachment Tips

- Compress the file with a .zip utility like WinZip (discussed in Chapter 12: Windows Add-Ons) before sending it. That way it won't take the recipient as long to download it from their ISP.
- Attach only one file to an e-mail message. If you're sending multiple files, save them in a single .zip file or send them as separate messages. This is especially true if you're sending them to someone on America Online, which sends all but the first into limbo.
- Never send an e-mail message with an attached image or document to someone who's not expecting it. There's nothing worse than twiddling your thumbs while your mail program downloads 500K of something you didn't ask for.
- Before sending a message with an attachment, always ask your recipient if there's a format or method by which they would prefer that you send the file. For instance, many people have difficulty receiving e-mail messages with attachments over Internet-linked corporate networks. Depending upon their situation they may prefer that the image or document be inserted inside an e-mail message as encoded text. Or they may want you to send the file as several small attachments.
- Never send a message with an attachment to a mailing list discussion unless that kind of thing is encouraged.

- When you reply to a message that came with an attached file, always make sure that the attachment is not going to be shipped back to the sender with your reply. Some mail programs will do this automatically unless you tell them not to.

Top Ten E-Mail Tips

Even compared with word processing, E-mail is probably the easiest application to learn and use. However, using e-mail *well* isn't as simple as it seems. Here are ten tips to get you from novice to expert ASAP:

1. **Create folders.** Many people new to e-mail print out all the messages they mean to keep, a silly habit that wastes paper and printer time. Instead, create named "folders" (see Figure 1) to store and organize your messages, something all major e-mail packages allow you to do.
2. **Manage your messages.** Don't let more than one screenful of messages accumulate in your inbox. Once you've read a message, delete it or store it in the appropriate folder. If you're too busy to read junk mail, move it to a "To read" folder.
3. **Stay cool.** Don't write a message in the heat of anger. Stop and think: Would you say this to the person's face? Would you print out the message and leave it on the recipient's desk?
4. **Think before you address.** Be careful when you use mailing lists or reply to messages with many addressees. If the "Everyone" list includes people at other branch offices, do they really want to know that the blood bank truck is in the parking lot?
5. **Blind copy.** If you want to send a query to a number of people but want the responses to go only to you, use "bcc" (for blind carbon copy) instead of "to" when addressing the message. The recipient can only reply to you, because that's the only name he or she will see. Great for party invitations. If your e-mail program insists on having an address in the To field, use your own.
6. **Make the subject clear.** Use descriptive headers for your messages. Instead of vague phrases like "A question" or "FYI," be specific: "Q1 figures ready yet?" or "FYI: laser printer out of service."
7. **What was the question?** Don't be too terse. If someone asks you a question by e-mail and you answer it a day later, a simple "yes" or "no" response may be incomprehensible. What was the question?
8. **Combine brief messages.** Everyone gets too many messages. So a whole message containing nothing but polite remarks ("Thanks," etc.) may not be appreciated. Try and fold them into a later message instead. ("Thanks for arranging today's meeting. Who's coming from your department?")
9. **Edit replies to group messages.** Group e-mail "discussions" can get confusing. Usually, a brief message copied to several people gets the ball

rolling. Then each participant adds comments, until everyone has to scroll through one huge message to reach the latest comment at the end. Instead of adding to the mess, try copying only a few relevant portions from earlier messages and leave out the rest when you add your two cents.

10. **Use common sense when sending e-mail to strangers you want to impress.** If you're writing to a stranger and your message can be written as text (as in apress release or resume) don't send it as a 1MB Adobe Acrobat document attachment. Similarly, don't bejewel it with HTML formatting when you don't know if their browser can display it properly.

How to Use E-Mail Filters

E-mail filters or rules are handy for automatically sorting the daily e-mail deluge. You can use filters to:

- Send messages from chronic spammers or obnoxious businesses to the trash.
- Automate replies to e-mail with form letters.
- Forward certain e-mail to other people or e-mail accounts.
- Send junk mail to the trash.
- Shuffle e-mail from mailing groups into a folder to read later at your leisure.
- Prioritize mail from designated people or businesses.
- Sound chimes or music when mail from a special someone arrives.

Outlook Express. One of the handiest uses of a mail filter is to automatically shuffle all the mail from one of those conversationally bloated special-interest mailing lists on the Internet into a special folder. You can then peruse it later at leisure. Outlook Express's Inbox Assistant, found in the Tools menu, is where you find the filtering dialog boxes (see Figure 9). This rule funnels all the messages from the majordomo list for squirrel lovers into a folder of the same name.

Netscape Messenger. To set up a mail-handling rule, choose Edit/Mail Filters (see Figure 10). The rule shown here will send to a review folder all e-mail that is not addressed specifically to the recipient (jack@bigmail.com). All those messages will most likely be spams. But in case they're not, and are addressed, for example, to an office mailing list, they can be reviewed later before being sent to the trash.

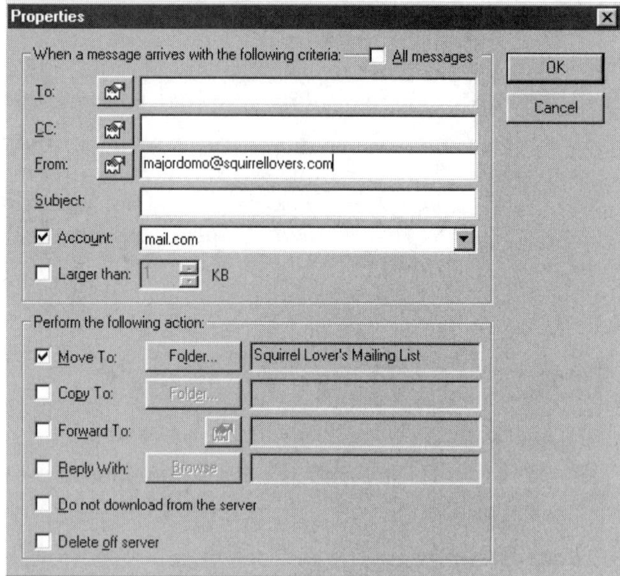

Figure 9

Outlook Express Inbox Assistant properties.

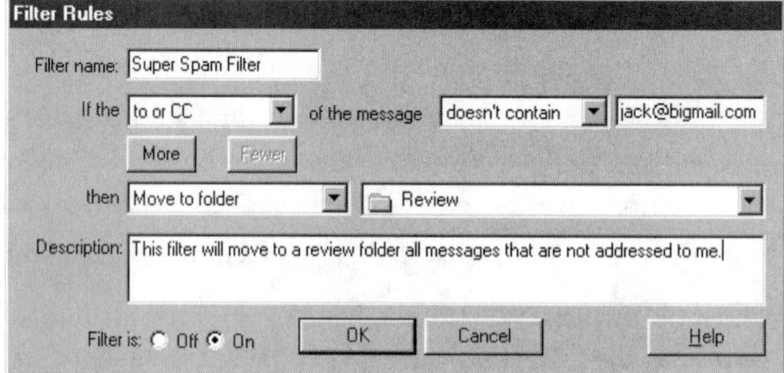

Figure 10

Netscape Messenger's Filter Rules.

Pegasus. Choose Tools/Mail Filtering Rules for the most extensive selection of mail filtering rules around. You can set up Pegasus to respond to particular types of e-mail messages with a form letter, send certain letters to the trash, run a program, respond with an e-mail messages, and a host of other things. You can also set conditions under which the rules will apply. You can even set it to, say, filter out mail from specific obnoxious people on a mailing list. The filter in Figure 11 plays a distinctive tune to alert the user of new mail from Melissa.

Eudora Light. The Tools/Filters dialog (see Figure 12) allows you to set up only the simplest mail filtering—transferring designated mail to folders or the trash, or setting it as a priority. If you pony up $39 for the commercial version of the program you get more options.

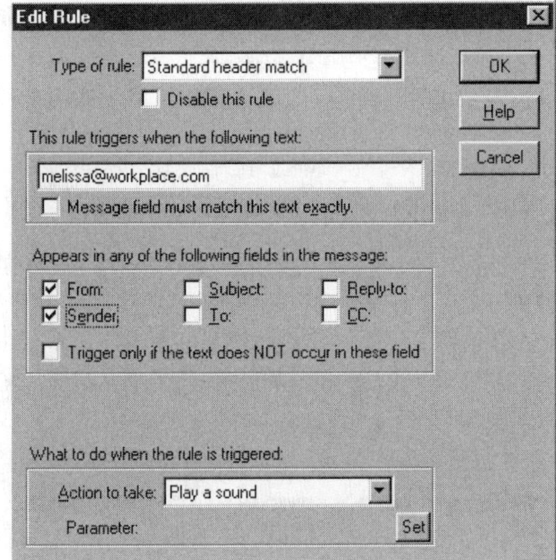

Figure 11

Editing a Pegasus mail-filter rule.

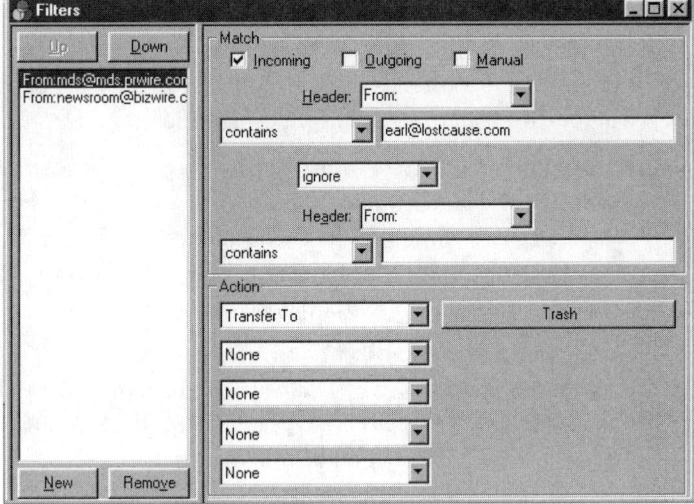

Figure 12

Eudora Light's Filters.

E-Mailing the Military

E-mail has become the preferred way for many military families to keep in touch with loved ones stationed abroad. It's faster and cheaper than long-distance phone calls. Plus, you can even e-mail ships at sea. Some branches of the service, including the United States Navy and the United States Army, routinely provide e-mail addresses to personnel stationed away from their families.

(Unfortunately, e-mail traveling between military installations and America Online often ends up MIA. Simply put, AOL has problems shuttling e-mail to and from the .mil domain in certain parts of the country. The solution is to use a commercial Internet service provider (ISP) or a free e-mail service like Juno.) Here are answers to the questions most frequently asked by military personnel and their families trying to stay in touch by e-mail:

How can I find local ISPs near military bases, either in the United States or abroad? This can be tough, since foreign ISP lists are often written in foreign languages. The List (**thelist.internet.com**) includes some foreign ISPs, but by no means all. The best way to find an ISP near an overseas base is word of mouth.

Is there a good alternative to America Online or an ISP for stateside family members or personnel? Juno (**www.juno.com**) offers free Internet e-mail through local numbers in many U.S. cities and is used by many people in the armed forces.

What e-mail solution best accommodates the nomadic military lifestyle? It's generally a good idea to use one of the free e-mail forwarding services like MilMail (**www.MilMail.com**) to establish a "permanent" e-mail address to give to friends and family. As one's duty station moves, the service will forward mail to your current e-mail address.

Where can I find the e-mail "white pages" directory for service personnel? There isn't one. Although some e-mail addresses of military personnel can be found in the Department of Defense's who-is database (**nic.ddn.mil**), in most instances the only way to obtain e-mail addresses of enlisted personnel is to ask them.

How can I e-mail a ship at sea? Through the Navy's SALTS project. To find out more head to (www_salts.icpphil.navy.mil. Many ships also have Web pages (**www_salts.icpphil.navy.mil/ships_choice.html**). Through them you can e-mail personnel on board.

How can I e-mail deployed forces? Through the Navy-Marine Corps MARS volunteer project **acan.net/~navymars**).

How can I e-mail a family member stationed overseas who does not have Internet access? The North American Center for Emergency Communications (www.nacec.org) offers free emergency and non-emergency e-mail delivery to enlisted personnel abroad who have no Internet access. There are some restrictions—non emergency mail can be sent only to Japan, Korea, Okinawa, Thailand, and bases in the United States. Emergency e-mail cannot be delivered to ships at sea.

Emergency e-mail can also be delivered through the Navy-Marine Corps MARS project (**acan.net/~navymars**). Mail can be sent to certain ships, deployed forces, and other military installations.

Can I track down my old army buddies through e-mail? Although the Department of Defense and the Veterans Administration offer some information online for veterans and their families, neither offers military records on the Internet. Military City Online on America Online offers a directory of reunion groups with e-mail addresses and Web links (keyword MCOMC). Military City on the Web (www.militarycity.com) offers a directory of over ten thousand active and retired military personnel. To access the site, you'll need to pay a $36 per year subscription fee.

How Private Is E-Mail?

You click the Send button and your mash note drops in the e-mailbox of its recipient within minutes, but how private is this mode of communication *really*? It's no more private than the old-fashioned postal system in which a letter dropped in the mail may pass through a hundred hands—all of whom are capable of wielding a letter opener—before arriving at its destination. Your e-mail may bounce through a dozen or more computers before it gets to where it's going on the Internet. And it may be stored in any of those computers for hours, minutes, even months. Your e-mail may also be stored on the disks of an office server—and everyone knows how private those are.

The moral is to never write in e-mail anything you don't want the rest of the world to know. That includes writing private information like credit card numbers.

What if you have to communicate something sensitive in e-mail? You can encrypt it. All the leading e-mail programs include tools to encode messages. Outlook and Netscape Messenger also let you add digital signatures to messages, which verify to the sender that you really are who you say you are. There is one catch to these James Bond desk accessories: your correspondent needs to know how to decrypt the message or authenticate the digital signature.

Adding Security Certificates to Messages

In order to sign e-mail cryptographically you first need to create a unique digital signature. You do so by heading a verification service like VeriSign (**`www.verisign.com`**) or BelSign (**`www.belsign.com`**). Netscape Messenger requires VeriSign signatures, but Microsoft Outlook can use signatures created by any verification service.

These sites usually let you create a trial signature that's good for 60 days or so. After that you need to pony up a fee—usually $10—for a permanent signature. You follow the prompts, type your name and a password. Once your digital signature is created, the service will e-mail you a PIN number. You must log back on to the site, paste in the PIN number, and retrieve the signature with your browser so that it can install it in its mail program. In order for this process to work you must be using the same computer and the same e-mail address you were using when you created the signature.

Encryption for the Masses

For e-mail programs that don't include encryption, download a copy of the freeware version of Pretty Good Privacy from **www.nai.com/products/security/freeware.asp**.

In order to use PGP you must encrypt your message and send it as a file attachment—a bit of a hassle, but the paranoid consider it well worth it. Some people post their PGP "public" keys on their Web pages so that correspondents can use them to encrypt messages; a matching "private" key allows them to decrypt the messages they receive. Some e-mail programs will flag encrypted messages you receive with a special icon (see Figure 13).

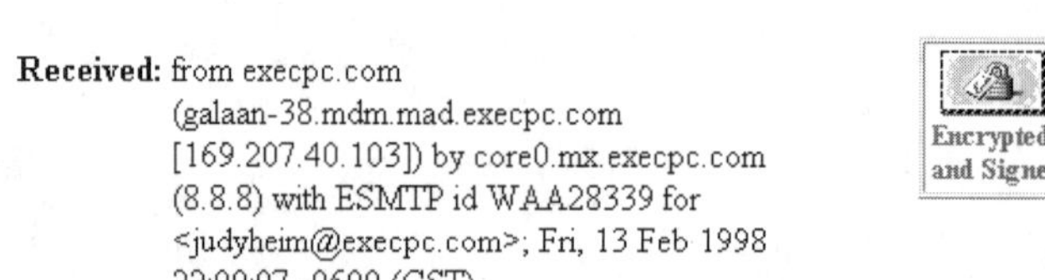

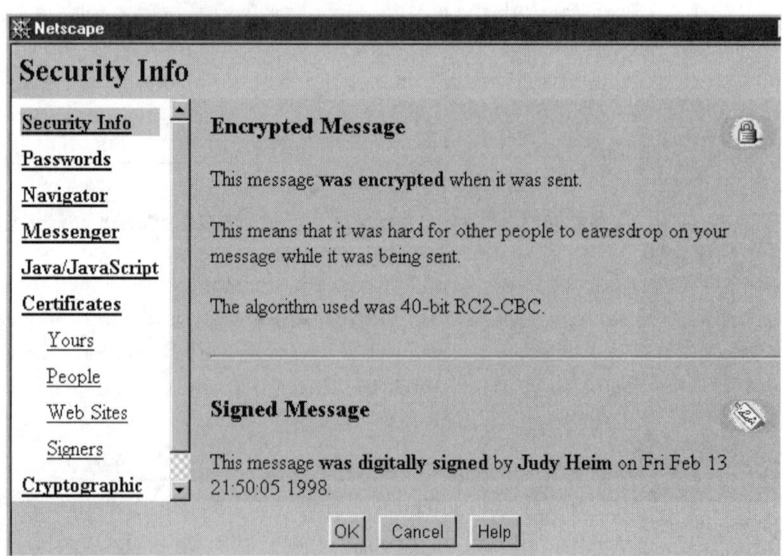

Figure 13

When you receive a message in Netscape Messenger that has been encrypted or digitally signed, a special icon appears at the top. Click the icon for details of how the message has been encrypted or signed.

Junk E-Mail: Battling the Spam Monster

Man: "Well, what've you got?"

Waitress: "Well there's egg and bacon, egg, sausage, and bacon, egg and Spam, bacon and Spam, egg, bacon, sausage, and Spam, Spam, bacon, sausage, and Spam, Spam, egg, Spam, Spam, bacon, and Spam, Spam, Spam, Spam, egg, and Spam, Spam, Spam, Spam, Spam, Spam, Spam, baked beans, Spam, Spam, Spam, and Spam, or lobster thermidor aux crevettes with a mornay sauce, garnished with truffled paté, brandy, and a fried egg on top, and Spam."

from The Complete Monty Python's Flying Circus: All the Words, Volume 2 *(Pantheon Books, ISBN 0679726489), or* The Final Rip Off *(Virgin Records double CD set).*

If you've had an e-mail account for a while, it's easy to see how that old Monty Python sketch about the pleasures of the British breakfast table came to refer to junk e-mail. Little by little, the ratio of junk to real e-mail increases until eventually your inbox is spam, spam, spam, spam, spam, spam, spam, e-mail you actually want to read, spam, spam, spam, and spam (see Figure 14).

Figure 14

"You've got mail"? You've gotta be kidding. That familiar AOL audio alert might more accurately be, "You've got spam."

How do spammers get your e-mail address? Mostly they use "spiders" which are a kind of programmed robot that trowels through message groups, Web pages, and anywhere else your e-mail address may be posted, to collect e-mail addresses. Here are spam myths, tips, and shocking realities.

Protecting Yourself Against Spam

- **Beware of Forms on Web Sites.** It's a fallacy that Web sites can simply nab your e-mail out of your Web browser—or off your hard disk. A Web site can, however, get your e-mail address if you submit a form to the site. Have you ever checked boxes, answered a survey, or entered a message of some sort into a Web site form? If you did you probably unknowingly e-mailed your address to the site. The moral: don't check any boxes or fill out forms on Web sites that you don't want to have your e-mail address.
- **Disable the FTP Password Setting in Your Browser.** There's one other way your browser might send your e-mail address to a Web site: if you have enabled the browser's setting to send your e-mail address as a password for anonymous FTP logons. In other words, if you log on to a site to download software, your browser might be sending the site your address. Disable this setting.
- **Use Separate E-mail Accounts.** One very effective way to protect yourself against spams is to use separate e-mail accounts for posting messages in public discussion groups, like Usenet newsgroups and AOL public forums, and for receiving private e-mail. AOL lets you set up multiple screen names, and many ISPs will also let you set up a second e-mail address for a small monthly fee, or for free.
- **Avoid Directories.** Don't post your e-mail address in directories on services like AOL.
- **Try the "No Spam" Approach in Public.** Some people set their mailer's Reply to: field to "No-spam." That way when they post a message in public, spammer "spiders" cannot collect their e-mail address simply by nabbing the contents of the Reply to: field in their message. They write their real e-mail address at the end of their message. But that makes it hard for people to respond to their messages.
- **Set Up Filters in Your Mailer.** The most effective way to filter spams is to set up an e-mail filtering rule in your mail program to send all e-mail that's not addressed specifically to you to a review folder, where you can later review and delete it. Most spams are not sent specifically to you but rather to an "undisclosed recipients" mailing list. Read on to learn more about setting up filters—and how to filter mail on AOL.

Complaining about Spam

- **Don't Answer.** Never answer a spam, whether it's to buy the advertised "1001 nude pix" or to complain. If you hit your mailer's reply button, your angry letter of protest may end up in the e-mail inbox of an innocent victim. Spammers often forge the Reply to: field in their messages so the replies go to a dead letter box or to some poor schmuck.
- **Forward the Message's Header.** If you're going to forward the message to your online service or ISP to complain, forward the message with its

full header. The ISP needs that to trace who sent the spam. To see a message's full header, in Netscape Messenger head, select View/Headers/All. In Outlook Express, open the message, then select File/Properties and click the Details tab. In Eudora click the Blah-Blah button at the top of the message. You may need to cut and paste the full header into an e-mail message.

- **Practice Effective Complaining.** In the past common wisdom held that you should complain to postmaster@thespammersisp.com, but sophisticated spammers often mask the domain where the message originated. It's better to complain to your ISP—or press Del. If you're on AOL, complain to TOSspam.

Spam Forensics 101: Reading E-Mail Headers?

It may look like gibberish—the trail of addresses, computer names, and I.D. numbers crowning a message. But it can tell you a great deal about where the message really came from. "Spam busters" at ISPs and online services are masters at deciphering message headers to uncover the fiends behind the obnoxious sales pitches. Here are a few of their secrets.

```
From: good_time_larry@thebigsalesblowout.com
```

Is this really the e-mail address of the person who sent the message? From: lines in messages can be easily forged.

```
Received: from my.mail.juxtaposition.com(my.mail.justaposition.com
[982.213.2.202])by big.juxtaposition.com (8.8.8) with ESMTP id DPT87271
for <peter@juxtaposition.com>; Tues, 5 Jan 1999 03:46:03 +0000 (CDT)
```

Let's say that the recipient of this spam message is named Peter and his ISP is called Juxtaposition.Com (peter@juxtaposition.com). Juxtaposition's mail server, code-named Big, received the spam message on Tuesday at 3:46 Greenwich Mean Time. It passed it on to the mail server named My.Mail, which deposited it in Peter's mailbox. The ESMTP I.D. is the message's mail protocol I.D.

```
Return-Path: <good_time_larry@thebigsalesblowout.com>
```

Spammers usually forge the address in the Return-Path, which ostensibly is supposed to tell you the path the message took on the Internet to get to you. In this case, the Return-Path doesn't tell us anything.

```
Received: from hortense.whatajerk.com (root@whatajerk.com [077.97.76.22])
by big.juxtaposition.com (8.8.8) with ESMTP id DPT87271 for
<peter@juxtaposition.com>; Mon, 4 Jan 1999 03:47:18 +000 (CDT)
```

Here we see that it was a computer code-named "Hortense" at an ISP with the domain name whatajerk.com that sent the spam to Juxtaposition's Big computer. The spam was not received from a computer in the domain of thebigsalesblowout.com, as the From: line might lead one to believe. Those numbers that follow the e-mail address of whatajerk.com (077.97.76.22) are the computer's domain name server address. Sometimes you can track down the real location of a spammer through this address.

```
Message-ID: <37373821k217@whatajerk.com>
```

The mail server the spam came from assigned the message this ID number. While spammers can forge From:, Return-path: and Reply-To: fields, it's harder to forge message IDs. Together with the information in the Received: field we can be fairly certain that the message originated at whatajerk.com.

```
Date: Tues, 05 Jan 1999 01:57:21
Reply-To: android@aol.com
```

If you hit the Reply button in your e-mail program to send an angry message in response to this spam, your message will go, not to the spammer, but to some innocent person on AOL named "android." Yes, spammers are really nasty sometimes.

Want to Remain Completely Anonymous in E-Mail? Try a Remailer

Want to send e-mail bearing no trace of your identity or whereabouts? Try an anonymous remailer, also known as an *alias server.* These are sites on the Internet where you can enter e-mail messages and they will be shuttled to their destinations bearing fake addresses, organization, and routing information. Don't think that because you're wearing the cyberspace equivalent of a fake nose and glasses no one can write back. Replies to your messages will be routed through the remailer.

There are lots of remailers. Some, like The Anonymizer (**www.anonymizer.com**), cost money. Others are free—but they seem to keep disappearing. They can require detective work to track down. For information try The Anonymous Remailer FAQ (**www.well.com/user/abacard/remail.html**) and The Nymserver (**www.nymserver.com**).

A handy $25 utility called John Doe lets you use remailers together with your favorite e-mail program. It works by setting up alias accounts on the remailers of your choice, using PGP encryption to ensure that no one else uses the remailer to send out mail with your alias. You can download a trial from Net Services (**www.cix.co.uk/~net-services/jdo.htm**).

America Online E-mail Tips

Automate Mail Retrieval and Sending. To set AOL's software to log on to the service, gather e-mail, send mail that you've written offline, then log off, you need to set its Flash Sessions feature. Choose Mail Center/Set Up/Automatic AOL (Flashsession). You can let AOL step you through the setup process, or you can click the Expert Set Up button to get this menu (see Figure 15). It's often good to set the software to download e-mail file attachments later. That way, you can check out what AOL is going to download to your computer before it spends 15 minutes doing so. Click the Schedule Automatic AOL to set the times when you'd like the software to dial mail. If you'd rather not (and many people don't) you can log on manually and, from the Mail Center menu, tell AOL to run the Flash Session on demand. That's often a more convenient way to gather mail.

Figure 15

Automatic AOL.

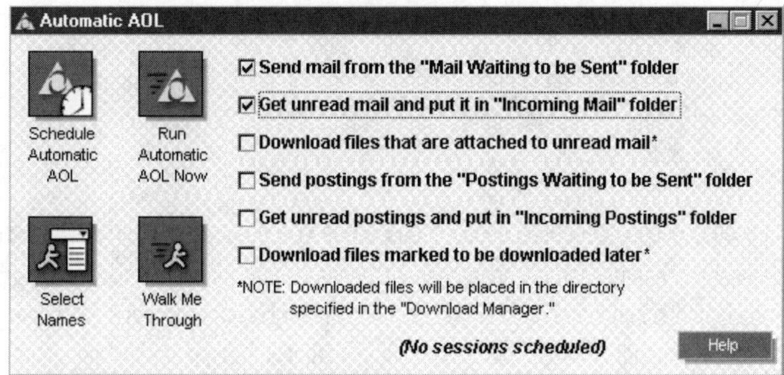

Keep Copies of Mail That You've Sent and Read. You can set AOL to retain copies on your hard disk of mail that you've sent and read by heading to Mail Center/Mail Preferences (see Figure 16). While you're there, set AOL to quote messages in Internet style (not AOL style, which will identify you as an AOL geek) and spell-check messages that you write. Click OK to make the settings permanent.

Figure 16

AOL Mail Preferences.

Mail Preferences
☑ Confirm mail after it has been sent
☑ Close mail after it has been sent
☑ Confirm when mail is marked to send later
☑ Retain all mail I send in my Personal Filing Cabinet
☑ Retain all mail I read in my Personal Filing Cabinet
☑ Perform a spell check before sending mail
☑ Use white mail headers
☑ Show addresses as hyperlinks
○ Use AOL style quoting: ⦿ Use internet style quoting:
<<This is an example of AOL style quoting>>
>This is an example
>of internet style quoting
Keep my old mail online 3 days after I read it
OK Cancel

(Don't) Add Snazzy Text and Pictures to Your Messages. You can use fancy fonts by clicking the buttons in the Write Mail dialog (Figure 17) or insert pictures in a message by clicking the Extras button—but reserve these embellishments strictly for other AOL users. If you use them with mail you send to other people, it may end up looking like digital ragout at their end (see Figure 7 earlier in this chapter).

Figure 17

AOL Write Mail.

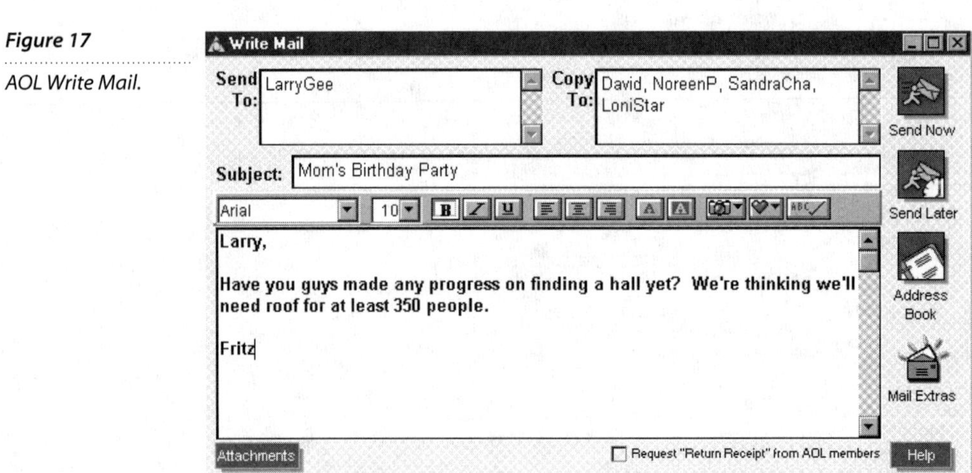

Filter Junk Mail. You can set AOL to filter out junk e-mail from Web sites or companies that send offensive mail. But if you use AOL regularly you may want to set it to accept e-mail only from people you correspond with often. You can also set it to filter e-mail that includes pictures (which are often offensive). To do so, head to the Mail Center/Mail Controls. Click Junk Mail. Add the AOL users, Internet addresses, and domain names from which you're willing to accept e-mail (see Figure 18). Click OK to make the settings permanent.

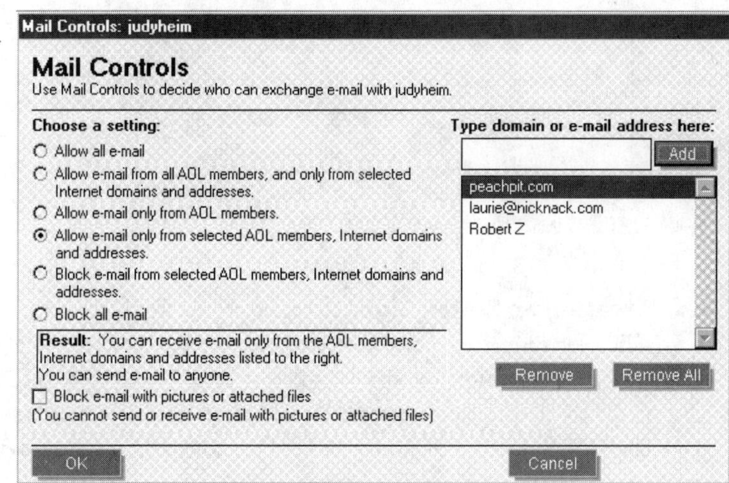

Figure 18

AOL Mail Controls.

Change Your AOL Screen Name. You can't change the "master" screen name—that is the name that you used to first log on to the service. But you can delete and change other screen names. AOL lets you create four screen names in addition to the master one, and you can have a separate e-mailbox for each. To create (or delete) a screen name, log on to AOL, click My AOL from the top menu bar, and select Screen Names. Select Create a Screen Name or Delete a Screen Name.

Outlook Express E-Mail Tips

Working with Folders. To create a new mail folder, right-click any existing folder and from the pop-up menu select New Folder. When prompted, type the name of the new folder, and select the folder you wish to make it a subfolder of (see Figure 19). You can drag and drop messages into folders. Or, right-click the messages and select Move to.

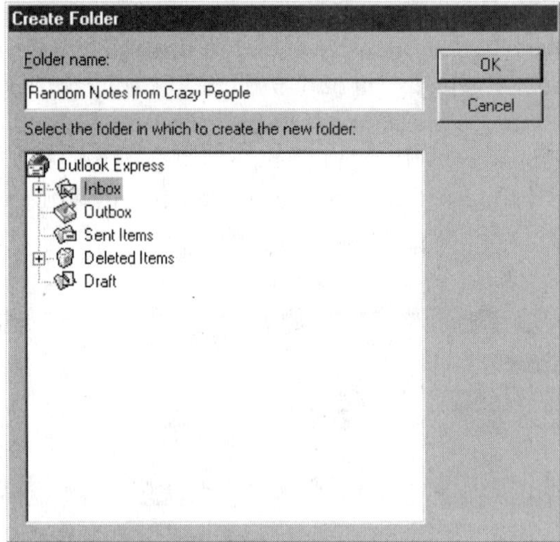

Figure 19

Outlook Express Create Folder.

Creating an E-Mail Signature. From the Tools menu select Stationery. Click the Signature button. In the dialog box that appears either type the text you want in your signature (see Figure 20) or select a text file. Click OK to make the settings permanent. To add your signature to an e-mail message, click the Signature button when you're composing the message.

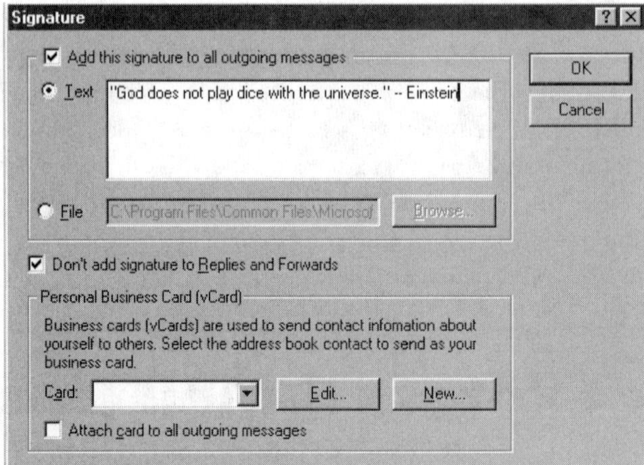

Figure 20

Outlook Express Signature.

Creating and Using Mailing Lists. To create a mailing list, click the Address Book icon, and then click New Group. In the dialog box that appears give your list a name, and then click the Select Members button in order to add e-mail addresses from your address book (see Figure 21). Click OK when you're finished. The mailing list will appear as an entry in your address book. To send a message to the list, address the message normally, and pick the group name from the Select Recipients list.

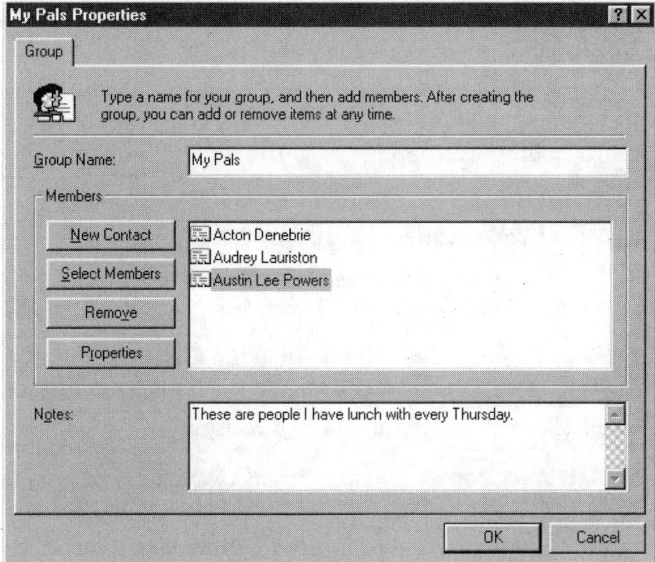

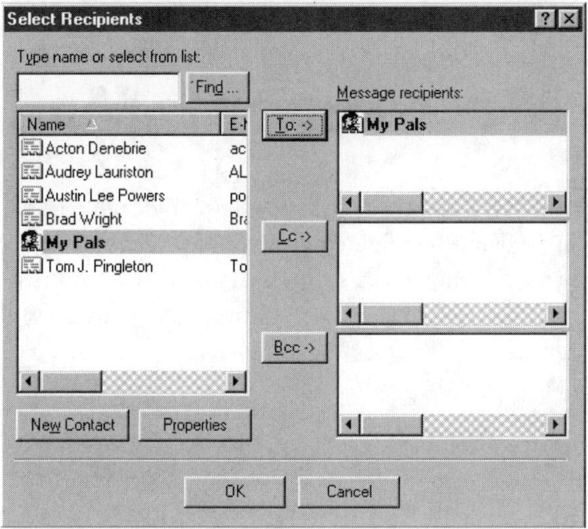

Figure 21

Outlook Express mailing lists.

Importing Address Books and Messages from Other Mailers. Use the File/Import submenu to import addresses or messages from Eudora, Netscape, or Microsoft Exchange. Outlook Express can also handle address books in LDIF/LDAP or comma-delimited text formats.

Sending Form Letters. There's no official form letter feature in Outlook Express. Instead you'll need to compose your form letter in a word processor and save it as a text file. When composing a message, select Insert/Text from File, then browse to the file you wish to insert in the message as a form letter.

Quickly Add E-Mail Addresses from Messages to Your Address Book. When someone sends you a message and you wish to add their address to your address book, open the message and click the e-mail address to send a reply message. When the New Message e-mail form pops up, right-click the e-mail address as it appears after To:. A menu should pop up. Click Add to Address Book.

Back Up Your Address Book and Mail. Your address book is stored in a file that's named: <*yourname*>.wab. You should find it in the c:\windows\profiles*yourname*\Application Data\Microsoft\Address Book folder.

Outlook Express stores your mail in the folder c:\windows\profiles\yourname\Application Data\Microsoft\Outlook Express\Mail. When you run your nightly tape backups, back up this entire directory.

E-Mail Web Pages. You can e-mail a Web page that you visit with Internet Explorer. From Explorer's File menu select Send/Page by E-mail. If you e-mail it to yourself, you can pick it up with Outlook Express, and Outlook will display the page just as you saw it on the Web. You can later print it or even fax it.

Netscape Messenger E-Mail Tips

Working with Folders. To create a new folder in Messenger in which to store e-mail, from the File menu select New Folder (see Figure 22). To file a message in a folder, right-click the message and from the pop-up menu select File Message (see Figure 23). Access your folders through the drop-down list on Messenger's top bar (see Figure 24).

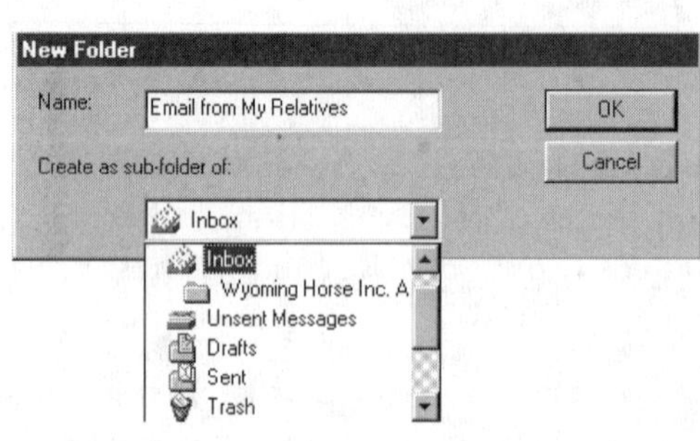

Figure 22

Netscape New Folders.

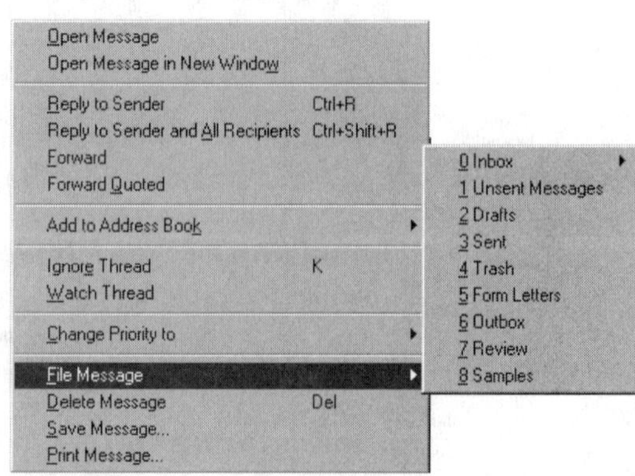

Figure 23

Netscape File Message.

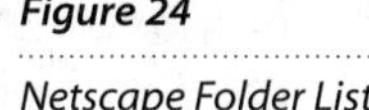

Figure 24

Netscape Folder List.

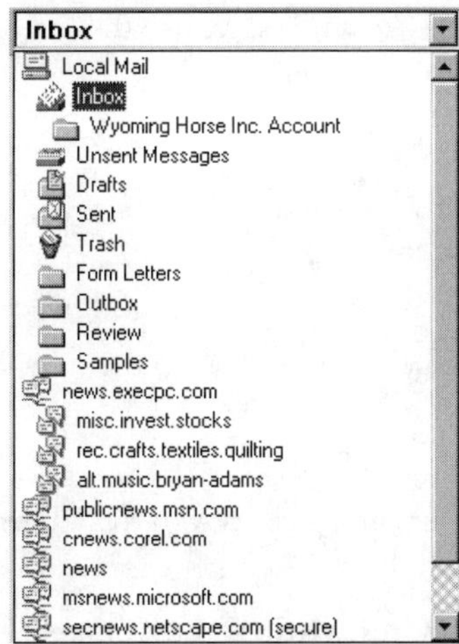

Create an E-Mail Signature. In your word processor or in Notepad, create a document that contains your name, title, e-mail address, and your business's name, its address, and fax number. Store it as a text file.

In Messenger, choose Edit/Preferences. Highlight and click Mail & Groups to expand it. Select Identity. In the menu screen that appears, click the Browse button to the right of the Signature File field, navigate to and select the file, click Open, then click OK to make the choice permanent.

Unfortunately, in Messenger you can have only one signature.

Create, Store, and Send Form Letters. While Netscape's Messenger lacks the ability to automatically reply to selected e-mail messages with a form letter, you can create form letters, store them in a special folder, and cut and paste their contents into replies.

The easiest way to do this is to head to the Message Center (Ctrl Shift 1), and from the File menu, select New Folder. Create it as a subfolder of your Inbox, and name it Form Letters. Click OK.

To create a form letter, create a new message (Ctrl M). Don't type in a recipient, but do type a subject that will identify the form letter. For example "Thank You For Your Request for Sales Information." Once you've finished writing your form letter, click the Save icon to save it in your draft folder. Close the message by clicking the X in the upper-right corner.

You now need to move the form letter from your Drafts folder to your Form Letters folder so that you can easily find it when you need it. Head to the Drafts folder, select the message, and click the File icon to move it to your Form Letters folder.

To send your form letter in reply to a message, use the forward feature or cut and paste its contents into a reply message.

Make a Mailing List

1. Open the address book. (You can launch it from the keyboard by pressing Ctrl Shift 2.)
2. Click the New List icon. Give the list a name and nickname if you wish.
3. Drag card icons from your address book onto the new list, or type in addresses.
4. Click OK.
5. To send a message to the list, just pick it from the address book the way you would a single user's address.

Send Mail from Windows Applications. You can use Netscape Messenger to send mail from applications like Word that support the Messaging Application Program Interface, or MAPI. From the Edit menu, select Preferences. Click on Mail & Groups to expand it and select Mail Server. From the Mail Server menu, click the More Options button.

Place a check beside "Use Netscape Messenger from MAPI-based Applications." But be careful of this setting. If you have other MAPI-compliant mail programs on your system, like Eudora, Netscape Messenger will interfere with them

Back Up Your Address Book and Your Mail. Netscape stores its address book in a proprietary-formatted binary file called abook.nab in your *user directory* (the folder Program Files/Netscape/Users/*yourname*). When you're running those quick late-night backups of critical files, you can set your backup software to back up abook.nab—or everything in your user directory if you wish to also back up mail and bookmarks.

You can export abook.nab other mail programs by choosing Save As from the File menu in the Address Book. You can also export it to an LDIF (Lightweight Directory Access Protocol Directory Interchange Format) file—an emerging standard that will supposedly make address books easily transportable between different mail programs. Unfortunately not many mail programs yet support LDIF.

Netscape stores your mail in the folder c:/program files/netscape/users/*yourname*/mail. You can back up that subdirectory at night. (In fact, it's recommended that you back up everything in the *yourname* subdirectory because that's where Netscape stores your address book, bookmarks, and user preferences.)

Or, you can move this directory to a spot that's easier to find when you're running "spot backups." Pull down the Edit menu and select Preferences. Click on Mail & Groups to expand it, and highlight and click on Mail Server. Hit the More Options button. You'll see the name of the directory where Netscape stores mail after "Local mail directory." To change it to someplace that's easier to find, click the Choose button and scroll to a directory of your choice. Click OK.

Quickly Add E-Mail Addresses from Messages to Your Address Book. Right-click the sender's e-mail address and from the pop-up menu select Add to Address Book.

Mail Management 101. When sorting through an inbox full of 500 messages, right-click each message's subject line to display a pop-up menu of quick-action selections (file, delete, reply, etc.).

Import Addresses from Other Versions and Other Mail Programs. You can import addresses from other e-mail programs into Netscape Messenger so long as those other programs are capable of exporting or saving their address books in LDIF format. In Netscape's address book, choose File/Import, then choose the file.

The trick to importing an address book from Netscape for Windows 3.*x* into Netscape for Windows 95 is to rename the LDIF file with a four-digit extension. For example: address.ldi should be renamed address.ldif.

Eudora Light Tips

Working with Mailboxes and Folders. You can organize your mail in nested folders and mailboxes in Eudora. (Folders hold mailboxes or other folders; mailboxes hold messages.) To get your mail in a mailbox you can: set up a filter to automatically deposit mail fitting certain criterion into certain mailboxes; drag and drop messages into a mailbox; or right click on a message, and from the pop-up menu select Transfer and then the mailbox (see Figure 25). To create a mailbox choose Mailbox/New, then type in a name in the dialog box. Remove the check beside "Make it a folder" to make it a mailbox and click OK. You can also create a new mailbox by right-clicking a folder and, from the pop-up dialog box, selecting New.

An Outbox Trick. To check the status of a message you've sent, open the outbox. An "S" beside the message means that the message has been sent. A "Q" means that it's queued and waiting to be sent. If you don't see any letter beside the message it's probably not queued, and it probably hasn't been sent. Open the message and click the Send button again.

Right-Click Messages for Quick Action!. Right-click a highlighted message to pop up a mini-menu from which you can reply to or delete the message or from which you can transfer it to a folder.

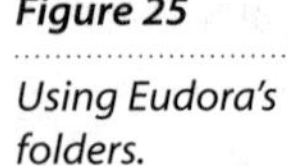

Figure 25

Using Eudora's folders.

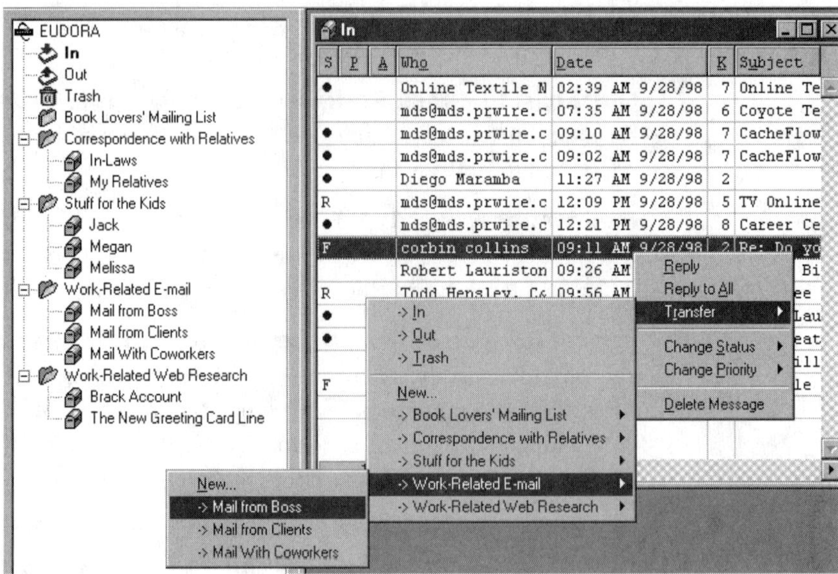

Add Your Signature to Messages. To create an e-mail message signature in Eudora, head to Tools/Signature. You can create a standard e-mail signature and an alternate one. When you click either Standard or Alternate, Eudora will pop up a scratch pad into which you can write your message. When you click the X to close the signature, Eudora will ask you if you want to save it. To use your signature, access the signature drop-down menu in Eudora's message creation toolbar, and pick your signature—or none.

Mini Scratch Pad. If you ever find yourself, in the course of composing a message, wishing you had a scratch pad to doodle on, head to the File menu and select New Text File. If the text file already exists on your disk, press Ctrl O to open it.

Give Eudora a Special Look. You can customize the fonts that Eudora uses, as well as its icons and toolbars, by heading to Tools/Options. Scroll to the Fonts & Display icon. When you're done making settings, click OK to make them permanent.

File Attachment Tricks. When you're composing a message, right-click the body of the message, and in the pop-up menu box, select Attach File to add an attachment. You can change the attachment setting from MIME (for recipients using PCs) to Binhex (for recipients using Macs) by clicking the Encoding drop-down menu at the top of the message creation toolbar. You can tell Eudora how to send file attachments by choosing Tools/Options and scrolling to the Attachments icon (see Figure 27). You can specify the directory on your hard disk where Eudora will deposit file attachments, as well as when the mailer will delete file attachments.

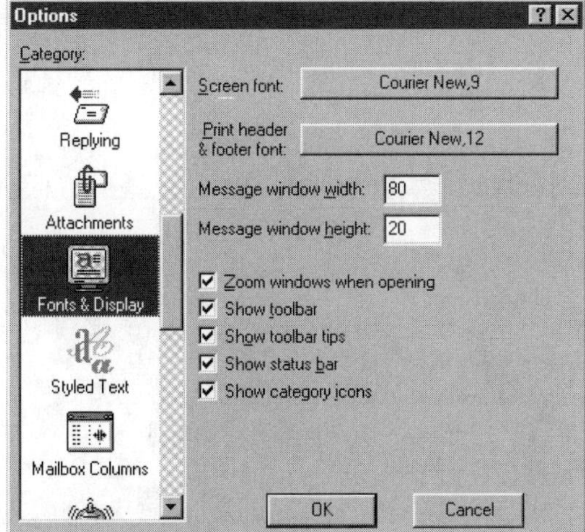

Figure 26:

Eudora font options.

Figure 27

Eudora attachment options.

Back Up Your Address Book and Mail. You'll find Mailbox files, which have an .mbx extension, in the C:\eudora directory. Folders are stored in subdirectories with an .fol extension. Message attachments are stored in the Attach subdirectory. In general, it's best to back up the entire contents of Eudora's directory, both files and subdirectories.

Add Addresses to Your Address Book. While a message is open, press Ctrl K to add the sender's address to your address book.

Search Your E-Mailboxes for That Certain Message. Can't remember where you filed that message from your Aunt Lou? Use Eudora's Find feature (Edit/Find) to search the contents of all your mailboxes. You can search through message headers, or the body of messages for a word—or e-mail address. If Eudora finds a message that matches, but it's not the one you're looking for, select Find Next to direct Eudora to find another match.

Keep Copies of Messages That You Send. To keep a copy of a message that you write, click the Copy button before or after you write the message (see Figure 28).

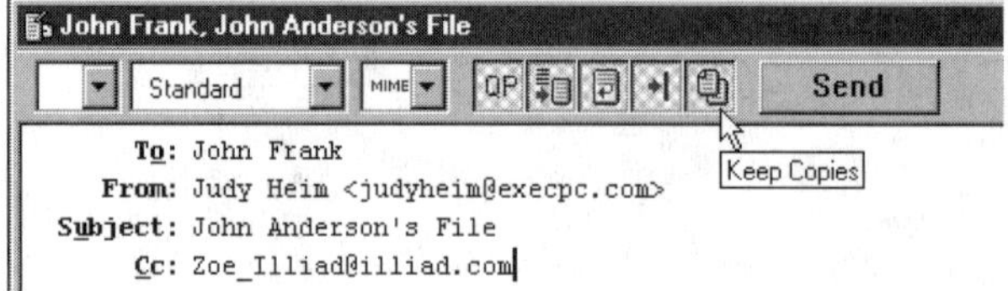

Figure 28

Eudora keeps copies.

Tell Eudora to Check for E-Mail Regularly. To set Eudora to check your ISP for mail at regular intervals choose Tools/Options and scroll to the Checking Mail icon (see Figure 29). Set the number of minutes and click OK. Be sure to tell Dial-Up Networking to remember your password and log on to your ISP automatically. But you'll need to remember to disconnect for yourself.

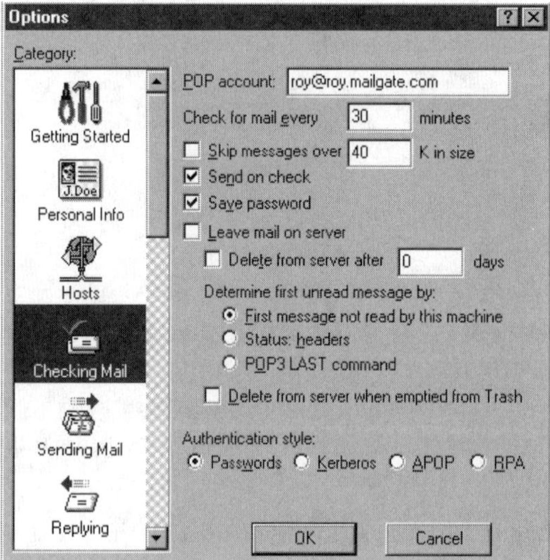

Figure 29

Eudora mail checking options.

E-mail Resources

mail-server@rtfm.mit.edu You can get a copy of the invaluable FAQ *Accessing the Internet by E-Mail* by sending a message to this address. In the body of the message type only the following:

```
send usenet/news.answers/internet-services/access-via-email
```

biz.mhv.net/drbob For tips on using the free e-mail service Juno, get a copy of *Juno: Free E-mail & More!* by Bob Rankin (San Francisco, No Starch Press, $14.95, 800/420-7240), or visit Bob's Web site.

www.tourbus.com If you're new to the Net, you can order a free e-mail newsletter from this site that is full of tips on e-mailing your way around. This site also includes an archive of past newsletters.

support.microsoft.com Microsoft's tech support Web site includes some great newsgroups devoted to Outlook and Outlook Express. In fact, if you have any questions or problems with the mailers you're more apt to find the answers here than anywhere else. But sometimes they can be hard to find. Head to Support Online and click "newsgroups." When asked to select a product category, head to the Microsoft Office Products.

help.netscape.com Netscape's tech support Web site offers lots of great advice, especially on bugs—and getting Netscape Messenger to do things you can't figure out otherwise.

www.aol.com You can download copies of America Online software and AOL mail-related freebies from AOL's Web site. But don't expect to find tech support. For that you'll need to go online on AOL. From the Welcome screen select Member Services, and then choose Help topics. Or, type **AOL help** in the keyword bar. An even better place to get help on AOL is in its member help forum: in the keyword bar type **members helping members**.

eudora.qualcomm.com/techsupport On Qualcomm's Web site you'll find a database of help files on Eudora Light and Pro.

eudora.qualcomm.com/techsupport/online.html The most useful section of Qualcomm's site, this page holds a list of elusive Internet FAQs, discussion groups, and mailing lists devoted to Eudora.

21

The Web and Browsers

by Robert Lauriston

In This Chapter

The growth of the Web has been remarkable. When the first edition of this book was published in 1994, most people had only heard of it, if that. Today, almost everyone who owns a PC surfs the Web, and an increasing percentage of us maintain our own Web sites as well. In this chapter, I'll briefly sketch the origins of the Web, tell you what to expect from a Web browser, compare the most popular browsers and search engines, point you to a few things you might not expect to find on the Web, and tell you where to find the information and tools to create your own site.

A Brief History of the Web

With plugs for Web sites now common in billboards, magazine ads, and TV commercials, it's hard to remember that just a few years ago only a handful of people had heard of the Web, and a couple of years before that, it hadn't even been invented. Would you believe that the first issue of that Web-happy magazine *Wired* didn't have *one word* about the Web?

The concept of the Web, HTML (the language used to create Web pages), and the original predecessor of today's browsers were invented in 1989 and 1990 by Tim Berners-Lee, who was at the time a software research fellow at CERN, an international particle-physics research center in Switzerland. Some of the ideas embodied in the Web were adapted from Enquire, a single-user program he'd written a decade earlier to organize random information.

Berners-Lee's Web software ran only on the NeXt computer, so at first most people couldn't use it, and the browser (see Figure 1) was text only, no graphics, further limiting the Web's appeal. As word got around, people started porting the tools to other computers and operating systems, but the Web still remained almost unknown outside of academic and computer-research circles.

The number of people using the Web grew steadily from its inception, but the Web didn't really take off until 1993, after a group of students working for the National Center for Supercomputing Applications at the University of Illinois developed an easier-to-use browser, Mosaic, and added support for graphics. What really sparked the Web explosion was the release of Macintosh and Windows versions of Mosaic: all of a sudden, anyone with a PC who could click a mouse could navigate the Internet.

Well, actually, it wasn't quite that simple; you also needed a direct connection to the Internet, which was then pretty much unheard of outside of universities and a handful of high-tech industries. Demand for such connections launched the Internet service provider (ISP) industry, which in turn sparked exponential growth in the business of producing routers, servers, and other Internet hardware. That "Internet gold rush" eventually absorbed or destroyed almost all of the existing modem-based online services: America Online, for example, had to turn itself into an ISP and switch to flat-rate pricing; CompuServe, once the king of online services, didn't handle the transition so well and is now a subsidiary of AOL.

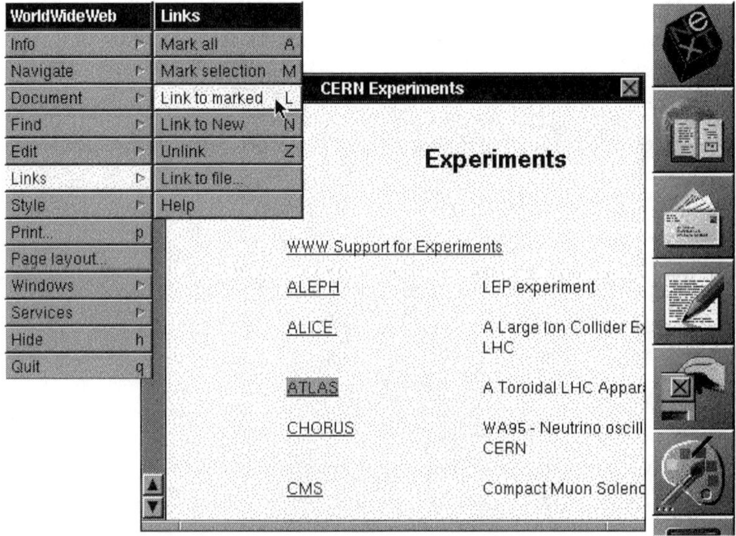

Figure 1

A version of WorldWideWeb, Tim Berners-Lee's original browser, running on a NeXt workstation. (This image has been edited to save space—you can see the full version at **`www.w3.org/History/1994/WWW/Journals/CACM/screensnap2_24c.gif`***.)*

Browser Basics

Just as the Web absorbed the online services that preceded it, Web browsers (see Figure 2) eventually absorbed most Internet software.

When I got my first direct dial-up account in 1994, my ISP sent me a whole collection of programs to handle various Net tasks: a TCP/IP stack, a PPP dialer, a Web browser, an e-mail program, an Archie program to search online file libraries, an FTP utility to download files, a newsreader to read newsgroups, another program to search Gopher databases, a somewhat awful Internet indexing system made obsolete by the Web. The first two functions are now handled by Windows; the rest can all be handled by my browser.

Figure 2

A typical Web browser.

Netscape Navigator, the most popular browser, is as good a choice as any to illustrate the features all browsers have in common. The main window displays the current Web page. The page's address (URL in Web jargon) is displayed in the Location menu, which you can also use to type in addresses from your PC's keyboard. A toolbar at the top lets you perform common tasks and also includes some buttons that are basically advertisements for Netscape sites. The Bookmarks menu stores addresses of pages you want to return to. The status bar displays information about the browser and current page: whether you're in online or offline mode, if the current page is secure, the status of downloads, and so on. (These concepts are all explained in "Browser Basics" later in this chapter.)

Today, for most people, their browser *is* the Internet. That makes the browser's job description simple: it has to take anything and everything that's out there on the Net and turn it into a form that you can use.

- Want to view a Web page? Your browser converts the HTML source code into formatted text, graphics, links, forms, and so on.
- Want to download a shareware program from a software library? Your browser handles the transfer from the library's server and stores the file on your hard disk.
- Want to tune into a live Internet audio or video broadcast? Your browser's Real Player plug-in connects to the Real server and makes your computer like a radio or TV.

- Want to shop online? Your browser encrypts your credit card number and other personal information so hackers can't intercept and abuse it and sends any forms you fill out to the appropriate server.
- Want to read an Internet newsgroup? Your browser has that covered, too.
- Want to communicate with friends and family? As discussed in Chapter 20, the e-mail programs bundled with browsers are not necessarily the best choice, but most people use them anyway.
- Want to see some advertisements? No? Too bad; that's the price of free software—your browser may let you shut off animations and sound, but that's about it.

Since a browser's job is to provide access to Internet services, its capabilities are limited mostly not by its own features, but by what's out there on the Net. If a browser doesn't flunk the basic test of letting you access the sites and services you're interested in, it's basically as good as any other similarly capable browser.

Beyond the basic compatibility issues, which browser will work best for you depends largely on personal preference. Here's a quick overview of some things to look at when comparing browsers. To give you a head start, I've noted basic differences between the three browsers discussed in detail in this chapter: Netscape Navigator, Microsoft Internet Explorer (MSIE), and Opera.

Navigation and Interface Design

At the most basic level, all browsers follow the same model introduced by Mosaic in 1993. Click a link, and the linked page replaces the current page; click the Stop button, and the page stops loading; click Back (or Previous), and you return to the linking page. Today's browsers consolidate these and other commands in right-click pop-up menus, so you don't have to constantly move the mouse up to the toolbar or drop-down menus.

The big difference is in keyboard shortcuts. Of the three browsers discussed here, Opera's the only one that's designed so you can control it as easily from the keyboard as you can with a mouse. MSIE and Netscape have keyboard shortcuts for some features, but not for everything.

When you first install any browser, it's set to go to the vendor's Web site automatically every time you open it. You can change that to any page you like, or to a blank page. In Navigator, choose Edit/Preferences; in MSIE, choose View/Internet Options; in Opera, choose Navigation/Set Home.

Toggling Graphics On and Off

Graphics take up a lot more space on disk than text. For example, those little banner ads you often see at the top of a Web page typically take up around 10K; load a text-only page of the same size into your browser, and you'd have to page down at least three times to read it all. When you're browsing one page after another in search of something specific, it speeds things up a lot if you turn off graphics (see Figure 3)—but you still want to be able to load graphics quickly when there's something worth looking at.

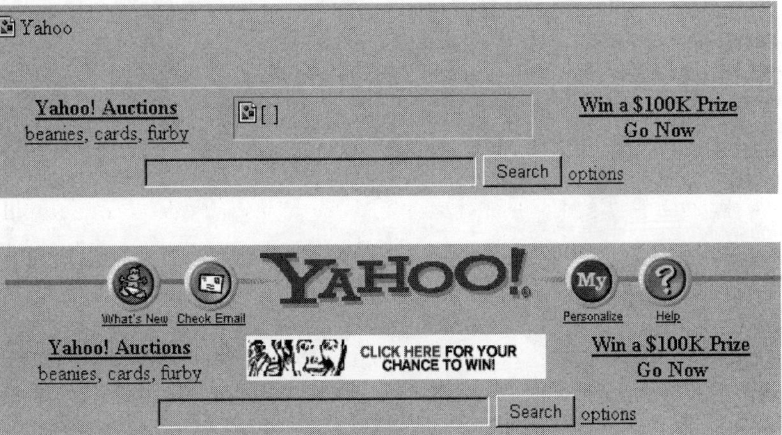

Figure 3

Toggling images. When you have images turned off, they're replaced by blank rectangles, which should (but, as here, often don't) contain text describing the images' contents.

In Navigator, when you turn image autoloading off, an Images button appears on the toolbar; click it, and the browser loads the images for the current page. Opera goes one better, providing a single button you can use to turn autoloading on or off or to load images for the current page. MSIE flubs this one: you can toggle images on or off, but the option's buried in an advanced Preferences dialog box, and when images are switched off, there's no button or menu command for loading the current page's images—though you can use the right-click menu to load individual images.

Bookmarks

Browser *bookmarks* (aka favorites or hot lists) let you save the address of the page you're browsing in a menu or desktop icon so you can easily return to it later. As you surf the Web, you may end up with *lots* of bookmarks, so a good browser will let you organize them into folders of related sites

All three browsers discussed here use similar hierarchical menus to organize their bookmarks. MSIE and Opera also offer a multipane approach similar to that in Windows Explorer, where bookmarks appear at the left and Web pages at the right. I like Opera's three-pane approach (see Figure 4) the best—it's particularly good if you're running the browser from the keyboard rather than with the mouse. The one drawback is that you can't *search* Opera's bookmarks as you can Navigator's and MSIE's—but if I'd been using Opera all along, I wouldn't have ended up with the disorganized mess of bookmarks I created in Navigator.

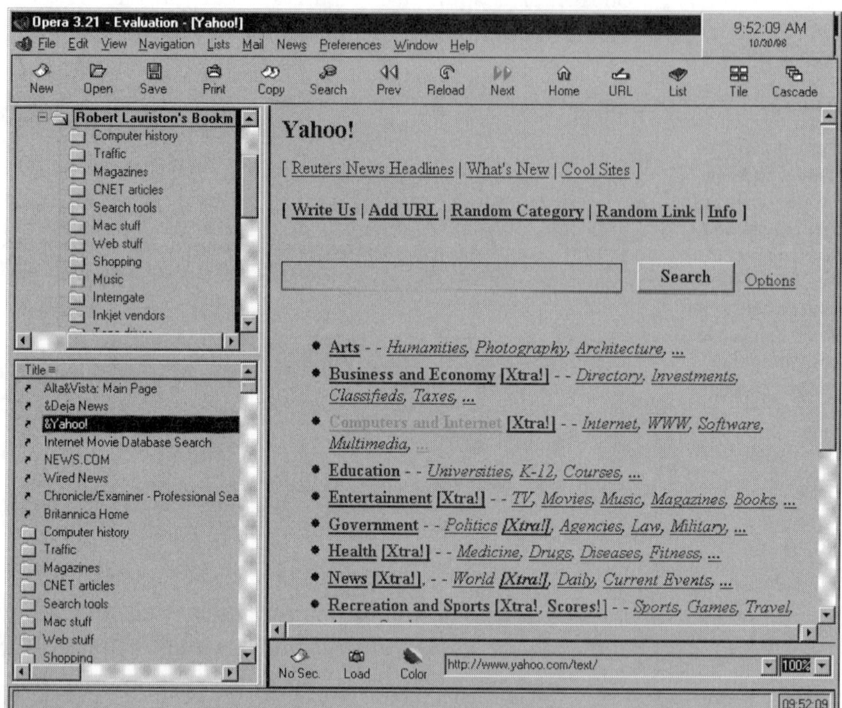

Figure 4

Using bookmarks. Opera's hot list (bookmarks) is set up for easy keyboard navigation: select a folder in the top-left pane and then a bookmark in the pane below it, and the page appears in the main window. Toggle the hot list off with Ctrl F2, and the Web page expands to fill the space.

History

A browser's *history* tracks the sites you visit, so at any time you can retrace your steps to a page you were looking at earlier, even if you neglected to bookmark it. (This is particularly helpful when you get lost in a large and confusing Web site and want to get back to the page where you made a wrong turn.)

In Opera, the history is just a list of page names with the dates you last visited. Navigator uses a similar approach, but tracks additional information, including how many times you've visited the site and the date of your first visit. MSIE's history is tops: it's organized into an easy-to-navigate set of folders organized by site and date (see Figure 5).

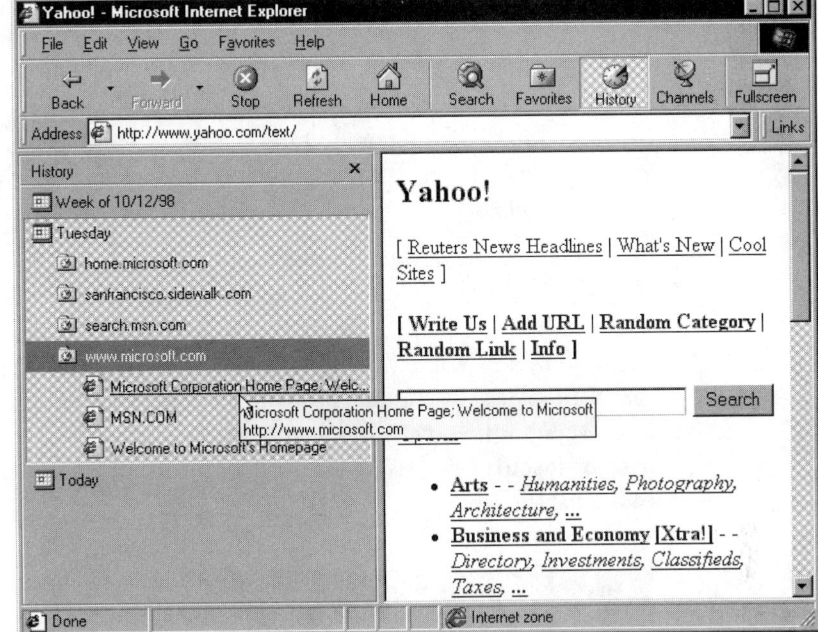

Figure

MSIE's history. Navigating MSIE's history is similar to navigating Windows Explorer's folder tree. Double-click a history entry, and it appears in the main window. You navigate MSIE's bookmarks (Favorites) similarly.

Cache and Offline Access

Web surfing involves a lot of redundant data. People frequently backtrack, reloading the same pages they loaded before, and many sites use the same set of graphics on many different pages. To avoid wasting time downloading the same thing twice, browsers *cache* pages—that is, they keep copies in memory or on disk, where they can be reloaded in a fraction of the time it would take to download them again from scratch. You can adjust the amount of disk space the cache uses in the browser's preferences, and the browser will automatically delete the least recently accessed pages from the cache as necessary to stay within that limit.

The browser's cache can also be used for *offline* access: the browser copies a set of pages to your hard disk, where you can access them whether or not you're connected to the Net. If you live in an area where connecting to the Internet carries significant per-minute charges, offline browsing will reduce your monthly bill. It's also useful with notebook computers: you can copy your favorite sites to your hard disk and read them when a Net connection isn't available.

Navigator provides offline access only for e-mail and newsgroups. In MSIE and Opera, you can view any page in the program's cache by choosing it from the history list.

MSIE also offers a subscription feature that will automatically download a selected page and up to three levels of links from that page for offline viewing.

That is, it will download all the pages the selected page is linked to, all the pages *those* pages are linked to, and all the pages *those* pages are linked to, as well as all the pages' graphics. By default, this feature blindly follows all links, which can snag a lot of irrelevant material. When I tested the feature at my own site, which takes up only a little over 900K on disk, it grabbed so much stuff from linked sites that the browser downloaded over 10MB before I gave up and canceled it.

To narrow the download to the selected site, choose Favorites/Manage Subscriptions, right-click the icon for the subscription, choose Properties, click the Receiving tab, click Advanced, and uncheck "Follow links outside this page's Web site." While you're in that dialog box (see Figure 6), you might also want to disable graphics, multimedia, and applets or impose a total download size limit. If you like this feature, check out WebWhacker ($49 shareware from **`bluesquirrel.com`**), which will work with any browser and has some additional features.

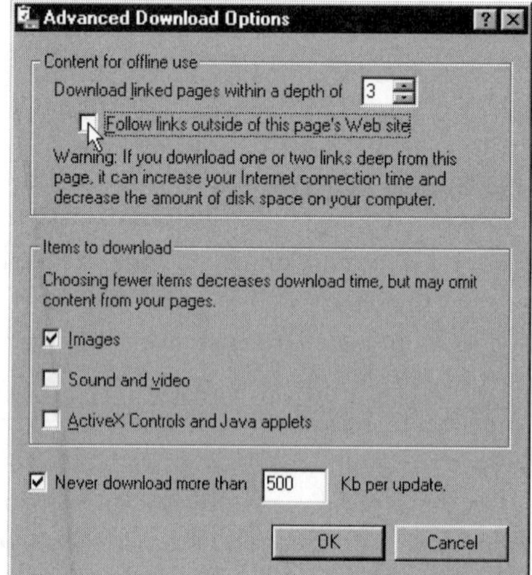

Figure 6

MSIE's advanced subscription settings.

Note that in any browser you can save Web pages to disk with File/Save As. Unlike offline browsing features, however, this won't snag graphics as well.

Security

Since the Internet is a public network, any information sent across it can potentially be intercepted and read by anyone with sufficient skill, time, and patience. To transmit private information across the Internet in a form that hackers can't read, browsers use *encryption*, a sort of secret code that turns your data into an incomprehensible mess that can be read only by someone who possesses the right key.

Standard encryption uses 40-bit keys, which are secure against garden-variety hacking but can be cracked easily by any hacker who can get control of a supercomputer or large network for a few hours. Thus, for really sensitive data, you should use 128-bit keys, which in theory, with current technologies, would take centuries to crack. As computers get faster, the time it takes to crack keys goes down, so it's anybody's guess how soon browsers will have to move to even longer keys to maintain the same level of security.

Since bigger keys slow things down, some sites use a mix of types. For example, one of my banks requires only 40-bit encryption to access information about my accounts and transfer money between them, but demands 128-bit encryption before it will let me pay bills. The bank also requires that my browser respond to commands from its server not to cache any information regarding my accounts, thus preventing a hacker from raiding the cache for passwords or personal information. Your browser may let you know when you have a secure connection through various visual clues or warning dialog boxes, or you can check the current document's security status manually (see Figure 7).

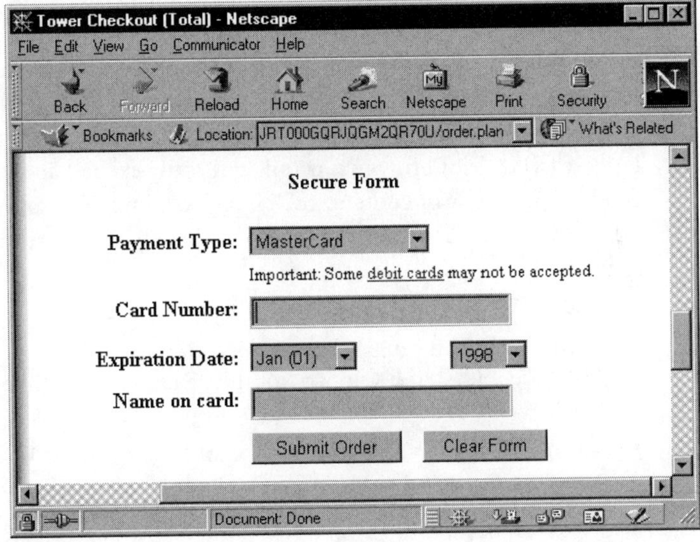

Figure 7

Secure browsing.

The little closed-padlock icon at the bottom-left corner of this Navigator window indicates that the form on the screen is secure, so you can enter private information and be sure it'll stay private. You can get more information about its security status by clicking the lock icon.

You can get both kinds of encryption in all three major browsers, though things are complicated by the U.S. government's bizarre classification of some types of encryption as munitions subject to export control by the State Department. That means that to avoid violating federal law, U.S. companies like Microsoft and Netscape have to produce separate 40-bit-only browsers for export—so make sure you download the 128-bit version. (I have yet to hear of anyone being arrested on federal charges of illegal arms trafficking for taking a laptop with a 128-bit browser out of the country, but it could happen.) Since Opera Software's a Norwegian company, Opera doesn't have to deal with that nonsense.

Performance

I've read reviews that found performance differences between browsers in benchmark tests, but in my experience, real-world delays are seldom the browser's fault. More often it's heavy traffic on the network, an overloaded Web server, the limited bandwidth of the connection to your ISP, or some other factor over which the browser has no control. On the other hand, the tendency of some browsers to eat up large amounts of memory may slow down your system, even when the browser's doing nothing. (That's one of the main reasons I switched from Navigator to Opera.)

Since Netscape's and Microsoft's browsers are free, and Opera offers a 30-day free trial, it doesn't cost you anything to compare them and judge their performance claims for yourself.

Multimedia

In the early days of browsers, people got really excited about the possibilities of adding all kinds of content to Web pages: animation, sound effects, music, motion video, etc., etc. As it turned out, there were several problems with that concept:

- Modem connections aren't fast enough to handle most of those kinds of media well. You can get halfway decent monophonic audio with the right software, but stereo's not so hot. Live video is more like a slide show, and the screen's the size of a postage stamp.
- Even with a faster connection, like an ISDN line or T1 line, the Internet itself often has traffic problems, so high-bandwidth media like video tend to be unreliable.
- Most people aren't interested in that stuff anyway: they're surfing the Web looking for information, not entertainment. There is *some* interesting stuff out there, however, particularly in the audio realm: see "What Else Is Out There" later in this chapter for some pointers.

Personally, I'm less interested in what kinds of multimedia my browser supports than in whether it lets me turn them all off. That's very easy in Opera and MSIE: check boxes in their preference dialog boxes let you turn animation, video, and sound playback on or off individually. (Opera also lets you disable automatic document loading, which some annoying Web sites use to load new advertisements every few seconds.)

Netscape doesn't let you disable anything except images. While Navigator has a View/Stop Animations command, you can't use it until after the page containing the animation has been loaded, since the Stop Animations command also stops downloading, just like the Stop button.

Java and ActiveX

Another item that was grossly overhyped in the early days of browsers is Java, a special programming language that allows software developers to create small programs (*applets*) that run in your browser, just as regular programs run in Windows. Java enjoyed a brief period of popularity as Web developers experimented with using it to do things they couldn't do with HTML (the Web's underlying language), like add custom navigation controls, but it turned out that there were almost always easier, more efficient, and more reliable ways to accomplish the same ends.

Since I found that Java tends to create problems, I keep it turned off (see Figures 8 and 9) in browsers that support it, and it's been a long time since I encountered a site where I had to turn it on. Don't confuse Java with JavaScript, a scripting language that allows programmers to embed simple commands in their HTML code–for example, to create a Send button to submit a filled-out form to a server application or to make buttons change appearance when you move the mouse over them. Navigator and MSIE have both Java and JavaScript built in. Opera has JavaScript only; Java support is available through a plug-in.

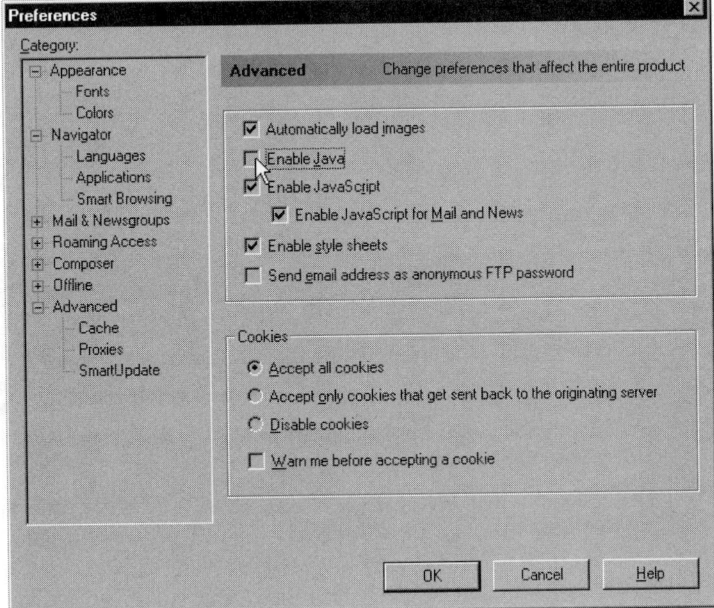

Figure 8

Turning off Java in Navigator. To get to the Java on/off switch, choose Edit/Preferences and click the Advanced tab.

Microsoft's ActiveX (formerly known as OLE) is to some extent a competitor to Java, in the sense that programmers can use it to add features to Web pages not supported by HTML. The key difference is that Java programs run in a *sandbox*, a sort of walled-off area in which they are isolated from other programs, Windows, and your hard disk, so you don't have to worry about whether they might be viruses: about the worst one could do would be crash your browser. In contrast, ActiveX applets are run by Windows, so they can do just about anything—crash your system, wipe out your hard drive, whatever. A system of *security certificates* is supposed to ensure that the ActiveX applets you download are safe, but the approach strikes me as inherently too insecure for casual use, so I keep ActiveX turned off (see Figure 9). (I can see using it on a private network, where you only allow users to run applets from your private servers.)

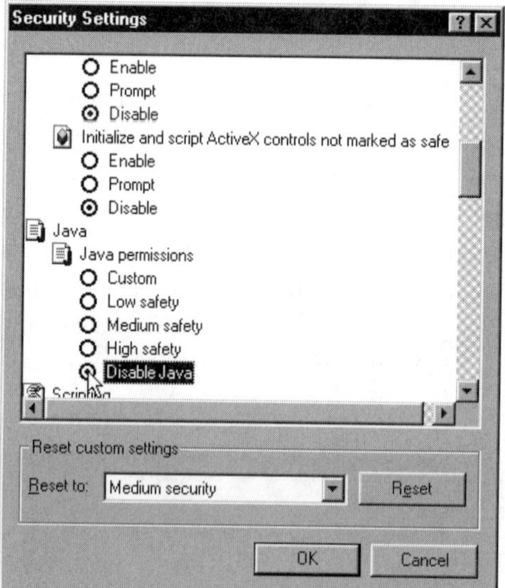

Figure 9

Turning off Java and ActiveX in MSIE.

Microsoft buries the Java and ActiveX on/off switches pretty deep. To find them, select View/Internet Options, click the Security tab, click the Custom radio button, and click Settings.

Plug-Ins

You can expand the basic capabilities of a browser almost indefinitely by adding plug-ins, programs that hook into the browser and add more features. There are lots of these add-ons out there, but you're likely to really need only a handful at most:

- **Real Player.** The standard for Internet audio and video broadcasts. (`www.real.com`)
- **Shockwave Flash.** Plays animations, product demos, and various other multimedia whatchamacallits created with Macromedia Director; very popular for kid-oriented sites. Personally, my browser crashed one too many times when attempting to load a "shocked" page, so I've given up

on it: I don't install it, and whenever a Web site displays a Get the Plug-In button, I click Cancel instead. (**www.macromedia.com/shockwave**)

- **QuickTime.** An Apple all-in-one multimedia player with capabilities similar to those in Real Player and Shockwave Flash, though since the data formats are mostly incompatible, you can't substitute one for the other. (**www.apple.com/quicktime**)
- **Adobe Acrobat.** While Acrobat is an essential tool, I don't see the point of installing its browser plug-in: it makes more sense to me to download files and read them in the more powerful and flexible stand-alone Acrobat Reader utility. For more information, see Chapter 12: Windows Add-Ons. (**www.adobe.com/acrobat**)

All of the preceding plug-ins are free and work with Netscape, Microsoft, and Opera browsers. Real Player and Shockwave flash, as well as an older version of QuickTime, are bundled along with Navigator in the Communicator suite.

Which Browser?

As I noted earlier, the key issue when choosing a browser is whether it lets you access the sites and services you're interested in. Unfortunately, there are only three browsers that are likely to come close to passing the compatibility test: Netscape Navigator (now part of the Communicator suite), Microsoft Internet Explorer (MSIE), and Opera.

I say "close to passing" because personally I have yet to find a browser that will work right with every site I try to click to. Whatever browser I try, once in a while I find a page that won't load, or that seems to load but never appears, or that appears but isn't formatted correctly, or that simply crashes or hangs the browser. Other heavy Web users I've talked with report similar experiences.

Consequently, like most people who surf the Web a lot, I keep several browsers on my system. In my main work environment, Windows NT, I'm in the process of switching to Opera 3.21 from my old main browser, Netscape Navigator 3.04, an old version that works better for me than later releases. (I'm hardly alone in that: on one Web site I visited recently, the server statistics showed that 38% of the users were using 3.x releases of Netscape or MSIE, versus 53% for 4.x versions.) I don't know Opera all that well yet, so I switch back and forth a lot, and since Opera doesn't have an e-mail program, I'll be keeping Navigator around for that.

When I encounter a page neither of those browsers can read, I fire up the newer version of Navigator in Netscape Communicator 4.5. (The main reason I keep the old Navigator around is that for some reason Netscape Messenger, the e-mail component of the Communicator suite, won't display all the entries in the large e-mail address book it shares with Navigator.) When Communicator doesn't work, I try MS Internet Explorer 2.0, which came on my Windows NT CD-ROM. If *that* can't handle the job, I reboot my PC to Windows 98 and try MSIE 4.0, though I'm happy to say I've had to do that only a couple of times.

Anyway, as I was saying, there are only three browsers that are likely to prove satisfactory. Let's take a quick look at each.

Netscape Navigator and Communicator

In the classic chicken-and-egg style of the computer industry, Netscape Navigator (now part of the Communicator suite) *is* the number 1 browser largely because it *was* the number 1 browser. Since Navigator has been the most popular browser for years, it's always a top priority for Web designers to make sure their sites look good in it. As a result, Navigator tends to do a good job of displaying most sites, and since that's the main thing people want in a Web browser, Navigator stays popular.

Navigator originally became top dog because early Web users widely considered it an upgrade to Mosaic, which, as discussed at the beginning of this chapter, was the first widely popular browser. Netscape was co-founded by Marc Andreessen, who was not only one of Mosaic's main programmers but also the guy who came up with and implemented the crucial idea of supporting graphics as well as text. Netscape was even called Mosaic Communications at first, though the name had to be changed after legal threats from the University of Illinois, which still owns Mosaic. The university's ownership didn't do it much good: most Mosaic users switched to Netscape as soon as the first version came out in 1994.

In the first few years of the browser wars, Netscape maintained its position largely through technical leadership. Navigator's popularity meant Netscape was able to extend the capabilities of the Web, adding now-familiar innovations like frames, tables, Java, and plug-ins that were quickly adopted by Web programmers. Competing browsers from Microsoft and now-forgotten companies like NetManage, Spry, Spyglass, and Wollongong often had trouble displaying pages that took advantage of Netscape's latest enhancements, so users naturally tended toward Navigator.

Microsoft eventually managed to catch up, more or less, and the two companies' browsers now seem roughly comparable in terms of compatibility. They read the vast majority of Web sites just fine, and screw up an equally small percentage of the time. As you can see from the preceding "Browser Basics" section, Netscape's fallen a little behind in terms of features, but it makes up for that by having a somewhat simpler interface and being *much* less intrusive to install than MSIE.

The version of Navigator in Communicator 4.5 (see Figure 10) struck me as being the first evidence that browsers are reaching maturity. Earlier releases often seemed less like products for users than salvos against Microsoft in a war for market share. Features of dubious value were tacked onto the menus where they fell, new modules were added until the program looked almost as complicated as Microsoft Office, and the rush to market meant a never-ending stream of bug-fixing minor updates.

Version 4.5, in marked contrast, simplified the jerry-built interface, eliminated several little-used modules, reorganized the commands into logical menus, and fixed some long-standing bugs (though it *still* drops entries from my old address book). The 4.5 release is actually *smaller* than its predecessor, 4.0, which may be a first among popular Windows apps. Most of Communicator 4.5's new features are in Messenger, the e-mail/newsreader module; the only major innovation in the browser is a What's Related button (see Figure 10), which compiles a list of related sites from a database maintained by Netscape.

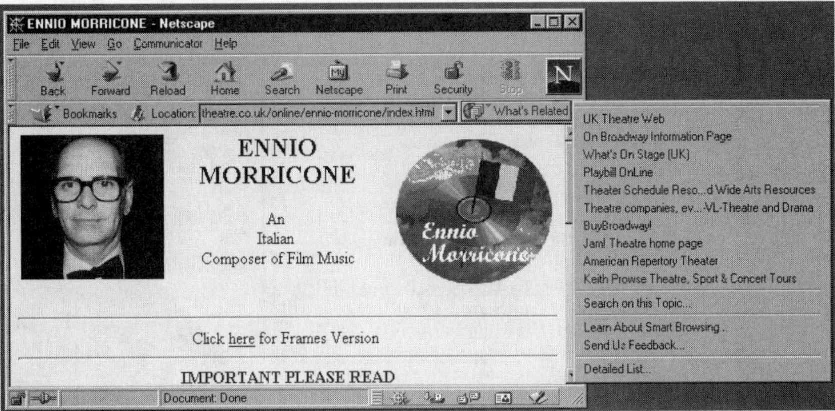

Figure 10

Related to what?

Navigator's What's Related feature is a great idea, but it's not always that useful. None of the supposedly related items here have anything to do with the subject of this page; they seem to have been picked based on the words in the location (URL) rather than the content of the page itself.

It's anybody's guess what's going to happen with future releases of Navigator and Communicator. Inspired by freeware programs like Linux, Netscape has switched to an open-source model of development, where volunteer programmers improve and revise the product in their spare time. Any programmer who wants to can use Netscape's code as a base for a new browser and give it away free; Netscape retains the right to fold the best into its own official releases. (For information, check out **mozilla.org**.)

Microsoft Internet Explorer

The good news is that MSIE is one of the best browsers around. In addition to the good stuff mentioned in the "Browser Basics" section, it has a unique full-screen mode that maximizes the space for displaying oversized Web pages, usually loads text before images so you can click through faster, and offers a clever interface to selected search engines like AltaVista and Lycos that lets you view your searches while keeping the search form in a small window (see Figure 11). In terms of features, its only big defect is that you can't toggle graphics on and off as easily as you can in competing browsers.

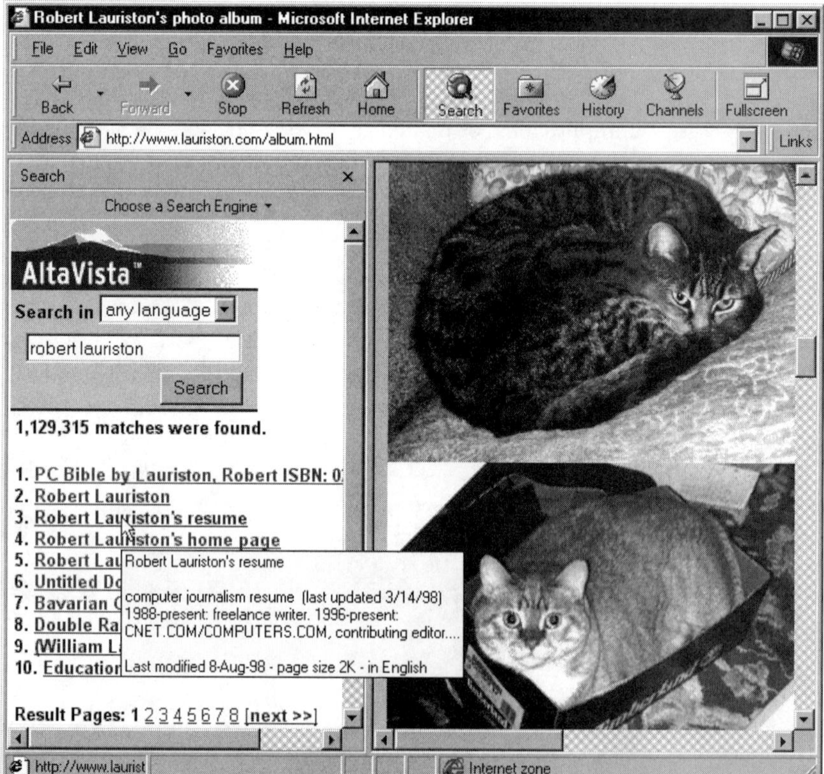

Figure 11

MSIE's two-pane search.

When you click the Search button in MSIE, you get this clever two-page interface. The search form stays on the screen, at the left, while the found pages you click appear at the right. The summary information that would appear under each link in a regular AltaVista search shows up here when you pause the mouse pointer over the link.

The bad news is that MSIE 4.0 and later releases blur the distinction between your browser and the operating system. This is good for Microsoft, which has been fighting antitrust lawsuits that hinge partly on whether it was barred from bundling MSIE with Windows 95 by a 1994 settlement of an earlier lawsuit. If MSIE and Windows 98 are not separate products, then there's no bundling, so the issue is moot. (For a little more on this topic, see the "Microsoft" section of Chapter 10: How to Choose and Buy Software.)

Fine for Microsoft, but what advantage is there for you and me in that deal? Do you really want to blur the distinction between your hard disk and the Web? I see my browser as a sort of bulletproof window onto the chaos of the Internet, and I like having a clear line between it and the other stuff on my PC. Most people seem to feel the same way: Microsoft was originally going to make Windows 98's interface even more browserlike, but so many beta testers complained that it made the most radical changes optional and turned off by default. (See the discussion of Active Desktop under "Customize the Desktop" in Chapter 11: Windows 95, 98, and NT.)

One result of erasing the boundaries between the browser and Windows is that MSIE is less an application than an operating system upgrade. Installing it makes all kinds of changes to Windows' interface and behavior, including major revisions to some of the dialog boxes in the Control Panel. As discussed in "Which Windows Is Right for You?" in Chapter 11: Windows 95, 98, and NT, installing MSIE 4.0 can even degrade performance when the browser's not running. Are these side effects really justifiable when all you're doing is installing a Web browser? Of course, if you're running Windows 98, this whole argument is moot: Microsoft designed it so MSIE 4.0 is automatically installed with the operating system, and it's almost impossible to remove it.

A more radical argument against MSIE is that by using it, you could be helping Microsoft destroy the culture of open standards that produced the Web in the first place. While to some extent embracing Internet standards like HTML and Java, Microsoft has consistently been peppering its Web-site creation tools, like FrontPage and J++, with proprietary extensions that work only with Microsoft browsers, and promoting the use of wholly proprietary alternatives, like Word and Excel viewers. When you use MSIE, you can't tell the difference between Web sites that stick to Internet standards and those created with Microsoft's proprietary stuff. Thus, the more people who use MSIE, the less pressure there will be on Web site designers to stick to the standards.

Opera

Though for the past few years it's sometimes seemed like Netscape and Microsoft were the only companies left in the browser market, there's at least one alternative browser worth considering: Opera.

It's different in several significant ways from its two better-known competitors. First, it's comparatively tiny: the download's under 1.2MB, small enough to fit on a floppy disk, and installed, the program takes up only about 3.5MB.

The small size makes it very fast to load, and according to published benchmark tests, it's also faster in operation, though as I said earlier, given the many delays the browser can't do anything about, it's kind of hard to notice. At least, it's hard for me to notice, but I'm lucky enough to have a 200MHz PC with 64MB of RAM. If you have an older PC with a 386 or 486 CPU, or 16MB or less memory, you might find Opera much faster than Navigator or MSIE.

The interface is also quite different. In other browsers, if you open multiple Web pages, they show up in separate application windows, like when you open multiple text files in Notepad. Opera instead opens each page as a separate document window in an application workspace (see Figure 12), just like Word or Excel. As in those applications, Opera has a zoom control: you can zoom in at up to 10X magnification or zoom out so the page is only 20% of its normal size. If you wish, you can save window settings when you exit Opera, and they're automatically reloaded the next time you start the program. Each window can have its own individual home page, so you can create separate windows for each of your favorite search engines and return to the search form at any time by pressing Ctrl Home. You can customize every aspect of the program, and, as I noted earlier, it's designed to be as easy to operate from the keyboard as with a mouse, and the bookmarks are particularly easy to navigate (see Figure 4 in the "Bookmarks" section earlier in this chapter).

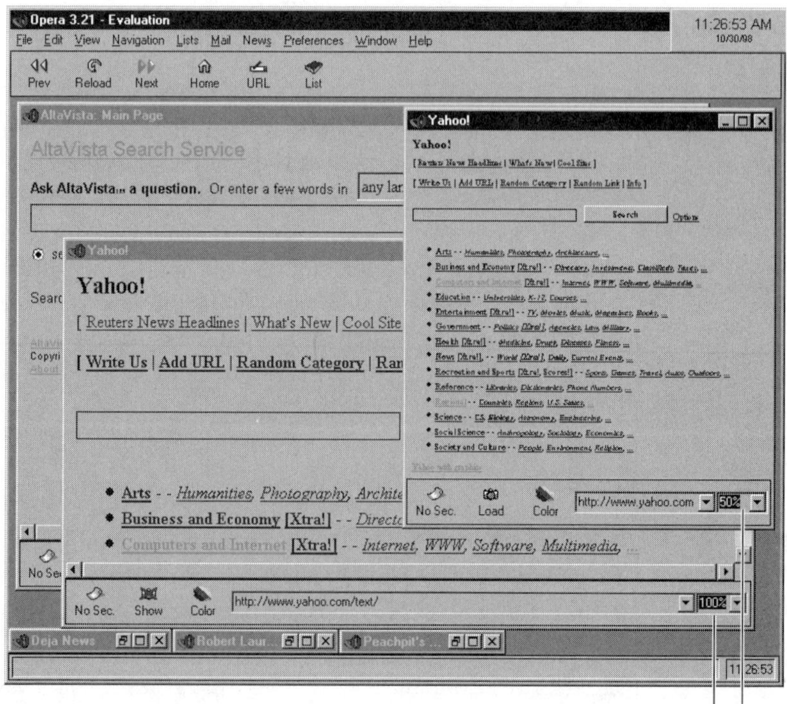

Figure 12

Opera.

Like Word or Excel, Opera can open multiple browser windows in an application workspace and zoom in or out on individual windows.

Opera has one significant limitation: it supports only official Web standards. As a result, it sometimes has trouble with pages created by Web developers who ignore the official standards and use the de facto standard of whatever-displays-well-in-both-Navigator-and-MSIE. However, such problems have been declining as the official standards expand to embrace popular programming practices, and as Opera grows in popularity, more Web developers will test their sites with it.

Since it's such a small download, there's not much reason for me to go on at length: if you're not totally satisfied with your current browser, why not just download Opera from **operasoftware.com** and try it for yourself? I strongly recommend downloading the current release rather than a beta of some future release: I've always found Opera's betas too buggy to use, which doesn't give a fair impression of the program.

If you do like Opera, there's one other difference: it's not free. After the 30-day trial, you have to pay $35 to keep using it.

Search Engines

The Web is huge—so huge that nobody's yet figured out how to measure it precisely. Recent estimates I've seen ranged from 320 million to 700 million pages, which sounds like a lot until you consider that there are around 40 million different domains (**peachpit.com**, **yahoo.com**, etc.) in use, and maybe 200 million people online worldwide.

Hence, the popularity of *search engines*, Web sites that help you sift through the seemingly infinite chaos of the Web and zero in on the stuff that interests you. The Web's so big that no search engine can cover it all. As this book goes to press, the two biggest, AltaVista and HotBot, claim to have indexed around 140 and 110 million pages, respectively, but those numbers change regularly as both sites beef up their hardware and software. (You can find the latest numbers at **searchengineguide.org**, a site devoted to evaluating and comparing the most popular search engines.)

In this section, I'll take a quick look at the best search engines and then offer some detailed tips on getting the best results from them.

Yahoo!

Most search engines work the same way. A *spider* program (so called because it crawls all over the Web) scans the Web, creating a database of keywords (or an *index*) that the engine uses to find pages that correspond to your search criteria.

Programmers constantly refine the spider and search software, but the actual indexing and searching are all computerized.

Strictly speaking, Yahoo (**yahoo.com**) is not a search engine at all: it's a catalog. Actual human beings choose what sites to include in the catalog and which of Yahoo's thousands of categories (see Figure 13) each site is filed under.

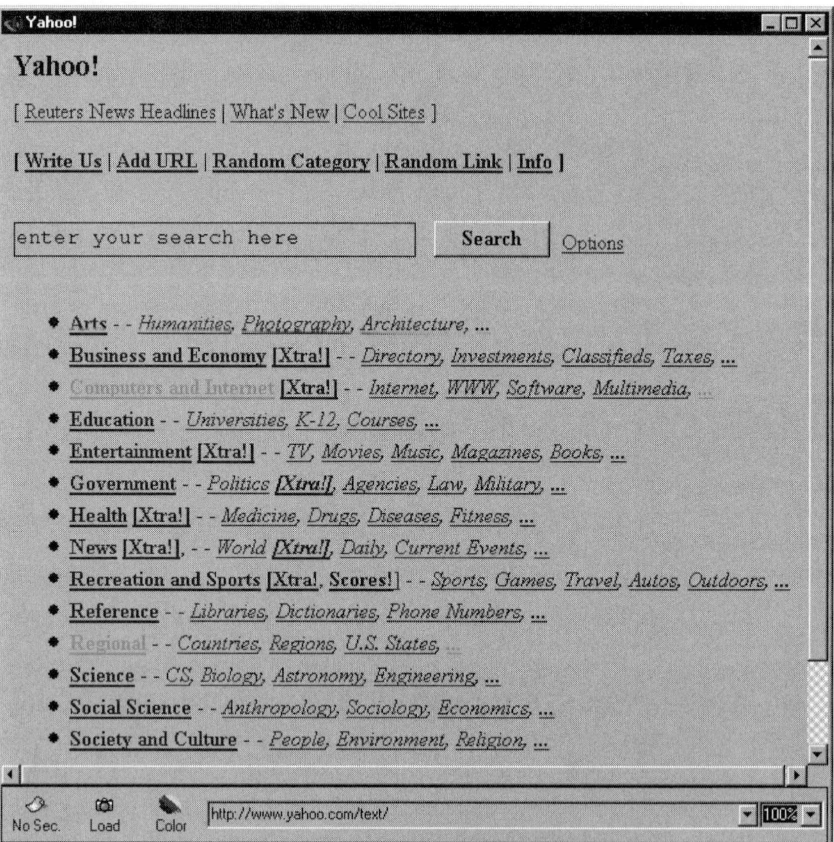

Figure 13

Yahoo.

The top level of Yahoo's hierarchy divides the whole universe up into a dozen categories. You can go directly to some of the second-level categories by clicking the italicized links.

This approach makes Yahoo the best choice when you're looking for sites rather than specific bits of information. For example, if you want to find beginners' guides to HTML, you can't beat Yahoo, but if you want to find out exactly how to use the `width` option in the `img src` tag, you're better off with a regular search engine.

Yahoo's also useful when you're unclear on exactly how to describe what you're looking for, or when the keywords you search for don't get you what you want. Just start with whichever of Yahoo's top-level categories works best and then navigate your way through the hierarchy until you find what you want. For example, if you want to learn about setting up your own Web site, you can click Computers and Internet, then World Wide Web, and then Page Creation, Tutorials, or FAQs.

When you click Yahoo's Search button and it doesn't find a match, Yahoo automatically passes the search to a regular search engine, which uses the same technology as HotBot. You can tell when that happens because the highlight on the menu bar over the search results switches from Categories to Web Pages (see Figure 14). Yahoo's search engine's not that great, so if you don't get any category or Web site matches, I recommend trying AltaVista instead.

Figure 14

Yahoo Categories versus Yahoo Web Sites.

The highlight in the toolbar over the search results tells you whether you're looking at entries from Yahoo's catalog or sites found by its search engine. Click the toolbar labels to switch to different kinds of results.

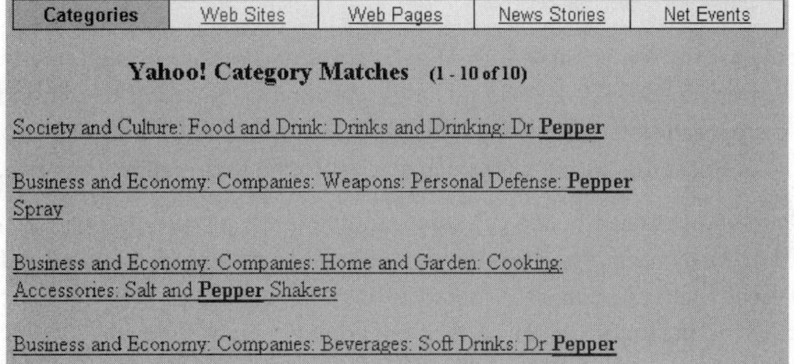

Categories | Web Sites | Web Pages | News Stories | Net Events

Web Pages (1-20 of 53357)

- Cookie Jars, Salt & **Pepper** Shakers, Collectible - Star Jars - Star Jars creates quality cookie jars, salt & peppers and other ceramic collectibles in the images of your favorite licensed characters from the movies, TV and the comics. *--http://www.starjars.com/indexa.html*
- A-1 **Self Defense Products** **Pepper** Spray, stun guns, self defense devices, knives, swords, batons, law enforcemant - A-1 Quality Self Defense Products, **Pepper** Sprays, Stun Guns, Knives, Swords, Law Enforcement Supplies, Batons, Online Encrypted Ordering, Image Catalog *--http://www.selfdefenseproducts.com/productinfo.htm*

The downside to Yahoo's reliance on human labor is that categories can get out of date. That often means that you won't find the latest sites, particularly in more obscure categories. Sometimes whole categories get out of date. For example, I tried to use Yahoo to find the statistics in the first paragraph of the previous section, but the relevant sites in the matching category (Computers and Internet: Internet: World Wide Web: Statistics and Demographics) were all years out of date.

To get a text-only version of Yahoo, use **`yahoo.com/text`**.

Portals

An unfortunate trend in recent years has been for any Web site that gets halfway popular to turn itself into a portal: a customizable page offering news, local weather, free Web e-mail, search engines, stock quotes, chat, and anything else that might hold people's interest. The idea is that you'll set the portal as your browser's home page (the one the browser goes to when you first launch it), and the site will make lots of money from the ads they stick on every page.

There's nothing inherently wrong with this approach: free stuff in exchange for putting up with advertisements is the American way. The problem is that companies keep trying to turn perfectly useful sites into portals.

Take **netscape.com**, for example. It used to be a normal company home page, where, with some effort, you could find and download the latest version of Communicator, or find links to compatible plug-ins, or read Netscape's press releases. Now it's a clone of Yahoo, and you have to figure out how to get past the portal before you can get to the information you want.

Many search engines have pulled the same stunt: they have you coming in to search for stuff, but they'd make more money if you stayed around longer and read more ads. This creates a conflict with their ostensible purpose: instead of helping you find you the information you want and get you to it, the site's main goal now is to get you to hang around and read more ads. The result, typically, is more and more clutter in the way of the search form and results, and constant plugs for more or less related sites and services offered by the portal itself or its partners (companies that pay for favorable placement).

My advice: avoid search engines that are constantly trying to distract you and stick with those that don't try to be anything else.

Note that the text-only versions of search engines often have a lot less extraneous clutter.

AltaVista

AltaVista (**altavista.com**), originally conceived as a demonstration of the power of Digital's Alpha servers, is the champ of brute-force search engines. It's not the most popular, but if you learn a few simple tricks, it will find more matches than its competitors. It also does a better job of figuring out which pages are the *best* matches and putting them at the top of the search results. Moreover, when an AltaVista search comes up empty for me, at least nine times out of ten the other search engines I try do so as well.

Here's one of many examples that formed that opinion. A while back I was looking for information on long pepper, a spice that was in common use in Europe prior to the introduction of chiles from America.

Using HotBot to search for documents that contained both the phrase "long pepper" and the word "history" turned up 45 pages. At the top of the list was the Web site of a Mexican restaurant in Austin, Texas. Among the other entries in the top ten were pages about hour-long orgasms and herbal medicine; none of the 45 matches included any historical information about long pepper. Other search engines did even worse.

The same search in AltaVista turned up 57 documents. At the top of the list? A history of long pepper (see Figure 15).

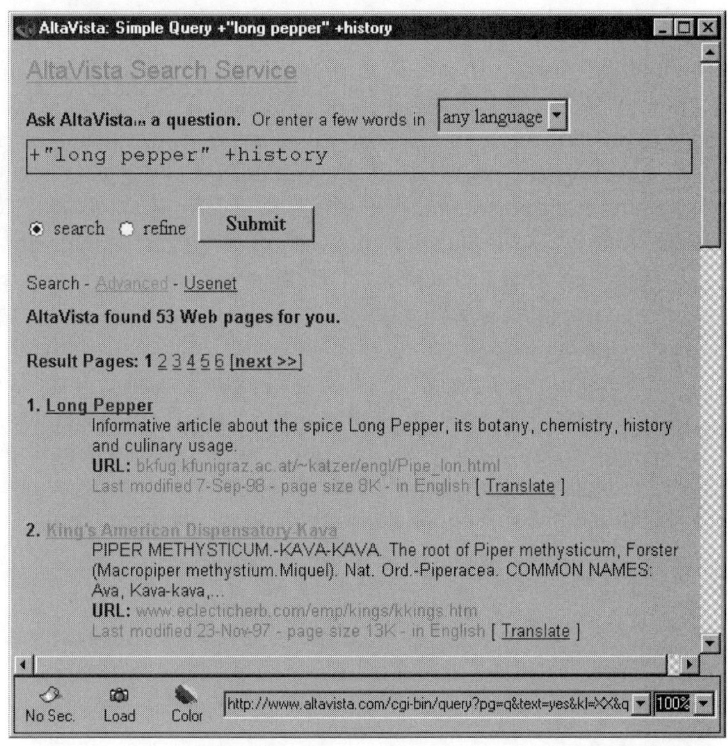

Figure 15

AltaVista.

The search form on AltaVista is nice and simple, but to make the most of it, you need to learn a few simple tricks, like the use of the plus symbols and quotation marks you see here. (See "Search Tips" later in this chapter for an explanation.)

Like I said, though, to get similar results, you need to learn a few tricks. See "Search Tips" later in this chapter for a detailed guide.

To get a text-only version of AltaVista, create a bookmark that points to **`altavista.com/cgi-bin/query?text`**.

Other Search Engines

If you're not as impressed with Yahoo and AltaVista as I am, here are a few competitors you might want to check out.

Northern Light. This relatively new search site takes sort of a hybrid approach, organizing pages found by its automatic search engine into a hierarchical set of Yahoo-style categories. You can navigate to a category and then search it, or search first and then select results by category. The site also has a bunch of extra material, not available on the Web, drawn from magazines, newspapers, and the like—though some of it costs extra. (**www.northernlight.com**)

LookSmart. The categories in this Yahoo knockoff aren't as thoughtful and well-organized as the original's, but the contents are sometimes better. Remember my earlier complaint about the lack of current material in Yahoo's Web statistics category? LookSmart's counterpart had just what I was looking for. On the other hand, its keyword searches aren't much help in finding the category you want: when I searched for `web statistics`, the category at the top of the list was Wound Management. (**looksmart.com**)

HotBot. While I'm not that impressed with the quality of HotBot's search results, it definitely has the best interface and the most flexible search tools around. It's better suited for beginners than AltaVista, since you can perform some fairly complex searches without having to format your search terms with any special characters. The basic search form has some really nice options: you can paste in a Web page's URL (address) and search for pages that link to it, use check boxes to include only pages that contain images, or restrict the search to pages updated within a set period of time. If that's not enough, click HotBot's More Search Options button for a more elaborate search form. You can use the Word Filter (see Figure 16) to perform complex searches like my "long pepper" example in the previous section or the other examples in the "Search Tips" section later in this chapter. (**hotbot.com**)

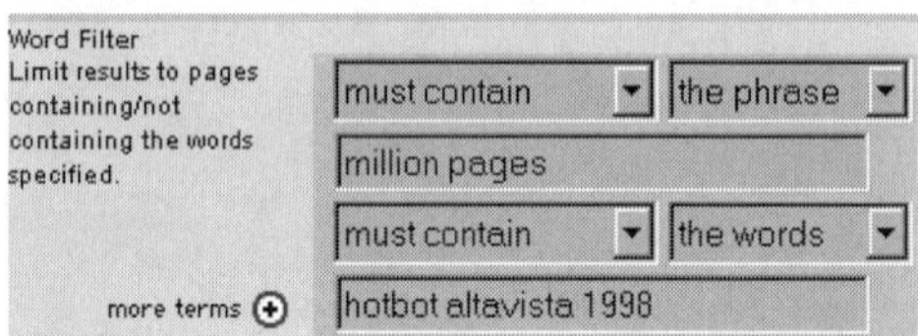

Figure 16

HotBot's Word Filter.

You can use this portion of HotBot's longer search form to set up complex searches. This example will find documents containing the words hotbot, altavista, *and* 1998, *as well as the phrase* million pages. *(I was trying to find the number of pages each search engine claimed to have indexed.)*

Lycos, Excite, and Infoseek. I check out these sites occasionally, but never get good enough results to encourage me to return soon. They're more popular than AltaVista, though, so I guess some people must find them satisfactory. (**www.lycos.com**, **excite.com**, **infoseek.com**)

Specialized Search Engines. There are thousands of smaller search engines on the Web that focus on particular topics. Yahoo's a good place to find them: for example, looking for `medical search` or `medical search engine` will turn up lots of sites devoted to helping you find health information, both on and off the Web.

Search Tips

Learning a few simple tricks will help you get the information you need faster and reduce the number of frustrating searches that don't find anything. Most of these tips focus on AltaVista, since I think you'll find it gives the best results, but the concepts are also applicable to most other search engines.

Don't Use Single-Word Searches. If you start with a single-word search, the search engine will probably find way too many pages: for example, if I search for `chocolate` on AltaVista, I get nearly a million hits. Adding more words will narrow things down: a search for `chocolate truffle` turns up only 1,500 pages.

Search for Phrases. While AltaVista assumes when you enter those two words that you want to find the phrase, other search engines, notably Yahoo, will find documents that simply contain both words. Most of those search engines let you change the search conditions to find pages containing the entire phrase, or any of the words in the phrase (for example, documents containing either *chocolate* or *truffle*), or choose other options (see Figure 17).

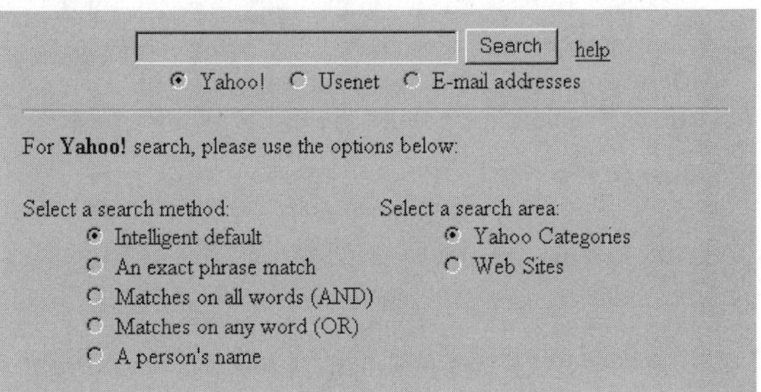

Figure 17

Yahoo search options.

Clicking Options (next to the Search button) in Yahoo brings up this dialog box. The Name option looks for common variations, like "Robert Lauriston" and "Lauriston, Robert."

You can also define a phrase manually, usually by enclosing it in double quotation marks (`"chocolate truffle"`). That's essential when you want to search for documents containing two phrases, like `"chocolate truffle" "raspberry truffle"`. On AltaVista, that particular search will find pages that contain either phrase; if you want only pages that have both, precede each phrase with a plus sign (`+"chocolate truffle" +"raspberry truffle"`).

Be aware that to save space and speed things up, search-engine databases typically exclude certain very common words (sometimes called *stop words*). These vary from one database to another, but typically include *an*, *and*, *by*, *for*, *from*, *of*, *the*, *to*, and *with*. Consequently, searching for "`market share`" will usually turn up *share of the market* as well.

Use Wildcards. With some search engines, a search for `truffle` will also find the plural, *truffles*, but not with AltaVista. To make AltaVista find plurals, too, you need to add an asterisk at the end of the word. The asterisk is a *wildcard*, a character that stands for any series of characters, so `truffle*` will find not just *truffle* and *truffles*, but *truffled* and *Truffler* as well. Thus, going back to the previous search, to find all pages that discuss both chocolate and raspberry truffles, you would search for `+"chocolate truffle*" +"raspberry truffle*"`.

Use wildcards freely at the end of your search terms to make them broad enough to catch any variations on the word. Say you're looking for articles about synchronizing databases: using the term `synchroniz*` will catch *synchronize*, *synchronizing*, and *synchronized*, but skip all variations on the British spelling, *synchronise*—so `synchroni*` is better. (Some search engines have options that will automatically search for all forms of a word.)

Exclude Words. Most search engines can find documents that contain some words but not others, which is often a great way to narrow your search down to the stuff you really want. For example, an AltaVista search for `"bobby's backdoor"` (my favorite rib joint) finds 24 pages, but the first 10 displayed are all from the same EonWeb restaurant guide. Refining the search to `"bobby's backdoor" -eonweb` gets rid of the duplicates. In HotBot, use the "must not contain" option in the Word Filter shown in Figure 16.

Search Indirectly. Searches involving extremely common words are tricky, since you often get zillions of irrelevant documents. For example, say you want to find comparisons of CD-ROM drives. Since the word *CD-ROM* is so common, any direct search is likely to turn up a lot of irrelevant stuff, like PC spec lists, software troubleshooting guides, etc. One way to weed out that stuff is to search for pages that mention two or more CD-ROM manufacturers and/or words or phrases that would be likely to come up when comparing drives, like *seek time* or *angular velocity*. For example, `+sony +teac +angular` will turn up mostly CD-ROM comparisons—even though the thing you're really searching for isn't one of the search terms.

Use Proximity Options. Many search engines have options or special words to tell the search engine to look for pages in which the specified words appear near or next to each other. The common "find a person" options, for example, find words that are next to each other in any order, so they find both *Robert Lauriston* and *Lauriston, Robert*. Sometimes you specify this option by putting ADJ between the search terms, like `robert ADJ lauriston`.

Some search engines have "near" options, which find words within a maximum distance of each other. Sometimes you can set the number of words apart the search items can be, and other times, a fixed number, like 10, is used. This option is usually used by putting NEAR, or N followed by the maximum distance, between the search terms. When available, use NEAR to make your net wide enough to catch various phrases referring to the subject you're interested in, but not so wide that you get every file that contains the particular words. For example, `share NEAR market` or `share N3 market` will find both *market share* and *share of the browser market*.

Downloading Software

There's an amazing amount of software on the Web: driver updates, program upgrades, freeware, shareware, trial versions of popular applications. Increasingly, you can even buy commercial software directly: just fill out a form, enter your credit card number, and download.

There's really nothing to downloading. I really just put this section in the chapter to reassure anyone who is worried that might not be the case.

The first step is to create a folder to hold your downloads—I use one called Download, in the root (top level) of my hard disk. This isn't absolutely necessary, but if you make a habit of downloading to the same place, you'll always know where to look.

When you find a Web page with a program you want, click whatever link starts the download. In some browsers, like Navigator, that will take you right to Windows' regular File/Save As dialog box; in others, like MSIE and Opera, you'll first see a dialog box confirming that you want to save the file (see Figure 18). After you click the Save button, you'll see a dialog box indicating that the download's progress (see Figure 19); this dialog box will stay on the screen until the whole file has been saved to your hard disk.

Once you've downloaded the file, you might want to check it with a virus scanner (see Chapter 9: Protect Your Data), though if you downloaded the file from a popular site like **`download.com`** or **`tucows.com`**, there's not much chance that it's infected.

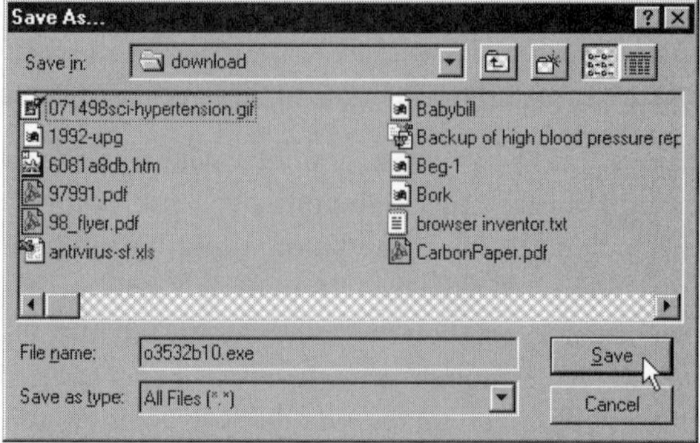

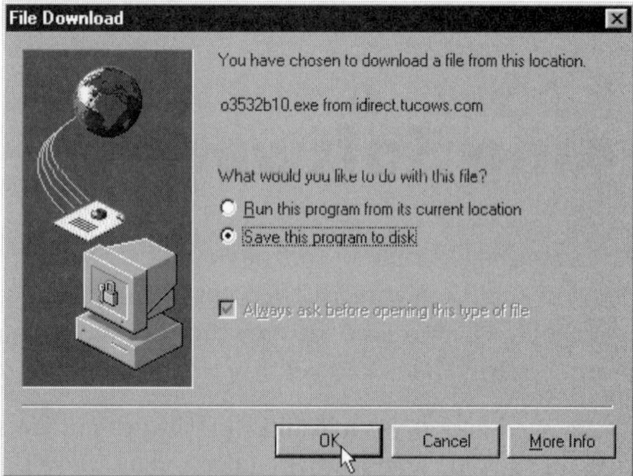

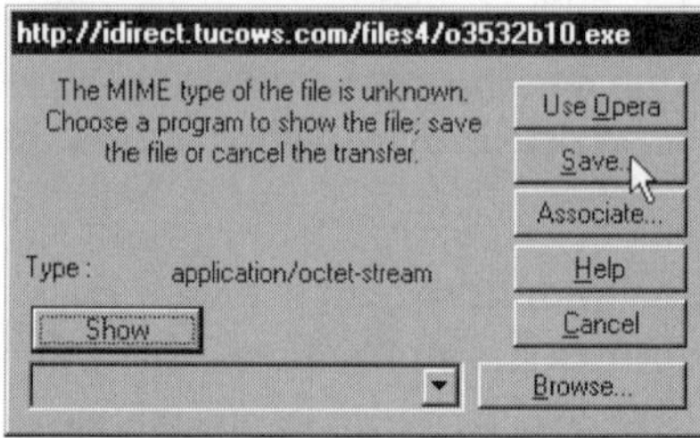

Figure 18

Downloading a file.

When you click a link that initiates a download, Netscape takes you directly to a Save As dialog box. So do MSIE and Opera, eventually, but first you have to confirm that you want to save the file. You may be able to eliminate such confirmation dialog boxes by fiddling with your browser's preferences.

Some downloadable programs are applications (.exe files): to install them, just double-click the new file in your download folder. That usually launches a setup routine, but sometimes it may create a bunch of other files in the download directory, in which case, you'll want to double-click the new Setup or Install application that appears.

Figure 19

Download progress.

Opera's progress window is the best of the three browsers discussed here. It stays on the screen after the download's done so you know it completed successfully.

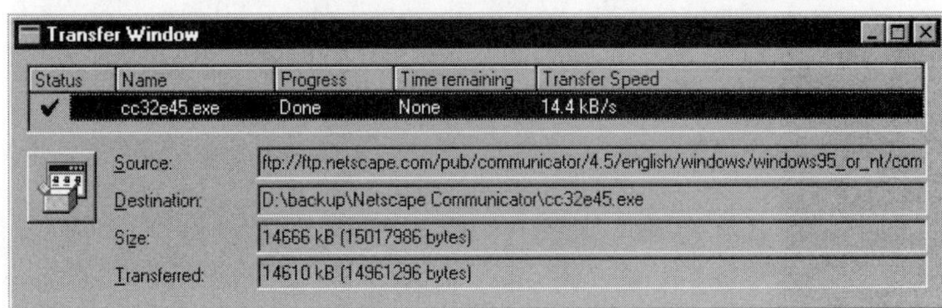

Other downloads are zip files. For instructions on installing them, see the WinZip section of Chapter 12: Windows Add-Ons.

Once you've installed the program, you can delete the file you downloaded. Alternatively, you may want to archive the download in case you need to reinstall it later. I have a Backup folder in which I create subfolders for all the freeware and shareware applications I download, so whenever I reinstall Windows or set up a new PC, I don't have to download them again (see Figure 20).

Figure 20

As you can see from the contents of my Backup folder, I have a fairly hefty selection of downloaded software archived in case I need to reinstall it. It's particularly important to back up software you've paid for—if the company should go out of business, you may not be able to download a replacement. You should also store a copy of any software license or registration number in the same folder.

What Else Is Out There?

So what can you find on the Web? With hundreds of millions of pages and more being added every day, practically anything.

Given the variety of stuff that's out there and how easy it is to find what you're interested in with search engines, I'm not even going to attempt an overview of the Web's contents. Instead, I'll just offer the following tips on places to start and mention a few things it may not have occurred to you would be out there.

- **Browse Yahoo's categories.** Yahoo's team of so-called ontologists (actually taxonomists) have created a great system for categorizing what's on the Web. Browsing your way down the **yahoo.com** category tree toward topics of interest is a great way to find sites of similar interest.
- **Search for your most obscure interests.** The global nature of the Internet means that no matter how obscure your interests, you can probably find like-minded souls, or helpful retailers, or obscure information on the Internet. Whether you want to talk shop with other ferret breeders, get a recipe for methyglyn, or complete your collection of Ennio Morricone soundtracks, the Net's got what you're looking for.
- **Hook up your speakers.** While generally the multimedia stuff on the Web's of little interest, there's a lot of great music out there. Web-based CD stores often have audio samples or whole tracks you can play to help figure out if you want to buy a new CD. Quite a number of radio stations offer Web "simulcasts" or archives of their programs: see **www.timecast.com/stations** for a guide. There are also Web-only broadcasters and jukeboxes: two of the best are **broadcast.com** and **spinner.com**. Most of these services use the RealAudio plug-in, which you can download from **www.real.com**.
- **Read the comics.** Most daily comic strips are on the Web, so if you have any favorites that aren't in your daily paper, look for them on **yahoo.com** at Entertainment: Comics and Animation: Comic Strips: Titles.
- **Check traffic conditions.** In many areas, you can get the latest traffic report on the Web instantly, without having to sit through a whole radio news cycle. Go to **yahoo.com**, click Regional, follow the links to your area, click Travel & Transportation, and click Traffic.
- **Do your banking.** If your bank has a Web site, you can probably get a special password that will let you check your balance, transfer funds between accounts, and maybe even pay bills, right from your Web browser. (I'm still waiting for the ATM you hook up to your PC.)
- **Visit the library.** Librarians were among the first to embrace the Web, and lots of libraries have their card catalogs online. If yours does, you will probably be able to see if the book you want is available; if it isn't, you may be able to reserve it.

- **Check TV listings.** You can find a bunch of online TV guides on **yahoo.com** at News and Media: Television: Schedules. Many TV stations and nearly all cable channels have their own Web sites, which usually have schedules. If you're a film buff and get Turner Classic Movies, check out **tcm.turner.com**, where you can skim schedules two or three months in advance. Look for other networks' sites on Yahoo at Business and Economy: Companies: News and Media: Television: Cable: Networks.

Creating Your Own Web Site

Does surfing the Web make you wish you had your own site? Creating one is easy.

First you need a host: a Web server where you can upload the files that create the site. Most Internet service providers include host services in the basic package; check with your ISP to find out how to upload your files. You'll need to know the name of the server and the directory path where you should upload the files.

If your ISP doesn't offer Web hosting, the best idea is to switch to one that does. Alternatively, you might check out the free hosts on **yahoo.com** at Business and Economy: Companies: Internet Services: Web Services: Free Web Pages. In exchange for the free site, these companies display ads on it, and usually the ads are annoyingly intrusive.

If you want your own domain name (like **lauriston.com**), you'll need to find an unused name, register it, and pay a registration fee (currently $70 for two years for .com domains, but that may change as companies start to compete to offer registration services.) Ask your ISP for help, or go to Yahoo and check out the Computers and Internet: Internet: Domain Registration category.

Once you have a host, there are a couple of ways you can go. The old-fashioned and totally free method is to build the site from scratch by typing HTML commands into a text editor, like Windows' Notepad, and then upload it to your server with an FTP utility or Windows' Web Publishing Wizard. Personally, I found this approach tedious, and was happy to give it up when there was an alternative—but then I don't much like programming. If you want to try it, check out some of resources on Yahoo at Computers and Internet: Internet: World Wide Web: Page Creation.

Personally, I much prefer managing my Web site with a *WYSIWYG* HTML editor. WYSIWYG (What You See Is What You Get) is an old acronym that traditionally referred to a program where what you saw on the screen looked like what came out of the printer. In the Web context, it just means that you lay out the Web page without programming, just as if you were working in your word processor.

For small personal sites, the best Web editor I've seen yet is Adobe PageMill (see Figure 21). Anyone who can use a word processor can easily learn to use it, and it makes tasks that would require fairly sophisticated programming skills painless. The HTML it creates is quite standard, so if a better program comes along and you want to switch, you won't be stuck or forced to re-create everything from scratch. Check out my site at **lauriston.com** to see what I was able to do with it, or download a free evaluation version from **www.adobe.com/prodindex/pagemill** to try it yourself.

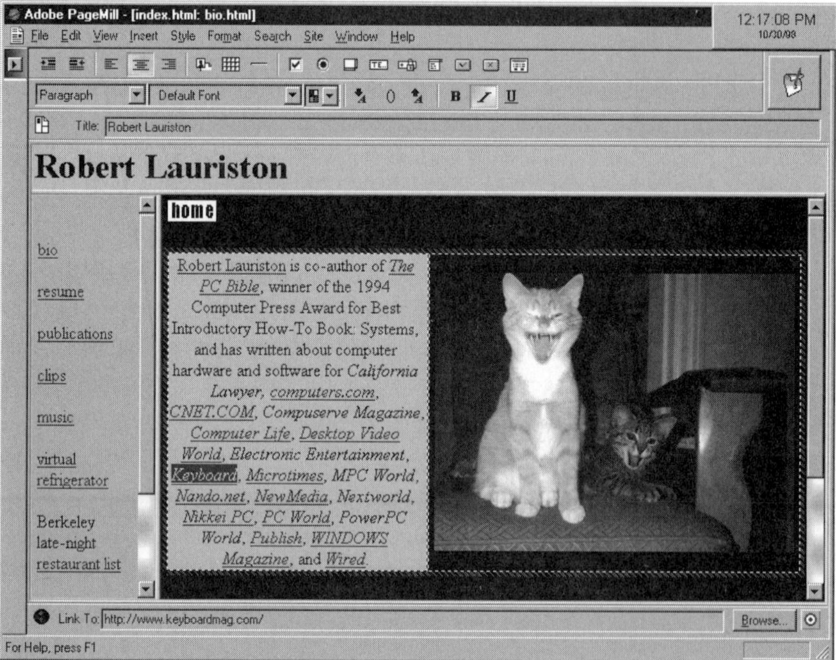

Figure 21

PageMill.

Here you see my personal Web site open for editing in Adobe PageMill. Tasks that would involve a lot of arcane manual coding back when I was working in HTML, like setting up the table that separates my short professional biography from the picture of Milo and Bernie or adjusting the position of the title and menu-bar frames, I can now handle with a few simple menu commands and mouse operations.

PageMill's main competitor is Microsoft FrontPage. Though at first FrontPage seems easier to use, it's based on a very rigid approach to site design. You can choose among scores of cosmetic variations on one basic site layout; if you don't like that layout, the program's not much use. Some of FrontPage's most attractive features, like its message boards (see Chapter 22: Online Discussions: Newsgroups, Etc.) are proprietary—that is, they'll work only with Microsoft's browsers and/or only if the Web server has Microsoft's FrontPage extensions loaded. It's unlikely that other Web editors will be able to read the proprietary codes, so if you start a site in FrontPage, it'll be harder to switch. As this book goes to press, Microsoft doesn't offer a free trial, but the company does offer a 30-day money-back guarantee if you're not satisfied.

Web Resources

Browsers

browsers.com This CNET site's the easiest place to find and download new browsers, upgrades, bug fixes, and plug-ins. It also includes pointers to reviews (the reviewers tend to be overly impressed by the latest gee-whiz features) and useful how-to articles.

browserwars.com This site consolidates browser reviews, tips, and other information from *PC Magazine*, *PC Week*, and other Ziff-Davis publications.

yahoo.com Search for `browser wars` and then click Full Coverage: Tech: Browser Wars for Yahoo's page of links to the latest browser news and reviews.

Search Engines

searchenginewatch.internet.com This online magazine covers search engines. Some articles are oriented toward users, others toward Web site operators trying to make their sites easier for users to find.

searchengineguide.org This site offers reviews of major search sites, a comparison table, and links to lesser-known search sites and all kinds of related information.

www.albany.edu/library/internet/syntax.html This somewhat geeky guide to search-engine syntax also includes pointers to a highly opinionated guide to search sites.

yahoo.com You can find a list of other pages that compare search engines on Yahoo at Computers and Internet: Internet: World Wide Web: Searching the Web: Comparing Search Engines.

Downloading Software

download.com I haven't found another site to compare with CNET's software download service. It seems to have pointers to every file in every software library on the Web, and its server rankings help minimize download time.

What Else Is Out There?

Here are a few of my favorite sites that I wasn't able to work into the chapter.

kcrw.org/c/jfrank/jfrank.html This site offers an archive of radio shows by Joe Frank, a surreal radio-theater artist.

www.harryshearer.com This is the Web site of Le Show, a satirical radio show produced by Harry Shearer (best known for his portrayal of Lenny, Ned Flanders, Rev. Lovejoy, Kent Brockman, Mr. Burns, Mr. Smithers, and dozens of other characters on *The Simpsons*).

imdb.com The Internet Movie Database offers an ever-growing, user-created database of movies and TV shows. Finally there's an easy way to answer the question, "Where have I seen that actor before?"

www.cs.virginia.edu/oracle The Oracle of Bacon at Virginia, an IMDB spinoff, lets you play the Kevin Bacon game against a computer. If you're unfamiliar with this game, click Instructions.

rs.internic.net/cgi-bin/whois Go to this site to find out who owns any domain name.

www.chezpanisse.com/downmenu.htm Look here for the weekly menu of Chez Panisse, the restaurant where California cuisine began.

22

Online Discussions: Newsgroups, Etc.

by Robert Lauriston

In This Chapter

If you can think of a topic, there's a conversation going on about it on the Internet right now. If that sounds like an exaggeration, consider that the Internet's primary discussion area, Usenet, has over 50,000 *newsgroups*. There's one for every imaginable topic, and then some: Windows NT device drivers, Tori Amos, home canning, professional wrestling, paving the entire earth.

Similar discussions go on in *mailing lists*, which take place in e-mail. There are also lots of newsgroup-like message boards on the Web, some of which have significant advantages over newsgroups and mailing lists.

In this chapter, we'll cover all three of these types of online discussions, which have one important feature in common: the participants take part whenever it's convenient for them. This means that it may take hours or days before anyone responds to your posts, but it also means that you can converse with people whose schedules are very different from yours. If you're looking for something more immediate, see the next chapter, which deals with chat and other forms of real-time Internet communication.

Newsgroups

Sometimes a newsgroup is like a collection of chain letters. One person posts a message—usually a question, request for advice, or provocative opinion (see Figure 1). Another participant in the group reads it and appends a response (or *post*). A third person adds another comment, and so on until everyone's had their say. A popular *thread* (newsgroup discussion) can go on for months or years, since once the thread's started, anyone can add to it at any time.

A newsgroup can contain any number of such threads, which means that it may start to resemble a transcript of all the simultaneous discussions at a cocktail party. Newsgroup *subscribers* (participants) can respond to any posting, not just the original, so discussions often split off in many different directions. One group of people may be carrying on a calm and intelligent discussion of a serious topic, while another group is making puns about a typo one of them made the previous week. Meanwhile, a pair of idiots is off in a virtual corner, exchanging insults no one else bothers to read.

Newsgroups don't have a single physical location: their messages are distributed among thousands of news servers (aka *NNTP servers*), most maintained by Internet service providers, all over the world. The news servers are linked by Usenet, a program created in 1979 by Jim Ellis, Tom Truscott, and Steve Bellovin at the University of North Carolina. Its original purpose was to automatically transmit news about various aspects of the UNIX world—hence the *news* in *newsgroups*.

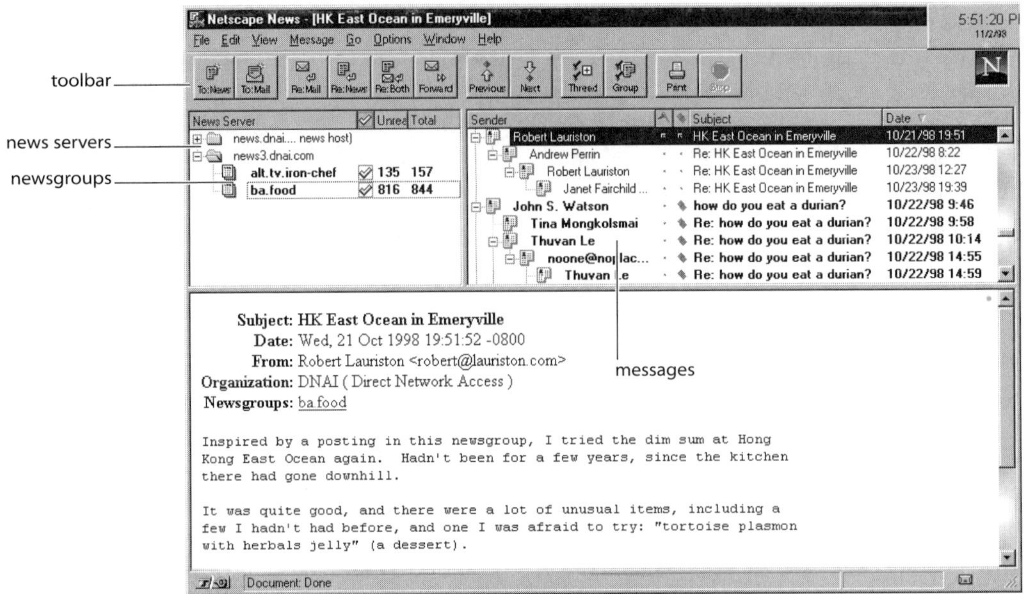

Figure 1

A typical newsreader.

The three-pane design of Netscape Messenger makes it easy to see the different elements involved in reading newsgroups. The upper-left pane shows two news servers, one of which is open to display two newsgroups. The messages in the selected newsgroup are displayed in a scrolling list in the pane at the right, which currently displays nine messages in two threads. Bold text indicates messages that haven't been read yet. The contents of the selected message appear in the bottom pane. The toolbar buttons let you navigate through the messages, create new threads, post and/or e-mail a reply to the displayed message, and forward or print messages.

Each news server keeps its own copies of every message, and whenever a server runs out of space, old messages are deleted to make room for new ones. Thus, when you first join a newsgroup, it's common to find that some of the posts are incomprehensible, since the discussion that led up to them has been deleted. (As discussed later in this chapter, however, you can always read the deleted posts at Deja News.) Due to variations in server capacity, some news servers have a larger backlog of messages, and thus fewer confusing tail-end discussions.

Newsgroup Types and Organization

Internet old-timers reminisce about the days when they could read all of Usenet in under an hour. Today, of course, things have grown far beyond that. Of over 50,000 newsgroups available today, only about 30 are devoted to discussing matters related to the UNIX operating system. Now there are groups devoted to every imaginable subject, everything from *The X-Files* to *The Rockford Files* to tips on brewing your own beer or using technical analysis to invest in the stock market.

To make that mass of messages manageable, some newsgroups are organized into a hierarchy along the lines of the one Yahoo uses to categorize the Web (see Chapter 21: The Web and Browsers). At the top level are general categories: **comp** for computers; **rec** for hobbies, sports, and other recreational activities; **de**, **fr**, **it**, and **no** for groups in German (Deutsch), French, Italian, and Norwegian—you get the idea (see Figure 2). You can find a master list of the official top-level categories at **magma.ca/~leisen/master_list.html**.

Figure 2

Liszt's top-level newsgroup category list.

This catalog page at the search site **liszt.com** *includes 29 of the most important top-level newsgroup categories, plus a link to a full list with over 17,000 entries.*

alt (3831)
Usenet alternative newsgroups

biz (43)
Usenet business newsgroups

comp (844)
Usenet computer newsgroups

misc (129)
Usenet miscellaneous newsgroups

news (29)
Usenet news

rec (649)
Usenet recreational newsgroups

sci (196)
Usenet science newsgroups

soc (242)
Usenet social issues newsgroups

talk (28)
Usenet talk newsgroups

all... (17,181)
View a different, longer menu

aus (110)
Australian and Australasian newsgroups

bit (234)
originating from BITNET (IBM mainframe)

cl (341)
/CL-Netz (German language newsgroups)

clari (575)
Clarinet News Service (commercial)

de (304)
International German language newsgroups

fido (159)
originating from Fidonet

finet (206)
Finland and Finnish language alternative newsgroups

fj (339)
Japan and Japanese language newsgroups

fr (125)
international French language newsgroups

it (161)
Italia

microsoft (373)
Microsoft newsgroups

no (128)
Norge (Norway)

pdaxs (123)
Portland Metronet, Oregon, USA

relcom (170)
Relcom, Commonwealth of Ind. States (ISP) (Cyrillic)

sfnet (231)
Suomi-Finland, Finland & Finnish language newsgroups

shamash (129)
Jewish newsgroups

tnn (221)
Japanese newsgroups

tw (285)
Taiwan

uk (171)
United Kingdom

z-netz (429)
originating from Z-Netz (German newsgroups)

Top-level categories are divided into subcategories. For example, under **rec** you'll find **rec.antiques**, **rec.aquaria**, **rec.arts**, and so on up to **rec.woodworking**. Subcategories can, in turn, be subdivided, so it's common to end up with long newsgroup names like **comp.os.ms-windows.nt.admin.networking**.

Usenet evolved in a fairly anarchic manner, so the hierarchy isn't entirely logical or consistent. For example, even though there's a top-level category called

sci, with a **sci.bio** subcategory for biology, there's also a top-level category called **bionet**. To make matters worse, lots of newsgroups ignore the official hierarchy: there are over 17,000 top-level categories listed on **liszt.com**. Luckily, many of these are not widely carried. (Note that ISPs, corporations, and universities often have their own private top-level categories found only on their own servers.)

Few news servers carry every newsgroup. Most carry a limited set simply to conserve disk space. In addition, many screen out those devoted to the pursuit of criminal activities, like exchanging pirate software or illegal pornography. In some places, such screening is required by law. For example, Germany bans Nazi-oriented newsgroups, and for a time, Canada banned a joke group ostensibly devoted to fans of accused serial killer Karla Holmolka due to a ban on press coverage of her trial.

Most newsgroups are completely uncensored: anyone with Internet access can post anything he or she likes. Some groups get along fine on this honor system; others are swamped with spam (see Chapter 20: E-mail) or disruptive, off-topic postings by *bozos* (Usenet slang for people whose postings are not worth reading) or *trolls* (a more pernicious subspecies of bozo whose posts are intended solely to provoke).

To deal with such problems, Usenet was revised to allow *moderated* newsgroups. Normally, when you post a message, the server makes it available to other users immediately, and within a few days it's passed along to the other servers around the globe. When you post to a moderated newsgroup, the server instead e-mails the message to the moderator, who decides whether or not to post the message. Some moderated newsgroups are indicated by .moderated at the end of the name; others aren't. (To find out more, check out the Moderated Newsgroup FAQ at **www.swcp.com/~dmckeon/mod-faq.html**.)

Reading and Posting to Newsgroups

There are two main ways you can follow and/or participate in newsgroup discussions. The traditional method is to use a *newsreader*, a program that connects to a news server, displays its groups and messages, and transmits your responses to the server. A newer alternative is to access newsgroups over the Web through a site like Deja News or SuperNews.

Using Newsreaders. The most popular newsreaders these days are the ones bundled with the most popular Web browsers: Netscape Messenger and Microsoft Outlook Express. Both programs integrate newsreading with e-mail, so you don't need to learn a new program from scratch—if you know how to read mail in your inbox, you know how to read messages in a newsgroup.

Before you can use your newsreader, you need to give it the name of your news (NNTP) server. If you're not sure what the server's name is, ask your ISP. Here's how to set it up in your browser' newsreader:

- In Netscape Messenger, choose Edit/Preferences. In the Category tree, click the + to the left of Mail & Newsgroups to expand this category and then select Newsgroup Server. Click Add, enter the name of your server, and click OK twice to save it.
- In Outlook Express, choose Tools/Accounts, click Add, select News, and then follow the prompts of the Internet Connection Wizard.

Once you've entered the server name, the next step is to *subscribe* to one or more newsgroups of interest. (See the next section for tips on finding such newsgroups.)

- In Netscape Messenger, choose Communicator/Newsgroups. Right-click the news server's icon (in the left pane of the Messenger window) and choose Subscribe to Newsgroups. Navigate the scrolling list of newsgroups (see Figure 3) just as you would the folder tree in Windows Explorer. (The first time you use the Subscribe command, the list may take a few minutes to appear.) When you find a newsgroup you're interested in, double-click it, and a check will appear in the Subscribe column.

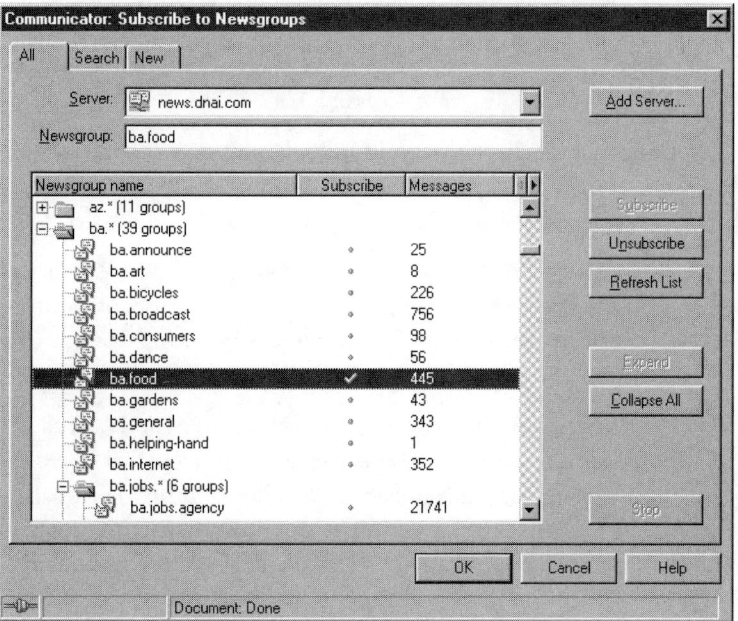

Figure 3

Subscribing to a newsgroup in Netscape Messenger.

- In Outlook Express, choose Tools/Newsgroups. Scroll down the list of newsgroups until you find one want; then select it and click Subscribe (see Figure 4).

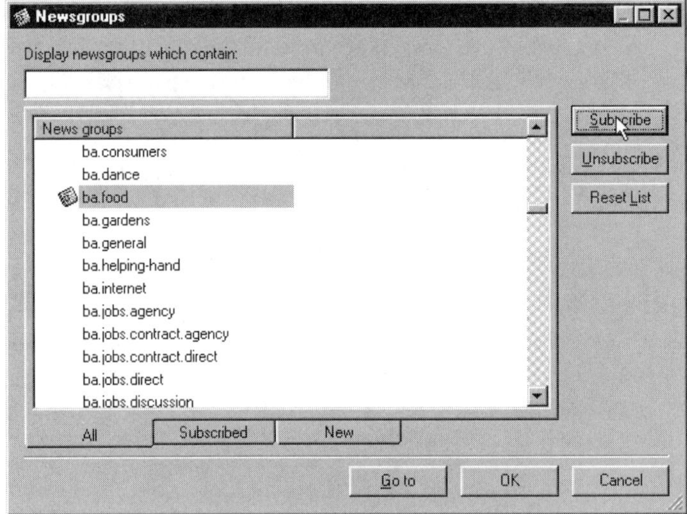

Figure 4

Subscribing to a newsgroup in Outlook Express.

Newsreader software not only lets you read and reply to postings; it also keeps track of the articles you've already read. More important, it can be set to follow the discussion thread and give you the messages in a given group in their order of posting. This makes it much easier to follow the online discussion of a particular subject. You can also download whole newsgroups for browsing offline—very useful if you live someplace where you have to pay by the minute for Internet access.

In both Messenger and Outlook, posting works almost exactly like sending e-mail. You can click a Reply button to respond to the message you're reading or click a New button to create a new thread for a new topic.

Using a Web Newsgroup Site. The downside to using a newsreader is that you have access only to the messages currently on your news server—which usually means only the last few weeks' or months' messages in a limited selection of newsgroups.

To get around that limitation, you can read and post to newsgroups through Deja News (**`www.dejanews.com`**), a Web site that offers a complete archive of most newsgroups back to early 1995 (and may eventually go all the way back to 1979). The site also filters out most spam, and protects your e-mail address so that junk e-mailers can't grab it from a newsgroup and spam your inbox. Unfortunately, Deja News is sometimes fairly slow, and even at its best, it's no match for an offline newsreader, which will let you flip through messages as fast as you can read.

Using Deja News to read and post is fairly self-explanatory: just click My Deja News to get started and follow the instructions. The first time you use the service, you'll need to fill out a registration form, but the service is free.

Be sure to make note of your user ID and password when you register, since if you switch browsers, they may be lost.

Deja News filters out binary attachments, which makes the site useless for newsgroups devoted to swapping files (often called *binary newsgroups*—binary is jargon for nontext data formats). You can access those groups through SuperNews (**supernews.com**).

Posting Tips

Over the years, a whole culture of Usenet "netiquette" has evolved. Here are a few general rules to follow, plus a few tips for making your experience as pleasant as possible.

- Before you post to a particular newsgroup for the first time, read the newsgroup's FAQ (Frequently Asked Questions file), if there is one, to see if there are any special rules about what people should post. A FAQ will typically be posted in its newsgroup every two weeks, and it theoretically should also be posted to the group news.answers. Perhaps the easiest place to find FAQs is on the Web site of The Internet FAQ Consortium (**www.faqs.org**).
- Look at the dates on the messages. If they're all old, the group may have no active participants, in which case, posting is probably a waste of time.
- Similarly, if all the messages are advertisements irrelevant to the newsgroup's stated topic, the group's probably been abandoned. There are thousands of newsgroups that never contain anything but spam and the occasional message from a confused newbie.

- Don't ask a question that's answered in the FAQ.
- Don't promote your business or offer items for sale in a newsgroup where commercial messages are banned.
- Get a sense of the newsgroup's content and dynamics before you post. Are some of the participants being ignored by almost everyone else? There may be a reason. Is there a lot of bickering and seemingly pointless arguments?
- Don't quote endlessly from earlier postings. (Many newsreaders automatically quote the message you're responding to, but your posts will be easier to read if you cut out everything that doesn't directly relate to your reply.)
- Make sure you understand your newsreader's commands. Most make it easy to send e-mail when you meant to post a message, or vice-versa.
- The bulk e-mail software used by spammers snags e-mail addresses out of newsgroup postings. If you don't want your inbox cluttered by spam, set a phony e-mail address in your newsreader's Identity settings. Of course, if you use a phony address, other subscribers won't be able to send you mail; if you browse a few newsgroups, you'll see some of the creative ways spam-hating newsgroup users have found to get around that.

For more netiquette tips, check out some of the links on **supernews.com/corporate/usenetlinks.html**. That page also has pointers to all sorts of other documents useful for newsgroup beginners.

Finding Newsgroups and Messages

Even if you prefer using a newsreader, you'll still want to access Deja News occasionally to catch up on the beginning of ongoing discussions. It's also useful for tracking down old posts when you remember having read something but can't recall the details and for general research purposes.

Deja News works pretty much like any other search engine: the instructions in the "Search Basics" and "Search Tips" sections of Chapter 21: The Web and Browsers, will help you master the process. The one trick with Deja News is that by default, it finds only relatively recent messages, typically only for the previous couple of months. To search the whole archive, enter a search; then when you get the results (or a message telling you that your search did not match any articles), change the Find option from "recent" to "past" (see Figure 5).

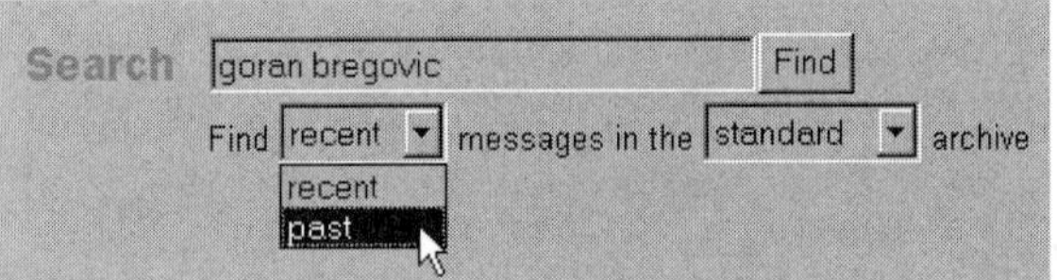

Figure 5

To find older messages with Deja News, change the Find option to "past."

For fancier searches, click Power Search. This more complicated form lets you restrict your search results to English-language posts, specify a range of dates, and limit the search to a specific newsgroup and/or a specific author.

Deja News's search engine is also one of the best tools for finding newsgroups to which you might want to subscribe. Just search for messages of interest and note what newsgroups they appear in. Deja News also offers an Interest Finder, which works just like the regular search engine except instead of bringing up a list of newsgroup messages, it brings up a list of newsgroups.

Another way to find newsgroups is to browse one of the many directories on the Web. Two of the best are the Usenet Info Center Launch Pad (**sunsite.unc.edu/usenet-i**) and Liszt's Usenet Newsgroups Directory (**liszt.com/news**). You can find additional directories at **yahoo.com** at Computers and Internet: Internet: Usenet: Newsgroup Listings.

Mailing Lists

Internet mailing lists are quite similar to newsgroups, except instead of browsing messages on a server, you read them from your e-mail inbox. Just like newsgroups, some are moderated—all messages to the list go first to a moderator, who decides whether or not to include them and may edit them for length or content.

The big advantage of mailing lists is that they can be private. Membership can be restricted to whoever the list creator or administrator chooses, and unless someone puts together an archive and makes it public, no one outside the list has access to the messages.

A major potential problem with mailing lists is that you may suddenly find your inbox jammed to overflowing with messages from list members. However, that's easily solved: just use the techniques described in the "How to Use E-Mail Filters" section of Chapter 20: E-Mail to automatically route messages from each mailing list to which you subscribe into their own folders. Then you can read all the messages whenever you feel like it, just as you would with a newsgroup.

Subscribing to a public mailing list is easy: typically, you just send an e-mail message containing a simple command, like SUBSCRIBE FILMUS-L, to the address of the mailing list server. There's no need to write an actual message, since under normal circumstances, it will never be read by another human being. If you find you aren't as interested in the topic as you thought and want to get off the list, a similar command (like UNSUBSCRIBE FILMUS-L) to the same address will halt the flood of messages.

The best resource for finding lists you might want to subscribe to is Liszt (**liszt.com**), which tries to do for mailing lists what Yahoo does for the Web. Liszt offers topic keyword searches on a claimed 90,000-plus lists (see Figure 6), plus a Yahoo-style hierarchical subject catalog of selected lists. Click "our intro" to get an overview of the site and pointers to lots more useful mailing-list resources.

Other mailing-list directories worth searching include Publicly Accessible Mailing Lists (**www.neosoft.com/internet/paml**), a Usenet tradition dating back to 1981; CataLyst (**www.lsoft.com/lists/listref.html**), a list of some 20,000 mailing lists managed by L-Soft International's LISTSERV software; and **tile.net/lists**, a site maintained by Lyris Technologies, one of L-Soft's competitors.

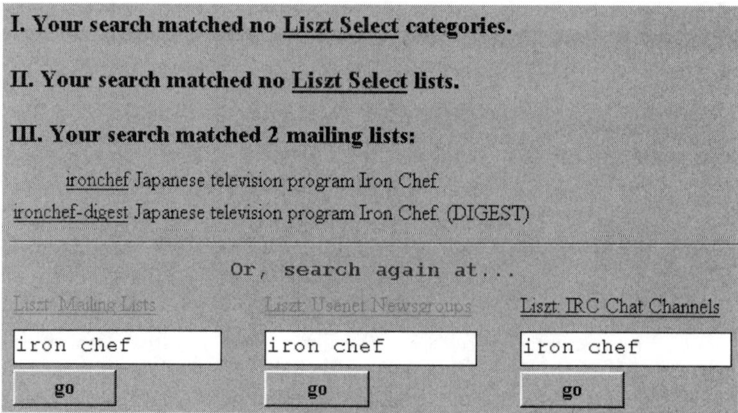

Figure 6

Liszt mailing-list search results.

A Liszt search for "iron chef" turned up two lists, one regular and one digest (an edited-down highlights version for people who don't have time to read all the messages). The search engine helpfully offers to search Liszt's newsgroup and chat databases as well.

Web Message Boards

Back in the dark ages before the Internet became ubiquitous—that is, up through 1994 or '95—most online discussions took place not in newsgroups or mailing lists but on private dialup systems like America Online, CompuServe, Genie, the Well, and thousands of bulletin board systems (BBSs) around the world. Every system had its own phone number, its own software, its own terminology, and (except for some BBSs) a steep hourly connect charge.

Flat-rate Internet access and the Web pretty much killed that system, but private systems are still around. America Online and CompuServe, for example, reinvented themselves as flat-rate Internet service providers, but they continue to offer the private discussion forums (and other special services) as extra goodies to differentiate themselves from the average ISP. The Well created a Web interface so people could join its discussions without having to learn how to use terminal emulation software and a lot of arcane UNIX commands.

Exactly how much discussion there is on the Web is anybody's guess. Newsgroups are easy to count, since they distribute themselves automatically all over the globe, but Web discussion sites are just sitting on their servers, waiting for users. Web developers have used hundreds, if not thousands, of different programs to add discussion features, so writing a program to count them automatically (like Liszt does for mailing lists) would be extremely difficult—and many of them aren't accessible without a password anyway. There's not even any standard term for these things: "message boards," "forums," "threads," "conversation area," "community," "boards," "bulletin boards," "conferences," "BBSs," "discussions," and "talk" are all in common use. (To avoid confusion, we'll just stick with "message boards" for the rest of this chapter, but remember that the Web sites in question could be called just about anything.)

So how do you find Web message boards on topics that interest you? As discussed in Chapter 21: The Web and Browsers, search engines usually make it easy to find what you're looking for on the Web. Unfortunately, this lack of common terminology, combined with the common practice of password-protecting message boards, makes most search engines fairly useless in this context.

For this task, Yahoo's the most useful of the search engines, since entries in its catalog are categorized by humans rather than indexed automatically. Thus, regardless of what term a site uses to describe its discussion area, Yahoo's description should call it a "message board." Message boards occasionally have their own subcategories, but more often they are dumped into "Chat and Forums" or "Chat" subcategories.

Since Web message boards aren't restricted to the capabilities of Usenet (or e-mail), some of them have significant advantages over newsgroups and mailing lists, or at least differences that have a significant influence on discussion. The design of the Well (**well.com**) is a good example: when a user starts a new topic in a conference (equivalent to starting a new thread in a newsgroup), each response is appended in chronological order, like a transcript of an orderly panel discussion (see Figure 7). There's no automatic deletion the way there is on a news server, so when new participants join the discussion, they can read it from the beginning if they wish. Since the old posts remain intact and in order, there's no need for all the quoting that clutters up many newsgroup discussions.

Naturally, this approach has its drawbacks—notably, that side discussions can't split off into their own threads the way they can in newsgroups. However, it provides a very different experience from newsgroups, one that appeals to several thousand people enough that they pay $10 to $15 a month for access. The online magazine Salon (**www.salonmag.com**) uses a somewhat similar interface in its free message boards, Table Talk.

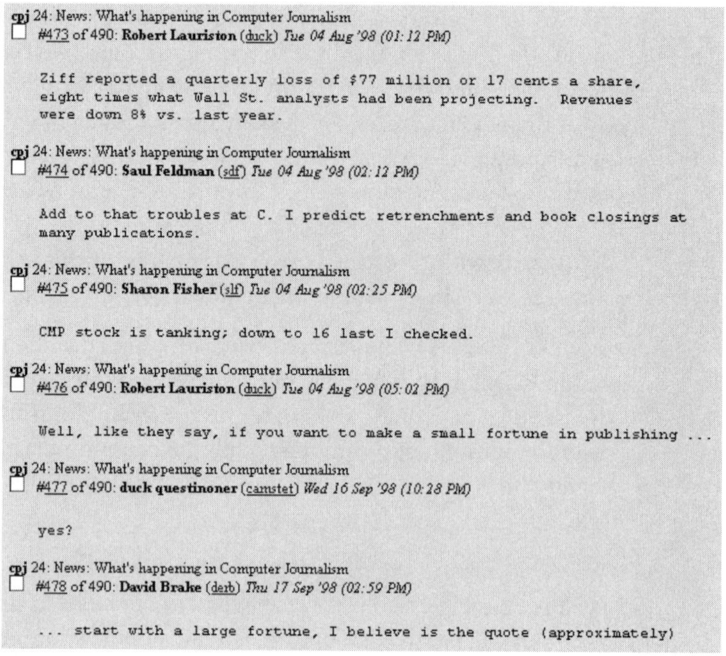

Figure 7

Conferencing on the Well.

This excerpt of a topic devoted to computer publishing industry gossip illustrates the Well's linear, transcriptlike discussions. This particular topic started in 1991, and all the posts since that date are still available in their original order.

cpj 24: News: What's happening in Computer Journalism
#473 of 490: **Robert Lauriston** (duck) *Tue 04 Aug '98 (01:12 PM)*

```
Ziff reported a quarterly loss of $77 million or 17 cents a share,
eight times what Wall St. analysts had been projecting.  Revenues
were down 8% vs. last year.
```

cpj 24: News: What's happening in Computer Journalism
#474 of 490: **Saul Feldman** (sdf) *Tue 04 Aug '98 (02:12 PM)*

```
Add to that troubles at C. I predict retrenchments and book closings at
many publications.
```

cpj 24: News: What's happening in Computer Journalism
#475 of 490: **Sharon Fisher** (slf) *Tue 04 Aug '98 (02:25 PM)*

```
CMP stock is tanking; down to 16 last I checked.
```

cpj 24: News: What's happening in Computer Journalism
#476 of 490: **Robert Lauriston** (duck) *Tue 04 Aug '98 (05:02 PM)*

```
Well, like they say, if you want to make a small fortune in publishing ...
```

cpj 24: News: What's happening in Computer Journalism
#477 of 490: **duck questinoner** (camstet) *Wed 16 Sep '98 (10:28 PM)*

```
yes?
```

cpj 24: News: What's happening in Computer Journalism
#478 of 490: **David Brake** (derb) *Thu 17 Sep '98 (02:59 PM)*

```
... start with a large fortune, I believe is the quote (approximately)
```

Resources for Online Discussions

The Virtual Community: Homesteading on the Electronic Frontier, Howard Rheingold (ISBN: 0201608707). This 1993 book paints portraits of a number of online communities around the world. It's out of print, but you can read it at Howard's Web site (**`www.rheingold.com`**). The brief history of the Internet in Chapter 3 stops in early 1993, before Mosaic launched the Web explosion that changed everything, but it provides a good summary of the events that led up to that historic moment and the personalities behind them.

Deeper: My Two-Year Odyssey in Cyberspace, John Seabrook (ISBN: 0684838737). *New Yorker* writer Seabrook took a couple of years off the job, dove into the Net, and came up with this book. If you can't comprehend what would motivate people to spend hours typing to each other online, Seabrook may offer some insight.

Newsgroups

`supernews.com/corporate/usenetlinks.html` A page with links to all kinds of documents that will be useful if you're getting started with newsgroups. There are also links to information about the SuperNews news server ($12 a month or $75 a year), which offers more groups and better performance than some ISPs' servers.

yahoo.com If you're not satisfied with your news server, go to Yahoo and check out the category Computers and Internet: Internet: Usenet: Public Access Usenet Sites, where you can find pointers to public news servers.

download.com Click Internet and then Newsreaders to get a list of alternative programs you can use to read newsgroups.

Mailing Lists

www.onelist.com You can use this site to create your own mailing list simply by filling out forms in your browser. You can make your list public or private, moderated or unmoderated, listed or unlisted, and you can choose whether to keep a public or private archive of messages.

Web Message Boards

www.delphi.com One of the old modem-dialup services that reinvented itself for the Web, Delphi Forums offers free Web-based message boards on thousands of topics. You can also create a free private forum (and associated chat room) for communicating with friends and family.

23

Internet Live: Chat, Etc.

by Alfred Glossbrenner

In This Chapter

Person-to-person communication is the essence of the Internet. Most of that communication takes place spasmodically: for example, you send an e-mail message tonight, the recipient replies tomorrow, you write back the next day, and so on.

But that's only part of the story. It's also possible to communicate over the Internet in real time. Chat software, for example, lets you enter a virtual room or channel where you can discuss issues of interest with other chatters, listen to and query experts or celebrities, or simply hang-out with cyberfriends.

Similar technology can be used to play real-time games, from online checkers to blackjack to the historical Raid on Schweinfurt game in which you and your online buddies join a squadron of B-17s in their assault on a Nazi ball-bearing factory. The Internet can even be used to make telephone and videophone calls, though neither of these applications yet delivers the quality of communication one hopes for.

This chapter will show you the landscape and give you the pointers you need to plug in, participate, and benefit from Internet chat and other forms of real-time online communication.

Getting into Chat

The desire to use the Internet to hold real-time conversations with other users has existed from the beginning. Think of it: It is 9:00 P.M. in Chicago. You're online at home, and your friend in India is online at the office. You could send each other e-mail back and forth, but wouldn't it be more like a real conversation if the messages you type appeared instantly on each others' screens?

A lot of Internet users have asked that question over the years, and numerous software solutions have been offered. Today, in fact, there are at least three kinds of chat: proprietary, Java-based, and Internet Relay Chat (IRC). All three offer essentially the same features, and all three operate the same way—but there are important distinctions.

Three Kinds of Chat

Subscribers to proprietary online services like America Online and CompuServe have been using chat since before most people had heard of the Internet. On these systems, the number of chat rooms and the number of people who can be in a room at the same time are typically limited. Since these are "family systems," chats may be monitored, and you may not be allowed to devote a chat room to certain topics. Nonetheless, this is a very popular feature. AOL, for example, estimates that many of its users spend as much as 25 percent of their online time in chat rooms.

Many Web sites offer chat rooms by downloading a Java applet to your browser. This is the approach used by Yahoo! Chat (**chat.yahoo.com**), Excite Chat (**talk.excite.com**), and other so-called portal sites that are trying to duplicate the popular appeal of America Online. (For more about Java and portals, see Chapter 21: The Web and Browsers.) There are also lots of special-interest Web sites with chat rooms devoted to everything from gourmet cooking to programming Java. As with chat on proprietary online services, there is no access to chat rooms hosted by other sites.

The third type of chat, Internet Relay Chat (IRC), is what most people mean when they refer to chatting on the Internet. IRC was developed in Finland in 1988 by Jarkko Oikarinen, and it has very few limitations. For example, the number of channels is limited only by the capacity of the chat server, and you can create a new channel any time you like. Doing so makes you the channel operator and endows you with the power to kick people off your channel at will. There are numerous IRC nets (groups of linked servers), the largest of which may have over 20,000 people chatting at the same time in over 12,000 chat rooms.

Getting the Software You Need

If you are a subscriber to America Online, CompuServe, or some other commercial system, you can begin chatting immediately. Chat is built into the software you use to log on, so all you need to do is enter a chat room, and it works automatically. The same is true for Java-based chat sites: all you need is a Web browser that can handle Java scripts (like 3.0 or later versions of the Netscape and Microsoft browsers).

IRC chat is quite different; it requires special software: either a stand-alone program or a browser add-on. These are the most popular IRC chat programs:

- **mIRC** (**www.mirc.co.uk/get.html**). This is the program to start with. Its features, including extensive help for IRC novices, and ease of use are unparalleled at the present time.
- **Microsoft Chat** (**microsoft.com/windows/ie/chat**). This serviceable program provides commands, menus, and controls that conform to the format used by most Microsoft programs. It's bundled with Windows 98 and sometimes with Microsoft Internet Explorer.
- **Netscape Chat** (**cws.internet.com/programs/nc3220b6.exe**). This good stand-alone program was originally supplied as part of the Netscape Power Pack in 1996, but it is no longer distributed by Netscape.

Connecting to IRC Networks

If you're going the IRC route, after you download and install your chat client program, it's time to connect to a chat server. There are easily over 100 IRC networks worldwide. Each consists of two or more servers, and each has its own set of channels and policies. The four largest networks are EFnet, Undernet, IRCnet, and DALnet, each of which can handle over 20,000 people at the same time.

To connect to a given network, you must tell your chat program to log you onto one of the servers that make up that network. Servers in the EFnet network, for example, include irc.cerf.net, irc.emory.edu, and irc.frontiernet.net. Lists of network servers (I'll show you how to find those in a moment) also include the port number you must set in your chat program before logging on; if none is specified, use 6667. One of the nice things about the mIRC client is that it is supplied with an address book packed with pre-entered server names and ports (see Figure 1). In general, you should try to select a server near to your geographical location whenever possible.

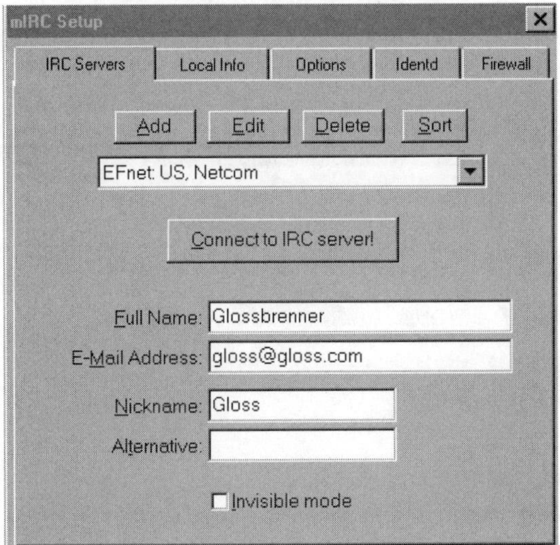

Figure 1

mIRC's server dialog box.

mIRC lets you pick from a drop-down list of IRC network servers. Here, we've chosen an EFnet server based in the U.S., but mIRC includes scores of other network server addresses.

How to Chat

Once you've made the connection, you'll be asked for the nickname (or "nick") you want to use during the session. Alternatively, you may be able to tell your chat program the name you prefer when you first install it and let it supply the nickname automatically when you connect. It's a good idea to select a distinctive name and stick with it since people will get to know you that way. However, there is no way to reserve a particular nickname for yourself (which means that any bozo can impersonate you).

The next step is to select a channel. Channel lists consist of the name of the channel, including the leading pound sign, the number of people currently logged onto the channel, and a one-line description of the channel's main topic. Your chat program will have a clickable button of some sort to call up a list of channels (see Figure 2), but you can also enter "`/list`" at any time in the same window you use to key in your chat remarks. Similarly, when you want to leave a given channel, you can enter "`/leave`."

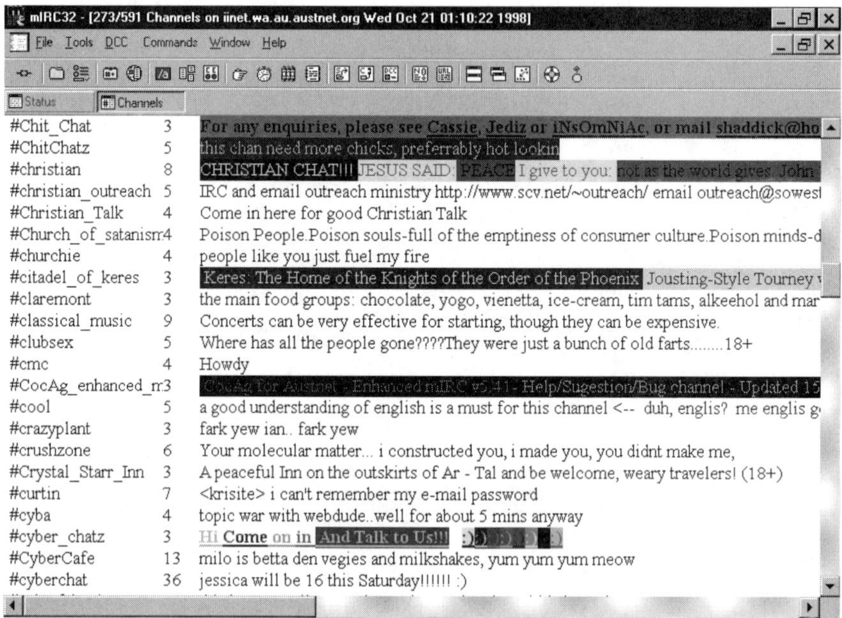

Figure 2

mIRC's channel list.

When you request a list of existing channels, you will see the channel name, the number of chatters currently logged onto that channel, and a one-line description prepared by the person who created the channel. To attract your attention, many channel creators use colored fonts, highlighting, and other gimmicks. When you find a channel that looks interesting, simply double-click its name to join.

Channel descriptions range from things like "A grin is a smile that burst" to "Bienvenidos a Cordoba Argentina!"—though the majority of channels are devoted to pornographic themes. To get started, connect to an EFnet server like one of those cited a moment ago and then specify one of the following channels, each of which is strictly G-rated:

```
#chat
#friendly
#new2irc
#IrcBar
#IrcNewbies
#chat4y
#beginner
```

Once you join a chat channel, you will see a screen like the one in Figure 3. As you might expect, IRC users, like their counterparts on AOL and other commercial systems, have developed a distinct culture. For example, it is considered good form to greet the group when you first log onto a channel. A simple "Hi, all," is fine.

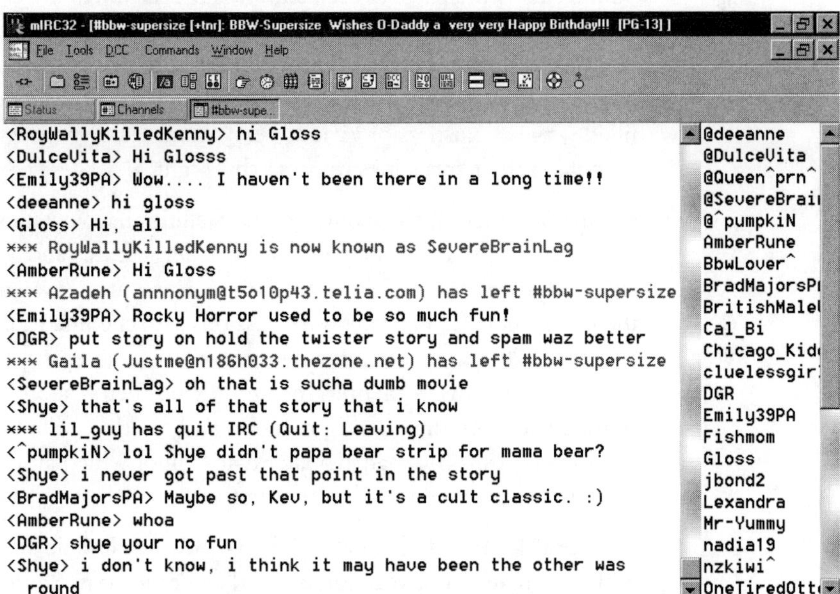

Figure 3

mIRC's chat window.

Each chatter's name is set off in angle brackets, and the list of chatters currently logged onto the channel is shown in an adjacent frame. Click any name in the frame to request profile information regarding the individual or to send a private message.

Regular chatters frequently use conversational abbreviations like ROTFL (rolling on the floor laughing), BTW (by the way), and YMMV (your mileage may vary). "Smileys" or "emoticons"—those facial expressions made up of letters and punctuation marks—are also common. The canonical smiley is `:-)`, which, if you look at it sideways, is two eyes, a nose, and a smile. There are hundreds of variations on the concept, like `:-(` (frown), `;-)` (wink), and `:^p` (sticking tongue out). See the "Internet Real-Time Resources" section at the end of this chapter for pointers to some guides to common and not-so-common acronyms and smileys.

On the darker side, some users will deliberately flood you with signals designed to force your server to disconnect you unless they're stopped by the channel's "op"—its operator (usually the person who created the channel).

You may be able to generate sounds as part of your conversations and even exchange files directly with other users. Certainly you will be able to make your personal interest profile available to anyone who is interested. And, depending on the chat system you are using, you may be able to have yourself represented by a photo or cartoon character of your choosing, with your chat remarks appearing in comic strip balloons over your image's head. (If this option is of interest, point your browser at **palacespace.com** and have a ball.)

Chat in Perspective

It's a personal opinion, but in my experience, no one should assume that online chat is the place to seek stimulating real-time conversation about anything. For one thing, scrolling through a list of channels with titles like "Teen Sex, Yes!" or "But the Little Girls Understand," each of which has only one occupant, is unsettling. It is the online equivalent of walking down a street filled with sex hustlers of various persuasions leaning against the buildings describing their specialties to passersby. Ugh!

On the other hand, chat/conferencing facilities have been used by America Online, CompuServe, and IRC sites to offer lectures and appearances by experts and celebrities from Iran-Contra prosecutor Lawrence Walsh to Koko the talking gorilla. Typically, such sessions are scheduled for a particular date and time. They are moderated by someone who accepts questions from participants and conveys them to the guest, who then responds. The transcripts of the session are then word processed and saved as a file that anyone can download, print, and read at a later date—all of which amounts to an excellent, life-enhancing use of online chat.

Chat can also broaden your circle of friends. It can help you make contact with soul mates you would never find any other way. Some years ago, for example, a man and a woman who had met on CompuServe's CB Simulator (the service's name for its chat feature) liked each other so much that they arranged to meet in person. True love blossomed, and they decided to get married—on CompuServe. Their respective parents were online in different states, the minister was online in a third, and the entire CompuServe CB community was logged on for the ceremony. When it was over, everyone hit their hyphen keys to simulate throwing rice (-- -- -- --).

Finding Channels and Chat Events

The best way to use chat, IMHO (in my humble opinion), is to check for announcements of guest appearances on whatever commercial system you use or check Yahoo!'s Net Events page at events.yahoo.com. The Yahoo! feature covers chats on other leading search engines (Excite, Lycos, etc.) and some IRC chats.

But don't stop there. If there's one site all new and experienced IRC users should visit it is **irchelp.org**. Here you will find a searchable database of files about IRC that can answer nearly every question you can think to ask. Click Network/Server List on the home page to be taken to a page from which you can locate all the servers on dozens of IRC networks, including EFnet, Undernet, IRCnet, and DALnet as well as smaller, often local nets worth checking out. The site also offers a feature called Channel List, which lets you perform a keyword search of all currently existing EFnet channels. The information that is searched consists of all the one-line channel descriptions.

Finally, the mother of all chat channel search sites is undoubtedly Liszt's IRC Chat Directory at **www.liszt.com/chat** (see Figure 4). As the site points out, this is the only place you can search for 36,193 IRC channels on 28 different IRC networks. You can get lists of the 100 most popular channels on each network (measured by the number of people currently logged onto a given channel), or you can narrow the focus to a given network. There's even a "naughtiness filter" you can switch on to exclude the porn channels from your search.

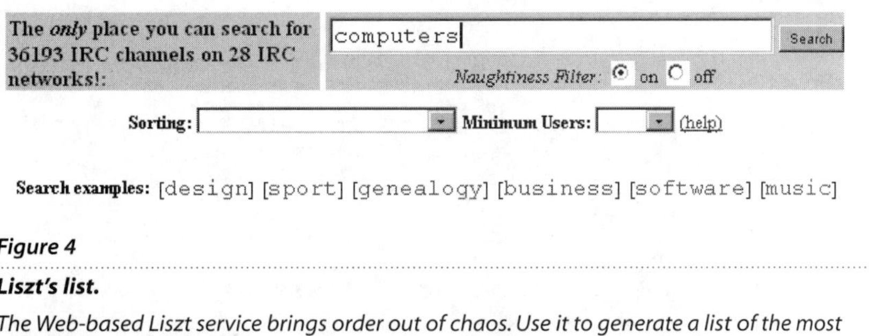

Figure 4

Liszt's list.

The Web-based Liszt service brings order out of chaos. Use it to generate a list of the most popular channels of the moment on nearly 100 IRC networks, or use it to search channel descriptions for keywords of interest.

Real-Time Games

Games have always been a part of computing, whether the machine involved was a mainframe, mini, or micro (personal) computer. Indeed, only three software packages were available for the original IBM PC back in 1981—BASIC,

VisiCalc, and the text-based game, Adventure. But Adventure, like Zork and its other imitators, was played against the computer. (In fact, Adventure began as an experiment in artificial intelligence.) Multiplayer games played against others logged onto the same computer system or commercial online system followed. On the Internet, text-based role-playing games called MUDs (multi-user dungeons) were developed based on the popular Dungeons and Dragons role-playing game.

Eventually, an entire universe of these multi-user games developed. By modern standards, these games are relics of the Internet's past, so we won't cover them here. However, they still have a devoted following, so if you'd like more information about this particular subculture, point your browser at **`geocities.com/TimesSquare/Alley/1185/scromud.html`** and click Mud FAQ. You should also go to **`handilinks.com`** and click Games.

Multi-user games have advanced far beyond the text-based games of the past. For example, you need only go to **`play.yahoo.com`**. to find backgammon, checkers, chess, bridge, blackjack, and many other games being played by thousands of people. The games are graphical and operate just like their real-life counterparts (see Figure 5). You can play other Internet users in real time, watch as others go at it, and even chat with players and opponents. Excite and other search engines offer similar game centers.

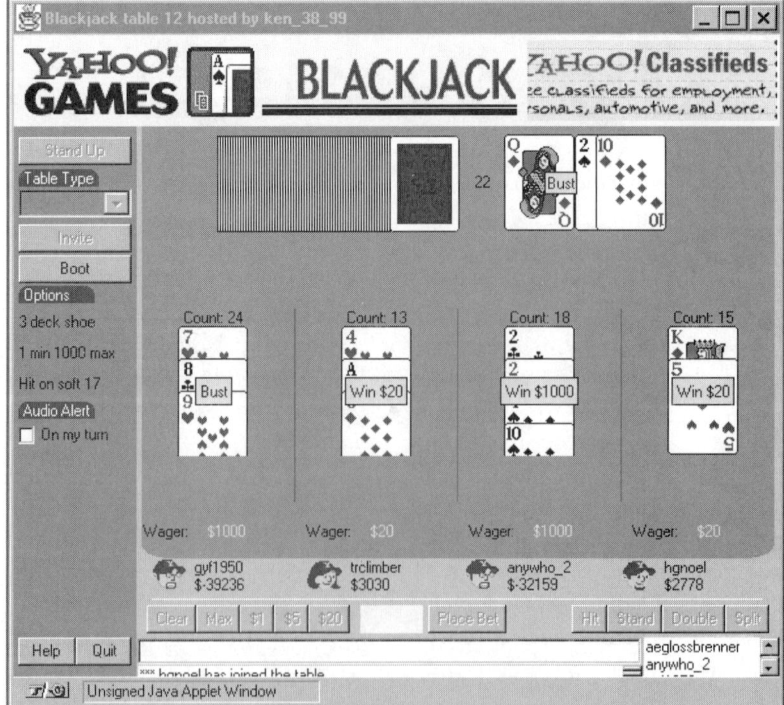

Figure 5

Yahoo's blackjack.

The money the players are betting is not real, but the competition is!

If you're willing to pay for your fun, there are much more sophisticated games available. Kesmai Studio's AirWarrior, for example, lets you climb into the cockpit of any of nearly 50 accurately modeled aircraft ranging from a Sopwith Camel or Fokker Dr. I (the Red Baron's plane) to an F-86F Sabre or the fabled Soviet MiG-15. You take off and engage in dogfights, bombing missions, and airfield defenses, all in real time against real opponents. The supervisors at AirWarrior regularly organize reenactments of historical air campaigns—though, of course, the outcomes online don't always match what actually happened. To play, go to **airwarrior.com** and click Join Now. Once you've signed up, you will be able to download the necessary software or request it on a free CD-ROM.

There are scores of similar games available online. You can find the best selection at the top three gaming sites: Microsoft's Internet Gaming Zone (**zone.com**), Interactive Magic (**imagicaonline.com/home.shtml**), and Gamestorm (**gamestorm.com**). Prices range from $2 an hour to $10 a month for unlimited access. For reviews of multiplayer games and tips for playing, check out CNET's **gamecenter.com** and Computer Gaming World's **gamespot.com**.

Internet Phone Calls and Videoconferencing

No discussion of real-time Internet-based communication would be complete without a nod toward the technology that makes it possible to place a long-distance phone call—or videophone call—over the Net. The reason for a nod instead of a full treatment is that neither of these applications is really ready for prime time yet.

Even if you have a fast connection, like an ISDN adapter or cable modem (see Chapter 19: Getting on the Internet), the Internet itself simply doesn't reliably provide enough bandwidth to dependably provide a voice connection comparable to what you get from a telephone. The result is that it can be hard to make a connection, once you connect the sound may have gaps or be distorted, and the link may break unexpectedly at any time. If you have friends or family living in places where you can't afford to call them as often as you'd like, by all means give Internet phone calls a try, but be prepared to be disappointed. For your best shot at a decent connection, try calling at times when net traffic is light at both ends; according to a recent survey by Inverse Network Technology, weekday traffic is lightest during morning automobile commute hours, before 8 A.M., and heaviest in the evening after 8 P.M.

Video calls require even more bandwidth, so Net traffic is a bigger obstacle. With an under-$200 videophone camera kit like the ones sold by 3Com, Creative Labs, Diamond, and Intel, typically you'll get a small, grainy image, updated every couple of seconds. Still, some people obviously think the fun factor outweighs the lousy quality: by some estimates, over one million camera kits shipped in 1998.

Some of these products support direct modem connections between PCs. Bypassing the Internet gives significantly better results—as you'd hope, since in that case, you'll be paying regular long-distance charges. The most popular software for making either phone or videophone calls over the Net is Microsoft NetMeeting. The program also includes a text chat window, a *whiteboard* (a shared window where you and the people you're talking with can sketch diagrams), and the ability to share applications, so you can collaborate on a document. It's bundled with Windows 98 and sometimes with Internet Explorer 4.0, and you can download it free from **microsoft.com/netmeeting**.

To use its phone capability, you'll need a sound card connected to a microphone and speakers or headphones, though with the chat and whiteboard, the program is useful even without sound. In theory, any video camera recognized by Windows' Multimedia control panel should be available for videophone calls, but getting videoconferencing set up is sometimes tricky. Note that you don't need to have a camera installed to receive a videoconference call. NetMeeting's phone and video features conform to Internet standards (H.323 and T.120), so in theory you should be able to connect with people using other software, but again the reality is sometimes more complicated than the theory.

Internet Real-Time Resources

delphi.com Founded in 1983, Delphi used to compete with CompuServe, Prodigy, and other online systems. Delphi has always done things a bit differently, so it isn't surprising that it now offers free chat services. (You have to register, but there is no cost.) This well-organized facility is a great place to get your feet wet.

chat.yahoo.com As search engines lard on the features in hopes of convincing you to make them your Internet starting point or portal, several have added chat features. Yahoo!'s is currently the best, with its easy-to-use Java Chat applet and its well-organized list of available chat rooms. One trick: to see how many people are in a given room, join any room and then click Change Room to produce a current list. Yahoo! also maintains a calendar of chat events and celebrity appearances scheduled at various sites around the Net.

www.pop.at/smileys This site offers over 650 smileys, compiled over the years from e-mail messages and news postings by David Sanderson, the "Noah Webster of Smileys" according to the *Wall Street Journal*.

czweb.com/smilies.htm Smilies Unlimited groups emoticons by theme.

www.pageblvd.com For a nice list of e-mail and chat expressions like IMHO or ROTFL, click "E-mail expressions and symbols."

onnow.com This site offers *TV Guide*–style listings of audio broadcasts, audio chats (you'll need a sound board and a microphone.), avatar chats, and audio broadcasts taking place at the moment. There is also an On Later feature that lets you click a calendar date and a time period to find out what events are scheduled. You can also search for events by keyword. One venue not covered, however, is the IRC networks. You may also want to visit Yack!, a site that also offers a guide to Internet events and chat (**yack.com**).

talkcity.com A sister site of OnNow, TalkCity is trying to make a business out of chat. Cleanly designed and quite well organized, TalkCity strives to create virtual communities by providing not only chat, but a bulletin board system and free home pages. In addition, it is strictly G-rated, and its code of conduct is enforced. That makes it yet another good place to start.

virtualquincy.com/quincy/internet/irc.html The IRC resources gathered here are excellent. Included are links to **irchelp.org** and Liszt's IRC Chat directory, two places everyone should visit before venturing into IRC.

24

Use Your PC as a Phone or Fax

by Robert Lauriston

In This Chapter

You probably know that your PC's modem can send and receive faxes, but did you know that some modems can also send and receive regular phone calls? In this short chapter I'll tell you what you need to take advantage of these special capabilities.

Using Your PC as a Fax Machine

Almost all modems sold in the past few years can double as fax machines. Check your modem's software bundle to see if it came with fax software—but don't try to install a fax program designed for a different version of Windows than you're running.

If you don't find any usable software, you don't necessarily have to buy anything: Windows 95 and 98 come with a basic program called Microsoft Fax. If you're running NT, or the software you've got isn't cutting it, check out WinFax Pro, which I'll discuss after I tell you how to install Microsoft Fax.

Note that cable modems don't have fax features. Neither do most so-called ISDN modems, though there are some models that combine ISDN adapters and conventional modems in one board: the best-known of these is the 3Com Courier I-Modem, which has a great reputation.

Microsoft Fax

The Microsoft Fax program that comes with Windows 95 and 98 is fairly limited compared with commercial software like WinFax Pro, but if you just want to send and receive the occasional fax, it's perfectly adequate.

In this section, I'll tell you how to install and use it. As you'll see, the process is a little trickier in Windows 98, since Microsoft doesn't officially support Microsoft Fax in that release. That means if something goes wrong, the company won't provide tech support. Microsoft says not to install Microsoft Fax if you're using Exchange Server Client 5.0.

Although with Windows 95 I've had no problems using Microsoft Fax, I was able to get the program working only halfway in Windows 98. I could send faxes fine, but no matter what I tried the modem wouldn't receive them. This may have had something to do with my having an ISDN adapter in the same machine, since MS Fax kept trying to use it instead of the modem—though deleting the ISDN drivers didn't help matters.

To install Microsoft Fax in Windows 95:

1. Run the Add/Remove Programs control panel, click the Windows Setup tab, and check Microsoft Fax. If prompted, click Yes to install Microsoft Exchange as well. Then click OK to start the installation.
2. When the Inbox Setup Wizard appears, click Next to indicate that you haven't installed Microsoft Exchange before.

Continue with step 5 in the next section.

To install Microsoft Fax in Windows 98:

1. Load your Windows 98 CD and navigate to the folder Tools\Oldwin95\Message\US.
2. Double-click the wms application (wms.exe). Click Yes twice and OK once to install. If prompted to reboot your computer, click No.
3. Double-click the awfax application (awfax.exe). Click Yes to install. When prompted, click Yes to reboot your computer.
4. After your computer reboots, double-click the Inbox icon on the desktop to bring up the Inbox Setup Wizard.
5. Uncheck everything but Microsoft Fax (see Figure 1) and click Next. (See Chapter 20: E-Mail for recommendations of better e-mail programs.)

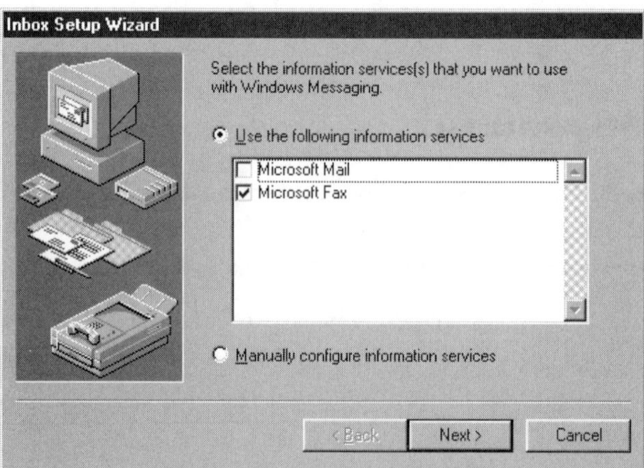

Figure 1

Installing Microsoft Fax.

6. If you have more than one modem in your system, select the one you want to use to fax, then click Next.
7. Select Yes or No depending on whether you want MS Fax to answer incoming calls automatically. If you choose Yes, set the number of rings you want it to wait before the fax picks up. (To change these settings later, right-click the modem icon on the taskbar, and choose Properties.) Then click Next.
8. Enter your name, choose your country from the list, and enter the telephone number of the line the fax modem's connected to (see Figure 2).

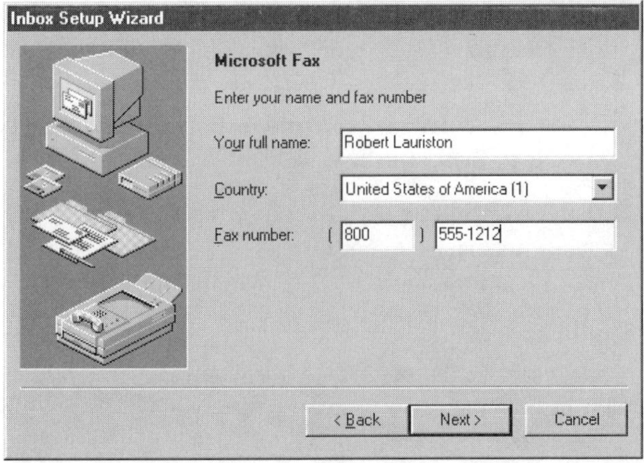

Figure 2

Giving Microsoft Fax your name and the number of your modem line.

9. Click Next twice to allow the wizard to create the MS Fax address book and folders in their default locations. If the wizard asks whether you want to add an icon to StartUp, choose No and click Next. Then click Finish.

To send a fax:

1. Print a document, from any application, to Microsoft Fax, just as if it were a printer. Note that some applications automatically print to the default printer. To fax from such apps, choose Settings/Printers from the Start menu, right-click on the Microsoft Fax icon, and choose Set As Default. Remember to change back to your regular default printer after you're through faxing.
2. The first time you send a fax, the Compose New Fax wizard will ask where you're dialing from. Unless you're on a notebook PC that you plan to use to fax from various locations, check "I'm not using a portable computer ..." to bypass this unnecessary step permanently. Then click Next.
3. Enter the name and fax number of the person to whom you're sending the fax (see Figure 3), then click Next.

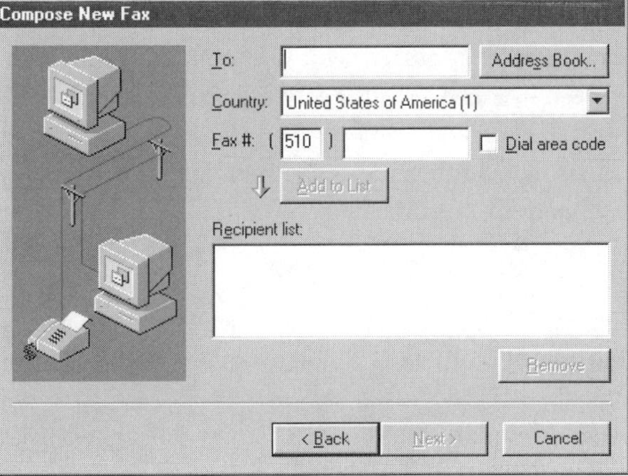

Figure 3

Enter the name and fax number of the person you're faxing.

4. Choose a cover page, if you want one. (See the next section for instructions on creating a custom cover.) Click Options if you wish to set MS Fax to send the fax later, when rates are lower. Then click Next.
5. If you wish, enter a subject and/or note to add to the cover page, then click Next, then Finish.

Note that if MS Fax has any problem sending the fax, it will not display an error dialog like a normal program. Instead, it will put what looks like an e-mail message from a phantom System Administrator in the Inbox (see Figure 4).

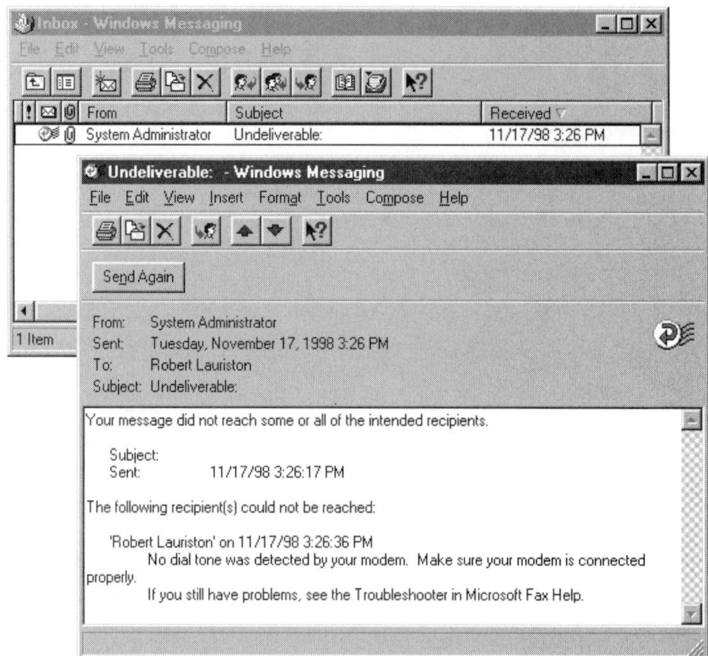

Figure 4

Instead of displaying a normal error message, MS Fax warns you of transmission problems by e-mail from an imaginary System Administrator. You can resend the fax by clicking Send Again.

If you're using Outlook, the e-mail program that comes with Microsoft Office—not to be confused with Outlook Express, which comes with Internet Explorer—you can find those messages in its inbox. Once you've installed Microsoft Fax, you'll be able to send Outlook messages to fax numbers in the address book. You can even address the same message to a mix of e-mail addresses and fax machines.

To create a custom cover page:

From the Start menu, choose Programs/Accessories/Fax/Cover Page Editor. This is kind of a confusing program, so rather than starting from scratch I suggest you start with one of MS Fax's cover pages and modify it. To do so, choose File/Open, navigate to the \windows directory, open one of the four cover page files (Generic, Urgent, Confidential, or For Your Information), then choose File/Save As and give the copy a new name.

Figure 5

MS Fax's cover page editor.

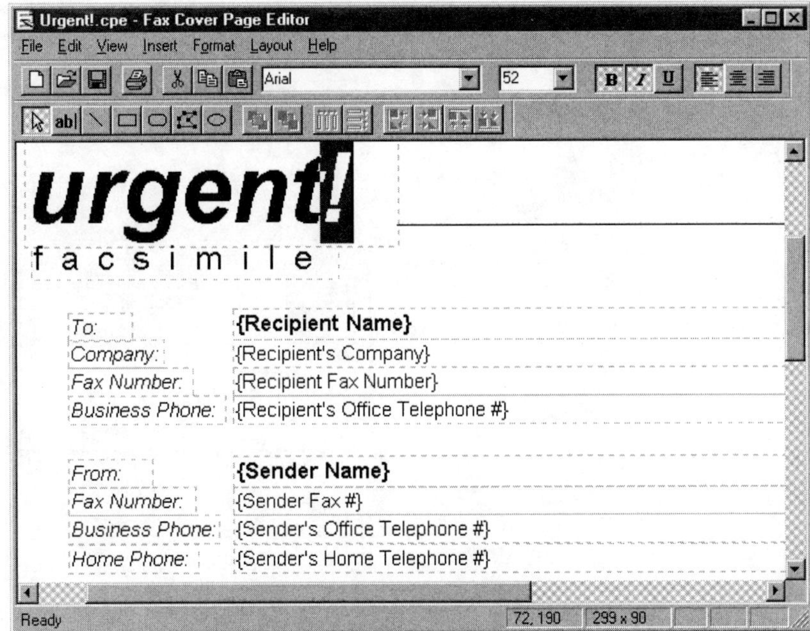

To read a received fax:

When Microsoft Fax receives a fax, it stores it in the Inbox, just as if it were a e-mail message. Open the Inbox and double-click on the fax icon to open it for reading.

If you're running Windows 95 OSR2 or Windows 98, you can add additional features to the fax viewer. From the Start menu, choose Programs/Accessories/Imaging. Then choose Tools/General options, click Imaging, click OK, and close the Imaging application. The next time you open a fax for viewing, you'll see a new toolbar that allows you to annotate received faxes with text, lines, and other elements.

WinFax Pro

If you can't run Microsoft Fax, or it doesn't fit your needs, check out Symantec's WinFax Pro (around $100). It's basically similar—you can fax by "printing" any document, and received faxes appear in the e-mail-like interface shown in Figure 6—but WinFax is a lot easier to use, and much more powerful.

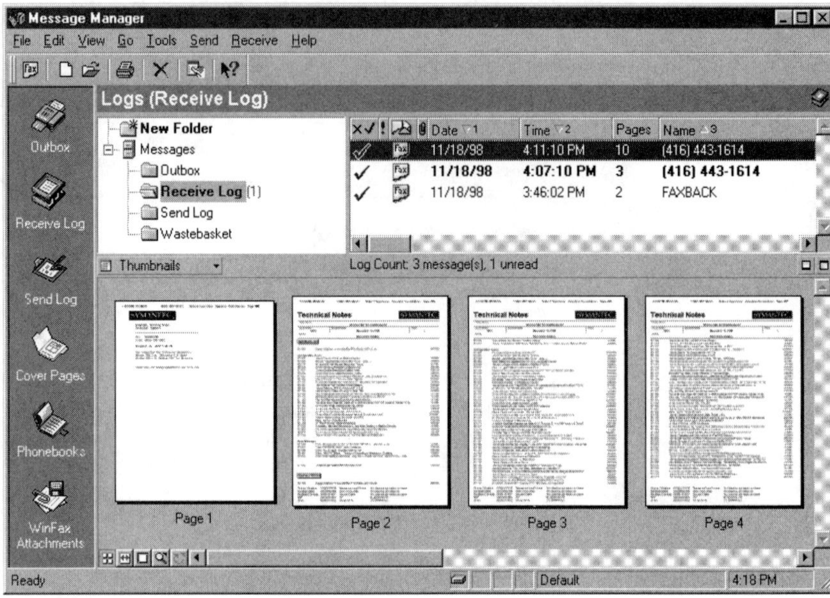

Figure 6

WinFax Pro.

The program includes over 200 cover sheets you can use as is or customize. It has much more sophisticated editing tools, so you can easily combine output from a number of applications into a single fax, rearrange and delete pages, and so on, and a preview mode so you can check out the fax looks before you send. If you have a compatible scanner, you can fax directly from hard copy. WinFax can share the address book of Outlook or ACT! (PIMs discussed in Chapter 16: Databases), or a contact list created in Microsoft Access, so you won't have to enter the same data twice.

When you receive a fax, WinFax can use the modem to send a message to your pager, forward the faxes to you at another location, or let you retrieve faxes to your notebook PC. An OCR module can convert received faxes back into editable text you can paste into any application.

For more info on WinFax Pro, see **symantec.com/winfax**. There you can read about other features, download a free 30-day trial version, or buy the program directly from Symantec (though you can find it cheaper elsewhere).

Using Your PC as a Speakerphone or Voicemail System

If you've got a *voice modem* (aka *data/fax/voice modem*) you can use your PC as a speakerphone, answering machine, and/or voicemail system. These devices are basically hybrids, a combination of a modem and a sound card. Prices start around $40 for brands you've never heard of and go up to around $150 for name models like the 3Com Sportster.

All voice modems I've seen, and all the PCs I've seen with voice modems installed, have been bundled with the necessary software. All the programs I've seen to date have worked basically the same way.

The speakerphone stuff is pretty straightforward. You just talk into your PC's microphone; when the person on the other end speaks into their handset, their voice comes out your speakers. When you receive a call, the speakers also play a ringing sound. An onscreen telephone book makes calling people easy (see Figure 7), and if you have Caller ID the phone program may display the number of incoming calls. Usually there's a dialing history, so you can retrieve recently dialed numbers, much like recently visited pages in a Web browser.

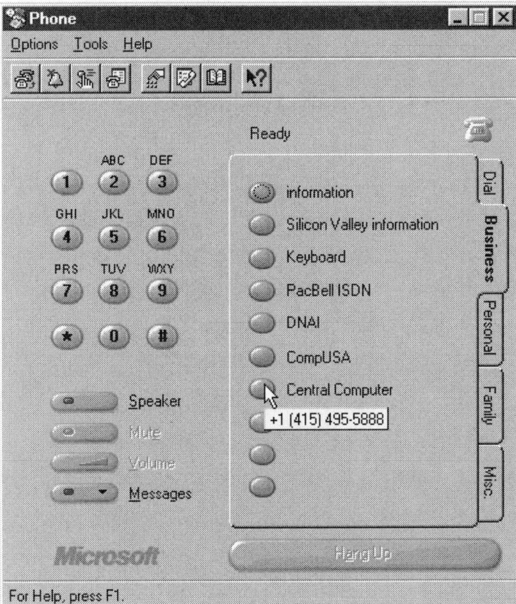

Figure 7

A typical onscreen dialer and phonebook. This one belongs to Microsoft Phone, a program that was bundled with a voice modem I bought a couple of years ago. I think it's since been discontinued. (It's hard to tell, because, like most voice-modem software, it was never sold retail, only bundled with voice modems.

Answering machine software and voicemail software are basically the same thing: the only difference is that the latter has a menu that stores messages in separate "boxes" for each user. I think this is the main attraction of voice modems: a voicemail system can avoid the lost messages that often result when roommates or family members share an answering machine, and if you already own a PC a voice modem is much cheaper than phone-company voicemail service. You should be able to screen calls as they come in, set the software to dial your pager number when a new message arrives (see Figure 8), or add fax-back services to the voicemail menu ("press 5 to have our server fax you a map and driving directions").

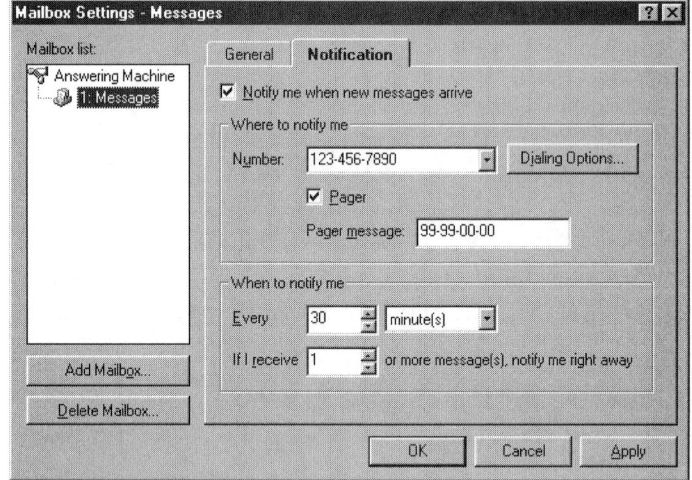

Figure 8

This dialog lets you set the phone software to page you when new messages arrive.

Voice modems can also be useful if you're having trouble getting phone, fax, and data dial-up services (like the Dial-Up Server described in Chapter 25: Networks: Connecting PCs) to share a single line. Most phone software supports *distinctive ring*, a phone-company service that routes calls to several numbers to a single line, which rings differently depending on which number you dialed. Just set your phone software to route the ring patterns appropriately (see Figure 9), and you've got most of the advantages of three phone lines without such high monthly bills.

Despite all those pluses, I'm not big on voice modems. Here's a quick list of some of the reasons why:

- Getting voice modems configured properly can be confusing. Windows often gets voice modems and sound cards confused, and getting such messes straightened out can be a real challenge, involving a lot of fiddling with settings and rebooting along the lines of what's described in the "Resolving Conflicts" section of Chapter 8: Upgrade It Yourself.

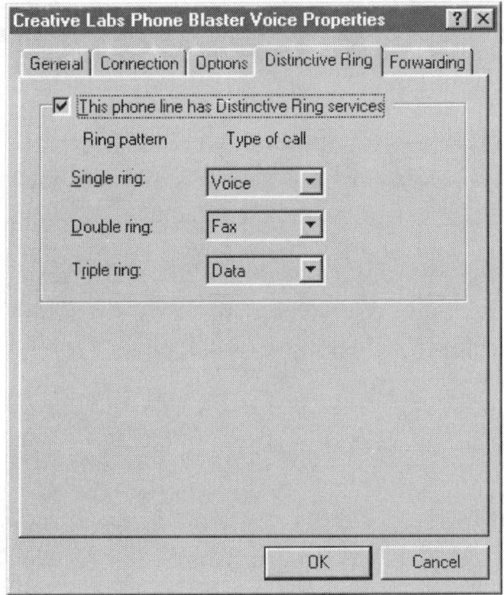

Figure 9

Setting the phone software to route calls based on distinctive ring patterns.

- Your PC has to be on for you to use the phone. Many newer PCs can "wake on ring," that is, automatically rouse themselves from power-saving sleep mode when the modem detects an incoming call, but I've seen a few where the wakeup sequence was slow enough that the phone software would sometimes miss calls.
- Unlike phone company voicemail systems, your PC's voicemail can't answer the phone when you're on it (unless you have another line for outgoing calls).
- Personally I couldn't live without separate lines for my phone and Internet connection. Sometimes research for articles I'm writing keeps me online for hours, while I'm expecting important phone calls, and when I get phone calls from associates asking if I got their urgent e-mail it's nice to be able to download and skim it while we talk.

If you do go for a voice modem, be sure to keep a real phone around for emergencies. Remember that regular phones will work during power failures, when PC phone software is dead.

TalkWorks Pro

If you find that your voice modem's software isn't all it should be, or if you just can't get it working right, check out TalkWorks Pro (around $150). This Symantec program combines speakerphone and voicemail features with the fax capabilities of WinFax Pro (described earlier). You can find out more about TalkWorks or download a free trial version from **symantec.com/talkworks**.

PC Phone and Fax Resources

faxtalk.com From this site, you can download a free trial version of FaxTalk Communicator, a program that combines fax and voice features, the way TalkWorks Pro does.

buy.trio.com Trio Communications sells DataFAX/Voice, a TalkWorks competitor that's bundled with many voice modems, for $50. Unforunately, as this book goes to print there's no free trial version.

yahoo.com The consensus of magazine reviews and users I've talked with is that WinFax Pro is the best fax program, and it's definitely the best I've seen, but if you want to check out its competitors for yourself, you can find some of them on Yahoo at Business and Economy : Companies : Computers : Communications and Networking : Software : Fax section.

25

Networks: Connecting PCs

by Lenny Bailes

In This Chapter

If you work in an office with other PC users, linking your computers into a network has a lot of advantages. You can exchange e-mail with each other, and use a group scheduling program to organize meetings and manage conference rooms. Everyone can share databases of useful information—customer contacts, inventory, billing, whatever's important to your business. Everyone in the office can easily share printers, scanners, or a single Internet connection.

Networks are even becoming popular among home users. In addition to the same practical benefits they offer in offices, a home network has entertainment value: you can use it to run multiplayer network games.

What a network means to you and how much you need to know (and worry) about it vary enormously depending on the kind of network you have and whether you or someone else is responsible for installing and maintaining the thing. Chances are you play one of these four basic roles:

1. user on a small network
2. cog in a big corporate network
3. qdministrator of a big corporate network
4. head user on a small network

If you fall into one of the first two categories, you might find this chapter informative, but the only portion that's likely to be of practical value is "Using Your Network." If you fall into group #3, you know most of this stuff already. This chapter is aimed mostly at #4, the poor sucker stuck with installing, managing, and troubleshooting a small network. If you fit that description, this chapter provides an overview of the decisions you'll need to make before taking the network plunge, a step-by-step guide to installation, and discussion of some issues that may become important as your network grows.

Why and When You Want a Network

You hardly notice the freeway you're driving on unless there's a traffic jam or a bump in the asphalt. Likewise, except for the people who maintain them, nobody cares about network cabling, interface boards, or the network operating system until the network misbehaves. What people who *use* networks really care about are the services provided by network *applications.* These applications provide the main motive for installing and running a network:

- **E-mail.** Goodbye telephone tag. As users quickly discover, e-mail often works better than a phone call, since you can send and reply to messages even when the person at the other end is busy. You can broadcast electronic messages to the whole office, replacing paper-wasting photocopied memos.
- **Multiuser databases.** For many organizations, the main motive for installing a network is to run a multiuser database application, such as an accounting program, order entry system, or customer contact list. See Chapter 16: Databases for tips on choosing between an off-the-shelf package and a custom application created with a database manager like FileMaker Pro or Microsoft Access.
- **Sharing files.** A network eliminates the need to carry documents from one location to another on floppies—instead, you can just "attach" a word processing, spreadsheet, or other file to an e-mail message to send a copy to a coworker electronically.
- **Sharing applications.** As networks get larger, it becomes more efficient to share a single copy of an application rather than installing separate copies on the hard disk of every PC whose user needs it. Note that with many applications you need to purchase additional licenses to avoid violating software piracy laws. License terms vary: some companies charge by the number of PCs on the network, some by the number of simultaneous users allowed to run the program, some by the total number of users who ever use the program.
- **Sharing printers and other hardware.** It's cheaper to share a few printers than to put one on every desk. A typical setup is a pair of laser or inkjet printers, one with letterhead, another with plain paper. Many companies set up shared dot-matrix printers to bang out multipart forms, like invoices or FedEx labels, and a network connection lets more people take advantage of an expensive color printer. Other useful devices often shared over networks include tape backup, CD-ROM jukeboxes, fax modems, and scanners.
- **Internet and Web access.** Providing a single Web connection for all the PCs on your network can be cheaper and easier than setting up modem dial-up accounts for everyone who needs access. Even if you don't care about Internet access, it can be useful to set up an in-house Web site for distributing information and files.
- **Other network applications.** Networked *project management* programs help schedule and track the work of hundreds of people collaborating on complex engineering projects, like designing an airplane or building an automobile prototype. *Document management* systems help businesses with thousands of documents in progress (such as law firms or large contractors) track revisions, control access, and record word processing time for client billing or departmental charge-backs.

Some of these network applications may, for performance or security reasons, need to run on one or more PCs devoted exclusively to that purpose. See "When You Need a Dedicated Server" later in this chapter for more on that issue.

Network Basics

So what is a network, exactly? Basically, any group of computers connected to share information. The simplest network is a pair of PCs connected by Ethernet to share files and a printer. The most complex is the Internet, the global network made up of tens of thousands of smaller networks. In this section, we'll quickly go through the basic concepts that underlie the practical tips that make up the rest of this chapter.

Network Design

There are various ways you can set up a network—which makes the most sense depends on how big it's going to be and exactly what you're going to do with it. The easiest way to understand the various approaches to network design is to consider these two extremes:

- **Total centralization.** In this model, all shared resources reside on *dedicated servers*, PCs *dedicated* exclusively to providing services to the other computers on the network. Dedicated *file servers* hold shared applications and data; print servers run shared printers; database servers run multiuser databases; gateway servers handle Internet access—you get the idea. Often a single PC plays multiple server roles. The servers, which no one touches except the network administrators, run industrial-strength operating systems like Novell NetWare, Windows NT Server, or Unix, which have features that allow all the other computers on the network to talk with each other, share files, and to access the Internet.
- **Total decentralization.** Shared applications, data, and printers can be located on any PC on the network; to put it another way, any PC can share its hard drive and printer with any other PC. Since each PC has an equal chance of being a server, this model is often called *peer-to-peer* networking. Windows 95, 98, and NT Workstation all have this kind of network capability built in.

In reality, larger networks are almost always a hybrid of these two models. Small networks like the ones we're focusing on in this chapter are sometimes purely peer-to-peer, but sometimes there are good reasons to use dedicated servers even on the smallest networks—for instance, if you've got a multiuser accounting package, you'll probably want to give it its own PC. See "When Do You Need a Dedicated Server?" later in this chapter for details.

Ethernet Hardware

A thorough discussion of the variety of network hardware currently in use could fill a book larger than this one, but for our purposes that's of only academic interest. Unless you're a network professional working for a large organization, the only kind of hardware you're likely to encounter is Ethernet. Here are the various components you'll need to build a basic small network.

- **Adapters.** A PC is connected to the network by its *Ethernet adapter*, a device that converts data into signals suitable for sending over the network's cables. Reliable adapter manufacturers include 3Com, Intel, Novell/Eagle, Hewlett-Packard, Xircom, and Standard Microsystems/Western Digital (SMC). You can get both ISA and PCI models; which makes most sense for you depends primarily on how many free slots you have and what other expansion cards you might want to install in the future. All else being equal, I recommend PCI.
- **Cables.** These days, the most popular flavors of Ethernet for PCs are 10BaseT and 100BaseT (a.k.a. Fast Ethernet), which use the same kind of wire telephones use but have slightly larger jacks and plugs (see Figure 1). Take care not to accidentally plug a telephone line into an Ethernet jack, as that can damage your equipment. In a small network, cables run from each PC's adapter to a central *hub*. In a large or older network, you may also encounter the old "thinnet" style of Ethernet. These adapters were usually *daisy-chained* by 3/16-inch round cables running from one to the next, like lights on a Christmas tree, though thinnet cables can also be connected to compatible hubs.

Figure 1

10Base-T cable and RJ-45 jack.

- **Hub.** In a small network, this is usually a small box, about the size of an external modem or paperback book, with a row of Ethernet jacks (also called "ports") on one side and, preferably, a few status lights for troubleshooting connection or performance problems (see Figure 2). Hubs start at under $100 for four-port models, and the price goes up as you add ports. More expensive hubs usually include an *uplink* port to connect to another hub, so when you've used up all the ports on one hub you can add another and keep adding PCs to your network indefinitely. On big networks, hubs are often mounted in racks, have all sorts of fancy features, and may have hundreds of ports.

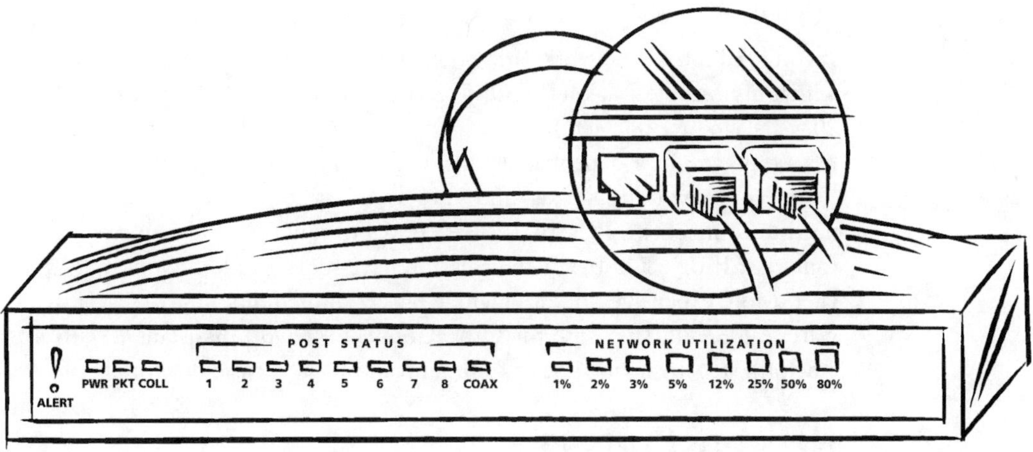

Figure 2

A typical network hub for a small business.

- **ISDN router.** An ISDN router is a good alternative to a standard hub. One of these boxes, which start at around $300, combines an Ethernet hub with an ISDN adapter that all the PCs on the network can share. (ISDN is a digital telephone line that gives you an Internet connection that's three to four times as fast as a V.90 modem. See Chapter 19 Getting On the Internet, for more details.)

For a small network, you need an Ethernet adapter for each PC, a hub or ISDN router with at least one jack for each PC, and cables to connect each PC to the hub. If you've got only two PCs, you don't need a hub: you can just connect the two directly. Note that a regular Ethernet cable won't work in that situation: you need a specially wired direct-connect cable.

If you're starting a new network from scratch, I recommend you use 100BaseT Ethernet hardware, which is much faster than the old 10BaseT products. The adapters cost about the same, and the faster hubs are only a little more expensive. Note that you can't use both 10BaseT and 100BaseT adapters on your network unless you have a dual-speed hub specifically designed to support such mixing.

It's generally best to buy adapters and hubs from established names in the industry, such as Xircom, Hewlett-Packard, or 3COM. The prices may be slightly higher than for "no-name" or off-brand models, but you have a reasonable guarantee that the stuff will work properly right out of the box, the first time you install it.

If you need reliable network cards and a hub to set up a small business network with a minimum of hassle, 3COM's starter kits are a good choice. Founded 20 years ago by Bob Metcalfe, the guy who invented Ethernet, the company has a reputation for dependable performance. The entry-level 4-Port Office Connect Networking Kit (around $110 on the street) includes everything you need to connect two PCs: two 10BaseT adapters, two 25-foot cables, and a four-port 10BaseT hub, which gives you have room to add two more PCs later. More expensive bundles include 8-port hubs and/or 100BaseT hardware. All the kits ship with the OfficeConnect Network Assistant CD-ROM, a helpful step-by-step guide to setting up and using a basic network.

Network Protocols

If you think of your Ethernet adapter as a mailbox and its hub as the central post office, transport protocols are the ZIP code system the network uses to tell where data's supposed to end up. When your PC sends a file across the network, it encodes the data into packets that bear distinctive destination signs. Actually, it's more complicated than that, since thanks to the anarchic evolution of PC networks there are a number of different protocols in common use, and there's a good chance your PC uses more than one of them.

You don't really need to know anything about protocols to use them. However, since you may see them in a dialog box and wonder what the alphabet soup's all about, here's a brief explanation of the three supported by Windows, plus one that comes into play if you've got Macs:

- **TCP/IP.** (Transport Control Protocol/Internet Protocol). The standard for the Internet, this protocol is increasingly popular on private networks as well, both to handle access to the Internet and to provide Internet-style local services, like in-house Web sites.

- **IPX/SPX.** The proprietary protocol used by Novell NetWare. It's a very efficient protocol for use with file servers, which is NetWare's forte. Generally, there's no need to install this protocol if none of the systems on your network are running NetWare, though there are occasional exceptions: the Direct Cable Connection utility, for reasons known only to Microsoft, uses it.
- **NetBEUI.** Microsoft's proprietary protocol. If you don't make a special effort to configure your network differently, this is what will be used for local services, like sharing hard drives and printers.
- **AppleTalk.** Macintosh computers use this proprietary protocol. Windows NT Server supports it, at least to the extent necessary to let Macs access files and share printers. (Apple formerly used the term AppleTalk to refer also to the low-speed network hardware that Macs once used, but when the company switched to Ethernet hardware it renamed the old hardware LocalTalk.)

Installing a Small Network

The trickiest part of most network installations is the cabling. If you're networking several PCs in the same room and you don't mind a few wires running along the floor, go ahead and do it yourself. But if you need to run cables through walls, or want to hide the wires for aesthetic reasons, hire a professional. In that case, you might as well contract out the whole cabling job.

While the other steps involved in setting up a network used to be pretty challenging, Windows 95, 98, and NT 4.0 make it pretty painless. The following guide will tell you just how to do it.

Do *not* attempt to follow these instructions on a PC that's running any other operating system, like DOS or Windows 3.1.

Install the Hardware

1. Power down each PC, open it up, install an Ethernet adapter in an available slot, and close up the PC. See "Installing Expansion Cards" in Chapter 8: Upgrade It Yourself, for more detailed instructions on that task.
2. Connect each PC to the Ethernet hub or ISDN router with Ethernet cables (see Figure 3).
3. Connect the hub's power supply and make sure that the power is switched on. (The hub should have a "power-on" LED status indicator.)
4. Switch the PCs back on.

In Windows 95/98, the operating system should detect and configure the network card automatically. If you're prompted to assign your computer to a workgroup, use the default name, "workgroup."

In Windows NT 4.0, you'll have to set up the adapter manually. Run the Network control panel, click the Adapters tab, click Add, choose the card from the list, and click OK. Follow any prompts to complete installation, then click OK to close the Network control panel, and click Yes to reboot the PC.

Figure 3

Connecting the hub.

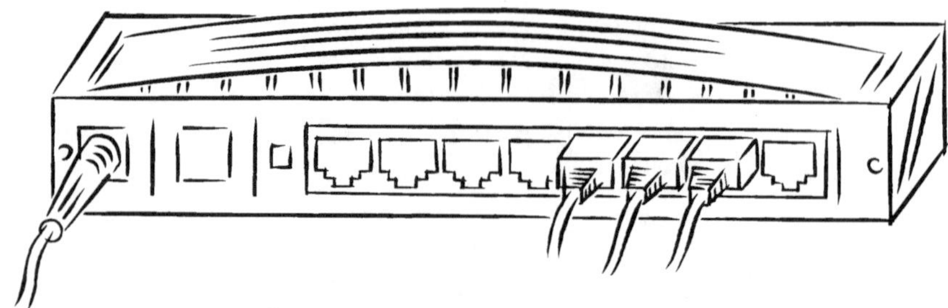

5. After your network card is set up and the machine reboots, right-click the Network Neighborhood icon on the desktop, choose Properties, and click the Identification tab. Make sure the Workgroup is "workgroup," and that each PC has a different "Computer name."

Figure 4

Network identification.

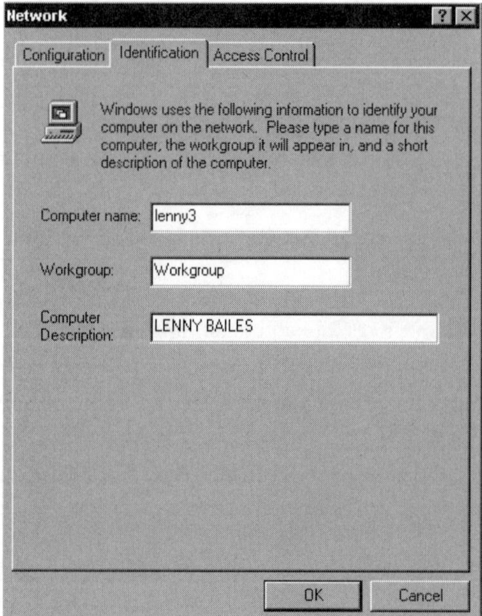

If Windows networking support is installed without a glitch, when you power up your network, the hardware connection will be negotiated automatically. Status LEDs on the network adapters and on the hub will generally flash green to indicate a functional network connection.

Troubleshoot Common Problems

If you see green status lights on your hub, and the Network Neighborhood icon is visible on the Windows desktop, you can skip this section of the chapter and proceed to the next. Your network hardware is working. The next section shows you how to confirm this by sharing a sample file resource.

However, if your hub doesn't show a green status light for one or more computers, or when you start Windows it reports a problem with the network adapter at startup, you can probably resolve the problem by adjusting hardware settings.

In Windows 95/98:

1. Open the System control panel and click the Device Manager tab.
2. Examine the Device Manager entry for Network Adapter. (If there's a + sign in front of the entry, click it to expand the tree to show the icon for the adapter itself.) A yellow exclamation point next to the listing for your adapter indicates a conflict with some other hardware device (see Chapter 8, Figure 4).
3. Select the network adapter in the device list and click the Properties button at the bottom of the window.
4. Select the Resources Tab in the Network Properties window and inspect the settings for "Interrupt Request" and "Input/Output Range." If conflicts are reported under "Conflicting device list," you can reassign either of these values on this screen.
5. If you don't find an entry for your network adapter in the Device Manager list, close this window. You can ask Windows to redetect your adapter by selecting the Control Panel/Add New Hardware applet. Choose the option that asks Windows to perform an automatic search. If the network adapter still isn't detected, shut down the computer, open the case and make sure the card is properly inserted in its motherboard slot.

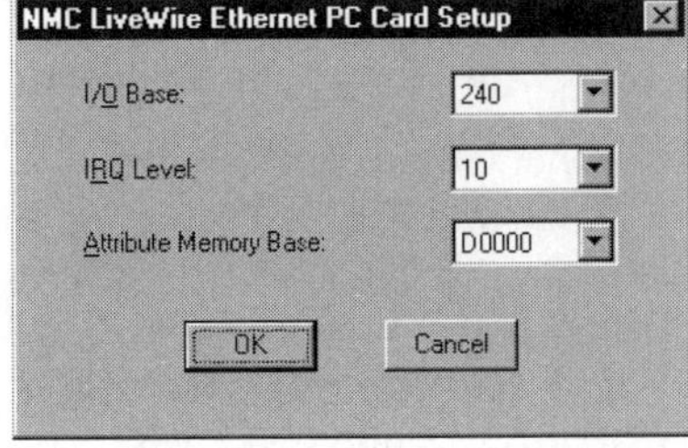

Figure 5

Windows NT 4.0 network card settings.

In Windows NT. Troubleshoot network error messages by examining reports in the Event Log (log on as an administrator and choose Programs/ Administrative Tools (Common)/ Event Viewer). To change the network adapter's configuration, open the Network control panel, click the Adapters tab, right-click the adapter icon, and choose Properties (see Figure 5).

Other troubleshooting techniques. If the foregoing procedures don't eliminate the error messages, turn on the green lights, and make Network Neighborhood appear on the Windows desktop, you may need to change the settings on the board itself.

Newer ISA and PCI network adapters generally let you change their settings using software, but unfortunately that software may have to run in DOS mode. You can switch to DOS mode in Windows 95 or 98 by choosing Shut Down from the Start menu, checking Restart in MS-DOS Mode, and clicking OK. If you're running Windows NT and your PC's not set up to dual-boot to Windows 95/98 or DOS, you can get to DOS mode by booting from a floppy. (See Appendix A: DOS Survival Guide for help dealing with DOS.) Once you're at the DOS prompt, run your network card setup/diagnostics program. This may show that the card is preset to use IRQ 5 and port address 0300, where the Windows Device Manager showed only IRQ10 and port address 0240 as available resources. You can generally use the DOS configuration software to change the presets of the network card to something that will make Windows happy.

With older ISA adapters, if there's no software you'll probably need to shut off the computer, open the case, and change a jumper on the card (see Chapter 8, Figure 11).

If Windows seems to think your network adapter is working properly, but the status light on the hub is not green, this may mean that your adapter is configured for an inappropriate cable type. For instance, you may have a 10Base-T network, but the adapter may be set for Coax/ThinNet. Generally, this setting can be corrected by running the configuration software that came with the card.

In rare circumstances, you may have to install an adapter manually in Windows 95/98. The process is similar to the one described for Windows NT, except that the Add button is on the Configuration tab.

Test the Network

If the status lights on your hub indicate network hardware is configured properly, you can confirm whether Windows 95/98 or Windows NT 4.0 Workstation has properly configured software settings with the following procedure:

1. Pick one computer on the network to be a test server. On that PC, right-click Network Neighborhood and choose Properties. In Windows 95/98, make sure File and Print Sharing are installed by clicking the File and Print Sharing button (see Figure 6); in Windows NT 4.0, make sure the Server component is installed in the Services list. Choose the Identification tab and verify or assign a Workgroup name (normally "workgroup"). If you're modifying or installing these services for the first time, you'll be prompted to restart the computer.

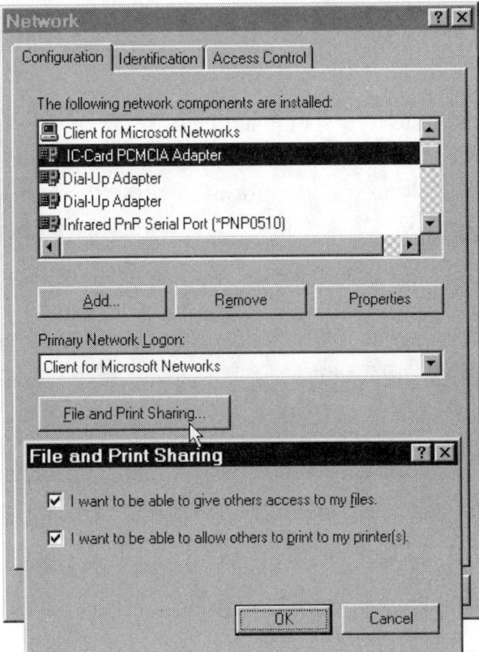

Figure 6

Installing file and print sharing.

2. After the computer restarts, test if the network's working by sharing a folder as described in "To Share a Folder or Drive" in the next section.
3. Double-click the Network Neighborhood icon on the test server's desktop, and you should see an icon for the computer you're working on (since it is now a server). Double-click the computer's icon, and you should see the folder you shared (see Figure 7).

Figure 7

Checking for the test server in Network Neighborhood.

4. Go around to the other PCs on your network and repeat step 3 on each. If the test server and shared folder appears on all of them, congratulations: your network is up and running.

If you *don't* see the test server listing in one or more of the Network Neighborhoods on the other workstations, make sure that they all have the same name in the Workgroup field of the Identification tab of the Network control panel (the dialog you get when you right-click Network Neighborhood and choose Properties).

Using Your Network

Now that you have your network up and running, it's time to take advantage of it. In this section I'll give step-by-step instructions for setting up the most common network services.

Sharing a Printer

To share a printer attached to one workstation among other members of your workgroup, follow this procedure under Windows 95/98 or Windows NT 4.0.

To share a printer connected to a PC by a printer cable:

1. Make sure the printer is working normally on that PC (the "print server") by printing any document. If not, resolve that problem before proceeding.
2. Choose Settings/Printers from the Start menu, right-click the printer, and choose Sharing. (If no Sharing option appears, turn on file and print sharing services as described in the previous section.)
3. Check Shared As (Shared in NT) and assign a Share Name, like "Lenny's LaserJet." On networks with multiple printers, it's important that the share name describe both the type of printer and its location. (In NT, you may need to enable some of the entries on the Alternate Drivers list.)

To share a printer connected to a network hub by an Ethernet cable. Make sure the printer shows up as available when you open Network Neighborhood. If it doesn't, consult the manual for the printer (or external print server) to determine which protocol (IPX-SPX, TCP/IP, etc.) its Ethernet port uses, and check the Network control panel to make sure that the same protocol is listed there; if not, add it. In the case of TCP/IP, it may be necessary to change the IP address of the printer so that it falls into the same range as the IP addresses of your network computers; a utility to make that change should be among the software bundled with the printer (or print server attachment).

To access the shared printer:

1. Go to any other PC on the network, choose Settings/Printers from the Start menu, and double-click the Add Printer button.
2. When the Add Printer Wizard asks how the printer is attached to your computer, choose Network and click Next.
3. Type the network path to the shared printer or select it through the Browse button. For example, if you've assigned a sharename of "Shared HP" to a printer connected to a computer named "Lenny1," the pathname to the printer would be \\Lenny1\Shared HP as shown. (The Connect to Printer screen for Windows NT 4.0 is similar, but not identical.)

Figure 8:

Mounting a shared network printer.

4. Follow the remainder of the prompts in the Add Printer Wizard, which will prompt you to select a driver, ask whether you want this printer to become the default output device and offer to let you print a test page. If you don't make the printer the default, you can still use it from most Windows applications by choosing it from the Printer Name list in the File/Print dialog.

Sharing a Folder or Drive

Any PC on a network can share any or all of its files with any other PC, but by default that option is turned off. To share files, in Windows 95/98 the File and Print Sharing option must be enabled, and in NT the Server component must be installed (as described in "Testing the Network" above).

To share a folder or drive:

1. Right-click the folder or drive in Windows Explorer and choose Sharing.
2. Click Shared As and assign a descriptive Share Name.

3. Set the kind of access you want to allow:

   In Windows 95/98, you can choose Read-Only (network users can open but not save or delete files), Full (network users can do whatever they want, just as if they were working on the PC), or Depends on Password, (gives users full or read-only access depending on which of the two passwords they enter, and denies all access to users who don't know either password). (See Figure 9.) This approach is called *share-level access control*.

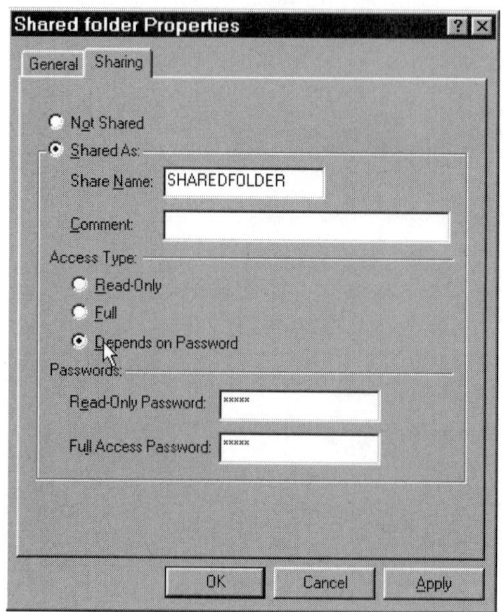

Figure 9:

Share settings in Windows 95/98.

   Windows NT uses a more complicated approach called *user-level access control* in which you assign access rights to groups of users (see Figure 10). Instead of having to enter separate passwords for each shared folder, the user just logs in once, and the server keeps track of which folders they get what kind of access to. User-level access is more work to set up, but as networks get larger it makes it much easier to manage security, since you can give new employees access to a whole set of access permissions by simply adding their names to a group list, and block all access simply by deleting a userid. NT security is unfortunately much too complicated to get into here—even a very basic treatment of the subject would take as much space as this chapter—but see the "Network Resources" section at the end of this chapter for recommendations of two books where you can learn how to set up and manage user accounts and access rights in Windows NT.

Once you turn on sharing for a folder or drive, it will appear in Windows Explorer under the Network Neighborhood section of the folder tree.

Figure 10

Share settings in Windows NT.

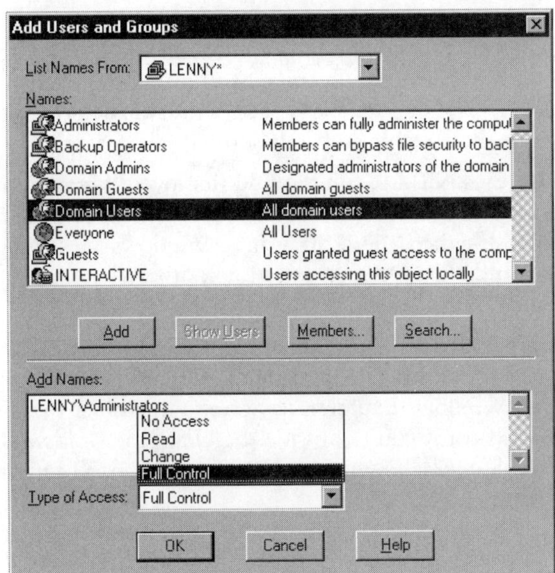

Windows 3.1 and DOS applications can't see Network Neighborhood, but they can access a shared folder if you "map" it to a drive letter. Under Network Neighborhood, right-click the shared folder or drive to which you want to assign a drive letter and choose Map Network Drive. Mapped drives look and act just like local, physical drives (C:, D:, etc.).

If the "Map Network Drive" command doesn't appear, try right-clicking the folder above it in the folder tree; if you still don't see the command, keep right-clicking your way up the tree until you find a folder where it does appear. Alternatively, you can go to the PC that's serving the folder, and follow the instructions above to define a separate Share Name, after which the "Map Network Drive" command should appear when you right-click that folder in Network Neighborhood.

If some of the PCs on your network don't have CD-ROM drives, you can use Windows' built-in networking to share one on another PC.

Exchanging E-mail

Windows includes "post office" software you can use to set up a private e-mail system on your local network. Setting it up is a little complicated. (See Chapter 20: E-mail for a discussion of Internet e-mail, which does not require a local postoffice.)

1. Install Microsoft Exchange or Windows Messaging on each PC on your network, starting with the PC you want to hold the "post office" files.

   In Windows 95, run the Add/Remove Programs control panel, click the Windows Setup tab, and double-click Microsoft Exchange. If either of the

two boxes is not checked, check it and click OK twice to install; otherwise, click Cancel twice to close the control panel. Users of the original release of Windows 95 should download and install the Exchange Update for Windows 95 from **microsoft.com/windows/downloads**. The updated version is more stable and adds some useful features.

In Windows NT 4.0, run the Add/Remove Programs control panel, click the Windows NT Setup tab, and double-click Windows Messaging, and click OK. If either Microsoft Mail or Windows Messaging is unchecked, check it and click OK twice to install; otherwise, click Cancel twice to close the control panel.

If you upgraded to Windows 98 from Windows 95, and there's an Inbox icon on your desktop, skip to step 2. Otherwise, load your Windows 98 CD, run Windows Explorer, navigate to the folder tree to \tools\oldwin95\message\us (or if you're outside the U.S., \tools\oldwin95\message\intl), and double-click the wms application (wms.exe) to install Windows Messaging.

Follow steps 2 through 5 only on the first PC you set up. For the rest of the PCs on the network, skip to step 6.

2. Follow the prompts to create a login profile and install the Microsoft Mail transport protocol. When the Inbox Setup Wizard asks you to enter the path to the postoffice, enter C:\WINDOWS.
3. After the Wizard finishes its work—again, on the first PC *only*—double-click the Microsoft Mail Postoffice control panel, choose Create a New Workgroup Postoffice, click Next, click Browse, select the Windows folder on drive C:, click OK, and click Next. When prompted, enter a mailbox name and password.
4. To create accounts for other mail users on your network, open the Post-office control panel again, click Next twice, enter your password, and click Next. Click the Add User button to create mailboxes and define addresses and passwords for each of the other people on your network (see Figure 11).
5. Run Windows Explorer , right-click the \WINDOWS\WGPO0000 folder and click the Sharing button on the popup menu. Click the Shared As button and assign a Share Name, as described in the last section; this will allow the other PCs on the network to access the postoffice files. You must allow full access. Password protection makes sense only if not everyone on the network has access to e-mail. (The e-mail system has its own password system to prevent users from reading each other's mail.)
6. Follow the prompts to create a login profile and install the Microsoft Mail transport protocol. When the Inbox SetupWizard asks you to enter the path to the postoffice, click Browse, navigate to the postoffice PC under Network Neighborhood, select the Windows\WGPO0000 folder, and click OK (see Figure 12).

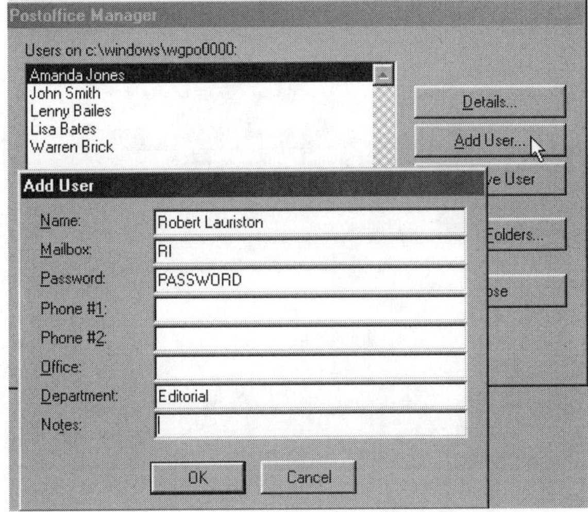

Figure 11

Adding user accounts to a Microsoft Mail postoffice.

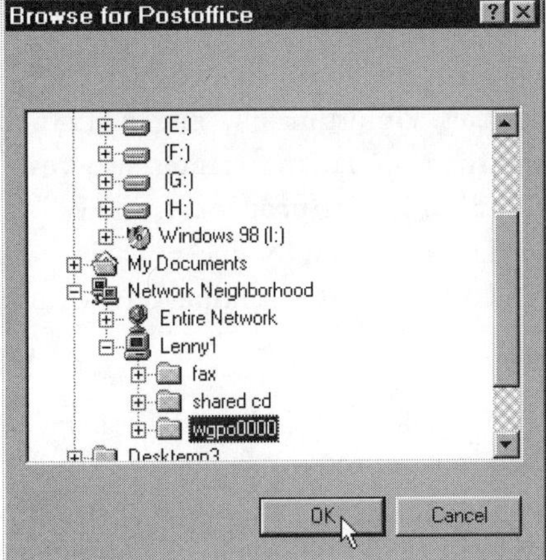

Figure 12

Choosing a Workgroup postoffice.

7. Once you've created the user accounts in the postoffice, and have installed Messaging or Exchange on each PC, your e-mail system should be ready to use. To test it, double-click the Inbox icon on the desktop, enter your password, and choose Compose/New Message. Click "To," select all the users in the list, click "To" (see Figure 13), and click OK. Type something in the Subject field and message area (the white space at the bottom), then click the Send button on the toolbar. When you open the Inbox on the other PCs on the network, each should have a copy of the message.

If for some reason one of the PCs can't see the postoffice, check to make sure it's pointing to the right directory. Right-click the Inbox icon on that PC, choose Properties, select Microsoft Mail in the list of services, and click Properties. Click Browse, navigate to the postoffice PC under Network Neighborhood, select its Windows\ directory, and click OK twice.

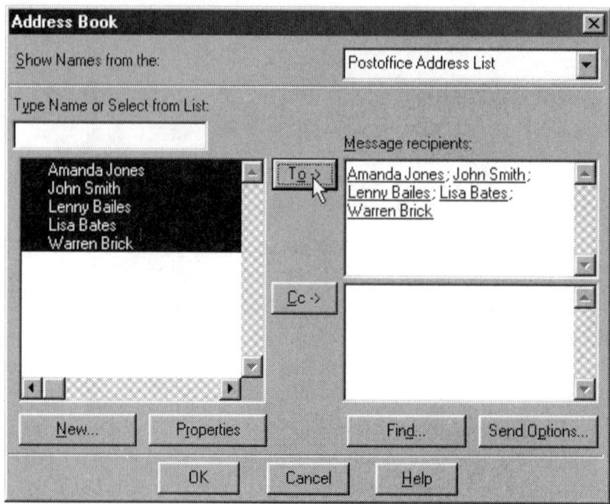

Figure 13

Addressing a message to everyone on the network.

Sharing a Fax Modem

Windows 95 and 98 will let everyone on a network except NT users share a single modem for sending faxes. Unfortunately, only the fax portion of the modem is shared: if you want to share a modem for Internet access, buy a copy of Artisoft's i.Share (**www.artisoft.com/products**), a program that will allow up to 32 PCs to share a single modem, ISDN line, or cable modem. i.Share's street price ranges from around $90 to $240 depending on the number of users.

To share a fax modem:

1. Set up a Microsoft Exchange or Windows Messaging e-mail system as described in the previous section.
2. Make sure Microsoft Fax is installed on the PC that has the modem (see Chapter 24: Use Your PC as a Phone or Fax), and that file sharing is turned on (see "Testing the Network" earlier in this chapter).
3. Double-click the Inbox, choose Tools/Microsoft Fax Tools/Options, and click the Modem tab.
4. Select the modem you want to share in the Available Fax Modems list. Click "Set as Active Fax Modem" and check "Let other people on the network use my modem to send faxes." If you get a dialog box asking which drive the network fax service should use, select the one where Windows is installed (see Figure 14).
5. Click the Properties button (to the right of the check box you enabled in the last step) and assign user access rights and passwords, as appropriate. (See step 3 in "To Share a Folder or Drive" earlier in this chapter.)
6. Click OK and close the Microsoft Fax Tools setup screen.

The shared fax modem will now be available to other workstations on the network.

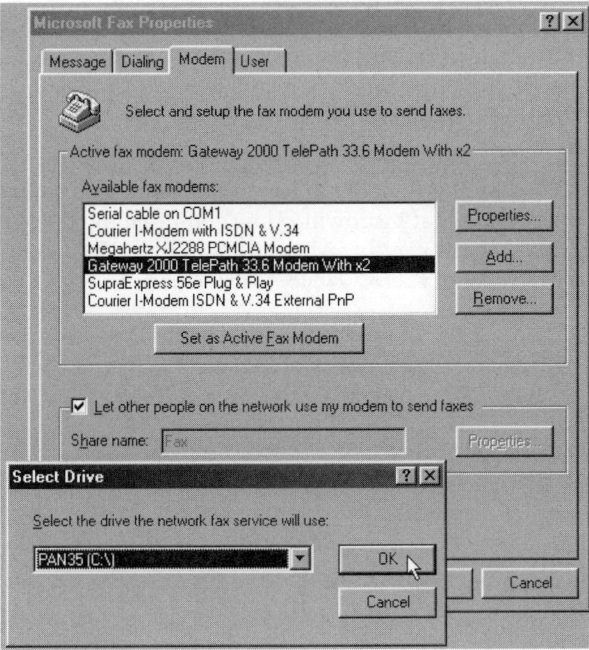

Figure 14

Sharing a Fax Modem.

To use a shared fax modem:

1. You need to know the name of the computer with the shared modem and the modem's share name. You can find them by browsing the Network Neighborhood tree in Windows Explorer.
2. Double-click the Inbox, choose Tools/Microsoft Fax Tools/Options, click the Modem tab, click Add, and double-click Network Fax Server.
3. Unfortunately the usual Browse button is missing from this dialog, so you have to type the path to the shared modem. The path has the form *computer name**share name*, for example, \\Lenny1\Fax. After you've typed the path, click OK to close the dialog.
5. Choose that modem in the Available Fax Modems list, click Set as Active Fax Modem, and click OK.
6. Click OK to exit to the Inbox.

Setting Up a Remote Access Server

If you set up the Remote Access Service (RAS) on one of the PCs on your network, users can connect to the network by modem to access their files. What other services are available depends on how the network is configured: any features that require TCP/IP (like Internet access, in-house Web pages, and some e-mail systems) will be available only if the remote-access server is running NT Server. You can even run applications across a RAS dial-up link, but performance is likely to be unacceptably slow.

To set up a Windows 95/98 PC as a remote-access server:

1. Run Windows Explorer and select Dial-Up Networking in the folder tree. (If you don't see it there, use the Windows Setup tab of the Add/Remove Programs applet to install it.)
2. Choose Connections/Dial-Up Server from the menu (see Figure 15). If you're running Windows 95 and the Connections menu doesn't have that command, add it by downloading and installing the Windows Dial-Up Networking 1.3 Performance and Security Upgrade for Windows 95 from **microsoft.com/windows/downloads**.

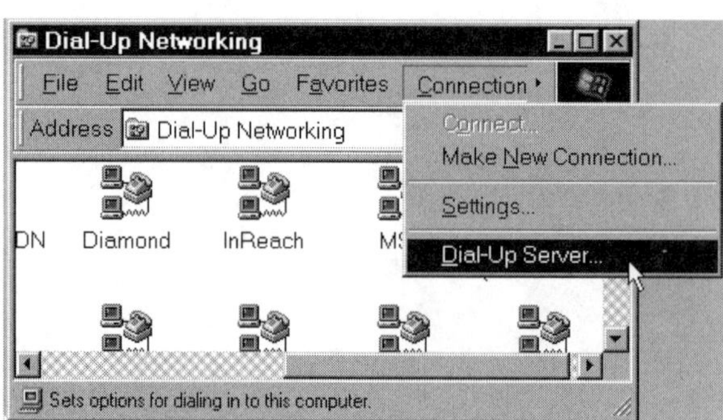

Figure 15

Windows 95/98 Dial-Up Server.

3. The Dial-Up Server window displays a series of tabs, each one representing an installed modem on your computer. If you've got more than one modem, choose the one you want to have handle remote access and click Allow Caller Access. Click Change Password and assign one to prevent any teenage hacker dialing numbers at random from gaining access to your network.

After you close the dialog, a small icon will appear in the taskbar's "tray" to let you know the Dial-Up Server feature is ready and waiting for calls.

To set up a Windows NT Workstation PC as a remote access server:

1. Open the Network control panel, click the Services tab, select Remote Access Service, and click Properties. (If Remote Access Service does not appear on the list, click the Add button and install it. Your PC will probably reboot; after it does, start over with step 1.)
2. Select the modem or other device you want to handle remote access and click Configure (see Figure 16). If you want to use the modem only for people to dial in, select "Receive calls only," if you also want to use to dial out to another remote access server or an Internet service provider, select "Dial out and Receive calls." Then click OK.
3. Click Network and select the protocols available for users dialing in. For each protocol enabled, click the Configure button, choose whether to allow users access to the whole network or only to the PC they're dialing into, and click OK. When you're finished with the Network settings, click OK, then click Continue and follow the prompts to complete setup.

Figure 16

Windows NT Workstation's Remote Access Setup.

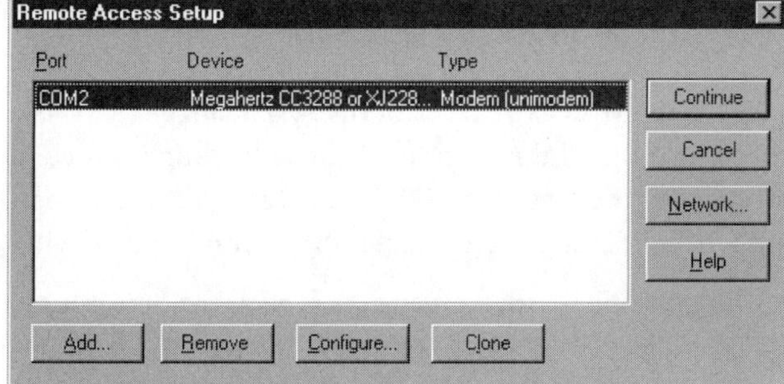

4. To enable dial-up access, run the User Manager (in the Administrative Tools section of the Start menu). Select the users you want to have access, choose User/Properties, click Dialin, check "Grant dialin permission to user," and click OK twice.

You don't have to define separate passwords; dial-up users just use the same passwords they use on the local network. If you haven't been using passwords on your local network, assign them before enabling dial-up access: otherwise the server's an open invitation to teenage hackers, who commonly random-dial numbers looking for insecure servers. Unfortunately a tutorial on using NT's User Manager is outside the scope of this book; see "Network Resources" at the end of this chapter for recommendations on a couple of other books that cover the subject well.

To connect to a remote access server. Setting up a PC to connect to a Dial-Up Server is almost identical to the process of creating a Dial-Up Networking connection to the Internet (described in detail in Chapter 19: Getting On the Internet). The only difference is that on Windows 95/98 computers you need to select NetBEUI and/or IPX/SPX on the Server or Server Type tab, since the Dial-Up Server supports TCP/IP only in Windows NT.

Accessing Your Network from the Internet

If at least one of the PCs on your network is running Windows NT, you can set it up so remote users can access the network from any Windows 95, 98, or NT PC with an Internet connection—a technique Microsoft calls *virtual private networking* (VPN). (That is, you're using the cheap public network of the Internet as a substitute for an expensive private network of leased lines.) This is supposed to be secure: all the data is encrypted and theoretically hacker-proof, or at least sufficiently hacker-resistant that it wouldn't be worth the time and expense to crack.

If you connect to the Internet via America Online or some other service that uses its own software rather than a Dial-Up Networking connection, VPN may not be available.

To set up PC running Windows NT Workstation as a VPN server:

Before you get started, download and install Windows NT 4.0 Service Pack 3, available from **microsoft.com/windows/downloads**. Microsoft recommends that you also install the Point to Point Tunneling Protocol update, discussed in **microsoft.com/support/kb/articles/q189/5/95.asp**. (If Microsoft decides to release a Service Pack 4, that second update will be unnecessary.)

1. Open the Network control panel, click the Services tab, and make sure that Remote Access Service is on the list. (If it's not there, click the Add button and install it. Your PC will probably reboot; after it does, open the Network control panel and continue with step 2.)
2. Click the Protocols tab, click Add, and double-click Point To Point Tunneling Protocol. Follow the prompts to install the driver from the Windows NT CD.
3. The PPTP Configuration dialog appears. Click OK to accept the default Number of Virtual Private Networks. (You might want to change the number if you want to use multiple VPN adapters, for example, for both channels of an ISDN adapter.)
4. Remote Access Setup will open automatically. Click Add, then click OK. This will add VPN1 to the list of ports (see Figure 17).

Figure 17

Enabling VPN in Windows NT.

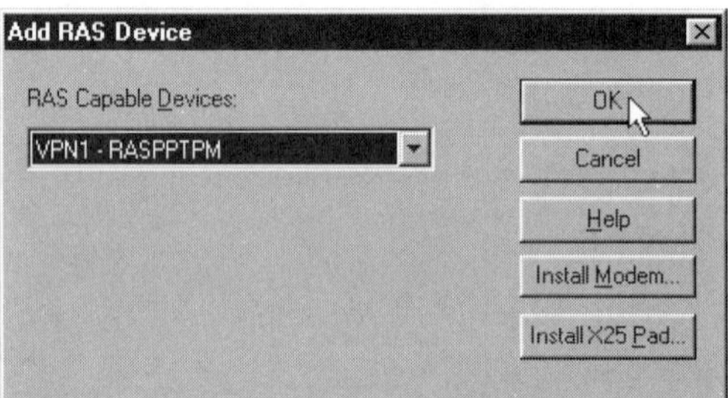

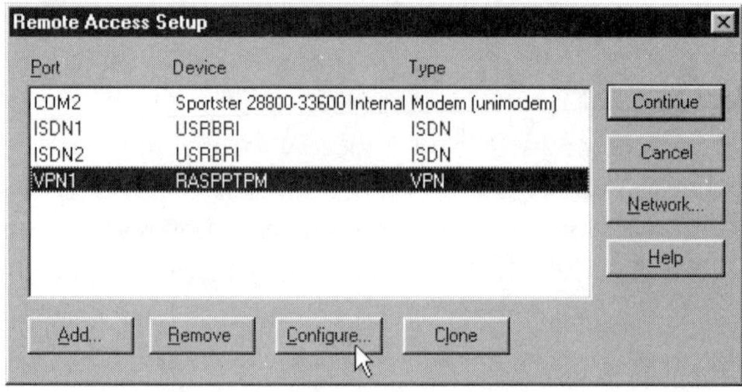

5. Click Configure. If you want to use this PC only as a VPN server to handle connections from the Internet, select "Receive calls only"; if also want to connect to other VPN servers from this PC, choose "Dial out and Receive calls." Then click OK.

6. Click Network, check all the protocols you need, and click OK. Note that users have to log in using NetBEUI or IPX in order to access the entire network; those logging in using only TCP/IP will be able to access only this PC.
7. Click Close. After NT reconfigures your network software, click Yes to let it restart the PC.

If you chose "Receive calls only" or "Dial out and Receive calls," then any time the PC is connected to the Internet the VPN server will be available to remote users who are allowed dial-in access. See step 4 of "To set up a Windows NT Workstation PC as a remote-access server" in the previous section for instructions on allowing access.

To log in, NT users will also need to know the VPN server's workgroup or domain name, and all users will need to know its IP address. If the PC has a permanent "24/7" connection to the Internet, your Internet service provider probably assigned it a fixed IP address when you set up the account. If it's a regular dial-up account, an IP number is probably assigned at random every time you connect; in that case, contact your provider about getting that changed to a fixed number (or an easy-to-remember name, like vpnserver.whatever.com).

To connect to a VPN server from a PC running Windows NT:

Initial setup:

First, follow steps 1–7 in the previous section, *except* in step 5, choose "Dial out only" or, if you also want to use this PC as a VPN server, "Dial out and Receive calls." Then continue with the following steps:

8. Run Dial-Up Networking and click New to create a phonebook entry for the VPN server. Enter an appropriate name (like "VPN server") in "Entry name," and the VPN server's IP number (or name) in "Phone number." Make sure "Use Telephony dialing properties" and "Use another port if busy" are unchecked (see Figure 18).

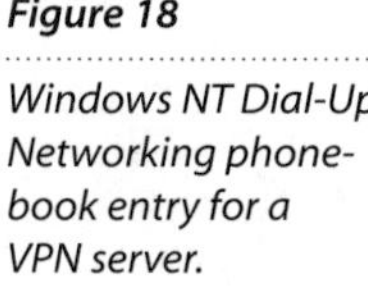

Figure 18

Windows NT Dial-Up Networking phonebook entry for a VPN server.

9. Click the Server tab. Check all the protocols you want to use, and uncheck all those you don't want to use. Note that if you check only the TCP/IP protocol, you'll have access only to the drives and other resources on the PC you're dialing into, at least if it's running NT Workstation. (VPN servers running on other operating systems, like NetWare or NT Server, may not have that limitation.) Click OK to save the phonebook entry.

Making a connection:

1. Connect to the Internet through your ISP with your regular Dial-Up Networking phonebook entry.
2. After the connection is established, choose the VPN connection you created in the previous section from the phonebook list, and click Dial. Enter your username and password, enter the VPN server's workgroup or domain name in the Domain field, and then click the Connect button (see Figure 19).

Figure 19:

Connecting to a VPN server in Windows NT.

To connect to a VPN server from a PC running Windows 95/98:

Initial setup:

1. If you're running Windows 95, open the System control panel. If the version number is 4.00.950 or 4.00.950a, download and install the upgrade discussed in step 2 of "To set up a Windows 95/98 PC as a remote access server" earlier in this chapter.
2. Open the Network control panel, click Add, and double-click Adapter. Select Microsoft in the left column (Manufacturers), Microsoft Virtual Private Networking Adapter in the right column (Network Adapters), and click OK twice. Follow the prompts to complete installation.
3. Open Dial-Up Networking, and double-click Make New Connection. Enter an appropriate name (like "VPN server") under "Type a name," and choose Microsoft VPN Adapter from the Select a Device list. Then click Next.
4. Enter the IP address (or name) of your VPN server (see Figure 20).

Figure 20

Setting up a VPN connection in Windows 95/98.

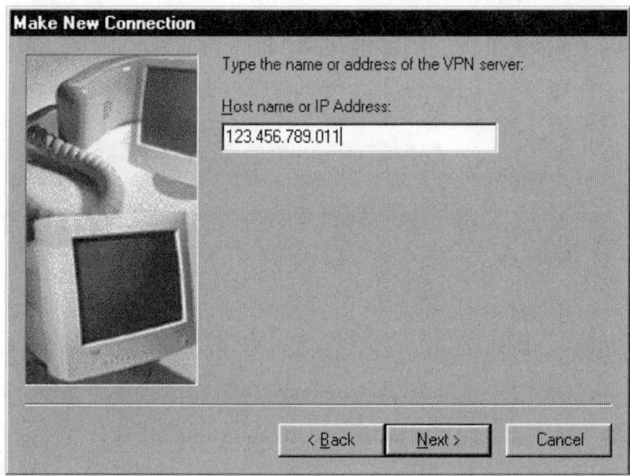

5. Click Next and Finish to add the VPN connection to the Dial-Up Networking folder.
6. Right-click the new connection, choose Properties, and click the Server Types tab. Check all protocols you want to use, and uncheck all those you don't want to use. Note that if you check only the TCP/IP protocol, you'll have access only to the drives and other resources on the PC you're dialing into, at least if it's running NT Workstation. (VPN servers running on other operating systems, like NetWare or NT Server, may not have that limitation). Click OK to save your changes.

Making a connection:

1. Connect to the Internet through your ISP with your regular Dial-Up Networking connection.
2. Open Dial-Up Networking and run the VPN connection you created in the previous section. Enter the username and password for your account on the LAN, then click the Connect button.

Troubleshooting VPN connections

VPN is very poorly documented and kind of flaky, so you may encounter problems. For example, when trying to connect to the VPN server I used for testing, occasionally I'd get an error message saying that the password was wrong—but I'd try again with the same password and get in. Currently, the only practical tip I can suggest is to experiment with the different protocols.

Microsoft's Web site has some information on using VPN. To look for it, go to **search.microsoft.com**, check Support & the Knowledge Base, type VPN under "Enter your search words," and click Search Now. (If you don't find any articles, try another browser, if you've got one, or try again another time.)

When Do You Need a Dedicated Server?

As noted earlier, certain applications benefit from, and others demand, a dedicated server: a PC devoted exclusively to providing network services. Here are the main reasons for setting up a dedicated server:

- **To run a multiuser database or accounting package.** Install a shared database on somebody's PC, and if that person's system crashes, the shared database goes down as well. Ditto if somebody forgets and flips the "off" switch. Installing the database on a dedicated server greatly reduces the likelihood of system crashes. In addition, server-based databases offer *transaction tracking,* which prevents half-completed operations from corrupting database files when crashes do occur.
- **To provide maximum network reliability.** Even if an operating system is fairly reliable, power outages, disk failures, and other unexpected events can still crash the network. The best way to prevent such disasters is to schedule frequent system backups and dedicate a server to running an operating system, such as Windows NT, that offers additional crash-protection features.
- **To simplify network administration.** It's often faster and easier to install a single shared copy of an application on a file server instead of installing a separate copy on each workstation. Ditto software upgrades. The bigger your network, the more time this approach will save.
- **To improve performance.** Dedicating a server to network applications keeps operations from slowing to a crawl, since no workstation will have to divide its energies by running shared databases and the e-mail system while simultaneously crunching the local user's huge spreadsheet file.
- **To provide Internet gateway, e-mail, and in-house Web services.** A single "intranet" server can act as an Internet gateway for all of the other computers on the network, and if you wish it can also provide Internet-style local services, like e-mail and a private Web site accessible only from your private network. Windows 95 and Windows 98 are not suitable for this task: it requires a more industrial-strength operating system like Linux, Windows NT, Novell NetWare, Solaris, or Warp OS/2 Server.
- **To connect with a wide area network.** Just as Ethernet links PCs into a local network (LAN), high-speed leased lines hook two or more LANs into a wide area network (WAN). Any workstation on any LAN in a WAN enjoys access to some or all of the other LANs' services, in effect creating a single network. Connecting to a WAN doesn't always require a separate server—sometimes the file server or a specialized piece of hardware called a *router box* can handle the job.

- **To run client-server applications.** This is definitely not do-it-yourself territory. Client-server databases like *Oracle* and *SQL Server* run on a dedicated *database server,* which might be a fast PC, but could just as easily be a high-end UNIX server or even a mainframe. Another client-server application that merits a dedicated server is *Lotus Notes*.

Server Operating Systems

If you do dedicate a server, you may want to install something more robust than Windows 95 or 98. Here's a brief guide to the most popular alternatives.

Windows 95 or 98. Plain old everyday Windows doesn't have any special server features, but it works fine, and the price is right. You don't have to pay per-user license fees the way you do with NT Server, and so far as I've been able to determine there's no software limit on how many users connect to a Windows 95/98 server (as there is in NT Workstation).

Windows NT Workstation. Despite its name, NT Workstation is actually excellent server for certain purposes, which isn't surprising considering that it's the exact same code as NT Server. For marketing reasons, Microsoft has disabled certain features in the Workstation version, and has coded some of its add-on packages, like its Web server and the high-end Exchange Server mail management application, so they will run only on NT Server—but other companies' server applications will, in many cases, run just fine.

The main restriction Microsoft's put on NT Workstation is a 10-client limit on file and print sharing. That is, no more than ten other PCs at a time can access it—which isn't a practical limitation until you get more than ten other PCs on your network. Some non-Microsoft server applications pay no attention to that limit and will handle any number of users, though that's a violation of NT Workstation's software license. (This is a fairly hypocritical practice, since it's impossible to use Microsoft's File and Print Services for NetWare without violating similar limitations in Novell's software license.)

Microsoft claims that NT Workstation won't perform well as a server, but independent tests have found it actually performs quite well. *PC Week*, for example, found that Netscape Enterprise Server 2.0 was only about 15% faster on NT Server than on NT Workstation.

Windows NT Server. This version of NT costs more, but it will run all of Microsoft's server applications, and you can buy additional licenses to expand the number of users who can access it. Another big plus is support for Macintoshes, including automatic translation of filenames so that PCs and Macs can share the same directories. NT Server has many features that make it easier to administer than NT Workstation; however, few of those differences will be very noticeable if your network's got only ten PCs. NT Server comes with Internet gateway software built in, so all PCs on a network can share a single net connection, though if you have no other reason for buying NT Server it's cheaper to use i.Share (see "Sharing a Fax Modem" earlier in this chapter).

NetWare. For large PC-based client-server networks, Novell's *NetWare* is a worthy competitor to Windows NT Server, particularly if your primary requirements are file and application sharing. Common wisdom among network professionals is that NetWare "scales better" than Windows NT. That is, in environments with hundreds of computers it tends to be more stable and easier to work with. NetWare's centralized network management tools make network administration efficient, but that doesn't mean it's easy: even the sharpest PC user faces a steep learning curve. To handle the job, most big companies hire an administrator, while smaller companies often hire a consultant or a service bureau—a significant, ongoing expense either way.

Linux. For Web and e-mail servers, a free version of UNIX called Linux is becoming extremely popular, largely because of its modest hardware requirements. Where a Windows NT or NetWare server might need a late-model Pentium with 64MB of RAM, a lot of Linux servers are running happily on old 16MB 386 and 486 PCs that might otherwise be gathering dust. Installing and configuring Linux is something of a black art, but it's frequently sold in "turnkey" servers that have all the necessary software preloaded and ready to run.

Bullet-Proofing Your Server

Nothing puts a whole office in a worse mood than a crashed server, so it's worth spending money to make it reliable. Here are some of the most common devices and techniques for protecting servers and their data:

- **Uninterruptible power supplies** use batteries to keep the server's juice flowing for a few minutes in the event of a power failure, while users are notified to save their work and log off. (See Chapter 9: Protect Your Data, for more info.)

- **Drive arrays** are multiple disks (four, typically) that act like a single big drive. If one disk breaks down, the others collectively "remember" all the data on the broken drive, so users can still access the information. In many cases you don't even have to turn off the server to replace the failed drive—you can just "hot-swap" a replacement. Drive arrays also perform better than single disks, so they can handle more users before performance starts to degrade.

- **Server mirroring**, the ultimate in fault tolerance, uses twin servers connected by a high-speed fiber optic link. When the primary server fails, the backup kicks in, and users can keep working without interruption.

PC to Mac and Back

Outside of the Macintosh file and print services built into NT Server, Windows networking pretty much ignores the Apple crowd. If your network includes both PCs and Macs, here are some products and tips to help get them connected.

Sharing Printers

The basic solution to sharing a printer among both PCs and Macs is to connect the printer to an Ethernet hub rather than to a PC's printer port. In that situation, the Mac can talk directly to the printer without Windows getting in the way. Some printers, particularly more expensive lasers, have Ethernet ports built in. If the printer you want to share doesn't have an Ethernet port, you can add one by buying a print server, like one of Hewlett-Packard's JetDirect boxes (**hp.com/net_printing/jetdirect**).

That leaves the question of where to get drivers. Most PostScript printers (discussed in Chapter 6: Printers) will come with both Windows and Mac drivers; the same goes for most Epson inkjets. For those PostScript printers that don't come with Mac drivers, you can usually get away with using one of the LaserWriter drivers that come with the Mac OS.

To access other PC printers from networked Macs, you'll probably need a copy of PowerPrint or PowerPrint Pro, Mac programs that include special drivers for PC printers. See **www.infowave.net/printing_solutions** for more information and a list of supported printers.

Sharing and Converting Files

If you've got NT Server, supporting Macs is no big deal. You can easily set up Mac services and make the server appear on Mac desktops just as it does on Windows PCs.

If you don't have NT Server, check out "Dave," a program that turns Macintoshes into equal citizens on Windows networks, letting Mac users access shared PC folders and printers, as well as Windows e-mail. It also permits Windows users to mount shared Mac/PC directories and print to Macintosh PostScript printers. You can download a trial version from **www.thursby.com**.

When you've got PCs and Macs on a network, the different file formats in use on the two platforms can sometimes lead to confusion. If you frequently run into such problems on the PC side, consider picking up a copy of DataViz Conversions Plus (**www.dataviz.com**), a utility that can convert Mac-only formats into something one of your Windows applications should recognize.

Without a Net

Macs purchased in recent years or upgraded to a recent version of Mac OS have no problem reading PC diskettes, but if you try to read a Mac floppy in your PC, Windows will find it unreadable and ask if you want to format it. If you'd like the convenience of reading Mac floppies on your PC, get a copy of MacOpener, also from DataViz.

Network Resources

Maximizing Windows 98, Lenny Bailes (ISBN: 0078825393). Around 60 pages of my 900-page book are devoted to more detailed and technical discussions of many of the subjects covered in this chapter, as well as more esoteric topics I didn't have room to get into here.

Windows NT 4.0 Connectivity Guide, Richard Grace (ISBN: 0764531603), ***Windows NT Workstation 4 in 24 Hours***, Martin Kenley et al. (ISBN: 0672310112). Either of these books can help you master Windows NT's somewhat complicated and confusing approach to network security.

Network Support

Finding good network support at a reasonable price can be difficult. If a consultant set up your network and then went out of business (unfortunately a common occurrence), you may not even know where to start looking. Fortunately, the Web can be a tremendously valuable network support resource, supplying you with hardware and software information, driver updates, bug fixes, and detailed technical information to resolve specific network configuration problems.

Here are pointers to useful network software, technical support and information resources for Windows 95/98, Windows NT, UNIX/Linux, and Novell networking.

`www.3com.com` 3Com's Web site contains a large catalog of network equipment that you can order directly online. This site also contains a glossary of networking terms and tutorials on setting up network hardware.

`microsoft.com/hwtest/hcl` This page on the Microsoft Web site contains a hardware compatibility database you can search to see whether a particular Ethernet card will work with your version of Windows.

`winfiles.com/howto` Scroll down to the "Windows Networking Articles" header, where you'll find useful tutorials on connecting to the Internet over a local network, networking over the Internet, setting up a dial-up server, sharing a single net connection among several machines, and other topics.

support.novell.com The homepage for technical support for Novell NetWare, including a technical reference database and pointers to support files, driver updates, and service upgrades.

linux.org Introduction to the Linux operating system with pointers to online Linux resources. (Don't confuse this site with **linux.com**.)

support.microsoft.com/support Choose Windows NT Server under "My search is about," type a few words describing the information you want under "My question is," and click Go. If you don't find what you're looking for, try again using different words—for some reason, Microsoft's search routine often fails to find relevant articles that are actually in the database.

26

Health and Safety

by Anita Amirrezvani, Robert Luhn, and Wendy M. Grossman

This chapter was originally written by Anita Amirrezvani and Robert Luhn, and updated for the third edition by Wendy M. Grossman.

In This Chapter

Living well is an art, and so is using computers. Most of this book focuses on the intricacies of choosing hardware and using software, but in this chapter we show you how to minimize the negative effects your PC can have on you and the environment.

If your workstation is poorly designed, using a PC can tire you, hurt you, or even result in debilitating physical ailments. The worst computer-related problems, like carpal tunnel syndrome and tendinitis, can cause severe pain in the hands and arms, requiring physical therapy or surgery and long absences from work. This chapter explains how to avoid such health hazards.

Then we turn to another pressing problem: the environment. Your personal computer may seem sleek and benignly high tech, but it contributes to our environmental woes by gobbling up power, paper, and other resources. Fortunately, it's pretty easy to use your PC in an environmentally sound way, and you can save money in the bargain.

This chapter shows you how to:

- avoid your monitor's radiation
- protect your hands and arms from cumulative trauma
- create an ergonomic workstation
- save paper and the environment
- reduce power consumption and costs
- find a happy home for orphan PCs

Health and Safety Guide

Is there more to safe, comfortable computing than following your mother's admonition to "sit up straight"? You bet. Good posture can mitigate back problems, but it won't help your eyes, nor will it save your wrists or hands from painful injury. Read on for some down-to-earth advice about protecting your whole body from the perils of the information factory.

Monitors: Preventing Eyestrain and Fatigue

We are a nation of viewers. The average American watches TV for an astonishing six hours per day; PC workers may spend even longer in front of a monitor. All that computer work can cause physical discomfort—blurred vision, headaches, fatigue, or muscle strain—if ergonomic considerations are ignored. Here are the key factors to keep in mind when using your monitor:

- **Make sure lighting is indirect.** Place your PC at a right angle to windows so the sun doesn't shine from behind or directly into your eyes. You may also need curtains or blinds to control light during the day; alternatively, you may be able to shade the screen with a partition or bookcase.
- **Control artificial lighting.** Standard office lighting is too bright for computing. To decrease lighting levels, you can buy overhead lighting with *parabolic louvers,* honeycomblike baffles that help diffuse light. If you're stuck with direct overhead lighting, arrange your work area so the computer is positioned between rows of overhead lights. If fluorescent lights are too bright, simply remove every other tube. With overall lighting levels lower, you may want to add bright task lighting, such as a desk lamp, to make it easy to read printed materials. (See Figure 1.)

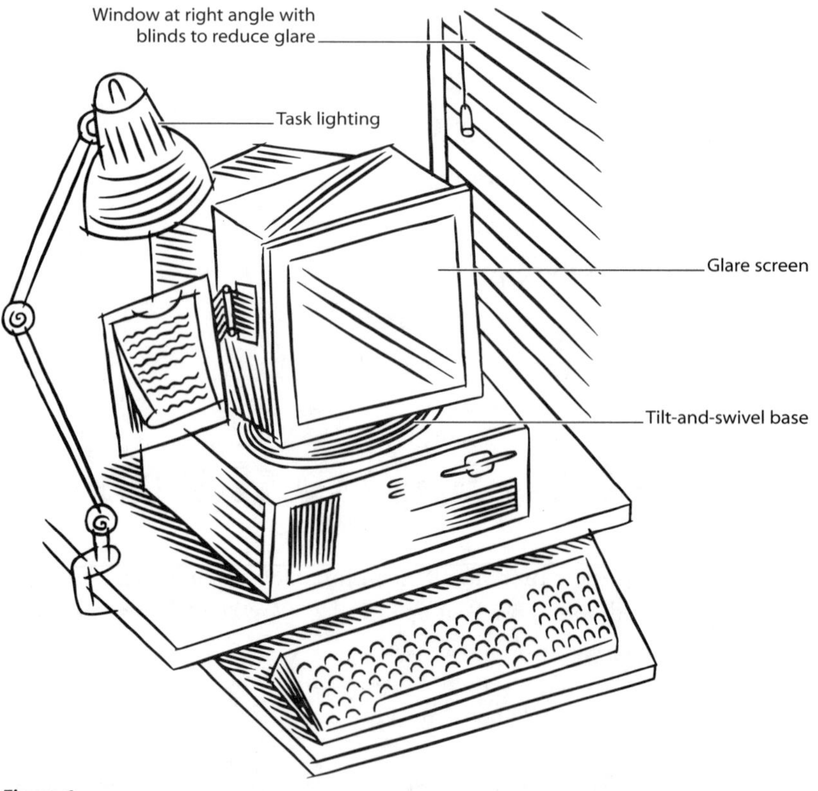

Figure 1

How to reduce eye fatigue.

Set your workstation up like this, and you can cut eyestrain significantly. One factor you may not be able to control is overhead lighting-if it's too strong, you might consider loosening a couple of fluorescent tubes.

- **Customize your display.** Buy a monitor that's big enough so that when you position it three feet away you can see the data on your screen clearly at the resolution you plan to use. While 21-inch and larger monitors are primarily appropriate only for people doing graphics-intensive work such as CAD-CAM and professional desktop publishing, 17-inch and 19-inch monitors are more reasonably priced and can make long hours staring at tiny details on the screen less stressful. Whatever your monitor size, experiment with screen fonts and the zoom features in software so you can read comfortably, and adjust the colors to combinations that give good contrast and are restful (for example, avoid red on blue because it makes the letters seem to float).
- **Avoid glare.** Most monitors (all-in-one machines like laptops and the iMac excepted) have a tilt-and-swivel base; take advantage of this to turn the screen away from glare and tilt the monitor to the most comfortable viewing angle. Look for anti-reflective and anti-glare coatings, which help ensure that your screen is clear and readable even in bright light. If possible, check monitors under a variety of lighting conditions before you buy. On older monitors lacking these coatings, glare screens, which mount on the front of a monitor, can be a big help. There are three types: mesh, plastic, and glass. Mesh screens are the least expensive, while glass filters are best at keeping the image sharp as they reduce glare. All types tend to darken your monitor, so you'll need to make appropriate adjustments in screen contrast, brightness, and other lighting.
- **Avoid fuzziness.** Your monitor should always display characters that are crisp and sharp. If you notice blurring or distortion that can't be eliminated with the brightness and contrast controls, you may need a new monitor, or you may need to adjust hidden controls. A handy utility called DisplayMate can help you identify and fix monitor problems (see "Give Your Monitor a Tune-Up with DisplayMate" in Chapter 5: Monitors, Etc.). Clean your screen occasionally using a soft, dry cloth to remove the dust and dirt that collects.
- **Avoid flicker.** Monitor flicker is caused by a slow *refresh rate* (the number of times the monitor repaints the screen per second). Sometimes flicker is undetectable, but it can still fatigue your eyes after a few hours. Look for a monitor and graphics card with a refresh rate of at least 70 Hz. Remember to check the refresh rate at all the resolutions you plan to use, since vendors use a lower refresh rate at higher resolutions. Whatever you do, never buy a monitor that uses interlaced scanning at your preferred resolution—this causes the worst flicker of all.

Staying Out of the Rays

The jury is still out on whether the low-frequency radiation emitted by monitors causes higher miscarriage or cancer rates. Nonetheless, just about all monitors now sold in the U.S. meet the Swedish government's MPR-II low-radiation standard. A new standard called TCO, also developed in Sweden, is even tougher, with tighter specifications for picture quality and controls, visual ergonomics, and electromagnetic emissions. The latest version, TCO99, was announced in October 1998 and requires massive reductions in magnetic and electric fields, reduced heat emission, lack of interference with the displayed image by external magnetic fields of other equipment or components in the same room, and reduced energy consumption and pollution. The first compliant models are available from Nokia and ViewSonic, but expect this standard to spread.

If you want to limit your exposure to ELF (extremely low frequency) or VLF (very low frequency) electromagnetic fields, here are some additional suggestions:

- **Keep your distance.** The strongest emissions come from the *back* of a monitor. Make sure you're not surrounded by an army of monitors directing their rays at you from their backs and sides. Also, since rays are most intense close to the monitor (remember how your mother told you not to sit right in front of the TV set?), try to sit at least three feet away from your monitor.
- **Use LCD screens.** The liquid crystal display screens that come on laptops and are now appearing on the market separately as space-saving flat screens do not give off the radiation common to TVs and monitors built with vacuum tubes. They also consume less power. However, LCD screens are still much more expensive, though prices are coming down.

Eye Care

The eye loves variety, but PC users usually spend most of their time focusing on a single object at close range. Here's how to reduce fatigue:

- **Look away from your PC often,** preferably into the distance. Blink frequently to moisten your eyes. To relax, close your eyes and cover them for a few moments with your palms.
- **Buy an antistatic cleaner or screen** to help repel the dust that gathers on your monitor, which can irritate your eyes as well as blur the display.

- **Get regular checkups** to ensure the health of your eyes, and keep your doctor informed about your working conditions. A growing number of optometrists understand the special problems of computer users and offer special glasses for those who do a lot of screen work and have poor vision.

Input Devices: Protecting Hands and Arms

The hand is a small miracle, precise enough to do the most intricate brain surgery or chisel a diamond out of a rock. But it also has limits. Any task involving awkward twisting, bending, repetition, or a fixed position—whether it's driving a screw, cutting meat, or typing data—can cause serious discomfort and even physiological damage.

Millions of Americans now work on computers, which explains the increasing prevalence of a group of occupational hazards called repetitive strain injuries (RSIs). Though RSI is not solely a condition of computer workers, the Bureau of Labor Statistics says that more days are lost to RSI than any other workplace injury, and most of those days are keyboard related. These injuries cause pain in the muscles, nerves, or tendons, and they can be disabling or even crippling. Some victims aren't able to hold their children, drive a car, or even lift a coffee cup. Workers suing for compensation, however, have had mixed results: The scientific evidence is still muddy, in part because many RSI claimants do not have easily identifiable tissue damage that can back up their claims. It is obviously much better to avoid the condition altogether.

Computer users suffer from several common RSIs, which usually affect the hand, wrist, or arm. Many professionals call these *cumulative trauma disorders* because they take time to appear, and they worsen if left untreated. See a doctor immediately if you feel pain, tingling, or numbness in the arms, wrists, or hands—and follow these precautionary measures to help stay injury-free.

- **Adjust your keyboard to fit your body.** Your wrists should always be in a neutral position (see Figure 2). To accomplish this, position your keyboard at a height that allows your wrists to remain straight; your hands should drop gently onto the keyboard as if you were a pianist. Many keyboards have feet that let you make adjustments to their height for maximum comfort; some radical variations on the standard keyboard design may also suit you (see the "Ergonomic Keyboards" section of Chapter 7: Input Devices, for some examples). Wrist rests—cushions that you place between you and your keyboard—can also help keep your wrists relaxed (as long as you don't use them while you type), but they're not for everyone. Resting your wrists and bending your hands upward can result in prolonged pressure or bending that can cause RSI.

- **Mouse carefully.** Most people don't realize how much tension and strain in the hand, arm, shoulder, and neck are caused by mouse use. If possible, learn to swap hands to even out the load. Also, try different shapes and consider other types of pointer devices such as a mouse pen, trackball, touchpad, digitizer tablet, or weirder options like Hunter Digital's foot-operated NoHands mouse, the joysticklike Anir ergonomic mouse, or Origin's HeadMouse, any of which may feel more natural and relaxed. Clean the mouse or tracker ball periodically to keep it moving smoothly and predictably.
- **Install a software program** such as RSI Rest (available from **`shareware.com`**), Typewatch, or RSI Break (both available from **`www.tifaq.com`**) that reminds you to take breaks at set intervals or after typing/mousing for a specified length of time. This helps not only in preventing RSI but in reducing eye and biomechanical strain.

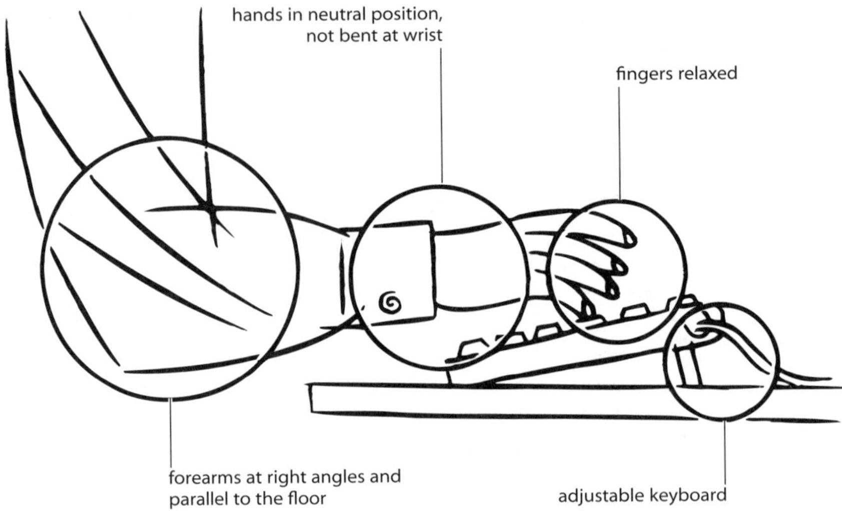

Figure 2

Keyboard common sense.

A good typing angle and an adjustable keyboard reduce wear and tear on the wrists and hands. Note that wrist rests are not a cure-all; if they make your hands bend at all, they can actually hurt.

- **Rest to avoid injury.** Most health professionals recommend a break every two hours—or if your work is keyboard intensive, every 45 minutes. Even while you're working, take advantage of opportunities to relax, such as while your PC is loading a program or recalculating a spreadsheet, or break up your workload by switching from one type of task to another (for example, making some phone calls between bouts of typing). Some workers rest their forearms on padded armrests to chill out.
- **Work more efficiently.** Learn your program's shortcut keys so you can navigate through your files with fewer keystrokes. If you use the same text frequently, such as your name and address, create boilerplate files or templates to avoid retyping the same information. Automate frequent program tasks with macros.
- **Get a headset.** Keep your body aligned properly by using a headset instead of a standard telephone handset. If you type while on the phone, use a speakerphone or a headset rather than squeezing the receiver between your head and shoulder. If those alternatives aren't available, get a shoulder rest to clip or stick to the handset (these are easily found in office supply stores), but that will only reduce the strain on your neck, not eliminate it.
- **Do simple exercises to reduce muscular tension.** Rotate your shoulders or make big circles with your arms to get circulation going. Massage your hands and forearms, gently flex your wrists up and down, or clench your fists for a few seconds and then stretch out your fingers.

- **Don't wait for problems to worsen.** At the first sign of discomfort in your hands, wrists, or arms, contact a knowledgeable medical professional. Waiting could cost you your livelihood.
- **Consider alternatives to typing, like speech recognition and scanning.** These can't yet supplant the keyboard entirely, but they can reduce the amount of time you have to spend typing. See Chapter 7: Input Devices, for more on these alternatives.
- **Check out alternative keyboard designs.** .In the future, we may be able to interact with computers solely by talking, but today some typing is unavoidable. Alternative keyboards may provide a solution if you're uncomfortable with standard designs. Some are radically different than typical keyboards and require learning a new way to type. Combined with exercises and a well-designed workstation, however, they may help keep debilitating RSIs at bay (for more on alternative keyboards, see the "Keyboards" section of Chapter 7: Input Devices).

Workstations: Saving Your Back and Neck

If we were all built the same, workstation design would be simple. But since human anatomy is so varied, each workstation needs to be individually tailored. That's the single most important factor in preventing musculoskeletal problems such as back, neck, or arm pain. When you find your perfect setup, make sure it also includes room to change positions and make adjustments: few people are comfortable for long hours in a fixed position. Think of your workstation as a whole system: Changing one element may mean having to adjust others so your whole body is comfortable.

When you use your PC, your neck should be straight, your shoulders relaxed, your elbows by your sides, your forearms and thighs approximately parallel to the floor, your wrists neutral and relaxed, not twisted or bent, your feet resting flat on the floor or on a foot rest. Here are some tips for positioning your equipment (see Figure 3) to maintain good working posture and reduce physical stress:

- **Position your monitor.** Make sure the top of your monitor is at eye level, or slightly below, to maintain a straight back and neck. If the monitor is too low, put a book underneath it, buy a stand, or raise the shelf if you have an adjustable workstation. The usual solution, placing the monitor on top of the PC's base, typically raises the monitor too high, straining the neck.
- **Purchase a document stand.** If you frequently refer to documents as you use your PC, maintain your alignment by positioning a stand at approximately the same height and distance as your monitor.
- **Position your keyboard.** Along with placing your keyboard so your wrists are relaxed and straight, when accessing faraway keys remember to move your entire hand rather than twisting your wrists. You should also keep

commonly used accessories like your telephone, Rolodex, or reference books within easy reach.

- **Don't ignore your legs.** The space underneath your desk is just as important as what's on top. Remove obstructions near your legs or feet; you don't want your thighs jammed against the desk or to be unable to stretch your legs.
- **Compensate for older desks.** Older desks are usually too high for computing. If you can't buy a new workstation with a lower shelf to hold the keyboard, try raising your chair or adding a keyboard drawer. A footrest can take pressure off your knees and back; even a phone book or a ream of paper can do the trick.

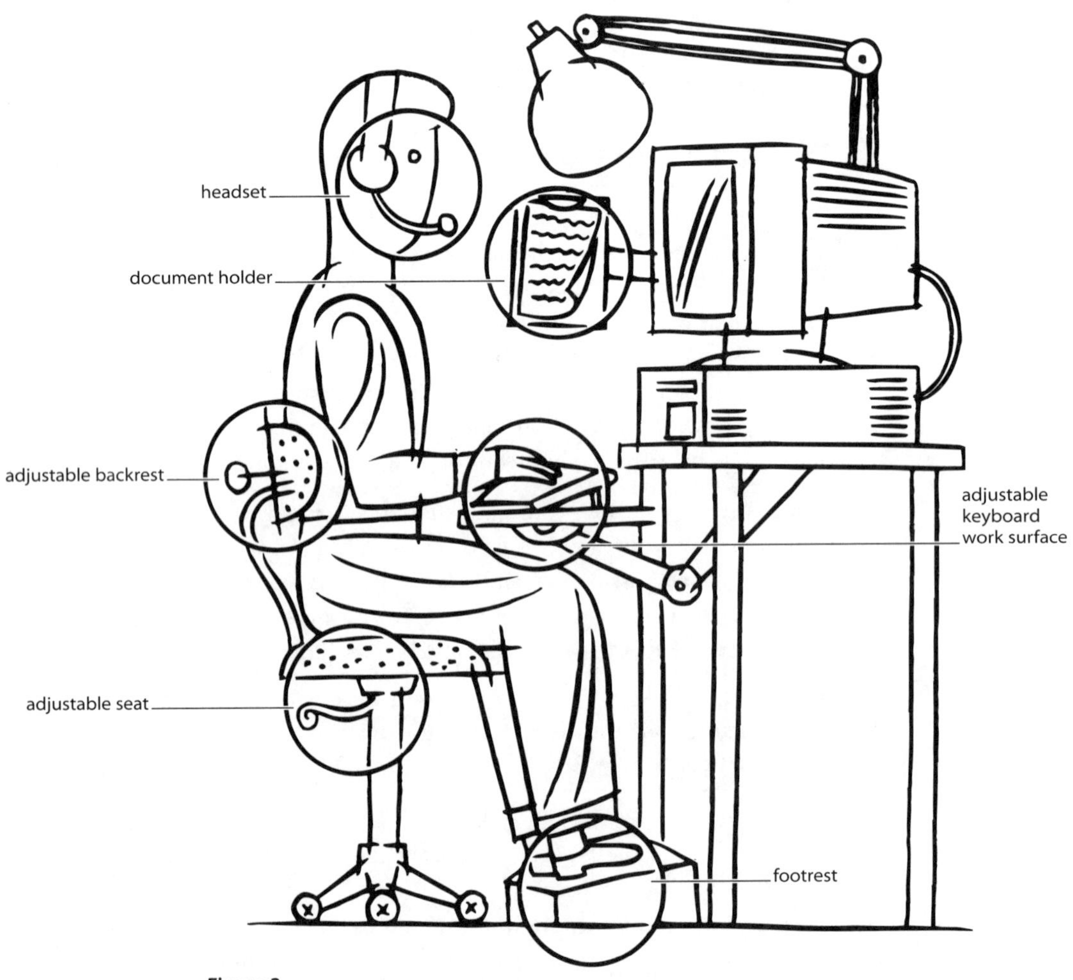

Figure 3

The well-designed workstation.

Yes, sitting up straight helps, but so does the right hardware. An adjustable chair and keyboard drawer help you tailor your workstation to fit your body. For your neck's sake, keep the top of your monitorís display area at eye level or a bit below.

I Think, Therefore I Sit

Your chair is critical. Look for good construction, good padding, and as many adjustable components as possible. For proper positioning of your hands on the keyboard, the chair should adjust easily up or down. A *pneumatic lift* is recommended so you can raise or lower your chair without getting up. The seat itself should be adjustable and padded; it's best if the front is rounded to take pressure off the backs of your knees. Armrests, if any, should be padded and should be adjustable in height or, ideally, flip out of the way altogether for extended periods of typing.

- **Support your back.** The best chairs for computing have an adjustable backrest, with plenty of support for your lower back. If your chair doesn't offer enough support, buy a lumbar support cushion to help out.
- **Move the chair instead of your body.** If your chair swivels, you won't have to twist your body to reach things. The chair should also be on wheels so you can travel with the chair instead of bending or twisting. Five-legged chairs are recommended for improved stability.
- **Test various chairs to get the perfect fit.** Since most large corporations buy several types of chairs, ask your facilities manager if you can test the options. If you're buying for yourself, look for a store that specializes in ergonomically designed chairs. If you need to cut costs, buy a cheap desk rather than compromise on the chair.
- **Buy a foot rest if your feet don't reach the floor**. Dangling feet strain your back and can lead to back problems. If the right height for typing means your feet can't rest flat on the floor, use a foot rest adjusted to a comfortable height.
- **Try standing.** Some people feel that standing reduces pressure on the back. In that case, put the PC on a stand on the floor and adjust shelving or work surfaces to accommodate the monitor and keyboard at appropriate heights. Movable arms that clamp to your desk and hold the monitor and keyboard separately allow you to switch between positions.
- **Exercise often.** Try to follow a regular exercise program that utilizes different muscles than those you use at work. Overall fitness helps your general health, counteracts stiffness, improves circulation, and makes your body better able to recover from the strain of being held still under stress for so many hours.

Other Hazards

Here are a few more miscellaneous tips on keeping you and your PC healthy.

- **Keep laser printers and photocopiers at a distance.** Both laser printers and photocopiers give off ozone formed in the laser's high-voltage printing process as well as paper and toner dust. Follow your manufacturer's instructions for maintaining internal filters and cleaning, and avoid sitting next to the machines' outlet vents.

- **Don't eat, drink, or smoke near your computer.** Smoke leaves a film on the computer screen that makes the display harder to read. Crumbs get into your keyboard's mechanism and gum it up, making it harder to type and sometimes causing keys to stick. Liquids can short out any piece of computer equipment, including your keyboard.
- **Keep your equipment well ventilated.** Do not block the vent holes on monitors or the fans on printers and computers. Overheating severely reduces the life of electronic components and can be a fire hazard.
- **Tidy up electrical cords and cables.** Masses of tangled cables can be dangerous; if you trip on them, both you and your computer can be damaged.

Health and Safety Resources

tco-info.com Lists monitors compliant with the tough TCO standard for emissions.

www.health.com/weight/exercise/index.html has a good collection of information on exercising, equipment buying advice, and a planner to help you design an exercise program.

misc.health.injuries.rsi, **misc**, **misc.health.injuries.rsi.moderated**, **sci.med.occupational** Newsgroups for the discussion of RSI and other occupational injuries. Experienced sufferers and medical personnel offer good help and advice and post the latest news and research. (See Chapter 22: Online Discussions: Newsgroups, Etc., for instructions on accessing newsgroups.)

www.rsinomore.com Illinois-based VDT Solutions offers training, newsletters, and archives of articles and information on ergonomics issues (especially RSI) and other resources. (*VDT* stands for *video display terminal,* an old-fashioned term for a computer keyboard and monitor.)

tifaq.com The Typing Injury page, with links to the RSI Newsletter, provides comprehensive information about health issues as well as buying guides for every type of office station device.

www.rsihelp.com Author Deborah Quilter's site provides help and advice on avoiding RSI and offers training services.

www.osha-slc.gov/SLTC/ergonomics The Occupational Safety and Health Administration's ergonomics pages highlight recent research and chronicle the agency's work on developing an ergonomics standard to help prevent musculoskeletal disorders, including RSI and computer-related conditions.

hfes.org The Human Factors and Ergonomics Society tracks new developments and sells a variety of specialist publications on ergonomics and human factors (the application of ergonomic principles to software design).

27

Help! Where to Turn When Things Go Wrong

by Robert Lauriston

In This Chapter

The good news: today's PCs are more reliable than ever before. The plug-and-play features that let them automatically resolve hardware conflicts have eliminated or greatly reduced many of the previously most common problems. The basic design hasn't changed in quite a while, and Windows 98 is only a modest revision of Windows 95, so much of the hardware and software has been around long enough that the manufacturers have gotten the kinks out.

The bad news: when something does go wrong, it's harder than ever before to figure out what to blame, and how to fix it. As I discussed in the "Resolving Conflicts" section of Chapter 8: Upgrade It Yourself, an unfortunate side effect of plug-and-play is that a conflict between two devices may manifest itself as a problem with a third. That's been the case with software for years—in Windows 3.1, a buggy video driver could cause any number of apparently unrelated problems—but troubleshooting has been getting thornier.

In this chapter, first I'll describe a bunch of things you can do yourself that solve common problems or, failing that, may at least help narrow the list of suspects so you can make a better guess about which company's tech support to call. Then I'll give you some tips on getting the most out of your available tech-support options and minimizing the time you have to spend navigating voicemail systems and listening to music-on-hold. At the end of the chapter, I've listed some troubleshooting and tech-support Web sites I've found particularly useful.

Do-It-Yourself Support

A lot of the calls computer users make to tech support lines are what support staffers call *RTMs*—that is, calls they think would be unnecessary if the users would just Read The Manual. Of course that sometimes helps, but there are a lot of other things you can do to fix problems on your own.

Danger Zone: When Files Disappear

One important warning for Windows 95 and 98 users: if valuable files have disappeared from your hard drive or are no longer readable, and you don't have backups, your best bet is to run Norton Disk Doctor, part of the Norton Utilities (discussed in Chapter 12: Windows Add-Ons). The less you do to your PC before running Disk Doctor, the better the chance that it will be able to recover the files — in particular, you don't want to save anything to the drive. If you don't have Disk Doctor and the files aren't important enough to justify buying a copy of Norton, try ScanDisk (discussed later in this section), which can sometimes recover missing files, though not as often as Disk Doctor.

Here are some things you can try, starting from the easiest and most basic troubleshooting tricks, and working up to some relatively advanced approaches you might not feel comfortable with.

- **Reboot.** If your PC seems to be frozen or is just acting weirdly in some way that prevents you from getting your work done, a lot of times you can snap it out of its trance by rebooting. Press Ctrl Alt Del and click Shut Down; if that doesn't work, press the reset button. If you find you need to reboot once every time you turn on your PC, but after that it works fine, you may have a component that doesn't work right until it warms up. That may be a sign of impending failure, or it may be just a chronic annoyance. I've had PCs with such problems for years without their getting worse—or, unfortunately, better.
- **Cold boot.** Occasionally, hardware may get into a weird state that's not cleared by rebooting. In that case, do a *cold boot*: turn the PC off, wait for five seconds, and turn it back on. With the new PCs you can only turn off from the Start menu, you may need to unplug the PC and plug it back in to do a real cold boot. With notebook PCs that don't have a power switch, there's usually a key combination (like Fn-suspend) that actually turns the system off, but if you can't find it, or it's not responding, you can always take the battery out.
- **Check Device Manager.** In Windows 95 or 98, check Device Manager as described in the "Resolving Conflicts" section of Chapter 8: Upgrade It Yourself to see if Windows has identified any problems.
- **Check the error log.** In Windows NT, from the Start menu choose Programs/Administrative Tools/Event Viewer. If any of the entries in the log begin with red stop-sign icons, double-click them to see if they give any clues to the problem.
- **Try Safe Mode.** In Windows 95 and 98, try booting to Safe Mode, or Safe Mode with Network Support. In Windows 95, restart the PC; when you see "Starting Windows 95," press F8 and hold it until you see a menu of start choices. In Windows 98, restart and hold down Ctrl until you see the menu. If whatever problem you've been experiencing goes away, that probably means it's a bad driver or a buggy application, not defective hardware.

  The closest thing to Safe Mode in NT is the VGA mode in its normal startup menu, which is worth trying. If the problem doesn't occur in VGA mode, your video card's driver is probably the culprit.
- **Run ScanDisk.** See the "Safety Check" section of Chapter 11: Windows 95, 98, and NT for instructions on running ScanDisk (or NT's equivalent, Check Disk). If you find yourself repeatedly fixing the same problem by running ScanDisk, that may indicate that your hard disk is wearing out. As usual with PCs, that's not the only explanation—if the problems always involve the same file or type of file, that's more likely a buggy application. If ScanDisk reports fixing any errors, reboot and see if the problem's fixed.

- **Run System Information.** If you have Windows 98, run Microsoft System Information (from the Start menu choose Programs/Accessories/System Tools/System Information) and run Tools/System File Checker and Tools/Registry Checker. These can resolve some common problems caused by buggy application setup programs. If they report fixing any errors, reboot and try to reproduce the problem.
- **Try Windows 98's troubleshooters.** I haven't found them particularly useful, but it can't hurt to try Win98's troubleshooting wizards. From the Start menu, choose Help, click the Contents tab, click Troubleshooting, and click Windows 98 Troubleshooters. Click on any that sound promising, and answer questions and follow instructions as prompted.
- **Check for viruses.** Run your antivirus utility in its most thorough mode. If you don't have an antivirus utility, download VirusScan from **`www.mcafee.com`** or F-Protect from **`datafellows.com`** and run it.
- **Check all the cables and switches.** Check the back of your PC to make sure all the cables are connected tight, and check the other end of each cable as well. Check any other switches that might be causing the problem, like the ones on your outlet strip or surge protector, printer, or monitor. If the problem's that the monitor's dark, check its controls to make sure that some clueless person didn't "shut it off" by turning the brightness all the way down.
- **Eliminate possibilities.** Think about the nature of the problem and see if you can eliminate some possibilities. For instance, if you can't do something in one program, like save files or find the font you want, see if you have the same problem in another application. If you don't, chances are very good the problem's in the first application. If you have access to another PC, try to replicate the problem there; if you can, it's likely a bug, or a virus that has infected both machines.
- **Undo the last thing you did.** If your problem started not too long after you installed a new piece of hardware or software, uninstall it and see if matters improve.
- **Upgrade your video driver.** If the problem is affecting the display, or if your PC is crashing or hanging a lot (which is sometimes caused by a bad video driver), check the video card manufacturer's Web site for an updated driver.
- **Check for weird stuff being loaded at startup.** Look in the Programs/StartUp folder on the Start menu to see if Windows is automatically loading anything at startup that might be causing the problem; if so, delete it, as described in the "Customizing the Start Menu" of Chapter 11: Windows 95, 98, and NT. In that same chapter, also see Figure 32 for pointers to other places where mysterious things can get loaded without your knowing about it.
- **Reseat the cards and blow out the dust.** This one's only for those who aren't afraid to get inside of their PCs. First, go to Radio Shack or an electronics supply store and buy a can of compressed air, and read the "Disassembly without Destruction" and "Installing Expansion Cards"

section of Chapter 8: Upgrade It Yourself. Then, open the PC's case, and use the compressed air to blow out all the accumulated air. (The traditional tech wisdom is that a vacuum cleaner may suck jumpers off your motherboard or dislodge other delicate parts.) Next, remove each of the expansion cards in turn. Check each card's contacts for signs of corrosion; if you see any, remove it with a pencil eraser, then use the compressed air to blow off any remains (don't let that schmutz fall into the PC); then reseat the card in its slot. Check to make sure that all cables on the motherboard, expansion cards, and drives are seated tightly. Close up the PC, plug it back in, and keep your fingers crossed.

- **Do a "verify reinstall" of Windows.** In Windows 95 and 98, if you insert the Windows CD, browse it in Windows Explorer, and double-click on Setup, you can run Windows Setup over your current installation, which will restore all files to their original state, a process Windows geeks call a "verify reinstall." This can make things worse, particularly if you've installed any updates, so it's something you probably don't want to try except as a last chance before wiping Windows off your disk and reinstalling from scratch.

Coping with Tech Support

Until you use a company's telephone tech support, there's no way to know what to expect. Some companies have knowledgeable techs who answer the phone promptly and always seem to have the answer, or at least know where to find it quickly. With any luck, you won't even have to pick up the phone, because the most common support questions are answered in an easy-to-find FAQ on the company's Web site.

Other companies throw up absurd obstacles to getting tech support, forcing you to navigate your way through a seemingly endless maze of voicemail menus before giving you the opportunity to describe your problem to an answering machine. Their Web sites follow a similar design: if there's a FAQ, it's buried a dozen links down from the site's "front door," and if there's a search engine any documents that might answer your question are buried in an avalanche of press releases, parts catalogs, and foreign-language promotional literature.

Most companies fall someplace in between those two extremes—sometimes various places, depending on which person you happen to talk with, or how recently the Web site has been redesigned. Since my work has required me to seek tech support on hundreds of products, I've picked up a few tricks for minimizing the pain. I hope you find them useful.

- **Check the Web site first.** Given how cheap it is to put documents on the Web, and how expensive it is to hire staff to answer the phones, it's not surprising that hardware and software companies, whose customers almost all have Internet access, usually have tech-support FAQs on their Web sites. Unfortunately, in most cases they don't seem to be updated very often, so in many cases you still have to phone to find fixes for bugs in the latest upgrade. Another common problem is that the FAQ is put together by the marketing department and answers useless questions like, "Why is our product the best?" instead of "What do I do when smoke's coming out the back?" If the site has a message board (aka forum, threads, community, bulletin board), check it out—sometimes you can find uncensored discussions among users and support staff that may cover precisely the problem you're experiencing.

- **Work around lousy search tools.** Many tech-support Web sites are so badly designed and have such awful search features that it's hard or impossible to find the information you need, even if you know it's there. Sometimes you can work around such problems with AltaVista (**`altavista.com`**): use the same search terms you were trying on the vendor's Web site, plus `+host:` followed by the name of the server that holds the tech-support documents. (Don't put a space between the colon and the server name.) For example, `+host:support.3com.com` will restrict AltaVista to searching 3Com's support site. To get the best results from AltaVista, see the "Search Tips" section of Chapter 21: The Web and Browsers. Unfortunately, this approach doesn't always work, because tech support sites often use database-generated pages that AltaVista can't index.
- **Check the newsgroups.** With many products, the best place to find out whether other people are having the same problem you are — and if so whether anyone has found a fix — is on Internet newsgroups. See "Searching Newsgroups with DejaNews" in Chapter 22: Online Discussions: Newsgroups Etc. for tips on finding relevant posts.
- **Be prepared.** If you're going to call tech support, often you can save time if you first gather the information that the company will need to diagnose your problem. In particular, if you've been getting some kind of error message, write it down, and also write down anything that appears in the title bar of the error dialog. You may need a serial or registration number to get support.
- **Bypass the fax-back system.** Some vendors don't let you talk with an actual human tech support person until you've navigated your way through a time-consuming voicemail menu of common problems, solutions for which you can receive by fax. However, there shouldn't be anything in the fax-back system that isn't on the Web site, so if you've already checked the latter it's a waste of time to sit through the menus. Sometimes pressing 0 or # will bypass the menus. If that doesn't work, sometimes you can zip through by pressing 1 or 2 repeatedly until you get to the end of the menu tree. Once you do get a human, ask them to give a direct number so if you get disconnected you won't have to wind through the menus again, or a problem ID number that you can enter at the main voicemail menu to be connected directly to a human.

- **Play by the script.** Phone staffers sometimes know little or nothing about the products they're supporting but are instead basically reading from a script. In such situations, don't expect creativity or snappy repartee, and don't confuse the tech by taking shortcuts. You'll get done faster if you just go along with the script, however slow and stupid it may seem, and follow the instructions to the letter.
- **Jump the tiers.** Many vendors have "tiered" tech support. The first level is typically a bunch of ill-paid people with no real experience. When problems aren't covered in their script, the first-level staffers pass the problem on to the next level, usually a professional support person with some first-hand knowledge of the program, who also has access to the programmers to resolve new or particularly tough problems. Many companies prefer to use the first-level support staff as a buffer so that more experienced staffers don't have to spend time dealing with the public directly, but if you're a good negotiator you may sometimes be able to talk your way up the tiers.

Troubleshooting and Tech Support Resources

yahoo.com In most cases, you can find a company's tech support Web site by sticking the company name between a www. and a .com, as in **www.microsoft.com** and **www.compaq.com**. In those cases where that doesn't work, a simple search on Yahoo will almost always lead you to the site.

dejanews.com As I mentioned earlier, Internet newsgroups are often the best place to find out if other people have experienced the same problem you have, and to find out whether there's a fix—and DejaNews is the best tool for searching newsgroups. See Chapter 22: Online Discussions: Newsgroups Etc. for instructions on finding newsgroups that are relevant to the product you're having trouble with and posting a request for assistance there.

fixwindows.com A clever site that uses flowcharts to help you diagnose and find solutions for many common Windows 95 and 98 problems. Not much help for NT users.

fixwindows.com/supnums.htm An extensive list of PC, peripheral, and software vendor tech support phone numbers.

www.annoyances.org/win95/faq.html The Windows 95 Annoyances site includes this useful FAQ, which has a lot of troubleshooting information.

annoyances.org/win98 Windows 98 Annoyances isn't as useful as its Win95 predecessor—it's more of an ad for the book of the same name—but it still has some useful information. Click on Troubleshooting or Frequently Asked Questions.

search.microsoft.com Microsoft's online tech-support library, the Microsoft Knowledge Base (MSKB), contains information about many companies' products—which makes sense, since any hardware or software that's not working right is in a sense a Windows problem. For tech-support info, be sure to choose Support & the Knowledge Base button before you click Search Now. (See the "Windows Resources" section at the end of Chapter 11: Windows 95, 98, and NT for more about this search engine.) You can also access the MSKB by e-mail: for details, send a message to mshelp@microsoft.com with the word "index" in the subject line (it doesn't matter what's in the body of the message).

support.microsoft.com/support/windows/faq Microsoft's tech support FAQs for Windows 95 and 98. As with the previous site I mentioned, there's stuff about third-party products that cause problems in Windows.

support.microsoft.com/support/NTWorkstation/faq Same deal, only for NT.

Glossary

Like the rest of this book, this glossary doesn't pretend to be fully comprehensive—but hey, a listing of almost a thousand words is nothing to sneeze at, either. Beginners will find many basic words here, but if you're new to computers and find yourself back here looking up elementary stuff too often, you're better off reading Chapter 1: For Beginners Only first. It's got pictures, for one thing.

You'll notice many cross references to other definitions here, but very likely if you don't understand one of the words *in* a definition you'll find it defined elsewhere in the glossary. If you don't find a word you think should be defined here, please put a note in the suggestion box on this book's Web site, **www.thepcbible.com**, and we'll consider adding it in the next edition.

1394 A type of high-speed (currently up to 400 mbps) serial port used by digital camcorders and other devices. The name comes from IEEE 1394, the official standard. Also has various trademarked names used by various manufacturers, like FireWire (Apple) and i.Link (Sony).

16-bit color This video mode displays over 65,000 colors. Unless you're a graphics professional, the only time you're likely to notice the difference between 16-bit and 24-bit modes is when looking closely at scanned photographs or other graphics with very subtle color gradations. Some Windows dialogs call this High Color.

24-bit color Synonymous with *photorealistic* color, this term describes printers, video cards, and monitors that use 24 bits of color information per pixel or dot, producing up to 16.7 million colors per image. Some Windows dialog boxes call this mode True Color.

286 An obsolete 16-bit CPU used in the original IBM AT and its clones. Incompatible with many contemporary applications and some Windows features.

3-D graphics accelerator A card or chip on a video card that improves display of 3-D graphics in game software.

32-bit color Most of the time, 32-bit color is functionally identical to 24-bit color. Some graphics applications may use the extra eight bits for special features.

386 Intel's first 32-bit CPU, now obsolete but still a key standard due to the millions of 386 systems in use and the ability of 486 and Pentium systems to run software written for the 386. The 386's optional *FPU* was a separate chip, the 387.

3-D graphics Usually refers to graphics containing shapes that can be rotated and otherwise manipulated in three dimensions. For example, you could "walk through" a 3-D drawing of a building. Also used to refer to true stereo 3-D images (which usually require that you wear special glasses). Loosely used to refer to 3-D graphics accelerators.

486 Created by Intel, the obsolete 486 was essentially a speeded-up 386 CPU with a built-in *FPU*and an 8K memory cache.

8-bit color This video mode displays only 256 colors, which is adequate for business use, not so good for games designed for 16-bit color, and downright lousy for displaying scanned photos.

8086 An obsolete 16-bit variation on 8088 used in a few XT clones.

8088 An obsolete 8-bit CPU, used in original IBM PCs and PC-XTs and their clones. Incompatible with most contemporary software, including Windows.

8514A A proprietary IBM graphics standard for interlaced 1024 by 768 resolution (see *interlaced*).

A

A-B roll system A video editing system that uses three decks, two for playback (A and B) and one for recording.

A/B switch A box that enables you to attach two printers to one PC port (or two PCs' ports to one printer) and switch between them as desired.

access control software A utility that blocks anyone without the proper password from accessing selected files on a PC's hard drive.

active-matrix display A brighter, sharper, and significantly more expensive alternative to *passive matrix* notebook displays (see *TFT*).

active window In Windows, the window you're currently working in.

adapter A device that connects one bus to another. *Expansion cards* are called adapters when they connect your PC's ISA or PCI bus to another bus, like Ethernet or ISDN.

add-on Any hardware or software designed to augment the capabilities of another product. In graphics programs, often called a plug-in.

Adobe Type Manager (ATM) A Windows utility that enables you to display and print PostScript Type 1 fonts from within any Windows application, whether or not you have a PostScript printer.

AGP Short for *Advanced Graphics Port*, a high-speed motherboard slot specifically for video cards.

algorithm A mathematical procedure for solving a problem, most often used to describe caching, compression, or encryption schemes.

alias A file that points to another file. Microsoft calls these *shortcuts*, an unfortunate term because it has another meaning.

allocation units To track data on disk, Windows divides disk space into groups of sectors called allocation units (also known as *clusters*). Depending on the size of the drive, allocation units range from 2K to 64K in size, but are always of equal size on any given drive. Windows' *file allocation table (FAT)* logs each allocation unit as available, damaged, or in use by a file. Only one file can use a particular allocation unit at one time (see *FAT, FAT32, sectors*).

alphanumeric The set of characters that includes all letters, numbers, and punctuation marks.

AMD An Intel competitor that makes Pentium-compatible CPUs that are usually more cost-effective than Intel's.

America Online Formerly the most popular online service, and now the most popular Internet service provider.

ANSI Short for the *American National Standards Institute,* which develops standards in many fields. ASCII, terminal emulation, and SQL are only three of the many standards ANSI has set for the computer industry.

ANSI.SYS A *device driver* used to control screen display and keyboard remapping. For DOS use only; pretty much obsolete.

antialiasing A technique that eliminates the jagged edges of text on screen or in a bitmapped graphic by replacing some of the black and white pixels around the edge of each character with a range of grays.

antivirus A type of program that scans your system and sounds the alarm if a computer virus is detected. Most antivirus programs also attempt to remove the infection (see *virus*).

aperture grille A set of thin strips of metal that are stretched across the inside of a monitor's screen. The aperture grille allows the CRT's electron beam to pass through and strike a selected pixel while blocking electrons that might strike neighboring pixels and cause the screen to appear fuzzy. This technology was formerly used only in Sony Trinitron monitors, but Sony's patent expired and it's now used by many companies (see *shadow mask, dot pitch*).

app Short for *application*.

applet A small application, usually referring to the mini apps that come with Windows, such as the Notepad, Clock, PIF Editor, and so on, or to small Java programs that run in your Web browser.

application Any program with a user interface designed to be *applied* to a specific set of tasks. Most often refers to such "productivity" software as word processors, spreadsheets, draw programs, and so on (see *program, user interface*).

application generator Several data management programs come with an application generator, which enables you to create custom database applications without programming (see *database application*).

application launcher A Windows utility program that makes organizing and starting applications easier.

archive Generally, any collection of data intended to be stored indefinitely and accessed infrequently (specifically, the type of file created by such compression utilities as WinZip—or the act of creating such files using these utilities. Archive files are also known as *library* files when composed of several files "packed" together by a compression utility; "unpacking" an archive file restores the original component files (see *compression*).

archive bit A file attribute used to indicate which files have been changed and which haven't since the last time you backed up your data (see *backup, file attribute*).

ASCII Short for the *American Standard Code for Information Interchange,* this is the international standard for turning characters (letters, numbers, and punctuation) into *binary* code. True ASCII uses only 7 bits of every byte for a total of 128 characters. However, a wide variety of 8-bit codes based on ASCII are used to support languages other than English and to create simple line graphics in character-based DOS programs.

ASIC Short for *application-specific integrated circuit,* an ASIC is a custom chip designed for a specific purpose. The size of motherboards has been radically reduced by the use of ASICs.

ASPI Short for *Advanced SCSI Programming Interface*, ASPI is a SCSI driver standard developed by Adaptec. In theory, any SCSI device that supports ASPI should work with any ASPI-compatible SCSI adapter card.

assembly language Also called *assembler*, the programming language closest to *machine language*, the only language understood by the CPU. Only crazy people write big programs in assembly language. These days, used mostly for fine-tuning the performance of programs written in easier, more sophisticated languages, such as C or C++.

asynchronous communications IBM-speak for using a modem.

AT See *IBM AT*.

AT drive Originally, a hard drive compatible with the *controller* used in the IBM PC-AT; also the basis of the contemporary *EIDE* standard.

audio compression A technique for reducing the size of sound files on disk. Depending on the compression scheme, it may reduce sound quality (see *lossless* and *lossy*).

audit trail Originally an accounting term, audit trail also applies to any log of a user's network or database activities.

auto-answer mode A setting that causes a modem to pick up incoming calls.

auto dialer A software utility that uses your modem to dial a phone number displayed on screen.

AUTOEXEC.BAT A batch file that contains DOS-prompt commands for Windows to execute during startup. Current versions of Windows do not usually need an AUTOEXEC.BAT, but some hardware and software still require it. (see *batch file, CONFIG.SYS*).

automatic backup A backup utility that uses a software timer to trigger backups at set times, or a network utility that backs up local hard drives to a server without users having to do anything.

autosave An option found in many applications that saves your work automatically at specified intervals. A nice feature if you forget to save manually and experience a crash.

autosizing A monitor automatically adjusting itself to the correct settings for the current video mode.

autotracing The imperfect process of converting *bitmapped graphics* (such as those created by paint programs and scanners) into *vector graphics*, which can be easily manipulated by drawing software.

average access time The average time it takes in milliseconds for a disk drive's read/write head (or a CD ROM drive's laser reader) to access any given point on a rotating disk. An important measure of hard disk performance.

average seek time The mean time it takes in milliseconds for a disk drive's read/write head (or a CD ROM drive's laser reader) to access any given point *along the radius* of a disk. Does not take into account the disk's rotation.

AVI Short for *Audio Video Interleaved*, Windows' standard file format for digital video.

B

background printing Printing while you continue to work in an application. We take this for granted nowadays, but back in the DOS days people actually bought software specifically to add this capability to their PCs.

backlighting Special lighting behind notebook *LCD* screens that increases contrast several times over; absolutely necessary for color LCDs (see *LCD, notebook computer*).

backup The process where you copy the contents of your hard disk to another medium, such as floppy disks or tape, in case the original data is lost or damaged (see *differential backup*, *full backup*, *incremental backup*).

backup set The disks or tapes on which you store your backup copies.

BAK file A backup copy of a data file. Many programs create files with a BAK extension automatically when you edit a file (for example, when you edit BUDGET.XLS, *Excel* creates a backup copy called BUDGET.BAK).

bandwidth The amount of information a piece of hardware (or a type of cable) can transfer during a given time interval.

bar chart A data chart designed to compare quantities at evenly spaced time intervals (by week, month, and so on). Bar charts emphasize each interval's *data point*, the individual numeric value represented by each bar's height (see *data chart*).

base memory See *conventional memory*.

BASIC Short for *Beginners All-purpose Symbolic Instruction Code*, a relatively simple programming language. Most versions of DOS included a BASIC interpreter (a program that lets you create and run BASIC programs). Current versions of Windows do not.

batch file A file containing a series of DOS-prompt commands, each on its own line, that executes automatically when you type the name of the file at the DOS prompt and press [Key Caps: Enter]. A batch file has the extension .bat and is described in Windows Explorer as "MS-DOS Batch File"

baud rate A technical term for modem speed that's best avoided. Some people use it interchangeable with *bits per second*, but that's incorrect.

bcc Short for "blind carbon copy," a typewriter-era term for a copy of a letter sent to someone whose name did not appear in the list of carbon copy (cc:) recipients below the signature. (For example, an attorney might send a paralegal a bcc for filing purposes.) Now used to refer to similar addressing options in e-mail programs.

benchmark A speed test performed under controlled conditions.

Bezier curve The technical term for the curved lines used in drawing programs that can be reshaped by moving *control points*.

bidirectional Primarily used to describe an older type of parallel port that can both send and receive data. Bidirectional ports were the predecessors of today's *enhanced parallel ports*.

binary The numerical system (also known as base 2) used by computers. Binary logic employs only two numbers (0 and 1), which correspond to the two states (off and on) of each bit in memory or on disk. All data—text, numbers, pictures, sound, video—must be converted to binary code before your computer can process or store it (see *bit*).

binary file Any file containing nontext data, such as a program file, a spreadsheet, or a graphics file.

BinHex If you get file attachments from Mac users, they may be encoded in BinHex, a format Windows normally identifies as "HQX File" and can't open. See the discussion of WinZip in Chapter 12: Windows Add-Ons for a pointer to a free program that sometimes can resolve this problem.

BIOS Short for *basic input/output system*, a small quantity of code used for controlling basic computer functions, stored permanently in a chip (or chips) on a PC's motherboard.

bit The smallest building block of computer data (see *binary, byte*).

bitmapped graphics Images stored as a grid of dots. Paint programs, scanners, and fax modems save data as bitmaps (see *vector graphics*).

bits per second (bps) The standard measure of modem speed. V.32bis modems run at a maximum speed of 14.4 kbps (kilobits per second), V.34 modems go up to 33.6 kbps, V.90 modems can, at least theoretically, download at up to 56 kbps. High-speed Internet connections are measured in mbps (megabits per second) or even gbps (gigabits per second). Do not confuse these measures with *megabytes per second* (MB/sec. or MBps), the common measure of hard disk throughput (1 MB/sec. equals 8 mbps).

bleed In design, layout, and desktop publishing circles, a bleed refers to any element (like a photo or a line of type) that runs off the edge of the page.

block copy Marking a block of text (in a spreadsheet or text document) and copying it to another location.

BMP Windows' own bitmapped graphics file format.

board See *expansion card.*

body text The main body of type in a book or article. It specifically *excludes* headlines, captions, and special graphic elements (see *display type*).

boilerplate Text or graphics that are created once and inserted, unchanged, into a series of letters, articles, reports, and so on. A form letter, exclusive of the salutation and any other personalized touches, is boilerplate text.

bold Short for boldface, a dark, heavy version of a type font used for emphasis; the word **bold** at the beginning of this paragraph is set in boldface.

bookmarks In a Web browser, icons or menu choices that let you keep track of Web pages you want to return to later. In a word processor, a feature that lets you move around rapidly in a long text document: insert several bookmarks in a document, and you can jump from one to the next instead of scrolling.

Boolean logic Refers to a set of logical commands (AND, OR, NOT, and so on) used in Internet search engines, database queries, and text searches.

boot The act of turning on your computer or of restarting it by pressing Ctrl Alt Del. Also refers to the moment when a PC finds the *operating system* on disk and loads it (see *cold boot, warm boot, operating system)*.

boot disk The hard disk that holds the files that load an operating system (with Windows, almost always C:), or a floppy disk you can use to boot your PC in emergencies (see *emergency disk*).

boot sector A small section of your hard or floppy disk in which Windows looks for instructions about how to start your computer.

bozo Internet slang for a person whose newsgroup or message board posts aren't worth reading.

bozofilter A program or feature that automatically filters out posts from people you have defined as *bozos* so you won't see them.

bps See *bits per second*.

branch When discussing disks and files, a branch is a subsection of the folder tree (that is, a folder and all the subfolders beneath it). In macros or programming, it refers to a point where two or more different things can happen depending on the circumstances: For example, a macro might look to see whether a folder contains a particular file and then either open that file or create a new one (see *macro*).

browser cache Temporary copies of recently-visited Web pages saved by Web browsers so that when you backtrack they don't have to download the same data again.

buffer Memory used to improve performance by creating a small reservoir of readily accessible data. For example, hard disks have buffers to hold data likely to be needed by the PC, while printers have buffers to hold information received from the PC (see *disk cache, memory buffer*).

bug A mistake a programmer made when writing software that shows up on your end as some unexpected event, usually an unpleasant one.

bullet A special character (like •) used to set off indented paragraphs or items in a list.

burst mode A special mode used by a disk drive or other device to quickly transfer a large block of data (see *bus)*.

burst transfer rate The speed (usually in MB per second) of a burst-mode transfer. With disk drives, the burst transfer rate usually reflects the best possible performance when sending a small amount of data under optimum circumstances; for a more realistic measure, look to the *sustained transfer rate.*

bus Any electrical circuit that transfers data. The term *bus* most often refers to the kind of slots (ISA, PCI, AGP)) found on a PC's expansion bus, but it may also refer to other connections within a PC: the memory bus, SCSI bus, USB bus, and so on.

bus arbitration The scheme by which a system prioritizes requests from multiple devices on the same expansion bus.

bus mastering When an intelligent expansion card enhances performance by taking control of the expansion bus, usually to transfer a large quantity of data in a short period of time without involving the CPU.

bus speed By itself, usually refers to the speed of the bus that connects a PC's CPU to its memory, which is the *external speed* of the CPU. For example, a Pentium II that runs at 450MHz internally communicates with memory at 100MHz. The term may also refer to the speed of any bus, for example, the PCI bus speed is normally 66MHz.

button A graphic representation of a push button with an icon on it, used by most Windows programs to provide easy access to commands; an array of buttons is usually called a *toolbar* or *button bar.* Also one of the two or three switches on your mouse.

byte The standard unit for measuring disk storage and memory. Each byte contains 8 bits. The characters you see on your computer screen are usually composed of 2 bytes, but if you're not a programmer you never have to worry about such matters.

C

cable modem A device that provides high-speed Internet access over a cable television system.

cache See *disk cache, memory cache, browser cache.*

CAD Short for *computer-aided design*. Essentially computerized drafting, CAD may also refer to programs that do complex materials analysis. CAD software ranges from $50 programs used mostly for space planning to engineering programs that cost hundreds of thousands of dollars. *AutoCAD* is far and away the most popular CAD program for PCs.

calculated field In database lingo, a field whose value is determined by using a formula that usually refers to data in another field. For example, in a payroll database, the net pay field might be calculated by subtracting tax and insurance from the gross salary.

card See *expansion card.*

CardBus A faster variant of the *PC Card* standard.

carpal tunnel syndrome One of the most common repetitive strain injuries (RSIs), carpal tunnel syndrome is an often painful compression of the median nerve in the wrist, caused by repeated bending of the wrist and/or by swelling of nearby tendons and their sheaths. Computer users are frequent victims of carpal tunnel syndrome (see *RSI*).

carriage return A term left over from typewriter technology, where the typewriter carriage had to be "returned" to start a new line. On a computer, a carriage return simply moves the cursor to the beginning of the next line (see *hard carriage return, line feed, text wrap*).

carrier detect (CD) When a modem connects with another modem, the CD light on an external modem lights up.

CASE Short for *computer-aided software engineering*. Using software to write software; that is, automated programming. Talked about far more often than it's done successfully.

CCITT Short for Comite Consultatif International Telephonique et Telegraphique *(International Telephone and Telegraph Consultative Committee)* (see *ITU*).

CD-I Short for *compact disk interactive,* a CD ROM standard used by the Philips CD-I player (a gadget you hook to your TV). Not relevant to PC CD ROMs.

CD-R Short for *Compact Disc-Recordable*. A write-your-own version of the CD-ROM format. You need a CD-R or CD-RW drive to create CD-Rs. This is a *write-once* format: once you copy a file to the disc, the space it takes up is gone forever, though you may be able to "delete" it in the sense that it won't appear when you browse the disc. Once you fill up a CD-R disc, it's as unwritable as a regular CD-ROM (see *CD-RW*).

CD-ROM Short for *Compact Disc-Read Only Memory*, which is not a type of memory at all, but the factory-produced CD format that almost all commercial software comes on. You need a CD-ROM drive to read CD-ROMs (see *read-only*).

CD-RW Short for *Compact Disc-Rewritable*. This relatively recent addition to the CD family is basically an erasable version of a CD-R. You can use a CD-RW disc over and over indefinitely, like a giant floppy. CD-RW drives can double as CD-R drives.

cellular modem A modem that connects to a cellular phone (see *modem*).

Celeron A variation on Intel's Pentium II processor.

CGA Short for IBM's first color video card, the *Color Graphics Adapter.* The CGA standard is long obsolete, offering a mere 320-by-200 resolution in four colors.

character A single letter, number, punctuation mark, or symbol.

chat room A virtual "place" on the Internet, an online service, or a Web site where people can exchange written messages in real time. Sometimes called a chat area or CB simulator.

checkboxes A group of boxes (usually found in Windows dialog boxes) that enable you to "check off" the options you want, letting you select all, none, or a few items from a list at one time.

chip Also called an *integrated circuit*, a chip refers to any complex combination of transistors and other circuitry etched onto a silicon die. Chips make computers possible, handling everything from data storage to number crunching. Chip is also slang for *CPU*.

click To press and release a mouse button—usually the left one. When you *click on* something (a menu item, a graphic, whatever), you move the pointer to it and click the left mouse button.

click and drag To hold down the left mouse button and move the mouse at the same time. Generally, you click and drag to move an object (such as a program icon) or to highlight a block of text (see *drag and drop*).

client-server Any network application (usually a database or accounting program) where most of the processing is done on the server, while workstations (clients) do relatively little work. By contrast, in conventional network applications, the file server holds the data files, but all the processing is done by the workstations (see *server*).

clip art Any collection of drawings or other ready-made images you can insert into your documents to liven them up.

Clipboard The place in Windows where text and graphics go when you cut or copy them. There they wait, ready to be pasted, until you cut or copy something else, in which case the previous contents are overwritten.

clock speed The speed of the CPU, measured in megahertz. A 450MHz Pentium II has a 450MHz clock speed; its bus speed, however, is only 100MHz.

clone An old-fashioned term that refers to an IBM-compatible PC. Sometimes used to refer to no-brand and house-brand PCs sold by small *clone shops*.

close To make a document or window disappear from the screen, for example by clicking the close box, the button with an X on it in the upper-right-hand corner of the window.

clusters See *allocation units.*

CMOS Short for *complementary metal oxide semiconductor,* a special kind of memory chip that requires very little power. Most PCs use battery-powered CMOS chips to store basic system configuration info, such as the type of hard disk and the amount of memory installed. You change those settings with a setup utility—hence the term *CMOS setup.*

CMYK Short for cyan, magenta, yellow, and key (usually black), the colors of the inks used in the four-color printing process. CMYK is one of several systems for combining primary colors to produce a full-color image.

cold boot When you turn your PC off and on, or press the reset button, you've just performed a cold boot, which is usually the last resort when a warm boot fails (see *boot, warm boot*).

color depth The number of colors your video card can currently display, described as "Colors" or "Color Palette" in Windows' Display control panel (see *8-bit color, 16-bit color, 24-bit color, 32-bit color*).

color matching A software and/or hardware system for making a PC's display approximate the colors of the final printed page. Some monitors have color matching features built in.

color separation A process used in desktop publishing for separating a color image into four single-color images, one for each ink (cyan, magenta, yellow, black) used in four-color printing.

color temperature A technical measure of the color displayed by a video tube. Variations in color temperature can give a monitor a slight yellow, blue, or red tint.

COM A file extension for a type of program file. Also used to designate a serial port, as in COM 1 and COM 2 (see *executable file, serial port*).

command An instruction you issue that tells your computer what to do. In Windows or most apps, you pick commands from menus, push a button on a tool bar, or hit a keyboard shortcut (like Ctrl C for Copy). At the DOS *command line*, commands are short words (COPY, MOVE, FORMAT) that you type at the C: prompt.

command line See *DOS prompt.*

command prompt See *DOS prompt.*

compiler Software that takes all the high-level instructions in a program and converts them wholesale into *machine language*, the language understood by the CPU. The compiled version of the program must then be *decompiled* for any modifications to be made (see *interpreter*).

compression The process of shrinking files to conserve disk space or reduce modem transmission time. Archiving utilities such as WinZip and disk-compression utilities such as DriveSpace compress files to approximately 65 percent of their original size on average, but the degree of compression varies widely depending on the file type. Programs that perform video and audio compression usually give you a choice of several compression ratios, depending on how much of the original quality you're willing to lose (see *archive, disk compression, lossy*).

CONFIG.SYS A file that contains instructions which tell Windows to load old DOS-style device drivers when your PC starts up. Generally unnecessary, but may be required by some older hardware (see *AUTOEXEC.BAT, device driver*).

configuration A general term for the process of setting up hardware or software the way you want it (for example, to configure Windows to work at a resolution higher than 640 by 480). Also refers to the specific combination of hardware installed in a PC..

contact manager A sophisticated program that keeps track of names, addresses, phone numbers, appointments, correspondence, and virtually everything else for people who make their living on the phone. It usually includes an electronic Rolodex, a powerhouse appointment calendar, and the ability to link information in various ways (see *PIM*).

continuous-form paper Also known as fan-fold paper, this is the folded stuff that feeds through old-fashioned dot matrix printers, with perforations between the pages and little holes on the outside (see *dot matrix printer, tractor-feed*).

Control Panel A Windows utility for setting a wide variety of options: selecting printers, changing the desktop's appearance, adjusting mouse response, and so on.

control point The small dots or boxes that appear when you select a line, curve, polygon, or other object in a drawing program. Dragging a control point with the mouse changes the object's shape and/or size.

controller The electronics that control the workings of a hard drive or a monitor. Strictly speaking, the controllers for today's hard drives are built into the drives themselves, and the EIDE or SCSI hardware on your motherboard or an expansion card is an *adapter*. The video controller is a chip, usually on a PCI or AGP card but sometimes on the motherboard.

conventional memory All memory under 640K (also known as *base memory*).

counter fields A database term used to describe a field that stamps a unique identification number on each record (see *field, record*).

cps Short for characters per second, a measure of dot-matrix printer speed. Has also been used as a measure of data communications speed, but that is conventionally measured by *bps*.

CPU Short for *central processing unit*, the chip that does most (if not all) of the computing in your PC. Many PC models derive their names from the name of the CPU inside the system (K6-2, Pentium II, and so on). The CPU is usually located on the motherboard, the main circuit board that lines the bottom of your PC (or the side, in a tower system).

crash A general term for a serious malfunction. In the most common type of crash, your computer *locks up* (synonymous with *hangs* or *freezes*) and refuses to accept keyboard or mouse input, so that you have to reboot in order to resume working. In some cases, only one of several applications will stop functioning, or Windows disappears and leaves you staring at a blue or black screen (system crashes obliterate any data not saved to disk).

CRC Short for *cyclical redundancy checking*, this is a common technique for detecting errors when transmitting data by modem.

crevettes (pronounced "cray-vet") French for shrimp. Very tasty with Spam.

cross-linked files When a disk error or system crash damages the *FAT*, one common result is that two files sort of merge into one big mess (kind of like a bad car wreck). ScanDisk can sometimes repair this problem, though if you have the Norton Utilities, its Disk Doctor will likely do a better job.

CRT Short for *cathode ray tube,* the picture tube in your monitor or TV set. Also jargony synonym for monitor.

cursor The small flashing rectangle, vertical line, or underline that shows you where the characters you type will appear. Not to be confused with the little arrow (called the *pointer*) or I-beam (called the *insertion point*) in Windows, both of which are controlled by the mouse.

cut and paste The term for a procedure used to move text or graphics from one place to another. In Windows, you can cut and paste data within the same file, between different files, or between applications (see *Clipboard*).

cut-sheet A single sheet of paper, like that used in most photocopiers and laser printers.

Cyrix An Intel competitor that makes Pentium-compatible CPUs that are usually more cost-effective than Intel's.

D

DAC Short for *digital-to-analog converter*, a chip used in sound cards, video cards, and other devices to transform digital signals into sound, video, and other things readily appreciable by humans.

daisy-chaining Hooking several devices (usually *SCSI* drives) together with a series of cables. The second device plugs into the first, the third plugs into the second, and so on, like strings of Christmas tree lights.

DAT Short for *digital audio tape*, a tape cassette format developed by the consumer electronics industry for use in tape decks for stereo systems, later adapted for use in tape backup drives for computers.

data A vague term that usually refers to the stuff you create or work with—text in a word processor, numbers in a spreadsheet, database records, and so on. Data may also refer to anything stored on disk or residing in memory.

data bits A basic modem setting that specifies the number of bits in the smallest unit of data exchanged (usually seven or eight bits).

data chart A term used to describe bar charts, line charts, pie charts, and other graphs based on numeric data.

data file The place where you keep your data—as opposed to a *program file*, which holds the programming code from which software is constructed.

data manager See *database program*.

data type In a database, refers to the kind of data stored in a field: text, date, number, logical, and so on. In programming languages, basic data types are integers (whole numbers), floating-point values (other numbers), and strings (usually text).

database Basically, any collection of information, but most often used to describe a file or a group of related files created by a data manager. Sometimes used as shorthand for *database manager*.

database application A complete custom program created using a database program. Usually written by a professional programmer to handle a specific task (such as order entry, billing, or sales tracking), the typical database application is designed to run on a network, so that an entire department or small business can enter and retrieve information.

database manager Any application, such as *Access* or *FileMaker,* that stores data in fields and records and enables users to retrieve that data using queries or reports. Also known as a *database* or *data manager* (see *field, record, query*).

database programming language The core of any programmable data manager, a database programming language is a set of commands that, used in specific combinations, can complete any database task, from sorting a group of records to creating a complex report. Most people use a database program's menus to accomplish simple tasks, while professionals employ a programming language to create database applications.

database server A server that does the processing in a client-server database (see *client-server*).

DBMS Short for for *data base management system* (see *database program*).

DDE A term describing a type of data link between Windows applications, now mostly supplanted by *OLE*.

dedicated server A PC used exclusively for supplying services (like communications or printing) to a network. Nondedicated servers provide services to the network but are also used as workstations.

default The computer equivalent of "factory settings," or how things will happen normally unless you decide otherwise. For instance, with most word processors, you insert text by default, and you must press the Ins key to overtype text. Usually, a menu enables you to change this default setting.

defragger See *disk defragmenter.*

Delete To remove or erase, usually by highlighting the thing to be deleted and pressing the Del key.

delimiter Usually a comma or tab, used to separate words in a text file into fields for use by a database program.

desktop A loose metaphor for the background of Windows and other graphical user interfaces, designed to make new computer users more comfortable. More obviously, the type of PC that goes *on* your desk as opposed to under it (see *tower system*).

desktop PC A PC designed to sit on your desk (see *tower system*); or, more generally, sedentary PCs as opposed to notebooks.

desktop publishing (DTP) The process of using word processing and page layout (desktop publishing) software—plus a laser printer or phototypesetter—to produce professional-looking reports, newsletters, brochures, and other publications. Windows word processors now include most of the DTP features that average users require, which means that using DTP software increasingly is an exclusively professional endeavor.

desktop video The process of recording and editing video on your PC.

device driver A small program than enables a specific peripheral device (such as a CD-ROM drive or a printer) to communicate with Windows and its applications (see , *peripheral*).

dialog box A window that pops up on screen in response to a command, system error, or alert, asking for input from the user. Dialog boxes can be as simple as two buttons (OK and Cancel), or they may contain dozens of buttons, checkboxes, list boxes, and sliders.

differential backup One of several kinds of daily backups. A differential backup makes copies of every file that has changed since the last full backup (see *backup)*.

digitize The process of converting analog input, such as photographs or sound waves, to digital output such as scanned images or audio CDs (see *scanner, sound card*).

DIMM Short for Double Inline Memory Module, the type of RAM used in most current desktop PCs (see *SIMM, SO-DIMM*).

dingbats Decorative typeface characters (also known as ornaments), such as arrows, stars, and yin-yang symbols, used to spiff up boring text. Look for Wingdings on the Windows' font menus; if you have a PostScript printer, also look for Zapf Dingbats.

DIP switch A tiny toggle switch mounted on expansion cards, motherboards, modems, and other devices. Used to configure hardware and avoid conflicts between devices.

direct memory access See *DMA*.

DirectCD An Adaptec format that allows you to access CD-R and CD-RW discs on the Windows desktop and from applications, just like floppy or hard drives. This format reduces the disc's capacity from its usual 650MB to 493MB.

directory See *folder*.

directory listing The old term for the contents of a folder, which in the DOS days was called a directory.

directory tree See *folder tree*.

disc An alternative spelling of *disk* usually reserved for CD-ROMs and other media that use laser rather than electromagnetic technology.

disk Any small discus-shaped medium for storing data. Usually refers to a *hard disk* (the disks are inside the hard disk casing) or *floppy disk*.

disk cache A software utility that speeds up performance by keeping recently accessed data in RAM instead of on disk.

disk compression A scheme in which all (or most of) the data on an entire disk is scrunched to gain more space, usually by Windows' DriveSpace. Disk compression compresses and decompresses files on the fly, without intervention from you (see *compression*).

disk defragmenter A program (also known as a *defragger*) that gathers up all the fragments of files that Windows has scattered across the surface of your hard disk and reassembles them, so that each file's data is contiguous. The defragging usually improves disk performance (see *full defrag*).

disk farm A particularly large drive array or set of drive arrays (see *RAID*).

disk mirroring A system where identical data is written to two separate drives in order to keep data safe and accessible if one drive dies. Usually used on servers (see *RAID*).

diskette See *floppy disk.*

display The monitor (or LCD panel on a notebook) that shows you the big picture. As a verb, it describes the PC's ability to show something on the screen (see *LCD, monitor*).

display type A design, layout, and desktop publishing term for headlines, subheads, pull-quotes, captions, and other prominent text (see *body text*).

dithering Simulating colors (or shades of gray) not available on a monitor or printer by mixing pixels or dots of other colors (or shades). For example, a monitor could simulate yellow-green by mixing yellow and green dots.

DLL Dynamic Link Library, a chunk of software that can be used by more than one program.

DMA Short for *direct memory access*, whereby an expansion card or other device accesses system memory directly, without involving the CPU.

DOC A file extension used by Microsoft Word and other word processors.

docking station An optional desktop platform for plugging in a notebook computer, so that connecting with a network, printer, full-size keyboard, desktop monitor, or any other peripheral can be accomplished all at once. Not all notebooks have optional docking stations (see *notebook computer*).

document When discussing files, any file created by an application. In other contexts, usually refers only those of such files that can be printed, such as a Word document or database report, but not the database itself or an Excel macro.

document management system A network application that helps large organizations track documents through many revision cycles. Most common in legal and corporate word processing centers.

documentation The manual and any other sheets of instructions that come with hardware or software, plus any software (tutorials, and so on) that helps you use the product in question.

DOS Short for *disk operating system,* DOS was the foundation on which Windows 3.1 ran. Current versions of Windows can emulate DOS as necessary to run old applications.

DOS prompt Also known as the command line or command prompt, the place on screen where you type in DOS commands (like COPY or DEL) and launch applications. It usually looks something like `C:\>`.

dot matrix printer A printer that uses tiny metal pins (usually 24 of them) and an inked ribbon to tap letters, numbers, and graphics onto the printed page. Dot matrix printers are the cheapest you can buy, and are still essential for multipart forms.

dot pitch A basic measure of monitor sharpness, the dot pitch is the distance, measured as a fraction of a millimeter, between phosphor dots of the same color on the inner surface of a CRT's screen. (On Trinitron and other aperture-grille monitors, which do not use phosphor dots, the equivalent measure is *aperture* (or *stripe*) *pitch*.)

double-click To tap the left mouse button twice in quick succession, usually to launch programs or execute commands (see *mouse*).

download Usually, to receive a file via modem from a Web site or online service. Also to send downloadable fonts, such as TrueType or PostScript fonts, from the PC to a printer (see *modem, upload*).

downloadable font A font that can be sent directly to a printer, without the PC having to create a bitmapped image of the text (see *bitmapped graphics, PostScript, TrueType*).

dpi (dots per inch) A measure of resolution used for printers, scanners, and other devices. Generally, the higher the dpi, the better a printed page or scanned image will look (see *resolution*).

DPMI Short for *DOS Protected Mode Interface*, a largely outdated specification developed to enable DOS applications to use memory beyond 640K.

draft mode A low-quality but generally fast mode for printing or displaying documents.

drag and drop A mouse move that usually refers to selecting text or graphics within a document, dragging it by holding down the left mouse button, and dropping it in a new location by releasing the button. Also refers to dragging a file icon and dropping it on an application (or command) icon to perform some action (see *click and drag*).

draw program An application that enables you to create and edit images—from simple lines and shapes to full-color illustrations—using lines, shapes, and patterns (see *vector graphics*).

drawing layer Some spreadsheets and word processors and many drawing programs enable you to draw on transparent overlays that "float" above the document (see *layers*).

drawing node See *control point.*

drive Generic term for peripheral device that handles data stored on disk or tape (see *disk, tape backup drive*).

drive arrays Clusters of network drives used to simulate a single drive (see *RAID*).

drive bay Space inside your computer reserved for holding a floppy drive, hard disk, CD ROM drive, or tape drive. Different computers accommodate different numbers and sizes of drives (see *form factor*).

drop cap A typesetting term for the first letter in a paragraph when set in extra-large or decorative display type, where the base of the letter drops below the rest of the line. Drop caps are typically used only to indicate the first page of a new chapter or the beginning of a new section.

DSL A high-speed Internet connection that uses conventional telephone lines and offers download speeds up to 1.5 mbps and upload speeds up to 350 kbps.

DSP Short for *digital signal processor,* a special kind of processor designed for ultra-fast manipulation of audio, video, and other analog data.

DSTN Short for *Dual-Scan Super-Twisted Nematic*, the most common type of *passive-matrix display*.

DTP See *desktop publishing*.

duplex printing The process of printing on both sides of a sheet of paper.

duty cycle The amount of time a piece of hardware is expected to be active. For example, if a printer has a 25 percent duty cycle, then the manufacturer expects it to be printing for 6 hours out of 24. Printer duty cycles are often expressed in pages per day or month.

DV Short for digital video, this is a standard format for digital videotapes, similar to the VHS standard for conventional analog videotapes.

DVD Short for *Digital Versatile Disc*, the movie equivalent of audio CDs, intended mostly for use in DVD players connected to TV sets. Most DVD-ROM drives can play DVD discs.

DVD-ROM Short for *Digital Versatile Disc-Read Only Memory*, which like CD-ROM is not memory at all but a storage format. This data counterpart of the format used in DVD video players is basically similar to CD-ROM, except it can hold four times as much data—up to 2.6GB.

Dvorak An alternative keyboard layout, named after its inventor, August Dvorak, that puts the most frequently used letters on the keys that are easiest to reach. (The standard *QWERTY* layout was designed to make the most frequently used letters hard to hit, so that fast typists wouldn't jam early mechanical typewriters.)

dye sublimation The best and most expensive color printing method used by desktop color printers.

E

ECC memory Short for *error correction code* memory, an expensive type of memory used mostly in expensive PCs intended for use as servers to help prevent crashes.

ECP See *Enhanced Parallel Port*.

EEPROM Short for *electronic erasable programmable read-only memory,* a special type of memory chip that holds information even when the PC is turned off. Can be erased by applying electric voltage; typically used for system BIOSs.

EGA Short for *Enhanced Graphics Adapter,* an obsolete IBM video card. The EGA standard is 640 by 350 resolution with 16 colors.

EIDE An augmentation of the IDE (Integrated Drive Electronics) standard, the most popular hard disk interface specification. Supports drives larger than 528MB, delivers increased performance, and lets one system handle up to four devices (see *IDE, UDMA*).

electron beam A stream of finely focused electrons that strike the inside face of the CRT, causing the color phosphors to glow.

electronic mail See *e-mail*.

ELF Short for *extremely low frequency*, which describes a type of electromagnetic radiation emitted by most electric and electronic devices, including computer monitors. May pose a health risk (see *VLF*).

e-mail Short for *electronic mail*, this term refers to private messages that can be sent and received over the Internet or a LAN.

embedded When applied to hardware, this term refers to built-in circuits such as the EIDE controllers built into hard disks. When applied to software, it refers to elements created by one program that have been saved within a document created by another (see *OLE*).

emergency disk A bootable floppy disk that contains data recovery utilities like ScanDisk, which you can use to boot up your computer if your hard disk becomes badly corrupted or infected with a virus. Windows 95 and 98 will automatically create an emergency disk for you (see *boot*).

EMI See *RFI*.

EMR Short for *electromagnetic radiation*, a broad term that refers to any radiation emitted at a frequency below that of light, including radio waves and monitor emissions.

EMS Short for *expanded memory specification,* a largely outdated specification developed to enable applications to use memory beyond 640K. Windows can emulate EMS for old applications that require it. Sometimes called LIM EMS for Lotus-Intel-Microsoft, the three companies that developed it.

emulated keys Notebook computer keyboards have fewer keys than a standard keyboard, so some of the keys must do double duty. For instance, if there's no [Key Caps: Page Up] key, the notebook may emulate that key by having you press [Key Caps: Fn] and [Key Caps: Home] simultaneously. [Maureen: Fn is a single key found on most notebooks. If there's no dingbat for it, use "the Fn key".]

encryption Protecting confidential files by turning them into gobbledygook. Encryption utilities let you assign passwords to encrypted files, so anyone who knows the password can restore the file to its original form.

Extended Capabilities Port See *EPP*.

Energy Star A set of specifications developed by the Environmental Protection Agency for energy-saving "green" PCs.

Enhanced IDE See *EIDE*.

Enhanced Parallel Port (EPP) A type of parallel port capable of sending data to and receiving data from printers, removable-media drives, and other devices at high speed. Enhanced Capabilities Ports (ECP) are similar. Cables for use with these ports are often labeled IEEE 1284, after the official standard.

EPROM Short for *erasable programmable read-only memory*. Like an *EEPROM*, except to erase the chip you must remove its cover and expose it to ultraviolet light. Generally used to produce small quantities of custom ROM chips (see *ROM*).

EPP See *Enhanced Parallel Port*.

EPS Short for *Encapsulated PostScript*, a high-quality, PostScript-based file format used by some drawing programs (see *PostScript*).

ergonomic A buzzword that means easy and comfortable to use.

error message Software's snippy way of telling you that you (or hardware or software) screwed up without giving you enough information to figure out what to do about it.

Ethernet The most popular kind of network card; also refers to the matching cables. The most common versions are 10BaseT and 100BaseT, which use the same kind of cable used by telephones, and similar plastic snap-in plugs. Older LANs may use thinnet (also known as Cheapernet or 10Base2), which uses thin coax cable and round metal snap-on connectors.

EXE A file extension used solely for executable files.

executable file Basically, a program that you can start yourself. When you choose a program from Windows' Start menu, , you're running an executable file. Most executable files end in an EXE extension, but some end in COM or BAT (see *program file*).

expanded memory See *EMS*.

expansion card Also known as an *expansion board*, an add-in circuit board that plugs into one of your PC's expansion slots and provides additional capability (as with a sound card), or supports a peripheral device such as a monitor or CD ROM drive (see *expansion slots, ISA, PCI, AGP*).

expansion slots The slots in your computer that hold expansion cards, known collectively as the *expansion bus*.

extended memory See *XMS*.

external memory cache See *L2 cache*.

F

fan-fold paper See *continuous-form paper*.

FAQ Short for *frequently asked questions*, Internet slang for a file or Web page containing answers to same.

Fast ATA See *EIDE*.

FAT Short for *file allocation table*, the tracking system Windows uses to monitor the status (available, in use, or damaged) of every *sector* on a hard or floppy disk (see *sectors*).

FAT32 An updated version of FAT that allows hard disks larger than 2GB to be formatted as a single C: drive.

fax-back An automated product-support system where you punch buttons on your touch-tone phone to order documents, which are sent to your fax machine.

fax modem A modem capable of sending and receiving faxes as well as the usual computer files. These days, it's probably impossible to find a modem that isn't a fax modem (see *modem*).

fax server A PC hooked to a network to provide fax modem services to workstations on a LAN. Sometimes tied in to an e-mail system.

FDDI Short for *Fiber Distributed Data Interface,* an *ANSI* standard for 100 mbps network adapters using fiber-optic cable.

featureitis The software equivalent of senility, where after a series of upgrades an application gets so overloaded with features that its overall quality or usefulness declines.

fiber-optic link Fiber-optic cables used as a faster alternative to Ethernet, most commonly to link servers (also known as a *network backbone*).

Fibre Channel A high-speed bus used mostly in servers with large drive arrays (see *RAID*).

field In databases, the basic building block of a data file. Each field holds a specific kind of information, such as a street address or a dollar amount. The contents of each field are called a *field value* (see *database, record*).

file The basic unit you use to store anything—text, data, computer instructions, all are saved in files (see *folder*).

file association A link established between a file extension and a particular application (for example, XLS with *Excel*, DOC with *Word*, and so on). Enables Windows to open files in the proper application when you double-click on them in Windows Explorer.

file attribute One of the four settings Windows uses to indicate whether a file is read-only (and cannot be deleted), an operating system file (like COMMAND.COM), a hidden file (that won't appear in Windows Explorer unless you change its default settings), or a file that has been backed up (see *archive bit*).

file extension The part of a file name that comes after the period, such as DOC or EXE (see *file, file name*).

file folder See *folder*.

file format A type of program or data file, often indicated by the file extension.

File Manager The Windows 3.1 counterpart of Windows Explorer

file name Windowsfile names have two parts separated by a period—though the period and the second part are hidden unless you change Windows' default settings. Windows uses part that comes after the period, called the *extension*, to identify file types. Applications' extensions are .exe (or sometimes .com), Word documents' are .doc, and so on.

file server A PC that stores data and program files for a network.

file transfer utility A program, such as *Laplink*, that lets you quickly copy files between two computers hooked together by a special cable connecting their parallel or serial ports.(see *parallel port, null modem cable*).

film recorder Primarily used by people who create professional presentations, film recorders transfer computer graphics output to 35mm slide film.

firmware Software that is permanently stored on a ROM or EEPROM chip, like your PC's BIOS. Firmware can be upgraded by replacing a ROM or running a special utility to load new software on the EEPROM.

flame Internet slang for an e-mail message or newsgroup or message board post that attacks the recipients in an unreserved and often vicious manner. By extension *to flame (someone)*, to send such a message; *to get flamed*, to receive one; *flamer*, someone who habitually sends flames; and *flame war*, an ongoing exchange of flames.

flash memory A type of memory chip, commonly used to create a kind of permanent RAM disk for notebooks, that can retain data after the system is turned off (see *RAM disk*).

flat file database A *data manager* that stores all its data in a single table (see *relational database*).

flat-panel display The kind of liquid crystal display (LCD) used in virtually all notebook computers.

flicker free A hyperbolic marketing term used by manufacturers to describe displays that run at *refresh rates* higher than 70 Hz to reduce perceived flicker.

floating point unit See *FPU*.

floppy disk A removable disk used to store computer data. The current standard floppy disk measures 3½" and holds 1.39MB (or 1.44 million bytes, which isn't the same thing). Older notebook PCs used 3½" floppies that held only 720K. Older desktop PCs used 5¼" floppies that held 1.2MB.

floppy drive The drive that reads and writes data to and from a floppy disk.

flowchart A diagram that uses lines, boxes, circles, arrows, and other shapes to demonstrate a process or other activity. Most popular presentation graphics programs let you create simple flowcharts.

Fn Short for *function*, on a notebook PC a key with this label is used in combination with other keys to access functions that do not have their own dedicated keys. On particularly cramped keyboards you may need to use the Fn key to access such keys as [Home] and [Enter].

folder The basic tool for organizing information on your hard disk, a folder is intended to hold related files, such as all the data files created with an application. Your hard disk is a filing cabinet, so logically files within it are grouped into folders. A folder inside another folder is called a *subfolder*. See *Windows Explorer, folder tree*.

folder tree A full listing of your hard disk's file structure, showing folders and subfolders as branches off the root. Shown in the left pane of Windows Explorer.

font Originally referred to a specific point size and weight of a particular typeface. In computer terminology, a font is an electronic file that contains a *typeface*.

font manager A utility that helps organize a large number of fonts.

footer Most word processors allow you to print a line or two of type at the bottom of every page called a footer. Footers may include text and/or a page number.

footprint The space a computer or a peripheral device takes up on your desk. If a computer is designed to stand on end, for instance, it is said to have a small footprint.

form In a database, a screen display that shows a subset of the database's fields, often with explanatory labels and instructions. Database applications typically include a variety of forms for various functions, such as entering data and browsing records.

form factor Most often used to refer to the size of an internal disk drive. The most common form factors are 3.5-inch and 5.25-inch, which describe the widths of the internal platters, not the widths of the drives themselves (which are actually closer to 4 and 6 inches wide, respectively). These are subdivided into full-height (takes up two drive bays), half-height (one bay), and third-height (fits a smaller bay that generally can hold only a floppy or superfloppy drive). By using an appropriate adapter, you can install a 3.5-inch drive in a 5.25-inch bay, or a third-height drive in a standard bay.

format To prepare a disk to receive data—or to apply fonts, indents, margins, colors, and so on to a document (see *file format*).

formatting The end result of creating a page layout and applying text attributes (see *desktop publishing, word processor*).

forum See *message board*.

FPU Short for *floating point unit*, a portion of your CPU that performs floating point calculations, as opposed to the integer calculations the rest of the chip performs.

fractal A mathematical formula that produces graphics that look like natural textures and shapes.

fractional T-1 A type of *leased line* that can carry amounts of data varying from 64 kbps up to 1.5 mbps.

frame In desktop publishing or word processing, a box that can be filled with graphics or text and positioned anywhere on the page. In video, one of many discrete images in a video sequence (broadcast standard is 30 frames per second).

frame grabber A video board and matching software that enable you to isolate individual frames in a video sequence and copy them into a graphics or page layout program.

freeware Free software, usually available through a Web page.

front end Usually just another way of saying user interface. Sometimes refers to the "client" end of a client-server network application (see *client-server, user interface*).

FTP Short for File Transfer Protocol, the standard for downloading files from *FTP servers*, the Internet's file libraries. When using a Web browser, you may not know whether or not you're using FTP.

full backup Making a safety copy of every file on your hard disk (see *backup*).

full-bleed A printer that can print all the way to the edges of the paper.

full defrag A mode used by a disk defragger, in which the scattered sectors used by each of your files are assembled in one place, all the empty spaces between them removed (see *disk defragmenter*).

full duplex A type of communications where data travels in both directions simultaneously. A full duplex speakerphone allows you to hear what the other person is saying while you're talking (see *half duplex*).

full-motion video Strictly speaking, TV-quality or better moving video images displayed in a window or full screen on your PC. Term often misused to refer to jerky, postage-stamp-size images.

function key The 12 (or fewer) "F" keys (F1, F2, etc.), usually lining the top of the keyboard. Different applications use them for different things, but F1 usually triggers the Help menu. May also refer to the the Fn key found on many notebook PCs.

G

gamer Someone who plays a lot of computer games; by extension, gamer PC, a computer that is optimized for game playing with a fast 3-D video board, a joystick, flightstick, or other alternative input device, and perhaps other unusual options.

gateway A PC or special box hooked to a network to connect it to another system, such as the Internet, a remote LAN, or a commercial e-mail system. See *server*.

GB See *gigabyte*.

gbps Short for *gigabits per second*. See *bits per second*.

geek A person with a profound understanding of computers or some particular technology. Sometimes used as a term of respect, e.g. "he's a hardcore Unix geek." By extension, *geeky*, to describe something that only a geek could understand or would appreciate.

GIF Short for *Graphic Interchange Format,* one of the standard graphics formats used on the Web.

gigabyte (GB) 1024 megabytes

glare screen An antiglare covering that goes over the front of your monitor to reduce eye-straining reflections.

glitch A small problem with hardware or software, usually less serious than a bug but annoying nonetheless.

glossary In word processing, a list of words that you can quickly insert into a document by typing only a short abbreviation.

graphics card See *video card*.

graphics controller The circuitry that produces the image you see on your screen, the graphics controller may reside either on a video card or on the PC's motherboard. Also used to refer to the single chip that does most of the work in producing an image.

graphics file Any file that holds an image rather than text, such as a drawing, a scanned photo, a bitmap, or clip art.

graphics mode See *video mode*. Also used to describe a display mode distinct from *text mode* (also known as *character mode*).

graphics tablet A flat panel (also known as a graphics pad) that enables you to draw using a stylus instead of a mouse. A pressure-sensitive tablet lets you vary the width or color of the line on screen by pressing harder, providing a close simulation of working with a pencil or brush.

grayscale A term used to describe an image containing a number of gray shades as well as black and white. Formerly used also to describe scanners that produced only grayscale images, but those are now rare if not entirely extinct.

green computing Using a PC with the environment in mind, typically involving computers and peripherals designed to use less power, plus a commitment to recycling paper, batteries, and toner cartridges.

Group III fax Supporting speeds up to 9600 bps, this is the standard to which almost every fax machine and fax modem conforms. With V.17 enhancement (supported by most modems but less common on fax machines), can go up to 14.4 kbps. Group I and II are long obsolete, while Group IV (which requires a *leased line*) is extremely rare.

GUI (graphical user interface) Back in the old DOS days, this unfortunate acronym, pronounced *gooey,* was what people used to describe environments like Windows in which you use your computer by mousing and clicking on icons and pull-down menus, instead of typing text-based commands. The term's not so useful now that almost everyone's running a GUI.

half duplex A type of communications where data travels in only one direction at a time. On a half-duplex speakerphone, when you're talking nothing the other person says comes through the speakers (see *full duplex*).

halftone A type of image produced using screens (patterns of dots) to simulate grays on black-and-white printers, or to simulate a full range of colors from the 3 or 4 inks used by color printers.

handle The nickname people use when they enter a chat room, used to preserve privacy and sometimes to adopt a strange persona.

hard carriage return Pressing the [Key Caps: Enter] key puts two invisible characters into a text file: a line feed and a carriage return. Together they are called a *hard carriage return*. They make the cursor move down one line and back to the left end of the new line.

hard copy A paper print out.

hard disk Also known as a *hard drive*, the basic data storage device in most computers, which stores gigabytes of data one metal platters coated with a magnetic medium (see *magnetic media*).

hard disk interface A term that variously refers to the circuitry employed by a hard disk to communicate with a PC; an expansion card containing that circuitry; or a hard disk connector either on the motherboard, an expansion card, or on the hard disk itself. EIDE and SCSI are the two hard disk interfaces currently in widespread use..

header A line or two of type at the top of every page, usually including a small amount of text and/or a page number (see *footer*).

Hertz (Hz) A standard measure of frequency, synonymous with cycles per second (cps). One megahertz (MHz) equals 1,000,000 Hz.

hibernation See *suspend to disk*.

hidden file See *file attribute*.

high-level programming language A *programming language* that's somewhat Englishlike, although only a programmer would think that. The ultimate *low-level* programming language is assembly language, which is kind of like programming with the 1s and 0s of binary math.

high memory area See *HMA*.

High Performance ATA A term used by Maxtor to identify a recent enhancement of the IDE hard disk interface standard (see *Enhanced IDE*).

HMA Short for *High Memory Area*, the first 64K of RAM above 1MB. Some old DOS programs need to use this particular chunk of memory; when necessary, Windows can let them, or at least fool them into thinking they are.

home page A somewhat outdated synonym for *Web site*. The Web's inventor, Tim Berners-Lee, imagined that users would create their own "home" pages from which they would navigate the Web, but as things turned out that role is played by search engines and Web browsers' bookmarks.

horizontal scan rate Measures how fast a video board or monitor can draw a line from one side of the screen to the other. The higher the horizontal scan rate, the higher the maximum resolution at a given *refresh rate*.

HPA Short for *High Performance Addressing*, a type of *passive-matrix display* that may have some minor advantages over improvement over the more common *DSTN* type.

hqx See *BinHex*.

HTML Short for *HyperText Markup Language*, the set of codes that format text for display in Web browsers.

I

IBM AT An ancient IBM personal computer, introduced in 1985 and built around Intel's 286 CPU (see *CPU*).

IBM PC The first IBM personal computer, released in 1981. Built around Intel's 4.77-MHz 8088 CPU, it originally shipped with 64K of RAM.

IBM XT The first IBM system with a hard disk, otherwise nearly identical to the IBM PC.

icon A little picture that represents an application, file, or command in Windows or another graphical user interface (see *GUI*).

IDE Short for *Integrated Drive Electronics,* a hard drive standard that predated *EIDE.*

IEEE Short for the *Institute of Electrical and Electronics Engineers,* a professional organization that (among other things) develops and publishes communications standards, notably including those for Ethernet, parallel ports, and 1394 serial ports.

image editor In desktop publishing parlance, an image editor is a tool used to touch up or enhance a *bitmapped* image, such as a scanned photograph.

imagesetter An expensive, high-resolution PostScript printer often used in desktop publishing (see *PostScript printer*).

incremental backup A backup that duplicates every file that has changed since the *last* incremental backup; usually performed every day (see *backup*).

infrared Light below the visible spectrum, used in some wireless mice, printer sharing devices, and network adapters.

INI An extension used by Windows 3.1 and its applications for the files used to store program initialization settings.

ink jet printer An inexpensive alternative to laser printers, an ink jet printer sprays liquid ink onto the paper. Ink jets are the least expensive color printers, though their quality to date has not matched that produced by more expensive *thermal wax* and *dye sublimation* printers.

insertion point The I-beam shaped mouse pointer that appears in Windows text documents.

instruction In programming, instructions are the equivalent of commands. Fundamentally, a program is simply a long list of instructions.

Intel The largest microprocessor manufacturer in the world, responsible for setting all the important standards in PC CPUs, including the 286, 386, 486, and Pentium lines.

interactive A buzzword in the computer gaming and multimedia business, it implies that your input will affect what's happening on the screen. But since that's true of almost all computer applications, including word processors, the term is a bit too general to be very useful.

interface A connector, such as a serial port or a hard disk interface; also any specification that enables hardware devices to communicate. When applied to software, a shortened form of *user interface* (see *hard disk interface, user interface*).

interlaced A video mode that draws the even lines on the screen in one pass, the odd lines on the next. Allows a higher resolution display than a monitor would otherwise be able to support, but usually results in an irritating flicker.

interleave Once upon a time, you had to set a hard drive's disk interleave (the number of rotations required to read a track from disk) to match the speed of the computer in which it was installed. With today's hard disk drives, this is a nonissue.

Internet The global network that connects an increasingly large percentage of the world's computers and LANs, and the infrastructure used by e-mail and the Web.

Internet backbone A high-speed network that connects major Internet service providers. Large companies, government agencies, and universities may also connect to the backbone instead of going through an ISP.

Internet connection The hardware that connects your PC to the Internet (see *modem, ISDN, cable modem, DSL, T-1, T-3*).

Internet service provider (ISP) A company that sells Internet access for a monthly or hourly fee.

interpolated resolution A technique used primarily by scanners to increase the sharpness of scanned images (see *scanner*).

interpreter Software that converts *high-level* programming instructions in a program into the *machine language* understood by your computer—on the fly, as the program is running. The so-called "virtual machine" that runs Java applets is an interpreter. A program that uses an interpreter is said to be *uncompiled*, and runs slower than one that's been compiled (see *compiler*).

interrupt A PC's hardware interrupts work a little like valves in a car's engine, routing the CPU's attention to various pieces of hardware as necessary. Most expansion cards need exclusive access to one or more of your PC's 15 interrupt request (IRQ) lines. There are also software interrupts, but only programmers need to mess with them.

interrupt conflict When two or more devices attempt to use the same IRQ.

I/O Computerese for *input/output*. The term *I/O port* describes any port on your PC, but is often used to refer specifically to a serial port (see *port, serial port*).

IPX The network protocol used on Netware LANs. Once ubiquitous, it is gradually being supplanted by TCP/IP.

IRC Short for **Internet Relay Chat** (see *chat room*).

IrDA Short for *Infrared Data Association*, an organization that gave its name to a standard for communicating between PCs, PDAs, printers, and other devices with the same kind of infrared light signals used by remote controls.

IRQ Short for *interrupt request line*, an exclusive communications channel between an expansion card and the CPU (see *interrupt*).

ISA Short for *Industry Standard Architecture,* the oldest and slowest of the three types of expansion slots commonly found in current PCs. Though verging on obsolecence, ISA slots are still standard equipment, since they're still the ones used by most modems and various other devices that don't need the higher performance of PCI slots (see *expansion slots*).

ISP See *Internet service provider*.

ISDN Short for *Integrated Services Digital Network,* a digital phone standard that enables high-speed data transmission. ISDN is available in most areas of the U.S., but not all. The "integrated services" part refers to ISDN's ability to handle telephones and data communications on a single wire, but to date ISDN lines are rarely used for anything except Internet access.

ITU Short for the *International Telecommunications Union,* the successor to the CCITT. This United Nations agency sets major modem and fax standards such as V.90 and Group III (see *Group III fax*).

J

jaggies Slang for the stairstep edges that result when curves and diagonal lines are displayed on screen or in bitmaped graphics (see *antialiasing*).

jargon What people who know something about computers use to intimidate others who know less.

joules See *watt*.

joystick A throttle-like input device that moves the cursor in computer games, usually outfitted with a couple of "fire" buttons and sensitivity controls.

JPEG Short for *Joint Photographic Experts Group* and the name of one of the standard graphics formats used on the Web.

jumper A bit of plastic a bit smaller than a match head containing a metal connector, designed to fit over a pair of pins on a circuit board. Many expansion cards, disk drives, and motherboards enable you to configure them by moving a jumper from one pair of pins to another pair (see *configuration*).

justified text Text that aligns perfectly on the right *and* left margins. Most word processors and desktop publishing programs can justify text with the click of a mouse.

K

K See *kilobyte*.

K6, K6-2, K6-3 AMD's competitors to Intel's Pentium family.

kbps Short for *kilobits per second* (ee *bits per second*).

kerning Adjusting the space between two adjacent letters so they look more pleasing to the eye.

keystroke A single key-press.

kilobyte (K, KB, or Kb) 1024 bytes. See *byte*.

kilohertz (KHz) One thousand cycles per second.

kioskware Slang term for multimedia applications run on terminals with touchscreens or membrane keyboards. Commonly found in museums, public transit hubs, and shopping malls.

L

L2 cache Short for *Level 2 cache*. All contemporary CPUs have a fast, built-in memory cache (the Level 1 or L1 cache). If the CPU can't find what it needs in its own cache, it tries the Level 2 or L2 memory cache—also known as *secondary* or *external* memory cache—an array of *SRAM* chips on the motherboard between the CPU and main memory. The idea is to keep the CPU from accessing main memory directly, which would slow things down (see *memory cache*, *CPU*).

LAN Short for *local area network*, a network connecting computers in your office or home, as opposed to the Internet, the big network that connects most of the computers in the world.

landscape orientation Printed sideways on a page, so the page is wider than it is tall (see *portrait orientation)*.

laptop Synonym for *notebook*, though some computer magazines use *laptop* for heavier models and *notebook* for lighter ones..

laser printer The most popular printer for getting sharp printouts, a laser printer produces one page at a time by scanning an image onto an electrostatically charged drum with a laser. Toner clings to the image and is fused to the page, similar to the way a photocopier produces copies.

LaserJet Hewlett-Packard's trade name for its popular line of laser printers.

layers In a graphics program, a stack of virtual transparent work surfaces. You can create, edit, and delete objects in one layer without affecting those in any other layer. Objects on the "top" layers obscure those underneath them. If you know how old-fashioned cel animation works, this is basically the same idea.

LCD Short for *liquid crystal display*, a flat panel of tiny cells, used on most mobile computers in place of a monitor. Each cell contains a substrate that blocks or admits light depending on the electric charge; together these cells produce the image on screen (see *passive-matrix display*).

LCD panel An LCD that sits atop an overhead projector, so images can be projected against a wall or screen. Plugs into any monitor connector (usually a notebook's, for convenience).

leading The amount of space, measured in points, between two lines of type. In the old days of manual typesetting, lines were divided by thin strips of lead—hence the name (and the pronunciation).

leased line Telephone line permanently connecting two locations, with a much higher *bandwidth* than a conventional phone line.

LED Short for *light-emitting diode*, an LED is a sort of tiny electronic light bulb. Used in a PC's front panel, external modems, smoke alarms, and so on.

ligature A character composed of two letters, as in the combination a/e in *encyclopædia.*

line chart A graph that shows continuous change over time, intended to emphasize trends rather than the individual values that make up the line.

line conditioner A device designed to protect your PC from such electrical problems as brownouts, surges, and spikes. More sophisticated and expensive than a *surge protector*.

line feed On a computer, a nonprinting character that moves the cursor down one line (see *hard carriage return*).

Linux A free version of Unix, designed for PCs, that's very popular for use on Web servers. May eventually become competitive with Windows for use by average users.

list boxes A Windows term for pull-down menus in dialog boxes.

lithium ion storage (LIS) Describes the better type of battery currently used in notebook PCs. Offers longer life than *nickel metal-hydride* batteries.

load A general term that refers to copying software or data from disk to memory. Synonymous with *start, run,* or *launch* when applied to programs; the same as *open* when applied to a data file. The only term used to describe copying a device driver from disk to memory.

local area network See *LAN*.

local network See *LAN*, a jargony term we've avoided using in this edition as it seems to be falling out of favor, a trend we're happy to encourage.

LocalTalk A network protocol used by Macintosh computers.

log in Synonymous with *log on*, to enter your name and password when you connect to the Internet, a LAN, an online service, or start a PC that's set up with multiple accounts so different users can store their settings.

logical drive A drive that Windows recognizes and identifies with a drive letter, as opposed to the actual, physical drive. For example, when some people buy a new hard disk, they split it into multiple logical drives (C:, D:, E:, and so on) of varying sizes using Windows' FDISK utility. Creating these drives is called *partitioning*.

logical format Preparing a disk to store data with Windows' Format commandcommand. Most people just say "format," for short (see *low-level format*).

logical operators See *Boolean logic*.

lookup tables A lookup table is a multi-column table used (primarily in spreadsheets and databases) to define correlations between different types of data. For example, you could use a lookup table to generate grades from test scores: The first column would contain break points for the scores (90 percent, 80 percent, and so on), while the second column would have the grades (A, B, and so on).

lossless A compression scheme that reduces file size without reducing the amount of information in the original file. See *lossy*.

lossy A compression scheme typically used with graphics, sound, and digital video that saves disk space by reducing the amount of information in the original file. High compression ratios result in smaller files but lower quality images or sound due to data loss (see *lossless*).

low-level format The lowest level of formatting, done at the factory, which must be in place before Windows can set up and format a hard disk.

lpi (lines per inch) A measure of the resolution of a printer when printing halftone images (see *halftone*).

M

M II Cyrix's competitor to Intel's Pentium II and Celeron processors.

macro A series of keystrokes, commands, and/or mouse actions that can be "played back" using a special key combination. Sometimes called a *script*.

macro language A simple programming language that goes beyond recording keystrokes and/or mouse actions, enabling you to add special features, such as branching (see *branch*).

macro recorder A feature found in many applications that records your keystrokes and/or mouse actions and saves them as a macro. This is the way most people create macros.

magic wand A tool in a paint program that selects a region of pixels with similar colors, such as the sky in the background of a landscape.

magnetic media Anything that stores information in magnetic form: diskettes, cassette tapes, reel-to-reel tapes in a recording studio, the strip on the back of your credit card.

magneto-optical (MO) drive A relatively unpopular type of removable-media drive.

mail merge A word processing feature that inserts information from a data file (usually a list of names and addresses) into pre-selected positions in a text file (such as a form letter) in order to print a series of customized documents. As its name implies, mail merge is most often used to create mass mailings.

main memory Also called *system memory*, the large block of memory chips in your PC where computing happens. When you start an application or open a file, that information is copied from its storage area on disk into main memory, the place where you create or change data (an e-mail message, a long report, whatever). When people say "memory" or "RAM," they usually mean main memory (see *memory*).

mainframe An old-fashioned computer that lives in its own air-conditioned tomb, attended by geek priests in lab coats. Now useful mostly for giant processing tasks like airline reservation systems and insurance claims processing.

mask In a database, a mask is used to ensure that data entered in a field is formatted in exactly the desired way. For example, a mask for a phone number might be (###) ###-####. The # characters will take only numbers, and the database will automatically add the parentheses, space, and hyphen.

master page An electronic page that holds the text and graphics you want to appear on every page of a desktop publishing document or on every slide of a presentation.

maximize To expand a window to fill the screen (see *restore*).

mbps Short for *megabits per second*. See See *bits per second*.

MCA Short for *Micro Channel Architecture,* an obsolete expansion bus standard employed in some PS/2s, an obsolete family of IBM computers.

mean time between failure (MTBF) A largely meaningless statistic suggesting how long a device, such as a hard disk or printer, will run before breaking down.

megabyte (MB) 1024 kilobytes or 1,048,576 bytes.

megahertz (MHz) One million cycles per second.

memory Usually refers to *main memory*, the biggest bank of memory chips in your PC—the place where data gets processed. Click a command in your word processor, and your computer shuffles 1s and 0s in memory at a frightening pace; turn off your PC, and everything in memory vaporizes, which is why you need to save any changes to disk before you turn off your PC. In the stricter, techier sense, memory refers to any chips that hold data or software in the form of minuscule electrical charges (see *main memory, RAM, ROM, storage*).

memory buffer This catchall term describes a small area of a memory on a wide range of devices, but it's most often used in conjunction with CD ROM drives and hard disks. Data immediately ahead of the drive's laser or read/write head is copied into the memory buffer for fast access. All things being equal, the bigger the memory buffer, the faster the data throughput (see *disk cache*).

memory cache A small chunk of fast RAM that holds a copy of whatever data the CPU most recently used. A PC's *main memory* is too slow for the CPU to access directly without incurring debilitating *wait states*; a memory cache keeps wait states to a minimum. Most CPUs have a small memory cache right on the chip (see *main memory, L2 cache, wait state*).

memory-resident Synonymous with *terminate and stay resident (TSR)*, describes an old type of DOS application or device driver that hangs around in RAM and "pops up" over other DOS programs at the press of a key or two. Made obsolete by Windows' ability to multitask applications and use large amounts of memory.

memory bus See *bus speed*.

memory speed A measurement in nanoseconds (ns) that indicates various types of memory (10ns, 60ns, 70ns). It's important not to use memory with a higher speed than your PC requires: for example, if the manual says the PC needs 60ns memory, you can't use 70ns. It's sometimes okay to use faster memory than your PC requires, though that will not make it run faster. Also refers to the speed at which memory operations can be performed, though that's more commonly referred to as *bus speed*.

menu A list of commands you choose from, as you'd choose an entrée.

menu bar The place at the top of a Windows application where the pull-down menus (File, Edit, and so on) are found.

message board A virtual "place" on the Internet, an online service, or a Web site where a group of people can exchange written messages. Similar to a chat room, except that participation is not in real time: participants post messages any time it's convenient, and they stay on the system for some time so that everyone can read all the posts. Other terms for message boards include forum, thread, conversation area, community, board, bulletin board, conference, BBS, and discussion area.

MGA Short for the long-dead *Monochrome Graphics Adapter,* IBM's first video card for the PC, which could only produce characters.

MHz See *megahertz*.

Micro Channel See *MCA*.

microprocessor Generally, a computer (or most of one) on a single chip. Many PCs contain several microprocessors: the CPU, the graphics controller, the controller built into the hard disk, the signal processor in the modem, and so on.

MIDI Short for *Musical Instrument Digital Interface,* this standard was created by musical instrument manufacturers. If you install MIDI-in and MIDI-out ports in your PC by attaching a *MIDI breakout box* or *MIDI interface*, you can hook up with any MIDI-compatible device (such as a synthesizer) and, with the aid of MIDI sequencer software, turn your PC into an electronic recording studio.

MIDI breakout box A box that hooks to a sound board's joystick port to add MIDI-in and MIDI-out ports.

MIDI interface A more sophisticated set of MIDI ports that will do more than the basic in and out of a breakout box.

mid-tower See *tower system*.

millisecond (ms) One thousandth of a second, a measurement often used to describe a disk drive's *average seek time*.

minicomputer A relatively expensive and powerful computer, such as an IBM AS/400 or Sun Enterprise servers, often used as a *database server* for PC networks. As PCs have gotten more powerful, the once-clear distinction between microcomputers (PCs and Macs), workstations (from Sun, IBM, and other manufacturers), and minicomputers has gotten fuzzy.

minitower See *tower system*.

MIPS Short for *million instructions per second*, an abstract (and therefore pretty useless) measure of CPU performance. Also the name of a company that tried to compete with Intel, and the CPUs it sold, which are still used by Silicon Graphics.

MLA Short for *Multi-Line Addressing*, a type of *passive-matrix display* that may have some minor advantages over the more common *DSTN* type.

mobile computer See *notebook*.

modem Short for *modulator/demodulator*, the device that enables your PC to connect to the Internet over the phone lines.

modem protocol See *protocol*.

monitor The TV-like box that shows you what's going on. Without one, you'd feel pretty dumb staring at the top of your computer. Alternatively referred to as the *display*.

monochrome Single-color video card or monitor that usually displays white, green, or amber characters against a dark background. Usually refers to the original IBM Monochrome Display Adapter (MDA) or Hercules Graphics Card (HGC).

monospaced A typeface, such as Courier, in which all the letters are spaced equally, no matter how fat or thin each letter is (the *i* gets as much space as the *w*). See *proportionally spaced*.

motherboard The main circuit board in your PC. Usually includes the memory, CPU, expansion slots, EIDE adapter, and circuits for serial, parallel, and USB ports. Less often may include video controller, Ethernet, sound chips, and/or SCSI adapter.

motion video A term used to distinguish TV-style moving pictures from computer "video" (video cards and monitors).

mouse A handheld device with at least two buttons and a taillike cord, which you slide around your desktop to move a pointer on screen.

mouse pointer The little arrow you move around the screen with your mouse.

mouse port A connector on the back of the PC where the mouse plugs in.

MPC Short for *Multimedia PC.* The original MPC specification suggested now-obsolete minimum hardware requirements for sound, motion video, CD-ROM, and other items used by games and other multimedia software. The succeeding MPC 2 spec is somewhat more realistic.

MPR II Concerned about health risks, the Swedish government established the MPR II standard, a maximum exposure level for electromagnetic monitor emissions. Most (but not all) new monitors come with specially engineered components that bring them in line with MPR II (see *VLF* and *ELF*).

MUD Short for *multiuser dungeon*, a text-based online virtual "environment."

multifrequency Describes a monitor that can handle more than one video mode. Except for a few cheap VGA-only monitors, pretty much every monitor on the market is multifrequency.

multimedia Probably the vaguest term in the PC industry, freely applied to anything that involves CD-ROM, sound, or motion video.

MultiRead A CD-ROM or DVD-ROM drive that can read CD-ROMs, CD-Rs, CD-RWs, and audio CDs.

multiscan See *multifrequency*.

multitasking Running more than one application at the same time. This capability is one of Windows' big advantages over its predecessor, DOS.

multiuser Network applications that enable more than one person to work on them at the same time.

N

nanosecond (ns) A billionth of a second, most often used to describe the speed ratings of memory chips.

NetBeui A network protocol promoted by Microsoft for use on LANs.

NetWare The most popular *network operating system*, still popular in large corporations but much less common than it was before Microsoft added basic networking capabilities to Windows..

network Generally used interchangeably with LAN, though the Internet is also a network.

network administrator The person who makes sure a LAN is working properly and who assigns access rights to users. Also the person you blame when something goes wrong.

network application Any application that requires a network to run—e-mail, multiuser databases, *Lotus Notes*, and so on.

network card The expansion card used to connect your PC with a LAN.

network node Synonymous with *network workstation*, a single PC on a LAN.

network operating system (NOS) Software (most often Netware) that used to be required to connect a group of PCs together into a *LAN*. Now that that capability's built into Windows, the term's largely obsolete.

network protocol See *protocol*.

network server See *server*.

newbie Internet slang for an inexperienced user. Often disparaging, e.g. "typical clueless newbie."

news reader A program for reading Internet newsgroups.

newsgroup One of the tens of thousands of discussion areas on Usenet, the Internet's main area for non-real-time discussions.

nickel-cadmium (NiCd) A type of battery formerly used in notebooks, now supplanted by LIS and NiMH..

nickel metal-hydride (NiMH) Formerly the most popular type of notebook battery, NiMH batteries seem to be on their way out since LIS batteries last longer.

nick Short for *nickname* (see *handle*).

noninterlaced See *interlaced*.

notebook PC A portable PC.

Notepad The simple text editor that comes with Windows (see *text editor*).

NT In Windows NT, this was originally short for *new technology* (see *Windows NT*).

NTFS Short for *NT File System*. An alternate disk format supported by Windows NT; more reliable than *FAT* or *FAT32*.

NTSC Short for *National Television Standard Committee.* Describes the U.S. standard for broadcast TV, which provides for 525 scan lines and 30 frames per second.

numeric keypad The 17 numeric keys on the right of most computer keyboards, arranged in a layout similar to that of an old 10-key adding machine. If you turn off Num Lock, these keys also do double duty as cursor movement keys (Pg Up, Home, Ins, and so on).

object In Windows or other graphical operating systems, an icon or other item on the screen that does something when you click on it with a mouse. In drawing programs, one of the basic building blocks of drawings, like a line, a rectangle, or a curve. In programming, a self-contained chunk of code that can be used in a variety of contexts without modification.

OCR Short for *optical character recognition,* a technology that takes a scanned image of a printed page and converts it into editable text, usually with a small percentage of errors.

OEM Short for *original equipment manufacturer*, the company that actually made the hardware as opposed to the company whose name is on it. Also used to refer to the *OEM market*—companies that buy and resell original equipment under their own name.

OLE Short for *Object Linking and Embedding,* a Windows standard for combining data from different applications. Creating an OLE link is like cutting and pasting between documents, except the pasted data is updated automatically to reflect any changes made to the original.

OLE automation A Widows standard that allows one application to control another, or a single macro written in a compatible language like Visual Basic to control more than one application.

online help Explanations and reference material for an application, which you can view on screen by pressing [Key Caps: F1] or choosing a command from the Help menu.

online service Once upon a time, services such as CompuServe and America Online were where PC users went for e-mail, message boards, chat, shareware, and other things we now get on the Internet. Today, online services are basically Internet service providers with a few extra private services thrown in.

on-site service If something goes wrong with your PC, the repair person will come to your door to fix it (or, worst case, pick it up for servicing).

operating system A program (usually Windows) that enables your PC to read and write data to and from disk, send pictures to your monitor, and accept keyboard commands. Without an operating system, your PC is just an expensive paperweight.

option buttons A standard dialog box element that enables you to pick only one choice from several entries (like a bank of car radio buttons that only allows you to choose one station). Also called *radio buttons*.

org chart A treelike diagram showing managerial responsibilities in a company, usually rendered with lines and boxes.

ornaments Also known as dingbats, ornaments are pictorial characters, as opposed to alphabetic or numeric characters.

orphan record A record in a database table that refers to information that has been deleted from another table (see *referential integrity*).

OS/2 An IBM operating system, functionally similar to Windows 95, that can run most of the same software Windows 3.1 could. Never popular, it's now essentially obsolete, since it can't run most current software.

overhead transparencies Paper-size sheets of clear plastic, which you write on or run through your printer and then plop on an overhead projector, which projects the text or graphics on a wall or screen.

overscanning Scanning at a higher resolution than that of the final output.

P

page layout The design decisions that affect the way a printed page will appear, including margins, columns, picture placement, typefaces, and so on. *Page layout program* means a desktop publishing program, like Pagemaker or Quark XPress.

paint program A graphics application that lets you create colorful images using your mouse or a drawing tablet. Unlike draw programs, paint images are saved as bitmaps, which makes them hard to edit (see *bitmapped graphics*).

palette Available screen colors; also, a grid showing these colors, which you can use to pick the colors you want. May also refer to groups of command buttons, such as the floating "icon palettes" in some Windows applications.

palmtop See *PDA*.

Pantone See *PMS*.

parallel port Sometimes called the *printer port,* the 25-pin socket on the back of your PC into which you plug a parallel cable (there's usually a printer on the other end). A PC can have a maximum of two parallel ports, referred to as LPT 1 and LPT 2 by Windows. Parallel ports move data 8 bits at a time (see *enhanced parallel port, serial port*).

passive-matrix display The most common and least expensive LCD, which uses an invisible grid of wires embedded in glass to send electrical pulses to individual liquid crystal cells, turning them on or off (see *active-matrix LCD, LCD*).

PC Card Three notebook expansion specifications (Type I, Type II, and Type III), which describe slots and expansion cards no larger in width and height than a credit card (but varying in thickness depending on the Type). Memory cards, modems, hard disks, and more have all been squeezed onto PC Cards. Formerly known as PCMCIA cards.

PCI bus A fast industry-standard expansion bus that runs at 33 MHz, common in Pentium systems but also used in some later 486 computers.

PCMCIA Short for *Personal Computer Memory Card International Association* (see *PC Card*).

PDA Short for *Personal Digital Assistant*, a general term for pocket-sized "palmtop" computers like the Palm Pilot, Pison, and HP 300LX.

PDF Short for Portable Document Format. Usually created by Adobe Acrobat, PDF files are the most popular format for distributing documents formatted for printing rather than on-screen reading over the Internet.

Pentium Intel's current processor family, successors to the 486, able to run virtually all software written for previous Intel CPUs. The original Pentium and Pentium Pro chips have been discontinued, or at least have all but disappeared from the market, supplanted by the Pentium MMX, Pentium II, Celeron, and Xeon. See also *K6* and *M II*.

Pentium II The successor to Intel's Pentium Pro chip, the Pentium II is potentially much faster, not so much because of its minor improvements to the basic design but because it can run at much higher clock speeds. The Celeron and Xeon chips are versions of the Penitum II.

Pentium MMX This minor variation on Intel's original Pentium chip runs faster due to its larger L1 cache.

peripheral Any hardware that installs in or connects to your PC, such as disk drives, monitors, modems, scanners, printers, CD ROM drives, and so on.

personal digital assistant See *PDA*.

phosphors A layer of phosphorescent material on the inside of your monitor's picture tube that glows when struck by an *electron beam*.

PhotoCD A digital alternative to conventional photographs: drop off your film, and pick up a CD you can read in your PC's CD-ROM drive.

photosensitive drum The key component of a laser printer. The laser draws the image of the page on the drum, creating a static charge that picks up toner only in the areas that are supposed to be black. In some laser printers, the drum is replaced separately from the toner; in others, the toner and drum are in a single replaceable cartridge.

pick list A database feature (or programming technique) that enables you to enter data in a field by picking entries from a list.

pie chart A circular data chart designed to show proportions (usually percentages) of a whole quantity.

PIM Short for *personal information manager*, an all-in-one program that keeps track of names and addresses, appointments, phone calls, to-do lists, and so on. Less powerful and expensive than a contact manager.

pixel Short for *picture element*, one of the tiny points of glowing phosphor that combine to create the image on your computer (or TV) screen.

pixelation The blocky appearance that results when a scanned image or video signal is displayed on screen or in a bitmap graphic.

plotter An output device that uses colored pens to literally draw on the page with a robotic arm. Used almost exclusively to produce engineering and architectural drawings; expensive models can draw full-size blueprints.

plug and play Automatic configuration of hardware, such as the automatic assignment of interrupts to PCI expansion cards. When capitalized (Plug and Play or *PnP*), refers to the way Windows 95 and 98 automatically configure peripherals and their drivers.

plug-in See *add-on*.

PMS Short for Pantone Matching System, this is a method of precisely selecting *spot colors* by referring to numbered samples, just like picking paint hues at a hardware store.

point The standard measure for type size. One point is approximately 1/72 of an inch.

pointer See *mouse pointer*.

pointing device A mouse, trackball, pointing stick, or touchpad used to move the mouse pointer.

polymorphic virus A computer virus that continually mutates, enabling it to avoid detection by antivirus software (see *virus*).

port A connector, usually on the back of your PC, through which data leaves and/or enters the computer, such as a serial port, parallel port, keyboard connector, or mouse port (see *parallel port, serial port*).

portable computer Synonymous with the umbrella term *mobile computer*, which applies to any PC designed to stray from the desktop. May also refer to the large, heavy mobile computers of yore that ran off AC power.

portrait orientation A page on which text and graphics are positioned normally—that is, the page is taller than it is wide (see *landscape orientation*).

PostScript The professional publishing standard for fonts and printers. Using PostScript fonts and a PostScript printer helps ensure that your printouts will closely match the eventual final output from an imagesetter or offset press.

power glitch A surge, spike, or other variation in line current that causes a problem for your PC (see *surge supressor*).

power management Software and hardware systems that conserve battery power by shutting down the hard disk, dimming the display, or idling the CPU when you're not using them.

power spikes A momentary jump in the amount of power a wall socket puts out. In some cases, power spikes can cause crashes or damage your hardware.

power supply The device in your PC that converts AC house current into the DC current your PC's innards need in order to function.

ppm Short for pages per minute, printer manufacturers' standard (and usually inflated) measure of their products' speed.

prepress The process of preparing documents for output on a printing press. Most often used in regard to color printing.

prescan A fast, low-resolution scan to create a preview image in the scanning utility.

presentation graphics Applications aimed at producing overhead transparencies or 35mm slides with graphics, display type, and lots of color. They can also be used to display "slide shows" on a PC monitor or LCD panel, often combining word and data charts with sound, music, and animation.

print buffer A small area of memory in a printer intended to speed up printing. Also a separate hardware device that can hold several print jobs in its memory, where they hang around in a queue until the printer is ready.

print spooler A part of Windows that takes over print jobs from applications, so you can continue working while a file prints. Print Manager is the print spooler built into Windows (see *background printing*).

printer port An informal name for the parallel port, the 25-pin female connector on the back of your PC to which you connect your printer.

private key See *public key encryption.*

process colors Colors produced by separating a color image into three or four colors, and then recombining those colors to reproduce the original hues (see *CMYK, color separation, PMS*).

processor Frequently used to refer to the main processor in a PC, the *central processing unit (CPU).* Actually, your PC has many little processors inside it (your microwave oven and TV also have a few), all of them carrying out their tasks based on instructions received from the CPU. Generally synonymous with the term *microproccessor.*

program A group of instructions that tell the computer what to do. Programs range from weeny *batch files* to huge Windows applications (which, strictly speaking, are collections of many small programs). More or less interchangeable with the term *software*.

program file A file that holds software instructions instead of your data.

programmable data manager A database program that includes (and usually requires extensive knowledge of) a programming language: for example, Microsoft Access.

programming code Programmers use different languages (BASIC, C, C++) to write the applications you use every day. Because these languages employ esoteric commands a cryptographer might balk at, the result is called code, or programming code.

project management software Timeline-based applications that help managers track complicated construction or engineering projects.

proprietary Denotes software or hardware features created by a company that are not compatible with industry standards.

proportionally spaced A typeface (such as the one you're reading) in which letters are spaced according to the width of each individual character.

protocol The code standards that allow modems to communicate with each other over telephone lines (V.34, V.90), or computers to communicate over a LAN or the Internet (TCP/IP, IPX, NetBEUI).

public key encryption An encryption scheme that uses two keys: a public key, which you distribute to anyone you wish, and a private key, which you keep to yourself. If someone wants to send you a secure message, that person encrypts it using your public key, resulting in a file that can be decrypted only by your private key.

pull-down menus In most applications, you can "pull down" a menu of choices by clicking your mouse on a menu bar at the top of the screen.

Q

query In databases, to ask a question about your data, usually by entering field values (a last name, an area code) in a blank record.

query by example (QBE) The most common method for finding data in a database. You define your query by entering the values (or ranges of values) in the appropriate fields. For example, to find all the checks you've written to the IRS since 1982, you'd enter `>1981` in the date field, and `IRS` in the payee field.

QWERTY Refers to the standard keyboard layout (look at the first six letters of the top row of letter keys).

R

radio button See option buttons.

RAID Short for *Redundant Array of Inexpensive Drives,* RAID refers to any of several methods where two or more disk drives are used to improve speed and/or reliability of network hard disk storage. Raid 1 is also known as *disk mirroring*.

RAM Short for *random access memory* (an archaic phrase not worth explaining), RAM usually refers to *main memory*, the large group of RAM chips where the computer does its computing. In the narrower, nerdy sense, RAM refers to the most common class of memory chip, which comes in several varieties (see *main memory, SRAM*).

RAM disk A section of system memory set up to emulate a super-fast disk drive. Data stored on a RAM disk disappears when you turn off the power.

Rambus A new memory technology widely expected to improve performance and reduce costs.

range In spreadsheets, this term refers to any group of (usually contiguous) cells.

RCA jacks The type of jacks used by most stereo equipment. They look like small raised cylinders shaped like a pencil eraser with a hole in the middle, often color-coded red for right channel, white for left.

readme file A file that installs alongside most applications and contains the latest information on troubleshooting and installation. You can use your word processor to read it.

read-only Describes any data that cannot be edited or deleted (see *file attribute*).

read/write head The part of every disk or tape drive that records data on the magnetic media and reads it back later.

real-time Communications like telephone conversations, chat, and videoconferencing, where participants respond to each other immediately, as opposed to non-real-time communications like e-mail, newsgroups, and message boards, where a message and a response to it may be composed hours or days apart.

reboot Restarting your computer, usually after a crash or to put into effect some change you've made to Windows' configuration. You can reboot by pressing Ctrl Alt Del simultaneously, by pressing the reset button, or by turning the power off and back on.

record A group of fields in a database that relate to a single entity: a person, an event, a place, a financial transaction, whatever. A record is like a single row in a table: a single product's name, description, and price on an inventory sheet, for example (see *field*).

referential integrity This ensures that users modifying a relational database cannot perform actions that would "orphan" data. For example, an inventory program might block you from deleting the account of a customer with pending orders. (Note that this is a gross simplification of an extremely complicated topic.)

refresh rate The number of times per second a monitor displays a complete screen of information. The faster the rate, the steadier the image, and the less likely you are to suffer eyestrain.

relational database A database with more than one table; by extension, any database management program that enables information in multiple tables to be linked. Sophisticated database programmers use a narrower definition.

remailer An Internet server that forwards e-mail, usually to allow users to send anonymous messages.

remote When two PCs are in communication, the distant one is the remote PC.

remote control software Applications that let you operate a remote PC via modem or over the Internet or a LAN, providing access to all files and applications.

removable media Any disk or drive designed to be removed without opening up a PC, including floppy disks, backup tapes, Zip disks, and so on.

repeater A device that amplifies (repeats) signals on a cable, allowing the data to travel longer distances.

report generator A database feature or separate utility that performs a query, then organizes and formats the results for printing.

repro paper A high-gloss paper used in phototypsetting machines. Often employed by professional printing services to print high-resolution master documents from which volume copies are reproduced.

resolution On a monitor, the dimensions of an image in *pixels*, the tiny dots that create what you see (VGA resolution is 640 by 480 pixels, for example). On the printed page, the sharpness of the printout measured in dots per inch (standard laser printer output is 300 dots per inch, for example).

resolution enhancement A technique used by some laser printers to make their printed characters sharper, smoother, and better-looking.

resource sharing Making a hard drive, printer, or other goodies available to users on a network.

restocking fee Even when a product is offered with a money-back guarantee, you may be stuck paying a small charge called a restocking fee, which supposedly covers the vendor's expense in replacing the unit you bought and then returned. Is this bogus or what?

restore To return a maximized window to its previous size (see *maximize*); also refers to copying a file from a backup onto your hard disk (see *backup*).

RFI Short for *radio frequency interference*, RFI is electrical noise—generated by computers, monitors, printers, and other electronic devices—that can interfere with radio, television, and cordless phone reception. An FCC Class B rating on a piece of equipment means its EMI emissions are low enough for use in residential areas. An FCC Class A rating means it's legal to use the equipment only in business and industrial areas.

RGB Short for red-green-blue, the primary colors used by monitors to create the images you see on screen. Sometimes refers to the obsolete CGA video standard.

RLE *Run-length encoding,* a lossless compression algorithm for bitmapped graphics.

RMA number Short for *return merchandise authorization,* this is the number you write on the box (and sometimes give to your credit card company) when you ship a piece of unsatisfactory or broken equipment back to the factory.

role-playing games A vague category of computer games defined primarily by what it *excludes*: shoot-em-up, kick-em-down arcade action. Role playing games include strategic war games, dungeon and dragon adventures, fantasy games, and a broad variety of interactive "movies" where the user pretends to be one or more characters in the game.

ROM Short for *read-only memory*, a type of memory that retains its information whether the computer is on or off. ROM chips are built into a variety of hardware devices and usually contain little pieces of software that give the hardware enough smarts to do its job. Your computer uses ROM to store basic start-up information, like where to look for an operating system and how to load it into RAM (see *BIOS*).

root or root directory The "top" level of a drive, where the folder tree begins.. Every logical drive (there can be more than one per hard disk—C:, D:, E:, and so forth) has its own root. On the C: drive, it contains the hidden system files required to boot your PC.

RS-232C The official spec (developed by the Electronics Industry Association) on which standard PC serial ports are based.

RSI Short for *repetitive strain injury*, one of several cumulative traumas resulting from repeated motion of the hands and forearms (you know, what you do with your keyboard and mouse every day). Includes tendinitis, tennis elbow, de Quervain's disease, tenosynovitis, and carpal tunnel syndrome. Computer users are frequent victims of RSI, which can be quite debilitating (see *carpal tunnel syndrome*).

rules Thin, straight lines used to set off blocks of text on a printed page.

run-time engine A stripped-down version of a program that can be distributed free without copyright violation, such as software than enables a database application to run on a PC that does not have the database manager program that created it installed.

S

sampling The process of turning sound into a digital audio file. The sampling rate is the number of times per second your sound board measures the amplitude of incoming sound. Typical sampling rates are 8 kHz (worst) to 48 kHz (best); 44 kHz is standard. The sampling resolution determines how much data is collected at each sampling interval. The two common *sampling resolutions* are 8 bit (lousy) and 16 bit (best).

sans serif Refers to a group of typefaces that lack the squiggles (used to make type more readable) you see in the body type here. The bold words in this glossary are sans serif. Arial is a typical sans serif typeface.

scalable font An electronic typeface that you can adjust in size, often from barely readable to poster size (see *font, PostScript, TrueType*).

scan lines The horizontal lines on a computer monitor.

scanner A device that takes a digital snapshot of a page (or part of one) and saves it as a graphics file. *Flatbed* scanners have photocopierlike windows and scan an entire page at one time; hand scanners are like little Dustbusters that you drag across the page (see *digitize, graphics file*).

screen saver Once upon a time, if the image on your monitor's screen didn't change often, the image would "burn in." To avoid this fate, screen saver programs notice when there's no keyboard activity and send a series of changing images to the screen: flying toasters, Captain Picard, kittens chasing butterflies. Modern monitors are reportedly not susceptible to the burn-in problem, but screen savers remain popular anyway.

script See *macro*..

scroll arrows The arrows at either extreme of a scroll bar. Click on one and hold down the left mouse button, and the contents of the window scroll past one line at a time. To scroll faster, click in the blank part of the scroll bar just next to the arrow, and the contents scroll a screenload at a time.

scroll bars The basic navigation system in Windows: Two bars, one at the bottom of a window and the other on the right, that enable you to move the contents of a window up and down or side to side with the mouse to reveal parts of a document not currently displayed.

scroll box The little square in the middle of a scroll bar—drag it with the mouse, and you can jump around a big document fast.

SCSI Pronounced *scuzzy,* but short for *Small Computer Systems Interface,* SCSI is the second-most popular interface standard for hard disks, though SCSI's also used by other things, like scanners and video capture devices. You can hook up as many as seven SCSI devices to a single SCSI interface card.

search engine A Web site that uses special software to create a database indexing thousands or millions of Web pages. By searching that database, you can (at least in theory) find the needle you're looking for in the haystack of the Web.

secondary memory cache See *L2 cache*.

sectors The basic units of disk storage. Windows groups sectors into *allocation units*, which are the lowest level of data storage you're ever likely to have to deal with.

self-extracting file A compressed file that decompresses automatically when you double-click on it (see *archive, compression*).

serial port Also known as a COM port, a 9-pin or 25-pin connector on the back of your PC usually used to connect an external modem or a mouse. A PC can have a maximum of four serial ports, but it's usually a pain in the butt to try using more than COM 1 and COM 2 (see *I/O*).

serif Refers to a group of typefaces, like the lighter-weight typeface in the text you're reading, whose characters end in little squiggles instead of clean lines. Also refers to the little squiggles themselves.

server A computer that shares files, printers, a database, Web pages, and so on with other computers on a LAN or the Internet. Sometimes more specifically identified by its function, as in file server, database server, print server, Web server. A server that shares an Internet connection, modem, or other communications device with a LAN is often called a *gateway*.

server mirroring Synchronizing two servers so that if the first one fails, the backup takes over automatically.

service bureau A shop that provides a variety of services for desktop publishing: scanners and fancy printers you can rent by the hour, Linotronic output, slide scanning, and so on.

service class A standard for fax communications with four successive variations—Group I, Group II, Group III, and Group IV—each one intended to supersede the previous one. Only Groups III and IV are currently in use (see *Group III fax*).

shadow mask A thin, finely perforated sheet of metal that covers the inside of a monitor's screen. The shadow mask allows the CRT's electron beam to pass through and strike a selected color dot while blocking electrons that might strike neighboring dots and cause the screen to appear fuzzy (see *aperture grille, dot pitch*).

share name The name assigned to a folder or printer when it's shared on a network.

shareware Software you can try out for free. If you like it, you're requested to send a small payment to the author. The most common way to get shareware these days is to download it from a Web site.

shortcut (1) Short for *keyboard shortcut*, a combination of keys that when pressed together execute a menu command (like [Ctrl][c]] for File/Copy). (2) Microsoft's term for an *alias*.

shovelware Disparaging slang term for huge quantities of marginally useful or useless software used as filler on commercial CD-ROMs.

SIMM Short for *Single In-line Memory Module,* the kind of memory used in virtually all 486 PCs and in older Pentiums. Although they have many different capacities, SIMMs come in two basic varieties: 30-pin and 72-pin (see *DIMM, SO-DIMM*).

SLED Short for *single large expensive disk,* this half-joking, half-serious term was coined to refer to the alternative to *RAID*.

sleep mode See *suspend mode*.

slot See *expansion slots*.

SMF Short for *Standard MIDI file*, a MIDI music file designed so it will play on any standard PC sound card (see *MIDI*).

sneakernet A joking name for the most popular alternative to Ethernet: put the file on a floppy and carry it to the PC where you want to use it.

SO-DIMM Short for Small Outline Double Inline Memory Module, the kind of memory currently used by most notebook PCs.

software piracy To make an unauthorized copy of commercial software.

sound card An expansion card that creates the sounds that come out of a PC's speakers, and converts microphone input into a digital format that your PC can handle. Sometimes these functions are handled by chips built into the motherboard.

Sound Recorder A standard Windows utility for recording digital audio (WAV) files.

spam Junk e-mail or newsgroup messages.

special interest group (SIG) See *message board*.

SPID Short for *service profile identifier*, telephone-company jargon for some long numbers you may have to enter into a dialog box to get an ISDN adapter working.

spot color A term used by desktop publishers to describe solid colors that can be produced without the multiple overlays required by *process colors*. Spot color can be reproduced on low-end color printers with good results.

spread A page layout term for two facing pages.

spreadsheet An application that performs a wide variety of mathematical, logical, financial, and statistical calculations, using an on-screen grid that looks a little like an accountant's paper spreadsheet. Spreadsheets are great for making complicated financial projections, but most people employ a fraction of their power and use them to maintain simple lists.

SRAM Short for *static random access memory*, static RAM is faster but more expensive than regular RAM. Mostly used for *L2 cache*.

standby mode The notebook computer equivalent of taking a nap. If you don't touch the keyboard for awhile, the little machine's screen goes dark, the hard disk stops spinning, and (in some cases) the CPU throttles down, giving you a few extra hours of battery life.

star topology A network layout where each workstation is connected to a central hub. 10-BaseT LANs use star topology (see *Ethernet*).

Start button The button that (assuming no one has rearranged things) Windows puts in the bottom-left corner of the screen. Click it to bring up the Start menu.

Start menu A menu from which you can launch applications, access Windows' control panel, reopen recently saved documents, search for files on your PC, or use Windows' online help.

static memory or static RAM See *SRAM*.

stealth virus A type of computer virus designed to defeat antivirus software by covering its tracks (see *virus, antivirus, polymorphic virus*).

stop bit Technically, a bit that divides data bits when communicating by modem. As a practical matter, it's a setting you seldom need to think about, since it's almost always set to 1 (as in N-8-1 or E-7-1).

storage Usually refers to your hard disk, but may also apply to floppy disks, tape cartridges, optical disks, or any other place where your data stays intact when you turn off your PC.

Structured Query Language (SQL) A standard language for database queries, supported by all client-server and most conventional database programs. Standard SQL is often ignored in favor of powerful proprietary variations or alternatives.

style In word processing and desktop publishing, a collection of formats (for example: bold, italic, 18-point Times Roman, 1/4-inch indent) that you can save together under a single name. Later, you can pick that name from a list and apply the style to any paragraph with a couple of mouse clicks.

stylus The penlike tool used with a *drawing tablet*.

subdirectory See *folder*.

subnotebook A very small *notebook PC*.

super VGA Video modes better than 640 by 480 at 16 colors, and the video cards and monitors that support those modes. Popular resolutions include 800 by 600, 1024 by 768, 1280 by 1024, and 1600 by 1200; the number of colors ranges from 256 to 16.7 million.

supercomputer A rare, expensive, and ultrapowerful computer with hundreds or even thousands of processors.

superfloppy Any of a number of inexpensive removable-media drives that are relatively inexpensive and hold more data than floppy disks.

surface scan Some diagnostic utilities check the surface of your hard disk, looking for—and marking off—physically damaged sectors.

surge suppressor A protective electrical device you put between your PC and the wall plug that keeps your PC from getting fried from sudden voltage spikes or power surges.

suspend mode A state of battery-saving hibernation that notebook and, increasingly, desktop PCs go into when you press a button, or after a period of inactivity. The screen goes dark, and Everything shuts down except for the trickle of power required to preserve data in memory, which may stay there intact for hours or weeks, or forever if the PC's connected to an AC outlet. Press the resume button, and after a few seconds you can pick up where you left off. (See *suspend to disk, notebook computer, power management*).

suspend to disk An extreme power-saving method (sometimes called hibernation) available in many notebook PCs. Similar to suspend mode, except that the contents of memory are saved to disk, and the notebook's power is shut off entirely. The computer can remain in that state indefinitely, and return to the point you left off the next time you turn it on.

sustained transfer rate The amount of data a device can transfer per second for sustained periods of time. An important measure of hard disk performance. See also *burst transfer rate*.

swap file The portion of your hard disk Windows uses as *virtual memory*.

swash characters Letters or numbers having one or more strokes ending in an extended flourish.

switches Things you add to a DOS command to change its behavior. For example, adding the /P switch to the DIR command results in a pause after each screenful of files. Switches are sometimes useful for modifying Windows programs; you can add them to the Target field in the properties of Start menu shortcuts.

sysop Short for *system operator;* the person in charge of a Web site or message board.

SYSTEM.INI Windows 3.1 configuration file, which stores mostly hardware-related settings. Still exists in current versions of Windows for compatibility with old applications.

system unit The PC itself—the main boxlike chassis to which the keyboard and monitor connect.

T

T-1 A type of *leased line* that carries 1.5 mbps of data, often used as a high-speed Internet connection or WAN link.

T-3 A type of *leased line* that carries 45 mbps of data, mostly used by Internet services providers and large organizations that connect directly to the Internet backbone.

tape backup drive A device reminiscent of a stripped-down car cassette player, designed to copy data from your hard disk to little cassette tapes for safekeeping (see *backup, restore*).

taskbar The gray bar that appears (unless you move it) at the bottom of the screen in Windows.

TCP/IP Short for *Transport Control Protocol/Internet Protocol*, the network *protocol* used on the Internet and increasingly on LANs as well.

tech support A telephone number, fax-back service, or Web site where you can get help, advice, and troubleshooting tips for an application or piece of hardware that isn't working right.

telecommunications In PCs, another word for modem communications over the phone lines.

telnet program A program that does *terminal emulation* over the Internet, allowing access to character-mode programs running on servers.

template A document where most of the layout and formatting decisions have been made for you, so all you need to do is enter data.

terminal A keyboard and monitor attached to a multiuser system, usually a minicomputer or mainframe.

terminal emulation The process of fooling a minicomputer or mainframe into believing your PC is one of the big guy's terminals, so you and the larger system can communicate over the phone lines using a modem or the Internet.

text editor A simple word processor designed for editing batch files, INI files, and other ASCII text files used by your computer. Windows' Notepad is a text editor (see *ASCII, batch file*).

text file A file containing plain text without formatting, also known as an ASCII file, which will usually have a .txt extension.

text mode A method of displaying images on your monitor, sometimes employed by full-screen DOS applications, which uses ASCII characters exclusively (see *ASCII*).

TFT Short for *thin film transistor,* the tiny device used to control a single cell in an *active-matrix LCD*, the best screen type available for notebook computers (see *LCD*).

thermal wax A popular method used by color printers to print color on plain paper, whereby colored wax is actually melted onto the page. Less expensive and lower quality than *dye sublimation.*

thinnet See *Ethernet*.

third-party Describes a piece of hardware or software designed to be used with another product, but sold by a different company.

TIFF Short for *Tagged Image File Format,* TIFF is the bitmapped graphics format of choice among graphics professionals.

tilt-and-swivel The ball-joint base of a monitor that allows you to adjust it for the most convenient viewing angle (see *monitor*).

TMP files Temporary files created by applications to hold scratch data.

toggle Derived from *toggle switch* (like a light switch), a toggle is a command or a key on the keyboard that turns something on or off. For example, the Ins key toggles between inserting and overtyping text.

tombstoning In design, layout, and desktop publishing circles, this refers to a bad layout in which boxed elements are lined up across the page.

toner cartridge Laser printers use replaceable cartridges containing a black powdered "ink" called toner; the cartridge saves you the messy task of refilling the toner by hand (see *laser printer*).

toolbars Many Windows applications place icons representing frequently used commands in a row of buttons along the top or side of the screen. This is a toolbar, and in most cases you can customize it easily.

ToolTip The explanatory text that appears in a little yellow box when you hold the mouse pointer over a toolbar button and various other objects on screen.

touchpad The touch-sensitive pad that substitutes for a mouse on most notebook PCs.

tower system *Desktop* computers are designed so the PC lies flat, on top of the desk. Tower systems are usually designed to stand on end and fit under the desk, using less space. *Full towers* are around 24 inches high; mid-towers are a few inches shorter, and minitowers are shorter still.

trackball A popular pointing device, sometimes described as a mouse "on its back." Instead of moving the pointer by rolling a mouse on your desk, you rotate a stationary ball with your fingers or the palm of your hand.

tracks The concentric rings in which data is stored on floppy and hard disks.

tractor-feed The sprocketed mechanism that feeds continuous-form paper through a dot matrix printer (see *dot matrix printer*).

transaction tracking A process that helps protect multiuser databases from becoming corrupted. If a database crashes in the middle of a transaction, its tables may no longer be synchronized (for example, an employee's withholding taxes might have been subtracted from the payroll table, but not yet added to the tax-paid table). Transaction tracking allows the database to be "rolled back" to the point before any incomplete transactions started or "rolled forward" to complete the transactions.

Trojan horse A program that pretends to be something nice (say, a game, or an update to a popular shareware utility) but is actually designed to do mischief. Often confused with a *virus*.

troll Internet slang for a person whose newsgroup or message board postings are intended only to provoke pointless argument.

True Color See *24-bit color*.

TrueType The scalable font format used by Windows, TrueType is much more popular on the PC than PostScript Type 1. Also the name for the *font rasterizer* in Windows that scales TrueType fonts and sends them to the printer.

TSR Short for *terminate and stay resident* (see *memory-resident)*.

typeface A complete set of letters, numbers, punctuation marks, and special characters in a particular style, such as Times Roman or Helvetica (see *font*).

U

UDMA Short for *Ultra DMA*, this is a faster variant of the EIDE hard disk interface. A *UDMA drive* is one that supports the standard.

undelete To recover an accidentally deleted file.

undo A function available in many applications than enables you to reverse your last action or series of actions.

unformatted text Plain text with no formatting: no bold, no italics, no font or size specified, etc.

uninterruptible power supply See *UPS*.

UNIX An operating system in some ways similar to Windows NT that's popular on network servers and large computers. The name isn't really an acronym; it's just an example of nerd humor.

unsaved A document that has not been saved to disk since it was last changed.

upgrade To buy a newer version of an application you already own, to add hardware that increases the performance or capacity of your PC, or to buy a new computer more powerful than your old one.

upload Any data that your PC sends out using your modem or other Internet connection, such as outgoing e-mail, e-mail attachments, or files you transfer to a Web server.

upper memory Memory between 640K and 1MB, reserved for drivers that control your video, hard disk, and so on.

UPS Short for *uninterruptible power supply*, a data protection device that you plug into the wall socket. Then you plug your PC into it. If the power fails, a built-in rechargeable battery will keep your computer running long enough for you to save your work and shut down safely. It also protects your PC from potentially destructive power surges.

USB Short for *Universal Serial Bus*, a relatively new kind of port found on virtually all new PCs and notebooks. USB ports can transfer data much faster than standard PC serial ports, making them suitable for a wide variety of devices including keyboards, mice, speakers, modems, and superfloppy drives. USB devices can be *daisy-chained*, so a single port can handle lots of peripherals.

Usenet See *newsgroup*.**user group** A kind of a computer club for people interested in computers in general, a particular type of computer, or a specific application. Memberships are often a wild mix of techies and beginners, all of them interested in learning more about PCs for work or play. Most user groups are nonprofits independent of any computer company; they have at times exerted substantial influence in the computer industry.

user interface The overall layout of software as it appears to the person who uses it—the arrangement of its menus, the positioning of its toolbars, the design of its dialog boxes. The user interface determines how easy a given application is to learn and use.

utility An inexpensive software tool that helps you accomplish some small but often important task, such as backing up your data, searching for files, tuning up your system in some way, and so on.

V.34 The standard for 28.8 and 33.6 kbps modems.

V.42 Widely accepted standard for modem error control. Includes the earlier error-control standards MNP 2, MNP 3, and MNP 4.

V.90 The latest modem standard. Basically the same as V.34, except it can download from an Internet service provider at a theoretical top speed of 56 kbps (though actual speed is more like 42 to 47 kbps). Uploads and modem-to-modem transfers are limited to 33.6 kbps, just as with V.34 modems.

vector graphics Easily edited graphics based on lines, curves, and shapes described by mathematical formulas. The type of graphics produced by draw programs.

vertical scan rate The speed at which the monitor's electron beam moves from the top of the screen to the bottom, measured in cycles per second (Hz). The higher the vertical scan rate, the faster the phosphors in the screen are "refreshed."

VESA Short for the *Video Electronics Standards Association,* a trade organization of graphics hardware manufacturers that devised and published the popular *VL Bus* specification used in 486 PCs and developed guidelines for video modes beyond standard VGA.

VGA Short for *Video Graphics Array,* the most widely accepted IBM graphics hardware standard and the lowest common denominator for all video cards and monitors manufactured in the last few years. All current video cards and monitors can handle resolutions higher than standard VGA's 640 by 480 at 16 colors (see *super VGA*).

video board See *video card.*

video capture device An expansion card or a box connected to your PC by a cable that enables you to convert analog video from a VCR or camera into digital video and store it on disk.

video card Also known as the graphics card or video board, an expansion card that contains the graphics controller. A connector on the card's rear bracket connects to the monitor.

video compression A technique for reducing the amount of data a video capture card sends to the PC and reducing the size of digital video files on disk.

video memory The memory on your PC's video card. In a few PCs, the video controller and CPU share the same memory, but that's a very rare design.

video mode Your video card's settings, a combination of *resolution*, *color depth*, and *refresh rate*.

video projector A device that accepts video input from a computer or VCR and projects it onto a large screen suitable for meetings.

virtual memory Not memory at all, but disk space treated as memory to enable you to run more applications than can fit in memory at once. Windows uses this technique automatically when it runs out of real, physical memory. Data in virtual memory is said to have been *swapped to disk*.

virus A nasty bit of software expressly designed to damage the data on your hard disk. A virus can infect your computer when you load new software, innocently accept a neighbor's floppy disk, or download a file via modem, and may lie quiet for months before becoming active (see *antivirus*).

VL bus The *VESA local bus*, a 486-era expansion bus that has been supplanted by PCI.

VLF Short for *very low frequency* radiation, a range of frequencies emitted by monitors and other devices. A possible health hazard (see *ELF*).

voice recognition A computer's ability to recognize and respond to spoken commands or to take dictation. Works OK...if...you...talk...like...this (and repeat yourself a few times).

voices The different instruments a sound board's synthesizer can imitate simultaneously.

volume Anything to which Windows assigns a drive letter (also known as a logical drive). Note that a single hard disk can be partitioned into multiple logical drives, or volumes.

wallpaper Windows' Display control panel lets you set a decorative pattern, or even a photographic image, as the background of the Windows desktop. This is called *wallpaper*.

WAN Short for *wide area network*, this refers to geographically dispersed LANs linked by *leased lines* or the *Internet*.

warm boot Restarting your computer by pressing Ctrl Ins Del or the reset button This has an effect similar to turning your PC off and on again, except it's a bit faster and easier on the power supply. You'll lose all unsaved data (see *boot, cold boot*).

watermark In desktop publishing, any image electronically "faded" and used as a background.

watt The standard measure of electric consumption, equal to one *joule* per second. A joule, the standard measure of work in the metric system, is roughly equal to the amount of energy expended moving one kilogram one meter.

wavetable A method used in some sound boards to store the sampled sounds of real instruments in ROM, resulting in better sounds than those produced by the usual cheesy synthesizer chip.

Web The usual term for the World Wide Web, a set of standards that allows people and organizations all over the world to make information and files easily available for reading or downloading over the Internet.

Web browser A program that lets you access the Web.

Web page One particular document on the Web.

Web server A server that makes Web documents available to the Internet.

Web site A collection of Web documents at a particular location.

weight A typesetting term that indicates the thickness of the lines that make up the characters in a font. A blocky, boldface font would be said to have more weight than a delicate italic character.

white space White space refers to margins and other parts of a printed page unoccupied by text or graphics.

wildcards In Windows' Find command, characters * and ? function as wildcards. They mean "all" and can be used to find a set of similarly named files. For instance, searching for *.BAK will find every file with a BAK file extension. You can also use these two wildcards at the DOS prompt.

Winchester drive An old-fashioned term for *hard disk*, reportedly named after the Winchester Mystery House, a local landmark not far from the IBM facility where the technology was invented.

window In Windows, applications run inside boxes called windows, which you can open, close, size, overlap, and otherwise have a ball with.

Windows NT Microsoft's high-end alternative to Windows 98. See Chapter 11: Windows 95, 98, and NT for a discussion of the differences between the two.

WIN.INI A Windows 3.1 configuration file, in which settings not directly related to hardware are stored. Still exists in current versions of Windows for compatibility with old applications.

WMF Short for *Windows metafile*, Windows' own vector graphics file format (see *vector graphics*).

word processor An application designed to let you create, edit, and print documents. These days, most word processors offer so many advanced formatting features they're hard to distinguish from desktop publishing programs (see *formatting, desktop publishing*).

word wrap In a word processor, when you type to the end of a line, the next line automatically begins flush with the left margin. That's word wrap. In Notepad, you can turn it on or off.

workgroup Marketing slang for a group of coworkers who share data on a LAN.

workgroup software Any application that couldn't run without a network, such as a group scheduler, or Lotus's popular *Notes* product.

worksheet A document created by a spreadsheet.

workstation Usually means a PC that's hooked to a network. Also used to describe high-end computers running UNIX or Windows NT. Sometimes just a synonym for PC.

write protected Describes a floppy disk that's been set up so you can only read its contents, not save anything. On 31/2-inch floppies, pushing up a little switch on one corner prevents the disk from being written to; on old 5¼-inch floppies, you need to cover a notch near one corner of the disk with tape.

write verification A scheme to check data after it's been written to disk to verify that no errors occurred.

WYSIWYG A silly acronym for "what you see is what you get"—that is, a representation on screen that closely approximates what you'll see in print. Once, only desktop publishing programs were WYSIWYG; now virtually all Windows programs are WYSIWYG.

XGA A high-end variation on Intel's Pentium II intended mostly for use in multiple-processor servers.

XGA Short for *Extended Graphics Array,* a proprietary IBM graphics standard for 1024 by 768 resolution.

XLS files The file name extension for Excel worksheet files (see *file extension*).

XMS Short for *extended memory specification*, the set of official rules that applications (and Windows) employ when they use extended memory. XMS is also a cool way of saying "extended memory"; it's one of those terms that makes it sound as if you know something (see *extended memory*).

Y-connector A Y-shaped cable that splits a source input into two output signals.

Z

ZIF socket Short for *zero insertion force* socket, a socket for CPUs that makes replacing a chip easy: Lift a little lever, and the chip comes out; push it back, and the chip is locked in tight. ZIF sockets are great for CPU upgrades.

ZIP file A file compressed with a zip utility like WinZip; has the file extension .zip.

Appendix A

DOS Survival Guide

by Robert Lauriston

In this Appendix

If you run DOS games, or for some reason you have to work on an old PC, or (knock on beige plastic) something weird goes wrong with your PC, you may find yourself in DOS. You'll know you're in DOS because instead of Windows' familiar cartoon-like interface, all you'll see is a blank screen plus something called the DOS prompt, which looks like this:

```
C:\>
```

This prompt is where you type in the commands that tell DOS to do your bidding. Your PC will sit there forever until you type a DOS command—that is, until you tell it to do something. In this emergency guide, we'll cover you the basics of navigating the DOS prompt. Then we'll tell you how to perform basic tasks in the DOS Cookbook, give a brief overview of the primitive operating system's capabilities in the DOS Command Guide, and offer some tips on editing CONFIG.SYS and AUTOEXEC.BAT.

DOS Prompt Basics

The DOS prompt is like your PC's basement. It's dark down here, and instead of Windows' pretty wallpaper patterns, you get a little sign glowing alone in the dark: the "C:\>" prompt. (If your prompt *doesn't* look like this, type `prompt $p$g` and press the Enter key.)

Loosely translated, DOS is saying, "Ready for orders, master." To tell DOS to do something, you type a *command,* and then press the Enter key.

Getting to Windows from DOS

If the only reason you're reading this appendix is to try to get from the DOS prompt into Windows, here are a few things to try, in this order:

1. Type `exit` and press Enter. If you got to a DOS prompt by using the TK command on the Shut Down dialog in Windows 95 or 98, this will take you back.
2. Type `win` and press Enter. Depending on how you got to the DOS prompt, this might take you into Windows 95 or 98. On an older computer, it might take you into Windows 3.1 (in which case see Appendix B: Windows 3.1 Survival Guide).
3. Type `cd \windows` and press Enter. Then repeat what you tried in (2): type `win` and press Enter. This may work if the *path* isn't pointing to Windows' directory.
4. Turn off your computer's power, wait ten seconds, and turn it back on.

If none of this works, and you're sure your PC *should* be booting to Windows, your Windows installation may have been damaged. See Chapter 27: HELP! Where To Turn When Things Go Wrong for tips on what to do next.

Displaying the Contents of the Current Directory

Let's start with the first DOS command everyone learns, the DIR command. This command displays a list of all file names and any directory names in your *current directory* ("`C:\>`" means you are currently in drive C:'s root directory). Type `dir`, and those three letters will appear to the right of the DOS prompt, like this:

```
C:\>dir
```

Press Enter, and you'll see a directory listing that looks more or less like this (exactly what you see depends on what's stored on your hard drive):

```
C:\>dir
 Volume in drive C is DOS-62
 Volume Serial Number is 1C8E-96EF
 Directory of C:\
DOS            <DIR>                01-10-94     2:57p
TEMP           <DIR>                01-10-94     3:03p
WINDOWS        <DIR>                03-22-94     9:13p
AUTOEXEC BAT                 629    03-28-94     6:15p
COMMAND  COM              54,619    09-30-93     6:20a
CONFIG   SYS                 572    03-28-94     3:25p
SCANDISK LOG                 461    04-16-94     1:37p
          7 file(s)                   56,281 bytes
                                      45,273,088 bytes free
```

Typing a DOS command and pressing Enter is commonly referred to as *entering* a command—when someone tells you to "enter" a DOS command, they mean "type it and press Enter." Same thing if someone tells you to "do" a command, as in "do a DIR."

You can modify the behavior of most DOS commands by adding *switches* to them. For example, try adding the /OD switch to the DIR command to display the files sorted by date:

```
C:\>dir /od
 Volume in drive C is DOS-62
 Volume Serial Number is 1C8E-96EF
```

```
 Directory of C:\
COMMAND  COM                     54,619 09-30-93 6:20a
DOS           <DIR>              01-10-94        2:57p
TEMP          <DIR>              01-10-94        3:03p
WINDOWS       <DIR>              03-22-94        9:13p
CONFIG   SYS            572      03-28-94        3:25p
AUTOEXEC BAT            629      03-28-94        6:15p
SCANDISK LOG            461      04-16-94        1:37p
        7 file(s)                  56,281 bytes
                                   45,273,088 bytes free
```

Changing Directories

Now let's try the CD (change directory) command: Enter `cd\dos` and the DOS prompt will change from `C:\>` to:

```
C:\DOS>
```

This indicates that you've changed your current directory from the root directory to the DOS directory. In so doing, you've taken a step along one limb of the directory tree, just as you could do by clicking on a different directory in Windows' File Manager. You just can't see what you're doing in DOS.

Enter `dir`, and you'll see a list of all files in the DOS directory. Enter `cd\` and the DOS prompt changes back to `C:\>`, indicating that you've moved back to the root directory.

Adding Paths or File Names to Commands

Paths, which are simply directory (folder) names preceded by a backslash, can be added to DOS commands to indicate where an action performed by a command should happen. For example, you can do a DIR on the DOS directory without leaving the root directory. Just type `dir`, a space, and the DOS directory's path, `c:\dos`. The root directory's DOS prompt, plus what you've typed, should look like this. Don't forget the space:

```
C:\>dir c:\dos
```

Press Enter and you'll see the same directory listing you saw when you entered DIR in the DOS directory.

Now let's see if a *specific file* named FORMAT.COM is in the DOS directory. Enter the same path as before, followed by a backslash and the file name.

What you've entered, plus the resulting partial directory listing, should look like this:

```
C:\>dir c:\dos\format.com
 Volume in drive C is DOS-62
 Volume Serial Number is 1C8E-96EF
 Directory of C:\DOS
FORMAT   COM                22,916            09-30-93   6:20a
         1 file(s)                      56,281 bytes
                                        45,273,088 bytes free
```

DOS Shortcuts

When working at the DOS prompt, there are several shortcuts you can use to avoid having to retype commands. Remember that you have to have entered the command for DOS to duplicate what you typed. Note that `w` and `d` work as they usually do, and that by default typing overwrites characters from the last command.

DOS Prompt Tricks

Recall last command	F3
Recall one character from last command	→
Recall series of characters from last command	F2, then first character *after* the portion you want to recall
Skip characters in last command	F4, then first character *after* the portion you want to skip
Insert characters, then recall rest of last command	Ins, type characters, then F3

You can really save time with these shortcuts. For example, if you just entered `md data\wp` to create a new directory, you could then simply type `c` and press F3 to get the command `cd data\wp`. Or if you just entered `dir c:\windows\*.ini`, you could press F2, type two periods, and add `cfg` to get `dir c:\windows\*.cfg`.

That's all the DOS you need to know to follow the instructions in the rest of this appendix. If you want to learn more, go through the Cookbook and experiment with the commands it describes, and read the guide to DOS commands.

DOS Cookbook

For those times when you can't avoid the DOS prompt, we offer the following Cookbook, which explains step by step how to perform 14 file, disk, and application tasks. Beginners who find any part of this Cookbook confusing should turn to the brief DOS introduction above.

File Tasks

To See What Files Are in a Directory

You need to see where a file is located before you open it in an application, move it, or otherwise manipulate it. Files live in directories, so that's where you look for them.

A list will scroll by showing the name and size of every file in the directory, along with the date and time it was last edited. To get a list of all files, sorted alphabetically (/o) one screenful at a time (/p), enter:

```
dir /o/p
```

To list all files, grouped by extension and then sorted alphabetically by name (/oen), one screenful at a time (/p), enter:

```
dir /oen/p
```

To list all files sorted by date (/od), enter:

```
dir /od
```

To list only those files with the TXT extension, enter:

```
dir *.txt
```

To see all files starting with the letter *d,* enter:

```
dir d*
```

To list files in a directory other than the current one, enter the full directory path name. For example, to see all the 1-2-3 data files in C:\WORK, you would enter:

```
dir c:\work\*.wk?
```

For more on the wildcards * and ?, see "To select multiple files..." a little later in this Cookbook.

Danger Zone: Hidden Files

Normally DOS does not list *hidden* files, which are special files that DOS, Windows, and some applications need to operate properly. There's a reason for hidden files' invisibility: If you rename, delete, or move them, you may lose data, crash your system, or both! The most likely reason you'd want to see hidden files is to discover how much disk space they're taking up. To reveal hidden files with the File Manager, select View//By File Type and check the Hidden Files check box; hidden files will be marked by an exclamation mark icon. To reveal them in a DOS directory listing, type `dir` followed by a space and /a, then press e.

To Move From One Directory to Another

The file you want to do something with often resides in a directory other than the one you're in—so you need to look in another directory to find the file.

Use the CD (for "change directory") command followed by the name of the destination directory to move from one directory to another. For example, to move to a different directory on the current drive (say, the DOS directory), enter:

```
cd\dos
```

To move to a directory on another drive—say, from C:\ to A:\DATA—you need to switch to the other drive before using the CD command:

```
a:
cd\data
```

To move to the root directory of the current drive, enter:

```
cd\
```

To move up one level—that is, from the current directory to the directory immediately above it on the directory tree—enter:

```
cd..
```

To move from one directory to another directory lower down on the same branch of the tree, just leave out the backslash. For example, to move from the Windows directory (C:\WINDOWS) to the Windows system directory (C:\WINDOWS\SYSTEM), enter:

```
cd system
```

To move between two subdirectories with the same parent directory—for example, from C:\WINDOWS\SYSTEM to C:\WINDOWS\MSAPPS—enter:

```
cd..\msapps
```

To Copy or Move Files or Directories

Copying and moving files and directories are part of routine disk housekeeping. There are a million reasons to perform either task—to copy files from your hard disk to a floppy so someone else can use them, to move files from a working directory to one that contains finished work, and so forth.

Use the COPY, XCOPY, or MOVE commands (the XCOPY command makes copying directories easier). As usual in DOS, you need to type not only the file name but at least one full directory path name to move or copy a file.

To copy a file named LETTER1.DOC from your current directory to a directory named \CORRESP on your C: drive, enter:

```
copy letter1.doc c:\corresp
```

To copy a file named LETTER1.DOC to your current directory from a directory named \CORRESP on your C: drive, enter:

```
copy c:\corresp\letter1.doc
```

To move LETTER1.DOC rather than copy it, simply substitute the MOVE command for the COPY command, as in:

```
move c:\corresp\letter1.doc
```

To copy the entire contents of your C:\WORK directory to a floppy, enter:

```
copy c:\work a:\
```

To copy a group of directories in one pass, you need to use XCOPY. For example, to copy C:\1994 and all the directories beneath it to W:\BACKUP, you would enter:

```
xcopy c:\1994 w:\backup\1994 /s/e/v
```

To copy all files with the DOC extension from your current directory to a floppy, enter:

```
copy *.doc a:
```

The /s switch specifies that all directories under C:\1994 containing files will be copied, the /e switch specifies that empty directories will also be copied, and the /v switch makes DOS verify that everything was copied correctly. Note that with XCOPY, you always need to enter the complete path for the source and target directories.

Danger Zone: Overwrite Confirmation

If you copy or move a file from one directory to another, and there's a file in the target directory that has the same name DOS will ask you whether you want to *replace* the file in the target directory, that is, if you want to overwrite the file in the target directory with the file of the same name from the source directory. If you don't want this to happen, you need to rename one of the files before proceeding (see "To rename files or directories..." in this Cookbook).

To Select Multiple Files

If you need to do the same thing (move, copy, delete, and so on) to a group of files or directories, you can often avoid time-wasting repetition by selecting all the files first and entering the command once.

Use wildcards, which are special characters that stand in for actual characters in a file name similar to the way jokers substitute for real cards in card games. The asterisk (*) represents multiple characters, while the question mark (?) represents a single character. Here are a few common examples using DOS's COPY command:

`copy *.*`	all files
`copy *.doc`	all files with the extension .DOC
`copy d*.*`	all files starting with d
`copy ??`	all files with one- or two-character names
`copy a??c`	all files with four-character names that begin with a and end with c (a24c, azbc, aaac, and so on)
`copy ??.w*`	all files with one- or two-character names and extensions starting with w

Note that DOS ignores any characters it finds after an asterisk (the period excepted). For example, if you mistakenly entered `*w.*`, DOS would read it as `*.*` without the w.

To Create a Directory

It's faster and easier to find files if you arrange them in directories. You may also need to create directories for programs that don't install automatically.

1. Change to the directory in which you want to create the new directory.
2. Enter md followed by a space and the name of the new directory. For example, to create the directory C:\WORK\AUGUST95, enter:

   ```
   c:
   cd\work
   md august95
   ```

   Feeling confident? Then you can create the directory from anywhere, without changing directories first, by entering:
   ```
   md c:\work\august95
   ```

To Delete Files or Directories

Old, useless copies of files often confuse matters and always take up disk space unnecessarily. The general rule: If you don't need it, delete it.

Deleting is about as straightforward as things get in DOS: Just enter `DEL` followed by a space and the file name. As usual, you need to include the path name if the file isn't in the current directory, along with wildcards if you want to delete multiple files. For example, to delete all TMP files in your C:\DOS directory, you'd enter:

```
del c:\dos\*.tmp
```

Now, here's a simple yet dangerous variation:

```
del c:\dos
```

In plain English, that means "delete everything in my DOS directory" (`del c:\dos\*.*` is an explicit way of saying the same thing using wildcards). If you actually try to enter this command, DOS is smart enough to come back at you with, "All files in directory will be deleted! Are you sure (Y/N)?" Good thing, too, since you'd have trouble running your computer without DOS.

To get rid of entire directories, use the DELTREE command, which is even simpler—and more dangerous. It removes the specified directory, all directories beneath it, and all of their files. For example, to get rid of the C:\TEMP directory, enter:

```
deltree c:\temp
```

Fortunately, as with wholesale attempts at deleting files, DOS asks you to confirm DELTREE operations. To bypass the confirmation—say, when you want to delete all the files and directories on a floppy—add the /y switch, as in:

```
deltree /y a:\
```

If DELTREE makes you nervous, you can use DOS's RD (for "remove directory") command instead. Enter `rd` followed by a space and the directory name, and the directory will disappear—but only if it's completely empty of files.

To Rename Files or Directories

The usual reason you need to rename a file or directory is to correct a typing mistake you made when you orginally named it. But there are a zillion other reasons—for example, to preserve an earlier version of a file.

To change a file's name, use the REN (for "rename") command followed by a space, the old file name, a space, and the new file name. For example, to change DRAFT.MAR to FINAL.DOC, enter:

```
ren draft.mar final.doc
```

To give a group of files with the same extension a different extension, use a wildcard. For example, to give all files with the SET extension the BAK extension, enter:

```
ren *.set *.bak
```

To change a directory name, you use the MOVE command, strangely enough. For example, to change C:\DATA\CIRREMT to C:\DATA\CURRENT, you'd enter:

```
move c:\cirremt current
```

You cannot use wildcards to rename multiple directories.

Danger Zone: Renaming Directories

Renaming program directories can cause big problems. Some programs expect to find files in certain places, and won't run properly, if at all, when you rename the directory in which they're stored. Unless you really know what you're doing, you should only rename directories that contain data files.

To Recover Accidentally Deleted Files or Directories

Sooner or later, all of us accidentally delete a file or directory. Fortunately, you can almost always recover files (and usually directories) easily.

1. Change to the directory in which you deleted the files (DOS only recovers files, not directories) and enter undelete.
2. Undelete will show you the names of the recoverable files one at a time. For each one, press y to undelete it or n to skip it. If prompted, enter the missing first character of each file you choose to undelete. If you don't know the missing character, pick whatever makes the most sense.

Disk Tasks

To Format a Floppy

You need to format a floppy disk before you can use it. Formatting lays down the basic information necessary for storing files.

Insert the floppy disk. Then enter one of the following commands. If the floppy is in the B: drive, substitute B: for A: in the command.

To format a brand-new floppy, enter:

```
format a:
```

To erase all files from an already-formatted floppy, enter:

```
format a: /q
```

To format a 720K floppy in a 3½-inch drive, enter:

```
format a: /f:720
```

To format a 360K floppy in a 5¼-inch drive, enter:

```
format a: /4
```

To create a system disk that you can boot your PC from, add /s to any of the above variations on the format command, as in:

```
format a: /s
```

Whenever you format a disk, DOS will prompt you to enter a descriptive label after it finishes formatting. If you don't want to bother, just press e.

To Copy a Floppy Disk

Sometimes you need to duplicate an entire floppy disk, either to make a backup copy or to give a copy to someone else.

1. Insert the disk you want to copy into the drive, and then enter the command:

   ```
   diskcopy a: a: (or diskcopy b: b:, as appropriate)
   ```

2. When you see the prompt, "Insert SOURCE diskette... Press any key to continue," press the space bar.
3. When you see the prompt, "Insert TARGET diskette... Press any key to continue," remove the disk you're copying from, insert the disk you want to copy to, and press the space bar.

In some cases you may have to repeat steps 2 and 3 several times, swapping the source and target disks in and out of the drive, before DISKCOPY is finished.

Application Tasks

To Install an Application

Before you can use an application, you have to install it on your hard disk. This takes some time, but usually all you need to do is follow prompts once you get started.

1. Change to the A: (or B:, if appropriate) drive.
2. Enter the command:

   ```
   dir read*
   ```

3. If the directory listing shows a README file with the extension BAT, COM, or EXE, check to see if there are any last minute changes to the installation instructions (if any) by entering the command:

   ```
   readme
   ```

4. If the directory listing shows a file with a name like README.TXT, READ.ME, or README.1ST, use MORE to read the file, as in:

   ```
   more < readme.1st
   ```

5. Enter the command to start the program's installation utility (usually `install` or `setup`), you'll probably be led step by step through an installation routine. However, in some cases, DOS programs need to be installed manually. It's easy: Just create a directory and copy the files from A:. For example, to install a hypothetical DOS utility called MemTest, you would enter the following:

   ```
   md utils\memtest
   cd utils\memtest
   copy a: *.*
   ```

To Start an Application

You have to start an application before you can use it.

There are three basic ways to start applications in DOS. Which one you choose depends primarily on whether or not the program is in your path, which is a list of directories following the PATH command in your AUTOEXEC.BAT file (see "Tuning CONFIG.SYS and AUTOEXEC.BAT" later in this appendix).

If the program's directory is in your path, just type the name of its EXE file without the extension. For example, you might enter q to start Quattro Pro, or wp to start WordPerfect.

If the program's directory is not in your path, type the full path and name of the EXE file. Start with the drive letter if it's not on your current drive, as in:

```
c:\apps\wp51\wp
```

for *WordPerfect*. Alternatively, you can change to the program's directory, then enter the command to start it, as in:

```
cd\apps\wp51
wp
```

To Open a File

To edit or (usually) to print a file, you need to open it.

You can instruct most DOS applications to load a file as they start up. The following examples assume that the applications in question are listed in your path:

To start WordPerfect and open the file MAR95.TAX in the C:\DATA\REPORTS directory, enter:

```
cd \data\reports
wp mar95.tax
```

To start 1-2-3 release 3.1 and open the file 1995EST.WK3 in the F:\TAXES\ directory, enter:

```
cd f:\taxes
123 f:1995est.wk3
```

To edit AUTOEXEC.BAT in the MS-DOS Editor, enter:

```
edit c:\autoexec.bat
```

To Print a File

There's no consistent way to print documents in DOS—some programs use File//Print, but there are many other alternatives. Check the application's on-line help or manual.

If you want to print a plain text file, you can copy it to the printer port. For example, to print a copy of your AUTOEXEC.BAT file, enter:

```
copy autoexec.bat lpt1
```

DOS Command Guide

Up through DOS 5, Microsoft shipped a decent manual with DOS, but after that the manuals started slimming down, and much of the information they used to contain is found only in the online help system—which is arguably an improvement, since it's fast and easy to use. At the DOS prompt, just enter `help` followed by the command you want to learn about (or enter `help` by itself if you just want to browse and see what's there). Another way you can sometimes get help is to type the command followed by `/?` —for example, `xcopy /?` will bring up a description of the XCOPY command syntax and options.

For easy reference, here's a list of the commands you're most likely to find useful (in some cases only in emergencies). We've also included a selection of essential warnings, tricks, tips, examples, and explanations that Microsoft left out of the help system. Exactly which commands are available will depend on which versions of DOS and/or Windows you've installed on your PC.

ANSI.SYS. Some old DOS applications might require that you add this to your CONFIG.SYS.

APPEND. This works just like the PATH command, only for data files instead of for programs. For example, if you enter the command APPEND C:\DATA, and that directory contains the file REPORT.TXT, entering the command EDIT REPORT.TXT would open the file, even if the current directory is not C:\DATA (unless there's a REPORT.TXT in the current directory, in which case that file would be opened instead).

ASSIGN. This command was removed from DOS 6. It's used to trick software that will only run from a particular drive into thinking that's where it is. For example, if you're installing an application from disks that fit your B: drive, but the setup utility is designed to work only from drive A:, the command ASSIGN B: A: will usually make it work properly. If your version of DOS has SUBST, enter `subst b: a:\` instead.

ATTRIB. HELP explains this command pretty well (you use it to hide files, make hidden files visible again, make files read-only, or make read-only files writable again), but neglects to mention that if you don't know what you're doing, using this command on hidden or system files can seriously screw up your system.

CD. This stands for "change directory" (see "To move from one directory to another..." above.

CHDIR. This is identical to CD, which you should enter instead because it's shorter.

CHKDSK. This checks disks for certain data errors and fixes some of them. ScanDisk is vastly superior, so use it instead if available.

COMP. This command was removed from DOS 6. It compares two files to see if they are identical, which you may want to do if, say, you've just copied a very important file to a floppy. FC is similar, but COMP is better if you just want to know if files are identical. For example, COMP C:\DOS \COMMAND.COM A: will check to see if the copy of COMMAND.COM in your DOS directory matches the one on a boot floppy.

COPY. Use this command to copy files (see "To copy or move files or directories..." above).

DEL. This commands deletes files (see "To delete files or directories..." above).

DELTREE. This deletes a directory, all directories underneath it, and all the files they contain (see "To delete files or directories..." above).

DIR. This displays a list of file names (see "To see what files are in a directory..." above).

DISKCOPY. This makes a copy of a floppy disk (see "To copy a floppy disk..." above).

DOSKEY. Improves the keyboard shortcuts available at the command line by letting you recall and edit the last few DOS commands you entered.

DOSSHELL. A DOS file manager, sort of a primitive version of Windows Explorer.

EDIT. A text editor, DOS's answer to Windows' Notepad.

EDLIN. This horrible antique editor was removed from DOS 6, and good riddance. Use EDIT instead.

ERASE. Use DEL, it's shorter.

EXPAND. EXPAND copies files from DOS's setup disks onto your hard drive. (HELP's example, EXPAND A:\SORT.EX_ C:\DOS\SORT.EXE, is unnecessarily complicated; you could drop the second file name and just use EXPAND A:\SORT.EXE C:\DOS.) EXPAND will look for A:\SORT.EXE; when it doesn't find it, it will look for SORT.EX_ instead, expand it as it copies it, and change the _ to an E in the expanded file. HELP mistakenly refers to "files," but in fact EXPAND can only work on one file at a time.

FDISK. This utility is used by DOS SETUP to create logical volumes on a new hard drive (see "How to Set Up a New Hard Disk" in Chapter 11: Windows 95, 98, and NT). Don't use FDISK if you don't know what you're doing, as it can erase everything on your hard drive. If you accidentally do wipe your drive screwing around with FDISK and don't have a backup, *do nothing* to the drive until you get your hands on a copy of Symantec's *The Norton Utilities*, which may be able to recover your data intact.

FORMAT. Use this command to prepare a new disk or erase an already formatted one (see "To format a floppy..." above).

INTERLNK AND INTERSVR. DOS's answer to Windows' Direct Cable Connection utility. You can use this pair of utilities to copy files between two computers over a file transfer cable connecting their serial or parallel ports (the latter is considerably faster). It's most often used for copying files between a desktop and a laptop. The DOS manual and on-line help explain both these commands well enough, but they don't do a great job of giving the big picture. First, decide which computer you want to work at; DOS calls this the "client," and the other computer the "server." Contrary to the DOS manual's advice, it's usually best to make the desktop the client and the laptop the server. Add the line `device=c: \dos\interlnk.exe` to the client's CONFIG.SYS, and reboot. On the server, enter the command `intersvr`. The server's drives then show up on the client as additional drive letters, and you can copy files using DOS commands, File Manager, or whatever file management tools you like.

JOIN. This not-so-useful command was removed from DOS 6. It "joins" the contents of a drive and a directory. For example, JOIN A: C:\UTILS would make the contents of A: appear in C:\UTILS. Enter the command `join /d` and A: and C:\UTILS resume their normal, separate roles.

MD. Short for "make directory," this command creates a directory immediately beneath the directory in which the command is entered (see "To create a directory..." above).

MEM. This command, for techies mostly, displays various information about your PC's memory. You can abbreviate MEM's switches—for example `mem /c/p` to page a moderately detailed display, or `mem /d/p` to page maximum details.

MKDIR. Use MD, it's shorter.

MORE. DOS HELP's example, TYPE CLIENTS.NEW | MORE, makes no sense, since it's more efficient to type MORE < CLIENTS.NEW. Use *command* | MORE to page command output, as in TREE | MORE, and MORE < *filename* to page files, as in MORE < AUTOEXEC.BAT.

MOVE. This command moves or renames files or directories (see "To copy or move files or directories..." above).

MSAV. This utility scans for and removes viruses. It's out of date; to check for viruses, download a newer utility from the Internet.

MSBACKUP. Backs up the hard disk to floppy disks.

MSD. Displays a wide variety of information about your system. Running MSD under Windows 3.1 sometimes interferes with applications currently using COM ports, such as a communications program performing a file transfer.

PATH. Tells DOS in which directories it can find commands. Enter `path` by itself to see where the path is currently set. If no path is set, you need to type the full path to each DOS command: for example, instead of just typing `path`, you'd have to type `c:\dos\path`. To add directories, enter `path` followed by the directories separated by semicolons, e.g.:

```
path c:\windows;c:\dos
```

PROMPT. One example missing from HELP is how to set the prompt to display the time. For the format (12:30) C:\DOS>, use the command prompt `($t$h$h$h$h$h$h) $p$g`.

RD. Deletes a directory, but only if it's empty (see "To delete files or directories..." above).

RECOVER. This command was removed from DOS 6. Better late than never: over the years, this badly designed data recovery tool has done far more harm than good. Don't try to use it.

REN. Use this command to rename files (see "To rename files or directories..." above).

RENAME. Use REN, it's shorter.

RMDIR. Use RD, it's shorter.

RESTORE. Restores backups created with DOS's BACKUP command.

SCANDISK. This tells DOS to search for and repair disk errors.

SETVER. Sometimes lets older apps work with newer versions of DOS by making them think they're running under an the older version of DOS they were designed for.

SHARE. Allows applications to share files; may be required by some DOS apps.

SMARTDRV. DOS's disk cache speeds up disk operations.

TREE. Presents a graphical display of the directories for the specified drive.

TYPE. Displays the contents of a file. Enter `more < filename` to see the file one screen at a time.

UNDELETE. This recovers files after you accidentally delete them (see "To retrieve accidentally deleted files or directories..." above).

VERIFY. This tells DOS whether to check if data is correctly written to disk. It slows operations a bit, so the default is OFF.

XCOPY. This copies entire directories—and the directories beneath them, if you like (see "To copy or move files or directories..." above).

Tuning AUTOEXEC.BAT and CONFIG.SYS

Running DOS games under Windows 95 or 98 sometimes requires creating or modifying CONFIG.SYS and AUTOEXEC.BAT files. These are text files containing a series of arcane commands and settings used to configure DOS. You may also need to deal with these files if for some reason you have to work with an old PC that runs DOS or Windows 3.1, or if something damages your Windows installation.

For the basic settings required to let DOS apps access your CD-ROM and/or sound card under Windows, you don't need the detailed info below. Just see the instructions in "Running DOS Applications under Windows" in Chapter 11: Windows 95, 98, and NT.

Editing these configuration files is more of an art than a science, so unfortunately I can't offer step-by-step instructions. The best I can do is walk through a couple of illustrative examples that should help you make sense of DOS applications' installation guides.

First, here are a few basic rules to follow:

1. Have a boot floppy handy in case you make a mistake that causes the PC to crash during boot.
2. Make a backup copy of the file before editing it, so you can return to the original settings if your changes cause problems.
3. To edit CONFIG.SYS and AUTOEXEC.BAT:

   In **DOS**, use the MS-DOS Editor—enter `edit c:\config.sys` or `edit c:\autoexec.bat`. Alternatively, you can use your favorite word processor; just be sure to save the file as text (also known as DOS text or ASCII) *without* line breaks. Never save a configuration file in a word processor format or as text with line breaks.

   In **Windows**, use the SysEdit utility. The latter is more convenient, as it automatically opens both CONFIG.SYS and AUTOEXEC.BAT along with Windows' two main configuration files, WIN.INI and SYSTEM.INI, all at once. To use SysEdit, choose Run from Program Manager's File menu and enter `sysedit`.

4. Every command or setting must go on a line by itself (a single CONFIG.SYS line is known as a statement).
5. To temporarily disable an entry for troubleshooting, insert `rem` at the beginning of the line.

Below you'll find a tour of fairly typical CONFIG.SYS and AUTOEXEC.BAT files for a DOS system running Windows 3.1. The lines appear in the order you normally see them listed, with explanations that can help you create and edit your own configurations. Note that you need to reboot before any configuration changes take effect.

DOS's Default CONFIG.SYS and AUTOEXEC.BAT

After installing DOS and Windows 3.1, CONFIG.SYS and AUTOEXEC.BAT will look pretty much like this. If you ever need to create a usable set of configuration files for a messed-up old DOS or Windows 3.1 PC from scratch, this is a reasonable place to start. To access the CD-ROM drive or sound card, you'll need to install their drivers from diskette—DOS and Windows 3.1 don't have them built in the way Windows 95, 98, and NT do. See the entries for cdromdrv.sys and mscdex.exe in the "CONFIG.SYS" and "AUTOEXEC.BAT" sections.

```
CONFIG.SYS
device=c:\dos\himem.sys
device=c:\dos\emm386.exe ram
buffers=15,0
files=30
dos=umb
lastdrive=H
fcbs=4,0
devicehigh=C:\dos\setver.exe
dos=high
stacks=9,256

AUTOEXEC.BAT
lh c:\dos\smartdrv.exe /x
@echo off
prompt $p$g
path C:\windows;c:\dos
set temp=c:\dos
```

The one objectionable setting here is the last line, `SET TEMP=C:\DOS`. Under some circumstances this can lead to your DOS directory getting cluttered with abandoned temp files. A much better approach is to create a directory dedicated to temporary files (so you'll know anything in it can be deleted), so you should replace this line with `SET TEMP=C:\TEMP`.

CONFIG.SYS

The CONFIG.SYS file is primarily a list of hardware *device drivers*—small programs that add capabilities to DOS or allow it to work with particular hardware. A few other basic DOS options are also set here, some by special commands that can be used only in CONFIG.SYS.

```
device=c:\dos\himem.sys
device=c:\dos\emm386.exe ram x=a000-c7ff
dos=umb
```

These three entries set up DOS's memory management. DOS's MemMaker (a utility that edits CONFIG.SYS and AUTOEXEC.BAT to conserve memory) usually creates these lines automatically, but sometimes you have to tweak them manually to troubleshoot software or hardware problems. The statement DEVICE= is the CONFIG.SYS command for loading a device driver.

HIMEM.SYS lets applications share *extended memory* (XMS). In practical terms, that means you need HIMEM.SYS to run Windows 3.1 or any DOS program that requires a 386. Some old PCs may have third-party memory manager like QEMM instead.

EMM386 does two things: It can emulate expanded memory (EMS) for older DOS applications that require it, and it can set up the upper memory area so you can use DEVICEHIGH and LH commands to make more conventional memory available (allowing you to run larger DOS apps and make Windows 3.1 run better). EMM386.EXE by itself does only the first; EMM386.EXE NOEMS does only the second; and EMM386.EXE RAM does both. (In DOS 5.0 and 6.0, you had to put a number after RAM indicating the amount of memory in KB you wanted to dedicate to EMS. Starting with DOS 6.2, EMM386 shifts memory between EMS and XMS on the fly.) Which setting is best depends on what programs you run; see the "Making More Memory Available" chapter of your DOS manual for tips on optimizing these settings.

DOS=UMB tells DOS to manage the upper memory area set up by EMM386. If you use EMM386 with the NOEMS or RAM options, you need "dos=umb" as well.

Windows 3.1 can emulate EMS for DOS applications, so if you don't need EMS outside of Windows, and you don't use DEVICEHIGH or LOADHIGH, you can leave EMM386 and DOS=UMB out of your CONFIG.SYS.

```
dos=high
```

This line moves some DOS code out of conventional memory and into the high memory area, making room in conventional memory for larger DOS applications and giving Windows 3.1 a little more elbow room to run more applications faster. DOS=HIGH requires HIMEM. You can combine DOS=HIGH and DOS=UMB into the single command DOS=HIGH,UMB.

```
devicehigh=c:\dos\setver.exe
```

The SETVER command fools older DOS apps into thinking that they're running under the version of DOS they expect to find. You may never run a program that needs SETVER, but you should include the statement just to be safe. DEVICEHIGH= works just like DEVICE=, except it loads device drivers into the upper memory area. Some drivers don't like it up there, so if MemMaker or a similar utility makes any of your hardware devices unusable, the first thing you should do is to find the CONFIG.SYS line that loads the driver for that hardware and try changing the command from DEVICEHIGH to DEVICE (see DOS Help for more on DEVICEHIGH).

```
buffers=4
```

This statement creates a sort of crude disk cache by telling DOS to copy a small quantity of data on disk into memory. If you use SmartDrive, you can save a little memory by setting it to a low value, like 4. (If you set it to 1, check to make sure it doesn't slow down floppy disk operations.) With no disk cache, 20 is usually adequate.

```
files=50
```

This controls how many files DOS can have open at once; 50 is a conservative setting if you're using Windows 3.1. If you're just using DOS, you can probably get away with 20. If you get an error message about "file handles" from DOS, Windows, or one of your applications, try raising this value.

```
lastdrive=F
```

DOS allocates a little memory for each potential drive letter. You can recover some of that by setting LASTDRIVE to the last drive letter in your system.

```
shell=c:\dos\command.com c:\dos\ /e:1024 /p
```

SHELL tells DOS where to look for COMMAND.COM, its *command interpreter* (the program that enables DOS to run commands and batch files). If you encounter the error message, "out of environment space," you can resolve it using the /e: switch to increase the amount of memory DOS sets aside to store the path and other variables displayed by the SET command.

```
device=c:\dos\smartdrv.exe /double_buffer
```

You probably won't need this, but under some circumstances it's required to use SmartDrive with some hard drives. For more information, see the Notes section of DOS Help for SMARTDRV.EXE.

```
fcbs=16
stacks=20,256
```

These arcane entries are required by some programs. If a program says it needs two numbers after FCBS, like FCBS=16,0, you can leave off the second number (unless you're using DOS 4 or an earlier version). If two programs need different STACKS settings, use the highest value for both numbers. For example, if one program wants STACKS=9,512 and another wants STACKS=32,256, set it to 32,512.

```
device=c:\bin\cdromdrv.sys /d:cdrom001
```

This loads the EIDE CD-ROM's device driver. The name and location of the driver file will vary depending on the brand and model of your CD-ROM.

Depending on what kind of hardware you have installed in your system, you may have a number of other device drivers installed in your CONFIG.SYS. Here are some from my old 386:

```
device=c:\apps\fax\satisfax.sys ioaddr=0350
device=c:\bin\cdromdrv.sys /d:cdrom001
device=c:\sb16\drv\ctsb16.Sys /unit=0 /blaster=a:220 i:5 d:1 h:5
device=c:\sb16\drv\ctmmsys.Sys
```

The first is used by my fax modem, the second by my CD-ROM drive, the last two by my sound card. There are thousands of drivers out there, so it's impossible to provide a guide to all of them. In most cases, installation software will add these statements automatically. Often the path will make clear what device is using the driver.

AUTOEXEC.BAT

The AUTOEXEC.BAT file loads memory-resident utilities, executes any commands that need to be run at startup, and sets various DOS options.

```
@echo off
```

This suppresses messages that would otherwise display on the screen as DOS executes the AUTOEXEC.BAT sequence.

```
prompt $p$g
```

Without this command, the DOS prompt won't show the path to the current directory.

```
path c:\windows;c:\dos
```

The PATH command lets you start programs just as if they were in the current directory. Simply add the program's directory name to the PATH, and DOS will search that directory and see if the command you entered at the DOS prompt starts anything.

```
set temp=c:\temp
```

The SET command followed by a \TEMP OR \TMP directory tells programs that need to create temporary files where to put those files. With DOS and Windows 3.1, it's a good idea to check that directory once in a while to make sure it's not accumulating garbage files and filling up your hard drive.

```
set wpc=/d–d:\temp
set sound=c:\sb16
set blaster=a220 i5 d1 h5 p330 t6
set midi=synth:1 map:e
```

Some applications and DOS commands use the SET command to store special settings. The WPC entry tells WordPerfect to store temp files in C:\TEMP, and the others have something to do with the sound card.

```
lh /L:0;1,45456 /s c:\dos\smartdrv /x
```

LH is shorthand for LOADHIGH (see DOS Help for more on this command). According to DOS Help, SmartDrive loads itself into upper memory without LOADHIGH's help, but MemMaker adds LH (and its /L: and /S switches) anyway. When you install DOS 6.2, it adds /X to turn off write-buffering, a measure that may keep you from losing data.

```
c:\bin\mscdex.exe /e /d:cdrom001 /L:r
```

DOS needs this to read CD ROM discs. The "/L:r" assignes the fixed drive letter R: rather than the default, which can vary if you add other drives to the system. MSCDEX should come after SMARTDRV in your AUTOEXEC .BAT—otherwise, SmartDrive won't speed up CD -ROM performance.

```
lh c:\windows\mouse.com
```

You need MOUSE.COM if you use a mouse with DOS applications outside of Windows. Some mouse drivers use upper memory automatically, even without LH, while others won't load high even *with* LH (in which case you should just leave LH out). Depending on what mouse you use, the driver may have a slightly different name (like LMOUSE for Logitech mice), or reside in a different directory. In some cases it may use a MOUSE.SYS driver in your CONFIG.SYS, instead.

As in your CONFIG.SYS, depending on what hardware and software you've installed, there are a seemingly infinite variety of entries that might show up in your AUTOEXEC.BAT. Here are a few from my old 386:

```
c:\utils\hercules\setcrt c:\utils\hercules\myscreen.crt
c:\apps\fax\casmgr.exe c:\apps\fax\casmgr.cfg
c:\sb16\diagnose /s
c:\sb16\sb16set /p /q
```

The first sets my super—VGA board's output to match my monitor's capabilities, the second loads some memory-resident (an old DOS concept) software used by my fax modem, and the last two do something to set up the sound card.

```
call pctools
```

CALL runs a batch file (in this case, PCTOOLS.BAT), and then continues with the rest of the commands in your AUTOEXEC.BAT. Without CALL, DOS would execute the commands in the batch file and stop without finishing the rest of the autoexec commands.

```
win :
```

This final entry loads Windows 3.1.

Appendix B

Windows 3.1 Survival Guide

by Robert Lauriston

In this Appendix

If you've never used it, working with Windows 3.1 (or NT 3.5, which has the same interface) can be a shock: it seems kind of like a really bad imitation of more recent versions. Most of the basic concepts are the same, but there are a few weird differences you may find confusing at first.

In this appendix, I'll first give you a quick rundown on those differences. After that, you'll find a step-by-step Windows 3.1 Cookbook for basic tasks that don't work the way they do in later versions.

If you're trying to get a malfunctioning Windows 3.1 PC running, take a look at the beginning of Appendix A DOS Survival Guide for ways to start Win31 if it doesn't launch automatically at startup. For tougher problems, see the the "Tuning AUTOEXEC.BAT and CONFIG.SYS" section of Appendix A: unlike Windows 95/98 and NT, which are self-contained, Windows 3.1 is layered on top of DOS, so if those configuration files aren't set properly Win31 may not run.

Windows 3.1 Basics

Windows 3.1's Desktop

In Windows 95/98/NT terms, Windows 3.1 doesn't *have* a desktop. There's something that looks like one, but you can't put files or folders on it.

In fact, the only things that appear on the Win31 desktop are minimized applications, which appear as small icons (see Figure 1). Double-clicking on one of these icons is like clicking on a program's button on the taskbar: if the window's minimized, it's restored, and the program comes to the front.

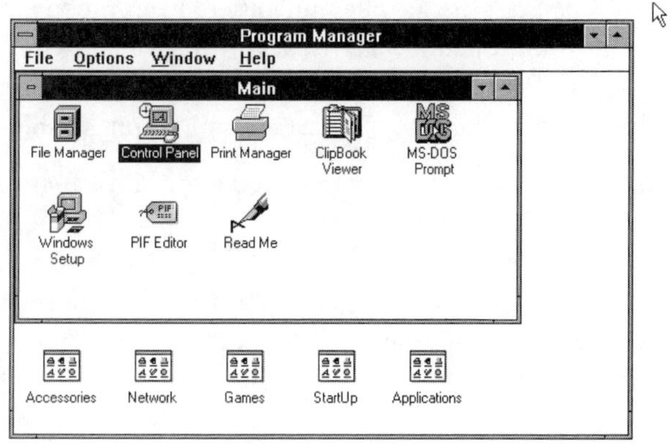

Figure 1

Windows 3.1 has no taskbar; instead, minimized applications appear on the desktop. This application is the Program Manager, 3.1's counterpart of the Start menu

Only minimized applications appear on the desktop. To see a list of all open applications, including those "hiding" behind others, press Ctrl Esc to bring up the Task List (see Figure 2).

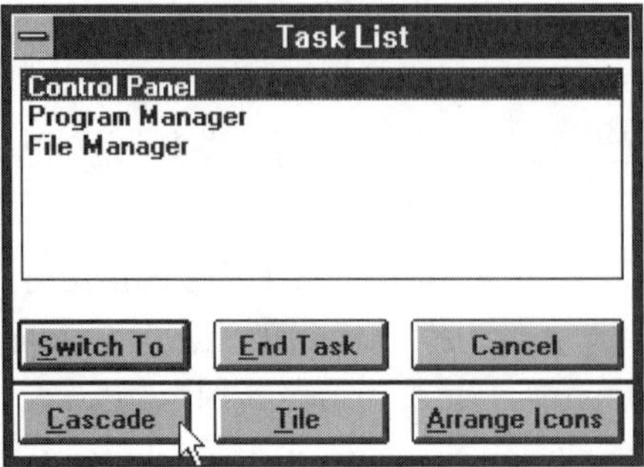

Figure 2

Windows 3.1's Task List is similar to the taskbar: all open applications appear here, whether or not they're visible on screen at the moment. Double-click on any program to bring it to the front. The Cascade and Tile buttons arrange application windows; the Arrange Icon button neatly arranges any minimized icons on the desktop.

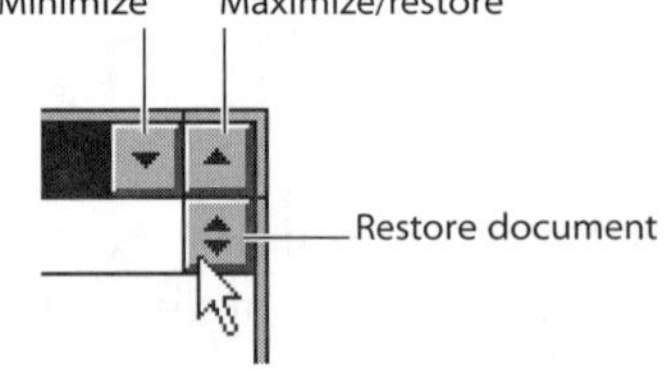

Figure 3

Windows 3.1's minimize and maximize/restore buttons look different, but they work the same way as the ones you're used to.

The minimize and mazimize/restore buttons (see Figure 3) look different than they do in later versions of Windows, but they work the same way. There is no close box; instead, when you want to close a window, *double*-click on the Control menu icon in its upper-right corner.

Program Manager and File Manager

Windows 3.1's Program Manager (see Figure 1 above) is functionally equivalent to the Start menu. The only difference is the interface: instead of the Start menu, Program Manager has an application window; instead of folders, it contains Program Groups, which you can open and minimize like documents in an application. To start an application, double-click on it.

The File Manager (see Figure 4) is the primitive ancestor of today's Windows Explorer. All operations are drag-and-drop: there's no Edit menu, no cut, copy, and paste commands, no Ctrl X, Ctrl C or Ctrl V. Each window shows only one drive's directories; if you want to copy or move files between disks, you must open a separate window for each disk. (See the Cookbook below for detailed instructions.)

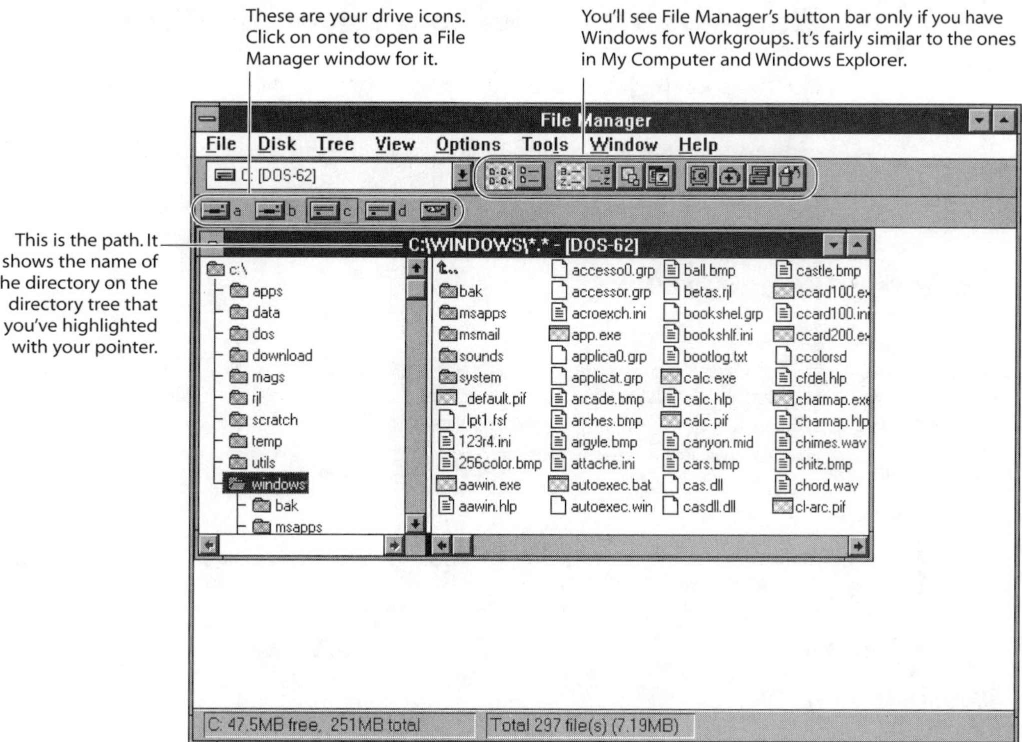

These are your drive icons. Click on one to open a File Manager window for it.
You'll see File Manager's button bar only if you have Windows for Workgroups. It's fairly similar to the ones in My Computer and Windows Explorer.
This is the path. It shows the name of the directory on the directory tree that you've highlighted with your pointer.
File Manager
File Disk Tree View Options Tools Window Help
C: [DOS-62]
C:\WINDOWS*.* - [DOS-62]
C: 47.5MB free, 251MB total
Total 297 file(s) (7.19MB)

Figure 4

Windows 3.1's File Manager has a radically different interface from Windows Explorer's.

That's all you really need to know to get started with Windows 3.1. You'll find more information in the Cookbook, below—but first, some keyboard and mouse shortcuts that may help speed up your work.

Windows 3.1 File Icons

Windows 3.1's file icons are relatively crude. They tell you which files are programs, which Win31 recognizes as documents (those you can double-click to open), and the rest just get a generic blank-page icon.

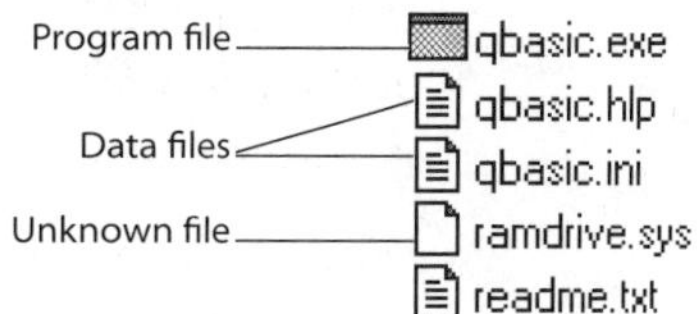

Windows 3.1 Mouse and Keyboard Shortcuts

How to do what you want with the least hassle is even less obvious in Windows 3.1 than in modern versions. This quick reference will help you out, whether you prefer the mouse or the keyboard. Note that right-clicking generally has no effect in 3.1.

Windows 3.1 Mouse Tricks

General	
Pop up Task List	Double-click on desktop
Close window	Double-click Control menu
Maximize window	Double-click on title bar
Program Manager	
Create new program item	Alt-double-click on blank area of group window
Change program item or group properties	Alt-double-click on icon
Save current Program Manager settings	Shift-click on File/Exit Windows
File Manager	
Move file(s) from one disk to another	Alt-drag and drop
Copy files from one directory to another on same disk	Ctrl-drag and drop
Copy files to another disk	Drag and drop on drive icon
Open new directory window	Double-click on drive icon
Expand to show all directories	Shift-click drive icon
Split window to show files and directories	Drag split bar from left edge of window
Tile windows side by side	Hold Shift while clicking Window/Tile

Windows 3.1 Keyboard Shortcuts

General	
Pop up Task List	Ctrl Esc
Close document window	Ctrl F4
Close application window	Alt F4
Switch document windows	Ctrl Tab
Switch application windows	Alt Tab
Program Manager	
Change program item or group properties	Alt Enter
Switch to another program group	Ctrl Tab
Close current group window	Ctrl F4
Select another program item	Tap first letter of icon label
Save current Program Manager settings	Alt Shift F4
Close Program Manager (and exit Windows)	Alt F4
File Manager	
Move to root directory in tree view	Home
Move up one level in tree view	Ctrl ←
Select adjacent files/directories	Hold Shift and use cursor keys
Select nonadjacent files/directories	Press Shift F8 and use Spacebar to tag items
Select all	Ctrl /
Deselect all	Ctrl \
Run program (or open file) minimized	Shift Enter]
Change directory windows	Ctrl Tab
Switch current directory window to another drive	Ctrl-[*drive letter*]
Open new directory window	Tab, select drive icon, Enter
Tile windows side by side	Shift F4

Windows 3.1 Cookbook

If for some reason you get stuck having to work in Windows 3.1, this Cookbook should come in handy. For those times when you can't avoid the DOS prompt, we offer the following Cookbook, which explains step by step how to perform TK file, disk, and application tasks. Beginners who find any part of this Cookbook confusing should turn to the brief DOS introduction above.

File Tasks

To See What Files Are in a Directory

You need to see where a file is located before you open it in an application, move it, or otherwise manipulate it. Files live in directories, so that's where you look for them.

1. Start the File Manager.
2. Click View on the File Manager's menu bar, and select the Tree and Directory option.
3. In the directory tree display (the left window), click on the directory folder you think contains the files you want. The files in that directory will appear in the right window.

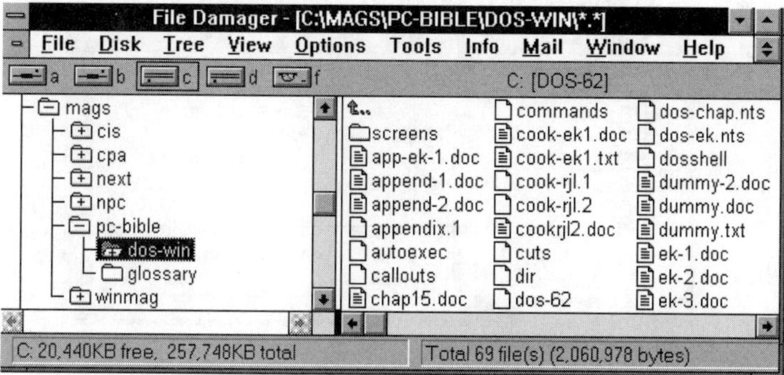

4. If there are more files in the directory than File Manager can show all at once, select View/Directory Only to omit the directory tree and see more files. You can also scroll, of course, or—for the biggest possible view—maximize the File Manager itself by clicking on the up arrow in the upper-right corner. (If there's still a small directory window within the maximized File Manager, then maximize that window in the same way.)

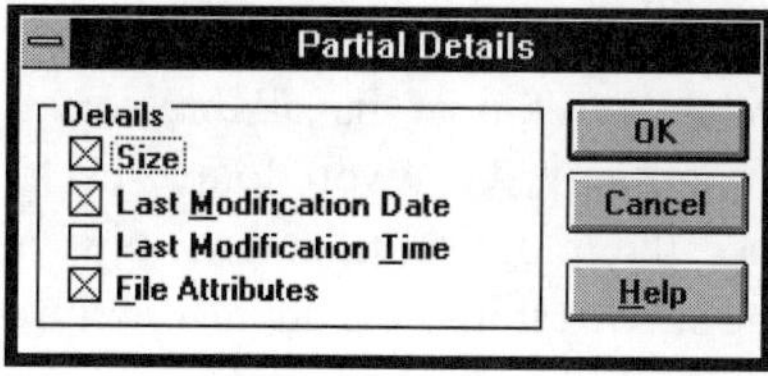

By default, File Manager displays only file names. If you want more information, select View/All File Details to display file size, the date and time the file was last saved, and the file attributes (select a file, choose File/Properties, and click on the Help button in the dialog box for more information on file attributes). Or select View/Partial Details, and check the boxes for only those details you want to see on screen.

By default, File Manager displays files in alphabetical order. If you want to change that, pick one of the Sort options from the View menu. The most useful option is Sort by Type, which groups files by their extensions—so if you want to quickly scroll through just the DOC files, for example, you'll find them all in one segment of the directory list.

To Move From One Directory to Another

The file you want to do something with often resides in a directory other than the one you're in—so you need to look in another directory to find the file.

In the File Manager:

1. Check the first letter on the title bar to make sure you're on the drive you want to be on. If not, click on the appropriate drive icon (just below the title bar) to change drives.

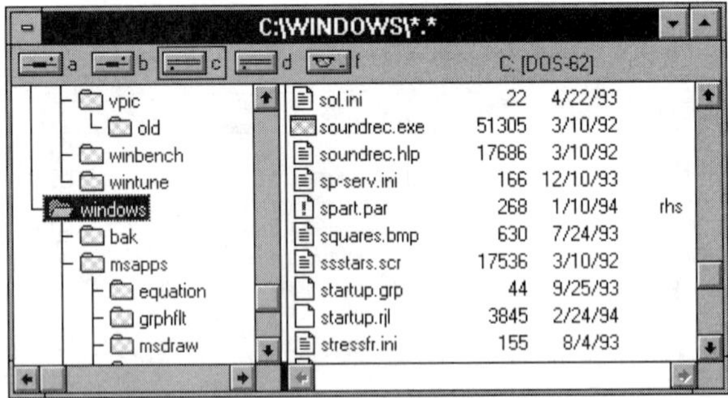

2. Select the View/Tree and Directory command.
3. Use the scroll bar in the middle of the File Manager window to scroll through the tree in the left Window until you find the folder icon for the directory you want. If you prefer, you can navigate using the keyboard's up and down cursor keys.
4. To display a directory's contents in the right window, click on its folder in the left window. If a directory folder appears in the right window and you want to display its contents, double-click on it.

If you select Tree/Indicate Expandable Branches, you'll note that all directories containing other directories have a plus sign on them. When you double-click on a folder to display its subsidiary directories, the folder opens and the plus sign turns into a minus sign. To reveal all the subdirectories on the drive without having to open folders, select Tree/Expand All.

In the File/Open and File/Save dialog boxes found in most Windows applications:

1. Select another drive from the Drives list if the dialog box displays the wrong drive.

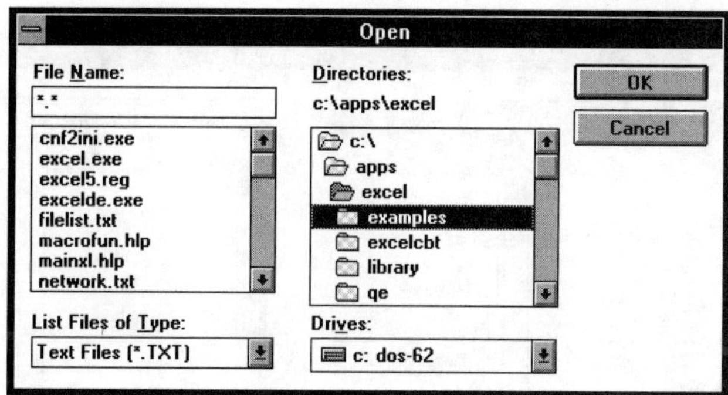

2. Instead of a full tree display, Windows' dialog boxes give you just the path for the current directory, both as text (C:\APPS\EXCEL in the example) and as a hierarchy of folder icons. Files are displayed in the left window.
3. To move to a different subdirectory, double-click on the folder icons. For example, to switch to C:\DOS, you'd double-click on C:\ to display the directories in the root directory, then double-click on the DOS folder.

To Copy or Move Files or Directories

Copying and moving files and directories are part of routine disk housekeeping. There are a million reasons to perform either task—to copy files from your hard disk to a floppy so someone else can use them, to move files from a working directory to one that contains finished work, and so forth.

1. Start the File Manager, and select Tree and Directory from the View menu.
2. If only one directory window in the File Manager is open, select Window/New Window, then press s$ to tile the two windows vertically.
3. In the left directory window, click the source directory, that is, the directory from which you want to copy or move a file.
4. In the right directory window, click the target directory, that is, the directory to which you want to copy or move a file.
5. Select the file(s) that you want to move or copy (see "To select multiple files..." later in this Cookbook).
6. To move the file between one hard disk directory and another, hold down the left mouse button, drag the file from the source directory to the target directory, and release the mouse button to drop the file, completing the action. To move the file between a hard disk directory and a floppy, hold down the s key as you drag and drop.

7. To copy the file between one hard disk directory and another, hold down both the left mouse button and the ? key, drag the file from the source directory to the target directory, and release the button to drop the file. To copy a file between your hard disk and a floppy, simply drag and drop without using the ? key.

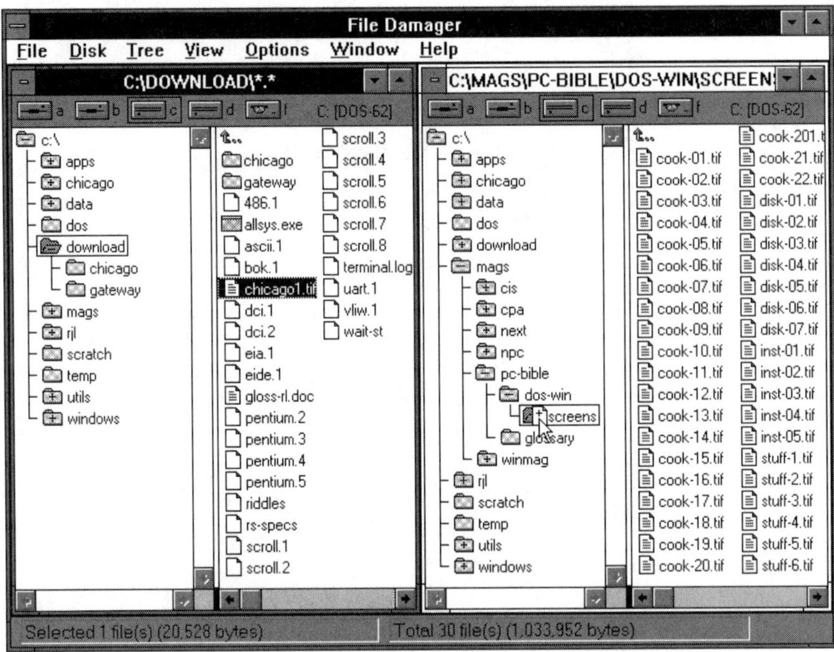

The procedure for moving and copying directories is identical to the one for files. Moreover, you can drop files or directories anywhere in a directory or on a folder in the tree display. You can even drop a file or directory on one of the drive icons at the top of the window—a handy method for copying files to floppy disks in your A: or B: drive.

To Select Multiple Files

If you need to do the same thing (move, copy, delete, and so on) to a group of files or directories, you can often avoid time-wasting repetition by selecting all the files first and entering the command once.

1. Start the File Manager and go to the directory containing the files you want to select.
2. To select several adjacent files (or directories) from the directory list, click the first file, hold down the s key, and then click the last file.

3. To select files (or directories) scattered throughout the list, click the first file, hold down ?, and click each additional file.

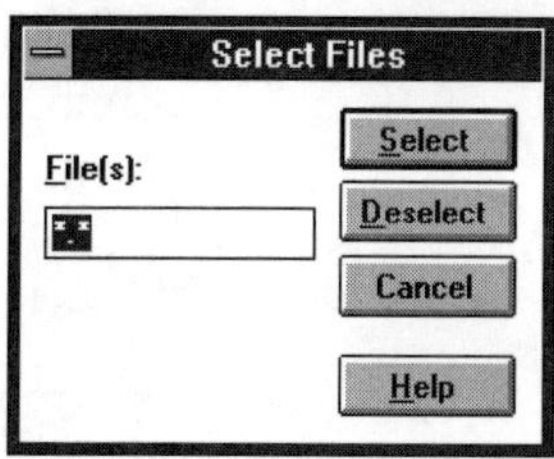

For other selection options—such as selecting all files in a directory—choose Select Files from File Manager's File menu and use DOS wildcards, described in the "To Select Multiple Files" section of Appendix A.

To Create a Directory

It's faster and easier to find files if you arrange them in directories. You may also need to create directories for programs that don't install automatically.

1. Start the File Manager and select the View/Tree and Directory command.
2. In the directory tree window, click on the directory folder in which you want to create the new directory. To create a directory at the topmost level (that is, in the root directory), press the 8 key to jump to the top of the tree, and click on the folder labeled only by the drive letter.

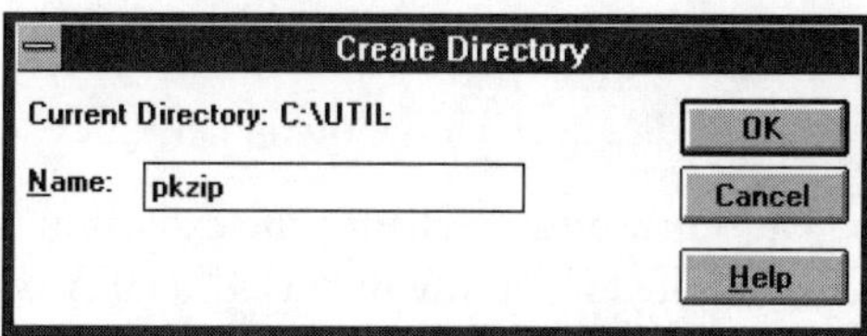

3. Select File/Create Directory.
4. Type the name you want to give the new directory and click OK.

To Delete Files or Directories

Old, useless copies of files often confuse matters and always take up disk space unnecessarily. The general rule: If you don't need it, delete it.

1. Start the File Manager, and select the file or directory you want to delete.
2. Press the Delete key, then click the Yes button (or Yes to All button, if you're deleting multiple files or directories).

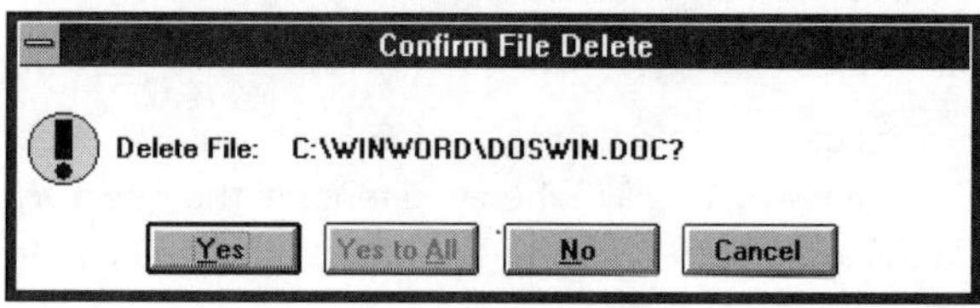

The way File Manager asks for confirmation every time you delete a file can be annoying. You can avoid that by selecting Confirmation on the File Manager's Options menu and unchecking File Delete in the resulting dialog box. While you're at it, you might as well eliminate other pointless interruptions by unchecking Mouse Action and Disk Commands. Deleting an entire directory is destruction on a mass scale, so you may want to leave that confirmation option checked. The same goes for File Replace, which helps prevent the common mistake of copying an old version of a file over a new one.

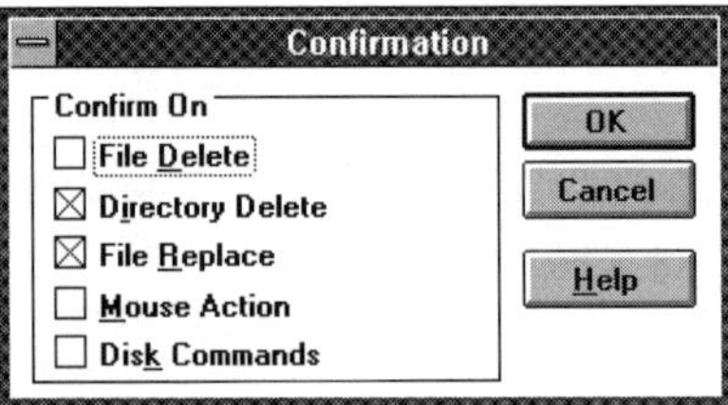

To Rename Files or Directories

The usual reason you need to rename a file or directory is to correct a typing mistake you made when you orginally named it. But there are a zillion other reasons—for example, to preserve an earlier version of a file.

1. Start the File Manager and select the file or directory you want to rename.
2. Select File/Rename.
3. Type the new file or directory name, then click OK.

Using wildcards, you can also easily change the extension for a group of files in a directory. For example, to give any file in a directory with a TXT extension a DOC extension instead:

1. Choose Select Files from the File Manager's File menu.
2. Enter *.txt in the File(s): box.
3. Select File/Rename, enter *.doc in the To: box, and click OK.

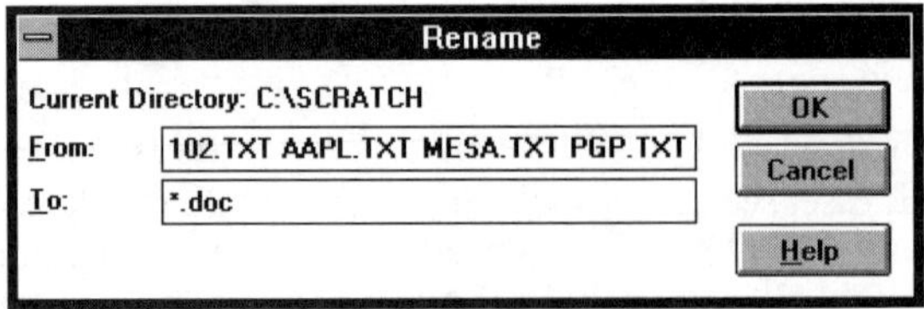

Danger Zone: Renaming Directories

Renaming program directories can cause big problems. Some programs expect to find files in certain places, and won't run properly, if at all, when you rename the directory in which they're stored. Unless you really know what you're doing, you should only rename directories that contain data files.

To Find a File

Unless you're better organized than anyone else, you'll occasionally forget where you saved a file.

1. Start the File Manager. If it doesn't display the contents of the drive you want to search, click the desired drive icon. (You can only search one drive at a time.)
2. To search the entire drive, press the 8 key to move to the top of the tree. To search only a particular directory, click on it.
3. Pick Search from the File Menu.
4. In the Search dialog box, type the name of the file you want to find after Search For:, or approximate the name with wildcards (for example, MO*.XL? to find all Excel data files that start with mo; see "To select multiple files..." for more on wildcards).

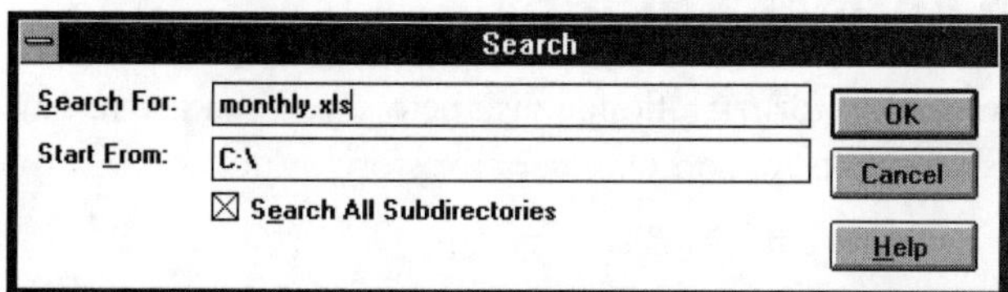

5. If you want to search only the current directory but not its subdirectories, uncheck Search All Subdirectories. Otherwise, leave it checked and click OK.

To Recover Accidentally Deleted Files or Directories

Sooner or later, all of us accidentally delete a file or directory. Fortunately, you can almost always recover files (and usually directories) easily.

1. Start the File Manager and select the directory that contained the deleted file or directory.
2. Select File/Undelete to start Microsoft Undelete. (If Windows 3.1 is running on top of an older version of DOS, Undelete may not be available. In that case, see the instructions in the "DOS Cookbook" in Appendix A: DOS Survival Guide.) If you're not sure which directory held the file or directory you deleted, click the Find button and enter the file or directory name (or the name as close as you remember it, with wildcards).
3. Scroll through the Microsoft Undelete list and click on each file or directory you want to recover. Notice that in place of the file or directory name's first character, a question mark may appear instead.
4. Click the Undelete button and replace the question marks with the first character of each file or directory name as prompted. If you don't know the missing character, pick whatever makes the most sense.

If you recovered a file or files in steps 1 through 4, you're done. If you just recovered a directory or directories, you're only half done, because recovering a directory does not automatically recover its files. Continue with the following steps to undelete a directory's files:

5. Click the Drive/Dir button.
6. Select the recovered directory from the Directories list in the Drives and Directories dialog box, then click OK.
7. Return to step 3.

Disk Tasks

To Format a Floppy

You need to format a floppy disk before you can use it. Formatting lays down the basic information necessary for storing files.

1. Insert the floppy disk.
2. Start the File Manager and select the Disk/Format Disk command.
3. Pick from the Disk In list the drive containing the floppy disk you want to format.
4. Adjust the Capacity setting if you're formatting a low-density disk (that is, a 720K disk in a 3½-inch floppy drive or a 360K disk in a 5¼-inch floppy drive).

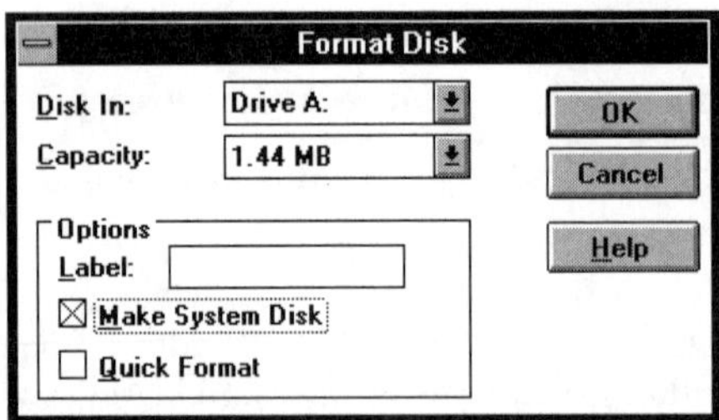

5. If you'd like a descriptive name for the disk to appear on File Manager's title bar, type up to 11 characters in the Label field.
6. Check Make System Disk only if you want to be able to boot your PC from the floppy.
7. Check Quick Format to quickly erase files from an already-formatted floppy.
8. Click OK to start formatting.

To Copy a Floppy Disk

Sometimes you need to duplicate an entire floppy disk, either to make a backup copy or to give a copy to someone else.

1. Start the File Manager and select Disk/Copy Disk.
2. If you have only one floppy drive, or one 3½-inch and one 5¼-inch floppy drive, insert the disk you want to copy into the drive and set both Source In and Destination In to that drive letter.
3. Click OK. When you see the "Insert source disk" prompt, click OK again.
4. When prompted to "Insert destination disk," remove the disk you're copying from, insert the disk you want to copy to, and click OK. Any files already on the second disk will be erased.

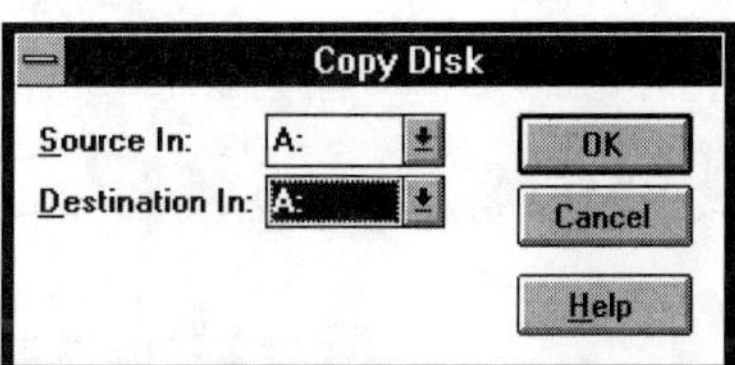

If you have two 3½-inch or two 5¼-inch drives, Insert the disk you want to copy in drive A: and the disk you want to copy to in drive B:. Set Source In to A:, Destination In to B:, and click OK.

Application Tasks

To Install an Application

Before you can use an application, you have to install it on your hard disk. This takes some time, but usually all you need to do is follow prompts once you get started.

1. Start the File Manager and click on the A: (or B:, if appropriate) drive icon.
2. If you see any files named README, READ.ME, README.TXT, README.WRI, or something similar, they may contain important information about installation. If their file icons show up as documents (pages with four horizontal lines), double-click to open and read them. If they show up as generic blank pages, drag them into Notepad. Print out the file and look for any instructions you should follow during installation.
3. Double-click on the installation program (usually SETUP.EXE; check the application's manual). An installation routine will start that should lead you through the whole process step by step. If you opt for custom installation and you're not sure which options to leave in or leave out, check the manual—don't guess!

To Start an Application

You have to start an application before you can use it.

Choose one of these four methods:

1. Double-click on the program's icon in the Program Manager.
2. Double-click on the program's EXE or COM file in the File Manager.
3. Double-click on one of the program's documents in the File Manager. This will start the application and open the document automatically.
4. Choose Run from the File menu in either the Program Manager or the File Manager, type in the program's startup command (click on Browse if you need to find the program's EXE or COM file), and click OK.

To Open a File

To edit or (usually) to print a file, you need to open it.

Normally, you choose Open from your application's File menu, select the file, and click OK.

If the application isn't running (or if you just want a change from the usual routine), try double-clicking on the file's icon in the File Manager. This way of opening a file works only if a file association has already been set up, so that Windows knows by the file's extension which application the file should be opened in. Most Windows applications establish these associations on installation—but some don't, and you may want to change associations anyway (so TXT files open in your word processor instead of Notepad, for example). To set up or change an association, do this:

1. Select a file with the extension whose association you want to create or change. (You can't define an association for files with no extension.)
2. Select File/Associate.
3. Scroll through the Associate With list until you find the program you want files with the extension to open in.
4. If the desired program isn't on the list, click the Browse button, select the program's EXE file from the directory display, and click OK.

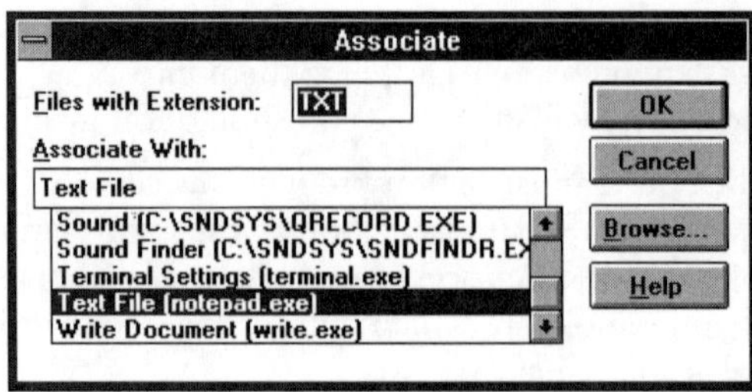

You can also try opening a file by selecting it in the File Manager, dragging the file across the desktop, and dropping the file on an application's minimized icon. The advantage to the drag-and-drop method is that Windows will open (or try to open) the file in the application no matter what file associations have been set up. Unfortunately, this method doesn't work with all programs.

To Print a File

In Windows, you "print" not only to get a hard copy of a document, but also to send faxes via fax modem.

Almost every Windows application has a File/Print command. You just set any options you want (like a page range) in the resulting dialog box and then click OK.

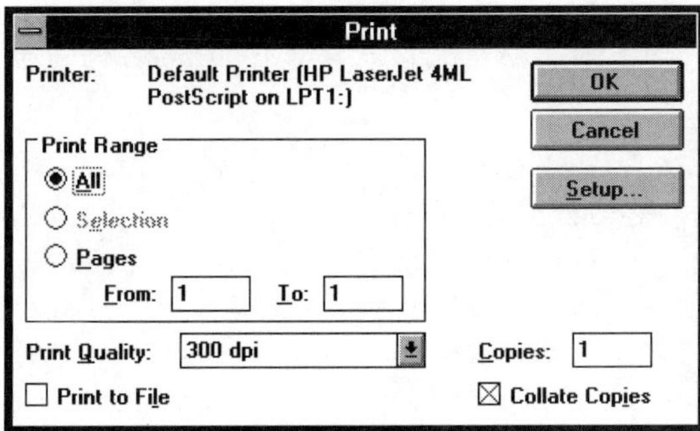

If you want to open a document, print it, and close it again, you need to select the document in the File Manager, choose Print from the File menu, and click OK. Alternatively, if the Print Manager is minimized on the desktop, you can drag the document's icon out of the File Manager and drop it on the Print Manager icon. However, this drag-and-drop move doesn't work with all programs.

To Switch Between Applications

DOS was designed to run just one application at a time. Windows is expressly designed to let you run multiple applications at the same time so that, for example, you don't have to close your word processor to read your E-mail.

There are five ways to move from one application to another in Windows:

1. If the application you're working in isn't maximized, one of the best ways to switch applications is to simply click on any part of another application window.

2. Pressing at takes you back to the last program you left—a fast way to switch back and forth between two programs.
3. Hold down a and press t repeatedly, and you can cycle through all the applications currently running.
4. Double-click anywhere on the Windows desktop (or press ?–), and the Task Lisk appears, which shows all programs currently running and enables you to switch to one by selecting it and clicking the Switch To button.
5. Give each application a keyboard shortcut, and switch to applications by entering their unique key combination. Just select the item in Program Manager, pick Properties from Program Manager's File menu, and enter the combination in the Shortcut Key box.

Index

Note: Page numbers in italic denote figures or screens

Numbers and Symbols

A

D

E

F

G

J

K

L

M

N

T

U

X

Y

Z